Women of
Classical Mythology

A BIOGRAPHICAL DICTIONARY

Athena. Bas-relief, circa 6th century B.C.

Women of
Classical Mythology

A BIOGRAPHICAL DICTIONARY

Robert E. Bell

OXFORD UNIVERSITY PRESS
New York   Oxford

Oxford University Press

Oxford   New York   Toronto
Delhi   Bombay   Calcutta   Madras   Karachi
Kuala Lumpur   Singapore   Hong Kong   Tokyo
Nairobi   Dar es Salaam   Cape Town
Melbourne   Auckland

and associated companies in
Berlin   Ibadan

First published in the United States 1991 by ABC-CLIO, Inc.
130 Cremona Drive, P.O. Box 1911
Santa Barbara, California 93116-1911

First issued as an Oxford University Press paperback, 1993

Oxford is a registered trademark of Oxford University Press

Library of Congress Cataloging-in-Publication Data
Bell, Robert E.
Women of classical mythology : a biographical dictionary / Robert
E. Bell.
p. cm.   ISBN 0-19-507977-9 (pbk.)
1. Mythology, Classical—Biography—Dictionaries. 2. Goddesses—
Dictionaries. 3. Women—Mythology—Biography—Dictionaries.
I. Title.
[BL715.B445   1992]
292.1'3'082—dc20   92-22754

2 4 6 8 10 9 7 5 3 1

Printed in the United States of America

DEDICATED TO

*the Tarrant City (Alabama) Public Library
and the Birmingham Public Library,
where this book had its beginning a half-century ago*

&

IN MEMORY OF
Georgia Airheart

Contents

Introduction

Women in classical mythology appear to have been somewhat neglected except for such headliners as Helen, Medea, Phaedra, Clytemnestra, Alcestis, Dido, Electra, and a few others who captured the creative imagination of ancient and modern writers. Goddesses, of course, have always received attention because of their role in religious history and, in due course, in works of art and architecture based on their worship. Curiously, an inordinate number of monsters were conceived by the ancients as female—the Theban Sphinx, the Furies, the Harpies, the Gorgons, Scylla and Charybdis, the Lamiae, the Chimaera, and even Chaos. By and large, however, mythology has been the province of gods and heroes, and women have been mentioned only in passing. Ask anyone, for example, the name of Achilles' wife. Who was the mother of the powerful Aeolian dynasty? Who were the daughters of Cadmus and what happened to them? What part did women play in the curse on the house of Pelops? Few can answer these questions.

There are reasons, of course, for this oversight. The ancient writers worked from oral traditions, which in turn could spin out male genealogies from Chaos to Caesar. Women were keepers of the house and the household gods. They were sisters, mothers, daughters, and wives of men who went on famous boar hunts, searched for the Golden Fleece, or stormed the walls of Thebes or Troy. So what has come down

is passing mention of most of them and little else. Perhaps another reason for the oversight was the regard in which women were held in ancient relationships. Men were constantly on the move and coupled with women where they stopped (e.g., Aegeus and Aethra, Heracles and the 50 daughters of Thespius, Achilles and Briseis, Apollo and Acacallis, etc.). Available nymphs roved the countryside, and adultery was not a cardinal sin. One can readily assess the situation by learning that Absyrtus was the son of Aeetes by Ipsia, Idyia, Asterodeia, Hecate, Neaera, or Eurylyte. Seldom do we encounter such a string of possible fathers. Then we have various versions of old stories, further complicated by later commentators. Fragments are cited out of context, and we find variant spellings (Hippolyte/Hippe or Antiope/Iope as wives of Theseus).

So why bother? Does it really matter? I believe it does. In attempting to look at the myths from a female perspective, I have found some interesting puzzles and maybe even answers, which I have enunciated. Having been occupied for several years with the geography of mythology, I find a number of inconsistencies. Women were not as mobile as men in those days, yet one can find the unquestioning statement that Achinoe, a daughter of the Nile River, was the mother of Pallene and Rhoeteia by the Macedonian king Sithon. It is unlikely that she migrated from Egypt to Macedonia, and there is no mention of Sithon's having gone to Egypt in search of a wife. This suggests that there was another Achinoe (also spelled variously as Achiroe and Anchiroe). There are several other such cases. Because these women had a more or less rooted station in life, one can also patch together itineraries of their men. Salmoneus, the father of Tyro and thus ancestor of important Thessalian and Messenian dynasties, migrated from Thessaly to Elis. He had to have detoured by way of Tegea in Arcadia, since that is where Alcidice, his first wife and the mother of Tyro, originated.

A very important reason for giving attention to women in mythology is the biological fact of the limited duration of childbearing capability, which has strong implications for chronologies. Alcippe, the daughter of Ares and Agraulos, has been called the mother of the great artisan Daedalus. She could not have been. Her mother and her aunts were put in charge of Erichthonius, the half-serpent ward of Athena, and were therefore considerably older than Erichthonius (Erechtheus I), who became the father of Pandion, who was the father of Erechtheus II, who was the father of Eupalamus, who was supposed to be Alcippe's husband. If Agraulos and her sisters committed suicide by leaping from the Acropolis when they saw the snaky baby, then Alcippe had already been born and was contemporary with Erechtheus I. This would make her roughly equivalent in age to a grandaunt of Eupalamus. Moreover, Daedalus has always been called one of the Metionidae, a descendant of Metion. Metion is sometimes called a son of Eupalamus, thus adding another two generations to the already yawning generation gap. Of course, we must take into account the vastly confused genealogy of the Athenian royal house, which for centuries has caused problems for mythologists.

In the case of Aethra, the mother of Theseus, we find that the question of the paternity of Agamemnon and Menelaus can more or less be determined by their relationship to her. Aethra was niece to Atreus, son of Pelops; if he had been the father of Agamemnon and Menelaus, she would have been their first cousin. But we learn from Plutarch that Theseus was about 50 when he abducted the very young

Helen to Aphidna. Therefore, by the time Helen became of marriageable age, several additional years had passed, so that Theseus was too old for the Trojan War. But Agamemnon and Menelaus, who married Helen, were at their prime, so it is rather certain that a generation intervened between Atreus and these heroes. Since several versions of the story record them as sons of Pleisthenes, who was the son of Atreus, others in the past must have come to a conclusion similar to mine, although I have never found anyone offering Aethra as possible evidence.

Still, does it matter? After all, in the world of myth nothing need be explained in realistic terms. I happen to belong to that persistent group that believes in a certain historical basis in certain of the epic accounts. I feel there are too many coincidences in time and place and circumstances. All the royal houses of cities such as Argos, Athens, Sparta, Mycenae, Pylus, Iolcus, Sicyon, etc., regardless of the chronicler, appear to have events so arranged that heroes and sons of heroes from places far apart come neatly together in the Trojan War or one of its prologues—the Calydonian boar hunt, the Argonaut, or the two wars on Thebes. Besides, scholars have speculated endlessly on the contradictions in the return route of the Argonauts, the itinerary of Odysseus, the mythological connection of the tholos tombs in Mycenaean cities, and so on. Why not the evidence from family trees and the women who can help provide this evidence? How many people know that Agamemnon and Menelaus were second cousins to Idomeneus (via their mother Aerope, whose father was a brother to Idomeneus' father)? Could this account for Crete's entrance into the Trojan War—a matter of family honor?

Not all the 2,600 names in this book provide clues to genealogical puzzles; only a few are involved in great epics. Most are just ordinary wives, sisters, or mothers; life happened mainly through their men. It may be claimed that too much space is given to a retelling of stories about men. Many times it was necessary to work from the barest mention of a woman's name. There was no way to talk about her, even briefly, without putting her into some kind of context via her father, husband, or son. But as sparse as the information might have been, I still wondered about some of these women and what they were like, how they might have been affected by the rush of destiny around them. Were they jealous of other women in their husbands' lives? How did they react to the glories or tragedies of their offspring?

Mythology offers a rich tapestry of human (and the humanly divine) condition. In its stories can be found many of the situations being dealt with today. Even the prevalence of present-day abortion had its ancient equivalent in the practice of infant exposure. The persistence of myth is accounted for in large part by the individuals who over the centuries could identify with Echo, Antigone, Acacallis, Callirrhoe, Atalanta, Byblis, and scores of others. Somehow it is all there, and this book attempts to look at the eternal woman, who still seeks solutions to problems that have followed her down the ages.

The book is arranged in dictionary form, since each individual here deserves a separate identity. If anyone should require a geographical context, my book, *Place-Names in Classical Mythology: Greece,* will be helpful. A certain amount of repetition is unavoidable, since some women appear in the accounts of others. Included with humans are divinities as well as female monsters and animals. There are even a couple of hermaphrodites and transsexuals who were included as part females and part-time females.

Cross-references are both direct and indirect. *See* references direct the user to a preferred spelling or an entry that will avoid repetition. Certain other entries point out in uppercase more commonly used names, to which the reader is directed for the principal information on an individual. The surnames and associated identifications under entries for goddesses are also cross-references. The special section following the main text is a cross-index of all the males (with relevancy to a particular entry) who are mentioned.

Citations to ancient writers appear at the end of most entries. Authors and their works are spelled out in full, using, where possible, the names of ancient works translated into English, a practice favored by Robert Graves and the editors of the Loeb Classical Library. Citations are not confined to works appearing in the Loeb

Classical Library (as was the case with my other volumes on mythology), since in order to be comprehensive I had to go to some rather obscure sources. Still, the largest percentage of these articles can be followed up in relatively accessible works in English translation. Spellings for the most part are uniform with those in my other two dictionaries, *Dictionary of Classical Mythology* and *Place-Names in Classical Mythology: Greece,* but where names appear for the first time here, I have used them as they appear in Loeb and other well-known translations. In certain cases I have used the form of a name more easily recognized from popularized spellings, such as Jason, Medea, Agave, and Hecuba, but I have retained Dice and Nice, since their names are basic to derivative names such as Eurydice, Demodice, Nicephorus, Nicippe, etc.

The works cited provided most of the needed material for this book, so there is no need for a formal bibliography. However, I did use dozens of reference works for obscure facts and for verification. The ones I found particularly useful were:

Ausführliches Lexikon der griechischen und römischen Mythologie. Herausgegeben von W. H. Roscher. 6 vols. and 3 suppls. Leipzig: B. G. Teubner, 1884–1937.

Crowell's Handbook of Classical Mythology. Edward Tripp. New York: Crowell, 1970.

The Dictionary of Classical Mythology. Pierre Grimal. Oxford: Basil Blackwell, 1985.

Dictionary of Greek and Roman Biography and Mythology. Ed. William Smith. 3 vols. London: Taylor, Walton, and Moberly; John Murray, 1849–1851.

Ethnika. Stephanus of Byzantium. Ed. August Meinek. Graz, Austria: Akademische Druck und Verlagsanstalt, 1958.

The Greek Myths. Robert Graves. Complete and unabridged edition. Mt. Kisco, NY: Moyer Bell, Ltd., 1988.

Hygini Fabulae. Hyginus. Ed. Herbert Jennings Rose. Leiden, Netherlands: A. W. Sijthoff, 1963.

Lexicon. Hesychius of Alexandria. Ed. Mauricius Schmidt. 5 vols. Amsterdam: Hakkert, 1965.

Pauly's Realencyclopädie der classischen Altertumswissenschaft. Herausgegeben von Wilhelm Kroll und Karl Mittelhaus. 68 vols., 15 suppls., register, and index. Stuttgart: Metzler, 1894–1962.

Suidae Lexikon. Suidas. Ed. Ada Adler. Stuttgart: B. G. Teubner, 1967–1971.

What Men or Gods Are These? A Genealogical Approach to Classical Mythology. Fred and Jeanetta Boswell. Metuchen, NJ, and London: Scarecrow Press, 1980.

Finally, I want to thank three individuals for their moral support as well as both direct and indirect assistance. They are Mark Hanrahan of Davis, California; Dr. Anna Strataridakis-Kylafis of the University of Crete at Rethymno; and Soula Philippatou of Athens, Greece.

Women of
Classical Mythology

ABANTIAS was a female descendant of Abas, the twelfth king of Argos and son of Lynceus and Hypermnestra. Thus Danae, granddaughter of Abas, was sometimes referred to as Abantias.

ABARBAREA was a Naiad and wife of Bucolion, the oldest but illegitimate son of Laomedon, king of Troy. Abarbarea bore him several sons, but only two, Aesepus and Pedasus, are named by ancient writers. Some writers do not mention this nymph, but Hesychius ("Abarbareae") mentions Abarbareae or Abarbalaeae as the name of a class of nymphs. [Homer, *Iliad* 6.22.]

ABIA was the nurse of Hyllus, a son of Heracles. She built a temple of Heracles at Ira in Messenia, for which the Heraclid Cresphontes afterward honored her in various ways, especially by changing the name of the town of Ira to Abia. [Pausanias 4.30.1.]

ABROTA was born in Onchestus in Boeotia. Her father was Onchestus, son of Poseidon and founder of the town of Onchestus, where the Onchestian Poseidon had a temple and a statue. She was the sister of Megareus and was said to be exceptionally intelligent and remarkably discreet. She married Nisus, a son of Pandion and king of Megaris. By Nisus she became the mother of Scylla. When she died she was mourned by all the Megarians. Wishing to perpetuate her memory for all time, Nisus ordered all the women to wear a garment of the same kind as Abrota had worn, called *aphabroma*, which was still in use in the time of Plutarch (*Greek Questions* 295). The writer said that when the Megarian women wanted to make a change in fashion, the gods prevented them by an oracle. [Pausanias 9.26.3.]

ACACALLIS was a daughter of Minos and Pasiphae. While she has not shared the fame of her sisters Ariadne and Phaedra, she did lead a most interesting life. She had children by the two handsomest of the Olympian gods and even by the father of the gods. Acacallis was Apollo's first love. With his sister Artemis he came to Tarrha from Aegialae on the mainland for purification after slaying the monster Python. Apollo stayed at the house of Carmanor, where he found Acacallis, a maternal relative of Carmanor; it was not long until he seduced her. Some say Minos banished Acacallis to Libya, where she became the mother of Ammon by Zeus. By Apollo she had two more sons, Amphithemis and Garamas. Amphithemis became the father of Nasamon and Caphaurus, or Cephalion, by the nymph Tritonis. Of Garamas little is known. Some say he was born in Libya when Acacallis fled there, but others say he was the first man ever to be born and therefore from a much earlier era.

Acacallis became the mother of Cydon by Hermes (others say the father was Apollo, and still others that it was Tegeates). Cydon grew up to found the town of Cydonia (modern Hania) in Crete. Some say that Acacallis had still another son (no father mentioned), Oaxus, or Oaxes, in Crete. Others say he was a son of Apollo by Anchiale. In Crete Acacallis was a common name for narcissus. Apollodorus (3.1.2) calls this daughter of Minos Acalle. [Pausanias 7.2.3, 8.53.2; Plutarch, *Agis* 9; Apollonius Rhodius 4.1490; Apollodorus 3.1.2; Stephanus Byzantium, "Oaxos"; Athenaeus 15.681; Hesychius, "Akakallis."]

ACALANTHIS was one of the nine PIERIDES, daughters of Pierus of Emathia in Macedonia.

ACALLE (*See* ACACALLIS)

ACASTE was one of the OCEANIDES. [Hesiod, *Theogony* 355.]

ACCA LARENTIA or LAURENTIA was a rather obscure Roman goddess sometimes identified with Luperca, the wife of Lupercus, who in the shape of a she-wolf nursed Romulus and Remus. She was the wife of Faustulus, the royal shepherd of Amulius who found Romulus and Remus as they were being nursed by the wolf and carried them to his wife to be brought up. Faustulus and Acca Larentia had 12 sons of their own, and Romulus and Remus were adopted and grew up with their foster brothers on the Palatine Hill. Later the college of the Fratres Arvales was founded in memory of the sons of Acca Larentia. She was thought to be connected with the worship of the Lares, not only from similarities of name but from the number of her sons, which corresponds with the number of the 12 country Lares. The day sacred to her also followed the one sacred to the Lares. According to some accounts, she was the she-wolf, *lupa,* that suckled Romulus and Remus.

Lupa was also a colloquialism for prostitute. That identity has to do with a separate story

about Acca Larentia—a story so different, in fact, from the first that there must have been two women of this name. During a festival in the reign of Ancus Martius, the keeper of the temple of Hercules challenged the god to a game of dice. The bargain was that the loser had to treat the other to a sumptuous meal and a beautiful woman, a bet that certainly must have appealed to Hercules' famous appetites. He won, of course, and got the meal and Acca Larentia, a very beautiful prostitute. When Hercules had his fill of her, he advised her to seek the affection of the first man she would meet. The man so met turned out to be a very wealthy Etruscan named Carutius, or Tarrutius, who married her. He died shortly afterward and left her his large estates near Rome, which she in turn bequeathed to the people of Rome. In gratitude for this handsome bequest Ancus, the fourth king of Rome, allowed her to be buried in the Velabrum and instituted an annual festival, the Larentalia, at which sacrifices were offered to the Lares. [Arnobius, *Adversus Nationes* 4.3; Livy 1.5; Massurius Sabinus on Gellius 6.7; Varro, *On the Latin Language* 5.85.]

ACHAEA (1) was a surname of Demeter, by which she was worshipped at Athens by the Gephyraei, a tribe who had emigrated there from Boeotia. [Herodotus 5.61; Plutarch, *Isis and Osiris* 378.]

ACHAEA (2) was a surname of Minerva at Luceria in Apulia, where the votive offerings and the arms of Diomedes were preserved in her temple. [Aristotle, *On Marvelous Things Heard* 117.]

ACHAMANTIS was one of the DANAIDES, daughter of Danaus, who on her wedding night murdered her husband Ecnominus, son of Aegyptus. [Hyginus, *Fables* 170.]

ACHELOIDES (1) were water nymphs, daughters of Achelous, who were sometimes the companions of the Pegasides (Muses). They belonged to a larger class of river nymphs, the Potameides, local divinities named after their rivers. [Columella, *On Country Matters* 10.263.]

ACHELOIDES (2) was a surname of the Sirens, the daughters of Achelous and Sterope, daughter of Porthaon. [Ovid, *Metamorphoses* 5.552,1487; Apollodorus 1.7.10.]

ACHELOIS was one of the seven MUSES said to be daughters of Pierus. [Tzetzes on Hesiod's *Works and Days* 6.]

ACHIROE, Anchinoe, or Anchiroe was a daughter of Nilus, the Nile River. Her history is somewhat confusing because of the different spellings of her name by ancient writers and tentative assignment to her of offspring in quite separate geographical locations. Achiroe, called Anchinoe by Apollodorus (2.1.4), was the wife of Belus, son of Poseidon and Libya, who ruled at Chemnis. By him she became the mother of Aegyptus and Danaus, thereby becoming grandmother to the 50 sons of the first and 50 daughters of the second. According to some, Cepheus and Phineus were also sons of Achiroe and Belus. According to one writer, Ares begot by her a son, Sithon, who became a king in Thrace and had two daughters, Rhoeteia and Pallene. At this point, things become a little muddled, since Egypt and Thrace are quite far apart. Not only that, but at least one writer called Rhoeteia and Pallene sisters of Sithon, not daughters. According to still another writer, Pallene was his daughter by Achiroe(!). It is quite reasonable to assume there might have been two Achiroes—one Egyptian and the other Macedonian—and that the Macedonian one was the mother, not the lover, of Sithon. [Tzetzes on Lycophron 583,1161.]

ACHLYS was the eternal night, said to have been the first being, even preexisting Chaos. Hesiod (*Shield of Heracles* 264), however, called her the personification of misery and sadness, and as such she was represented on the shield of Heracles. She was pale and emaciated, and her teeth constantly chattered while she wept. She had long fingernails, swollen knee-joints, bloody cheeks, and dust-covered shoulders. It is interesting that deep space and misery were thus equated, and that both were conceived as female.

ACHOLOE was mentioned as one of the HARPIES. [Hyginus, *Fables: Preface* 15, *Fables* 14.]

ACIDALIA was a surname of Venus; according to Servius, a commentator on the *Aeneid,* the name derived from the spring Acidalius near Orchomenus, in which Venus used to bathe with the Graces. Others connect the name with the Greek *akides,* i.e., cares or troubles. [Virgil, *Aeneid* 1.720.]

ACIDUSA was the wife of Scamander, son of Deimachus and Glaucia. Scamander obtained a tract of land in Boeotia across which flowed two rivers. He named one of the rivers Glaucia in honor of his mother and the other Scamander, not only after his own name but also that of his maternal grandfather, the river-god Scamander in the plain of Troy. Acidusa benefited from her husband's habit of naming places after his family—he commemorated her by naming a Boeotian spring Acidusa. By Scamander, Acidusa had three daughters, who for one reason or another came to be regarded as minor divinities and were worshipped under the name of "the Maidens." [Plutarch, *Greek Questions* 4.]

ACME was, according to Hyginus (*Fables* 183), one of ten HORAE.

ACMENES was a surname of certain nymphs worshipped at Elis, where a sacred enclosure contained their altar, together with those of other gods. [Pausanias 5.15.4.]

ACRAEA (1) was a daughter of the river-god Asterion near Mycenae, who, together with her sisters Euboea and Prosymna, acted as nurse to Hera. A hill called Acraea opposite the temple of Hera near Mycenae derived its name from her. [Pausanias 2.17.2.]

ACRAEA (2) was an attribute given to several goddesses whose temples were situated upon hills, including Hera, Aphrodite, Athena, and Artemis. The male counterpart was Acraeus. Acraea was a designation used for Athena as protectress of towns, fortresses, and harbors, particularly during wartime. When abandoned by Jason, Medea killed her children by him and fled to Athens in a chariot drawn by winged dragons. Previous to her flight, she placed her younger children on the altar of Hera Acraea as suppliants, but the Corinthians took them away and put them to death. [Apollodorus 1.9.16.]

ACRISIONEIS was a patronymic of Danae, daughter of Acrisius. Homer (*Iliad* 14.319) uses the form Acrisione. [Virgil, *Aeneid* 7.410.]

ACTAEA (1) was one of the NEREIDES, a daughter of Nereus and Doris. [Homer, *Iliad* 18.41; Apollodorus 1.2.7; Hyginus, *Fables* 7.]

ACTAEA (2) was one of the DANAIDES, one of six daughters of Danaus and Pieria. The sons of Aegyptus cast lots for these six, and Periphas got Actaea. [Apollodorus 2.1.5.]

ADAMANTEIA was the name given by Hyginus (*Fables* 139) to Amaltheia, the nurse of Zeus.

ADIANTE was one of the DANAIDES, the daughter of Danaus by Herse. She was paired with Daiphron, one of the youngest sons of Aegyptus. She and Hippodice were the only daughters of Danaus by Herse. [Apollodorus 2.1.5.]

ADICIA was the personification of injustice. Dice, the personification of justice, was represented on the chest of Cypselus as a handsome goddess dragging Adicia, an ugly woman, with one hand, while holding in the other a staff with which she beat her. [Pausanias 5.18.2.]

ADITE was one of the DANAIDES, one of the six daughters of Danaus by Pieria. Six sons of Aegyptus cast lots for them, and Menacles thus acquired Adite as his wife. [Apollodorus 2.1.5.]

ADMETE (1) was one of the OCEANIDES. [Hesiod, *Theogony* 349.]

ADMETE (2) was the daughter of Eurystheus and Antimache or Admete. Eurystheus, cousin of Heracles, succeeded to the throne of Mycenae by being born before Heracles through Hera's manipulation. He also was in charge of selecting the labors Heracles had to perform as penance for the murder of Megara and his children by her. It was at the insistence of Admete that

Heracles was required to perform his ninth labor. Hippolyte, queen of the Amazons, possessed a magnificent girdle, or belt, given to her by Ares. Admete had heard about this splendid belt and had always longed to own it, so she persuaded Eurystheus to have it brought to her as one of Heracles' labors. Heracles was therefore sent to fetch it and, accompanied by a number of volunteers, he sailed out. According to one writer, Admete accompanied him on this expedition.

In another tradition, Admete was originally a priestess of Hera at Argos. She fled with the image of the goddess to Samos. The Argives hired pirates to bring the image back, but the ship on which they loaded the image would not move out of the harbor. They unloaded it and left. When the Samians found it, they tied it to a tree, but Admete purified the image and restored it to the temple of Samos. The Samians celebrated an annual festival, Tonea, to commemorate this event. It is likely that this story was invented by the Argives to prove their worship of Hera was older than that of Samos. It is curious that Admete was selected as the motivator, unless her status as a princess gave a special prestige to the Argive claim. In other respects, the office of priestess seems incongruous with an obviously spoiled daughter who sent a cousin on a perilous mission for the sake of personal vanity. [Tzetzes on Lycophron 1327; Athenaeus 15.447.]

ADMETE (3) was the wife of Eurystheus and mother of Admete (2). According to some, the mother of Admete (2) was Antimache.

ADRASTE (1) was one of the HYADES, usually mentioned with her sisters Eidothea and Althaea. [Hyginus, *Fables* 182.]

ADRASTE (2) was one of the companions of Helen when Telemachus came to Sparta seeking news of Odysseus. When Helen appeared to greet him, Adraste placed a chair for her, and Alcippe brought a rug of soft wool. [Homer, *Odyssey* 4.124.]

ADRASTEIA (1), Adrastea, or Adrastia was a daughter of King Melisseus and Amaltheia of

Crete. When Rhea was pregnant with Zeus, she left Arcadia and went to Crete. She delivered him in a cave on Mount Dicte, then gave him to Adrasteia to rear. In this office Adrasteia was assisted by her sister Ida and by the Curetes, whom a commentator on Callimachus called her brothers. They fed the infant Zeus on the milk of the goat Amaltheia, and the bees of the mountain provided him with honey. This would have been an awesome experience and responsibility for two simple mountain nymphs, as they are usually described. Being daughters of a king rather changes the effect, but we have to wonder how they explained their absence from home. Maybe the king was privy to the undertaking, or perhaps his wife Amaltheia wet-nursed the baby and was somehow confused with the goat. The princess role, however, makes more sense when we read in Apollonius Rhodius (3.132) that Adrasteia gave to the infant Zeus a beautiful globe (*sphaira*) to play with. On some Cretan coins Zeus was represented sitting on a globe. [Apollodorus 1.1.6; Callimachus, *Hymn to Zeus* 47; Diodorus Siculus 5.70; Ovid, *Fasti* 5.115.]

ADRASTEIA (2) was a surname of Nemesis. The name has a meaning close to "unyielding."

ADRASTINE was a female patronymic from Adrastus. Aegiale or Aegialeia was a daughter of Adrastus or of Aegialeus, the son of Adrastus, and thus bore the name of Adrastine. [Homer, *Iliad* 5.412.]

ADRYADES, nymphs of trees, were believed to die together with the trees that had been their abode and with which they had come into existence. They were called Dryades, Hamadryades, or Adryades from *drys*, which signifies not only an oak but any wild-growing lofty tree. They seem to be of Arcadian origin and never appear together with any of the great gods. (*See also* NYMPHS.) [Pausanias 8.4.2; Apollonius Rhodius 2.477; Antoninus Liberalis 31,32; *Homeric Hymn to Aphrodite* 259.]

AEA, a huntress of Colchis, was metamorphosed into the fabulous island bearing the same name in order to rescue her from the pursuit of Phasis, the river-god. [Valerius Flaccus 5.425.]

AEAEA (1) was a surname of Medea derived from Aea (another name for Colchis), the country where her father Aeetes ruled. [Apollonius Rhodius 3.1135.]

AEAEA (2) was a surname of Circe, the sister of Aeetes. Her son Telegonus is likewise mentioned with the surname Aeaeus. [Homer, *Odyssey* 9.32; Apollonius Rhodius 4.559; Propertius 2.23.42.]

AEAEA (3) was a surname of Calypso, who was believed to have inhabited a small island named Aeaea in the straits between Italy and Sicily. [Pomponius Mela 2.7; Propertius 3.10.31.]

AEDON (1) was another case of an evil plan backfiring and plunging its perpetrator into tragedy. Aedon was a daughter of Pandareos of Ephesus. According to Homer (*Odyssey* 19.517), she was the wife of Zethus, king of Thebes, and the mother of Itylus. Zethus' twin brother, Amphion, was married to Niobe; by her he fathered six sons and six daughters. Aedon was insanely envious of Niobe, since she herself had but one son. She eventually devised a plot to kill Amaleus, one of Niobe's sons, but in the dark mistook her own son for her nephew and killed him. One writer adds that she did kill Amaleus, then killed Itylus from fear of Niobe. It is not further explained how this would make a difference, but it may be that such an action might prove her insane and perhaps spare her own life. In any case, Aedon was so grief-stricken that Zeus took pity on her and changed her into a nightingale, whose melancholy song recalls her lamentations for Itylus. Aedon was the word for nightingale in Attic Greek.

Robert Graves in his *Greek Myths* calls the intended victim Sipylus, not Amaleus. While Sipylus was said to be the eldest son of Amphion and Niobe, there is no evidence that he was connected with the Aedon story. Graves also refers to Aedon as the sister of Niobe.

Astute readers will recognize in this story some of the elements of the myth of Procne and Philomela. The name of the slain son, Itys, is almost the same, and one of the sisters was changed into a nightingale, which to this day mourns the death of Itys. [Eustathius on Homer's *Odyssey* 1875.]

AEDON (2) was, according to Antoninus Liberalis (11), the wife of Polytechnus, an artist of Colophon. When she boasted that she lived more happily with her husband than Hera with Zeus, in revenge Hera ordered Eris, the goddess of discord, to induce Aedon to enter into a contest with her husband. Polytechnus was at that time engaged in making a chariot and Aedon a piece of embroidery, and they agreed that whoever finished their work first would receive from the other a female slave as the prize. When Aedon won the contest, Polytechnus went to his wife's father and told him that Aedon was eager to see her sister Chelidonis, and took her with him. On his way home he raped her, dressed her in slave's attire, threatened her into absolute silence, and gave her to his wife as the promised prize. After some time, thinking she was alone, Chelidonis lamented her fate. She was overheard by Aedon, and the two sisters conspired against Polytechnus. They killed his son Itys, whom they served to Polytechnus for dinner. Aedon fled with Chelidonis to her father who, when Polytechnus came in pursuit, had him bound, smeared with honey, and exposed to ants and other insects. Aedon then took pity on him, and her relatives were about to kill her for her display of mercy. About this time, Zeus changed Polytechnus into a pelican, her father into a sea eagle, Chelidonis into a swallow, and Aedon herself into a nightingale. This story is almost identical to that of Procne and Philomela.

AEDOS was the personification of shame or, as some prefer, modesty. We hear of her in only two connections in mythology. When Odysseus married Penelope, her father, Icarius, begged her to remain at Sparta. He even followed the chariot in which the newlyweds were driving away. Not pleased with this situation, Odysseus turned to Penelope and said words to the effect: "Which will it be?" Penelope's only reply was to lower her veil. Icarius had to concede; afterward he raised on that spot a statue of Aedos, which Pausanias (3.20.2) saw about 6 kilometers from the city of Sparta.

Nemesis, the personification of moral reverence for the order of things, of deterrence out of fear of wrongful action, and of conscience, is often mentioned along with Aedos. [Hesiod, *Theogony* 223, *Works and Days* 183.]

AEETIAS, Aeetine, and Aeetis were names sometimes used for Medea, as the daughter of Aeetes, by Roman poets. [Ovid, *Metamorphoses* 79,296, *Heroides* 6.103; Valerius Flaccus 8.233.]

AEGA, or Aegia, is one of those persons of ancient myth whose identity is obscured by variant versions of a story. According to one tradition, she was a daughter of Olenus, son of Hephaestus, and sister of Helice. The sisters are said to have nursed Zeus in Crete, and Aega was later changed by him into the constellation Capella. Another tradition made her the daughter of Melisseus, king of Crete, and she was chosen to suckle the infant Zeus. She could not manage this, so the goat Amaltheia was brought into service. Still others say that Aega was a daughter of Helios and, as the daughter of the sun, dazzling in appearance. She therefore frightened the Titans who were assailing Olympus, and they begged Gaea, their mother, the earth, to remove her from their sight. Gaea accordingly confined her in a cave in Crete, and there she became the nurse of Zeus. Later on, while fighting Titans, Zeus was commanded by an oracle to cover himself with Aega's skin (*aegis*); he did so and raised her among the stars. So, even with three separate fathers assigned by different writers, we can see that in all the stories Aega was regarded as a nurse of Zeus. No attempt seems to be made to combine her office in this matter with the services of Adrasteia and Ida, who are usually called the nurses of Zeus (they too were daughters of Melisseus). The entity of Aega, like that of Amaltheia, seems to be confused between human being and goat. One would hope that it was the goat identity from which Zeus obtained his *aegis*.

By some kind of mythological teleportation Aega became the wife of Arcadian Pan. Never missing an opportunity, Zeus became the father of Aegipan by her, although some claim that Zeus coupled with a goat to produce him. Again there is this strong identification with goats, and it is probably safe to say that the name Aega was translated as "goat," even though some have contended that "gale of wind" might be better, since the rise of the constellation Capella brings storms and tempests. [Hyginus, *Poetic Astronomy* 2.13; Aratus, *Phenomena* 150.]

AEGERIA, or Egeria, was one of the Camenae in Roman mythology. The Camenae were prophetic nymphs often identified with the Greek Muses. Numa, the early Roman king, turned to them for advice about religious worship, and Aegeria became more than just an adviser—she became his lover. In the grove where they met for advice and lovemaking ran a spring that Numa dedicated to the Camenae. This grove was probably near the city of Rome at the Porta Capena at the foot of the Caelian Hill in the valley later called Caparella. When Numa died, Aegeria fled to the valley of Aricia to another grove sacred to her. She was so loud in her lamentations that she disturbed the worship of Diana, which had been brought from Tauris by Orestes and from Greece by Hippolytus.

In one version of the Hippolytus story, Asclepius restored him to life at the request of Artemis, who then carried him to her sanctuary on the shore of Lake Nemi in Italy. When Aegeria fled to Aricia she met Hippolytus, by whom she became the mother of Virbius. Some say that Virbius was a hero-king of Aricia and a favorite of Diana, who, when he died, restored him to life and put him under the care of Aegeria. Still others claim that when Hippolytus was restored to life, Artemis/Diana concealed him in Aricia, changed his name to Virbius, and married him to Aegeria. In his precinct no horses were allowed, and only runaway slaves could be priests. Aegeria was regarded not only as a prophetic divinity but also as a giver of life, and for this reason she was invoked by pregnant women. [Virgil, *Aeneid* 7.761; Servius on Virgil's *Aeneid* 7.761; Ovid, *Metamorphoses* 15.532, *Fasti* 6.745.]

AEGESTA (*See* EGESTA)

AEGIA (*See* AEGA)

AEGIALE (1), or Aegialeia, can be considered almost stereotypical of unfaithful and vindictive wives. She was a daughter of Adrastus and Amphithea and, from her father, often called Adrastine. She had two older sisters, Argeia and Deipyle, who married Tydeus and Polyneices, two principals in the war of the Seven against Thebes. Her brothers were Cyanippus and

Aegialeus, the second of whom was one of the Epigoni. She herself married Diomedes, son of Tydeus and also one of the Epigoni. By this marriage Aegiale became the daughter-in-law of her own sister Deipyle, and one wonders if this circumstance had anything to do with her subsequent behavior. Shortly after the expedition of the Epigoni, in which Aegiale's brother Aegialeus was the only fatality among the seven leaders, Diomedes went off to the Trojan War, in which he was greatly distinguished. Among other glorious achievements he even wounded Aphrodite, and this act was believed to have set in motion his future woes, for Aphrodite was capable of far worse wounding. To help her carry out her revenge was Nauplius, whose son Palamedes had been stoned to death at Troy for a false report of treason. Nauplius spread the report that several of the Greek heroes, including Diomedes, were returning home with Trojan concubines who would replace their wives. Aegiale consequently took a series of lovers and was living with Cometes, son of Sthenelus, when Diomedes returned home. Either of his own accord or expelled by the adulterers, he went to Aetolia. He eventually returned to Argos with Oeneus, his grandfather, but again was forced to leave when he learned that Cometes and Aegiale were planning to murder him. He settled in southern Italy, where he founded several colonies. The subsequent fate of Aegiale is not known. [Homer, *Iliad* 5.412; Apollodorus 1.8.6,9.13; Tzetzes on Lycophron 602.]

AEGIALE (2) was the mother of Alcyone by Aeolus, according to some, although Alcyone's mother is usually given as ENARETE.

AEGINA was the daughter of the god of the Asopus River, which flows from Phliasia through Sicyonia into the Corinthian Gulf. Asopus married Metope, daughter of the river-god Ladon, and had by her two sons, Ismenus and Pelagon, and twenty daughters, one of whom was Aegina. Since she was very beautiful, she attracted the attention of Zeus, who abducted her and carried her from her home in Phlius to the island of Oenone or Oenopia, afterward called Aegina. A little tired of having his beautiful daughters carried away by lustful gods (Poseidon and Apollo were other examples), Asopus went in search of Aegina. At Corinth he learned from Sisyphus, the king (perhaps in exchange for supplying the Acrocorinthus with a spring), the facts about Aegina's disappearance. Asopus then pursued Zeus until the god, by hurling thunderbolts at him, sent him back to his original bed. Pieces of charcoal found in the riverbed in later times were thought to be residue from the stormy struggle. For his interference in the affair, after his death Sisyphus received special punishment in the lower world.

Aegina became by Zeus the mother of Aeacus. His youth was marked by the progressive disappearance of the island's population by a plague or a dragon sent by the ever-jealous Hera. When Aeacus eventually became king, he had almost no subjects to govern, so Zeus restored the people by changing ants into human beings. Aeacus went on to become such a just king that his counsel was sought even by the gods, and after his death he was made one of the judges of the lower world.

After her affair with Zeus, Aegina married Actor, son of Deion, and became by him the mother of Menoetius, who became the father of Patroclus, the famous friend of Achilles. In fact, it was through Aegina that Patroclus and Achilles were related, one being her grandson and the other her great-grandson by the separate lines begun by her two husbands. One commentator (Pythaenetos, quoting the scholiast on Pindar's *Olympian Odes* 9.107) said Menoetius was Actor's son by Damocrateia, a daughter of Aegina and Zeus. This makes sense in terms of putting Patroclus and Achilles in the same generation. In that case, also, Aegina's sexual encounters with the greatest of the gods would have remained inviolate, unless we consider the single account that she was the mother of Sinope (usually called her sister) by Ares. Even here she at least kept with the immortals for lovers. [Apollodorus 3.12.6; Pausanias 2.5.1; Scholiast on Apollonius Rhodius 436.]

AEGINAEA was a surname of Artemis, under which she was worshipped at Sparta. It means either the huntress of chamois or the wielder of the javelin (*aiganei*). [Pausanias 3.14.3.]

AEGLE (1), the most beautiful of the NAIADES, was the daughter of Zeus and Neaera. According to some, by Helios she was the mother of the Charites, but their mother more often was called EURYNOME. [Virgil, *Eclogues* 6.20; Pausanias 9.35.5.]

AEGLE (2) was a sister of Phaethon, and daughter of Helios and Clymene. In her grief at the death of her brother she and her sister HELIADAE were changed into poplars. [Hyginus, *Fables* 154,156.]

AEGLE (3) was one of the HESPERIDES. [Apollodorus 2.5.11; Servius on Virgil's *Aeneid* 4.484.]

AEGLE (4) was a daughter of Panopeus, the Phocian hero. Her distinguished father went with Amphitryon against the Taphians. He took an oath not to embezzle any of the booty but did so. Consequently, his son Epeius was lacking in martial spirit and probably effeminate. Panopeus was also listed among the Calydonian hunters. Aegle was said to be the one for whom Theseus deserted Ariadne. It is difficult to imagine what she was doing on the island of Naxos, which is where Theseus abandoned Ariadne. It is conceivable she was one of the seven maidens intended for sacrifice to the Minotaur. [Plutarch, *Theseus* 20; Athenaeus 13.557.]

AEGLE (5) was one of the daughters of Asclepius by Lampetia, the daughter of Helios, or by Epione. Her name means "Brightness" or "Splendor," and she might have personified the glowing healthfulness of the human body. At least, with the exception of Podaleirius and Machaon, her other brothers and sisters seemed to be personifications of the powers ascribed to their father (e.g., Alexanor, Hygieia, Panaceia).

AEGLEIS was one of the HYACINTHIDES. [Apollodorus 3.15.8.]

AEGOPHAGOS, Goat-Eater, was a surname of Hera at Sparta. In his campaign against the sons of Hippocoon, Heracles did not receive the usual interference from Hera, so he built a shrine to her at Sparta. Having no other victim at hand, he sacrificed goats to her. Sparta was the only place giving this surname to Hera.

AELLA was an Amazon prominent in the story of Heracles' labor involving the fetching of the girdle of Hippolyte. The Amazons were arrayed against the main body of the followers of Heracles, and the most honored of the women were drawn up opposite Heracles himself. The first to join battle with him was Aella, who had been given this name because of her swiftness, but she found her opponent more agile than herself and was killed by him. [Diodorus Siculus 4.16.]

AELLO, or Aellopos, was one of the HARPIES. [Hesiod, *Theogony* 267.]

AELLOPOS was a surname of Iris, the messenger of the gods, by which she is described as swift-footed like a storm wind. [Homer, *Iliad* 8.409.]

AENETE (also called Aenippe) was a daughter of Eusorus and sister of Acamas. Both Eusorus and Acamas, Trojan allies from Thrace, were killed in the war by the Telamonian Ajax. Aenete became the wife of Aeneus, a son of Apollo and Stilbe, and bore to him Cyzicus, who founded the town in Asia Minor by this name. [Apollonius Rhodius 1.950; Orphica, *Argonautica* 502.]

AENIPPE (*See* AENETE)

AEOLIA was the daughter of Amythaon, son of Cretheus and Tyro, and sister of Bias and Melampus. Their mother was Eidomene; she was also their first cousin, since Amythaon married his brother's daughter. Aeolia married Calydon, by whom she became the mother of Epicaste and Protogeneia. Since Calydon was the founder of the town of Calydon, Aeolia can be considered the mother of the Calydonian dynasty. [Apollodorus 1.7.7.]

AEOLIS is the patronymic designating the female descendants of Aeolus. Canace and Alcyone, his daughters, were sometimes referred to

by this name. [Ovid, *Metamorphoses* 11.573, *Heroides* 11.5.]

AERO was the daughter of Oenopion loved by Orion. (*See* MEROPE.)

AEROPE (1) was a daughter of Catreus, king of Crete, and granddaughter of Minos. From the very start, fortune did not smile on her. Catreus learned from an oracle that one of his children would kill him. His son Althaemenes left Crete voluntarily, taking with him one of his sisters, Apemosyne. The other two daughters, Clymene and Aerope, Catreus gave to Nauplius to sell in a foreign land. Nauplius married Clymene and gave Aerope to Pleisthenes, the son of Atreus. By him she became the mother of Agamemnon, Menelaus, and Anaxibia. Pleisthenes was sickly and died young; Atreus then married Aerope, and adopted and reared his grandchildren. Thyestes, the younger brother of Atreus, seduced Aerope. About the same time, the rule of Mycenae became available through the death of Eurystheus, and an oracle said a son of Pelops should be chosen king. Atreus had found in one of his flocks a lamb with golden fleece; instead of dedicating it to Artemis as he had promised, he hid the fleece in a chest. Aerope found it and secretly gave it to her lover. Thyestes proposed that the rule of Mycenae should go to the possessor of the fleece, and the unsuspecting Atreus readily agreed. So Thyestes was declared king, but the gods intervened. It was agreed that if the sun changed its course, Atreus would be king.

Then the sun set in the east, and Thyestes' exceedingly short reign was over. So was his residence in Mycenae, since Atreus promptly exiled him for the theft of and deception about the golden fleece. Atreus found out about the adulterous affair and exacted a terrible revenge. He recalled Thyestes from exile, pretending to forgive him, but meanwhile he had killed Thyestes' three sons, Aglaus, Callileon, and Orchomenus. He had them dismembered, boiled, and served to Thyestes during a feast. After Thyestes had eaten, the grisly heads were brought in. Once more Atreus drove Thyestes from the country, then turned his attention to Aerope, whom he drowned. Interestingly, this was a fate originally intended for her back in

Crete, according to some, when she had been caught by her father in bed with a lover.

Aerope is noteworthy not only for her tempestuous career but for being the blood link between the royal lines of Mycenae and Crete. Few people ever stop to consider that Agamemnon and Menelaus were great-grandsons of Minos and thereby second cousins of Idomeneus. This could even account for the entrance of Crete into the Trojan War. [Apollodorus 3.2.2; Euripides, *Orestes* 5, *Helen* 397; Hyginus, *Fables* 87.]

AEROPE (2) was the daughter of Cepheus and by Ares the mother of a son, Aeropus. She died at the moment she gave birth to the child; Ares, wishing to save it, caused the child to derive milk from the breast of its dead mother. This wonder gave rise to the god's surname, Aphneius (Abundant). Under this name Ares had a temple on Mount Cresius near Tegea.

AEROPE (3), a daughter of Oenopion and Helice, is also called Haero, Maerope, and MEROPE.

AEROPE (4) was, according to one writer, the mother of Circe by Hyperion. [Orphica, *Argonautica* 1215.]

AESA was a personification of destiny. By some she was considered one of the Moirae, or Fates. Some made her an exclusively Argive divinity, and others identified her with Ate. Aeschylus (*Libation-Bearers* 647) describes her as bearing a sword.

AESCHREIS was one of the THESPIADES, a daughter of Thespius and Megamede, by whom Heracles became the father of Leucones. [Apollodorus 2.7.8.]

AESYLE was called one of three HYADES by Eustathius (on Homer's *Iliad* 1156). The usual number given was seven.

AETAE (*See* LITAE)

AETHERIA was a daughter of Helios and Clymene, and one of the HELIADAE or Phaethontiades.

AETHILLA (*See* AETHYLLA)

AETHRA (1) was a daughter of Pittheus of Troezen and therefore sometimes called Pittheis. Pittheus was one of the sons of Pelops and therefore a brother to Atreus and Thyestes. His wife's name is never mentioned. We do know that Aethra had one sister, Henioche. Pittheus emigrated to this region of the Argolid peninsula with another brother, Troezen. Troezen incorporated the cities of Hyperes and Anthea into a single city, and the two brothers shared the reign with Aetius, who had inherited the throne from his father Anthas. Pittheus outlived the other two and became the sole ruler. He named the merged cities after his brother and founded there the temple of Apollo Thearius, said to be the oldest Greek temple. He was considered a wise king and was famous for his eloquence. He is said to have written a book on public speaking.

When Aethra reached marriageable age she was courted by Bellerophon, but he was banished from Corinth before the nuptials could take place, and there was little hope of his return. Pittheus became concerned that his daughter might have trouble presenting him with an heir, so when Aegeus, king of Athens, paid a visit to Troezen, Pittheus contrived to bring Aegeus and Aethra together. Aegeus had been married twice but still was childless, probably, he decided, because of some slight to Aphrodite, whose worship he introduced at Athens by way of conciliation. He visited Delphi to consult the oracle about begetting heirs, and the Pythia gave him a characteristically obscure answer: "The bulging mouth of the wineskin, o best of men, loose not until thou hast reached the height of Athens." On his way back to Athens, he took a complicated detour by way of Troezen. He might have done so for two reasons. Along with other attributes, Pittheus had a reputation for being a seer and might therefore be able to interpret the oracle. Also, Pittheus had close relatives in Attica who might have talked about their spouseless royal cousin in Troezen. In any case, Aegeus was a guest at the palace and revealed to Pittheus the message of the oracle. Pittheus saw at once that the message said "Don't drink till you get home," and correctly interpreted it to carry the implicit complement "unless you want to father an illegitimate heir." The message he gave to Aegeus, however, probably did not go beyond telling him that he would become the father of a famous son. Pittheus proceeded to start his own prophecy in motion by getting Aegeus drunk and into Aethra's bed. Later in the night, Athena came to Aethra in a dream and told her to go to the tomb of Sphaerus, one of Pelops' charioteers, and pour libations.

Aethra did so at once, not bothering to question this rather curious command. She waded from the mainland to the island of Sphaeria, where she proceeded to perform the holy rite. She was interrupted by Poseidon who, with the help of Athena, had contrived to lure Aethra to the island. He enjoyed her and went his way, leaving Aethra baffled by the events of the night. Presumably a virgin, in a single night she was deflowered by a drunken Athenian king and then raped by the god of the sea. After being violated by the god, she returned to bed with Aegeus. Upon waking and seeing where he was, he begged Aethra that if she should give birth to a male child she bring him up without saying who the father was. Otherwise, he said, the boy would be in danger from the sons of Pallas, who contended for the throne of Athens. Before sailing back to Athens in time to celebrate the Panathenaea, he hid a sword and his sandals under a rock on the road from Troezen to Hermione. Upon becoming of age, the boy would be shown the rock. If he could lift it and recover the sword and sandals, he was to be made acquainted with the circumstances of his birth and sent to Athens.

There was always doubt whether or not Poseidon really was the father of Theseus. On the one hand was Aegeus' earlier inability to produce an heir, and on the other was the Pythian warning he had defied. Aethra *had* gone to Sphaeria on the night of her coupling with Aegeus, so who was to say? In any case, Aethra had the island renamed Hiera, or Holy, and founded on it a temple of Athena Apaturia (Deceitful). She also established a tradition that every Troezenian girl should from that time dedicate her girdle to the goddess upon getting married. This action was a curious one, and it is hard to think of reasons. Did Aethra secretly suspect that Poseidon had ennobled her womb and, therefore, was this an act of gratitude to Athena for her assistance in the matter? Or was this an ironical gesture, wherein virgins capitulated their virginity (symbolized by the girdle) at the altar of a deceiving goddess?

At a tiny place called Genethlium near the harbor of Troezen, Aethra gave birth to Theseus. No explanation has been given as to why she was here rather than at the palace for this event. It might have been for reasons of safety from Aegeus' enemies, except that Theseus was then brought up at Troezen, with Connidas as his tutor, with no seeming concern for danger. The years passed, and apparently Aethra kept her promise about bringing up the boy in secret, for not even Aegeus appears to have been informed of the existence of Theseus, in spite of the relatively short distance by water from Troezen to Athens. One might assume he was at least curious, but during this time he had married Medea, who promised him a royal son. Aethra, meanwhile, did not marry and seemed content to attend to the rearing of her son, who might or might not have been half-divine.

When Theseus had developed sufficiently, Aethra led him to the rock under which the tokens had been left. It is conceivable that rumors of his divine conception had reached Theseus, but even if he believed such reports he could still claim a mortal father as well, particularly one so highly placed as king of Athens. Theseus moved the rock with ease and recovered the sword and sandals. After that he went to Delphi and sacrificed some of his hair to the god. Upon his return, he insisted on setting out at once for Athens. Emulating Heracles, he chose to go by land, even though Aethra and Pittheus begged him not to, since the route was notorious for its brigands and monsters.

His adventures along the way are not relevant to this account, except that he made Aethra a grandmother by producing a son, Melanippus, with Perigune, daughter of Sinis, one of the isthmian robbers he slew. He also killed Sciron, another brigand and his first cousin, son of Aethra's sister Henioche.

He was happily received by Aegeus, who was still without an heir. His arrival in Athens was not welcomed by Medea or by the Pallantidae, who were in line for the throne. Medea tried to poison him on his first night at the palace and was exiled by Aegeus. Theseus had to overcome the Pallantidae in a battle. He then went against the Marathonian bull and conquered it. He volunteered as one of the youths sent in tribute to Crete for sacrifice to the fearful Minotaur. He killed the monster and fled Crete with Ariadne, daughter of Minos, abandoning her on the island of Naxos. Some say he left her because of his love for Aegle, daughter of Panopeus. Believing Theseus to be dead, Aegeus killed himself. It seems very likely that Aethra never again saw Aegeus after conceiving Theseus.

More than likely Theseus visited home after his Cretan triumph. We know he was in Troezen long enough to abduct a woman named Anaxo, rape her two daughters, and kill her sons, but we do not know the reason for this violent behavior. Somewhat later he married Periboea, daughter of Alcathous of Megara, before she married Telamon. He went either alone or with his cousin Heracles to the country of the Amazons and received Antiope as reward for his valor. While on the campaign he founded Pythopolis on the Euxine Sea. The Amazons retaliated for the abduction of Antiope by marching on Athens, but were repelled at the very gates; Antiope was killed in the battle. Earlier she had borne Theseus a son, Hippolytus. After that, he married Phaedra, the sister of Ariadne, and this was perhaps a political marriage. After bearing two sons to Theseus, Acamas and Demophon, Phaedra fell in love with Hippolytus, her stepson, and brought about his death, after which she killed herself. Theseus is also recorded as being married to Iope, daughter of Iphicles, and to Hippe. Some writers have taken these names to be shortened forms of Antiope and Hippolyte (for some have said that Theseus was married to Hippolyte instead of Antiope).

This vastly abbreviated sketch of Theseus' life is an effort to show the succession of Aethra's daughters-in-law and grandchildren. There is no record that she ever became part of Athenian court life. She and Pittheus, it seems, remained in Troezen, where Hippolytus had been sent for rearing and educating.

When he was 50 years of age, Theseus and his friend Peirithous abducted Helen from Sparta when she was still a young girl. It is likely that Theseus planned to marry her when she came of age, for the two friends had vowed to marry daughters of Zeus. He secreted her at Aphidna, a town about 26 kilometers north of Athens, and summoned Aethra from Troezen to superintend her. After that, he and Peirithous journeyed to Epeirus to one of the entrances of the underworld in order that Peirithous might abduct Persephone. They were apprehended and imprisoned, but Theseus was later freed by his cousin Heracles.

During the absence of Theseus, the Dioscuri had come with an army to Aphidna and freed their sister, taking her back to Sparta. They also took Aethra, who by now was in her mid- to late sixties, and Thisadie, sister of Peirithous, who was at Aphidna with Aethra. Aethra remained with Helen, voluntarily it is said, during her relatively short marriage to Menelaus and through the birth of Hermione. It is interesting that no effort was made by Theseus to secure the release of his mother. Perhaps she had sent word to him that she chose to remain in Sparta. It was disclosed that she even encouraged Helen to leave Menelaus and go with Paris. When this happened, Aethra was taken along to Troy as Helen's slave.

Theseus meanwhile had returned to Athens to a miserable political situation. In despair he sent his sons to his friend Elephenor in Euboea and went into exile, but this decision must have come after two or three years of effort to restore things. Theseus ended up in Scyros, where the king, Lycomedes, probably fearing so powerful a man, pushed him from a cliff.

Acamas, Theseus' son, went with Diomedes to Troy before the war to try to recover Helen. He recognized his grandmother and also fell in love with Laodice, one of Priam's daughters. A son, Munitus, was born to them, and Aethra brought him up. Both Acamas and Demophon went to the Trojan War, and after the fall of Troy, Acamas, Aethra, and Munitus set out to return home. Munitus died from a snakebite on the way, but Acamas and Aethra reached Attica safely, and Acamas reassumed the throne. Some say that Aethra killed herself when she learned of Theseus' death, but this is not too likely. According to even clumsy reckoning, he had been dead for ten years, and Aethra had not seen him for perhaps another five prior to her going to Troy. It is more likely that she died of old age.

Aethra is most interesting, not only in a near-historical context but also for the long chronology she helps to establish. Remarkably she is involved with four generations—Aegeus, Theseus, Acamas, and Munitus. It is even more remarkable that she is separately involved in two of the greatest stories in mythology—the Theseus saga and the Trojan War—which are not closely related. As a person, she appears for most of her life as subservient to other people, either as a nurse, companion, or slave, enjoying no independence or power even though she was part of two royal families. From a mythographic perspective she is important, since she more or less establishes that Menelaus and Agamemnon were sons of Pleisthenes rather than of Atreus, since otherwise they would be of her generation. Even so, Theseus was as much as 20 years older than Agamemnon—too old to participate in the Trojan War, even if he had lived to do so.

Aethra was represented in bondage to Helen on the chest of Cypselus and in the painting of Polygnotus in the Lesche at Delphi. [Ovid, *Heroides* 10.31; Plutarch, *Theseus* 3,4; Apollodorus 3.15.7; Pausanias 1.14.6, 2.31.12,32.7, 4.19.1, 10.25.2.]

AETHRA (2), one of the OCEANIDES, was the mother of the Hyades and Hesperides by Atlas. The Pleiades have also been called her daughters, although their mother is usually called Pleione, hence their name. [Ovid, *Fasti* 5.169; Eustathius on Homer's *Iliad* 1155.]

AETHUSA was a daughter of Poseidon and the Pleiad Alcyone, and sister of Hyrieus, Hyperenor, Hyperes, and Anthas. Hyperes and Anthas were kings of Troezen, probably concurrently, and had neighboring towns named for them. Hyrieus was the founder of Hyria in Boeotia and father of Orion. Aethusa was loved by Apollo and became by him the mother of Eleuther. According to one account, she was also mother by him of Linus, but most accounts call his mother Psamathe. Eleuther grew up to found Eleutherae in Boeotia. He is credited with having erected the first statue of Dionysus and with

spreading the worship of the god. His grandson Poemander—and thus Aethusa's great-grandson—founded Tanagra. [Apollodorus 3.10.1; Pausanias 9.20.2.]

AETHYIA was a surname of Athena, under which she was worshipped in Megaris. The word *aethyia* signifies a diver and figuratively a ship, so the name must have reference to the goddess teaching the art of shipbuilding or navigation. The tomb of Pandion was shown in the territory of Megara near the rock of Athena Aethyia on the seacoast. [Pausanias 1.5.3; Lycophron 359; Tzetzes on Lycophron 359.]

AETHYLLA was a daughter of Laomedon and sister of Priam, Tithonus, Lampus, Clytius, Hicetaon, Bucolion, Hesione, Cilla, Astyoche, Medesicaste, and Procleia. When Troy fell, Aethylla, Astyoche, Medesicaste, and other women were taken captive. It is not clear why, but the vessel carrying them ended up in southern Italy in a river near the present-day city of Crotone. It is likely that the Greek ships were blown off course or had gone astray. Dreading to contemplate the rest of their lives as slaves, the Trojan women set fire to the ships, and from this act the river was called Navaethus (or Neaethus), which means "burned ships." The women were later referred to as Nauprestides. Having lost their vessels, the Greeks settled there and married their captives. This story is not only interesting in its own right but also because it introduces Trojan ancestry to Italy prior to the arrival of Aeneas.

Another version of the story has Aethylla becoming the captive of Protesilaus. On the way home he landed at the Macedonian peninsula of Pallene. When he went ashore in search of water, Aethylla and the other captive women burned his ships. Protesilaus had to remain on Pallene, where he founded the city of Scione. It is doubtful that he or anyone else married Aethylla, since she must have been advanced in age by this time. This version suggests that later residents of Scione needed a noble heritage and invented the story. Protesilaus was, according to most accounts, the first Greek to die at Troy. [Tzetzes on Lycophron 232,467,921,1075; Conon, *Narrations* 13; Strabo 6.1.12.]

AETNA was a Sicilian nymph, a daughter of Gaea by Uranus or Oceanus, or of Briareus, the giant. When Hephaestus and Demeter disputed the possession of Sicily, she acted as arbitrator. Her decisions must have been favorable to Hephaestus, since she became by him the mother of the Palici. These Sicilian demons, however, were most often called twin sons of Zeus by Thaleia, the daughter of Hephaestus. Mount Aetna in Sicily was believed to have derived its name from her. Zeus buried a few giants under Mount Aetna, and it was here that Hephaestus and the Cyclopes forged thunderbolts for him. Both these circumstances helped the inhabitants explain the rumblings and eruptions. [Servius on Virgil's *Aeneid* 9.584; Euripides, *Cyclops* 296; Propertius 3.15.21; Cicero, *On Divination* 2.19.]

AETOLE was a surname of Artemis by which she was worshipped at Naupactus. In her temple was a statue representing her as throwing a javelin. [Pausanias 10.38.6.]

AGAMEDE (1) was a daughter of Augeas and wife of Mulius. Her husband was acquainted with the pharmaceutical properties of all the plants that grew on earth, but apparently he was unable to find one that could overcome his sterility. Agamede, however, managed to provide three sons—Belus, Actor, and Dictys—by Poseidon, and it is unfortunate that we know nothing else about the circumstances. It is remarkable, though, that Poseidon returned to her again and again; usually with the gods it was a one-time affair with mortal women. Mulius' scientific knowledge was snuffed out by Nestor in a war between the Pylians and the Epeians. [Homer, *Iliad* 11,738–739; Hyginus, *Fables* 157.]

AGAMEDE (2) was a daughter of Macaria, the daughter of Heracles. Agamede, a place in Lesbos, was said to have derived its name from her. [Stephanus Byzantium, "Agamede."]

AGANIPPE (1) was a daughter of the river-god Permessus. She was a nymph of the spring of the same name at the foot of Mount Helicon in Boeotia. This spring was considered sacred to the Muses and had the power of inspiring those who drank of it. For this reason the Muses are some-times called Aganippides. [Pausanias 9.29.5; Virgil, *Eclogues* 10.12.]

AGANIPPE (2) was the wife of Acrisius and, according to some accounts, the mother of Danae, although EURYDICE is usually called her mother. [Hyginus, *Fables* 63; Scholiast on Apollonius Rhodius 4.1091.]

AGANIPPIDES was a name sometimes given to the Muses, so-called from the fountain Aganippe at the foot of Mount Helicon, which was considered sacred to them. [Pausanias 9.29.5.]

AGAVE (1) was a daughter of Cadmus and Harmonia, who along with her sisters seemed to be born under an evil star. Her sisters were Autonoe, Ino, and Semele, and she had one brother, Polydorus. She married Echion, one of the Sparti who had sprung from the dragon's teeth sown by Cadmus at the founding of Thebes, and their only child was Pentheus. Echion helped Cadmus build Thebes, and he also dedicated a temple to Cybele in Boeotia.

When Semele, during her pregnancy with Dionysus, was destroyed by the splendor of Zeus, Agave and her other sisters spread the report that Semele had been promiscuous and was trying to conceal her guilt by pretending divine fatherhood for her unborn child. They said she deserved what she got as punishment for her deceitfulness. This malicious gossip was a big mistake, and the sisters met with various calamities as a result, even though retribution took many years. Pentheus, for example, had time to grow to manhood and acquire the throne of Thebes. Some say he directly succeeded Cadmus, who abdicated to migrate to Illyria. Others say that Pentheus usurped the throne from Polydorus, his uncle and the only son of Cadmus. In any case, he was ruling when Dionysus came home after traveling over the world teaching viticulture and establishing himself as god of wine. As was his custom, Dionysus immediately set out to recruit the women of the region as followers, and soon crowds of them began celebrating his riotous festivals on Mount Cithaeron. Pentheus was not happy with these drunken orgies that put a considerable segment of his population beyond his control, but he was also curious. Spying on the proceedings by climbing a tree, he was observed by Agave. Inflamed with wine and Dionysiac frenzy, she thought he was a wild beast. Agave and her sisters pulled him from the tree and tore him to pieces. The women were afterward commanded by an oracle to locate the tree and to worship it like the god Dionysus himself. Two carved images of the god were accordingly fashioned from the tree and venerated from that time.

After such a grisly crime it was customary for the perpetrator to commit suicide, but it seems Agave followed her father to Illyria, where she married Lycotherses, the king. (There is no record of what happened to Echion, but it is safe to assume he died many years before.) Agave later killed Lycotherses in order to gain the kingdom for her father. [Apollodorus 3.4.2,5.2; Ovid, *Metamorphoses* 3.714–725; Hyginus, *Fables* 184,240,254; Theocritus, *Idylls* 26; Euripides, *Bacchanals*; Pausanias 2.2.6.]

AGAVE (2) was one of the NEREIDES, daughters of Nereus and Doris. [Apollodorus 1.2.7.]

AGAVE (3) was one of the DANAIDES, one of the four daughters of Danaus by Europa. She was drawn by lot by Lycus, son of Aegyptus. [Apollodorus 2.1.5.]

AGAVE (4) was one of the AMAZONS. [Hyginus, *Fables* 163.]

AGDISTIS was a hermaphrodite, but for purposes consistent with the theme of this book will be referred to as female. She came into being when Zeus had an involuntary nocturnal emission, which impregnated Gaea (the earth, his grandmother). From this most curious union came Agdistis, who had sexual organs of both genders. Even the gods feared the superhuman strength of this strange being and apparently agreed the creature was safer without male organs, which they cut off. From the severed penis grew an almond tree. Nana, the daughter of the river-god Sangarius, happened by one day and put one of the almonds in her vagina. At once she became pregnant with Attis. She exposed the boy when he was born, but he was suckled by goats and later raised by shepherds. When he

grew up, he was of such startling beauty that Agdistis fell in love with him. His relatives became anxious about this and sent him to the city of Pessinus in Galatia, where he became betrothed to the king's daughter. During the opening of the wedding ceremony, Agdistis appeared, and Attis went into a fit of madness. He fled to the mountains where he castrated himself and bled to death. His spirit entered a pine tree, and violets sprang from his blood.

Agdistis begged Zeus, her father, to keep the body of her beloved from decomposition, and he agreed. A tomb was built for the incorruptible body on Mount Dindymas in the sanctuary of Cybele. From that time, the priests of the temple had to undergo emasculation in memory of Attis. Cybele and Agdistis became identified, and a festival was held each spring to honor Attis and Cybele Agdistis. A pine tree was covered with violets and carried to the shrine of Cybele. Then with wildly raucous music and rites of abandoned sorrow, the population sought and mourned for Attis on the mountains. On the third day he was found again, and the image of the goddess was purified for her part in his death. After that, a riotous feast of joy was celebrated. It should be mentioned that Rhea, the mother of Zeus, was called Agdistis in Pessinus; she was also identified with Cybele. [Pausanias 7.17.10; Hesychius, "Agdistis"; Strabo 12.5.3; Arnobius, *Adversus Nationes* 9.5.4.]

AGELEIA, or Ageleis, was an epithet of Athena, meaning "Driver of Spoil" or "the Forager," and these meanings had to do with her warlike nature, particularly in her role as protectress of the people. [Homer, *Iliad* 4.128, 5.765, 6.269, 15.213, *Odyssey* 3.378.]

AGLAIA (1) was one of the CHARITES and therefore a daughter of Zeus and Eurynome. Her sisters were Thaleia and Euphrosyne; Aglaia was the youngest of the three. She was a wife of Hephaestus and lived in his palace. [Hesiod, *Theogony* 945; Homer, *Iliad* 2.672.]

AGLAIA (2) was the wife of Charopus, king of Syme, and by him the mother of Nireus. Nothing further is known of her or her husband, but next to Achilles, Nireus was the handsomest Greek at Troy—so handsome, in fact, that his beauty became proverbial. He was unwarlike but made up for this by bravado, since he led a small number of men from the tiny island of Syme in three ships against Troy. In the war he killed Hiera, wife of Telephus, in Mysia and was later killed by Telephus' son Eurypylus before the walls of Troy. His tomb was in the Troad. Before the war he had been one of Helen's suitors. [Homer, *Iliad* 2.671; Diodorus Siculus 5.53; Lucian, *Dialogues of the Dead* 9.]

AGLAIA (3), according to some, was mother of Melampus and Bias by Amythaon. Others say their mother was EIDOMENE or Rhodope. [Diodorus Siculus 4.68.]

AGLAIA (4), a daughter of Mantineus, was the wife of Abas, king of Argos, and therefore the mother of the Perseid dynasty. She was sometimes called Ocaleia. Abas was the only heir of the mass wedding of the sons of Aegyptus with the daughters of Danaus because Lynceus, his father, was the only Aegyptid spared by the Danaid brides on that bloody wedding night. Aglaia and Abas produced twin sons, Acrisius and Proetus, who quarreled even in the womb, and a daughter, Eidomene, who married Amythaon and became the mother of Melampus and Bias. Abas turned over the kingdom to his twin sons and migrated to Phocis, probably accompanied by Aglaia, where he founded the town of Abae. While still at Argos he had a mistress by whom he produced Lyrcus, founder of Lyrceia near Argos. [Apollodorus 2.2.1; Pausanias 2.12.2,16.2, 10.35.1; Scholiast on Euripides' *Orestes* 953.]

AGLAIA (5) was one of the THESPIADES, daughter of Thespius and Megamede, who became by Heracles the mother of Antiades. [Apollodorus 2.7.8.]

AGLAOPE was one of the SIRENS; her two sisters are usually called Peisinoe and Thelxiepeia. [Tzetzes on Lycophron 712; Apollodorus, *Epitome* 7.18.]

AGLAOPHEME was one of two SIRENS. [Eustathius on Homer's *Odyssey* 1709.]

AGLAOPHONOS was one of three SIRENS, the other two being Thelxiope, or Thelxione, and Molpe. [Scholiast on Apollonius Rhodius 4.892.]

AGORAEA was an epithet given to Athena and Artemis as protectors of the assemblies of the people in the agora. [Pausanias 3.11.8, 5.15.3.]

AGRAEA (*See* AGROTERA)

AGRAULOS (1) was a daughter of Actaeus, the first king of Athens. By her husband Cecrops she became the mother of Erysichthon, Agraulos (2), Herse, and Pandrosos. This might have presented certain difficulties since Cecrops, an autochthon, most often has been described as having the body of a serpent from the waist down. Apart from the physiological problem, there are other reasons not to accept a literal interpretation of this story. While some women in mythology might have coupled now and then with bulls, swans, and other animals (usually gods in animal forms), they did not deliberately marry men with animal parts. Also, with a half-serpent father, Agraulos (2), Herse, and Pandrosos would not have gone insane from fear at the sight of the infant Erichthonius. Two of these daughters had offspring by gods, and both began lines of prominent families—the Daedalids and the Ceryces. The son, Erysichthon, died while still quite young during a journey back from Delos, where he had gone to bring back a statue of Eileithyia, the goddess of childbirth. There is something about this half-told story that triggers the historical imagination, since it seems to gain significance from its lack of relatedness to the main story. [Apollodorus 3.14.2; Pausanias 1.2.5.]

AGRAULOS (2) was a daughter of Cecrops and Agraulos (1), and sister of Herse, Pandrosos, and Erysichthon. The three daughters occupied a dwelling on the Acropolis; their brother had died on a religious mission to Delos. Agraulos became the mother of Alcippe by Ares and, according to some, of Ceryx by Hermes. From Ceryx arose the priestly family of the Ceryces. This second liaison might account for her jealousy of her sister Herse, with whom Hermes fell in love while visiting their home during a celebration of the Panathenaea. Agraulos tried to prevent the god from entering the house, but he changed her into stone and proceeded to have his way with Herse, which resulted in the birth of Cephalus. One is tempted to believe that Agraulos was only temporarily immobilized, because it makes it easier to fit in the most famous story of the sisters.

Hephaestus, the blacksmith god, became aroused one day when Athena visited his shop, and he attempted to force her. She sidestepped his thrust so that he ejaculated on her leg; she wiped away the sperm with a piece of wool and threw it on the ground. A child grew up from this union of sperm and earth. This was Erichthonius, who had the lower body of a serpent. Apparently accepting at least a tiny part in the maternity of the child, Athena adopted him and put him in a closed basket, which she placed under the care of the daughters of Cecrops with a stern warning not to peer inside. She might as well have shown them Erichthonius from the start, since they did not waste any time looking into the basket. When they saw the snaky baby they promptly went mad and jumped from the highest point of the Acropolis. This must have been Athena's intention, since the baby would have been hissing for food before too long, and the sisters would have had to open the basket to feed him. The child crawled off into the shield of Athena and grew up to be one of the fathers of the city.

Another story makes Agraulos a heroine. Athens was being besieged, and an oracle declared that the city would be victorious if someone would sacrifice his or her life. Agraulos came forward and threw herself from the cliff of the Acropolis, and the grateful Athenians built a temple to her on the Acropolis. It became a custom for young Athenians on receiving their first suit of armor to take an oath that they would defend Athens to the very last. One of the demes of Attica was named for her, and a festival was celebrated at Athens in her honor. According to one writer, she was also worshipped in Cyprus, where human sacrifices were offered to her. [Pausanias 1.18.2; Hyginus, *Fables* 166; Ovid, *Metamorphoses* 2.710; Herodotus 8.53; Plutarch, *Alcibiades* 15; Stephanus Byzantium, "Agraule"; Porphyry, *On Abstinence* 1.2.]

AGRIOPE (1), according to some, was the mother of Phoenix by Agenor. Most writers call his mother TELEPHASSA.

AGRIOPE (2) was, according to some, a nymph married to Orpheus. After a visit to Egypt, Orpheus joined the Argonauts and sailed to Colchis. On his return he married Eurydice, whom some called Agriope, and settled among the Thracian Cicones. [Diodorus Siculus 4.25; Hyginus, *Fables* 164.]

AGROTERA, the Huntress, was a surname of Artemis. When Artemis arrived on the mainland from Delos, she was believed to have hunted first at Agrae, just across the Ilissus River from Athens. Here a temple was erected to Artemis Agrotera and within it was a statue of her carrying a bow. Agrotera means the same thing as Agraea (cf. Apollo Agraeus). She was also worshipped under this name at Aegeira. At Megara there were temples of Artemis Agrotera and Apollo Agraeus built by Alcathous, son of Pelops, in gratitude for his success in slaying the Cithaeronian lion and thus obtaining Euaechme and succession to the throne. At Ambracia the people of the city in gratitude erected a statue to Artemis Agrotera for having ridded them of the tyrant Phalaecus. She caused him to discover a lion cub while he was hunting. When he picked it up, its mother came forth and tore him to pieces. [Homer, *Iliad* 21.471; Pausanias 1.19.7, 7.26.2; Antoninus Liberalis 4.]

ALALCOMENEIS was a surname of Athena, derived from the hero Alalcomenes, or from the Boeotian village of Alalcomenae, where she was said to have been born. In times of war, fortresses, towns, and harbors were under her special protection, so others derive the name from the verb *alalkein,* "to defend strongly." [Homer, *Iliad* 4.8; Stephanus Byzantium, "Alalkomenion."]

ALALCOMENIA was one of the PRAXIDICAE.

ALCAEA was a daughter of Hypseus, a king of the Lapithae, and Chlidanope, and sister of Cyrene, Themisto, and Astyageia. While her sisters were quite well known, nothing whatsoever has been written of Alcaea. It is likely she died as a young girl.

ALCANDRA was the wife of Polybus at Thebes in Egypt. Polybus gave hospitality to Menelaus and Helen while they were in Egypt. Alcandra gave Helen a golden distaff and a basket with wheels. [Homer, *Odyssey* 4.126.]

ALCATHOE, or Alcithoe, was one of the MINYADES.

ALCE (1) was a daughter of Rhea Cybele by Olympus, and sister of Midas and Nicaea. [Diodorus Siculus 3.57, 5.49.]

ALCE (2) was one of the female DOGS of Actaeon.

ALCEIS was a daughter of Antaeus, a king of Irasa, a town in the territory of Cyrene. He promised his exceedingly beautiful daughter to whoever could conquer him in a footrace. The prize was won by Alexidamus. Some call her Barce. [Pindar, *Pythian Odes* 9.108.]

ALCESTIS, or Alceste, is one of the most admirable women in mythology. She is almost symbolic of connubial devotion and sacrifice. She was the loveliest of the daughters of Pelias and Anaxibia, and was probably quite young when her father connived to send Jason, her stepcousin, on the perilous quest known as the Argonaut. Her brother was Acastus, and her sisters were Peisidice, Pelopeia, Hippothoe, Medusa, Euadne, Amphinome, and Asteropeia.

When the *Argo* returned to Iolcus with most of its crew alive, two major events shook Alcestis' life. One was her wooing by Admetus, the son of Pheres; he was half-brother to her father and king of nearby Pherae. Admetus had been on the Calydonian boar hunt as well as the Argonaut and now had become king after his father's death. He was well favored, even to having in his service during this time the god Apollo, who was obliged to serve a mortal for one year for having slain one of the Cyclopes (and who also was probably in love with him). Admetus asked Pelias for the hand of Alcestis, but

his uncle agreed to such a union only if Admetus would come to her in a chariot drawn by lions and boars. Admetus was able to accomplish this with the assistance of Apollo, and Pelias was obliged to make good his bargain. On his wedding day Admetus forgot to sacrifice to Artemis, and when he went into the bridal chamber he found a knot of snakes in the bed. He again appealed to Apollo, who interceded with his sister, and she removed the curse. He also managed to persuade the Fates to grant Admetus deliverance from death when it came time for him to die, if he could find a family member to die in his stead.

Meanwhile, the other event took place. Back from Colchis with Jason, Medea sought revenge for the outrages Pelias had committed against Jason. In the presence of his daughters, the Peliades, she cut up an old ram and boiled it in a cauldron with magical herbs and incantations. At the end of this ritual, a lamb emerged from the cauldron. Medea swore that the daughters could do the same thing for the aged Pelias. They quickly agreed and performed the ceremony, but Pelias did not emerge as a young man. He stayed quite dismembered and quite dead. Alcestis alone had refrained from taking part in the bloody business, even though her father had consented. Her sisters then went into exile in Arcadia.

The fateful day finally arrived when Admetus was scheduled to die. He had enough warning to try to find a relative to die for him. His parents refused, as apparently did his children. Finally, just before the Moirae snipped the final vital cord of life, Alcestis took poison and died. She was transported to Hades, where Persephone, her usually unrelenting heart touched by this unprecedented act of devotion, conducted her back to the upper world. Others say that Heracles arrived on the day of mourning and went to Hades to fetch her back.

Nothing is recorded about her life after the grave. We do know she bore Admetus two children—Eumelus and Perimele. Perimele married Argos, the son of Phrixus, and bore him Magnes. Eumelus went to Troy with 11 ships and warriors from Pherae, Boebe, Glaphyrae, and Iolcus. He took the horses Apollo had tended for Admetus, and with them won a victory at the funeral games of Patroclus. He apparently survived the war and was married to Iphthima, the daughter of Icarius.

Lacking any evidence to the contrary, Alcestis died eventually from old age. No one has ever speculated on what happened to Admetus after his initial brush with death. Did he enter a kind of immortality, or did he have a succession of death dates on which he had to find replacements? Alcestis was represented on the chest of Cypselus as participating in the funeral solemnities of Acastus. [Apollodorus 1.9.10,15, 3.10.4; Pausanias 5.17.4; Euripides, *Alcestis;* Diodorus Siculus 4.53; Callimachus, *Hymn to Apollo* 47–54; Hyginus, *Fables* 50; Scholiast on Euripides' *Alcestis* 2; Fulgentius, *Mythology* 1.27.]

ALCIBIA was one of the AMAZONS. [Quintus Smyrnaeus 1.54.]

ALCIDAMEIA was the mother of Bunus by Hermes. Bunus obtained the government at Corinth when Aeetes went to Colchis. He built a temple to Hera there, from which she derived the surname Bunaea. [Pausanias 2.3.10,4.7.]

ALCIDICE, daughter of Aleus, was the first wife of Salmoneus. She died giving birth to their daughter Tyro. Salmoneus originally lived in Thessaly but migrated to Elis, where he built the town of Salmone. During this time he must have visited Alea near Tegea, for that is where Alcidice resided. Alcidice lived only a short time after going with her husband to Salmone, but by producing Tyro she became, in effect, the progenitor of some of the greatest royal houses of Greece—the Thessalian dynasties of Pherae and Iolcus, and the Messenian royal house at Pylus. [Apollodorus 1.9.8; Diodorus Siculus 4.68.]

ALCIMACHE (1), Defender in Battle, was a surname of Athena derived from her warlike character. [*Greek Anthology* 6.124.]

ALCIMACHE (2), daughter of Aeacus, by some was called the mother of Medon by Oileus. Medon's mother was usually called RHENE. Alcimache was also called the mother of Ajax, but his mother was more often called ERIOPIS. [Scholiast on Homer's *Iliad* 13.694.]

ALCIMACHE (3) was a Maenad from Lemnos who accompanied Dionysus to India. [Nonnos, *Dionysiaca* 30,192,210.]

ALCIMEDE, a daughter of Phylacus and Clymene, was sometimes called the mother of Jason by Aeson. Jason's mother was usually called POLYMEDE.

ALCINOE (1) was a daughter of Sthenelus, son of Perseus, and Nicippe, daughter of Pelops, and sister of Medusa, Iphis, and Eurystheus. Nothing else is known about her or Medusa, but Eurystheus was the taskmaster in the famous labors of Heracles. Sthenelus ruled over Mycenae, as did Eurystheus, who succeeded him. Iphis was one of the Argonauts and perished in Colchis during a battle with Aeetes. It is tempting to think of the two sisters as spinsters who moved around the heights of the walled city of Mycenae observing the exotic deliveries made by Heracles beyond the Lion Gate. Both their father and Eurystheus were killed by the Heraclids, and Mycenae fell to Atreus, their uncle. They probably were part of his court and lived to witness some of the horrors arising from the curse on the house of Pelops. [Apollodorus 2.4.5.]

ALCINOE (2) was a woman of Corinth and wife of Polybus, son of Dryas. She needed to have some spinning done and hired a woman to do the work. Afterward, she refused to pay the contracted amount, and the woman called on Athena, the patron goddess of spinning and weaving. Athena caused Alcinoe to go mad. In this state she fell in love with a visitor from Samos. When the man, Xanthus, left to go home, she abandoned her husband and children and pursued him. Before they reached Samos she came to her senses and, crying for her family, threw herself overboard and drowned. [Parthenius, *Love Stories* 27.]

ALCINOE (3) was one of the nurses of the infant Zeus as represented on the altar of Athena Alea at Tegea. [Pausanias 8.47.3.]

ALCIPPE (1) was the daughter of Ares and Agraulos, the daughter of Cecrops. She was one of the many females in Greek mythology whose name was derived from *hippos*, or horse. In her case, her name is translated "Mighty Mare." There appears to be no good reason for this except, perhaps, for being a daughter of Ares, the god of war, who certainly was the patron of battle horses. Alcippe came close to being an immortal, not only from her father but from her grandfather Cecrops, who was a son of Gaea according to the common interpretation of autochthon. She was part of the royal family at Athens, although the main branch stemmed from Erichthonius (Erechtheus I).

While Alcippe was still a maiden, Halirrhothius, the son of Poseidon, tried to rape her and was killed by her father. Poseidon accused Ares before the court of the gods, and Ares was acquitted. This event was thought to have been the origin of the Areiopagus, the seat of justice in Athens.

Alcippe's later history unfortunately is obscured by the complicated genealogy of the Athenian royal houses. She has been generally acknowledged as the mother of Daedalus, the famous artisan and builder of the Cretan labyrinth. His father was either Metion or Eupalamus. In order for Alcippe to have had a child by either, he would have to have been a son of Erechtheus II. That would be stretching it because Agraulos would have had to give birth to Alcippe prior to jumping in panic from the Acropolis with her sisters after seeing the half-serpent baby Erichthonius (Erechtheus I). That would make Alcippe contemporary with Erechtheus I and equivalent in age to a great-grandaunt of the sons of Erechtheus II. Perhaps Agraulos somehow survived the fall and lived a long time afterward before sacrificing herself for Athens. If she had Alcippe quite late in life (but would Ares have been interested?), say at age 40, then, at a correspondingly late age, Alcippe might have borne Daedalus to a son of Erechtheus II, provided the Erechthid males fathered sons while in their late teens. This would have made Alcippe around 40 and her husband half her age. Diodorus calls Daedalus one of the sons of Metion, and Metion a son of Eupalamus and grandson of Erechtheus. Alcippe would have been 60 by then. Apollodorus calls Eupalamus a son of Metion and father of Daedalus by Alcippe. This is also most improbable. Since

Daedalus was called one of the Metionidae, it is most likely that young Metion was a son of Erechtheus II and cohabited with his 40-year-old aunt, who bore him Daedalus. This would not be too unusual, since there was a tendency in the Athenian royal house for the males to marry older relatives. Alcippe was not exactly a relative, but she was a member of the older royal line. With her marriage to Metion she joined the old and new royal lines, but it is interesting that these lines appeared to be joined by numbering Cecrops II among the sons of Erechtheus II. In addition to Daedalus, Alcippe had two other sons, Eupalamus and Sicyon. Some writers have called the mother of Daedalus Iphinoe, Merope, or Phrasimede. [Apollodorus 3.14.2,15.1,5,6,8–9; Pausanias 1.5.3, 2.6.3; Diodorus Siculus 4.76; Euripides, *Electra* 1261; Pindar, *Olympian Odes* 1173; Pherecydes, quoted by the scholiast on Sophocles, *Oedipus at Colonus* 472.]

ALCIPPE (2) was a Macedonian maiden whose brother Astraeus had sex with her, unaware she was his sister. When he learned the truth, he threw himself into a river, which was afterward called Astraeus (and still later the Caicus). It is tantalizing to know so little of this story. How did it come about that Astraeus did not know Alcippe was his sister? Did she know he was her brother? How did she react to his suicide? Incest, accidental or deliberate, is a recurrent theme in classical myth, and invariably dire things happened to the participants. Apparently incest was the province of the gods but not a good idea for anyone else. [Pseudo-Plutarch, *On Rivers* 21.]

ALCIPPE (3) was one of the ALCYONIDES. [Eustathius on Homer's *Iliad* 776; Suidas, "Alkyonides."]

ALCIPPE (4) was a daughter of Oenomaus and the mother of Marpessa by Euenus, a son of Ares. Since Ares was also the father of Oenomaus, he was both father-in-law and grandfather to Alcippe. Marpessa was a beautiful young woman and had many suitors. Euenus, however, was not happy to see his daughter yielding her virginity to a husband and invited each aspirant to compete with him in a chariot race, which he always won. This was not exactly an unfamiliar situation to Alcippe, who had seen her father do the very same thing in regard to her sister Hippodameia. Both Apollo and Idas, son of Aphareus, fell in love with Marpessa, and Idas managed to conquer Euenus in the race. Alcippe more than likely felt relief that these chariot races obsessing the men in her life were over even though, in disgust and frustration at having lost the race, Euenus drowned himself in the Lycormas River, afterward called the Euenus. [Plutarch, *Greek and Roman Parallel Stories* 40; Eustathius on Homer's *Iliad* 9.557; Apollodorus 1.7.8.]

ALCIPPE (5) was an Amazon who fell during the battle of the Amazons against Heracles when he came to seize the girdle of Hippolyte. Alcippe had taken a vow to remain a virgin, and it was confirmed when she lost her life. [Diodorus Siculus 4.16.]

ALCIPPE (6) was one of the companions of Helen when Telemachus went to Sparta seeking information about Odysseus. When Helen appeared to greet him, Adraste placed a chair for her, and Alcippe brought a rug of soft wool. [Homer, *Odyssey* 4.124.]

ALCIS (1), the Strong, was a surname of Athena, under which she was worshipped in Macedonia. [Livy 42.51.]

ALCIS (2) was a daughter of Antipoenus. (*See* ANDROCLEIA.)

ALCITHOE, or Alcathoe, was one of the MINYADES.

ALCMENA was one of the most interesting and important women in mythology. Not only was she the mother of the greatest hero of ancient times, Heracles, but through him and her other son, Iphicles, she was ancestor of the whole Heraclid dynasty, which was part of the famous Dorian invasion and also linked myth to history through its long line of kings. Alcmena was a granddaughter of Perseus, daughter of Electryon and Anaxo, and is sometimes called Electryone (and also Mideatis from her father's kingdom). Her mother was also her first cousin and, later, sister-in-law, since Amphitryon was Anaxo's

brother. This made her husband, also a grandchild of Perseus, her first cousin as well as her uncle. Others have called Alcmena's mother Lysidice or Eurydice, daughter of Pelops, which would make her a cousin of Theseus, Agamemnon, and Menelaus. She had ten brothers, including her half-brother, Licymnius, son of Electryon and Media, a Persian slave. During Electryon's reign, his kingdom at Mycenae was raided by the Taphians (some say the sons of Pterelaus, but this would have been quite a feat, since they would have been great-great-grandnephews of Electryon). It is more likely that Taphius, the grandson of Electryon's brother Mestor, came with allies to claim the kingdom of Mestor, who had preceded Electryon on the throne. Subsequent versions of the story introduced the sons of Pterelaus, who were two generations later. In any case, Electryon rebuffed the Taphians, who then proceeded to drive away his cattle. A battle ensued in which all of Electryon's sons were killed except Licymnius. The surviving Taphians took the cattle aboard their ships and dropped them off at Elis for safekeeping with King Polyxenus. Amphitryon, son of Aleus, was by now in love with his cousin/niece Alcmena and, seeking to ingratiate himself with her and her father, was able to ransom the cattle from Polyxenus. When he returned, Electryon was just setting out to avenge the death of his sons. Realizing that Amphitryon could be trusted, he placed his kingdom and Alcmena in Amphitryon's charge until his return. He had Amphitryon swear an oath to leave Alcmena a virgin during his absence. It is not altogether clear why, but it was probably Alcmena's idea; she apparently wanted to see her brothers avenged before settling into married life. This display of willfulness might have brought her to Zeus' attention.

Amphitryon was spared this moral trial. While unloading the cattle, one of them charged, and he threw a club at her. The club bounced off the cow's horns and crushed Electryon's skull. It is easy enough to think this was not quite an accident, and that is what Sthenelus, Electryon's brother and next heir to the throne, used as a convenient excuse to exile Amphitryon and claim the throne for himself. Amphitryon took Alcmena and her half-brother,

Licymnius, to Thebes. Alcmena still wanted revenge for the death of her brothers; although she had married Amphitryon, she would not allow him to consummate the marriage until he accomplished this task. So he set out, enlisting the help of Creon, king of Thebes, as an ally against the Taphians. During this time Licymnius married Perimede, Amphitryon's sister, as if to further complicate the already confusing family relationships.

Shortly before Amphitryon's return from his successful campaign, Zeus, disguised as her husband, visited Alcmena. He related to her how he had avenged her brothers, and thereby succeeded in ending her virginity. One does not question motives of the gods, but it is interesting to speculate on Zeus' reasons for choosing Alcmena. She was certainly beautiful enough to persuade a man to fight a war for her. She was stubborn and determined. Zeus must have seen in her a perfect vessel for his divine seed to produce the greatest of Greek heroes. Whatever his motives, he enjoyed the experience enough, it is said, to cause the night with Alcmena to last for a period equivalent to three. It was also claimed that Alcmena was the last mortal woman with whom he had sexual relations.

Amphitryon returned the following day and repeated to her exactly what Zeus had said. Somewhat baffled, she bedded down for what she thought was a second night with her husband, who was unaware of what a performance he was following. Alcmena was impregnated by him as she had been by Zeus the night before. Puzzled by her reaction to him, Amphitryon consulted Teiresias, the great Theban seer, who told him the real story. Amphitryon's first impulse was to punish Alcmena, but he was forced to bow to the divine force of destiny. Carrying this one step further, he is reported never to have had sexual relations with her again, fearing the possibility of divine jealousy and reprisal.

It is said that on the day Heracles was to be born, Zeus boasted that he was about to become the father of a man who would rule over the heroic dynasty of Perseus. Hera, bitterly jealous of Alcmena, persuaded him to take an oath that would give the rule to the first male descendant of Perseus born from that moment. She knew that Nicippe, the wife of Sthenelus, son of

Perseus and uncle to both Amphitryon and Alcmena, was several months along in pregnancy. Hera promptly did two things. First, with the help of Eileithyia, her daughter and goddess of childbirth, she delayed the birth of Heracles (and, incidentally, Iphicles). With similar assistance she caused premature delivery of Eurystheus, Nicippe's son.

Apparently this was not enough. The labor of Alcmena was prolonged, with delivery prevented by Eileithyia, her assistants, the Pharmacidae, and the Moirae, or Fates. Galinthias, or Historis, a friend of Alcmena, finally managed to break the spell by rushing in with the false report that Alcmena had given birth to a son. Thus Alcmena brought into the world two boys—Heracles, the son of Zeus, and Iphicles, Amphitryon's son, who was one night younger than his fraternal twin. There was an account that Alcmena, now aware of Hera's feelings and her power, exposed Heracles in a field near Thebes. Athena and Hera passed by; struck by the child's great beauty, Athena persuaded Hera to take the child to her breast. Forever young and forever able to lactate, it seems, Hera nursed the child until he could be returned to Alcmena.

Lulled into a sense of security, Alcmena proceeded to rear the children, but when they were about eight months old, Hera sent two serpents that twined around the babies in their cradle. Heracles promptly strangled them, leaving no lurking doubt with Amphitryon which child was his. Alcmena consulted the seer Teiresias, who predicted Heracles' future glories and recommended the sacrifice of a boar at Zeus' altar in order to purge the house of the evil effects of the serpents.

So Heracles grew older and, unlike Iphicles, was somewhat unmanageable. He eventually killed his tutor, Linus. Although Amphitryon pardoned him, Heracles was sent away from home, during which time he learned the skills necessary to heroic exploits. This is not, however, the place to deal with these events. We do not know how often he came into contact with Alcmena during the apex of his career, but we do know he provided her generously with grandsons (and a granddaughter or two). In little more than a fortnight, 50 grandsons were born from his unions with the 50 daughters of Thespius. He killed his children by Megara, but made up for the loss by fathering children by Astyoche, Parthenope, Epicaste, Auge, Chalciope, and a half-dozen others. Alcmena's most illustrious grandson was Hyllus, son of Heracles and Deianeira.

After Amphitryon died, Alcmena rejoined Heracles just at the time that he, Iphicles, and Iphicles' son Iolaus were attempting to wrest Tiryns from Eurystheus. Their attempt failed, and they withdrew. Alcmena, however, remained in Tiryns with some of her grandchildren. She was there when Heracles died and was apotheosized. Afraid that Eurystheus, no longer having a need to fear Heracles, would attempt to stamp out the whole race of Heraclids, she fled with her grandsons to Trachis, where other grandsons had already taken refuge. Eurystheus threatened Ceyx, king of Trachis, who feared him, so Alcmena and the Heraclids went to Athens, where they were protected by Demophon, son of Theseus. Eurystheus demanded they be expelled; when Demophon refused, a battle ensued. Eurystheus and his sons were killed near the Scironian Rocks, and Hyllus cut off Eurystheus' head and brought it to Alcmena, who gouged out the eyes with hairpins.

Some say she married Rhadamanthys, son of Zeus. He had fled Crete out of fear of his brother Minos, and settled at Ocaleia in Boeotia. It is hard to fit Rhadamanthys into Alcmena's chronology. We never see him mentioned in the struggle between Eurystheus and the Heraclids, and it makes sense that if Alcmena married him, she did so after the defeat of Eurystheus. Also, he is not mentioned in accounts of Alcmena's death. In any case, at Haliartus a tomb was pointed out that was said to be the burial place of Alcmena and Rhadamanthys.

However, the more common account says that Alcmena died at a very old age at Thebes. Zeus directed Hermes to steal the body from the coffin the Heraclids were carrying to the grave. He transported Alcmena to the Isles of the Blessed, leaving a stone in place of her corpse. In the Isles of the Blessed she was revived and rejuvenated, and became the wife of Rhadamanthys, which makes far more sense than the Boeotian version. When the Heraclids discovered the stone in the coffin, they set it in a sacred grove at Thebes, where Alcmena was worshipped as a goddess. There are others who believe she died in Megara on the way from Argos to Thebes and was buried there at the command of the Delphic oracle. She was also worshipped as a goddess at Athens, and was represented on the chest of Cypselus.

As stated at the beginning, Alcmena was extremely important. She places Heracles in a chronological context, and through her we can establish that he belonged to the same generation as Agamemnon, Helen, and Theseus. Like Theseus, however, he was early enough in the generation to miss the Trojan War and was even, it seems evident, already dead when it began. The next great event after the Trojan War was the beginning of the so-called Doric invasion, and Alcmena can be said to have been the mother of the long line of Heraclids that extended into historical times. It is seldom remarked that Alcmena could be called the stepmother of Helen, just as Heracles could be called her half-brother, but congress with the gods probably precluded these mortal considerations. At any rate, from her original status as daughter of a herdsman king she went a long way. Mixed with her beauty were stubbornness, courage, and fierce loyalty to family. It is no wonder she was selected by the father of the gods to become the mother of the greatest Greek hero. [Apollodorus 2.4.5–11,8.1; Diodorus Siculus 4.9; Pausanias 1.41.1, 2.25.8, 5.17.4,18.1, 9.11.2,16.4; Ovid, *Amores* 1.13.45, *Metamorphoses* 9.273; Hyginus, *Fables* 29; Lucian, *Dialogues of the Gods* 10; Homer, *Iliad* 19.95; Plutarch, *On the Sign of Socrates* 578; Hesiod, *Shield of Heracles* 1–56,80; Theocritus, *Idylls* 13,24.]

ALCYONE (1), or Halcyone, was one of the PLEIADES, a daughter of Atlas and Pleione. By Poseidon she became the mother of Aethusa, Hyrieus, Hyperenor, Hyperes, and Anthas. Aethusa became by Apollo the mother of Eleuther, who founded Eleutherae. Hyrieus became king of Hyria and started the royal line that produced Amphion and Zethus, the builders of Thebes. Hyperes, who is probably the same as Hyperenor, and Anthas built the two cities of Hypereia and Antheia, which were united to form Troezen. Thus, Alcyone can be regarded as the mother of the founders of some of the most important cities of ancient times. [Apollodorus 3.10.1; Pausanias 2.30.7; Plutarch, *Theseus* 2.]

ALCYONE (2) was a daughter of Aeolus and Enarete or Aegiale. She and her sisters were often called Aeolis from their father. Her brothers were Sisyphus, Cretheus, Athamas, Salmoneus, Deion, Magnes, Perieres, Macareus, Aethlius, and Mimas; her sisters were Canace, Peisidice, Calyce, and Perimede. This Thessalian family was one of the most distinguished in mythology, the wellspring of royal houses in Magnesia, Corinthia, Boeotia, Elis, Messenia, and Phocis. She herself was married to Ceyx, a son of Eosphorus (Hesperius). Ceyx, being half-divine, was so happy with his life that he prevailed on Alcyone to call him Zeus, while he called her Hera. This was not wise, for the two of them were soon changed into birds, the halcyon and the ceyx (kingfisher and gannet). Another story says that Ceyx drowned in a shipwreck while on the way to consult an oracle. In deep grief Alcyone threw herself into the sea, and the gods changed both of them into birds. It was said that during the winter-solstice nesting period of the kingfishers, the sea remained calm, so from this circumstance we get the term "halcyon days."

Some modern writers (e.g., Robert Graves) have combined the Ceyx of this story with the Ceyx of Trachis, a friend of Heracles. Once more, genealogy comes to the rescue, since the children of Aeolus were seven generations (about 150 years) older than Heracles and his contemporaries. Graves also calls Alcyone's father, Aeolus, the guardian of the winds. Again, the Thessalian Aeolus was eight generations older than the wind king, who figured in the wanderings of Odysseus. There are many versions of the Alcyone/Ceyx story, and it is easy enough to get confused. [Apollodorus 1.7.3; Hyginus, *Fables* 65; Ovid, *Metamorphoses* 11.410–750.]

ALCYONE (3) was the real name of CLEOPATRA, wife of Meleager.

ALCYONE (4) was a daughter of Sthenelus and Nicippe (others say Antibia or Archippe), and sister of Eurystheus and Medusa, thus a granddaughter of two of the greatest heroes of ancient myth, Perseus and Pelops. She undoubtedly witnessed the results of the labors of Heracles, and she herself was indebted to the hero when he killed Homadus the Centaur, who had attempted to rape her. [Apollodorus 2.4.5; Scholiast on Homer's *Iliad* 19.119; Tzetzes, *Chiliades* 2.172,192.]

ALCYONIDES were the daughters of the giant Alcyoneus. In the battle between the gods and giants, Alcyoneus remained immortal as long as he was in his native country. Heracles, whose assistance as a mortal was necessary in overcoming the giants, eventually dragged Alcyoneus out of his country and killed him. After their father's death, the daughters threw themselves into the sea and were changed into ice birds. Their names were Phthonia (probably Chthonia), Anthe, Methone, Alcippe, Pallene, Drimo, and Asteria. [Eustathius on Homer's *Iliad* 776; Suidas, "Alkyonides."]

ALEA was a surname of Athena in her worship at Alea, Mantineia, and Tegea. She probably derived this name from Aleus, son of Apheidas, who built the oldest of her temples at Tegea. This temple burned in 394 B.C., and Scopas, the famous sculptor and architect, superintended its rebuilding. The result surpassed in size and splendor all other temples in Peloponnesus. Surrounding it was a triple row of columns of different orders. Endoeus, another famous sculptor, created in ivory the statue of the goddess, which was later carried to Rome by Augustus for a prominent place in his Forum. The front pediments featured the Calydonian boar hunt, and Atalanta appeared among the hunters. The back pediment showed Telephus fighting Achilles on the plain of the Caicus River. The temple functioned as an asylum, and many persons sought refuge there. The priests were boys who had to leave the office when they reached puberty. There was also a wooden image of Athena Alea on the road from Sparta to Therapne. [Pausanias 2.17.7, 3.5.6,7.8, 5.19.1, 8.23.1,45.4,7.]

ALECTO was one of the three EUMENIDES (Furies). Her sisters were Tisiphone and Megaera. They are usually conceived with a collective identity, but Alecto was singled out on one occasion by Hera/Juno to stir Turnus to fight against Aeneas, who had landed in Italy and sought the hand of Lavinia, already betrothed to Turnus. [Virgil, *Aeneid* 7.408.]

ALETIS was a surname of ERIGONE, daughter of Icarius, the man who introduced the cultivation of the vine into Attica. She also had a brother called Aletes. *Aletis* was also the name of a song sung in her honor. [Athenaeus 14.618; Pollux 4.55; Apollodorus 3.10.6.]

ALEXANDRA was a name by which CASSANDRA, daughter of Priam, was also known. Under this name she had a sanctuary and statue at Amyclae. A temple and statue of Alexandra also existed at Leuctra in Laconia. [Pausanias 3.19.6,26.5.]

ALEXIDA was a daughter of Amphiaraus, the seer, who was skilled in the medical arts as well. From her the Elasii were said to be descended. They were minor divinities who averted epileptic seizures. [Plutarch, *Greek Questions* 23.]

ALEXIRRHOE, whose name appears three or so times in obscure works, poses unanswerable questions. There might have been more than one person by this name, but it is more than likely that the three very brief mentions of her can all be related, since they at least coincide geographically. She was a daughter of the Granicus River, or of Antandrus. Her short history seems fraught with tragedy. By three lovers she had three sons, and they all died young, two by their own hand. According to some, by Priam she had Aesacus (although his mother was more often called Arisbe), who would have nothing to do with his father's court and lived in the forests of a mountain (Ida?). He fell in love with Hesperia, daughter of Cebren, and pursued her. One time as he followed her, she was bitten by a snake and died. Aesacus was so grief-stricken he threw himself into the sea and was changed by Thetis, the Nereid, into an aquatic bird. Another son, Carmanor, whom she had by Dionysus, was killed by a wild boar on a mountain that came to bear his name, Mount Carmanor (later Tmolus). Still another son, Sagaris, whom she bore to Mygdon, was driven insane by Rhea, the mother of the

gods, for neglecting her mysteries and insulting her eunuch priests. He threw himself into the Xerobates River, after which time it was called the Sagaris.

Even with the brevity of these fragments we can still put together a possible chronology for Alexirrhoe. She was a nymph and more likely the daughter of the Granicus River than of the otherwise totally unknown Antandrus. She was encountered first by Priam, perhaps during a hunt, and made pregnant by him. She most likely never saw him again and married Mygdos, one of the kings of Phrygia, by whom she had a second son. When Dionysus wandered the world spreading his worship, a great number of married women flocked to his drunken orgies. Perhaps Alexirrhoe was one of these and mated with the god to produce still another son. Then all her sons perished, leaving her childless. Had they lived, they undoubtedly would have been Trojan allies in the invasion by the Greeks. [Servius on Virgil's *Aeneid* 4.254; Ovid, *Metamorphoses* 11.750; Pseudo-Plutarch, *On Rivers* 7.5., 12.1; Scholiast on Homer's *Iliad* 24.497.]

ALGEA was the daughter of Eris, goddess of discord, and personification of sorrow and grief. [Hesiod, *Theogony* 227.]

ALIMEDE was one of the NEREIDES. [Hesiod, *Theogony* 256.]

ALITTA, or Alilat, was the name given to Aprodite Urania by the Arabs. [Herodotus 1.131, 3.8.]

ALOPE of Eleusis, daughter of Cercyon, paid a penalty for her great beauty. The god of the sea, Poseidon, was filled with lust for her, and Alope responded. She was yet another example of an unfortunate liaison with a deity. To make matters worse, she had a cruel brute of a father. This Cercyon was, according to some, also her stepson, since he was a son of Poseidon. This, of course, made her lover her grandfather, so Alope was indeed in trouble from the beginning. She had a son and, knowing her father, she promptly exposed the boy. The child was suckled by a mare until found by shepherds. The shepherds quarreled over the baby's costly garments, and the dispute was brought before Cercyon. He recognized the dress and realized the situation. He had Alope imprisoned in order to have her put to death, then he himself exposed the child. The infant was suckled again and found once more by shepherds, who named him Hippothoon. Alope was put to death with no further ado, and Poseidon finally arrived in time to change her into a fountain with the same name. There was a monument erected to her on the road from Eleusis to Megara on the spot where she was believed to have been killed. The town of Alope in Thessaly was thought to have derived its name from her, although there seems to be no good reason.

Cercyon, it may be remembered, challenged travelers crossing the Isthmus and invariably killed them until he was finally overcome by Theseus. In spite of a bad beginning, Hippothoon fared rather well. He ended up with a hero shrine at Athens, and one of the Attic tribes was called Hippothoontis after him. (Robert Graves confuses both Cercyon and Hippothoon with an Arcadian dynasty, wherein Cercyon was a son of Agamedes and Hippothous was son of Cercyon.) [Pausanias 1.5.2,38.4,39.3.]

ALOS was a serving-maid to Athamas, the unfortunate son-in-law of Cadmus. Athamas' wife Ino was plotting to kill his children by his first wife Nephele. He was able to prevent this through information provided by Alos. When he was exiled and had settled in Phthiotian Thessaly, he named one of the cities he founded in her honor. [Stephanus Byzantium, "Alos."]

ALPHAEA, Alpheaea, Alpheionia, or Alpheiusa was a surname of Artemis, which she derived from the river-god Alpheius. Alpheius was enamored of the virtuous goddess and once pursued her. She fled to Letrini in Elis, where she and her nymph companions covered their faces with mud so Alpheius could not tell who was who. He withdrew, and this was the occasion of the building of a temple to Artemis Alphaea at Letrini. Another version says Artemis fled to the island of Ortygia (near Syracuse in Sicily), where she later had a temple under the name of Alphaea. There was also an allusion to Alpheius'

love of Artemis at Olympia, where the two divinities had one altar in common. [Pausanias 5.14.5, 6.22.5; Strabo 8.3.12; Scholiast on Pindar's *Pythian Odes* 2.12, *Nemean Odes* 1.3.]

ALPHEIAS was a name by which Ovid (*Metamorphoses* 5.487) designates the nymph of the Sicilian fountain of Arethusa on the island of Ortygia near Syracuse, because it was believed to have a subterranean communication with the Alpheius River in Peloponnesus. (*See also* ARETHUSA.)

ALPHESIBOEA (1) was the mother of Adonis by Phoenix, according to Hesiod (quoted by Apollodorus 3.14.4). The usual story calls his mother MYRRHA (or Smyrna).

ALPHESIBOEA (2) was a daughter of Phegeus, who married Alcmaeon. She is more often called ARSINOE.

ALPHESIBOEA (3) was, according to Theocritus (*Idylls* 3.45), a daughter of Bias and the wife of Pelias. The wife of Pelias, however, is usually called ANAXIBIA.

ALPHESIBOEA (4) was a nymph of Asia. Dionysus, promoting his worship in this country, fell in love with her but was not able to seduce her. Eventually he changed himself into a tiger, and she was so frightened that she allowed him to carry her on his back across the Sollax River, after which he (presumably) changed back to the form of a god and had his way with her. From this union a son, Medus, was born, and when he grew up he named the river Tigris to commemorate the circumstances of his unusual conception. [Pseudo-Plutarch, *On Rivers* 28.]

ALSEIDES was the name of a species of nymphs of forests, groves, and glens, who were believed to sometimes appear to and frighten solitary travelers. [Apollonius Rhodius 1.1066.]

ALTA was the mother of Ancaeus by Poseidon, according to some, while others say the mother was ASTYPALAEA.

ALTHAEA (1) was famous in mythology for causing the death of her son Meleager, which in turn caused her own death. She was one of the daughters of the Aetolian king Thestius and Eurythemis, and sister of Iphiclus, Euippus, Prothous, Plexippus, Eurypylus, Hypermnestra, and Leda. Through her family life, Althaea enjoyed considerable prestige. Thestius was king of Pleuron, and most likely the son of Agenor and grandson of Pleuron, his claim of divine origin notwithstanding. Althaea and Leda were sometimes called by the patronymic Thestias. Her brother Iphiclus took part in both the Argonaut and the Calydonian boar hunt. Laocoon, her brother-in-law, was also an Argonaut. Her sister Hypermnestra married Oicles and was the mother of Amphiaraus, the famous warrior and seer. Leda, of course, became the mother of the beautiful Helen, who changed the course of events forevermore.

Althaea was married to Oeneus, king of Calydon, by whom she became the mother of Toxeus, Thyreus, Clymenus, Meleager, Gorge, and Deianeira. (Some writers added sons Agelaus and Periphas as well as Eurymede, Melanippe, and other daughters, who were metamorphosed into birds on Meleager's death.) According to one rumor, Althaea was the mother of Meleager by Ares and of Deianeira by Dionysus. In the case of celebrated heroes such as Meleager, it was often difficult for ancient storytellers not to assign divine fathers. Ares was already Althaea's paternal grandfather, according to some, but since there had been an intervening mortal generation, perhaps the divine blood needed to be replenished.

Future tragedy in Althaea's life was omened by the appearance of the Moirae, or Fates, to her when Meleager was only a few days old. They warned her that the boy would die as soon as a certain piece of wood burning on the hearth should be entirely consumed. Althaea at once extinguished the flame and put the piece of wood in a chest so it could not be accidentally burned. This made Meleager invulnerable, so much so that he came through the voyage of the Argonauts and numerous skirmishes with the hostile Curetes of Calydonia unscathed.

Tragedy started early enough for Althaea. Toxeus, her firstborn, was killed by his father for what appears to have been an act of youthful defiance, when the son leapt over a fortification ditch that Oeneus was digging. During Oeneus' reign the kingdom of Calydon was under constant defense against the Curetes, and Althaea saw her sons go out in battle against them. Meleager was still quite young when he joined the adventurers who journeyed to Colchis to fetch the Golden Fleece. On this voyage he met the exciting but aloof young huntress Atalanta, who was the only woman on the trip. He returned safely and married Cleopatra, the daughter of Idas and Marpessa. Idas had also been a member of the Argonaut, and it is highly likely that an arrangement was made before the two returned from the voyage.

The offensive from the Curetes continued, and Meleager was a valuable asset to the defenders since he was invulnerable. In sacrificing the first fruits of the annual crops, Oeneus inadvertently neglected Artemis. In revenge she sent a monstrous boar to ravage the Calydonian countryside. It frightened planters from the fields, and killed cattle and even some people. Eventually Oeneus sent out a call for help to the noblest men of Greece and promised the animal's hide as the trophy. Of course, for those to whom such a contest appealed, the skin was secondary to the glory. They came from almost everywhere in Greece, and not all accounts agree on exactly who participated. A total of about 40 can be rounded up from all sources, but the ones who are agreed on both by Apollodorus and Ovid are: Meleager, Dryas, Idas, Lynceus, Castor, Polydeuces, Theseus, Ancaeus, Jason, Peirithous, Peleus, Telamon, Eurytion, Amphiaraus, Hyleus, the sons of Thestius, and Atalanta. It can be seen that this event acted in part as a reunion of some of the shipmates of the *Argo*. One can recognize, too, several fathers of heroes of the Trojan War soon to follow.

Althaea's shining son did not draw first blood when the beast was sighted; his friend Atalanta had that honor. It was Meleager, however, who brought down the monster, and he gallantly presented the hide to Atalanta. Behind the gallantry was lust for the huntress and a desire to father a child by her. Atalanta's presence at the boar hunt was opposed by two or three of the hunters, and when she was given the trophy,

Althaea's brothers were very much offended. They contested the award and argued about who first drew blood. At least, they said, they deserved the prize, by right of blood, if Meleager did not choose to accept it. Meleager flew into a rage and killed his uncles. Althaea was devastated by this turn of events and cursed Meleager for his violent action.

According to some, the Curetes renewed their offensive about this time. It has never been made clear whether or not Althaea's brothers were somehow allied with these traditional enemies, but Apollodorus seems to suggest this. In any case, Meleager, smarting from his mother's curse, withdrew from battle, and the victorious Curetes were pressing Calydon very hard. The elders of the city begged him to relent and even made promises of reward, but he was deaf to them and to his friends. Eventually he yielded to the entreaties of Cleopatra and before long put the Curetes to flight. After that, he left Calydon and never returned.

But the usual story is that Althaea threw the long-preserved piece of wood into the fire as soon as she learned of the death of her brothers, and Meleager died instantly. Doubly heartbroken, she hanged herself, as did Cleopatra, who probably felt responsible. Cleopatra might not have been so ready to do this had she realized Meleager had made advances to Atalanta, who more than likely complied, since it was later rumored that Parthenopaeus was her son by Meleager. Althaea, on the other hand, was better off dead, since her daughters wept so hard over their brother's death (and Althaea's, presumably) that Artemis changed them into guinea hens and transported them to the island of Leros. Deianeira survived to marry Heracles, giving some credibility to the otherwise unsupported claim that he participated in the boar hunt. Gorge, the other remaining daughter, was thought to have become the mother of Tydeus by her own father, and it would be well to think this took place after Althaea's death.

Althaea is a fascinating study in moral dilemma. By being left by fate with the power of life or death over her son, she shared something in common with the immortal gods. However, their often human emotions—such as the fit of pique that caused Artemis to send the

Calydonian boar—could not result in their own destruction. Althaea's anger toward Meleager was such that she must have known his end would be hers as well. The whole story raises the question of whether or not she had a real choice. Had he outlived her, and had she carefully enough secured the splinter of wood, he would have been immortal. This was not the way of the Fates. They knew in advance how things would work out and gave her the unhappy role of seeing that they accorded with destiny. [Apollodorus 1.7.10,8.1–3; Hyginus, *Fables* 31,33,99,129; Ovid, *Metamorphoses* 8.445,532; Homer, *Iliad* 9.527–600; Antoninus Liberalis 2; Diodorus Siculus 4.35.]

ALTHAEA (2) was one of the HYADES, sister of Eidothea and Adraste. [Hyginus, *Fables* 182.]

AMALTHEIA (1) was the famous goat that suckled the infant Zeus. Rhea gave birth to Zeus in a cave on Mount Dicte or Mount Ida in Crete and entrusted him to the Curetes and the nymphs Adrasteia and Ida, daughters of Melisseus and Amaltheia (not to be confused with the goat). Another daughter named Aega was chosen to suckle the god, but she was unable to, and it was necessary to call in the goat for this service. Some say Hermes fathered Pan on the goat Amaltheia. One way or another one of the goat's horns was broken off, and either the nymph Amaltheia or Zeus filled it with the bounties of the harvest, so that its possession assured the owner of plenty even in the midst of famine. Zeus also placed the horn and the goat Amaltheia among the stars.

The horn continued to turn up in other stories, and it is represented in works of art even today as the symbol of plenty. When Heracles and the river-god Achelous fought for possession of Deianeira, Achelous assumed various shapes, including a bull. While he was in this state, Heracles broke off one of his horns and withheld it until Achelous exchanged it for the horn of Amaltheia. What Achelous was doing with the horn has not been revealed. In artistic representations we find that Sosipolis, an Elean hero, was shown as a boy in a military cloak carrying in his hand the horn of Amaltheia. Some say that during his twelfth labor, Heracles carried the horn filled with Hesperidean fruit to the underworld as a gift for Plutus, the god of wealth, who was the assistant of Tyche, goddess of fortune. At Smyrna, the statue of Tyche by Bupalus held in one hand the horn of Amaltheia. Also at Aegeira in Achaia she was represented with the cornucopia. [Apollodorus 1.1.6,8.1, 2.7.5; Ovid, *Metamorphoses* 9.8,87; Pausanias 7.26.3; Diodorus Siculus 5.70; Hyginus, *Poetic Astronomy* 2.13; Aratus, *Phenomena* 163; Callimachus, *Hymn to Zeus* 49.]

AMALTHEIA (2) was a nymph, the wife of King Melisseus of Crete. Her daughters by him were Ida and Adrasteia, and, according to some, Aega. Amaltheia was sometimes called the daughter of Melisseus. The stories about the Cretan birth of Zeus are confusing, and Amaltheia the goat plays a prominent part. Amaltheia the nymph is understandably identified with the goat; it can be conjectured that the family of Melisseus was entrusted with the rearing of the god and that part of this office consisted of providing the services of the family goat, which for some reason was named for the mother of the house. One writer calls her Adamanteia. [Hyginus, *Fables* 139; Scholiast on Homer's *Iliad* 21.194; Eratosthenes, *Star Placements* 13; Apollodorus 2.7.5; Lactantius 1.22.]

AMALTHEIA (3) was a daughter of Haemonius. The Libyan king Ammon married her and gave her a very fertile tract of land shaped like a bull's horn, which then became known as the horn of Amaltheia. One tradition calls Dionysus the son of this couple and says that Ammon carried the child to a cave on Mount Nysa to be raised. [Diodorus Siculus 3.67, 4.35.]

AMALTHEIA (4) was one of the SIBYLS. She is sometimes identified with the Cumaean Sibyl, who sold to King Tarquinius the celebrated Sibylline books. She might also have been considered as a teacher of Zeus. [Lactantius 1.6; Servius on Virgil's *Aeneid* 6.72; Lydus, *On the Months* 4.34.]

AMATA was the wife of Latinus, a king of Latium. Her husband was a son of Faunus and the nymph Marica, and brother of Lavinius. Amata and Latinus had a daughter, Lavinia, whom they named after her uncle. Amata was semidivine, being the sister of Venilia, a goddess of winds and the sea who was married to Daunus. Turnus, king of the Rutulians and the son of Venilia and Daunus, was nephew to Amata. Lavinia became the wife of Aeneas when he arrived in Italy, and bore to him Ascanius and Silvius. [Virgil, *Aeneid* 6.761, 4.47, 12.138; Livy 1.1.; Dionysius of Halicarnassus, *Roman Antiquities* 1.70.]

AMATHEIA was one of the NEREIDES. [Hyginus, *Fables: Preface* 8.]

AMATHUNTIA (*See* AMATHUSIA)

AMATHUSA was the mother of Cinyras, and the town of Amathus in Cyprus was believed to have derived its name from her. The mother of Cinyras is usually called PAPHOS. [Stephanus Byzantium, "Amathus."]

AMATHUSIA, or Amathuntia, was a surname of Aphrodite, derived from the town of Amathus in Cyprus, one of the most ancient seats of her worship. [Tacitus, *Annals* 3.62; Ovid, *Amores* 3.15.15; *Appendix Virgiliana: Ciris* 242; Catullus 68.51.]

AMAZONS (1) were a warlike tribe of women in Asia Minor who captured the imagination of ancient writers so completely that generations of readers have wondered whether or not there might have been some historical basis. Particularly is this true in regard to the Amazonian invasion of Attica, which not only would have represented an audacious undertaking for the women but also for the ancient chroniclers of the event, since the quasi-historical Theseus was involved.

Because no rational explanation has ever been advanced for this mysterious race, we can look at them only in their mythological context. They were descendants of Ares and had come from the country around the Caucasus Range. They settled on the bank of the navigable Thermodon River near the point at which it entered the Euxine (Black Sea). There they founded the town of Themiscyra (probably modern Therme or Terme). Their principal pursuits were war, hunting, and the agricultural activity necessary for their sustenance. They were said to have been the first humans to ride on horseback. Their rule was entirely by women, and any men in their community were in servile positions. The women mated for a short period each year with the neighboring Gargarean men for purposes of continuing their race. Male children were sent to the Gargareans or exterminated. Female children had their right breast (or both breasts) seared so that this part of the anatomy would not inhibit the customary pursuits when they became adult Amazons. They worshipped Ares, Cybele, and the Taurian Artemis.

We encounter them first, in mythological chronology, when gadfly-driven Io, wandering the world in the form of a heifer, found them inhabiting the region around the Thermodon. Several generations later, when Bellerophon was exiled to the Lycian court of Iobates, who was instructed to dispose of him, the king sent him on a series of dangerous missions. One of them was a fight against the Amazons, in which he was victorious. We next hear of them via the Argonauts, who sailed past their country en route to Colchis, which was not a great distance beyond. So the territory was not entirely new to Heracles, who returned to the land of the Amazons very soon after the Argonaut in conjunction with his ninth labor.

Admete, the daughter of Eurystheus, coveted the girdle of Hippolyte, the queen of the Amazons, so the ninth labor imposed on Heracles by Eurystheus was obtaining this emblem of royal dignity, a gift from Ares to his daughter. Heracles fought with the Amazons and killed Aella, Philippis, Prothoe, Eriboea, Celaeno, Eurybia, Phoebe, Deianeira, Asteria, Marpe, Tecmessa, and Alcippe. He allowed Melanippe to live in return for the girdle and gave Antiope to Theseus, his cousin.

The stories involving Theseus are somewhat confusing. Some accounts say Theseus accompanied Heracles on the trip and thus received Antiope as a reward of friendship. It is more likely Theseus went on his own, probably very shortly after Heracles' visit. He abducted Antiope and carried her back to Athens. Soon afterward, the Amazons invaded Attica. They appear to have conquered the countryside around Athens, for they pitched their camp and staged attacks within the city itself. Antiope fought at Theseus' side and was killed by Molpadia. This battle continued for three months, and apparently it was more than a local affair. There are references to the Amazons penetrating Peloponnesus as far as Pyrrichus in Laconia. Apollo Amazonius had a temple at Pyrrichus. So did Artemis Astrateia, who was supposed to have stopped the progress of the Amazons there. A treaty was eventually signed, and the Amazons left. Some say they were defeated and that Hippolyte fled to Megara, where she died of grief. Her tomb, which was later shown there, had the form of an Amazon's shield.

Priam, later king of Troy, assisted Mygdon and Otreus, two Phrygian kings, in another war against the Amazons. It is hard to know when this war took place in Amazonian chronology. It is likely that it was before the invasions of Heracles and Theseus, which had to precede the Trojan War by as much as 20 years. Theseus married Phaedra not long after Antiope's death, and his sons by her, Demophon and Acamas, were old enough to fight in the war.

The Amazons apparently did not hold this long-past hostility against Priam, for they emerged as Trojan allies during the invasion of the Greeks. Perhaps the Amazons had good reason to hate Greeks more than Trojans. Penthesileia led them to battle, and we have their names from Quintus Smyrnaeus (1.20–46): Clonie, Polemusa, Derinoe, Euandre, Antandre, Bremusa, Hippothoe, Harmothoe, Alcibie, Derimacheia, Antibrote, and Thermodosa. They were entirely wiped out by the Greek warriors. Penthesileia herself was killed by Achilles.

After this time we hear nothing further of the Amazons. From writers other than Diodorus Siculus, Quintus Smyrnaeus, and Plutarch, we have names of Amazons so far not mentioned: Anaea, Andro, Andromache, Euryale, Gryne, Hippo, Iphito, Lysippe, Marpesia, Molpadia, Myrina, Myrto, Mytilene, Smyrna, and Thalestris. Hyginus (Fables 163), fond of making lists, submitted Ocyale, Dioxippe, Iphinome, Xanthe, Hippothoe, Otrera (mother by Ares of certain Amazons), Antioche

(Antiope?), Laomache, Glauce, Agave, Theseis (wife of Theseus?), Clymene, and Polydora. His list included Hippolyte and Penthesileia as well.

The persistence of stories about these warrior women is in itself a fascinating consideration. How had the idea arisen in the first place? Was there perhaps a Black Sea people among whom ordinarily masculine pursuits were practiced by the women as well? Was there a cult of Artemis Tauropolos or of Cybele that for a short period grew strong enough to allow females the sovereignty? Had there been some kind of insurrection such as that on Lemnos in which all the males had been put to death? We shall probably never know. But the myth of the Euxine Amazons was so persuasive that at least one historian even conjectured that by planned intermarriage with the Scythians the Amazons created a tribe called the Sauromatians, who eventually blended in with other Scythians north of the Euxine. In this way the Amazons were reabsorbed into a male-dominated society, one from which they undoubtedly sprang.

The Amazons were frequently represented in works of ancient art. The battle between the Athenians and Amazons was the subject of a painting in the Stoa Poecile at Athens. The Amazons were shown also on the shield of Athena in the Parthenon and on the footstool of the Olympian Zeus by Pheidias. They were carved by Alcamenes on the pediment of the temple of Zeus at Olympia. [Apollodorus 2.5.9; Diodorus Siculus 4.16; Hyginus *Fables* 30; Plutarch, *Theseus* 27,31,33; Pausanias 1.17.2,41.7, 5.10.2; Tzetzes, *Posthomerica* 182; Servius on Virgil's *Aeneid* 4.345; Herodotus 4.110–117; Quintus Smyrnaeus 1.18–47.]

AMAZONS (2) were a race of women preceding the more famous Amazons of the Black Sea. They were located in western Libya, and figured in accounts about Dionysus, the Argonauts, and Perseus. Their kingdom was on an island called Hespera, located in the marsh Tritonis, named for the Triton River, which emptied into the (Atlantic) ocean nearby. The mountain overlooking the whole region was Mount Atlas. In most respects their life-style was like that of the Asian Amazons except that males among them seemed to fare somewhat better.

These Amazons subdued all the cities on the island. Their queen was Myrina, and she collected an army of 30,000 foot soldiers and 3,000 cavalry. Their breastplates, shields, and helmets were made from the skins of large snakes. They invaded the land of the Atlantians and razed the city of Cerne. They treated the inhabitants with such ruthlessness that the other Atlantian cities quickly capitulated, after which time Myrina treated them well and founded on the site of the destroyed city a new one that she named after herself. The Atlantians then requested her to invade the land of the Gorgons (another tribe of women, it appears), their traditional enemies. Myrina did so, and the Amazons again were victorious, taking 3,000 prisoners and killing many more. But the captives were able to overpower their captors and butchered many of them before they could be stopped. Myrina raised great heaps of earth as tombs, which were called "Amazon Mounds." When the Gorgons grew strong again, Perseus arrived to subdue them (a neat example of twisting pure myth into pseudohistory).

The Amazons, led by Myrina, swept across Libya, which meant everything from the Atlantic Ocean to Egypt, and crossed into that country and made a treaty. Later they crossed to Asia, warred on the Arabs, and subdued the Syrians. They also conquered the races in the Taurian region and then descended along the Mediterranean coast, declaring the Caicus River their boundary. Myrina founded cities and named them for women who held outstanding commands—Cyme, Pitana, and Priene. They also seized certain islands along the coast, such as Lesbos, on which Myrina founded the city of Mytilene, which she named for her sister, who took part in the campaign. During this campaign, Myrina was washed away by a storm and landed on an uninhabited island on which she set up altars to Cybele. She named it Samothrace, and it later became famous for its mysteries and its reputation for offering right of sanctuary.

Eventually these Amazon colonists were overcome by Mopsus the Thracian and Sipylus the Scythian, and Myrina was slain. The surviving Amazons withdrew again into Libya.

Another reference to these Libyan Amazons concerns Dionysus, son of Ammon and Amaltheia. Dionysus united the Amazons to fight against the Titans and Cronus, who had expelled Ammon from his dominions. Later, on his return from India, Dionysus opposed the Amazons. It is not clear which group of Amazons these were (Pausanias 7.2.7 called them the women from the Thermodon), since the battle-ground was the territory that the Libyan Amazons had colonized. The temple of Artemis at Ephesus, for example, was the place in which the Amazons took refuge. Pindar (quoted by Pausanias 7.2.4) said that the temple was founded by the Amazons on their march to Athens. This would be a most curious route, especially since there is never mention of a navy in connection with the Themiscyran Amazons. In any case, Dionysus pursued these particular Amazons to the death on the island of Samos; so many were killed, the battlefield was called Panhaema. The descendants of the Amazons who remained in Ephesus endured for many generations as protectors of the temple. They, like their northern counterparts, blended with the general populace.

The Amazons who returned to Libya were finally destroyed along with their enemies the Gorgons by Heracles when he went west to set up his famous pillars. Perhaps these famous landmarks could serve today as monuments to a combination of chauvinism and genocide, since Heracles slaughtered these women in the belief that in his role as savior of mankind he could ill afford to let any nation be under the rule of females. [Diodorus Siculus 3.52–70.]

AMBOLOGERA, from *anaballo* and *geras,* "delaying old age," was a surname of Aphrodite, who had a statue at Sparta under this name. [Pausanias 3.18.1; Plutarch, *Table-Talk* 36.]

AMBRACIA (1) was a daughter of Phorbas, son of Helios, and mother by Mesolas of Dexamenus. The Ambracian tribe of the Dexamenae was named for Dexamenus. [Stephanus Byzantium, "Dexamenai."]

AMBRACIA (2) was a daughter of Melaneus, son of Apollo, Dryopean king, and conqueror of all Epeirus. She was the sister of Eurytus, the famous archer who taught Heracles to shoot.

Their mother is usually called Stratonice, although a Messenian tradition says she was Oechalia, for whom the town of Oechalia was named. The city of Ambracia was said to have been named for Ambracia. [Antoninus Liberalis 4.]

AMBRACIA (3) was a daughter of Augeas. She grew up adjacent to the dirty stables of her cattle-baron father and witnessed Heracles cleaning them. When her father refused to pay, Heracles made war on him. Phyleus, her brother, was exiled to the Taphian Islands for siding with Heracles. [Stephanus Byzantium, "Ambracia"; Eustathius on Dionysius Periegeta 492.]

AMBROSIA was one of the HYADES, according to Hyginus (*Poetic Astronomy* 2.21). Her sisters were Eudora, Pedile, Coronis, Polyxo, Phyto, and Thyene, or Dione. According to Eustathius (on Homer's *Iliad* 1156) there were three Hyades: Ambrosia, Eudora, and Aesyle.

AMBULIA was a surname under which the Spartans worshipped Athena. The meaning of the name is uncertain, but it has been supposed to derive from *anaballo* and to designate the goddess as one who delayed death.

AMEIRACE was the original name of PENELOPE. Nauplius is said to have cast her into the sea in retaliation for the death of Palamedes (in which Odysseus had a part). She was rescued by sea birds (*penelopes*), from which she derived her name. [Didymus, quoted by Eustathius on Homer's *Odyssey* 1422.]

AMMONIA was a surname under which Hera was worshipped in Elis. From the earliest times the inhabitants of Elis had been in the habit of consulting the oracle of Zeus Ammon in Libya. [Pausanias 5.15.7.]

AMNISIADES were the nymphs of the Amnisus River in Crete. They were mentioned in connection with the worship of Artemis as her attendants, mainly devoted to caring for the sacred deer of the goddess. [Callimachus, *Hymn to Artemis* 15.162; Apollonius Rhodius 3.881.]

AMPHICOMONE was one of the DANAIDES, a daughter of Danaus, who married Plexippus, son of Aegyptus. [Hyginus, *Fables* 170.]

AMPHICTYONE was the mother of Dotis by Elatus. She was not married to him, since his wife's name was Laodice, by whom he had four sons. Dotis, who was the mother of Phlegyas by Ares, gave her name to the Dotian Plain in Thessaly. [Stephanus Byzantium, "Dotion."]

AMPHICTYONIS was a surname of Demeter, derived from Anthela, where she was worshipped under this name because it was the place of meeting for the amphictyons of Thermopylae, and because sacrifices were offered to her at the opening of every meeting. [Herodotus 7.200; Strabo, 9.4.17.]

AMPHINOME (1) was the wife of Aeson and mother of Jason, according to some, but Jason's mother is usually called POLYMEDE.

AMPHINOME (2) was one of the PELIADES, sister of Alcestis and Euadne.

AMPHINOME (3) was one of the NEREIDES. [Homer, *Iliad* 18.44.]

AMPHIRHO was one of the OCEANIDES. [Hesiod, *Theogony* 358.]

AMPHISSA (1), daughter of Macareus and granddaughter of Aeolus, was loved by Apollo and is said to have given her name to the town of Amphissa in Phocis, where her memory was perpetuated by a splendid monument. Her paternity poses a bit.of a problem, since Macareus had an incestuous relationship with his sister Canace and killed himself when she became pregnant. Canace's baby was thrown to the dogs, so it is difficult to see where Amphissa could fit into this picture. The only explanation is that Macareus got someone else pregnant before doing the same for his sister. [Pausanias 10.38.4.]

AMPHISSA (2) was another name for METOPE, daughter of Echetus.

AMPHITHEA (1) was a daughter of Pronax. He was a son of Talaus and Lysimache, and brother to Adrastus, whom Amphithea married. According to some accounts, the Nemean games were instituted in honor of Pronax. By Adrastus she was the mother of Aegiale, Aegialeus, Argeia, and Deipyle. Argeia married Polyneices, son of Oedipus, and Deipyle married Diomedes, so he was both her grandson and son-in-law. Aegialeus was the only one of the Epigoni who fell in the war against Thebes, and he was worshipped as a hero at Pegae in Megaris, where his body was brought from Thebes. Amphithea had a brother, Lycurgus, who fell in the battle of the Seven against Thebes, and he is mentioned among those whom Asclepius brought back to life. [Pausanias 1.44.7, 3.18.7; Apollodorus 3.10.3.]

AMPHITHEA (2) was married to Autolycus. (Homer, *Iliad* 19.394, calls his wife Neaera.) She must have led an exciting but lonely life since Autolycus, son of Hermes, was the famous robber of Mount Parnassus. They had two daughters, Anticleia and Polymede. Anticleia married Laertes and became the mother of Odysseus. When Odysseus was an adolescent, he came to visit his grandparents. During a hunt with Autolycus he was wounded by a boar, and it was by the scar of this wound that he was later recognized by his old nurse when he returned to Ithaca from Troy. Polymede, the other daughter, was the mother of Jason, according to some. [Apollodorus 2.4.9.]

AMPHITHEA (3) was married to Lycurgus, brother of Admetus and king of Nemea. They were parents of Opheltes. On their expedition against Thebes, the Seven heroes stopped at Nemea to take in water. Opheltes' nurse left the child alone while showing the way to the Seven. The child was killed by a snake in the meantime, and subsequently buried by the Seven. Amphiaraus saw in this accident an omen boding destruction to him and his companions, and they called the child Archemorus, the Forerunner of Death, instituting the Nemean games in honor of him. Amphithea's name was occasionally seen as Eurydice. [Apollodorus 3.6.4; Pausanias 2.15.3.]

AMPHITHOE was one of the NEREIDES.

AMPHITRITE was the wife of Poseidon and goddess of the Mediterranean Sea. She is usually called one of the NEREIDES, but she also could have been one of the OCEANIDES. In either case she was Poseidon's first cousin, since Gaea was mother to Nereus, Oceanus, and Cronus, the father of Poseidon. She and her sister Thetis shared a surname, Halosydne, which means "the sea-born." As an immortal, her long history extended from the founding of things; she was present at the birth of Apollo and Artemis, and she was aunt to Achilles.

When Poseidon sought to embrace her in marriage, she fled from him, but one of his spies, Delphineus, told where she was hiding; he also pleaded Poseidon's suit so eloquently that Amphitrite conceded. After consummating the marriage, the grateful Poseidon placed Delphineus among the stars. Amphitrite became by Poseidon the mother of Triton, Rhode, and Benthesicyme. Rhode was called by some the wife of Helios, and the mother of Phaethon and the Heliades (but see RHODOS). Triton had two daughters—Pallas, whom Athena loved, and Triteia. Benthesicyme lived in Ethiopia and raised her bastard half-brother Eumolpus, son of Poseidon and Chione, who had been thrown into the sea by Chione out of fear of her father, Boreas, the god of the north wind.

In fact, Chione was only one of Poseidon's infidelities. In spite of what appeared to be a scene of domestic bliss in a golden palace under the sea with hordes of sea deities blowing on conches, Poseidon fathered a vast number of children both by divinities and mortal women. Amphitrite, on the other hand, appeared to be a faithful and dutiful wife, even assisting Poseidon in hitching his horses to his chariot. Only once did she rebel, and that was in the case of Scylla, a beautiful maiden being visited by Poseidon. Amphitrite put poisonous herbs into Scylla's bathing pool and changed her into a monster with six heads.

Amphitrite plays a part in two legends. The Penthelides, first settlers of Lesbos, received an oracle from her commanding them to sacrifice a bull to Poseidon and a virgin to her. They complied, and Phineis, the daughter of Phineus, was chosen by lot. When she was about to be thrown into the sea, her lover Enalus grasped her and leapt with her into the waves, where they were rescued by dolphins. The other story involves Theseus. When Minos threw a ring into the sea to test Theseus' claim of divine paternity (Poseidon), Theseus dove in and recovered not only the ring but a jeweled crown given to him by Amphitrite.

Amphitrite was a frequent subject in ancient art. She was often represented with a net over her hair and crab claws on her forehead. Sometimes she was shown riding on marine animals or being drawn by them in a chariot. She had a celebrated statue in the temple of Poseidon on the Isthmus of Corinth. She appeared in the sculptural group in the temple of Apollo at Amyclae and in the temple of Zeus at Olympia. She can be viewed even today on the arch of Augustus at Rimini. She was also represented on coins of Syracuse. [Homer, *Iliad* 20.207, *Odyssey* 4.404; Hesiod, *Theogony* 930; Apollodorus 1.4.6, 3.15.4; Apollonius Rhodius 1.1158, 4.1325; Hyginus, *Poetic Astronomy* 2.17; Euripides, *Cyclops* 702; Pausanias 1.17.3, 2.1.7, 5.2.3,26.2.]

AMYMONE was one of the DANAIDES, daughter of Danaus and Europa. With the exception of Hypermnestra, who with Lynceus started the royal house of Argos that extended to historical times, Amymone was the only other Danaid to achieve special distinction. When Danaus with his 50 daughters arrived by ship at Argos, there was a severe drought, and he sent Amymone out to look for water. First, we have to wonder why Amymone was chosen or why a whole search party from his plentiful supply of daughters was not sent. Next we wonder at what point in their itinerary this took place. Amymone found water at Lerna, about 7.5 kilometers from Argos. It is more likely she went inland to Lerna from Apobathmi (modern Kiveri), the landing place of Danaus, which was not over 2 kilometers.

Amymone was self-sufficient. Perhaps her prowess in the outdoors made her a good choice for the mission. She had brought along her bow and arrows. Encountering a stag, she shot at it but instead grazed the body of a sleeping satyr, who rose and chased her. Poseidon, who had a habit of turning up unexpectedly even on dry land, appeared and rescued her from the amorous satyr. He threw his trident, which stuck in a rock, and the satyr fled. Poseidon then turned his attentions to Amymone. We have no record as to how she reacted to this turn of events. But after he had finished, he told her to pull out the trident from the rock; when she did, a triple spring gushed forth. It was known afterward as the spring of Amymone, running freely even during droughts.

When the sons of Aegyptus followed the Danaides to Argos with professions of love and good intentions, Danaus was still certain they were there to usurp his new kingdom. He consented to the collective marriage of the 50 sons and daughters, but arranged to have the daughters kill the bridegrooms on their wedding night. Amymone, the only nonvirgin—and pregnant—Danaid, drew by lot for a husband Enceladus (or Midamus), whom she killed later that night. According to one or two accounts, she did not kill her husband, and this would have shown a certain amount of good sense, since she now faced the prospect of single parenthood.

The son of her union with Poseidon was Nauplius, a famous navigator and father of Proetus and Damastor. He discovered the constellation of the Great Bear and also founded the town of Nauplia. Proetus was the ancestor of the later Nauplius, who took revenge on the Greeks in the Trojan War for treacherously murdering his son Palamedes. Damastor was grandfather of Polydectes, who sent Perseus on his quest for the Gorgon's head. [Apollodorus 2.1.5; Hyginus, *Fables* 170; Lucian, *Dialogues of Sailors* 6; Pausanias 2.37.1, 4.35.2; Apollonius Rhodius 1.136.]

ANADYOMENE was a surname of Aphrodite referring to her being born from the foam of the sea. Apelles, the famous Greek painter, made a painting of Aphrodite Anadyomene drying her hair with her hands as she rose from the waves. He did the painting for the inhabitants of the island of Cos, who displayed it in the temple of Asclepius. Augustus later removed it to Rome. By the time of Nero it had deteriorated and was withdrawn. [Strabo 14.2.19; Pliny, *Natural History* 35.36.12,15; Pausanias 2.1.7.]

ANAEA (1) was one of the Amazons, from whom the town of Anaea in Caria derived its name (Stephanus Byzantium, "Anaea"). She was not mentioned by any of the main chroniclers of the Amazons (Diodorus Siculus, Pausanias, or Quintus Smyrnaeus), and it is interesting to speculate how this town became identified by name with an unrecorded Amazon. One begins to suspect that Stephanus Byzantium made such assignments in an arbitrary manner. After all, Caria was Amazon territory, so why should not such and such a place have been named for a long-dead warrior, if its name could not be otherwise explained?

ANAEA (2) was a name by which the Asiatic divinity Anaitis was sometimes called. This divinity was sometimes identified with Artemis and sometimes with Aphrodite. [Pausanias 3.16.6; Plutarch, *Lucullus* 24.]

ANAITIS, sometimes written Anaea, Aneitis, Tanais, or Nanaea, was an Asiatic divinity representing the creative powers of nature. She was worshipped in Armenia, Cappadocia, Assyria, Persia, and other parts of Asia. She had slaves often taken from prominent families as attendants in her temples. The female slaves were temple prostitutes, and the males were priests and keepers of the land adjoining the temples. Anaitis was identified by Greek writers with Aphrodite for rather obvious reasons and with Artemis for somewhat more obscure reasons. [Strabo 11.8.4, 12.3.36, 15.3.15, 16.1.4; Plutarch, *Artaxerxes* 27, Pausanias 3.16.6; Clement of Alexandria, *Exhortation to the Greeks* 43.]

ANANKE was the goddess of necessity. According to some, she was the mother of the Moirae, or Fates, although this distinction is usually given to THEMIS. [Plato, *Republic* 617.]

ANATOLE was one of the HORAE. [Hyginus, *Fables* 183.]

ANAXANDRA was the daughter of Thersander, Heraclid king of Cleonae. She and her twin sister Lathria were married to the twin-born kings of Sparta, Eurysthenes and Procles, sons of Aristodemus. The two brothers were in continual strife, although they ruled jointly, but they joined forces on one occasion with the son of Temenus to restore Aepytus, the son of Cresphontes, to Messenia. By Procles, Anaxandra became the mother of the Eurypontid line of Spartan kings. An altar sacred to Anaxandra and Lathria, as well as their tomb, was seen at Sparta by Pausanias. This marriage of twin sisters to twin brothers may be the only occurrence in mythology. [Pausanias 3.16.5; Herodotus 6.51, 8.131.]

ANAXARETE was a beautiful maiden of Cyprus, a descendant of Teucer. In vain Iphis professed his love to her and lamented that she did not return it. Finally, in despair he hanged himself at the main entrance to her house. While his funeral was going on, Anaxarete watched with indifference, but Venus punished her by changing her into a stone statue. This statue was preserved at Salamis in Cyprus in the temple of Venus Prospiciens. Antoninus Liberalis (39) tells the same story about Arsinoe and her lover Arceophon. [Ovid, *Metamorphoses* 14.698.]

ANAXIBIA (1) was a daughter of Bias and Pero, and sister to Talaus, Areius, and Leodocus. Her father and his brother Melampus shared the rule of two-thirds of the kingdom of Argos. Her brothers were counted among the Argonauts; one of them, Talaus, was also father of the hero Adrastus, one of the Seven against Thebes. She married Pelias, son of Poseidon and Tyro. Some writers called her Phylomache or Alphesiboea. Pelias was twin brother to Neleus, and when the two were grown, Pelias took over the government of Iolcus and exiled Neleus. Anaxibia bore Pelias several children—Acastus, Peisidice, Pelopeia, Hippothoe, Alcestis, Medusa, Amphinome, Euadne, Asteropeia, and Antinoe. It is interesting that her son, Acastus, accompanied the Argonauts, since her husband was certain all the crew were doomed to die. That was, of course, his reason for sending Jason on the perilous voyage.

Anaxibia saw Pelias send Jason on the quest for the Golden Fleece, and she witnessed his killing of his half-brother Aeson, Jason's father, and his nephew Promachus, Jason's brother. When the Argonauts returned, Medea deceived the Peliades, or daughters of Pelias, by assuring them that their old father could be rejuvenated by dismembering him and boiling his limbs in a cauldron with magic potions. It is not known whether or not Anaxibia was around during these gruesome events. It is not likely, since Medea might have suggested boiling the mother too, so as to match her with her rejuvenated husband.

In that case she would not have seen the celebration by her son, Acastus, of the funeral games for Pelias and the expulsion of Jason and Medea from Iolcus. Neither would she have seen the sacrifice Alcestis was willing to make for her husband, Admetus. Alcestis, incidentally, was not party to the murder of Pelias. [Apollodorus 1.9.10; Apollonius Rhodius 1.118; Hyginus, *Fables* 24; Diodorus Siculus 4.53; Pausanias 5.8.1, 8.11.2.]

ANAXIBIA (2) was a daughter of Cratieus, about whom absolutely nothing is known, and was the first wife of Nestor. He was a son of Neleus and Chloris of Pylus in Messenia, and had a most distinguished and heroic career from an early age. He took part in the fight of the Lapithae against the Centaurs, was a Calydonian hunter, and sailed with the Argonauts. Consequently, he was of an advanced age when he led 60 ships against Troy.

He married Anaxibia, who became by him the mother of Peisidice, Polycaste, Perseus, Stratichus, Aretus, Echephron, Peisistratus, Antilochus, and Thrasymedes. Modern lexicographers have indicated that Eurydice, daughter of Clymenus, could have been the mother of these children, citing Homer as evidence, but there is absolutely no foundation for this. Eurydice was married to Nestor when Telemachus came seeking news of Odysseus, but Nestor most likely married her on his return from Troy.

Nestor was probably in his mid-forties when he married Anaxibia. During the next dozen or so years Anaxibia produced nine children, with Antilochus and Thrasymedes being the eldest. She was probably pregnant with either Polycaste or Peisistratus when Nestor left for the war. Antilochus might have been the eldest son, but he was among the youngest of the Greeks at Troy. He and his brother were probably 18 and

19, and they had joined the war after it had been going on for five years. This explains why Nestor's other sons did not participate in the war; they were too young.

Nestor and Thrasymedes returned from the Trojan War. Antilochus did not, having been killed by Memnon and buried with Achilles and Patroclus. Peisistratus, the youngest son of Nestor and Anaxibia, became a friend to Odysseus' son Telemachus, whom he accompanied on a journey to the court of Menelaus in Sparta to further inquire about Odysseus. Polycaste, the younger of his two sisters, became by Telemachus the mother of Perseptolis. Anaxibia, though considerably younger than Nestor, died while he was in Troy or shortly after his return. After that he married Eurydice and, still reigning at Pylus, watched his sons and daughters raise families. He must have been around 80 when his long, eventful life ended. [Apollodorus 1.9.9; Homer, *Odyssey* 3.451; Hyginus, *Fables* 97, 252.]

ANAXIBIA (3) was a daughter of Pleisthenes and Aerope, and sister of Agamemnon and Menelaus. Atreus is often called her father, and she herself was also called Cydragora, Cyndragora, or Astyoche. She was married to Strophius, king of Crissa, and mother by him of Pylades and Astydameia.

When Aegisthus and Clytemnestra killed Agamemnon on his return from the Trojan War, they also planned to kill Orestes, the son of Agamemnon and Clytemnestra. But Electra, his sister, secretly entrusted him to a slave who carried him to Strophius at Crissa (modern Hrisa, which is adjacent to Delphi) at the foot of Mount Parnassus. Pylades and Orestes grew up together and formed a friendship that has become proverbial. They were already first cousins, and when Pylades married Electra they also became brothers-in-law. Orestes' marriage to Hermione, Menelaus' daughter, further strengthened the family bond since she was first cousin to each of them. Pylades' children were Hellanicus, Medon, and Strophius.

Anaxibia was in most respects a fortunate woman. She escaped the curse hanging over the House of Atreus, except for the murder of her brother Agamemnon. But both her son Pylades and Orestes, her nephew and foster son, lived to rule kingdoms, in spite of Orestes' final fulfillment of the curse when he committed matricide. [Pausanias 2.16.5,29.4; Euripedes, *Orestes* 804; Apollodorus 2.2.2; Pindar, *Pythian Odes* 11.23,35; Hyginus, *Fables* 117.]

ANAXIBIA (4) was one of the DANAIDES, a daughter of Danaus by an Ethiopian woman. She married Archelaus, son of Aegyptus. [Apollodorus 2.1.5.]

ANAXIROE was the daughter of Coronus, who might have been the same as the Sicyonian king of that name. She was, according to some, the wife of Epeius, son of Endymion. Epeius succeeded his father to the throne in Elis by winning a contest at Olympia over his brothers Paeon and Aetolus. Thus Anaxiroe was queen of the Elean territory. Her only child was Hyrmine, and through her Anaxiroe was grandmother of Augeas of the famous stables; Actor, father of the famous Moliones; and Tiphys, the pilot of the *Argo*. [Pausanias 5.1.6; Hyginus, *Fables* 14.]

ANAXITHEA was one of the DANAIDES. By Zeus she was the mother of Olenus, from whom the town of Olenus in Achaia derived its name. She is not mentioned in the usual lists of the Danaides. [Stephanus Byzantium, "Olenos"; Eustathius on Homer's *Iliad* 883.]

ANAXO (1) was a daughter of Alcaeus and Astydameia. Other writers called her mother Hipponome, Laonome, Lysidice, or Eurydice. Alcaeus was a son of the hero Perseus and Andromeda. Anaxo married Electryon, her uncle, who was king of Mycenae. They had nine sons— Stratobates, Gorgophonus, Phylonomus, Celaeneus, Amphimachus, Lysinomus, Chirimachus, Anactor, and Archelaus—and one daughter, Alcmena. Electryon also produced a bastard son, Licymnius, by a Phrygian woman.

Anaxo saw all her sons die in a battle with the sons of Pterelaus, a claimant to the Mycenaean throne, and she saw her husband killed accidentally by her brother and son-in-law, Amphitryon. Her daughter, Alcmena, who was also her first cousin, became her sister-in-law as well when she married Amphitryon. Anaxo had the distinction of being the grandmother of Heracles, whose original name was Alcaeus, from her father. [Apollodorus 2.4.5; Pausanias 2.25.8, 8.14.2.]

ANAXO (2) was a woman of Troezen whom Theseus was said to have carried off. After slaying her sons, he raped her daughters. It is most unfortunate that no more details are available on this uncharacteristic action by Theseus. [Plutarch, *Theseus* 29.]

ANCHIALE (1) was a daughter of Iapetus and mother of Cydnus, who was believed to have founded the town of Anchiale on the Cydnus River in Cilicia. This is the only reference to this Anchiale in mythology, although as daughter of Iapetus she was a sister of Prometheus, Epimetheus, Menoetius, and Atlas. She has the distinction of being the mother of a river-god, for these marine divinities were almost always the offspring of Oceanus and Tethys. There is nothing to say she could not have been the mother of a river by her uncle Oceanus.

Her son, half-man, half-river in form, was loved by a maiden called Comaetho. One of their sons, Parthenius, gave the surname Parthenia to the city of Tarsus, which lay on the Cydnus River. [Stephanus Byzantium, "Anchiale"; Nonnos, *Dionysiaca* 40.143.]

ANCHIALE (2), a nymph, was the mother of the Idaean Dactyls, who were born to her in a cave on Mount Ida near Oaxus. These mysterious beings were skilled in working with their hands and were said to have discovered the art of metallurgy. There were ten of them, five of each sex. The names of the males were Heracles, Epimedes, Idas, Paeonius, and Iasus. The names of the females, who settled in Samothrace, were a well-guarded secret. Anchiale was sometimes called also the mother by Apollo of Oaxus, founder of the Cretan city by this name, but usually his mother is called Acacallis. [Servius on Virgil's *Eclogues* 1.66; Diodorus Siculus 5.64; Cicero, *On the Nature of the Gods* 3.16.]

ANCHINOE (1) was the wife of Proteus and mother of Cabeiro, who in turn was the mother of Cadmilus by Hephaestus. Proteus was the famous marine deity who could assume various shapes, but if someone persisted in holding onto him through all his changes, Proteus had to reveal the future to him. Cadmilus was the father of the Samothracian Cabeiri and the Cabeirian nymphs, although some have called him one of the Cabeiri themselves. They were mystic divinities who were at the center of a cult worship surpassed only by the Eleusinian mysteries. [Stephanus Byzantium, "Kabeiria"; Scholiast on Apollonius Rhodius 1.917.]

ANCHINOE (2) was, according to some, the mother of Danaus and Aegyptus. She more often is called ACHIROE.

ANCHIROE (1) was a daughter of the river-god Erasinus and sister to Byze, Melite, and Moira. They lived in Argos and hospitably received Britomartis when she arrived there from Phoenicia. [Antoninus Liberalis 30.]

ANCHIROE (2) was the wife of the Messenian Penthilus and mother by him of Borus. Borus' son was Andropompus, whose son was Melanthus, father of Codrus. Codrus became king of Athens and sacrificed his life for Athenian victory over the Peloponnesians. Her grandson, Andropompus, was credited with the founding of Lebedus. [Pausanias 2.18.8; Strabo 14.1.3.]

ANCHIROE (3) was a daughter of the Libyan river-god Chremetes and wife of Psyllus. By him she became the mother of the Libyan Crataigonus, who played a role in the confusing saga known as the Indian Wars, a monumental struggle by the god Dionysus to drive the Indians out of Asia. Psyllus is called "the harebrained" and also the "gods' enemy." These two tantalizing pieces of information are all we are ever likely to know. There has been a suggestion that Anchiroe and Psyllus were the ancestors of a race called Psylloi, an African people of whom it was said that snakes would not harm them. [Nonnos, *Dionysiaca* 13.380.]

ANCHIROE (4), according to some, was the mother of Aegyptus and Danaus. She is more often called ACHIROE.

ANDRO was an Amazon, a companion of Penthesileia at Troy. [Tzetzes, *Posthomerica* 179.]

ANDROCLEIA was a daughter of Antipoenus and sister of Alcis. When Heracles mutilated the emissaries of Erginus and sent them back to Orchomenus, Erginus declared war on Thebes. Heracles armed every Theban of fighting age, taught them the use of weapons, and assumed command himself. An oracle promised him victory if the noblest born person in Thebes would take his own life. All eyes turned expectantly toward Antipoenus, a descendant of the Sparti; when he grudged dying for the common good, his daughters Androcleia and Alcis gladly did so in his stead. They were afterward honored as heroines in the temple of Artemis Eucleia. [Diodorus Siculus 4.10; Pausanias 9.17.1.]

ANDRODAIXA was a leader of the Amazons at Troy and was killed by Achilles. [Tzetzes, *Posthomerica* 179.]

ANDRODICE is mentioned as the mother of Thestius by Ares. (*See* DEMONICE.)

ANDROGENEIA was the mother of Asterius by Minos. Asterius was slain by Theseus. Both Androgeneia and Asterius are very mysterious individuals. Asterius seems to have been invented by Nonnos (*Dionysiaca* 222–252) as a Cretan leader in the forces Dionysus raised in the Indian Wars. Androgeneia was from Phaestus in southern Crete and coupled with Minos in Cydonia, bearing as a result the noble Asterius. In most of the other accounts of a being by this name, Asterius was the real name of the Minotaur, of which Minos was certainly not the father. [Pausanias 2.31.1; Apollodorus 3.1.4.]

ANDROMACHE is one of the noblest and saddest women in Greek literature. She was a daughter of Eetion, king of Thebae in Cilicia. She was already married to Hector, son of Priam, when the Greeks invaded Troy; otherwise, she might have met the fate of other women whose towns in the vicinity of Troy were captured by the foraging Greeks. In fact, Thebae was seized by Achilles, who slew Andromache's father, Eetion, and her seven brothers. Her mother was freed by Achilles after paying a ransom, but later killed by Artemis for some reason.

Andromache and Hector were very happily married, and they had two sons, Astyanax (Scamandrius) and Laodamas. Hector was the most distinguished warrior of the Trojans. The lines in the *Iliad* involving him and Andromache are among its most beautiful and moving passages. When finally Hector was killed by Achilles, she cradled his head at his funeral ceremony and lamented that their life together had ended so soon. She unknowingly predicted the fate of Astyanax when she feared that some Achaean would throw him from the wall of the city in revenge for a friend or relative killed by Hector. This is ultimately what happened.

Neoptolemus, son of Achilles, received Andromache and her children as his share of the Trojan spoils. The Greek council meanwhile debated what should be done with Astyanax. No mention was made of Laodamas. Homer mentions only one son, while Dictys mentions two. Odysseus held that all Priam's descendants should be put to death. Calchas, the seer, sealed Astyanax's fate by saying that if he lived he would avenge his parents and his city, so at the last moment Astyanax was killed. Neoptolemus had meanwhile given the two boys to their uncle Helenus, so Astyanax must have been seized from him. Why this did not happen with Laodamas as well cannot be answered. Perhaps Calchas' prophecy applied only to Astyanax. The identity of the one who murdered Astyanax is uncertain. Some say Odysseus carried out the deed; others say Neoptolemus did. In Euripides' *Trojan Women,* Talthybius takes him away from Andromache and returns with the dead body, but the actual killer is not identified.

Despite being on opposite sides of the war, Helenus and Neoptolemus became friends, because Helenus had earlier made prophecies favorable to the Greeks and especially to Neoptolemus. When the Greeks were busy debarking from Troy, Helenus, seeing the perils awaiting some of the returnees, advised Neoptolemus to travel overland. Phthia was still under the rule of the sons of Acastus, so Helenus advised Neoptolemus to build a city where he would find a house with foundations of iron, walls of wood, and a roof of wool. In Epeirus

Neoptolemus found some people living in tents made by upright spears thrust in the ground with their shafts draped over with blankets. This location was Lake Pambotis (modern Lake Ioanina) near the Dodonaean oracle. Neoptolemus and Andromache settled there, and Neoptolemus was able to overcome the Molossians who occupied that territory. Helenus, to whom Neoptolemus gave his mother Deidameia, settled in Chaonia, another part of Epeirus, in a city that he founded. Aeneas visited Epeirus and found Andromache offering a sacrifice at a shrine of Hector that she had erected.

By Neoptolemus Andromache became the mother of Molossus, Pielus, Pergamus, and Amphialus. After a few years Neoptolemus was able to return to Phthia, but for some reason he left Andromache, his sons, and his stepson Laodamas in Epeirus. Perhaps he had elected to settle the affairs of state in Phthia and yield the rule to relatives so he could return to Epeirus, although that is highly doubtful. His real reason must have been to seek out Menelaus, who at Troy had promised him his daughter Hermione. Hermione, inheritor of her mother's beauty, was already betrothed to her cousin Orestes. This did not deter Neoptolemus, who married her in accordance with the promise and presumably took her with him to Phthia. After a year or so, he journeyed to Delphi to inquire of the oracle why Hermione was not getting pregnant. At the altar of Apollo he was stabbed at the order of Orestes and buried under the edge of the temple.

Before leaving Epeirus he had undoubtedly conferred with Helenus about disposal of his property in the event of his death. We cannot know what happened to Deidameia, but when news of Neoptolemus' death reached Molossia, at his prior direction Andromache married her former brother-in-law, and became by him the mother of Cestrinus.

Molossus succeeded Helenus on the throne of Epeirus. Pielus began the line from which the historical Pyrrhides sprang. Cestrinus went northwestward to found Cestrine (modern Filiates), just north of the Thyamis River. Nothing further is known of Amphialus, and the fate of Hector's son Laodamas is also unknown. After Helenus' death, Andromache went with Per-

gamus to Asia Minor, where he joined Grynus of Mysia against his enemies. He built a town in commemoration of the victory, calling it Pergamus, and erected a sanctuary of his mother.

Andromache has been reported by a modern writer (Pierre Grimal, *The Dictionary of Classical Mythology*, Oxford: Blackwell, 1986) as a "tall, dark woman with a dominating character." This description certainly does not fit the picture presented in the *Iliad* and other sources. Perhaps strength of character was viewed by some as dominating. After all, seeing her beloved husband's body being dragged behind a chariot before the walls of Troy, having her little boy viciously hurled to his death, enduring the hardship of a long voyage to western Greece, being forced into sex with the son of her husband's killer and bearing his children, losing this husband (with whom she probably had fallen in love) to a much younger and more beautiful woman, and eventually being given to her former brother-in-law as property might have hardened anyone. But it would seem she had little opportunity to dominate anyone. All things considered, she was a most admirable individual, and she was important, as well, as the mother of founders of cities and royal lines. With Astyanax she was painted by Polygnotus in the Lesche at Delphi. [Homer, *Iliad* 6.390–502, 22.460, 24.725; Ovid, *Metamorphoses* 13.415; Pausanias· 1.11.1; Apollodorus 3.12.6, *Epitome* 6.12–14; Virgil, *Aeneid* 3.295; Dictys Cretensis 6.7; Hyginus, *Fables* 123.]

ANDROMEDA was the wife of Perseus and the mother of the royal Perseid line. She was the daughter of the Ethiopian king Cepheus, son of Belus and Achiroe, and Cassiepeia, daughter of Hermes' son Arabas. In an obscure account, Cassiepeia is called Iope, daughter of Aeolus, and the setting is Joppa in Phoenicia, which was named for her.

Andromeda was very beautiful, so much so that Cassiepeia boasted that her daughter outshone the Nereids in this respect. This was an unwise action, since the Nereids were sisters-in-law to Poseidon as well as part of his court. He sent a flood that devastated the land and a sea monster that harried ships. Cepheus consulted the oracle of Ammon and learned that the people would be delivered from these calamities only if Andromeda were given to the monster. When the people learned of this, they demanded the terms be met, so Andromeda was chained to a rock by the side of the sea.

Sent by his uncle on a perilous journey to fetch the head of the Gorgon Medusa, Perseus had successfully completed his task and was returning home, when from the air he observed Andromeda's dreadful predicament. With the assistance of his winged sandals, his helmet that rendered him invisible, and the petrifying head of Medusa, he was able to overcome the monster by turning it into a stony reef. He untied Andromeda, promptly fell in love with her, and asked for her hand in marriage. Overcome with gratitude, Cepheus and Cassiepeia readily agreed, forgetting that she had already been promised to Phineus, Cepheus' brother. Instead of being grateful that Perseus had saved his niece and fiancée from becoming the sea monster's lunch, Phineus raised an army and interrupted Perseus and Andromeda's wedding. What had worked for the sea monster worked also for Phineus and his followers, for they too were turned to stone by the Gorgon's head. Perseus and Andromeda stayed in Ethiopia long enough for Andromeda to have her first child, Perses, whom they left with Cepheus and Cassiepeia to bring up.

Perseus took Andromeda with him to the island of Seriphos, from where he had set out. He used the by-now-familiar means of dealing with his enemies and left Seriphos strewn with more stones than it already possessed by showing the fatal head to the tyrant Polydectes. He returned to Hermes the magical implements that had made the mission possible, and he gave Medusa's head to Athena, who mounted it on her shield. Next he enthroned as king of Seriphos the gentle Dictys, who had originally pulled him and Danae, his mother, from the sea. Then with Andromeda and Danae he sailed for Argos.

It is a mystery why Perseus and Danae returned to Argos. After all, they were aware that Acrisius had tried to kill them by setting them adrift in the sea. Maybe they thought sufficient time had elapsed to erase whatever the old problem had been. When Acrisius learned Perseus was coming to Argos, he was both shocked that his grandson still lived and terrified that the prophecy of his death at the hands of Perseus was

still in effect. He hastily departed for Thessaly, presumably leaving his kingdom in the hands of regents. Perseus and company arrived and took up residence in the city, most likely as honored guests. Both Danae and Perseus learned, perhaps for the first time, why they had been condemned and why Acrisius was not there to greet them. They must have lived in these circumstances for some time, at least until Perseus was comfortable enough in their new surroundings to journey to Larissa to compete in funeral games for King Teutamides' father. During the pentathlon, in throwing the quoit, he struck Acrisius and killed him, thus fulfilling the prophecy.

He was ashamed to return to Argos to succeed on the throne the man he had killed, so he struck a bargain with Megapenthes of Tiryns to swap kingdoms. He and Andromeda thus became king and queen of Tiryns, and had the neighboring cities of Mycenae and Midea fortified. Here Andromeda bore him several children—Alcaeus, Heleius, Sthenelus, Mestor, Electryon, Gorgophone, and Autochthe (all their names sounding like attributes of their father, except for Heleius).

The Perseid line was highly distinguished. Perses, who had been left in Ethiopia, was described as the founder of the Persian nation. Alcaeus and Electryon were progenitors of the Heraclids. Mestor was the ancestor of the Taphians, and Heleius received dominion over them when he helped Amphitryon in his war against them. Gorgophone became by Perieres the mother of a distinguished family that included Tyndareus, Icarius, and Leucippus. Sthenelus was the only one whose career was not especially glorious. He was the father of Eurystheus, who was in charge of imposing and monitoring the labors of Heracles. Of Autochthe nothing at all is known.

Andromeda is usually thought of as the "Chained Lady" in astronomy for she, along with Cepheus and Cassiepeia, was placed among the stars. Most people who know about the constellation and the nebula are unaware of her role in mythology as mother of several very important royal lines. We get few or no clues to her personality from the brief references available. It is too bad that two or three plays about her known once to exist disappeared in early times.

Marks left by the chains that bound Andromeda are pointed out even today on cliffs near Joppa. The petrified bones of the sea monster were shown in the city until one of the aediles had them transferred to Rome. [Apollodorus 2.4.3,5,7;. Hyginus, *Fables* 64; Ovid, *Metamorphoses* 4.663; Aratus, *Phenomena* 198; Eratosthenes, *Star Placements* 17.]

ANEITIS (*See* ANAITIS)

ANEMOTIS, the Subduer of the Winds, was a surname of Athena, under which she was worshipped and had a temple at Methone in Messenia. It was believed to have been built by Diomedes because the goddess answered his prayers to relieve the storms that devastated the countryside. [Pausanias 4.35.5.]

ANESIDORA, the Sender of Gifts, was a surname given to Gaea and to Demeter, the latter of whom had a temple under this name at Phlius in Attica. [Pausanias 1.31.2; Hesychius, "Anesidora"; Plutarch, *Table-Talk* 745.]

ANGELOS was a surname of Artemis, under which she was worshipped at Syracuse, and, according to some accounts, the original name of Hecate. [Hesychius, "Angelos"; Scholiast on Theocritus 2.12.]

ANGERONA was a Roman divinity of somewhat uncertain attributes. By some she was regarded as the goddess of anguish and fear, both producing these states in man and also relieving them. Her statue, with its mouth bound, was in the temple of Volupia near the Porta Romanula close to the Forum. This representation has been interpreted as expressing the value of keeping one's troubles private or of discouraging the bad luck attendant on giving voice to personal anxiety. Placement of a statue of anguish in a temple of joy could mean a number of things but was generally accepted as exposing sorrow to the contagion of joyfulness. Sacrifices to Angerona were made by persons suffering from a disease called *angina* (not the same as our modern ailment).

Other writers referred to Angerona as the goddess of silence (cf. Muta, Tacita). Some believe her worship was introduced at Rome to prevent the sacred and secret name of Rome from being known. Her statue with a silencing finger on the lip represented security as long as this secret was kept, and therefore Angerona came to be regarded as the protecting divinity of Rome. Her festival was called Angeronalia and celebrated in Rome every year on December 12. [Macrobius, *Saturnalia* 1.10, 3.9; Varro, *On the Latin Language* 6.23; Verrius Flaccus on Macrobius' *Saturnalia* 1.10.]

ANGITIA, or Anguitia, was a goddess worshipped in the area around Lake Fucinus by the Marrubians and Marsians. Once living in this region, she had taught the people remedies against snakebite; her name came from her ability to kill serpents by incantations (*anguis*=serpent). The goddess appears to have been of Greek origin, and some thought that Angitia was a name given to Medea by the Marsians, for it was recorded that Medea had gone to Italy eventually and taught the people magical remedies. Angitia had a temple and a treasury, according to inscriptions. The forest of Angitia near Lake Fucinus was named for her. She has been identified with the Bona Dea of the Romans. [Servius on Virgil's *Aeneid* 7.750; Silius Italicus 8.498; Solinus 2.]

ANIGRIDES were nymphs of the Anigrus River in Elis. A grotto near the mouth of the river was sacred to them and visited by persons suffering from skin diseases. Those afflicted prayed and offered sacrifices to the nymphs and bathed in the river. [Pausanias 5.5.6; Strabo 8.3.19; Eustathius on Homer's *Iliad* 880.]

ANIPPE was a daughter of the Nile River. She was the mother of Busiris, king of Egypt, by Poseidon. Others say his mother was LYSIANASSA, daughter of Epaphus.

ANNA PERENNA was an ancient Roman divinity whose identity seems to have been composed from three different legends and most likely three separate individuals. According to one story she was a daughter of Belus and sister of Dido. After Dido committed suicide, Anna fled to Italy when Carthage fell to the native king

Iarbas. The ship she took was wrecked on the shore of the town of Laurentum, where Aeneas ruled, and Anna was hospitably received by him. From her he learned of Dido's sad demise and lamented her. As a guest in his palace, Anna was bitterly resented by Aeneas' wife, Lavinia, who was preparing to do harm to her. But Dido appeared in a dream to warn Anna, who fled. She encountered Numicius, the god of the nearby river, and he took her to his bed. When Aeneas' servants came to search for her, they were informed by a water spirit that Anna had become the nymph of the stream and that her new name was Perenna, meaning eternal. The servants immediately established a festival of Anna Perenna.

Another manifestation of Anna Perenna was in a legend having to do with the plebs and their migration to the Mons Sacer because of political strife. Here they faced famine, and to help relieve them an aged woman named Anna Perenna came every day from nearby Bovillae. She distributed cakes among the hungry, and when eventually they were able to return to Rome they paid their benefactress divine honors and erected a temple to her.

Finally, it seems that Mars, the war god, fell in love with Minerva, the goddess of wisdom, but could not make her show any return of interest. He enlisted the help of the aged Anna, who, knowing the goddess would never succumb, led him on mercilessly, until one night she actually disguised herself as Minerva. Just when Mars was sufficiently worked up, she lifted her veil and ridiculed him. He riddled her with strong language, and this was the origin perhaps of the obscenities sung at the festival of Anna Perenna on every March 15.

Her festivals were joyful and merry, and betokened the return of spring. She was regarded as a giver of life, health, and abundance. As usual for divinities associated with the cycles of the seasons, she was identified with other beings, such as Luna, Themis, Io, and even the nymphs who nursed Jupiter. [Ovid, *Fasti* 3.517,657; Virgil *Aeneid* 4 passim; Macrobius, *Saturnalia* 1.12.]

ANTAEA was a surname of Demeter, Rhea, and Cybele, probably signifying a goddess whom man may approach in prayers. [Apollonius Rhodius 1.1141; Hesychius, "Antaea."]

ANTANDRA was one of the AMAZONS. [Quintus Smyrnaeus 1.43.]

ANTEIA was a daughter of the Lycian king Iobates (called Amphianax by some). Anteia was also called sometimes by a different name, Stheneboea. She had a sister named Anticleia. When Proetus was expelled by his twin brother, Acrisius, from Argos, he went to the court of Iobates and was hospitably received. Iobates gave him Anteia in marriage, then with an armed force helped him regain part of the Argolid rule. Tiryns was taken and fortified by the Cyclopes, who were loyal to Proetus. Acrisius finally was forced to share the kingdom with his brother, and Proetus became ruler of Tiryns, the Heraion, Midea, and the coast of Argolis.

Anteia's children by Proetus were Maera, Iphianassa, Lysippe, Iphinoe, and Megapenthes. Perhaps life grew dull on the stark heights of the walled city of Tiryns, and maybe the cares of motherhood weighed heavily, for when the young, dashing, and tantalizingly handsome Bellerophon arrived from Corinth to be purified from a murder he had committed, Anteia fell in love with him. She tried desperately to seduce him, but he rejected her advances. With injured pride and perhaps fear of being found out, she told Proetus that their young guest had made indecent proposals to her and that she wanted him put to death. Though enraged by this reported affront, Proetus could not bring himself to violate the strict rules of hospitality by murdering a guest. Instead he sent him to his father-in-law on one pretext or another, bearing a sealed message directing Iobates to put him to death.

Anteia must have paid for this when three of her daughters went insane, probably as a result of rejecting the worship of Dionysus. This reason makes sense in view of the fact that ironically the three in their madness almost mimicked the orgiastic wanderings of the followers of the god. Melampus the seer eventually cured them, but at a heavy price—two-thirds of the kingdom for himself and his brother, Bias. Iphinoe died while being pursued by Melampus and his assistants. Iphianassa and Lysippe married Bias and Melampus, and consequently became queens in the territories owned by the brothers.

Megapenthes succeeded Proetus as king of Tiryns, but later traded Tiryns for Argos after the return of Perseus. The remaining daughter, Maera, was one of the many conquests by Zeus and bore him a son, Locrus, who helped Amphion and Zethus build Thebes.

By no means can Anteia be called an admirable character. Her behavior toward Bellerophon (not to mention toward her husband) was unconscionable. We never hear from her after the Bellerophon incident, and perhaps it is safe to assume she learned her lesson. Or maybe word got out and young, handsome heroes went elsewhere for purification or other needs. [Apollodorus 2.2.1; Homer, *Iliad* 6.160; Eustathius on Homer's *Odyssey* 1688; Pausanias 2.16.2.]

ANTEVORTA, also called Porrima or Prorsa, and Postvorta, or Postverta, were described as companions of the Roman goddess Carmenta. Or, they might have been attributes of the goddess. Carmenta possessed the gift of prophecy, and the two names could represent her ability to look backward and forward in time. Carmenta was also a divinity of procreation, and she was invoked by pregnant women. In this connection, Prorsa and Postvorta might mean "head first" or "feet first," the two positions in which a child can be born. In later times, however, Antevorta and Postvorta were regarded as two distinct beings, companions to Carmenta. They had two altars at Rome and received prayers and sacrifices from expectant mothers. [Ovid, *Fasti* 1.633; Macrobius, *Saturnalia* 1.7; Gellius 16.16.]

ANTHE was one of the ALCYONIDES. [Eustathius on Homer's *Iliad* 776; Suidas, "Alkyonides."]

ANTHEA was one of the THESPIADES and bore Heracles a son, whose name has disappeared. [Apollodorus 2.7.8.]

ANTHEDON was a nymph from whom the Boeotian town of Anthedon derived its name. [Pausanias 9.22.5.]

ANTHEIA, the Blooming, or the Friend of Flowers, was a surname of Hera, under which she had a temple at Argos. Before this temple was the mound under which were buried the women who had come with Dionysus from the Aegean islands and had fallen in a contest with the Argives and Perseus. Antheia was used at Cnossus as a surname of Aphrodite. [Pausanias 2.22.1; Hesychius, "Antheia."]

ANTHEIS was one of the HYACINTHIDES. [Apollodorus 3.15.8.]

ANTHELIA was one of the DANAIDES, daughter of Danaus and Polyxo. She was married to Cisseus, son of Aegyptus. [Apollodorus 2.1.5.]

ANTHIPPE was one of the THESPIADES, and by Heracles became the mother of Hippodromus. [Apollodorus 2.7.8.]

ANTHRACIA was an Arcadian nymph, probably a nurse of Zeus. She was represented at Megalopolis along with Anchiroe, Hagno, Myrtoessa, and Nais. [Pausanias 8.31.2.]

ANTIA (*See* ANTEIA)

ANTIANEIRA (1) was a daughter of the Aeolid Pheres, who was the founder of Pherae in Thessaly. This made her a sister of Admetus, Eidomene, Lycurgus, and Periopis. She is seldom heard of in the usual accounts, but she was one of Apollo's many conquests. By him she gave birth to Idmon on the banks of the Amphrysus River. It was by this river that Apollo tended the flocks of Admetus, and this association provided the opportunity for the liaison. Apollo's sexual interest in her might have been gratuitous, since he was probably in love with her brother Admetus.

Idmon was one of the soothsayers who accompanied the Argonauts. He joined the expedition knowing he would die before its completion. He was killed in the country of the Mariandynians by a boar or a serpent. He had a shrine at Heracleia that Apollo had commanded to be built. The mother of Idmon has also been called Asteria or Laothoe. [Scholiast on Apollonius Rhodius 1.139,140,143,443, 2.815; Orphica, *Argonautica* 185,721; Hyginus, *Fables* 14; Apollodorus 1.9.23.]

ANTIANEIRA (2) was a daughter of Menetus and therefore called Meneteis. By Hermes she was the mother of twin sons, Eurytus and Echion. Some call their mother Laothoe. The twins were born at Alope in Thessaly. They took part in the expedition of the Argonauts (Apollodorus lists only Eurytus) and in the Calydonian boar hunt (although they are absent from the lists of both Apollodorus and Ovid). During the Argonaut they used the cunningness they had inherited to great advantage. It is too bad we do not know more of this story, such as why Antianeira was selected by Hermes. His progeny were not all that many, and in contrast to Zeus, Apollo, and Poseidon, he appeared almost chaste. His sexual partners were not run-of-the-mill, so it would be interesting to know what attracted him to Antianeira. [Apollonius Rhodius 1.56; Hyginus, *Fables* 14; Pindar, *Pythian Odes* 4.179; Ovid, *Metamorphoses* 8.311.]

ANTIBIA was a daughter of Amphidamas, wife of Sthenelus, and mother of Eurystheus. The mother of Eurystheus is usually called NICIPPE. [Didymus, quoted by scholiast on Homer's *Iliad* 19.116.]

ANTIBROTA was one of the AMAZONS. [Quintus Smyrnaeus 1.45.]

ANTICLEIA (1) was a daughter of Autolycus and Amphithea or Neaera. Her sister was Polymede, who became the mother of Jason. The sisters were granddaughters of Hermes, and their father had inherited his father's talents for thievery and cunning. Autolycus was also one of the Argonauts (and not everyone will remember that he was grandfather to Jason, the captain).

Anticleia was seduced by Sisyphus, king of Corinth, when her father rustled some cattle from him and was found out after Sisyphus set a trap. When Sisyphus came to Parnassus to retrieve his cattle, he managed, while Autolycus was diverted by the Corinthian cadre, to sneak into Anticleia's quarters and have sex with her. This might appear to some as possible rape, but given the lonely mountain existence, with her sister gone for many years, it is not surprising

that Anticleia willingly succumbed to a handsome and aggressive king from the sophisticated city of Corinth. Later writers claimed that this coupling was responsible for the conception of Odysseus, and that Anticleia, already betrothed to Laertes, shortly married him and passed the child off as his.

Laertes was more likely the father of Odysseus. His own brilliant career anticipated that of his more renowned son. He was the son of Arceisius in Ithaca, and participated in both the Calydonian boar hunt and the Argonaut. It makes good sense that Autolycus saw a good prospect for a son-in-law in this fellow crew member of the *Argo*. Shortly after Odysseus was born, Autolycus visited Ithaca and named the baby at the request of Eurycleia, the nurse. As a boy, Odysseus visited Autolycus and went on a hunt with his uncles, during which he was wounded on the leg by a boar. It was this wound by which Eurycleia recognized him on his secret return to Ithaca.

Anticleia had a daughter, Ctimene, by Laertes. She also had a kind of foster child in Eumaeus, the swineherd, whom she brought up with Ctimene and treated as her own child. This kindness paid off when Odysseus returned, since Eumaeus was his principal ally against the suitors. Ctimene married Eurylochus, who later accompanied Odysseus in the war and on the fearful voyage home. He died after the sacrilege of killing the cattle of Helios.

Anticleia died from grief at the imagined fate of her son. When Odysseus returned to Ithaca, he was advised of this fact by Eumaeus. But this was only confirmation of what he already knew, since he had seen the shade of his mother in Hades. By this time Laertes lived in rural retirement, devoted to agricultural pursuits and attended by one ancient female slave.

Anticleia was an admirable person. She led an isolated existence during her youth. Her sister, Polymede, was considerably older, since her son, Jason, was old enough to lead the expedition of the Argonauts, on which he was accompanied by Laertes, who later became Anticleia's husband. There were probably several brothers in between, the ones who took the young Odysseus on the boar hunt. Anticleia's indiscretion with Sisyphus was only a brief interlude and had no impact on the rest of her life, unless we consider that Odysseus was a result of this hasty liaison. She was a very kindly person, exemplified by the fact that she raised Eumaeus with her own children. It is possible, of course, that his royal blood (for he was the son of Ctesius, king of the island of Syros) had something to do with this. The strength of her devotion to her family is indicated by her dying from grief at Odysseus' apparent death. [Pausanias 8.4.3; Homer, *Odyssey* 4.755, 11.85, 15.362, 16.118, 19.394; Apollodorus 1.9.16; Eustathius on Homer's *Odyssey* 1791; Ovid, *Metamorphoses* 13.32, *Art of Love* 3.313; Plutarch, *Greek Questions* 43; Hyginus, *Fables* 243.]

ANTICLEIA (2), who some suggest may be the same as (1), was the mother of Periphetes by Hephaestus or Poseidon. Periphetes, surnamed Corynetes (Club-Bearer) because of the brazen club he used to bash out his victims' brains, was a robber at Epidaurus. On his journey by foot from Troezen to Athens, Theseus was waylaid by Periphetes. He took the club from his assailant and beat him to death.

It is almost certain that this Anticleia is not the same as the daughter of Autolycus. Unfortunately, people with the same name in mythology were often identified as one person. This Anticleia had to be at least 15 to 20 years older than her son, Periphetes, and his slayer, Theseus. Theseus, we learn, was between 55 and 60 at the beginning of the Trojan War. That would make Anticleia about 75. Odysseus was at his prime at the start of the war—30 or younger. This would mean his mother was 45 or older when she bore him, not a very likely circumstance if we remember the seduction by Sisyphus and the fact that young heroes like Laertes were not prone to marry women in their forties if they hoped to produce heirs. [Pausanias 2.1.4; Apollodorus 3.16.1; Hyginus, *Fables* 38; Plutarch, *Theseus* 8; Ovid, *Metamorphoses* 7.437.]

ANTICLEIA (3) was the daughter of Iobates, king of Lycia. Because of a false report by his wife that Bellerophon had tried to seduce her, Proetus, the king of Argos, sent the young hero to the court of his father-in-law in Lycia. Choosing not to kill him outright, Iobates sent him on the perilous mission of killing the fearful Chimaera. When Bellerophon accomplished this, Iobates sent him on other dangerous missions. But Bellerophon survived these as well, even an ambush by the bravest and strongest of the Lycians. Seeing that it was hopeless to get rid of the hero by putting him to adventurous tasks, Iobates showed him the message he had received from Proetus. He gave him his daughter Anticleia (some call her Philonoe or Cassandra) in marriage and made him his successor on the throne. We do not know how Anticleia felt about all this. Chances are she was quite willing to be matched with this dashing and handsome young hero. The reputation that preceded him as seducer of her sister probably added interest to the arrangement. In any case, the two were married, and they became parents of Isander, Hippolochus, and Laodameia. Isander was killed by Ares in a fight with the Solymi. Hippolochus was father of Glaucus, the Lycian prince. Laodameia became by Zeus the mother of Sarpedon. For some reason she was killed by Artemis while engaged in weaving. Glaucus and Sarpedon commanded the Lycian forces that assisted the Trojans, and both were killed in battle. Earlier than this, probably while the children were still infants, Bellerophon had fallen out of favor with the gods and wandered from home, avoiding other people. He tried to recapture his great triumphs by attempting to scale heaven while astride Pegasus, but was dashed to earth and became lame or blind. He was worshipped as a hero in Corinth, where he had a sanctuary in the grove of Craneion. The subsequent history of Anticleia is not known. If she reached old age, she did so quite alone, for her husband and children were gone. Glaucus, however, had founded the Lycian dynasty, and perhaps she found a home with her grandchildren. [Homer, *Iliad* 6.197–205; Apollodorus 2.3.2; Pindar, *Olympian Odes* 13.82; Pausanias 2.2.4.]

ANTICLEIA (4) was a daughter of Diocles. She married Machaon, a son of Asclepius, who appropriately was a physician. He was surgeon to the Greeks in the Trojan War but also, with his brother Podaleirius, commander of men from Tricca, Ithome, and Oechalia in Thessaly, who had sailed from Greece in 30 ships. He cured Philoctetes, was himself wounded, and was one of the men concealed in the wooden horse. He was killed by Eurypylus, and his remains were carried to Messenia by Nestor. His tomb was in Gerenia, but it is likely his ashes were buried at Tricca with those of Podaleirius, since they had a joint sanctuary there.

Before he left for the war, Machaon fathered several children by Anticleia—Gorgasus, Nicomachus, Alexanor, Sphyrus, and Polemocrates. Diocles, king of Pharae (modern Kalamata), was a wealthy vassal of the Atreidae; upon his death, his grandsons Gorgasus and Nicomachus succeeded to the kingdom. They practiced the healing art as their father had done and were accorded almost divine honor. Their sanctuary at Pharae was founded by Isthmius, the son of Glaucus and grandson of Aepytus.

The other sons were notable as well. Alexanor built a temple to Machaon at Titane in Sicyonia, and he himself was worshipped there also. Polemocrates had a sanctuary at Eua in Cynuria, and Sphyrus founded the sanctuary and temple of Asclepius in Argos.

It is easy enough to figure out a possible series of events in the case of Anticleia. Machaon ruled the cities of Tricca, Ithome, and Oechalia, while Anticleia grew up in Pharae in southern Peloponnesus. How did they happen to come together? Machaon was one of the suitors of Helen of Sparta. Perhaps seeing that the suit was futile, he crossed the mountain to Pharae and courted Anticleia. Undoubtedly she accompanied him to his kingdom, because he departed from there for the Trojan War and never returned. After his death, Anticleia returned to Pharae, since her own brothers were killed in the war and the throne of Pharae would be vacant upon Diocles' death. She would need to be there to advance the cause of her own sons. As for the throne in Tricca, there were the heirs of Podaleirius to consider. This worked out to her advantage and also explains why Nestor brought Machaon's ashes back to Messenia.

Anticleia appears as a woman of considerable intelligence, aware of the affairs of state and able to predict the uncertain political tides. She probably lived comfortably in Pharae until her death, celebrated as the mother of a far-reaching

medical fraternity. [Homer, *Iliad* 2.728, 11.515; Apollodorus 3.10.8; Hyginus, *Fables* 81; Pausanias 2.11.6,23.4,38.6, 3.26.7, 4.3.2,6,30.2.]

ANTIGONE (1) was one of the two daughters of Oedipus by his mother Iocaste, thus making her also half-sister to him. Her sister was Ismene, and her brothers were Eteocles and Polyneices. When the terrible truth was learned about the incestuous marriage of the parents, Oedipus blinded himself and Iocaste killed herself. In Sophocles' *Oedipus the King,* Oedipus called in the daughters, who were still children, for a farewell. At this point the sons were only babies, so it would appear.

Creon assumed control of Thebes, and Oedipus was expelled. Antigone undertook to guide her father, although she was still virtually a child. She accompanied him on years of wandering until he came to Attica, where he eventually died at Colonus just outside Athens. After his death, Antigone returned to Thebes and lived with Ismene. There is no record of how long she was away, but it was long enough for her brothers to become adults and assume the rule of Thebes. Polyneices was subsequently denied his term of alternate rule and fled to avoid assassination. He went to Argos and enlisted the assistance of Adrastus and others against his brother. Meanwhile, Antigone became betrothed to Haemon, the son of Creon. From all appearances her relationship with Eteocles was amiable.

When the seven chiefs, including Polyneices, marched against Thebes, her brothers killed each other in battle, and the rule of Thebes reverted for the third time to Creon. His first act of office was to forbid the burial of any of the invaders, especially the treasonable Polyneices. Antigone was horrified at this order and sneaked out to strew dust over her brother's body. (Some say that with the help of Argeia, Polyneices' Argive wife, she secretly burned the body on Eteocles' funeral pyre.) Here was an extreme case of civil disobedience, for which the penalty of capital punishment had been clearly established. Antigone had no case, even though devotion to family and the divine sacrament regarding disposal of the dead were on her side.

She was sentenced to death, and Creon placed her, alive, in the crypt with her brother's body, or in a subterranean cave. Haemon came to her, and finding that she had hanged herself, fell on his sword and died by her side. Another version of the story says Haemon secretly released her and that she lived a pastoral life outside Thebes while she raised their son. In time the son grew up and went to Thebes, where by a birthmark he was recognized by Creon and killed, whereupon Haemon killed both Antigone and himself.

Antigone is one of the saddest people in the old tragedies. It is easy to pity Iocaste, but after all, her awareness of the sad state of affairs endured for perhaps less than an hour, because she killed herself immediately upon learning the horrible truth. But Antigone's grief was only beginning. She sacrificed what was left of her childhood and also her adolescence to become companion and guide to her helpless father. Could a day have passed that she did not also remember he was her half-brother as well? The years of companionship must have developed a very strong bond, so that Oedipus' death was doubly sorrowful for her. Then to return to Thebes and find her brothers in political strife must have been painful. The war and resulting deaths of the brothers, followed by Creon's decree, were shocking. Her violation of the decree out of her strong conviction that she was obeying deep familial and even divine imperatives was a final reaction to a life of grief that had been thrust upon her. Death must have been welcome to her. She is one of the totally admirable women in mythology. [Apollodorus 3.5.8,7.1; Hyginus, *Fables* 72; Sophocles, *Oedipus the King* and *Antigone*.]

ANTIGONE (2) was a daughter of Eurytion of Phthia. Son of Actor, he was one of the Argonauts and a Calydonian hunter. On the Argonaut he met Peleus, son of Aeacus, and they became friends. After the voyage was over, Peleus returned to Aegina, where he became involved in a plot that resulted in the death of Phocus, his half-brother. He was exiled and went to his friend Eurytion in Phthia for refuge and purification. In addition, Eurytion gave him Antigone in marriage and she became by him the mother of Polydora. Peleus also ruled over one-third of the kingdom. Not long afterward, the two men were united in another heroic adventure, when they joined the famous

Calydonian boar hunt. Unhappily, Peleus, while casting a javelin at the boar, accidentally killed Eurytion. Although inadvertent, the act assumed another dimension when it followed that Peleus and Antigone would inherit the entire kingdom. Peleus at once went into a kind of voluntary exile, during which time he would be purified before officially claiming the kingdom. He went to the court of Acastus, another old Argonaut friend, at Iolcus and was purified, a process that must have taken some time. He was there long enough for Astydameia, Acastus' wife, to fall in love with and offer herself to him. He rejected her, and she told her husband that Peleus had tried to rape her. As if that were not enough, she also wrote to Antigone, telling her Peleus was about to marry Sterope, Acastus' daughter. Acastus did not kill Peleus outright but, pretending he had no knowledge of the affair, took him hunting on Mount Pelion and left him weaponless as he slept. Peleus nearly lost his life to hostile Centaurs but managed to escape. He returned home to the sad news that Antigone had hanged herself.

Polydora, Antigone's daughter by Peleus, married Borus, the son of Perieres, but had a son by the river-god Spercheius. This was Menesthius, who fought with Achilles, his (far younger) uncle, at Troy. [Apollodorus 3.12.2,13.1–3; Eustathius on Homer's *Iliad* 321.]

ANTIGONE (3) was a daughter of Laomedon and sister of Priam, Lampus, Clytius, Hicetaon, Bucolion, and Tithonus (who was kidnapped by the goddess of the dawn because of his beauty). She also had sisters—Hesione, Cilla, Astyoche, Aethylla, Medesicaste, and Procleia. Antigone made the grievous mistake of boasting that she was better-looking than Hera. Sensitive about her appeal to the philandering Zeus, Hera punished this presumptuous behavior by changing Antigone into a stork. [Ovid, *Metamorphoses* 6.93.]

ANTIGONE (4) was a daughter of Pheres and sister of Admetus, Lycurgus, Periapis, and Eidomene. Her father, son of Cretheus, founded Pherae in Thessaly. She married Pyremus or Cometes and became the mother of Asterion, the Argonaut. There is little of importance about Antigone except that she was surrounded by participants in the Argonaut. Jason was her first cousin, Admetus her brother, and Asterion her son. Perhaps, like so many women in mythology, she serves as a kind of anchor in the convergence of events that preceded the Trojan War. [Homer, *Odyssey* 11.259; Apollodorus 1.9.11,14, 3.10.4; Apollonius Rhodius 1.35; Orphica, *Argonautica* 161; Hyginus, *Fables* 14.]

ANTIMACHE was the mother of Admete and Perimedes by Eurystheus. Admete's mother is usually called also ADMETE. Her father was Amphidamas, a son of Lycurgus. [Apollodorus 2.8.1.]

ANTINOE (1) was a daughter of Cepheus, son of Aleus, and had twenty brothers and one sister, Sterope. Antinoe was sometimes called Cleophile or Eurynome. At the command of an oracle she led the inhabitants of Mantineia from the original site of the city to a new one. The old site is not known, but we know it was founded by Mantineus, the son of Lycaon. She accomplished this enterprise by following a snake. The river in the vicinity of the later Mantineia was consequently called the Ophis (Snake). A monument at Mantineia commemorated this event. Her tomb, called the Common Hearth, was near the theater. This is all we know of Antinoe, but it is probable she was the wife of Lycurgus, the brother of Cepheus, since marriage between nieces and uncles was fairly common. Lycurgus was designated as an Arcadian king, and his kingdom could have been Mantineia, since Cepheus already held Tegea. He also killed Areithous in a battle near Mantineia, which suggests he was defending the city. This would help explain what Antinoe was doing in Mantineia in the first place. Being wife of the king would give her sufficient credibility to be followed from one town site to another. Her children by Lycurgus were Ancaeus, Epochus, Amphidamas, and Iasus.

Ancaeus was an Argonaut and Calydonian hunter; he was killed on the hunt. He was also father of Agapenor, founder of Paphus in Cyprus. Amphidamas was the father of Antimache (usually called Admete), who married Eurystheus. Iasus, who had a statue at Tegea, was the father of the Arcadian Atalanta. Epochus was

represented on one of the pedestals of the temple of Athena Alea at Tegea. [Apollodorus 2.7.3, 3.9.1; Pausanias 8.9.5.]

ANTINOE (2) was one of the PELIADES. [Pausanias 8.11.2.]

ANTIOCHE (1) was a daughter of Pylon and married to Eurytus, by whom she became the mother of Iphitus, Clytius, Molion or Deion, Toxeus, and Iole. She was also called Antiope. Nothing is known of her father and consequently her lineage, but chances are they were Thessalians from Oechalia or one of its neighboring cities.

Antioche's lot was not a happy one. Her husband, Eurytus, son of Melaneus and Stratonice, was a skillful archer and was said to have instructed Heracles in the art. If this was true, it proved to be his undoing. Their daughter, Iole, was exceptionally beautiful and had many suitors. However, Eurytus was not ready to yield her to just anyone, and this reluctance was coupled with an opportunity to demonstrate his prowess with the bow. He offered Iole to anyone who could outshoot him and his sons. Nobody could come close to matching him until Heracles came back to Oechalia. He quite easily bested Eurytus and claimed Iole. Remembering that Heracles had slaughtered his wife, Megara, and his own children by her in a fit of madness, Eurytus refused to give him Iole and, with the exception of Iphitus, his sons stood behind him. Heracles consequently marched on Oechalia and killed Eurytus and his sons Molion and Toxeus. He then took Iole with him, and Iphitus followed them. It is likely that Iphitus was one of Heracles' many male lovers. They had met on the Argonaut, during which Antioche's other son, Clytius, was killed by Aeetes.

So Antioche was left quite alone, unless Heracles carried her along as Iole's companion. We never hear of her again, but it is more than likely that she remained in Oechalia to minister to the memory of her husband. His remains were preserved in a grove in Oechalia, and sacrifices were offered to him in the Messenian Oechalia, which shared the reputation of being the scene of the whole occurrence. [Apollonius Rhodius 1.86; Hyginus, *Fables* 14; Diodorus Siculus

4.37; Apollodorus 2.4.9; Pausanias 4.3.6, 27.4,33.5.]

ANTIOCHE (2) was one of the AMAZONS. [Hyginus, *Fables* 163.]

ANTIOPE (1) was a daughter of Nycteus and Polyxo (or, some say, the river-god Asopus in Boeotia). Nycteus was a son of Hyrieus, and brother to Lycus and Orion. Nycteis was a patronymic that could be applied to Antiope, but there seems to have been a sister whose real name was Nycteis—the wife of Polydorus, son of Cadmus, and mother of Labdacus. Thebe was a name also used occasionally for Antiope. She was very beautiful, and she attracted the attention of Zeus, who soon slept with and impregnated her.

Epopeus, a son of Poseidon and Canace, was king of Sicyon. There is confusion about the role he played in this story. About half the accounts say he carried Antiope off from Thebes. The others say she fled to him when she discovered she was pregnant, and this would indicate they had some prior acquaintanceship. One writer even maintains she was married to her uncle Lycus and that Epopeus seduced her away from him. Whatever the situation, Epopeus was said to have married her. According to some, Nycteus killed himself; others relate that he went in hot pursuit of his daughter and killed Epopeus, who also killed him. Whether by suicide or mortal battle wounds, Nycteus had time enough to exact a deathbed promise from Lycus that he would recover Antiope. This Lycus did, and returned to Thebes. When they reached Eleutherae, Antiope gave birth to twin sons. Lycus promptly exposed the babies on Mount Cithaeron, but they were found by a goatherd and brought up by him.

Antiope meanwhile was carried back to Thebes and kept imprisoned by Lycus and his wife, Dirce. Dirce was jealous of her, and this lends some credibility to earlier accounts of a liaison between Antiope and her uncle. At any rate, Dirce was not happy with her husband's role as protector of his dead brother's beautiful daughter. This situation continued until the twins Amphion and Zethus, named by the goatherd, had grown up. Amphion was a musician; Zethus loved hunting and tending the flocks.

They fortified the town of Entresis near Thespiae and made their home there. It is hard to figure what took place with Antiope all these long years. Had she become a kind of servant under everyone's watchful eye, or was she actually manacled? It seems evident there was some kind of restraint, since she wasted no time in escaping her uncle and his wife at the first opportunity.

For some reason she made her way to Entresis, where she came to her sons' cottage. She asked asylum, and before long they recognized each other from the coincidences of the past. The sons immediately set about avenging the wrongs done to their mother. They went to Thebes and killed Lycus; they tied Dirce to a bull and had her dragged to death, after which they threw her body into a spring. They then took possession of Thebes and married, Zethus to Thebe and Amphion to Niobe.

Antiope's woes were not quite over. Dionysus threw her into a state of insanity because of the vengeance her sons had taken on Dirce. She wandered all around Greece and eventually came to Phocis, where Phocus, the grandson of Sisyphus, cured her and married her. It is not known whether or not she kept in touch with her sons. If so she would have had the additional shock of learning of the deaths of Amphion's 12 children. She and Phocus were buried in a common tomb in Tithorea. Amphion and Zethus were buried together in Thebes at a later time. It became a custom for the Phocians to try to steal earth from the burial mound at Thebes and place it on the grave of Antiope and Phocus. This was done at a certain time of year and was carried out to increase the fertility of Phocis, even if it was at the expense of the Thebans, who always set a guard in the grove of Amphion and Zethus.

Antiope is one of the exceptional cases of extended punishment for promiscuity. In addition to her impregnation by Zeus, she had an affair with Epopeus, probably before they married. It is pretty evident that Lycus had more than avuncular interest in her, and Dirce had probable cause to be jealous. Interestingly, though, the promiscuity was carried on at a very young age. She had to pay, not only to man but also to the gods, for her own indiscretions and then, by association, for a crime committed by her sons. Her whole life seemed characterized by unfair treatment except for her final years in Phocis. We cannot even be sure of that period, for it would have been then that she might have learned of the slaughter of her grandchildren. [Apollodorus 3.5.5,10.1; Homer, *Odyssey* 11.260; Apollonius Rhodius 1.735; Pausanias 9.17.4; Hyginus, *Fables* 7.]

ANTIOPE (2) was one of the AMAZONS, a sister of Hippolyte and Melanippe. As with anybody or anything connected with the mysterious Amazons, her history is shrouded with conflicting accounts and ambiguity. One writer called her a daughter of Hippolyte; another said she was a daughter of Ares. Some say Theseus received her as a present from Heracles. Others say he abducted her; still others claim Theseus killed her in consequence of an oracle.

The usual story is that Theseus went alone (that is, accompanied only by his own men) to the country of the Amazons, where he was welcomed. Antiope, one of the queens, brought him presents and came aboard his ship. As soon as she did, he confined her and set sail. There is nothing to say that she might not have gone with him willingly. They were pursued by her sisters, Hippolyte and Melanippe, and a host of their subjects. No one has been clear on how long the Amazons took to reach Athens after the abduction, but certainly there had been time enough for Antiope to fall in love with Theseus and to bear a child to him. It is not unlikely that the child could have been conceived the very first night after the ship pulled away from Themiscyra. After his birth, Hippolytus was probably shipped to Troezen for safekeeping with his grandmother Aethra before the Amazons arrived in Athens.

The Amazons camped right at the foot of the Acropolis and on neighboring hills. Their attack lasted for about three months, during which time Antiope was killed by Molpadia while fighting at her husband's side. Hippolyte was conquered and fled to Megara, where she died from grief.

So the battle on the walls of Athens ended the short life of Antiope, who was probably less than 20 despite being an Amazonian queen and briefly queen of Athens. She was the only Amazon known to marry, since her sisters and companions cohabited only out of desire and the necessity for perpetuating the race. It is regrettable that we know so little of Antiope, one of the most mysterious women in mythology. [Pausanias 1.2.1; Hyginus, *Fables* 241; Plutarch, *Theseus* 27; Diodorus Siculus 4.16.]

ANTIOPE (3), a daughter of Pylon, was married to Eurytus, by whom she became the mother of the Argonauts Iphitus and Clytius. She is also called ANTIOCHE. [Hyginus, *Fables* 14.]

ANTIOPE (4) was called by some a daughter of Aeolus and mother by Poseidon of Boeotus, Aeolus, and Hellen. Other writers called their mother ARNE. [Hyginus, *Fables* 157.]

ANTIOPE (5) was one of the THESPIADES, daughter of Thespius by Megamede. By Heracles she was the mother of Alopius. [Apollodorus 2.7.8.]

ANTIOPE (6) was the mother of Aloeus by Helios. Nothing is known of this Antiope. She was one of the conquests of the all-seeing sun, so she must have been lovely indeed. Nothing further is known of her son, Aloeus, except that Helios gave him sovereignty over the region of Asopia (the plain of Sicyonia), at the same time giving his other son, Aeetes, rule over Corinth. Later, Epopeus, the son of Aloeus, gained the throne to both when Aeetes' appointee died. Thus Antiope was the mother of the Sicyonian and Corinthian dynasties.

She has also been called the mother of Aeetes, but most accounts call his mother Perseis. It was not uncommon for a bastard son to inherit equally with a legitimate son. [Pausanias 2.1.1,3.8; Scholiast on Pindar's *Olympian Odes* 13.74; Tzetzes on Lycophron 174.]

ANTIOPE (7) was a daughter of Belus and mother of Cadmus by Agenor, according to one of the accounts that makes Cadmus a native of Egypt. His mother is most often called TELEPHASSA. [Scholiast on Euripides' *Phoenician Maidens* 5.]

ANTIOPE (8), according to some, was a Pimpleian nymph who became by Pierus the mother of nine daughters named after the Muses. She was also called Euippe. Pierus was an autochthon, king of Emathia. He insisted on giving his daughters the same names as the Muses, and encouraged them to enter a contest with the real Muses. Not only did they lose the contest, but they were metamorphosed into various birds. [Antoninus Liberalis 9; Pausanias 9.29.2; Ovid, *Metamorphoses* 5.295.]

ANTIOPE (9) was the wife of Laocoon of Troy. He had been a priest of Thymbraean Apollo, whom he had angered by marrying and begetting children despite a vow of celibacy. Worse, he lay with his wife in sight of the god's image. Laocoon warned the Trojans when they decided to drag the wooden horse into the city. He also thrust his lance into the side of the horse. While Laocoon was preparing to sacrifice a bull to Poseidon, suddenly two fearful serpents were seen swimming toward the Trojan coast from Tenedos. They rushed towards Laocoon; while everyone took flight, he remained standing by the altar of the god with his two sons. The serpents first entwined the two boys and then the father, who went to the assistance of his children, and all three were killed. [Virgil, *Aeneid* 2.199–227.]

ANTIPHATEIA was the wife of Crisus, son of Phocus, who founded Crissa. The worship of the Delphinian Apollo was also founded here, and Crissa became an important holy city until overshadowed by Delphi. Antiphateia was the mother of Strophius, who became the father of Pylades. Consequently, Orestes, sent to the court of Strophius after Agamemnon's murder, grew up in this household and was in effect a foster son. Anaxibia, Agamemnon's sister, was married to Strophius. [Pausanias 1.29.4.]

ANTIPHERA was an Aetolian slave belonging to Athamas. Ino, his second wife, went mad from jealousy of her and killed her own son Melicertes, after which she and her son were changed into the marine divinities Leucothea and Palaemon. Plutarch recognized an allusion to that story in a ceremony observed at Rome in the temple of Matuta, who was identified with Leucothea; no female slave was allowed to enter the temple of Matuta at her festival, with the exception of one, who received a box on the ears from the matrons present. [*Roman Questions* 13.]

AOEDE was one of four MUSES called the daughters of Zeus and Plusia. She was also one of the original three Muses, whose worship was introduced on Mount Helicon by the Aloeidae, Otus and Ephialtes.

APANCHOMENE, the Strangled Goddess, was a surname of Artemis at Caphyae. Near Caphyae was a place called Condylea, in which there was a grove sacred to Artemis Condyleatis. Some small boys were once playing in the grove and put a string noose around the throat of the statue, saying they were strangling the goddess. The boys were observed at this innocent play and stoned to death. Immediately, the women of Caphyae began having premature births with stillborn children. The condition persisted until the boys were honorably buried and annual sacrifices to them instituted. This was directed by an oracle of Apollo, along with a change of surname from Condyleatis to Apanchomene. [Pausanias 8.23.5.]

APATURIA (1), the Deceitful, was a surname of Athena for her part in the rape of Aethra, the princess of Troezen, by Poseidon. Athena had appeared to her in a dream while she was in bed with Aegeus, king of Athens, directing her to go to the island of Sphaerus to offer sacrifices at the tomb of Pelops' charioteer. As a consequence, the paternity of Theseus was never entirely certain, and he was able to claim Poseidon as father when the occasion required. Aethra introduced among the maidens of Troezen the custom of dedicating their girdles to Athena Apaturia on the day of their marriage. This seemingly pious gesture was probably ironic. Athena Apaturia apparently never looked at it as sacrilege. [Pausanias 2.33.1,11.]

APATURIA (2) was a surname of Aphrodite at Phanagoreia and other places in the Taurian peninsula. In the war with the giants, Aphrodite was attacked by them and called Heracles to come to her assistance. He hid in a cavern, while she sat seductively at its entrance. When the giants approached her, she sidestepped, and Heracles bashed out their brains as they sprawled into the cave. For this violent little scheme she earned the surname of Apaturia, the Deceitful. [Strabo 11.2.10; Stephanus Byzantium, "Apatouron."]

APEMOSYNE was one of the three daughters of Catreus of Crete, son of Minos. Her sisters were Aerope and Clymene, and her brother was Althaemenes. An oracle told Catreus he would die at the hands of one of his children. He got rid of Clymene and Aerope by having them sold abroad. Althaemenes left Crete voluntarily, taking Apemosyne with him. They landed at a place in Rhodes and settled there, naming it Cretenia, probably out of nostalgia. On nearby Mount Atabyris, Althaemenes founded an altar to Zeus, the god of his fathers. Not long afterward he became the murderer of his sister. Hermes, particularly discriminating about his lovers, saw Apemosyne and was filled with lust for her. She fled from him, and he was unable to catch her. Eventually he spread fresh hides on the path she used to bring water to her house. She slipped and was raped by the god. When she came home in tears, her brother, doubting her claim of rape, especially by a god, kicked her to death. Althaemenes turned out to be his father's murderer as well. [Apollodorus 3.2.1.]

APHACITIS was a surname of Aphrodite, derived from the town of Aphace in Coele-Syria, where she had a celebrated temple with an oracle, destroyed by the command of the emperor Constantine. [Zosimus 1.58.]

APHAEA was the name under which BRITOMARTIS was worshipped on the island of Aegina. The Aeginetan Aphaea was probably a goddess of the moon. The temple of Aphaea on the northeast corner of Aegina is one of the most impressive ruins found in Greece.

APHRODITE, one of the 12 Olympian divinities, was the goddess of love and beauty.

NATIVITY: Born from foam of the sea. Daughter of Zeus and Dione, Cronus and Euonyme, or Uranus and Hemera.

LOVERS: Hephaestus (husband), Adonis, Anchises, Ares, Butes, Dionysus, Hermes, Poseidon, Zeus.

CHILDREN: Eros, Golgos, Beroe, Aeneas, Lyrus (or Lyrnus), Eryx, Harmonia, Hermaphroditus, Hymen, Priapus, Phobos, Deimos, Anteros, Rhodos, Herophilus.

PRINCIPAL SEATS OF WORSHIP: Cythera, Cyprus, Cnidus, Mount Ida (Troas), Cos, Abydos, Athens, Thespiae, Megara, Sparta, Sicyon, Corinth, Eryx (Sicily).

SACRED TO HER: Myrtle, rose, apple, poppy, sparrow, dove, swan, swallow, iynx, tortoise, ram, planet Venus, April.

COMPANIONS: Eros, Genii, Himerus, Peitho, Horae, Charites, Hebe, Harmonia, Muses, Pothos, Tychon, Priapus.

IDENTIFIED WITH: Alitta, Anaitis, Astarte, Daeira, Cabeiri, Faula, Gamelii, Libitina, Marica, Syria Dea, Venus.

SURNAMES: Acraea, Amathusia, Ambologera, Anadyomene, Antheia, Apaturia, Aphacitis, Apotrophia, Aracynthias, Areia, Argennis, Callipygos, Cnidia, Colias, Ctesylla, Cypria, Cythera, Delia, Despoena, Dionaea, Epidaetia, Epitragia, Erycina, Genetyllis, Hecaerge, Hippodameia, Idalia, Limenia, Mechanitis, Melaenis, Melinaea, Migonitis, Morpho, Nicephoros, Pandemos, Paphia, Peitho, Philia, Urania, Zephyritis, Zerynthia.

Aphrodite was the embodiment of the Greek ideal of love and beauty, the immortal blend of heavenly perfection and mortal fallibility. The cosmic nature of such beauty could only have been conceived from something as ineffable and ethereal as the foam of the sea. This foam was created when Cronus severed the sex organs from his father Uranus and threw them into the sea, so even at that early date her being was touched with elements of mortality and eroticism. Others claimed for her slightly more conventional parentage of Cronus (Time) and Euonyme (epithet for earth) or Uranus (Heaven) and Hemera (Day). Most often, though, she was considered the daughter of Zeus by his aunt Dione, one of the Titans. Others call her one of the Oceanides, which origin more closely corresponds with a foamy conception. The sea-birth version has Aphrodite stepping ashore on Cythera, the island at the tip of Peloponnesus, where her son Aeneas founded a temple to her after the Trojan War. She left Cythera and relocated at Paphus on the island of Cyprus, and it appears that she maintained dual residence between there and Mount Olympus.

She was one of the Olympian goddesses and the only one, it appears, with any active sexual life. Hera had produced divine children by Zeus, most of them Olympian gods, and then apparently stopped. Demeter had one daughter by Zeus and one or two children by others, but she mainly rejected any advances. Hestia, Artemis, and Athena were staunch virgins. Perhaps in an effort to curb his daughter's amorous proclivities, which, after all, were appropriate to her fated role, Zeus arranged for Aphrodite to marry her half-brother Hephaestus, the god of fire and smithy to the gods. This was an odd combination, since Hephaestus was ugly and lame, and probably not very congenial. If they had anything in common, it was the great sense of beauty he demonstrated in turning out wonderful and intricate works of art for the gods. Hephaestus was not sterile, since he produced children by others, so he must have been largely discouraged from sharing Aphrodite's bed. This was not the case with all the other Olympian males, except Apollo, curiously. But her favorite lover was Ares, the god of war.

The liaison of Aphrodite and Ares is perhaps the most inspired in all mythology. Here is beauty coupled with hatred and carnage, a true case of the attraction of opposites. To the more gender-conscious it would represent extreme virility paired with utter femininity. Whatever the situation, the couple carried on their affair right under everyone's noses, producing children—Phobos, Deimos, Anteros, and Harmonia—most certainly passed off as fathered by Hephaestus. But this fine arrangement had to end. Once, the lovers slept too late; Helios, the sun, observed them and told Hephaestus, who contrived to trap them. He rigged Aphrodite's bed with a bronze net, and she and Ares shortly were caught in naked embrace with all the Olympians as witnesses. She remained married to Hephaestus, but the sight of her voluptuous body tangled in the net probably ignited the passions of her father, her uncle, and her half-brother. According to most reports, she became the mother of Eros by Zeus, and of Rhodos and Herophilus by Poseidon. Undeniably she was the mother of Hermaphroditus by Hermes. A final divine connection was with Dionysus, another half-brother (and for that matter, her great-grandson, via Harmonia and Semele), with whom she produced Priapus. Some say she and Dionysus were also parents of Hymen, the god of marriage.

Her son by Hermes took a bath in a pool and was welded with the nymph of the spring into a body with both sexes, from which circumstance we get the word *hermaphrodite*. Her son by Dionysus was an ugly dwarf with a huge phallus. Some called Priapus her son by Adonis, but in either case the monstrous child was said to be a punishment sent by Hera on Aphrodite because of her promiscuity. Priapus was another inspired creation in mythology, a most unbeautiful offspring of two extraordinarily beautiful parents. In Aphrodite, however, there appeared always to be a contest between divinely inspired love (Aphrodite Uranus) and earthly love (Aphrodite Pandemos). Priapus symbolized naked animal and human lust, and thus became the god of fertility as well as protector of crops and livestock. Statues of him with a perpetual erection were placed in fields and gardens. We get from his name the words *priapic,* meaning phallic, and *priapism,* an abnormal and persistent state of penile erection. Conversely, Hymen, often called the son of Aphrodite and Dionysus, was exceptionally beautiful and, although bisexual (his male lovers included Apollo, Thamyris, and Hesperus), he was invoked to bless marriages.

Aphrodite's favors were not limited to the gods. She once punished Smyrna, a Syrian princess, for neglecting her sacrifices or for comparing her beauty to Aphrodite's. Smyrna fell in love with her father and managed to sleep with him while in disguise. When he learned of this he tried to kill her, but the gods changed her into a myrrh tree, from which Adonis, Smyrna's son (and brother), was born. Aphrodite adopted him, placing him in Persephone's care, but the infernal goddess fell in love with her beautiful charge when he reached adolescence and refused to return him to Aphrodite. It was eventually decided that he could spend part of each year with each. By him Aphrodite became the mother of Golgos and Beroe. Some claim Ares caused his rival to be killed by a boar. His death was celebrated thereafter, and cults of his worship spread throughout the Mediterranean. An obvious question might be why Aphrodite waited so long to reclaim Adonis. Perhaps time had no meaning for the gods, but more likely she had forgotten about leaving him with Persephone until she saw what a beautiful man he turned out to be.

Zeus sought to temper Aphrodite's wanton games with mortals by having her fall in love with one—Anchises, son of Capys, in the Troad. His beauty, it was said, equaled that of the gods. Aphrodite visited him in the disguise of a Phrygian princess. On parting from him she revealed herself and told him he would be father by her of a son, Aeneas, and she commanded him, under threat of death, to say the child was from a nymph. Of course, he bragged about sleeping with the goddess of love and, though not put to death, was lamed. Aphrodite also had a second son, Lyrus, by him, and one wonders whether his conception was before or after the laming. Anchises was saved by Aeneas during the sack of Troy, but died soon after his arrival in Sicily and was buried on Mount Eryx.

Aphrodite had a famous temple on Mount Eryx, which was built by Eryx, her son by Butes, the only Argonaut who leapt overboard when passing the island of the Sirens. Aphrodite saved him and carried him to Lilybaeum, where he later became king.

Aphrodite's lovers ranged from the heights of Olympus all the way down to sailors, soldiers, and pretty Syrian boys. She was generous with favors other than her body, as well. She gave Meilanion the golden apples that enabled him to overtake Atalanta in a footrace and thereby gain her for his wife. She inspired Medea with passion for Jason so that she helped him overcome Aeetes, her father, and acquire the Golden Fleece. She rescued Pallene when her father tried to burn her on the funeral pyre with her rejected lover, in whose murder she had conspired. Melus and his wife had killed themselves when Adonis died, and Aphrodite changed them into an apple tree and a dove; she helped young Melus found a colony on Delos and taught him to make cloth from wool. She gave Orion's daughters great beauty and changed them into comets when they died for their country. She also helped nourish the orphaned daughters of Pandareos and arranged for their nuptials. She adorned Pandora with beauty. She restored youth and beauty to Phaon, an aged boatman at Mytilene, for rowing her across the sea. She breathed life into the ivory statue carved by Pygmalion.

Just as readily, though, she brought misfortune to those who neglected sacrifices to her, compared their beauty to hers, or denied the power of love. She caused the mares of Glaucus to bolt and throw him from his chariot during a race, after which they ate him. He had despised Aphrodite's power and would not allow his mares to breed. She caused the Sirens to grow wings as a punishment for wishing to remain virgins. She supported the murder by the Maenads of Orpheus, since he condemned their promiscuity and advocated homosexual love. She instilled in dawn-goddess Eos, a rival for Adonis' affection, an insatiable desire for beautiful young men, so that she was constantly kidnapping them. In addition, she herself carried off Phaethon, son of Eos and Cephalus, to be guardian of one of her temples. She was insulted by six of Poseidon's sons and struck them mad, so that they gang-raped their mother. She willed Scylla to fall in love with Minos so that she brought about her father's death and the fall of Megara. She caused Aegeus to be childless until he introduced her worship in Athens. She caused Himerus, son of Lacedaemon, unwittingly to deflower his sister Cleodice on a night of promiscuous revelry, after which he drowned himself. She caused Pasiphae to crave sexual relations with the Cretan bull. When the women of Astypalaea proclaimed their beauty was above hers, she caused them to grow cow horns. For a slight from Tyndareus she took revenge by making all his daughters notorious as adulteresses—Clytemnestra, Helen, and Timandra. So it was very unwise to trifle with the power of love—its sensual pleasures could be rapidly transmuted to ingenious and fearful tortures.

Aphrodite's role in the Trojan War was a very central one. From the moment she, Hera, and Athena claimed the apple inscribed "To the Fairest," thrown among the guests at the wedding of Peleus and Thetis by the uninvited goddess of discord, events moved inexorably toward that fateful climax of Greek mythology. The movement was very slow, since the product of that particular wedding, Achilles, had yet to be born and grow to sufficient age to be the greatest hero in that war. So if the three goddesses took the apple immediately to Paris on Mount Ida to have him judge which was the fairest, at least 18 years had to pass before Achilles arrived at Troy. In any event, the judgment of Paris, Priam and Hecuba's supposedly dead son, was swayed by the awesome force of love when, over bribes of power and wisdom, he chose the love of the most beautiful woman in the world—Helen of Sparta. Aphrodite helped Paris prepare for the abduction and paved the way for him. In appreciation he founded the shrine of Aphrodite Migonitis on or near the island of Cranae, where he and Helen consummated their elopement.

Aphrodite was, of course, on the side of the Trojans. Priam swore never to surrender Helen as long as she remained under Aphrodite's protection. She saved Paris when Menelaus was dragging him to the Greek camp. While assisting her son Aeneas she was wounded by Diomedes and fled to Olympus to her mother Dione. Her revenge was complete when Diomedes' wife Aegialeia left him for Cometes, then with her new lover plotted to kill her husband, so that he was obliged to leave the country. When Hector was killed, she kept Achilles from throwing his body to the dogs, and instead had him embalmed in ambrosia and protected by a cloud.

Aphrodite's worship reached throughout the Mediterranean world. Probably Assyrian in origin, it traveled via Syria to Cyprus. The introduction of her worship in Cyprus was reportedly by Paphus, a son of Cephalus and Eos, who is often confused with Paphus, the son of Pygmalion and his statue Galateia, who founded the city of Paphus. The first Paphus is called the father of Cinyras, the father of Adonis, which appears to be an attempt by the Cypriots to appropriate everything relevant to Aphrodite to Cyprus. The Adonis story has traditionally been set in Syria. The Cephalus connection additionally ties the Cyprian worship to the Athenian royal house, even though Aegeus was the first king who officially introduced the worship in Athens. Porphyrion, said to have been the most ancient king of Attica, installed it in the peninsula many years earlier. Phaedra built a temple to Aphrodite Calascopia at Troezen. Theseus dedicated a wooden image of Aphrodite at Delos that had been made for Ariadne by Daedalus. A stone image of her stood at Lerna. Two Ephesian lovers, Meliboea and Alexis, were favored by the goddess and dedicated a sanctuary to Aphrodite Automate and Epidaetia. There were carved images at Argos believed to be the work of Epeius, the builder of the wooden horse of Troy. She had temples or sanctuaries at Thebes, Megara, Sicyon, Thespiae, Sparta, and many other cities. At Corinth a great number of *hierodules* were dedicated to her service as temple prostitutes.

She was identified with a number of other divinities. Her worship had arisen from that of Astarte but developed almost exclusively Greek characteristics as time went on. In fact, she seemed to be involved with just about every aspect of Greek life. She had an altar in the temple/hospital of Amphiaraus at Oropus. At Hermione she had a temple dedicated to her under the names of Pontia and Limenia, perhaps suggesting sponsorship of sea travelers. She was identified with the Genetyllides, a class of divinities presiding over generation and birth, and with the Gamelii, divinities who protected and presided over marriage. She was identified as well with two of the principal cults of ancient times—the Eleusinian mysteries and the Cabeirian mysteries. As Aphrodite Erycina, she entered Italy via Sicily, from where her worship spread onto the mainland and into Rome at the beginning of the second Punic War. By this time the Roman identity of Venus had emerged.

Aphrodite's role as an Olympian goddess was celebrated in accounts of the other divinities.

Hera sometimes borrowed her famous girdle to focus Zeus' wandering passions. Aphrodite gave to Thetis a wedding present of a golden crown created by Hephaestus. As earlier stated, she gave generously to those who were placed under the protection of the gods, such as Pandora and the daughters of Pandareos. She even did a little pandering for her former bedfellows, as in the case of Dionysus, when she inspired in Aura, a virginal companion of Artemis, a desire for the god. She presented her daughter Harmonia with the famous golden necklace made by Hephaestus for Zeus to give to Europa. It conferred irresistible beauty on its wearer but, as all too often with love and beauty, there was a darker side to this fatal piece of jewelry, and it brought despair to its wearers all the way into historical times.

There is a curiosity, mentioned earlier, in regard to Aphrodite and Apollo. To most it would seem that theirs would have been an ideal match—beauty, love, poetry, song, pastoral pursuits—particularly since both were the most beautiful of the Olympians. Perhaps they were too much alike to be interesting to the Greek poets and playwrights, who saw the perfect dramatic irony of love and war instead. We do know that Artemis and Aphrodite were enemies, although this is seldom given much attention. Aphrodite supposedly brought about the death of Hippolytus because he vowed celibacy. Artemis was said to have been involved in Adonis' death in retaliation. Not only would Apollo be expected to take his sister's side (although he himself was far from chaste), he himself had reason to hate Aphrodite in his own right. Apollo's son Erymanthus had seen Aphrodite bathing and was struck blind, so some claimed that Apollo, too, participated in Adonis' death. Finally, while Zeus, Poseidon, Hermes, and Dionysus might have played around with a boy or two, they were heterosexuals, and Ares was not connected with a single homosexual liaison. Apollo, on the other hand, must certainly be called bisexual, and this behavior could only be offensive to Aphrodite.

Zeus and Aphrodite were readily assimilated into the religion of Rome, for they were both ancestors of the Trojans who founded and settled Rome. In fact, their line could be traced to Julius Caesar. Perhaps Aphrodite more than any of the other Olympian gods retained her nature when eventually she was identified with Venus. Her earlier associations with marriage, generation, and birth were retained, and the ancient spirit of Aphrodite Pandemos was passed along in temple prostitution and the licentiousness for which, Rome became famous. [NATIVITY: Hesiod, *Theogony* 190,353; Homer, *Iliad* 5.370, 20.105; Cicero, *On the Nature of the Gods* 3.23; Natalis Comes 4.13; *Homeric Hymn to Aphrodite* 2.5; Apollodorus 1.1.3; Hyginus, *Fables: Preface* 19—LOVERS: Cicero, *On the Nature of the Gods* 3.23; Apollodorus 1.9.25; Hyginus, *Fables* 58,242; Diodorus Siculus 4.83; Homer, *Odyssey* 8.266–358—CHILDREN: *Appendix Virgiliana: Ciris* 134; Scholiast on Theocritus 15.100; Antoninus Liberalis 23; Servius on Virgil's *Aeneid* 4.127, *Eclogues* 8.30; Pindar, *Olympian Odes* 7.24; Tzetzes on Lycophron 923; Apollodorus 3.12.2—CHARACTERISTICS: Strabo 9.2.24; Homer, *Iliad* 5.305,405, *Odyssey* 19.518, 20.67; Ptolemaeus Hephaestion 1.306; Hyginus, *Fables* 92; Servius on Virgil's *Aeneid* 1.724; Ovid, *Metamorphoses* 10.243; Aelian, *Various Narratives* 12.18—WORSHIP: Virgil, *Aeneid* 5.760; Livy 22.9,10, 23.30, 40.34; Ovid, *Fasti* 4.871, *Remedies of Love* 549, *Heroides* 15.57; Horace, *Odes* 1.2.33; Dio Chrysostomus, *Orations* 7.568; Aristophanes, *Thesmophoriazusae* 130; Pausanias 1.1.4,2.5, 14.6,34.2,43.6; Alciphron, *Letters* 3.2; Lucian, *Goddess of Surrye*.]

APIA was the daughter of Phoroneus and Peitho, and sister of Aegialeus. Phoroneus was a son of the Inachus River and married to the nymph Laodice, by whom he became the father of Niobe, Apis, and Car. Laodice was regarded as his second wife, while Peitho was his first. He was the first to offer sacrifices at Argos. He united the people into a city. Some say he discovered the use of fire, but that is perhaps taking the national Argive pride a little too far. Nothing is known of Apia. It is not unreasonable to guess that she might have been confused with her half-brother Apis, after whom the country later known as Peloponnesus was originally called. [Pausanias 2.19.5,20.3; Scholiast on Euripides' *Orestes* 920.]

APOLLONIS was one of three MUSES recognized at Delphi. [Tzetzes on Hesiod's *Works and Days* 6.]

APOTROPHIA, the Expeller, was a surname of Aphrodite, under which she was worshipped at Thebes. This name described her as the goddess who expelled lust and carnal recollections from men's minds. Her daughter Harmonia was believed to have begun her worship under this name in conjunction with the contrasting manifestations of Aphrodite Urania and Aphrodite Pandemos. [Pausanias 9.16.2.]

APPIADES were nymphs of the Appian Spring (Appia Aqua) in Rome, which was in the vicinity of the temple of Venus Genetrix in Julius Caesar's Forum. The fountain was surrounded by statues of nymphs called Appiades; an individual nymph was an Appias. Several of these have been unearthed in modern times. [Ovid, Remedies of Love 659, Art of Love 1.81, 3.451.]

APSEUDES was one of the NEREIDES. [Homer, Iliad 18.48.]

APTEROS, the Wingless, was a surname under which Nice (Nike), the goddess of victory, had a sanctuary at Athens. Nice was usually represented as winged, as at Samothrace, and the wingless state was meant to express the idea that victory could never retreat from Athens. Aegeus was said to have thrown himself down from the roof of this temple when Theseus failed to raise a white sail, thus signaling a safe return, on coming back from Crete. [Pausanias 1.22.4.]

ARACHNE was the daughter of Idmon of Colophon in Lydia. Colophon was famous for its purple dye, and Idmon was a famous dyer. Arachne was highly skilled in weaving and was so sure of her preeminence in the craft that she dared to challenge Athena to a contest. Arachne outdid herself, producing a piece of cloth depicting the love life of the gods. When Athena could find no flaw in the work and had to admit its perfection, she tore the piece to shreds. In terror and despair at this unfair treatment Arachne hanged herself. Athena undid the rope and saved the girl's life but, still smarting from the insult to her divine status, changed the rope into a web and Arachne into a spider. Once more it was demonstrated that the gods were not to be com-

promised when it came to human pride. [Ovid, Metamorphoses 6.1–145; Virgil, Georgics 4.246.]

ARACYNTHIAS was a surname of Aphrodite derived from Mount Aracynthus. The location of this mountain is uncertain. There is a range by this name north of Pleuron in Aetolia, but there were also mountains by this name in Boeotia and Attica, more than likely on their common border. [Strabo 2.10.4; Rhianus, with Stephanus Byzantium, "Arakynthos."]

ARAETHYREA was the daughter of Aras, the autochthonous founder of Arantes, the oldest town in Phliasia. Along with her brother, Aoris, she was devoted to hunting and warlike activities. These pursuits indicate she had a masculine nature, but her sexual orientation appears to have been unaffected by her tomboy exterior. Somehow she met Dionysus, the young god who wandered extensively promoting his status as god of wine, and became pregnant by him. Maybe Araethyrea participated in the orgies that characterized his worship, and perhaps Dionysus as father of her son was used figuratively. One writer calls the boy's father Ceisus. This son was Phlias, an Argonaut and the father of Androdamas.

When Araethyrea died, her devoted brother named the region Araethyrea after her. After his death, monuments were erected to him, his sister, and their father. These were round pillars, and suppliants always faced the monuments when they invoked Aras or his children. Phlias changed the name of the region and the town to his own. [Homer, Iliad 2.571; Strabo 8.6.24; Pausanias 2.12.4–6; Stephanus Byzantium, "Phlious" and "Araithyrea."]

ARCADIA (1) was the wife of Nyctimus. He was a member of the infamous family of Lycaon, all of whom except Nyctimus were either changed into wolves or drowned in the Deucalionian flood. Arcadia bore to Nyctimus a daughter, Phylonome, who became a companion of Artemis. Not true to her vows of chastity, Phylonome slept with Ares and became the mother of twins—Lycastus and Parrhasius. From fear of her father and probably Artemis, she threw the babies into the Erymanthus River. They were carried by the river-god to safety in a hollow oak tree, where a she-wolf suckled them until they were found by a shepherd.

Arcadia must have existed in an atmosphere of perpetual uncertainty. Her sinister in-laws, although colonizing much of Peloponnesus, practiced unspeakable rites, including human sacrifice. Then undoubtedly she had to endure the terror of the flood; even after the waters subsided, life was not peaceful. We do not learn what happened to Phylonome, but believing that she killed her own babies could not have left her very well adjusted. Perhaps Arcadia lived to see her grandsons seize the power in Arcadia, but then again she would have had no way of knowing they were her grandsons. Arcadia is probably a personification of the region. Her nephew Arcas, son of Callisto, her sister-in-law, was the eponymous hero of Arcadia. [Plutarch, *Greek and Roman Parallel Stories* 36.]

ARCADIA (2) was one of the DANAIDES and married to Xanthus, son of Aegyptus. [Hyginus, *Fables* 170.]

ARCE was a daughter of Thaumas, son of Pontus and Gaea. Her sisters were the unlikely combination of Iris, the rainbow, and the Harpies. Like her sisters, she was winged; probably she too represented some primeval element or force. It is not clear which, however, and her name fails to offer a clue. In the war of the gods against the Titans, she sided with the Titans and was thrown with them into Tartarus by Zeus. First, though, she was deprived of her wings. Zeus was said to have presented them to Thetis as a wedding present. She in turn attached them to Achilles' heels, thus earning for him the nickname of Podarces (Swift-Footed). [Ptolemaeus Hephaestion 6.]

ARCENA was one of the female DOGS of Actaeon. [Apollodorus 3.4.4.]

ARCHE was mentioned as one of four MUSES, daughters of Zeus and Plusia. Her name signified "beginning." [Cicero, *On the Nature of the Gods* 3.21.]

ARCHIA, according to some the wife of Inachus, was probably a variant spelling of ARGEIA.

ARCHIPPE was, according to some, a daughter of Pelops and wife of Sthenelus, by whom she became the mother of Alcinoe, Medusa, and Eurystheus. Others call her NICIPPE, Leucippe, or Astydameia. [Apollodorus 2.4.5.]

ARCHIROE (*See* ANCHIROE)

ARDALIDES, or Ardaliotides, was a surname of the Muses at Troezen. They were thus called from Ardalus, a son of Hephaestus, who was said to have invented the flute and to have built a sanctuary of the Muses at Troezen. [Pausanias 2.31.3; Hesychius, "Ardalides."]

AREGONIS was the wife of Ampycus and mother of Mopsus. She is more often called CHLORIS. [Orphica, *Argonautica* 127.]

AREIA (1), the Warlike, was a surname of Aphrodite when represented in full armor like Ares, as was the case at Sparta. [Pausanias 3.17.5.]

AREIA (2), the Warlike, was a surname of Athena, under which she was worshipped at Athens. Her statue, together with those of Ares, Aphrodite, and Enyo, stood in the temple of Ares at Athens. Her worship under this name was instituted by Orestes after he had been acquitted by the Areiopagus of the murder of his mother. He had fled from land to land, pursued by the Erinyes. On the advice of Apollo he took refuge with Athena at Athens. The goddess afforded him protection and appointed the court of the Areiopagus to decide his fate. The Erinyes brought forward their accusation, and Orestes made the command of the Delphic oracle his defense. When the court voted and was equally divided, Athena cast the deciding vote in Orestes' favor, and he was acquitted. He therefore dedicated an altar to Athena Areia. [Aeschylus, *Eumenides* 753; Pausanias 1.8.4, 28.5.]

AREIA (3) was a daughter of Cleochus, by whom Apollo became the father of Miletus. Miletus was one of the most extraordinarily beautiful men in Greek mythology. Minos, the stern ruler of Crete, fell in love with him; so did Minos' brother Sarpedon. Miletus decided to stay with Sarpedon, but the two of them had to flee to Asia Minor. There Miletus founded the city of Miletus, which became one of the most important cities of the ancient world. [Apollodorus 3.1.2.]

AREIA (4) was, according to some, the mother of Byblis by Miletus. The mother of Byblis is usually called TRAGASIA.

ARENE was a daughter of Oebalus by Gorgophone. She married her half-brother Aphareus. He was a son of Perieres and Gorgophone. Some called his wife Polydora, Laocoosa, or Arne. Her brother and sister were Tyndareus and Peirene. Her half-brothers were Aphareus, Icarius, Leucippus, and Hippocoon, the last being the illegitimate son of Oebalus by the nymph Bateia.

It is small wonder that problems of succession arose when Oebalus died. Tyndareus was scheduled to succeed his father to the throne of Sparta, but Hippocoon usurped the power and forced Tyndareus and Icarius into exile. Aphareus and Leucippus, being considerably older, had already succeeded Perieres to the throne of Messenia, where they ruled jointly. For the most part, they were removed from the contest, which Heracles finally solved by killing Hippocoon and his sons and restoring Tyndareus to the throne along with his new wife, Leda, whom he married during his exile in Aetolia. Arene's sympathy was certainly with her brother Tyndareus. A Messenian tradition said that Tyndareus came to Aphareus and Arene when he was exiled.

Arene became the mother of twins Idas and Lynceus, and Peisos, of whom nothing whatsoever is known; a reasonable assumption is that he died as a child. Idas and Lynceus, on the other hand, we know a great deal about. They were Argonauts and Calydonian hunters. They were also betrothed to their cousins Phoebe and Hilaeira, daughters of Leucippus, but their other cousins, Castor and Polydeuces, carried the

women off and married them. This set up a bitter rivalry, resulting in the death of Idas, Lynceus, and Castor (Polydeuces was immortal).

Arene's marriage to Aphareus may well be the only case of incest among mortals not punished in some way by the gods, who themselves practiced it widely. The interesting thing here is that the marriage was open and apparently legal. Maybe their having different fathers allowed for this. It is probably just as well that Idas and Lynceus were prevented from further genetic risk-taking when they were not able to marry their first cousins.

Aphareus founded a town in Messenia, which he named Arene. He and Arene received Neleus, who had fled from Iolcus, and assigned him a tract of land that became the basis of the great Neleid kingdom. They also received Lycus, son of Pandion, and from him they learned of the orgies of the great gods. [Apollodorus 1.9.2,9.16, 3.10.3,11.2; Pausanias 3.1.4, 14.6,15.2, 4.2.3; Aristophanes, *Plutus* 210.]

ARETE was the wife of Alcinous, king of the Phaeacians. She was also his niece, since her father was Rhexanor, Alcinous' only brother, who died early. He was called the "godlike" Rhexanor, but nothing else is known of him. Alcinous and Rhexanor were sons of Nausithous and therefore grandsons of Poseidon. Under the leadership of Nausithous the Phaeacians had come from Hypereia in Thrinacia to escape the Cyclops, an interesting circumstance for which we have no further details. The island of the Phaeacians was first called Drepane because of its resemblance to a sickle. The name was later changed to Scheria; we know it today as Kerkira or Corfu.

Arete had five sons and a daughter by Alcinous. We know the names of three of the sons—Halios, Laodamas, and Clytoneus. The daughter was Nausicaa.

Alcinous and Arete appear in two different epics, and it is necessary to accept at least a 25-year gap between these two appearances. Therefore, when the Argonauts landed at Drepane, Arete must have been around the age of 20. When Odysseus was cast ashore on Scheria, she was 45 or so. In both cases, the island and its rulers represented a safe haven.

The Argonauts stopped there and were hospitably received on their return from Colchis. Not long after their arrival, the pursuing Colchians landed, demanding that Medea be delivered to them. Alcinous declared he would deliver her, but only if she and Jason were not married. There would appear to be little question that they had already slept together, but perhaps this physical union needed to be formalized. Arete immediately sent word to warn the lovers, who quickly had a ceremony. Thus the Colchians were forced to leave without Medea, although some of them remained, fearing the wrath of Aeetes. So the Argonauts were able to leave and did so laden with presents.

Odysseus swam to shore here after his raft was overturned, and was discovered by Nausicaa. He was welcomed by Alcinous and Arete, and honored with feasts and contests. He related his story since the fall of Troy and was eventually transported to Ithaca by the Phaeacians. Later writers represented Nausicaa as the wife of Telemachus, by whom she became the mother of Persepolis or Ptoliporthus.

In the *Odyssey,* Arete is described as dutiful, wise, and honorable. The Phaeacians looked upon her as a goddess. She settled domestic quarrels among her subjects and was loyal to her friends.

In looking at the two stories, we can only conclude that Drepane/Scheria must have been regarded as a kind of paradise, with a benevolent royal family ruling over loyal subjects. It stands in sharp contrast to the scenes of violence witnessed by the Argonauts and by Odysseus. Arete emerges as the most entirely gracious queen in mythology, maybe the most gracious individual. [Homer, *Odyssey* 6.12,62,310, 7.65,123,142, 170, 8.116,119,130,370; Apollonius Rhodius 4.990–1225; Eustathius on Homer's *Odyssey* 1796; Dictys Cretensis 6.6.]

ARETHUSA (1) was one of the NEREIDES and a follower of Artemis in Elis. Once, she bathed nude in the Alpheius River, and the river-god fell madly in love with her. He pursued her relentlessly, even changing himself into a hunter in order to follow her on land. Eventually he caught her, but her frantic prayers to Artemis caused the goddess to change her into a spring. Alpheius immediately returned to his river form and tried to mingle his waters with hers. Artemis prevented this by leading the transformed Arethusa through a subterranean passage all the way to the island of Ortygia off the coast of Syracuse in Sicily. There another spring burst forth. As time went on, it seems that Alpheius prevailed. The popular belief that there was a natural subterranean connection between the Alpheius River in Elis and the fountain of Arethusa in Ortygia was extended to include the preposterous notion that a cup thrown into the Alpheius would make its appearance in the Ortygian spring.

Arethusa was elevated to the rank of a divinity who inspired pastoral poetry. The Syracusans used the image of her head on many of their coins. Her hair was netted, and she was surrounded by dolphins. [Virgil, *Eclogues* 4.1, 10.1; Strabo 6.2.4; Pausanias 5.7.2,3.]

ARETHUSA (2) was one of the HESPERIDES. [Apollodorus 2.5.11; Apollonius Rhodius 4.1427.]

ARETHUSA (3) was one of the female DOGS of Actaeon. [Hyginus, *Fables* 181.]

ARETHUSA (4) was a daughter of Herileus (Hesperus? Nereus?) and by Poseidon the mother of Abas, after whom Euboea was called Abantis. [Hyginus, *Fables* 157; Stephanus Byzantium, "Abantis."]

ARETHUSA (5) was the daughter of Abas, and sister of Alcon and Dias, who founded the city of Athenae Diades in Euboea. The spring of Arethusa in Chalcis was probably named after her, as was one of the same name in Euboea. [Stephanus Byzantium, "Athenai."]

ARETHUSA (6) was a woman from Ithaca. Her son Corax was crushed by a rock during a hunt, and the rock was subsequently called the Rock of Corax. Arethusa hanged herself in grief, and a nearby fountain was named for her. [Scholiast on Homer's *Odyssey* 13.408.]

ARETHUSA (7) was the wife of Thersander, a Cretan. By him she became the mother of Hyllus on the Lethaeus River in Crete. Hyllus was slain by Aeneas in the Trojan War. Nothing further is known of any of these individuals. [Quintus Smyrnaeus 10.79–82.]

ARGANTHONE was a lovely huntress in Mysia who hunted by herself in the fields and forests. Rhesus, the Thracian hero, heard about her and traveled to meet her. He joined her in the chase and succeeded in winning her love. After they were married, he had to go away to the Trojan War as an ally to Troy. He was famous for his pure white horses, which were swift as the wind. He had fought for only a single day, taking a great toll among the Greeks, when he was killed in his sleep by Diomedes and Odysseus. Arganthone died of grief when she got the report. [Parthenius, *Love Stories* 36; Stephanus Byzantium, "Arganthonis."]

ARGE (1), according to some, was the mother by Zeus of Dionysus. His mother is usually called SEMELE. [Diodorus Siculus 3.62,74; Scholiast on Pindar's *Pythian Odes* 3.177; Pseudo-Plutarch, *On Rivers* 16.]

ARGE (2) was a Hyperborean maiden who, together with Upis, carried an offering, which had been vowed for the birth of Apollo and Artemis, to Eileithyia at Delos. Hyperborea was a distant and mysterious country, not unlike the areas from which came the Magi in New Testament accounts. [Herodotus 4.35.]

ARGEIA (1) was a surname of Hera, derived from Argos, the principal seat of her worship. [Pausanias 3.13.6.]

ARGEIA (2), one of the OCEANIDES, was according to some the mother of Io by her brother Inachus. The wife of Inachus was usually called a Melian nymph. Inachus' great-grandson (times five), Iasus, was called most often the father of Io. [Hyginus, *Fables* 145.]

ARGEIA (3) was the wife of Polybus and mother of Argus, the builder of the *Argo*. Argus was also one of the Argonauts.

ARGEIA (4) was a daughter of Adrastus and Amphithea. Her sisters were Deipyle, Hippodameia, and Aegialeia. Argeia had a rather exciting life. The kingdom of Argos was ruled by three families, and this situation led eventually to serious trouble. During a riot, Amphiaraus from one of the royal houses killed Talaus, the girls' grandfather from a rival royal house. Fearing for his and his family's safety, Adrastus fled to Sicyon, where his maternal grandfather ruled. Argeia and her sisters were probably born there. As king of Sicyon, Adrastus decided it was to his advantage to be reconciled with his cousin Amphiaraus. He gave him his sister Eriphyle in marriage and returned to Argos to resume the joint rule.

One night, Tydeus of Calydon and Polyneices of Thebes, both fugitives from their countries, met at Argos and through a misunderstanding were about to do battle with each other. Adrastus intervened and shortly realized that they were, according to the creatures depicted on their armor, the lion and boar that an oracle had promised as husbands for two of his daughters. Thus Argeia became the wife of Polyneices, the exiled Theban king and son of Oedipus.

Polyneices was bent on regaining the throne of Thebes and exacting revenge on his brother Eteocles. He persuaded Adrastus to join him and bribed Deipyle, the wife of Amphiaraus, to hold her husband to a promise to let her decide any issue on which he disagreed with Adrastus. The expedition of the Seven against Thebes was undertaken, but Adrastus was the only one of the Seven who survived.

Argeia lost Polyneices, for the sons of Oedipus killed each other. Creon, their uncle, who became king, refused to allow the attackers to be buried. Antigone, Argeia's sister-in-law, defied the order and managed to give at least a symbolic burial to Polyneices by sifting dust over him. Some say Argeia assisted her in slipping his body onto the funeral pyre of Eteocles.

Argeia's troubles were not over. Thersander, her son by Polyneices, was one of the Epigoni, or sons of the Seven, who went to avenge their fathers. This time, the Argives were successful, and Thersander became king of Thebes. He went on the first expedition against Troy and was killed in Mysia by Telephus.

Thus Argeia was part of the court life at three of the most important cities of ancient

Greece—Sicyon, Argos, and Thebes. There is no evidence she went to Thebes with Thersander, but there is also no reason to suppose she did not, if she still lived. The family was one of the strongest bonds in the Greek world, and the elderly were protected and revered. [Apollodorus 1.9.13, 3.6.1; Pausanias 3.15.4, 7.3.1, 9.5.7, 10.10.3; Hyginus, *Fables* 69,70.]

ARGEIA (5) was a daughter of Autesion, who was a son of Tisamenus, grandson of Thersander, and great-grandson of Polyneices. Autesion was a native of Thebes and would have succeeded his father as king, but an oracle told him to go to Peloponnesus and join the Dorians, which he did to escape the curse of Oedipus, which still pursued him.

It appears that Argeia did not accompany him on this relocation. By that time she had married the Heraclid Aristodemus, great-great-grandson of Heracles. Some accounts say he was killed at Naupactus or Delphi on his way to Peloponnesus, but others say he was able to occupy his Laconian allotment. The second circumstance makes more sense, since Argeia would have accompanied him to his new kingdom but might have remained in Thebes, had he never arrived in Sparta. He died shortly after becoming king and establishing the royal line. A few weeks after his death, Argeia bore twin sons, Eurysthenes and Procles.

The succession to the throne presented a problem, since Argeia professed not to know which twin was the elder. The Lacedaemonians sought the assistance of the Delphic oracle, which instructed them to make both kings but give greater honor to the older one. They set a watch on Argeia and discovered she bathed and fed Eurysthenes first, displaying customary attention to the firstborn. The boys grew up under the guardianship of Argeia's brother Theras, who was also regent of the kingdom.

We do not know what happened to Argeia. She was still relatively young when her sons assumed the throne. She most certainly remained in the palace as long as she lived, associating with her daughters-in-law, twin sisters from Cleonae. This association might have been difficult for all concerned, since the brothers were in constant strife. [Herodotus 4.147, 6.52;

Pausanias 3.1.5,15.4, 4.3.3., 9.5.8; Apollodorus 2.7.2,8.2; Strabo 8.3.19.]

ARGELE was one of the THESPIADES, daughter of Thespius and Megamede. By Heracles she became the mother of Cleolaus. [Apollodorus 2.7.8.]

ARGENNIS was a surname of Aphrodite, derived from Argennus, a son of Peisidice. Agamemnon lusted after him and pursued him until Argennus threw himself into the Cephissus River and drowned. In remorse Agamemnon built a sanctuary of Aphrodite Argennis. [Stephanus Byzantium, "Argennis"; Athenaeus 13.603.]

ARGIOPE (1) was a Parnassian nymph. She loved Philammon, the son of Apollo, an artist and poet. He liked taking her to bed but had no intention of settling down, especially when he learned she was pregnant. For some reason she wandered to Thrace and settled among the Odrysians, and there Thamyris was born.

Thamyris inherited his father's talents and good looks but also his less desirable characteristics. He was arrogant, presumptuous, and oversexed. He challenged the Muses to a musical contest, offering sexual intercourse with each as his prize. (This is especially interesting, since Thamyris is credited with being the first man to be enamored of other males.) He lost the contest and was blinded by the Muses. Thamyris was also deprived of his talent for song, a truly cruel penalty. He was afterward represented with a broken lyre in his hand. Argiope must have taken care of him as long as he lived. [Apollodorus 1.3.3; Pausanias 4.33.3, 9.30.2, 10.7.2; Euripides, *Rhesus* 901,925; Homer, *Iliad* 2.595.]

ARGIOPE (2), a daughter of the Nile River, was the mother by Agenor of Cadmus, according to some. She is most often called TELEPHASSA. [Scholiast on Euripides' *Phoenician Maidens* 5; Hyginus, *Fables* 6,178,179.]

ARGIOPE (3) was the mother by Branchus of Cercyon. This Branchus, of whom nothing is known, should not be confused with the Carian Branchus who founded an oracle near Miletus.

Nothing further is known of Argiope, except that she produced a villainous son. Cercyon became king at Eleusis, and we know him from two stories. One concerns his daughter Alope, whom he killed when she gave birth to a child fathered by Poseidon. Cercyon also exposed the child, which was, in the usual fashion, suckled by beasts and rescued by shepherds. Using his kingly powers to evil advantage, Cercyon was also a robber. He accosted travelers and forced them to fight with him. When he invariably defeated them, he murdered them and took their possessions. Finally, Theseus passed by on his way to Athens from Troezen and made short work of Cercyon, after which he put Alope's son, Hippothoon, on the throne of Eleusis. On the road between Eleusis and Megara was an area known as "the Wrestling Ground," where Cercyon attacked and killed his victims. Argiope probably lived to see evidences of Cercyon's villainy. How did she feel about his murders of travelers, and did she try to interfere when he killed her granddaughter? There are many unanswered questions, notably one concerning the royal lineage, and how Cercyon ended up as king of Eleusis. [Plutarch, *Theseus* 11,29; Apollodorus, *Epitome* 1.3; Pausanias 1.39.3; Scholiast on Plato's *Laws* 7.796.]

ARGIOPE (4) was the daughter of Teuthras, king of Mysia. As a young man he had offended Artemis by killing a sacred boar and almost died for his impiety. Mount Teuthrania, the scene of his misadventure, was named for him. Perhaps this fateful event softened him, for he welcomed Auge when she was sold by Nauplius.

Auge had a son by Heracles and was sold into slavery by her father, who had been warned that any son of hers would usurp the kingdom. The child, Telephus, was exposed, suckled, and saved, and grew to manhood in Arcadia. He learned from an oracle the whereabouts of his mother and went to Mysia. Teuthras, who had meanwhile married Auge, received her son kindly and later adopted him. He also gave Argiope in marriage to Telephus; therefore, Auge was both stepmother and mother-in-law to Argiope. When Teuthras died, Telephus became king. He was king when the Greeks invaded Mysia, believing they had arrived at Troy. He was

wounded by Achilles, who later healed him in exchange for directions to Troy. He did not participate in the war, but his and Argiope's son Eurypylus led a Mysian contingent to help Priam. [Pausanias 1.4.9; Apollodorus 3.9.1; Diodorus Siculus 4.33; Pindar, *Olympian Odes* 9.112, *Isthmian Odes* 5.52.]

ARGO was one of the female DOGS of Actaeon. [Hyginus, *Fables* 181.]

ARGYPHIA was a woman of royal blood who bore to Aegyptus two sons, Lynceus and Proteus. They married the DANAIDES Hypermnestra and Gorgophone. [Apollodorus 2.1.5.]

ARGYRA was the nymph of a spring in Achaia. She fell in love with Selemnus, a handsome shepherd who fed his flocks nearby. She came out of the water and had sex with him, quite often at first, then lost interest and returned to her watery element for good. Thus deserted, Selemnus pined away in grief, and Aphrodite changed him into the Selemnus River. Even as a river he could not forget the faithless Argyra, so Aphrodite gave him a further gift, which was oblivion to the memory of the nymph. Bathing in the Selemnus was rumored to slake the passions or remove the sorrows of love. [Pausanias 7.23.2,3.]

ARIADNE was a daughter of Minos II and Pasiphae. Minos, son of Lycastus and Ida, was king of Crete. Pasiphae was a daughter of Helios and Perseis and sister to Aeetes, king of Colchis, and Circe, the famous enchantress. Ariadne's brothers and sisters were Catreus, Deucalion, Glaucus, Androgeus, Acacallis, Xenodice, and Phaedra. She had about a dozen half-brothers through Minos' extramarital relations. She also had another half-brother that people spoke of only in whispers. This was the fearful and loathsome Minotaur, offspring of Pasiphae and a bull, kept imprisoned in the celebrated labyrinth built by Daedalus and fed on human flesh.

Early Cretan genealogy is complex, since the son of Zeus and Europa was called by some the first Minos. According to them, Ariadne was his daughter, but this would have made her three generations older than Theseus. So we have to accept that Ariadne was the daughter of a different Minos, although most early writers considered only one.

In any case, Minos made war on Megara and subdued it. He would have done the same for Athens had the people not agreed to send at regular intervals a tribute of seven youths and seven maidens to be fed to the Minotaur. This was compensation for the mysterious and probably treacherous death of Minos' son Androgeus in Attica. Theseus decided to put a stop to this gruesome practice and volunteered the next time the tribute came due. When the ship reached Crete and discharged its forlorn cargo, Ariadne spied Theseus and was immediately smitten.

No account has ever dealt with the duration of the Athenians' stay in Crete. It becomes apparent that it was a rather extended time. How was the succession of victims determined? Certainly the Minotaur could not eat nearly a ton of meat all at once. It might seem obvious that Theseus would volunteer to go first into the labyrinth, since he had put himself forward as the deliverer from this dreadful carnage. There might have been some kind of ritual involved, during which the victims were fattened and indulged, even given permission to move about freely. It could well be that Ariadne and Theseus had ample opportunity to become lovers. She exacted a promise from him to take her with him if and when he should leave Crete. On that condition she gave Theseus a ball of twine to unwind as he penetrated the labyrinth, since even if he killed the Minotaur he could still starve to death by not being able to find his way out of the maze.

Once inside the labyrinth Theseus soon located the Minotaur and killed it with his bare hands. Following the thread, which he had unwound, he made his way back to the entrance and, with the intended victims and Ariadne, seized a ship and fled from Crete.

They reached Naxos eventually and apparently were not pursued. Several questions arise in connection with Naxos, the principal one being in relation to Theseus' abandonment of Ariadne. There were those who said that Ariadne bore twin sons, Staphylus and Oenopion, to Theseus on Naxos. This would have meant either the Athenians remained on Crete for almost the duration of a pregnancy that started almost

as soon as they arrived or that they remained on Naxos for several months. Neither seems very likely.

The big question asked over the centuries is why Theseus left Ariadne. None of the answers are very good ones. Homer said she was killed there by Artemis on being denounced by Dionysus, and this denunciation appears to have been because Theseus and Ariadne made love in a grotto sacred to the god. Most accounts, though, say Theseus left her alive on the island. Some say Dionysus fell in love with her and carried her away. Others say Dionysus appeared to Theseus in a dream and demanded Ariadne for himself. Still others claim Theseus had fallen in love with Aegle, daughter of Panopeus of Phocis. Was Aegle the girl he left behind? In that case, he never loved Ariadne in the first place but only used her to accomplish his purpose. Though not a native Athenian, Aegle might also have been one of the victims, with whom a love affair slowly developed.

A most ingenious explanation was used by the modern novelist Mary Renault in *The King Must Die* (New York: Pantheon, 1958). Ariadne, she claimed, was a priestess of the Mother Dia, a fertility goddess. When the escapees arrived in Naxos, the annual ceremony was just taking place during which last year's king was being replaced by the new one, who would guarantee a harvest for the year to come. Ariadne joined the bacchanalian ritual, which consisted of falling into a drunken frenzy and hunting down the king whose year had ended and tearing him to pieces. At dawn the next day Theseus found Ariadne still in a drunken slumber, clutching the mutilated king's sexual organs in her hand. In disgust Theseus immediately set sail, leaving her behind.

Symbolically, this makes sense as well. She was taken over by Dionysus, the god of wine. Perhaps it would be carrying things too far to suggest that Ariadne was an alcoholic and that her marriage to Dionysus was a figurative one.

According to the older stories, though, Theseus left her on Naxos. Some say she killed herself in despair, but most stories say that Dionysus happened along and was overcome with her beauty. He married her and raised her among the immortals. He also placed his wedding present to her, a crown, among the stars. By her he became the father of Thoas, Peparethus, Latramys, Euanthes, Tauropolis, and the disputed Staphylus and Oenopion (whose names alone should leave no doubt as to their father's identity). Phlias, the founder of Phlius, was also said to be their son.

Two other accounts involving Ariadne are of interest. When Daedalus fled from Crete (not on wings but in a merchant vessel) to Athens, Minos pursued him but was swept off course and perished in Sicily. Deucalion, who succeeded his father, demanded the return of Daedalus. Otherwise, he said, he would put to death the Athenian hostages he was currently holding. Theseus put him off and meanwhile built a fleet, which when completed sailed on Crete. He killed Deucalion at the gate of the labyrinth and then married Ariadne, who had become queen upon the death of her brother.

When Theseus and Ariadne left for Athens, they were driven to Cyprus by a storm. Fearing she would miscarry the child she had conceived with Theseus, Ariadne wanted to be put ashore at Amathus. He just managed to put her ashore when he and his whole fleet were swept back out to sea. The women of Amathus treated her well, even pretending to convey messages from Theseus. She died in childbirth, and the women gave her a lavish funeral, burying her in a grove in Amathus. The accounts that follow the traditional story say she was buried in the temple of Dionysus Cresius in Argos. [Plutarch, *Theseus* 15,19,20; Cleidemus, quoted in Plutarch's *Theseus* 19; Hyginus, *Fables* 42,43, *Poetic Astronomy* 2.5; Homer, *Odyssey* 11.324; Diodorus Siculus 4.61, 5.51; Pausanias 1.20.2,27.9,44.5, 9.40.2, 10.29.2; Ovid, *Metamorphoses* 7.456, 8.175, *Heroides* 10; Scholiast on Apollonius Rhodius 3.996,997; Stephanus Byzantium, "Phlious"; Apollodorus 3.15.8.]

ARICINA was a surname of Artemis from the town of Aricia in Latium, where she was first worshipped in Italy. There was a tradition that Hippolytus, son of Theseus, upon being restored to life by Asclepius, was transported to Italy by Artemis and ruled over Aricia, where he dedicated a grove to her. This goddess was the Taurian Artemis, and her statue was considered to be the one Orestes and Iphigeneia brought from Tauris. The priest of this temple was always a runaway slave. As a challenge, a runaway slave would snap a branch off a certain tree, and the presiding priest, himself a former slave, was obliged to fight with the challenger. If he lost the battle, the challenger became his successor, and on and on. [Pausanias 2.27.4; Servius on Virgil's *Aeneid* 2.116; Strabo 5.3.12; Hyginus, *Fables* 261; Ovid, *Fasti* 3.260; Suetonius, *Caligula* 35.]

ARISBE (1) was a daughter of Merops, king of Percote on the Hellespont. Her father was a celebrated soothsayer, which gift he passed to his sons, Amphius and Adrastus. Arisbe's sister Cleite married Cyzicus, the founder of the city of Cyzicus on the Propontis (Sea of Marmara). Arisbe was the first wife of Priam, king of Troy, and bore to him one son, Aesacus. This marriage, most probably a thing of extreme youth, did not last long. Priam fell in love with Hecuba and gave Arisbe to Hyrtacus, a Trojan nobleman. Hyrtacus already had a son, Nisus, from an affair with a nymph. Nisus and Asius, his son by Arisbe, were called Hyrtacides.

Apparently Aesacus remained with his father when his mother was deposed from the queenship. From his grandfather he had learned the art of interpreting dreams and was able to give a dire interpretation to one of Hecuba's dreams. Hecuba dreamed she was giving birth to a firebrand, and Aesacus explained that she would give birth to a son who would be the downfall of the city of Troy. Aesacus married Asterope, daughter of Cebren, who died very young. On the point of dying from grief, Aesacus was changed into a bird.

The Trojan War took its toll on Arisbe. Her son, Asius, was killed, as were her brothers, Amphius and Adrastus. The Trojan town of Arisbe was said to have derived its name from her. [Stephanus Byzantium, "Arisbe"; Apollodorus 1.12.5; Homer, *Iliad* 2.831; Apollonius Rhodius 1.975; Strabo 13.1.7; Virgil, *Aeneid* 9.177.]

ARISBE (2), a daughter of Teucer, was called by some the wife of Dardanus. She was a native of Crete, and some traditions stated that it was this Arisbe who gave the name to the town of Arisbe.

According to others, BATEIA was the wife of Dardanus. [Stephanus Byzantium, "Arisbe"; Lycophron 1308.]

ARISBE (3) was a daughter of Macareus, a priest of Dionysus at Mytilene in Lesbos. The name Macar, or Macareus, carried an evil reputation, and this Macareus was no exception. As priest he committed an act of sacrilege by appropriating some gold left in trust at the temple, then killing the owner when he came to reclaim the treasure. Even worse, he killed him in the sanctuary, and the god took a terrible revenge. Arisbe's small brothers were playing in the temple and imitated their father's actions during a just-completed sacrifice. The elder stabbed his brother with the sacred knife, then burned him on the still-flaming altar. In frenzied shock the mother killed the elder son, and Macareus killed her.

It was little wonder that Arisbe saw fit to leave this unhappy scene, despite the fact that someone, probably her father, had elected to give her name to the town of Arisbe (modern Arisvi) in Lesbos. She went to the mainland and eventually settled on the slopes of Mount Ida. She was the first wife of Paris. Some writers have confused her with Arisbe, daughter of Merops, but such a combination would mean that Paris' first wife would also have been his father's first wife. Even if Arisbe had been 15 when she married Priam, she would have been double Paris' age when he reached maturity—she in her thirties and he in his teens. This marriage did not last long, since Paris left her for Oenone, whom he in turn left for Helen of Sparta.

When Paris was killed, Helenus and Deiphobus quarreled for Helen's hand. Deiphobus eventually took her by force. Helenus left the city and went to live with Arisbe on the slopes of Mount Ida, but this arrangement did not last long. Arisbe did not do well with Priam's sons. When Troy fell, Helenus went to Epeirus with Neoptolemus and Andromache, whom he later married. [Stephanus Byzantium, "Arisbe"; Eustathius on Homer's *Iliad* 894; Apollodorus, *Epitome* 5.9; Tzetzes on Lycophron 168; Servius on Virgil's *Aeneid* 2.166; Aelian, *Various Narratives* 13.2.]

ARISTE, the Best, was a surname of Artemis at Athens. [Pausanias 1.29.2.]

ARISTIPPE was one of the MINYADES.

ARISTOBULE, the Best Adviser, was a surname of Artemis at Athens. Themistocles built a temple there under this name and in it dedicated his own statue. [Plutarch, *Themistocles* 22.]

ARISTODEME (1) was a Sicyonian woman who, according to a local tradition, was the mother of Aratus by Asclepius. He was said to have impregnated her in the form of a dragon (serpent). There was a painting of her and the dragon at Sicyon in the temple of Asclepius. Aristodeme was a real person and does not belong in this book except for this strange cohabitation with a god. This juxtaposition of history and myth was not all that uncommon. We have only to remember a similar claim made by Olympias, the mother of Alexander the Great. [Pausanias 2.10.3, 4.14.5.]

ARISTODEME (2) was a daughter of Priam, but not by Hecuba. She was one of four illegitimate daughters, the others being Medusa, Medesicaste, and Lysimache. Nothing whatsoever is known about her, but as always it is interesting to speculate as to why she was mentioned at all. [Apollodorus 3.12.5.]

ARNACIA, or Arnaea, according to some was the original name of PENELOPE. [Tzetzes on Lycophron 792.]

ARNE (1) was a daughter of Aeolus. This sounds simple enough, but both Arne and Aeolus are names that have become increasingly confused over the years. There is no point in reviewing all the variations; the simplest method is to accept the genealogy of Diodorus Siculus (4.67). The Aeolus referred to here was the great-grandson of Aeolus I, son of Hellen. Aeolus II was a son of Hippotes and Melanippe and the grandson of Mimas. Arne was one of the daughters of Aeolus II. To further confuse things, she was also called Antiope or Melanippe.

Arne had sex with the ubiquitous Poseidon, and she told her father she was pregnant by the god. Apparently it had become a commonplace for unwed girls to tell their families they had become pregnant by gods and just as much a commonplace for outraged fathers not to believe them and have them killed or sold into slavery. In this case Arne was telling the truth, but Aeolus did the usual outraged-father scene and gave her to a stranger from Metapontum in Italy. Not long afterward Arne gave birth to twin sons, Boeotus and Aeolus III. An oracle instructed the Metapontan to adopt the boys, which he promptly did. He was already married to Autolyte, but the marriage was childless. The boys grew up, and it seems rather certain that Arne remained with them as a kind of nurse/mother/slave. The brothers eventually seized the throne of Metapontum during a revolution. This suggests a favorable turn of events for Arne and her boys, and it is too bad that it could not have lasted. When Arne and Autolyte had a dispute, the brothers killed their foster mother and had to flee with their mother from Metapontum.

Even though they were twins and had been inseparable all their lives, Boeotus and Aeolus went separate ways. Or it is conceivable that Boeotus and Arne first settled with Aeolus in the Aeolian Islands in the Tyrrhenian Sea, where he built the city of Lipara. Wishing to have his own colony, Boeotus might have decided to leave. In any case, he went to the region of Aeolis in Thessaly and settled there. He was considered the ancestor of the Boeotians. It seems likely Arne went with him, since the town of Arne (later Cierium) in Thessaly was named for her, as well as the town eventually called Chaeroneia. [Thucydides 1.12; Pausanias 9.40.5; Diodorus Siculus 5.7.]

ARNE (2) was a princess of the island of Siphnos. When Minos, king of Crete, sought to enlist support of the islands of the Aegean against Athens, some of the islands volunteered, but others, such as Siphnos, were not very willing. While being entertained at the palace, Minos discerned Arne's love for gold and bribed her to betray the island. She was not able to enjoy this particular gold, however, since the gods turned her into a jackdaw, which to this day is attracted to shiny things and steals them to hide in its nest. [Ovid, *Metamorphoses* 7.460–8.6.]

ARNE (3) was the wife of Aeson and mother of Jason, according to some. Most accounts call the

mother of Jason POLYMEDE. [Tzetzes on Lycophron 872.]

ARNE (4) was called by some the mother of Idas and Lynceus by Aphareus. Others call their mother Polydora, Laocoosa, or ARENE.

ARNE (5) was the nurse of Poseidon. When Cronus searched for Poseidon to devour him, Arne declared she did not know where he was. The town of Arne in Boeotia was said to have been named for her. [Tzetzes on Lycophron 644.]

ARRHIPPE was a huntress and chaste attendant of Artemis on Mount Carmanor in Lydia. Tmolus, son of Ares and husband of Omphale, saw Arrhippe while he was hunting and fell in love with her. She repulsed him, but he persisted; she fled from him and took sanctuary in the temple of Artemis. Tmolus was so filled with lust that he raped her then and there on the goddess' couch. Arrhippe invoked the goddess, then hanged herself from a beam of the temple. Artemis set a raging bull on Tmolus, which killed him. Mount Carmanor was renamed Mount Tmolus by Tmolus' son. [Apollodorus 2.6.3; Pseudo-Plutarch, *On Rivers* 7; Tacitus, *Annals* 2.47.]

ARSALTE was one of the DANAIDES. She was married to Ephialtes. [Hyginus, *Fables* 170.]

ARSINOE (1), also called Alphesiboea, was the daughter of Phegeus, king of Psophis (modern Tripotamo) in Arcadia. Her brothers were Pronous and Agenor. After Alcmaeon killed his mother, he went temporarily insane and fled from Argos. Pursued by the Erinyes he went from place to place. Finally he came to Phegeus in Psophis for purification. This process took some time, during the course of which Alcmaeon fell in love with Arsinoe and married her. When he had murdered his mother, he took from her the necklace and robe of Harmonia, with which she had been bribed to convince Amphiaraus to enter the war of the Seven against Thebes. These he gave to Arsinoe as a wedding gift. They had a son, Clytius. Unfortunately the gods were not through with Alcmaeon, and Psophis was the scene of a famine, which lifted only when

Alcmaeon left the city. An oracle told him to go to Achelous, the river-god, where he could settle in a land (a river island) formed since his matricide. This he did, probably planning to have Arsinoe follow him. But Achelous wanted him for a son-in-law, so he gave him Callirrhoe, his daughter. Either Alcmaeon made the mistake of telling her about the necklace and robe, or its fame was already known to her. She wanted these items and persuaded Alcmaeon to go and fetch them from his former wife. He came to Psophis and asked for the jewels and robe under the pretext that he planned to dedicate them at Delphi in order to be free from his madness once and for all. Phegeus complied but learned from a servant immediately after Alcmaeon left that the treasures were for Callirrhoe. He sent his sons, Pronous and Agenor, after Alcmaeon, and they killed him in ambush just north of Psophis and buried him at that spot.

Although Arsinoe had been abandoned by Alcmaeon, she still loved him enough to severely criticize her brothers for their action. Displeased at being upbraided for something they did in her behalf, they imprisoned Arsinoe in a chest and conveyed her to Tegea, where she was given as a slave to Agapenor. They told Agapenor she herself had killed Alcmaeon. Word must have traveled fast to Callirrhoe about what had happened. She was having a covert affair with Zeus, and she begged him to make her two sons by Alcmaeon grow up at once. This was done, and Callirrhoe must have sent them immediately to Tegea to intercept the sons of Phegeus. It is stated that the sons of Phegeus were on their way to dedicate the heirlooms at Delphi, so this must have been planned in conjunction with depositing Arsinoe. Otherwise it makes no sense that they were in Tegea, since Tegea is a considerable distance southeast of Psophis, while Delphi is roughly the same distance northeast. According to the common account, Alcmaeon's sons met Arsinoe's brothers at Agapenor's house and killed them. They took the jewels and went to Psophis, where they killed Phegeus and his wife. They were pursued by the Psophidians and fled back to Tegea, where they were saved by the Tegeans and some Argives. They returned to Callirrhoe and were instructed by Achelous to dedicate the necklace and robe at Delphi.

As usual, much is left out of this story. Arsinoe is not mentioned again. One wonders how she was treated by Agapenor, if she was indeed enslaved. Why is Tegea the scene of so much of this story? Why did the Tegeans protect the sons of Alcmaeon when they were pursued by the Psophidians? After all, they were Aetolians, and the sons of Phegeus were fellow Arcadians. Had Arsinoe perhaps intervened in their behalf? Most of all, why did the young brothers flee to Tegea rather than toward their home in the north?

Even with its puzzles this is an interesting account. Arsinoe comes through as a forgiving wife, even after her husband left her for another woman, with whom he fathered children. She opposed her brothers when they killed him, even though she might have known the possible consequences. She was the only one connected with the infamous necklace who showed any strength of character. [Apollodorus 3.7.5; Pausanias 8.24.4.]

ARSINOE (2) was the nurse of Orestes. Some accounts call her Geilissa or Laodameia. When Aegisthus and Clytemnestra murdered Agamemnon, they also intended to kill Orestes, who was still only a boy. Arsinoe anticipated this and managed to sneak him out of the palace. Some say she put her own son to bed in Orestes' place, so that Aegisthus believed he had killed Orestes and had no reason to search further. This allowed Arsinoe time to smuggle him out of Argolis, and she took him to Strophius in Crissa. Strophius was married to Anaxibia, the sister of Agamemnon, and they were the parents of Pylades. Nothing further is known of Arsinoe. She probably lived out her days in Crissa, unable to return to Mycenae. If indeed she substituted her own child for Orestes and he was her only child, she probably had no reason to return. [Pindar, *Pythian Odes* 11.17,25,54; Scholiast on Pindar's *Pythian Odes* 11.25; Aeschylus, *Agamemnon* 877, *Libation-Bearers* 732; Euripides, *Electra* 14.]

ARSINOE (3) was a daughter of Leucippus and Philodice, and sister of Hilaeira and Phoebe, the wives of the Dioscuri. Leucippus was a son of

Perieres and Gorgophone, and brother of Aphareus. He was one of the Calydonian hunters and was prince of the Messenians. The Messenian town of Leuctra was said to have been named for him.

Not to be outdone by her sisters and their divine husbands, Arsinoe slept with Apollo and became by him the mother of Eriopis. The Messenians also claimed she was the mother of Asclepius by him. There were other claims for this honor, and eventually an oracle was called upon to settle the question. The decision was that Asclepius had been born in the territory of Epidaurus, so this ruled out Arsinoe, who had never been out of Messenia. It is not clear whether she made this claim for herself or whether it was another evidence of national propaganda.

Nothing is known of Eriopis, which is unusual considering she was the offspring of Apollo. Arsinoe had a sanctuary at Sparta and was worshipped as a heroine, probably because of her reputation as the mother of Asclepius. [Apollodorus 3.10.3; Pausanias 2.26.6, 3.12.7; Cicero, *On the Nature of the Gods* 3.22; Scholiast on Pindar's *Pythian Odes* 3.14; Ovid, *Metamorphoses* 8.306.]

ARSINOE (4) was one of the MINYADES.

ARSINOE (5) was a maiden of Cyprus, loved by Arceophon, a son of Minnyrides of Salamis in Cyprus. The story about her is identical to one told about ANAXARETE and Iphis.

ARSINOE (6) was called by some the mother of Podaleirus and Machaon by Asclepius. Others call her EPIONE.

ARSIPPE was one of the MINYADES.

ARTEMICHA was another of those unfortunate people caught up in consequences of actions not of their own doing. She was the daughter of Cleinis and Harpe, and sister of Lycius, Ortygius, and Harpasus. They lived near Babylon in Mesopotamia. Cleinis was apparently very desirable both physically and spiritually, since

Apollo and Artemis loved him greatly. Cleinis wanted to please Apollo and, having heard that the Hyperboreans sacrificed asses to the god, he tried to introduce the custom in Babylon. Apollo was not happy with this change from the usual sheep, goats, and heifers, and prohibited the practice. Lycius and Harpasus, however, defied the order and continued to sacrifice asses. Highly indignant, Apollo drove the asses insane so that they attacked Cleinis and his family. The gods took pity and changed the family members into different birds. This curious story is a kind of parable with no really clear meaning, unless it is a warning to give the gods only what they ask for. The names of at least three of the family had reference to birds even before the metamorphosis. [Antoninus Liberalis 20.]

ARTEMIS, one of the 12 Olympian divinities, was the goddess of the hunt, virginity (though a goddess of childbirth as well), the moon, and the natural environment.

NATIVITY: Daughter of Zeus and Leto, twin sister of Apollo. Daughter of Persephone and Zeus. Daughter of Dionysus and Isis. Daughter of Upis and Glauce.

LOVERS: Britomartis.

CHILDREN: None. Cicero (*On the Nature of the Gods* 3.23) said she was mother of Eros (Cupid) by Hermes (Mercury).

PRINCIPAL SEATS OF WORSHIP: Delos, Arcadia (especially Mount Erymanthus and Mount Maenalus), Tauris, Sparta, Mount Taygetus, Troezen, Hermione, Brauron, Ephesus, Crete, Sicily, southern Italy.

SACRED TO HER: Laurel, fir tree, fish, stag, bear, boar, dog, goat, bee, and other animals.

COMPANIONS: Apollo, Nymphs, Oceanides, Aura, Amarynthus, Maera, Orion, Phylonome, Pleiades, Upis, Theia, Arhippe.

IDENTIFIED WITH: Britomartis, Dictynna, Eileithyia, Diana, Taurica Dea, Anaites,

Bendis, Bubastis, Brimo, Callisto, Iphigeneia, Gamelii, Hecate, Hestia, Juno, Persephone, Selene.

SURNAMES: Acraea, Aeginaea, Aetole, Agoraea, Agrotera, Alphaea, Angelos, Apanchomene, Aricina, Ariste, Aristobule, Astrateia, Brauronia, Britomartis, Calliste, Caryatis, Chitone, Chrysaor, Cnagia, Colaenis, Condyleates, Cordaca, Coryphaea, Coryphasia, Corythallia, Curotrophos, Daphnaea, Delia, Delphinia, Derrhiatis, Diana, Dictynna, Eileithyia, Ephesia, Eucleia, Eurynome, Gaeeochos, Genetyllis, Hecaerge, Hegemone, Hemeresia, Heurippe, Hymnia, Iphigeneia, Issoria, Laphria, Leogeneia, Leucophryne, Limenia, Limnaea, Locheia, Loxo, Lyceia, Lycoatis, Lygodesma, Lysizona, Melissa, Munychia, Mysia, Oenoatis, Orthia, Ortygia, Parthenia, Peitho, Pheraea, Phoebe, Phosphoros, Pitanatis, Saronia, Sarpedonia, Soteira, Stymphalia, Tauropolis, Thoantea, Triclaria, Upis.

Artemis was the most complex of the Olympian deities, paradoxically compassionate and vengeful, nurturing and destructive, pacific and bloody. Like the other gods and goddesses, her worship had evolved from several eastern and Mediterranean divinities. In her case some of these had been orgiastic and involved human sacrifice. Coming together finally into a goddess called Artemis, these earlier characteristics had to be distinguished by surnames reflective of the older identities. We can quickly conclude that the Arcadian Artemis, the Brauronian Artemis, and the Ephesian Artemis were quite different, even though the basic and contrasting attributes of chastity and fertility still obtained. Perhaps some of these earlier identities were responsible for the various versions of her birth, particularly the one that made her the daughter of Dionysus and Isis. Her darker side might have been re-

flected in assignment of Zeus and Persephone as parents, thereby giving her an infernal aspect.

Artemis as the sister of Apollo probably came later than the rather terrifying identities stemming from Middle Eastern mother goddesses, for the Delos connection firmly secured her place in the Greek pantheon. Some accounts of Apollo's birth, such as its having taken place in Tegyra in Boeotia or Zoster in Attica, do not include Artemis. One account has her born separately by Leto at Corissus. An interesting tie-in with her earlier worship in Asia Minor and that of the purely Greek Apollo places their birth in the grove of Ortygia near Ephesus. The name "Ortygia" provides a bridge to Delos, for which Ortygia was an earlier name. So finally we come to the birth of the twins at Delos, where their mother, Leto, had fled to escape Hera's persecution. This took the physical form of the monster Python, which pursued her from place to place. Even there, however, the real event was the birth of Apollo; Artemis seemed like an afterthought. Some even represented her as born first and establishing her midwife identity by immediately helping Leto deliver Apollo. But most accounts have them born together, with other divinities such as Eileithyia and Dione in attendance.

There is a blank spot after their birth. Apollo was nursed by Themis, while the nymph Upis reared Artemis. These arrangements apparently did not last long, since deities tended to mature rapidly. It was not long before Apollo and Artemis were off to avenge Leto by killing Python and the giant Tityus, both of whom had persecuted her. Artemis accompanied Apollo to Aegialeia and Tarrha for purification after killing Python. Then, just as she had appeared rather superfluous in the birth stories, she tended to disappear from any abiding association with Apollo. We find her coming together with him to address some wrong, usually a slight to their mother, but then they go their separate ways. While Artemis was counted among the Olympian goddesses, it is difficult to think of her as even a part-time resident of the sacred mountain. She is universally familiar as the free-roving huntress of the mountains and forests of Arcadia. She is also regarded by most people as goddess of the moon, although this attribute was a result of her later identity with earlier moon goddesses, mostly foreign. In addition, well-read individuals can associate her with the more somber elements of her worship found in the Taurian Artemis, who appeared in Greece as the Brauronian Artemis and later the Orthian Artemis, and eventually in Italy as the Arician Artemis/Diana. The human sacrifice connected with the Taurian goddess came to be symbolized by the ritual scourging of Spartan boys at the altar of Artemis Orthia. The Arcadian Artemis, the one most closely associated with the pastoral Apollo, retained some of this vengeful vigor in her power to send plagues or sudden death by her arrows.

At the same time, Artemis was the protectress of children and sucking animals. She was skilled in midwifery. In Ephesus she was associated with fertility. Statues there represented her equipped with what were thought to be multiple breasts but recently were found to be bull testicles. It can be seen that her worship was most complex, making her a kind of universal goddess with almost limitless power. Her virginity made her even more awesome than Hera, Aphrodite, or Demeter. It made her less human as well, a characteristic she shared with Athena.

As if to soften this image somewhat, we are given the story of Britomartis, the Cretan divinity of hunters and fishermen. Artemis loved her, and saved her from the lustful Minos. It is probably safe to assume they were lovers in the total sense. Artemis certainly had an undeniably masculine nature in all her manifestations, but even so she was an object of male desire on more than one occasion. Alpheius the river-god pursued her, but she eluded him by covering herself and her nymphs with mud so he could not distinguish them. At Olympia, she and Alpheius had an altar in common. Otus, one of the giant Aloeidae, sued for her hand, for which presumptuousness he paid with his life. Some have hinted that she was attracted to Orion, the handsome Boeotian hunter, but her basic nature could not tolerate anything further, and she ended up killing him. Actaeon, another hunter, saw her bathing. She changed him into a stag, which was immediately torn to pieces by Actaeon's hunting dogs. One account said he was in love with her and suggested that he deliberately spied on her.

Buphagus, an Arcadian hunter, was killed when he pursued her (an especially unwise act, considering that he was married). Artemis simply did not care for men. She made an exception for Hippolytus, son of Theseus, who swore himself to chastity and the service of the goddess. When his stepmother, Phaedra, became responsible for his death out of unrequited love for him, Artemis had him resurrected and conveyed to Aricia in Italy, where he became the god Virbius and established her worship.

A few other men directly or indirectly received benefits from her. Orestes was spared his life at Tauris, but most certainly because of Artemis' love for Iphigeneia. She warned the Telchines of an impending tidal wave in Rhodes, so they had time to flee. She advised Hypermnestra to save Lynceus, when the rest of the Danaides slew their husbands on their wedding night. There was one account that said she assisted Theseus in getting to Hippolytus' side before he died so Theseus could be reconciled with his son. She helped heal Aeneas when he was wounded by Diomedes.

By and large, though, men did not fare well with her, particularly those who neglected sacrifices to her. Admetus, husband of Alcestis, forgot to offer her thanks during his wedding and found snakes in the bridal bed. Aesymnetes violated her temple at Aroe, and for many years thereafter handsome youths and beautiful maidens had to be sacrificed to Artemis Triclaria. For killing one of her sacred stags, Agamemnon was forced to sacrifice Iphigeneia. Phalaecus, tyrant of Ambracia, was torn to pieces by a lioness for playing with a lion cub. She sent the famous Calydonian boar to plague Oeneus, who forgot to sacrifice to her. She caused the dispute between Meleager and his uncles over the spoils from the boar hunt, which led to his death. She caused Narcissus to fall in love with himself. She made Procris spy on Cephalus, thus causing her death and eventually his. Because he refused to honor her, she drove Broteas mad and he burned himself to death. She was involved in the hideous events concerning the house of Atreus; it was she who sent the golden lamb that set off the deadly rivalry between Atreus and Thyestes. She cruelly punished Tmolus for the rape of her companion Arhippe. She inflicted the plague of leprosy on

Teuthras for killing one of her sacred boars. She killed Ischys, the lover of Coronis, mother of Asclepius.

Although Artemis favored women, she was swift in her vengeance when one of them, in her terms, failed her. She killed Coronis along with Ischys, although infidelity to her brother Apollo was only suspected. Some say she killed Ariadne in Naxos. She metamorphosed the sisters of Meleager into guinea hens. Chione, daughter of Daedalion, was killed by Artemis for finding fault with the goddess's beauty. Gerana, daughter of Nicodamas and mother of Mopsus, was turned into a crane because she hated Artemis. The goddess even risked the wrath of Zeus by killing one of his lovers, Maera, who had once been one of her companions. Ethemea, wife of Merops, was killed by the goddess for neglecting sacrifices to her. And, of course, there is the story of the dreadful carnage by Artemis and Apollo on the children of Niobe. Even the innocent did not escape the arrows of this vengeful goddess. Nor did she always need a reason for her actions; both Andromache's mother and Laodameia, the mother of Sarpedon, were killed by her for no ostensible crime. Finally, Artemis was even accounted by one writer as demanding the sacrifice of Helen and Menelaus when they went ashore at Tauris.

The worship of Artemis was as complicated as her many identities and attributes. The Hyperboreans carried offerings to her and Apollo at Delos. Philammon, the mythical poet, established a chorus of girls who sang hymns to celebrate Leto, Artemis, and Apollo. Otrera, the wife or daughter of Ares, built the temple of Artemis at Ephesus, where Amazons were priestesses and attendants. The Amazons also built shrines to Apollo and Artemis at Pyrrhichus, the farthest southern point to which they advanced on their invasion of Greece. Theseus built a temple of Artemis Soteira in Troezen, and Hippolytus, his son, built one for Artemis Lyceia. A temple of Artemis Britomartis at Olus in Crete was ascribed to Daedalus. The Lacedaemonians dedicated a temple of Artemis Caryatis. Alcathous built a temple of Artemis Agrotera at Megara. According to the rumor that Iphigeneia was the daughter of Helen and Theseus, on the way home from Aphidna Helen dedicated a sanctuary to Artemis in gratitude for a safe delivery. A curious ceremony took place in Tegea at the festival of Apollo Agyieus, in which a priestess of Artemis pursued a man to commemorate the pursuit and slaying of Leimon, son of Tegeates, who slew his brother Scephrus. The Taurian, Brauronian, Orthian, and Arician identities have already been mentioned as steps in the evolution from human sacrifice.

Well-known names in mythology were connected with her worship. The famous huntress Atalanta, who had been suckled by a bear (a symbol of Artemis), was dedicated to her service. Taygete, one of the Pleiades, refused to yield to Zeus, and Artemis changed her into a cow. Taygete showed her gratitude by dedicating to her the Cerynitian hind with golden antlers. Heracles narrowly escaped her wrath when he captured the animal. Some say he sacrificed it on the goddess's altar on Mount Artemisium. Erigone, daughter of Clytemnestra and Aegisthus, was saved from Orestes by Artemis, who made her a priestess. Hilaeira, wife of Castor, had been a priestess of Artemis; presumably this office ended when she married. Achilles hastily sacrificed to Artemis when he killed the Amazon Penthesileia. In her attempt to seduce Hippolytus, Phaedra claimed she had joined a cult of Artemis.

In spite of some of her more frightening attributes, most people conceive of Artemis as a slender, nymphlike huntress or ethereal moon goddess. Art over the ages has most often shown her in hunting attire with bow and arrows, often in the company of deer or in a chariot drawn by stags. It is difficult to identify this pastoral maiden with the testicle-festooned Ephesian goddess or the bloody Taurica Dea. [NATIVITY: Tacitus, *Annals* 3.61; *Homeric Hymn to Apollo, Homeric Hymn to Delos,* Scholiast on Callimachus' *Hymn to Artemis* 240; Apollodorus 1.4.1, 3.8.2; Hyginus, *Fables* 181, *Poetic Astronomy* 2.1; Stephanus Byzantium, "Korissos"; Hesiod, *Theogony* 918; Pausanias 8.37.3; Herodotus 2.156; Scholiast on Pindar's *Nemean Odes* 1.1; Diodorus Siculus 5.72—LOVERS: Pausanias 2.30.3, 3.14.2, 8.2.4, 9.40.3; Diodorus Siculus 5.76; Callimachus, *Hymn to Artemis* 3.191; Antoninus Liberalis 40—CHARACTERISTICS: Statius, *Thebaid* 2.203; Apollodorus, 1.9.15;

Euripides, *Iphigeneia in Aulis* 90, *Iphigeneia in Taurica* 15; Pausanias 2.21.1,25.4,31.1, 3.5.6,18.9, 5.14.5, 6.22.5, 7.19.1, 8.13.1,9.2.3; Callimachus, *Hymn to Artemis* 13,15,81,90,162; Servius on Virgil's *Aeneid* 1.539; Horace, *Odes* 2.4.72; Antoninus Liberalis 4; Pindar, *Olympian Odes* 3.51,53; Homer, *Iliad* 6.197–205, *Odyssey* 11.325—WORSHIP: Herodotus 2.32,35, 4.103; Plutarch, *Theseus* 33; Hyginus, *Fables* 79; Tzetzes on Lycophron 995; Ovid, *Metamorphoses* 5.329; Antoninus Liberalis 28; Servius on Virgil's *Eclogues* 8.30; Pausanias 2.7.4,19.6,22.7,35.1, 3.16.6, 7.2.4, 8.12.1,14.6,35.7.]

ASCRA was the mother of Oeoclus by Poseidon. Oeoclus, in conjunction with the Aloeidae, is said to have founded the town of Ascra in Boeotia. Poseidon was indeed far-wandering and often distant from his watery element. On this foray into Boeotia, he must have impregnated both Iphimedeia, the mother of the Aloeidae, and Ascra. Thus the giant twins and Oeoclus were half-brothers. [Pausanias 9.29.1.]

ASIA (1) was a surname of Athena in Colchis, the land of the Golden Fleece and home of Aeetes and Medea. Her worship was believed to have been carried from there by Castor and Polydeuces to Laconia, where a temple was built to her at Las. [Pausanias 3.24.5.]

ASIA (2), one of the OCEANIDES, was called by some the mother of Atlas, Prometheus, Epimetheus, and Menoetius by Iapetus. Most sources call the wife of Iapetus CLYMENE. According to some, she gave her name to the continent of Asia. [Hesiod, *Theogony* 359; Apollodorus 1.2.2; Herodotus 4.45.]

ASIA (3) was the wife of Prometheus, and it is entirely possible that she was the same as the Oceanid above. As the wife of Prometheus she saw the birth of mankind. Although it is never stated anywhere, she must have been the mother of Deucalion, who with his wife Pyrrha repeopled the earth after the flood. She saw her husband bring fire to mortals and suffer the consequences by eternal torture. In that ancient time identities were uncertain, and many beings were personified sources of energy and forces of nature. Asia came

from the sea and was matched with Prometheus, a heavenly figure; together they were responsible for the formulation of the human clay, first destroyed and then recovered. [Herodotus 4.45; Stephanus Byzantium, "Asia."]

ASIA (4) was one of the NEREIDES. [Hyginus, *Fables: Preface* 8.]

ASINE was a daughter of Lacedaemon and Sparta, and sister of Amyclas and Eurydice. Lacedaemon, son of Zeus and Taygete, was king of the country he called Lacedaemon after his own name. Nothing further is known of her, but there were three towns in Peloponnesus that bore her name. [Stephanus Byzantium, "Asine."]

ASOPIS (1) was one of the THESPIADES, who became by Heracles the mother of Mentor. [Apollodorus 2.7.8.]

ASOPIS (2) was a daughter of the river-god Asopus. Asopus made his home in Phlius, where he was married to Metope, the daughter of the river Ladon. By her he had two sons, Pelasgus and Ismenus, and 12 daughters. His daughters were very beautiful, and he had problems with their being abducted, mainly by the Olympian gods. [Diodorus Siculus 4.72.]

ASOPO was one of the PIERIDES. [Tzetzes on Hesiod's *Works and Days* 6.]

ASPALIS was a daughter of Argaeus. In the town of Melite ruled a tyrant named Tartaros. Every time he heard someone praise the beauty of a maiden in the area, he had her seized for his pleasure before she could marry. Aspalis was one of these unfortunate objects of his lust. When she learned of what was about to happen to her, she hanged herself prior to the arrival of the soldiers who came to look for her. Before the news of her death was even announced, her young brother Astygetes swore to punish the tyrant before burying his sister. Hurriedly he dressed in her garments, hid a sword under his gown, and passed the palace guards undetected. He found the tyrant unarmed and killed him. The people of Melite crowned Astygetes and held a procession, after throwing Tartaros' body in a river, which they afterward called Tartarus. They searched in vain for the body of Aspalis in order to hold funeral services. The body had disappeared, and in its place appeared a statue of Artemis. The people gave the statue the name of Aspalis Ameilete Hecaerge, and every year the virgins of the country hanged a young unmated female goat in memory of Aspalis. [Antoninus Liberalis 13.]

ASSA was the mother of Sithon by Poseidon. Sithon was married to the nymph Mendeis, by whom he became the father of Pallene and Rhoeteia. He was king of the Hadomantes in Macedonia and Thrace. His daughters, grand-daughters of Assa, gave their names to two peninsulas in the north Aegean. [Tzetzes on Lycophron 1356.]

ASSESIA was a surname of Athena, derived from the town of Assesus in Ionia, where she had a temple. [Herodotus 1.19.]

ASTERIA (1) was a daughter of the Titans Coeus and Phoebe, and sister of Leto. She was an inhabitant of Olympus, probably part of the booty from the overthrow of the Titans by the Olympian gods. Not surprisingly Zeus fancied this beautiful cousin, and she had to flee to escape his embraces. It appears that Zeus sought to usurp the bed of another cousin—Perses, son of the Titan Crius and Eurybia—for he was married to Asteria and by him she was the mother of Hecate. But Zeus was the powerful ruler of heaven and earth, and there was no choice for them except Asteria's flight. First she changed into a quail; still pursued, she threw herself into the sea. There she was metamorphosed into the island Asteria, or Ortygia (quail), afterward called Delos. At this early time it was a floating island, but became anchored when Leto arrived there to bear Apollo and Artemis. [Hesiod, *Theogony* 377,409; Apollodorus 1.2.2,4.1; Athenaeus 9.392; Hyginus, *Fables* 53; Callimachus, *Hymn to Delos* 37, *Hymn to Artemis* 35,37,191; Servius on Virgil's *Aeneid* 3.73.]

ASTERIA (2) was one of the ALCYONIDES. [Eustathius on Homer's *Iliad* 776.]

ASTERIA (3) was one of the DANAIDES, a daughter of Danaus and Atlantia or Phoebe. She was married to Chaetus, son of Aegyptus. [Apollodorus 2.1.5.]

ASTERIA (4), occasionally called Asterope, was a daughter of Atlas and one of the PLEIADES. She was, according to certain accounts, the mother of one of the most unpleasant individuals in ancient story. This was Diomedes, king of the Bistones in Thrace. She bore him to Atlas, her own father. While incest was not uncommon among the gods, it did not seem to work too well in this case. Diomedes' stables were infamous, since they housed mares that he fed on human flesh. One of Heracles' labors involved bringing these animals to Mycenae. Diomedes was killed during this horse-rustling episode. [Hyginus, *Fables* 250; Apollodorus 2.5.8; Servius on Virgil's *Aeneid* 1.756.]

ASTERIA (5) was a daughter of Hydis and became by Bellerophon the mother of Hydissus, the founder of Hydissus in Caria. We know quite a lot about Bellerophon, such as that after his fall from heaven he became something of a derelict and died in Caria. We know nothing more about Asteria, Hydis, or Hydissus. Stephanus Byzantium, the author of this information, seldom gave sources, and all too often he seemed to be dignifying a place with the name of a hero. On the other hand, he might have had access to bodies of literature that have long since disappeared. [Stephanus Byzantium, "Hydissos."]

ASTERIA (6), the daughter of Coronus, was said to be the mother of Idmon by Apollo. Idmon's mother is more often given as ANTIANEIRA. [Scholiast on Apollonius Rhodius 1.139.]

ASTERIA (7) was the daughter of Teucer and Eune. She was born on Cyprus, the home of her mother. Teucer had gone there as a result of an oracle of Apollo. When he had returned from the Trojan War, he was rejected by his father, Telamon, king of Salamis, because he had not avenged the death of his half-brother Ajax nor brought back with him Ajax's wife and son. Teucer was kindly received in Cyprus and given land by Belus, the king of Cydon. He married

Eune, the daughter of Cyprus, and became the father of Asteria. He founded the town of Salamis, named for his native island. Nothing else is known of Asteria. [Tzetzes on Lycophron 447,450; Pindar, *Nemean Odes* 4.60; Aeschylus *Persians* 896; Euripides, *Helen* 87,146; Pausanias 2.29.4; Horace, *Odes* 1.7.21.]

ASTERIA (8) was one of the AMAZONS killed in the battle with Heracles while he was attempting to fetch the girdle of Hippolyte. She fell at the same time as her companions Deianeira, Marpe, Tecmessa, and Alcippe. [Diodorus Siculus 4.16.]

ASTERIA (9) was the wife of Phocus, by whom she was the mother of Panopeus and Crisus. She is usually called ASTERODEIA.

ASTERODEIA (1) was called by some the mother by Endymion of Aetolus, Paeon, and Epeius. Their mother is most often called NEIS. [Pausanias 5.1.2.]

ASTERODEIA (2) was named by some as the wife of Icarius, son of Perieres, but his wife is usually called POLYCASTE. [Pherecydes, quoted by the scholiast on Homer's *Odyssey* 15.15.]

ASTERODEIA (3) was the mother of Absyrtus by Aeetes, king of Colchis, according to the principal chronicler of the expedition of the Argonaut. Others, with less authority, have called her Ipsia, Idyia, Hecate, Neaera, and Eurylyte. Absyrtus was therefore Medea's young half-brother, since her own mother was Idyia (or sometimes Hecate, although this dark goddess might have been named to enhance Medea's evil reputation). We don't know who Asterodeia was, but when in doubt we usually say an otherwise unidentified woman was a nymph. Nymphs usually had hasty liaisons and left the progeny, especially male, with the more stable father to raise. If Asterodeia did come out of the forests to dwell in the royal house, she would have seen the Argonauts arrive, achieve their purpose of acquiring the Golden Fleece with Medea's help, and leave with her and with Absyrtus as hostage. She would have seen the Colchian pursuers return with the dismembered youth, since Medea

killed him and threw parts of him into the sea to slow her father's ships. It is more likely that Asterodeia never knew or really would not have cared all that much. Having borne Absyrtus she returned to the forests of the Caucasus Range and was never heard from again. [Apollonius Rhodius 3.241.]

ASTERODEIA (4) was a daughter of Deion, king of Phocis, and Diomede, daughter of Xuthus. Thus she was part of the early Aeolian dynasty, since her grandparents were Aeolus and Enarete. Her father assisted in starting the Messenian branch of the vast family by taking the daughter of his brother Salmoneus into his house and marrying her to Cretheus, another brother. Asterodeia's brothers were Aenetus, Actor, Phylacus, and Cephalus. This made her the aunt of Menoetius, Actor's son, and therefore grandaunt of Patroclus. This careful attention to minor relatives in the tributary stories that flow into the eventual stream of events culminating in the Trojan War lends credibility to literary evidence for the war. The fact that Asterodeia is never mentioned again poses the question of why she was mentioned at all. [Apollodorus 1.9.4.]

ASTERODEIA (5), sometimes called Asteria, was the mother of Panopeus and Crisus by Phocus. It is tempting to regard her as the preceding Asterodeia, daughter of Deion, since her husband migrated to and extended the territory of Phocis, and her sons founded two important cities there. But the evidence seems to point to an Aeginetan origin, since Phocus was a son of Aeacus and Psamathe in Aegina. Her husband was murdered by his jealous half-brothers Peleus and Telamon when he returned from Phocis. After his death, the sons migrated to Phocis to found the towns named for them. [Hesiod, *Theogony* 1094; Pindar, *Nemean Odes* 5.23; Tzetzes on Lycophron 53,939; Apollodorus 3.12.6; Pausanias 2.29.]

ASTEROPE (1), one of the OCEANIDES, was the mother of Acragas by Zeus. The foundation of the town of Acragas (Agrigentum) in Sicily was ascribed to Acragas. [Stephanus Byzantium, "Acragantes."]

ASTEROPE (2), sometimes called Hesperia, was the daughter of the river-god Cebren. She was the wife of Aesacus, the son of Priam and his first wife, Arisbe. Aesacus learned the art of interpreting dreams from his mother's father, Merops. It was he who divined the meaning of Hecuba's dream about giving birth to a firebrand. Unhappily, Asterope died while very young, and Aesacus lamented her death so intensely that he was pitied by the gods and changed into a sea bird. The death of Asterope calls for an examination of the concept of immortality among the ancients. Apparently having a river-god for a parent did not guarantee everlasting life. [Apollodorus 3.12.5.]

ASTEROPE (3) was sometimes called a daughter of Atlas and mother by him of Diomedes, king of the Bistones. She was probably identical with ASTERIA.

ASTEROPE (4) was the wife of Hippalcimus, or Hippalmus, and mother by him of Peneleus. Nothing further is known about Asterope or her husband, but their son fitted into a rather common pattern for his particular time. He was an Argonaut, a suitor of Helen, and then a leader of the Boeotians in the Trojan War. He was killed in the war but left a son, Opheltes, who became the father of Damasichthon, a postbellum king of Thebes. [Apollodorus 1.9.16, 3.10.8; Pausanias 9.5.8; Diodorus Siculus 4.67.]

ASTEROPEIA was one of the PELIADES. After they were deceived into killing their father, they fled to Arcadia. Asteropeia and Antinoe were the only two identified when the painter Micon inscribed their names on their portraits. [Pausanias 8.11.2.]

ASTRAEA was a daughter of Zeus and Themis, or of Astraeus and Eos. She was one of the nebulous heavenly beings who coexisted on earth with mortals during the period called the Golden Age. As time went on, mankind became progressively corrupt, and this innocent age came to an end. Astraea was called the last of the immortals to leave the "blood-soaked" earth. [Ovid, *Metamorphoses* 1.150; Hyginus, *Poetic Astronomy* 2.25; Eratosthenes, *Star Placements* 9.]

ASTRATEIA, Invasion Stopper, was a surname of Artemis, under which she had a temple near Pyrrhichus in Laconia. It was there she was believed to have halted the advance of the Amazons. The warrior women from Thermodon left there a wooden image of the goddess. [Pausanias 3.25.2.]

ASTYAGEIA was a daughter of Hypseus, son of the Peneius River and the Naiad Creusa. Her sisters were Cyrene, Alcaea, and Themisto. Astyageia was not as famous as her sisters Cyrene and Themisto, who migrated to other places. She remained among the Lapithae and married Periphas, son of Lapithes. Her son by Periphas was Antion; he in turn fathered the infamous Ixion, who spawned the Centaurs. Ixion's famous son was Peirithous, the great friend of Theseus and author of the celebrated battle between the Lapiths and Centaurs. [Diodorus Siculus 4.69; Pindar, *Pythian Odes* 9.13; Scholiast on Pindar's *Pythian Odes* 2.39; Apollodorus 1.9.2; Pausanias 9.34.5.]

ASTYANASSA was a daughter of Musaeus, the quasi-legendary poet from the age of Heracles. She was said to have been one of Helen's slaves and to have composed pornographic poems. It is unfortunate we have so very little knowledge of this woman who was certainly ahead of her time. [Suidas, "Astyanassa"; Photius, *Library* 142.]

ASTYCRATEIA (1) was a daughter of Polyidus, the Corinthian soothsayer, and sister of Euchenor and Manto. Polyidus was particularly famous for having restored Glaucus, son of Minos, to life. His children apparently never gained any particular renown, although they were descendants of Melampus, perhaps the greatest seer in antiquity. The tombs of the two sisters were shown at Megara near the entrance of the sanctuary of Dionysus, which their father had erected. [Pausanias 1.43.5; Pindar, *Olympian Odes* 13.104; Homer, *Iliad* 13.663; Apollodorus 3.3.1.]

ASTYCRATEIA (2) was one of the daughters of Amphion and NIOBE killed by the arrows of Artemis.

ASTYDAMEIA (1) was the wife of Acastus. Some have called her Hippolyte, or Cretheis, daughter of Cretheus and Tyro. Acastus was the son of Pelias, who sent Jason on the perilous voyage to seek the Golden Fleece. Pelias was probably unpleasantly surprised when his own son enlisted as an Argonaut with his cousin Jason. Most likely the cousins were close companions on the voyage and became enemies only on their return to Iolcus, when Medea tricked the daughters of Pelias into carving up their father and boiling him on the false assumption that he would be rejuvenated. Acastus and Astydameia immediately exiled his sisters, as well as Jason and Medea. They buried what was left of Pelias and held funeral games for him.

Acastus had earlier participated in the Calydonian boar hunt, where he became friends with Peleus, who would later become the father of Achilles. They had also been companions on the Argonaut. During the boar hunt Peleus accidentally killed his father-in-law, Eurytion, and afterward came to Acastus at Iolcus to be purified. Astydameia took an interest in the dashing young adventurer during this time. (He had also helped kill his brother Phocus, which apparently made him deliciously dangerous and desirable.) Her own husband, busy with the affairs of state, lacked the glamor of his friend, so when Peleus reappeared to participate in the funeral games of her father-in-law, Astydameia fell obsessively in love with him. For all his sins Peleus was not promiscuous. He was in love with his wife Antigone, and rejected the overtures of his hostess. Astydameia must have been especially lovely, at least in her own estimation, since she was outraged at his spurning of her. Had she been pockmarked or squinting, she probably would not have told her husband that Peleus had tried to seduce her.

Acastus, unlike his father, was a decent man. He didn't go into a blind rage at the report from his wife. He liked Peleus and maybe even had a notion of the real truth. Nevertheless, he was obliged to do something to appease his vengeful wife. He took Peleus on a hunt on Mount Pelion and slipped away with all the weapons while Peleus slept. Peleus was almost killed by Centaurs but was saved by Cheiron. He came back to Iolcus, and some say he killed Acastus and Astydameia at once. It is more likely he did so after learning Astydameia had written to Antigone that Peleus was about to marry Sterope, Acastus' daughter, causing Antigone to hang herself. The more dramatic story is that Peleus, with the help of Jason and the Dioscuri, besieged Acastus. He killed Astydameia and trampled her to pieces when he marched over her body on entering the city. [Hyginus, *Fables* 14,24,273; Apollodorus 1.9.27, 3.13.1–3; Pausanias 3.18.9, 5.17.4, 6.20.9; Pindar, *Nemean Odes* 4.57,90,91, 5.26; Scholiast on Pindar's *Nemean Odes* 3.55; Apollonius Rhodius 1.91.]

ASTYDAMEIA (2) was a daughter of Amyntor, king of the Dolopians in Ormenium in Thessaly, by Cleobule. Her brothers were Crantor, Euaemon, and Phoenix. Amyntor was something of a tyrant, and Astydameia grew up in a house where her father lived openly with a mistress. Cleobule persuaded Phoenix to seduce the mistress; he did, and was exiled. When conquered in a war with Peleus, father of Achilles, Amyntor gave Crantor, another son, as a hostage. Heracles visited the kingdom and found Astydameia very desirable. Knowing something of Heracles' record with women, Amyntor refused to surrender her. As might be expected, Heracles made war on the city and killed Amyntor. He carried off Astydameia, who bore him Ctesippus (not to be confused with another of his sons by Deianeira). Some say she was also mother by him of Tlepolemus, but most say his mother was Astyoche. [Homer, *Iliad* 9.434; Apollodorus 2.7.7,8, 3.13.7; Pausanias 2.19.1, 3.16.5.]

ASTYDAMEIA (3) was a daughter of Pelops and Hippodameia, and sister of Atreus and Thyestes. She was married to Alcaeus, and by him the mother of Amphitryon, Perimede, and Anaxo. This made her both mother-in-law and grandmother to Alcmena, mother of Heracles. Astydameia lived in an exciting time. Her father was one of the great heroes, and from him southern Greece, or Peloponnesus, received its name. Her husband was a son of the famous hero Perseus. Her brothers were involved in one of the deadliest feuds in ancient myth. Her son fought battles with the raiding Taphians. Her granddaughter was mother by Zeus of the greatest of the heroes and through him the Heraclid dynasty. Some have said that Laonome, daughter of Guneus, or Hipponome, daughter of Menoeceus, or Lysidice, daughter of Pelops, was the wife of Alcaeus. Some also said that Astydameia was the wife of Sthenelus, son of Perseus, but his wife was more often called Nicippe, another daughter of Pelops. [Apollodorus 2.4.5; Scholiast on Thucydides 1.9.]

ASTYDAMEIA (4) was the daughter of Strophius and Anaxibia, and sister of Pylades. Her mother was sister to Agamemnon and Menelaus, and her father was the son of Crisus, from whom Strophius had inherited the kingdom of Crissa. Orestes, her cousin, was sent there for protection after Agamemnon was murdered, and he grew up with Pylades and Astydameia. It is unfortunate we know nothing further of her. Depending on her age, she might have been an important part of Orestes' adolescence. [Scholiast on Euripides' *Orestes* 33.]

ASTYDAMEIA (5), daughter of Phorbas, was the wife of Caucon, son of Celaenus. Caucon carried the orgies of the Eleusinian mysteries to Messene, where later he was worshipped as a hero. His tomb was shown at Lepreum. His son by Astydameia was Lepreus, founder of the town of Lepreum in Triphylia. Somehow Lepreus got the notion that he was a grandson of Poseidon (and one or two writers support this) and became quite overbearing. He foolishly advised Augeas to put Heracles in chains when the hero asked to be paid for cleansing the famous stables. Astydameia urged Lepreus to offer Heracles hospitality and beg his forgiveness. So all was forgiven, and Heracles good-naturedly challenged Lepreus to a series of contests such as throwing the discus, swilling buckets of water, and eating an ox. Heracles easily won the discus throw and managed to drink Lepreus under the table, but Lepreus ate his part of the ox first. Not content to leave well enough alone, he challenged Heracles to a duel. Heracles promptly clubbed him to death. For some reason his remains were buried at Phigalia. [Pausanias 4.1.4,27.4, 5.5.4; Aelian, *Various Narratives* 1.24.]

ASTYMEDUSA was said to be the last wife of Oedipus. She was probably a daughter of Sthenelus, the son of Perseus, being identical with Medusa. This made her, of course, the sister of Eurystheus, who belabored Heracles. Her connection with Oedipus is full of problems, since it breaks the dramatic plot line of the tragedians. But the story is worth telling to illustrate the capacity of later commentators for embroidering on perfectly sound accounts. It seems that Iocaste was the first wife of Oedipus, by whom he had sons Phrastor and Laonytus. Next he married Euryganeia and had the four children usually attributed to Iocaste. Finally, he married Astymedusa, who developed an immediate hatred for her stepsons Eteocles and Polyneices. She accused them of spying on her and pursuing her, and for this allegation Oedipus laid a curse on them. How all this fitted in with the usual story is hard to say, particularly the incest part. Astymedusa seems to have shared the evil disposition of her brother, and the stature of Oedipus is not improved with this version. [Pausanias 9.5.5; Scholiast on Euripides' *Phoenician Maidens* 63.]

ASTYNOME (1) was the daughter of Chryses, priest of Apollo, which accounts for her more familiar name, Chryseis. When Achilles conquered the cities allied with Troy, he overcame Lyrnessus and took many prisoners. These included Astynome, who had been sent there for protection by her father from the island of Chryse. When the spoils were allotted, she fell to Agamemnon. Achilles got Briseis, also from Lyrnessus. Apollo was quite unhappy with the abduction of the daughter of one of his priests and sent a plague on the Greek camp. Calchas the seer explained the reason for the pestilence, and Odysseus returned the young woman to her father—not, however, before she was made pregnant by Agamemnon. She delivered a boy and, unhappy with his paternity, announced he was a son of Apollo, not by any means improbable. To reinforce this claim, she named him Chryses. Regardless, he was still half-brother to Orestes, Iphigeneia, and Electra, as well as to the ill-fated twins of Cassandra. As the daughter of a high-ranking priest and protected by Apollo himself, Chryseis was perhaps something of a snob, apparently unimpressed with being mistress to the leader of the Greeks at Troy. But who can blame her for not wanting to be a chattel in a filthy army camp? One wonders what would have happened, though, if Achilles had kept her for himself. [Homer, *Iliad* 1.10,398; Eustathius on Homer's *Iliad* 77,118; Dictys Cretensis 2.17.]

ASTYNOME (2) was one of the daughters of NIOBE and Amphion killed by Artemis.

ASTYNOME (3) was the daughter of Talaus, king of Argos, and Lysimache (or Eurynome or Lysianassa). Her brothers were Adrastus, Parthenopaeus, Pronax, Mecisteus, and Aristomachus, and her sisters were Eriphyle and Metidice. Her father had been an Argonaut and was buried with heroic honors at Argos. Adrastus was the leader in the famous battle of the Seven against Thebes. Parthenopaeus was also one of the Seven, and some add Mecisteus. Astynome married Hipponous, king of Olenus in Achaia, and was mother by him of Capaneus. Thus, she had more close relatives in the war of the Seven than any other woman—two or three brothers, a nephew, and a son, along with a brother-in-law, Amphiaraus. All were killed except Adrastus. Capaneus was not a victim of the foe but of Zeus himself, who struck him from a scaling ladder with a bolt of lightning for saying that not even Zeus could keep him from entering the city. Nothing else is known of Astynome. She probably continued to rule with her husband at Olenus and lament the deaths in her family. She was called by some Laodice. [Hyginus, *Fables* 70; Pausanias 8.25.5; Apollodorus 3.6.1–8.]

ASTYOCHE (1), sometimes called Astyocheia, was a daughter of Actor, son of Azeus of Orchomenus. She came from a heritage of war, since her grandfather and granduncles had waged war on Thebes for the murder of their father Clymenus. It is somehow appropriate that she was the lover of Ares, to whom she bore two sons, Ascalaphus and Ialmenus (meaning that the affair lasted for at least two years, unless the boys were twins, which is not so recorded). Her sons were typical Minyans of Orchomenus. They were both Argonauts, and they also lined up with all the others who sought to marry the beautiful Helen of Sparta. As a result of this they were also pledged to fight for her honor, so they led the Minyans of Orchomenus against Troy in 30 ships. Astyoche thus became another war mother, but fortunately lost only one son, Ascalaphus. After the destruction of Troy, Ialmenus wandered about with the Orchomenians on the Euxine Sea and founded colonies on the coast of Pontus. One wonders whatever happened to Astyoche. As a past lover of Ares did she receive benefits, or did she die alone and lonely? Did the ever-youthful gods give any attention to their aging lovers? The mother of Ialmenus was sometimes called Pernis. [Homer, *Iliad* 2.512, 13.519, 15.110; Eustathius on Homer's *Iliad* 272; Pausanias 9.37.3; Apollodorus 1.9.16, 3.10.8; Strabo 9.2.42.]

ASTYOCHE (2) was a daughter of Phylas, king of Ephyra in Thesprotia. Ephyra was a sinister place near the mouth of the Acheron River, where the Acherusian lake emptied into the sea. This lake was considered the principal entrance to the underworld. Astyoche undoubtedly led a lonely existence, with potential suitors probably kept away because of superstition. So it was not surprising that she had a liaison with Heracles when he came with an army of Calydonian in-laws to invade Thesprotia. Of course, she may have had no choice, but chances are she succumbed willingly to this glamorous hero, made even more attractive because of his very recent marriage to Deianeira, princess of Calydon. By Heracles Astyoche became mother of Tlepolemus.

Tlepolemus accidentally killed Lycimnius, Heracles' uncle, and fled to Rhodes, where he founded the cities of Ialysus, Cameirus, and Lindus. From there he joined the Greeks against Troy with nine ships. He was killed very early in the war, and funeral games were held in his honor. [Apollodorus 2.7.6,8,8.2; Homer *Iliad* 2.658, 16.180; Tzetzes on Lycophron 911.]

ASTYOCHE (3) was a daughter of Laomedon by Strymo. Her brothers were Priam, Tithonus, Lampus, Clytius, Hicetaon, and Bucolion; her sisters were Hesione, Cilla, Aethylla, Medesicaste, and Procleia. (This is a roundup from a number of writers who gave various combinations of Laomedon's children.) Her young life was colored by a series of events. Her father had refused to pay Apollo and Poseidon for their involuntary services to him, such as the building of the walls of Troy, and Poseidon sent a sea monster to which the Trojans had to sacrifice a maiden from time to time. Astyoche's sister Hesione eventually was staked out for sacrifice but rescued by Heracles. Laomedon refused to pay the price for this heroic act, and Heracles sailed on Troy and killed Laomedon and all his sons except Priam. (Tithonus had already been abducted by Eos, lover of beautiful boys.) Hesione became the property of Telamon, and her other sisters married or remained at home. Astyoche married Telephus, son of Heracles and Auge, and moved with him to Mysia. The wife of Telephus was also called Hiera.

When the Greeks sailed on Troy, they landed in Mysia, and Telephus drove them back. He was wounded by Achilles before the Greeks discovered he was one of them by birth. They sought to enlist him on their side, but he said he must remain neutral since his wife was a member of the Trojan royal family. After the Greeks left, his wound became infected and would not heal. Later the Greeks returned when they learned it had been prophesied that they must seek his advice. They in turn were able to cure his wound with rust from the sword that had inflicted it. He accordingly set them on the correct course. Later Telephus was worshipped as a hero at Pergamus and on Mount Artemisium, where he was born.

Eurypylus, son of Astyoche and Telephus, was inclined to join his father in remaining out of the war, but Priam sent Astyoche presents to induce him. This she did, and Eurypylus led an army of Mysians to the aid of Troy. He killed Machaon, the famous physician, but was himself killed by Neoptolemus, son of Achilles.

There is one report that counts Astyoche among the prisoners taken by the Greeks. She was said to have been one of the women, led by her sister Aethylla, who set fire to the ships beside the river Navaethus in Sicily. If this is true, she ended her days in Sicily as wife to one of her Greek captors. [Apollodorus 1.8.6, 3.12.3; Hyginus, *Fables* 112; Pausanias 3.26.7, 5.13.2, 8.34.5; Tzetzes on Lycophron 232,467,921.]

ASTYOCHE (4) was the daughter of the river-god Simois. This river rises in Mount Ida and flows through the plain of Troy to join the Scamander. Hieromneme was the sister of Astyoche. It was rather common for daughters of the rivers of this area to marry residents of Troy, and Astyoche and Hieromneme were no exception. Astyoche married Erichthonius, son of Dardanus, and bore him Tros, apparently an only child. Erichthonius was the wealthiest of all mortals and owned 3,000 mares. They were so beautiful that Boreas, the north wind, fell in love with them and increased the herd by impregnating several. Erichthonius is mentioned as a king of Crete, but this may be a reference to hereditary holdings from his grandfather Dardanus, who was supposed to have resided there at one time.

Tros succeeded his father to the throne and gave his name to the whole Phrygian peninsula, calling it the Troad. His offspring were Ilus, Assaracus, Ganymede, and Cleopatra. Astyoche saw her grandson Ganymede traded to Zeus for horses. She saw Ilus found Troy, where he and Assaracus both ruled, apparently at different times. Most surprisingly, Assaracus married Astyoche's sister Hieromneme, becoming by her the father of Capys. This made for a most complex set of relationships. Assaracus became not only her grandson but her brother-in-law, and Capys was both great-grandson and nephew to Astyoche. [Apollodorus 3.12.2; Virgil, *Aeneid* 5.261; Servius on Virgil's *Aeneid* 8.130; Homer, *Iliad* 5.774, 12.22, 20.220,230; Pausanias 5.24.1.]

ASTYOCHE (5) was a daughter of Amphion and NIOBE. [Apollodorus 3.5.6.]

ASTYOCHE (6) was the wife of Iphiclus, the son of Phylacus, and mother of Podarces and Protesilaus. Most call her DIOMEDEIA. [Homer, *Iliad* 2.705, 13.698; Apollodorus 1.9.12; Hyginus *Fables* 103.]

ASTYOCHE (7) was said to be one of the DANAIDES. However, she was not included in the lists of either Apollodorus or Hyginus. She was reported to be the mother of Chrysippus by Pelops. If she was a Danaid, in the literal sense, she was probably old enough to be the grandmother of Pelops, since he was more or less contemporary with Perseus, the great-great-great-grandson of Danaus, the father of the 50 Danaides. Actually, Danaid was probably used in this case in the broad sense of belonging to a race or tribe. [Scholiast on Pindar's *Olympic Odes* 1.44; Plutarch, *Greek and Roman Parallel Stories* 33.]

ASTYOCHE (8), or Astyocheia, was sometimes called a sister of Agamemnon and Menelaus, and mother of Pylades. The sister is more often called ANAXIBIA. [Scholiast on Euripides' *Orestes* 5; Hyginus, *Fables* 117.]

ASTYPALAEA was a daughter of Phoenix and Perimede, the daughter of Oeneus. She was also called sister to Europa, and her name was given by some as Alta. Phoenix settled in the country that later would be called Phoenicia for him.

Astypalaea was one of Poseidon's amatory conquests, and with him one can never be sure whether the liaison was willingly entered into or forced. In the few cases in which more than one child resulted, it was probably by mutual agreement. Astypalaea was the mother of Ancaeus and Eurypylus by the god. She was also rewarded by having the island of Astypalaea named for her, and her sons were treated favorably as well. Ancaeus became king of the Leleges in Samos and produced several sons. Eurypylus became king of Cos and fared well until he was killed by Heracles, who was attacked by the inhabitants under the misapprehension he was a pirate. In fact, another account says he was, since he attacked the island in order to obtain possession of Chalciope, the daughter of Eurypylus. [Apollodorus 2.7.1,8; Pausanias 7.4.2; Apollonius Rhodius 2.866; Hyginus, *Fables* 178; Scholiast on Pindar's *Nemean Odes* 4.40.]

ATALANTA, the famed huntress, has presented a puzzle to writers for centuries. The confusion arose mainly over the question of whether there were two Atalantas—an Arcadian one and a Boeotian one—later blended into one story or whether there was one whose story so impressed early writers that two separate localities claimed

her and assigned to her different parents and a different husband. A rather good case can be made for an Arcadian origin with Iasus, son of Lycurgus, as her father. Her mother was Clymene, the daughter of Minyas, and herein may lie a clue to the connection, if any, between the two versions of her story, for Clymene provided a blood link between Arcadia and Boeotia. In other words, Atalanta was a Minyan on her mother's side, and the Minyans were the principal participants in the two major adventures prior to the Theban wars and the Trojan War—the Argonaut and the Calydonian boar hunt.

In any case, Iasus very much wanted a son, and when Atalanta was born he exposed her on Mount Parthenium. She was suckled by a she-bear and grew up in the forests. She lived a life of virginity, pursuing game and fending off amorous centaurs. At some point she went north to the area of Iolcus, where encounters with Centaurs make more sense. On her way there she had to pass through Boeotia. Maybe by that time she had learned of her parentage and decided to call on her Orchomenian relatives. She might have met Schoeneus, son of Athamas and Themisto, an older cousin to Jason, and somehow come under his sponsorship. (One commentator even calls Athamas a son of Minyas, which would make Schoeneus her first cousin.) All this could explain how Atalanta might have been able to become one of the Argonauts. Here is another matter for dispute: Apollodorus and Diodorus Siculus count her among the crew of the *Argo*, but Apollonius Rhodius, Ovid, Valerius Flaccus, and Hyginus do not. It seems scarcely likely she would have been allowed to go on the expedition, but then again such things are the stuff of myth and modern fiction. After all, Medea was aboard the ship on the return voyage. In his novel *Hercules My Shipmate*, Robert Graves goes along with Apollodorus and Diodorus Siculus, also including Theseus and Peirithous, who were in Hades at the time according to most writers. If she did go on the trip, no great exploits have been attributed to her. After the return of the Argonauts, Pelias, the author of the trip, was butchered by his daughters at the instigation of Medea, and Atalanta participated in the funeral games. She even bested Peleus, the future father of Achilles, in racing (some say wrestling, but this is unlikely since wrestling was always done in the nude).

Where there might have been a question about the Argonaut, there certainly was none in regard to the Calydonian boar hunt. The hunters were not happy to have her participate, but Meleager, who had fallen in love with her, insisted. She inflicted the first wound on the monster, but Meleager dealt the death thrust. He gave the boar's skin to her, but his uncles, the sons of Thestius, claimed it, whereupon Meleager killed them, thus bringing about his own death.

If Atalanta went on the voyage of the Argonauts, she and Meleager must have been well acquainted. The claim is made by many that the hero Parthenopaeus was their son. This brings a new element into the next part of her curious history.

After the hunt she appears to have returned to Arcadia to become reconciled with her father, Iasus. He wanted her to find a husband and settle down. Maybe he even suspected she was pregnant, although fathers usually killed their daughters under these circumstances. Atalanta had no intention of marrying; perhaps she had seen enough of men during her adventures in northern Greece. She agreed to accept any man who could outrun her in a footrace, because she knew none could. She further reserved the right to kill the losers and usually did so by spearing them at the finish line, where she had arrived long before. Finally, her cousin Meilanion (the Boeotian version calls him Hippomenes), with divine assistance, thought of slowing her down by throwing golden apples one at a time into her path. Curiosity forced her to stop for each of them, and thus by a narrow margin she was beaten by Meilanion. This race was said to have taken place at Schoeneus, an area near Methydrium in Arcadia.

Once she lost her independence, she apparently also abandoned her earlier inhibitions concerning men. She and Meilanion were discovered having sex in a sacred grove of Zeus (the Boeotian version says in the temple of Cybele), and the two were metamorphosed into lions. The offspring from their union was said to have been Parthenopaeus, one of the principals in the expedition of the Seven against Thebes. His father was also called Meleager, as mentioned, or the god Ares. It is more likely

Parthenopaeus was one of the brothers of Adrastus, for as the son of Atalanta he had little reason to be involved in a war with the Thebans.

Atalanta is one of the most interesting women in mythology. Her masculine nature permitted her into companies of male heroes no other woman would dream of entering. At the same time, she was desirable enough to men that many were willing to risk their lives to possess her. She was bunkmate and fieldmate to many of the most renowned persons in Greek legends. Her exploits are so implausible that one can almost suspect some historical foundation, stories that came via the oral tradition of a famous woman hunter. While her inclusion as an Argonaut seems contrived and her footrace wooing somehow imitative, the Calydonian boar hunt has a ring of authenticity, whether real or fictitious.

A spring near the ruins of Cyphanta in Laconia was thought to have gushed forth when Atalanta struck a rock with her spear. She was represented with the Calydonian hunters on the pediment of the temple of Athena Alea at Tegea. She also appeared with Meilanion on the chest of Cypselus. [Aelian, *Various Narratives* 13.1; Hyginus, *Fables* 99,185; Callimachus, *Hymn to Artemis* 216–221; Pausanias 3.24.2, 5.9.1, 8.45.4; Apollodorus 3.9.2; Servius on Virgil's *Aeneid* 3.313; Ovid, *Metamorphoses* 8.318, 10.565.]

ATE was the personification and goddess of error. She was a daughter of Eris (some say of Zeus), and led gods and men to rash and inconsiderate acts. She was the one who deceived Zeus at one point into making the oath granting preeminence to the next born of the line of Perseus. This was Eurystheus, who thus became taskmaster of Zeus' son Heracles. For this act Ate was thrown from Olympus and fell to earth on the hill where Troy was later built, thus, it would seem, ensuring its ultimate downfall. In the great age of Greek literature, Ate came to be viewed more in the light of avenger of evil deeds than creator of them. In this respect she resembled Nemesis or the Erinyes. Nevertheless, she was still banned from heaven, and mankind had to accept the fact that it could not escape error. [Hesiod, *Theogony* 230; Homer, *Iliad* 9.503, 10.391, 19.85,126; Aeschylus, *Libation-Bearers*

381; Tzetzes on Lycophron 29; Apollodorus 13.12.3.]

ATHENA was one of the great Olympian divinities, goddess of reason in war and peace alike, intelligent activity, arts and literature, and useful arts.

NATIVITY: Daughter of Zeus and Metis. Daughter of Zeus only. Daughter of Pallas. Daughter of Poseidon and Tritonis. Daughter of Itonus. Daughter of Hephaestus.

LOVERS: None, but strong attachment to Pallas, daughter of Triton, and to Myrmex.

CHILDREN: None, but in late times she was called mother of Apollo by Hephaestus.

COMPANIONS: None, except for brief periods of friendship with Pallas and Myrmex.

PRINCIPAL SEATS OF WORSHIP: Athens and Attica, towns on Lake Copais, Lindus, Corone, Troy, Tegea, Argos, Megara, Sparta.

SACRED TO HER: Olive, serpent, owl, cock, lance, crow.

IDENTIFIED WITH: Minerva.

SURNAMES: Acraea, Aethyia, Ageleia, Agoraea, Alalcomeneis, Alcimache, Alcis, Alea, Amublia, Anemotis, Apaturia, Areia, Asia, Assesia, Axiopoenos, Boulaia, Budeia, Chalinitis, Chryse, Cleidouchos, Colocasia, Coryphasia, Cydonia, Ergane, Glaucopis, Hellotia, Hippia, Hippolaitis, Hygieia, Iasonia, Itonia, Laosos, Laphria, Larissaea, Lindia, Longatos, Magarsia, Munychia, Narcaea, Nedusia, Nice, Onca, Ophthalmitis, Optiletis, Oxydercis, Paeonia, Pallas, Pallenis, Panachaea, Pareia, Parthenos, Phrygia, Polias, Poliuchos, Polyboulos, Promachorma, Pronaea, Pylaitis, Saitis, Salpinx, Sciras, Soteira, Telchinia, Triton, Xenia, Zosteria.

Athena was purely a Greek goddess, unless the story of her birth in Libya suggests her worship spread from the African continent. We do not find any foreign goddesses from whom she was borrowed, however, as in the case of Artemis and Aphrodite. Evidence of her strong Greek identity was demonstrated in her association with the Greek warlike spirit and patriotism. Her benefits to early inhabitants were endless, and she was champion of many of their most glorious heroes.

Most stories make her the daughter of Zeus. Some go so far as to say she sprang from his head without the benefit of woman or womb. The barely more plausible account concerns Metis, a daughter of the Titans Oceanus and Tethys, who was said to be the first wife of Zeus. Most of the Oceanides were prophetic; although she was said to be the personification of prudence, Metis foolishly revealed that if she bore a son he would replace Zeus. Zeus knew about these things, since he had overthrown his own father Cronus, as Cronus had earlier overthrown Saturn. It did not take him long to figure out a solution: He simply swallowed the pregnant Metis. He did not reckon with later events. As time went on he developed a headache and was finally obliged to appeal to Prometheus to split open his head to relieve the pressure. Athena emerged (some said fully armed, but this suggests a latter-day declaration of militaristic patriotism). This event is supposed to have taken place on the shore of the Triton River in Boeotia.

Another tradition called Athena the daughter of Pallas, a winged giant of Attica. He tried to rape her, and she killed him, later using his skin for her shield and his wings to fasten to her feet. Still another account of her birth set the event in Libya, where she was born to Tritonis and Poseidon.

She was educated by the river-god Triton together with his daughter Pallas. The persistent references to Triton, gaining for her the variously interpreted surname of Tritogeneia, caused many places with a Triton river or lake to claim to be her birthplace.

Finally, two other stories assign different parents. One was Itonus, son of Amphictyon, who is credited with founding the cult of Athena Itonia. Athena was said to have accidentally killed Iodama, his daughter and her sister. This story makes little sense, since the Olympian gods were firmly established before the flood, and Amphictyon, son of Deucalion, was of the first generation to appear after the flood. The tradition that she was a daughter of Hephaestus might be explained because of their being great patrons of both useful and elegant arts.

This juxtaposition of Athena and Hephaestus went even further. When the worship of Apollo was introduced into Attica, he was called their son, making for an ideal artistic trinity. Another son, Lychnus, was also claimed for them. A more acceptable story in connection with Hephaestus had to do with his attempted rape of Athena, during which his semen fell on her leg. When she wiped it off and let it fall to the ground, it impregnated Gaea, the earth, Hephaestus' great-grandmother. From this incredible union the half-serpent child Erichthonius was born. Apparently Athena accepted some small part in this freakish birth and consequently took the child under her protection. She left him in the temporary custody of Cecrops' daughters, warning them not to open the chest in which she had concealed him. They disobeyed her and promptly went insane, throwing themselves from the Acropolis. The serpentine baby crawled into Athena's shield, meaning perhaps that he accepted her as something close to a mother. He grew up under her guidance to be king of Athens.

Athena's identification with Athens started even before Erichthonius, however. Cecrops, an autochthon said by some to be the first king of Attica, gained Athena's favor when he witnessed for her in her dispute with Poseidon over the possession of Athens. Poseidon had opened a well on the Acropolis, and Athena had planted an olive tree. Her gift was judged to be more important, so she became the protectress of Athens. After that she fortified the Acropolis. It was reported that the news of the death of Cecrops' daughters so startled her that she dropped the huge rock she was carrying to strengthen the fortification. This was Mount Lycabettus.

She became the patron divinity of the state, not only at Athens but in other parts of Greece as well. She promoted prosperity by encouraging agriculture and other kinds of industry. She maintained law and order internally and protected the state from external enemies. In times of war she protected fortresses, harbors, and towns. Though she was frequently represented in armor, her warlike attributes were geared more to protectiveness than to aggression, a quality she was content to leave to Ares and Enyo. Her principal role was the strengthening of the state from within and the civilization of its people. She invented the plough, the rake, the bridle, numbers, the chariot, and navigation. She also invented the trumpet, the flute, and domestic arts such as weaving.

It does not take long to realize that Athena was almost entirely a benevolent goddess. She had very few ulterior or selfish motives, and for the most part was totally ethical. She seldom did anything spiteful, but turned Arachne into a spider for outspinning her and Myrmex into an ant for claiming invention of the plough. She dealt severely with the giants, but this was evidence of her patriotism. She was totally unhappy with the judgment of Paris and consequently sided with the Greeks in the Trojan War. But even then she punished some of them, such as the two Ajaxes and Menelaus, for impiety and sacrilege. It is not too much to say that if someone incurred her wrath and received punishment, he or she usually more than deserved it.

Starting very early, Athena was the champion of heroes, far more than anyone else in the Olympian family. She assisted Cadmus in the founding of Thebes, notably in directing him to plant the dragon's teeth, which created the nobility of the city when men sprang from them. She helped Bellerophon capture Pegasus and bridle him. She was especially helpful to Perseus, who might have perished at any point in cutting off the Gorgon's head. She was of vast assistance to the Argonauts. Athena was ready to confer immortality on Tydeus as he lay dying in the battle of the Seven against Thebes but withdrew when he ate the brains of one of the enemy. Above all, she was the protectress of Heracles. She even tricked Hera into nursing him when he was first born, and ran interference on most of his labors. She protected Orestes; when he came before the court of the Areiopagus for his crime of matricide, she cast the deciding vote in his favor and then placated the Eumenides so they ended their pursuit of him. She had a special affection for Diomedes and protected him when he returned from the Trojan War with the Palladium. He founded a temple to her in Argos, and she followed him to Italy, where he established several colonies. Eventually she conferred on him the immortality she had intended for Tydeus, his father. She was tremendously valuable to Odysseus on his return to Ithaca. When his raft disintegrated, she guided him to the island of the Phaeacians. When he reached Ithaca, she came in disguise to him and assisted him in disguising himself. She sent Telemachus back from Sparta to assist his father. She accompanied Odysseus to the banquet hall and, remaining invisible or disguised as a swallow, helped him dispatch every last suitor. She made Laertes, the father of Odysseus, young again to battle the Ithacans after the slaughter of the suitors, then helped impose a truce between Odysseus and the rebellious islanders. Earlier she had disguised herself as Mentes and Mentor, loyal supporters of Odysseus, to assist Telemachus in dealing with the interlopers and in gaining knowledge of his father.

Athena's worship was closely interwoven with reverence for the state. Her temples and statues on the Acropolis could be called the center of the political universe. One of these statues could be seen as far away as Cape Sunium, itself dedicated partially to her. Alalkomenes, a Boeotian autochthon, was said to have brought up Athena and to have introduced her worship. Anyone traveling today from Athens to Delphi can have the experience of visiting the tiny town of Alalkomenes, about 2 kilometers north of the highway. From there her worship spread around nearby Lake Copais, where Cecrops had founded two cities, one of which was Athenae. When it was flooded, he must have carried her worship next to Attica, where he founded Athens, naming it for the earlier Boeotian town. Her priests and priestesses were numerous, and many were important in their own right. The priestly family of the Butadae came from Butes, who obtained office of priest of Athena when his father, Pandion, died. Theano, wife of Antenor the Trojan elder, was a priestess. So was Phoebe, who became the wife of Polydeuces, one of the Dioscuri and conse-

quently Athena's half-brother. Auge, mother of Telephus by Heracles, was a priestess but foolishly concealed her baby in the temple of Athena Alea and caused a famine to ensue. Tritaea, a priestess and daughter of Triton, became by Ares the mother of Melanippus, who founded a town in Achaia he named for his mother. It is not clear whether or not chastity was a job requirement, or if these women lost their office when they mated. It would appear not, since sacrifices were offered to both Tritaea and Ares in the temple of Athena in Tritaea.

The curious story concerning Aethra, the mother of Theseus, deserves a brief examination. On the night Theseus was conceived, Aethra was in bed with Aegeus, the king of Athens, a situation arranged by her father, Pittheus of Troezen. Athena came to Aethra in a dream and directed her to sacrifice at the tomb of Sphaerus. While Aethra was thus engaged, she was surprised by Poseidon, who raped her. This circumstance gave rise to the question of the paternity of Theseus, and it certainly caused confusion to Aethra. She later instituted the custom of having brides-to-be leave their girdles at the altar of Athena Apaturia (the Deceitful). Aethra's irony aside, why did Athena deceive her? She and Poseidon certainly did no favors for each other. They had quarreled over possession of Athens, which Athena won, and also Troezen, which they had to share. The only plausible explanation is that Athena wanted to guarantee a semidivine successor to Aegeus in Athens. Poseidon, moreover, had been a strong contender, proving he indeed held Athens in high esteem. If anything, the legend of Athena Apaturia is the strongest proof that Theseus was the son of Poseidon. A later political festival at Athens called the Apaturia might have had a distant connection with this mythological event.

Athena's temples were edifices that promised security for the cities in which they were built, as well as places of refuge for individuals. Persons and whole populations dedicated precious items to her in these usually magnificent structures. Daedalus carved a wooden statue of the goddess at Cnossus, and another by him stood in the temple of Athena Polias at Athens. Epopeus dedicated a temple to her at Sicyon. Theseus dragged the Marathonian bull up the

Acropolis and sacrificed it to Athena. He also introduced the Panathenaea and the worship of Athena Polias. The sons of Alcmaeon eventually dedicated the fatal necklace of Harmonia in the temple of Athena Pronaea at Delphi. The Hyacinthides were sacrificed to the goddess to deliver Athens from famine and plague during the war with the Eleusinians. Idomeneus built a temple of Athena in Calabria when he was expelled from Crete. Menelaus dedicated Helen's necklace before the siege of Troy to Athena Pronaea. And so the list goes on.

Essentially gentle, Athena was quick to wrath when anyone interfered with her worship or her person, or violated someone under her protection. The city of Epidaurus had to offer sacrifices to Athena Agraulos for allowing two virgin maidens to be stoned to death during an insurrection. For Ajax's rape of Cassandra the Locrians had to pay penance for years by sending girls to serve in Athena's temple in Troy. (One account says they provided human sacrifices and that the practice lasted into historical times.) Panopeus, king of Panopeus in Phocis and an ally of Amphitryon against the Taphians, broke an oath to Athena, and she caused him to produce a cowardly son. She was seen naked by young Teiresias of Thebes, and immediately struck him blind. Her actions were irreversible, even if later she had second thoughts about their severity. To Epeius, the son of Panopeus, she brought glory by having him engineer the building of the wooden horse that proved the downfall of Troy. In the case of Teiresias, she supplied him with a staff that enabled him to function as though he had vision, and she caused him to understand the voices of birds, thus making him one of the greatest seers in the ancient world.

A substantial part of the worship of Athena had to do with the mysterious Palladium. This was an image of the goddess, usually an ancient one, and there were more than one. Its possession by a city served as a kind of pledge of the safety of the place, and it was kept in a highly secret location to prevent its theft by an enemy. As can be expected, its origin was obscure but probably stemmed from the incident in Athena's maidenhood in which she accidentally killed her dearest companion, Pallas, daughter of Triton. Athena caused an image of the girl to be made.

After she took on the identity of Pallas and added her name to her own—Pallas Athena—the image came to be hers as well. At first the image was placed beside the image of Zeus on Olympus, but when the Pleiad Electra fled to the image of Pallas after being raped by Zeus, he was outraged and threw the image from Olympus. It landed at the spot where Troy was to be built, and a sanctuary was constructed around it, making it the center of the new city. It was said to measure 3 cubits (about 54 inches) in height. Its legs were together; it held in its right hand a spear, and in its left a spindle and a distaff. To touch the image was forbidden. Ilus, the king of Troy, once rushed in to rescue the statue during a fire, and was struck temporarily blind.

The Palladium remained at Troy until Odysseus and Diomedes carried it away. After that, various stories grew around its eventual resting place. Athens and Argos claimed it, as did Rome, Lavinium, Luceria, and Siris. Aeneas was said to have brought the real Palladium to Italy from Troy; the one removed by Odysseus and Diomedes was said to be an imitation. It makes sense that something guaranteeing a city's security would be not only carefully guarded but even provided with decoys. However, since Troy did indeed fall, the real Palladium must have left with the Greeks.

In spite of the care and attention provided by Troy to the Palladium through many years, Athena's outrage at the judgment of Paris overcame any sense of loyalty to the Trojans. She was very pro-Greek, but might not this have been so in any case since, in effect, she was their national goddess long before the Trojan War? She assisted the Greeks directly and indirectly during the war. She was instrumental in Hector's demise, since she assumed the appearance of Deiphobus and urged him to face Achilles. She was the author of the idea of the wooden horse and supervised Epeius in its construction. Epeius consecrated the horse to her, and the Trojans accepted it largely because it was dedicated to her. To the Trojans who opposed bringing in the horse, Sinon, the Greek spy, said the Greeks forfeited Athena's support when they stole the Palladium and that they left the horse as a placatory gift to her. Still unconvinced, Laocoon, a priest of Apollo, threw a spear into the horse's side, as a result of which two serpents were sent from the sea to strangle him and his two sons. In fear of Athena, Priam then dedicated the horse to Athena and brought it into the city; Troy's doom was sealed.

It is not easy to get a picture of Athena. In spite of her kindnesses to the great heroes and her beneficial improvements for the welfare of mankind, she remains in the imagination as stern and formidable. Representations of her probably account for this unapproachable quality, since she is usually shown as armed and masculine in appearance. She might be compared to a kind of humorless aunt living in a family, kindhearted but starchy and independent. Even though she partook of certain attributes of other Olympian goddesses—notably Demeter, Hera, and Hestia—she was unique and, more than that, uniquely Greek. [NATIVITY: Homer, *Iliad* 5.880; Hesiod, *Theogony* 886,924; Pindar, *Pythian Odes* 4.20, 12.19, *Olympian Odes* 7.35; Scholiast on Pindar's *Olympian Odes* 7.66; Apollodorus 1.4.2,6, 3.12.3; Tzetzes on Lycophron 355,519; Cicero, *On the Nature of the Gods* 3.23; Herodotus 4.180; Hyginus, *Fables* 165; Pausanias 1.24.1, 9.33.5,34.1—CHARACTERISTICS: Homer, *Iliad* 1.199, 2.547, 5.736,840, 10.244, 21.406; Eustathius on Homer's *Iliad* 1076; Homer, *Odyssey* 13.394, 16.172, 18.190, 23.160; Tzetzes on Lycophron 520; Hesychius, "Hippia"; Servius on Virgil's *Aeneid* 4.402; Pindar, *Olympian Odes* 13.79; Livy 7.3; Pausanias 1.24.3,28.5; *Homeric Hymn to Aphrodite* 4.7; Plutarch, *Cimon* 10; Ovid, *Fasti* 3.833, *Heroides* 5.36; Aeschylus, *Eumenides* 753; Apollodorus 1.6.1, 3.6.7,14.6; Horace, *Odes* 1.12.19—WORSHIP: Pausanias 1.2.4,23.5,24.3,7,28.2,31.3, 4.34.3, 6.26.2; Plutarch, *Isis and Osiris;* Hyginus, *Fables* 164; Suidas, "Poine," "Tauropolos"; Homer, *Iliad* 2.550; Ovid, *Metamorphoses* 4.754.]

ATHENAIS was the wife of Alalcomenes, a Boeotian autochthon. He and Athenais are said to have brought up the goddess Athena, who was born at the site on which Alalcomenes founded a town he named for himself. He introduced the worship of Athena there, which later spread to Attica and other parts of Greece. In those days men walked with gods and, in the case of Alalcomenes, even advised them. Zeus applied to

him once when Hera accused him of infidelity. He advised the god to dress a wooden statue in bridal clothes and pretend he was taking another wife. Hera's jealousy turned to embarrassment when she tore the image from the chariot. The son of Alalcomenes and Athenais was Glaucopus; like the name Athenais, Glaucopus (meaning blue-eyed) later was a reference to the goddess. Her identification with this family and this part of Greece was very ancient. [Pausanias 9.3.3,33.4; Stephanus Byzantium, "Alalkomenion"; Plutarch, *Fragments* 5.]

ATLANTIA was a Hamadryad nymph, by whom Danaus was the father of some of the following ten daughters: Hippodameia, Rhodia, Cleopatra, Asteria, Hippodameia, Glauce, Hippomedusa, Gorge, Iphimedusa, and Rhode. The others had Phoebe for their mother. It is not known which were which, although it is likely that each had a daughter named Hippodameia. [Apollodorus 2.1.5.]

ATLANTIDES were the daughters of Atlas and Hesperis, and are consequently known by this patronymic or the more usual HESPERIDES. [Diodorus Siculus 4.27.]

ATLANTIS was a patronymic of MAIA from her father, Atlas. From her mother, Pleione, she is sometimes called Pleias.

ATROPOS was one of the three MOIRAE.

ATTHIS, or Attis, was a daughter of Cranaus, king of Attica, and Pedias. Her sisters were Cranae and Cranaechme. Cranaus reigned at the time of the Deucalionian flood but was deprived of his kingdom by Amphitryon, his son-in-law and Deucalion's son. Atthis died a virgin by most accounts, but some say she was by Hephaestus the mother of Erichthonius. In a way, this would be an improvement over the Athena/Hephaestus story, since the line of kings would then extend unbroken from Cranaus. The land, originally called Acte, was renamed Attica by Cranaus in memory of his young daughter. [Apollodorus 3.14.5,6; Pausanias 1.2.5,31.2.]

AUGE (1) was a daughter of Aleus and Neaera. Aleus founded the town of Alea and the first temple of Athena at Tegea. Auge's brothers were Cepheus, Lycurgus, and Amphidamas. Both Amphidamas and Cepheus took part in the Argonaut. Auge became a priestess of Athena. When Heracles once visited the kingdom, he was entertained by Aleus; he repaid him by seducing Auge. Auge managed to conceal her pregnancy, but when the child was born she had to hide him. She secreted him in the temple, and it was not long before a famine came to Tegea. An oracle of Athena revealed that something unholy was profaning the temple of the goddess. Aleus soon found the child and exposed it on Mount Parthenium. As for Auge, he turned her over to his friend Nauplius, who was instructed to drown her. Nauplius, however, saw that he could turn a profit, and he sold her to Teuthras, king of Mysia.

Subsequent events could easily have supplied the plot for an opera. Auge was settled quite comfortably as queen of Mysia with her husband and stepdaughter, Argiope. Teuthrania in Mysia was named for her husband. Meanwhile, the abandoned son had been nursed by a hind and raised by shepherds, who named him Telephus (Deer). He grew up wondering about his origins and eventually consulted an oracle. Directed to Mysia, he was reunited with his mother and married to his stepsister. He eventually inherited the kingdom and was of considerable help to the Greeks when they landed to invade Troy.

Another version of the story has Teuthras purchasing Auge as a slave and giving her to Telephus as a reward for service to him. First Auge tried to kill Telephus, not knowing who he was, and when he learned of her plan he started to kill her. They were stopped in time, and returned to Greece.

Auge was one of the fortunate women in mythology. Although she broke a vow to Athena and disgraced her family, she ended up a queen in a foreign land, loved by her husband and reunited with her long-lost son. She probably lived long enough to see Telephus inherit the throne in Mysia. One version of the story had her dragged from the temple of Athena while still pregnant. At one point she fell to her knees and delivered the baby, after which they were put in a chest and cast adrift. They still ended happily, for Teuthras found the chest, married Auge, and adopted Telephus. Auge was buried in Pergamus in Mysia. She was represented by Polygnotus in the Lesche of Delphi. [Apollodorus 2.7.4, 3.9.1; Pausanias 8.4.3,6, 10.28.4; Apollonius Rhodius 1.163; Hyginus, *Fables* 14.]

AUGE (2) was one of the HORAE, according to Hyginus (*Fables* 183).

AULIS was one of the PRAXIDICAE.

AULONIADES were nymphs of forests, groves, and glens, and were believed to sometimes appear to and frighten solitary travelers. [Apollonius Rhodius 1.1066,1227; Theocritus, *Idylls* 13.44; Ovid, *Metamorphoses* 15.490; Virgil, *Georgics* 4.535.]

AURA (1) was a daughter of Lelantos and Periboea. She was one of the fleet-footed companions of Artemis and therefore sworn to chastity. The god Dionysus lusted for her and, mindful only of his own desire, pursued her. She always outran him, until he enlisted Aphrodite's help. Not looking beyond the pleasure of arranging a carnal liaison, Aphrodite caused Aura to fall in love with the handsome young god. Neither Dionysus nor Aphrodite had reckoned with the quickly vengeful nature of Artemis. When Aura bore twin sons, she was seized with madness and tore one of her babies to pieces, after which she threw herself into the Sangarius River. [Nonnos, *Dionysiaca* 48.243–943.]

AURA (2) was one of Actaeon's DOGS. [Hyginus, *Fables* 181.]

AURORA was the Latin name of EOS, the goddess of the dawn.

AUTOCHTHE was the daughter of Perseus and Andromeda, and sister of Alcaeus, Sthenelus, Heleius, Mestor, Electryon, and Gorgophone. She was one of the wives of Aegeus. Aegeus had trouble conceiving an heir. He married at least two women before his encounter with Aethra finally, according to most accounts, produced Theseus. This marriage with Autochthe might have been political as well, since marriage with one of the Perseids would mean alliance between Argos and Athens. [Apollodorus 2.4.5; Tzetzes on Lycophron 494, *Chiliades* 5.677.]

AUTODICE was one of the DANAIDES. She was married to Clytus. [Hyginus, *Fables* 170.]

AUTOLYTE, also called Theano, was the wife of the Metapontan to whom Aeolus had given his daughter Arne when she became pregnant by Poseidon, a story Aeolus did not believe. The man from Metapontum was childless, so he adopted the twins Boeotus and Aeolus that Arne produced. There is no evidence that the Metapontan displayed any physical interest in Arne, but certainly the presence of Arne and her sons must have been a constant reminder of what Autolyte could not provide for her husband. It is likely that she barely tolerated Arne's presence for all the years it took the twins to grow up, and they must have quarreled on more than one occasion. One day the women had a serious disagreement, and Arne's sons killed Autolyte. For this act they and their mother had to leave Metapontum. The stepfather must indeed have loved his adopted sons to let them off so easily. [Diodorus Siculus 4.67.]

AUTOMATE (1) was one of the DANAIDES; she killed Busiris on their wedding night. She later married Architeles, the son of Achaeus, who migrated from Phthiotis in Thessaly to Argos with his brother, Archander. Architeles and Archander had waged an unsuccessful war on Lamedon at Sicyon and more than likely found it to their advantage to leave the area. In Argos they met the two Danaides Automate and Scaea, who along with their sisters had had trouble in finding husbands. [Apollodorus 2.1.5; Pausanias 2.6.2, 7.1.3.]

AUTOMATE (2) was the wife of Achaeus and mother of Architeles and Archander. Achaeus, son of Xuthus and Creusa and brother of Ion and Hellen, was one of the eponymic heroes of the Greek race. The Achaeans regarded him as the ancestor of their race and derived their name from him as well as the name Achaia, which until

then had been called Aegialus. Achaeus also migrated to Phthiotis when his uncle Aeolus died and gave his name to that area as well— Phthiotan Achaia. The sons engaged in a territorial dispute with Lamedon over the area that later became Sicyon, but were unsuccessful. They went on to Argos and married Automate and Scaea, daughters of Danaus. Automate, the mother, most certainly accompanied her husband to Thessaly. [Pausanias 2.6.2, 7.1.2; Apollodorus 1.7.3; Strabo 8.7.1.]

AUTOMATIA was a surname of Tyche (Fortuna). The name suggests that chance, rather than an individual's merits or demerits, determines the way things happen. Under this name, Timoleon, the master of Syracuse, built a sanctuary to the goddess in his house. [Plutarch, *On Praising Oneself Inoffensively* 542; Nepos, *Timoleon* 4.]

AUTOMEDUSA was a daughter of Alcathous and Euaechme, and sister of Echepolis, Callipolis, Iphinoe, and Periboea. Alcathous, son of Pelops, was the famous killer of the Cithaeronian lion for Megareus, king of Megara. This deed earned him the daughter of Megareus and succession to the throne of Megara. As king he rebuilt Megara after the Cretans sacked the city. Automedusa's brother Echepolis went on the Calydonian boar hunt and was killed. The younger brother heard the news first and rushed to inform his father, who was performing a sacrifice to Apollo on the Megarian citadel. Alcathous thought the boy was being deliberately sacrilegious and struck him with a burning log, killing him. One of Echepolis' companions on the boar hunt was Iphicles, the half-brother of Heracles. Possibly he came to Megara to pay his respects to his dead friend's family or to take part in funeral ceremonies. He fell in love with Automedusa, and they were married.

Their only child was Iolaus, who consequently was a nephew of Heracles. He became his uncle's charioteer, companion, and probably lover. Heracles eventually sent Iolaus to head a colony in Sardinia of his 50 sons by the daughters of Thespius. Iolaus was afterward honored as a demigod by the Sardinians.

No one knows what happened to Automedusa. We know Iphicles married again, this time the youngest daughter of Creon. Whether or not this meant he was a widower is impossible to say, but in those days the death of one wife was not prerequisite to taking another. [Pausanias 1.41.4,42.1,7, 4.43.4; Apollodorus 2.4.11, 3.12.7.]

AUTONOE (1) was one of the four ill-fated daughters of Cadmus and Harmonia. Her sisters were Agave, Semele, and Ino. When Semele was destroyed by the sight of the splendor of Zeus, her sisters spread the report that she had endeavored to conceal her guilt by pretending that Zeus was the father of her child, and that her destruction was a just punishment for her deceitfulness. It is a little hard to understand how they fitted the miraculous birth of Dionysus into this picture, and how they explained their own actions when later they joined the orgiastic worship of Dionysus. In any case, they had to pay for their accusation, although the retribution was many years in coming. Pentheus, the son of Agave, tried to stop the Dionysiac celebrations on Mount Cithaeron and was torn to pieces by Agave and other wine-crazed women, including Autonoe and Ino.

Autonoe married the god Aristaeus, son of Apollo. He was one of the most beneficent divinities in ancient mythology, worshipped as the protector of flocks and shepherds, vines, and olive trees. He taught men to hunt and keep bees, and how to protect crops. In spite of Autonoe's earlier crime, it appeared she had achieved an ideal situation. She and Aristaeus had sons, Charmus, Calaicarpus, and Actaeon, and a daughter, Macris. Actaeon, probably the youngest, was a handsome hunter who regularly roved the forests. One day he observed—no one is sure whether unintentionally or deliberately— Artemis bathing in a stream. She changed him into a stag, which was immediately torn to pieces by the 50 hounds that had belonged to Actaeon. After this happened, Aristaeus left Thebes and went alone to Ceos.

Autonoe also left Thebes. The series of tragedies sent her into deep depression, and she wandered to Erineia in Megaris, where she died. Her tomb was shown there until a late date. She and her sisters appeared to be somewhat spoiled, perhaps by the prestige available to them through their powerful father. They engaged in spiteful gossip and, probably out of boredom, took up the emotional religion associated with their nephew Dionysus. [Apollodorus 3.4.2,5.2; Pausanias 1.44.8, 10.17.3; Ovid, *Metamorphoses* 3.513; Euripides, *Bacchanals* 1215.]

AUTONOE (2), the daughter of Peireus, was the mother of Palaemon by Heracles. Some call Palaemon's mother Iphinoe, daughter of Antaeus. Unfortunately, nothing further is known of Peireus, Autonoe, or Palaemon, except that Palaemon was sometimes used by Heracles as a surname. [Apollodorus 2.7.8; Tzetzes on Lycophron 662.]

AUTONOE (3) was one of the NEREIDES, daughter of Nereus and Doris. [Apollodorus 1.2.7; Hesiod, *Theogony* 258.]

AUTONOE (4) was one of the DANAIDES, daughter of Danaus and Polyxo. She was married to Eurylochus. [Apollodorus 2.1.5.]

AUTONOE (5) was one of the companions of Penelope in the court of Ithaca. [Homer, *Odyssey* 18.182.]

AUXESIA was a maiden who came with a companion, Damia, from Crete during an insurrection at Troezen. Why they came is not known, although later writers concluded they were Persephone and Demeter in human form. The maidens were stoned to death, and afterward the Troezenians had to pay them divine tribute, instituting a festival called Lithobolia. Perhaps the two goddesses used this ploy as a means of introducing their worship at Troezen.

The worship spread, first up the coast from Troezen to Epidaurus. Epidaurus was struck by famine, and the Delphic oracle instructed the Epidaurians to erect statues of the two women. These had to be made of olive wood and apparently from a sacred tree, since the Epidaurians had to beg the Athenians for the proper wood. The Athenians agreed on the condition that every year the Epidaurians would offer sacrifices to Athena Agraulos and Erechtheus. All this took place, and Epidaurus bloomed again.

In historical times Aegina separated from Epidaurus. Since they held sacred objects in common, the Aeginetans took away the statues of Auxesia and Damia and erected them at Oea, where they sacrificed to them and celebrated mysteries(!). The Epidaurians did not resist this confiscation, probably relieved they no longer had to fulfill their promise to Athens. The Athenians then demanded the statues from the Aeginetans, who refused to surrender them. The Athenians threw ropes around the statues and started to drag them away, but a fierce thunderstorm arose coupled with an earthquake. The Athenians engaged in taking the images went mad and killed one another. The Aeginetans also claimed that while they were being dragged away, the statues fell to their knees and remained forever after in that position.

Auxesia became a surname of Persephone, and the goddess thus identified granted growth and prosperity to the fields. [Pausanias 2.30.5,32.3; Herodotus 5.82–86.]

AUXO (1) was one of ten HORAE listed by Hyginus (*Fables,* 183).

AUXO (2) was an ancient Attic divinity worshipped together with Hegemone under the name of CHARITES.

AVERNA was a Roman name of PERSEPHONE, referring to her as the queen of the shades. The Erinyes were said to have been her daughters by Pluto. [Virgil, *Aeneid* 6.138; Ovid, *Metamorphoses* 14.114.]

AVERNALES were NYMPHS of the underworld river Avernus. [Ovid, *Metamorphoses* 5.540, *Fasti* 2.610.]

AXIEROS was a daughter of Cadmilus, son of Cabeiro and Hephaestus. She was one of the three Samothracian Cabeiri and was identified with Demeter. [Paris-scholia on Apollonius Rhodius 1.915–921.]

AXIOCERSA was a daughter of Cadmilus and Cabeiro, and one of the three Samothracian

Cabeiri. She was identified with Persephone. [Paris-scholia on Apollonius Rhodius 1.915–921.]

AXIOCHE, also known as Danais, was a nymph by whom Pelops became the father of Chrysippus. This made Chrysippus a half-brother to Alcathous, Atreus, and Thyestes. Pelops favored Chrysippus, however, and it was a relief to the other brothers when Laius of Thebes (father of Oedipus) carried him away because of his beauty. Pelops was able to recover him, much to the displeasure of Hippodameia, the boy's stepmother. She eventually persuaded Atreus and Thyestes to kill him, which they did, tossing his body into a well. Hippodameia and her two sons were forced to flee. This event was the first in the series of tragedies that followed the curse pronounced on the house of Pelops by his charioteer, whom he betrayed.

One wonders what happened to Axioche. Apparently in liaisons involving nymphs, the mothers disappeared, leaving the children to be cared for by the fathers and their families. Axioche very likely never knew of the fate of Chrysippus. [Apollodorus 3.5.5; Hyginus, *Fables* 85,271; Pausanias 6.20.4.]

AXIOPOENOS, the Avenger, was a surname of Athena. Under this name Heracles built a temple to the goddess at Sparta, after he had slaughtered Hippocoon and his sons for the murder of Oeonus. [Pausanias 3.15.4.]

AXIOTHEA was, according to some, the mother of Deucalion by Prometheus. Others say CLYMENE or Hesione was the mother. [Aeschylus, *Prometheus* 560; Tzetzes on Lycophron 1283; Scholiast on Apollonius Rhodius 1086.]

AZESIA was a surname of Demeter and Persephone at Troezen as goddesses of the harvest. They were associated with AUXESIA and Damia in the same place and in the same role. [Hesychius, "Azesia"; Zenobius 4.20; Suidas, "Azesia."]

BABO (*See* BAUBO)

BACCHAE (*See* MAENADES)

BACCHANTES (*See* MAENADES)

BACCHE was one of the HYADES.

BARBATA, the Bearded, was a surname of Venus among the Romans. In Amathus in Cyprus, a statue of Venus was found representing the goddess with a beard but in female attire. This curious combination of genders in the most feminine of the goddesses might have had its origin in an Attican festival in which men and women dressed in one another's clothes to sacrifice to Selene, whose statue exhibited characteristics of both sexes. [Servius on Virgil's *Aeneid* 2.632; Macrobius, *Saturnalia* 3.8; Hesychius, "Aphroditos."]

BARCE (1) was the nurse of Sychaeus, the husband of Dido. After Sychaeus' murder, Barce accompanied Dido to Carthage. Just before she killed herself, Dido sent Barce with a message to her sister Anna to bring sacrifices and gifts of atonement. [Servius on Virgil's *Aeneid* 4.632.]

BARCE (2) was, according to some, the daughter of Antaeus, king of Irassa in the territory of Cyrene. She is usually called ALCEIS.

BARGE was the mother of Bargasus by Heracles. The details have disappeared, but it appears that for one reason or another Lamus, the son of Heracles by Omphale, was obliged to expel Bargasus from the kingdom. This suggests Heracles had been unfaithful to Omphale while he lived with her. Barge was more than likely a nymph, who characteristically left the child to be reared by the father. Perhaps Omphale tolerated the boy until he was able to fend for himself. Bargasus went on to found the city of Bargasa in Caria. [Stephanus Byzantium, "Bargasa."]

BASSARAE were among the women who nursed the infant Dionysus. They were Maenads who were called Bassarae or Bassarides from the long robes worn by them and by the god. The name of the garment seems to be connected with, or rather the same as, *bassaris* (a fox), probably

because it was originally made of fox skins. [Hesychius, "Bassarai."]

BATEIA (1) was a daughter of Teucer, son of the Scamander River, and Idaea. Teucer was the first king of Troy. His daughter has also been called Arisbe or Myrina, a native of Crete. She married Dardanus from Samothrace, whose first wife, Chryse, had died. Teucer gave him Bateia and part of his kingdom. After Teucer died, Dardanus inherited the entire country and called it Dardania, naming a city in the Troad after his wife. He built the citadel of Troy and initiated the people into the Samothracian mysteries. Bateia had three children by him— Erichthonius, Ilus, and Idaea. Ilus died childless and left his part of the kingdom to Erichthonius, who became the wealthiest of mortals. Bateia's fate after the death of Dardanus is not known, but she probably remained in the royal household as long as she lived and served as a priestess in the mysteries introduced by her husband. [Apollodorus 3.12.1; Homer, *Iliad* 20.220; Eustathius on Homer's *Iliad* 894; Diodorus Siculus 4.75; Tzetzes on Lycophron 1298.]

BATEIA (2) was a Naiad and a lover of Oebalus of Sparta, who was married to Gorgophone, daughter of Perseus. Nobody has ever agreed on the complicated genealogy associated with the early Spartan lineage, but it seems Gorgophone had two husbands—Oebalus and Perieres, by whom she had sons and daughters variously assigned to one or the other. They were Icarius, Tyndareus, Peirene, Arene, Aphareus, and Leucippus. While she was married to Oebalus, he had intercourse with the Naiad Bateia, who bore him Hippocoon. Hippocoon grew up to usurp the kingdom from his half-brother Tyndareus, which suggests that Tyndareus, at least, was the son of Oebalus. These events are treated elsewhere. If she was like her sister nymphs, Bateia abandoned the child to Oebalus and disappeared. She was also called Nicostrate. [Apollodorus 1.9.5, 3.10.4, who says in one place that Bateia was also the mother of Tyndareus and Icarius; Pausanias 3.1.4.]

BAUBO was a woman from Eleusis involved in a curious way with the development of the

Eleusinian mysteries. She was married to Dysaules, and the couple received Demeter hospitably when she came to Eleusis in search of Persephone. Baubo offered Demeter a drink, but the goddess was so grieved that she refused it. Baubo was a jolly woman and resorted to an extreme diversion to amuse the goddess. She threw her skirt over her head and exposed her bare backside. This caused the boy Iacchus, who had either accompanied Demeter or was just standing by, to break into laughter. So did Demeter; the sorrowful mood thus broken, the goddess drank. This incident apparently was the basis for part of the mysteries in which the celebrants traded bawdy jests. Some have called Baubo the nurse of Demeter, and some have attributed similar activities to Metaneira, wife of Celeus and mother of Triptolemus. It must be said that the beginnings of the mysteries are shrouded by time and the very nature of their great secrecy. [Clement of Alexandria, *Exhortation to the Greeks* 2.20; Arnobius, *Adversus Nationes* 5.25; Pausanias 1.14.2; Suidas, "Dysaules."]

BAUCIS was a Phrygian woman, wife of Philemon. Their story, very often told, was a moral tale centering on hospitality. Jupiter and Mercury were traveling, and had been turned away by everyone in that vicinity when they applied for food and shelter. Baucis and Philemon, an elderly and very poor couple, shared what little they had, and the grateful gods not only saved them from a flood but made them priests in Jupiter's temple. They also granted the couple's wish that they might die at the very same time. When the time arrived, they were changed by Jupiter into trees that grew side by side. [Ovid, *Metamorphoses* 8.620–724.]

BEBRYCE was one of the DANAIDES. The Bebryces in Bithynia were believed to have derived their name from her. [Eustathius on Dionysius Periegeta 805; Apollodorus 2.1.5 calls her BRYCE.]

BELLONA was the Roman goddess of war, equivalent to the Greek Enyo. Like Enyo, she was a fearful goddess delighting in the riot and carnage of battle. Her companions were Mars, Discordia, and the Furies. It is said that human sacrifice, or even cannibalism, might have accompanied her worship. In 47 B.C., while destroying by decree a temple of Isis, workers also pulled down the walls of the adjoining temple of Bellona and found pots filled with human flesh. Bellona was sometimes described as the wife of Mars. [Gellius 13.23; St. Augustine, *City of God* 6.10; Plautus, *Amphitryon* 42; Statius, *Thebaid* 5.155.]

BENDIS was a Thracian moon goddess. From Thrace her worship was introduced to the island of Lemnos, and later carried to Attica by Thracian aliens. In the time of Plato, the Bendideia, a public festival, was celebrated at Peiraeus every year. It featured torch races and a solemn procession. In Samothrace her worship became involved with the celebrated mysteries. Bendis was identified with the Brauronian Artemis, with Hecate, with Persephone, and even with Rhea. [Proclus, *Platonic Theology* 353; Hesychius, "Bendis"; Plato, *Republic* 1.1; Strabo 10.3.18; Dionysius of Halicarnassus, *Roman Antiquities* 30.45.]

BENTHESICYME was a daughter of Poseidon and Amphitrite, and sister of Triton and Rhodos. She was married to Enalus in Ethiopia and was the mother of several daughters. Benthesicyme was also half-sister to Eumolpus, son of Poseidon and Chione. Fearing the wrath of her father, Boreas, when Eumolpus was born, Chione threw the baby into the sea. Poseidon rescued him and gave him to Benthesicyme to bring up and educate. Benthesicyme was devoted to him and arranged to have him marry one of her daughters. However, he soon took a fancy to one of his sisters-in-law and tried to rape her. For this rash act Benthesicyme threw him out; he went to Thrace, from where he later left to become a leader of the Eleusinians in their war against Athens.

Enalus, her husband, does not seem to be connected with the hero of the same name from Lesbos, even though his exploits had to do with the sea and the worship of Poseidon and Amphitrite. [Apollodorus 1.4.6, 3.15.4; Hesiod, *Theogony* 930.]

BERECYNTHIA was a surname of Cybele derived from Mount Berecynthus in Phrygia, where she was particularly worshipped. Mount Berecynthus in turn received its name from Berecynthus, one of Cybele's priests. [Callimachus, *Hymn to Artemis* 3.246; Servius on Virgil's *Aeneid* 9.82, 6.785; Pseudo-Plutarch, *On Rivers* 10.]

BEROE (1) was the aged wife of Doryclus, one of the companions of Aeneas. She was from the promontory of Rhoeteia in Thrace and accompanied her husband on the voyage with Aeneas in quest of a new Troy. Still smarting from the 20-year-old slight in the judgment of Paris, Hera sent Iris, the goddess of the rainbow, to incite the Trojan women to burn the ships and force a settlement on Sicily. Iris disguised herself as Beroe, but as a younger version. The disguise was discovered, but the women set fire to the ships anyway, only to have them doused by a rainstorm. Beroe meanwhile was in her sickbed and knew nothing of the ruse. [Virgil, *Aeneid* 5.620.]

BEROE (2) was the aged nurse of Semele. Semele, the daughter of Cadmus, had Zeus for a lover, and Hera knew about this infidelity. She assumed the appearance of Beroe and persuaded Semele to beg Zeus to appear to and make love to her in the same splendid and majestic way he did to Hera. Zeus finally gave in to her nagging and embraced the pregnant Semele in his full glory, as a result of which she was burned to a crisp. Zeus managed, however, to save the unborn Dionysus and bring him to full term in his own body. [Apollodorus 3.4.2; Hesiod, *Theogony* 940; Diodorus Siculus 4.2; Ovid, *Metamorphoses* 3.259.]

BEROE (3) was a daughter of Aphrodite and Adonis, and sister of Golgos. She was loved by Dionysus and Poseidon, who contended for her affection. Poseidon won out, to the satisfaction of Beroe, it is said. Her brother was the founder of Cyprian Golgi, and the town of Beroe (Beryton) in what is now Lebanon was named for her. [Nonnos, *Dionysiaca* 41.155; Scholiast on Theocritus 15.100; Diodorus Siculus 4.83.]

BEROE (4) was one of the OCEANIDES. [Virgil, *Georgics* 4.341.]

BEROE (5) was one of the NEREIDES. [Hyginus, *Fables: Preface* 8.]

BIA was the personification of force or mighty strength. She is described as the daughter of the Titan Pallas and Styx, and sister of Zelus (Zeal), Cratus (Power), and Nice (Victory). When the Olympian gods engaged in battle with the Titans, Styx brought her children to Zeus as allies. He was so pleased he allowed them to live on Olympus forever after. Thus Bia became one of his ministers; when Prometheus failed to carry out the will of Zeus, he was chained to a rock by Hephaestus with Bia and Cratus as witnesses. It is interesting that the ancients personified force and victory as women, with zeal and power as men. [Hesiod, *Theogony* 385; Aeschylus, *Prometheus* 12; Apollodorus 1.2.2; Pausanias 7.26.5.]

BIADICE was by some called the wife of Cretheus who accused her nephew Phrixus of trying to rape her. Usually she is called DEMODICE. [Hyginus, *Poetic Astronomy* 2.20; Scholiast on Pindar's *Pythian Odes* 288.]

BITHYNIS was the mother of Amycus by Poseidon. Others said his mother was the Bithynian nymph Melia. Nothing is known of Bithynis and her affair with Poseidon, and not a great deal about her son. He was ruler of the Bebryces, and when the Argonauts landed in his territory he challenged the bravest of them to a duel. Somewhat unfairly his challenge was met by Polydeuces, the immortal one of the Dioscuri, and Amycus was killed quite quickly. Amycus had a history of troublemaking and had done battle with Heracles in a war with Lycus. It was said that even in death his quarrelsome spirit endured, for on his tomb grew a species of laurel that incited crew members on a vessel to incessant strife until the offending plant was thrown overboard. [Apollodorus 1.9.20, 2.5.9; Hyginus, *Fables* 17; Apollonius Rhodius 754.]

BLIAS (?) was the mother of Menephron, an Arcadian. She lived in an incestuous relationship with her son. One writer said Menephron also slept with his daughter Cyllene, but he probably confused the name of the place in Arcadia, where the mother and son lived, with the name of a person. It is unfortunate that nothing whatsoever is known about this close-knit family, especially whether or not the arrangement was by common agreement. [Ovid, *Metamorphoses* 7.386; Hyginus, *Fables* 253.]

BOEOTIA was sometimes called the mother of the HYADES by Hyas. [Hyginus, *Poetic Astronomy* 2.21.]

BOLBE, a nymph, was the mother of Olynthus by Heracles. Mother and son were yet two more minor events in the roving life of the hero. We know nothing of Olynthus except that the Thracian town of Olynthus and the Olynthus River in Chalcidice were thought to have received their names from him. [Stephanus Byzantium, "Olynthus"; Athenaeus 8.334; Conon, *Narrations* 4.]

BONA DEA was a Roman goddess, daughter (or sister or wife) of Faunus. She was also called Fauna, Fatua, or Oma. In all her relationships with Faunus she maintained purity and chastity. One version of their story has him as her father trying to violate her, in the process of which he changed her or himself into a serpent. When she became deified, serpents were involved in her worship. Her worship was confined entirely to women, and men were not even allowed to know her name. Her oracles were not available to men. Her sanctuary was a cave in the Aventine Hill, but she had another sanctuary between Aricia and Bovillae. Her worship eventually became important enough so that her festival involved sacrifices on behalf of the entire Roman people. These state occasions were conducted by Vestals, and only women—mostly from the nobility— were allowed to participate. No males, regardless of rank or status, could enter the consulate where these celebrations took place; even portraits and statues of men were covered over. Only one case is recorded of a male's having witnessed the ceremony. That was Publius Clodius, who entered in the disguise of a woman.

In preparation for the festival, women abstained from sexual intercourse. The consulate was decorated with flowers and foliage except myrtle, for in the versions that made Bona Dea wife of Faunus, he beat her to death with myrtle switches when she became intoxicated on wine. Consequently, wine was forbidden to be brought in by the celebrants. However, a wine-filled vessel stood in the room. But what it held was called milk instead of wine. The first part of the ceremony was a sacrifice, probably hens of various colors except black. After the sacrifice, Bacchic dances were performed, and wine was consumed. The festivities took place only at night.

Bona Dea was conceived as a goddess of healing, characterized by serpents being part of her worship, and medicinal herbs were sold in her temples. She was identified with Semele, Medea, Hecate, or Persephone among the Greeks. She was almost identical with the Marsian goddess Angitia. [Servius on Virgil's *Aeneid* 8.324; Macrobius, *Saturnalia* 1.12; Varro on Lactantius 1.22; Dio Cassius 37.45; Juvenal 6.3.14,4.29; Seneca, *Letters* 97; Plutarch, *Caesar* 9, *Roman Questions* 20; Cicero, *De Harispicum Responsis* 17, *Pro Milone* 31, *Letters to Atticus* 1.13, 2.4, *Paradoxa Stoicorum* 4.]

BORYSTHENIS was one of three MUSES at Delphi, her sisters being Cephisso and Apollonis. Their names characterized them as the daughters of Apollo. [Tzetzes on Hesiod's *Works and Days* 6; Servius on Virgil's *Eclogues* 7.21; Diodorus Siculus 4.7.]

BOULAIA was a surname of Athena, referring to her role in upholding the authority of the law. To her was attributed the founding of the ancient court of the Areiopagus. In cases in which the vote of the judges was tied, she cast the deciding vote in favor of the accused. She did this in the trial of Orestes. [Aeschylus, *Eumenides* 753.]

BRAESIA was a daughter of Cinyras by Metharme, daughter of Pygmalion, king of Cyprus. She was a sister of Oxyporus, Orsedice, Laogore, and Adonis. Cinyras was the son of Sandacus, king of Syria. He founded Paphos in Cyprus. The daughters cohabited with foreigners and ended their lives in Egypt. This tantalizing statement about the three sisters is all we know of them. The writer implies that cohabitation with foreigners somehow caused them to end their lives in Egypt. Were they abducted or exiled? Or did they find Egypt a more profitable place to cohabit with foreigners? [Apollodorus 3.14.3.]

BRAURONIA was a surname of Artemis from the deme of Brauron on the east coast of Attica. She had an important temple there featuring the ancient image brought by Orestes and Iphigeneia from Tauris. She also had a sanctuary at Athens with a statue made by Praxiteles. [Pausanias 1.23.8.]

BREMUSA was one of the AMAZONS. [Quintus Smyrnaeus 1.43.]

BRIMO, the Angry or Terrifying One, occurs as a surname of several goddesses such as Hecate, Persephone, Demeter, and Cybele. She was also a goddess in her own right, it appears, who was worshipped principally in places that had the worship of the Cabeiri. [Apollonius Rhodius 3.861,1211, Tzetzes on Lycophron 1171; Arnobius, *Adversus Nationes* 5.170.]

BRISA was one of the nymphs said to have brought up Dionysus. From her he derived one of his surnames, Brisaeus. [Stephanus Byzantium, "Brisa"; Scholiast on Persius' *Saturae* 1.76.]

BRISEIS (1) was the patronymic of HIPPODAMEIA from her father, Briseus.

BRISEIS (2) was the beautiful daughter of Calchas who was loved by Troilus. She had been left behind in Troy by her father; since she had played no part in his defection, she continued to be treated with courtesy. Knowing that Troy must fall, Calchas persuaded Agamemnon to ask Priam for her on his behalf, lest she be made a prisoner of war. Priam generously gave his assent, and several of his sons escorted Briseis to the Greek camp. Although she had sworn undying fidelity to Troilus, Briseis soon transferred her affections to Diomedes the Argive, who fell passionately in love with her and did his best to kill Troilus whenever he appeared on the battlefield. [Benoit, *Le Roman de Troie*.]

BRITOMARTIS was originally a Cretan goddess of hunters and fishermen. She was the daughter of Zeus and Carme, the daughter of Eubulus. In spite of the staccato sound of her name, it probably meant "sweet maiden." And a maiden she was. She was loved by Artemis but by no man. Minos lusted after her and pursued her; she fled from him until once he was on the point of catching her. She then leapt from Mount Dictynnaeus into the sea, where she became tangled in fishing nets. About to drown, she was saved by her lover, Artemis. Artemis made her a goddess, who was from that time worshipped in Crete and afterward in Aegina. In Crete she had the surname Dictynna, and in Aegina she was known as Aphaea. Her magnificent temple in Aegina can be seen today.

Another tradition gives Britomartis a Phoenician origin and makes her a granddaughter of Phoenix. She went to Argos and was received hospitably by the daughters of Erasinus. Then she went to Cephallenia, where she was worshipped under the name of Laphria, and from there she went to Crete, where the preceding events occurred. A sailor, Andromedes, carried her to Aegina and upon landing tried to rape her, but she escaped once more by the intervention of Artemis.

Her identification with Artemis became so strong that some even called her mother Leto. Like Artemis she was a goddess of the moon. Both goddesses were also included in the mystic worship of Hecate. A wooden statue of Artemis Britomartis existed at Olus in Crete. [Pausanias 2.30.2, 3.14.2, 9.11.2,3; Antoninus Liberalis 40; Callimachus, *Hymn to Artemis* 3.189; Diodorus Siculus 5.76; Euripides, *Iphigeneia in Tauris* 126.]

BRIZO was a goddess worshipped on the island of Delos. She was a prophetic deity who revealed the meaning of dreams. The Delian women put sacrifices to her in vessels shaped like boats. The sacrifice to her of fish was forbidden. Although her protection was sought for various activities, she was invoked mainly to protect ships. [Athenaeus 8.335; Eustathius on Homer's *Odyssey* 1720; Hesychius, "Brizomantis."]

BROME, or Bromie, was one of the nymphs who brought up Dionysus on Mount Nysa. Some claim that the god's surname Bromius was derived from her. [Hyginus, *Fables* 182; Servius on Virgil's *Eclogues* 6.15.]

BRYCE was one of the DANAIDES, a daughter of Danaus and Polyxo. She was married to Chthonius, the son of Aegyptus. She was also called Bebryce. [Apollodorus 2.1.5; Eustathius on Dionysius Periegeta 805.]

BUBASTOS was the name of the deified Parthenos, daughter of Staphylus. (*See* MOLPADIA.)

BUBONA was a Roman goddess who protected oxen and cows. She was associated with Epona, who protected horses. As joint protectors of stables, figures of the goddesses were placed in niches of the walls of these buildings. Sometimes their likeness or a symbolic rendering was painted over mangers. [St. Augustine, *City of God* 4.34; Tertullian, *Apology* 16; Apuleius, *Golden Ass* 60; Juvenal 8.157.]

BUDEIA (1) was an epithet of Athena, having reference to her teaching people to yoke oxen to the plough. [Eustathius on Homer's *Iliad* 1076; Stephanus Byzantium, "Boudeia."]

BUDEIA (2) was the wife of Clymenus, the king of Orchomenus in Boeotia. She is considered identical with Byzyge (probably a nickname), a daughter of Lycus. Her principal distinction was that the Boeotian town of Budeion was named for her. By Clymenus she had five sons—Stratius, Arrhon, Pyleus, Azeus, Erginus—and two daughters—Eurydice and Axia. Erginus, the eldest, had been an Argonaut. In Lemnos he contended successfully in the funeral games of Thoas but was ridiculed by the Lemnian women because, although quite young, he had gray hair. When Clymenus was killed at a festival of the Onchestian Poseidon by a stone cast during a scuffle with the visiting Thebans, Erginus raised an army and marched on the Thebans, defeated them, and forced them to pay an exorbitant annual tribute. He was later killed by Heracles. Nothing is known of the other sons except Azeus, whose granddaughter Astyoche produced sons by Ares who led the Minyans against Troy. Eurydice became the wife of Nestor, and Axia

gave her name to a town in Ozolian Locris. [Eustathius on Homer's *Iliad* 1076; Scholiast on Apollonius Rhodius 1.185; Pindar, *Olympian Odes* 4.29, with the scholiast; Apollodorus 2.4.11; Pausanias 9.37.1,2.]

BUNAEA was a surname of Hera derived from Bunus, the son of Hermes and Alcidameia, who is said to have built a sanctuary to Hera on the road that led up to Acrocorinthus. [Pausanias 2.4.7,3.8.]

BURA was a daughter of Ion, the ancestral hero of the Ionians, and Helice. From her the Achaian town of Bura derived its name. [Pausanias 7.25.5; Stephanus Byzantium, "Bura."]

BYBLIS was a daughter of Miletus and Tragasia, and lived in the town of Miletus in Crete with her parents and brother, Caunus. She conceived a passion for her handsome brother, and the obsession grew to the point that she sent a servant to him with a lengthy written declaration of her love. She cited examples of sibling liaisons among the gods themselves and begged him to share her couch. Caunus read the confession of love with horror and anger, and sent the servant back to his mistress in terror. Caunus promptly decided to leave, and did so as soon as he could. Byblis was devastated at his rejection and obvious revulsion. After he left, she followed him through Caria, Lycia, and other places, until at length she fell exhausted and dissolved in tears over her impossible love. She was changed into a spring, which was called by her name. The city of Byblos in Phoenicia was also said to have derived its name from her.

Other versions of the story had Caunus falling in love with her and fleeing before things could get worse. In one version she followed him and hanged herself with her girdle. In another version she was on the point of jumping from a cliff but was rescued by Hamadryads, who transformed her into one of them. Even in the story that makes Caunus the one with incestuous desires, there is a strong suggestion that Byblis would have reciprocated the love. [Parthenius, *Love Stories* 11; Conon, *Narrations* 2; Antoninus Liberalis 30; Ovid, *Metamorphoses* 9.446–665; Stephanus Byzantium, "Byblis."]

BYZE was one of the daughters of Erasinus. With her sisters, Melite and Moira, she hospitably received Britomartis when she arrived in Argos. [Antoninus Liberalis 30.]

BYZYGE (See BUDEIA)

CABEIRIA was a surname of Demeter at Thebes. In addition to the better-known Cabeiri of Samothrace, Lemnos, and Imbros, there were also Boeotian Cabeiri. Near the Neitian gate of Thebes there was a grove of Demeter Cabeiria and Kore, where only the initiated were allowed to enter. About 1.5 kilometers beyond was a major sanctuary of the enigmatical Cabeiri, where mysteries were celebrated as late as the time of Pausanias. [Pausanias 4.1.5.]

CABEIRIAE were the so-called Cabeirian nymphs, daughters of Cadmilus, son of Hephaestus and Cabeiro. The Cabeiriae are merely mentioned; there is never a clue as to their function. Obviously they had some role in the celebration of the Cabeirian mysteries, but the extreme secrecy in which these rites were conducted allowed for no details. It is not unlikely that they were originally attendants at the ceremonies on Samothrace, where they were born. Later, sacred rites were held in their honor. [Strabo 10.3.21; Acusilaus on Strabo 10.3.21; Scholiast on Apollonius Rhodius 1.917.]

CABEIRO was the daughter of Proteus and Anchinoe and mother of Cadmilus, Eurymedon, and Alcon by Hephaestus. Proteus was the marine deity familiarly called the Old Man of the Sea. Consequently, Cabeiro must have been a sea nymph. When thrown from heaven Hephaestus fell to earth on the island of Lemnos, and it was here that Cadmilus was probably born. [Nonnos, Dionysiaca 14.22; Cicero, On the Nature of the Gods 3.21.]

CABYA, or Cambyse, was a daughter of Opus, son of Zeus and Protogeneia, daughter of Deucalion. She was the wife of Locrus, son of Physicus and grandson of Amphictyon, thus placing the couple only four generations from the famous flood. Her husband was also her cousin a few times removed. The son of Cabya

and Locrus was Locrus II, the mythical ancestor of the Ozolian Locrians. His son was Opus II, ancestor of the Opuntian Locrians. [Plutarch, Greek Questions 15; Pindar, Olympian Odes 9.86; Eustathius on Homer's Iliad 277.]

CACA, or Cacia, was the sister of Cacus, the early Italian cattle rustler. He stole the cattle of Hercules and dragged them to his cave by their tails so they would not leave hoofprints. Caca was not pleased with her brother's activities and told Hercules where the cattle were concealed. Hercules killed her brother and saw to it that Caca was rewarded; she was even paid divine honors. In her sanctuary a perpetual flame was kept burning. One account made Cacus and Caca son and daughter of Vulcan, and described Cacus as a fearful giant who terrorized the land. [Lactantius 1.20.36; Servius on Virgil's Aeneid 8.190; Livy 1.7.]

CAECILIA, or Caia, was the real name of TANAQUIL.

CAENIS was the daughter of Atrax, a Lapith, and sister of Hippodameia. She was quite beautiful and had several suitors, but seemed reluctant to marry. One day she was surprised by Poseidon, who raped her and was quite satisfied with the experience. He promised her any gift she might name. To his astonishment she asked to be changed into a man. This transformation took place, and Caenis became Caeneus, sometimes called Atracides after his father. As a man Caeneus loved to wage war and became so successful in battle that he was elected king of one of the Lapith tribes. He even married and fathered a son, Coronus. He stuck a spear in the marketplace and had the people sacrifice to it, probably not thinking beyond its merely military symbolism. Caeneus also was one of the Argonauts, which must have made for interesting shipboard discussion among those who knew the facts. About this time his sister, Hippodameia, married Peirithous, which became the occasion for the famous battle between the Lapiths and Centaurs. Caeneus was in his element and slaughtered many of the Centaurs, even though he was taunted about his original gender by another of the Lapiths. Part of

Poseidon's gift had included invulnerability to weapons, so Caeneus was impervious to the blows from the enemy. Eventually they mobbed him and buried him under logs and branches until they smothered him. From the piled logs flew a small bird, which the seer Mopsus declared to be the soul of Caenis/Caeneus. It was said that the corpse was that of a woman. [Antoninus Liberalis 17; Ovid, *Metamorphoses* 12.190–531; Apollonius Rhodius 1.57–64; Apollodorus 1.9.16, 2.7.7 and *Epitome* 1.22; Hyginus, *Fables* 14.]

CAIA (*See* CAECILIA)

CAIETA was the nurse of Aeneas and, according to others, also the nurse of Creusa or Ascanius. The promontory of Caieta, as well as the port and town of this name on the western coast of Italy, were believed to have been named for her. [Virgil, *Aeneid* 7.1; Servius on Virgil's *Aeneid* 7.1.]

CALAENE was one of the PROETIDES, according to one writer. [Aelian, *Various Narratives* 3.42.]

CALAMETIS, one of the THESPIADES, was a daughter of Thespius and Megamede, and mother of Astybies by Heracles. [Apollodorus 2.7.8.]

CALCHINIA was the daughter of Leucippus, king of Sicyon. She became one of the amatory conquests of Poseidon and bore a son, Peratus. Peratus was brought up by Leucippus, who at his death passed the kingdom to his grandson. The Sicyonian line almost ended with Calchinia's grandson Plemnaeus, all of whose children died the first time they cried. Demeter finally took pity and came to Sicyon in the disguise of a foreign woman and reared Plemnaeus' son Orthopolis, who carried on the royal line. [Pausanias 2.5.7.]

CALE (1) was by some called one of the CHARITES. It was related that Aphrodite and the three Charites—Pasithea, Cale, and Euphrosyne—disputed about their beauty with one another. When Teiresias, the Theban seer, awarded the prize to Cale, he was changed by Aphrodite into an old woman, but Cale rewarded him with a beautiful head of hair and took him to Crete. This story seems somehow unfinished. It is hard to understand how beautiful hair and a trip to Crete could possibly compensate for being changed into an old woman. The record does not show at what point in the career of Teiresias this took place. He had been changed into a woman another time by Athena, so the experience of being a female was not entirely new. [Eustathius on Homer's *Odyssey* 1665.]

CALE (2) was one of the NEREIDES. [*Corpus Inscriptionum Graecorum* 4.8406.]

CALIADNE, a Naiad, was the mother by Aegyptus of 12 sons: Eurylochus, Phantes, Peristhenes, Hermus, Dryas, Potamon, Cisseus, Lixus, Imbrus, Bromius, Polyctor, and Chthonius. All were killed by their brides, the DANAIDES, on their wedding night. [Apollodorus 2.1.5.]

CALIGO was the personification of darkness. She was the mother of Chaos, by whom she became the mother of Aether, Nyx, Hemera, and Erebus. Usually Chaos was considered a female and the mother of the darkness of space, but cosmogonies differed on this point. [Hyginus, *Fables: Preface* 1.]

CALLIANASSA was one of the NEREIDES. [Homer, *Iliad* 18.6; Hyginus, *Fables: Preface* 29.]

CALLIANEIRA was one of the NEREIDES. [Homer, *Iliad* 18.4.]

CALLIDICE (1) was a queen of the Thesprotians. After Odysseus slew the suitors of Penelope, he journeyed, as directed by Teiresias, to a land where men knew not the sea. He came to Thesprotia and propitiated Poseidon with sacrifices. Callidice urged him to stay, and he did so, reigning over the kingdom. He led the Thesprotians against the Brygians, who had made war on them. By Odysseus, Callidice became mother of Polypoetes. When she died, Odysseus turned the kingdom over to their son and returned to Ithaca. [Apollodorus, *Epitome* 7.34.]

CALLIDICE (2) was one of the DANAIDES, a daughter of Danaus by Crino. She was married to Pandion, son of Aegyptus. [Apollodorus 2.1.5.]

CALLIGENEIA was a surname of Demeter herself as the mother of Kore (Persephone) or of Demeter's nurse and priestess. [Aristophanes, *Thesmophoriazusae* 298, with the scholiast; Hesychius, "Kalligeneia"; Photius, *Library* 127.9.]

CALLIOPE was one of the nine MUSES. As Muse of epic poetry she appears with a tablet and stylus, and sometimes with a scroll. Although she shared a great deal in common with her eight sisters and joined them most of the time in dancing and singing on Olympus and in their sacred groves on Mount Helicon, she led a most interesting private life. She was called at one time or another the mother of the Corybantes by Zeus, of Hymen by Apollo, of Ialemus by Apollo, of Linus by Apollo, of Rhesus by the Strymon River, of the Sirens, and of Orpheus by Oeagrus. It makes good sense that she was considered the mother of these famous poets and musicians (except for Rhesus). Hymen was the god of marriage and the author of the songs performed at weddings. Ialemus was the inventor of a special kind of song sung on melancholy occasions. Linus was the personification of lamentation; he invented dirges and songs in general. Orpheus was the most famous poet and musician who ever lived. The Corybantes were the attendants of Rhea Cybele and accompanied her with wild dancing and music. The Sirens, of course, were the women with beautiful voices who lured sailors to their death with their songs. As for Rhesus, the Thracian prince who went to the Trojan War, there is little reason for assigning him a Muse for a mother, and it seems this was done by later writers perhaps to lend poetic enhancement to his early and tragic death.

Calliope also took a fancy to Achilles and taught him how to cheer his friends by singing at banquets. She was called by Zeus to mediate the quarrel between Aphrodite and Persephone over possession of Adonis. She settled the dispute by giving them equal time, providing Adonis some much-needed free time to himself.

Calliope is somehow easier to picture than the other Muses, with the possible exception of Terpsichore. One can think of a voluptuous woman with a beautiful face and a pleasant manner. In spite of being credited with mournful sons who met unhappy ends, she may even be conceived as light-spirited. [Hesiod, *Theogony* 77; Philostratus, *Heroicus* 19.2; Hyginus, *Fables* 14, *Poetic Astronomy* 2.7; Catullus 61.2; Nonnos, *Dionysiaca* 33.67; Apollodorus 1.3.2,4; Pausanias 1.43.7, 2.19.7; Conon, *Narrations* 45; Apollonius Rhodius 1.23; Servius on Virgil's *Aeneid* 5.364; Zenobius 4.39.]

CALLIPYGOS was a surname of Aphrodite. Callipygos means "Beautiful Buttocks." It was related that a farmer of Syracuse had two lovely daughters, who fell into an argument as to which had the more beautiful behind. One day a young man, son of a wealthy landowner, passed by. Asking him to decide, they turned around and upped their skirts. He decided in favor of the older girl and also fell in love with her. He told his younger brother of this incident, and the boy went to see for himself. He judged in favor of the younger sister and fell in love with her. Their father was not too satisfied with their desire to marry these country girls but finally agreed, and the two couples were married. The sisters, who had come into such good fortune because of their lovely backsides, founded the temple of Aphrodite Callipygos. [Athenaeus 12.554.]

CALLIRRHOE (1) was a daughter of Oceanus and Tethys. By Chrysaor she became the mother of Geryones and Echidna. Chrysaor was a son of Poseidon by Medusa. When Perseus cut off Medusa's head, Chrysaor and Pegasus came forth, Chrysaor brandishing a golden sword. Perhaps he was not particularly monstrous-looking when he mated with Callirrhoe; the Oceanides usually managed to have presentable fathers for their children. However, the offspring from this union reverted to the type represented by their grandmother Medusa. Geryones was three-headed, and Echidna had a serpentine lower body. Both these monsters figured in the stories of Heracles. Callirrhoe had more normal children by other men. She had a daughter, Chione, by the Nile River and by Poseidon a son, Minyas, the ancestor of the Minyans. Callirrhoe was also said to be the mother of Cotys by Manes, the first king of Lydia. [Dionysius of Halicarnassus, *Roman Antiquities* 1.27; Hesiod, *Theogony* 280,351,981; Apollodorus 2.5.10; Hyginus, *Fables* 151; Servius on Virgil's *Aeneid* 4.250; Tzetzes on Lycophron 686.]

CALLIRRHOE (2) was a daughter of the Achelous River. She is part of the story of the fatal necklace and peplus (robe) of Harmonia. Alcmaeon, the prince of Argos, had killed his mother, Eriphyle, who had been bribed by Polyneices of Thebes with the necklace and peplus to force her husband, Amphiaraus, to join the campaign of the Seven against Thebes, although Amphiaraus, with prophetic certainty, had told her he would perish in the battle. He exacted a promise from Alcmaeon to avenge him, which he did ten years later after the campaign of the Epigoni that Eriphyle also induced him to join. Alcmaeon went to Psophis to be purified by the king, Phegeus, and married his daughter Arsinoe, giving her the Theban heirlooms as a wedding present. A plague came on Psophis for harboring a matricide, and Alcmaeon had to leave. An oracle directed him to a place that had not existed—and was therefore free of the curse—when he killed his mother: a portion of land that came into existence when the Achelous River formed an island in the territory later called Acarnania. Achelous, the god of the river, was pleased to welcome Alcmaeon and give him his daughter Callirrhoe in marriage.

Callirrhoe also enthusiastically welcomed the tragic young man. The lower valley of the Achelous was a lonely place, and she happily bore him two sons, Amphoterus and Acarnan. After two or three years of domestic bliss she learned of the necklace and peplus, and was determined to have them. She nagged at Alcmaeon to fetch them for her, but he refused until she resorted to denying him sexual relations with her. He eventually broke down and journeyed to Psophis; he convinced Phegeus that only by dedicating the treasures at Delphi could he be free of the pursuing Erinyes and the curse of matricide. Phegeus granted this request with the consent of Arsinoe, who still loved Alcmaeon and believed he would return to her after the curse was lifted.

Alcmaeon was scarcely out of the palace before one of his servants revealed the truth, and Phegeus sent his sons to ambush and murder him.

Whether or not Callirrhoe ever saw the fatal items is a question. When she learned that her covetousness had resulted in her husband's murder, she was devastated. She prayed to Zeus, her intermittent lover, to allow her small sons to become fully grown in order to avenge the murder. So Amphoterus and Acarnan went to Psophis and killed Phegeus and his wife, and later at Tegea the two sons of Phegeus as they were setting out to dedicate the treasures at Delphi. From this point the story, already complicated, grows even more vague. Did the brothers return to Callirrhoe with the necklace, or did they proceed to Delphi, where they eventually dedicated it and the peplus? The story has it that Achelous requested them to dedicate it, so they must have journeyed from Tegea to the territory later named after Acarnan. Callirrhoe must have possessed the heirlooms for a short time. Her father, in his divine wisdom, would have recognized by then their lethal properties and wanted to be rid of them for once and all. Both the sons returned to the Achelous valley and resided in the region where they had been born and robbed of their boyhood and adolescence. [Apollodorus 3.7.5–7; Ovid, *Metamorphoses* 9.413; Thucydides 2.102; Strabo 10.2.25–26; Pausanias 8.24.4.]

CALLIRRHOE (3) was a daughter of the Scamander River in the Troad. Like other daughters of rivers in the vicinity, she married into the royal family of Troy. Her husband was Tros, a son of Erichthonius and Astyoche. Erichthonius was among the wealthiest of mortals, so Callirrhoe married quite well. The city of Troy, as well as the entire area called the Troad, was named for her husband. Callirrhoe had four children by him—Cleopatra, Ilus, Assaracus, and Ganymede. Except for Cleopatra, about whom nothing is known, the other three achieved fame for ages afterward. Ilus continued the royal line of Troy and was the grandfather of Priam. He was said to have founded Troy, which he named for his father. However, Ilium, from his own name, was used almost as frequently for the name of the city. Assaracus was the ancestor of the line that produced Aeneas, so the Romans could trace their origin back to him. Ganymede, the youngest son, was extraordinarily beautiful, so much so that Zeus (some say in the form of an eagle) carried him away, ostensibly to make him cupbearer to the gods. (Later generations doubted if this abduction had anything to do with cupbearing, and indeed the Romans corrupted Ganymede's name to Catamitus to designate a passive homosexual.) It would be interesting to learn how Callirrhoe viewed this abduction, whether she considered it an honor to have her son become a favorite of the supreme deity or whether she was horrified at this flagrant early example of child sexual abuse. Perhaps any protest from her might have been silenced by her husband, who received in compensation a pair of divine horses. Had she lived long enough, she might have considered any anguish on her part small price for the ultimate honor accorded Ganymede by his divine lover. Zeus placed him among the stars as the constellation Aquarius. [Apollodorus 2.5.9, 3.12.2; Homer, *Iliad* 20.232, 5.266; Pindar, *Olympian Odes* 1.44; *Homeric Hymn to Aphrodite* 202; Pausanias 5.24.1; Eratosthenes *Star Placements* 26; Hyginus, *Fables* 224, *Poetic Astronomy* 2.29.]

CALLIRRHOE (4) was a Calydonian maiden. She was deeply loved by Coresus, a priest of Dionysus, but rejected all his overtures to her. His manly pride wounded, Coresus prayed to Dionysus to punish this arrogant young woman. Always inclined to overdo things, Dionysus brought a plague of madness on the citizens of Calydon. The oracle at Dodona declared that the only release from the calamity would be the sacrifice of Callirrhoe or a substitute. Callirrhoe was finally dragged to the altar, but Coresus, upon seeing her helplessly awaiting her fate, felt his love revive and impulsively sacrificed himself in her stead. Seeing the price this rejected lover was willing to pay, Callirrhoe killed herself. Near the site of her suicide ran a spring, which from that time was given her name. It is not difficult to believe that Callirrhoe got unfair treatment. There are stories similar to this one, all of them carrying a hint of male chauvinism. Perhaps Callirrhoe was totally unattracted to Coresus and found his persistence annoying; maybe she loved someone else. Her suicide could

well have been committed with the knowledge of how she would be treated afterward by the townspeople or by Dionysus, who might well have taken vengeance on behalf of his priest. [Pausanias 7.21.1.]

CÁLLIRRHOE (5) was a daughter of the Maeander River. By Car, the ancestral hero of the Carians, she was the mother of Alabandus and Idrieus. Alabandus was worshipped as the founder of Alabandus in Caria, and Idrieus gave his name to the Carian city of Idrias. [Stephanus Byzantium, "Alabanda," "Idrias."]

CALLIRRHOE (6) was the daughter of Lycus, king of Libya. She fell in love with Diomedes when, having incurred the wrath of Aphrodite during the war, he was driven by a storm onto the Libyan coast on his return from Troy. King Lycus was on the point of sacrificing him to Ares, as was the custom of the country with foreigners. However, Athena protected him by having Callirrhoe help him escape. He repaid this loving and merciful act by abandoning her. Either out of frustrated love or the very real fear of reprisal by her father, she hanged herself. [Plutarch, *Greek and Roman Parallel Stories* 23.]

CALLIRRHOE (7) was a name shared by a succession of priestesses of Hera at the Heraion near Argos. The chronological table of these priestesses was headed by Io, who was considered the founder of the worship of Hera in Argos. Callithyia was an alternate form of this honorary title.

CALLIRRHOE (8) was a daughter of Peiranthus, a son of Argus and Euadne. Her brothers were Argus, Arestorides, and Triopas. Her uncle was Iasus, whom many regard as the father of Io. The foregoing entry names Io as the first in a succession of priestesses at the Heraion near Argos. There is a strong possibility that there was a connection between Io's cousin and this honorary title. Perhaps Callirrhoe died and was thus commemorated. It is not unlikely that the cousins were confused (Io had more than one genealogy) and that Callirrhoe was indeed the one who founded the worship of Hera in this place. [Apollodorus 2.1.2; Hyginus, *Fables* 145; Scholiast on Euripides' *Orestes* 932.]

CALLIRRHOE (9) was a daughter of Nestus, the Thracian River. Nothing else is known of her. [Stephanus Byzantium, "Bistonia."]

CALLIRRHOE (10) was the daughter of Phocus of Glisas. She was so beautiful she had 30 suitors, all young and well placed, from the surrounding region. Phocus kept delaying the day when she would announce a selection, then finally said he would leave the choice to the Delphic oracle. The young men were outraged by this proposal, since each one fancied he would be Callirrhoe's choice. They set upon Phocus and killed him outright. The horrified Callirrhoe fled, but was soon pursued. She hid in various places until the festival of the Pamboeotia. Then she went to Coroneia and, from the altar of Athena, Itonia told of the heinous act of the suitors; in addition, she recited their names and whereabouts. The Boeotians resolved revenge for her sake, and when her pursuers learned the tide had turned against them, they sought refuge first in Orchomenus and then in Hippotae. The Thebans demanded the surrender of the men, but the people of Hippotae refused to deliver them. The Thebans and other Boeotians amassed an army under the command of Phoedus and besieged the village. They seized the murderers and stoned them to death, and made slaves of the villagers. They razed the town and divided its land between Thisbe and Coroneia. There is no record of what happened to Callirrhoe. It is possible to construct many different scenarios. Perhaps she had already made a selection before her father was killed. Maybe his death was an accident from being shoved or struck, but one must admit something menacing in Callirrhoe's being pursued by the entire mob. After the execution of the men, how was she regarded? Was she considered bad luck, or did her beauty continue to outweigh negative considerations? Then again, the series of horrible events could have sent her into a temple of Artemis or Athena as a priestess for the rest of her life. [Plutarch, *Love Stories* 4.774–775.]

CALLISTE was a surname of Artemis, under which she was worshipped at Athens and Tegea.
CALLISTO was a companion of Artemis, and some have tried to explain that the two were joined in much the same way as Artemis and Britomartis. Callisto's tomb was the site of a temple of Artemis, and the bear into which Callisto was changed was a symbol of the goddess. This kind of merging of identities was not uncommon in ancient religion, since local heroines assumed almost divine status. Eventually their worship tended to blend into the worship of the major deity with whom they had been associated. [Pausanias 1.29.2, 8.35.7.]

CALLISTO (1) was the daughter of Lycaon, Nycteus, or Ceteus, or she might have been an ordinary nymph. She was also called Megisto or Themisto. She was a companion of Artemis and thereby sworn to chastity. Zeus found her highly desirable and eventually succeeded in sleeping with her, some say in the disguise of Artemis, which raises some interesting speculations. The eternally potent god made her pregnant but made haste to hide the evidence from Hera by changing Callisto into a bear. One wonders how Hera would have decided an Arcadian nymph's pregnancy was the doing of Zeus, but somehow Hera did learn of the deception and had Artemis arrange for Callisto to be killed during a hunt. Artemis had her own reason for being involved. According to one account, she had discovered Callisto's condition while they were bathing together and changed her into a bear, which she then hunted down. Another writer had Hera's revenge take many years—until Arcas, the offspring from the union, grew up. Then Hera turned Callisto into a bear and had Arcas, a hunter, encounter her during the chase. Zeus came along just in time to prevent this urso/matricide by changing bear and son into the constellations Ursa Major and Minor.

An obvious question is whether or not Arcas was born while Callisto was in her bear state. Probably he was, since the whole purpose of her metamorphosis had been to hide her condition. Maybe she resumed human form when she was killed, and delivered the baby at the very instant of her death. Zeus gave Arcas to his one-time lover Maia to bring up. Maia already had a connection with Callisto, since Maia's son Hermes supposedly had fathered Pan by her. One has to doubt this story, since this event would have made Callisto unchaste before Zeus came along and thus cancel Artemis' outrage over the second pregnancy. Even with his bad start in life, Arcas turned out to be quite important. He was the ancestor of the Arcadians; he succeeded Nyctimus in the government of the country, and taught the useful arts to the population. [Apollodorus 3.8.2,9.1,10.2; Ovid, *Metamorphoses* 2.410; Pausanias 8.9.2, 10.9.3; *Homeric Hymn to Hermes* 3; Hesiod, *Theogony* 938; Hyginus, *Poetic Astronomy* 2.1; Scholiast on Theocritus 1.3.]

CALLISTO (2) was a sister of Odysseus. She was also called Phace. [Eustathius on Homer's *Odyssey* 1572; Athenaeus 4.158.]

CALLISTO (3) was a priestess of Athena at Troy at the time of the fall of the city. [Tzetzes, *Posthomerica* 776.]

CALLITHEA was the daughter of Choraeus. She married Atys, son of Manes, king of the Maeonians, and became mother by him of Lydus and Tyrrhenus. Lydus was called the ancestor of the Lydians, and Tyrrhenus led a colony from Lydia into Umbria in Italy and called the new inhabitants Tyrrhenians. [Herodotus 1.7.94; Dionysius of Halicarnassus, *Roman Antiquities* 1.27.]

CALLITHYIA was a daughter of Inachus, the founder of the worship of Hera at Argos, or of Iasus or Peiren. (*See also* CALLIRRHOE 7.)

CALVA, the Bald, was a surname of Venus at Rome. Its meaning has been disputed, but the likeliest explanation is that the temple was dedicated as a monument to the patriotic act of the Roman women during a siege of the Gauls. They were said to have cut off their hair to provide bowstrings for the Roman soldiers. Afterward it became the custom for women to cut off a lock of hair on their wedding day and sacrifice it to Venus Calva. [Persius, *Saturae* 2.10, with the scholiast; Servius on Virgil's *Aeneid* 1.724; Lactantius 1.20.]

CALYBE (1) was a nymph by whom the Trojan king Laomedon became the father of Bucolion, the eldest of his sons. Bucolion fell in love with the nymph Abarbarea and had twin sons by her.

These sons, Aesepus and Pedasus, were killed together in the Trojan War. [Apollodorus 3.12.3; Homer, *Iliad* 6.23.]

CALYBE (2) was a priestess of Juno at Ardea. At the command of Juno, Alecto, one of the Furies, appeared to Turnus in a dream in the guise of the highly respected Calybe. She incited him to fight against Aeneas after his landing in Italy. [Virgil, *Aeneid* 7.419.]

CALYCE (1) was a daughter of Aeolus and Enarete. Her family tree produced some of the greatest heroes and heroines in mythology, since her brothers were Cretheus, Sisyphus, Athamas, Salmoneus, Deion, Magnes, Perieres, and Macareus. She did well in her own right. She married Aethlius, son of Zeus and Protogeneia and grandson of Deucalion. By him she became the mother of the famous Endymion, who was not only the lover of the moon goddess Selene but also king of Elis and ancestor of the Aetolians, Epeians, and Paeonians. By report, she had 50 half-immortal granddaughters by the union of Selene with her sleeping son, but this phenomenon is discussed elsewhere. [Apollodorus 1.7.2,3.5; Pausanias 5.1.2,8.1, 10.31.2.]

CALYCE (2), or Calycia, was the daughter of Hecaton. She was seduced by Poseidon and became the mother of Cycnus. Others called her Harpale or Scamandrodice. Cycnus was carried to full term in secrecy, for Calyce feared her father, and then she exposed the child on the seashore. Shepherds saw a swan descending on him and intervened, calling him Cycnus. He grew up to become king of Colonae in the Troad and married Procleia, a daughter of Laomedon, by whom he became the father of Tenes and Hemithea. Calyce probably never learned what became of him but perhaps hoped his father, Poseidon, would protect him. [Hyginus, *Fables* 157.]

CALYPSO was the famous nymph of the *Odyssey*. Her nativity is uncertain; some make her parents Oceanus and Tethys, others Nereus and Doris, and still others Atlas and Pleione. Of course, there could have been three different Calypsos. One account even calls her a daughter of Helios, which would make her a sister of

Circe, with whom in certain respects she has been sometimes confused. She inhabited the island of Ogygia, somewhere in the extreme western Mediterranean. Some writers have assigned her to the island of Aeaea between Italy and Sicily, and she even had a surname from the island, but this represents one of the points of confusion with Circe, who was said to be the inhabitant of Aeaea.

The wreck of Odysseus' last ship cast him alone on Ogygia, where he was warmly received by Calypso. Her island was an idyllic place, with gardens and forests and fountains. She entertained Odysseus for several years—seven according to Homer—and he might have stayed even longer had the gods not insisted that she allow him to continue his journey homeward. He stayed long enough to have two sons, Nausinous and Nausithous, by her.

The lonely Calypso had promised him eternal youth if he would remain with her. Had he decided to do so, the will of Zeus might have been deflected, but his longing for Ithaca caused him to refuse her offer repeatedly. Eventually Zeus sent Hermes with a command for Calypso to relinquish her gentle spell, and Hermes helped Odysseus construct a raft. It must have been painful for her to watch the days narrow down until his departure from her and their children. Finally he finished the raft, and had a favorable wind and current. But he waited one more day, and some have pondered about his delay. Perhaps he wanted to prolong the leave-taking from a woman who had shown him great kindness and given him sons. One irreverent opinion was that perhaps he was taking "one for the road." Whatever the reason, he set off the next day and was seen by Calypso no more.

Some accounts gave Calypso additional sons by Odysseus—Telegonus and Auson—but again this represented confusion with Circe. The circumstances were, in fact, similar: an enchanted island with an immortal woman loving him and producing children with him. The main difference was in the nature of the women. Circe was an enchantress from a family that included Pasiphae, Medea, and Phaedra, women with less than savory reputations. She changed Odysseus' men into swine and used spells to hold him on her island. Calypso was like the other, brighter

side of a coin, and indeed this might have been the contrast Homer sought in placing them close together in Odysseus' series of adventures. [Hesiod, *Theogony* 359,1017; Apollodorus 1.2.7; Homer, *Odyssey* 1.50, 4.28, 7.254, 12.127,260; Eustathius on Homer's *Odyssey* 1796; Pomponius Mela 2.7; Propertius 3.10.31; Tzetzes on Lycophron 44,696.]

CAMBYSE was the wife of Locrus and mother of Locrus, the ancestor of the Ozolian Locrians. She is usually called CABYA. [Plutarch, *Greek Questions* 15.]

CAMEIRA (1) was one of the DANAIDES. According to one writer, when Danaus stopped at Rhodes, his daughters built the temple of Athena at Lindus. Later Tlepolemus, son of Heracles, built the towns of Cameirus, Lindus, and Ialysus and named them for three of the Danaides. According to another writer, three of the daughters of Danaus died while at Rhodes. Presumably the towns might have been named for them. [Herodotus 2.234; Diodorus Siculus 5.58; Strabo 14.2.8.]

CAMEIRA (2) was a daughter of Pandareos and sister to Clytia. Pandareos, son of Merops of Miletus, stole the golden dog Hephaestus had made for the temple of Zeus in Crete and left in the keeping of Tantalus. The god retrieved the dog, and punished Tantalus and Pandareos. In fact, Pandareos perished in Sicily with his wife, Harmathoe; thus, the two daughters were orphaned. The goddesses of Olympus for some reason took them as a collective enterprise and did everything possible to make them happy. Hera gave them beauty and wisdom above all women; Artemis gave them dignity; Athena gave them skill in arts. When Aphrodite went to Olympus to prepare for their nuptials, the Harpies snatched up the women, and they were never seen again. Some say they were carried to the Erinyes, who made them suffer for the sin of their father.

This strange story seems rather pointless, and again it would appear that the gods vacillated between compassion and cruelty in an arbitrary manner. Why did the goddesses go to all this trouble over these particular orphans? There had been many before them just as deserving. Did Zeus suspect they had collaborated with their father in the unforgivable theft? Or was their abduction by the Harpies a warning from Zeus that punishment for a crime did not end with the perpetrators but included their families as well? The daughters are also called Merope and Cleodora. [Homer, *Odyssey* 19.518, 20.67; Eustathius on Homer's *Odyssey* 1875.]

CAMENAE were Roman divinities whose name was connected with *carmen* (oracle or prophecy). They were prophetic nymphs possibly introduced into Italy from Arcadia. The various names assigned to them were Antevorta, Postvorta, Prorsa, Proversa, and Carmenta. Carmenta, a healing divinity, had a temple at the foot of the Capitoline Hill. Aegeria was also called one of the Camenae. They were loosely equivalent to the Muses. They were also identified with the Molae, divinities who presided over mills. Plutarch considered Tacita, the Silent, as one of the Camenae and said that her worship was introduced at Rome by Numa, who considered her the most important of the Camenae. [Plutarch, *Numa* 8; Gellius 13.22; Servius on Virgil's *Aeneid* 8.51,336; Dionysius of Halicarnassus, *Roman Antiquities* 1.15,32.]

CAMILLA was a daughter of Metabus, king of the Volscian town of Privernum. Her father was expelled by his subjects and fled with the infant Camilla. On reaching the Amasenus River he realized he could not swim across with the baby, so he lashed her to his spear and hurled it across the river. He then swam across and found her uninjured. He had her suckled by a mare and brought her up dedicated to the service of Diana. She was swift-footed and devoted to the chase and warlike activities. In the war between Aeneas and Turnus she was allied with Turnus and was slain by Aruns. In revenge Diana sent Opis to kill Aruns and rescue the body of Camilla. [Virgil, *Aeneid* 7.803, 11.432,543,558,648; Hyginus, *Fables* 252; Dionysius of Halicarnassus, *Roman Antiquities* 2.21.]

CAMPE was the jailor of Tartarus. When the battle between the Olympian gods and the Titans had lasted for ten years, Gaea, his grand-mother the earth, promised Zeus victory if he would free the Cyclopes and the Hecatoncheires, the hundred-handed giants, from Tartarus. Zeus had to kill Campe in order to do this. The Cyclopes then provided him with thunderbolts, which turned the tide in this cosmic clash. [Apollodorus 1.2.1; Nonnos, *Dionysiaca* 18.237; Diodorus Siculus 3.72; Ovid, *Fasti* 3.799.]

CANACE was a daughter of Aeolus and Enarete, and from her father she was sometimes called Aeolis. Her distinguished brothers were Cretheus, Sisyphus, Athamas, Salmoneus, Deion, Magnes, Perieres, and Macareus. Her sisters were Alcyone, Peisidice, and Calyce. Nearly all her brothers and sisters initiated or were involved in royal houses that branched off the main Aeolian stem. Through union with Poseidon, Canace produced Aloeus, Epopeus, and Triopas, who were famous in Boeotian, Sicyonian, and Carian protohistory, respectively.

But Canace is mainly known for her incestuous liaison with her brother Macareus. She was strongly attracted to him and finally seduced him. She became pregnant but managed to conceal this from everyone. The baby was born, and there was an attempt to smuggle it out of the palace. Unfortunately it cried out, and the plan was thwarted. Aeolus threw the baby to the dogs and sent a sword to Canace. She killed herself, as did Macareus.

These two accounts about Canace offer a real puzzle, particularly when we learn that Macareus was reported to be the father of Amphissa. The usual reaction is to regard such an incestuous relationship as the product of youthful passion and inexperience. In this case, however, both brother and sister were already parents, unless we can believe that neither committed suicide. Assuming they were already parents puts a different light on the affair. There is no doubt that Canace was strikingly beautiful. Why else would Poseidon have slept with her often enough to produce three sons? She was certainly experienced, so much so, perhaps, that her physical needs sought satisfaction beyond the intermittent visits from the god. One suspects that Macareus was somewhat younger than Canace and that, in spite of his alleged affair, which produced a daughter, he was probably naive. Possibly the affair was a quick coupling with a nymph while he was on a hunting trip. Whatever the situation, the two began to engage in sexual relations, although perhaps their liaison could have been a one-time experience. When Canace realized she was pregnant, she had a perfect opportunity to pass the child off as another fathered by Poseidon. Apparently she had not shared the information with Macareus, since he probably would have killed himself sooner or fled the country.

It can be seen that the story has many twists and turns. Maybe the best scenario would be the young couple's refusal to commit suicide. After a tryst or two with the resulting pregnancy and birth, they tried to smuggle out the baby but failed. Macareus might have left word that he drowned himself, and Canace could simply have fled. Afterward they both went separate ways, with Canace becoming Poseidon's lover. If this were the situation, it would make better sense that Canace could not represent the child as being that of Poseidon. It is also more likely that frightened teenagers would break down and confess their guilt rather than put the blame on, say, a neighborhood acquaintance. [Apollodorus 1.7.3; Hyginus, *Fables* 238,242; Ovid, *Heroides* 11.]

CANENS, daughter of Venilia and Janus, was the wife of Picus, a Latin prophetic divinity. In some traditions he was called the first king of Italy. He was a soothsayer and used a woodpecker in his augury. The fate of Canens is not known, but Picus eventually fell in love with Pomona, the goddess of fruit. He in turn was loved by Circe, who changed him into a woodpecker for not reciprocating her love. As a woodpecker he retained his prophetic powers, and the woodpecker became sacred to Mars. [Ovid, *Metamorphoses* 14.320–346, *Fasti* 3.37,291; Virgil, *Aeneid* 7.48,190; Plutarch, *Roman Questions* 21; Tzetzes on Lycophron 1232.]

CAPHEIRA was one of the OCEANIDES. With the nymphs Telchiniae she was entrusted by Rhea with the bringing up of Poseidon. [Diodorus Siculus 5.55; Pausanias 9.19.1.]

CAPTA, or Capita, was a surname of Minerva at Rome. Under this name she had a chapel at the foot of the Caelian Hill. The origin of the name is uncertain. It could mean "superlative," or perhaps it could have to do with the goddess springing forth from the head of her father. [Ovid, *Fasti* 3.837.]

CARDEA was a Roman divinity who protected the hinges of doors (*cardines*). She was loved by Janus, the god of thresholds; when she returned his love, he gave into her keeping the hinges of doors, with the extended power of keeping evil spirits from entering houses. She was particularly invoked to protect children in their cradles against formidable night birds—witches in disguise—who plucked them from their beds and sucked out their blood. Cardea used white thorn and other magic substances in performing this office. She initiated this special power first in the case of Procas, prince of Alba. [Ovid, *Fasti* 6.101; Tertullian, *De Corona Militis* 13.]

CARME was a daughter of Eubulus, son of Carmanor. She became by Zeus the mother of Britomartis. Britomartis was the Cretan nymph later immortalized by Artemis. [Pausanias 2.30.2.]

CARMENTA, or Carmentis, was one of the CAMENAE. She was a healing divinity with a temple at the foot of the Capitoline Hill and altars near the Porta Carmentalis. Some traditions said her original name was Nicostrate and that her prophetic powers earned her the name of Carmenta. Other names by which she was known were Themis, Tiburtis, and Timandra. She supposedly had set out from Arcadia in Greece with Euander, her son by Hermes. They had fled to Italy because of a foolhardy attempt Euander had made on Hermes' life at the instigation of his mother. In Italy Carmenta lost no time in going into the oracle business. Euander killed her at the age of 110. Nobody has given a reason for this; perhaps in some curious way it was a means of being immortalized. In fact, thereafter Carmenta received divine honors. She was considered the inventor of 15 characters of the Roman alphabet from the Greek alphabet Euander brought from Arcadia. Antevorta and Postvorta were said to be her companions, although some considered them attributes of

Carmenta. [Servius on Virgil's *Aeneid* 8.51,336; Dionysius of Halicarnassus, *Roman Antiquities* 1.15,31,32; Hyginus, *Fables* 277; Gellius 16.16; Ovid, *Fasti* 1.633; Macrobius, *Saturnalia* 1.7.]

CARNA was a Roman divinity who protected the physical well-being of man. She presided over the vital organs. Junius Brutus dedicated a sanctuary to her on the Caelian Hill. A festival, the Calendae Fabrariae, was celebrated to her on June 1, and during this time beans and bacon were offered to her. [Macrobius, *Saturnalia* 1.12.]

CARPO was one of the two HORAE at Athens. She was the Hora of autumn, while Thallo was the Hora of spring. They were worshipped from very early times. The two Horae had a temple at Athens, which contained an altar of Dionysus Orthus; they were likewise worshipped at Argos, Corinth, and Olympia. In works of art the Horae were represented as blooming maidens, carrying the different products of the seasons. Hyginus listed Carpo among ten Horae. [Athenaeus 2.38; Pausanias 5.15.3; Hyginus, *Fables* 183.]

CARPOPHORI, the Fruit-bearers, was a surname of Demeter and Kore, under which they were worshipped at Tegea. Demeter Carpophoros appears to have been worshipped in Paros also. [Pausanias 8.53.3.]

CARYA was a daughter of Dion, a king of Laconia, and Iphitea, a daughter of Prognaus. Iphitea had offered hospitality to Apollo, who rewarded her by giving her three daughters—Orphe, Lyco, and Carya—the gift of prophecy. He did this with the conditions that they should not betray the gods or seek to know forbidden things. This agreement worked very well until Dionysus paid a visit to the house of Dion. He too was hospitably received, and he and Carya fell in love. He returned later to consummate the affair, but Lyco and Orphe guarded their sister. Dionysus told them they were betraying the gods; when they persisted in protecting their sister (perhaps with good reason), they went mad and climbed to the heights of Mount Taygetus. Here they were changed into rocks. Carya, however, was metamorphosed into a nut tree. Artemis

informed the Laconians of this happening, and they dedicated a temple to Artemis Caryatis. [Servius on Virgil's *Eclogues* 8.30; Pausanias 3.10.8, 4.16.5.]

CARYATIS was a surname of Artemis derived from the town of Caryae in Laconia. The statue of the goddess stood in the open air, and maidens celebrated a festival to her every year with dances. Caryatides, the name of the female statues used as columns, is probably derived from this name as well as the festival Carya. [Pausanias 3.10.8, 4.16.5; Servius on Virgil's *Eclogues* 8.30.] (*See also* CARYA.)

CASPERIA was the second wife of Rhoetus, king of the Marrubians in Italy. Anchemolus was her stepson, and he was reported to have dishonored her. This is another one of those tantalizingly abbreviated accounts, and "dishonored" could mean a number of things. Did she seduce him? Did he rape her? Did she want him and he refused her? Whatever happened, he had to flee from the kingdom to the realm of Daunus, the Rutulian king. [Servius on Virgil's *Aeneid* 10.388.]

CASSANDRA (1) was a daughter of Priam and Hecuba. She was also called Alexandra. She was very beautiful, but her family and the people of Troy considered her a little unbalanced. This came about because of her gift of prophecy. When she was a child, she and her brother Helenus were left overnight in the temple of the Thymbraean Apollo. No reason has been advanced for this night in the temple; perhaps it was a ritual routinely performed by everyone. When their parents looked in on them the next morning, the children were entwined with serpents, which flicked their tongues into the children's ears. This enabled Cassandra and Helenus to divine the future. After Cassandra grew up, she again spent a night in the temple. This time the god appeared and tried to get her to yield to his desire, but she refused. For this affront to him he punished her by causing her prophecies, though true, to be disbelieved. This curse failed to be effective on only one occasion. When Paris appeared as an adult at the court of Priam, Cassandra declared him her brother. It had been accepted by everyone that he had died in infancy from being exposed.

After the war began, Cassandra continued to predict the calamities in store for the Trojans. Nobody believed her but, perhaps deciding she was bad for the war effort, Priam concealed her in a locked chamber, where she was guarded like a madwoman. Mad though she might have been considered, she was still highly regarded for her beauty. During the war, both Othryoneus of Cabesus and Coroebus, son of Mydon, asked for her hand, but both were killed in the war. When Telephus reinforced the Trojans with an army of Mysians, Priam betrothed Cassandra to his son Eurypylus. He was also killed. Cassandra's curse of not being heeded came to a climax when she announced there were men in the wooden horse. Only Laocoon believed her, but he was soon silenced, and this seemed to confirm that Cassandra was merely raving again.

It probably would not have mattered whether or not she was married to one of her unfortunate suitors, as things turned out. At the taking of Troy, she fled to the temple of Athena and embraced the statue of the goddess as a suppliant. The Lesser Ajax found her there and, violating one of the most powerful interdicts in ancient religion, dragged her from the temple. Some said he raped her in the sanctuary. She never learned that he paid the supreme price for his great violence and short pleasure.

When the spoils of Troy were allotted, Cassandra was given to Agamemnon. Some said he had spread the report that Ajax had raped her so he could have her to himself. Others say he tried to save Polyxena from being sacrificed on Achilles' grave, again to ingratiate himself with Cassandra. He carried her with him to Mycenae, but she was scarcely in his hands before he forced her into sexual relations. As a result of this union she became pregnant and bore twins— Teledamus and Pelops. This poses a question. The trip to Mycenae could not in Agamemnon's case have taken a great deal of time since, unlike several of the other Greeks, he had no difficulties in reaching home. Therefore, he must have stayed in Troy for a few more months as leader of the Greek army of occupation. Even adding a month or so for the voyage, he must have taken the better part of a year in getting to Mycenae.

There is the possibility that the twins were born on shipboard or even after arrival in Mycenae, but all accounts seem to suggest that Cassandra arrived with the babies.

Agamemnon, expecting to arrive home in glory, was murdered by Clytemnestra and her lover, Aegisthus, shortly after his arrival. Cassandra was murdered by Clytemnestra, and the twins were killed by Aegisthus. Agamemnon's bringing Cassandra back with him is repeated often as a principal motive for the slaughter, but Clytemnestra had reasons enough without Cassandra. Some say that the murders took place at Amyclae, although nobody gives a reason. This claim allowed the Amyclaeans to say that Cassandra was buried there. She also had a statue at Amyclae and at Leuctra in Laconia. Mycenae, however, had the best reason for saying her tomb was there, and Schliemann, the archaeologist, was certain of this when he found the remains of a woman and two infants in one of the circle graves at Mycenae.

The story of Cassandra is one of the most poignant of all the stories of women in the Trojan War. Possessing the divine gift of prophecy carried with it an obligation, and the principal responsibility would have been the protection of homeland and the whole Trojan race. Not being taken seriously would have been frustrating and heartbreaking enough under any circumstances, but with the safety of a whole nation at stake, Cassandra must occasionally have approached the borders of the insanity with which she was labeled. It is not difficult to think of her as a beautiful but disheveled young woman, wild-eyed and shrill. It is not too much of an exaggeration to compare her with modern-day fanatics who claim the world is ending on such and such a day. We cannot be sure that, along with everything else, she might not have developed a reputation for being obnoxious with her superior knowledge. The tendency is to regard her as a victim of circumstances, someone severely wronged by men and gods alike. Her tragedy was knowing the unhappy truth and revealing it, something highly unwelcome then as now. [Pausanias 2.16.5, 3.19.5,26.3, 10.27.1; Hyginus, *Fables* 93; Aeschylus, *Agamemnon* 1207,1260; Apollodorus 3.12.5; Homer, *Iliad* 24.700, 13.363; Eustathius on Homer's *Iliad*

663; Homer, *Odyssey* 11.420; Virgil, *Aeneid* 2.344,425; Servius on Virgil's *Aeneid* 2.247.]

CASSANDRA (2), according to some, was a daughter of Iobates, king of Lycia. Most accounts call his daughter ANTICLEIA. [Scholiast on Homer's *Iliad* 6.155.]

CASSIEPEIA, or Cassiopeia, was the daughter of Arabus, eponymic founder of Arabia, and wife of Cepheus. They ruled in Ethiopia at the time Perseus went on his perilous mission to fetch the head of Medusa. She was also called the mother of Phineus by Phoenix, the mother of Libya and Lysianassa by Epaphus, and the mother of Atymnius by Zeus. The wife of Cepheus has sometimes been called Iope. It is difficult to fit these genealogies together, and perhaps the effort is uncalled for since other, more appropriate parentage is assigned to the offspring in question. Iope was a daughter of Aeolus, and little evidence can be supplied that transports her to north Africa. She has been confused probably with a shortened form of Cassiopeia.

Cassiepeia and Cepheus were parents of the exceedingly beautiful Andromeda. So beautiful was the girl that her mother boasted her daughter's beauty excelled that of the Nereids. Cassiepeia should have known better than to disparage anyone with any degree of divinity. The Nereids went directly to Poseidon and decried this insult. He promptly sent a sea monster to ravage the seacoast and through oracles announced that sacrifice of Andromeda was the only way to get rid of the monster.

Andromeda was chained to a rock (some say at Joppa) and left for the monster. Perseus came along in time to turn the monster into stone by giving it a glimpse of Medusa's snaky head. Cepheus and Cassiepeia only grudgingly welcomed Perseus as their son-in-law, since Phineus, the brother of Cepheus, had a prior claim to her hand. Cassiepeia should have considered that without Perseus there would have been no Andromeda to quarrel over. While the wedding was in progress, Phineus appeared with an army. Perseus turned the army to stone and disabled Phineus. Perseus and Andromeda stayed long enough in Ethiopia to leave an heir to the throne, Perses; then they proceeded back to Seriphos and Argos.

Cepheus and Cassiepeia became constellations, and Andromeda in recent times became a nebula. At certain times of the year the vain Cassiepeia turns upside down in the sky. [Aratus, *Phenomena* 187; Apollodorus 1.9.21, 2.1.3–5, 3.1.2; Stephanus Byzantium, "Iope"; Scholiast on Apollonius Rhodius 2.178; Manilius, *Astronomica* 1.355.]

CASSIPHONE was the daughter of Odysseus by Circe and sister of Telegonus. The sister and brother grew up on the enchanted island and probably heard stories of their illustrious father from Circe, who still had fond memories of him. Finally Circe sent Telegonus in search of him. Telegonus was shipwrecked on the coast of Ithaca and began to plunder the fields in search of food. Odysseus and Telemachus went out to confront the stranger, and Telegonus thrust a spear through his father before he knew who he was. Ever the guardian of Odysseus, Athena commanded the two half-brothers to take the body to Aeaea. Accompanied by Penelope they did so, and buried their father on the island. Some say Circe restored Odysseus to life, but if so he did not live very long. Cassiphone married Telemachus, her half-brother, and Telegonus married Penelope, his stepmother. At some later time Telemachus quarreled with Circe and killed her (a remarkable feat, considering that Circe was supposed to be immortal), and Cassiphone in turn killed him. But these violent actions occurred after Cassiphone had borne a daughter to her brother by the name of Roma. Roma ended up in Italy and was, among others, married to Aeneas. [Tzetzes on Lycophron 795,808; Servius on Virgil's *Aeneid* 1.273, 10.167.]

CASSOTIS was a Parnassian nymph from whom was derived the name of the spring Cassotis at Delphi. The water of this spring gave the priestess the power of prophecy. [Pausanias 10.24.5.]

CASTALIA was a daughter of the Achelous River. She was pursued by Apollo and threw herself into a spring at Delphi on the slope of Mount Parnassus. The spring was named for her, and few people have ever conceived of it as a natural monument to virtue preserved.

[Pausanias 10.8.5; Lutatius on Statius' *Thebaid* 1.697.]

CASTALIDES were the Castalian nymphs, by which name the Muses are sometimes designated. The Castalian spring was sacred to them. [Theocritus, *Idylls* 7.148; Martial 7.11.]

CEGLUSE was, according to some, the mother of the river-god Asopus by Poseidon. Asopus was married to Metope, the daughter of the river-god Ladon, by whom he had two sons and twelve or, according to some, twenty daughters. Several of these daughters were carried off by gods. Asopus was usually called a son of Oceanus and Tethys.

CELAENO (1) was one of the PLEIADES. By Poseidon she was the mother of Lycus and Eurypylus. According to some, she was mother of Lycus and Chimaereus by Prometheus, who was considered to be her husband. Others call her also mother of Triton, but that distinction is usually Amphitrite's. Nothing is known of Lycus except that he was transferred by his father to the Isles of the Blessed. Eurypylus was among the heroes of Hyria. He went to Cyrene in Libya, where he became connected with the Argonauts. It was he who gave Euphemus a clod of earth when the Argonauts passed through Lake Tritonis. Possession of this clod later established the right to rule over Libya. Eurypylus was married to Sterope, the daughter of Helios, by whom he became the father of Lycaon and Leucippus. [Apollodorus 3.10.1; Ovid, *Heroides* 19.135; Scholiast on Apollonius Rhodius 4.1561; Tzetzes on Lycophron 132,902.]

CELAENO (2) was named as one of the HARPIES. [Apollodorus 1.9.21; Servius on Virgil's *Aeneid* 3.209; Hyginus, *Fables: Preface* 14.]

CELAENO (3) was a daughter of Erginus, son of Poseidon, and mother of Euphemus, Lycus, and Nycteus by Poseidon. The mother of Euphemus is usually called EUROPA, daughter of Tityus. The mother of Lycus and Nycteus is usually called CLONIA. [Hyginus, *Fables* 157.]

CELAENO (4) was a daughter of Hyamus. She was mother of Delphus by Apollo, who was also her great-grandfather, thus making Delphus both son and great-great-grandson of Apollo. Delphi received its name from Delphus, and his son Pythes supposedly gave his name to the oracle. Celaeno was called Melaena by some. [Pausanias 10.6.2,3.]

CELAENO (5) was one of the DANAIDES. According to Apollodorus, her mother was Crino, and she married Hyperbius, son of Aegyptus. According to Hyginus, she was married to Aristonous. [Apollodorus 2.1.5; Hyginus, *Fables* 170.]

CELAENO (6) was one of the AMAZONS. In the battle with Heracles, she, Eurybia, and Phoebe attacked the hero together. They were companions of Artemis in the hunt and invariably struck their prey, but they did not even graze their single target. Heracles cut them down as they stood as one, shoulder to shoulder. [Diodorus Siculus 4.16.]

CELEDONES, the Soothing Goddesses, were frequently represented by the ancients in works of art and were believed to be endowed, like the Sirens, with a magic power of song. Hephaestus was said to have made their golden images on the ceiling of the temple at Delphi. [Athenaeus 7.290; Philostratus, *Life of Apollonius of Tyana* 6.11; Pindar, *Fragments* 25.568.]

CENCHREIS was the wife of Cinyras of Cyprus. Their daughter was Smyrna, or Myrrha. Cenchreis was very proud of her daughter and made the mistake of bragging that Smyrna excelled Aphrodite in beauty. Aphrodite caused Smyrna to fall in love with her father and crawl into his bed. In the belief that she was one of his mistresses, he had intercourse with her and impregnated her. When the truth was learned, he pursued her with a sword until she was changed into a myrrh tree. Cinyras split the tree, and Adonis came forth. Cenchreis was both grandmother and stepmother to him. It is not known whether or not she knew of the incestuous affair or the birth of Adonis. She was also called Metharme or Oreithyia. [Ovid, *Metamorphoses* 10.435; Hyginus, *Fables* 58; Lactantius 10.9.]

CENCHRIS was one of the PIERIDES.

CEPHISSO was one of three MUSES originally recognized at Delphi. The other two were Apollonis and Borysthenis. They were daughters of Apollo. [Tzetzes on Hesiod's *Works and Days* 6.]

CER was the personification of the inevitability of death. In the plural—Ceres—the meaning may refer to the various forms that dying can take. In Homer the word in both singular and plural was not usually a proper noun. With some writers the Ceres assumed a more definite form. They were said to be daughters of Nyx and sisters of the Moirae, or Fates, Thanatos, Hypnos, Oneirata, and similar beings. They were fearful in appearance, formidable, dark, and hateful. During battles they wandered about with Eris and Cydoimes in bloody garments and quarreled over the wounded and dead. They also avenged the crimes of men, and it is not clear where their role in this ended and where that of the Erinyes began. They even were viewed sometimes as the personification of epidemic diseases. It appears that Cer or the Ceres were vague entities who shared parts of the attributes of the Fates, the Furies, Discord, and Death. [Hyginus, *Fables* 211,217,756,904; Cicero, *On the Nature of the Gods* 3.17; Homer, *Iliad* 2.302,859, 3.454, 12.326, 18.535; Aeschylus, *Seven against Thebes* 1055.]

CERCEIS was one of the OCEANIDES. [Hesiod, *Theogony* 353.]

CERCYRA, or Corcyra, was a daughter of the Phliasian river-god Asopus and the Arcadian nymph Metope. The island of Corcyra (Corfu) was named for her after she bore to Poseidon a son, Phaeax, on the island. From Phaeax the Phaeacians derived their name. The famous king of Corcyra (called Scheria in the *Odyssey*) was Alcinous, a son of Phaeax. [Diodorus Siculus 4.72; Stephanus Byzantium, "Phaiax"; Conon, *Narrations* 3.]

CERDO, according to some, was the wife of Phoroneus. Others called her Teledice or PEITHO. [Pausanias 2.21.1.]

CERES was the Roman equivalent of DE-METER. The Romans received her worship from Greece via Sicily. It is somewhat curious that her Greek name was not adopted as well, since it was very close in sound and meaning in both places. It is likely that Ceres was an extinct goddess, perhaps with very similar attributes, from Etruscan times.

The first temple of Ceres at Rome was dedicated in 496 B.C. for the purpose of averting a famine. The worship of Ceres soon assumed considerable political importance, and gifts of property were assigned to her temple. Senatorial decrees were deposited there, as well, for public inspection.

Worshipped in conjunction with Ceres were Liber and Libera, divinities presiding over the vine and fertility of the fields and called children of Ceres. They could rather easily be equated with Persephone and Dionysus (particularly in his mystic identification with Iacchus). The Greek goddess Hera was occasionally identified with her, as was the Sabine divinity Vacuna. [Valerius Maximus 1.1.1; Dionysius of Halicarnassus, *Roman Antiquities* 6.17,79,89; Tacitus, *Annals* 2.49; Servius on Virgil's *Aeneid* 2.325; Pliny, *Natural History* 34.4.59; Livy 2.41; Cicero, *On the Nature of the Gods* 2.24.]

CEROESSA was a daughter of Zeus by Io. She was born where Byzantium (modern Istanbul) was later built. By the time Io, metamorphosed by Zeus into a cow, reached this point she must have been traveling for a really considerable time, having moved at a plodding pace from Argos up through mainland Greece, through Macedonia and Thrace, northward around the Euxine to the Caucasus Mountains, and then through Amazon country and along the southern Euxine coast. Zeus must have impregnated her in her metamorphosed form, probably, but not necessarily, assuming the form of a bull to accomplish this. This means also that Ceroessa was delivered by a cow. This circumstance also explains why she was brought up by a nymph of the area rather than by Io, who probably had to move along to fulfill her destiny. Ceroessa was visited by Poseidon and bore Byzas, the founder of Byzantium. [Stephanus Byzantium, "Byzantion"; Diodorus Siculus 4.49.]

CERTHE was one of the THESPIADES, daughter of Thespius and Megamede. By Heracles she became the mother of Iobes. [Apollodorus 2.7.8.]

CETO (1) was a daughter of Pontus and Gaea. She was a sister of Thaumas, Phorcys, Nereus, and Eurybia. Ceto was probably monstrous in appearance, judging from her offspring by her brother Phorcys. These were the Graeae and Gorgons, familiar through the myth of Perseus, as well as the Hesperian dragon Ladon. Some have called her and Phorcys parents of the Hesperides, but these handsome women were more likely the daughters of Atlas and Hesperia, as usually stated. [Hesiod, *Theogony* 237,270; Apollodorus 1.2.6.]

CETO (2) was one of the NEREIDES. [Apollodorus 1.2.7.]

CHALCIOECOS, the Goddess of the Bronze House, was a surname of Athena at Sparta. It was derived from the chief building on the acropolis, the temple of Athena Chalcioecos. This temple was said to have been begun by Tyndareus but not completed until many years later. It was covered with plates of bronze on which were represented in relief the labors of Heracles, the exploits of the Dioscuri, Hephaestus releasing Hera from her chains, and other scenes from mythology. A festival held in honor of the goddess was called Chalcioecia. [Pausanias 3.17.3, 10.5.5; Polybius 4.22.]

CHALCIOPE (1) was a daughter of Rhexenor. She was the second wife of Aegeus and, like the first wife, unable to bear a child to him. Nothing further is known of Chalciope or her father, but she serves an important purpose. She lends credibility to the claim that Poseidon was the father of Theseus. Aegeus was almost certainly sterile, being unable to produce heirs by his first two wives and fathering no children after the event of Theseus' birth. [Apollodorus 3.15.6; Athenaeus 13.556.]

CHALCIOPE (2) was the daughter of Eurypylus. He was a son of Poseidon and Astypalaea, and king of the Meropes on the island of Cos. When Heracles and Telamon landed there on their return from Troy, Heracles fell in love with Chalciope. When Eurypylus refused to give her up, Heracles killed him. As in similar cases of slaughter and seizure by Heracles, we do not know the circumstances. Unless her father had been cruel to her or unless she was attracted to Heracles to the extent that she would surrender everything, she must have been miserably unhappy to have to yield physically to a man who had just slain her father. She would have been unhappier still if she had known that Heracles and Telamon were lovers. Since Telamon was newly occupied with Hesione of Troy, whom he had received as booty from Heracles, there was no suggestion of such a relationship. Chalciope became by Heracles the mother of Thessalus. It seems evident that once his appetite was satisfied, Heracles left Chalciope on Cos and sailed away. Thessalus grew up to occupy the throne, and he sent two sons to the Trojan War. After the war they settled in the country they called Thessaly after their father. [Apollodorus 2.7.8; Homer, *Iliad* 2.676, 14.250, 15.25; Scholiast on Pindar's *Nemean Odes* 4.40.]

CHALCIOPE (3), sometimes called Iophossa, was a daughter of Aeetes, king of Colchis, and Idyia. She was the sister of Medea and half-sister of Absyrtus. She was a princess at the royal court when the young Phrixus flew in from Thessaly on the ram with the golden fleece. He was adopted by Aeetes and grew to manhood in the palace. He married Chalciope, who bore him five sons—Argus, Melas, Phrontis, Cytissorus, and Presbon (others call the sons Autolycus, Phronius, Demoleon or Deileon, and Phlogius). The brothers joined Heracles in his expedition against the Amazons. Deileon and Phlogius got lost and lived at Sinope until they joined the Argonauts and thus returned home. Melas became the father of Hyperes, for whom a famous fountain at Pherae was named. Cytissorus traveled to Halus in Thessaly in time to rescue his grandfather Athamas from being sacrificed to the gods for his accumulated sins. Phrixus died in old age at Colchis, although some said he was murdered by Aeetes in response to an oracle. Still others said he returned to the country of the Minyans, where he was born.

There is no record that Chalciope was tainted with the evil genetic strain that ran through her family. Like his brother, Perses, and his sisters, Circe and Pasiphae, Aeetes was touched with sinister enchantment. Medea was a veritable sorceress, skilled in poisons and lacking in compassion when anyone stood in her way. One can only speculate about the relationship between Chalciope and Medea, and how Chalciope reacted to the Argonauts and Medea's treasonable support of them. It is possible that one or two of her sons went in pursuit of the Argonauts only to return with the dismembered parts of their uncle Absyrtus. [Apollonius Rhodius 2.955, 1115,1151–1158; Apollodorus 1.9.1,28; Hyginus, *Fables* 3.14; Valerius Flaccus 5.115; Scholiast on Pindar's *Pythian Odes* 4.221; Pausanias 9.34.5.]

CHALCIOPE (4) was the daughter of Phalerus. He was a son of Alcon, son of Erechtheus, and one of the Argonauts. He founded the town of Gyrton in Thessaly; later he migrated from Attica to Chalcis in Euboea, taking Chalciope with him. His father demanded that he be sent back, but the Chalcidians would not let him return. This brief announcement begs for more details, but that is all we have. We do know that the port of Phalerum (Faliro) near Athens derived its name from Phalerus and that an altar was dedicated to him there. Of Chalciope we know nothing else whatsoever. [Pausanias 1.1.4; Orphica, *Argonautica* 144; Scholiast on Apollonius Rhodius 1.97.]

CHALCIOPE (5) was the wife of Thessalus, son of Heracles and Chalciope (2). By him she was the mother of Antiphus and Pheidippus. The brothers joined the Greeks with 30 ships and commanded the men of Carpathos, Casus, Cos, and other islands. They returned intact from the war and migrated to the country they called Thessaly after their father. There is no record of what happened to their parents. [Homer, *Iliad* 2.675–679; Apollodorus 2.7.8.]

CHALCIS was one of the daughters of the river-god Asopus and Metope. The town of Chalcis in Euboea derived its name from her. According to some, she was the mother of the Corybantes; the

Curetes of Euboea, the earliest inhabitants of Chalcis, were somehow associated with them. [Eustathius on Homer's *Iliad* 279; Scholiast on Homer's *Iliad* 14.291; Strabo 10.1.9.]

CHALCOMEDUSA was the wife of Arceisius, son of Zeus and Euryodeia, or of Cephalus and a bear. If Chalcomedusa indeed had a bear for a mother-in-law, she was not alone (Callisto was also changed into a bear). Chalcomedusa's chief distinction, though, was being the mother of Laertes, He anticipated the glory of his son Odysseus by conquering Nericum while still in his teens and then participating in both the Calydonian boar hunt and the Argonaut. [Homer, *Odyssey* 4.755, 14.182, 16.118, 24.270; Eustathius on Homer's *Odyssey* 1796,1961; Apollodorus 1.9.16; Ovid, *Metamorphoses* 13.145; Hyginus, *Fables* 189.]

CHALINITIS, Horse-Bridler, was a surname of Athena, under which she had a temple at Corinth. It was here that she helped Bellerophon bridle Pegasus. The name could mean she bridled the horse, or it could have reference to Athena as inventor of the bridle. [Pausanias 2.4.1.]

CHAMYNE was a surname of Demeter at Olympia. Some derived the name from *chanein*, meaning a gaping of the earth to receive the chariot of Hades during the abduction of Persephone. More probably it had reference to Chamynus, a Pisan who opposed Pantaleon, despot at Pisa, and was killed by him. From his property a sanctuary was built to Demeter. [Pausanias 6.21.1.]

CHAOS was the vacant and unfathomable abyss preceding creation of the world. Out of this emptiness all things eventually arose, including gods and men. Some described Chaos as a confused mass containing the elements of all things finally formed from it. It is difficult to conceive of Chaos as having gender, but apparently Hesiod thought this infinite nothingness needed a sex in order to produce offspring, and he called Chaos female. It was perhaps easier for him to believe that such children as Nyx (Night) and Erebus (Impenetrable Darkness) emerged from a womb, even though it was unfertilized and cosmic in dimension. Some cosmologies included Eros and Gaea as born from Chaos. [Hesiod, *Theogony* 116,117,120,123,125; Ovid, *Metamorphoses* 1.1.]

CHARIBOEA, sometimes called Curissia or Periboea, was one of the two great sea serpents that swam to land to crush Laocoon and his sons. The other serpent was Porcis. Sent by Apollo, they came from the direction of Tenedos and the Calydnian Islands. Laocoon, a priest of Apollo, had warned of Troy's approaching doom and had thrown a spear into the wooden horse. Apollo did not send the snakes because of Laocoon's disagreement with the prevailing opinion but rather because Laocoon had once defiled the god's temple by having sexual intercourse in sight of the altar. The serpents did not confine themselves to Laocoon; they also crushed to death his sons Antiphas and Thymbraeus. The creatures then crawled to the citadel; one wound around the feet of the statue of Athena, while the other crept into her shield. [Hyginus, *Fables* 135; Apollodorus, *Epitome* 5.18; Tzetzes on Lycophron 347.]

CHARICLO (1) was a daughter of Apollo. She was the wife of Cheiron the Centaur. He was the wisest and most just of the Centaurs, and was famous as instructor of Achilles, Jason, and other heroes. He lived with his wife and his mother Philyra on Mount Pelion. Unhappily, he was forced to leave when the Lapithae exiled the Centaurs because of their savage behavior at the wedding of Peirithous and Hippodameia. Presumably Chariclo and Philyra accompanied him.

It is only natural to wonder what physical form Chariclo took. As a daughter of Apollo she certainly must have been human. But Cheiron was human only from the waist up, the rest of him taking the form of a horse. This situation undoubtedly posed a few problems that needed inventive solutions. Solutions were indeed reached, since the marriage produced Carystus, from whom Carystus in Euboea derived its name. According to some, it also produced Endeis, who became the mother of Peleus and therefore grandmother of Achilles (but *see* CHARICLO 2). [Ovid, *Metamorphoses* 2.636;

Apollodorus 3.12.6; Homer, *Iliad* 11.831; Eustathius on Homer's *Iliad* 281; Scholiast on Pindar's *Pythian Odes* 4.181.]

CHARICLO (2) was a daughter of Cychreus of Salamis. She was the wife of Sciron, son of Pylas and grandson of Lelex. She was the mother of Endeis, who in turn was the mother of Peleus by Aeacus. In spite of the fact that Plutarch cited a Megarian historian for this particular lineage, it seems apparent that this was probably an attempt to give Peleus and Achilles historical respectability. Otherwise, Endeis would have been the daughter of a Centaur, and the greatest Greek hero at Troy would have been the great-grandson of a half-horse being. [Pausanias 2.29.7; Plutarch, *Theseus* 10.]

CHARICLO (3) was a nymph who married Eueres. He was a descendant of Udaeus, one of the Sparti sprung from the dragon's teeth sown by Cadmus. Phorbas, son of Lapithus, has also been called her husband. Chariclo's son was one of the most important persons in the history of Thebes—Teiresias, the great seer. At a very young age Teiresias had accidentally observed Athena naked in her bath, and she instantly blinded him. Chariclo begged the goddess to reverse this affliction since, after all, the boy had not been deliberately spying. Athena was unable to change what was destined, but she did make it possible for him to understand the voices of birds in order to make predictions, and she gave him a staff that allowed him to function as though he had full vision.

Chariclo is most interesting, not only as the mother of one of the greatest seers of antiquity but because she was one of the very few nymphs who did not disappear as soon as her child was born. She also appeared to be on speaking terms with the Olympians, and this was quite unusual. Nymphs were shy and elusive; they were most often sought out by lustful gods, heroes, and kings for quick and easy sexual gratification and then seen no more. [Apollodorus 3.6.7; Callimachus, *Hymn to Athena* 67, *Bath of Pallas* 75.]

CHARIS, called Gratia by the Romans, was the personification of grace and beauty. She was described as the wife of Hephaestus in the *Iliad,* but in the *Odyssey* the wife of Hephaestus is Aphrodite. It appears that Homer made such a positive connection between the goddess of beauty and the personification of beauty that this change was scarcely an oversight. As in the case of Aphrodite, the marriage of the lame and ugly god to the beautiful and graceful Charis seemed most incongruous; but apart from purposes of contrast, the union was quite appropriate, considering the delicate and exquisite workmanship performed by the god. Hesiod called Hephaestus' wife Aglaia, and she was identified as the youngest of the CHARITES, for by that time the personification had been pluralized. [Homer, *Iliad* 18.382, *Odyssey* 8.270; Hesiod, *Theogony* 945.]

CHARITES were personifications of aspects of grace and beauty. They were assigned a variety of different parents. Usually Zeus was considered their father, but their mother has been called Hera, Eurynome, Eunomia, Eurydomene, Harmonia, or Lethe. According to others, they were daughters of Apollo and Aegle or Euanthe, or of Dionysus by Aphrodite or Coronis. The most commonly accepted parentage was Zeus and Eurynome, a daughter of Oceanus.

Usually three Charites are named—Euphrosyne, Aglaia, and Thaleia. However, certain places in Greece held onto earlier established numbers and names for them, probably from the time the concept moved from singular to plural. Sparta had two Charites, Cleta and Phaenna. The Athenians had Auxo and Hegemone, but in later times Peitho was added. One story tells of a dispute among three Charites—Pasithea, Cale, and Euphrosyne—and Aphrodite about who was most beautiful. The contest was decided by Teiresias, which suggests that these particular Charites were worshipped by the Thebans.

Whatever their names or wherever their habitat, the Charites were characterized by their role as spreaders of joy and enhancers of enjoyment of life. Social intercourse, manners, and culture were their domain, and they gave visibility to artists and poets. It is to be expected that for companions they chose the Muses. The Muses inspired, while the Charites applied the artists' products to the embellishment of life.

Other companions were Hera, Hermes, Eros, Aphrodite, the Horae, and Apollo. Dionysus was a companion in his early life, but as his worship spread, his companions and celebrations took on a drunken and orgiastic aspect, something quite unacceptable to the Charites, who advocated moderation in everything.

Eteocles, son of the Cephissus River or of Andreus and Euippe, was credited with founding their worship at Orchomenus in Boeotia. At first they were worshipped in the form of rude stones supposed to have fallen from heaven. Later, a festival, the Charitesia, was celebrated there and at Paros. Statues of them were erected in various cities of Greece, such as Sparta, Athens, Elis, and Hermione. They were represented in temples in Crete as well. In the earliest images they were clothed, but eventually they were always shown nude. This is one way they can be identified, but another is that they usually carried some object, such as a musical instrument or a wreath.

It is remarkable that none of the Charites seems to have had a sexual liaison. Even the Muses have been credited with offspring. Here were two or three splendid women, their youthful bloom fully displayed, bringing joy and elegance to the lives of everyone, yet not partaking of one of the greatest joys of all. [Hesiod *Theogony* 64,907; Apollodorus 1.3.1, 3.15.7; Pindar, *Olympian Odes* 13.8, 14.7,15; Statius, *Thebaid* 2.286; Pausanias 4.24.5, 9.35.1,38.1; Horace, *Odes* 3.21,22, 19.15; Seneca, *De Beneficiis* 1.3; Theocritus, *Idylls* 16.104.]

CHARYBDIS was said to be the daughter of Poseidon and Gaea. She was a voracious woman who stole cattle from Heracles. For this crime Zeus struck her with a thunderbolt and hurled her into the sea. She inhabited a rock on which grew a huge fig tree. Three times a day she sucked in most of the water of the sea and then vomited it up again, thereby causing dangerous currents and whirlpools. Opposite her rock was the rock of Scylla, a hideous, multiheaded monster who plucked men from ships and ate them. The choice of one who commanded a vessel was whether to sail closer to Charybdis and perhaps lose his entire ship, or closer to Scylla and lose a few sailors. Jason was spared from making this decision since Thetis and the Nereides conducted him safely between the monsters. Odysseus was not so fortunate—he had to pass them twice. The first time, he steered too near Scylla, and six of his men were eaten in full view of their companions. After his men had killed and eaten some of the cattle of Helios, their ship was wrecked and only Odysseus survived. Clinging to a raft he was swept into the maelstrom but escaped just in time by clutching a branch of the overhanging fig tree. He held on for several hours until his raft was regurgitated from the whirlpool; then he was able to paddle away from the perilous area. Aeneas also had to pass this fatal spot, but managed without incident.

The story attached to Charybdis' involvement with Heracles is terribly contrived and was probably the product of a late period. This applies to her parentage as well, but since virtually everything and everybody in mythology was obliged to have parents, a grandson/grandmother union probably seemed grotesque enough to account for the unpleasant characteristics of Charybdis. It is easier to think of her simply as the personification of a whirlpool. [Apollodorus 1.9.25; Apollonius Rhodius 4.789,825,923; Virgil, *Aeneid* 3.418,428,555; Homer, *Odyssey* 12.73,235.]

CHEDIAETROS was one of the female DOGS of Actaeon.

CHELIDONIS was the sister of AEDON.

CHELONE was a nymph with a haughty and rebellious disposition. When Zeus and Hera's wedding was about to take place, Hermes was responsible for inviting everyone—gods and goddesses, men and women, and animals. Chelone alone refused to show up, choosing to remain in her house, which stood on the bank of a river. Hermes returned and toppled her and the house into the water, where she was changed into a tortoise. Her house fell all around her and was converted into a shell, which she had to carry forever on her back. This story, straight out of the Golden Age when men and gods walked together, appears to be a story for children. It has a moralizing hint that even suggests Aesopian influence. [Servius on Virgil's *Aeneid* 1.505.]

CHERA was a surname of Hera. Temenus, the son of Pelasgus, who educated her, erected three sanctuaries to her at Stymphalus. One was called Hera Pais (as a maiden), another Hera Teleia (as wife of Zeus), and the third was Hera Chera (the widow, alluding to a time when she and Zeus were briefly separated). [Pausanias 8.22.2.]

CHIMAERA (1) was the fearful fire-breathing monster, daughter of Typhon and Echidna. It is not surprising that Chimaera was so terrible, since her parents were among the most devastating and loathsome in ancient story. Their other offspring were Cerberus and Orthrus, hell-dogs, the Hydra, and the Sphinx (although some call her the daughter of Chimaera and her brother Orthus). Chimaera's forebody was that of a lion, her midbody that of a goat, and her hindquarters those of a dragon. She had three heads, one to match each body part. The dragon head apparently breathed the flames, since that is what dragons do. This monstrosity was said to have been brought up as a pet by Amisodarus of Caria, but later the creature roamed free and terrorized the land.

When Bellerophon was sent to Iobates to be killed, Iobates thought he could not survive an encounter with the Chimaera and sent him to conquer the monster. Mounted on the winged horse Pegasus and with Athena's assistance, Bellerophon shot arrows into Chimaera and killed her. He dealt the deciding blow with his lance, which was tipped with lead. The lead melted when the lance was driven into the fiery mouth and caused Chimaera to strangle. Her shade joined the monsters at the entrance of Hades. The battle between her and Bellerophon was thought to have taken place in Lycia, where there is a volcanic valley. [Homer, *Iliad* 6.180, 16.328; Eustathius on Homer's *Iliad* 634; Ovid, *Metamorphoses* 9.646; Apollodorus 1.9.3, 2.3.1; Virgil, *Aeneid* 6.288.]

CHIMAERA (2) was the daughter of a Sicilian king. She chanced to behold the incredibly handsome young shepherd Daphnis and set about seducing him. Meanwhile Daphnis had pledged to the nymph Nomia that he would never sleep with another woman, especially since

Nomia had let him know she would blind him if he did. Chimaera finally got the youth drunk and had her way with him. True to her word, Nomia blinded him. [Diodorus Siculus 4.84; Parthenius, *Love Stories* 29; Servius on Virgil's *Eclogues* 8.68.]

CHIONE (1), sometimes called Deiope, was a daughter of Boreas, god of the north wind, and Oreithyia. She was sister to Cleopatra, Zetes, and Calais. She became pregnant by Poseidon but somehow managed to escape detection until the child was born. Then, fearing her father, she threw the infant into the sea. She was not being entirely heartless by throwing the baby into the sea, since she probably assumed that Poseidon would protect his own. She was right, for the child Eumolpus was saved by Poseidon, who gave him to his daughter Benthesicyme to raise. Eumolpus went on to make a reputation for himself in the war of the Eleusinians against Athens. He later founded the Eleusinian mysteries and was the first priest of Demeter and Dionysus. [Apollodorus 3.15.2,4; Pausanias 1.38.3.]

CHIONE (2) was a daughter of Daedalion. She was very beautiful and was visited by both Hermes and Apollo. She conceived by both of them at the same time and gave birth to twins—Autolycus, the son of Hermes, and Philammon, the son of Apollo. Inheriting his father's cunning, Autolycus became the famous thief of Mount Parnassus. However, some said that Daedalion, his grandfather, was also his father. Philonis, Leuconoe, and Telauge are other names given his mother. Philammon was a great poet and musician, also inheriting from his father. He passed along the tradition to his son Thamyris. His mother has also been called Philonis or Leuconoe.

Chione was vain over having produced children by the two handsomest gods. She once criticized Artemis' beauty and was killed by her. Her father (and possibly lover as well) threw himself from a cliff on Parnassus. In falling he was changed by Apollo into a hawk. [Ovid, *Metamorphoses* 11.300; Hyginus, *Fables* 161,200,201; Eustathius on Homer's *Iliad* 804; Apollodorus 1.3.3; Pausanias 4.33.3.]

CHIONE (3) was a daughter of the Nile River by Callirrhoe. Her sister was Memphis. Her half-brother Minyas was, like her, human in appearance, but her other half-brother Geryones and her half-sister Echidna were monsters. Chione was not in her element on land; as if to confirm this, she was taken advantage of and raped by a peasant. At the command of Zeus, Hermes transported her to the clouds, and snow sifted down on the hostile land. *Chione* is the Greek word for snow. [Hesiod, *Theogony* 351,981; Servius on Virgil's *Aeneid* 4.250.]

CHIONE (4) was, according to some, the mother of Priapus by Dionysus. Priapus was the demigod who presided over agricultural pursuits and fertility. He was quite ugly and had unusually large genitals. His mother is usually called APHRODITE. [Scholiast on Theocritus 1.21.]

CHITONE was a surname of Artemis. The name either referred to her as a huntress with her chiton (loose garment) tucked up for freedom of movement or to the village of Chitone in Attica, where she had a festival, the Chitonia. The clothes in which newborn children were dressed were sacred to her, so that reference, too, was also a good possibility for the derivation of the name. [Callimachus, *Hymn to Artemis* 225; Scholiast on Callimachus' *Hymn to Zeus* 77.]

CHLIDANOPE, a Naiad, was the mother of Cyrene, Alcaea, Themisto, and Astyageia by Hypseus. He was the son of the Peneius River and king of the Lapiths. Astyageia married Periphas, and from them came Ixion and the Centaurs. Themisto was the third wife of Athamas and tragically murdered her own children. Alcaea probably died as a child. Cyrene was the only one to achieve lasting fame. Apollo abducted her and carried her to Libya, where the city of Cyrene derived its name from her. She was the mother by him of Aristaeus, the beneficent demigod. Some say Peneius was the father of Chlidanope's children. [Pindar, *Pythian Odes* 9.5.13; Diodorus Siculus 4.81; Apollodorus 1.9.2; Pausanias 9.34.5; Apollonius Rhodius 1.500; Hyginus, *Fables* 161.]

CHLOE, the Blooming, was a surname of Demeter as protectress of green fields. She had a sanctuary at Athens together with Gaea Curotrophos. A festival in her honor was called Chloeia. The name Demeter Euchlos was probably a variation on the appellation of Chloe. [Pausanias 1.22.3; Sophocles, *Oedipus at Colonus* 1600.]

CHLORIS (1) was a daughter of Amphion and NIOBE. Niobe was ruthlessly punished for bragging that she had twelve children while Leto had only two. Quick to punish any slight or insult to their mother, Apollo and Artemis killed Niobe's children, Apollo bringing down the males while they hunted on Mount Cithaeron and Artemis shooting the females while they were engaged in everyday chores. Some accounts say that all the sons and daughters were thus slaughtered, but the usual tradition has it that one daughter and one son were spared. Perhaps the avenging twins decided that by leaving two alive they could even the count and prevent any further boasting by Niobe. The surviving daughter was Chloris, but it was said that the name was given to her after the horrible incident, during which she turned white from terror. Her original name was said to be Meliboea.

Chloris and her brother Amyclas left Thebes and relocated in Argos, where they built the temple of Leto. This temple also contained a statue of Chloris, perhaps a reminder that the goddess would hear the prayers of suppliants. This same Chloris was reported to have won the prize in a footrace at Olympia during the festival of Hera. Competition in this race was confined to virgins, so up to that point Chloris had not married, although some authors confused her with Chloris, the wife of Neleus.

In a way Chloris represents victory over adversity, as well as stubborn independence. After the death of her brothers and sisters she probably left home in disgust at a tragic event brought about by vanity. She further tried to make amends by helping build a temple to the offended goddess. Finally, she demonstrated that she had an indomitable spirit by winning the race at a sacred festival. It seems rather evident that her unhappy experience caused her to turn her attention to religious pursuits. [Pausanias 2.21.10, 5.16.2–3.]

CHLORIS (2) was a daughter of Amphion, king of Orchomenus, by Persephone, daughter of Minyas. Chloris married Neleus, son of Poseidon and twin brother of Pelias. Early in their career the twins had a falling-out, and Neleus was banished. He went to Pylus in Messenia, taking Chloris with him. After settling at Pylus they had 12 sons—Taurus, Asterius, Pylaon, Deimachus, Eurybius, Epilaus, Phrasius, Eurymenes, Euagoras, Alastor, Nestor, and Periclymenus. Their daughter was the beautiful Pero. Neleus drove out the Leleges and raised Pylus to fame and glory. Unfortunately he incurred the disfavor of Heracles, whom he refused to purify of the murder of Iphitus. Heracles went away but returned with an army and destroyed all the sons of Neleus and Chloris except for Nestor, who escaped by being absent during the devastating reprisal. Later he became a favorite of Heracles.

Chloris was yet another victim of the rather commonplace violence of the day. Most accounts say Neleus was also slain in the war with Heracles, so Chloris was left with a daughter and a son. Her daughter did well, securing the royal alliance by marrying Bias, joint ruler of Argos. Chloris was probably dismayed by her son's affair with Heracles, which was described as more intense than the ones with Hylas and Abderus. Yet, if she lived to see it, she could well be proud of the great city that grew out of Nestor's inheritance, the distinguished sons he produced, and the universal respect he commanded. [Apollodorus 1.9.9,15; Homer, *Iliad* 11.692, *Odyssey* 3.413,452,464, 11.281,285; Pausanias 10.31.2,36.4.]

CHLORIS (3) was the wife of Zephyrus and the goddess of flowers. Zephyrus was the personification of the west wind. He lived with his brother Boreas, the north wind, in a palace in Thrace. The brothers appeared to lead a carefree and rapacious existence. Boreas had abducted Oreithyia from Athens. Zephyrus had coupled with Podarge, one of the Harpies, to produce the two magnificent horses of Achilles. After that, Zephyrus abducted Chloris and settled down with her. Their son was Carpus (Fruit). Zephyrus had an altar on the Sacred Way between Athens and Eleusis. Chloris was more or less identical with the Roman Flora. [Ovid, *Fasti* 5.195; Hesiod, *Theogony* 579; Homer, *Iliad* 9.5, 16.150, *Odyssey* 5.295; Pausanias 1.37.1.]

CHLORIS (4) was a nymph who became by Ampycus (or Ampyx), son of Pelias, the mother of Mopsus. Some called his mother Aregonis or Himantis. Mopsus was one of the Lapiths of Oechalia and a Calydonian hunter. He was also a combatant in the battle between the Lapiths and Centaurs at the wedding of Peirithous. He was most particularly the famous prophet among the Argonauts. On the return from Colchis he died from a snakebite in Libya and was buried there. Chloris' son became an oracular hero, but it is unlikely she was ever aware of his great fame. He, by the way, should not be confused with Mopsus the son of Manto, daughter of Teiresias. [Hyginus, *Fables* 14,128; Apollonius Rhodius 1.80,1083, 4.1518; Tzetzes on Lycophron 881; Orphica, *Argonautica* 127.]

CHLORIS (5) was a daughter of Teiresias. We hear of her in only one reference, although other daughters, especially Manto, are mentioned rather often. Chloris was the mother of Periclymenus by Poseidon. In the war of the Seven against Thebes he killed Parthenopaeus by throwing a stone down on him from the city wall. He also pursued Amphiaraus, but when he overtook him, Amphiaraus was swallowed up by the earth. When the Epigoni returned to Thebes and captured it, causing Teiresias and other residents to flee, there was no mention of Chloris. Perhaps she had died during the ten-year interval. [Euripides, *Phoenician Maidens* 1157; Pindar, *Nemean Odes* 9.57, with the scholiast.]

CHLORIS (6) was one of the PIERIDES.

CHROMIA was the mother of Aetolus by Endymion, according to Pausanias (5.1.2). She is usually called NEIS.

CHRYSE (1) was a daughter of Pallas, one of the sons of Lycaon. When Chryse married Dardanus, son of Zeus and Electra, Pallas assigned to his son-in-law the care of various Arcadian sacred objects, among which was the

Palladium. Chryse bore to Dardanus two sons, Deimas and Idaeus. They grew up to reign over the Arcadian kingdom founded by their great-grandfather Atlas. It is not clear what Dardanus was doing during this time. He was probably only about 40, but he might have been already dabbling in the mysteries with which he and Chryse were later deeply involved, leaving the governing to his sons. The Deucalionian flood, however, changed the course of history for them, and the brothers separated. Deimas stayed in Arcadia, while Idaeus accompanied his father and mother to Samothrace, where they introduced the mysteries. Chryse was a priestess of the new cult, which featured worship of the Cabeiri, the mysterious divinities often referred to as the Great Gods. Dardanus and Chryse colonized Samothrace and called the island Dardania.

From Samothrace Dardanus went to Phrygia at the invitation of his friend Teucer. Chryse went with him, as did Idaeus, who parted from his family there and instituted the worship of the Phrygian mother of the gods in the Idaean Mountains, which he named for himself. Dardanus set about founding a city in Phrygia and learned that this city would be invincible as long as the Palladium should be preserved. The city, of course, was Troy. This rendering, vastly simplified, does not take into account the miraculous appearance of the Palladium that supposedly fell from heaven and provided the cornerstone around which Troy was built. This event, like so many others, has to be accepted on an allegorical level. Tradition allowed for a more conventional introduction of the sacred object.

About this time Chryse died. She was not really very old, but certainly beyond childbearing. Dardanus married Bateia, the daughter of Teucer, and had children by her, thus beginning the royal Trojan line. Interestingly enough, there was already a bilateral family line established by Chryse's cousin Euander in Italy, thus making for a family connection long before the Trojan refugees arrived with Aeneas. [Dionysius of Halicarnassus, *Roman Antiquities* 1.61; Diodorus Siculus 5.48; Conon, *Narrations* 21; Homer, *Iliad* 20.21; Lycophron 72; Tzetzes on Lycophron 72; Apollodorus 3.12.1, 3.15.3; Virgil, *Aeneid* 3.167, 7.206, 8.134; Servius on Virgil's *Aeneid* 2.3.25, 3.15,167,170, 7.207, 9.10.]

CHRYSE (2) was a daughter of Halmus. Her father was a son of Sisyphus and founder of the Boeotian town of Halmones. Chryses' sister was Chrysogeneia. Observing that the names of the daughters have to do with gold, it appears Halmones might have been obsessed with riches. Chryse was one of the lovers of Ares, and their son was Phlegyas. Phlegyas succeeded to the throne of Orchomenus when his cousin Eteocles died without issue. He called the kingdom Phlegiantis after himself. Phlegyas was the father of Coronis, the mother of Asclepius. [Pausanias 2.4.3, 9.35.5,36.1; Apollodorus 3.5.5.]

CHRYSE (3) was a surname of Athena on the island of Chryse, where Philoctetes was bitten by a snake on his way to the Trojan conflict. This pivotal event happened when the devout Philoctetes pointed out to his companions the altar of Athena and came too near the serpent guarding her temple. [Sophocles, *Philoctetes* 1327.]

CHRYSE (4) was a nymph on the island of Chryse off the shore of Lemnos. When Philoctetes landed there, she fell in love with him, but he rejected her advances. He was busy clearing away debris from the neglected altar of Athena Chryse when Chryse sent a viper to bite him and render him incapable of sailing further with the Greeks to Troy. It would be interesting to know what happened when he was left alone with her after his companions were forced to sail without him. [Tzetzes on Lycophron 911.]

CHRYSEIS (1) was the patronymic of ASTYNOME, as daughter of the priest Chryses of Lyrnessus.

CHRYSEIS (2) was one of the THESPIADES, a daughter of Thespius and Megamede. By Heracles she became the mother of Onesippus. [Apollodorus 2.7.8.]

CHRYSEIS (3) was one of the OCEANIDES. [Hesiod, *Theogony* 357.]

CHRYSIPPE (1) was one of the DANAIDES, a daughter of Danaus by Memphis. She was married to Chrysippus, son of Aegyptus by Tyria. [Apollodorus 2.1.5.]

CHRYSIPPE (2), the daughter of Irus, was the wife of Phthios and mother of Hellen, the mythical founder of the Thessalian town of Hellas. Hellas was a small district of Phthiotis, which itself was named for Phthios. Apparently this Hellen was local and not to be confused with the son of Deucalion and Pyrrha, and father of the Greek nation. [Stephanus Byzantium, "Ellas"; Strabo 9.5.6.]

CHRYSOGENEIA was a daughter of Halmus, son of Sisyphus and the founder of the Boeotian town of Halmones, and sister of Chryse. While Chryse was becoming the great-grandmother of Asclepius, Chrysogeneia was not sitting idly by. By Poseidon she was the grandmother of Minyas and through him the ancestor of the Minyans, including Jason among others. It must not be overlooked that both Chryse and Chrysogeneia were lovers of the great gods Ares and Poseidon. In order to create so powerful a race of heroes as the Minyans, an infusion of the divine seed seemed to be called for. After this impetus, the succeeding generations apparently settled down to a more mortal heritage. [Pausanias 9.34.5, 2.4.3]

CHRYSONOE was a daughter of Cleitus and wife of Proteus, son of Poseidon and king of Egypt. She is usually called TORONE. [Conon, *Narrations* 32.]

CHRYSOPELEIA was a Hamadryad and mother by Arcas of Elatus, Apheidas, and Azan. Their mother is usually called ERATO. [Apollodorus 3.9.1; Tzetzes on Lycophron 480.]

CHRYSORTHE was the daughter of Orthopolis and the mother of Coronus by Apollo. Coronus was king of Sicyon and father of Corax and Lamedon. Corax died without issue; before Lamedon could assume the throne, the kingdom was usurped by Epopeus of Thessaly. Epopeus was killed in the battle over Antiope, and Lamedon then acquired the kingdom. He passed the rule to his son-in-law Sicyon, after whom the territory came to be called Sicyonia. Chrysorthe was merely a milestone in the line of Sicyonian kings, giving the line divine sanction through her sexual intercourse with Apollo. This was almost a convention in a recital of royal successions. [Pausanias 2.5.8.]

CHRYSOTHEMIS (1) was a daughter of Agamemnon and Clytemnestra, and sister of Iphigeneia, Electra, and Orestes. Chrysothemis is a silence in the whole tragedy of Agamemnon. She played no role in the saga of revenge engendered by Electra; she seemed totally withdrawn from the events that placed Iphigeneia in Tauris. She extended no sympathy, it seems, to her matricidal brother in his agony with the Eumenides. Clytemnestra, troubled with horrible dreams, once sent her to Agamemnon's tomb with libations, but otherwise Chrysothemis is an unknown element in the entire drama. Why was she so passive? She was at least as old as Orestes, who was a child when his father left for the Trojan War. It is entirely possible that Chrysothemis was either mentally retarded or so totally dominated by her mother's aggressive personality that she was virtually immobilized. The strength of Electra's passion and Orestes' vacillating resolve seemed to impress her not at all. Her mother ran things, and her uncle Aegisthus probably extended kindnesses to her. [Sophocles, *Electra* 47–50,320,417,1223.]

CHRYSOTHEMIS (2) was one of the DANAIDES, married to Asterides, son of Aegyptus. [Hyginus, *Fables* 170.]

CHRYSOTHEMIS (3) was the wife of Staphylus. He was the son of Dionysus and Ariadne (some say Theseus and Ariadne, but that makes very little sense, for reasons expressed elsewhere). Staphylus was one of the Argonauts, and on his return he married Chrysothemis and became the father of three daughters. These three daughters were from the very first a little awkward and odd. Rhoeo, the pretty one, was soon spotted by Apollo, her granduncle, who without ceremony took her to bed. It was not long before her father discovered she was pregnant and, turning a deaf ear to her claim that his uncle made her do it, threw her in a chest and cast her into the sea. Apollo not only guided the chest to Delos, where she gave birth to Anius, but got her pregnant again with Zarex. So much

for Rhoeo, who seemed to be well-protected by her lover.

Parthenos and Molpadia were not quite as fortunate. They were commanded to guard their father's wine but fell asleep. The swine, which they were also supposed to be watching, got into the wine, spilled it, then spoiled it while lapping it up. The sisters awoke and took flight, remembering how their father handled frustration. They climbed a hill and threw themselves over a cliff. Apollo, probably in deference to their sister, his lover, resurrected them. (Hyginus, *Poetic Astronomy* 25; Diodorus Siculus 5.52,62; Tzetzes on Lycophron 570,580; Apollodorus 1.9.16; Plutarch, *Theseus* 20; Parthenius, *Love Stories* 1.]

CHTHONIA (1), the Subterranean or Goddess of the Earth, was a surname of the infernal divinities such as Hecate, Nyx, and Melinoe. It was used especially in reference to Demeter. In her case, it had reference to protectress of the fields. [Apollonius Rhodius 4.148,978; Herodotus 2.123; Orphica, *Hymns* 2.8, 3.19, 35.9, 70.1.]

CHTHONIA (2) was a daughter of Phoroneus. She and her brother Clymenus founded at Hermione a sanctuary of Demeter, whom they called Chthonia. (*See also* CHTHONIA 3.)

CHTHONIA (3) was a daughter of Colontas. When Demeter in her wanderings came to Argolis, she was ill received by Colontas. Chthonia was very unhappy with her father's conduct and even approved when the goddess set fire to his house. Demeter carried Chthonia to Hermione, where the women built a sanctuary to Demeter Chthonia and instituted the festival of Chthonia in her honor. Chthonia would be regarded today as a bit fanatical. Indeed she had good reason to object to her father's treatment of the disconsolate Demeter, but cheering on the demolition of her father's house was a little extreme. Colontas would not be the first to question the introduction of a new religion to his domain; he might have had good reason. [Pausanias 2.35.3.]

CHTHONIA (4) was a daughter of Erechtheus II. Erechtheus was a son of Pandion by

Zeuxippe, so he was a brother of Butes, Procne, and Philomela. After his father died, he succeeded him as king of Athens. He was married to Praxithea, by whom he became the father of Cecrops, Pandarus, Metion, Orneus, Procris, Creusa, Oreithyia, Chthonia, Otiona, and others. The daughters agreed among themselves to die together if one of them was to die. When Eumolpus, a son of Poseidon who assisted the Eleusinians in the war against the Athenians, had been killed, Poseidon (or an oracle) demanded the sacrifice of one of the daughters of Erechtheus. When one was drawn by lot, the others voluntarily accompanied her in death, or so the story goes. But Procris had a curious on-again, off-again relationship with her husband, Cephalus, Oreithyia was snatched away by Boreas, the north wind, and Creusa had a smoldering affair with Apollo in the caves under the Acropolis. So only a handful of sisters joined Otiona in her self-sacrifice. Chthonia married her uncle Butes and started the line of the Butadae. [Apollodorus 3.15.1; Hyginus, *Fables* 46,238; Plutarch, *Greek and Roman Parallel Stories* 20; Pausanias 2.25.5; Ovid, *Metamorphoses* 6.676.]

CHTHONIAE referred to a class of nymphs connected with certain races or localities, Nymphae Chthoniae. They usually had a name derived from the places with which they were associated, as Nysiades, Dodonides, Lemniae, etc. [Apollonius Rhodius 2.504.]

CHTHONOPATRA was the wife of Amphictyon. He was the son of Deucalion and Pyrrha, and therefore the first of the new generation to appear after the flood. Chthonopatra was probably his first wife when the waters subsided and, as with Noah's ark, a good question is where she came from. By her he had a son, Physcus, who became the father of Locrus, although some call Physcus a grandson. Amphictyon is further reported to have married Cranae, daughter of Cranaus, in Attica and to have usurped the throne. He was also supposed to have introduced the custom of mixing wine with water and to have dedicated altars to Dionysus. This makes no sense, since Dionysus was not born at this time. Chthonopatra was

probably precedent to Amphictyon's involvement with the Attican royal house. [Apollodorus 3.14.5; Pausanias 1.2.5; Eustathius on Homer's *Iliad* 277,1815.]

CHTHONOPHYLE was the daughter of Sicyon and Zeuxippe. Sicyon was a son of Marathon and the eponymic founder of Sicyon, which before him was called Mecone or Aegialeia. Zeuxippe was the daughter of Lamedon, of the royal Sicyonian lineage. Chthonphyle first slept with Hermes and produced Polybus, a king of Corinth who brought up Oedipus. Others say Polybus was king of Sicyon and father of Lysianassa, whom he gave in marriage to Talaus, king of the Argives. Chthonophyle later married Phlias, son of Dionysus and Araethyrea, and bore to him Androdamas. The women in these recitals of lineage appear to be almost invisible, but provide links in a chain of rulers. It is interesting that Hermes is listed in this king list. He was seldom claimed as an ancestor of a race. [Pausanias 2.1.1,6.3,12.6, 6.2.3; Apollodorus 3.5.7; Sophocles, *Oedipus Rex* 770; Apollonius Rhodius 1.115; Valerius Flaccus 1.411; Hyginus, *Fables* 14; Stephanus Byzantium, "Phlious."]

CIDARIA was a surname of the Eleusinian Demeter at Pheneus in Arcadia. The name was derived either from an Arcadian dance called *cidaris* or from a royal headdress of the same name. [Pausanias 8.15.1.]

CILLA was a daughter of Laomedon and Strymo. Others call her mother Placia, Leucippe, Rhoeo, Thoosa, or Zeuxippe. As one might expect, the Trojan genealogy was complicated. Cilla was a sister of Priam, and her other brothers were Tithonus, Lampus, Clytius, Hicetaon, and Bucolion. Her sisters were Hesione and Astyoche. Other sons and daughters were bastards and offspring of the liaisons mentioned above. Aethylla, Medesicaste, and Procleia were probably half-sisters.

Cilla grew up in a strange, half-formed environment of doubt and hesitation. With varying ambitions for control of the kingdom, her brothers waited for their father's death, and her sister Hesione had been taken away by Heracles.

Astyoche had married Telephus and was trying to get him to enter the Trojan War against his fellow Greeks. Cilla had a secret union with Thymoetes and conceived by him a son, Munippus.

Priam managed to achieve the throne, mainly because Heracles had killed all the other contenders in his private war against Troy. Somewhat shaken by the turn of events, Priam came to the throne and was soon confronted with an oracle that said Troy would be destroyed if a mother and son were not put to death. Assaracus, the seer, meant Hecuba and Paris, but Priam preferred to think he meant his sister Cilla and her newborn son Munippus. He ordered them to be killed, then buried them in a secret precinct of the city.

Cilla and Munippus were thus victims both of coincidence and politics. It was certainly unlikely that Priam would kill his own wife and son to fulfill an oracle (although he soon took the precaution of having Paris exposed on Mount Ida). The real irony was that Cilla and her son died in vain. They were not entirely unavenged, since Thymoetes was among those who insisted on bringing the wooden horse into Troy. [Apollodorus 12.3,8; Tzetzes on Lycophron 224,232,467,921.]

CINXIA was a surname for Juno. Cinxia alluded to her invocation by newly married people.

CIRCE was a daughter of Helios by Perse. Her brothers were Aeetes and Perses, and her sister was Pasiphae. Aloeus was a half-brother, being a son of Antiope, and was king of Asopia. Perses was a king in Tauris, while Aeetes was king of Colchis. Pasiphae had married Minos and was queen of Crete. Circe lived on the island of Aeaea, from which she derived the surname Circe Aeaea. The island was enchanted, as was its owner. Circe probably chose to live on this island because it was near Thrinacia, the island on which her father, Helios, lived with his white cattle. Circe's island was probably off the coast of Italy near present-day Terracina.

After Odysseus escaped with only one ship from the Laestrygones, he went to Aeaea and sent his men ashore to explore. They were impressed with the tameness of the wild animals that abounded on the island but found out soon enough why this was so. Circe appeared and prepared food for them that had been drugged; they lapsed into unconsciousness and awoke as swine. Eurylochus had not entered Circe's palace, so he escaped to tell Odysseus the awful facts. Odysseus was instructed by Hermes to ingest the antidotal herb *moly* so he could resist Circe's magic. He forced her to restore his men; afterward she offered all of them genuine hospitality with no threat of further harm. Her hospitality was so warm, in fact, that Odysseus remained with her for an extended time.

Sources vary on how long Odysseus stayed with Circe. Some accounts say as much as a year, but two children are attributed to her by him—Telegonus and Cassiphone—and this would be trimming things rather close. Later writers add several other children—Anteias, Ardeas, Auson, Latinus, Agrius, Romus, and Casiphones—but most of these were involved with the founding of Roman cities and may be considered eponymic heroes. It was tempting for places to claim so distinguished a heritage.

Eventually the time came when Odysseus wanted to resume his voyage. Circe was not happy at losing him, but wisely insisted he go first to the underworld to learn the best way to proceed back home. Odysseus did this, consulting Teiresias, the Theban seer whose long life had finally come to an end. Teiresias' main advice was to leave the cattle of Helios alone on the return trip. The company returned from Hades and bade Circe farewell. She saw them off with parting advice for escaping dangers still awaiting, then turned back to the lonely business of rearing her small children.

This, then, was the extent of Circe's involvement with Odysseus in the *Odyssey* (except that Homer did not mention any children). Later writers, not content to let well enough alone, had Telegonus and Cassiphone grow up. Circe had never ceased to long for her valiant lover, who had presumably made it back home successfully many years before. She finally sent Telegonus to find him if possible. Telegonus, mistaken for a pirate, killed his father before he knew who he was. He, Telemachus, and Penelope brought Odysseus' body to Aeaea to be buried. No reason was given, just as none has been advanced for having Penelope accompany the body. Some wrote that Circe resurrected him. Others wrote that Telemachus was induced by Athena to marry Circe and that he became by her the father of Latinus. Still other accounts say he married his half-sister Cassiphone. Meanwhile Telegonus was supposed to have married the widowed Penelope. Telemachus was said to have killed Circe during an argument and to have been killed by Cassiphone in return. Where were Circe's magical powers during these events; what happened to her immortality?

Circe's story is a fascinating one because of her change from one personality to another. It is no wonder that she has often been confused with Calypso, the gentle enchantress with whom Odysseus was ultimately involved. Circe's family included more than one sorcerer. She had cast evil spells on others besides Odysseus' companions. Picus, the prophetic divinity who loved and was loved by Pomona, was changed by Circe into a woodpecker for not returning her love. Circe loved Glaucus also, but Glaucus was in love with Scylla and turned a deaf ear to Circe's overtures. So the sorceress mixed noxious herbs in the water of the fountain where Scylla bathed, and the nymph was turned into the hideous monster that lurked in the cliff overlooking the strait between Italy and Sicily. The Argonauts were forced to visit Circe for purification after Medea had killed her brother Absyrtus. Medea was her niece; except for this, Circe might well have turned Jason and his companions into swine.

Some writers identified Circe with Marica, the mother of Latinus by Faunus. Others even associated her with Aphrodite. [Homer, *Odyssey* 10-12; Hyginus, *Fables* 125,127; Hesiod, *Theogony* 1011; Ovid, *Metamorphoses* 14.9,346; Apollonius Rhodius 4.599; Virgil, *Aeneid* 3.386, 7.47,190; Servius on Virgil's *Aeneid* 7.47, 12.164; Pausanias 2.1.6.3.8; Dionysius of Halicarnassus, *Roman Antiquities* 1.72; Stephanus Byzantium, "Anteia"; Suidas, "Ausonion"; Tzetzes on Lycophron 44,696,795,808.]

CIRRHA was a nymph from whom the town of Cirrha in Phocis was believed to have derived its name. [Pausanias 10.37.4.]

CISSA was one of the PIERIDES.

CISSEIS was one of the NYSEIDES, the nymphs of Nysa, who were said to have reared Dionysus.

CISSIA was the mother of Memnon, according to some. By most, however, Memnon's mother was EOS, the goddess of the dawn.

CITHAERONIDES were nymphs of Mount Cithaeron.

CLEIA, or Cleeia, was one of the HYADES. Her sisters were Phaesyle, Coronis, Phaeote, and Eudora. [Hesiod, quoting Theon on Aratus' *Phenomena* 171.]

CLEIDOUCHOS was one of the epithets of Athena, referring to her warlike character.

CLEIO (*See* CLIO)

CLEIS was one of the HYADES in Naxos who were nurse to the infant Dionysus. He was carried there by Zeus. The other two were Philia and Coronis. [Diodorus Siculus 3.69, 5.52.]

CLEISITHYRA was the daughter of Idomeneus of Crete. Idomeneus was one of the heroes of the Trojan War but another of the victims of Nauplius, who sought revenge for the treacherous murder of his son Palamedes. Nauplius persuaded Idomeneus' wife Meta to take Leucas as a lover. Leucas, the son of Talos, was Idomeneus' foster son and already betrothed to Cleisithyra. Leucas had inherited a pathological nature from his father and killed not only Meta but her children as well, including Cleisithyra. [Lycophron 1222; Tzetzes on Lycophron 1218,1222, *Chiliades* 3.294.]

CLEITE (1) was a daughter of Merops, king of Phrygian Percote on the Hellespont. He was a celebrated soothsayer and father of Arisbe, Amphius, and Adrastus, as well as Cleite. She had just married Cyzicus, the son of Aeneus, who ruled the land on the peninsula of Arcton, when the Argonauts landed. Cyzicus and Heracles were friends, and the Argonauts were warmly welcomed to share in the marriage feast. Later the Argonauts left but were driven by a storm back to the peninsula. Not recognizing their recent guests, the army of Cyzicus attacked them, and Cyzicus was killed along with most of his men. Cleite, the new bride who had scarcely tasted the joys of marriage, went insane over the news and hanged herself. The nymphs of the grove where she killed herself wept so copiously over the sad event that their tears created a fountain known thereafter as the fountain of Cleite. [Apollonius Rhodius 1.967,975,1063; Conon, *Narrations* 41.]

CLEITE (2) was one of the DANAIDES, daughter of Danaus and Memphis. She was married to Cleitus, son of Aegyptus and Tyria. They and two other couples were wed without drawing lots because of the similarity of their names. [Apollodorus 2.1.5.]

CLEO was one of the DANAIDES. She was married to Asterius. [Hyginus, *Fables* 170.]

CLEOBOEA (1) was a daughter of Criasus and Melantho, and sister of Phorbas and Ereuthalion. Nothing further is known of her. It is tempting to make her identical with the mother-in-law of Thestius, but geography and chronology make this a problem. Cleoboea was part of the Argive family that produced Argus Panoptes. [Scholiast on Euripides' *Phoenician Maidens* 1123.]

CLEOBOEA (2) was the mother of Eurythemis, who married Thestius and produced, among others, Leda, mother of Helen of Sparta, and Althaea, mother of Meleager. She is therefore only a name in a line of Aetolian kings and queens; however, being grandmother to Leda and Althaea makes her name a distinguished one. These same granddaughters were children in the palace in which she was an honored elder. [Apollodorus 1.7.10.]

CLEOBULE (1) was the wife of Amyntor, a son of Ormenus of Eleon in Thessaly. He is mainly known as the owner of the beautiful helmet that was stolen by Autolycus and ended up in the hands of Meriones, who wore it in the war against Troy. By Cleobule, Amyntor was the father of Crantor, Euaemon, Astydameia, and

Phoenix. Amyntor had a mistress, Phthia, with whom he lived openly. Cleobule, sometimes called Hippodameia, resented her very much and prevailed on her handsome son Phoenix to seduce his father's lover. Phoenix did this (although some claim that the mistress took a fancy to him and, when her affection was not returned, accused him of trying to seduce her). Amyntor was swift in reprisal and blinded his son. Some say he merely called down a curse of sterility on him. Phoenix fled to Peleus, who had previously conquered Amyntor, and was received kindly. The blindness, if that indeed happened, was cured by Cheiron the Centaur, and Phoenix became an honored friend of Peleus as well as of his son Achilles, whom he accompanied to Troy.

In a way Cleobule got her revenge by exposing Phthia, but Amyntor is not recorded as having taken any action against Phthia, so the untenable situation probably continued. Cleobule's other son, Crantor, had been given as a hostage when Peleus invaded the territory of Amyntor and probably remained with Peleus. Astydameia was courted by Heracles, who became by her the father of Ctessipus. It seems that both Amyntor and Phoenix took part in the Calydonian boar hunt. Phoenix (probably confused with an earlier Phoenix) was said to have invented the alphabet. [Homer, *Iliad* 9.434; Lycophron 417, Apollodorus 2.7.7, 3.13.7,8; Hyginus, *Fables* 257; Ovid, *Heroides* 3.27.]

CLEOBULE (2) was the mother of Cepheus by Aleus. Usually her name is given as NEAERA.

CLEOBULE (3), or Polybule, was the wife of Alector. The only thing known about this couple is that they were parents of Leitus, an Argonaut and a leader of the Boeotians against Troy. He took the remains of Arcesilaus, another Boeotian hero, back from Troy. He was the father of Peneleus, also a hero in the war. The tomb of Leitus was pointed out at Plataea. [Apollodorus 1.9.16, 3.10.8; Homer, *Iliad* 17.602; Pausanias 9.4.3,39.3.]

CLEOBULE (4), the daughter of Aeolus or Aetolus, was the mother of Myrtilus by Hermes. Others call her Clytia, Phaetusa, Myrto, or Theobule. It is not really surprising that Hermes' lover is so obscure. Unlike Apollo, Poseidon, and Zeus, he was secretive about his affairs even though he had no permanent attachment. In spite of being a son of a god, Myrtilus had a menial position as charioteer of Oenomaus, the father of Hippodameia. It might be interesting to pursue the reasons. His story is well known. When Oenomaus forced suitors for the hand of Hippodameia to compete with him in a chariot race, which he invariably won, he put them to death. Pelops came along and accepted the challenge, but this time Hippodameia persuaded Myrtilus to tamper with the nails in the wheels of her father's chariot. Some say Myrtilus loved Hippodameia himself and that she had promised to sleep with him. Others say Pelops was in on the plan and promised him a substantial reward. Pelops did not keep his part of the bargain, and treacherously threw Myrtilus into the sea. As he died Myrtilus put a curse on the house of Pelops, and the record of the subsequent tragedies testifies to its efficacy. Hermes placed his son among the stars as the constellation Auriga. Myrtilus was also worshipped as a hero and honored with nocturnal sacrifices. Cleobule's parentage is vague (it was easy for ancient writers to assign someone to the huge dynasty of Aeolus). Chances are she was a nymph who, in the tradition of her sisters, left Myrtilus a foundling to be raised by Oenomaus. That might explain his lowly career as a charioteer. [Hyginus, *Poetic Astronomy* 2.13; Scholiast on Apollonius Rhodius 1.752; Pausanias 6.20.8, 8.14.7.]

CLEOCHAREIA was the mother of Eurotas by Lelex. Lelex was one of the original inhabitants of Laconia, which at first was called from him Lelegia. By the Naiad Cleochareia, or Peridia or Taygete, he became the father of Myles, Polycaon, and Eurotas. All these developed the Laconian royal line, but Eurotas was prominent. He dug a canal in the plain of Lacedaemon and diverted water to the sea. This waterway was called Eurotas, which is even today the principal river of Sparta. He was the father of Sparta, who married Lacedaemon and started the royal house of Sparta. [Apollodorus 3.10.3; Pausanias 3.1.1, 12.4, 4.1.2.]

CLEODICE was the daughter of Lacedaemon and sister of Himerus. In some way Himerus

offended Aphrodite, who caused him to get very drunk one night and take Cleodice to bed with him. When he learned the next day what he had done, he leapt into the Eurotas River, which for a time was called by his name. One always speculates in these kinds of stories about the role of the one debauched. Did Cleodice get drunk with her brother, or did he barge into her room to consummate a long-smoldering passion? Did she encourage the act, or did she confront him with a threat of telling all? There is no suggestion that anyone else in the family knew about the affair. [Pseudo-Plutarch, *On Rivers* 17.]

CLEODORA (1) was a daughter of Pandareos. (*See* CAMEIRA.)

CLEODORA (2) was the wife of Cleopompus and mother of Parnassus. He was the founder of the town of Delphi (not the oracle), and he anticipated the prophetic nature of the place by being a seer in his own right. He could foretell the future by watching birds in flight. He also gave his name to Mount Parnassus. [Pausanias 10.6.1.]

CLEODORA (3) was one of the DANAIDES, daughter of Danaus and Polyxo. She was married to Lixus. [Apollodorus 2.1.5.]

CLEODOXA was one of the daughters of Amphion and NIOBE. [Apollodorus 3.5.6.]

CLEOLA, daughter of Dias, was the first wife of Atreus. By him she became the mother of Pleisthenes. The genealogy of the house of Atreus is quite complex, but for reasons stated elsewhere (*see* AEROPE), Cleola was the most likely candidate as mother of Pleisthenes. She has also been called the wife of Pleisthenes and mother of Agamemnon, Menelaus, and Anaxibia. [Scholiast on Euripides' *Orestes* 5.]

CLEOMESTRA was the wife of Aesyetes and mother of Antenor. Antenor was married to Theano. He was one of the wisest among the elders at Troy, and received Menelaus and Odysseus into his house when they came to Troy as ambassadors. He also advised his fellow citizens to restore Helen to Menelaus. [Homer, *Iliad* 3.146,203, 7.348.]

CLEONE was one of the daughters of Asopus, from whom the town of Cleone in Peloponnesus was believed to have derived its name. Cleone exists today and is the site of a temple of Heracles. [Pausanias 2.15.1; Diodorus Siculus 4.74.]

CLEOPATRA (1), also called Alcyone, was the daughter of Idas and Marpessa of Messenia. Idas was one of the famous sons of Aphareus and Arene. It is not altogether curious that Idas' daughter ended up in Calydon married to Meleager. Idas and Meleager had been shipmates in the famous Argonaut, and some of the participants arranged marriages for their sisters and daughters during their extended association.

Cleopatra went to Calydon and became the wife of Meleager, heir to the throne. By him she became the mother of Polydora. She was a faithful wife and a loving mother. It could only have been painful to her that Meleager fell in love with the glamorous Atalanta, who shared the honors with him at the celebrated Calydonian boar hunt. It is not clear whether or not Atalanta went also on the journey of the Argonauts, but certain accounts say that she did and later bore a son to Meleager.

Meleager, however, had to pay not only for his treatment of Cleopatra but for his rashness in killing his mother's brothers, either in a fight over the trophy of the hunt or in a battle against the Curetes, to which tribe his uncles belonged. If the second situation was true, then Cleopatra was partially responsible, since she urged her husband to emerge from his fit of pique over his mother's curse for killing her brothers and enter the war against the Curetes. The usual story, though, is that his mother, Althaea, threw into the fire a brand which the Fates had told her would keep her son alive as long as it remained unconsumed. When he did die as a result of the burning of this piece of wood, both his mother and Cleopatra hanged themselves. [Apollodorus 1.8.2,3, 3.10.3; Hyginus, *Fables* 171,174; Homer, *Iliad* 9.556; Eustathius on Homer's *Iliad* 776; Orphica, *Argonautica* 157; Diodorus Siculus 4.35; Ovid, *Metamorphoses* 8.450,531.]

CLEOPATRA (2) was one of the DANAIDES, a daughter of Danaus and one of the Naiads, Atlantia or Phoebe. She married Agenor, son of Aegyptus. Her sister was also Cleopatra. [Apollodorus 2.1.5.]

CLEOPATRA (3) was one of the DANAIDES, a daughter of Danaus and Polyxo. She married Hermus. [Apollodorus 2.1.5.]

CLEOPATRA (4) was one of the DANAIDES and married to Metalces. [Hyginus, *Fables* 170.]

CLEOPATRA (5) was a daughter of Tros and Callirrhoe and sister of Ilus, Assaracus, and Ganymede. Nothing else is known of her. She might have died early, or she might have remained unmarried. Her brothers meanwhile had interesting careers, which she might well have observed. It is always provocative to find a dead end in a succession of heirs and heiresses, since the Greeks (and Trojans) were fascinated with genealogy. [Apollodorus 3.12.2.]

CLEOPATRA (6) was the daughter of Boreas, the north wind, and Oreithyia. Her brothers were the famous Boreades, Zetes and Calais, who had winged feet and could fly through the air. Chione, mother of Eumolpus, was also called their sister. Cleopatra was married to the blind seer Phineus, son of Agenor and king of Salmydessus in Thrace. He had elected blindness over a short life and gave prophecies in this remote place. Cleopatra bore to him sons Oryithus (Oarthus) and Crambis. Others add Parthenius, Plexippus, Gerymbas, Polydectus, Pandion, Aspondus, and Polydorus. Later generations of commentators perhaps felt that there should be some compensation for blindness.

Unhappily this large number of sons proved insufficient, and Phineus took a mistress, Idaea, daughter of Dardanus, a fellow mystic. Idaea had two sons by him, Thynus and Mariandynus. She was insanely jealous of Cleopatra and contrived a story that two of Cleopatra's sons had tried to seduce her. Without pursuing the validity of this accusation, Phineus blinded the sons. Others say he exposed them to be devoured by wild beasts or that he scourged them and half-buried them in the earth. Cleopatra was thrown into prison with her sons, although the reason for this is not quite clear.

About this time the Argonauts arrived. Zetes and Calais, Cleopatra's brothers, wasted no time in liberating their sister and giving their nephews the kingdom. They sent Idaea back to her own country.

Most people will recall that Phineus was plagued by the Harpies and that the Argonauts routed these monsters. It is difficult to bring these two stories into conjunction, even though the Harpies were said to have been sent as punishment for the way Phineus treated his sons. Perhaps it was considered that Phineus had paid for his sins and that semiexile and old age were punishment enough. Cleopatra probably continued to live in comfort with her sons until she died, most likely consigning Phineus to deserved anonymity in the royal court. [Apollodorus 3.15.3; Scholiast on Apollonius Rhodius 2.140,178,207; Scholiast on Sophocles' *Antigone* 9.73; Ovid, *Ibis* 273; Scholiast on Pindar's *Pythian Odes* 4.324; Hyginus, *Fables* 14; Diodorus Siculus 4.44; Orphica, *Argonautica* 671.]

CLEOPHEMA was the daughter of Malus and the Muse Erato. Malus was called one of the sons of Amphictyon. Cleophema married Phlegyas, a native of Epidaurus, and they had a daughter, Aegla, more often known as Coronis. Coronis was mother of Asclepius by Apollo. [Isyllus 43.]

CLEOPHILE was the mother of Ancaeus, Epochus, Amphidamas, and Iasus by Lycurgus. She is more often called ANTINOE.

CLEOTHERA was a daughter of Pandareos and sister of Merope. She more often was called CAMEIRA.

CLESO was a maiden of Megara, daughter of Cleson and sister of Tauropolis. The sisters found and buried the body of Ino, which had been washed up on the coast of Megara. When in her madness Ino leapt with Melicertes into the sea, both she and her son were changed into the sea divinities Leucothea and Palaemon. However, there were mortal remains, and those of Ino were discovered and buried by the sisters. [Pausanias 1.42.7.]

CLETA (1) was one of the two CHARITES worshipped in Sparta; her sister was Phaenna.

CLETA (2) was the wife of Eurotas, the early king of the country later called Sparta. Eurotas created a canal system to drain the stagnating waters from the Laconian plain, and the resulting flow was called the Eurotas River from him. Cleta's daughter by Eurotas was Sparta, who married Lacedaemon and started the royal Spartan line. [Apollodorus 3.10.3; Pausanias 3.1.3.]

CLETA (3) was the nurse of the Amazon Penthesileia. When she heard that Penthesileia had fled to Troy after the death of Hippolyte, she set out in search of her but was driven by contrary winds to Italy, where she settled and founded the city of Clete. [Tzetzes on Lycophron 995.]

CLIO was one of the nine MUSES. She was the Muse of history and is usually shown sitting with a scroll of paper or an open chest of books. As with certain of the other Muses, there were efforts on the part of writers to link her with poets and musicians. She has been called the mother of Hyacinthus by Pierus, and of Linus, Ialemus, and Hymenaeus by Magnes. [Apollodorus 1.3.3; Tzetzes on Lycophron 831; Scholiast on Hesiod's *Works and Days* 1.27.]

CLOACINA, or Cluacina, was a surname of Venus, under which she was worshipped at Rome. It was derived from the verb *clorare* or *cluare*, to wash, clean, or purify. After Titus Tatius and Romulus had waged war over the rape of the Sabine women, the two ordered their subjects to purify themselves with sacred myrtle branches on the spot afterward occupied by the temple of Venus Cloacina. Venus Cloacina later was regarded as the goddess who presided over and purified sexual intercourse in marriage. [Livy 3.48; Pliny, *Natural History* 15.29,36; Lactantius, *On False Worship* 1.20.]

CLODONES were a group of Bacchantic women who accompanied Dionysus in his expeditions and travels. They are represented in works of art as raging with madness or enthusiasm, in vehement motion, their heads thrown back with disheveled hair, and carrying in their hands ivy-entwined thyrsus staffs, cymbals, swords, or serpents.

CLOELIA, a Roman virgin, was one of the hostages given to Porsena, the Etruscan lord who occupied part of Rome briefly. She escaped from the Etruscan camp and swam across the Tiber to Rome, but was sent back to Porsena by the intimidated Romans. Porsena was so impressed with her defiant spirit that he set her free and even allowed her to take some of the hostages with her. He also gave her a fine horse and had the Romans erect a statue of her on horseback on the Sacred Way. [Livy 2.13; Dionysius of Halicarnassus, *Roman Antiquities* 5.33; Valerius Maximus 3.2.2; Virgil, *Aeneid* 8.651.]

CLONIA (1), sometimes called Celaeno, was a nymph, wife of Hyrieus. He was a son of Poseidon and Alcyone, and king of Hyria in Boeotia. Clonia became by him the mother of Nycteus, Lycus, and Orion. Orion, a handsome rover, left home early and had a series of unhappy amatory adventures culminating in his being killed by Apollo and Artemis. Nycteus married Polyxo and became the father of Antiope. Antiope either willingly eloped with Epopeus, king of Sicyon, or was abducted by him. Nycteus, by then guardian of the underage heir to the throne, Labdacus of Thebes, raised a Theban army and marched on Sicyon. He was mortally wounded and before his death exacted a promise from Lycus to avenge him.

Clonia was somewhat unusual in that, although she was a nymph, she remained with Hyrieus to bear three children by him. Nymphs usually bore only one child to a lover and then left it for him to bring up. Clonia, then, was probably present during the misfortunes that beset the family. [Apollodorus 3.10.1; Hyginus, *Fables* 7,8,195; Antoninus Liberalis 25; Pausanias 2.6.2.]

CLONIA (2) was one of the AMAZONS. [Quintus Smyrnaeus 1.42.]

CLOTHO was one of the MOIRAE, or Fates. She spun the thread of one's life. She was involved in only one story that did not include her sisters. When Tantalus, the favorite of the gods, served the flesh of his son Pelops to the gods, they knew what he had done and refused to eat. In her grief over Persephone, Demeter consumed

the shoulder. The gods ordered Hermes to put the limbs in a cauldron and restore life and former appearance to Pelops. When this was done, Clotho took him out of the cauldron; seeing that the shoulder was missing, Demeter replaced it with one of ivory. The descendants of Pelops were believed to have a shoulder as white as ivory. [Pindar, *Olympian Odes* 1.37; Tzetzes on Lycophron 152; Hyginus, *Fables* 83; Virgil, *Georgics* 3.7.]

CLYMENE (1) was one of the OCEANIDES, a daughter of Oceanus and Tethys. By her uncle Iapetus she was the mother of Atlas, Prometheus, Menoetius, and Epimetheus. Iapetus was regarded as the ancestor of the human race, although it was his son Prometheus who fashioned men out of clay.

It is to be expected that there was confusion in the genealogies of the beings involved in setting up the world. Clymene was also called the mother by Prometheus of Hellen and Deucalion. This mother/son liaison would not be particularly unusual in the confusing descent of the gods, but Prometheus' wife was usually called Celaeno. Somewhere along the way, probably after the confinement of Iapetus in Tartarus with other Titans, Clymene married Merops, a king of the Ethiopians. Clymene was unfaithful to him and gave herself to her cousin (and brother-in-law) Helios, the sun. By him she had the Heliades and Phaethon.

Clymene's children were pivotal in the contest of the gods against the Titans and in the development of the human race. Atlas and Menoetius were both punished for their roles in the conflict with the Olympians. Atlas was condemned to bear the heavens on his head and shoulders, but not before he became father of the Pleiades, the Hyades, the Hesperides, and other beings. Menoetius was struck by Zeus with a thunderbolt and thrown into Tartarus. Prometheus and Epimetheus were the parents of Deucalion and Pyrrha, respectively, and these offspring were responsible for repopulating the earth after the great flood. For going contrary to the will of Zeus in regard to the human race, Prometheus was punished atop Mount Caucasus by having his liver pecked out daily by an eagle and having it restored each successive day. Pandora, the wife of

Epimetheus, let loose all the troubles of the world by opening a forbidden chest.

Phaethon, the son of Clymene and Helios, almost caused the destruction of the world. He begged his father to let him drive the chariot of the sun across heaven. He proved too weak to handle the dazzling horses, and the chariot fell toward the earth. Zeus struck him from the chariot, and he plummeted to earth. Helios recovered the reins in time to keep the earth from burning to a cinder. Phaethon's mother was also called Merope, Prote, or Rhode. [Hesiod, *Theogony* 351,507; Hyginus, *Fables* 156; Apollodorus 1.2.3; Ovid, *Metamorphoses* 1.763, *Tristia* 3.4.30.]

CLYMENE (2) was a daughter of Minyas (some say Iphis) and the wife of Phylacus, son of Deion. By him she became the mother of Iphiclus and Alcimede. Some call her the mother also of Phaethon by Helios, but this is obviously a confusion with another Clymene, one of the Oceanides.

Phylacus was the founder of the town of Phylace in Thessaly. Their son, Iphiclus, was a typical young hero. He was an Argonaut and renowned for his swiftness in racing. After his return from the voyage he married Diomedeia or Astyoche and became wealthy in cattle. Alcimede is often called the mother of Jason, but most writers call his mother Polymede.

Phylacus apparently died early, for we find that Clymene was also called the mother of Atalanta by Iasus. He was an Arcadian, son of Lycurgus. He participated in the first Olympic games and won a prize in the horse race. There was a statue of him at Tegea. Atalanta, of course, was the famous huntress who shared honors with Meleager at the celebrated Calydonian boar hunt. Clymene provided a link between the Arcadian Atalanta and the Boeotian one, connecting the athletic maiden with Minyan relatives. Under these circumstances Iphiclus would be Atalanta's half-brother.

Clymene probably had an affair with her brother-in-law Cephalus. Some said Iphiclus was his son rather than Phylacus'. This would not be too surprising. The handsome Cephalus was a sexual opportunist. He was married to Procris but had had an affair with Eos, the goddess of

the dawn. He was even on the point of taking to bed a pretty male hunting companion in exchange for a dog and a spear, when the companion turned out to be his wife in disguise. Clymene's affair with Cephalus had certainly ended by the time Procris came into the picture, and Clymene probably passed off Iphiclus as Phylacus' son. [Apollodorus 1.9.4,12, 3.9.2; Apollonius Rhodius 1.45; Aelian, *Various Narratives* 13.1; Hyginus, *Fables* 48,99; Callimachus, *Hymn to Artemis* 216; Pausanias 5.8.1,4; Homer, *Iliad* 2.705; Eustathius on Homer's *Iliad* 323.]

CLYMENE (3) was a relative of Menelaus. She was kept at the court of Sparta as a companion to Helen. When Helen was carried off by Paris, Clymene was taken along as well, probably at Helen's request. When Troy fell and the spoils were distributed, Clymene was given to Acamas, the son of Theseus. She was portrayed in the Lesche of Delphi as a captive. [Homer, *Iliad* 3.144; Dictys Cretensis 1.3, 5.13; Pausanias 10.26.1.]

CLYMENE (4) was a daughter of Catreus, king of Crete, successor to his father, Minos. Catreus received an oracle that declared he would die at the hands of one of his children. His son, Althaemenes, and daughter, Apemosyne, learned of the prediction and went to Rhodes to protect their father from either of them. Obsessed with the ominous prophecy, Catreus gave the remaining daughters, Clymene and Aerope, to Nauplius to sell in a foreign land. Instead, Nauplius kept Clymene for his wife and gave Aerope to Pleisthenes of Mycenae. Nauplius was king of Euboea; by him Clymene became the mother of Palamedes, Oeax, and Nausimedon. Some have called Nauplius' wife Philyra or Hesione, and it is not inconceivable that he was married to her before Clymene, maybe even having one of his children by her. She might have died in childbirth or, if a nymph, she might have disappeared. Palamedes and his brothers are usually attributed to Clymene, however. Nothing is known of Nausimedon, but Oeax and Palamedes were prominent in the Trojan War. Palamedes was an especially talented young man. He was an inventor, but the war interrupted his career, which already included the invention of lighthouses, numbers, scales, the discus, dice, certain letters of the alphabet, and the art of regulating sentinels.

His military service proved his downfall. Prior to the war he was part of an envoy to persuade Helen to return to Sparta. When war proved inevitable, he tricked Odysseus into joining the Greek forces. He also discovered Achilles hidden in women's clothes at Lycomedes' court on Scyros. After hostilities were opened, he was a good soldier, boosting morale and generally proving superior in ethics and leadership. But Odysseus, still smoldering from Palamedes' cunning ruse to force him into the war, planted incriminating evidence of treason in Palamedes' quarters, and Agamemnon had him arrested. Odysseus and Diomedes are said to have stoned him to death at the bottom of a well.

Oeax, who accompanied Palamedes to the war, carved the message of what had happened on an oar and threw it in the water, trusting that his father would find it. Nauplius did indeed find the message and took revenge by setting up signal lights in areas of particularly treacherous waters, so that the Greeks returning from the war would crack up their vessels on the rugged coastline of Euboea. He also sent messages to Greek wives that their husbands were bringing home Trojan concubines (often the case, unknown to him), causing the wives to take lovers or to commit suicide. Meanwhile, Oeax advised Clytemnestra to kill Agamemnon when he returned. He himself was later killed by Pylades, when countervengeance was carried out.

Though taking no direct part in all these vendettas, Clymene was very much central to what went on. She was aunt to Agamemnon and Menelaus. In fact, Menelaus was attending the funeral ceremonies of Catreus in Crete when Helen eloped with Paris. Clymene was seriously wronged by Catreus, and she and her family were deeply injured by his grandson Agamemnon, who, without investigation, sealed the fate of Palamedes. She might have taken some comfort from the fact that her son was honored with a sanctuary and statue on the coast of Asia Minor opposite Methymna in Lesbos. [Apollodorus 2.1.4, 3.2.2; Philostratus, *Heroicus* 10.11, *Life of Apollonius of Tyana* 4.13; Euripides, *Orestes* 432; Scholiast on Euripides' *Orestes* 422; Tzetzes on Lycophron 384; Hyginus, *Fables* 116; Eustathius on Homer's *Iliad* 24; Pausanias 1.22.6, 2.20.3, 10.31.1.]

CLYMENE (5), a nymph, was the wife of Parthenopaeus. According to some, he was the son of Atalanta and Meilanion, but more likely a brother of Adrastus. He was one of the Seven against Thebes. He was killed in the war, just as Athena had warned he would be, falling at the hands of Periclymenus. By Clymene he had a son, Promachus (or Tlesimenes or Stratolaus), who took part in the expedition of the Epigoni. Like most nymphs, Clymene was virtually invisible and seemed to play no role except sexual partnership and resultant motherhood in relation to her handsome husband. [Apollodorus 1.9.13, 3.7.2, 9.2; Pausanias 3.12.7; Eustathius on Homer's *Iliad* 489; Hyginus, *Fables* 71.]

CLYMENE (6) was the wife of Pheres and mother by him of Admetus. She was more usually called PERICLYMENE. [Apollodorus 1.8.2, 9.14.]

CLYMENE (7) was one of the NEREIDES. The Athenians had a precinct sacred to Perseus and an altar of Dictys and Clymene, who were called the saviors of Perseus. [Pausanias 2.18.1.]

CLYMENE (8) was one of the AMAZONS. [Hyginus, *Fables* 163.]

CLYTEMNESTRA is one of the most unforgettable women in Greek mythology. She is complex and controversial, viewed most often as a cold-blooded murderess and unfaithful wife to one of the glorious heroes of the great Trojan War. Any attempt to do her justice in these respects must take into account an examination of her and her husband's unusual relationship, all events prior to and after the war, and the role of their children in these various interactions. That is a big order and deserving of studies beyond the scope of this one.

Clytemnestra was the daughter of Tyndareus and Leda; she was the sister of Castor, Timandra, and Philonoe, and half-sister of Helen and Polydeuces. This is not the place to go into the strange circumstances of her conception and that of Helen and the Dioscuri except to say tradition has it that Zeus and Tyndareus impregnated Leda on the same night, so that she produced two mortal and two immortal children at one time. By the simplest reckoning this would make Leda mother of quadruplets. We hear of the twins—the Dioscuri, one mortal and one immortal—but Helen and Clytemnestra are never mentioned as twins. But indeed they must have been if the Dioscuri were.

Zeus, of course, made his entrance and exited, leaving Tyndareus to bring up this improbable brood. We do not get a picture of Leda during these years; probably the royal children were reared by nurses. It is fascinating to think of their early years and how they reacted to each other, how the touch of divinity might have affected Helen and Polydeuces in the everyday business of growing up. We know Castor and Polydeuces were extremely close, but what about Helen and Clytemnestra? When Helen was still very young—not yet of marriageable age—she was abducted by Theseus and secreted at Aphidna. Castor and Polydeuces went there and delivered her, in spite of the fact that they themselves were only adolescents. What about Clytemnestra during this time? She was left alone for a considerable time, since the liberation of Helen involved a small war.

Clytemnestra married young, possibly as soon as Helen returned to Sparta from Aphidna. Her husband was Tantalus, son of Thyestes. He was considerably older than she, and did not live long after the marriage. He was killed either by his uncle Atreus or by his cousin Agamemnon, who wanted Clytemnestra for himself.

Some say Agamemnon peacefully succeeded Thyestes on the throne of Mycenae, but others say he usurped the throne. He married Clytemnestra, thus joining the royal families of Mycenae and Sparta, and proceeded to become the most powerful ruler in Greece. This made Clytemnestra the most powerful woman of her time, but we do not see much evidence that she used this extraordinary influence. We look more often at Helen as the spoiled wielder of power to gain for herself what she desired.

Clytemnestra seemed content to stay at home and bear four children to Agamemnon—Electra, Orestes, Iphigeneia, and Chrysothemis. There is no reason to believe she was not happy with her lot. There is never the slightest hint that she resented the enormous popularity of her twin sister, who was courted far and wide by almost every noble red-blooded bachelor in Greece. One can even imagine conversations between her and her sister regarding the attributes of one or another of the suitors.

Helen married Clytemnestra's brother-in-law Menelaus, and Clytemnestra was more than likely pleased at the match. Menelaus was not exactly the most glamorous of the possible choices, but he was politically correct and, after all, her own husband's brother. She probably approved Odysseus' rather presumptuous pledge that all the suitors would subsequently rally to defend Helen's honor.

When that challenge came, Clytemnestra saw her husband rally the princes of Greece to recover the delinquent beauty. By then Clytemnestra realized her sister had succumbed to a glorious debauch with the charming son of Priam in faraway Troy. She even sent word to her sister by the emissary Palamedes to come back and make everything right. Of course, Helen did not return, and the Trojan War got under way.

Agamemnon and the Greek forces convened at Aulis. According to the common story, Agamemnon killed a stag in the sacred grove of Artemis. As a result, the Greek fleet was held up by a deadly calm. The seer Calchas affirmed that the only thing that would appease the goddess would be the sacrifice of Iphigeneia. Agamemnon said absolutely not, but Odysseus and Diomedes went to fetch her anyway, on the pretext that she was marrying Achilles. Iphigeneia came to Aulis (in some accounts accompanied by Clytemnestra), and it was not long before the terrible truth came out. Iphigeneia was sacrificed but, according to most accounts, saved at the last minute by Artemis. It has never been clear whether or not her parents were aware of this miraculous rescue, since Artemis tended to do things with great flourish. There was probably a thunderstorm, general confusion, and finally a vacant altar or one with a substituted sacrifice. The storm signaled the arrival of the wind that would carry the Greek fleet to Troy. With a heavy heart and deep loathing, Clytemnestra turned homeward to Mycenae. Even if she had been convinced that Iphigeneia had been spared, the fact remained that Agamemnon had allowed her to be sacrificed.

The days of the war must have been bitter ones for Clytemnestra. She had the children to provide for. Orestes was a baby when Agamemnon left. In fact, Clytemnestra might have been pregnant with him when her husband went to war, which means Agamemnon never laid eyes on his only son. Inasmuch as Iphigeneia was of marriageable age and Electra was probably next eldest, there was quite a spread in the ages of the four children.

When Agamemnon left, the temporary rule of the kingdom shifted to Aegisthus, the son of Thyestes. Aegisthus had his reasons to hate Agamemnon. His father had been served the flesh of his brothers by Atreus, grandfather of Agamemnon. In addition, Agamemnon had done away with Tantalus, another brother, to gain Clytemnestra. It certainly is not clear why Agamemnon left the kingdom in the hands of someone who had so many reasons to despise him. But Agamemnon was obsessed with recovering the lost Helen; one almost suspects he himself was in love with her.

Aegisthus started to lust after Clytemnestra. She was, after all, the twin sister of the most beautiful woman in the world. She was also the queen of Mycenae and the satellite governments of the whole Peloponnesus. Looking over the brown hills of her kingdom, Clytemnestra wondered about a future with a husband cruel enough to allow the sacrifice of a beautiful daughter for a cause so inglorious as the retrieval of his wanton sister-in-law, her sister.

He succeeded. She lay with Aegisthus and conceived by him. Some say this coupling was a result of Nauplius' gossip about the concubines of the returning Greeks. For other Greek wives it was so, perhaps, but Clytemnestra was already under the curse of Aphrodite, along with her sisters Helen and Timandra. Their father had once neglected an important sacrifice to Aphrodite, and she resolved that all three of his daughters would be adulteresses.

But mere adultery was not the essential force that drove Clytemnestra. She hated her husband for his role in the sacrifice of Iphigeneia. We ordinarily look at Aegisthus as an arrogant individual who took the vulnerable Clytemnestra by force and brought her to his own murderous intentions. He was probably bored with the great clamor over Helen. He did not go to the war, and nobody has ever asked why he did not. Too old immediately leaps to mind, but there is no substantiation of this. After all, Nestor went to the war, and he was quite old, a veteran of both the Argonaut and the Calydonian boar hunt. Aegisthus was Agamemnon's father's cousin, but as families went in those days, he was possibly as young or even younger than Agamemnon. He was probably quite good-looking. Maybe Aegisthus was needed to leave a force in Greece in case the invading army failed. There are many possibilities.

Clytemnestra bore him a daughter, Erigone, who was later to become by her half-brother Orestes the mother of Penthilus. Clytemnestra and Aegisthus lived as husband and wife for the years it took Agamemnon to finish up the war and return home. Aegisthus had kept spies out against this day. When signal fires along the coast of Greece announced the return of the conquering hero of the Trojan War, Aegisthus was ready for him. Word had come along, probably this time by Nauplius, the vengeful father of Palamedes, that Agamemnon was bringing with him the Trojan princess Cassandra, who had recently produced twins by him.

Agamemnon and his companions received the public welcome granted to returning heroes. Aegisthus then invited him to a grand feast, which Agamemnon never lived to see. While he prepared himself for the banquet he was slain by Aegisthus. Clytemnestra murdered Cassandra, and Aegisthus arrived in time to guarantee that the twin sons of Agamemnon and Cassandra would never rule in Mycenae. The deed was done.

But not entirely—there was the matter of Orestes. It was part of the plan that he should die along with Agamemnon. It is difficult to understand why Clytemnestra had agreed to this scheme. Judging from her reaction to the sacrifice of Iphigeneia, she was fiercely devoted to her children. She had ample motives for participating in the murder of Agamemnon. He had sacrificed their daughter and then at the end of the war brought home with him a Trojan princess who had borne him two children. But

Orestes was still a boy and had had no part in the sins of his father. Perhaps it was Electra who was responsible for turning mother against son. She herself loathed Aegisthus and probably inflamed the teenaged Orestes against the usurping cousin. Or maybe Aegisthus had persuaded Clytemnestra that Orestes would be an ever-present threat after the assassination of Agamemnon.

Electra anticipated the threat to Orestes and had him spirited away by a servant to Phocis to the court of Strophius, whom Agamemnon's sister Anaxibia had married. There he grew up with his cousin Pylades. When he reached manhood Orestes was commanded by Apollo to avenge his father's death by killing Aegisthus and Clytemnestra. With Pylades he went to his father's tomb in Argos and dedicated a lock of his hair. By this token Electra and Orestes were reunited in person, although they had kept in touch by messages, mainly pleas from Electra for Orestes to avenge the wrong, by then seven years in the past.

Orestes finally took action by appearing at Aegisthus' court with an urn full of ashes, which he claimed were those of Orestes sent by Strophius. Clytemnestra was relieved at the news, since Orestes would, she thought, pose no further problem. Electra was, after all, half-demented and could be handled. Even while she was thinking this, Aegisthus arrived on the scene and was hastily felled by Orestes. Clytemnestra fell to her knees and begged Orestes, who she then realized was her son, to spare her, who had given birth to him and suckled him. Orestes wavered, but Pylades, who accompanied him, urged him to fulfill Apollo's divine will, and he thrust his sword into his mother.

Thus ended the bitter drama of Clytemnestra's life. Her sister's profligacy had taken an even greater toll than anyone could have predicted. The question is really how harshly Clytemnestra should be judged. Could she be held too accountable for turning her back on a husband who was so obsessed with a war involving the honor of his wife's self-indulgent sister that he was willing to kill his own daughter? And, if that was not enough, how could he expect to come home to the way things were, bringing with him a beautiful young mistress and two children by her? The intended murder of Orestes is about the only charge that can be leveled against her, even though conspiracy in the murder of one's husband is not exactly the most admirable of pursuits. In all respects Clytemnestra was a victim, not only of her insensitive husband and her scheming lover, but of her own wounded vanity and self-esteem. [Apollodorus 3.10.6; Homer, *Iliad* 9.145,287, 13.365, 24.299; *Odyssey* 1.28,30,298, 3.263, 4.365,518,524, 11.400,422, 24.96; Dictys Cretensis 1.20; Pausanias 2.16.5,18.5,22.4; Aeschylus, *Agamemnon* 1260,1492, *Libation-Bearers* 732,931; Euripides, *Orestes* 26,162,804, *Electra* 1245; Sophocles, *Electra* 11,35,296, 530,1346,1405; Tzetzes on Lycophron 1099; Hyginus, *Fables* 77.]

CLYTIA (1), the mother of Myrtilus, was more often called CLEOBULE.

CLYTIA (2) was a daughter of Pandareos and sister of CAMEIRA.

CLYTIA (3), daughter of Amphidamas, was sometimes called the mother of Pelops. More often his mother was called DIONE, daughter of Atlas. [Scholiast on Euripides' *Orestes* 5.11; Tzetzes on Lycophron 52.]

CLYTIA (4) was the mistress of Amyntor. She is usually called PHTHIA.

CLYTIA (5) was a nymph who loved Helios, the sun. From his great advantage of height and light, Helios could survey the most beautiful of women as they performed their daily functions. He loved, among others, Leucothoe, daughter of the Babylonian king Orchamus. Jealous Clytia betrayed the fiery love of Helios and Leucothoe to Orchamus, who buried his daughter alive. Clytia accomplished nothing by this cruel action and pined away, sitting all day watching the object of her desire cross the heavens in his radiant splendor. She was eventually changed into a sunflower, which, like her, exposed its face to the sun. [Ovid, *Metamorphoses* 4.208.]

CLYTIA (6) was one of the OCEANIDES. [Hesiod, *Theogony* 351.]

CLYTIPPE was one of the THESPIADES, daughter of Thespius and Megamede, and mother of Eurycapys by Heracles. [Apollodorus 2.7.8.]

CLYTODORA was the wife of Minyas, according to some. Usually his wife is called EU-RYANASSA.

CNAGIA was a surname of Artemis at Sparta. It came from Cnageus, a Laconian, who accompanied the Dioscuri to Aphidna in order to recover Helen from Theseus. Cnageus was captured and sold as a slave to Cretans, who put him in service in the temple of Artemis. He escaped and, with one of the priestesses of the goddess, brought her statue to Sparta. [Pausanias 3.18.3.]

CNIDIA was a surname of Aphrodite from the town of Cnidus in Caria. Praxiteles made for Cnidus the famous statue of the goddess. The so-called Medici Venus was considered a copy of the Cnidian Aphrodite. [Pausanias 1.1.3; Pliny, *Natural History* 36.5; Lucian, *Amores* 13.]

CNOSSIA, a nymph, was the mother of Xenodamus by Menelaus. Menelaus was in Crete attending his grandfather's funeral ceremonies when Helen was abducted. Some believe that his delay in getting home from Crete gave Helen and Paris ample time to leave without pursuit. Menelaus' extended visit with his bereaved relatives was only part of the story apparently, but it seems hardly likely that he would have delayed long enough for a son to be born. Nothing further is known of Cnossia or of Xenodamus. [Apollodorus 3.11.1.]

COCCYMO was, according to some, one of the PLEIADES. [Scholiast on Theocritus 13.25.]

COCYTHIAE were a class of nymphs of Elis, among whom was Mintha, the beloved of Hades.

COLAENIS, a surname of Artemis in the Attic deme of Myrrhinus, was derived from a mythical king, Colaenus, who was believed to have reigned even before the time of Cecrops. [Pausanias 1.31.3.]

COLIAS was a surname of Aphrodite, who had a statue on the Attic promontory of Colias. Strabo places a sanctuary of Aphrodite Colias in the neighborhood of Anaphlystus. [Pausanias 1.1.4; Strabo 9.1.21.]

COLOCASIA was a surname of Athena at Sicyon. When Thyestes fled from Atreus to King Thesprotus at Sicyon, where his daughter Pelopia was a priestess, he consulted the Delphic oracle and was advised to beget a son by his own daughter. Thyestes found Pelopia sacrificing by night to Athena Colocasia. He waited for her and ravished her while she was cleansing herself. Pelopia did not recognize him but contrived to steal his sword and carry it back to the temple, where she hid it under the pedestal of Athena's image. Thyestes found the sword missing and, fearing detection, escaped to Lydia. [Apollodorus, *Epitome* 2.14; Hyginus, *Fables* 87; Scholiast on Euripides' *Orestes* 14.]

COLYMBAS was one of the PIERIDES. [Antoninus Liberalis 9.]

COMAETHO (1) was the daughter of Pterelaus, king of the Taphians. When Electryon was reigning at Mycenae, the sons of Pterelaus invaded his territory and drove away his oxen. Electryon set out to avenge this act, but the task had to be completed by his son Amphitryon. While Amphitryon was doing battle with the Taphians, Comaetho fell in love with him. Pterelaus bore a golden lock of hair on his head and was invincible as long as the lock remained intact. Willing to gain Amphitryon by any means, Comaetho cut off the golden hair while her father slept. Amphitryon at once gained the victory, but Comaetho's desperate act availed her nothing except death, for Amphitryon had her killed as soon as he took the city. He must have learned of her perfidious and unpatriotic act, otherwise she certainly would have been taken captive. [Apollodorus 2.4.6,7; Pausanias 9.10.4; Herodotus 5.9.]

COMAETHO (2) was a priestess of Artemis Triclaria at Patrae in Achaia. Melanippus loved her and she him, but they could not get their parents to consent to a wedding. Perhaps it was a disgrace for a young woman to leave the service of Artemis for a man. Deprived of a legal means of consummating their love, the couple had sex in the temple of the goddess. One hopes their moment was sublime, for Artemis killed them instantly. She also brought a plague and famine on the whole country and could be appeased only with the sacrifice each year of the handsomest youth and most beautiful maiden. [Pausanias 7.19.2.]

CONCILIATRIX was a surname of Juno at Rome. Jupiter and Juno were the guardians of the bond of marriage; when the harmony between husband and wife was disturbed, it was restored by Juno Conciliatrix, who had a sanctuary on the Palatine Hill. [Festus, "Conciliatrix"; Valerius Maximus 2.1.6.]

CONCORDIA, a Roman divinity, was the personification of concord. She had several temples in Rome, the earliest of which originally served as a meeting place for the senate. It fell into decay but was restored by Livia, the wife of Augustus. It later burned, but again was restored in the reign of Constantine. Other temples were built as time went on. A statue of Hygieia, the goddess of health, stood in one of her temples.

Concordia was represented on coins as a matron. Sometimes she held a cornucopia or an olive branch. She was worshipped in conjunction with Pax, Janus, and Salus on April 30 in a public ceremony. [Plutarch, *Camillus* 42; Ovid, *Fasti* 1.639, 3.881; Suetonius, *Tiberius* 20; Dio Cassius 55.17; Livy 22.33; Cicero, *On the Nature of the Gods* 2.23.]

CONDYLEATES was a surname of Artemis at Caphyae. (*See* APANCHOMENE.)

CONSERVATRIX was a surname of Juno. (*See* FORTUNA.)

CORA (*See* PERSEPHONE)

CORCYRA (*See* CERCYRA)

CORDACA was a surname of Artemis at Pisa in Elis. The name came from a dance, probably lascivious, that the followers of Pelops brought with them from Asia Minor. They performed the dance in honor of the goddess after every victory. [Pausanias 6.22.1.]

CORONIDES were daughters of Orion. Their names were Menippe and Metioche. After Artemis killed their father, they were reared by their mother. As if in compensation for the death of their father, the goddesses Athena and Aphrodite bestowed special favors on them. However, Aonia, their home, was visited by a plague, and the oracle of Apollo Gortynius ordered the inhabitants to propitiate the Erinyes by the sacrifice of two maidens who would give themselves to be offered. Menippe and Metioche volunteered after invoking the gods, and bashed their brains out with their shuttles. The gods of the underworld changed them into comets. The Aonians built a sanctuary to them near Orchomenus, and youths and maidens offered sacrifices to them every year. [Ovid, *Metamorphoses* 13.685; Antoninus Liberalis 25; Scholiast on Homer's *Iliad* 18.486.]

CORONIS (1) was a daughter of Phlegyas, son of Ares and Chryse and king of the Lapiths. He succeeded Eteocles to the throne and called the district of Orchomenus after himself Phlegyantis. Coronis was overpowered by Apollo and became pregnant by him. Phlegyas was enraged at this and, god or no god, set fire to the temple of Apollo. For this, of course, he paid with his life, and he was further condemned to especially severe punishment in the underworld.

What Phlegyas perhaps did not know was that Coronis had been carrying on a passionate affair with Ischys, a son of Elatus, and probably would have ended up pregnant anyway. It did not take long for Apollo to learn of this act of "unfaithfulness" on the part of Coronis. Some say he was informed of this by a raven he had set to watch her. Others say he divined the situation by his own prophetic powers. In any case, he sent Artemis to kill her, and Ischys as well. The avenging goddess did so without hesitation. The deed was carried out at Lacereia in Thessaly on the shore of Lake Boebe. Some writers claim

Apollo himself was the avenger. He was on hand when the body of Coronis was burned, for he saved the premature infant from the flames. The infant was Asclepius, and Apollo took him to Cheiron the Centaur, who later instructed him in the art of healing. Some writers have Asclepius born in Tricca or in Epidaurus. In the Epidaurus version he was suckled by a goat and guarded by a dog until found by a shepherd.

Coronis was one of the very few women who chose a mortal lover over a divine one. Marpessa, the daughter of Euenus, was given a choice between Idas and Apollo, and chose Idas because she feared Apollo would desert her when she grew old. However, she did not have sexual relations with the god. Coronis was also said by one writer to have been the mother of Machaon by Asclepius. This would, of course, have meant an incestuous relationship. Another Coronis was probably intended, since the mother of Machaon was Epeione, according to most accounts. [Apollodorus 3.10.3; Pindar, *Pythian Odes* 3.14; Ovid, *Metamorphoses* 2.605; Hyginus, *Fables* 97, *Poetic Astronomy* 2.40; Pausanias 2.26.5.]

CORONIS (2) was a daughter of Coroneus, king of Phocis. She was pursued by Poseidon and prayed for the protection of Athena. The goddess changed her into a crow. [Ovid, *Metamorphoses* 550.]

CORONIS (3) was one of the HYADES. [Hyginus, *Fables* 182, *Poetic Astronomy* 2.21; Diodorus Siculus 5.52.]

CORONIS (4) was a Naxian nymph who, with her sisters Philia and Cleis, helped rear Dionysus. Butes, the son of Boreas, went with a band of colonists from Thrace to Naxos. They had no women except for the resident nymphs, so they made predatory excursions to the mainland. For himself, Butes was happy with Coronis, but she invoked Dionysus to protect her. He struck Butes with madness, so that he threw himself into a well. [Diodorus Siculus 5.50.]

CORONIS (5) was, according to some, the mother by Dionysus of the Charites. Their mother most often was called EURYNOME. [Nonnos, *Dionysiaca* 48.555.]

CORYCIA, a nymph, became by Apollo the mother of Lycorus, or Lycoreus. The Corycian cave on Mount Parnassus derived its name from her, while the village of Lycoreia in the neighborhood of Delphi derived its name from her son. [Pausanias 10.6.2,32.2.]

CORYCIAE were the daughters of the Pleistus River. They were mountain nymphs named for the Corycian cave they inhabited. However, Ovid placed them on the island of Ceos, where they had lived until frightened away by a lion, after which they lived in Carystus. It is not clear how this geographical disparity came about. It is known that the Phocian area sent colonists to Ceos, and perhaps the worship of the nymphs was transported. [Apollonius Rhodius 2.710; Ovid, *Metamorphoses* 1.320, *Heroides* 20.221.]

CORYPHAEA, the Goddess of Summits, was a surname of Artemis, under which she had a temple on Mount Coryphum near Epidaurus. [Pausanias 2.28.2.]

CORYPHASIA was a surname of Athena derived from the promontory of Coryphasium in Messenia, where she had a sanctuary. [Pausanias 4.36.2.]

CORYTHALLIA was a surname of Artemis at Sparta. At her so-called "nurse" festival, the Tithenidia, the nurses took the male children into the country and before the temple of Artemis Corythallia provided for them a special feast, a kind of picnic. [Athenaeus 4.139.]

COS was the daughter of Merops and the nymph Ethemea. Merops was king of the island of Cos, which he named for his daughter. The inhabitants were called Meropes. Cos did not have a very happy life. Ethemea neglected to worship Artemis and was killed by her. In despair Merops tried to end his life but was changed into an eagle by Hera, who placed him among the constellations. Nothing further is known of Cos. [Hyginus, *Poetic Astronomy* 2.16; Antoninus Liberalis 15.]

COTHONEA was the wife of Eleusis. He was a son of Hermes and Daeira, one of the Oceanides; the town of Eleusis in Attica was named for him. Some said Triptolemus was the son of Eleusis and Cothonea, but the mother of Triptolemus was usually called METANEIRA. The wife of Eleusis has also been called Cyntinia or Hyona. [Hyginus, *Fables* 147; Servius on Virgil's *Aeneid* 1.19.]

COTYS, or Cotytto, was a Thracian divinity. Her worship was connected with that of Rhea, Demeter, Bendis, and other fertility goddesses, but most particularly with that of Cybele. Her festivals were celebrated on the hills with riotous and licentious proceedings. In later times her worship was introduced at Athens and Corinth and connected with that of Dionysus, featuring sexual abandon. The worship eventually spread as far as Italy and Sicily. Those who celebrated her festivals were called *baptai* from the purifications evidently suggested by the purgative effects of the orgiastic festivals. [Strabo 10.3.16; Hesychius, "Kotys"; Horace, *Epodes* 17.56; Juvenal 2.92.]

CRANAE was a daughter of Cranaus, king of Attica, and Pedias. Her sisters were Cranaechme and Atthis. Cranaus ruled at the time immediately after the flood of Deucalion. Deucalion's son Amphictyon came to Attica and married Cranae. Amphictyon usurped the kingdom and ruled for 12 years until he was expelled by Erichthonius (Erechtheus I). He founded the amphictyony of Thermopylae. Cranae has no history of her own, but almost certainly she shared the fate of her exiled husband and died in Thermopylae. [Apollodorus 3.14.5; Pausanias 1.2.5,31.2.]

CRANAECHME was a daughter of Cranaus, king of Attica, and Pedias, and sister of Cranae and Atthis. She was totally insignificant. Cranae married Amphictyon in the first generation after the flood. From Atthis the territory of Attica was named. But of Cranaechme we know nothing; this is surprising since in the new Attica it was a time for beginning dynasties. She might have died at a very early age. [Apollodorus 3.14.5; Pausanias 1.2.5.]

CRANE was an ancient form of CARNA. [Ovid, *Fasti* 6.101.]

CRANTO was one of the NEREIDES. [Apollodorus 1.2.7.]

CRATEIS was the mother of the monster Scylla by Phorcys according to some, and by Poseidon according to others. Phorcys was a son of Pontus and Gaea, and routinely fathered monsters. By others he was father of the Gorgons, the Graeae, and the Hesperian dragon. The genealogy of Scylla is disputed, and there are various accounts of how and why she became a monster. Her mother was sometimes referred to as Hecate Crateis. [Homer, *Odyssey* 12.124; Ovid, *Metamorphoses* 13.749; Hesychius, "Krateis"; Hesiod, *Theogony* 237,270; Apollonius Rhodius 4.828.]

CRENAIAE were a class of freshwater nymphs belonging to the general order known as Naiades, who inhabited rivers, lakes, brooks, and fountains.

CRENEIS was one of the NEREIDES. [Hyginus, *Fables: Preface* 8.]

CRETE (1) was a daughter of Asterius, king of Crete. She was said to have been the wife of Minos, although most accounts call PASIPHAE his wife. This disagreement is somewhat mediated by the view that the Minos of the Theseus legend was the grandson of Minos, the son of Zeus and Europa. Crete, then, would have married her foster brother, and Pasiphae would have been her granddaughter-in-law. To complicate things further, though, other writers have called Crete the mother of Pasiphae by Helios, and still others have called Ariadne, Androgeus, Catreus, and their brothers and sisters the children of Minos and Crete. [Apollodorus 3.1.2; Diodorus Siculus 4.60; Pausanias 8.53.2.]

CRETE (2) was a daughter of Deucalion, sister of Idomeneus, and half-sister of Molus, a bastard son of Deucalion.

CRETE (3) was a daughter of one of the Curetes. Cronus, the leader of the Titans, made war on Ammon. Being sorely pressed, Ammon fled to the island of Crete. The Curetes were ruling there at this time, and Ammon married Crete. Afterward he gained the sovereignty of the whole island and changed its name from Idaea, by which it had been called up to that time, to Crete, the name of his wife. Crete the island was called symbolically the nurse of Zeus. [Diodorus Siculus 3.71; Virgil, *Aeneid* 3.104; Dionysius Periegeta 501.]

CRETHEIS was a patronymic of Hippolyte, daughter of Cretheus and the wife of Acastus. The wife of Acastus is usually called AS-TYDAMEIA. [Pindar, *Nemean Odes* 5.26.]

CREUSA (1) was a daughter of Oceanus and Gaea. By her half-brother Peneius, son of Oceanus and Tethys, she became the mother of Hypseus, Stilbe, and Daphne, who were also called the children of Phillyra. Peneius was the river that flowed through Thessaly, and it is fitting he was the father of the royal line that started in the territory. Hypseus was king of the Lapithae and the father of Cyrene, who by Apollo became the mother of the god Aristaeus. Stilbe, also a lover of Apollo, was mother of Lapithes and Centaurus. Daphne was pursued by Apollo, but was changed into a laurel tree. It is no wonder the valley of the Peneius River became sacred to Apollo. [Diodorus Siculus 4.69; Pindar, *Pythian Odes* 9.13,26; Apollodorus 1.9.2; Pausanias 9.34.5; Hyginus, *Fables* 161, 203.]

CREUSA (2) was a daughter of Erechtheus (II) and Praxithea. Erechtheus was a grandson of Erichthonius (Erechtheus I), son of Pandion by Zeuxippe, and brother of Butes, Procne, and Philomela. He succeeded to the kingship of Athens when Pandion died. By Praxithea he became the father of Cecrops, Pandorus, Metion, Orneus, Procris, Chthonia, Oreithyia, and Creusa, to whom were added by various writers Thespius, Eupalamus, Alcon, Protogeneia, Pandora, and Otiona. It is well that there were additional daughters, for it was reported that the daughters had agreed they would all die together. It is hard to imagine why, but that is the story. When Eumolpus, son of Poseidon, assisted the Eleu-

sinians in a war against Athens and was killed, Poseidon demanded the sacrifice of one of the daughters. It is said that all of them volunteered and died. Oreithyia did not; she was kidnapped by Boreas, the north wind. Procris did not; she was killed by her husband, Cephalus. Creusa did not; she married Xuthus, son of Hellen. So the alleged collective sacrifice must have included only Chthonia, Protogeneia, Pandora, and Otiona.

Xuthus had been expelled from Thessaly by his brothers and went to Athens, where, having married into the royal family, he assumed considerable importance. He was chosen arbitrator after the death of Erechtheus and adjudged the kingdom to his brother-in-law Cecrops. For doing so he was expelled by Cecrops' brothers and settled at Aegialus in Peloponnesus.

While all these political events were taking place, Creusa was living her own life. Her husband, busy with affairs of state, probably neglected her or had trouble satisfying her physical needs. He was also unable to produce children by her. Apollo observed Creusa walking near the Acropolis and took her into a cave below the Propylaea, where he impregnated her. She was able to conceal her condition from her husband, which gives some idea about the frequency of their sexual relations. Of course she could have passed off the unborn child as his (some say he was indeed the father) and then claimed a miscarriage. In any case, she delivered the baby in the same cave in which it was conceived and left it there to die from exposure. Apollo rescued the child and had it conveyed to Delphi, where it was brought up and educated by a priestess. The child was named Ion.

Creusa did not know the child was saved and went about her days in the court of Pandion. Xuthus continued to fret about having no heirs, but apparently he was a man slow to action. Some 18 or so years after Creusa's affair with Apollo, he decided to check with the Delphic oracle about his (or more probably, to his way of thinking, his wife's) inability to conceive children.

With Creusa he journeyed to Delphi. The oracle, more direct than usual, told Xuthus that the first human being he should meet on leaving the temple would be his son. Xuthus left the temple and immediately encountered Ion, the temple aide. He embraced the young man and declared him his son, meanwhile running through his mind all the possible occasions on which he might have sired him. Totally baffled, Ion tentatively agreed to be adopted by this seemingly long-lost father. Xuthus presented Ion to Creusa, who at once decided he was the product of her husband's long-ago infidelity (forgetting her own, apparently). That afternoon she presented her new "stepson" with a congratulatory cup she had generously laced with the venom of a serpent. A pious youth, Ion escaped death by first pouring a libation to the gods. A pigeon drank from the lethal brew and died on the spot. Pursued by Ion, Creusa fled to the altar of Apollo, but Ion dragged her away and was about to strangle her when a priestess intervened and explained to them their peculiar relationship. Even though Ion had every right to complete the action he had started, considering that Creusa had left him to die as a baby and then tried to poison him, he forgave her, and mother and son became reconciled. With good reason they decided to keep their secret to themselves, especially since the oracle promised Xuthus other sons by Creusa.

This indeed proved to be the case. Although she was in her mid- to late thirties, Creusa produced for Xuthus two sons, Dorus and Achaeus, eponymic ancestors of two Hellenic dynasties. Ion married Helice, daughter of Selinus, king of Aegialus, and succeeded him to the throne. He was also, according to some, an interim king of Athens, fathering four sons—Geleon, Aegicores, Argades, and Hoples—whose names were given to the four classes of Athenian citizens.

Creusa's clandestine passion in the Acropolian cave was thus never found out. She was lacking in ethics, not just for her understandable efforts to conceal her adultery but also because of her self-righteous outrage at the imagined infidelities of Xuthus. He perhaps remembered more promiscuities than he actually committed. One writer makes Creusa the mother of Cephalus by Hermes. Cephalus was the exceptionally beautiful young man kidnapped by Eos, goddess of the dawn. [Apollodorus 1.7.3, 3.14.8,15.1; Pausanias 1.5.3, 2.25.2–5, 7.1.1–3; Ovid, *Metamorphoses* 6.676; Plutarch, *Greek and Roman Parallel Stories* 20.]

CREUSA (3), occasionally called Eurydice, was the eldest daughter of Priam and Hecuba. She married Aeneas, a distant cousin, who was the son of Anchises and Aphrodite. Theirs was a fine marriage, and they produced a son—Ascanius, or Iulus. According to one writer, Creusa had previously had a son, Anius, by Apollo, but the rumor was probably founded on the god's insatiable appetite for young women, particularly those who needed a divine infusion for the sake of the nobility of their race. Anius' mother is usually called Rhoeo.

When Troy fell, Aeneas fled the city with his crippled father and his son. Creusa was supposed to accompany them, but in the confusion she got separated. Actually, she was detained by Aphrodite (or perhaps by Cybele). Aeneas came back searching for her but failed to find her. Instead he encountered her shade—even though she was not dead—which consoled him and revealed his future destiny. She told him to continue his flight, that she was held back by the Great Goddess and had no choice but to remain.

In the Lesche of Delphi she was depicted among the captive women of Troy, but she really never left Troy. Aeneas remarried more than once and established the lines of Roman nobility. Ascanius went on to found the Julian line in Italy, from which the Caesars sprang. [Apollodorus 3.12.5; Conon, *Narrations* 41; Virgil, *Aeneid* 2.725,738,752,769,775; Pausanias 10.26.1.]

CREUSA (4) was a daughter of Creon, king of Corinth, who married Jason. In most accounts she is known as GLAUCE.

CREUSA (5) was the wife of Cassandrus, a Trojan ally from Caria, and mother of Menes, who was slain by Neoptolemus. Nothing else is known of this family, but the mention of them brings up the idea that there probably was an oral tradition in Caria paralleling that used by Homer in writing the *Iliad*. [Quintus Smyrnaeus 8.81.]

CRINO (1) was the mother of the Danaides Callidice, Oeme, Celaeno, and Hyperippe. Danaus had several wives, and all his 50 daughters were produced before he left Egypt. There is no revealing information about Crino. [Apollodorus 2.1.5.]

CRINO (2) was the only daughter of Antenor and Theano. Nothing is known of her except that she was depicted by Polygnotus in the Lesche at Delphi. She was shown holding a baby with her father. Theano was also shown with two of her sons, probably the only surviving ones from the Trojan War. Antenor betrayed the Trojans and was protected by the Greeks when they took Troy. [Pausanias 10.27.3.]

CRITOMEDEIA was one of the DANAIDES and was married to Antipaphus. [Hyginus, *Fables* 170.]

CTESYLLA was a lovely young woman of Ceos. Antoninus Liberalis (1) relates a story of her and Hermochares almost identical to one related by other writers of CYDIPPE and Acontius. Some say Ctesylla might have been an attribute of some goddess worshipped there. We do know Aphrodite Ctesylla was worshipped at Ceos, where she might have had a love affair with a mortal.

CTIMENE was the daughter of Laertes and Anticleia. Her father was a glorious adventurer, conqueror, and participant in both the Argonaut and the Calydonian boar hunt. Her brother Odysseus was even more famous. Ctimene was the wife of Phyleus, the son of Augeas, who had been exiled by his father because he supported Heracles in his demand for payment for cleaning the Augean stables. Phyleus went to Dulichium, a neighboring island of Ithaca, where he married Ctimene. Some writers called her Timandra or Eustyoche. Their son was Meges, often called Phyleides, who led forces from Dulichium and the Echinades Islands against Troy. He was a casualty in the war. [Homer, *Iliad* 2.625, 13.692; Dictys Cretensis 3.10.]

CUBA, Cunina, and Rumina were three Roman divinities worshipped as protectors of infants asleep in their cradles. Libations of milk were offered to them. *Cunae* was the word for cradle, while *ruma* in ancient Latin meant a mother's breast. These divinities were related to Edulica

and Potina, who blessed food and drink of children. [St. Augustine, *City of God* 4.10; Lactantius 1.20,36; Arnobius, *Adversus Nationes* 3.25.]

CUNINA (*See* CUBA)

CUPRA was a surname of Juno in Etruria. Some have derived the name from a town, but others have connected it with the Sabine word *cyprus,* which, according to Varro (*On the Latin Language* 5.159), signified good.

CURA was the personification of care. She fashioned man from clay. Jupiter appeared and agreed to give her image life. Cura wanted to give it her name, but Jupiter said no. Tellus, the earth, agreed Cura should name her creation but that the name should be *homo,* since he was made from *humus.* Saturn decided Jupiter should take man after death and that Cura should possess him as long as he lived. Care was an essential concept in man's existence and meant, among other things, his own anxious effort. [Hyginus, *Fables* 220.]

CURISSIA, according to some, was one of the great sea serpents sent by Apollo to destroy Laocoon and his sons. The other was Porcis. Curissia is more often called CHARIBOEA or Periboea. [Tzetzes on Lycophron 347.]

CUROTROPHOS, Nurse of Youth, was a surname of Gaea at Athens, where she had a sanctuary jointly with Demeter Chloe. It was also a surname of Artemis as huntress and protector of youth. Under this name she was identified with Hecate. [Pausanias 1.22.3.]

CYANE (1) was a Sicilian nymph and playmate of Proserpina. Through grief at the loss of Proserpina she was changed into a well. The Syracusans celebrated on that spot an annual festival, which Hercules was said to have instituted. A bull was sunk into the well as a sacrifice. [Diodorus Siculus 5.4; Ovid, *Metamorphoses* 5.412.]

CYANE (2) was a daughter of Liparus, son of Liparus. He had fled from Italy to the island that he named for himself. He founded a city of the same name and later brought under cultivation Lipara and neighboring islands. After Liparus had reached a great age, Aeolus, son of Hippotes, came to the island with several companions. He married Cyane and formed a government. He helped Liparus set up a retirement kingdom at Surrentum, where he ruled with great esteem until his death. This Aeolus, keeper of the winds, was the one involved with Odysseus, who came to Lipara during his wanderings. [Diodorus Siculus 5.7.]

CYANE (3) was a daughter of the Maeander River and, according to some, the mother of Byblis and Caunus. Their mother is more often called TRAGASIA. [Hesiod, *Theogony* 339.]

CYBELE, the principal goddess of the Phrygians, was often referred to as the Mother of the Gods. Although initially a foreign goddess and one with a separate identity, she became incorporated into the Greek pantheon by eventual identification with other goddesses having to do with the entirety of nature and the powers of growth. Among her surnames were Antaea, Berecynthia, Brimo, Dindymene, Genetrix, Idaea, Pessinuntia, and Phrygia. Her principal identification was with RHEA, particularly in connection with Rhea's relationship to Dionysus. Rhea was said to have purified Dionysus and taught him the mysteries. Under the name of Cybele we find her worship on Mount Sipylus and Mount Coddinus in Phrygia. She was also called the mother of Sabazius, the mystic Dionysus, because she brought him up as she had done in the case of Zeus. In any event, the worship of Dionysus became interwoven with that of Rhea/Cybele. The same orgiastic rites, the same sexual masochism accompanied their sacrifices.

Central to the worship of Cybele were the stories involving her relationship with the beautiful, doomed, hermaphroditic Atys. Son of Nana, a daughter of a river-god, he was conceived when his mother masturbated with almonds that had sprung from a tree under which were buried the severed genitals of the terrifying Agdistis. Cybele fell in love with the beautiful young man when he grew up, and made him a

priest in her worship. He was sworn to chastity but had a final fling with the nymph Sagaritis, daughter of Sangarius. Cybele drove him mad, and in this state he emasculated himself. When he recovered his senses he wanted to kill himself, but Cybele changed him into a fir tree, which became sacred to her. After that, she ruled that all her priests had to be eunuchs. Another version of the story made her a daughter of Maeon, a Phrygian king, and Dindyme, secretly marrying Atys against her family's will. Her father killed Atys and, maddened with grief, Cybele roamed the countryside with loud lamentations and the sound of cymbals. She apparently also prevented interment of the corpse. A plague came, and an oracle demanded Atys should be buried. His body had already decayed too far, so funeral honors were paid to an image of him, and Cybele was accorded divine recognition. Still another story had Cybele entranced with the stunning young man, so a jealous Zeus sent a boar to kill him. He was buried at Pessinus under Mount Agdistis, and the worship of Cybele was established. He was worshipped in her temples along with her. A final story says Atys was a priest of Cybele and that a Phrygian king fell desperately in love with him. Atys warded off his advances until one day he was cornered and had no choice but to succumb or fight. In the struggle he deprived the king of his testicles. Before dying the king did the same for Atys. Atys bled to death before Cybele could save him. She instituted annual lamentations and required all her priests to undergo self-inflicted emasculation.

It can be seen that Cybele had a colorful history before she was taken up by the impressionable Greeks. They were fascinated with her amorous adventures and stood in awe of her, males especially, since it might not prove wise to get too involved with her mysteries. Nevertheless, she was worshipped as an extension of Aphrodite on Samothrace. She was identified with Demeter and Hecate. She had ties with the reverence paid Marsyas and Misa. Her mysteries were fostered by Idaeus, who instituted her worship in the Troad, and Echion, who gave impetus to her worship in Boeotia. All her identifications fit in well with the universal awe-inspiring mother-goddess types who had been revered in the Mediterranean for centuries. Not surprisingly her worship spread to Rome. The ships used by Aeneas were said to have been constructed from her sacred pines. In late Roman times, a temple was built to her on the Palatine Hill. [Apollodorus 3.12.6; Apollonius Rhodius 1.985,1092–1152; Hyginus, *Fables* 191,274; Hesychius, "Agdistis," "Misatis"; Arnobius, *Adversus Nationes* 4; Diodorus Siculus 3.58; Pausanias 3.22.4, 5.13.4, 7.17.5; Ovid, *Metamorphoses* 10.686, 14.536; Virgil, *Aeneid* 7.139, *Fasti* 3.47; Lucian, *Dialogues of the Gods* 22; Aristophanes, *Birds* 873.]

CYDIPPE (1) was a beautiful Athenian maiden who went once to Delos to celebrate an annual festival of Artemis. She attracted the attention of a splendid-looking youth, Acontius from Ceos. He was immediately desperate to have her—to his credit, in marriage. He thought of a way and inscribed a message on an apple, which he tossed to her nurse-companion. The message simply said: "I swear by the sanctuary of Artemis to marry Acontius." Cydippe looked at the message and threw the apple away. Unhappily for her, the goddess had taken note. Later in Athens when Cydippe's father wanted to give her in marriage to a series of suitors, she was always taken ill before the nuptials could take place. Acontius learned of the occurrences and went to Athens. When the truth was learned he was given Cydippe in marriage.

Acontius was clever; he could have had almost anybody by this ruse. Was Artemis so insensitive that she allowed Cydippe to fall into the hands of anyone to whom she was appealing? Perhaps Cydippe had other intentions. Maybe the arranged marriages were unacceptable. Was she ever consulted? The records seem to indicate she had no choice. [Ovid, *Heroides* 20,21, *Tristia* 3.10.73; Antoninus Liberalis 1, who tells the same story about Ctesylla and Hermochares.]

CYDIPPE (2) was a priestess of Hera at Argos. Once, on her way to the Heraion, the oxen meant to draw her carriage did not arrive. Her sons Cleobis and Biton came to the rescue and dragged her chariot all the way to the temple, a distance of 18 kilometers. Cydippe asked the gods to give to her sons the greatest gift available to mortals. The gods had them fall asleep in the temple, never to awaken again. The Argives made statues of them, and even today they can be seen at the Museum of Delphi. [Herodotus 1.31; Cicero, *Tusculan Disputations* 1.47; Valerius Maximus 5.4.]

CYDIPPE (3), or Lysippe, was the daughter of Ochimus and Hegetoria. Ochimus, a Rhodian king, gave his daughter in marriage to his younger brother Carcaphus. By him she became the mother of Cameirus, Ialysus, and Lindus; they founded the three towns named for them in Rhodes. [Diodorus Siculus 5.51; Pindar, *Olympian Odes* 7.74,135; Plutarch, *Greek Questions* 27.]

CYDIPPE (4) was one of the NEREIDES. [Hyginus, *Fables: Preface* 8.]

CYDONIA was a surname of Athena, under which she had a temple at Phrixia in Elis. Before entering the race with Oenomaus for the hand of Hippodameia, Pelops sacrificed to the Cydonian Athena. The temple was built by Clymenus of Cydonia. [Pausanias 6.21.5.]

CYDRAGORA was a daughter of Pleisthenes and Aerope, and sister of Agamemnon. She is more often called ANAXIBIA.

CYLLA (*See* CILLA)

CYLLENE (1) was a nymph who became the mother of Lycaon by Pelasgus. Pelasgus was the mythical ancestor of the Pelasgians, the earliest inhabitants of Greece. He established the worship of the Dodonaean Zeus, of Hephaestus, and of the Cabeiri. He was a son of Zeus and Niobe, daughter of Phoroneus. Their son Lycaon was the father of 50 sons, most of whom colonized Greece, naming the colonies for themselves. Lycaon is sometimes called pious and the author of many improvements in the social welfare of his subjects. By others he was regarded as a tyrant who among other things tried to feed Zeus with human flesh and was changed into a wolf. The dark worship he fostered included human sacrifice. His mother was also called Meliboea or Deianeira. [Apollodorus 3.8.1; Dionysius of Halicarnassus, *Roman Antiquities* 1.11,13; Scholiast on Euripides' *Orestes* 1642.]

CYLLENE (2) was the daughter of Menephron. Her father was said to have lived in incestuous intercourse with both her and his mother, Blias. One can only wonder where his wife was at this time and whether Menephron's somewhat diverse sexual appetite took in three generations. Some believe his mother was his main preoccupation and that Cyllene refers to the location of their curious relationship. Menephron might even have been a bachelor. [Ovid, *Metamorphoses* 7.386; Hyginus, *Fables* 253, who calls him Menophrus.]

CYLLO was one of the DOGS of Actaeon. [Hyginus, *Fables* 181.]

CYMATOLEGE was one of the NEREIDES. [Hyginus, *Fables: Preface* 8.]

CYMO was one of the NEREIDES. [Apollodorus 1.2.7.]

CYMODOCE was one of the NEREIDES. [Homer, *Iliad* 18.42.]

CYMOTHOE was one of the NEREIDES. [Apollodorus 1.2.7.]

CYNDRAGORA was by some called the mother of Pylades. More often his mother was called ANAXIBIA.

CYNOSURA was an Idaean nymph and with Helice one of the nurses of Zeus. The two nymphs, along with Zeus, were pursued by Cronus. Zeus changed them into the constellations of Ursa Major and Ursa Minor, and himself into the constellation Draco. A place in Crete near Histoi was named for Cynosura. [Hyginus, *Poetic Astronomy* 2.2; Aratus, *Phenomena* 35; Servius on Virgil's *Georgics* 1.246.]

CYNTHIA was a surname of Artemis, which she derived from Mount Cynthus on the island of Delos, her birthplace. For the same reason her twin brother, Apollo, was surnamed Cynthius. [Callimachus, *Hymn to Delos* 10; Horace, *Odes* 1.21.2, 3.28.12.]

CYNTINEA, or Cyntinia, was the wife of Eleusis and, according to some, the mother of Triptolemus. Usually Triptolemus is called the son of Celeus and METANEIRA. The wife of Eleusis is more often called COTHONEA. [Servius on Virgil's *Georgics* 1.19.]

CYPRIA, Cypris, Cyprigeneia, or Cyprogenes were surnames of Aphrodite, who was born on the island of Cyprus, which was also one of the principal seats of her worship. [Homer, *Iliad* 5.458; Pindar, *Olympian Odes* 1.120, 11.125, *Pythian Odes* 4.383; Tibullus 3.3.34; Horace, *Odes* 1.3.1.]

CYPRIDOS was one of 11 HORAE mentioned by Hyginus (*Fables* 183).

CYRENE was a daughter of Hypseus by Chlidanope. Hypseus was a son of the Peneius River and the Naiad Creusa, and king of the Lapiths. Cyrene's sisters were Alcaea, Themisto, and Astyageia. Themisto married Athamas, and Astyageia became the grandmother of Ixion. Cyrene was not interested in marriage and devoted herself to hunting on Mount Pelion. Aroused once by watching her wrestle with a lion, Apollo carried her off and made her a queen in Libya. From her the city of Cyrene derived its name.

By Apollo she became the mother of Aristaeus. Apollo found her desirable enough to visit again, and she bore to him Idmon. Aristaeus early displayed a talent for hunting and an interest in agricultural pursuits. When he grew up he went to Boeotia, where he married Autonoe, a daughter of Cadmus. He learned from Cheiron the Centaur and from the Muses the arts of healing and prophecy. He left Boeotia after the death of his son Actaeon, and lived in Sardinia and Sicily. Afterward he went to Thrace, where he disappeared. He was worshipped as a god by the Thracian barbarians and by the civilized Greeks as well.

Idmon was one of the soothsayers who accompanied the Argonauts. He divined before the journey that he would not live to return, and it proved true when he was killed in the country of the Mariandynians by the bite of a serpent. Apollo commanded the founders of Heracleia on the Black Sea to build the town around the tomb of Idmon and worship him as the protector of the place.

Cyrene was also said to be by Ares the mother of Diomedes. He was king of the Bistones in Thrace and raised mares, which he fed with human flesh. One of the labors of Heracles was to return these mares to Greece. After the mares ate Heracles' lover Abderus, he killed Diomedes and fed him to the animals.

Cyrene returned to Boeotia at one point, probably because Aristaeus was there, and gave him advice on various matters. Later, for some reason she returned to Libya, and when Aristaeus left Boeotia she outfitted him with a fleet to go to Italy.

Cyrene's history is really unusual. All her children were by gods. Two of them were worshipped, even though they died like other mortals. It is hard to fit the villainous Diomedes into the picture after Cyrene had produced two benevolent sons. Perhaps the difference in fathers could account for the disparity. [Pindar, *Pythian Odes* 9.5; Apollonius Rhodius 1.500, 2.846; Diodorus Siculus 4.15,69,81; Hyginus, *Fables* 161; Apollodorus 1.9.2, 2.5.8; Pausanias 9.34.5.]

CYRIANASSA was the wife of Melampus, according to some. His wife, was usually called Iphianassa, one of the PROETIDES.

CYTHERA, Cythereia, and Cytherias were different forms of a surname of Aphrodite, derived from the town of Cythera in Crete, or from the island of Cythera, where the goddess was said to have first landed when she rose from the sea. She also had a celebrated temple there. [Homer, *Odyssey* 8.288; Herodotus 1.10.5; Pausanias 3.23.1; Horace, *Odes* 1.4.5.]

DAEIRA was a daughter of Oceanus, sometimes called a sister of Styx. By Hermes or Ogygus she became the mother of Eleusis. Her name meant "the Knowing," and she was connected with the Eleusinian mysteries. She was often identified with Aphrodite, Demeter, Hera, or Persephone. Her son gave his name to the town of Eleusis. [Pausanias 1.38.7; Apollodorus 1.5.2; Apollonius Rhodius 3.847; Hyginus, *Fables* 147.]

DAETO was the mother of Enorches by her brother Thyestes. Enorches was born from an egg. He later built a temple of Dionysus, who took his name as a surname in Samos. A dance

from the mysteries of the god was also called *enorches*. This curious brief reference tells us very little. Thyestes was from the first an unsavory character, eventually committing adultery with his brother's wife. He also slept with his daughter, Pelopeia, to produce Aegisthus. How Daeto happened to produce an egg is never explained. Thyestes' grandnephews Agamemnon and Menelaus married sisters who emerged from eggs, but there seems to be no connection between these events. [Tzetzes on Lycophron 212; Hesychius, "Daito."]

DAMIA was the companion of AUXESIA.

DAMOCRATEIA was, according to some, the mother of Menoetius by Actor. The mother of Menoetius is usually called AEGINA. [Scholiast on Pindar's *Olympian Odes* 9.107.]

DAMONE was one of the DANAIDES and married to Amyntor. [Hyginus, *Fables* 170.]

DANAE had the distinction of being the mother of one of the greatest heroes of Greek mythology. She was the daughter of Acrisius, king of Argos, and Eurydice. She grew up in the luxury attending the daughter of a king, but while still pubescent was molested by her uncle Proetus, her father's twin brother. A short time after this family scandal, Acrisius learned, while consulting an oracle about his own ability to father a son, that his grandson would kill him. Fearing Danae might be pregnant from her seduction by his brother, he locked her in a brazen tower. There the beautiful girl was visited by Zeus in the form of a golden shower (probably sunlight entering the off-limits area). She became pregnant, and Acrisius believed the culprit was his brother, although Danae vowed Proetus had never actually completed his incestuous effort and that she had become pregnant by the father of the gods. Daughters were accustomed to claiming divine insemination when they dallied with relatives or mortal lovers, but it is questionable how Danae knew the identity of her strange lover.

Acrisius could not bear to kill his own daughter and her newborn son, Perseus, so he put them in a chest and cast them out to sea. Poor Danae, who had spent the last year in confinement, continued her destiny in yet another claustrophobic space. Some say the little ark floated to Italy, where she was found by Pilumnus, who married her and later founded the city of Ardea. This same tradition states that she was the mother of Daunus, who was an ancestor of Turnus. But most accounts say she floated east and washed onto the shore of the island of Seriphos. Here she was discovered by Dictys, a fisherman who was also the brother of Polydectes, king of the island. Accounts vary on her treatment at the hands of Polydectes. Some say he married her and had Perseus brought up in the temple of Athena. Most accounts say she was made a slave by Polydectes, who repeatedly tried to seduce her. He sent Perseus on the perilous quest for the head of Medusa, claiming the head would be a wedding present for his intended bride, Hippomedeia. He meanwhile continued to force himself on Danae, and when Perseus successfully completed his dangerous mission, he found Danae and Dictys cowering in the temple of Athena as suppliants.

Perseus showed the fatal head of Medusa and changed all the adversaries to stone. He put Dictys on the throne, and returned to Argos with Danae and Andromeda. In the usual unexpected way he indeed killed his grandfather and became the father of a dynasty that produced, among others, Heracles.

Danae was a perpetual victim until her son finally grew up and redressed all the wrongs done to her. She came back with him to Argos and probably died an old woman in his court. After accidentally killing his grandfather, Perseus had chosen to relocate his kingdom to Tiryns. One cannot help but wonder why Danae did not remain in Seriphos with Dictys, who undoubtedly loved her. She had no further role in the rise of the Perseids, and the only conclusion one can reach is that she did not love Dictys, in spite of the protection he offered her, and was happier living in the large shadow of her son. [Apollodorus 2.2.1,4.1; Pausanias 2.5.6,16.2, 3.13.6; Hyginus, *Fables* 63; Virgil, *Aeneid* 9.4, 410; Servius on Virgil's *Aeneid* 7.372, 8.345, 9.148; Pindar, *Pythian Odes* 12.21; Ovid, *Metamorphoses* 5.238; Tzetzes on Lycophron 838.]

DANAIDES were the 50 daughters of Danaus. Their story is certainly one of the most curious and provocative in all mythology. Danaus and his twin brother Aegyptus were sons of Belus and Anchinoe, and grandsons of Poseidon and Libya. When the twins grew up, Belus gave the territory of Libya to Danaus, and Arabia to Aegyptus, but Aegyptus also subdued the Melampodes and added Egypt to his domains. This annexation more than likely was the cause of a quarrel over the brothers' inheritance when Belus died.

Danaus had meanwhile produced 50 daughters by various wives, and Aegyptus had produced 50 sons. Aegyptus decided that perhaps a good way to settle their differences would be a mass marriage of all his sons to all the daughters of Danaus. Danaus suspected ulterior motives in this sweeping gesture and had his suspicions confirmed by an oracle: Aegyptus was planning to have his sons murder their wives. Acting on further advice from the oracle, Danaus hastily had a ship built and left from Chemmis in the Egyptian Thebaid. The ship arrived first at Rhodes, where Danaus set up an image of Athena Lindia. Some say the Danaides built the famous temple of Athena at Lindus.

From Rhodes they sailed to the coast of Greece, landing at a place they called Apobathmi, not far from Lerna. Danaus soon sent word to Gelanor, the king of Argos, that he was planning to take over the rule of Argos, since this action was divinely ordained. Gelanor did not take this claim at all seriously, but his disbelief changed to awe when the superstitious Argives interpreted a wolf's killing an ox during the same night as a sign from heaven.

So Danaus became king of Argos, and if one could accept even the remotest historical connection here, one would have to accept the introduction of an Egyptian dynasty into Argive history. Danaus undertook many improvements for the city and its inhabitants. He built the acropolis; more importantly he provided water by digging wells. Thus the flight from Egypt and the government takeover had worked very well.

But the old threat was revived when the sons of Aegyptus turned up at Argos, assuring their uncle of their peaceful intentions and renewing their suit for the hands of his daughters. Danaus was not at all convinced, and his reasons had a great deal of validity. Why would his 50 nephews come all the way from Arabia to marry his daughters? Surely all these young men were not in love with their cousins. Danaus obviously had given up his claim to Libya when he fled to Peloponnesus, so what did the sons of Aegyptus have in mind? The old territorial dispute no longer existed, so the suitors had to be interested in the new kingdom he had taken over in Greece.

Danaus knew that some action was called for to settle the question for once and all. He decided on a violent and grisly plan, one suggested to him by the fate originally planned for his daughters, if the old oracle could be believed. He consented to the mass marriage, distributing his daughters by lot to their suitors, or by similarity of names. (This chance allotment of brides speaks again to a lack of burning passion on the part of the suitors.) The pairing was thus arranged, and we have the lists of Apollodorus and of Hyginus:

These lists, composed of some of the most beautiful names in ancient story, were made up by two writers who were enamored of lists of people. They do not correspond except in a half-dozen or so instances in both the male and female lists. The list of Apollodorus has a ring of a little more authenticity—via oral tradition, perhaps?—because he repeats three female names—Euippe, Cleopatra, and Hippodameia—which might have happened with different mothers. The list of Hyginus is very corrupt, but even so it suggests he probably enjoyed inventing a whole body of names to carry out a story. The work attributed to Apollodorus, incidentally, came later than that of Hyginus, and it is curious but not unusual that he did not accept the names Hyginus had provided. Endless variations in names of the same people seemed to be a pastime among ancient writers. It should be noted that Hyginus' list falls short by three in the pairing of the 50 couples.

Apollodorus		*Hyginus*	
Hypermnestra	Lynceus	Hypermnestra	Lynceus
Gorgophone	Proteus	Midea	Antimachus
Automate	Busiris	Philomela	Panthius
Amymone	Enceladus	Amymone	Midanus
Agave	Lycus	Scylla	Proteus
Scaea	Daiphron	Amphicomone	Plexippus
Hippodameia	Istrus	Demoditus	Chrysippus
Rhodia	Chalcodon	Hyale	Perius
Cleopatra	Agenor	Cleopatra	Metalces
Asteria	Chaetus	Trite	Enceladus
Hippodameia	Diocorystes	Damone	Amyntor
Glauce	Alces	Hippothoe	Obrimus
Hippomedusa	Alcmenor	Myrmidone	Mineus
Gorge	Hippothous	Arcadia	Xanthus
Iphimedusa	Euchenor	Phila	Philinus
Rhode	Hippolytus	Hipparete	Protheon
Pirene	Agaptolemus	Chrysothemis	Asterides
Dorium	Cercetes	Pyrante	Athamas
Phartis	Eurydamas	?	Armoasbus
Mnestra	Aegius	Glaucippe	Niauius
Euippe	Argius	Euippe	Agenor
Anaxibia	Archelaus	Demophile	Pamphilus
Nelo	Menemachus	Autodice	Clytus
Cleite	Cleitus	Polyxena	Aegyptus
Sthenele	Sthenelus	Hecabe	Dryas
Chrysippe	Chrysippus	Acamantis	Ecnominus
Autonoe	Eurylochus	Arsalte	Ephialtes

continued

Apollodorus		_Hyginus_	
Theano	Phantes	Monuse	Eurysthenes
Electra	Peristhenes	Helice	Euidea
Cleopatra	Hermus	Cleo	Asterius
Eurydice	Dryas	Eurydice	Canthus
Glaucippe	Potamon	Polybe	Iltonomus
Anthelia	Cisseus	Helicta	Cassus
Cleodore	Lixus	Electra	Hyperantus
Euippe	Imbrus	Eubule	Demarchus
Erato	Bromius	Erato	Eudaemon
Stygne	Polyctor	Daplidice	Pygnones
Bryce	Chthonius	Hero	Andromachus
Actaea	Periphas	Europome	Athletes
Podarce	Oeneus	Pyrantis	Plexippus
Dioxippe	Aegyptus	Critomedeia	Antipaphus
Adite	Menalces	Pirene	Dolichus
Ocypete	Lampus	Eupheme	Hyperbius
Pylarge	Idmon	Themistagora	Podasimus
Celaeno	Hyperbius	Celaeno	Aristonous
Adiante	Daiphron	Itea	Antiochus
Oeme	Arbelus	Oeme	Polydector
Callidice	Pandion		
Hippodice	Idas		
Hyperippe	Hippocorystes		

Danaus provided each of his daughters with a dagger, which he instructed them to use on their wedding night. They also were told to behead their husbands after killing them. One can only imagine the scene of carnage that followed. It is miraculous that not one thrust proved inadequate, allowing a dying Aegyptid to sound an alarm. Or that not one of the sisters reconsidered her pledge after experiencing the ecstasy of a wedding night. Or that some of them simply could not bring themselves to kill. Even to imagine this night of gore is difficult. On first reading, one tends to sympathize with the slaughtered males, visualizing the barrows that collected the headless bodies when the next day dawned. Given, though, the persistence of this band of suitors, one has to agree that perhaps the victims could as easily have been the Danaides. They simply might have beaten the Aegyptides to the draw.

All the sons of Aegyptus were thus murdered except Lynceus. He was spared by Hypermnestra because, according to some, he allowed her to keep her virginity intact. (This interesting circumstance will be treated else-

where.) The Danaides buried the heads of their murdered husbands under a monument on the way to the citadel and their bodies at Lerna. They were later purified by Hermes and Athena at the command of Zeus. There was a tradition at Patrae that Aegyptus came to Greece and died at Aroe from grief at the fate of his sons. The temple of Serapis at Patrae had a monument to him.

Some say Lynceus returned from Lyrceia, where he had fled, and killed Danaus and his daughters. But most accounts have them remain alive. Danaus was now saddled with the responsibility of 49 widows, some of them undoubtedly pregnant from their sole sexual experience. He was confronted with the problem of finding husbands for them, since understandably they did not have suitors flocking to their door. He organized public contests with his daughters as prizes, and little by little managed to marry them off. From them and their father the succeeding generations of Argives took the name Danaians.

As might be expected, there are discrepancies in the chronicle of the Danaides. Writers other than Apollodorus and Hyginus mentioned the infamous sisters. Pindar (*Pythian Odes* 9.117) stated that only 48 bridegrooms were murdered because, according to him, Hypermnestra and Lynceus were already married, and Amymone had been the lover of Poseidon and was mother of his son. Pausanias (7.1.3) said that Automate and Scaea were married to Architeles and Archander, sons of Acaeus, but he might have been talking about their history subsequent to the murders. Twelve Danaides appearing on neither of the lists have been identified. Hesione was the mother of Orchomenus by Zeus. Phylodameia was the mother of Pharis, founder of Phares, by Hermes. Polydora was the mother of Dryops by the Peneius River. Side had a town in Laconia named for her. Anaxithea was the mother of Olenus by Zeus. Physadeia had a spring near Argos named for her. Some said Oenomaus was begotten on Eurythoe by Ares. Myrtilus, according to some, was a son of Hermes by Phaethusa. Chrysippus was the son of Pelops by Astyoche, according to some. Then there was the matter of the three Danaides who were supposed to have died in Rhodes. Their names, from which the Rhodian cities of Cameirus, Lindus, and Ialysus were said to have been derived, would therefore be Cameira, Linda, and Ialysa. Maybe the shortage on Hyginus' list can be explained by their not being counted. It is entirely possible that Hesione, Phylodameia, Anaxithea, Physadeia, Polydora, Side, Eurythoe, Phaethusa, and Astyoche were children conceived by Danaus after his arrival in Argos. We never find out how old he was, but if he was young enough and energetic enough to oust Gelanor and assume power at Argos, he certainly was potent enough to produce more daughters. The fact that he produced no son is attested by Lynceus' taking the throne after the death of Danaus. Danaus was buried at Argos.

Although the Danaides were purified of the mass murder of their husbands, they were punished in the afterlife by having to pour water into a vessel full of holes. [Apollodorus 2.1.5; Pindar, *Nemean Odes* 10.7; Scholiast on Pindar's *Pythian Odes* 9.200; Scholiast on Euripides' *Hecuba* 869,886; Ovid, *Metamorphoses* 4.462, *Heroides* 14; Hyginus, *Fables* 170; Herodotus 2.91; Eustathius on Homer's *Iliad* 37,461; Pausanias 2.19.3,6,24.3,38.4, 7.21.6.]

DANAIS, according to some, was the mother of Chrysippus by Pelops. Usually his mother was called AXIOCHE. [Plutarch, *Greek and Roman Parallel Stories* 33.]

DAPHNAEA was a surname of Artemis at Hypsi in Laconia. The name was derived from *daphne*, a laurel, which was sacred to Apollo, who was called Daphnaeus. It is not clear why she was called by this surname, although she and Apollo frequently had matching names (Cynthia-Cynthius, Delphinia-Delphinius, etc.). The reference could have been a local one, referring to the wood from which her statue was made. [Pausanias 3.24.6; Philostratus, *Life of Apollonius of Tyana* 1.16.]

DAPHNE (1) was a daughter of Teiresias, usually called MANTO. [Diodorus Siculus 4.66.]

DAPHNE (2) was a daughter of the Peneius River in Thessaly and Creusa. Her brother was Hypseus and her sister was Stilbe. Stilbe became by Apollo the mother of Lapithes and Centaurus, and the god was therefore brother-in-law to Daphne. During his visits to Stilbe he became attracted to Daphne, who as a perhaps younger sister blossomed into a most desirable young woman. He made overtures to her, which she rejected. Finally, caught up in an insatiable lust, which for gods must have been many times stronger than for men, he pursued her in the valley of Tempe. When he had her almost in his grasp, she prayed to Gaea, mother earth, to deliver her. She was consequently swallowed up by the earth or changed into a laurel tree, which Apollo impotently embraced. From that time on, the laurel tree was sacred to him. Every ninth year the Delphians sent to Tempe a procession of well-born youths. Their leader plucked a branch of laurel and brought it back to Delphi. On this occasion a solemn festival, in which the inhabitants of the neighboring regions took part, was celebrated in Tempe in honor of Apollo Tempeites. [Ovid, *Metamorphoses* 1.568, *Amores* 3.6.31; Diodorus Siculus 1.69; Hyginus, *Fables* 203.]

DAPHNE (3) was a daughter of the Ladon River in Elis (there is also a Ladon River in Arcadia). She was extremely beautiful, and Leucippus, the son of Oenomaus, king of Pisa, fell in love with her and followed her at a distance when she hunted with her sisters along the riverbank. He finally hit on a plan to better woo her. Being young and beardless, he dressed in the garments of the hunting parties and accompanied Daphne wherever she went. Daphne became attached to her beautiful young friend, and they spent many happy hours together. One hot day, one of the nymphs suggested they stop by the river and swim. Leucippus had to undress, and almost as soon as he displayed male genitals was run through with the spears of the huntresses.

This story is a most unhappy one. Leucippus was killed because he loved enough to take a serious risk. Daphne might have loved him—or who she thought he was—enough to have saved his life. Apparently the women were followers of Artemis, who did not bother to question circumstances. Some say Apollo loved Daphne and arranged the whole tragic event, but this would be confusing two different stories in two different geographical locations. [Pausanias 8.20.2.]

DAPHNE (4) was the daughter of Amyclas. She was probably the same as Pasiphae, an oracular goddess at Thalamae in Laconia. Pasiphae was believed to be a daughter of Atlas, but is also identified with Cassandra. People slept in her temple for the purpose of receiving revelations in dreams. [Plutarch, *Agis* 9; Cicero, *On Divination* 1.43; Parthenius, *Love Stories* 15.]

DAPLIDICE was one of the DANAIDES and married to Pygnones. [Hyginus, *Fables* 170.]

DEA ROMA (*See* ROMA)

DEIANEIRA (1) was a daughter of Althaea by Oeneus, and sister of Toxeus, Agelaus, Thyreus, Clymenus (or Periphas), Meleager, Gorge, Eurymede, Melanippe, and others. It was rumored that Meleager's father was Ares and that Deianeira's was Dionysus, but it was common practice to claim divine parentage for outstanding offspring, and both Meleager and Deianeira were very special. Meleager's heroic deeds ended in his early death; not only did Althaea kill herself, but Meleager's sisters mourned until

they were changed into guinea hens. Only Deianeira and Gorge were spared this metamorphosis, since Dionysus intervened; this could be the reason some thought he had fathered Deianeira.

She was left then in the rocky kingdom of Calydon with her sister Gorge, several brothers, and an aging father. Gorge became pregnant by her father, and Deianeira must have been relieved when two powerful suitors contested for her hand: the god of the Achelous River and Heracles. They finally came to physical violence. Achelous could assume any form he wanted, so he changed into a serpent and then a bull, but each time Heracles overcame him. While he was in the form of a bull, Heracles deprived him of a horn. Eventually Heracles routed Achelous and claimed Deianeira.

He lived with Deianeira at Calydon for some time, using the place as a base for his various excursions. It is not certain where Calydon fitted into his complicated chronology. Finally, he had to leave because of an incident in the atmosphere of violence that seemed to follow him. He accidentally killed the boy Eunomus, son of Architeles, and went into voluntary exile, taking Deianeira with him.

They came to the Euenus River, which flows near Calydon. Here Nessus, a Centaur, awaited them. He provided a kind of ferry service for travelers by carrying them across on his back. Heracles had no need of him, but gave him Deianeira to carry across while he himself swam. Most certainly unaware he was dealing with the greatest of Greek heroes, Nessus became excited by the scent of the lovely woman he was transporting and attempted to rape her on the opposite shore. Deianeira's screams brought Heracles near enough to shoot Nessus with one of the poisoned arrows he had dipped in the blood of the Hydra. In the seconds he had left to live, Nessus soaked a cloth in the contaminated blood that flowed from his wound and pressed it into Deianeira's hand. With this, he told her, she could guarantee the love of her husband forever.

Deianeira needed this assurance. From the lonely outpost of Trachis Heracles pursued his brilliant career, coming home only long enough to ready himself for other sojourns and to leave her pregnant. She became the mother of Hyllus,

Ctesippus, Glenus, Hodites, and Macaria. Heracles meanwhile assisted Aegimus against the Lapithae, and later killed Cycnus and Amyntor. He also spent over a year in Lydia playing reversed sex roles with Omphale, the Lydian queen. He returned from there to Oechalia to take vengeance on Eurytus and his sons, and this time he carried off Iole, the beautiful daughter of Eurytus. Word preceded him that he was bringing home a new bride, and Deianeira, though by now accustomed to his amorous adventures, thought about the long-ago remedy for dying love. She was getting old, and the idea of sharing her husband with a young and beautiful woman in their house was more than she could bear. She soaked a shirt in a vat with the desiccated blood of the Centaur and dried the new white garment. She kept it in readiness to restore her husband's love.

On his return from Oechalia Heracles stopped at Cenaeum, a promontory of Euboea, and prepared to sacrifice to his father, Zeus. Lichas, a servant, was sent to Trachis for a white garment, and confided to Deianeira that indeed Heracles had with him the lovely Iole. Deianeira then knew it was time to use the magic formula Nessus had given her, so she sent the shirt back with Lichas. Heracles dressed in the fatal shirt and soon was consumed in agony. He tore at the shirt but brought away handfuls of flesh where the shirt adhered to his body. In his agony he threw Lichas into the sea. Afterward, Heracles was conveyed back to Trachis. On seeing what she had unwittingly done, Deianeira hanged herself. Heracles raised a pile of wood on Mount Oeta, ascended it, and ordered it set on fire.

In spite of being the author of her husband's death, Deianeira was more sinned against than sinning. Wooed and won in the lonely hills of Calydon, the scene of tragedies for her family, she went with Heracles to Trachis. While not as remote as Calydon, it was a place where she experienced loneliness. There she reared her children, the oldest, Hyllus, still in adolescence when both she and Heracles died. While Deianeira had only five children of her own, she was stepmother to at least 65 sons of Heracles by other women. [Apollodorus 1.8.1,3, 2.7.5,6.7; Hyginus, Fables 129,171,174; Apollonius Rhodius 4.543; Ovid, Metamorphoses 8.445,

9.8,201; Pausanias 1.21.6, 2.19.1, 10.38.1; Sophocles, Trachiniae 555–558; Seneca, Hercules Oetaeus 496.]

DEIANEIRA (2) was the daughter of Dexamenus, king of Olenus in Achaia. After his battle with the Moliones, Heracles was hospitably entertained at the house of Olenus and characteristically seduced the king's daughter. Curiously this did not seem to disturb Dexamenus, who probably stood in awe of the hero. Upon departing, Heracles promised to return and marry Deianeira. In his absence, which in all likelihood was an extended one, Eurytion the Centaur asked for Deianeira's hand in marriage. Again proving somewhat spineless and intimidated by the physically superior Centaur, Dexamenus agreed to the arrangement. Deianeira, seemingly with no say in the matter, was on the point of being mated with the half-human creature, probably only half-aware of the unthinkable physical demands that would ensue. Fortunately, Heracles arrived on the wedding day and slew Eurytion. It is not recorded whether or not Heracles then married her. In fact, the whole story probably arose out of a confusion with the story of Deianeira, the sister of Meleager. Other writers called her Mnesimache or Hippolyte. Diodorus Siculus, who called the woman Hippolyte, had a variation on the story that somehow removed the confusion about the other Deianeira. According to him, Heracles was entertained by Dexamenus at the same time the daughter was being married to Azan, son of Arcas. At the wedding the Centaur Eurytion made advances toward Hippolyte, and Heracles slew him and later went his way. [Hyginus, Fables 33; Apollodorus 2.5.5; Diodorus Siculus 4.33.]

DEIANEIRA (3) was a daughter of Lycaon, son of Azeus. She was said by some to be the mother of the famous Lycaon, king of Arcadia. His mother is more often called CYLLENE.

DEIANEIRA (4) was one of the AMAZONS. She was part of the sixth wave of attack against Heracles when he came for the girdle of Hippolyte, but fell with Asteria, Marpe, Tecmessa, and Alcippe. [Diodorus Siculus 4.16.]

DEIANEIRA (5) was one of the NEREIDES. [Apollodorus 1.2.7.]

DEIDAMEIA (1) was a daughter of Bellerophon and Anticleia. Homer calls her Laodameia. She grew up in the household of the great slayer of the Chimaera with her brothers Isander and Hippolochus. She married Euander, the son of Sarpedon of the Minoan dynasty, who had migrated to Lycia from Crete. Hippolochus was the father of Glaucus. Being the eldest of Bellerophon's grandsons, Glaucus should have been king when Bellerophon died, but Isander and Hippolochus disputed over the succession. They decided to settle the argument with a contest. Deidameia's infant son Sarpedon was made the innocent arbiter by having placed on his chest a ring through which his uncles would try to shoot. Deidameia was either a fatalist or really wanted to see the argument settled. One wonders why some other child might not have been selected, but maybe having a royal nephew placed in jeopardy was part of the test. In any case, the contest did not take place, and maybe Deidameia knew it would not when she volunteered Sarpedon for the contest. The brothers were so impressed with her bravery that they declared Sarpedon king (when he grew up and if no more such contests were held).

Deidameia's valor was apparently hereditary. Sarpedon distinguished himself in the Trojan War but was slain by Patroclus. The rumor that Zeus was, in fact, his father seemed to be substantiated when the god commanded that Sarpedon's body be cleansed and anointed with ambrosia and buried with great honor in Lycia. There was a sanctuary to him at Xanthus. Deidameia had two other sons by Euander— Clarus and Themon. [Diodorus Siculus 5.79; Apollodorus 3.1.1; Virgil, Aeneid 10.125; Homer, Iliad 6.197; Eustathius on Homer's Iliad 894; Appian, Civil Wars 4.78.]

DEIDAMEIA (2) was a daughter of Lycomedes, a king of the Dolopians on the island of Scyros near Euboea. When Achilles had reached the age of nine, the seer Calchas declared that in the looming war with Troy the city could never be taken without Achilles. Knowing the war would prove fatal to her son, Achilles' mother, Thetis,

disguised him as a girl and, apparently with the agreement of Lycomedes, placed him among the daughters of the king. He was treated with affection by the daughters, especially Deidameia, who became by him, as soon as he reached puberty, the mother of Pyrrhus (later called Neoptolemus). Seemingly undisturbed by an illegitimate grandson, Lycomedes called him Pyrrhus, probably because Pyrrha had been the name of Achilles while he remained in disguise.

Odysseus discovered his place of concealment and caused Achilles to reveal himself by displaying weapons, which the boy instinctively reached for. Achilles then promised his assistance to the Greeks, and left Deidameia and his new son on Scyros. Pyrrhus grew up in the house of Lycomedes and was himself eventually called to the war. He entered very late in the war, but although still an adolescent he distinguished himself under the name Neoptolemus, by which he was called when he arrived in Troy. At the taking of Troy he killed Priam and sacrificed Polyxena on the tomb of his father. He received Andromache as his part of the booty and, although she was considerably older than he, had by her several children.

As for Deidameia, some claim Achilles formally married her after landing at Scyros on the way to Troy. She was reported to have had a second son, Oneirus, by him. After the war Helenus, Priam's son, and Neoptolemus became friends, and Neoptolemus gave Deidameia to Helenus as a wife for his new kingdom in Molossia. [Apollodorus 3.13.7,8, Epitome 6.13; Ptolemaeus Hephaestion 3; Hyginus, Fables 96; Statius, Achilleid 2.200; Homer, Odyssey 11.491,508, Iliad 19.326; Eustathius on Homer's Iliad 1187; Virgil, Aeneid 2.263,547, 3.296; Servius on Virgil's Aeneid 2.469; Pausanias 4.17.3,10.27, 10.26.1.]

DEIDAMEIA (3) was called by some the wife of Peirithous. She is commonly called HIPPO-DAMEIA. [Plutarch, Theseus 30.]

DEIDAMEIA (4) was the wife of Thestius, according to some. Others, however, call her EURYTHEMIS. [Scholiast on Apollonius Rhodius 1.146,201.]

DEIMA was the personification of fear. She was represented in the form of a fearful woman on the tomb of Medea's children at Corinth. [Pausanias 2.3.6.]

DEINO was one of the GRAEAE. [Apollodorus 2.4.2.]

DEIOIS (See DEIONE)

DEIONE (1), Deiois, Deoine, i.e., the Daughter of Demeter, is used as a name for Persephone. Deo was another name for Demeter. [Ovid, Metamorphoses 6.114; Athenaeus 10.449.]

DEIONE (2) was the mother of Miletus. Most accounts call her AREIA. [Ovid, Metamorphoses 9.442.]

DEIOPE was a daughter of Triptolemus. Her father was famous in the story of the beginning of the Eleusinian mysteries. He was granted honors and lasting tribute by Demeter because of his family's hospitality to her while she searched for Persephone. Nothing is known of Deiope except that she has been called both the mother of Triptolemus himself and of Eumolpus. The mother of Triptolemus is most often called METANEIRA, and the mother of Eumolpus, CHIONE. [Scholiast on Sophocles' Oedipus at Colonus 1108; Aristotle, On Marvelous Things Heard 143,291.]

DEIOPEA (1), a fair Lydian nymph, belonged to the suite of Hera, who promised her as a reward to Aeolus if he would assist her in destroying the fleet of Aeneas. [Virgil, Aeneid 1.72.]

DEIOPEA (2) was one of the NEREIDES. [Hyginus, Fables: Preface 8.]

DEIPHILE (See DEIPYLE)

DEIPHOBE was a daughter of the seer Glaucus. Glaucus was more than a seer, actually; he was a sea-god who had been metamorphosed from a mortal. One of his daughters was the most celebrated of the so-called SIBYLS. She was the Cumaean Sibyl, who acted as Aeneas' guide to the underworld. [Virgil, Aeneid 3.441, 6.10,36; Servius on Virgil's Aeneid 6.36.]

DEIPYLE was a daughter of Adrastus and Amphithea. Adrastus was a son of Talaus, king of Argos, and Lysimache. He had quarreled with his cousin Amphiaraus and was driven from Argos, only to return years later with his family to share in the government of Argos. He gave his sister Eriphyle to Amphiaraus in marriage.

Tydeus of Calydon and Polyneices of Thebes, both exiled from their countries, once happened to meet near the palace of Adrastus. They quarreled over right-of-way and had almost come to blows when Adrastus emerged and immediately recognized the fulfillment of an old prophecy that two of his daughters would marry a boar and a lion. These symbols the two men bore on their shields. Consequently, he gave Argeia to Polyneices and Deipyle to Tydeus, and promised to get his two new sons-in-law reinstated in their kingdoms. This promise led to the famous war of the Seven against Thebes.

Not only did Deipyle give up her husband to the war, but also her father, brother-in-law, uncle, uncle by marriage, and cousin. With the exception of her father, Adrastus, all were killed. Tydeus was under the protection of Athena and would have survived, except that when wounded he was brought two remedies—one from Athena, which would have made him immortal, and one from Amphiaraus, the brains of Melanippus. In blood lust Tydeus ate part of his enemy's brains; in horror Athena withheld the healing potion, and Tydeus died.

Deipyle's son, Diomedes, was still a boy when Tydeus died. He grew up to become one of the great heroes of two wars. He married Aegiale, his mother's sister, so Deipyle was both mother and sister-in-law to him. Diomedes was recruited by Adrastus for the second battle against Thebes, the expedition of the Epigoni. He survived the battle to become one of the heroes of the Trojan War, leading Argos against Troy in 80 ships.

Deipyle knew nothing but adversity and war all her life except during the time the Epigoni were coming of age. Her earliest memories must have been exile from Argos and the resentment between her family and that of

Amphiaraus. Her husband spent their entire married life preparing for the expedition of the Seven. Her son went off with the Epigoni when he was not much more than a boy. Afterward he sailed to Troy and returned in glory. If Deipyle lived to welcome him back, she saw adversity continue with the adultery and murderous plot by her sister Aegiale. Her life could not have been a happy one. [Apollodorus 1.8.5,9.13, 3.6.1; Hyginus, *Fables* 69,70; Pausanias 1.4.3, 9.18.2; Homer, *Iliad* 2.406, 14.115.]

DELIA was a surname of Artemis in the same way Apollo was called Delius, from Delos, their birthplace.

DELIADES were the nymphs of Delos. The name also was applied to divinities worshiped in Delos, such as Demeter, Aphrodite, Artemis, and Apollo. Glaucus, the marine deity, was also said to live in Delos in the company of the nymphs, and there he gave oracles. [Aristophanes, *Thesmophoriazusae* 333; Callimachus, *Hymn to Artemis* 169, *Hymn to Delos* 323; *Homeric Hymn to Apollo* 157.]

DELPHINIA was a surname of Artemis at Athens. This name, like several other of her surnames, was a feminine version of names given to her brother. The name originally might have had to do with his slaying of the dragon Delphine (or Delphyne), usually called Python or the mate of Python. More likely it concerned the colonization of Delphi, when Apollo in the form of a dolphin led Cretans there. [Pollux 10.119; Tzetzes on Lycophron 208.]

DELPHYNE, or Delphine, was the dragon who guarded the oracle at Pytho (later Delphi). She is usually called Pytho, and in that case considered male. Robert Graves (*Greek Myths*, p. 76) compromises by calling Delphyne both mate and sister of Python.

Delphyne appeared early in cosmologies. When the gods overcame the giants, Gaea was enraged and created Typhon in Cilicia. Typhon pursued the gods to Egypt, but Zeus was able to rout him with thunderbolts and chased him as far as Mount Cassius in Syria. In hand-to-coil combat Typhon deprived Zeus of his sinews and hid them in the Corycian cave in Cilicia, setting the she-dragon Delphyne to guard them. Hermes and Aegipan stole the sinews and refitted them to Zeus. Restored, Zeus again pursued the monster and buried him under Mount Aetna in Sicily.

Meanwhile, Apollo set out to avenge the wrongs done by Python to Leto, the mother of Apollo and Artemis. This time the scene shifted to the Corycian cave on Mount Parnassus. Apollo killed the monster, most often called Python but occasionally called Delphyne, which must certainly be a confusion of Zeus' battle with Typhon and Apollo's battle with the evil force at Delphi. [Nonnos, *Dionysiaca* 1.481; Apollodorus 1.6.3.]

DEMETER, one of the 12 Olympian divinities, was the goddess of the earth, of agriculture, and of fertility in general.

NATIVITY: Daughter of Cronus and Rhea.

LOVERS: Zeus, Poseidon, Iasion, Mecon.

CHILDREN: Persephone, Artemis, Parius, Dionysus, Hecate, Iacchus, Plutus, Philomelus, Areion, Despoena.

PRINCIPAL SEATS OF WORSHIP: Crete, Delos, Argolis, Paros, Attica (particularly Eleusis), west coast of Asia, Sicily and Italy.

SACRED TO HER: Livestock and agricultural products, especially wheat; poppy; narcissus; crane.

COMPANIONS: Hecate, Persephone, Triptolemus.

IDENTIFIED WITH: Axiocersa, Daeira, Hecate, Isis, Rhea, Saturnus, Hestia.

SURNAMES: Achaea, Amphictyonis, Anesidora, Antaea, Azesia, Brimo, Cabeiria, Calligeneia, Carpophoros, Chamyne, Chloe, Chrysaor, Cidaria, Delia, Demo, Deo, Despoena, Eleusinia, Epipole, Erinys, Europa, Hercyna, Lernaea, Mycalessia, Mysia, Panachaea, Pelagia, Prosymna, Rharias, Sito, Thesmia.

Demeter belonged to a tradition of earth-mother goddesses associated with the Mediterranean world. When a Greek cosmogony was eventually designed, she fitted quite well among the offspring of Cronus and Rhea, inheriting, as it were, most of her mother's characteristics. She could even be compared in a distant way with her grandmother Gaea, but Gaea was the earth itself, while Demeter came to represent the products of soils and seasons, and the generative forces that directed their abundance.

Her sisters were Hestia and Hera. She has occasionally been identified with Hestia, even though Hestia was a virgin goddess and confined to a narrower area of responsibility. Her brothers were Zeus, Poseidon, and Hades. Along with her brothers and sisters (with the exception of Zeus), she was devoured by her father and later regurgitated. After the cataclysmic battle with the Titans, Demeter became by her brother Zeus the mother of Persephone and, some say, of Dionysus and Hecate. Others add Iacchus, but more often he was regarded as the son of Zeus and Persephone. Knowing Hera's vengeful resentment of all her husband's mistresses, it is hard for us to understand why she failed to take some kind of action against Demeter. It is likely that Zeus slept with Demeter before he married Hera. One account even calls Artemis her daughter, presumably by Zeus.

Persephone was the apple of Demeter's eye, so to speak. The relationship between mother and daughter was the glory of the worship of Demeter in the Greek and Roman world since it symbolized death, regeneration, and the cycle of life.

Demeter's gloomy brother Hades, whose inheritance was the sunless underworld, had, unlike Zeus and Poseidon, a severely deprived sexual life, because no woman was content to share his morose kingdom. However, his bright, cheerful niece excited his affections, and for some reason Zeus agreed to help him kidnap her. One day while Persephone gathered flowers, Hades appeared in his dark chariot and snatched her from the earth. About a dozen places laid claim to the scene of her abduction, including Eleusis.

Demeter was devastated at the disappearance of her daughter and roamed the earth for nine days without eating, drinking, or bathing.

She changed the daughters of Melpomene into Sirens for not being willing to help her in her search. On the tenth day Hecate told her that Persephone had been kidnapped but that only the all-seeing Helios (Sun) knew by whom. Helios revealed that Hades was the abductor but in effect felt Persephone could have done worse.

Demeter was not comforted and continued to wander, refusing to return to Olympus. In human form she roamed in frustration, not caring how she looked. As if she were not already miserable enough, her brother Poseidon tried to rape her in Arcadia. Demeter changed herself into a mare and grazed with the horses of Oncus at Onceium near Thelpusa. Not at all deterred by this disguise, Poseidon turned himself into a stallion and mounted her in a furious frenzy. Apparently this event produced almost at once the horse Areion (and presumably the Arcadian goddess Despoena, who may be considered a counterpart of Persephone; her role is never made clear, but her nature was probably revealed in the later mysteries of the goddess). Demeter's anger at this rape caused her to be called Erinys at Thelpusa, and under this name a temple was built to her on the Ladon River. She shut herself in a cave on Mount Elaeus near Phigalia, where she was later discovered by Pan and placated by the Moirae, or Fates. During her stay there she probably gave birth to Areion and Despoena. She left Areion the horse with Oncus and gave Despoena to Anytus to bring up. Areion later was owned by Heracles and then Adrastus, whose life was saved by the valiant horse in the battle of the Seven against Thebes. Despoena became an Arcadian divinity worshipped especially in the country around Phigalia.

The most common account, though, had Demeter continuing her wanderings in anger and frustration, hoping to find a way to regain Persephone. In her roaming she put the ancient laws of hospitality to the test. Where she met with rejection of any kind, she was quick to punish; where she was kindly received, she bestowed favors. In this ambivalent state she came to Eleusis. Most of what happened to her there became the basis of the mysteries developed there.

First of all, at a well she encountered Baubo, a cheerful woman, who tried to get her to drink. Demeter would not react to her in any way, so finally Baubo turned around and threw up her skirts to reveal her ample, naked behind. This brought a smile from Demeter, who then drank from the offered vessel. Demeter's initial refusal to drink might have had to do with an earlier experience in her wanderings, when she once drank thirstily and was ridiculed by a young man named Ascalabus. Unceremoniously she changed him into a lizard. In Eleusis, Demeter claimed to be a Cretan woman carried off by pirates; when the daughters of King Celeus came to the well to draw water, they felt sorry for her and invited her to the palace. Metaneira, the queen, welcomed her but could not shake Demeter out of her despondency. One of the members of the court named Iambe induced her to smile at her jokes. Soon Demeter was accepted into the household and made the nanny of Demophon, one of the king's sons.

The goddess became very fond of Demophon, probably in partial compensation for the loss of her daughter. She decided to confer immortality on him, and over several nights she held him in the fire to accomplish this. Metaneira walked in one evening on the unsettling scene and screamed in terror, thereby causing the spell to be broken and Demophon to be consumed by the flames. Demeter assumed her own majestic appearance and revealed herself at once. To compensate for the loss of Demophon, she conferred honor on Triptolemus, the other son, and gave him the sacred mission of distributing grain to all parts of the earth. She also acquainted Celeus and his family with the rituals accompanying her worship, and these grew into the celebration of the great Eleusinian mysteries. Interestingly, incorporated into these mysteries were the recent happenings at Eleusis, such as bawdiness recalled from the incident with Baubo and the hilarity inspired by Iambe. Celeus became the first priest of Demeter at Eleusis. Eumolpus has been called the founder of the Eleusinian mysteries, but more likely he was responsible for their spread to other parts of Greece.

Demeter's experience at Eleusis by no means ended her anger over the abduction of Persephone. Her conferral on Triptolemus of minister of agriculture did not deter her from visiting one place and another with famine. She threatened to withhold fertility from the entire earth until she could see her daughter again. Afraid that the race of mortals might become extinct if she carried out her threats, Zeus eventually relented and sent Hermes to bring Persephone to Eleusis. The reunion was a joyful one, except that Persephone's complete divorce from Hades depended on whether or not she had partaken of any food while in the underworld. This brings up a most interesting point. Demeter looked for her for quite a long time, during which she underwent deprivation of food and drink, suggesting she was accustomed to partaking of them. Although against her will, she even managed to produce two children, during which time she had grazed in the fields of Oncus. At some point she even absentmindedly consumed the shoulder of Pelops, whom Tantalus, his father, had served to the gods. (She later replaced the shoulder with an ivory one, which gave the Pelopids a distinctive birthmark.) But poor Persephone was not expected to eat anything if she was to be delivered fully from the nightmarish world of the shades. Alas, she had consumed a few pomegranate seeds, so she was required to spend the wintry parts of each year in the lower world, then was reunited with her mother at the beginning of every spring. The information about her overindulgence in pomegranates was given out by one Ascalaphus, who paid for his loose tongue by being buried under a huge rock in the underworld by Demeter. He was later changed into an owl when Heracles rolled the rock away.

Demeter's love life was not restricted to her brothers; like Aphrodite, she slept with mortals. She loved Mecon, an Athenian, but for some reason changed him into a poppy, which flower remained sacred to her. Her great love was Iasion. He was a son of Zeus and Electra, and Demeter met him at the wedding of Cadmus and Harmonia. (According to the Samothracian tradition, Harmonia was a daughter not of Aphrodite and Ares but of Zeus and Electra, thus making her a sister of Dardanus and Iasion.) Demeter at once fell in love with him and gave herself to him, appropriately in a thrice-plowed field. The result of this union was Plutus, the god of wealth. A second son, Philomelus, invented the chariot and was placed among the constellations as Bootes. A third son, Parius, was also mentioned. Iasion accompanied Dardanus and helped him establish the Samothracian mysteries, and he traveled to various countries teaching the people the fundamentals of Demeter's worship.

Demeter can generally be regarded as a kindly goddess, not only through her offices as benefactress of mankind but also in her dealings with individuals. In spite of outbursts of temper, particularly those associated with her loss of Persephone, she repaid people well for even small favors. She rewarded Cabarnus of Paros for first revealing that Persephone had been carried off. She conferred on Pandareos of Miletus the benefit of never suffering from indigestion. She rewarded Phytalus of Eleusis with a fig tree and the honor of being the ancestor of the prominent Athenian family the Phytalidae. She reared Orthopolis, son of Plemnaeus of Aegialeia. Her vengeance on individuals, while severe in some cases, never approached the excesses one found in the bloody retributions by goddesses like Artemis. She punished Erysichthon, son of Triopas, with insatiable hunger for deliberately cutting down trees in her sacred grove. She turned Lyncus, a king of Scythia, into a lynx for attempting to murder Triptolemus. And, finally, one can certainly condone her action concerning Mintha, a Cocythian nymph. Mintha was having an affair with Hades, probably during the spring and summer months while Persephone stayed with her mother. After all she had been through with her loss and recovery of Persephone, Demeter was not going to sit by and watch her son-in-law betray her beloved daughter—Mintha was promptly metamorphosed into a mint plant.

The worship of Demeter was fundamental. While worship of some of the other divinities dealt in abstractions such as love and beauty, or inspiration and political might, hers had to do with perpetuation of the food supply for large populations. Priests and priestesses of the goddess could well have been agricultural advisers. Her worship at Eleusis was interlinked with the Samothracian mysteries, which at first had to do with lesser divinities such as the Cabeiri, who were ministers of the greater gods, but later the worship of the Cabeiri became inseparable from that of Demeter. Their common worship was

even carried back to the mainland, where near Thebes there was a grove and temple of Demeter Cabeiria and Kore (Persephone). We continue to encounter the names of some of her priests and priestesses, such as Cychreus, son of Poseidon; Euander, son of Hermes; Hercyna, founder of the worship of Demeter at Lebadeia; Lycus, who carried her worship from Attica to Andania; Messene, who introduced the mysteries in Messenia; Mysia, an Argive, who built a sanctuary to her between Argos and Mycenae. Iasion was supposedly responsible for planting her worship in Sicily.

It is interesting that at one time Demeter vied with Hephaestus for possession of Sicily. Evidence suggests Hephaestus was the winner since he slept with Aetna, the nymph who acted as arbitrator. But in the long run, Demeter probably gained Sicily far more firmly than Hephaestus ever managed. In Italy her worship resembled that of Saturnus, who had the same attributes as Demeter except he was male and married to Ops, the goddess of plenty. Generally, though, Demeter is identified with Ceres, probably a very early Roman goddess, whose worship was fused with and absorbed by that of Demeter.

In passing, it should be mentioned that there were the usual attempts to reconcile the account of the rape of Persephone and her recovery with convoluted historical explanations. One such occurs in Plutarch's history of Theseus. [NATIVITY: Hesiod, *Theogony* 137,452; Apollodorus 1.1.3—LOVERS: Servius on Virgil's *Aeneid* 3.15,167, 7.207; Diodorus Siculus 5.48; Callimachus, *Hymn to Demeter* 45,133; Pausanias 8.25.4, 9.25.5—CHILDREN: Pausanias 1.2.4,37.3, 8.25.4,37.3; Hyginus, *Poetic Astronomy* 2.4; *Homeric Hymn to Demeter* 491; Plutarch, *Theseus* 33.35; Eusebius, *Chronicles* 27—CHARACTERISTICS: Pausanias 1.31.2,38.3, 2.14.2, 8.53.3; Apollonius Rhodius 1.1141, 4.986–990; Arnobius, *Adversus Nationes* 5.170; Hesychius, "Kalligeneia"; *Homeric Hymn to Demeter* 101,161; Stephanus Byzantium, "Eleusis"; Callimachus, *Hymn to Demeter* 34; Ovid, *Metamorphoses* 5.650; Antoninus Liberalis 11—WORSHIP: Livy 1.5; Pausanias 1.38.6, 8.15.1–4,25.2–7,37.6,42.1–13, 9.39.4; Lycophron 153, with note of Tzetzes; *Homeric Hymn to*

Demeter 202; Apollodorus 1.5.1–3, 2.5.12; Hyginus, *Fables* 141,146,147; Herodotus 2.171, 6.16; Aristophanes, *Thesmophoriazusae* 303.]

DEMO (1) was an alternate name of DEMETER. [Suidas, "Demo."]

DEMO (2) was a name of the Cumaean Sibyl. [Pausanias 10.12.1] (*See* SIBYLS.)

DEMO (3) was a daughter of Celeus and Metaneira, king and queen of Eleusis. She and her sisters hospitably received Demeter at the spring of Callichorum and invited her to their home as a guest. [*Homeric Hymn to Demeter* 109.]

DEMODICE, sometimes called Biadice, was married to Cretheus before he married Tyro. Very likely quite young, since Cretheus liked women far younger than himself, she became enamored of Phrixus, the adolescent nephew of Cretheus. He ignored her overtures of affection, and she finally told her husband that Phrixus had made advances to her. Highly enraged, Cretheus persuaded Athamas, his brother and Phrixus' father, to have the young man put to death. Nephele, Phrixus' half-immortal mother, procured the ram with golden fleece, which rescued Phrixus in the nick of time. We do not know what happened to Demodice. In view of her conduct with her nephew-in-law, she was afflicted with a wandering eye, and it was only a matter of time until her husband should discover her adulterous tendencies. This might have happened, and soon, since Cretheus married his niece Tyro as soon as she became of age. [Hyginus, *Poetic Astronomy* 2.20; Scholiast on Pindar's *Pythian Odes* 4.288.]

DEMODITAS was one of the DANAIDES and married to Chrysippus. [Hyginus, *Fables* 170.]

DEMODOCE (*See* DEMONICE)

DEMONASSA (1) was the wife of Irus, son of Actor. By him she became the mother of Eurydamas and Eurytion, both of whom were Argonauts. Eurytion befriended Peleus on the trip, and when Peleus was exiled for complicity in the murder of his brother, he went to Eurytion's court at Phthia. Eurytion not only purified him but gave him his daughter Antigone in marriage along with part of the kingdom as dowry. Peleus and Eurytion went to the Calydonian boar hunt, and Peleus inadvertently shot and killed his father-in-law. Peleus tried to soothe Irus by offering him his flocks. Irus, probably in agreement with Demonassa, would not accept them, and an oracle commanded that the sheep should roam free. A wolf devoured the sheep but was changed into a stone, which was pointed out in later times on the frontier of Locris and Phocis. Demonassa and Irus were old and probably died soon after, with Eurydamas sharing the kingdom with Peleus. [Hyginus, *Fables* 14; Apollonius Rhodius 1.71,74; Scholiast on Apollonius Rhodius 1.71; Apollodorus 3.13.1; Antoninus Liberalis 38; Tzetzes on Lycophron 175.]

DEMONASSA (2) was a daughter of Amphiaraus and Eriphyle. Her father had been an Argonaut and one of the Calydonian hunters. He had reigned at Argos in common with his cousin Adrastus, but a feud broke out between them, and Adrastus fled to Sicyon. The two later became reconciled, and Adrastus gave Amphiaraus his sister Eriphyle in marriage. Demonassa and Eurydice were their daughters, and Alcmaeon and Amphilochus were their sons. The offspring of Amphiaraus saw him forced to bend to their mother's will regarding his participation in the Argive campaign against Thebes, even though as a seer he knew he would not return from the war. Demonassa's brothers vowed to avenge their father should he fall. The war followed, and indeed Amphiaraus was a casualty, as was everyone else who stormed Thebes except for Adrastus.

Demonassa married Thersander, son of her cousin Argeia, the wife of Polyneices. As one of the Epigoni, or sons of the original Seven, Thersander was a principal in the campaign of the Seven against Thebes. This time the battle was successful, and Thersander became king of Thebes. He accompanied Agamemnon to Troy, but was slain and buried there. Consequently, Demonassa lost a father in one war, lived through the trauma of another, and finally lost her husband in a third. Her son by Thersander was Tisamenus, who succeeded her husband as king of Thebes.

Demonassa occupies a special place in the history of the heroic age, providing in a sense a continuity from the Argonaut through the Trojan War. People tend to forget how closely these events followed each other. [Pausanias 3.15.6, 7.3.1, 9.5.8, 10.10.2; Apollodorus 3.7.2.]

DEMONASSA (3) was, according to some, the mother of Aegialeus by Adrastus. More often his mother was called AMPHITHEA. [Apollodorus 1.9.13; Hyginus, *Fables* 71.]

DEMONASSA (4) was the wife of Poeas, son of Thaumacus. She is sometimes called Methone. Poeas was one of the Argonauts and was sometimes credited with killing Talos, the formidable brazen man in Crete. Demonassa became by him the mother of Philoctetes. Both father and son were famous for their role in lighting the funeral pyre of Heracles on Mount Oeta. Both were given credit for the merciful act, and they might have carried it out jointly. Just before Heracles died, he bequeathed his famous quiver, bow, and arrows to Philoctetes. The subsequent fate of Poeas is not known, but Philoctetes went on to become one of the prominent characters in events connected with the Trojan War. In spite of her illustrious son, who went on after the war to found a town in Italy, Demonassa was never mentioned again. [Apollodorus 1.9.16,26, 2.7.7; Hyginus, *Fables* 97,103.]

DEMONASSA (5) was the wife of Hippolochus, a son of Bellerophon. By him she was the mother of Glaucus, a Lycian ally of Troy. Nothing further is known of this final remnant of the famous Bellerophon's family. [Scholiast on Homer's *Iliad* 6.206.]

DEMONICE, sometimes called Androdice, was a daughter of Agenor and Epicaste, and sister of Porthaon. Agenor was a son of Pleuron and grandson of Aetolus, and Epicaste was the daughter of Calydon. The family was well established in Aetolia, and it is difficult to imagine how it reacted to an extended love affair between Demonice and the god Ares. We do not read much about the amorous life of Ares, but it is understandable that he frequented the territory of Aetolia, in which there seemed to be constant strife, and took advantage of the opportunity to sleep with a Pleuronian princess whenever he chose. Their long-term relationship resulted in four sons—Euenus, Molus, Pylus, and Thestius. We know Euenus as the father of the beautiful Marpessa, who was fought over by Apollo and Idas. Thestius was even more famous, since he fathered Hypermnestra, Althaea, and Leda. Demonice's granddaughters established important links with Argolis, Messenia, and Laconia, thereby setting the stage for a kind of national unity demonstrated by the Greeks in the war against Troy. [Apollodorus 1.7.7,9.16, 3.10.5; Pausanias 3.13.5; Hyginus, *Fables* 14.]

DEMOPHILE (1) was one of the DANAIDES and married to Pamphilus. [Hyginus, *Fables* 170.]

DEMOPHILE (2) was one of the names of the Cumaean Sibyl. (*See* SIBYLS.)

DENDRITIS, the Goddess of the Tree, was a surname of Helen on the island of Rhodes. A legend told that after the death of Menelaus, Helen was exiled by her stepsons and took asylum in Rhodes with her friend Polyxo, the widow of Tlepolemus. Polyxo pretended friendship but held Helen accountable for the death of her husband, who had been killed in the Trojan War. Once while Helen was bathing, Polyxo sent out her servants disguised as Erinyes. They hanged Helen on a tree. Beneath this tree later grew a magical plant that was supposed to be a remedy against snakebite. The Rhodians afterward built a sanctuary to Helen Dendritis. [Pausanias 3.19.10.]

DEO was another name for Demeter. The matronymic form of it, Deiois, Deoine, or Deione, was often given to Persephone. [*Homeric Hymn to Demeter* 47; Sophocles, *Antigone* 1121; Ovid, *Metamorphoses* 6.114; Athenaeus 10.449.]

DERIMACHEIA was one of the AMAZONS. [Quintus Smyrnaeus 1.45.]

DERINOE was one of the AMAZONS. [Quintus Smyrnaeus 1.42.]

DERO was one of the NEREIDES. [Apollodorus 1.2.7.]

DERRHIATIS was a surname of Artemis, which she derived from the town of Derrhion on the road from Sparta to Arcadia. [Pausanias 3.20.7.]

DESPOENA (1) was the daughter of Demeter and Poseidon Hippius. When Demeter wandered the earth searching for Persephone, she was at one point pursued by Poseidon for sexual purposes. She sought to elude him by changing herself into a mare and grazing with the herds of Oncus near Thelpusa. Undeceived, Poseidon changed himself into a stallion, mounted the mare, and doubly impregnated her. From this brutish coupling came what had to be twins, since the incident occurred only once. Areion the horse and Despoena, presumably in human form, were born from the union. The twins either were born very quickly, as could sometimes be the case with supernatural beings, or they were born when Demeter resumed her regular form and secreted herself in a cave near Phigalia. Areion was left with Oncus and later became the property of Heracles, who then gave him to Adrastus.

Despoena was given to the Titan Anytus to rear. The upbringing must have been in Arcadia, for Despoena was an Arcadian goddess, her worship particularly strong around Phigalia. Despoena was a cult name since the real name of the goddess could never be mentioned outside the secret rites. The name was so well guarded that even today there is no record of it.

Many writers have tried to make Despoena identical with Kore (Persephone's cult name at Eleusis) and indeed there were many similarities, particularly in the cult rituals. Even in modern Greek, *despoinis* and *kore* are words for a young woman or girl. It is understandable that with the Greeks' flair for elaborating on their myths they might have been considered responsible for creating a variation on the Persephone story. However, Despoena was worshipped as a separate goddess. She had temples in Arcadia, in at least one of which Anytus, her guardian, appeared in armor with her and Demeter. [Pausanias 8.37.1–10, 8.42.1; Apollodorus 3.6.8.]

DESPOENA (2), the Mistress, occurs as a surname of several goddesses, such as Aphrodite, Demeter, and Persephone. [Theocritus 15.100; Aristophanes, *Thesmophoriazusae* 286; Pausanias 8.37.6.]

DEVERRA was one of a trio of Roman divinities invoked at the birth of a child; the other two were Pilumnus and Intercidona. These symbolic beings were importuned to protect the child from the malevolence of Silvanus, the god of deep dark forests. The night after the birth of a child, three men walked around the house. One man struck the threshold of the house with an ax, another knocked on the door of the house with a pestle, and the third swept the inside with a broom. All these motions were believed to prevent Silvanus from entering the house. Perhaps these actions symbolized movement from nomadic existence to a civilized agricultural life. [St. Augustine, *City of God* 6.9.]

DEXAMENE was one of the NEREIDES. [Homer, *Iliad* 18.46.]

DEXITHEA was the mother of Euxanthius by Minos. Nothing further is known of Dexithea and little more of Euxanthius. He was said to be the father of Miletus, though Apollo is usually called his father. The Euxanthides appear to have been a Milesian patrician family. [Apollodorus 3.1.2.]

DIA (1) was a daughter of Deioneus, who was sometimes called Eioneus. Ixion, son of Phlegyas, courted her and made extravagant promises of a dowry to Deioneus. After he married Dia, he failed to keep the bargain, and Deioneus kept pressing him. Finally, Ixion invited him to his house and pushed him into a pit of fiery coals. As a result of this, Ixion became an outcast, very likely in his own house as well as abroad. Dia was said to be by him the mother of Peirithous, but her husband's treatment of her father might have caused her to succumb to Zeus' attempts to seduce her. He was said to have changed himself into a horse and to have run in a circle around Dia. Many claimed this action as the basis of Peirithous' name.

Ixion could find no man willing to purify him for the wanton murder of his father-in-law, for his was a violation of a sacred code.

Eventually Zeus took pity on him—perhaps in exchange for the favors extended him by Dia—and purified him. A congenital scoundrel, Ixion repaid the kindness by trying to seduce Hera. Learning of this, Zeus set up a phantom of his wife; Ixion had sex with it and became father of the Centaurs. The inevitable question here is whether or not the Centaurs were formed at the moment of Ixion's ejaculation or whether they were carried to full term by the cloud-like phantom. Zeus caught Ixion at his moment of ecstasy and consigned him to the underworld where he was chained to a fiery wheel, a punishment somehow in keeping with the means he used to kill Dia's father.

Peirithous, by one or the other father, turned out to be one of the great Thessalian heroes. If Ixion was his father, he had Centaurs for half-brothers. If Zeus was his father, he was half-brother to Heracles and many other godlike heroes. His marriage to Hippodameia provided the scene for one of the great themes of ancient art—the battle between the Lapiths and Centaurs.

Dia was accounted in some records as the mother of the Centaurs by Zeus. If indeed he courted her in the form of a horse, there could have been foundation for this belief. [Diodorus Siculus 4.69; Eustathius on Homer's *Iliad* 101; Servius on Virgil's *Aeneid* 8.293; Nonnos, *Dionysiaca* 16.240, 14.193; Pindar, *Pythian Odes* 2.39; Scholiast on Euripides' *Phoenician Maidens* 1185; Lucian, *Dialogues of the Gods* 6.]

DIA (2) was a surname of Hebe, or Ganymeda, the goddess of youth, who had temples under this name at Phlius and Sicyon. [Strabo 8.6.24; Pausanias 2.13.3.]

DIA (3) was a daughter of Lycaon. Lycaon was the Arcadian king who was changed into a wolf because of his impiety. Before this happened, Dia became pregnant by Apollo. Managing somehow to conceal her condition, she eventually bore a boy and hid the newborn baby in a hollow oak tree. From this circumstance she called him Dryops. He grew up to become ancestor of the Dryopians. [Tzetzes on Lycophron 480.]

DIA (4) was the second wife of Phineus. She was usually called IDAEA.

DIA (5) was by Pelops the mother of Pittheus. Pittheus was king of Troezen, father of Aethra, and grandfather of Theseus. When Theseus married Phaedra, Pittheus took Hippolytus, the son of Theseus and Antiope, into his house. His tomb and the chair on which he sat in judgment were shown at Troezen down to a late time. He is said to have taught the art of speaking and even to have written a book on the subject. (Pausanias 1.22.2, 2.32.3,4.]

DIA (6) was the mother of Thersites by Agrius, son of Porthaon. Nothing is known of Dia except that she bore six sons to Agrius—Onchestus, Prothous, Celeutor, Lycopeus, Melanippus, and Thersites. These sons drove Oeneus from his throne in Calydon and were killed, with the exception of Thersites, by Diomedes. Thersites went on to the Trojan War, in which he played an inglorious part. He helped lead a revolt against Agamemnon but reacted in a cowardly fashion when apprehended. He dug out the eyes of the beautiful Amazon Penthesileia after she had been killed by Achilles, and in fury Achilles beat him to death. Thersites' looks did not help, since he was said to have been the ugliest Greek at Troy. [Scholiast on Homer's *Iliad* 2.212.]

DIANA was the Roman equivalent of Artemis, but from available evidence she had been a Latin and Sabine divinity from an older era. Once installed at Rome, her principal worshippers were the plebeians, who were mainly of Latin and Sabine stock. Servius Tullius built a sanctuary to her on the Aventine Hill, and every year thereafter slaves of both sexes celebrated Dies Servorum, the Day of Slaves, since Diana was the protectress of slaves.

With Artemis she shared a preference for out-of-the-way groves and springs, and remained a virgin. Although she inspired men, she dreaded the sight of them, and males were not allowed to enter her temple. She was also a goddess of the moon.

Even though she detested males, she made an exception for Virbius. Through one of those trans-Adriatic connections frequently made in the evolution of Roman gods, Virbius was a reincarnation of Hippolytus, who had been precious to Artemis because he embraced chastity and even died as a result of his steadfastness. Somehow he got transported to Rome and established Diana's worship, probably picking up from the point at which the Taurian goddess had been brought from Asia Minor to Greece. Diana entrusted him to the care of the nymph Aegeria in the vicinity of Aricia, and the two lived happily ever after.

The Roman goddess was not clearly defined. There was no distinct brother-sister relationship such as that between Artemis and Apollo, unless we consider as analogous the association between Fauna, or Fatua, with whom she was sometimes identified, and Faunus. She was further identified with Vacuna, Jana, Luna, and other early divinities. One of her surnames was Fascelis and could have had to do with one tradition that claimed her image was brought by Orestes from Tauris in a bundle of sticks (*fascis*). A bloody reminder of the possible Taurian origins of her Italian worship was the fact that her priest at Nemi could be slain, if possible, by anyone who wanted to take his place. [Plutarch, *Roman Questions* 3,4,100; Martial 12.67; Livy 2.32, 3.51.54; Virgil, *Aeneid* 761; Servius on Virgil's *Aeneid* 2.116, 7.657,761; Dionysius of Halicarnassus, *Roman Antiquities* 3.43; Varro, *On the Latin Language* 5.74, *Country Matters* 1.37; St. Augustine, *City of God* 7.16; Ovid, *Metamorphoses* 15.431,545.]

DICE (Dike) was the personification of justice. She was a daughter of Zeus and Themis, and sister of Eunomia and Eirene. The three daughters were considered the HORAE, but their names and roles were not always the same. Dice was in charge of justice and protected its wise administration. She was connected with the Erinyes, except that she not only punished injustice but rewarded virtue. She was an attendant and counselor of Zeus, and her assistant was Poena, the personification of retaliation. She was the mother of Hesychia, the personification of tranquillity. On the chest of Cypselus she was represented as dragging Adicia (Injustice) with one hand while beating her with a staff. [Pindar, *Pythian Odes* 8.1; Apollodorus 1.3.1; Sophocles, *Oedipus at Colonus* 1377; Aeschylus, *Agamemnon* 773; Hesiod, *Theogony* 901; Diodorus Siculus 5.72; Pausanias 5.18.2.]

DICTE was a nymph from whom Mount Dicte in Crete received its name. (*See* BRITOMARTIS.)

DICTYNNA (1) (*See* BRITOMARTIS)

DICTYNNA (2) was one of the titles of the Taurian ARTEMIS.

DIDO, the legendary founder of Carthage, is best known for her love affair with Aeneas, which ended in her being abandoned by him and her resulting suicide. The story of Dido has always posed problems for mythographers and historians, because there were really two quite separate accounts of her, creating, in effect, a double anachronism. Virgil took a quasi-historical tradition from the eighth century B.C. and moved it to the twelfth century B.C. to coincide with events on which he based the *Aeneid*.

The near-historical Dido, more properly called Elissa, was the daughter of Mutto(n), king of Tyre. Her brother, Pygmalion, still an infant, was recognized as king when Mutto died. Until Pygmalion grew up, the kingdom was in the hands of Mutto's brother Acerbas, priest of Heracles and the second most important authority after the king. Dido meanwhile married Acerbas. When Pygmalion reached adulthood he became king, but shortly afterward he had Acerbas assassinated in order to seize his wealth. Dido was horrified and, accompanied by several Tyrians who had been loyal to Acerbas, managed to escape with most of her husband's fortune. They were pursued but managed to elude Pygmalion's henchmen. They stopped in Cyprus, where they picked up a priest of Zeus and his family, along with 80 young women to provide wives for the colonists.

The refugees landed safely in a bay on the coast of Africa and decided to settle there. Dido concluded a crafty, if rather absurd, real estate deal with Hiarbas, the king of the adjoining territory. Hiarbas agreed to a price for as much land as a bull's hide would cover. Surely Hiarbas did not believe he was selling a few square feet. Dido had the hide cut in exceedingly small strips, so that when it was stretched out it covered a sizable area. Dido called this area Byrsa, naming it from the hide of the bull.

Soon commerce began to flourish, and people from adjoining areas swelled the population. The city of Carthage was built on the spot where a horse's head was found. King Hiarbas soon became anxious about the rivalry he experienced in domination of the territory. Summoning Carthaginian nobles, he suggested, or rather demanded, a blending of the countries by his marriage to Dido. The emissaries were reluctant to tell Dido of Hiarbas' threats if she failed to comply. At first they told her Hiarbas wanted someone to live among the Libyans and instruct them in the manners of a civilized life. Dido declared this was not unreasonable; a person should be willing to sacrifice everything for the common good. Then they told her the truth. She was committed by her own strong statement. At length she agreed to marry Hiarbas but asked for time to settle her affairs. During the next few months she raised a funeral pyre. After sacrificing many animals, she ascended the pyre with sword in hand. As the fire was lighted, she plunged the sword into her chest.

In Virgil's story, Dido was a contemporary of Aeneas. When he came to Africa on his voyage, she fell in love with him. Although Aeneas lived with her while in Carthage, he was not seriously in love with her. He was still following a destiny that did not end in Africa. When instructed by the gods to continue his journey, he did so without question and with only mild concern for how this would affect Dido. She was deeply affected and shortly had a pyre built on which she immolated herself.

The two stories of Dido are possibly based on a distant historical event surrounding the Phoenician colonization of Carthage. Elissa (Dido) and Anna, her sister, could even have been early Phoenician divinities. Be that as it may, Virgil's treatment conferred a far more lasting immortality, for subsequently the tragic Dido became a theme for poetry, opera, and painting. [Justinus 18.4,6; Virgil, *Aeneid* 1.335–756, 4.1–705, 6.450–476; Servius on Virgil's *Aeneid* 1.343,363,670,674, 4.459,682, 5.4; Macrobius, *Saturnalia* 5.17, 6.2; Silius Italicus 1.81.]

DINDYME was the wife of Maeon, an ancient king of Phrygia and Lydia. The territory Maeonia was named for him. Dindyme, about whom virtually nothing is known, became by him the mother of Cybele. [Diodorus Siculus 3.58.]

DINDYMENE was a surname of Cybele, derived either from Mount Dindymus in Phrygia, where the Argonauts built a temple to the goddess, or from Dindyme, her mother. Dindymene was also one of the names by which Rhea was designated. Some say Zeus was born at Thebes, where a temple of the Dindymenian mother was built by Pindarus. [Apollonius Rhodius 1.985, with the scholiast; Diodorus Siculus 3.58; Pausanias 9.25.3.]

DINOMACHE was one of the DOGS of Actaeon. [Hyginus, *Fables* 181.]

DIOGENEIA (1) was a daughter of the Cephissus River (in Attica) and wife of Phrasimus, who was probably a provincial king of Attica. Their daughter was Praxithea, who married Erechtheus. Therefore, Diogeneia was at the head of the long line of individuals who shaped the mythological history of Athens. Among her descendants were Cecrops, Pandion, Aegeus, and Theseus. [Apollodorus 3.15.1.]

DIOGENEIA (2) was the daughter of Phorbas, son of Lapithes and Orsinome. Phorbas was famous for having delivered the island of Rhodes from snakes, as a result of which he was honored with heroic worship and after his death placed among the stars as the constellation Ophiuchus. Another tradition had him going from Thessaly to Olenus in order to help Alector, king of Elis, against Pelops. Alector shared his kingdom with Phorbas and married Diogeneia. Their son Amarynceus later shared in the government with his relative Augeas, who needed allies against Heracles. [Diodorus Siculus 4.69; Eustathius on Homer's *Iliad* 303; Scholiast on Apollonius Rhodius 1.172; Pausanias 5.1.8; Apollodorus 2.5.5; Ovid, *Metamorphoses* 11.414, 112.322.]

DIOGENEIA (3) was one of the daughters of Celeus and Metaneira, king and queen of Eleusis. Her sisters were Pammerope and Saesara, and some add Demo. The sisters befriended

Demeter when she came to Eleusis in her search for Persephone. The goddess became nurse to their baby brother, Demophon, who was killed when Demeter sought to make him immortal. Their other brother, Triptolemus, was made a minister of the goddess. [Pausanias 1.38.3; *Homeric Hymn to Demeter* 109.]

DIOMEDE (1) was the daughter of Phorbas of Lesbos. Achilles carried her off to replace Briseis, whom Agamemnon had appropriated. She shared his tent along with Patroclus and his lover Iphis of Scyros. This menage makes for interesting speculation, since Achilles and Patroclus were generally regarded as lovers. Diomede was incorporated in a painting in the Lesche at Delphi along with Briseis and Iphis. [Homer, *Iliad* 9.665; Pausanias 10.25.4.]

DIOMEDE (2) was the daughter of Xuthus, son of Hellen, and sister to Achaeus and Ion. Expelled from Thessaly by his brothers Dorus and Aeolus, Xuthus went to Athens, where he married Creusa, the daughter of Erechtheus. After the death of Erechtheus, he was chosen arbitrator for the disputed throne, and he assigned the kingdom to Cecrops. In consequence, he was expelled by the other sons of Erechtheus and had to leave Athens. He took his family to Aegialeia (Sicyon) in Peloponnesus, where he became king.

Diomede married her cousin Deion, son of Aeolus; apparently the old family feud had subsided. Deion was king in Phocis, so Diomede was queen of the beautiful but rugged country overlooked by the great mass of Mount Parnassus. Here she gave birth to five children—Actor, Aenetus, Cephalus, Phylacus, and Asteropeia—all of whom, with the exception of Aenetus, had descendants famous in the Trojan War. Actor was grandfather of Patroclus. Cephalus was great-grandfather of Odysseus. Phylacus was the grandfather of Protesilaus. Asteropeia was grandmother of Epeius, who built the wooden horse.

Some of Diomede's children were interesting in their own right, as well. Phylacus founded the town of Phylace; his son Iphiclus was celebrated for his fleetness and could run across the tops of grain in the field without breaking the stalks. Cephalus was extraordinarily handsome

and was abducted while still an adolescent by the goddess of the dawn, Eos, and had a son by her. He left her eventually and had a romantic entanglement with his sister-in-law Clymene, Phylacus' wife. He was more than likely the father of the aforementioned Iphiclus.

Besides her own children, Diomede reared Tyro, the daughter of her brother-in-law Salmoneus. Tyro was seduced by Poseidon and bore the twins Pelias and Neleus. She later married her uncle Cretheus; their famous grandson was Jason.

Though we do not get a clear picture of Diomede, we can sense the dynamic flow around her of humans and events later to be incorporated in the Trojan War. To her it might have seemed a long way from the slopes of Parnassus to the plains of Troy, but some of the energy expended in the war had passed through her to some of the principals. [Apollodorus 1.9.4,16, 3.10.8; Pindar, *Olympian Odes* 9.75; Homer, *Iliad* 11.785, 16.4; Eustathius on Homer's *Iliad* 323; Pausanias 1.37.4, 10.29.2; Hyginus, *Fables* 48.]

DIOMEDE (3) was the daughter of Lapithes of Sparta. She married Amyclas, the son of Lacedaemon and Sparta. Amyclas was king of Amyclae, which he founded adjacent to the city later known as Sparta. Diomede bore him four children—Cynortas, Argalus, Hyacinthus, and Laodameia (whom some call Erato, Meganeira, or Leaneira). Hyacinthus grew into an extremely handsome young man. Not only did Zephyrus, the west wind, and the poet Thamyris fall in love with him, but also Apollo. He bestowed his favors on Apollo, and once while the lovers were taking turns hurling a discus, the jealous Zephyrus caused Apollo's discus to swerve and strike Hyacinthus a fatal blow to the head. Diomede's lamentations were joined by others, for Hyacinthus was from that time worshipped at Amyclae as a hero; a great festival, the Hyacinthia, was celebrated in his honor.

Diomede probably outlived Amyclas as well as her oldest son, Argalus, who died childless after a short reign following his father's death. Cynortas inherited the throne and became the father of Oebalus, who is generally regarded as the progenitor of the Spartan dynasty, which continued into historical times. Laodameia married Arcas and became mother by him of Triphylus, Apheidas, Elatus, Azan, and Diomeneia. [Apollodorus 3.10.3; Pausanias 3.1.3; Scholiast on Euripides' *Orestes* 447; Lucian, *Dialogues of the Gods* 14.]

DIOMEDEIA was, according to some, wife of Iphiclus, son of Phylacus. She is more often called ASTYOCHE.

DIOMENEIA was a daughter of Arcas, the ancestor and eponymic hero of the Arcadians, and Erato (some say Leaneira, Meganeira, or Laodameia). Her brothers were Apheidas, Elatus, Azan, and Triphylus. Actually, Apheidas and Elatus were probably half-brothers, and her mother one of the women other than Erato, since nobody seems to agree on the mother of Arcas' offspring. Diomeneia was remembered many years after her death since a bronze statue of her stood in the marketplace at Mantineia. Nobody knows anything about her or why a statue was erected to her. Pausanias, who saw the statue, fails to say why it was there. [Pausanias 8.9.9.]

DIONAEA was a matronymic form of Dione and applied to her daughter Aphrodite. The name was also given to things that were sacred to her, such as the dove. [Statius, *Silvae* 3.5.80; Virgil, *Aeneid* 3.19.]

DIONE (1) has always presented a problem in the genealogy of the Greek gods. She most often has been described as a Titan, daughter of Uranus and Gaea, but some have called her an Oceanid, daughter of Oceanus and Tethys. Others have said she was the daughter of Aether and Gaea, and still others, of Cronus and Euonyme or Uranus and Hemera. If a Titan, she would add one more to the traditional number of 12 (six males and six females), but this did not disturb the prevailing opinion. It would make a certain amount of sense that she came from either Uranus or Gaea in liaison with another god, since in that case she would be only half-Titan.

Dione became by Zeus the mother of Aphrodite, the legend of Aphrodite's sea-foam birth notwithstanding, for those requiring conventional uterine deliveries. As either a Titan or half-Titan, Dione was Zeus' aunt; consequently his daughter by her was also his cousin. Zeus and Dione have also been called parents of Dionysus, but there has certainly been no wide acceptance of this notion.

Dione played insignificant parts in the stories of the gods and goddesses. She was present at the birth of Apollo and Artemis in Delos. During the Trojan War when Diomedes wounded Aphrodite in the hand, Aphrodite abandoned her son Aeneas and fled to Olympus, where Dione was installed, to seek the comfort of her mother, for which she was ridiculed by Hera and Athena.

Dione was worshipped in conjunction with Zeus at Dodona and a few other places. There was also a temple of Aphrodite at Dodona, thus bringing the worship of mother, father, and daughter together in one place. [Apollodorus 1.1.3; Hesiod, *Theogony* 353; Homer, *Iliad* 5.370–416; *Homeric Hymn to Delos* 93; Diodorus Siculus 3.62,74.]

DIONE (2) was one of the NEREIDES. [Apollodorus 1.2.7.]

DIONE (3) was one of the daughters of Atlas. By Tantalus she became the mother of Pelops. Tantalus was the son of Zeus and Pluto, another daughter of Atlas, who was therefore both mother-in-law and sister to Dione. Tantalus was a very wealthy king of Phrygia and a favorite nephew or cousin of the other Olympian gods, therefore frequently invited to their feasts. He was soon spoiled by their attention and pressed his advantage in scandalous activities. He lied to Zeus about a magic dog entrusted to him by Pandareos, who had stolen it from Zeus. He also stole ambrosia and nectar from the table of the gods and shared them with his mortal friends. He revealed divine secrets. He even served the gods the flesh of his son Pelops, but happily for Dione the gods realized what he had done and restored Pelops to life. So Dione saw her powerful but insane husband condemned by Zeus to various tortures in the underworld, such as eternal hunger and thirst, with food and drink immediately at hand but moved away when he would reach for them.

In spite of his shaky start in life, Pelops turned out to be very successful. He left Asia Minor and went to southern Greece, called Peloponnesus after him, where he founded the dynasty that included Atreus, Agamemnon and Menelaus. The mother of Pelops was also called Clytia, Euryanassa, Eurythemistra, Eupryto, or Linos.

Dione had other children by Tantalus, including Broteas and Niobe. Broteas carved the most ancient statue of Cybele on the face of a cliff near Mount Sipylus, but destroyed himself when Artemis drove him insane for refusing to worship her. Insanity appeared to be a family curse. Niobe boasted of her 12 children by Amphion, saying that Leto had only two. Artemis and Apollo quickly made her regret her bragging, for they killed ten of the children.

Dione, although herself half-divine, had an unhappy life. Her husband was a scoundrel. Her son Pelops left home and dwelled with the gods for a while, probably as Poseidon's lover. He then incurred a curse on his line for a treacherous slaying. Broteas went insane and burned himself alive. Niobe lost most of her sons and daughters and wept herself to death. [Hyginus, *Fables* 9,11,82,83; Ovid, *Metamorphoses* 6.146–312; Pausanias 1.21.3, 3.22.4; Homer, *Iliad* 11.582–592, 24.605–617.]

DIONE (4) was one of the HYADES.

DIOXIPPE (1) was one of the DANAIDES, daughter of Danaus by Pieria. Her husband was Aegyptus, son of Aegyptus and Gorgo. [Apollodorus 2.1.5.]

DIOXIPPE (2) was one of the HELIADES. [Hyginus, *Fables: Preface* 154.]

DIOXIPPE (3) was one of the AMAZONS. [Hyginus, *Fables* 163.]

DIOXIPPE (4) was one of the DOGS of Actaeon. [Hyginus, *Fables* 181.]

DIRAE was a Roman name for the EUMENIDES or Erinyes.

DIRCE (1) was a daughter of Helios and the wife of Lycus. True to his promise to his dying brother Nycteus, Lycus had brought Nycteus' daughter Antiope back from Sicyon, where she had fled to escape her father's wrath over her pregnancy by Zeus. Dirce hated Antiope. Some claimed that Antiope was married to her uncle before he married Dirce. Dirce had Antiope put in chains, but Zeus helped her escape to Mount Cithaeron, where she gave birth to Amphion and Zethus. The twins were brought up by shepherds, but Antiope was recaptured and spent her life in servitude and squalor. Finally she escaped, found her sons, and revealed to them the misery she had endured. The sons went to Thebes and killed Lycus. They tied Dirce by her hair to a bull, which tossed and dragged her until she died in agony. They threw her body into a stream on Mount Cithaeron, afterward called the spring of Dirce. Some say she was engaged in a Bacchic revelry on Mount Cithaeron when snatched up by the twins. A small river flowing on one side of Thebes was also called Dirce. [Hyginus, *Fables* 7,8; Pausanias 9.25.3; Apollodorus 4.5.5.]

DIRCE (2) was the mother of Lycus of Euboea by Poseidon. Lycus attacked Thebes during a time of sedition, killed King Creon, and usurped the throne. Believing Heracles was dead, Lycus tried to seduce Megara. She resisted him, and he was about to kill her when Heracles returned and killed him. Thereupon Hera, whose favorite Lycus was, drove Heracles mad so that he killed Megara and his own sons. [Hyginus, *Fables* 32.]

DISCORDIA was the Roman goddess of war and discord. She was similar to the Homeric Eris. The companions of Discordia were Mars, Bellona, and the Furies. [Virgil, *Aeneid* 8.702.]

DODONE was one of the OCEANIDES, from whom the oracle of Dodona was believed to have been named. Dodona was one of the most ancient centers of worship of Zeus. [Stephanus Byzantium, "Dodone"; Scholiast on Homer's *Iliad* 16.233.]

DODONIDES were the nymphs, according to some, who brought up Zeus. They were identified with the Hyades. The Dodonaean Zeus possessed the most ancient oracle in Greece at

Dodona in Epeirus on Mount Tomarus. At Dodona he was mainly a prophetic god, and the oak tree was sacred to him. [Scholiast on Homer's *Iliad* 18.486; Hyginus, *Fables* 182; Ovid, *Fasti* 6.711, *Metamorphoses* 3.314.]

DOGS of Actaeon. Actaeon was another member of the ill-fated family of Cadmus. He was the son of Aristaeus, son of Apollo, and Autonoe, daughter of Cadmus. He inherited from his father a love of the fields and forests, and learned the sport and industry of hunting from Cheiron the Centaur, under whose guardianship he was early placed. Perhaps Actaeon learned so much about hunting that he became arrogant enough to compare his ability with that of Artemis. Rumor also was current that he lusted after his aunt Semele, who was the mistress of Zeus. Either of these transgressions could have proved fatal to him, but he had so far escaped punishment. Perhaps Artemis was biding her time for the right moment. It came one day when she stopped to bathe in a stream in the valley of Gargaphia near Plataea. Actaeon had been out hunting with his 50 hounds and had decided to rest atop a boulder. He saw the goddess in her naked glory, and she realized she had been seen. Fearing Actaeon would brag about this, she promptly changed him into a stag; when he leapt from the rock, his hounds fell on him and tore him to pieces. Some of the female dogs ate the dismembered body.

The names of the female dogs were: Arethusa, Argo, Aura, Chediaetros, Cyllo, Dinomache, Dioxippe, Echione, Gorgo, Harpyia, Lacaena, Leaena, Lynceste, Melanchaetes, Ocydrome, Ocypete, Oresitrophos, Orias, Oxyrhoe, Sagnos, Theridamas, Theriope, Theriphóne, Uolatos, and Urania. (In the process of copying and handing down the list, some of the copiers probably confused gender and misspelled some of the names. Also, the total number of dogs varied.)

After killing their master, the dogs sought him throughout the forest, howling so piteously that eventually Cheiron found them and made a statue of Actaeon to soothe them. As a side note, there was speculation that Actaeon had brought the calamity on himself by deliberately spying on the goddess.

One might ask why Actaeon needed 50 dogs for a hunt. A fraction of that number should have been sufficient to smell out and help bring down even the largest quarry. One of the later commentators, following the fashion of trying endlessly to tie stories together regardless of the sense, stated that Actaeon's dogs were later changed into the beings known as Telchines, who are identified with the island of Rhodes. Pausanias claimed to have seen the rock where the tragedy occurred. [Apollodorus 3.4.4; Ovid, *Metamorphoses* 3.138–252; Hyginus, *Fables* 180,181; Pausanias 9.2.3; Eustathius on Homer's *Iliad* 771.]

DOMIDUCA was a surname of Juno, as Domiducus was a surname of Jupiter. Under these names they were gods of marriage and were believed to conduct the bride into the house of the bridegroom. [St. Augustine, *City of God* 7.3, 9.6.]

DORIPPE (1) was the mother of Melampus. His mother, however, is more often called EIDOMENE. [Dieuchidas, quoted by the scholiast on Apollonius Rhodius 1.121.]

DORIPPE (2) was the mother by Anius of the Oenotropae and Andron, king of Andros. Anius was a son of Apollo by Rhoeo, daughter of Staphylus. When Staphylus discovered his daughter was pregnant, he cast her afloat in a chest. The chest floated to Delos, and when the child was born he was consecrated to the service of Apollo, who endowed him with prophetic powers. Dorippe was probably a Delian nymph, and since Delos is quite a small island, she remained with Anius and bore four children by him. The daughters were Oeno, Spermo, and Elais, the so-called Oenotropae, who could produce at will any quantity of wine, wheat, or oil. When Agamemnon tried to carry them to Troy to function as a veritable commissary, they were changed into doves by Dionysus. [Ovid, *Metamorphoses* 13.628–704; Virgil, *Aeneid* 3.80–83; Apollodorus, *Epitome* 3.10.]

DORIS (1), one of the OCEANIDES, was the wife of Nereus, son of Pontus and Gaea. Their kingdom was the Mediterranean, more particularly the Aegean Sea. Nereus fathered 50 daughters by Doris; they were the Nereides, nymphs of the sea, who became mothers of various heroes by mortals. Thetis, the mother of Achilles, was a Nereid. Nereus was the prophetic old man of the sea and could assume any shape he chose. While Doris can be conceived as mermaid-like, Nereus had seaweed for hair, eyebrows, and beard. The name Doris was sometimes applied to the sea itself. [Apollodorus 1.2.2; Hesiod, *Theogony* 240; Ovid, *Metamorphoses* 2.269; Virgil, *Eclogues* 10.5.]

DORIS (2) was one of the NEREIDES. [Homer, *Iliad* 18.45.]

DORIUM was one of the DANAIDES, daughter of Danaus and an Ethiopian woman. She was married to Cercetes. [Apollodorus 2.1.5.]

DORODOCHE, daughter of Orsilochus, was married to Icarius according to some. Most say, however, that the wife of Icarius was POLYCASTE; others say Asterodeia. [Scholiast on Homer's *Odyssey* 15.16.]

DOTIS was the illegitimate daughter of Elatus, son of Arcas, by Amphictyone. Her half-brothers were Stymphalus, Aepytus, Cyllen, Pereus, and possibly Ischys. Dotis was probably born after Elatus left Arcadia and settled in Thessaly. The Dotian Plain was named for her. When Dotis grew up, she was seduced by the god Ares and became the mother of Phlegyas. Phlegyas inherited his father's warlike nature and became ruler of the region that would later be called Orchomenia, which he named Phlegyantis. Phlegyas was the father of Coronis, who by Apollo became the mother of Asclepius.

After Phlegyas was killed by the Theban kings Nycteus and Lycus, Dotis married Ialysus of Rhodes. How this came about is impossible to say. Women did not journey very far in those days without very good cause, so perhaps Ialysus journeyed to Thessaly for some reason. In any case, they had a daughter, Syme, who was abducted by Glaucus and taken to an island near Rhodes off the coast of Caria. Glaucus named the island in honor of his new wife. [Apollodorus 3.5.5,9.1; Stephanus Byzantium, "Dotion"; Pausanias 8.4.2; Athenaeus 7.296.]

DOTO was one of the NEREIDES. [Apollodorus 1.2.7.]

DRACONTIS was one of the PIERIDES.

DRIMO (1) was one of the ALCYONIDES. [Eustathius on Homer's *Iliad* 776; Suidas, "Alcyonides."]

DRIMO (2) was one of the NEREIDES. [Hyginus, *Fables: Preface* 8.]

DRYADES were nymphs of trees. They were also called Hamadryades or Adryades. Their name, although derived from *drys*, or oak, meant any lofty tree. Nymphs of fruit trees were called Melidae, Meliades, Epimelides, or Hamamelides. These nymphs were particularly shy and did not venture far from the trees to which they were attached in a life-and-death association. When a tree died, its nymph died with it. We hear of Dryades as individuals very infrequently. The town of Phigalia in Arcadia was believed to have derived its name from a Dryad of the same name. Dryope, originally an ordinary mortal, was changed into a Hamadryad. Aristaeus, son of Apollo and Cyrene, was once instructed by his mother how to remove a curse from his bees. He had to build four altars in the woods, dedicating them to Dryades. Otherwise, we must realize that when a nymph was mentioned without qualification, she may have been a Dryad as well as any other type of nymph. [Pausanias 8.4.2,39.2; Apollonius Rhodius 2.477; Antoninus Liberalis 31,32; *Homeric Hymn to Aphrodite* 259.] (*See also* NYMPHS.)

DRYOPE (1) was a daughter of Eurytus or, according to others, of Dryops. Iole, the beloved of Heracles, was said to be her half-sister. She tended her father's flocks on Mount Oeta, where she was a playmate of the Hamadryades. They taught her hymns to the gods and how to dance. Apollo happened along once and saw this beautiful, simple girl frolicking with the nymphs. He changed himself into a tortoise, and the delighted nymphs played with the creature. Dryope took it in her lap, but suddenly it changed into a serpent. The Hamadryades were frightened away, which was what Apollo had in mind as he leisurely assumed his usual appearance and enjoyed the young woman before she could recover from her astonishment.

Shortly afterward she married Andraemon, son of Oxylus, probably in time to have him believe that Apollo's son was his doing. The son was Amphissus, who grew up possessed with extraordinary strength. He built the town of Oeta and a temple of Apollo. One day when Dryope was in the temple, her old playmates, the Hamadryades, came looking for her and carried her off. In the temple they left a fountain, and afterward a poplar tree grew rapidly on the spot. Dryope became a Hamadryad. Amphissus appeared to be aware of this and erected a temple to the nymphs, which no woman was allowed to enter. Games were celebrated in the vicinity of the temple for many years. [Ovid, *Metamorphoses* 9.325,363; Antoninus Liberalis 32; Stephanus Byzantium, "Dryope."]

DRYOPE (2) was a nymph and the mother of Tarquitus by Faunus. Tarquitus was one of the princes slain by Aeneas in his war with Turnus. Overcome, Tarquitus begged for his life, but Aeneas beheaded him and denied burial of the corpse. [Virgil, *Aeneid* 10.550–515.]

DRYOPE (3), a Phoenician, was the mother of Chromis. Chromis was born during a Bacchanalian revelry when Dryope was dragging a bull to the altar of Dionysus. In the war of the Seven against Thebes, while urging the Thebans forward Chromis was struck in his open mouth with a spear and died almost instantly. [Statius, *Thebaid* 2.615–630.]

DRYOPE (4) was one of the Lemnian women present during the visit of the Argonauts. There is no record of which of the Argonauts slept with her in the women's effort to repopulate the island with men. They had slaughtered all the males on the island before the arrival of the Argonauts, but decided to review the situation when the finest men of Greece dropped anchor on Lemnos. [Valerius Flaccus 2.174.]

DRYOPE (5) was a kind of patronymic instead of a real name, since the person in question was the daughter of Dryops, an Arcadian king.

According to some, she became the mother of Pan by Hermes. The mother of Pan was called by various names, such as Hybris, Oeneis, and Thymbris. Some even named Callisto or Penelope. Others said he was the offspring of a goat and a man, a report probably spread to frighten young goatherds.

Pan was a half-man, half-goat individual. He was bearded and horned, his body was hairy, and he had cloven hooves. He was agile and swift, and endowed with boundless sexual energy. There were various stories about him and his affairs with nymphs, such as Pitys and Echo. He was the god of fields and flocks, and the principal seat of his worship was Arcadia. As god of everything connected with pastoral life, he was fond of music and was the inventor of the syrinx or shepherd's flute. Sacrifices were offered to him in common with Dionysus and the nymphs.

Dryope was never heard of again. There is no good explanation of why Hermes and Dryope should have produced such a strange-appearing child, but it may be recalled that Hermes was also the father of Priapus by Aphrodite. Perhaps there was a connection. [*Homeric Hymn to Pan;* Apollodorus 1.4.3, *Epitome* 7.38; Cicero, *On the Nature of the Gods* 3.56.]

DYNA was a daughter of Euander, and sister of Pallas and Roma. Several years before the Trojan War, Euander, who was a son of Hermes, migrated from Pallantium in Arcadia to Italy. There be built the town of Pallantium, later included as a part of Rome. He taught his neighbors much useful information, especially the art of writing. He also introduced the worship of Pan, Demeter, Poseidon, Heracles, and Nice (Nike). He formed an alliance with Aeneas when the Trojan hero arrived in Italy. His son Pallas was killed in a battle with Turnus. Dyna had a son, whom she called Pallas, fathered by the ubiquitous Heracles. Some claimed the Palatine Hill was named for him, but it could have been equally named for his uncle. [Dionysius of Halicarnassus, *Roman Antiquities* 1.32; Virgil, *Aeneid* 8.104.]

DYNAMENE was one of the NEREIDES. [Homer, *Iliad* 18.43.]

DYSIS was one of the HORAE. [Hyginus, *Fables* 183.]

ECECHEIRIA was the personification of the armistice or truce. She was represented at the entrance of the temple of Zeus at Olympia in the act of crowning Iphitus, the Eleian lawgiver and reviver of the Olympic games. During the games a period of cessation of hostilities was supposed to be in effect. [Pausanias 5.10.3,26.2.]

ECHENAIS was a Naiad who fell in love with the Sicilian shepherd Daphnis. Most writers called her NOMIA. [Pausanias 8.38.11.]

ECHIDNA is somehow the epitome of the female monster in classical myth. It would perhaps be worthwhile to investigate the reason the Greeks and Romans made the majority of their monsters female. Perhaps this was a downside to fertility, fate, justice, retribution, and other things personified by women. If women presided over those things that were necessary and good, then why should they not personify as well the malevolence and destruction that characterized the legion of monsters identified in the Mediterranean world?

Echidna's genealogy, as might be expected, was confusing. She was the daughter of either Chrysaor and Callirrhoe, Peiras and Styx, or Tartarus and Gaea. It is easy to see how confusion was inevitable, since in those primordial eras of cataclysmic coupling it must have been difficult to determine who was doing what to whom. Tartarus and Gaea were the most likely parents. Their other offspring included the giants and Typhon.

Echidna was half-woman and half-serpent in appearance, and her eyes were black and fearful. She mated with her brother Typhon, who personified the destructive hurricane but was described as a fire-breathing giant. Not surprisingly, the two of them produced some of the most terrifying beings in mythology, such as the hell-dogs Orthrus and Cerberus, the Lernaean Hydra, Chimaera, and the Sphinx. Some added the Gorgons, the Nemean lion, Scylla, the Crommyonian sow, and the eagle that consumed the liver of Prometheus.

The Greeks on the Black Sea believed that Typhon and Echidna lived in a cave in Scythia, but others consigned them to the country of the Arimi, a remote desert place somewhere in central Asia. It was in the vicinity of one or the other of these habitats that Heracles happened to pass when he was driving home the oxen of Geryones. While he slept one night his horses disappeared, and he scoured the country for them. He found them in the country of the Hylaea, a peninsula in the northern part of the Black Sea, in the possession of Echidna, who had them hidden in her cave. She agreed to give them up if he would have intercourse with her. One always wonders about the physiological accommodations where scaly monsters are concerned, but Heracles knew his way around and managed to carry out his part of the bargain. Typhon was apparently off blowing an ill wind somewhere. From this improbable union triplets were born—Agathyrsus, Gelonus, and Scythes. Heracles left certain instructions with Echidna for the son or sons he knew she would bear. Consequently, when the three grew up, Scythes became king of the Scythians. In accordance with the old instructions, he was the only son who could wield the bow Heracles left behind, and the only one who could wear his father's belt.

The foregoing story is really a story about Heracles and not Echidna. The tale was most probably written in late classical times as an addition to earlier descriptions of the hero's sexual prowess, as if any were needed. The account tended to humanize Echidna somewhat, giving her emotions and even a sense of duty (i.e., she did not eat her children, who were probably human in appearance, but allowed them to grow up and vie for the rule of Scythia). Her history up until then had consisted mostly of destruction and the spawning of loathsome creatures with multiple heads.

After her encounter with Heracles she was killed in her sleep by Argus Panoptes. This reported incident is perhaps the most baffling in Echidna's already strange career. Argus, the great-grandson of the eponymic hero of Argos, was said to have multiple eyes, which made him valuable as a watchman. There is no report that he ever left Peloponnesus, so Echidna must have stirred herself from her Scythian lair and gone to

Peloponnesus, where she plagued travelers. The larger question is how Argus could have killed her, since she was supposed to be immortal. Immortal monsters could be restrained and immobilized, but they could not be killed. Even her son the Lernaean Hydra was not entirely put down by Heracles—his immortal head was buried under a boulder. [Apollodorus 2.1.2, 3.1,5.10, 3.5.8, 5.10.11; Hesiod, *Theogony* 295, 306,307,311,351,981; Pausanias 8.18.1; Hyginus, *Fables* 151; Herodotus 4.8–10.]

ECHIONE was one of the DOGS of Actaeon. [Hyginus, *Fables* 181.]

ECHO was an Oread, or mountain nymph. Because she had a reputation among her companions for garrulity, she was often posted to detain Hera while Zeus had sexual relations with her sister nymphs. While Echo continued her chatter, the nymphs would slip away undetected. Hera learned of this deception and punished Echo so that she could only repeat the final words spoken to her. She had no power of initiating a conversation.

Before this happened she had been seduced by Pan, the great god of flocks and shepherds. By him she had two daughters, Iambe and Iynx. After she bore the daughters to him he lost interest in her. It was probably during the time these daughters were growing up that as a fellow matron she engaged Hera in the long, gossipy conversations. After she had lost her voice she happened one day to encounter the beautiful youth Narcissus. She fell immediately in love with him and began following him. Narcissus was not capable of loving anyone and had been cruel to his would-be lovers, mostly male. He considered Echo a nuisance, particularly since she had what he must have thought a weird habit of repeating what he said. He turned coldly away from her each time she came near. Echo pined away until finally she disappeared altogether; only her voice remained. At the same time she was pining away so was Narcissus, since one of his rejected lovers had prayed to Nemesis to punish the self-centered youth. Nemesis caused him to fall in love with his reflection in a pool, and thereafter he could not bear to leave the beautiful youth staring up at him from the

depths. In this way he, like Echo, disappeared; in his accustomed place by the pool, a flower grew that was named for him. [Ovid, *Metamorphoses* 3.356–401; Tzetzes on Lycophron 310.]

EDULICA, or Edusa, was a Roman divinity worshipped as the protectress of children. She was believed to bless their food, just as Potina and Cuba blessed their drinking and their sleep. [St. Augustine, *City of God* 4.11; Arnobius, *Adversus Nationes* 3.25.]

EGERIA (*See* AEGERIA)

EGESTA, or Segesta, was the daughter of Phoenodamas of Troy. When a sea monster invaded the Troad as a result of Laomedon's refusal to pay Poseidon and Apollo for building the city walls, Phoenodamas was ordered to expose one of his three daughters. However, he incited the Trojans to protest this order and compel Laomedon, whose actions had brought the monster into the country in the first place, to expose his daughter Hesione. For this treasonable action Phoenodamas was slain by Laomedon, and the three daughters were sold to Sicilian merchants. There is no record of what happened to the other sisters in Sicily, but Egesta excited the attention of the river-god Crimisus. He assumed the shape of a dog and mounted her. One quickly asks why a dog and why not a human. Maybe Egesta had been raped by the sailors during the voyage and hated men, or perhaps she was fond of animals. We must accept that Crimisus knew what he was doing. From this curious union Egestus (Aegestus or Acestes) was born, and fortunately he inherited the appearance of his mother. According to one writer, she returned to Troy and married Capys, by whom she became the mother of Anchises, but this notion probably originated in efforts by commentators to strengthen ancestral ties between Rome and Troy. Egestus did go to Troy and took part in the war. He returned to Sicily in time to receive Aeneas hospitably in the town he had built and named for his mother (and himself), Egesta (later Segesta). He went on to found the cities of Eryx, Entella, and Asca. [Virgil, *Aeneid* 1.195,550, 5.36,711; Servius on Virgil's *Aeneid* 1.550,554, 5.30,73; Tzetzes on

Lycophron 471,951,953,963; Dionysius of Halicarnassus, *Roman Antiquities* 1.52.]

EIDO was the daughter of Proteus, who fell in love with the steersman of Menelaus in Egypt. She was usually known by the name THEONOE. [Euripides, *Helen* 11; Aristophanes, *Thesmophoriazusae* 897; Homer, *Odyssey* 4.363.]

EIDOMENE, or Idomene, was a daughter of Pheres, son of Cretheus and Tyro, and Periclymene. Her brothers were Admetus and Lycurgus, and her sister was Periapis. Pheres founded the town of Pherae in Thessaly. In one place Eidomene was referred to as the daughter of Abas. She married Amythaon, her uncle, thus becoming not only a cousin but also aunt of Jason, since Amythaon was brother to Aeson, Jason's father. By Amythaon she became the mother of sons Bias and Melampus, and a daughter, Aeolia. She was sometimes called Aglaia or Dorippe. Amythaon migrated to Messenia and settled at the court of Neleus, his half-brother. He started the Olympic games after the sons of Pelops left Elis. He went back to Thessaly to greet Jason when his nephew appeared at the court of Pelias. Bias and Melampus went on to become joint rulers in Argos because they were able to cure the insanity of the daughters of Proetus. Melampus was able to accomplish the cure through his combined gift of prophecy and medical knowledge. Eidomene probably lived with her sons in Argos after Amythaon died and they had acquired their part of the kingdom. [Apollodorus 1.9.11, 2.2.2, 3.10.4,13.8; Diodorus Siculus 4.68; Homer, *Odyssey* 11.259; Pausanias 5.8.2; Pindar, *Pythian Odes* 4.124.]

EIDOTHEA (1) was a daughter of Proteus. She was called Eurynome by one writer. Her sister was Cameiro. When Menelaus and Helen were on the final part of their voyage home, they were driven by winds to the island of Pharos off the coast of Egypt. Here was one of the habitats of Proteus, the old man of the sea, who could change himself into any form he desired. He used this ability particularly when someone wanted him to foretell the future, which he was reluctant to do. Menelaus was eager to question him about getting back to Sparta and also about

the fate of his brother. Eidothea befriended the wanderers and advised Menelaus how to make her father reveal what he wanted to know. Menelaus lay in wait for Proteus and grasped him tightly while the old man changed into a lion, a serpent, a panther, a boar, a tree, and even water. Eventually the god resumed his regular form and told Menelaus what he needed to know. [Homer, *Odyssey* 4.365; Dionysius Periegeta 259.] (*See also* THEONOE.)

EIDOTHEA (2) was the mother of Byblis and Caunus, according to some. More often she was called TRAGASIA. [Antoninus Liberalis 30.]

EIDOTHEA (3) was the second wife of Phineus, and mother of Thynus and Mariandynus. She is usually called IDAEA. [Apollodorus 3.15.3.]

EIDOTHEA (4) was the mother of Terambus by Euseirus. Nothing further is known of her or Euseirus, but Terambus was an excellent musician both on the lyre and the syrinx. The nymphs loved him, and he undoubtedly loved them, since he was unwilling to cease frolicking with them when Pan warned him once that a severe winter was coming to Mount Othrys. Terambus further made insolent remarks about Zeus and the nymphs. When the predicted winter came, his flocks perished, and he was changed into a beetle called *cerambux*. [Antoninus Liberalis 22.]

EIDOTHEA (5) was, according to some, one of the OCEANIDES. Others called her and her sisters Althaea and Adraste HYADES. In any case, she was one of the nurses of Zeus. [Hyginus, *Fables* 182.]

EIDYIA (*See* IDYIA)

EILEITHYIA, Eleithyia, Eilethyia, or Eleutho was the goddess of birth. She assisted women in labor, and when she approved of the circumstances surrounding a birth, she caused the delivery to be an easy one. However, if a woman had been unchaste or got pregnant too frequently, Eileithyia delayed the birth and made labor long and painful.

Originally Eileithyia was used in the plural, but eventually only one goddess was designated.

She was a daughter of Zeus and Hera, and sister of Ares, Hestia, and Hebe. She was believed to have been born in a cavern in Crete near Cnossus. From there her worship spread to Delos and Attica. The Delians said she came from the country of the Hyperboreans to assist Leto in the birth of Apollo and Artemis. In Attica she had a sanctuary containing three carved images of her, all of which were covered from head to toe. Two of these were said to have been brought from Crete by Phaedra, the second wife of Theseus. The third was brought from Delos by Erysichthon, son of Cecrops and Agraulos. Eileithyia had sanctuaries as well in Sparta, Cleitor, Messene, Tegea, Megara, Hermione, and other places. Her surname at Athens was Lysizona, i.e., the Goddess Who Loosens the Girdle.

Like Artemis, with whom she was frequently identified, she was a virgin, although an early hymn to her referred to her as the mother of Eros. Some said she was also the mother of the mysterious Sosipolis, an Eleian hero. Following the advice of an oracle, the sorely beset Eleians placed Sosipolis, only moments after being born, in front of the advancing Arcadians. He was changed into a serpent, causing the Arcadians to flee. On this spot, at the foot of the hill of Cronus at Olympia, the Eleians built a sanctuary to him and his supposed mother, Eileithyia. No one could approach the altar except a priestess with her head covered. Oaths taken in the name of Sosipolis were especially solemn and binding.

Eileithyia was present at the birth of Heracles and, persuaded by Hera, helped delay his birth so that Eurystheus could be born first. She was considered a companion of the Moirae, since they spun the thread at the beginning of one's life and prophesied the fate of the newly born.

She was associated with Artemis, Hera, and the Elionia in Greece. In Rome she was identified with Juno and Nascio. She also had a counterpart, Bubastis, in Egypt. [Homer, *Iliad* 11.270, 16.187, 19.103,119; *Odyssey* 19.188; Pausanias 1.8.15,44.3, 3.14.6,17.1,25.4, 6.20.2, 8.21.2, 9.2.27; *Homeric Hymn to Delos* 98; Hesiod, *Theogony* 922; Apollodorus, 1.3.1.; Herodotus 4.35; Plutarch, *Roman Questions* 49; Ovid, *Amores* 2.13; Catullus 34.13; Dionysius of Halicarnassus, *Roman Antiquities* 4.15.]

EIONE was one of the NEREIDES. [Apollodorus 1.2.7.]

EIRENE (1) was the goddess of peace and one of the three HORAE, daughters of Zeus and Themis. Her sisters were Dice (Justice) and Eunomia (Order). After Timotheus was victorious over the Spartans, altars were built to Eirene at Athens at public expense. One of her statues at Athens stood beside that of Amphiaraus, and she was depicted carrying Plutus, the god of wealth, in her arms. This seemed to symbolize peace as a source of wealth. Another statue of her stood in the Prytaneion near that of Hestia. She often appeared holding a cornucopia or an olive branch. Sometimes she was represented as burning a pile of arms. She had a counterpart, Pax, in Rome, where Vespasian built a magnificent temple to her. [Cornelius Nepos 2; Plutarch, *Cimon* 13; Hesiod, *Theogony* 901; Diodorus siculus 5.72; Suetonius, *Vespasian* 9.]

EIRENE (2) was a daughter of Poseidon and Melanthea. In early times the island of Calaureia (modern Paros) was called Eirene after her. [Plutarch, *Greek Questions* 19.]

ELACHIA was one of the THESPIADES. By Heracles she became the mother of Buleus. [Apollodorus 2.7.8.]

ELAEIRA (*See* HILAEIRA)

ELAIS was one of the OENOTROPAE.

ELARA was a daughter of Minyas (some say Orchomenus). Her father was among the early Minyan kings, which line produced many of the great heroes. Elara was a conquest of Zeus, and when she became pregnant by him, he concealed her beneath the earth out of fear of Hera's jealousy. It is curious that Zeus always worried after the numerous seductions rather than before. Also, it is a mystery why he believed Hera would recognize a particular bastard as his. Perhaps there was an identifying aura that characterized his offspring. In this case, the child that forced its way to the surface of the ground as soon as it was born was nothing to be proud of—he was the monstrous Tityus. Although with typical

Greek exaggeration he was said to cover acres, he probably was a victim of a glandular abnormality such as gigantism. After all, he later mated and had a daughter, and finding a wife big enough to accommodate his massive proportions would have been quite an undertaking.

Hera was not long in discovering the truth of the matter, and used her disproportionate stepson to her advantage. She induced him to try to rape Leto, another of Zeus' lovers, when she came through the mountain pass at Panopeus on her way to Delphi. Artemis and Apollo promptly dispatched him, and he was cast into Tartarus, where vultures devoured his liver. His gigantic tomb was shown afterward at Panopeus. The fate of Elara was never disclosed. Undoubtedly she died when Tityus was born, either from suffocation underground or by what must have been a horrible and mutilating delivery. It should be remarked that Zeus made no effort to come to the rescue of Elara. or his grotesque son. [Apollodorus 1.4.1; Apollonius Rhodius 1.181,762; Hyginus, *Fables* 55; Pausanias 10.11.1,29.2; Ovid, *Metamorphoses* 4.457, *Ex Ponto* 1.2.41; Pindar, *Pythian Odes* 4.160.]

ELASII were divinities who averted epileptic fits. They were said to have been descendants of Alexida, daughter of Amphiaraus. The family of Amphiaraus was noted for its medical knowledge and skill. [Plutarch, *Greek Questions* 23.]

ELATE was the daughter of Aloeus and Iphimedeia, and half-sister of the gigantic Otus and Ephialtes. She herself was a giantess. When her brothers were killed, she wept so unceasingly that she was metamorphosed into a spruce tree. [Libanius 34.1110.]

ELECTRA (1) was one of the OCEANIDES. She married Thaumas, the son of Pontus and Gaea, thereby becoming not only cousin but also sister-in-law to a variety of marine divinities. Her own children by Thaumas, however, were divinities of the air, the Harpies and Iris. The Harpies were personified storm winds, but they also snatched up criminals for punishment by the Erinyes. They were generally considered horrible to behold and to be avoided at all costs.

Iris, on the other hand, was the personification of the rainbow and the messenger of the gods. [Hesiod, *Theogony* 237,265–269; Apollodorus 1.2.2,6; Homer, *Odyssey* 20.77–78, 22.66,77; Apollonius Rhodius 2.298.]

ELECTRA (2) was a daughter of Atlas and Pleione, and one of the seven PLEIADES. Her story is a confusing one. Zeus fell in love with her and carried her to Olympus, a rather daring thing to do, considering the perennial jealousy of Hera. He succeeded in raping her, but she managed to escape in midrape and as a suppliant embraced the sacred Palladium, which Athena had established. Since she had been sullied, the divinity of her attacker notwithstanding, she was considered a defiler of the sacred object, and it was hurled from Olympus to land in Ilium (Troy), where it was revered as the city's principal security.

Through her unwelcome encounter with the father of the gods, she became the mother of Iasion and Dardanus. They must have been twins, although this fact was never particularly emphasized. (According to an Italian version of her story, she was the wife of Corythus, king of Tuscia, and had Iasion by him and Dardanus later by Zeus.) When Dardanus and Iasion migrated to Samothrace from Arcadia (or Italy or Crete), they carried the Palladium with them. This is contrary to the story of its celestial origin, but there might have been two such images. Electra appears to have followed or accompanied her sons, for we find her on Samothrace. She was even said to have been the mother of Harmonia by Zeus in Samothrace, although Harmonia is nearly always called the daughter of Aphrodite and Ares. In keeping, though, with the accounts of the origin of the Samothracian mysteries, the presence of Harmonia appeared to be called for in establishing a connection between the Samothracian and Theban Cabeiri. It seems hardly likely that Electra voluntarily would have submitted to Zeus after her first unfortunate experience with him.

Thoroughly instructed in the mysteries by Demeter, his lover, Iasion passed on their knowledge to numerous heroes. He later married Cybele, according to some. Dardanus went to the Troad and was hospitably received by Teucer, the king of the region, who gave him part of the kingdom and his daughter Bateia. He built the city of Dardania (later Troy) and initiated the inhabitants into the mysteries of the gods of Samothrace. He introduced the cult of Cybele into Phrygia.

Electra went with him to the Troad, and she brought the Palladium along from Samothrace. Again we have a conflicting account. Here is the very person who allegedly contaminated the Olympian Palladium, so that it was cast out of heaven, now bringing it to the city whose site was determined by the landing place in the earlier account. Apparently there needed to be an explanation for the introduction of the mysteries into Troy. Although the Palladium was connected with Athena, who had no strong role in the mysteries, its function of guaranteeing the safety of the city was perhaps given more credibility by having Dardanus and Electra heavily involved in worship of the Cabeiri.

Electra remained in Troy until its fall, according to some writers. Even though the Pleiades had a kind of second-class immortality, being daughters of a Titan, this would have made Electra well over 100 years old. According to the story, she watched the city founded by her son perishing in flames and tore out her hair in grief; she was placed among the stars as a comet. Other accounts say she and her sisters were already among the stars as the seven Pleiades and that Electra's brilliancy dimmed when Ilium was destroyed. [Apollodorus 3.10.1, 12.1.3; Servius on Virgil's *Aeneid* 1.32,384, 2.325, 3.167, 7.207, 10.272; Tzetzes on Lycophron 29; Diodorus Siculus 5.48; Scholiast on Euripides' *Phoenician Maidens* 1136; Eustathius on Homer's *Iliad* 1155.]

ELECTRA (3) was a sister of Cadmus, from whom the Electrian gate at Thebes was said to have received its name. It is curious that we know nothing further about her. The story of Cadmus is rich in variations, and his brothers and sisters from Phoenicia have their own histories. It is conceivable that the names of Cadmus and Electra, associated at Samothrace as son-in-law and mother-in-law, might have been transported to Thebes in a different relationship. [Pausanias 9.8.3; Scholiast on Apollonius Rhodius 1.916.]

ELECTRA (4), also called Laodice, was a daughter of Agamemnon and Clytemnestra. Her sisters were Iphigeneia and Chrysothemis, and her brother was Orestes. Orestes was the youngest of the four, and it is reasonable to assume that Electra was about ten years older. In that case, she was probably about 11 when Iphigeneia was taken to Aulis and sacrificed. Consequently, she grew up in the shadow of her mother's anger and eventual infidelity. She loathed Aegisthus and made no effort to conceal her bitterness. One can only speculate about her feelings for Agamemnon and why his role in Iphigeneia's sacrifice did not turn her against him. Perhaps her mother's openly adulterous relationship was to her young mind an even worse thing. When Aletes and Erigone were born to the impious couple, Electra was even more outraged and alienated.

By the time the news arrived that Agamemnon was returning home, Electra was about 20. Apparently she looked with tolerance on the news preceding him that he was bringing home a mistress and twin sons by her. Surely she knew also of the famous impasse between him and Achilles over Briseis. She might even have heard that Agamemnon had made a deal to give her to Polymestor, Priam's son-in-law, in exchange for the murder of Polydorus, the last of Priam's sons. (This plan, however, was thwarted, and Electra might never have learned of it.) In spite of all these facts and rumors, she most certainly believed her father would come back to set things right and punish the wrongdoers. Even so, a doubt must have arisen in regard to his safety, since Clytemnestra showed no signs of pushing Aegisthus out of palace or bed. Nearer home, however, was the matter of Orestes, who was now 11 or 12. In the event anything happened to Agamemnon, Orestes would be a threat to the succession of Aegisthus and, later, Aletes. Electra made emergency plans for him through the loyal servants.

When Agamemnon was cut down almost as soon as he returned, Orestes was spirited away to Phocis, and just as well, since Aegisthus indeed had planned to kill him along with his father. In fact, Electra was fortunate to have escaped death, since she could have borne a successor to the throne. She had been betrothed to her uncle

Castor, but after the murder she was locked away to prevent her from deliberately seeking to produce an heir or incite trouble from a populace that had grown to accept Aegisthus.

For the next seven or eight years Electra remained under close surveillance. She managed to keep in touch with Orestes, and after he reached manhood her messages became urgent that he avenge their father's murder. Finally Orestes came with his cousin Pylades to Mycenae, having been ordered by Apollo to carry out the revenge Electra so desperately wanted. With Pylades he went to the tomb of Agamemnon and dedicated a lock of his hair. Electra, who regularly visited the tomb, recognized the hair and took it as a pledge of Orestes' intention.

Shortly afterward, Orestes, abetted by Pylades, carried out the dictates of his destiny: the murder of his mother and stepfather. Immediately he was pursued by the Erinyes and, although purified by Apollo himself, had to answer to his conscience and to the laws of man. Only a formal trial could help alleviate the madness into which the Erinyes had plunged him. He was freed by the court of the Areiopagus with Athena casting the deciding vote. During this time Electra was at his side against the hostility of the people and the vengeful Erinyes. There is an extension of the story that says Orestes, Pylades, and Electra, thinking they were condemned to die, plotted to kill Helen, the author of their plight. They even abducted Helen's daughter, Hermione, to this purpose, but Apollo intervened.

Orestes' madness persisted, however, and Apollo advised him to go to Tauris in search of a certain statue of Artemis. He and Pylades were almost sacrificed to the Taurian goddess, and would have been had not the long-lost Iphigeneia intervened. Through some kind of exchange or token, the brother and sister recognized each other, and the three escaped. Rumors reached Electra that they had perished and that the head priestess at Tauris was responsible. Though still quite young, Aletes assumed the throne. Electra went to Delphi to inquire about the circumstances and encountered Iphigeneia, who had come there with Orestes and was pointed out as the murderer of her brother. Electra seized a firebrand from the altar and was about to blind her sister, whom she of course did not recognize. About that time Orestes appeared, and the truth was made known. Iphigeneia went to Brauron as a priestess of Artemis Brauronia, and Electra returned with Orestes to Mycenae, where he killed Aletes. Electra then married Pylades, and in spite of the matricide in which she had played a major role, her life ended happily. She accompanied Pylades back to Phocis, where he became king, and bore him two sons, Medon and Strophius.

There are several unanswered questions about Electra. Her obsession with revenge appeared to be well under way before the murder of Agamemnon. His murder gave this obsession a sharp focus, which did not diminish over the years. Her father was not really an admirable person, and one wonders how she juggled values to account for the intensity of her hatred for her mother, who in many ways had justification for what she did. Was there a deep psychological reason for her unquestioning loyalty to her father? What if he had survived to depose Aegisthus and Clytemnestra and then lived in adultery with Cassandra? Would Electra have turned her hatred on her stepmother? In her favor it can be said that after revenge had been carried out on her mother and Aegisthus, she did not let Orestes suffer alone. This devotion proved to be her redemption, since her consuming hatred was destructive to her as well as to its victims. [Sophocles, *Electra* 326,417,1405; Aeschylus, *Libation-Bearers* 130,931; Pausanias 2.16.7; Hyginus, *Fables* 109,122,240; Servius on Virgil's *Aeneid* 1.653, 11.268; Euripides, *Electra* 19,60–64,253,312.]

ELECTRA (5) was a servant of Helen. In the Lesche at Delphi she was shown kneeling forward to fasten Helen's sandals. Polygnotus, the painter, gave her 700 or more years of immortality she otherwise would not have had. Thousands of people viewed her in this act of servitude and friendship. [Pausanias 10.25.4.]

ELECTRA (6) was one of the DANAIDES, daughter of Danaus and the Naiad Polyxo. She married Peristhenes, son of Aegyptus and the Naiad Caliadne. According to Hyginus, she married Hyperantus. [Apollodorus 2.1.5; Hyginus, *Fables* 170.]

ELECTRYONE (1) was the daughter of Helios and Rhodos, and one of the Heliades, her brothers being the seven sons of Helios. The sons—Cercaphus, Actis, Macareus, Tenages, Triopas, Candalus, and Ochimus—became founders of cities and kings, and were knowledgeable about astronomy. Nothing else is known of Electryone except she did not marry. One modern writer speculates that she was identified with the goddess of the moon. [Diodorus Siculus 5.56; Scholiast on Pindar's *Olympian Odes* 7.24; Robert Graves, *The Greek Myths*, Mt. Kisco, NY: Moyer Bell Limited, 1988, p. 155.]

ELECTRYONE (2) was a patronymic for Alcmena from Electryon, her father. [Hesiod, *Shield of Heracles* 16.]

ELEGE was, according to one writer, one of the PROETIDES. [Aelian, *Various Narratives* 3.42.]

ELEIONOMAE referred to NAIADES who inhabited marshes. [Theocritus 5.17.]

ELEITHYIA (*See* EILEITHYIA)

ELEOS was the personification of pity or mercy. She had an altar in the agora at Athens, the only city in which she was worshipped. Anyone seeking to enlist Athens as an ally first approached her altar as a suppliant. [Apollodorus 2.8.1, 3.7.1; Pausanias 1.17.1.]

ELEPHANTIS was the mother by Danaus of Gorgophone and Hypermnestra. [Apollodorus 2.1.5.]

ELEUSINA, or Eleusinia, was a surname of Demeter and Persephone derived from Eleusis in Attica, the principal seat of their worship. When Heracles attacked Sparta to punish the sons of Hippocoon, he was wounded and fled to the shrine of the Eleusinian Demeter near Mount Taygetus, where Asclepius hid him and healed his wounds. [Pausanias 3.15.5,20.5; Virgil, *Aeneid* 1.163; Stephanus Byzantium, "Eleusis."]

ELEUTHO (*See* EILEITHYIA)

ELIONIA was a goddess of birth worshipped at Argos. She was probably the same as EILEITHYIA. [Plutarch, *Roman Questions* 49.]

ELIS (*See* HALYS)

ELISSA (*See* DIDO)

ELPIS was the personification of hope among the Greeks. The story goes that when Pandora uncovered the vessel from which all the evils of the world escaped, only Elpis remained. In the very few representations of her she was youthful and fully clothed, and usually carried flowers. Her Roman counterpart was Spes.

EMATHIDES was another name for the PIERIDES, daughters of Pierus.

EMPANDA, or Panda, was a Roman goddess who had a sanctuary near the Pandana gate, which led to the Capitoline Hill. Her temple offered asylum and was always open. Food bought from temple funds was given to suppliants. Empanda and Panda were possibly surnames of Juno. [Festus, "Pandana"; Varro, *On the Latin Language* 5.42.]

EMPUSA was yet another female monster. She was in the train of Hecate and originally was sent out to frighten travelers. She was supposed to have one leg of brass and one of an ass. This absurd combination lends a certain comical effect rather than one of horror. Moreover, a traveler could rout the monster with insulting words, causing her to flee with a shrill shrieking. Naughty children were threatened with visits from this awkward creature.

But the Empusae (plural for Empusa) were not comical at all when it came to their real design—luring men, especially young ones, to bed. For this purpose they could turn themselves into beautiful women, in which shape they sucked the blood from their victims and ate their flesh. In this respect they were related to the Lamiae and Mormolyceia. [Aristophanes, *Frogs* 294, *Ecclesiazusae* 1094; Philostratus, *Life of Apollonius of Tyana* 2.4, 4.25; Suidas, "Empusa."]

ENARETE, though not generally recognized when mentioned, was one of the great women in mythological dynastic history. She was the mother of the important royal lines that reached down the generations to and beyond the Trojan War. She was a daughter of Deimachus, about whom nothing is recorded, and her mother was never identified. She married Aeolus, the son of Hellen, in the first generation after the flood, so it would not be too presumptuous to guess that her father might have been an older cousin of Aeolus, a hitherto unmentioned son of Melantheia, Amphictyon, or Protogeneia. It was customary in those days for women to marry cousins, uncles, or even half-brothers.

Aeolus was described as the ruler of Thessaly and regarded as the founder of the Aeolian branch of the Greek nation. He is not to be confused with his descendant considered the keeper of the winds. Enarete bore Aeolus 13 children. The eight sons were Cretheus, Sisyphus, Athamas, Salmoneus, Deion, Magnes, Perieres, and Macareus. The daughters were Canace, Alcyone, Peisidice, Calyce, and Perimede.

Cretheus was the grandfather of Jason. Sisyphus was the grandfather of Bellerophon. Athamas was an ancestor of the Minyans. Through his daughter Tyro, Salmoneus started the Messenian royal line, which included Nestor. Deion was the father of Actor, Phylacus, and Cephalus; he was also the great-grandfather of Jason as well as Jason's cousins Protesilaus and Podarces, heroes in the Trojan War. Magnes was father of Dictys and Polydectes, who were prominent in the adventures of Perseus. By Gorgophone, daughter of Perseus, Perieres was father of Aphareus and Leucippus, who were famous in Messenian history. Finally, Macareus, probably the youngest son, was the only one without a distinguished career. He and his sister Canace committed incest and, according to some accounts, killed themselves after their terrible secret was revealed. Other versions have Canace as mother of several children by Poseidon. From her the Sicyonian royal house developed.

Two of the other daughters contributed to the distinguished history of this important family. Calyce was the mother of Endymion and therefore ancestor of the Aetolians. Peisidice was married to Myrmidon, ancestor of the Myrmi-

dons. Perimede and Alcyone produced no outstanding heroes. Indeed, Alcyone probably died childless, since she and her husband were changed into aquatic birds for comparing their newlywed happiness with that of the gods.

It is difficult to assign a personality to Enarete. From her marriage to middle age she was involved in childbearing. As much as 20 years separated her oldest from her youngest child. She had many occasions for grief, as in the case of Macareus and Canace and their child, whom Aeolus threw to the dogs. Alcyone was changed into a bird. Salmoneus was killed by Zeus for blasphemy. Athamas went mad and killed his son by Ino. Sisyphus was an unscrupulous tyrant who eventually incurred the wrath of the gods. Even so, her offspring provided the fabric from which a very large part of mythological history was woven. [Apollodorus 1.3.3,7.1,3,5,9.1,4,6; Hyginus, *Fables* 242,288; Pausanias 4.2.2,3.3; Callimachus, *Hymn to Demeter* 100.]

ENDEIS was a daughter of Sciron and Chariclo. This Sciron has always been a controversial figure. According to the common account, he was the brutal brigand who robbed travelers and cast them from the so-called Scironian Rocks into the sea. He was later killed in the same fashion by Theseus. The Megarians claimed, though, that he was a respectable king with good credentials. Theseus, who was related to him, did kill him but for a different reason, it was claimed, and then established the Isthmian games in compensation.

Endeis married Aeacus, son of Zeus and Aegina. Aeacus was held in the highest esteem by men and gods alike. Endeis might have been already present on the island of Aegina when Zeus answered Aeacus' prayer by turning ants into men to populate the island. They were called Myrmidons, as were their descendants, who included Achilles and Neoptolemus. Endeis became the mother of Peleus and Telamon (although some of the earliest accounts assign the latter a different parentage).

Though never stated, it appears Endeis died while her sons were still children, perhaps even in childbirth. Aeacus married Psamathe and had Phocus by her. Phocus was sufficiently close in age to Telamon and Peleus that they were jealous of his athletic prowess and killed him. For this act they were exiled. Endeis was grandmother to both Ajax and Achilles. [Apollodorus 3.12.6; Pausanias 2.29.7; Homer, *Iliad* 24.535; Plutarch, *Theseus* 10.]

ENTELLA was the wife of Egestus (Acestes). Egestus was the son of the god of the Crimisus River, who assumed the form of a dog for the coupling, and Egesta. Egestus founded several cities; one was Entella, which he named for his wife. [Tzetzes on Lycophron 953.]

ENTORIA was a daughter of a Roman farmer. The god Saturn was hospitably entertained by him, and the hospitality included access to Entoria's bedroom. The relationship lasted for at least four years, and Entoria bore Saturn four sons: Janus, Hymnus, Faustus, and Felix. In appreciation for the family's attention to him, Saturn taught his father-in-law the cultivation of the vine and the chemistry of wine making, suggesting his relative share this knowledge with his neighbors. The neighbors drank their new beverage and became drunk. They were certain they had been poisoned and stoned Entoria's father to death. The grandsons hanged themselves in grief. Afterward, the Romans had a plague and learned from an oracle that the pestilence was a result of their treatment of Entoria's father. The plague ceased when Lutatius Catulus caused a temple to be erected to Saturn on the Tarpeian Rock. The temple contained an altar with four faces. Saturn meanwhile changed the entire family into a constellation. This story is identical to the story told of the Greek Icarius and his daughter Erigone. [Plutarch, *Greek and Roman Parallel Stories* 9.]

ENYO (1) was the goddess of war, who took delight in carnage and the destruction of towns. She was usually considered the daughter of Ares, whom she accompanied in battles. By him she became the mother of Enyalius, who was little more than a personification of war except in Sparta, where youths sacrificed puppies to him. At Thebes and Orchomenus, a festival called Homoloia was celebrated in honor of Zeus, Demeter, Athena, and Enyo. Zeus was said to have received his surname Homoloius from

Homolois, a priestess of Enyo. A statue of Enyo stood in the temple of Ares at Athens. [Suidas, "Homolois"; Homer, *Iliad* 5.333,592; Eustathius on Homer's *Iliad* 140; Pausanias 1.8.5.]

ENYO (2) was one of the GRAEAE.

EONE was one of the THESPIADES. By Heracles she became the mother of Amestrius. [Apollodorus 2.7.8;]

EOS was the goddess of dawn, daughter of the Titans Hyperion and Theia (some say Euryphaessa), and sister of Helios and Selene. One or two writers claimed Pallas was her father. In later times she was identified with Hemera, and similar stories were related of her. She was the "rosy-fingered dawn" familiar to readers of Homer, and not only did she announce the coming of the sun but was conceived as accompanying Helios on his daily swing across the heavens.

The appearance of dawn evokes a mysterious and almost mystical feeling. Its personification can be thought of in only the most delicate and evanescent way. The fragile beauty of the chromatic displays of this goddess seem almost incompatible with the carnal nature ascribed to her.

She was initially considered the wife of Astraeus (the Starry), son of the Titan Crius and Eurybia. By him she became the mother of the evening star Eosphorus (Hesperus), other stars, and the winds Boreas, Zephyrus, Notus, and, according to some, heavenly Astraea. This did not prevent her, however, from trying out the bed of Ares, perhaps out of curiosity. Discovered in the act, she gained the great displeasure of Aphrodite, who cursed her with insatiable lust for handsome young men.

She carried off Clytus, son of Mantius and grandson of Melampus. We do not know what his ultimate fate was, only that he dwelled for a time on Olympus. She carried away Orion, the handsome young Boeotian giant, but the gods were unhappy with her and caused him to be killed by Artemis, who was always available for such services. Eos then snatched Cephalus, son of Hermes and Herse, from atop Mount Hymettus and carried him away to Syria. Some accounts say Eos became the mother of Phaethon by him, but Phaethon was more often considered the son of Helios. Cephalus eventually abandoned Eos and returned to Attica. Years later she fell in love with another Cephalus, son of Deion, and caused his wife to be unfaithful to him in order to gain her own purpose. But Artemis in turn revealed his infidelity to his wife, and Eos had to withdraw when the score was thus evened. Eos was even credited with carrying off Ganymede before Zeus did and then making a deal with Zeus to grant immortality to Tithonus, Ganymede's grandnephew, in exchange for Ganymede. This is a dubious claim, since it would be difficult to bring the two young men close enough in age to be attractive to both Zeus and Eos at about the same time. It can be worked out that they could have been not much older than 15 at approximately the same time.

Tithonus was the great love of her life, in spite of her former abductions known and unknown. He was one of the sons of Laomedon and brother of Priam. Some made him a brother of Laomedon, which would make it easier to accept the story of Eos' bargain with Zeus. As mentioned, by one means or another Eos obtained from Zeus the gift of immortality for Tithonus. There must have been a sublime moment when she realized that for all eternity she could experience physical ecstasy with this superbly beautiful young man. Then it dawned (!) on her that she had overlooked the most important thing: she had forgotten to ask for perpetual youth. Before the effects of this oversight started to become apparent she bore him two sons, Memnon and Emathion. Tithonus grew old as all mortals do, but was unaffected by life-destroying infirmity. He just shriveled away until he was metamorphosed into a cricket.

His immortality was not inherited by his sons, even though they were half-brothers to the winds and stars. Emathion was king of Arabia and slain by Heracles in his journey through northern Africa. Memnon, king of Ethiopia, assisted his uncle Priam in the Trojan War and was killed by Achilles after slaying Achilles' close friend Antilochus. Eos, so it is said, persuaded Zeus to grant immortality to Memnon in the afterworld. She wept over his mortal remains so profusely that, forever after, her tears have

appeared each morning as dew. Memnon's tomb was on the bank of the Hellespont, and birds called the Memnonides gathered there annually to lament his death and fight until half of them were destroyed. A huge pair of statues of Amenhotep III were erected in the Valley of the Kings in Egypt and called the Colossi of Memnon. The first rays of the sun were supposed to cause one of the statues to emit sweet music, as if Memnon were greeting his mother's daily appearance.

Eos has been called a nymphomaniac for her repeated abductions of handsome young men. The symbolism of these actions should not be overlooked, however. Young men represented dawn of adult life, while old men represented sunset. Stealing youths in their glorious prime was a brief respite from the inexorable march of years among mortals, most poignantly set forth in the story of Tithonus. Eos (or Hemera) was represented in the Stoa Basileius in Athens in the act of carrying away Cephalus. She was also shown in the same act on the throne of the Amyclaean Apollo. At Olympia she was represented in the act of praying to Zeus for Memnon. In works of art she appeared most often winged or in a chariot drawn by four horses. Two of these horses were Lampus and Pegasus. [Hesiod, *Theogony* 371,378,984; *Homeric Hymn to Helios* 2; *Homeric Hymn to Aphrodite* 218,219; Ovid, *Metamorphoses* 7.703, 9.420; Homer, *Odyssey* 5.390, 10.144, 15.250; Eustathius on Homer's *Odyssey* 1780; Pausanias 1.3.1,3, 3.18.7, 5.22.2; Apollodorus 1.4.4,9.4, 2.5.11, 3.12.4,14.3; Horace, *Odes* 1.22.8, 2.16.30; Virgil, *Aeneid* 3.384; Hyginus, *Fables* 125,160,189,270.]

EPAINE, the Awesome, was an appropriate surname of Persephone. [Homer, *Odyssey* 9.457.]

EPEIONE (*See* EPIONE)

EPHESIA was a surname of Artemis, but the goddess thus designated was really quite different from the Arcadian sister of Apollo or even the Taurian Artemis. She seems to have been a personification of the nourishing powers of nature, and her worship was early established in Asia Minor. This worship was said to have been established in Ephesus by the Amazons, but if so, they brought the religion from a far older culture, since the Amazons were contemporary with a fairly late period in mythology—i.e., a generation immediately before and one during the Trojan War.

This Asiatic divinity, once recognized as having some features identifiable with those of Artemis, especially the more somber ones, assumed some of the attributes of the Greek goddess. Her mother became Leto, but her birth took place in the vicinity of Ephesus. But like some modern religions superimposed over older ones, certain characteristics from the older worship persisted. For one thing, the priests were eunuchs, which was a kind of Asiatic convention. The goddess herself was equipped with what appeared to be multiple breasts but have recently been identified as a necklace of bull testicles. Her mummylike figure was crowned, and the lower part of her body came to a point. Her symbol of divinity was a bee.

The magnificent temple of the Ephesian Artemis was one of the seven wonders of the ancient world, but hardly a trace of it remains today. Two streams, both called Selenus, flowed on either side of the temple in opposite directions. [Strabo 14.1.23; Pausanias 2.7.4, 4.31.6, 7.5.2, 8.21.1; Hesychius, "Essin."]

EPHYRA (1) was a daughter of Oceanus and Tethys and was the first to live in the area named Ephyra for her. Another source calls her the daughter of Epimetheus. Still another writer calls her the daughter of Myrmex and wife of Epimetheus. What all the versions have in common is the application of her name to Ephyra, the town that later became Corinth. [Pausanias 2.1.1; Virgil, *Georgics* 4.343; Scholiast on Apollonius Rhodius 4.12.12.]

EPHYRA (2) was one of the NEREIDES. [Hyginus, *Fables: Preface* 8.]

EPICASTE (1) was a name by which IOCASTE, mother of Oedipus, was occasionally called.

EPICASTE (2) was a daughter of Calydon and Aeolia, and sister to Protogeneia. Her father, son of Aetolus and Pronoe, was regarded as the founder of Calydon. Thus Epicaste grew up in the stony forest area overlooking the Euenus valley. The kingdom of Calydon lay not far from that of Pleuron, whose king was the brother of King Calydon. Epicaste and her sister, Protogeneia, more than likely knew well and associated with their cousins Sterope, Stratonice, Laophonte, and Agenor. This frequent association apparently provided occasions for a ripening love affair between Epicaste and Agenor, and they were married, probably while quite young. Their children were Porthaon and Demonice. Some add Thestius, but he more frequently is called the son of Demonice. The family of Epicaste became quite prominent through the offspring of Porthaon, which included Oeneus and Meleager. Through her daughter she was grandmother of Leda and great-grandmother of Helen. [Apollodorus 1.7.7; Stephanus Byzantium, "Kalydon"; Pausanias 3.13.5, 4.35.1, 6.20.8,21.7; Hyginus, *Fables* 175.]

EPICASTE (3) was the daughter of Augeas, and sister of Phyleus and Agasthenes. Augeas is a familiar figure because of his filthy stables and the deal he made with Heracles to clean them. When this was accomplished, Augeas refused to pay Heracles for the job on the grounds that the hero was not supposed to be paid for the labors imposed by Eurystheus. During these negotiations Heracles, in his usual fashion, seduced Epicaste. He was probably sleeping with her brother as well, since Phyleus took Heracles' side and even publicly witnessed against his father. Epicaste bore Thestalus as a result of this union. Nothing else is known of him. She was certainly abandoned by the hero but perhaps saw him from time to time since he kept in touch with Phyleus, who straightened out the affairs of the kingdom after the death of Augeas. Epicaste's other brother, Agasthenes, became king, and she probably lived out her days with him in the royal palace. [Apollodorus 1.9.16, 2.5.5,7.8,9; Homer, *Odyssey* 11.701; Pausanias 5.1.9,2.1.]

EPICASTE (4) was the wife of Clymenus, son of Teleus at Argos. They had two sons, Idas and Therager, and an exceptionally beautiful daughter, Harpalyce. Clymenus succumbed to a consuming passion for his daughter and eventually had sex with her. He attempted to remove the temptation by marrying her off to Alastor, one of the Neleids, but later took her back. Epicaste probably was unaware of what was happening until Clymenus lived with Harpalyce openly. At this point, Harpalyce killed her younger brother and served his flesh to their father. She was changed into a bird, and Clymenus committed suicide. The fate of Epicaste is not known. [Hyginus, *Fables* 242,246,255; Parthenius, *Love Stories* 13.]

EPICASTE (5) was the wife of Agamedes, son of Stymphalus and great-grandson of Arcas. By him she was the mother of Cercyon. Sometime earlier Epicaste had borne Trophonius, a son of Apollo. Some said Agamedes was Apollo's son by Epicaste and that he was the father of Trophonius. Most commonly, however, Agamedes and Trophonius were brothers and sons of Erginus, king of Orchomenus. It is not certain whether or not Epicaste was part of the Orchomenian tradition. In all the traditions, however, Agamedes and Trophonius were distinguished architects, having constructed the temple of Apollo at Delphi, the temple of Poseidon in Arcadia on the Mantineia/Tegea road, and the treasury of Hyrieus at Hyria in Boeotia. [Pausanias 8.4.5,5.3.]

EPILAIS was one of the THESPIADES and by Heracles mother of Astyanax. [Apollodorus 2.7.8.]

EPIMELIDES was another name of the Maliades, nymphs who were worshipped as the protectors of flocks and fruit trees. [Theocritus 1.22.]

EPIONE was married to Asclepius, the god of medicine and healing. Her father might have been Merops or even Heracles, although it is generally accepted that he had only one daughter. By Asclepius, Epione had Ianiscus, Alexanor, Aratus, Hygieia, Aegle, Iaso, and Panacea. These names are mostly personifications or attributes of Asclepius. Epione's two more earthy sons were Machaon and Podaleirius. They were occasionally called sons of Arsinoe. They went to Troy with 30 ships, commanding the men from

Tricca, Ithome, and Oechalia. Machaon was the surgeon of the Greeks at Troy; among other services, he cured Philoctetes. He was killed in the war, and Nestor brought his body to Messenia. At Gerenia a sanctuary was dedicated to him, and served as a kind of hospital. Podaleirius, also skilled in medicine, survived the war and settled on the coast of Caria, where he had been shipwrecked on his way home. He was also worshipped as a hero. [Scholiast on Pindar's *Pythian Odes* 3.14; Pausanias 1.34.2, 2.10.3; Homer, *Iliad* 2.728, 11.515,614.]

EPIPOLE (1) was a daughter of Trachion of Carystus in Euboea. She was drawn to masculine pursuits and joined the Greeks against Troy in the disguise of a soldier. There were a few instances in which women fought in the war, but they were all Trojan allies (e.g., Penthesileia and her Amazons and Hiera, the wife of Telephus, who commanded the Mysian women). Epipole was the only known woman among the Greek forces. Unfortunately her patriotism did not pay off; her sex was discovered by Palamedes, and she was stoned to death by the Greek army. Several questions need to be asked. How did Palamedes discover her gender? She must have known the risks and been especially careful up until then. Did Palamedes—thinking she was a handsome, beardless boy—forcibly undress her? Why did the Greeks react so violently? Was it an affront to their masculinity to have a woman fighting at their side? Was her presence considered taboo or bad luck? A saner and certainly more humane action would have been to send her back to Greece. [Ptolemaeus Hephaestion 5.]

EPIPOLE (2) was a surname of Demeter at Lacedaemon. The name had to do with her wandering in search of Persephone. [Hesychius, "Epipola."]

EPIPYRGIDIA, On the Tower, was a name under which Hecate had a sanctuary at Athens on the Acropolis near the temple of Nice (Nike). [Pausanias 2.30.2.]

EPITRAGIA was a surname of Aphrodite. Before Theseus left for Crete on his mission to slay the Minotaur, the Delphic oracle advised him to take Aphrodite as his guide. He sacrificed to her as he departed, and the she-goat he offered developed male genitals during its death spasm. Consequently, Aphrodite Epitragia had given the sign that she would be in attendance to the enterprise. [Plutarch, *Theseus* 18.]

EPONA was the protectress of horses among the Romans. Her counterpart was Bubona, protectress of oxen and cows. Small figures of these divinities were placed in niches in stables. [St. Augustine, *City of God* 4.34; Tertullian, *Apology* 16; Apuleius, *Golden Ass* 60.]

EQUESTRIS was a surname of Venus. Its origin is unknown. There appears to be no Greek equivalent. [Servius on Virgil's *Aeneid* 1.724; Macrobius, *Saturnalia* 3.8.]

ERATO (1) was an Arcadian nymph who was said to be a prophetic priestess of Pan in his temple at Acacesium. It is not clear whether or not this office continued after she married Arcas. Most likely it did, although rearing three sons while managing a temple might have been difficult. Her sons were Elatus, Apheidas, and Azan. Her husband, Arcas, had succeeded Nyctimus, son of Lycaon, to the throne of Pelasgia (later Arcadia), where he was the fourth king. He was a benevolent ruler and taught his subjects useful arts. Undoubtedly Erato assisted him in these endeavors, since a priestess of Pan would certainly know uses of the land. Before his death Arcas divided the kingdom among his three sons. Apheidas obtained Tegea and the surrounding area. Azan obtained the territory called Azania after him. He was the first in Greece for whom funeral games were celebrated. Elatus acquired Mount Cyllene. Later he went to Phocis and founded Elateia. His son, Erato's grandson, inherited the Arcadian property of Elatus and Azania as well.

Since Erato was a prophetic nymph, she probably served in Pan's temple for the rest of her life. A perpetual flame burned on the altar of this temple. The wife of Arcas was also called Leaneira, Meganeira, Chrysopeleia, or Laodameia. [Pausanias 5.16, 8.4.1,9.2, 27.9,37.8; Apollodorus 3.9.1; Stephanus Byzantium, "Azania."]

ERATO (2) was one of the nine MUSES. She was the Muse of erotic poetry and mimic imitation. She is sometimes shown with a lyre. By Malus she was the mother of Cleophema. [Apollodorus 1.3.1,2.6.]

ERATO (3) was one of the NEREIDES. [Apollodorus 1.2.7; Hesiod, *Theogony* 247.]

ERATO (4) was one of the NYSEIDES or HYADES.

ERATO (5) was one of the THESPIADES. By Heracles she was the mother of Dynastes. [Apollodorus 2.7.8.]

ERATO (6) was one of the DANAIDES, daughter of Danaus and Polyxo, and married to Bromius. According to Hyginus, she was married to Eudaemones. [Apollodorus 2.1.5; Hyginus, *Fables* 170.]

ERGANE, or Ergatis, the Worker, was a surname of Athena, who was believed to preside over and instruct man in all kinds of arts. At Thespiae there was a statue of Athena Ergane with Plutus as her child, symbolizing work as a source of wealth. Plutus was the personification of wealth. [Pausanias 1.24.3, 5.14.5, 9.16.1, 26.5; Hesychius, "Ergane"; Plutarch, *On the Fortune or the Virtue of Alexander* 99.]

ERIBOEA (1) was the wife of Aloeus. His first wife had been Iphimedeia, mother of the notorious Aloeidae. These were twin giants, sons of Poseidon. Their stepfather, also a son of Poseidon, was half-brother to Iphimedeia's sons. Consequently, Eriboea was sister-in-law to the twins and their stepmother by adoption, since Aloeus claimed the pair as his own. Otus and Ephialtes, as they were called, had reached gigantic proportions by the time they were adolescent, and they gave the gods no end of trouble. Occasionally they did something admirable; for example, they rescued their sister Pancratis and their mother from pirates, who had carried the women to Naxos. Not long afterward Iphimedeia died, and Aloeus married Eriboea. It was at her house that the twins captured Ares and kept him imprisoned in a large brazen cauldron for several months. Eriboea secretly informed Hermes, who set him free. Artemis ultimately tricked the twins into killing each other. [Homer, *Iliad* 5.385, *Odyssey* 305; Apollodorus 1.7.4; Hyginus, *Fables* 28; Servius on Virgil's *Aeneid* 6.582.]

ERIBOEA (2) was one of the AMAZONS. When Heracles went for the girdle of Hippolyte, the Amazons arrayed themselves against him. He overcame Aella, Philippis, and Prothoe, and then turned to Eriboea. She had boasted that because of the manly bravery she displayed in contests of war she had no need of anyone to help her, but she was quickly overcome by Heracles. [Diodorus Siculus 4.16.]

ERIBOEA (3) was, according to some, one of the maidens among the victims sent with Theseus from Athens to Crete as a tribute to Minos. She was more often called PERIBOEA, daughter of Alcathous and mother of Ajax by Telamon. [Plutarch, *Theseus* 29.]

ERIGONE (1), sometimes called Aletis, was a daughter of Icarius and Phanothea. They were Athenians and lived in the reign of Pandion. Icarius hospitably received the often-rejected Dionysus when the god was promoting his own worship throughout Greece. Dionysus showed his gratitude by teaching Icarius the principles of viticulture. After seducing Erigone he departed, leaving behind several wine-filled bags as a gift of appreciation. Icarius took pleasure in sharing these with his neighbors, but some shepherds became intoxicated and thought they had been poisoned. They killed Icarius and buried him under a tree. Erigone did not know where her father had disappeared and searched everywhere for him. Maera, Icarius' faithful dog, at length found the grave. Overcome with grief, Erigone hanged herself on the tree. Dionysus placed Erigone, Icarius, and Maera among the stars. The god then punished the Athenians with a plague in which Athenian maidens hanged themselves as Erigone had done. The plague was eventually lifted, and a festival called Aiora or Aletides was instituted in honor of Erigone. [Ovid, *Metamorphoses* 6.125; Hyginus, *Fables*

130; Gellius 15.10; Clement of Alexandria, *Miscellanies* 1.366.]

ERIGONE (2) was one of the three children of Aegisthus and Clytemnestra. Her brother was Aletes, and her sister was Helen. When Orestes killed his mother and stepfather, Tyndareus, Clytemnestra's father, wanted revenge for the death of his daughter. Joined by Erigone and the Eumenides, he brought the charge before the Areiopagus. Orestes was acquitted, and some said Erigone hanged herself. Others said that when Orestes finished the job by killing Aletes, who had acquired the throne, he also planned to kill Erigone. Artemis, however, removed her to safety in Attica and made her a priestess. Still others said Orestes married Erigone after Hermione and fathered Penthilus.

It is hard to imagine Erigone as the wife of her half-brother, one who had murdered her father and their mother. What could have changed her mind about Orestes? We have to consider that her growing up had none of the recriminations that dominated her half-sister Electra. She was probably a devoted and happy daughter, exempt from the politics of usurpation and plotted murder of her stepfather. Penthilus led a colony of Aeolians to Thrace and was the father of Echelatus and Damasias. [Dictys Cretensis 6.4; Pausanias 2.18.5, 3.2.1, 5.4.2, 7.6.2; Hyginus, *Fables* 122; Tzetzes on Lycophron 1374; Aristotle, *Politics* 5.18,13.]

ERIGONE (3) was a daughter of Themis and personification of righteousness. Nothing further was heard about her. [Servius on Virgil's *Eclogues* 4.6.]

ERIMEDE was the daughter of Damasiclus and wife of Elatus, son of Icarius. She was the mother of Taenarus, for whom the town and promontory at the tip of Laconia were named. [Scholiast on Apollonius Rhodius 1.102; Stephanus Byzantium, "Tainaros."]

ERINYES (*See* EUMENIDES)

ERINYS was a surname of Demeter. This name was given to her because of the fury she experienced when, in the form of a mare, she tried to hide from her brother Poseidon but was raped anyway when he changed himself into a stallion. [Pausanias 8.25.4.]

ERIOPIS (1) was the daughter of Pheres and married to Oileus, son of Hodoedocus and Laonome. By him she became the mother of Ajax (known by his companions as the Lesser in order to distinguish him from Ajax the Greater, son of Telamon). His mother was also called Alcimache or Rhene. Oileus was king of the Locrians and a hero in his own right, having gone on the Argonaut. Oileus also had a bastard son, Medon, by the nymph Rhene. When Medon grew up he was banished from Phylace for killing the brother of Eriopis. Ajax was born in Naryx in Locris, and was sometimes referred to as the Locrian Ajax. He was described as one of the great heroes among the Greeks in the Trojan War. He frequently fought in conjunction with the Telamonian Ajax, who probably looked upon him as a kind of scrappy younger brother. The Locrian Ajax was small in stature and intrepid. He was especially skilled in throwing the spear and, next to Achilles, the fastest runner at Troy. He was lightly armed, wearing only a linen cuirass.

Unfortunately he was a person of mean character—quarrelsome, irreligious, and arrogant. He incurred the disfavor of the gods by violating Cassandra in the temple of Athena, where she had sought sanctuary, and was thus drowned in a shipwreck on his return from Troy by Poseidon. Eriopis could not for long be proud of her illustrious son, who she thought had died in service for Greece. The Locrians were required to send two girls each year to Troy to atone for the violation of Cassandra. When they landed, these girls were met by the population, who tried to stone them to death. Those who made it safely to the temple of Athena spent their entire lives as temple priestesses. [Homer, *Iliad* 2.527–530, 13.697,701, 14.520, *Odyssey* 4.499; Scholiast on Homer's *Iliad* 13.697, 15.333,336; Hyginus, *Fables* 97; Philostratus, *Heroicus* 8.1; Apollodorus 5.10.8.]

ERIOPIS (2) was the daughter of Apollo by Arsinoe, daughter of Leucippus and Philodice. Nothing is known of Eriopis. She has been referred to as the sister of Asclepius; this is true only because Apollo was father to both of them.

Her mother was sister of Hilaeira and Phoebe, wives of the Dioscuri, and had a sanctuary at Sparta. [Pausanias 3.12.8; Scholiast on Pindar's *Pythian Odes* 3.14.]

ERIOPIS (3) was a daughter of Jason and Medea, and sister of Medus, according to a commentator who assigned only two children to them. Usually several children were mentioned, and Medus was considered the son of Medea and Aegeus (even though there is rather good evidence that Aegeus was sterile). Eriopis was mentioned by one commentator only, and even he made no further reference to her. (Cinaethon, quoted by Pausanias 2.3.7.]

ERIOPIS (4) was, according to some, the wife of Anchises and by him the mother of Hippodameia. The references did not make it clear whether or not Anchises was married to Eriopis during his glorious affair with Aphrodite. If Eriopis came later, she had the disadvantage of having a crippled husband, since Aphrodite had disabled Anchises for talking about his affair with her. Lameness seemed not to interfere too seriously with his sex life. While married to Eriopis he had a mistress and became by her father of a son, Elymus. [Servius on Virgil's *Aeneid* 5.73.]

ERIPHA (1) was one of the mares of Marmax, the first suitor of Hippodameia killed by Oenomaus. Marmax's mares, Eripha and Parthenia, were butchered and buried beside the river Parthenia, where their tomb was shown for many years. [Pausanias 6.21.7.]

ERIPHA (2) was one of the NYSEIDES, or nymphs of Nysa, who were said to have reared Dionysus. [Nonnos, *Dionysiaca* 21.81.]

ERIPHYLE was the central figure at the beginning of the history of the fatal necklace of Harmonia. This necklace, fashioned by Hephaestus, had been a present from Cadmus to Harmonia on their wedding day. The gods smiled on the presentation of this exquisite jewelry, which was accompanied by an elegant peplus, or robe.

Eriphyle was a daughter of Talaus and Lysimache, and sister of Adrastus, Parthenopaeus, Pronax, Mecisteus, Aristomachus, Astynome, and Metadice. Talaus had led a distinguished life, having been among other things an Argonaut, and was finally king of Argos. But early in Eriphyle's life her father was killed by Amphiaraus, his cousin who ruled jointly with him. The family of Adrastus was exiled, and they went to Sicyon to seek sanctuary with King Polybus. Adrastus succeeded Polybus on the throne and not long afterward became reconciled with Amphiaraus. He gave him Eriphyle in marriage and returned the family to Argos, where he ruled jointly with his relative. The two kings made an agreement that Amphiaraus would abide by the decision of Eriphyle on any point in which he should differ in opinion with Adrastus.

Meanwhile Eriphyle bore to Amphiaraus two sons, Alcmaeon and Amphilochus, and two daughters, Demonassa and Eurydice. Amphiaraus was a descendant of Melampus and had inherited the family's prophetic powers. Therefore, when he was approached about joining with Adrastus, along with Polyneices of Thebes and Tydeus of Calydon, the sons-in-law of Adrastus, in a proposed war against Thebes, he could predict not only the unsuccessful outcome of such a venture but even his own death. His refusal to join the campaign was short-lived, since Eriphyle held him to the old sworn agreement with Adrastus.

Eriphyle had a good reason for forcing Amphiaraus to accept Adrastus' plans. Polyneices had inherited the famous necklace of Harmonia. He promised this treasure to Eriphyle if she would insist on enforcing the old contract, in which her decision would be final. Amphiaraus told her he would die if he went to war, but she either did not believe him or did not want to. So Amphiaraus was compelled to enter the planning for this lost-cause expedition. Alcmaeon and Amphilochus were still boys, but Alcmaeon was old enough to understand his father's anger and to take a pledge of vengeance against Eriphyle if Amphiaraus did not return.

Amphiaraus did not return. Events moved slowly from that time forward. We are not sure just how long the campaign of the Seven lasted, but from the end of the war until the expedition of the Epigoni was a period of ten years. The memory of the promise to Amphiaraus probably dimmed in Alcmaeon's mind as he encountered the everyday urgencies of growing up. He was barely an adult when Thersander, the son of Polyneices, came to Argos seeking to launch another campaign against Thebes, this time with the sons of the Seven. Alcmaeon and Amphilochus declined the invitation to join the force, but Thersander, using his father's ploy, now offered Eriphyle the splendid peplus, or robe, which was the perfect accompaniment to the necklace already in her possession. She used her most eloquent persuasion, and her two sons reluctantly agreed to join the enterprise. Only later did Alcmaeon learn the reason, not only for her role in recruiting him and Amphilochus but also in the earlier case of his father. He realized she had been willing to surrender her husband and now was ready to do the same in regard to her sons for the sake of her vanity, and his old promise to Amphiaraus came back in full force.

After the battle of the Epigoni, as the sons of the Seven were called, Alcmaeon went to the Delphic oracle and received a somewhat ambiguous statement about the guilt of his mother. Taking the answer at face value, he went back to Argos and killed her. Some said Amphilochus assisted him. Alcmaeon was pursued by the Erinyes and suffered many hardships because of his matricide. The story of the fatal necklace and peplus was continued by the wives of his two marriages. Amphilochus, inheriting his father's gifts, founded oracles in various places. He was a seer in the Trojan War and was worshipped with his father at Oropus. He also founded Argos Amphilochium on the Ambracian Gulf.

Eriphyle had no redeeming qualities, it seems. Amphiaraus must have been foolishly in love with her when he made the rash promise of abiding by her decision. At this point one can only think the men in his family were hopelessly naive, even stupid. It is difficult to believe he could not have suspected that his old enemy Adrastus would use this promise against him. The sons, especially Alcmaeon, were even worse. Alcmaeon was not held by any such promise. His mother had already hastened his father to his death. How much proof did he need that Eriphyle was a scheming and self-centered woman? Alcmaeon's subsequent history proved he was slow-witted, and Eriphyle most certainly was aware of this. One can imagine her sitting before a mirror, dressed in her jewels and robe, posturing and preening for an unseen audience. [Homer, *Odyssey* 11.326, 15.247,248; Apollodorus 1.9.3, 3.6.2,7.2; Hyginus, *Fables* 73; Pindar, *Nemean Odes* 9.57, *Olympian Odes* 6.21; Plutarch, *Greek and Roman Parallel Stories* 6; Pausanias 1.34.2, 3.15.6, 5.17.4.]

ERIS was the goddess of discord. She was the sister of Ares, therefore a daughter of Zeus and Hera. Some called her a daughter of Nyx, thus making her a kind of primordial abstraction. She fitted more neatly, however, into the glorious scheme of the *Iliad* and its background where, as an immortal with the mortal fallibilities of the rest of the Olympian family, she was angry when she was not invited to the nuptials of Peleus and Thetis. One of the really perfect revenges occurred to her. An apple inscribed "To the Fairest" was thrown among the guests, and this seemingly innocent gesture was the cause of the Trojan War.

Eris delighted in war and lurked around the battlefield after the heroes and gods had withdrawn. She was obsessed with bloodshed, havoc, and suffering. Her role and that of Ares in relation to war was that she called forth war, and he carried out the action.

Eris had several children—Ponus, Lethe, Limus, Algea, Ate, and Harcus. These abstract concepts—sorrow, forgetfulness, hunger, pain, error, and the oath—appeared to be fatherless. It is not unreasonable to suggest that Ares was the father; after all, the parents of Ares and Eris were brother and sister. Moreover, Ares had produced a son with his daughter Enyo, so incest was a way of life in his branch of the family.

The counterpart of Eris in Roman mythology was Discordia. She appeared in the company of Mars, Bellona, and the Furies. [Homer, *Iliad* 4.441,445, 5.518, 11.3,73, 20.48; Hesiod, *Theogony* 225; Virgil, *Aeneid* 8.702; Herodotus 6.86; Tzetzes on Lycophron 93; Euripides, *Iphigeneia at Aulis* 1302; Pausanias 5.19.1; Lucian, *Dialogues of the Gods* 20.]

ERSA was a daughter of Zeus and Selene, and sister of Pandeia and Nemea. Nothing at all is known of these three sisters. [*Homeric Hymn to Selene* 32.14.]

ERYCINA was a surname of Aphrodite. She had a famous temple on Mount Eryx in Sicily, said to have been built by Eryx, her son by Butes. The building of the temple was also ascribed to Aeneas. Aphrodite Erycina had another temple in Psophis, said to have been founded by Psophis, a daughter of Eryx. The worship of Aphrodite (Venus) Erycina was introduced at Rome around the beginning of the second Punic War, and in 181 B.C. a temple was built to her outside the Porta Collatina. [Diodorus Siculus 4.83; Virgil, *Aeneid* 5.760; Pausanias 8.24.3; Livy 22.9,10, 23.30, 40.34.]

ERYMANTHE was the mother of the Hebrew (Babylonian or Egyptian) Sibyl, Sabba, by Berosus. [Pausanias 10.12.5.] (*See* SIBYLS.)

ERYMEDE (*See* ERIMEDE)

ERYSIPTOLIS, Protecting the City, was a surname of Athena. In times of war, towns, fortresses, and harbors were under her special care. [Homer, *Iliad* 6.305; *Homeric Hymn to Athena* 11.1, 28.3.]

ERYTHEIA (1) was one of the HESPERIDES, and her sisters were Aegle, Hestia, and Arethusa. [Hesiod, *Theogony* 215.]

ERYTHEIA (2) was the daughter of Geryones, the three-headed giant of the island of Erythia. This island, obviously named for Erytheia, was probably off the coast of Spain. On the island, Geryones raised large herds of cattle, guarded by a formidable herdsman and a monstrous dog. Stealing the cattle of Geryones was one of the labors of Heracles. Erytheia was visited by Hermes. Presumably she did not inherit her father's grotesque appearance, since Hermes was discriminating about his sexual partners. From this union came Norax, who grew up on the island and then led an Iberian colony to Sardinia, where he founded Nora, the oldest city on the island. [Pausanias 10.17.4.]

ETEOCLYMENE, daughter of Minyas, was more often called CLYMENE.

ETHEMEA was the wife of Merops, king of Cos, which was named for his daughter. He and Ethemea were also parents of Eumelus. The inhabitants of Cos were called Meropes. Ethemea was killed by Artemis because she had neglected to worship her. Grief-stricken, Merops tried to kill himself but was changed into an eagle and placed among the stars. [Hyginus, *Poetic Astronomy* 2.16; Antoninus Liberalis 15; Eustathius on Homer's *Iliad* 318; Euripides, *Helen* 384.]

ETHODAIA, also called Neaera, was one of the daughters of Amphion and NIOBE, and was killed by Artemis. [Apollodorus 3.5.6.]

EUADNE (1) was a daughter of Poseidon and Pitane. For reasons not stated Pitane sent Euadne directly to Aepytus, son of Elatus, in Arcadia as soon as she was born. Aepytus brought up the girl as his own daughter and was immensely disturbed when Euadne turned out to be the mother of a beautiful boy found on the banks of the Alpheius. The baby, which had been fed with honey by serpents, was brought back to the palace, and Euadne named him Iamus. She would not reveal that the father was Apollo (unlike many maidens who were only too ready to claim, true or not, a god as the father of a bastard), so Aepytus journeyed to Delphi and learned the truth from the oracle. He was told that the boy would grow up to be a celebrated prophet and the ancestor of a great family of prophets. This turned out to be the case, after Iamus sought verification from Apollo himself. His descendants, the Iamidae, were distinguished seers at Olympia. [Pindar, *Olympian Odes* 6.28,30,43,46; Hyginus, *Fables* 175; Pausanias 6.2.3; Cicero, *On Divination* 1.41.]

EUADNE (2), or Ianeira, was a daughter of Iphis, son of Alector, and a sister of Laodice and Eteoclus. Iphis, a king in Argos, was the one who had advised Polyneices to bribe Eriphyle with the necklace of Harmonia to induce Amphiaraus to take part in the campaign of the Seven against Thebes. Eteoclus was called one of the Seven by some, but he does not appear in the usual lists. He was, however, a casualty in the war. Euadne married Capaneus, the son of Astynome and nephew of Adrastus, and became by him the mother of Sthenelus.

Capaneus was one of the Seven in this odd war, which really had little to do with the Argives except that Adrastus' daughter had married Polyneices, contender for the Theban throne. The participants were all related in one way or another, so it became a matter of family honor. Euadne's own father, as mentioned, had an indirect role and gave up a son to the cause and, as it turned out, a son-in-law as well.

Capaneus was stationed at the Ogygian (some say Electrian) gate of Thebes. He and his force were in the process of scaling the wall, and such was the fervor of Capaneus that he declared not even the fires of Zeus could prevent his entering the city. Zeus could not let this challenge go unanswered and struck Capaneus with a flash of lightning as he neared the top of the wall on a ladder. Creon, regent of Thebes, decreed that the bodies could not be buried, but the Athenians under Theseus interceded. The body of Capaneus became sacred when he was divinely struck down and should have been buried in a special enclosure. Instead, along with the other fallen, he was burned. Euadne had hastened to Thebes when the news reached her that Capaneus had died. While his pyre was burning she threw herself into the flames and was consumed.

Sthenelus inherited the throne, since there were no other heirs left. He was one of the Epigoni and also commanded the Argives in the Trojan War under Diomedes, his friend and companion. He was also one of the Greeks concealed in the wooden horse. [Euripides, *Suppliants* 983,985,1034; Apollodorus 3.6.6, 7.1,10.3,8; Hyginus, *Fables* 70,243,256; Pausanias 2.18.4, 9.8.3; Plutarch, *Theseus* 29; Aeschylus, *Seven against Thebes* 423; Ovid, *Art of Love* 3.21; Homer, *Iliad* 2.564, 4.367, 23.511.]

EUADNE (3) was a daughter of the river-god Strymon and Neaera. Strymon was a river in Thrace and was also called a king. In addition to his children by Neaera, he had a son, Rhesus, by one of the Muses. An ally of the Trojans, Rhesus was treacherously murdered in his sleep by Diomedes and Odysseus. It should be noted that

Rhesus was at least ten generations later than Euadne, but river-gods were immortal and could reproduce endlessly. Euadne married Argus, the third king of Argos. Some called his wife Peitho. It is puzzling that a young woman from Thrace ended up in Argos, a really great distance even today. There is no known connection between her father and Argus.

By Argus she became the mother of Peiranthus (or Peiras), Epidaurus, Criasus, Tiryns, and Ecbasus. Peiranthus was father of Triopas. Epidaurus was the founder of Epidaurus, and Tiryns, the founder of Tiryns. Ecbasus was the father of Agenor (or Arestor). Criasus inherited the throne of Argos from his father.

It should be pointed out that the Argive genealogy was very complicated. Epidaurus and Tiryns were considered by some as sons of Pelops, again a tremendous forward leap in time. The names of Agenor and Triopas occurred in several family trees. [Apollodorus 1.3.4, 2.1.1,2; Hesiod, *Theogony* 339; Conon, *Narrations* 4; Antoninus Liberalis 21; Euripides, *Rhesus* 347; Pausanias 2.16.1,22.6,26.3,34.5; Hyginus, *Fables* 145.]

EUADNE (4) was one of the PELIADES. She was married to Canes, son of Cephalus of Phocis.

EUAECHME (1) was the daughter of Megareus and Iphinoe, king and queen of Megara. Her brothers were Euippus and Timalcus, and some add Hippomenes. She grew up in tragic surroundings. First, Euippus was killed by the monstrous Cithaeronian lion that constantly menaced hunters and herdsmen. Timalcus was killed in the battle at Aphidna, when Helen was liberated by the Dioscuri. Megareus offered his kingdom and the hand of his daughter to anyone who would slay the lion. Several people came forward but either fled from the beast or were killed by it.

Alcathous, son of Pelops, finally conquered the lion and obtained the kingdom of Megara and the kingdom of Orchomenus as well. This sudden glory caused him to abandon Pyrgo, his wife, and to take Megareus' offer of marriage to Euaechme. Alcathous had five children, but it is never made clear whether these were by Pyrgo or Euaechme, or some by each. They were Echepolis (Ischepolis), Callipolis, Iphinoe, Periboea, and Automedusa. The two sons lived with their father in Megara.

In gratitude for his success in slaying the Cithaeronian lion, Alcathous built temples to Artemis Agrotera and Apollo Agraeus. He also restored the walls of Megara, which had been destroyed by the Cretans when Minos invaded Attica.

Euaechme witnessed the untimely deaths of her stepsons (or maybe sons). Echepolis went to the Calydonian boar hunt and was killed. Callipolis heard the news first and went to the acropolis, where Alcathous was sacrificing to Apollo. Callipolis interrupted the sacrifice to announce the death of his brother; Alcathous, thinking the boy was being sacrilegious, struck him with a firebrand and killed him. The entire family had tombs at Megara. [Pausanias 1.39.5,41.5,42.1,2,7,43.2,4; Apollodorus 2.4.11, 3.15.8; Ovid, *Metamorphoses* 10.605; Hyginus, *Fables* 157; Plutarch, *Greek Questions* 16.]

EUAECHME (2) was the daughter of Hyllus, the son of Heracles. The oldest of Heracles' sons by Deianeira, Hyllus was the first leader of the Heracleidae, or descendants of Heracles, who sought to recover Peloponnesus. Euaechme married Polycaon, a son of Butes, but nothing further is known of them. [Pausanias 4.2.1.]

EUAGORE was one of the NEREIDES. By Sangarius or Dymas she was said to be the mother of Hecuba, although this claim was made also for Glaucippe, Eunoe, Telecleia, and Metope.

EUANDRA was one of the AMAZONS. [Quintus Smyrnaeus 1.43.]

EUANTHE, daughter of Asopus and beloved of Nilus, was, according to some, the mother by Apollo of the CHARITES. Their mother was more often called EURYNOME.

EUARETE was a daughter of Acrisius and, according to some, the mother by Oenomaus of Leucippus, Hippodamus, Dysponteus, and Hippodameia. The wife of Oenomaus is usually identified as STEROPE. [Hyginus, *Fables* 84, *Poetic Astronomy* 2.21; Pausanias 4.22.2, 8.20.2; Diodorus Siculus 4.73.]

EUARNE was one of the NEREIDES. [Hesiod, *Theogony* 259.]

EUBOEA (1) was a daughter of Asopus, from whom the island of Euboea was believed to have derived its name. She was loved by Poseidon and was the mother of a son, Tychius. Nothing else is known of mother or son. [Eustathius on Homer's *Iliad* 278; Hesychius, "Euboia."]

EUBOEA (2) was a daughter of the river-god Asterion near Mycenae who, together with her sisters Acraea and Prosymne, acted as nurse to Hera. The Heraion near Mycenae was at the foot of Mount Euboea, which was named for her. [Pausanias 2.13.3.]

EUBOEA (3) was the mother of Glaucus by Polybus. Glaucus was a fisherman who consumed an herb that made him immortal. He built the *Argo*, according to some, and went on the Argonaut as steersman. There was a belief in Greece that once each year Glaucus visited all the coasts and islands, accompanied by marine monsters, and made prophecies. Fishermen and sailors paid particular reverence to him and watched his oracles, which they believed were very accurate. [Athenaeus 7.48; Claudian, *Epithalamium of Honorius and Maria* 10.158.]

EUBOEA (4) was one of the THESPIADES. She became by Heracles the mother of Olympus. [Apollodorus 2.7.8.]

EUBOEA (5) was the wife of Phorbas. According to some, Phorbas was a son of Argus and brother of Peirasus. Euboea's son by Phorbas was Triopas, and her daughter was Messene. Triopas founded the city of Cnidus. Messene and her husband, Polycaon, settled Messenia and established the capital at Andania. They instituted the worship of Demeter and Persephone and were later worshipped as divinities themselves. [Pausanias 2.16.1; Apollodorus 1.7.4; Diodorus Siculus 5.61.]

EUBOTE was one of the THESPIADES. By Heracles she became the mother of Eurypylus. [Apollodorus 2.7.8.]

EUBULE (1) was one of the LEONTIDES. [Aelian, *Various Narratives* 12.28.]

EUBULE (2) was one of the DANAIDES and married to Demarchus. [Hyginus, *Fables* 170.]

EUCLEIA (1) was a kind of invented divinity worshipped at Athens. She had a sanctuary financed by the spoils taken at the battle of Marathon and became the personification of glory in battle. She was described by some as the daughter of Heracles and Myrto, daughter of Menoetius. She was said to have remained a virgin all her life and to have died in Boeotia, where she had an altar and statue in most marketplaces. She was similarly worshipped in Locris. Persons about to marry offered sacrifices to her, and it is curious that a virgin goddess was chosen for such ceremonies. It is not clear whether or not there was a connection between the Attic worship and that of Boeotia and Locris. [Pausanias 1.14.4, 9.17.2; Plutarch, *Aristides* 20.]

EUCLEIA (2) was a surname of Artemis at Athens. There seemed to be a connection between the minor goddess Eucleia and Artemis Eucleia, the latter of whom had a temple at Thebes. [Pausanias 9.17.1.]

EUCRANTE was one of the NEREIDES. [Apollodorus 1.2.7.]

EUDORA (1) was one of the NEREIDES. [Hesiod, *Theogony* 244; Apollodorus 1.2.7.]

EUDORA (2) was one of the HYADES.

EUDORA (3) was one of the OCEANIDES. [Hesiod, *Theogony* 360.]

EUDOXA was one of the daughters of Amphion and NIOBE. [Hyginus, *Fables* 11.]

EUIPPE (1) was one of the DANAIDES, daughter of Danaus and an Ethiopian woman. She was married to Argius, according to Apollodorus

(2.1.5), and to Agenor, according to Hyginus (*Fables* 170), who does not mention a mother for her.

EUIPPE (2) was one of the DANAIDES, daughter of Danaus and Polyxo, and married to Imbrus. [Apollodorus 2.1.5.]

EUIPPE (3) was a daughter of Daunus, a king in Apulia. He had been forced to flee from Illyria, his native land. He named a portion of Apulia after himself, Daunia, and became king of the region. The Trojan War hero Diomedes, fleeing from Argos, was shipwrecked on the coast of Daunia. Daunus received him graciously but asked for his assistance in a war against the Messapians, promising him his daughter Euippe and part of his kingdom in return. Diomedes and his Dorian companions defeated the Messapians. He gained Euippe and had a son, Diomedes, by her. Afterward he became quite Italianized. He even assisted the Trojans, his former enemies, against Turnus. He also built several cities, including Brundisium. He died in Daunia at an advanced age and was buried on one of the islands off Cape Garganus. These islands were thereafter called the Diomedean Islands. As usual, there were other accounts of his ultimate fate. Some said he was killed by Daunus or returned to Argos or just disappeared. The subsequent fate of Euippe is not known. [Pliny 3.11; Servius on Virgil's *Aeneid* 8.9; Antoninus Liberalis 37; Tzetzes on Lycophron 602,618; Strabo 6.3.9.]

EUIPPE (4) was another name for HIPPE, daughter of Cheiron.

EUIPPE (5) was a daughter of Leucon and granddaughter of Athamas. Her brother was Eurythrus. She married Andreus but, according to some, bore a son to the Cephissus River in Boeotia. This son was Eteocles, known for being the first to offer sacrifices to the Charites at Orchomenus. [Pausanias 9.34.5,35.1; Theocritus 16.104; Hyginus, *Fables* 157; Apollodorus 1.9.2.]

EUIPPE (6) was the daughter of Tyrimmas of Epeirus. Odysseus came to Epeirus to consult an oracle. He was kindly received by Tyrimmas and entertained very cordially, even to the extent that he had no trouble in seducing Euippe. The son born of this union was Euryalus. When he grew up, his mother sent him to Odysseus with certain tokens by which his father could identify him. Odysseus was away from home, and Penelope, to whom Odysseus had revealed the affair, welcomed the young man as a guest. When Odysseus returned she did not tell him who the visitor was; instead, she convinced him that the young man was part of a plot to kill him. Before Euryalus had a chance to make himself known to his father, he was killed by him. Euippe never learned the fate of her son, for Odysseus himself was killed not long after by another of his sons. [Eustathius on Homer's *Odyssey* 1796; Parthenius, *Love Stories* 3.]

EUIPPE (7) was the wife of Pierus and mother of the nine daughters he named for the Muses. More often the wife of Pierus was called ANTIOPE.

EULIMENE was one of the NEREIDES. [Apollodorus 1.2.7.]

EUMENIDES, or Erinyes, were the daughters of Gaea, the earth, who conceived them from the drops of blood that penetrated her from the severed genitals of Uranus (Heaven). Some said they were daughters of Cronus and Euonyme, and sisters of the Moirae, or Fates. Others called them daughters of Nyx (Night) or of Scotus (Darkness) and Gaea. Still others said they were daughters of Persephone and Hades.

Originally, the sisters might have been conceived as a personification of curses following a criminal. Later they were thought of as goddesses who actually pursued wrongdoers. They did not actually punish in the sense of bringing ruin or death to individuals, but they made evildoers wish they were dead. Their endless pursuit could bring on insanity, as it often did, and they followed their victims even after death. In addition, the curse of fathers could be visited upon their offspring. The crimes that particularly summoned them were disobedience toward parents, ill-treatment of the elderly, murder, violation of the law of hospitality, and improper conduct toward suppliants.

They eventually came to be three in number and were called Alecto, Megaera, and Tisiphone. Their original appearance was Gorgonlike, with bodies covered with black garments, serpents twined in their hair, and blood dripping from their eyes. Later they were represented with a less fearful appearance, as solemn maidens dressed as huntresses, with a band of serpents around their heads and torches in their hands. Their abode was Tartarus, where they stayed in readiness to come to the surface of the earth and pursue criminals.

Their office overlapped that of several other goddesses. Some of these were identified with them or were their companions, such as the Ceres, Dice (Dike), Eris, the Harpies, the Inferi, the Maniae, the Moirae, Nemesis, the Orphic Pandora, and Poena. They were older than the Olympian gods and therefore not under the will of Zeus, but they paid respect to him and he to them. Once a person incurred their wrath and had become their quarry, the pursuit was relentless. No pleading, prayer, tears, or sacrifice could move them.

No one was exempt from being haunted by the vengeful sisters, but they were particularly severe on the mighty who had fallen. Some of their famous victims were Alcmaeon, Alpheius, Meleager, Oedipus, Theseus and his friend Peirithous, Pandareos' daughters, and especially Orestes. Alcmaeon was a matricide and could find peace of mind only when he settled in a place that had not existed at the time of his crime. Alpheius, a son of Helios, according to some killed his brother in a contest and, pursued by the Eumenides, leapt into the Nyctimus River, which later bore his name. Meleager killed his uncles and was relentlessly dogged by the sisters. Oedipus, perhaps unfairly, was pursued for unwitting parricide followed by incest. Theseus and Peirithous were tortured in the underworld when they tried to abduct Persephone. The daughters of Pandareos were punished for the sins of their father.

Orestes was their most challenging assignment. After he killed his mother, Clytemnestra, and her lover Aegisthus, he was followed constantly by the Eumenides. He wandered far and wide trying to elude them, but they were tireless. Periodically he went insane, and during one of these attacks even bit off one of his fingers. He sought help from the Delphic oracle and was sent to Tauris to bring back an ancient image of Artemis. He and his friend Pylades came close to being sacrificed to the Taurian Goddess, but escaped with the help of the long-thought-dead Iphigeneia. Back in Greece he was brought to trial before the Areiopagus in Athens at the insistence of Clytemnestra's family and the Eumenides. Apollo acted as counsel for the defense, asserting that Orestes was directed by the Delphic oracle to avenge his father. The vote was equal, but Athena, ever the friend of heroes, cast the deciding vote in his favor. The Eumenides were furious but soothed when Athena arranged for them to have a sanctuary on the rock of the Areiopagus. Thus mollified, they abandoned their persecution of Orestes. It was said they received their name of Eumenides from that time forward. Eumenides was a euphemism meaning the Kindly Ones, since people were afraid to address them in terms of the terrifying beings they really were. They were also called the Venerable Goddesses.

They were utterly sexless, apparently, none of them producing offspring to further their vengeful missions. There is one vague reference to one of them being the mother by Ares of the dragon killed by Cadmus when he founded Thebes. Sacrifices to them consisted of black sheep and nephalia, or honey mixed with water. Somewhat inappropriately, it seems, white doves and the narcissus were sacred to them. A festival called the Eumenideia was celebrated in their honor near their grotto in Athens. Their worship, of course, was transported to Rome, where they were called the Furies or Dirae. [Aeschylus, *Eumenides* 107,231,321,384,499,511,918, *Agamemnon* 69, *Libation-Bearers* 1055; Pindar, *Olympian Odes* 245; Cicero, *On the Nature of the Gods* 3.18; Sophocles, *Oedipus at Colonus* 37,40,106,128; Suidas, "Eumenides"; Homer, *Iliad* 9.454,571, 15.204, 19.259, 21.412, *Odyssey* 2.136, 11.280, 15.234, 17.475; Virgil, *Aeneid* 4.469, 12.848; Pausanias 1.28.6, 2.11.4; Euripides, *Iphigeneia in Tauris* 290,970, *Orestes* 317.]

EUMOLPE was one of the NEREIDES. [Apollodorus 1.2.7.]

EUNE was a daughter of Cyprus on the island of Cyprus. She was married to Teucer, son of Telamon and Hesione. Upon his return to Salamis from Troy, Teucer was denied a welcome by his father because he had not avenged the death of his brother Ajax nor brought his remains home. He had also left behind Tecmessa and Eurysaces, Ajax's Phrygian wife and son. On the advice of Apollo, Teucer searched for a new home. He went to Cyprus, which Belus, king of Sidon, gave to him. He married Eune and became by her the father of Asteria. The first town he founded he nostalgically called Salamis. [Tzetzes on Lycophron 447,450; Pindar, *Nemean Odes* 4.60; Aeschylus, *Persians* 896; Pausanias 2.29.4.]

EUNICE was one of the NEREIDES. [Apollodorus 1.2.7.]

EUNOE was the mother of Hecuba by Dymas. Others call her mother Telecleia, Metope, or Glaucippe. [Scholiast on Homer's *Iliad* 16.718.]

EUNOMIA (1) was one of the HORAE. [Hesiod, *Theogony* 901.]

EUNOMIA (2) was by some called the mother of the Charites. Their mother was usually called EURYNOME.

EUNOSTE was a nymph of Boeotia who brought up the Tanagran hero Eunostus, a son of Elisus and Scias. Ochne, the daughter of Colonus, fell in love with him, but he avoided her. She falsely accused him before her brothers of attempted seduction, and they killed him. Afterward she confessed and threw herself from a cliff. Eunostus had a sanctuary at Tanagra in a sacred grove, which, understandably, no woman was allowed to approach. [Plutarch, *Greek Questions* 40.]

EUNOSTOS was a goddess of mills, whose image was set up in mills. She was believed to keep watch over the just weight of flour. [Hesychius, "Eunostos."]

EUONYME was a mysterious divinity. She was mentioned in very few connections by ancient writers but appeared to be part of the Titan regime. She was said to be the mother of the Eumenides by Scotus, although more often she was said to have borne them to Cronus along with the Moirae (Fates) and Aphrodite. Nothing else is known of her. She could have been any one of a number of abstract beings in the beginning of things. It is possible that her name was another name for Gaea. [Epimenides, quoted by Tzetzes on Lycophron 406; Scholiast on Sophocles' *Oedipus at Colonus* 42.]

EUPHEME (1) was the nurse of the Muses. She had a son, Crotus, by Pan. She brought up her son with the Muses, with whom he sang, danced, and hunted. He was a skillful shooter, and at his death the Muses requested that he be placed among the constellations as the Archer. Eupheme herself was commemorated with a statue in the grove of the Muses near Mount Helicon. [Hyginus, *Fables* 224, *Poetic Astronomy* 2.77; Pausanias 9.29.3.]

EUPHEME (2) was one of the DANAIDES, married to Hyperbius. [Hyginus, *Fables* 170.]

EUPHROSYNE was one of the CHARITES.

EUPOLEMEIA was the daughter of Myrmidon. By Hermes she became the mother of Aethalides, the herald of the Argonauts. Aethalides had a phenomenal memory, inherited from his father. He retained this gift even in Hades, and perhaps because of this he was allowed to live alternately in the upper and lower worlds. His soul meanwhile migrated from his body to that of Euphorbus, next to that of Hermotimus, then to that of Pyrrhus, and at last to that of Pythagoras, who could remember the former migrations. There is no record of where the soul migrated after Pythagoras. Eupolemeia's soul, presumably migratory as well, was not chronicled. [Apollonius Rhodius 1.54,640; Hyginus, *Fables* 14; Diogenes Laertius 8.1.4; Valerius Flaccus 1.437.]

EUPOMPE was one of the NEREIDES. [Hesiod, *Theogony* 261.]

EUPORIA was one of the HORAE. [Hyginus, *Fables* 183.]

EUPRYTO was called by some the wife of Tantalus, son of Zeus. More commonly the wife of Tantalus was called DIONE. [Apostolius 18.7.]

EUROPA (1) was a surname of Demeter at Lebadeia, where she was said to have been the nurse of Trophonius. At the oracle of Trophonius, the suppliant had to purify himself several days beforehand and sacrifice to Trophonius, Demeter Europa, and other deities. [Pausanias 9.39.4,5.]

EUROPA (2) was one of the OCEANIDES, although some have called her a daughter of Oceanus and Parthenope, and sister of Thrace. [Tzetzes on Lycophron 894; Hesiod, *Theogony* 356.]

EUROPA (3) was the daughter of Tityus, son of Zeus and Elara. Tityus was a giant from Panopeus whose size was probably vastly exaggerated by ancient writers. He married and had a daughter, so he must have been somewhere within the range of human proportions. He was killed by Artemis and Apollo for attacking Leto as she passed through Panopeus. His gigantic tomb was shown there in later times. Europa, who is never described, grew up in the somber hillside village of Panopeus with the reputation of her father surrounding her. This did not keep her from catching the eye of Poseidon and producing by him a son, Euphemus, who was the helmsman of the *Argo* and a Calydonian hunter. He was also able to walk on water. Europa and Euphemus were also ancestors of Battus, the founder of Cyrene. The mother of Euphemus was sometimes called Celaeno, Mecionice, or Oris. [Pausanias 3.18.9, 10.11.1,14.4,29.2; Apollonius Rhodius 1.182; Hyginus, *Fables* 55.]

EUROPA (4), the Phoenician princess, has stirred historic and artistic imagination for centuries. She has been viewed as the mythological version of Phoenician expansion and colonization, the mother of the Minoan dynasty, and even indirectly responsible for the creation of the Greek alphabet. She was the mother of two (or three) judges of Hades. She could be said to

have inspired the Cretan bull worship. From her the continent of Europe received its name.

Europa was the daughter of Agenor and Telephassa, according to the common tradition, but Homer called her a daughter of Phoenix, the ancestor of the Phoenicians. Agenor was a son of Poseidon and Libya, and a twin brother of Belus. By Telephassa he became the father of Cadmus, Phoenix, Cilix, Thasus, Phineus, and Europa.

The story is that as a young woman Europa was frolicking with companions on the seashore of Tyre. Zeus, not limited by geography in his seemingly endless quest for sexual partners, had observed her and lusted for her. To accomplish his purpose he awaited an opportunity and changed himself into a snow-white bull, which lumbered onto the beach from the sea. The maidens were delighted with the beautiful animal and festooned it with garlands. Europa was even persuaded to climb on the back of the gentle beast, and from that moment her life changed. The bull entered the water and swam to Crete, not a short distance; one wonders about the rate of speed the white bull managed.

The bull came ashore, probably on the southern coast of Crete, and made its way to Gortyna in the middle of the island. There under a plane tree Zeus resumed his usual appearance and ravished the thoroughly bewildered young woman. This union probably was responsible for the conception of Minos. Things are somewhat confused from that point. Zeus had fathered children all over the Greek mainland and islands, and he usually departed after his desire was satisfied. In the case of Europa, we find five children attributed to her and Zeus. This is quite unusual, but suggests Zeus found her desirable enough to visit over half a decade. As a rule, we hear only about the first three children—Minos, Rhadamanthys, and Sarpedon. The usual story says that, after Zeus left, Europa married Asterius, who adopted the three boys.

Asterius was the son of Tectamus, who had come to Crete with a colony of Aeolians. There he married a daughter of Cretheus and had Asterius and other children by her. Asterius fell in love with the abandoned Europa and, unable to have children by her, adopted her three sons by Zeus. Minos succeeded him and married Itone, daughter of Lyctius, by whom he had a son,

Lycastus. By Ida, daughter of Corybas, Lycastus became father of a second Minos, who was contemporary with Theseus.

We have very little information on Europa's other children credited to Zeus, Carneius and Dodon. Carneius was a favorite of Apollo, and brought up by him and Leto. Apollo received his surname Carneius from him. Dodon gave his name to the oracle at Dodona. But we do not know when or where these sons were born. There is a suggestion that Zeus returned to visit Europa after she was married, which in his case would not be too surprising. Perhaps Asterius thought the sons were his, or, even if he suspected otherwise, he might have decided he was already rearing three of Zeus' sons and that two more would not matter.

After this time we leave Europa, but it is necessary to look briefly at the events set in motion by her kidnapping. Agenor ordered his sons to set out in search of their sister, and they did so, taking different directions. Telephassa was said to have accompanied Cadmus as far as Thrace, where she died. Cadmus eventually abandoned his search and founded Thebes. Cilix settled in a country he called Cilicia. Phoenix went to Africa and gave his name to Phoenician colonists there. Thasus discovered the island of Thasos.

Europa's three eldest sons quarreled among themselves. Minos and Sarpedon fell in love with Miletus, a son of Apollo, and Sarpedon had to flee to Asia Minor when the youth chose him over the powerful Minos. Rhadamanthys also left Crete out of fear of Minos and went to mainland Greece, where he was said to have married Alcmena, the mother of Heracles, although he must have been quite old, even though he might be considered half-immortal.

Europa is one of those felicitous fictional characters whose story, absorbing in its own right, blends with fanciful historical speculation. Then when archaeological evidence of real history is presented at Thebes, Thasos, Carthage, Cnossus, and Gortyna, the essence of the story returns to us, and it is not hard to imagine a bull coming from the sea with a beautiful woman on its back. [Homer, *Iliad* 14.321, *Odyssey* 4.564; Apollodorus 2.1.1,4.11, 3.1.1,2; Hyginus, *Fables* 178; Pausanias 3.13.3, 7.4.1, 9.19.1; Ovid,

Metamorphoses 2.839; *Homeric Hymn to Apollo* 251; Herodotus 1.173, 4.45, 7.173; Pindar, *Olympic Odes* 137; Diodorus Siculus 4.60, 5.49,80; Stephanus Byzantium, "Dodona."]

EUROPA (5) was the second wife of Phoroneus and mother of Niobe, according to some. The wife of Phoroneus was more often called LAODICE.

EUROPA (6) was a name by which AEROPE, daughter of Catreus, was sometimes known. [Lactantius on Statius' *Thebaid* 3.306.]

EUROPA (7) was the mother by Danaus of the DANAIDES Automate, Amymone, Agave, and Scaea. [Apollodorus 2.1.5.]

EUROPOME was one of the DANAIDES, married to Athletes. [Hyginus, *Fables* 170.]

EURYALE (1) was, according to some, the mother of Orion by Poseidon or by Hyrieus. We know nothing of Euryale. If she was the wife of Hyrieus, she was also the stepmother of Lycus and Nycteus, whose mother was Clonia.

Orion was a giant huntsman, extraordinarily handsome and prodigiously strong. In spite of his exceptional attributes he was unlucky in love. His wife was destroyed because of her vanity. He went to Chios, where he fell in love with Merope, the daughter of Oenopion, who was opposed to their marriage. Orion got drunk one day and tried to rape Merope, and Oenopion blinded him. He was eventually cured, only to be carried away by Eos, goddess of the dawn, who had a weakness for beautiful young men. This affair was short-lived, since for one reason or another Artemis brought about the death of Orion. [Apollodorus 1.4.2; Homer, *Iliad* 18.486, *Odyssey* 5.121, 11.572; Hyginus, *Poetic Astronomy* 2.34; Eratosthenes, *Star Placements* 7.32; Virgil, *Aeneid* 10.763.]

EURYALE (2) was one of the GORGONS.

EURYALE (3) was a princess of the AMAZONS. The Amazons were allies of Aeetes against the Scythians. The warrior Euryale drove a chariot and was described by Aeetes as trampling the corpses of enemies in her wind-swift chariot. He said she was terrible in battle with her uplifted battle-ax and shield. He said he considered her as dear as one of his own daughters. During a battle between the Argonauts and Scythians, Canthus was slain by Gesander, who tried to take his body, and a fierce struggle ensued. Finally, his companions rescued his body and put it in the chariot of Euryale, who took him beyond the reach of the enemy. [Valerius Flaccus 5.612, 6.370.]

EURYANASSA (1) was sometimes called the mother of Pelops by Tantalus, but usually the mother of Pelops was called DIONE. [Tzetzes on Lycophron 52; Scholiast on Euripides' *Orestes* 5.11.]

EURYANASSA (2) was a daughter of Hyperphas and wife of Minyas, the founder of the race of Minyans who inhabited Orchomenus and surrounding regions. The wife of Minyas was also called Clytadora, Phanosyra, or Trigoneia. Minyas was either a son or grandson of Poseidon. Euryanassa bore him several children: Orchomenus, Cyparissus, Leucippe, Arsippe, Alcithoe, Elara, Araethyrea, and Clymene. All of them achieved distinction of one sort or another. Orchomenus succeeded his father on the throne and gave the region his name. Cyparissus gave his name to a town in Phocis. Leucippe, Arsippe, and Alcithoe were the so-called Minyades, who were turned into bats for not adopting the worship of Dionysus. Elara became by Zeus the mother of Tityus. Araethyrea was the mother of Phlias by Dionysus. Clymene was the wife of Phylacus and, according to some, the grandmother of Jason. [Pausanias 9.36.4, 10.29.6; Scholiast on Homer's *Iliad* 2.511, 22.227; Scholiast on Pindar's *Isthmian Odes* 1.55; Scholiast on Apollonius Rhodius 1.45; Tzetzes on Lycophron.]

EURYBIA (1) was a daughter of Pontus and Gaea, and sister to Thaumas, Phorcys, Nereus, and Ceto. She was therefore aunt to the Graeae, Scylla, the Gorgons, and the Hesperian dragon. Her own children by the Titan Crius—Astraeus, Pallas, and Perses—were more genteel. Astraeus by Eos was father of the winds and stars. Pallas by Styx was father of Zelus, Cratos, Bia, and Nice. Perses by Asteria was father of Hecate. [Hesiod, *Theogony* 375,376,377,409; Apollodorus 1.2.2,4; Pausanias 7.26.5.]

EURYBIA (2) was one of the THESPIADES and mother by Heracles of Polylaus. [Apollodorus 2.7.8.]

EURYBIA (3) was one of the AMAZONS who fought against Heracles when he came for the girdle of Hippolyte. She, Celaeno, and Phoebe were described as companions of Artemis whose spears invariably found their mark. In this brief combat their spears did not even graze the hero, and they were cut down as they stood shoulder to shoulder against him. [Diodorus Siculus 4.16.]

EURY[CE], or Eury[te], was one of the THESPIADES and mother by Heracles of Teleutagoras. The name is uncertain because of illegibility of the manuscript. [Apollodorus 2.7.8.]

EURYCLEIA (1) was a daughter of Athamas and Themisto. Athamas' first two marriages had been disastrous, and his union with Themisto must have been welcome after the pain and bereavement of the others. Not content with seeing anyone die happy, the tragedians came up with a version that had Themisto plot the deaths of Ino's children. However, the common story was that Athamas settled in a region he called Athamania and married Themisto, daughter of Hypseus, having by her four sons—Leucon, Erythrius, Schoeneus, and Ptous—and a daughter, Eurycleia. Eurycleia was, of course, half-sister to Phrixus, Helle, Learchus, and Melicertes, three of whom died before she was born.

She married her nephew Melas, a son of Phrixus and Chalciope. He had been one of the lords in the court of Aeetes at Colchis and participated in the contest against the Argonauts. Phrixus was reported to have returned to Boeotia, and Melas seems to have accompanied him. The son of Eurycleia and Melas was Hyperes; a spring near Pherae was named for him. [Scholiast on Pindar's *Pythian Odes* 4.221; Apollodorus 1.9.1; Apollonius Rhodius 2.1158; Valerius Flaccus 5.461, 6.196,197,199.]

EURYCLEIA (2) was the famous nurse of Odysseus. She was a daughter of Ops and had been purchased by Laertes as a nurse for Odysseus. When Odysseus finally returned home, Eurycleia recognized him even though he had been gone 20 years and was in the disguise of a beggar. She was able to do this because of a scar from a wound he had received as a child while boar hunting with his grandfather on Mount Parnassus. She later faithfully assisted him against the suitors by identifying the women servants who had collaborated with them. Odysseus made them clean up the blood from the slaughter and then hanged them. [Homer, *Odyssey* 1.429, 4.742, 19.385, 22.23.]

EURYCLEIA (3), according to some, was the mother of Oedipus by Laius. She was the daughter of Ecphas. For some reason, perhaps a prophecy of future parricide, Oedipus was thrown into a chest and cast into the sea when still an infant. The chest floated to Sicyon and was found by Polybus. The story continued more or less the same from there, with Oedipus killing his father and marrying Iocaste, who in this version would be his stepmother. [Scholiast on Euripides' *Phoenician Maidens* 13.26.]

EURYCYDE was the daughter of Endymion and the mother by Poseidon of Eleius. Eleius was king of the Epeians and father of Augeas. Her brothers were Aetolus, Paeon, Epeius, and Naxus, all founders of places and tribes. [Pausanias 5.1.6.]

EURYDICE (1) was a nymph who was married to the poet Orpheus, son of Oeagrus and Calliope. She was sometimes called Agriope. She and Orpheus were very happy and well adjusted to the savage surroundings of Thessaly, where they had settled. Once, Eurydice was pursued by the god Aristaeus, who tried to rape her. In her efforts to elude him she stepped on a poisonous serpent, which bit her. She died and was within hours transported from a blissful state to the gloomy caverns of Hades.

Orpheus was disconsolate and went in search of her. He entered the underworld from Thesprotia, and whenever he found his way blocked he played his lyre and sang plaintive songs that suspended activity and opened doors to him. He charmed Charon, the ferryman; Cerberus; the judges of the dead; and even Persephone. He finally was granted his prayer, and the infernal deities told him to walk back to the upper world and that Eurydice would follow him. On no condition, however, must he look behind him until both had fully gained the sunny upper reaches. Everything went well for a while, but Orpheus began to have doubts that Eurydice really was behind him, or perhaps he heard threatening noises. Finally he looked behind him, and Eurydice instantly vanished. This time nothing could move the stony hearts of the guardians of the shades. Orpheus was even barred from entering, and the implacable infernal spirits were impervious to his lyre.

With Eurydice gone, Orpheus fell from the popularity he had enjoyed. The women of the region resented his obsession with her. Orpheus rejected women and turned to men; he was even said to have invented pederasty. The women eventually fell upon him and tore him to pieces. [Diodorus Siculus 4.25; Hyginus, *Fables* 164,251; Athenaeus 1.3.7; Ovid, *Metamorphoses* 10.1; Apollodorus 1.3.2; Moschus 3.124; Conon, *Narrations* 45; Pausanias 9.30.6.]

EURYDICE (2) was one of the DANAIDES, daughter of Danaus and Polyxo, and married to Dryas. According to Hyginus she was married to Canthus. [Apollodorus 2.1.5; Hyginus, *Fables* 170.]

EURYDICE (3) was a daughter of Adrastus. She was not mentioned in the usual list of his children by Amphithea (i.e., Argeia, Hippodameia, Deipyle, Aegialeia, Aegialeus, and Cyanippus), so it is likely she was illegitimate. Be that as it may, she quite successfully married Ilus, who founded and built Troy. Ilus was a son of Tros and Callirrhoe, and brother of Assaracus, Ganymede, and Cleopatra. It is not known under what circumstances Eurydice happened to come to Troy or at what stage in the family history of the house of Tros. She was by some called Leucippe. By Ilus she became the mother of Laomedon and Themiste.

Eurydice was probably still alive when Laomedon succeeded Ilus as king. He continued to build Troy, and employed Apollo and Poseidon to assist him. His problems started when he refused to pay them. Themiste married Capys, and some say she was the mother of Anchises. [Apollodorus 3.12.3; Scholiast on Homer's *Iliad* 20.236.]

EURYDICE (4) was a daughter of Lacedaemon and Sparta. Lacedaemon was the eponymic hero of the region of the Lacedaemonians later called Sparta. He was a son of Zeus by Taygete and married to Sparta, daughter of the Eurotas River. By her he became father of Amyclas, Asine, and Eurydice. He built the first shrine of the Charites in Laconia. A shrine was erected to him near Therapne.

Eurydice, sometimes called Aganippe, became the wife of Acrisius in neighboring Argos. Their daughter was Danae, who was locked in a tower to prevent her having sexual relations with anyone, since an oracle had predicted that a son born to her would kill Acrisius. Zeus, however, solved the problem of access by changing himself into a shower of gold (a ray of sunlight?) and entering the chamber through a window. Eurydice saw her daughter and Perseus, her grandchild, cast into the sea in a chest. Years later, if she still lived, she saw Perseus and Danae return to Argos, and she saw the oracle fulfilled when Perseus accidentally killed his grandfather. She probably accompanied Perseus, Danae, and Andromeda when Perseus abandoned his inherited rule at Argos in exchange for the kingdom of Tiryns. [Apollodorus 2.2.2, 3.10.3; Pausanias 3.13.6,20.2; Hyginus, *Fables* 63.]

EURYDICE (5) was a daughter of Clymenus and wife of Nestor, according to some. She was usually called ANAXIBIA, daughter of Cratieus. [Homer, *Odyssey* 3.452.]

EURYDICE (6) was the wife of Lycurgus and mother of Archemorus. She was more frequently called AMPHITHEA. [Apollodorus 1.9.14.]

EURYDICE (7) was the wife of Creon, king of Thebes, and the mother of Megara, Haemon, Henioche, and Pyrrha. She was also called Henioche, the same name as her daughter. Creon was the son of Menoeceus and brother of

Iocaste. Eurydice saw many upheavals in the world around her. Her brother-in-law Laius was killed by a stranger. The horrible Sphinx arrived to plague the residents of Thebes until Oedipus came along and guessed its complex riddle. He was rewarded with the kingdom and Iocaste's hand in marriage. Then, after Oedipus had fathered four children by Iocaste, it was revealed that he had killed Laius and committed incest with his mother, and that his children were also his half-brothers and sisters. He blinded himself and died in exile; Iocaste killed herself.

Creon resumed the government of Thebes. He had earlier appeared to be a gentle man, but after the war of the Seven against Thebes he refused to allow burial of the fallen invaders. When Antigone defied his orders, she was buried alive. Haemon, son of Creon and Eurydice, chose to die with Antigone, whom he loved. Her daughter Megara was married to Heracles, who went mad and killed his children by her and some say Megara as well. So Eurydice's life was spent in turmoil and unhappiness. Her daughters Henioche and Pyrrha were commemorated with statues at the entrance to the temple of the Ismenian Apollo at Thebes, but Eurydice probably did not live to see this honor conferred. Some said she committed suicide when Haemon died. [Pausanias 9.10.3; Apollodorus 3.5.8,7.1; Sophocles, *Antigone* 1180.]

EURYDICE (8) was, according to some, the wife of Aeneas. His wife was more frequently called CREUSA. [Pausanias 10.26.1, citing Lescheos, author of the epic poem *Cypria*.]

EURYDICE (9) was, according to some, a daughter of Pelops and mother of Alcmena by Electryon. Alcmena's mother was most frequently called ANAXO. [Diodorus Siculus 4.9.]

EURYDICE (10) was a daughter of Actor and by Peleus mother of Polydora. Polydora's mother was most often called ANTIGONE. [Staphylus, quoted by the scholiast on Homer's *Iliad* 16.175.]

EURYDICE (11) was a daughter of Amphiaraus and Eriphyle, and the sister of Alcmaeon, Amphilochus, and Demonassa. Nothing further is known of her. It would not be unreasonable to guess that she might have been confused with Eurydice, the daughter of Adrastus, who became the wife of Ilus of Troy. The name could easily have been shifted in transcribing the genealogy of these closely related families. [Pausanias 5.17.4.]

EURYDICE (12) was one of the NEREIDES. [Hyginus, *Fables: Preface* 8.]

EURYDOMENE, according to some, was the mother of the Charites by Zeus. Their mother was more commonly called EURYNOME.

EURYGANEIA was called by some the mother of Eteocles, Polyneices, Antigone, and Ismene by Oedipus. Apparently the notion of sex with one's mother and children by her was so repugnant to some commentators that they sought endlessly to circumvent the incestuous legacy of the Theban royal house. Some of their alternatives were quite imaginative. Euryganeia was said to be the second wife of Oedipus. Iocaste had been, the first wife, and the incestuous products of this marriage were Phrastor and Laonytus, totally obscure individuals who could be depended on not to vitiate the royal line. Their fate was never disclosed. Oedipus finally married Astymedusa, a daughter of Sthenelus. According to a similar tradition, Euryganeia was a daughter of Hyperphas and mother of Oedipus' only children. He had married Iocaste earlier as a reward for killing the Sphinx, but there were no children by her. (See also EURYCLEIA.)

EURYLYTE was the mother, according to some, of Absyrtus by Aeetes. His mother was more frequently called ASTERODEIA.

EURYMEDE (1) was the wife of Glaucus and mother of Bellerophon. Some said the parents of Bellerophon were Poseidon and Eurynome. Eurymede's lot was not a happy one. First of all, her husband was a strange individual—not surprisingly, since he was a son of Sisyphus. He and Eurymede lived at Potniae in Boeotia between Thebes and Plataea. It is reported that he hated the power of Aphrodite and prevented his mares

from breeding so they would be stronger for the race track. Some said he tried to increase their competitiveness by feeding them on human flesh. Aphrodite, probably with the concurrence of the other gods, took revenge. When Acastus celebrated funeral games for Pelias at Iolcus, Glaucus entered the chariot race with four of the mares, which became frightened and upset the chariot. Some say they had gone mad from drinking from a sacred well or eating an herb called *hippomanes*. Whatever the cause, they tore Glaucus to pieces after the chariot overturned. Since Glaucus was born in Corinth, some associated his ghost with the race course on the isthmus. A spot on the track called *taraxippus* caused horses to shy. Such was Glaucus' monument.

Eurymede was unfortunate in her offspring as well, even though Bellerophon was considered one of the great Greek heroes. He killed his brother Deliades (some say Alcimenes or Peirin, and others a man called Bellerus). He had to flee and ended up being sent to overcome the dreaded Chimaera. Later he drew upon himself the hatred of the gods and wandered alone over the countryside. Some say he tried to fly with Pegasus to heaven but was thrown off and fell to earth, and became lame or blind in consequence. To make Eurymede's plight even worse, both her grandson Isander and her great-grandson Glaucus were killed in the Trojan War. Her granddaughter Laodameia became by Zeus the mother of Sarpedon and was herself killed by Artemis. Sarpedon was also slain in the Trojan War, thus ending the unfortunate line. [Apollodorus 1.9.3,28, 2.3.1; Pausanias 3.18.9, 5.17.4.]

EURYMEDE (2) was one of the MELEAGRIDES.

EURYMEDUSA was a daughter of Cleitor. She was seduced by Zeus in the disguise of an ant and bore Myrmidon. This unqualified statement has always been fascinating. One can without too much imagination see an ant crawling beneath the clothes of Eurymedusa and finding her external sexual organs. But the idea of sufficient seminal emission to effect a pregnancy is ludicrous. It is easier to believe that once the target was centered, Zeus resumed his usual appearance and accomplished his purpose in the approved manner. Still, the son was called Myrmidon (from *myrmex,* an ant), so the association with an ant persisted. Myrmidon was the ancestor of the Myrmidons in Thessaly, which line included Achilles. [Apollodorus 1.7.3; Apollonius Rhodius 1.5.6.]

EURYNOME (1) was one of those beings who seemed to turn up in a variety of connections but never with any real presence. She was called a daughter of Oceanus and Tethys. It is said that she ruled with Ophion over the Titans previous to the time of Cronus and Rhea. This means she had to be older than her uncle Cronus, who was the brother of Oceanus. She and Ophion were overthrown by Cronus, and she sank into the ocean. There she associated with Thetis, and the two of them received Hephaestus when he was expelled from Olympus. He stayed for several years in their grotto and made for them many intricate and beautiful ornaments. He also made the golden chair in which he later temporarily imprisoned his mother. This might have been at the instigation of Eurynome, who was strongly out of favor with Hera.

Hera certainly was not happy with the hospitality Eurynome extended to the Olympian outcast. Eurynome was herself a deposed Titan, and these were inferior beings. Eurynome had also become the mother of the Charites by Zeus, and that certainly was not kindly received by Hera. The Asopus River, according to some, was also a son of Zeus by Eurynome, although rivers were generally called the sons of Oceanus and Tethys, thus making Asopus her brother rather than her son.

It appears that Eurynome was a product of a time when the great cosmic symbols were being recorded, and her role was not as yet clearly drawn. Her liaison with Zeus to produce the Charites was perhaps the most solid part of her identity. The Charites were also called daughters of Eunomia, Eurydomene, Harmonia, Lethe, Hera, Aegle, Euanthe, Aphrodite, or Coronis. [Hesiod, *Theogony* 908; Apollodorus 1.2.2, 3.12.6; Homer, *Iliad* 14,302, 18.395,398, *Odyssey* 10.139; Pindar, *Olympian Odes* 13.66; Apollonius Rhodius 1.503; Hyginus, *Fables* 157.]

EURYNOME (2) was, according to Hyginus (*Fables* 69), mother by Talaus of Adrastus. His mother was usually called LYSIMACHE.

EURYNOME (3) was the wife of Lycurgus and mother of Ancaeus, Epochus, Amphidamas, and Iasus. Their mother was more often called ANTIGONE. [Apollodorus 3.9.1.]

EURYNOME (4) was the daughter of Iphitus, son of Naubolus by Hippolyte. Iphitus was a prince of Phocis and an Argonaut. His sons Schedius and Epistrophus commanded the Phocians in 40 ships during the Trojan War. Eurynome is never mentioned again. As in other cases, she could have remained unmarried, therefore contributing no heirs to the royal line, or she could have died young. [Homer, *Iliad* 2.518,564; Pausanias 10.4.1; Apollodorus 1.9.6; Apollonius Rhodius 1.207.]

EURYNOME (5) was the wife of the Babylonian king Orchamus and mother of Leucothoe. The daughter was loved by Helios but was betrayed by the jealous Clytia to her father, who buried her alive. Helios metamorphosed her into an incense shrub. It is always interesting to speculate in such cases. What was the role of the victim's mother? Did she intercede, or did she accept the authority of her husband even in such a life-and-death matter? [Ovid, *Metamorphoses* 4.208.]

EURYNOME (6) was, according to Zenodotus (citing Eustathius on Homer's *Odyssey* 1500), the daughter of Proteus, the old man of the sea. Homer calls the daughter EIDOTHEA.

EURYNOME (7) was a surname of Artemis at Phigalia in Arcadia. Her sanctuary, which was surrounded by cypresses, was opened only once each year, and sacrifices were offered to her. She was represented as half-woman and half-fish. [Pausanias 8.41.4.]

EURYNOME (8) was a daughter of Nysus and by Poseidon the mother of Bellerophon. His mother was more often called EURYMEDE. [Hyginus, *Fables* 157.]

EURYNOME (9) was a faithful housekeeper in the palace of Odysseus. Guided by Athena, she advised Penelope to show herself once more to the suitors in order to bring greater glory on her son and husband when they should take revenge. [Homer, *Odyssey* 168–186.]

EURYODIA was quite obscure, but not too obscure to be courted by Zeus. By him she was the mother of Arceisius and the grandmother of Laertes, the father of Odysseus. [Homer, *Odyssey* 14.182, 16.118; Eustathius on Homer's *Odyssey* 1796; Apollodorus 1.9.16.]

EURYPHAESSA was, according to the Homeric hymn on Helios, the mother by Hyperion of Helios the sun-god. Usually he was called the son of Hyperion and THEIA, and brother of Selene and Eos. [*Homeric Hymn on Helios* 2.]

EURYPYLE was one of the THESPIADES, and by Heracles the mother of Archedicus. [Apollodorus 2.7.8.]

EURYSTERNOS, the Goddess with the Broad Chest, was a surname of Gaea, under which she had a sanctuary with a very ancient statue on the Crathis River near Aegae in Achaia. [Pausanias 5.14.8, 7.25.8.]

EURYTE (1) was a daughter of Hippodamas and thus the granddaughter of the Achelous River and great-granddaughter of Aeolus. She married Porthaon, son of Agenor and king of Pleuron and Calydon. She bore him six children— Oeneus, Leucopeus, Agrius, Alcathous, Melas, and Sterope. Agrius and Oeneus were the only really noteworthy sons. Alcathous died young as a result of being one of Hippodameia's suitors, and thus killed by her father Oenomaus. Euryte was elderly when Agrius and his sons deposed Oeneus from the throne to which he had succeeded on the death of Hippodamas. This usurpation took place when Oeneus himself was middle-aged, since he had reared a sizable family, including Meleager, in Calydon. Euryte was also the grandmother-in-law of Heracles, since Deianeira was one of the daughters of Oeneus. By the time Diomedes restored Oeneus to his kingdom, Euryte had probably died of old age.

[Apollodorus 1.7.10,8.5; Diodorus Siculus 4.65; Pausanias 2.25.2; Antoninus Liberalis 2.]

EURYTE (2) was a nymph and the mother of Halirrhothius by Poseidon. Halirrhothius tried to rape Alcippe, the daughter of Ares by Agraulos, and Ares unceremoniously killed him, nephew or not. Poseidon called Ares before a tribunal of the gods, and he was acquitted. The hill on which the gods convened was called thereafter the Hill of Ares, or the Areiopagus. Euryte probably disappeared as soon as she bore Halirrhothius. He had very likely been reared by foster parents. [Apollodorus 3.14.1; Euripides, *Electra* 1261; Pindar, *Olympian Odes* 11.73.]

EURYTELE was one of the THESPIADES and mother by Heracles of Leucippus. [Apollodorus 2.7.8.]

EURYTHEMIS, a daughter of Cleoboea, was mother by the Aetolian king Thestius of Althaea, Leda, Hypermnestra, Iphicles, Euippus, Plexippus, and Eurypylus. Her family was a distinguished one. Thestius was part of the Aetolian dynasty established by Aetolus. Iphicles took part in the Calydonian boar hunt, as did Euippus, Plexippus, and Eurypylus; he was also an Argonaut. Althaea was the wife of Oeneus, and mother of Meleager and Deianeira, who as Heracles' wife established a line that extended into historical times. Hypermnestra was the mother of Amphiaraus, and her son not only was prominent in the war of the Seven against Thebes but was the progenitor of an important family of medical seers. Leda, of course, was the most famous of the offspring of Eurythemis, since by Zeus she produced Helen and Polydeuces, and by Tyndareus of Sparta Castor and Clytemnestra.

Eurythemis experienced much sadness. Her grandson Meleager killed three of her sons and was in turn caused to die by his mother Althaea, who then destroyed herself. Althaea's widowed husband slept with his own daughter Gorge, Eurythemis' granddaughter, and had a son by her, according to rumor. Gorge's sister Deianeira had an unhappy life with her husband, Heracles, and unintentionally killed him, afterward killing herself. Her grandson Amphiaraus was killed in the battle of the Seven. Leda's daughters turned out to be adulteresses, but then so had their mother been. It is not known how many of these tragic situations Eurythemis lived to see. Certainly she could not have lived to see the devastation caused by the Trojan War, but she probably knew about the abduction of Helen by Paris of Troy. The wife of Thestius was also called Deidameia, Laophonte, Leucippe, or Lycippe. [Apollodorus 1.7.10,8.3, 3.10.6; Pausanias 2.21.2; Homer's *Odyssey* 24.199; Ovid, *Metamorphoses* 8.445.]

EURYTHEMISTRA, daughter of the river-god Xanthus in Lycia, was, according to some, the mother by Tantalus of Pelops, Niobe, and Broteas. Tantalus' wife was more often called DIONE.

EURYTHOE was a daughter of Danaus and, according to some, the mother of Hippodameia by Oenomaus. Hippodameia's mother was more frequently called STEROPE. [Apollonius Rhodius 1.752; Tzetzes on Lycophron 156.]

EURYTIA was, according to some, the second wife of Phineus, son of Agenor and king of Salmydessus. Most accounts referred to this wife as IDAEA. By this second wife he had two sons, Thynus and Mariandynus.

EURYTIONE was a daughter of Timander and sister of Hellotia. When Corinth was burned by the Dorians, the sisters were destroyed in the temple of Athena. (*See* HELLOTIA.)

EUSTYOCHE was the wife of Phyleus, son of Augeas. She was also called Timandra but more often CTIMENE, daughter of Laertes and sister of Odysseus.

EUTERPE was one of the MUSES. She was the Muse of lyric poetry and usually represented with a flute. She was said to be the mother of Rhesus by the Strymon River.

EUTYCHIA was the Greek personification of happiness. In Roman myth she was called Felicitas.

EXOLE was one of the THESPIADES and mother by Heracles of Erythras. [Apollodorus 2.7.8.]

FAMA was the Latin personification of rumor or report. She was a daughter of Terra, born after Coeus and Enceladus. She had a great number of eyes and mouths and moved from one place to another. She lived in a palace of bronze that had a thousand openings, which every voice could penetrate. From there she kept watch over the whole world, surrounded by Credulitas, Error, Laetitia (Unfounded Joy), Timores (Terror), Seditio, and Susurri (False Rumor). Her Greek name was Ossa.

FASCELIS was a surname of Diana in Italy, which she was believed to have received from the circumstance of Orestes having brought her image from Tauris in a bundle of sticks (*fascis*), but it could also allude to the usual representation of the goddess with a torch (*fax*) in her hand. [Servius on Virgil's *Aeneid* 2.116; Solinus 1,2; Silius Italicus 14.260.]

FATUA (*See* BONA DEA)

FAULA, or Fauna, was, according to some, a concubine of Hercules in Italy; according to others, she was the wife or sister of Faunus. Latinus, called a son of Hercules by a concubine, was probably considered to be the son of Faula, but the common tradition described him as a son of Faunus. Faula was identified by some of the ancients with the Greek Aphrodite. [Varro, *On the Latin Language* 7.36; Servius on Virgil's *Georgics* 1.11; Macrobius, *Saturnalia* 1.12; Dionysius of Halicarnassus, *Roman Antiquities* 1.33.]

FELICITAS was the personification of happiness, to whom a temple was erected by Lucullus in 75 B.C.; however, it burned down in the reign of Claudius. Felicitas is frequently seen on Roman medals in the form of a matron, with the staff of Mercury and a cornucopia. Sometimes she had other attributes, according to the kind of happiness she represented. The Greeks worshipped this personification under Eutychia. [Pliny 34.8; St. Augustine, *City of God* 4.18,23.]

FERONIA was an ancient Italian divinity introduced to the Romans by the Sabines and Faliscans. Her exact nature is not clear. She was basically an earth goddess, one with perhaps infernal attributes, since her son Eurylus had three souls and consequently had to be killed three times by Euander. The principal seat of her worship was the town of Feronia at the foot of Mount Soracte, and she and the divinity Soranus shared certain things in common. Soranus, another infernal divinity sometimes identified with Apollo, had a cult called the Hirpini, who walked barefooted on glowing coals and carried in their hands the entrails of the sacrificial victims. Anxurus was another divinity worshipped in conjunction with Feronia, and in joint ceremonies they were identified with a youthful Jupiter and Juno.

Some consider that Feronia was also the goddess of liberty, since at Terracina slaves were set free in her temple. She also was thought to protect commerce because of trading transactions carried out at her festivals.

Greek writers described Feronia as Greek in origin, her worship having been brought to Italy by Lacedaemonian colonists who came to the vicinity of Feronia during the time of Lycurgus and built a temple to the goddess Feronia. [Dionysius of Halicarnassus, *Roman Antiquities* 2.49, 3.32; Virgil, *Aeneid* 3.564, 11.786; Servius on Virgil's *Aeneid* 7.799, 8.465, 11.785; Livy 22.1, 26.11, 27.4; Silius Italicus 5.174, 13.84; Varro, *On the Latin Language* 5.74.]

FIDES was the personification of fidelity or faithfulness at Rome. She had a temple on the Capitoline Hill along with one for Jupiter and one for Victoria. This proximity was based on Jupiter's sovereignty over all transactions, which in turn were based on faithfulness and justice. Fides was represented as elderly, wearing an olive wreath and carrying fruit or other produce. [Cicero, *On the Duties of Office* 3.29, *On the Nature of the Gods* 2.23,31, *On Laws* 2.8,11; Dionysius of Halicarnassus, *Roman Antiquities* 2.75.]

FLORA was the goddess of flowers and spring. Like many other Roman goddesses, she had been a Sabine divinity, and her worship was introduced by Titus Tatius. The month of April, or its Sabine equivalent, was dedicated to her, and the accompanying festival, the Floralia, was carried out with extravagant merriment and lasciviousness. Certain writers maintained she had been a courtesan who had inherited property during her active years and then left it to the city of Rome. Perhaps this accounted for the participation of courtesans in the games accompanying the Floralia.

Flora figured in a myth about Juno. She provided the goddess with a special flower that brought on pregnancy without male assistance. Juno had been jealous that Jupiter had produced Minerva from his head, and thus with Flora's help she produced Mars. It is not recorded whether Mars sprang from her head or came through the regular channels.

Flora was identified with the Greek Chloris, who was abducted by Zephyrus, the west wind, and given dominion over flowers. [Varro, *On the Latin Language* 5.74; Tacitus, *Annals* 2.49; Ovid, *Fasti* 5.195.]

FLUONIA, or Fluviona, was a surname of Juno, under which she was invoked by newly married couples to stop the menstrual flow and thus allow conception. [Arnobius, *Adversus Nationes* 3.30; Martianus Capella 2.149.]

FORNAX was a Roman goddess thought to preside over the process of providing bread, from the ripening of grain to its baking in an oven (*fornax*). Her festival was the Fornacalia. She was identified with Vesta. [Ovid, *Fasti* 2.525; Festus, "Fornacalia."]

FORTUNA was the Roman goddess of luck or chance, worshipped in Greece as Tyche. Her worship in Rome was introduced by Servius Tullius, who according to report was the king most favored by Fortuna, even to the point of physical relationship. When she went to Rome she took off her wings and shoes, since she intended to remain there. Servius Tullius built two temples to her, and her popularity was impressive. She had several epithets, such as Redux, Conservatrix, Publica, and Privata. She was portrayed often with a cornucopia and a rudder, the latter symbolizing the course she steered for man. Fortuna Virginensis was invoked by newly married women, who dedicated their virgin garments in her temples. Fortuna Virilis had a following of married women, who asked her to preserve their sex appeal so they could keep their husbands happy. She was generally represented as blind. [Plutarch, *On the Fortune of the Romans* 4,5,10; Dionysius Halicarnassus, *Roman Antiquities* 4.27; Livy 10.46; Ovid, *Fasti* 4.145, 6.570; St. Augustine, *City of God* 4.11.]

FURIAE were the Roman equivalent to the Greek EUMENIDES. They were almost identical, except for Latin epithets such as Patrii Dii, designating them as avenging the death of parents. [Cicero, *Against Verres* 2.1,3.]

FURINA, or Furrina, was an ancient Roman divinity who had a sacred grove and spring on the right bank of the Tiber at the foot of the Janiculum Hill. She was considered one of the Furies, and she even had an annual festival, the Furinalia. Her worship declined, and the shrine was taken over by Syrian colonists for other purposes. Eventually her name was almost forgotten. [Cicero, *On the Nature of the Gods* 3.18, *Letters to His Brother Quintus* 3.1.]

GAEA, or Ge, was the earth. At the beginning of things were the vast elemental entities such as Chaos, Nyx, and Erebus, and the ancient cosmologists found it necessary to arrive early at a stage on which these primordial interactions could take place. The earth was conceived by them as female, a mother whose vast womb could be fertilized by heaven, air, ocean, sun, and even infernal forces. By some she was considered the first being to emerge from Chaos, followed closely by Eros (Love), Nyx (Night), and Erebus (Darkness). Eros inspired the union of his brothers and sisters with one another, and allowed unilateral spontaneous generation where there was no convenient partner. Partners were soon enough provided by Gaea's own sons, Uranus (Heaven) and Pontus (Sea), whom she bore without male assistance.

By Uranus she had the Titans—Oceanus, Coeus, Crius, Hyperion, Iapetus, Cronus, Theia, Rhea, Themis, Mnemosyne, Phoebe, Tethys—and the Cyclopes and the Hecatoncheires (Hundred-Handed)—Brontes, Steropes, Arges, Cottus, Briareus, Aegaeon, Anax, Porphyrion, and Gyges.

Uranus forced all these offspring to remain hidden in the earth, and Gaea resolved to avenge this wrong. She persuaded Cronus, the youngest of the Titans, to disable his father, and for the purpose she provided him with an exceedingly sharp sickle. The next time Uranus had intercourse with Gaea, Cronus cut off his father's testicles, which fell on the bosom of his mother, causing her to produce the Eumenides, the Giants, and the Melian nymphs. Various writers mentioned other children by Uranus and Gaea before his enforced retirement from fatherhood. These were Cratus, Aristaeus, Dione, the Muses, Pan, Adanus, Demeter, Ostasus, Andes, Olymbrus, Anytus, and Saros, although some of these were given entirely different parents in other myth cycles.

The Titans then ruled heaven and earth, with Cronus as their leader. It is not clear whether or not the castration proved fatal to Uranus. That does not appear to be the case, since he was said to have joined Gaea in warning Zeus to beware of any son Metis might bear, thus causing Zeus to swallow his first wife and produce Athena. Earlier they had also advised Rhea to go to Crete to give birth to Zeus in order to prevent Cronus from swallowing him as he had done with Rhea's other children.

Gaea certainly did not drop out of sight when her children gained control of the universe. As already stated, she gave advice to them and to her grandchildren, who in turn overturned the supremacy of the Titans. She also was the earliest holder of the oracle that later became the province of Apollo at Delphi, and her prophecies were said to have been even better than the ones that followed. Her oracle was guarded by the monster Python, who was also her son.

Gaea was also busy in other ways. When it came to sexual partners, she seemed universally available. By her brother Pontus she had Aetna, Eurybia, Nereus, Phorcys, Ceto, and Thaumas. By another brother, Aether, she bore Atlas, Aphrodite, and Tartarus, although the first two were given other parents in later myths. Oceanus was the only one of her Titan sons with whom she had intercourse. He fathered, according to some, the Moirae, or Fates, and Triptolemus by her. It is curious that she did not have sex with Cronus, since offspring from Earth and Time would seem to be most appropriate. By her son

Tartarus she had a series of monsters—Echidna, Typhon, Enceladus, and the Giants, who joined in battle against her grandchildren, the Olympians.

Gaea did not stop at brothers and sons for lovers. By Helios, her grandson, she had Acheron; some said he was her son by Oceanus. She was accustomed to intercourse with oceans, since she had children by her brother Pontus and her son Oceanus. Why should she stop there? By Poseidon, her grandson, she produced Charybdis and Antaeus. Charybdis will be remembered as the famous whirlpool of the Argonaut and the wanderings of Odysseus; Antaeus, as Heracles' adversary, who remained invincible as long as he was in contact with mother earth. Her sexual contact with Zeus was rather bizarre. He had an involuntary nocturnal emission that fell on the ground and caused Gaea to produce the terrifying hermaphrodite Agdistis. The contact with her great-grandson Hephaestus was stranger still. He tried to rape Athena, but his semen ended up on the ground, and Erichthonius was the result. It must have been necessary to have divine seed in order to thus impregnate the earth, since countless mortals must have deliberately dropped their sperm in countless secret places.

Apart from all these children, there were those regarded by the ancients as autochthonous, or born from the earth. This term was usually reserved for those who started dynasties but could not be traced to gods. They sprang from the earth because they had to have a beginning. They included Pelasgus, Argus Panoptes, Cranaus, and Amphictyon, although some of these were later assigned proper fathers and mothers. In addition, there were those whom Gaea was said to have borne without insemination: Areion (usually said to be Demeter's son), Hyllus, the Oneirata (Dreams), Python, the Sirens, Tityus, and the dragon Ladon. Again, some writers gave different parentage to some of these beings. But when in doubt, one could always assign motherhood of anyone to the earth. In the long run, this would be a correct assignment, since everyone did ultimately arise from the earth.

Gaea was understandably regarded as one of the divinities presiding over marriage. She was all-producing and all-nourishing. She had temples or altars at Athens, Sparta, Delphi, Olym-
pia, Bura, Tegea, Phlius, and several other places. We know the exact location of some of these sites, but there appear to be no remains, thereby attesting to the ancientness of her worship. At Rome she was worshipped under the name of Tellus. [Homer, *Iliad* 3.104,278, 15.36, 19.259, *Odyssey* 5.124, 7.324, 11.576; Apollonius Rhodius 1.762, 3.716; Hesiod, *Theogony* 117,125,232; Apollodorus 1.1.1; Aeschylus, *Eumenides* 2; Pausanias 1.22.3,24.3,31.2, 5.14.8, 10.5.3; Philostratus, *Life of Apollonius of Tyana* 6.39; Ovid, *Metamorphoses* 7.196; Thucydides 2.15.]

GAEEOCHOS, Holder of the Earth, was a surname of Artemis at Thebes. [Sophocles, *Oedipus the King* 160.]

GALATEIA (1) was one of the NEREIDES. She loved the youth Acis, son of Faunus and Symaethis. Polyphemus, one of the Cyclopes, was jealous of him and crushed him under a boulder. The blood that flowed from under the rock was changed by Galateia into the Acis River at the foot of Mount Aetna. She was identified by some with Galene, the personification of the calm sea. [Ovid, *Metamorphoses* 13.750; Homer, *Iliad* 18.45; Hesiod, *Theogony* 251.]

GALATEIA (2) was a daughter of Eurytius and married to Lamprus, son of Pandion, at Phaestus in Crete. She was pregnant by him, and he ordered her to kill the baby if it should not be a son. Galateia gave birth to a daughter but could not bear to kill the infant. How she managed to disguise its sex is a mystery, since Lamprus was the sort of tyrant who would have demanded a view of the child's genitals to be sure that his will was carried out. Maybe Galateia was able to substitute a boy baby born at the same time to a servant. She was advised by dreams and soothsayers to pass the baby off as a boy, whom she called Leucippus. The girl grew up in this disguise, and this is also a mystery, since fathers and sons must have undressed in each other's presence after athletic exercise or the hunt. With this ever-present risk, Galateia finally went to the temple of Leto and prayed to the goddess to change the girl into a boy. This was granted, and from that time the Phaestians sacrificed to Leto

Phytia (the Creator) and celebrated a festival called the Ecdysia in commemoration of the girl's having put off her female attire. The modern term for stripteaser, *ecdysiast*, can be traced back to this event. [Antoninus Liberalis 17.]

GALATEIA (3) became the wife of Pygmalion, a talented sculptor. He made an ivory statue so beautiful that he fell in love with it and caressed it in bed. He prayed repeatedly for Aphrodite to give it life. Eventually she did so, and Pygmalion became by the newly created Galateia the father of Paphus and Metharme. [Ovid, *Metamorphoses* 10.243.]

GALAXAURE was one of the OCEANIDES. [Hesiod, *Theogony* 353; *Homeric Hymn to Demeter* 423.]

GALENE, a personification of the calm sea and perhaps identical with Galateia, one of the NEREIDES, was called by Hesiod (*Theogony* 244) a daughter of Nereus and Doris.

GALINTHIAS, or Galinthis, was a daughter of Proetus of Thebes (after whom one of the gates of Thebes was named) and a friend of Alcmena. The familiar story of the birth of Heracles involved Galinthias. Hera, the Moirae (Fates), Eileithyia (the goddess of birth), and the Pharmacides (Sorceresses) were endeavoring to delay Heracles' birth, even though Hera's purpose of allowing Eurystheus to be born first had already been accomplished. Galinthias rushed into the place where the goddesses were assembled to announce that Alcmena had given birth. The goddesses were so surprised that they relaxed their birth-inhibiting postures and broke the spell; immediately Alcmena was enabled to deliver Heracles. The deceived goddesses changed Galinthias into a weasel or a cat and condemned her to a life of skulking in dark corners. It is said Hecate took pity on Galinthias and made her one of her attendants. At Thebes, when sacrifices were offered to Heracles, it was customary to first pay tribute to Galinthias. Some attributed this friendly act to Historis, a daughter of Teiresias. [Ovid, *Metamorphoses* 9.285–306; Antoninus Liberalis 29; Aelian, *On the Characteristics of Animals* 12.5, 15.11; Pausanias 9.8.4,11.1–2.]

GAMELIA was a surname of Hera in her role as goddess of marriage. [Plutarch, *Advice to Bride and Groom* 27.]

GANYMEDA was a surname of Hebe, under which she was worshipped in a sacred grove at Sicyon and Phlius. [Pausanias 2.13.3.]

GEILISSA, according to some, was the nurse who rescued Orestes on the evening Agamemnon was murdered. She is usually called ARSINOE.

GENETRIX, the Mother, was a surname of Cybele. It was also a surname of Venus, to whom Julius Caesar dedicated a temple at Rome as the mother of the Julian family. The name was also said to be a surname of Elissa (Dido), the founder of Carthage. [Ovid, *Metamorphoses* 14.536; Suetonius, *Lives of the Caesars: Deified Julius* 61,78,84; Silius Italicus 1.81.]

GENETYLLIDES, or Gennaides, were a class of divinities presiding over generation and birth. They were companions of Aphrodite Colias. The name is often seen in the singular. [Aristophanes, *Thesmophoriazusae* 130; Pausanias 1.1.4.]

GENETYLLIS, Protectress of Births, occurred as a surname of Aphrodite. It was also a name of Artemis, to whom women sacrificed dogs. [Aristophanes, *Clouds* 52, *Lysistrata*; Hesychius, "Genetyllis."]

GERANA was a woman from the curious race of dwarfs called Pygmies, who were mentioned in the *Iliad*. This race lived in Egypt or India and engaged in perpetual struggle with the storks. Gerana, or Oenoe, as she was sometimes called, was a Pygmy and very beautiful. She despised the gods, especially Artemis and Hera. She married Nicodamas, one of the Pygmies, and had by him a son, Mopsus; the people brought gifts to celebrate his birth. However, Hera finally decided to take action because of the young woman's bad attitude, and changed her into a stork. Though now a stork, Gerana tried to recover her son, but the Pygmies drove her away. From that time on, the Pygmies were at war with the storks (some said cranes). According to some, Gerana bore a tortoise to Nicodamas. Apparently this was a famous legend as early as Homer's time and probably an example of the tall tales told around the campfires during battle. [Homer, *Iliad* 3.3; Eustathius on Homer's *Iliad* 1322; Aelian, *On the Characteristics of Animals* 15.29; Athenaeus 9.393; Ovid, *Metamorphoses* 6.90; Antoninus Liberalis 6.]

GLAUCA was the wife of Ajax the Greater. His wife is most frequently called TECMESSA. [Dictys Cretensis 5.16.]

GLAUCE (1) was one of the NEREIDES and the personification of the color of the sea. [Homer, *Iliad* 18.39.]

GLAUCE (2) was one of the DANAIDES, daughter of Danaus and Atlantia or Phoebe. She was married to Alces. [Apollodorus 2.1.5.]

GLAUCE (3) was an Arcadian nymph who appeared on the altar of the temple of Athena Alea at Tegea. Accompanying her were Neda, Theisoa, and Anthracia, standing on one side of Rhea and the nymph Oenoe, who held the baby Zeus. On the other side were Ida, Hagno, Alcinoe, and Phrixa. There were also images of the Muses and of Memory. [Pausanias 8.47.3.]

GLAUCE (4) was the wife of Upis and mother of the third Diana (the first being the daughter of Jupiter and Proserpina and mother of Cupid, and the second being the daughter of Jupiter and Latona). [Cicero, *On the Nature of the Gods* 3.23.]

GLAUCE (5) was the daughter of Creon, king of Corinth. Creon's reign at Corinth poses a mystery. There is no provision for his reign in the royal line since Marathon, son of Epopeus, divided his territory between his sons Corinthus and Sicyon. When Corinthus died without heirs, the Corinthians invited Medea from Iolcus (as the daughter of Aeetes, the original heir of Corinth) to take over the government. Thus her husband, Jason, obtained the sovereignty. Perhaps Creon was an interim ruler after the death of Corinthus. His father's name was Lycaethus, but nothing else is known of his background. He

is often confused with Creon of Thebes, son of Menoeceus.

In any case, even after Jason and Medea came to Corinth, Creon was still referred to as king. Perhaps as king of Iolcus Jason let Creon continue in the responsibilities of office in Corinth, or maybe he even shared the government with the older man. This seems a good possibility, since after ten years (while his young daughter grew up?) Creon offered Jason his daughter in marriage. None of the accounts say that he offered succession to the throne, which certainly suggests Jason already shared the throne in some capacity. It is not clear what Creon thought Jason should do with the wife he already had, one who had borne him several children. Jason was no longer young, and a pretty adolescent wife must have been very appealing. One can only speculate on what basis Jason presented Creon's offer to Medea. In all probability it had to do with the politics of the kingdom, the good of the state. Somehow Medea came to accept the proposition, or appeared to.

Creon and Glauce could not be expected to understand Medea's nature. Although her life with Jason had been a happy one, there must have been occasions when she invoked charms and used potions, if for no other reason than to stay in practice. Her father, Aeetes, his sisters Circe and Pasiphae, and his brother Perses all had a reputation for wizardry and enchantment. Medea was especially skilled in the manufacture and use of poisons. Certainly Jason knew her dark capabilities.

So it is astonishing that none of them seemed troubled when Medea gave in so easily to what amounted to a divorce. It is even more puzzling that Glauce would accept a present, a golden crown and a robe, from Medea and wear them on the day of her wedding. The crown and robe were, of course, poison-laden, and Glauce immediately was consumed in flames even though she plunged into a fountain, as was Creon, who tried to extinguish the fire. Jason managed to escape but not soon enough to prevent Medea's murdering some of their children.

The brief story of Glauce does not allow for any particularly good notion of her. It is not difficult to suppose that Creon arranged the marriage between her and Jason at her request, but it is easier to suspect that she did what her father wanted. She was probably vain, hastening to put on the handsome presents Medea sent to her, with perhaps a smug satisfaction in taking the sender's husband, a renowned hero, away from her. [Apollodorus 1.9.28; Diodorus Siculus 4.55; Hyginus, *Fables* 25.]

GLAUCE (6) was a daughter of Cychreus of Salamis, who married Actaeus and became by him the mother of Telamon. Telamon's parents are usually called Aeacus and ENDEIS. According to one account, Telamon married Glauce, the same woman later writers called his mother, and afterward married Periboea, a daughter of Alcathous, by whom he became the father of Ajax. [Apollodorus 3.12.7; Diodorus Siculus 4.72.]

GLAUCE (7) was a daughter of Cycnus, who was slain by the Greeks in the Trojan War, whereupon Glauce became the slave of the Telamonian Ajax. [Dictys Cretensis 2.12.]

GLAUCE (8) was an Amazon (also called HIPPOLYTE or Melanippe), who was accidentally shot by her sister Penthesileia, either while hunting or in the fight that followed Theseus' wedding with Phaedra. [Quintus Smyrnaeus 1.18; Apollodorus, *Epitome* 5.1–2; Lesches, *Little Iliad*, quoted by Pausanias 3.26.7.]

GLAUCIA was the daughter of the Scamander River. Deimachus, a Boeotian and one of Heracles' companions in his war against Troy, fell in love with the lovely woman. Deimachus was unfortunately slain before Glaucia gave birth to their child. She appealed to Heracles, who took her with him to Greece and presented her to Cleon, the father of Deimachus. When the child was born, she named him Scamander, probably out of homesickness for her father. Scamander grew up and obtained in Boeotia a tract of land surrounded by two streams. He named one of them Scamander and the other Glaucia. He married Acidusa and had by her three daughters. The Boeotian fountain Acidusa was named for his wife, and their three daughters were worshipped under the name of "the three Maidens." [Plutarch, *Greek Questions* 41.]

GLAUCIPPE (1), the daughter of Xanthus, was, according to some, the mother of Hecuba. Others called Hecuba's mother Eunoe, Telecleia, or Metope. [Strabo 13.1.48.]

GLAUCIPPE (2) was one of the DANAIDES, daughter of Danaus and Polyxo, and married to Potamon. According to Hyginus, her husband was Niauius. [Apollodorus 2.1.5; Hyginus, *Fables* 170.]

GLAUCONOME was one of the NEREIDES. [Hesiod, *Theogony* 256; Apollodorus 1.2.7.]

GLAUCOPIS, With Gleaming Eyes, was a surname of Athena. As the goddess who made so many inventions necessary and useful in civilized life, she was characterized by various epithets and surnames, expressing the keenness of her sight or the power of her intellect. [Homer, *Iliad* 1.206, *Odyssey* 1.44,156.]

GORGE (1) was one of the daughters of Althaea and Oeneus. Her sisters were Phoebe, Eurydice, Menesto, Erato, Antiope, Hippodameia, and Deianeira. Her glorious brother was Meleager. Gorge grew up with the knowledge that Meleager, the favorite son of Oeneus and Althaea, would dominate the lives of her and her sisters. Her sisters were fawning and somewhat in awe of their brother, who was, according to report, a son of Ares. The sisters accepted this report as they did the one that made Deianeira a daughter of Dionysus. Her other brothers were Toxeus, Thyreus, and Clymenus. When Toxeus was a young man, he had been killed by Oeneus for jumping over a ditch his father was digging. Her other two brothers were nondescript.

Meleager led a charmed life—more than Gorge knew, in fact—since he was indeed invulnerable as long as a certain piece of wood in the possession of Althaea remained unburned. He was the winner in the festival-like boar hunt organized by Oeneus. It must have been an exciting day for Gorge and her sisters when handsome and brave young men came from all over Greece to vie for the honor of being the killer of the monstrous boar.

When Meleager killed his uncles, Althaea's brothers, she threw the wood splinter into the fire, and Meleager died. Althaea killed herself over her rash action against her shining son. All his sisters except Deianeira and Gorge mourned themselves to death and, probably unknown to Gorge, were metamorphosed into guinea hens.

The stony hills and valleys of Calydon must have appeared desperately barren with everyone gone. Though vacuous and childish, her sisters had brought laughter and life to the now grim palace. Meleager and his brothers, busy with the war with the Curetes, had banged in and out of the house with their war gear and bold conversations.

Now Oeneus leaned on her and Deianeira for solace and company. He was not really old, probably no more than 45. More and more he grew closer to Gorge. Deianeira was more or less aloof, probably taking comfort in her belief that she was only partially related to this woebegone family. It was no great shock to Gorge when one night Oeneus came into her bed. She bore a son by him, one most people thought was by his second wife Periboea. This son was Tydeus, who grew up to become one of the principals in the war of the Seven against Thebes. He became also the father of Diomedes, a hero both in the campaign of the Epigoni and in the Trojan War.

No doubt guilt-ridden at what he had done, Oeneus soon married Periboea and found a husband for Gorge—Andraemon, probably a wellborn Aetolian. Some 20 years later when Diomedes freed Oeneus from the sons of his brother Agrius, Diomedes gave the kingdom to Andraemon and Gorge since Oeneus was too old to rule effectively. In spite of her unhappy adolescent years, Gorge was happily married. Andraemon was a fine husband and gave her a stout son, Thoas, who brought glory to Aetolia by going with 40 ships to the Trojan War. Gorge was buried in the same tomb with Andraemon at Amphissa; Andraemon's kingdom apparently expanded to include this Locrian capital. Thoas carried a bronze statue of Athena to Amphissa from Troy. [Antoninus Liberalis 2; Ovid, *Metamorphoses* 8.532; Apollodorus 1.7.10,8.1,3,6; Pausanias 5.3.5, 10.38.3; Homer, *Iliad* 2.406,638.]

GORGE (2) was one of the DANAIDES, daughter of Danaus and either Atlantia or Phoebe, and wife of Hippothous. [Apollodorus 2.1.5.]

GORGO (1) (*See* GORGONS)

GORGO (2) (*See* MEDUSA)

GORGO (3) was the mother by Aegyptus of Periphas, Oeneus, Aegyptus, Menalces, Lampus, and Idmon. Her sons were all murdered by their brides on their wedding night. [Apollodorus 2.1.5.] (*See* DANAIDES.)

GORGO (4) was one of the DOGS of Actaeon. [Hyginus, *Fables* 181.]

GORGONS were the loathsome serpent-haired creatures that Perseus was sent to find. His special assignment was to bring back the head of Medusa, one of the accursed trio.

Originally there was only one Gorgon, it seems, and she was a fearful phantom in Hades. Her head was mounted on the shield of Athena. But the expansive Greeks were not content with one. After all, they conceived of three fates, three furies, and three graces, so it was understandable that one horror multiplied by three was ultra-horrible. They even decided on parents, Phorcys and Ceto, who were in the habit of producing monsters to plague ancient heroes. Others said they were daughters of Typhon and Echidna, also celebrated monster-producers. The Gorgons—Stheino, Euryale, and Medusa—inhabited a remote place. When in doubt about appropriate locales for obnoxious creatures, the ancients said the western ocean, the neighborhood of Nyx, Hyperborea, or Libya. The Gorgons' heads were entwined with serpents so that their hair seemed to be made of snaky locks. They had tusks instead of teeth, and hands of bronze for gripping and tearing. They had wings and could fly. Most of all, their gaze was able to turn anyone to stone who looked directly at them.

A variation on the origin of the hideous trio made Medusa mortal. According to some legends, she had once been a beautiful maiden but was caught having sex with Poseidon in one of Athena's temples, whereupon she was transformed into the famous monster.

Perseus had great difficulty killing her, but he received help from the gods, especially Athena, who still hated Medusa. Perseus accomplished his mission with the help of magic sandals that enabled him to fly, a helmet that made him invisible, a sharp scimitar for the decapitation, a bag to carry the head, and last but not least a mirror in which to look while carrying out the action so he would not run the risk of eye contact with the fearful woman. He accomplished the task, but it is just as well he had not been directed to dispatch all three of the Gorgons, since the other two were immortal. From the stump of Medusa's neck sprang two beings—Pegasus, the winged horse, and Chrysaor, a mysterious warrior with a golden sword, about whom nothing further is recorded. Some say both beings came from the union of Poseidon and Medusa when she was still mortal.

Most accounts related that Medusa's head became the boss of Athena's shield, but some said the head was buried in the agora at Athens. Some also said Athena gave one of the snaky Medusan locks to Heracles, which he kept concealed in an urn. A lock of the monster's hair, while it did not turn people to stone, could throw an entire army into panic, as was the case when Heracles gave the lock to Sterope to protect Tegea.

Diodorus Siculus, one of the Greek writers who specialized in trying to put myths into pseudohistorical context, claimed the Gorgons were a race of savage women who lived in Libya and waged war with the Amazons. They were defeated by them but rose again to oppose Perseus and were finally killed by the ubiquitous Heracles.

Regardless of their ancestors and the explanatory stories that arose, the Gorgons were very real to the superstitious Greeks in pre-Homeric times. They undoubtedly were employed in threats to unruly children. Snakes for hair was an especially effective image in a setting where the bite of a poisonous snake in the days before antidotes was more often than not fatal. [Homer, *Iliad* 5.741, 8.349, 11.36, *Odyssey* 11.633; Euripides, *Ion* 989; Hesiod, *Theogony* 278,287; Aeschylus, *Prometheus* 793,797; Pindar, *Pythian Odes* 12.24; Ovid, *Metamorphoses* 4.792, 5.230; Apollodorus 2.4.2,7.3; Herodotus 2.91; Pausanias 2.21.6, 5.12.2,18.1, 8.47.4; Athenaeus 5.64; Diodorus Siculus 3.55.]

GORGOPHONE (1) must have been named when her father, Perseus, was in a whimsical or nostalgic mood. Naming a baby, especially a female baby, Gorgon-killer would otherwise suggest perversity. Gorgophone was Perseus' daughter by Andromeda, and her brothers and sister were Alcaeus, Sthenelus, Heleius, Mestor, Electryon, and Autochthe, all of them with reasonably normal names for the time.

Happily Gorgophone did not have to live up to her name, but she was certainly the sister and mother of heroes. Her two marriages have presented problems for centuries of genealogists. She was supposedly the first woman ever to remarry after the death of a husband. Ancient writers had a talent for creating variations in family histories, and for modern writers attempting to thread through the confusing possibilities it is often necessary to select a reasonable chronology and follow it. With that in mind, one can accept perhaps the chronology that follows.

Gorgophone's first husband was Perieres, a son of Aeolus and Enarete. By him she had Aphareus, Icarius, and Leucippus. When Perieres died, Gorgophone married Oebalus, son of Cynortas. He had previously had a son, Hippocoon, by the nymph Bateia. Oebalus was called by some a son of Perieres, presumably by an earlier marriage, and this would mean Gorgophone married her stepson. By Oebalus she had Peirene, Arene, and Tyndareus. Some say Icarius was also her son by Oebalus and not by Perieres.

Icarius and Tyndareus came to rule jointly at Sparta but were expelled by their half-brother Hippocoon. Both took refuge in Aetolia, but Tyndareus was later restored to the throne of Sparta by Heracles. Icarius remained in Acarnania and became the father of Penelope. Tyndareus became the father of Clytemnestra, Castor, Timandra, and Philonoe, and foster father of Helen and Polydeuces. Aphareus went to Messenia and was followed by his half-sister Arene, whom he married; their sons were Idas and Lynceus. Leucippus co-ruled in Messenia with Aphareus. His daughters were Arsinoe, Hilaeira, and Phoebe. The sons of Aphareus wanted to marry Hilaeira and Phoebe, but the maidens were stolen by the Dioscuri. This event and a quarrel over cattle provoked the famous battle between the Dioscuri and the Aphareidae, in which Idas, Lynceus, and the mortal Castor were killed.

Gorgophone's brothers Alcaeus and Electryon were both grandparents of Heracles. Sthenelus was father of Eurystheus, taskmaster to Heracles. Mestor was ancestor of the Taphians. Gorgophone's children and grandchildren were prominent in Peloponnesian lore. She probably led a long life, watching events unfold on all sides. Her tomb was shown at Argos in the marketplace. [Apollodorus 1.7.3,9.5, 2.4.1–5, 3.10.3,11.2; Pausanias 2.2.3,21.6–8, 3.1.3,15.7,26.3, 4.2.4; Ovid, *Metamorphoses* 8.306.]

GORGOPHONE (2) was one of the DANAIDES, daughter of Danaus and Elephantis, and married to Proteus. [Apollodorus 2.1.5.]

GORGYRA was the mother of Ascalaphus by Acheron. Some called her Orphne. When Demeter finally persuaded Zeus and Hades to allow Persephone to return to the upper world, permission was granted on the condition that she had not eaten anything during her stay in the lower world. Ascalaphus, whose station is not made clear, was apparently some kind of hanger-on in Hades, his father being one of the infernal rivers and his mother probably an Acherusian or infernal nymph. He revealed that indeed Persephone had nibbled at a pomegranate. This condemned her to part-time residence in the underworld, and it condemned the informer to burial under a huge rock by Demeter. Years later, the rock was removed by Heracles, and the still-vengeful Demeter then changed Ascalaphus into an owl. [Apollodorus 1.5.3, 2.5.12; Ovid, *Metamorphoses* 4.462.]

GRAEAE, the Old Women, were the three daughters of Phorcys and Ceto, and sisters of the Gorgons as well as a few other terrifying creatures. They appear in mythological accounts mainly in the story of Perseus and Medusa, but Io was said to have encountered them on her wanderings. They were born old but became older and older as time went on, so that they had remaining to them only one eye and one tooth, which they took turns in using. The tooth might have been employed in chewing, although a single tooth would be next to useless. The eye was for guarding the Gorgons, when they were home, by sounding an alarm if anything threatening took place. There was certainly no other service the old crones could offer, since two of them were blind at all times. Their names were Pephredo (sometimes written Pemphredo), Deino, and Enyo. One writer listed Perso instead of Deino.

Perseus was directed to seek from them the location of certain nymphs who would outfit him for his encounter with the Gorgons. He found the Graeae, two asleep and one keeping watch. He slipped up on them and when it came time to pass the eye, he intercepted it and left all three blind. They could have sounded an alert at that time but getting their eye back was more important, so they were willing to listen to Perseus' conditions. Perseus needed certain items to help him assail the Gorgons, since two of them were immortal and all three could by their gaze turn one to stone. The Graeae knew the location of the nymphs who could supply the needed implements, and Perseus told the sisters he would not give them their eye unless they revealed the whereabouts of these nymphs. They told him, but he did not return the eye, throwing it instead in Lake Triton. So the career of the Graeae was ended in terms of being at all menacing. Perhaps the single tooth was a comfort to them.

Since several members of the family of Phorcys and Ceto were marine divinities, some have speculated that the Graeae were such, perhaps a collective personification of the white foam, or whitecaps, on the waves of the sea. [Hesiod, *Theogony* 270; Apollodorus 2.4.2; Scholiast on Aeschylus' *Prometheus* 793,794; Hyginus, *Poetic Astronomy* 2.12, *Fables: Preface* 9; Ovid, *Metamorphoses* 4.742,774, 5.230.]

GRATIAE was the Roman name of the CHARITES, or Graces.

GRYNE was an Amazon from whom the Gryneian grove in Asia Minor was believed to have derived its name, for it was said that Apollo had there embraced her. [Servius on Virgil's *Aeneid* 4.345.]

GYMNASIA was one of the HORAE. [Hyginus, *Fables* 183.]

GYRTONE was a daughter of Phlegyas, a son of Ares. He was a king of the Lapithae and succeeded to the government of Orchomenus, which he called Phlegyantis. He was the father of Coronis, who became the mother of Asclepius by Apollo. Outraged at his daughter's lover, he set fire to one of the temples of Apollo and was promptly killed by the god. Unlike her sister, Gyrtone had no great love affair, but the town of Gyrtone on the Peneius River was named for her. [Apollodorus 2.26.4, 3.10.3; Scholiast on Apollonius Rhodius 1.57.]

HAERO was another name for MEROPE, daughter of Oenopion.

HAGNO was an Arcadian nymph who was said to be one of the nurses, with Neda and Theisoa, of the infant Zeus. According to some, Zeus was brought up in the vicinity of Mount Lycaeus. On the mountain was a spring sacred to Hagno. When the country was suffering from drought, a priest of Zeus, after offering prayers and sacrifices, would touch the surface of the spring with an oak branch. Immediately clouds were supposed to form, and rain would come. Hagno was represented at Megalopolis along with Archiroe, Myrtoessa, Anthracia, and Nais, other nurses of Zeus. She was shown carrying a pitcher in one hand and a platter in the other. [Pausanias 8.31.2,38.3,47.2; Callimachus, Hymn to Zeus 38.]

HALCYON (See ALCYONE)

HALIA (1) was one of the NEREIDES. [Homer, Iliad 18.42; Apollodorus 1.2.6.]

HALIA (2) was a sister of the Telchines in Rhodes. The Telchines were mysterious beings who were artisans, magicians, and ministers of Zeus. Poseidon slept with Halia on more than one occasion and produced by her six sons and a daughter, Rhodos. The sons turned out to be impious and malicious, and eventually insulted Aphrodite, who caused them to go mad and gang-rape Halia. Poseidon struck them down and thrust them underground. In despair Halia threw herself into the sea and was thereafter worshipped by the Rhodians under the name of Leucothea as a divine being. [Diodorus Siculus 5.55.]

HALIAE was a name for marine nymphs in general. [Sophocles, Philoctetes 1470; Callimachus, Hymn to Artemis 13.]

HALIMEDE was one of the NEREIDES. [Hesiod, Theogony 255; Apollodorus 1.2.6.]

HALSODYNE, the Sea-Fed or Sea-Born, occurs as a surname of Amphitrite and Thetis. [Homer's Odyssey 4.404, Iliad 20.207.]

HAMADRYADES were virtually the same as DRYADES, but the latter was perhaps a more general term. One legend called them daughters of Oxylus by his sister Hamadryas. We find two women who became Hamadryades—Byblis and Dryope—so being metamorphosed into a Hamadryad, a feat these nymphs seemed able to accomplish in special situations, was apparently an honor and simultaneous conferral of immortality (as long as the tree lived to which the conferee was inextricably bound). [Pausanias 8.4.2; Apollonius Rhodius 2.477; Antoninus Liberalis 30,31,32; Homeric Hymn to Aphrodite 259; Athenaeus 3.78; Stephanus Byzantium, "Dryope"; Ovid, Metamorphoses 9.325.]

HAMADRYAS was the sister of Oxylus, son of Oreius. She lived with her brother as a wife and bore him Carya, Balanos, Craneia, Morea, Aegeiros, Ptelea, Ampelos, and Syke. They were called Hamadryad nymphs, and from them many trees derived their names. [Athenaeus 3.78.]

HAMAMELIDES, nymphs of fruit trees, were more or less a class of DRYADES.

HARMONIA (1), one of the inspired conceptions of some long-forgotten writer, was a tribute to the ability of the Greeks to create an ideal balance. She was the daughter of Love (Aphrodite) and War (Ares). Her brothers were Deimos (Terror) and Phobos (Fear), both mainly thought of in terms of war. Again, as if to balance things, some called Eros and Anteros full brothers as well, but in any case they were half-brothers.

After Cadmus founded Thebes, Zeus gave him Harmonia as a wife. This was a union favored by all the gods and goddesses of Olympus, especially Athena, who was the self-appointed protectress of Cadmus. All the Olympians attended the wedding, and rich presents were given, the most opulent being a necklace of exquisite design studded with precious stones. Fashioned for him by Hephaestus, this was the groom's gift to the bride, along with a handsome peplus, or robe. Some said the necklace was presented to her by Aphrodite or Athena. Some said Cadmus had received it from his sister Europa, who had earlier received it from Zeus, but this would make no sense, since Cadmus never saw Europa again after her abduction. In fact, his fruitless search for her had resulted in his founding Thebes.

This beautiful jewelry, whatever its origin, came with a curse as it was passed from generation to generation. The results of its attraction culminated in the battle of the Seven against Thebes and the subsequent campaign of the Epigoni. Even in Harmonia's possession, its virulence seemed to spread like poison over the family. The children of Harmonia by Cadmus were Autonoe, Ino, Semele, Agave, and Polydorus. While they were small, Harmonia seemed to lead a rather idyllic life. Undeniably immortal herself, she spent time in the company of other immortals such as the Charites (Graces), Hebe (the goddess of youth), the Horae (Seasons), the Muses, Apollo, and her mother Aphrodite. Some even claimed that the Charites were her daughters by Zeus, who was already her grandfather and later would become her son-in-law as well.

The mellow life enjoyed by Harmonia came to an end when her daughters grew up. Ino's husband went insane and tried to kill her, but she leapt into the sea and became a sea divinity. Autonoe married the god Aristaeus, but he left her when their son Actaeon was turned into a stag, then killed and eaten by his hunting dogs. Semele was burned alive when she forced her lover Zeus to appear to her in his full splendor. He managed to save the child she was carrying, which turned out to be Dionysus. This grandchild did not help things when later he converted his aunts to his worship. One day the three of them got drunk and, mistaking him for a wild beast, tore Agave's son, Pentheus, apart with their bare hands. Only Polydorus, the son, turned out reasonably well, if we do not dwell

on the fact that he was the great-grandfather of Oedipus.

Cadmus and Harmonia left Thebes even before the death of Pentheus. Their leaving has never been explained; perhaps the tragedies of the other daughters caused them to go to a remote place. There was a prophecy among the Enchelean people in northern Greece that if Cadmus would lead them against their enemies, the Illyrians, they would be victorious. Cadmus did so, and the prophecy was fulfilled. He and Harmonia then ruled in Illyria. Although grandparents, they produced another son, Illyrius. Afterward, the gods changed them into dragons and transported them to Elysium, or the Isles of the Blessed.

A variation on this account calls Harmonia the daughter of Zeus and Electra, daughter of Atlas. She was therefore sister to Dardanus and Iasion. She and her brothers lived on the island of Samothrace, where they had gone from Arcadia. When Cadmus went there searching for Europa, he fell in love with Harmonia. In this version also, the gods smiled on the marriage and attended the wedding celebration on Samothrace. Then Cadmus took Harmonia to Thebes, and the two stories merged at that point. The second version might have arisen in conjunction with the strong Cabeirian influence in Theban worship (the Cabeiri were the divinities worshipped on the islands of Lemnos and Samothrace). Dardanus and Iasion taught the mysteries in the Aegean and Asia Minor, and it would seem appropriate that Harmonia introduced them on the Greek mainland. [Apollodorus 3.4.2,5.4; Diodorus Siculus 1.68, 4.48; Pindar, *Pythian Odes* 3.94,167; Statius, *Thebaid* 2.266; Euripides, *Bacchanals* 1233, 1350; Ovid, *Metamorphoses* 4.562–602; Pausanias 9.5.1,12.3; Hyginus, *Fables* 6,184,240; Ptolemaeus Hephaestion 1; Apollonius Rhodius 4.517.]

HARMONIA (2), a Naiad, was by some called the mother of the Amazons by Ares. Their mother was most often called OTRERA. [Pherecydes, quoting the scholiast on Apollonius Rhodius 2.992.]

HARMOTHOE (1) was the wife of Pandareos. He was the son of Merops, a native of Lydian (or

Cretan) Miletus—or it could have been Ephesus. He stole the golden dog that Hephaestus gave to Rhea to guard the infant Zeus; it later guarded Zeus' temple at Dicte. Pandareos took it to Tantalus for safekeeping on Mount Sipylus, but when he asked for its return, Tantalus said he had never heard of it. Hermes recovered the dog by force or by stratagem, and Zeus crushed Tantalus under Mount Sipylus. Pandareos and Harmothoe fled to Athens and from there to Sicily, where they perished miserably. [Antoninus Liberalis 11,36; Eustathius on Homer's *Odyssey* 19.518; Pausanias 8.7.3, 10.30.1.]

HARMOTHOE (2) was one of the AMAZONS. [Quintus Smyrnaeus 1.44.]

HARPALE, according to some, was the mother of Cycnus by Poseidon. The mother of Cycnus is usually called CALYCE.

HARPALYCE (1) was a daughter of Harpalycus, king of the Amymnaeans in Thrace. Her mother died when she was a baby, and her father, who would have preferred a son, trained her in masculine pursuits. She lived up to his expectations to the extent that she even saved him once from the Myrmidons. After he died she became a robber and was so adept in eluding pursuers that she could outstrip the horses of those who sought to apprehend her. Finally she was caught in a snare by shepherds, who killed her. [Servius on Virgil's *Aeneid* 1.321; Hyginus, *Fables* 193.]

HARPALYCE (2) was a maiden who pined away and died because the object of her affection, Iphiclus, or Iphis, did not return her love. According to some, he was a son of Phylacus (or Cephalus) and Clymene, daughter of Minyas. He was one of the Argonauts and celebrated for his fleet-footedness. As a young man he was struck with impotence, and it might have been during this time that he rejected Harpalyce. Later he was cured, got married, and fathered children. In commemoration of the fate of Harpalyce, a contest in songs, called Harpalyce, was celebrated by maidens of Phylace. [Athenaeus 14.619.]

HARPALYCE (3) was the daughter of Clymenus and Epicaste. Her father had a passion for her and committed incest with her against her will, probably starting when she was still a child. When she came to marriageable age, he gave her to Alastor, son of Neleus and Chloris, possibly in an effort to remove temptation. But thoughts of her plagued him, and he took her away from Alastor and slept with her again. Harpalyce took her son (and brother) by Clymenus, dismembered him, and served his flesh to her father. When he learned the nature of his dinner, he hanged himself. The gods turned Harpalyce into a bird. [Hyginus, *Fables* 242,246,255; Parthenius, *Love Stories* 13.]

HARPE was the wife of Cleinis, a Babylonian who was a favorite of Apollo and Artemis. Their children were Lycius, Ortygius, Harpasus, and Artemicha. Cleinis was a priest of Apollo, and when he heard that the Hyperboreans sacrificed asses to the god, he decided to imitate them. Apollo was quite displeased and said that only sheep, goats, and heifers were acceptable. Cleinis ceased the practice, but his sons Lycius and Harpasus persisted in sacrificing asses. Apollo was infuriated and caused the sacrificial asses to go mad and attack the family. The gods intervened in time to save them by turning them into birds. This story could pass for early evidence of religious intolerance and some of the risks of denominationalism. [Antoninus Liberalis 20.]

HARPIES, the Snatchers, at first might have personified storm winds, but little by little they assumed a distinct physical identity. Their number grew, one at a time, from Homer, who conceived of only one Harpy (Podarge). By Zephyrus, the west wind, she was the mother of Xanthus and Balius, the swift horses of Achilles. According to Hesiod, there were two, Aello and Ocypete, and they were daughters of Thaumas by the Oceanid Electra and sisters of Iris the rainbow. Initially they were described as fairhaired and winged, surpassing birds and the winds in their speed of flight, which would make them somehow more acceptable as sisters of the resplendent Iris, but later they were conceived as ugly and disgusting creatures, having the heads of young women but the bodies of birds. Their faces were pale, and they had long claws for snatching food or individuals.

As was usual in the case of monsters, different parents came to be assigned to the Harpies. Perhaps Thaumas and Electra were too tame to be considered father and mother of these loathsome beings. Some called them daughters of Pontus, Poseidon, Terra, Typhon, or even Phineus, whom they tortured in the Argonaut story. Not only was their parentage variously recorded but, as time went on, their number increased. Podarge, Aello, and Celaeno were generally named as Harpies, but later writers added Aellopos, Nicothoe, Ocythoe, Ocypode, and Acholoe. Except in the case of Podarge, they did not reproduce, which is just as well, though one account says that one of them was the mother of the famous horse Areion. However, he was almost always called the offspring of Demeter and Poseidon.

The Harpies are principally known for two stories. One involved the daughters of Pandareos. He had sinned against the gods and was accorded his own punishment. His daughters, Clytia and Cameira, were adopted by the gods and given all kinds of favors, but for some reason they were snatched up by the Harpies one day and carried away to some unknown place to be tortured by the Eumenides.

The most famous account of the Harpies was told in conjunction with the Argonaut. The voyagers lost their bearing on their voyage to Colchis and stopped in Thrace to ask directions from Phineus. This Phineus was probably a son of Phoenix, in which case he would have to be quite old to be contemporary with the Argonauts. Phineus, who was a blind seer, had been married to Cleopatra, the sister of the Boreades Zetes and Calais, who were aboard the *Argo*. He had abandoned her for another wife, who caused him to mistreat cruelly his sons by Cleopatra. For this crime he was plagued by two Harpies, Aello(pus) and Ocypete. They were progressively starving him by suddenly swooping down to snatch the food from his table or, when sated, by defecating on his dinner. The Argonauts arrived, and Zetes and Calais were understandably most outraged by Phineus' treatment of their sister and nephews. Some say they blinded him at that time in retaliation for his having blinded his sons, though most accounts say he was

already blind. However, the Boreades were put in the position of becoming Phineus' salvation, since Phineus was apparently the only one who could give the Argonauts the necessary directions to reach their destination.

An ancient oracle had foretold that the Harpies would die at the hands of the sons of Boreas or, failing that, the Boreades themselves would die. So in addition to providing a service for Phineus, Zetes and Calais had their own destiny to consider. Consequently, the next time the evil winged sisters flew through the palace windows, Zetes and Calais sprang into the air in pursuit. The chase was a long one, all the way across northern Greece and across the Ionian Sea. The Harpies finally reached the Strophades Islands, which some writers incorrectly called the Echinades. (The Echinades were formed from alluvial deposits at the mouth of the Achelous River in Acarnania, while the Strophades lay about 55 kilometers south of Zacynthus off Peloponnesus.) Here they fell down from fatigue.

Again there were variations on the story. Some said the Boreades were on the point of killing the monsters but were commanded by Hermes and Iris to set them free. Some said both the Harpies and the Boreades died. Others said the Harpies turned around at these islands—hence the name, the Turning Islands—and flew back to the mainland, where one of them fell from the sky into a river afterward called the Harpys. The remaining one was overtaken and made to promise she would not bother Phineus again.

The persistent theme of immortality enters into these stories. The Harpies, like their sister, Iris, were immortal, so it is questionable that they should have had to flee from the sons of Boreas. Of course, we cannot examine too closely the logic of these accounts, but there should perhaps be a certain consistency even in the illogical. [Homer, *Odyssey* 1.24, 14.371, 20.66,77, *Iliad* 16.149; Hesiod, *Theogony* 267; Apollodorus 1.2.6,9.21; Virgil, *Aeneid* 3.210,216, 6.289; Servius on Virgil's *Aeneid* 3.209; Hyginus, *Fables* 14, *Fables: Preface* 15; Valerius Flaccus 4.428,516; Apollonius Rhodius 2.298; Ovid, *Metamorphoses* 7.4, *Fasti* 6.132.]

HARPINNA (1) was one of the many daughters of Asopus, the Peloponnesian river that flows into the sea near Sicyon. Asopus had a problem with his daughters because they were constantly being kidnapped by amorous gods. Harpinna was no exception, and her abductor was Ares, the god of war.

The son of this union was Oenomaus, who certainly inherited his father's belligerent nature. He was the king of Pisa in Elis, and he married one woman, the Pleiad Sterope, but loved two others, his mother and his daughter. He named the town of Harpinna in Elis for his mother, and also one of his swift mares, a gift from his father. He was sexually attracted to his daughter Hippodameia and caused her many suitors to race with him, the prize being Hippodameia and the penalty decapitation. Harpinna saw quite a mound of skulls built up before Pelops won the race by deception and gained Hippodameia. Oenomaus was either killed in the race or committed suicide. The fate of Harpinna was never disclosed. [Pausanias 5.10.2,22.5, 6.21.6; Apollodorus 3.10.1.]

HARPINNA (2) was one of the mares of Oenomaus. Oenomaus never failed to conquer his daughter's suitors in a chariot race because his chariot was drawn by the wind-begotten mares Psylla and Harpinna, which Ares had given him. They were the best in Greece, even swifter than the north wind. [Lycophron 166.]

HARPYIA was one of the DOGS of Actaeon. [Hyginus, Fables 181.]

HEBE was the goddess of youth. She was the daughter of Zeus and Hera, and sister of Ares, Hephaestus, and Eileithyia. All of Zeus' many illegitimate offspring were, of course, her half-brothers and sisters, such as Artemis, Apollo, Aphrodite, Dionysus, Hermes, and Persephone. As if to earn her keep, Hebe had some routine chores around Olympus. She helped Hera hitch horses to her chariot, she bathed and dressed Ares, and she was the herald of Aphrodite. Her most frequent activity was acting as cupbearer to the other gods, filling their cups with nectar and ministering to their daily needs. But she was not all work. Befitting her role as goddess of youth, she frolicked with the Charites, Harmonia, Aphrodite, and the Muses. All in all, she was the

perfect picture of industrious and fun-loving youth.

When Zeus went off to the Phrygian Troad and abducted the beautiful Ganymede, Hebe was replaced as cupbearer. This substitution infuriated Hera; forced to put up with Zeus' endless affairs with mortal and immortal women, she now had to watch his boy lover pour nectar. But in the timelessness of the gods, it was not long before attention was directed to the newcomer to Olympus—the great Heracles, who became immortal when he immolated himself on Mount Oeta. Even his former enemy Hera welcomed him, and her aversion to Ganymede might have been responsible.

Hebe was given to Heracles as his divine wife, and she bore him two sons, Alexiares and Anicetus. Both Hebe and Heracles were worshipped at Athens, having almost adjacent altars in the Cynosarges just outside the city. Under the name of Ganymeda (!) or Dia, Hebe was worshipped in sacred groves at Sicyon and Phlius. Part of the attention paid to her had to do with her alleged ability to make the old young again. As might be expected, her worship was carried to Rome, where she was called Juventas. [Apollodorus 1.3.1; Homer, *Iliad* 4.2, 5.722,905, *Odyssey* 11.603; Ovid, *Metamorphoses* 9.400; Pausanias 2.13.3; Diodorus Siculus 4.75; Hesiod, *Theogony* 949.]

HECABE (1) was one of the DANAIDES and married to Dryantis. [Hyginus, *Fables* 170.]

HECABE (2) was the proper form of the Romanized HECUBA, which is more commonly used than the Greek name.

HECAERGE (1) was a daughter of Boreas and one of the Hyperborean maidens who introduced the worship of Artemis in Delos. The great event on Delos of the birth of Artemis, even overshadowed as it was by the simultaneous birth of Apollo, should have been sufficient introduction, but there appeared to have been a need for validation from travelers from afar, much in the nature of the Magi in the Christian tradition. The Hyperborean maidens were commemorated in historical times by the custom of Delian brides dedicating a lock of hair to Hecaerge and her companion Upis. [Callimachus, *Hymn to Delos* 292; Pausanias 1.43.4, 5.7.4; Herodotus 4.35; Antoninus Liberalis 13.]

HECAERGE (2), Hitting at a Distance, was a surname of Artemis, describing her attribute of marksmanship. It was also a name given to Aphrodite, who dealt in a different form of marksmanship, at Iulis in Ceos. [Antoninus Liberalis 1,13.]

HECALE, or Hecalene, was an impoverished old woman who offered hospitality to Theseus when he came to find the ferocious Marathonian bull. She went even further and vowed to offer Zeus a sacrifice for the safe return of this very young man, for whom she developed a great tenderness. She died before he completed the job of killing the bull, but Theseus, who called her by the diminutive nickname Hecalene, did not forget her. After he came to power, he decreed that the inhabitants of the Attic tetrapolis should offer sacrifices to her and Zeus Hecaleius. [Plutarch, *Theseus* 14; Callimachus, *Fragments* 40; Ovid, *Remedies of Love* 747.]

HECAMEDE was a maiden of Tenedos and daughter of Arsinous. When Achilles took the island, Hecamede was given to Nestor as a slave. Her ultimate fate is not known. It is not likely that Nestor took her home with him, as many of his companions might have done, since his homecoming and final years have been described as happy ones. It is likely, however, that Hecamede shared his bed at Troy. [Homer, *Iliad* 11.622, 16.6.]

HECATE was perhaps the most complex divinity in Greek mythology, mainly because she represented a blending of a very ancient worship with one practiced in much later times, indeed historical times. She was originally a Thracian divinity, and when the Olympian succession was established, she was conceived as a Titan. Her parentage consequently was more or less assigned, and variously she was called the daughter of Perses and Asteria, or Zeus and Pheraea, daughter of Aeolus. Her parentage has also been linked to both Leto and Tartarus. Some writers, disregarding her reasonably plausible connection with the Titans, suggested Zeus and Demeter or even Zeus and Hera as parents. This last would make no sense, since being a Titan and being respected by the Olympians for the powers achieved by her in an older age would have to be overlooked. Perses and Asteria make far more sense as parents since Perses was related to Aeetes and Circe, two powerful magicians, and magic and sorcery were two of Hecate's most widely acknowledged attributes. She assisted the gods against the giants and killed Clytius single-handedly, thus earning even more esteem among the Olympians.

She was quite powerful and was able to confer wealth, victory, and wisdom on mortals. She brought good luck to sailors and hunters. However, she could withhold these blessings if they were undeserved, so fear became a motivating factor in her worship. Her diverse powers caused her to be identified with Demeter, Rhea, Cybele, and especially Artemis. Her worship also became involved with that of the Cabeiri, and she became a mystic goddess in Samothrace. In Aegina she was identified with Aphaea, the extension of the Cretan Britomartis. Inevitably she became connected with the Eleusinian mysteries. It was she who observed the abduction of Persephone and, torch in hand, accompanied Demeter in her search for her. When Persephone was found, Hecate remained with her as attendant and companion.

From this association with the queen of the underworld, she herself became identified with the infernal regions and had a share in ruling over the souls of the departed. She was invoked in purification rites and could grant expiation. Because of her unearthly aspect she came to be regarded as a kind of queen of witches, high priestess of the occult. At night she sent forth demons and spectral beings to prey on and startle unwary passersby. Her name was most likely used as a warning to unruly children. Her ministers lurked at intersections of roads, at graves, and near spots where blood had been spilled in commission of murders. She herself often wandered with the disembodied, and her approach was signaled by the whining and howling of dogs. She sometimes was accompanied by

Stygian dogs and sometimes a cat. When Galinthias, who helped Alcmena when she was trying to give birth to Heracles, was changed into a cat, Hecate took pity on her and made Galinthias her attendant.

It is hard to visualize Hecate. Typical Greek exaggeration sometimes gave her multiple heads and bodies (usually three), but she was also represented as fairly human in appearance. She was not so repulsive that she did not attract men to her couch, according to some writers. By her uncle Aeetes she was said to be mother of Absyrtus and Medea, but their mother is more usually called Idyia. Also by Aeetes, Hecate was called by some the mother of Circe, but Circe was more often regarded as Aeetes' sister. By Phorcys she was said to be the mother of Scylla, but Scylla's mother was more often called Crateis. Although Phorcys regularly fathered monsters, Scylla was supposed to be an exception and only turned into a monster by Poseidon or Aphrodite. It could be that Hecate remained a virgin, either by choice or because of her appearance. However, if her powers were all they were claimed to be, she was perfectly capable of changing her appearance to suit any lover she might choose.

Besides Samothrace and Aegina, we find her worship at Argos and at Athens, where she had a sanctuary adjacent to the temple of Nice (Nike) on the Acropolis. Small statues of her, called Hecataea, were set up at the entrance of houses to ward off evil. They also appeared at places where two roads met. At the end of each month food was set out at crossroads, where it served not only as an offering to the goddess but as food for the poor. Sacrifices to her consisted of dogs, honey, and black female lambs. Her surnames included Angelos, Brimo, and Chthonia. [Apollodorus 1.2.4,6.2; Apollonius Rhodius 3.478,529,1211, 4.829; Lycophron 77,1175; Tzetzes on Lycophron 1175; Hesiod, *Theogony* 411–452; Pausanias 1.43.1, 2.30.2; Virgil, *Aeneid* 4.609, 6.257; Orphica, *Argonautica* 975; Pseudo-Plutarch, *On Rivers* 5; *Homeric Hymn to Demeter* 25; Ovid, *Heroides* 12.168, *Metamorphoses* 14.405; Diodorus Siculus 4.45; Plutarch, *Roman Questions* 49; Homer, *Odyssey* 1467, 1714,1887; Eustathius on Homer's *Iliad* 1197; Euripides, *Medea* 396.]

HECUBA, or more properly Hecabe, was the daughter of Dymas and the second wife of Priam, king of Troy. She and Helen were the most prominent women in the Trojan War. Each in her way contributed to the cause of the conflict, and most of the principals in the war interacted with one or the other.

Hecuba's parents were never satisfactorily established. Some said her father was the Phrygian king Dymas, the son of Eioneus. Her brothers in that case were Asius, Otreus, and Meges. Her mother's name was thought to be Eunoe, but this was never definitely stated. Others called her a daughter of Cisseus, a king of Thrace. Still others said her father was the Sangarius River. It was always safe to call someone the daughter or son of a river when in doubt. Euagore, Glaucippe, Telecleia, or Metope were also named as her mother. Dymas and Eunoe were the most likely, because Priam had early been associated with the family. He accompanied Otreus on a looting expedition among the Amazons and thus set up one of those comradeships that sometimes resulted in marriage into a family.

Priam was already married to Arisbe and had by her a son, Aesacus, but when he married Hecuba he gave Arisbe to Hyrtacus, a Trojan nobleman and friend. So Hecuba became queen of Troy when Priam inherited the kingdom. She immediately began producing children by him, and not surprisingly the number of children she bore was subject to gross exaggeration. Euripides claimed 50, but even in mythology this is preposterous. A somewhat more realistic figure was 19, but the 14 suggested by Apollodorus seems quite reasonable. In that case, she had ten sons and four daughters.

The daughters were Creusa, Laodice, Polyxena, and Cassandra. The sons were Hector, Paris (called Alexander), Deiphobus, Helenus, Pammon, Polites, Antiphus, Hipponous, Polydorus, and Troilus. Later writers added Polydamas. In the usual fashion, one of her sons, Troilus, was attributed to a secret rendezvous with a god, Apollo in this case. Without too much calculation, it readily can be seen that Hecuba was pregnant most of her life. Only Helenus and Cassandra were twins.

Hector was the eldest son, and Paris was next. When Hecuba was on the point of giving birth to Paris, she dreamed she gave birth to a firebrand that set the whole city on fire. Led by Aesacus, Hecuba's stepson, soothsayers were summoned and conferred about the rather obvious meaning of the dream. They concluded that the child about to be born would bring destruction on the city and that he should be exposed. It is not unlikely Aesacus took a grim satisfaction in this development. Paris was sent with the royal shepherd Agelaus to Mount Ida, where he was left to die. Agelaus returned there five days later to find the child alive, suckled by a bear. Taking this as a sign from heaven, he reared the boy as his own. Paris grew up helping his foster father tend Priam's livestock.

The tragedians were not quite content with that version. Instead, they maintained Priam had been warned that a child born on a certain day would cause the ruin of the city and that he and his mother should be put to death. Paris was born on that day, but so was Munippus, the son of Priam's sister Cilla. Hecuba and Priam kept quiet about the birth of Paris and ordered the execution of Cilla and her baby. For tragic purposes, the blame for the Trojan War could then be assigned to Priam and Hecuba.

Going with the version in which Paris was exposed, though, we see that Hecuba was unaware her second son was still alive. He returned to the city, accompanying a favorite bull selected for a prize at funeral games for the dead son (Paris himself) that had been observed annually for years. Paris competed in the games, hoping to win the bull. He won all events, in which his brothers were the principal contenders. Deiphobus, a poor loser, drew his sword and was about to use it on the handsome stranger. Paris fled to the altar of Zeus, where his sister Cassandra, through her gift of clairvoyance, acknowledged him (even though she had not been born when Paris was exposed). The dire prophecy about the fall of Troy was forgotten as Priam, overjoyed, welcomed him and gave him his proper place in the royal house.

Happy at being reinstated and spoiled by everyone, Paris almost forgot the visit to him while still a shepherd by three stately and beautiful women, who claimed to be goddesses. They were accompanied by a young man who said Paris had been chosen to decide which of the women was the fairest. Each goddess promised him great rewards for his vote, such as power, strength, and wisdom. One of them, quite truly the fairest, offered him the love of the most beautiful woman in the world. He did not hesitate to select the last offer and named Aphrodite the fairest.

Paris found occasion to go to Sparta, for that is where the most beautiful woman lived. Hecuba and Cassandra knew of his intentions and, ever mindful of the old prophecy, begged him to desist, but he ignored them and set out on the fateful mission, accompanied by Aeneas, his brother-in-law and cousin.

Meanwhile, Hecuba's other sons and daughters were growing up, marrying, and producing children. Cassandra and Helenus, the twins, did not marry. As children they had been endowed with the gift of prophecy by sleeping in the temple of Apollo and having their ears licked by serpents. In later years the god tried to seduce Cassandra while she worshipped in his temple; when she refused him he allowed her to retain her gift, but invalidated it by having all her prophecies disbelieved. Hector married Andromache and became by her the father of Astyanax and Laodamas. Creusa married her cousin Aeneas and became by him the mother of Ascanius and Iulus. And so on. Hecuba had many other grandchildren, not to mention the stepchildren fathered by Priam on various concubines, several of whom came freely into the palace. It appears Hecuba regarded Priam's sexual extravagances as a normal exercise of privilege and power by an Asiatic king. Many of Hecuba's grandchildren were, of course, born after the Trojan War began.

And war it was, just as the ancient dire prediction had warned, for Paris came back to Troy with the incredibly beautiful Helen, queen of Sparta, who as a maiden had been courted by dozens of Greek citizens. These princes had taken a vow that they would rally to the defense of the one she finally selected, if anyone should ever dare dishonor the couple in any way. Soon enough the couriers were taking the news to all parts of Greece.

First, though, Hecuba saw the visit of Menelaus, Odysseus, and Acamas, who came to try to recover Helen. The Trojans would not yield her, and Hecuba, who was delighted with her, was as stubborn as the other citizens. It is curious that she was not terrified to see what was happening. But then 20 years had passed, and the prophecy had been made by Aesacus, her stepson. It had later been verified by Cassandra, but nobody believed her ravings. And, if rumors were true that Priam's sister and nephew had been killed on the prescribed day, then the prophecy was canceled. Most of all, she and the rest of the Trojans did not want to believe any evil could come from the elopement of two such beautiful people. How could the city be destroyed by such perfect love? Hecuba was a champion of love. She was not distressed when Acamas, the handsome son of Theseus, and one of the Greek ambassadors, impregnated her daughter Laodice, who later became by him the mother of Munitus.

The war began in earnest, and Hecuba could watch its progress from the lofty walls. Reality began to penetrate as first one son and then another fell before the enemy, followed by deprivation and monotony. After several years, the accustomed scene over the wall could scarcely arouse any excitement. There was only the daily ritual of death and burial on all sides.

The war has been endlessly written about, and there were individual stories about all the members of Hecuba's family. Her most staggering loss during the war was the glorious Hector, and the sight of his body being dragged before the walls of the city must have been devastating. Other sons died one by one. Even the fateful Paris was finally shot down. Only Deiphobus, Polites, Helenus, and Polydorus were left at the end of the war.

After ten years the Greeks took Troy. The remaining male members of the family were killed. Old as he was, Priam was ready to fight to the death, but Hecuba persuaded him to take refuge with her and her daughters as suppliants at the altar of Zeus Herceius. While they huddled together, Polites was pursued into the temple by Neoptolemus. Polites died at the feet of his father, and when Priam rose against Neoptolemus he was killed by him as well. Deiphobus, who had inherited Helen when Paris was killed, was slain and mutilated by Menelaus. Cassandra was torn from the altar of Athena

and raped by Ajax the Lesser. She became the property of Agamemnon when the spoils were distributed.

Hecuba herself fell to Odysseus, perhaps to his dismay, since she was too old to be of much use to him. There was considerable delay at getting away, and Hecuba witnessed three further tragedies in her family. First, Astyanax, her young grandson by Hector, was thrown from the city walls, a final act of brutality to finish off Hector's line once and for all. Then Polyxena, with whom Achilles had fallen in love during the last days of his life, was sacrificed on his grave. Finally, the body of Polydorus washed up on the shore of the plain of Troy near the tents of the captive women. Still a boy at the start of the war, Polydorus had been sent to his half-sister Iliona, who had married Polymestor, king of the Chersonese. Polymestor had received part of the Trojan treasury to be held in trust for Polydorus. When Polymestor saw the way things were going, he decided to appropriate the treasure for himself and killed Polydorus, throwing the body into the sea. Hecuba quickly sent a message to Polymestor, who was unaware of her discovery, telling him she knew where more treasure was hidden and that he should recover it for her son. When Polymestor arrived with his two sons, Hecuba's companions murdered the boys while Hecuba tore out the eyes of Polymestor. Agamemnon pardoned her for this act, probably conceding that Polymestor deserved what he got.

There were several versions relating to Hecuba's death, all of which had her remaining in the area of the Thracian Chersonese (Peninsula). Some said she was stoned to death by the vengeful Greeks for her murder of Polymestor, who had become a collaborator. Others said she was changed into a dog when pursued by Polymestor's companions. Still others said she leapt overboard from Odysseus' ship and was changed into a bitch at a place called Cynosema. In this form she howled through the country for a long time.

Hecuba was one of the truly tragic figures in mythology, for by her own acts she contributed to the destruction of her family, herself, and Troy. Her first act was standing by and allowing Cilla and Munippus to be killed. Understandably she did not want to die, but she might have protested more strongly the sacrifice of her sister-in-law and nephew. If she believed deeply enough in her dream to have Paris exposed, she might have required evidence of his death. Paradoxically, this would have dehumanized her and made her a murderess, regardless of her patriotic motive. It would also have deprived centuries of readers and playgoers the glories of the Trojan War. And, finally, she might have turned her back on Helen and joined those who wanted to deport the superlative beauty. Whatever her degree of guilt, she paid the penalty many times over. Symbolic of her total descent from a noble and favored position was being changed into one of the lowliest of animals, a furtive and whimpering wild dog. [Homer, *Iliad* 2.817, 16.716, 22.234, 24.495; Eustathius on Homer's *Iliad* 1083; Apollodorus 3.12.5,8; Euripides, *Hecuba* 3,40,1050, *Daughters of Troy* 17; Thucydides 8.104; Ovid, *Metamorphoses* 13.423–575; Hyginus, *Fables* 91,111; Hesiod, *Theogony* 344; Virgil, *Aeneid* 7.720; Servius on Virgil's *Aeneid* 3.6,80, 5.535; Cicero, *Tusculan Disputations* 3.26; Dictys Cretensis 2.18,22,27, 3.20, 5.13; Parthenius, *Love Stories* 16; Pausanias 2.24.5, 4.17.3; Quintus Smyrnaeus 13.240; Tzetzes on Lycophron 224,340.]

HEGEMONE (1), the Leader or Ruler, was a surname of Artemis at Sparta and in Arcadia. The name was also used for her at Ambracia (modern Arta) in Thesprotia, where in historical times the tyrant Phalaecus ruled. Once while hunting, he found a lion cub, which Artemis had placed in his path. He picked up the cub, and its mother rushed from her den and tore him to pieces. The people of Ambracia, thus rid of the tyrant, propitiated Artemis Hegemone. [Antoninus Liberalis 4.]

HEGEMONE (2) was one of the Athenian CHARITES. When the Athenian youths took their civic oath, they invoked Hegemone. She was worshipped jointly with Auxo. [Pollux 8.106; Pausanias 9.35.1.]

HEGETORIA was a Rhodian nymph married to Ochimus, son of Helios and Rhodos. Ochimus was the eldest of the Heliadae, the sons of Helios and earliest inhabitants of Rhodes, and he was also king. As in the case of the other Aegean islands, the nymphs were omnipresent and had been there for time out of memory. Hegetoria bore a daughter, Cydippe, or Cyrbia, to Ochimus. This daughter married Cercaphus, the brother of Ochimus, and bore him three sons, Lindus, Ialysus, and Cameirus, who succeeded to the supreme power and founded the three major cities of Rhodes, which they named after themselves. [Diodorus Siculus 5.56,57; Plutarch, *Greek Questions* 27.]

HEIMARMENE was the personification of fate. This highly abstract being was referred to in a more general sense than the more familiar Fates, Clotho, Atropos, and Lachesis. In fact, they were apparently included, along with Tyche, Ananke, Eunomia, Dice, Nemesis, and others, in a kind of collective sense of inevitability called by this name. [Plato, *Phaedrus* 115a.]

HELARA (*See* ELARA)

HELEN (1) of Sparta was perhaps the most inspired character in all literature, ancient or modern. A whole war, one which lasted for ten years, was fought over her. Not only that, nearly all the myths of the heroic age were threaded together in such a way that this most idealized of all wars was the culmination of various exploits, including the Argonaut, the Theban wars, and the Calydonian boar hunt. It is as though this event was in the destiny of every dynasty formed from the beginning of things.

Helen, the face that launched a thousand ships, was a tantalizing enigma from the very first. She was flesh and blood certainly, but she was also immortal, since her father was none other than Zeus. Her mother was the beautiful Leda, queen of Sparta, who was ravished by the father of the gods in the form of a swan. Leda's husband was Tyndareus, who later the same night, unaware of his feathered predecessor, also impregnated his wife. She produced two eggs, one of which yielded Helen and Polydeuces and the other of which contained Castor and Clytemnestra. While a swan's egg can be accepted for the sake of myth, it has never made much sense that the part of her pregnancy initiated by Tyndareus should produce an egg as well. This most curious of births has been subjected to all manner of combinations over the years. As delicious as the story of Leda was, some commentators even went so far as to suggest that Helen and the Dioscuri were conceived at Rhamnus in Attica by Zeus and Nemesis, the usually rather stern and sexless goddess whose job it was to curb excesses. Nemesis, not happy with being raped by a swan, laid an egg and left it. Leda found it, and when the egg hatched it produced Helen and the Dioscuri. In that case, Clytemnestra was not even a sister of Helen.

It is difficult to imagine the childhood of the famous egg-born quartet. Two of them could be injured, perhaps, but not fatally; two had special gifts that made them physically and mentally superior. Apparently there was no jealousy among them. Castor and Polydeuces were so closely attached they swore to die together, even if Polydeuces could not hope to fulfill this resolve. The relationship between Helen and Clytemnestra was not so simple. Helen was stunningly beautiful, and this must have caused Clytemnestra some wistful moments when inevitable comparisons were made.

When the sisters reached puberty, Helen was kidnapped. Both the aging Theseus, king of Athens, and his friend Peirithous, king of Larissa, wanted to have sex with one of Zeus' daughters before they died. Theseus chose Helen, whose remarkable beauty was already talked of far and wide. The abductors took her to Aphidna, a small city north of Athens, and left her in the safekeeping of one of Theseus' vassals. He put his mother, Aethra, with her as a guardian and companion. Inevitably, stories arose that Theseus took her into safekeeping to do Tyndareus a favor. One of Tyndareus' nephews was persistently pursuing her as a suitor, even at her very young age. Another story said the sons of Aphareus, Idas and Lynceus, stole her, which caused the famous fatal battle between them and the Dioscuri. There can be little question that Theseus took Helen's virginity. After all, that was the object of the kidnapping. Some suppose that he planned to keep her intact until she reached marriageable age. But the more realistic writers even gave the couple a child. Interestingly, but improbably, the child was Iphigeneia.

We cannot know how long Helen was at Aphidna. Theseus had accomplished his goal, so he left her and went with Peirithous to Hades to steal Persephone. This was foolhardy as it turned out, for both were imprisoned, Peirithous forever. The Dioscuri meanwhile raised an army and marched on Athens. The Athenians knew nothing of the outrage to their sister, but one Academus had knowledge of the facts and revealed the hiding place. The brothers razed Aphidna and delivered Helen, whom they carried home to Sparta, along with Aethra and Peirithous' sister as personal slaves to their sister.

Clytemnestra married during this time, first to Tantalus, son of Thyestes, and later to Agamemnon, who killed Tantalus. If Helen did bring a baby back from Aphidna, it made good sense for Clytemnestra to adopt it, since Helen was still considered a virgin. If the child was Iphigeneia, some of the drama of sacrifice at Aulis would be diminished, and Clytemnestra's revenge motive would not be as strong. It is probably best to go with the common story that Helen had no child by Theseus and that Iphigeneia was the daughter of Agamemnon and Clytemnestra.

Upon Helen's return to Sparta, an avalanche of suitors started to arrive. It would be interesting to explore the dynamics of this mass courting. Every red-blooded male in Greece who had heard of the gorgeous Helen dreamed of possessing her. But acting on such ambition had a price tag. One had to be able to afford an impressive appearance, complete with attendants, gifts, and other evidence of affluency. It must be pointed out that the suitors were really wooing Tyndareus, not Helen. Their expense was nothing to what the process cost the father. The suitors and their attendants had to be lodged and entertained, and the laws of hospitality probably did not allow for limits on the duration of one's stay.

The roll call of suitors shows that they came from all parts of Greece and represented the finest stock of heroes and heirs to property and wealth. They were Odysseus, son of Laertes; Diomedes, son of Tydeus; Antilochus, son of Nestor; Agapenor, son of Ancaeus; Sthenelus, son of Capaneus; Amphimachus, son of Cteatus; Thalpius, son of Eurytus; Meges, son of Phyleus; Amphilochus, son of Amphiaraus; Menestheus, son of Peteos; Schedius and Epistrophus, sons of Iphitus; Polyxenus, son of Agasthenes; Peneleus, son of Hippalcimus; Leitus, son of Alector; Ajax, son of Oileus; Ascalaphus and Ialmenus, sons of Ares; Elephenor, son of Chalcodon; Eumelus, son of Admetus; Polypoetes, son of Peirithous; Leonteus, son of Coronus; Podaleirius and Machaon, sons of Asclepius; Philoctetes, son of Poeas; Eurypylus, son of Euaemon; Protesilaus and Podarces, sons of Iphiclus; Menelaus, son of Pleisthenes (or Atreus); Ajax and Teucer, sons of Telamon; Patroclus, son of Menoetius; and Idomeneus, son of Deucalion. There were other lists, of course, with considerable variation in the names. In later years it was probably socially advantageous for one to be able to claim an ancestor who had been one of Helen's suitors, in much the way descendants of the Argonauts could probably have filled three ships with their ancestors.

It is interesting to learn that some of the suitors did not appear in person but sent representatives with offers of handsome dowries. Ajax the Greater promised considerable property, some of it not his own but to be acquired if he was chosen. Odysseus took no gifts, not expecting to win. Idomeneus of Crete appeared in person, depending on his extraordinary good looks to overcome the competition. Tyndareus was at a loss as to how to proceed, because he feared reprisal from the unsuccessful. Happy to settle for Tyndareus' niece, the wily Odysseus offered a solution in exchange for Penelope, a match Tyndareus was able to arrange with his brother Icarius. Odysseus suggested that each suitor swear an oath to stand behind whomever Tyndareus selected and be ready at any time in the future to defend the favored bridegroom against any wrong done to him in respect to the marriage. Everyone agreed to these terms, and Tyndareus promptly chose Menelaus, whom he had probably had in mind all along.

It may be important to realize that Helen really had little say-so in this arrangement. Menelaus was a political choice on her father's part. He had wealth and power, mainly through his brother Agamemnon, but for Helen he did not offer the good looks and glamor of some of her other suitors. It was her lot to grace the palace and the kingdom Menelaus soon inherited.

She gave birth to Hermione, Aethiolas, Maraphius, and Pleisthenes, and, according to some, Nicostratus, although many claimed he and Megapenthes were the sons of Menelaus by Pieris, a slave. In that case, we can look at an additional reason for her own infidelity. (She had no way of knowing about another amorous adventure Menelaus was having in Crete during the time he was attending his grandfather's funeral.)

According to some writers, Sparta experienced a plague during the early years of their marriage, and Menelaus was advised by an oracle to go to Troy to observe propitiatory rites at the graves of Lycus and Chimaereus, sons of Prometheus, who were buried there. Menelaus did so and was accompanied on his return by Paris, who had accidentally killed his best friend in an athletic contest and needed purification. The two arrived in Sparta, and during the several days necessary for the purification ceremony, Paris had many opportunities to see the gorgeous woman who had been promised to him. About the time the absolution was completed, Menelaus had to leave unexpectedly for Crete to attend funeral ceremonies for his grandfather Catreus. Ingenuously he left the handsome visitor to be entertained by his wife. Helen had been utterly charmed by the stranger. He was by nature already handsome, but Aphrodite, as if to guarantee the success of her project, had made him even more irresistibly beautiful. In addition, he possessed manners and charm, and it was impossible for Helen not to fall in love with this superb young man. He, of course, had fallen under her spell the instant he laid eyes on her.

Menelaus had not been gone long before the lovers departed. Some say they left the very next night, but some preparation must have been necessary. Paris had his own ship, and certainly he had retainers with him befitting his royal status. Helen required her own attendants, who included Aethra, the mother of Theseus; Thisadie, sister of Peirithous; and Astyanassa, Clymene, and Electra, servants. According to some reports, Paris helped himself to the royal treasury. It does not speak too well for Menelaus' authority that his security forces would have allowed this flagrant plundering. He must have left a considerable army behind when he went to Crete. It is likely Helen had a sufficiently large number of loyal subjects that she could come and go without question. Undoubtedly many of the palace guards were secretly in love with her.

Inevitably there were the stories that sought to make Helen look sinned against rather than sinning. According to these, she was taken by force. One silly version even suggested that Aphrodite deceived her by giving Paris the appearance of Menelaus. It was Aphrodite herself, though, who had pronounced a curse on Tyndareus that his daughters Clytemnestra, Timandra, and Helen would be adulteresses, and she probably did not allow for such an excuse as involuntary adultery.

At Gythium, the port of Sparta, they embarked after Paris dedicated a sanctuary to Aphrodite Migonitis in appreciation for her assistance. They were barely under way before they stopped at the island of Cranae, still within view of Gythium. So far the couple had not been to bed together, even though there was ample opportunity after Menelaus left. Perhaps Paris felt comfortable in robbing the treasury of his host but not further violating the code of hospitality by sleeping with his wife in his own house. For some similar moral reason, Helen may have held him off until they had left the mainland. Or maybe it made good sense to erect the sanctuary at Gythium to Aphrodite, who might otherwise give them trouble at a later time. Paris could have had in mind to make for Onugnathus, farther down the Laconian Gulf and more or less out of immediate range of any pursuers, but biological urgencies probably forced him to cast anchor immediately. The consummation stuns the imagination. What a sublime moment for Paris, who now lay with the most desired woman in the entire world. Undoubtedly his passion was heightened by Aphrodite, who must have considered this her most inspired achievement. As for Helen, there could have been a bittersweet response to the great moment. Until then she had experienced sex with only the aging Theseus and the prosaic Menelaus. This virile young man must have given her bliss she had not imagined, but certainly the shadow of her infidelity and the abandonment of her children must have cast itself across the love couch.

The trip thereafter has been variously described. The temptation to embroider on the already rich tapestry was too strong to resist. The ship went to Egypt and Phoenicia. According to one account, Proteus, king in Egypt, took Helen from Paris and gave him a phantom image of her, restoring the real Helen to Menelaus on his return from Troy. This inane account would then make the Trojan War a total mockery. Another similarly tiresome account had Paris robbing the king of Sidon, who had offered the party hospitality on their way up the coast. Already disgraced in most eyes, Paris would then have been little more than a pirate.

Whatever minor adventures befell them, the company came at last to Troy. The Trojans, even those who had criticized the rashness of Priam's son, could only marvel at the divine beauty who stepped off the ship. A wedding ceremony took place, and it was as though Helen was marrying Troy, since her destiny became at that moment interlocked with the destiny of the city. Even Priam was fully won over and vowed to protect her as long as she wanted to remain.

The lovers had barely left Sparta before couriers were running swiftly to all parts of Greece. The unthinkable had happened. Menelaus came swiftly back from Crete, where his loitering with a nymph had allowed the elopers ample time to outdistance any possible pursuit. Agamemnon was furious. Not only was his family dishonored, but he took the insult almost personally. One suspects he himself was in love with his sister-in-law. Swift action was taken. Menelaus, Odysseus, and, according to some, Acamas, the son of Theseus, went to Troy to demand that Helen be returned. Incidentally, this above all would seem to silence the versions that had Paris and Helen taking months to reach Troy. Though counseled by such advisers as Antenor and Aeneas to surrender Helen, Priam stubbornly held to his promise to her. Moreover, he recalled the reverse situation when his sister Hesione had been kidnapped by Heracles and Telamon, and the Greeks had turned deaf ears to entreaties for her return.

The envoys returned to Greece, and preparations for war began. The former suitors of Helen were reminded of the oath they had sworn. Armies were recruited and ships were built. Men who had been boys when Helen married came forward to enlist in a cause that had become not so much a personal insult as one of national honor.

The *Iliad* described the tenth year of the war, and major and minor writers for years thereafter added parts and pieces, so that a whole epic literature was developed about this singular war. Helen played little part in the *Iliad* and its satellites. The war became bigger than Helen; the *Iliad* is about the wrath of Achilles, not of Menelaus. It is true that one is always aware of Helen behind the towering walls. We learn that by Paris she became the mother of Bunomus, Aganus, Idaeus, and Helen. All the sons were killed when a roof collapsed at the taking of Troy. Menelaus and Paris fought in single combat, but their duel was inconclusive, displaying a lack of resolve on both sides. Helen was glimpsed periodically. Later writers kept trying to give her more presence in the war.

Achilles, for example, saw her one day on the wall and fell in love with her. He called to her to display herself, and she proudly and tantalizingly complied. According to some accounts, Priam's young son Polydorus was stoned to death by the Greeks, and his battered body was sent to Helen with a message to Priam, asking him if he still felt so strongly about not giving up Helen. Odysseus found an audience with Helen, who revealed she was ready to go home. Hecuba observed them in this meeting but did not sound an alarm. She must many times have wanted Helen to leave. According to one story, Helen knew the warriors were in the wooden horse and taunted them by imitating the voices of their wives. Helen also had time for an affair with Paris' son Corythus. The youth's mother, Oenone, had instigated the liaison, but unhappily the young man was killed by his jealous father. When Paris was killed, his brothers Deiphobus and Helenus quarreled for Helen's hand, and the dying Paris designated Deiphobus. Deiphobus had very little time to enjoy his inheritance, for Troy fell shortly after.

On the fall of Troy, Menelaus sought Helen with every intention of killing her. He and Odysseus found her and Deiphobus together, and Menelaus killed and mutilated (it is probably safe to say castrated) Deiphobus. One account says he was assisted by Helen. This would make good dramatic sense, since she obviously was terrified

for her own safety. When Menelaus saw her after all the many years—and she had made certain her bare breasts were revealed—his resolve was shattered, and he simply took Helen with him. They were among the first to leave Troy.

The satellite writers were not content to let the story end there. The body of literature referred to as the Returns included the difficult journey of Menelaus and his crew back to Sparta. It took them about eight years, as preposterous as that sounds. Storms plagued them, and their steersman died. They reached Egypt and roamed for years trying to get back to Sparta. Menelaus finally seized Proteus, the old man of the sea, and made him reveal a means of getting home. Next to Odysseus, Helen and Menelaus were the last of the Greeks to reach their destination.

They arrived on the very day Clytemnestra and Aegisthus were being buried. Ashamed to mourn in public because of her indirect involvement, Helen sent Hermione with locks of her hair to place on Clytemnestra's grave. Even this ostensible act of devotion was reported to be insincere, since vanity prevented her from cutting off more than the barest minimum.

If, as it appears, everything about Helen was anticlimactic after the commencement of the Trojan War, then her final years were even more so. The ingenious Greek and Roman writers and their myriad commentators had trouble finding a way to get rid of her. One writer said Orestes and Pylades killed her as the author of all the ills that had befallen the house of Agamemnon, and that the gods had removed her body. Another had her and Menelaus follow the advice of an oracle and visit Tauris, where Iphigeneia sacrificed them to Artemis. Still another had Helen outlive Menelaus and suffer exile by her bastard stepsons. In this version, she went to live with an old friend, Polyxo, on the island of Rhodes. Polyxo pretended friendship and hospitality but secretly hated Helen, since her own husband had died in the war. Therefore she disguised her servants as Erinyes and had them hang Helen from a tree. From this incident Helen was called Dendritis, Goddess of the Tree, and worshipped under that name by the citizens of Rhodes.

Most accounts, though, had her living out her life in peace, comfort, and prosperity until the gods transported her to Elysium. This was the most fitting end of the story since Helen was, after all, immortal. Consequently, Menelaus could scarcely have carried out his intention of killing her when he was reunited with her at Troy. Immortal or not, her physical remains and those of Menelaus were supposed to be buried at Therapne in a temple dedicated to them. Writers even followed her into the afterworld, where they had her marry Achilles, making him her fifth husband, following Theseus, Menelaus, Paris, and Deiphobus. From there she was even said to have blinded the poet Stesichorus for writing unflattering things about her; she restored his vision when he recanted and composed a poem in her praise.

The most fascinating thing about Helen was her story. It was far better than she was. We do not see any real character development in her and have to regard her as a pawn of the gods. The larger story is involved with the people around her, their rise and fall. She herself seemed almost oblivious to the horrors that surrounded her. She displayed very little emotion and no remorse. She seemed removed and largely unaffected by the outcome of the war. In most accounts of her final years she was not even made to pay for her part in the calamity that touched virtually every family in Greece. It is small wonder some writers contrived alternative versions in which she was made to pay a debt to society. [Apollodorus 3.10.5,6,8,12.6, *Epitome* 1.24, 2.16, 6.29; Hyginus, *Fables* 77,79,81; Pausanias 1.17.6,33.7,41.5, 2.22.7, 3.19.2,9,22.2; Homer, *Iliad* 1.159, 2.589, 3.46,144, 174,351,445, 6.291, 7.470, 11.125, *Odyssey* 4.11,228, 11.469; Eustathius on Homer's *Iliad* 215,521, *Odyssey* 1946; Conon, *Narrations* 18,22,23,34; Parthenius, *Love Stories* 34; Antoninus Liberalis 27; Plutarch, *Theseus* 31; Euripides, *Helen* 33,46,243,584,670, *Daughters of Troy* 939, *Electra* 1280; Callimachus, *Hymn to Artemis* 232; Tryphiodorus, *Sack of Troy* 463–490; Dictys Cretensis, 1.5, 2.18,22.27, 5.5; Lycophron 110,113,132; Tzetzes on Lycophron 57,93,112,143,183,820; Servius on Virgil's *Aeneid* 2.166; Herodotus 2.112–120.]

HELEN (2) was the daughter of Helen and Paris. According to scattered accounts, Helen of Troy bore Paris three sons, Bunomus, Aganus, Idaeus (some added Corythus), and a daughter, Helen. Still infants, the boys died during the sack of Troy when a roof collapsed. Helen was said to have been killed by Hecuba. These tantalizing mentions are very brief, and it is possible they referred to now-lost longer works or were perhaps notes for works that never got written. [Tzetzes on Lycophron 851; Dictys Cretensis 5.5; Ptolemaeus Hephaestion 4.]

HELEN (3) was a daughter of Clytemnestra and Aegisthus. Her brother was Aletes, and her sister was Erigone. It is somehow touching that Clytemnestra would name her daughter for the sister who caused her such grief. But it is more likely that she gave the name as ironic expression to her hatred of Agamemnon, who had every reason to despise the child's namesake. When Orestes killed his mother and stepfather, he also killed little Helen, his half-sister. [Ptolemaeus Hephaestion 4, quoted by Photius, *Library* 479.]

HELEN (4) was a daughter of Epidamnius. She was an attendant of Aphrodite and herself honored as a goddess by the Epidamnians, who believed she provided food for the hungry. Epidamnus, later Dyrrhachium, was a city on the coast of Illyria, and the later Roman inhabitants were debauched and vicious. Their worship of Venus was a typical transition from the earlier Aphrodite. [Ptolemaeus Hephaestion 4; Catullus 34.11.]

HELEN (5) was a daughter of Faustulus, the shepherd who brought up Romulus and Remus. Her mother was Acca Larentia, and she had 12 brothers. Unfortunately nothing beyond this is known of her. [Ptolemaeus Hephaestion 4.]

HELEN (6) was a daughter of Tityrus, an Aetolian. She fought with Achilles and wounded him, but he killed her. This is all we know about her. Undoubtedly this fragment came from a larger work long since lost. [Photius, *Library* 149.]

HELIADAE were the female descendants of Helios, the god of the sun. (The males were called Heliades, although the designations were usually interchangeable.) The name was applied particularly to his children by Rhodos. Rhodos was a daughter of Poseidon by Halia or Amphitrite, and her children were Cercaphus, Actis, Macareus, Tenages, Triopas, Candalus, Ochimus, and Electryone. Confusingly, there were two sets of Heliades, since Helios' children by Clymene were known by this name as well. They were Aegle, Aetheria, Dioxippe, Merope, and Phaethon. We are most familiar with Phaethon, the Shining, a name given to him by his father. He was brother to four of the Heliadae and half-brother to Electryone. His father doted on him, as did his sisters. Phaethon usually got his way, and one day he begged his father to let him drive the chariot of the sun across heaven. Helios said no, but Phaethon kept nagging until he succeeded. His sisters were delighted that their splendid brother would have a chance to show off, and they yoked the horses to the chariot. It was not long before Phaethon realized he had taken on more than he could handle. He was too weak to check the powerful horses, which came down the sky and swung perilously near the earth, nearly setting it on fire. The sisters watched in horror as Zeus struck the boy from the chariot with a flash of lightning. Helios somehow managed to recover the reins and save the world, but Phaethon fell from the sky and drowned in the Eridanus River. His sisters, who felt they had a part in his death, wept so hard that the gods changed them into poplar trees and their tears into amber. As a result of this event, they were also called Phaethontiades. [Apollonius Rhodius 4.598; Lucian, *Dialogues of the Dead* 25; Hyginus, *Fables* 152,154; Virgil, *Eclogues* 6.62, *Aeneid* 10.190; Ovid, *Metamorphoses* 1.755.]

HELICE (1) was a daughter of Lycaon and loved by Zeus, by whom she became the mother of Arcas. She is more commonly called CALLISTO, granddaughter of Lycaon. The versions calling her Helice state that after she was changed into the constellation of the Great Bear, she was able by reason of her vantage point in the heavens to assist Demeter in locating Persephone. [Servius on Virgil's *Aeneid* 1.138; Ovid, *Fasti* 4.580.]

HELICE (2) was a daughter of Selinus, a son of Poseidon and king of Aegialus (later Achaia). Aegialus had been the refuge of Xuthus, a Thessalian, after he had been expelled from Athens by the sons of Erechtheus when, acting as arbitrator, he awarded the head of government to Cecrops. In Aegialus he ruled a colony of settlers from the mainland. The original inhabitants were Pelasgians, or Aegialeans. When Xuthus died, his son Achaeus returned to Thessaly, and his stepson Ion prepared to march against the Aegialeans. Before hostilities were entered, Selinus decided on an unusual tactic. He offered Helice in marriage to Ion. Since Ion accepted, he realized a war against his in-laws might appear ridiculous; besides that, he became at once the heir to the kingdom. When Selinus died, Ion assumed the throne and called the inhabitants Ionians. He built a principal town, which he called Helice after his wife. When Erechtheus died, Ion also became king of Athens, according to Strabo. Helice bore him four sons and a daughter. The four sons gave their names to the four occupational classes of Athens—Geleon, Aegicores, Argades, and Hoples. The daughter, Bura, gave her name to the Achaian town of Bura, near the site of an oracle of Heracles Buraicus. [Pausanias 7.1.2,25.5; Apollodorus 1.7.2; Eustathius on Homer's *Iliad* 292; Strabo 8.7.1.]

HELICE (3) was one of the DANAIDES. She was married to Euideas. [Hyginus, *Fables* 170.]

HELICE (4) was a daughter of Olenus, a descendant of Hephaestus, and sister of Aega. The two sisters are among those said to have brought up Zeus. [Hyginus, *Poetic Astronomy* 2.2,13.]

HELICE (5), a nymph, was the wife of Oenopion in Chios. She was the mother of Thalus, Euanthes, Melas, Salagus, Athamas, and Merope. Nothing is known of her sons except that they migrated with Oenopion and Helice from Crete to Chios. It is likely they were engaged in wine making or cultivation of the vine. Merope, however, was the beloved of the handsome giant Orion, who had come to Chios and fallen in love with the beautiful girl. In his fervor he cleared the island of wild beasts, bringing Merope the spoils of the chase. Oenopion was not totally impressed with the young man and kept deferring any notion of the couple's marriage. As was so often the case, he himself might have been half in love with his daughter or at least highly overprotective. One day Orion, pushed to the limit of his need for Merope, became intoxicated and raped her. For this outrage Oenopion blinded him. Helice observed the usually passive role in these proceedings. Orion left and wandered for a long time in his blinded state but was eventually healed; he returned to take vengeance on Oenopion, who was able to hide and escape. There is no evidence that Orion ever saw Merope again. [Apollodorus 1.4.3; Hyginus, *Poetic Astronomy* 2.34; Parthenius, *Love Stories* 20.]

HELICTA was one of the DANAIDES and married to Cassus. [Hyginus, *Fables* 170.]

HELIOCONIS was one of the THESPIADES. By Heracles she became the mother of Phalais. [Apollodorus 2.7.8.]

HELLE (1) was the daughter of Athamas and Nephele, and sister of Phrixus. Athamas was one of the sons of Aeolus and Enarete. He had been commanded by Hera to marry Nephele. Nephele, which means Cloud, was by some considered to be the phantom created in the form of Hera by Zeus to deceive Ixion, who lusted after Hera. By Nephele Ixion produced the Centaurs. After this multiple foaling, Nephele must have roamed around Olympus in a kind of disembodied state until Hera decided, perhaps out of a misplaced sense of obligation, to have her wed to Athamas. Somehow this was not fair to Athamas, but he nevertheless managed to father by his ethereal wife a son, Phrixus, and a daughter, Helle. It is seldom commented on that the two had Centaurs for brothers.

Athamas meanwhile had fallen in love with Ino, the daughter of Cadmus, who was flesh-and-blood reality. She bore him two sons, Learchus and Melicertes. Discouraged by his greater affection for Ino and his obvious favoritism for Ino's sons, Nephele disappeared. Ino then contrived to get rid of Nephele's children. By sabotaging the grain production she caused a famine, then bribed messengers to bring back from the Delphic oracle a report that Phrixus was causing the scarcity and would have to be sacrificed. A more believable reason for Phrixus' downfall was the charge that he had attempted to seduce Demonice, his uncle Cretheus' wife, when in fact she had attempted to seduce him. When the bewildered adolescent did not respond to her advances, she charged him before her husband, who persuaded his brother to kill his son. Whichever was the case, Phrixus was about to be sacrificed when Nephele sent a ram with golden fleece, which nudged both Phrixus and Helle onto its back and then flew away toward Colchis.

The ram sailed high over the Aegean, but between Sigeium and the Thracian Chersonese, Helle fell into the sea, which was thereafter called the Hellespont. Apparently Helle did not die when she fell into the water; the omnipresent Poseidon seems to have rescued her. Perhaps he converted her into a sea deity, for she became by him the mother of Paeon and Almops. Paeonia and Almopia in Macedonia were named for these sons. Whether she was a mortal or a divinity, Helle's tomb was afterward shown near Pactya on the Hellespont. [Apollodorus 1.9.1; Apollonius Rhodius 927; Ovid, *Fasti* 4.905, *Metamorphoses* 11.195; Hyginus, *Poetic Astronomy* 2.20, *Fables* 3; Stephanus Byzantium, "Almopia."]

HELLE (2) was a daughter of Xuthus, after whom Hellas was named. More often we read that Hellen, her grandfather, was the source of the name.

HELLOTIA (1) was one of the daughters of Timander, the last pre-Dorian king, who fled into the temple of Athena when Corinth was burned by the Dorians. She and her sister Eurytione died in the fire. Not much later a plague began at Corinth, and the oracle declared it should not cease until the souls of the maidens were propitiated. It said also that a sanctuary should be erected to Athena Hellotia. [Scholiast on Pindar's *Olympian Odes* 13.56.]

HELLOTIA (2) was a surname of Athena at Corinth. The name might have been given to her by the Hellotians at Corinth for her assistance to Bellerophon, who built a temple to her. Or it could have been associated with the word for swamp (*helos*), for she had a temple by this name near Marathon. [Pindar, *Olympian Odes* 13.56.]

HELLOTIA (3) was a surname of Europa in Crete, where also a festival, Hellotia, was celebrated to her. There were various explanations for the name, such as its being a Phoenician word for maiden. [Athenaeus 15.678; Stephanus Byzantium, "Gortyn."]

HEMERA (1) was the personification of day. She was the daughter of Erebus and Nyx, who were brother and sister. Her own brother was Aether, by whom she became the mother of Thalassa, the personification of the Mediterranean Sea. In the ancient cosmogonies she was a kind of forerunner of Eos, goddess of the dawn. She is often identified with Eos, even being called by some the mother of Memnon and Phaethon. She was also said to have carried off Cephalus, son of Hermes and Herse, although most accounts name Eos as the one responsible. It is somehow surprising there are so few references to her. [Pausanias 1.3.1, 3.18.7; Hesiod, *Theogony* 123,986; Hyginus, *Fables: Preface* 2; Lucian, *Dialogues of Sailors* 11.]

HEMERA (2) was a nymph and mother by Zeus, according to some, of Iasion. His mother is usually called ELECTRA. [Apollodorus 3.12.1; Servius on Virgil's *Aeneid* 1.384; Hesiod, *Theogony* 970.]

HEMERESIA, the Soothing Goddess, was a surname of Artemis, under which she was worshipped at the spring Lusi in Arcadia. [Pausanias 8.18.3; Callimachus *Hymn to Artemis* 236.]

HEMITHEA (1) was the daughter of Cycnus and Procleia. Cycnus was a son of Poseidon, and Procleia was the daughter of the Trojan king Laomedon. They lived at Colonae in the Troad, where Hemithea and her brother Tenes grew up. After they had reached postadolescence, Procleia died and Cycnus remarried. His new wife was Philonome, and before long she fell in love with

her handsome stepson. She made herself available to him but he retreated. When this happened once too often, she told Cycnus that Tenes had tried to seduce her. Cycnus was enraged; he threw Tenes and Hemithea into a chest and set them adrift in the sea. It is not clear why he included Hemithea; perhaps she had defended her brother and accused Philonome of lying.

The chest floated westward to the island of Leucophrys. Tenes and Hemithea became honored citizens, and the inhabitants eventually made Tenes their king for services rendered to them. He named the island Tenedos. About that time, Cycnus learned the truth about the alleged seduction and went searching for his son and daughter. He located them but Tenes, on learning of his identity, refused to let him land. He even cut the moorings of his father's ship.

When Achilles landed at Tenedos on his way to Troy, Tenes and his subjects hurled stones at the ships, and Tenes was slain by Achilles. Some say he was killed when he tried to stop Achilles from raping Hemithea. Others say Hemithea was swallowed up by the earth when Achilles pursued her. A temple of Tenes was built by the people of Tenedos. Anyone entering the temple was forbidden to mention the name of Achilles, and no flute player could enter, since a flute player named Molpus had been bribed by Philonome to say he had observed Tenes trying to rape her. [Pausanias 10.14.2; Plutarch, *Greek Questions* 28; Diodorus Siculus 5.83.]

HEMITHEA (2) was the deified name of MOLPADIA, daughter of Staphylus.

HENICEA was, according to Hyginus (*Fables* 90), a daughter of Priam. There is no mention of her by any other writer, even under the more likely spelling, Henioche.

HENIOCHE (1) was one of the daughters of Creon of Thebes. Her sister was Pyrrha, and her brother was Haemon. She was present during the tragedies that came to Thebes during the reign of Oedipus and later during the siege of the Seven. She and her sister were not involved in any of the events, according to available literature. However, there was something significant enough about the sisters for statues to be erected to them at the entrance of the temple of the Ismenian Apollo at Thebes. [Pausanias 9.10.3.]

HENIOCHE (2), Charioteer, was a surname of Hera at the oracle of Triphonius in Lebadeia. [Pausanias 9.39.4.]

HENIOCHE (3) was the wife of Creon of Thebes. More often she was called EURYDICE. [Hesiod, *Shield of Heracles* 83.]

HENIOCHE (4) was one of the daughters of Pittheus, thus making her one of the distinguished family of Pelops. She was the sister of Aethra, the mother of Theseus, and grew up in Troezen. She married Canethus (not to be confused with the father of the Argonaut Canthus from Euboea). The son from this marriage was the infamous Sciron. This psychopath lived at the northern end of the Corinthian isthmus and robbed travelers who had to take the rocky pass into Attica. He forced his victims to wash his feet, and while they were doing so he pushed them over the cliff into the sea, where an enormous turtle tore them to pieces. On his way to Athens Theseus was waylaid in the same manner, but made short work of Sciron by throwing him from the cliff known thereafter as the Scironian Rocks. Theseus later returned and founded the Isthmian games as an atonement for the murder of his cousin. Henioche was not heard from again, but through Endeis, her granddaughter, she was the great-great-grandmother of Ajax and Achilles. [Plutarch, *Theseus* 25.]

HENIOCHE (5) was a daughter of Armenius, a descendant of Admetus. She married the Neleid Andropompus and became by him the mother of Melanthus, who as king of Messenia was driven out by the Heracleidae. Melanthus later became king of Athens as a result of overthrowing Xuthus, who had usurped the kingdom from the last of the line of Theseus. During his reign the Ionians were expelled from Achaia and settled in Attica. Henioche's grandson was Codrus, son of Melanthus and king of Athens after his father, who deliberately tricked the invading Peloponnesian Dorians into killing him, since they were warned by an oracle not to kill the king. They withdrew after that. Unable to find a worthy successor to this great hero, the Athenians abandoned a monarchical form of government in favor of rule by archons. [Hellanicus, quoted by the scholiast on Plato 376; Herodotus 5.76; Pausanias 4.5.4,7.2.]

HEPHAESTINE was the mother of Pandion by Aegyptus. Her son was killed by his wife, Callidice, one of the DANAIDES. [Apollodorus 2.1.5.]

HEPTAPORA was, according to some, one of the MUSES. [Arnobius, *Adversus Nationes* 3.37; Tzetzes on Hesiod's *Works and Days* 6.]

HERA, one of the 12 Olympian divinities, was the goddess of marriage and the birth of children.

NATIVITY: Daughter of Cronus and Rhea.

LOVERS: Zeus (husband), Jason (unconsummated).

CHILDREN: Ares, Hebe, Hephaestus, Eileithyia(e), Hecate (?), Charites (?), Eris.

PRINCIPAL SEATS OF WORSHIP: Argos, Mycenae, Sparta, Samos, Corinth, Sicyon, Epidaurus, Heraea, Olympia.

SACRED TO HER: Peacock, immortelle, pomegranate, lily, cuckoo.

COMPANIONS: Hebe, Horae, Charites, Eileithyia(e).

IDENTIFIED WITH: Juno, Ceres, Diana, Proserpina, Daeira.

SURNAMES: Acraea, Aegophagus, Ammonia, Antheia, Argeia, Bunaea, Chera, Gamelia, Henioche, Hippia, Hypercheiria, Imbrasia, Pais, Parthenia, Pelasga, Pharygaea, Prodromia, Samia, Telchinia, Zygia.

Hera was the supreme goddess of the Greeks, finally replacing her predecessors Rhea and Gaea, who shifted to more universal roles on the ascension of their respective daughter and granddaughter. Hera was the daughter of Cronus and Rhea, the eldest according to some, and a twin of Zeus according to others, which would make her the youngest. She was said to have been swallowed by Cronus along with

Demeter, Hestia, Poseidon, and Hades. This, of course, means she would not have been Zeus' twin sister, because he delivered those already swallowed and at a considerably later time, since he had to have time to grow up. An interesting riddle might be whether or not the ingested children continued to mature while they were in their father's stomach. If they did not, then Zeus, though the youngest born, would be the oldest in years of maturity.

This might have been the case. Various beings have been named as Hera's guardians or nurses—Tethys, her aunt; Temenus, the son of Pelasgus; Euboea, Prosymne, and Acraea, the three daughters of the Asterion River; and the Horae. Argos and Samos laid principal claim to being her birthplace, but it is not clear whether Rhea gave birth to her in one of these cities or whether Cronus vomited her up in one of them.

Hera married Zeus. It was her first and only marriage but his third, for he had been married first to Metis, his cousin, and then to Themis, his aunt. A sister was the next expected step. Incest was the norm among the gods, and the evasive problem of immortality might have been the reason, since only by coupling with another divinity could immortality by guaranteed in the offspring. Two or three places claimed to be the scene of the marriage, notably Euboea, Cnossus, and Mount Thornax in Argolis. If a formal ceremony took place on Mount Thornax, it was an anticlimax, since it was there that Zeus changed himself into a cuckoo and, when fondled by Hera, took quick advantage of the situation. Zeus was by that time the supreme being, and by marrying him Hera assumed a corresponding, even if subordinate, role to his.

Hera became by Zeus the mother of Ares, Hebe, and Hephaestus. The children of Cronus established dominions such as heaven, earth, sea, and underworld, while the next generation of Olympians would set up realms of the spirit, such as love, war, youth, wisdom, and artistic achievement. The Eileithyiae, or childbirth divinities (later considered only in the singular) were also daughters of Hera and Zeus. Hecate and the Charites were considered by some as their daughters. Eris was a kind of afterthought in a conception of war, which needed discord as a complement, so she too was called one of their daughters. Since Zeus produced Athena from his head, Hera was said by some to have produced Hephaestus, without impregnation, from her thigh. Later, when Hephaestus had developed his extraordinary genius for craftsmanship, he invented a chair with a manacling device in which he trapped Hera until she revealed to him his beginning. Otherwise, he always took Hera's part, and for doing this once too often was thrown from heaven by Zeus. Hera showed this son little affection, even after for her sake he had become a cripple from the fall.

In fact, we do not see her showing affection to too many of her family. She was not particularly amiable and had a quarreling disposition. Her domestic rows with Zeus and her vendettas against his lovers and illegitimate offspring provide most of what we know of her. Although her principal role was goddess of marriage, her actions made it appear to be a tempestuous and highly uncertain state, one in which jealousy, pettiness, and disharmony seemed routine. Her tantrums were not without provocation, but instead of taking a dignified and philosophical view of Zeus' infidelities, she punished him by her often cruel behavior toward the children he thus produced. The lovers were lucky if they could be changed into bears, heifers, and other beasts to escape her detection.

One can draw up a rather extensive list of the individuals Hera punished because of Zeus' amorous adventures. She punished the nymph Aegina by sending a plague to the whole island of the same name. She had Leto pursued from land to land, island to island, to prevent her from finding a place to give birth to Apollo and Artemis. She set the hundred-eyed Argus to guard the heifer into which Io had been changed, and when Argus was killed she had Io tormented by a gadfly that followed her over three continents. She caused Semele to be burned alive and then brought calamities on Athamas and Ino for helping rear Dionysus, Semele's son. She had Artemis shoot the bear into which Zeus changed Callisto. She kidnapped the children of Lamia, causing her to turn into a compulsive kidnapper.

Her largest-scale punitive project, however, was directed against Heracles. Although quite innocent in the affair between Alcmena and Zeus, he was hounded by Hera his entire life. For that matter, Hera did not take into account that Alcmena herself was innocent, since Zeus slept with her in the assumed appearance of her husband. What probably inspired Hera's vindictiveness most was the fact that Zeus enjoyed the lovemaking with Alcmena so much he caused the night to last for the equivalent of three. Hera also knew Heracles would live to become the most glorious of Greek heroes.

Therefore she pulled out all the stops. With the help of her daughter Eileithyia, who presided over women in labor, she delayed Heracles' birth even longer than necessary since she had already engineered the birth of Eurystheus, holding Zeus to his promise that the first of the race of Perseus born that day would hold dominion. When Galinthias, a faithful friend of Alcmena, broke the birth-delaying spell, Hera turned her into a cat. Heracles became a kind of obbligato in Hera's life. She unwittingly nursed him when Alcmena, out of fear, exposed him. Even with all the impediments she planted in his way, he overcame them. He not only accomplished the 12 labors but managed to do so brilliantly. In spite of Hera's hostility, Heracles was the sort of son she would have loved to have. When he finally was apotheosized and went to Olympus, she gave him her daughter Hebe in marriage and forever after loved him like a son. In fact, she appeared to shower on him the affection she had always denied her own sons Ares and Hephaestus.

Hera was exceedingly vain (the peacock was not her symbol for nothing). Her endless vigilance regarding Zeus' amorous straying was rooted in her own self-image. Whenever a mortal presumed to set her beauty or happiness above Hera's, the result was predictable. Proetus' daughters were said to have been driven mad by her for comparing their beauty with hers. Side, the wife of Orion, was sent immediately to Hades for a similar offense. Gerana, one of the Pygmies, had only to be extremely beautiful to incur the disfavor of the goddess and be changed into a crane. Rhodope and her husband, Haemus, were so happy that they compared their estate with that of Zeus and Hera and were changed into mountains. Alcyone and Ceyx did the same thing and were changed into sea birds. Hera was so anxious about her sexuality, her

desirability to Zeus, she once borrowed the belt from Aphrodite that guaranteed restoration of physical charms of a wife to a husband. She went once a year to the spring of Canathus to renew her virginity. She fell in love with the handsome Jason and assisted him in many ways, only interested, it appears, in his adoration of her.

Consequently, it is no wonder she claimed the famous apple of discord cast by Eris onto the banquet table at the wedding of Peleus and Thetis. The other claimants were Athena and Aphrodite, and one cannot help but think Athena was out of her league, especially in the matter of vanity. Extravagant rewards were offered the bewildered young shepherd for his choice of the fairest of the three goddesses, but Athena's promise of wisdom and Hera's of power could not deter the vote for Aphrodite in exchange for the most beautiful woman on earth. Hera was totally incensed, and only the pledge to Paris of immunity in spite of his choice saved him from instant destruction. But Hera took out her spite on various other individuals in the Trojan conflict. It goes without saying that she championed the Greeks and that the Trojans, no matter how remote from Paris and his fatal judgment, were punished in direct and subtle ways. Hera gave special support to Menelaus and Achilles.

Hera is an enigma when it comes to imagining her. One thinks immediately of a middle-aged matron, someone rather testy and unafraid to speak her mind. She had a great deal of power, but as it was so often confined to domestic situations, one comes to think of it as capricious. Whatever one imagines, it is hard to consider Hera as a sexual being. If it is difficult to imagine the bearded, august Zeus in bed, it is even more so to imagine Hera with him. She was obsessed with sexuality in general, as disclosed in the well-known story regarding Teiresias, the seer of Thebes. Once Zeus and Hera argued about whether a man or a woman derived more pleasure from the sexual act, Hera maintaining that men did, in view of their infidelity and promiscuity. They sought out Teiresias who, having been both a man and a woman, was in a position to know. Without hesitation Teiresias answered that women received many times the pleasure, and for this unsatisfactory answer Hera struck him blind. In spite of her intimidating mien, she was more than once a sexual object. Ixion fell in love with her but unknowingly expended his sperm in a phantom of Hera created by Zeus. By this phantom he became the father of the Centaurs. Endymion was reported to have been sent into his eternal sleep for lusting after her. One of the Aloeidae wanted to take her to bed, but ended up killing his brother and being killed by him. It was not wise to lust after the queen of the gods.

In a way it seems that ancient writers sought to project in Hera a stereotypical shrew, full of insecurities, petty revenges, and even self-elected martyrdom. She represented the battered wife, the coaddictive (sexual addiction in this case), the enabler. She found it perversely satisfying to punish the victims instead of the victimizer. As a supreme ruler she fell miserably short because she failed in the most important responsibility of all, the rule of herself.

The worship of Hera was widespread and intense, in spite of—or maybe because of—her all too human characteristics. She could bestow the gift of prophecy, an attribute considerably revered by the Greeks. She had an oracle near Pagae. She vied with Poseidon for the rule of Argos and was the victor, so that her reverence was confirmed there, even though Poseidon dried up all the rivers in protest. Phoroneus, one of the early kings, founded her worship in Argos, which culminated in the great temple called the Heraion between Argos and Mycenae. Her temple was in effect a small city. Her priestesses included Io, on whom she took special revenge when the young woman slept with Zeus. Another priestess had two sons, Biton and Cleobis, who once pulled their mother's chariot to a festival of Hera. They were rewarded with eternal sleep, as well as immortality in the present-day museum of Delphi, where their statues can be seen. Hippodameia, the wife of Pelops, organized the Heraean games at Olympia in gratitude to Hera. The site of the temple of Hera can be seen today at Olympia. Halesus, who founded Phaleron, taught the mysteries of Hera. In the strange relationship between Hera and Heracles we find that he built shrines to the goddess in Sparta and elsewhere, often in gratitude for her not thwarting him in various enterprises. The

Argonauts founded a temple of Hera at Leucania. [NATIVITY: Homer, *Iliad* 14.20, 16.432; Apollodorus 1.1.5; Pausanias 2.7.1, 13.3, 8.22.2; Plutarch, *Table-Talk* 3; St. Augustine, *City of God* 6.10—CHILDREN: Apollodorus 1.3.1; Hesiod, *Theogony* 921; Homer, *Iliad* 1.585, 5.896, 11.271, 19.118, *Odyssey* 11.604—CHARACTERISTICS: Apollodorus 1.4.3, 9.8; Diodorus Siculus 20.41; Homer, *Iliad* 2.15, 4.21, 24.519—WORSHIP: Homer, *Iliad* 4.51; Apollodorus 1.9.28; Pindar, *Nemean Odes* 10; Aeschylus, *Suppliant Maidens* 297; Herodotus 3.60; Plutarch, *Roman Questions* 74; Pausanias 2.4.7, 3.8, 11.2, 15.5, 17.22, 24.1, 5.15.7, 7.4.4, 8.26.2; Euripides, *Helen* 1097; Servius on Virgil's *Aeneid* 1.51, *Georgics* 1.5.]

HERCYNA (1) was a daughter of Trophonius, son of Erginus, king of Orchomenus. Her father was a famous architect, and attributed to him was the construction of several great buildings, such as one of the temples of Apollo at Delphi and the temple of Poseidon at Mantineia. After his death a celebrated oracle was established in his honor at Lebadeia.

Once Hercyna was playing with Persephone in the grove of Trophonius. She had a pet goose, and it managed to elude her and hide in a cave under a rock. When Persephone pulled the goose from its hiding place, a spring gushed forth. The spring was called Hercyna, and a statue of the maiden was erected on the bank of the stream. In the cave, next to a statue of Trophonius, she was also commemorated with a statue holding a staff entwined with serpents. Hercyna founded the worship of Demeter at Lebadeia. She herself was worshipped there in common with Zeus, and sacrifices were offered to both of them. [Pausanias 9.39.2; Lycophron 153, with the note of Tzetzes; Livy 45.27.]

HERCYNA (2) was a surname of Demeter at Lebadeia, where Hercyna, daughter of Trophonius, founded her worship. [Lycophron 153, with the note of Tzetzes.]

HERMAPHRODITUS qualifies only partially as a woman in mythology. He was originally a young man, son of Hermes and Aphrodite and consequently a great-grandson of Atlas, from whom he was occasionally called Atlantiades. He inherited the beauty of his parents and was brought up by the nymphs of Mount Ida. When he was 15, for some reason he went to Halicarnassus, and one day happened to rest near a spring called Salmacis. The nymph of the spring fell desperately in love with the beautiful youth and tried in vain to win his affection. While he was bathing in the spring, Salmacis embraced him and begged the gods to unite them forever. The gods granted this request, and the youth and the nymph became involved in a single body, which had external sexual organs of both genders. When Hermaphroditus realized what had happened, he prayed that anyone bathing in the spring in the future should be metamorphosed as he was.

Both the prayers of Salmacis and Hermaphroditus seem presumptuous. How were the gods so easily persuaded in the case of Salmacis? Why did she have the right to ruin someone else's life? Hermaphroditus was even worse, since his/her prayer could have affected any unwary passerby. Why did he/she want others to be hermaphrodites? [Ovid, *Metamorphoses* 4.368; Diodorus Siculus 4.6; Lucian, *Dialogues of the Gods* 15.2; Hyginus, *Fables* 271.]

HERMIONA (*See* HARMONIA)

HERMIONE (1), occasionally called Ledaea from her grandmother, was the only daughter of Helen and Menelaus. Her brothers were, according to some writers, Aethiolas, Maraphius, and Pleisthenes, but Homer says she was the only child of Menelaus and Helen. Nicostratus and Megapenthes were her half-brothers by a slave named Pieris. Hermione was only nine years old when Helen eloped with Paris, and she went to live with her aunt Clytemnestra in Mycenae when Menelaus went off to the war.

Hermione inherited much of her mother's beauty, and her cousin Orestes, who grew up with her in the same household, fell in love with her. Even though he was five or six years younger than she, it was taken for granted the two were engaged. In fact, Menelaus had promised his daughter to Orestes before leaving for Troy, it is said, but both must have been preadolescent at the time.

Orestes was spirited away to Phocis to the court of Strophius when he was about 12, and his long stay there of course interrupted any plans of an early marriage to Hermione. Meanwhile, Menelaus also promised her to Neoptolemus while they were together at Troy. Neoptolemus left Troy after the war, taking Andromache, Hector's widow, with him, and went to Epeirus, where he had three sons by her. Later he decided to hold Menelaus to his promise, and went to Sparta. It must be remembered that several years had gone by, since Menelaus and Helen took a long time returning from Troy. Orestes meanwhile had killed his mother and stepfather and was driven mad by the Eumenides. There was a story that Electra held Hermione hostage to protect Orestes against the wrath of the Argives, who wanted to lynch him for the double homicide.

The marriage between Hermione and Neoptolemus took place, and Orestes came back to claim Hermione. He was repulsed by Neoptolemus, who said Orestes was under a curse and unfit for marriage. After a time it developed that Hermione was unable to conceive children by Neoptolemus, and he went to Delphi to inquire of the oracle the reasons. There he was killed by unknown assailants, but the consensus was that Orestes contracted the murder. Orestes took Hermione back to Mycenae from Phthia, where she had lived with Neoptolemus, and married her. By that time the curse had been lifted from him.

Hermione proved fertile after all, for she became by Orestes the mother of Tisamenus. Orestes had a successful reign as king of Sparta and Argos, and we can assume Hermione had some years of pleasure after all the unhappiness she had seen and experienced. Orestes eventually died of a snakebite, and Tisamenus held the throne until he was deposed and slain when the Heracleidae invaded Peloponnesus. A statue of Hermione was dedicated by the Lacedaemonians at Delphi.

Like her mother, Hermione appeared rather passive. She was promised to two different men, probably without any consent on her part. It is easy enough to believe she favored her cousin, for they had known each other all their lives. One rather obscure account had her encouraging Orestes to kill Neoptolemus, since he was able to give Andromache, a mere slave, three sons and her none. This was the only evidence that she fought against forces in her male-dominated world. [Homer, *Iliad* 3.175, 7.470, 10.37, *Odyssey* 3.188, 4.4,5,11–14, 11.469; Scholiast on Homer's *Iliad* 3.175; Euripides, *Andromache* 33,891,1085; Pindar, *Nemean Odes* 7.43; Hyginus, *Fables* 123; Apollodorus 2.8.2,3; Pausanias 1.3.1,33.7, 2.18.5,38.1, 3.25.1,26.5, 7.6.2; Virgil, *Aeneid* 3.327,330, 11.264.]

HERMIONE (2) was a surname of Persephone at Syracuse. [Hesychius, "Hermione."]

HERMIONE (3), wife of Phorbas and sister of Alector, is usually called HYRMINE.

HERMIPPE was the daughter of Boeotus. He was one of the sons of Poseidon and Arne, and the ancestral hero of the Boeotians. Hermippe grew up in Boeotia to become the wife of Orchomenus. Orchomenus presents another all-too-common puzzle. He was called both the father and son of Minyas, the eponymic hero of the Minyans. As father, he was the son of Zeus or Eteocles by Hesione, daughter of Danaus. As son, he briefly held the throne of Orchomenus, gave his name to the city, and died without issue. Hermippe consequently becomes even more obscure, particularly in the second case, in which the claim cannot even be made that she was the mother of the Minyan race. [Pausanias 11.1.1; Scholiast on Apollonius Rhodius 1.135,230; Tzetzes on Lycophron 874.]

HERO (1) was one of the DANAIDES. She was married to Andromachus. [Hyginus, *Fables* 170.]

HERO (2) was a daughter of Priam. That is all we know about her. Hyginus, the source of this information, was enamored of lists, and many of them have the appearance of having been padded. If Hero was a daughter of Priam, she was one of his many illegitimate children. [Hyginus, *Fables* 90.]

HERO (3) was the subject of one of the most beloved legends ever passed down. She was a priestess of Aphrodite at Sestus, a Thracian city on the Hellespont. Across on the Asian side was Abydus, home of Hero's lover, Leander. The strait at this point was less than 2 kilometers wide, and Leander, apparently an athlete in more than one respect, swam across nightly to visit the beautiful Hero. He was guided across the treacherous currents by the lighthouse at Sestus. One night a storm extinguished the light; miscalculating the distance and usual landing place, Leander was swept away by the current and drowned. His body was washed onto the coast of Sestus, and when Hero saw the white, battered corpse she threw herself into the swift-running stream. [Ovid, *Heroides* 18.19; Statius, *Thebaid* 6.535; Virgil, *Georgics* 3.258.]

HEROPHILE was one of the SIBYLS. She resided at Troy, where she was a priestess of the Sminthian Apollo. She was born on Mount Ida, daughter of a nymph and a mortal. Her influence later spread to Erythrae, Clarus, Samos, Delos, Delphi, and finally Italian Cumae. Her grave was in Troy in the temple of Apollo Smintheus. When Hecuba delivered Paris, Herophile and other seers urged Hecuba to kill the child. [Pausanias 10.12.5; Suidas, "Herophila."]

HERSE (1) was one of the wives of Danaus and mother by him of Hippodice and Adiante. [Apollodorus 2.1.5.]

HERSE (2) was one of the three daughters of Cecrops and Agraulos. Her sisters were AGRAULOS and Pandrosos, and she also had a brother, Erysichthon. The sisters lived on the Acropolis; as daughters of the king they had important roles in the celebration of the Panathenaea. Once Hermes went to Athens during this sacred festival and fell in love with Herse. Agraulos was jealous of the liaison. Rumor had it that she already had a son, Ceryx, by Hermes (others said the boy's mother was Pandrosos). She tried to prevent Hermes from entering the house and was turned into stone by the impatient god. The offspring of this union was Cephalus, who grew up to be so beautiful that he was kidnapped by Eos, the goddess of the dawn.

Hermes' spell apparently meant only temporary immobilization, since Agraulos recovered sufficiently to be involved in the fatal incident in which the half-serpent baby Erichthonius was placed in the charge of her and her sisters by Athena. Warned not to look in the covered basket in which he was delivered to them, they did so and promptly went insane, throwing themselves over the cliff.

At Athens, sacrifices were offered to Herse. The maidens who carried the vessels containing the libation were called Arrephoroi. [Pausanias 1.2.5,27.3; Apollodorus 3.24.2,6; Ovid, *Metamorphoses* 2.710.]

HERSE (3), or Ersa, was a daughter of Zeus and Selene, and sister of Pandeia and Nemea. She was said to be the wife of Taus, but nothing about him can be located. [Plutarch, *Table-Talk* 3.10.3; Alcman, *Fragments* 39.]

HERSILIA was the only married woman among the Sabine women who were abducted by the Romans. Her husband Hostilius was killed in the war that broke out over the incident. Later, it seems she married another Hostilius, one of Romulus' followers, and had by him a son, Hostus, thus beginning a noble line. During the war between the Sabines and Romans she served as mediator, having interests on both sides. Through her efforts, peace was brought about.

Another legend had Hersilia becoming the wife of Romulus and bearing to him two children, Prima and Aollius (later called Avilius). When Romulus was deified, becoming the god Quirinus, so was Hersilia. Her name became Hora Quirini. [Gellius 13.22; Ennius, *Annals* 1; St. Augustine, *City of God* 4.16; Livy 1.11; Plutarch, *Romulus* 14,19.]

HESIONE (1) was one of the pivotal individuals in the epic history of ancient Greece because of her role in the first Trojan war, which contributed to the second, greater war. She was one of the daughters of Laomedon, king of Troy, and Strymo. Her brothers were Tithonus, Lampus, Clytius, Hicetaon, Bucolion, and Priam. Her sisters were Cilla and Astyoche, and some writers added Aethylla, Medesicaste, and Procleia.

Her father was not an especially honorable individual. The gods Poseidon and Apollo, because of a treasonable action against Zeus, were required to work for wages for a mortal for a certain period. This servitude was carried out by working for Laomedon in building the walls of Troy. When the task was completed, Laomedon refused to pay them their due, so Poseidon sent a marine monster into the Troad, and the whole region was terrorized by the beast. The Trojans had to sacrifice a maiden periodically in order to keep the monster at bay. They were about to sacrifice one of the daughters of Phoenodamus, a nobleman, but he rebelled and said that Laomedon, who had caused the calamity, should be made to pay with one of his daughters. Thus compelled, Laomedon had Hesione chained to the rock to which the creature usually came.

To Hesione's good fortune, Heracles happened along about that time. He was just returning from one of his labors, the expedition against the Amazons. He was informed of the unhappy state of affairs and promised to deliver Hesione and rid the country of the monster. His price for doing so was the horses Zeus once gave Tros, Laomedon's grandfather, in payment for Ganymede. This agreed, Heracles killed the beast as it was about to devour Hesione. Characteristically, Laomedon refused to pay and backed up his refusal with a small army, knowing that otherwise Heracles would have killed him on the spot.

Heracles continued on his journey, delivered Hippolyte's girdle to Eurystheus, and proceeded to build a small armada of six ships, with which he sailed against Troy. He killed Laomedon and all his sons except for Priam, whom Hesione ransomed with her veil. Heracles gave Hesione to Telamon, his lover, who had accompanied him both on the expedition against the Amazons and on this campaign against Troy.

So Hesione went with Telamon to Salamis. The Trojans, under their new king, protested the abduction. Antenor and Anchises, two of the chief counselors, were sent by Priam to petition the surrender of Hesione, but the entreaty fell on deaf ears. This incident was claimed to be one of the causes of the Trojan War, for it was later cited by Priam when an envoy came to Troy demanding the return of Helen.

Hesione became by Telamon the mother of Teucer. She was desperately unhappy, and during her second pregnancy she fled to Miletus. Arion, the king of the city, found her and her newborn son, Trambelus. He married Hesione and reared Trambelus as his own son. When Achilles came to Miletus on one of his sorties, he killed Trambelus but was most remorseful when he discovered that he was the son of Telamon. Since Hesione was not mentioned in connection with this incident, we can assume she had died by then. [Apollodorus 2.5.9,6.4, 3.10.8,12.3,7; Diodorus Siculus 4.32,42,49; Homer, *Iliad* 5.265,640,649, 6.23, 20.236, 21.441; Scholiast on Homer's *Iliad* 3.250; Dares of Phrygia 4,5; Tzetzes on Lycophron 18,232,467,921; Hyginus, *Fables* 89; Horace, *Odes* 3.3.21; Pindar, *Nemean Odes* 3.65.]

HESIONE (2) was a daughter of Danaus. She does not appear on the usual list of the DANAIDES, but if Danaus was young enough to rule the city of Argos, he was certainly able to father daughters in addition to the ones he arrived with from Egypt. By Zeus or Eteocles she was said to be the mother of Orchomenus, although he is sometimes called the son of Minyas by Phanosura. [Scholiast on Apollonius Rhodius 1.230; Eustathius on Homer's *Iliad* 272; Pausanias 9.36.6.]

HESIONE (3) was the wife of Nauplius and the mother of Palamedes, Oeax, and Nausimedon. Usually the wife of Nauplius was called CLYMENE. [Apollodorus 2.1.5.]

HESIONE (4) was the wife of Prometheus and mother by him of Deucalion. Most writers called Deucalion's mother CLYMENE. [Aeschylus, *Prometheus* 560; Tzetzes on Lycophron 1283; Scholiast on Apollonius Rhodius 2.1086.]

HESPERA, Hesperie, or Hesperia was one of the HESPERIDES.

HESPERIA was the name given by Ovid (*Metamorphoses* 11.769) to ASTEROPE, daughter of the river-god Cebren, who was loved by Aesacus, son of Priam.

HESPERIDES were the guardians of the golden apples Hera received from Gaea at her marriage to Zeus. They were variously called daughters of Nyx, Phorcys and Ceto, Hesperus, Zeus and Themis, or, most often, Atlas and Hesperis. Their number varied as well. In addition to the usual four—Aegle, Erytheia, Hestia, and Arethusa—we find Hespera or Hesperia. They were generally regarded as comely and talented in singing. The location of the famed garden of the Hesperides was also a mystery, just as well since the golden apples were valuable enough to be coveted. For this reason the security system included the dragon Ladon, son of Phorcys and Ceto. The garden was generally thought to be located in the extreme west. To the ancients that meant the western boundary of the Mediterranean. Others placed it as far east as Libya, and some thought it to be far north beyond the land of the Hyperboreans.

The acquisition of the apples was one of Heracles' most difficult assignments, for he had no idea where to find them. He eventually made a bargain with Atlas to fetch them while he took over Atlas' job of carrying the heavens on his shoulders. Atlas brought the apples, but did not want to reassume his burden and had to be tricked by Heracles into doing so.

The garden of the Hesperides and the Hesperides themselves were symbols of the unattainable, perhaps a kind of ever-retreating reward to keep men reaching forward. [Diodorus Siculus 4.26,27; Virgil, *Aeneid* 4.480; Servius on Virgil's *Aeneid* 4.484; Apollonius Rhodius 4.1399,1427,1996; Statius, *Thebaid* 2.281; Hesiod, *Theogony* 215,334,518; Euripides, *Madness of Hercules* 394; Apollodorus 2.5.11; Pliny, *Natural History* 6.31,36.]

HESPERIS was a daughter of Hesperus. He was the brother of Atlas and regarded by many as the personification of the evening star. By Atlas, her uncle, Hesperis was the mother of the HESPERIDES, who were also called Atlantides. [Diodorus Siculus 4.27; Servius on Virgil's *Aeneid* 1.530.]

HESTIA (1) was one of the 12 Olympian gods. She was the goddess of the hearth or, more accurately, the flame burning on the hearth, the center of the household. Consequently, she was also the goddess of domestic life. She was the eldest daughter of Cronus and Rhea, and therefore the first of the children swallowed by Cronus. Like Artemis and Athena, she was a virgin goddess. This circumstance was not from lack of attractiveness to the male sex. Both her brother Poseidon and her nephew Apollo wanted to marry her or at least have sexual intercourse with her, but she swore by the head of Zeus to remain forever a virgin. Once, she nearly lost her virginity when Priapus tried to rape her at a festival.

In her role as goddess of home life she dispensed domestic happiness and blessings, and was said to be the inventor of domestic architecture. She was believed to dwell in the inner part of every house and to preside over all sacrifices. When sacrifices were offered, she was invoked first, and the first part of the sacrifice was offered to her.

Hestia was also worshipped as the goddess of the community of citizens, and the public hearth was usually in the prytaneion of a town. Here the goddess had a special sanctuary under the name of Prytanitis. A statue and constantly burning flame were features of the sanctuary, which the prytanes guarded as part of their office. Suppliants could find asylum at these public hearths, and the state usually received ambassadors and other visitors there. Colonists carried fire from the place they were leaving. If fires were accidentally extinguished, they had to be re-lighted with a burning glass or by friction, and not from another flame.

The idea of a perpetual flame to represent the center of one's ordinary life in home and village took on more universal significance to embrace the notion of centricity in the earth and even the universe. Consequently, Hestia shared some attributes of the goddesses of the earth and underworld, such as Cybele, Gaea, Demeter, Persephone, and Artemis.

The worship of Hestia, while universal in Greece, featured very few special temples, probably because virtually every prytaneion was a sanctuary, in which Hestia was honored with the first portion of sacrifices. She had an altar at Hermione, but it was not even adorned with a statue. Her sacrifices consisted of first fruits,

water, oil, wine, and year-old cows. Her Roman equivalent was Vesta, but their worship differed in several ways.

One can best visualize Hestia as stately but not formidable, pretty but not beautiful, sweet-faced but distant. Her manner would be modest and gentle. Her flowing garments might well conceal voluptuousness, but only the truly lascivious would pursue the thought of the fleshly hills and valleys beneath. Hestia was mentioned very infrequently in stories of the gods and goddesses. She did not join the conspiracy to overthrow Zeus, nor did she take part in disputes or wars such as the battle against the giants or the Trojan War. When Dionysus came to Olympus, she yielded her seat at the high table to him. Of all the Olympians she appeared to be the mildest, most upright, and most charitable. [Hesiod, *Theogony* 453; Apollodorus 1.1.5; *Homeric Hymn to Aphrodite* 22,24,30; Pausanias 2.35.2, 5.14.5,26.2, 10.5.3,11.3; Callimachus, *Hymn to Delos* 325, *Hymn to Demeter* 129; Diodorus Siculus 5.68; Homer, *Odyssey* 14.159; Eustathius on Homer's *Iliad* 735, *Odyssey* 1579; Pindar, *Nemean Odes* 11.1,5,6; Plato, *Cratylus* 401; Dionysius of Halicarnassus, *Roman Antiquities* 2.65; Plutarch, *Numa* 11; Parthenius, *Love Stories* 18.]

HESTIA (2) was one of the HESPERIDES.

HESYCHIA was one of the THESPIADES and mother of Oestrobles by Heracles. [Apollodorus 2.7.8.]

HEURIPPE, Finder of Horses, was a surname of Artemis, under which Odysseus was said to have built her a temple in common with Poseidon Hippius at Pheneus, where at length he found his lost horses. [Pausanias 8.14.4.]

HIERA was, according to some, the wife of Telephus. She was better known by the name of ASTYOCHE.

HIEROMNEME was the daughter of the god of the Simois River. The Simois flowed from Mount Ida and joined the Scamander in the plain of Troy. Simois was also the father of Astyoche, who married Erichthonius, son of

Dardanus, and bore him a son, Tros. Tros, the eponymic hero of Troy, in turn had three sons—Assaracus, Ilus, and Ganymede. Hieromneme married Assaracus, her grandnephew, and this means her marriage took place a minimum of 35 years after that of Astyoche. It also means her sister was her grandmother-in-law.

The son from Hieromneme's marriage was Capys, and he in turn sired Anchises, the lover of Aphrodite and father of Aeneas. Hieromneme therefore had a significant part in the shaping of the events leading to the Trojan War. It will be noticed that river nymphs figured prominently in Trojan genealogy. [Homer, *Iliad* 5.774, 12.22, 20.232,239; Apollodorus 3.12.2; Virgil, *Aeneid* 5.261, 6.768; Diodorus Siculus 4.75.]

HILAEIRA (1) was one of the LEUCIPPIDES.

HILAEIRA (2), the Shining, was a surname of Selene, goddess of the moon. [Hesychius, "Hilaeira."]

HIMALIA was a nymph and mother of Cronius, Spartaeus, and Cytus by Zeus. They were early inhabitants of Rhodes, and they or their offspring survived the flood foreseen by the Telchines. [Diodorus Siculus 5.55.]

HIMANTIS was the mother by Apollo of Mopsus, according to some. The parents of Mopsus were usually called Ampycus and CHLORIS. [Hesiod, *Shield of Heracles* 181; Valerius Flaccus 1.385.]

HIMERA (*See* HEMERA)

HIPPARETE was one of the DANAIDES and married to Protheon. [Hyginus, *Fables* 170.]

HIPPE (1) was a nymph of Mount Tmolus, who nursed Dionysus. [Orphica, *Hymns* 47.4.]

HIPPE (2) was a wife of Theseus. [Hesiod, *Catalogues of Women* 76, quoted by Athenaeus 13.557.]

HIPPE (3) was a daughter of Danaus. She is not mentioned in the lists of Apollodorus and Hyginus. [Hesychius, "Hippeion."]

HIPPE (4) was a daughter of the Centaur Cheiron. Hippe (earlier called Thetis) was seduced on Mount Pelion by Aeolus, son of Hellen. She fled when she was about to give birth but was followed by Cheiron. She beseeched the gods to allow her to bear her child in secret. The gods changed her into a constellation in the shape of a horse. The child's name was Melanippe. Hippe was also called Euippe. [Hyginus, *Poetic Astronomy* 2.18; Eratosthenes, *Star Placements* 18.]

HIPPE (5), or Hippeia, was the wife of Elatus, prince of the Lapiths at Larissa in Thessaly. She had two sons by him, Caeneus and Polyphemus. Caeneus was born a female but prayed successfully to be changed into a male. Some say he was killed by Centaurs, but others claim he was one of the Argonauts. His brother, Polyphemus, was certainly an Argonaut. He was married to Laonome, a sister of his friend Heracles, with whom he traveled on the *Argo*. When Heracles lost his lover Hylas in Mysia, Polyphemus tried to help locate him, so both were left behind and did not complete the journey. After Heracles had gone his own way, Polyphemus founded Cius in Mysia and later fell in battle with the Chalybes.

It is unfortunate that women were given such brief mention in most stories. Surely Hippe's reaction to having a daughter turn into a son must have produced a strong emotional reaction. The son was also reported to exhibit exaggeratedly masculine characteristics, which moved him even further away from Hippe's domestic world. [Hyginus, *Fables* 14; Ovid, *Metamorphoses* 12.497; Homer, *Iliad* 1.264; Scholiast on Apollonius Rhodius 1.40,1241, 4.1470; Virgil, *Fasti* 1.457; Apollodorus 1.9.16,19.]

HIPPIA, Horse Goddess, was a surname of Hera at Olympia, where she had an altar in the Altis. It was also a surname of Athena at Athens, Tegea, and Olympia. Athena Hippia was said to help Bellerophon overcome the Chimaera. [Pausanias 1.30.4,31.3, 5.15.6; Pindar, *Olympian Odes* 13.66.]

HIPPO (1) was one of the THESPIADES and mother by Heracles of Capylus. [Apollodorus 2.7.8]

HIPPO (2) was one of the AMAZONS, one of the queens who helped found the cities of Ephesus, Smyrna, Cyrene, and Myrina. At Ephesus the Amazons set up an image of Artemis under a beech tree, where Hippo offered sacrifices, after which her followers performed a shield dance with rattling quivers, beating the ground in unison to the accompaniment of pipes. The temple of Ephesian Artemis, later built around this image and unrivaled in magnificence even by that of Delphian Apollo, was included among the seven wonders of the ancient world. Some believe Hippo was a shortened form of Hippolyte. [Callimachus, *Hymn to Artemis* 239,266.]

HIPPO (3) was one of the OCEANIDES. [Hesiod, *Theogony* 349.]

HIPPOCRATE was one of the THESPIADES and mother by Heracles of Hippozygus. [Apollodorus 2.7.8.]

HIPPODAMEIA (1) was one of the great names in the literature of the heroic cycles that included Heracles, the Theban wars, and the Trojan War. She was the daughter of Oenomaus and the Pleiad Sterope. The belligerent Oenomaus was the son of Ares and Harpinna, a daughter of the Asopus River. He was king of Pisa, which was about 1 kilometer from Olympia on the Alpheius River.

Hippodameia grew into an exceptionally beautiful woman, and the report of her loveliness reached far and wide. Oenomaus was already a rather joyless man. He had lost his only son, Leucippus, who, falling in love with a nymph, Daphne, disguised himself as a nymph and was killed by Daphne's companions when his sex was discovered. Oenomaus was therefore suspicious of everyone and checked with oracles to learn of his fate and that of Hippodameia. One of the oracles foretold that if his daughter should marry, he would die. Instead of removing Hippodameia from view and discouraging anyone from approaching her, he took a morbid pleasure in showing her off and inviting suitors for her hand. The only catch was that those who presented themselves had to contend with him in a chariot race from Pisa to the altar of

Poseidon on the Corinthian isthmus. The contenders had before them the delectable prize of Hippodameia, but anyone who lost the race would lose his head as well.

Oenomaus let a suitor start and then he took his time making a sacrifice to Zeus Areius. After that, he armed himself and set off in pursuit in his chariot drawn by four swift horses given to him by his father. Myrtilus, his charioteer, guided them over the increasingly familiar route. Needless to say, the suitors did not stand a chance. Oenomaus brought back the chariot and horses of the losers as well as the bodies of the victims, which he buried in a common tomb. It was whispered about that there had been no oracle, that Oenomaus was himself in love with Hippodameia and had devised the race for the pleasure of killing and robbing and of holding on obsessively to something others wanted badly enough to risk death.

In spite of the staggering odds, young men continued to pursue the nearly impossible dream of possessing Hippodameia (and, with her brother Leucippus out of the way, succession to the throne of Pisa). We have the names of some of these suitors but not always their parents or native lands. The first was Marmax, whose mares Parthenia and Eripha were buried with him. After him came Alcathous (son of Porthaon), Euryalus, Eurymachus, Crotalus, Acrias, Capetus, Lycurgus, Lasius, Chalcodon, Tricolonus (descendant of Tricolonus, son of Lycaon), Aristomachus, Prias, Pelagon, Aeolius, Cronius, Erythras (son of Leucon), and Eioneus (son of Magnes). One commentator added a Pelops of Opus, perhaps for dramatic effect, considering the ultimate resolution of the one-sided contests. They were, as stated, buried in a common tomb, and their skulls decorated the facade of Oenomaus' house.

The twentieth suitor was Pelops, a son of Tantalus and Dione. A widely circulated report said he came from Phrygia or Paphlagonia, but he most recently had resided in Arcadia. He arrived in Pisa with a strong determination to win Hippodameia. His resolution was reinforced by two considerations. One was a certain divine assistance, since he had been a lover of Poseidon. The other was the sight of the heads of the conquered stuck above the door of Oenomaus.

He knew he would have to use his head while it was still attached to his body. Consequently, he enlisted the support of Myrtilus, the charioteer of Oenomaus, and some claimed he even promised to let him sleep with Hippodameia when the contest was over. Others said the promise was for half the kingdom. Myrtilus, son of the wily Hermes, probably agreed to the plan, thinking he might get part of the kingdom as well as occasional access to Hippodameia, about whom he constantly fantasized. The plan was for him to tamper with the fastenings on the wheels of Oenomaus' chariot so it would overturn during the race. He must have made sure he would be able to jump clear of the wreckage. Some said Hippodameia desperately wanted Pelops to win the race and helped convince Myrtilus to assist them.

The plan succeeded, and Oenomaus was killed in his fall from the chariot. Before dying he pronounced a curse on Myrtilus, who he realized belatedly was responsible for the wreck. The curse was not long in being effected. Myrtilus expected to be paid for his complicity in the victory but was thrown into the sea by Pelops. The Myrtoan Sea, the alleged site of his drowning, was supposedly named for him, but the sea is far from any place that Myrtilus or Pelops would have had a reason to be. One reason advanced for Pelops' treachery was that Myrtilus tried to force himself on Hippodameia, probably as part of the promised payment. In any case, as Myrtilus drowned he pronounced a curse on Pelops and his house. In effect, then, there was a double curse on the race of Pelops before he ever consummated his marriage.

Very shortly Pelops tried to atone for the murder of Myrtilus by founding the first temple of Hermes in Peloponnesus. He also erected a monument to the unsuccessful suitors and later observed annual sacrifices to them. By that time he had assumed the government of Pisa, and it was not long before he added neighboring kingdoms to his domain. He also restored the Olympic games.

Hippodameia bore him many sons and daughters. In fact, it appears she spent her next 15 or 20 years in childbed and nursery. According to most accounts the children were Atreus, Thyestes, Dias, Cynosurus, Corinthus, Hippalmus (also called Hippalcmus or Hip-

palcimus), Hippasus, Cleon, Argeius, Alcathous, Aelius, Pittheus, Troezen, Nicippe, Astydameia, and Lysidice. Some also added Sciron and Epidaurus.

Not satisfied with a perpetually pregnant wife, Pelops had affairs on the side, and one of these resulted in a son, Chrysippus, by the nymph Axioche. Hippodameia was obliged to rear him along with her increasingly large brood. She did so grudgingly since Chrysippus was Pelops' favorite. She probably felt vindicated when Laius of Thebes lured the boy away and took him home with him. Outraged, Pelops went to Thebes and recovered his son. At that point Hippodameia plotted to get rid of Chrysippus. She induced Atreus and Thyestes to kill him, probably playing on the homophobia they had perhaps already demonstrated in taunting their half-brother not only for being a bastard but also for being the plaything of a pederastic king. They hid his body in a well, but their deed was discovered and they had to flee, accompanied by Hippodameia, who feared for her life. Pelops did not stop until he had expelled all his sons, who dispersed all over Peloponnesus. Rumors persisted, probably started by the guilty parties, that Chrysippus had killed himself in shame. Thus part of the curse of Myrtilus was fulfilled.

Hippodameia went with Atreus and Thyestes to Mycenae to the court of Sthenelus, who had married Nicippe, daughter of Pelops and Hippodameia. He gave them the small dependent city of Midea. From there Atreus and Thyestes later vied for the government of Mycenae, and there Hippodameia ended her days, most say by her own hand. Later, an oracle commanded Pelops to bring her bones back to Olympia, where they were buried in a sanctuary to her in the Altis, or sacred grove. Only women had access to the shrine. A bronze statue of her was also placed at one of the turns of the racecourse.

Hippodameia is especially interesting because of her active participation in what happened to her. Her father was preventing her from marriage, so she helped plan for his overthrow. She persuaded her sons to dispose of her stepson, then went to another place to protect them and herself. While her actions were not exactly commendable and certainly not wise in the second case, at least she was not content to sit by and accept her lot in life without resorting to efforts to change things. Her offspring, even though under a curse, were among the greatest names in the two generations before the Trojan War. [Apollodorus 2.4.5, 3.5.5,10.1; Pausanias 5.10.2,14.5,15.5,20.3,22.5, 6.20.10,21.3–7; Hyginus, *Fables* 84,85,253,271; Diodorus Siculus 4.73; Tzetzes on Lycophron 156; Scholiast on Euripides' *Orestes* 5.]

HIPPODAMEIA (2) was the eldest daughter of Anchises and Eriopis, and the favorite of her parents. She grew up in a famous household. Her father had been the lover of Aphrodite, and Hippodameia had two half-brothers from that union, Aeneas and Lyrus (or Lyrnus). Hippodameia was accustomed to handsome men; her father, though lamed by Aphrodite for bragging of his affair with her, was still stunningly handsome. Her half-brothers were also well above average in this respect. It is not surprising she sought someone similarly endowed when she reached marriageable age. She did not have to look far. Her half-brother Aeneas had been educated in the house of Aesyetes along with Alcathous, the son of Aesyetes. Alcathous, later called one of the handsomest among the Trojans, must have met Hippodameia's standards, for she married him. Their marriage was not very old when the Greeks landed. Alcathous was one of the bravest among the Trojans, but he was no match for the god Poseidon, who blinded and paralyzed him so that Idomeneus could deal him a death blow. It would be interesting to know how Hippodameia fared after the fall of Troy. It must not be forgotten that the Greeks came in many ships, and that all of them carried spoils home. This was probably the fate of the beautiful daughter of Anchises. There is no record that she escaped with Aeneas, Ascanius, and Anchises. [Homer, *Iliad* 12.93, 13.427–433, 20.208; Scholiast on Homer's *Iliad* 13.429; Apollodorus 3.13.2.]

HIPPODAMEIA (3), commonly called Briseis from her father Briseus, was the maiden captured by Achilles when he plundered Lyrnessus during the tenth year of the Trojan War. She was the reason for the celebrated quarrel between Achilles and Agamemnon.

When Agamemnon was obliged to give up his lovely prisoner Chyseis to her father, he threatened to take Briseis away from Achilles. Athena persuaded Achilles to let him have her, which Achilles did, but he promptly shut himself up in his tent and refused to have anything further to do with the war. As a result the Greeks began suffering defeats, and finally Agamemnon sent a mission to Achilles, promising him the return of Briseis and a handsome reward. Achilles remained obstinate. Only when Patroclus, Achilles' friend and (most probably) lover, borrowed Achilles' armor, reentered the battle (he had stayed with Achilles in the tent up until then), and was killed did Achilles emerge from his tent and rejoin the conflict. Briseis was returned to him inviolate, according to Agamemnon, who claimed he had taken her in the first place out of anger rather than lust. Achilles went on from one glorious victory to another, not the least of which was the slaying of Hector. He himself was killed by Paris later on.

One wonders how Briseis managed to endure these events. She had been married to Mynes, a son of Euenus of Lyrnessus. When Achilles took the town, he killed Mynes. The couple had probably been married only a short time, and there were so far no children. She came into a scene of violence, a world of men at war. She had to share Achilles' tent with Patroclus, and privacy for ordinary physical needs must have been nearly impossible. Escape was out of the question. Just when she might have made some adjustment to her lamentable situation, Agamemnon took her away. And finally she was returned to Achilles. Agamemnon's claim that he had not slept with her most certainly went uncontested by her, since in that atmosphere of violence her life was worth little more than her body. She had been passed back and forth like a piece of merchandise at a bazaar.

We can only guess at her ultimate fate. Undoubtedly she was given to one of Achilles' comrades-at-arms just as his armor had been. It is rather surprising we do not have a play that followed her after the fall of Troy. [Homer, *Iliad* 1.184, 2.689,692, 9.119, 19.291; Scholiast on Homer's *Iliad* 1.184; Eustathius on Homer's *Iliad* 322; Dictys Cretensis 2.17.]

HIPPODAMEIA (4) was a daughter of Atrax and sister of Caenis. Atrax was a son of the Peneius River and Bura, and the town of Atrax in Histiaeotis was named for him. Hippodameia was quite a bit younger than her sister, Caenis. She did not have this sister long, since at Caenis' own request she was changed by Poseidon into a man and became Caeneus.

Hippodameia, occasionally called Deidameia, became the wife of the hero Peirithous, the famous friend of Theseus. Peirithous governed the Centaurs, who were half-brothers to him via their common father, Ixion. The Centaurs wanted a share in their father's kingdom, which was a stronghold of the tribe of the Lapithae, and skirmishes arose between the two family branches. With difficulty Peirithous was able to keep the situation under control.

When he married Hippodameia, he invited these relatives to the ceremony and festivities. Things went well at first, but the Centaurs had no head for wine and became first rowdy and then sexually frenzied. Eurytion, one of the Centaurs, tried to rape Hippodameia, and others straddled women and boys. Theseus, a guest of honor, and Peirithous cut off Eurytion's ears and nose, and several individuals on both sides were killed or injured. Caeneus, Hippodameia's brother (former sister), was killed in the fight that lasted until nightfall. As a result of this insurrection, the Centaurs were expelled and settled in Malea.

Hippodameia bore a son to Peirithous. He was Polypoetes, who later commanded the men of Argissa, Gyrtone, Orthe, Elone, and Oloosson in the Trojan War. After the fall of Troy he and his cousin Leonteus (grandson of Caeneus) founded the town of Aspendus in Pamphylia.

Hippodameia became a kind of widow after many years of marriage to Peirithous. He and Theseus had vowed to have sons by daughters of Zeus, so they successfully kidnapped Helen of Sparta and then went to Hades to try to capture Persephone. They were trapped by the infernal gods and put through tortures. Theseus was eventually released by Heracles, but Peirithous ended his days imprisoned in the lower world. He was later worshipped at Athens as a hero along with Theseus. [Stephanus Byzantium, "Atrax"; Antoninus Liberalis 17; Ovid, Meta-

morphoses 12.190,210,224; Plutarch, Theseus 30; Homer, Odyssey 11.630, 21.295, Iliad 1.263, 12.128,181; Eustathius on Homer's Iliad 334; Diodorus Siculus 4.70; Pausanias 1.7.2,30.4, 5.10.8, 10.29.2; Apollodorus 1.8.2, Epitome 1.21.]

HIPPODAMEIA (5) was, according to some, the wife of Amyntor and mother of Phoenix. Usually the wife of Amyntor was called CLEOBULE. [Homer, Iliad 9.450; Eustathius on Homer's Iliad 762.]

HIPPODAMEIA (6) was the wife of Autonous, by whom she was the mother of Anthus. Anthus was torn to pieces by his father's horses and changed into a bird that imitated the neighing of a horse but always fled from the sight of one. [Antoninus Liberalis 7; Pliny, Natural History 10.57.]

HIPPODAMEIA (7) was the name of two of the DANAIDES, daughters of Danaus, one by Atlantia and the other by Phoebe. One married Diocorystes and the other Istrus, sons of Aegyptus. [Apollodorus 2.1.5.]

HIPPODAMEIA (8) was one of the MELEAGRIDES. [Eustathius on Homer's Iliad 774.]

HIPPODAMEIA (9) was a maidservant of Penelope. When her mistress showed herself a last time to the suitors, she asked Hippodameia and Autonoe to stand with her, since she did not want to face the unwelcome guests alone. [Homer, Odyssey 18.182.]

HIPPODAMEIA (10) was one of the companions of Theseus on his return from Crete. [Corpus Inscriptionum Graecorum 8185b.]

HIPPODAMEIA (11) was the wife of Diomedes, the king of the Bistones in Thrace. Her husband owned flesh-eating mares, which Heracles in one of his labors was supposed to deliver to Eurystheus in Mycenae. This he did, but at the cost of his lover Abderus, who was eaten by the mares. In revenge Heracles fed Diomedes to the mares. One can only believe that Hippodameia was relieved to be rid of such a ruthless and bloodthirsty husband, but on the other hand she might have been an enthusiastic horsewoman, as her name (Horse-Tamer) suggests. She was called Cyrene by some writers. [*Etymologicum Magnum* 480.]

HIPPODAMEIA (12) was a surname of Aphrodite. [Hesychius, "Hippodameia."]

HIPPODICE was one of the DANAIDES, daughter of Danaus and Herse, and sister of Adiante. She was married to Idas, son of Aegyptus. [Apollodorus 2.1.5.]

HIPPOLAITIS was a surname of Athena at Hippola in Laconia. Hippola was located a little northwest of the promontory of Taenarum and contained a temple of Athena Hippolaitis. [Pausanias 3.25.9.]

HIPPOLYTE (1), queen of the AMAZONS, has for centuries presented problems to mythographers. Part of the problem has been her name, which turned up in various accounts regardless of inconsistencies in time and place. The name might have been a dynastic name like Minos.

The Hippolyte most of us know was the owner of the famous girdle that was the object of Heracles' ninth labor. She was a daughter of Ares and Otrera, and her sisters were Antiope and Melanippe. She was queen of the Amazons, but it appears her sisters also shared in the government. Hippolyte, however, was the supreme ruler by virtue of the girdle, the emblem of dignity she had been given by Ares. The city in which she ruled was Themiscyra on the Thermodon River.

Admete, the daughter of Eurystheus, had somehow heard of this royal belt and wanted to own it, so its acquisition became one of the labors of Heracles. With the exception of the cattle of Geryones and the apples of the Hesperides, this labor took him the greatest distance, unless one can say how far Hades was. Themiscyra was on the southern coast of the Euxine Sea on the way to Colchis.

Heracles arrived unexpectedly, and although men were *personae non gratae* at Themiscyra, he was hospitably received by Hippolyte. The Amazons were impressed with strength, and Heracles almost symbolized that attribute. Although Amazon mating was rather well regulated and seasonally observed, Hippolyte had the authority to

break the rules when the need or opportunity arose. She was attracted to the muscular hero and, upon learning of the object of his mission, even promised him the girdle as a love gift.

Hera, omnipresent nemesis of Heracles' fortunes, was ready, though, to upset these plans. She disguised herself as an Amazon and spread the report that the queen had been robbed by the stranger. The Amazons promptly rose to Hippolyte's assistance. Believing she had plotted against him from the very beginning, Heracles killed her, took the girdle, and departed.

The story might have ended there, but some writers presented a variation and others an entirely separate story. Some said Theseus accompanied Heracles on his quest and that Heracles gave him Antiope as a reward for his valor. Others said Theseus went alone at a later date to the land of the Amazons and was kindly received by Antiope. He abducted her and thus launched the attack of the Amazons on Athens.

In the second account, Hippolyte is not mentioned, so it is not certain whether or not she was assumed dead. One writer said that in the fourth year of the war, peace was brought about by Hippolyte. He called her the wife of Theseus instead of Antiope. So did Euripides, who made her the mother of Hippolytus.

Another tradition had Hippolyte leading the march of the Amazons into Attica (and into Peloponnesus as well). The invaders were conquered by Theseus, and Hippolyte fled to Megara, where she died in grief and was buried. Her tomb was shown there in later times and was distinctive because it was shaped like an Amazon's shield.

So the various accounts are conflicting. This is not surprising, since all the reports of this curious race were shrouded in mystery. A reasonable chronology might be the visit of Heracles, who would receive the girdle but depart peacefully. After him would come Theseus, who would abduct Antiope and be pursued by the Amazons, led by Hippolyte. After that, the Amazons would be defeated and Hippolyte would die in Megara. [Hyginus, *Fables* 30; Pausanias 1.41.7; Plutarch, *Theseus* 26,27; Apollodorus 2.5.9; Apollonius Rhodius 2.968; Scholiast on Aristophanes' *Frogs* 873; Tzetzes on Lycophron 449,1329,1332; Euripides, *Hippolytus*.]

HIPPOLYTE (2), daughter of Cretheus and Tyro, was the wife of Acastus, according to some. His wife was usually called ASTYDAMEIA. [Apollodorus 3.13.3; Pindar, *Nemean Odes* 4.57, 5.26.]

HIPPOLYTE (3) was, according to some, the daughter of Dexamenus. She was also called DEIANEIRA. [Diodorus Siculus 4.33.]

HIPPOLYTE (4) was the wife of Iphitus, son of Naubolus. He was from Phocis and one of the Argonauts, but had no further distinction. He and Hippolyte were parents of Schedius, Epistrophus, and Eurynome. The two sons commanded the Phocians in the Trojan War, leaving Greece in 40 ships. Epistrophus seems to have survived the war, but Schedius was killed by Hector. His remains were carried from Troy to Anticyra in Phocis. He was represented in the Lesche at Delphi. [Pausanias 10.4.1,30.2,36; Apollodorus 1.9.16, 3.10.8; Homer, *Iliad* 2.517, 17.306.]

HIPPOMEDUSA was one of the DANAIDES, daughter of Danaus and a Hamadryad named either Atlantia or Phoebe. She was married to Alcmenor. [Apollodorus 2.1.5.]

HIPPONOE (1), more often called Iphinoe, was one of the PROETIDES.

HIPPONOE (2) was one of the NEREIDES. [Apollodorus 1.2.7.]

HIPPONOME, daughter of Menoeceus of Thebes, according to some was married to Alcaeus and the mother of Amphitryon and Anaxo. More often, though, their mother was called ASTYDAMEIA. [Apollodorus 2.4.5.]

HIPPOTHOE (1) was one of the NEREIDES. [Hesiod, *Theogony* 251; Apollodorus 1.2.7.]

HIPPOTHOE (2) was one of the DANAIDES and married to Obrimus. [Hyginus, *Fables* 170.]

HIPPOTHOE (3) was one of the AMAZONS. [Hyginus, *Fables* 163.]

HIPPOTHOE (4) was one of the PELIADES. [Apollodorus 1.9.10.]

HIPPOTHOE (5) was a daughter of Mestor and Lysidice. Her parents represented the merging of two vastly important dynasties: Mestor was a son of Perseus, and Lysidice was a daughter of Pelops. Hippothoe was a lovely maiden, and attracted the attention of the easily aroused Poseidon. At the first opportunity he abducted her and took her to the Echinades Islands. A son, Taphius, was born to her. When he grew up, he led a colony to Taphos and called the inhabitants Teleboans. At a later time the descendants of Mestor waged a war against Electryon because they felt they had been cheated of their share of the Mycenaean kingdom. Hippothoe was probably part of the Teleboan colony founded by Taphius. The citizens were notorious cattle rustlers. [Apollodorus 2.4.5; Pausanias 8.14.2.]

HISCILLA was the mother of Phorbas by Triopas. Usually he is called son of Lapithes and ORSINOME. [Hyginus, *Poetic Astronomy* 2.14.]

HISTIAEA was the daughter of Hyrieus and the nymph Clonia. Hyrieus was a king in Boeotia. Histiaea's brothers were Nycteus, Lycus, and Orion. This made her the aunt of Antiope, whose sons Zethus and Amphion built the walls of Thebes. Histiaea herself seems not to have married. Her only distinction was having a town in Euboea named for her, and what the connection was between her and the town of Histiaea is not known. [Apollodorus 3.10.1; Hyginus, *Fables* 195; Scholiast on Homer's *Iliad* 18.486.]

HISTORIS, daughter of Teiresias, was sometimes credited with distracting the goddesses who were delaying the birth of Heracles. More often this kindly friend was called GALINTHIAS. [Pausanias 9.11.2.]

HOMOLOIS (1) was a daughter of NIOBE and Amphion. Some say the Homoloian gate of Thebes was named for her. [Pausanias 9.8.3; Scholiast on Euripides' *Phoenician Maidens* 1126; Tzetzes on Lycophron 520.]

HOMOLOIS (2), or Homoloa, was a priestess of Enyo at Orchomenus. This name was connected with the surname of Enyo, meaning "warlike." At Thebes and Orchomenus, a festival called Homoloia was celebrated in honor of Zeus, Demeter, Athena, and Enyo. Zeus was said to have received the surname Homoloius from Homolois. [Photius, "Homoloios Zeus"; Apostolius 14.40.]

HORA was a Roman goddess connected with boundaries of time or space. (*See* HERSILIA.)

HORAE were goddesses of the seasons and the orderly procession of things in general. The unvarying annual cycle suggested an ideal order in the affairs of men, so these goddesses also came to be the collective personification of justice. Without mentioning their individual names, Homer considered them Olympian divinities of weather and ministers of Zeus. They guarded the doors of Olympus, and from its height kept watch over the fertility of the earth and sent down the proper amounts of rain and sun. The Hora of spring accompanied Persephone every year on her ascent from the lower world. Horae adorned Aphrodite when she rose from the sea.

The names and number of the Horae varied from writer to writer, time to time, and place to place. Hesiod, who saw them as givers of law, justice, and peace, called them daughters of Zeus and Themis, and gave them the names of Eunomia (Discipline), Dice (Justice), and Eirene (Peace). The Homeric concept ran more to their role in seasonal change, especially spring and autumn. At Athens two Horae, Thallo and Carpo, were worshipped from very early times. They represented budding and maturity of growing things, and it was easy enough to regard Thallo as a protectress of youth. Consequently, when the Athenian youths took their ephebic oath in the temple of Agraulos, Thallo was mentioned, among other gods.

As in the case of the winds, some writers got carried away with the idea and included parts of seasons and even hours in the ranks of the Horae. Hyginus, a dedicated list-keeper, named the following: Titanis, Auxo, Eunomia, Pherusa, Carpo, Dice, Euporia, Eirene, Orthosia, Musia, Gymnasia, Nymphes, Mesembria, Sponde, Telete, Acme, Cypridos, Dysis, Thallo, Auge, and Anatole. It can be seen that some thought of them as a large company of joyous maidens in a perpetual dance of the hours, accompanied by the Charites, Hebe, Harmonia, Aphrodite, and the Muses, while others looked upon them as guardians of ethical notions.

Thallo and Carpo had a temple at Athens that contained an altar of Dionysus Orthus. They were worshipped at Argos, Corinth, and Olympia as well. [Homer, *Odyssey* 2.107, 10.469, 24.343, *Iliad* 5.749, 8.393, 21.450; Theocritus 15.104,105; Apollodorus 1.3.1; Pindar, *Olympic Odes* 4.2, *Nemean Odes* 4.34; Horace, *Odes* 4.7.8; Ovid, *Metamorphoses* 2.118; Pausanias 2.20.4, 3.18.7, 5.11.2,15.3, 9.35.1; Hesiod, *Works and Days* 65; Lucian, *Dialogues of the Gods* 10; Hyginus, *Fables* 183.]

HORME was the personification of energetic activity, who had an altar dedicated to her at Athens. [Pausanias 1.17.1.]

HYACINTHIDES were daughters of Hyacinthus, a Lacedaemonian. An oracle commanded him to take his daughters to Athens and sacrifice them on the tomb of the Cyclops Geraestus. Athens was suffering from a famine and plague during its war with Minos, and according to the oracle this was the only means of relief. Hyacinthus obeyed the command and sacrificed the maidens to Persephone or Athena. Their names were usually Aegleis and Antheis, but Lusia, Lytaea, and Orthaea were also mentioned as Hyacinthides. The ways of the gods were indeed strange. Why should Spartan maidens have to die for Athens, a city with which their native city had always had an uneasy relationship? Where were all the Athenians who took oaths to die for their city if necessary? Moreover, their deaths were in vain since the pestilence continued. When consulted by the Athenians, the Delphic oracle told them to give Minos whatever satisfaction he required. Minos then exacted the tribute of youths and maidens to be sacrificed to the Minotaur.

Some accounts make the Hyacinthides daughters of Erechtheus and say they got their collective name from the village of Hyacinthus, where they were sacrificed when

Athens was attacked by the Eleusinians. These versions are further complicated because there were two kings named Erechtheus, and both had daughters who sacrificed themselves. Patriotic suicide came to look almost fashionable in Athens. [Apollodorus 3.15.8; Hyginus, *Fables* 238; Suidas, "Parthenai"; Demosthenes, *Funeral Speech* 1397.]

HYADES are still another group of nymphs with an indefinite significance. It seems that theirs is a case in which the ancients took a heavenly constellation (cf. Pleiades) and invented a story to accommodate it. Their name, which means Rainy, was also of uncertain origin. It could have been taken from their brother Hyas, who was killed by a boar and for whom they wept incessantly until they were changed into stars. It might have been from Hyes, a mystical name of Dionysus, whom they reportedly helped nurse. It could have been from their father, who, according to some, was named Hyas.

Their parents were Atlas and Aethra, Atlas and Pleione, Hyas and Boeotia, Oceanus, Melisseus, Cadmilus, or Erechtheus. Melisseus connects them with Crete, and Cadmilus connects them with Samothrace. They were identified both with the Nyseides, the nymphs who brought up Dionysus, and the Dodonaean nymphs who brought up Zeus. It can be seen that there was considerable confusion over their basic identity, as was the case with their number. A list of their names was contributed to by several writers: Ambrosia, Eudora, Aesyle, Eidothea, Althaea, Adraste, Philia, Coronis, Cleis, Phaesyle, Cleia, Phaeo, Pedile, Polyxo, Phyto, Thyene, Bacche, Macris, Nysa, Erato, Brome, and Dione. The common number was seven, and the usual tradition was that Zeus placed them among the stars in gratitude for their having saved Dionysus. Later they were also made young by Medea at the request of Dionysus.

The more reasonable number and etymology came from the constellation of the Hyades and the word for rainy, since the simultaneous rising of the Hyades with the sun announced rainy and stormy weather. In modern times their immortality has been guaranteed by Tennyson's famous lines: " . . . and when / Thro' scudding drifts the rainy Hyades / Vext the dim sea. . . . " [Hyginus, *Fables* 182,192, *Poetic Astronomy* 2.21; Ovid, *Fasti* 5.167–169,181, *Metamorphoses* 3.314, 7.295; Servius on Virgil's *Aeneid* 748, *Georgics* 1.138; Apollodorus 3.4.3; Diodorus Siculus 5.52; Eustathius on Homer's *Iliad* 1155.]

HYALE (1) was a nymph belonging to the train of Diana. [Ovid, *Metamorphoses* 3.171; Virgil, *Georgics* 4.335, with note of Servius.]

HYALE (2) was one of the DANAIDES and married to Perius. [Hyginus, *Fables* 170.]

HYBRIS was the mother of Pan by Zeus, according to some. His mother was usually called DRYOPE and his father Hermes.

HYGIEIA (1), Hygea, or Hygia was a daughter of Asclepius, and the goddess of health. Inevitably she was called also the wife of Asclepius, and one writer, for a reason known only to himself, thought she should be the daughter of Eros (Love) and Peitho (Persuasion). As a daughter of Asclepius, her mother was Epione, and her brothers and sisters were Machaon, Podaleirius, Ianiscus, Alexanor, Aratus, Aegle, Iaso, and Panaceia. With the exception of Machaon and Podaleirius, who were surgeons in the Trojan War, the rest of her siblings appeared to be attributes of Asclepius. She herself was almost pure symbol. There are no stories in mythology that make her flesh and blood. She was most often depicted as a virgin and usually in the company of her father. She had a separate identity in some famous works of art, but her worship was usually observed jointly with Asclepius. Her attribute was a serpent, the symbol of perpetual renovation. She was mainly the goddess of physical health, but this role included mental health as well, and thus she might have been identified with Athena Hygieia. She was worshiped along with Asclepius in temples at Argos, Athens, Corinth, Gortys, Sicyon, and Oropus. Her image bespoke the serenity attendant on physical and mental well-being. The Roman goddess Salus corresponded to Hygieia. [Pliny, *Natural History* 39.19; Aeschylus, *Eumenides* 522; Scholiast on Pindar's *Pythian Odes* 3.14; Pausanias 1.23.5,31.5,34.2, 2.4.6,11.6,23.4, 3.22.9, 8.28.1; Lucian, *Slip of the Tongue in Greeting* 5.]

HYGIEIA (2) was a surname of Athena as the protectress of mental health. She was thus identified with Hygieia, the daughter of Asclepius. [Pausanias 1.23.5.]

HYLE was a daughter of Thespieus from whom the town of Hyle in Boeotia was believed to have derived its name. Nothing further is known of Hyle or her father. [Eustathius on Homer's *Iliad* 267.]

HYLONOME was the wife of the Centaur Cyllarus. Female Centaurs had a reputation for being very beautiful, and Hylonome was among the most beautiful. She and Cyllarus attended the wedding feast of Peirithous as guests. Cyllarus did not participate in the drunken debauch of his fellow Centaurs, but was killed anyway. Hylonome, who was very deeply in love with him, fell on the spear that killed him. [Ovid, *Metamorphoses* 12.393–428.]

HYMNIA was a surname of Artemis, under which she was worshipped throughout Arcadia. She had a temple between Orchomenus (in Arcadia) and Mantineia, and at first her priestess was always a virgin; after the time of Aristocrates, who raped one of the priestesses, it was decreed that she should be a married woman. [Pausanias 8.5.8,12.3,13.1,4.]

HYONA was, according to some, the mother of Triptolemus by Eleusis. His parents were usually called Celeus and METANEIRA. [Servius on Virgil's *Aeneid* 1.19.]

HYPATE was one of the MUSES worshipped at Delphi, where her and her sisters' names were identical with those of the lowest, middle, and highest chord of the lyre—Nete, Mese, and Hypate. [Plutarch, *Table-Talk* 9.14.]

HYPERCHEIRIA, the Goddess with Protecting Hands, was a surname of Hera. A sanctuary had been erected to her at Sparta at the command of an oracle when the country was inundated by the Eurotas River. [Pausanias 3.13.6.]

HYPERIPPE (1) was the wife of Endymion, according to some, and also the mother of Aetolus. Endymion's wife was usually called NEIS. [Pausanias 5.1.2.]

HYPERIPPE (2) was one of the DANAIDES, daughter of Danaus and Crino, and wife of Hippocorystes. [Apollodorus 2.1.5.]

HYPERMESTRA was another name for MESTRA, daughter of Erysichthon, son of Triopas. [Antoninus Liberalis 17.]

HYPERMNESTRA (1) was a daughter of Thestius and Eurythemis. Her family was a distinguished one, for her sisters were Althaea and Leda. She married Oicles and was the mother of Amphiaraus. He grew up to become a principal in the war of the Seven against Thebes. Prior to that he was both an Argonaut and a Calydonian hunter. He perished at Thebes, and his sons Alcmaeon and Amphilochus avenged his death on their mother, Eriphyle, Hypermnestra's daughter-in-law.

Hypermnestra has no special story of her own, but she served an important purpose in the chronology relevant to the Trojan War. The war was the fifth heroic event in a line of heroic expeditions, and their succession is vital to an understanding of the ages and backgrounds of the participants. It is then apparent that Hypermnestra was married and bore Amphiaraus when Leda was but a child. Since Amphiaraus was an Argonaut and a Calydonian hunter, the second of these events had to follow the first almost immediately. Althaea's son Meleager also participated in both. Not long after the hunt came the war of the Seven, since ten years had to intervene between it and the expedition of the Epigoni, in which Alcmaeon, Hypermnestra's grandson, was prominent. Meanwhile, Hypermnestra's sister Leda became the wife of Tyndareus and bore Helen. Helen would have been a contemporary of Amphiaraus had the sisters been close in age. Helen was scarcely even a contemporary of Alcmaeon, the son of Amphiaraus, so she must have been born very late. All the sons and even grandsons of Helen's aunts—Amphiaraus, Alcmaeon, and Meleager—were gone by the time she eloped to

Troy, and about the only descendant of Thestius who fought in the war was Diomedes, the grandson of Helen's niece. Her own brothers had been killed by her nephew Meleager as far back as the boar hunt.

Hypermnestra's tomb was at Argos, and this is reasonable since Amphiaraus was king in Argos, as were his successors. Also, there is reason to believe that Hypermnestra's husband, Oicles, lived long enough in retirement in Arcadia to receive his grandson Alcmaeon. [Apollodorus 1.7.10,8.2,3; Pausanias 1.8.3,34.2, 2.21.2; Hyginus, *Fables* 73; Homer, *Odyssey* 15.244.]

HYPERMNESTRA (2) was one of the DANA-IDES, daughter of Danaus and Elephantis. If one had to pick one of his or her favorites in mythology, Hypermnestra would stand a good chance of being the one. She came from Egypt with her 49 sisters in a boat built by their father. This curious flight was supposed to have been occasioned by Danaus' belief that his brother Aegyptus and his 50 sons, who had proposed marriage to the 50 maidens, were intent on slaughtering them. They fled from Egypt, stayed for a time in Rhodes, and landed finally at Apobathmi, a small port at the entrance of the Argolic Gulf. Danaus rapidly took over the kingdom of Argos by an ingenious coup d'état and moved into the palace with his 50 daughters. The sons of Aegyptus arrived shortly and reopened their suit for the hands of the maidens. Certain his acquisitive brother was bent on colonizing Argos, Danaus consented to a mass marriage but secretly ordered each daughter to kill her husband on the wedding night. In spite of all that could have gone wrong with such a plan, it succeeded, and Argos was full of corpses the morning after the great wedding.

Hypermnestra alone did not kill her husband (Lynceus), and no good reason has ever been given. Perhaps it was out of pity, or maybe she could not bring herself to commit murder. She might have disagreed with her father, whose authority was certainly strong enough to cause the other daughters to kill unquestioningly. One rather silly commentator suggested she was grateful to Lynceus for sparing her maidenhead. Conversely, he might have pleased her to such an extent that she refused to deny herself future

pleasure from him. Last of all, she was probably hopelessly in love with him. Whatever the reason, she not only spared Lynceus but helped him escape to a city later called Lynceia (Lyrceia) just north of Argos. They had previously arranged a signal to show he had arrived safely, since no doubt Danaus had soldiers to back up his terrible order. Lynceus sent her the signal with a torch, and Hypermnestra returned the sign from the citadel of Argos. This event was celebrated for many years by the Argives with a festival of torches.

Inevitably stories grew that Lynceus slew Danaus and all Hypermnestra's sisters in revenge for his brothers. Some said Danaus kept Hypermnestra in confinement for her disobedience but was afterward prevailed upon to give her to Lynceus. We will never know what the intent of the slain brothers was. Perhaps Danaus was right; maybe his daughters would have been the victims. Lynceus apparently lived among the assassins for years while Danaus tried to raffle them off to men all over the country. He succeeded Danaus on the throne of Argos, and Hypermnestra became the mother of Abas. The tombs of Hypermnestra and Lynceus were shown at Argos, where they were considered heroes. They also had a temple at Delphi, a present from the Argives.

Hypermnestra is especially interesting because she refused to subscribe to the hysteria of her father and sisters. We cannot know whether or not she had any appreciable acquaintance with Lynceus prior to the fateful night, but it speaks well for her that she was willing to take a chance. She was able to make decisions for herself, and her intuition proved correct. She and Lynceus reigned effectively in Argos and were the progenitors of the Perseids, which line reached into historical times. [Ovid, *Heroides* 14; Hyginus, *Fables* 168,273; Apollodorus 2.1.5, 2.1; Pausanias 2.16.1,19.6,21.2,25.4, 10.10.2; Apollonius Rhodius 1.125; Servius on Virgil's *Aeneid* 10.497.]

HYPEROCHE, according to Delian tradition, was one of the Hyperborean maidens who went to Delos to bring their sacred offerings at the birth of Artemis. These offerings were enclosed in stalks of wheat. The maidens died in Delos and were honored with special ceremonies. [Herodotus 4.33–35.]

HYPSIPYLE was the daughter of Thoas and Myrina on the island of Lemnos. Her half-brother was Sicinus. The Lemnian women had neglected sacrifices to Aphrodite, and the touchy goddess punished them by giving them an unpleasant odor so that their husbands avoided them. The women did not take kindly to this neglect, and much in the manner of the Amazons they killed the men on the island. Myrina the queen was already dead, so Thoas' fate hung in Hypsipyle's hands. She could not bring herself to kill her father, so she helped him escape.

Lemnos was the first landing place of the Argonauts after leaving Iolcus, and they arrived not too long after the massacre took place. Hypsipyle had meanwhile become queen, and at first it looked as if she and her subjects were not going to let the Argonauts land. However, she listened to the advice of her old nurse, Polyxo, who told her that without men there would soon be no population left. Hypsipyle then hospitably received the young men, who like sailors everywhere were bursting to come ashore after many days at sea. Hypsipyle even arranged to have them celebrate funeral games for Thoas.

Just about all the women of childbearing age were impregnated by one or another of the Argonauts, and descent from these heroes must have been claimed by Lemnians for centuries. Jason's contribution to repopulation was a set of twins by Hypsipyle herself, Euneus and Nebrophonus (sometimes called Thoas). Euneus was useful to the Greeks during the Trojan War since he supplied them with wine for the duration of the campaign. He also was the ancestor of the Euneidae, a famous family of cithara players in Lemnos.

Eventually Hypsipyle's treasonable act of sparing her father was discovered, and she had to flee for her life. She was found by pirates and sold as a slave to Lycurgus, king of the country around Nemea, where she was made nurse of the king's child, Opheltes. When Amphiaraus and his men came through on their way to attack Thebes, they stopped and asked where they could get water. Hypsipyle left the child unguarded for a moment while she pointed the

way, and a huge snake crawled forth and killed the boy. Lycurgus wanted to put Hypsipyle to death, but about that time her sons, who had searched far and wide for her, arrived and with Amphiaraus' help persuaded Lycurgus and his wife to spare Hypsipyle. Amphiaraus changed the boy's name to Archemorus and instituted the Nemean games in his honor. Hypsipyle returned to Lemnos with her sons.

It is obvious that the parts of the story after the visit of the Argonauts were tacked on, much in the manner of present day spin-offs from successful dramatic entertainments. It is foolish to think the Argonauts hung around awaiting the births of the children they fathered. One account says the twins sailed with the Argonauts when they were about a year old. That would mean the heroes lingered in Lemnos for nearly two years, which is hard to imagine. Then if Hypsipyle was found out and had to flee for her life, the Lemnian women certainly held grudges for inordinate periods of time. In other words, nearly two decades had to be accounted for from the time the Argonauts left until the sons found their mother. If Lycurgus bought her from the pirates as a nurse for his infant son, she must not have served very long with him, since the boy died while still an infant. There was also a long spin-off on the later adventures of Thoas, so there was no end of raw material for the ancient hack writers. It is curious nobody ever followed the fate of Hypsipyle's half-brother, Sicinus, who was the son of Thoas by Oenoie, after he fled from Lemnos. [Pindar, *Olympian Odes* 4.29, with the scholiast; Homer, *Iliad* 7.468, 23.741; Eustathius on Homer's *Iliad* 1327; Hyginus, *Fables* 15; Apollodorus 1.9.17; Pausanias 2.15.3; Apollonius Rhodius 1.668; Valerius Flaccus

HYPSO was the wife of Hyperasius, son of Pelles of Pellene, by whom she became the mother of Amphion and Deucalion (or Asterius), the Argonauts. The city of Hyperesia in Achaia was named for her husband. [Valerius Flaccus 1.366; Apollonius Rhodius 1.176.]

HYRIA, or Thyria, was a daughter of Amphinomus and the mother of Cycnus by Apollo. Cycnus and his mother lived in the district between Pleuron and Calydon, and Cycnus hunted for a living. He was very handsome, quite vain about his looks, and probably spoiled rotten by his doting mother. Many yearned for him, but he turned everyone away. One suitor named Phyllius persevered, and finally Cycnus agreed to consider him as a lover if he accomplished three labors. The labors were extremely difficult, but Phyllius managed to do them and even received a bull as a prize in the final contest. When the time came for Phyllius to collect his reward, Cycnus wanted the prize bull. Perhaps tired of the self-centered demands, Phyllius refused to give it to him. Cycnus was infuriated that he had been spurned, and in hysteria leapt into Lake Canope and drowned. Hyria was devastated and jumped in behind him. Some claimed Cycnus died another way and that Hyria's tears created the lake, which was thereafter called the Cycnean Lake. According to the usual story, both Cycnus and Hyria were metamorphosed into swans. [Antoninus Liberalis 12; Ovid, *Metamorphoses* 7.371.]

HYRMINE, sometimes called Hermione or Iphiboe, was a daughter of Epeius and Anaxiroe. Her brother was Alector, who followed his father as king of Elis. Alector once solicited assistance against Pelops, and Phorbas came from Thessaly to help him. Phorbas seemed to be a kind of professional adventurer. He had earlier been invited to Rhodes to clear the island of snakes and consequently was extended heroic worship there. Alector and Phorbas became close friends, and Phorbas gave his daughter Diogeneia in marriage to Alector. Alector in return gave Hyrmine to Phorbas, who must have been a widower.

Hyrmine was the mother by Phorbas of Augeas, Actor, and Tiphys. All these sons made a name for themselves. By Molione, Actor became the father of the Molionidae, Cteatus and Eurytus. According to more than one report, they were joined at the waist, but this deformity did not seem to diminish their effectiveness as soldiers. Augeas was famous for his dirty stables that were finally cleaned as one of Heracles' labors. Augeas failed to pay the hero and was killed by him along with his nephews, the Molionidae, whose help he had solicited. Tiphys was the helmsman of the *Argo*. Augeas also went on the Argonaut.

Hyrmine was honored by her son Actor, having the city of Hyrmine (or Hormine) named for her. Phorbas continued as an adventurer in his later years, and was described as a bold boxer. His final exploit was the plundering of the temple of Apollo at Delphi along with the Phlegyes, but he was defeated by Apollo in this enterprise. [Pausanias 5.1.4,8, 8.14.6, 9.32.3; Scholiast on Apollonius Rhodius 1.105,173; Eustathius on Homer's *Iliad* 303; Hyginus, *Fables* 14; Diodorus Siculus 5.58; Apollodorus 1.9.22, 2.5.5,7.2; Ovid, *Metamorphoses* 11.414, 12.322.]

HYRNETHO was the daughter of Temenus, one of the Heracleidae. Her brothers were Ceisus, Cerynes, Phalces, and Agraeus. Temenus was one of the leaders of the Heracleidae into Peloponnesus, and after the conquest of the peninsula, he received Argos as his share. His sons had every reason to think succession to the throne was clearly established.

However, Hyrnetho married Deiphontes, son of Antimachus, another Heraclid leader. Temenus was especially fond of his daughter, and he admired Deiphontes very much. Consequently, he turned most of his attention to the couple and gave rather strong indications that he wanted to pass the government to them. Before a formal declaration of this intent could be made, the sons killed Temenus. Although there was strong sentiment that Deiphontes and Hyrnetho were the rightful successors, Ceisus, the eldest son, succeeded Temenus.

Deiphontes and Hyrnetho left Argos and lived at Epidaurus, where Deiphontes remained militarily active and even gained the throne of the Ionian king Pityreus. Hyrnetho bore him four children—Antimenes, Xanthippus, Argeius, and Orsobia. Things went well for some time, but her brothers, who had long envied Deiphontes, knew that the only way they could cause him grief would be through their sister. They also had an eye on the territory acquired by their brother-in-law. Ceisus sent Cerynes and Phalces alone, since Agraeus disapproved of what they were doing. The brothers came to Epidaurus and enticed Hyrnetho outside the walls to talk to her. They tried to convince her that she had married beneath herself and that they could do better for her if she would return with them to Argos. She scorned them as murderers of their father and turned to leave. They seized her and threw her in their chariot. One of the Epidaurians had alerted Deiphontes, who arrived in time to see them pull away with his wife. He gave chase and, overtaking them, shot Cerynes but could not do the same with Phalces, who was holding Hyrnetho. In his effort to elude Deiphontes and the pursuing Epidaurians, Phalces dragged Hyrnetho about so roughly that he killed her, since she was pregnant. He must have thrown the body from the chariot when he realized what he had done, since there is no record that he was caught or that any reprisal was taken on him and his brothers.

Hyrnetho was buried at a place eventually named the Hynethion. A shrine was built there, and the custom was established that no one should ever carry from the spot anything shed from the surrounding trees, since everything in the area was sacred to Hyrnetho. [Apollodorus 2.8.5; Pausanias 2.19.1,23.3,26.2,28.3.]

IAERA (1) was one of the NEREIDES. [Homer, Iliad 18.42; Hyginus, Fables: Preface 8.]

IAERA (2) was a wood nymph who was the mother of Pandarus and Bitias by Alcanor of Mount Ida in the Troad. Pandarus and Bitias were twins and companions of Aeneas. They were slain by Turnus. [Virgil, Aeneid 689–780.]

IALYSA was called by some one of the DANA-IDES, although her name and those of her sisters Cameira and Lindia do not appear in the usual lists of the famous sisters. Tlepolemus built the towns of Lindus, Ialysus, and Cameirus and, according to some, called them thus after the names of the three Danaides. It must be remembered that Tlepolemus, a son of Heracles, came many generations after the Danaides, and it is not at all clear why he chose to name the cities for them. Other accounts say the cities were named for three sons of Carcaphus and Cydippe. [Strabo 14.2.8.]

IAMBE was a daughter of Pan and Echo, and a slave in the house of Celeus and Metaneira. When Demeter in her wanderings came to Eleusis and was received hospitably by Celeus, no one seemed able to cheer the mournful goddess. Iambe was able finally to make her smile by her joking and dancing. These diversions came to be incorporated into the festivals of Demeter and accounted for their extravagant hilarity. Iambe's jokes were not well received by everyone, and their cutting edge seems to have offended someone to the extent that Iambe hanged herself. She was believed to have given the name to iambic poetry. [Homeric Hymn to Demeter 202; Apollodorus 1.5.1; Diodorus Siculus 5.4; Eustathius on Homer's Odyssey 1684.]

IANASSA was one of the NEREIDES. [Homer, Iliad 18.49; Hyginus, Fables: Preface 8.]

IANEIRA (1) was one of the NEREIDES. [Apollodorus 1.2.7.]

IANEIRA (2), daughter of Iphis, was more often called EUADNE. [Scholiast on Pindar's Olympian Odes 6.46.]

IANEIRA (3) was one of the OCEANIDES. [Hesiod, Theogony 354.]

IANTHE (1) was one of the OCEANIDES and a playmate of Persephone. [Homeric Hymn to Demeter 418; Hesiod, Theogony 349; Pausanias 4.30.3.]

IANTHE (2) was a daughter of Telestes of Crete, and the beloved of Iphis. Iphis, daughter of Ligdus and Telethusa of Phaestus, was brought up as a boy because previous to her birth her father had ordered that if a girl was born to Telethusa she should be killed. Telethusa passed the baby off as a male, and thus the maiden grew up. She was betrothed to Ianthe by their families. Ianthe did not suspect a thing and was eager for the marriage to take place. Iphis had fallen deeply in love with Ianthe, and went through the agony of homosexual guilt in addition to knowing that the truth would have to be revealed and she would be rejected. Telethusa kept postponing the wedding, but knew she could hold out no longer. She finally went to the temple of Isis and prayed for a solution. Isis obliged by changing Iphis into a man. Her unisexual name remained the same, so no one except Iphis, Telethusa, and, of course, Isis was any the wiser. The wedding went off without a hitch, and everyone lived happily ever after. On his votive offering to the goddess, the newly sexed young man wrote: "The boy pays what the girl vowed—Iphis." This same story was told of GALATEIA and her daughter, who was called Leucippus. The goddess in their case was Leto. [Ovid, *Metamorphoses* 670–797.]

IARDANIS was a patronymic of Omphale from her father, Iardanus, king of Lydia. [Apollodorus 2.6.3; Ovid, *Heroides* 9.103.]

IASO, the personification of recovery, was a daughter of Asclepius, and sister of Hygieia and Panaceia. In the temple of Amphiaraus at Oropus a part of the altar was dedicated to her in common with Aphrodite, Panaceia, Hygieia, and Athena Paeonia. [Pausanias 1.34.2; Aristophanes, *Plutus* 701, with the scholiast.]

IASONIA was a surname of Athena at Cyzicus. The Argonauts acquired a new anchor at Cyzicus and left their old one. The inhabitants later placed it in Athena's temple as a sacred stone. Iasonia, of course, refers to Jason, who was assisted by Athena during the Argonaut. [Apollonius Rhodius 1.960.]

ICHNAEA, the Tracing Goddess, occurred as a surname both of Themis and Nemesis. In the case of Themis the name could have been derived from the town of Ichnae in Phthiotis, where she was worshipped. [*Homeric Hymn to Delphian Apollo* 94; Lycophron 129; Stephanus Byzantium, "Ichnai."]

IDA (1) was the daughter of Corybas; nothing is known of him. There were dwellers on Crete prior to Zeus' arrival with Europa, some of them certainly dating back to the time when Zeus was born on the island. King Melisseus and his daughters had descendants, as was probably the case with the attendant Curetes and Corybantes. A colony had also come to Crete from Aetolia led by Tectamus. Ida married Lycastus, son of Minos and Itone. Lycastus succeeded Minos as

king of Crete, and the town of Lycastus was named for him. A son was born to Ida by Lycastus. He was called Minos after his grandfather, and he was king during the period of Daedalus, the Minotaur, and Theseus. Consequently, Ida was grandmother of Ariadne and Phaedra. [Apollodorus 2.1.3; Stephanus Byzantium, "Lykastos."]

IDA (2) was one of the daughters of Melisseus, an ancient king of Crete. Her mother was Amaltheia (not to be confused with the goat Amaltheia that suckled Zeus). Ida and her sister Adrasteia were entrusted by Rhea to bring up the infant Zeus. The Curetes, who also assisted in this sacred endeavor, were called her brothers. Ida and other nymphs involved in this duty were represented on the altar of Athena Alea at Tegea. [Pausanias 8.47.1; Apollodorus 1.1.16; Hyginus, *Poetic Astronomy* 2.13; Callimachus, *Hymn to Zeus* 47.]

IDA (3) was one of the Idaean nymphs. By her Zeus became the father of the Idaean Dactyls, according to some. This would make little sense because they are generally accepted as part of the retinue that watched over Zeus during his infancy. Ida still might be considered their mother, however, and in that case she would be Phrygian and not Cretan. The Dactyls were noted for working with metals, but they had other attributes as well. They were skilled in music and magic. They were credited with the spread of the mysteries and the organization of the first Olympic games. [*Etymologicum Magnum* 465; Strabo 10.3.22; Pausanias 5.7.6; Diodorus Siculus 5.64; Apollonius Rhodius 1.1129.]

IDA (4) was a nymph who was loved by Hyrtacus. Hyrtacus was probably part of the family of the Hyrtacus who married the first wife of Priam. Ida's son by him was Nisus, who with his lover, Euryalus, was a companion of Aeneas. When Aeneas was away seeking alliance with Euander, the forces under Turnus surrounded the Trojan stronghold. Nisus and Euryalus sneaked out in the middle of the night and slaughtered many of the enemy. They were apprehended and cut off from escape. Euryalus was killed by Volscens; arriving on the scene moments later, Nisus killed Volscens, then threw himself across the body of his lover and died from his own wounds. [Virgil, *Aeneid* 9.176–450.]

IDAEA (1) was a nymph from Mount Ida in the Troad. She coupled with the god of the Scamander River and produced Teucer, who was the first king of Troy. Dardanus landed there, became friends with Teucer, and married his daughter Bateia. From them the line and its branches reached through the Trojan War and to the colonization of Italy. [Tzetzes on Lycophron 29.]

IDAEA (2) was a surname of Cybele. [Virgil, *Aeneid* 10.252; Hesychius, "Idaia."]

IDAEA (3) was the daughter of Dardanus and Bateia, and sister of Ilus, Erichthonius, and Zacynthus. Her father built the citadel of Troy and initiated the Trojans into the mysteries of the Samothracian Cabeiri. Idaea became the second wife (but more likely the mistress) of Phineus, son of Agenor and king of Salmydessus. She was also called Dia, Eidothea, or Eurytia. Phineus' first wife was Cleopatra, daughter of Boreas, the god of the north wind. When Phineus took Idaea into his house, he rejected Cleopatra, but her continued presence in the palace caused tremendous resentment on Idaea's part. She was particularly unhappy with having to tolerate the sons of Phineus, who posed a threat to the succession of her own sons by him, Thynus and Mariandynus.

She eventually accused his two eldest sons, Plexippus and Pandion, of having tried to seduce her. Phineus dealt harshly with them. Some say he half-buried them in the ground and then scourged them, that he exposed them to be devoured by wild animals, or that he blinded them. Cleopatra was imprisoned, probably on the charge that she had instigated the attempted seduction.

Fortunately the Argonauts arrived in time to deliver the young men and their mother. Two of the Argonauts, Zetes and Calais, were brothers to Cleopatra. The Argonauts also delivered Phineus from the daily raids of two Harpies, who had been sent as a punishment for his treatment of his wife and sons. The truth finally came out

that Idaea had falsely accused her stepsons; Phineus restored his sons to favor and sent Idaea back to her father.

Idaea's accusation was unusual in that it was a result of a power play and not of an unrequited passion for someone who rejected amorous advances. There is no record of her subsequent history, but her sons must have accompanied her when she was exiled by Phineus. Mariandynus became the ancestral hero of the Mariandyni, a Bithynian tribe. Thynus was the eponymic hero of Thynia. [Scholiast on Apollonius Rhodius 2.140,178; Apollodorus 3.15.3; Diodorus Siculus 4.44.]

IDALIA was a surname of Aphrodite derived from the town of Idalion in Cyprus. [Virgil, *Aeneid* 1.680,692, 5.760, 10.86; Ovid, *Art of Love* 3.10.6.]

IDOMENE was a daughter of Abas, king of Argos. She was sometimes called the wife of Amythaon, and mother of Bias and Melampus. Most often the wife of Amythaon was called EIDOMENE, daughter of Pheres.

IDOTHEA (*See* EIDOTHEA)

IDYIA was one of the OCEANIDES, a daughter of Oceanus and Tethys. She was a wife of Aeetes, who was a son of Helios and Perseis, and brother to Circe, Pasiphae, and Perses. He was given the kingdom of Corinth by his father but for some reason went to Colchis, a country at the eastern end of the Black Sea. In Colchis he ruled over Aea, a kingdom within Colchis, and his capital was Phasis on the banks of the Phasis River. His wife's name was recorded inconsistently, and a good reason may be that he had more than one. Some of their names were Eurylyte, Neaera, Asterodeia, and even Hecate. Idyia was mentioned more than any others as the mother of Medea and Chalciope, but Asterodeia, a nymph, appeared to have a better claim as mother of Absyrtus.

When Phrixus flew in on the ram with golden fleece, Aeetes gave Chalciope, the older daughter, to him in marriage. Idyia then saw the fame of the Golden Fleece spread and, as a result, the arrival of the Argonauts. Since she was an

Oceanid and also the wife of Aeetes, she was not unduly impressed with the exploits of the enchanted voyage of the adventurers, nor did the phenomena of guardian dragons and fire-breathing bulls employed by her husband seem extraordinary. Her second daughter, Medea, had inherited the ability to cast spells and manufacture potions and poisons, and her love affair with Jason could have been abetted by Idyia. It is doubtful she went so far as to condone the slaughter of her stepson Absyrtus when Medea fled with Jason from Colchis.

In his later years Aeetes was said to have been dethroned by his brother Perses. As his principal wife, Idyia probably accompanied him in exile. Medea reportedly came in disguise to Colchis after the end of her marriages with Jason and Aegeus. 'She had Perses killed and gave the kingdom back to her father, who probably at that point forgave her for stealing the Golden Fleece and carving up his son. [Hyginus, *Fables* 25; Hesiod, *Theogony* 352,960; Apollonius Rhodius 3.234; Apollodorus 1.9.1,23,26.]

ILAEIRA (*See* HILAEIRA)

ILIA was a name frequently given to RHEA SILVIA, the mother of Romulus and Remus.

ILIONA was the oldest daughter of Priam and Hecuba, but her name is left off most of the lists of the Trojan royal family. She married and left home before some of her brothers and sisters were born. Her husband was Polymestor, king of the Thracian Chersonesus (Peninsula). Polydorus was the youngest son of Priam and Hecuba, and only an infant when the Trojan War commenced. Iliona and Hecuba delivered sons at the same time, and Iliona agreed to take Polydorus for safekeeping during the conflict. Her son by Polymestor was Deipylus, but she passed him off as her younger brother, and her brother as her son. She did this in order to guarantee that if one of them died or was killed the other would retain his right of succession to the throne. Somehow she kept this knowledge even from her husband, and one suspects she might quite early have decided he could not be trusted.

Ten years passed, and the war ended. The victorious Greeks wanted to wipe out the entire race of Priam, so Agamemnon promised Polymestor his daughter Electra if he would kill Polydorus. Polymestor was greedy. He knew that marrying Electra would mean a share in the kingdom of Mycenae. So he complied, but unknowingly he killed his own son. And so the matter rested there for several years. No further mention seems to have been made concerning Agamemnon's promise to Polymestor. But then it is all too clear why Agamemnon could not keep his end of the bargain. Iliona, now the only one alive who knew the secret, remained with Polymestor for reasons of her own. Surely she knew of the aborted agreement about Electra, and she was certainly now aware of what a despicable man she had married. Troy was no more; she had no place to go, so her only hope was for Polymestor to die and have Polydorus succeed him.

Polydorus meanwhile grew up and once had occasion to go to Delphi. While there he consulted the oracle and learned that his parents were dead and his native city was in ruins. He was totally baffled by these statements and would have dismissed them as typical of the often obscure messages given out by the oracle had not Iliona told him the truth when he revealed to her what he had heard in Delphi. He instantly sought revenge and urged the passive Iliona into action. She blinded Polymestor, and Polydorus then killed him.

There were several other stories about Polymestor, including a principal variation on the above account. Polymestor was bribed by the Greeks to kill Polydorus. He threw the body into the sea, and it was found by Hecuba, who lured Polymestor to Troy with the promise of treasure and then gouged out his eyes. Iliona did not figure in any of the other stories about Polydorus. [Hyginus, *Fables* 109,240; Horace, *Satires* 2.3.64; Servius on Virgil's *Aeneid* 1.653; Cicero, *Tusculan Disputations* 1.44.]

ILISSIADES was a surname of the MUSES, who had an altar on the Ilissus River in Attica. [Pausanias 1.19.6.]

ILITHYIA (*See* EILEITHYIA)

IMBRASIA was a surname of Hera derived from the Imbrasus River in Samos, on the banks of which some say the goddess was born. [Apollonius Rhodius 1.187; Pausanias 7.4.4.]

IMENARETE was the mother of Elephenor and Chalciope by Chalcodon, a son of Abas from Euboea. He was killed by Amphitryon during a battle with the Thebans, who were trying to rid themselves of a tribute imposed by the Euboeans. Elephenor, prince of the Abantes, was a suitor of Helen and went against Troy in 40 ships. He took with him the young sons of Theseus, who had been entrusted to his care; his sister Chalciope was stepmother of Theseus. Before the commencement of the war Elephenor had unintentionally killed Abas, his grandfather, and had to flee Euboea. Consequently, he assembled his forces from beyond the island. He was killed by Agenor, according to most accounts, but some said he survived and went to the island of Othronos near Sicily but, driven from there by a dragon, ultimately settled in Amantia in Illyria. There is no further record of Imenarete. The spelling of her name was probably corrupt. By one writer she was called Melanippe. [Plutarch, *Theseus* 35; Pausanias 1.17.6; Hyginus, *Fables* 97; Homer, *Iliad* 2.540, 4.463; Tzetzes on Lycophron 1029.]

INACHIA, Inachis, or Inachione frequently occurs as a surname of Io, the daughter of Inachus. He was a river-god in Argolis, whose judgment as to who should possess Argos was unfavorably received by the loser, Poseidon, who caused the waters of Inachus to dry up during summer. [Aeschylus, *Prometheus* 591; Callimachus, *Hymn to Artemis* 254; Virgil, *Georgics* 3.153.]

INFERNA was a surname of Proserpina as goddess of the underworld. This surname was interchangeable with Juno Inferna. [Virgil, *Aeneid* 6.138.]

INO was one of the four ill-fated daughters of Cadmus and Harmonia. Her story was complicated in its sequences and variations, for it was popular with ancient writers, who kept adding chapters in a kind of soap opera style to what might have been an otherwise rather straightforward account.

Ino's problem began when she and her sisters Agave and Autonoe spread the rumor that their other sister, Semele, only claimed a sexual relation with Zeus, when really she got pregnant by one of her mortal admirers, and that Zeus punished her by incinerating her. This malicious gossip was not well received by the father of the gods, nor, in fact, by Dionysus, the product of Zeus' affair with Semele, when he grew up.

Ino married Athamas, one of the many sons of Aeolus, but she came into a household with two adolescent children from Athamas' first marriage. He had been married to Nephele, a phantomlike woman created by Zeus, and she had borne him two children, Phrixus and Helle. Ino immediately hated them and devised ways to get rid of them. She sabotaged the grain crop and bribed messengers to the Delphic oracle to say that the sacrifice of Phrixus was the only salvation from drought. Athamas took her seriously; the children were saved only by flying away on the back of a miraculous ram with golden fleece sent by Nephele. Ino even reinforced her claim that Phrixus was a ne'er-do-well by charging that he had tried to sleep with his aunt Demodice, who in fact had tried to seduce her young nephew.

Even before Phrixus and Helle were gone, Ino and Athamas had become foster parents of Dionysus. Zeus apparently decided to forgive Ino for her calumny of Semele. The Nyseides, who had nursed Dionysus, were no longer adequate for his education, so Dionysus grew up in the household of Ino and Athamas much to Hera's displeasure. As soon as he was old enough, he left to wander for several years in an effort to establish himself as the god of wine. His worship caught on and spread back to his native city. His foster mother and her sisters embraced the new religion. His aunt Agave, queen of Thebes, was a principal adherent and sponsored bacchanalian orgies on the nearby mountains. Once, her son, Pentheus, sought to investigate these activities; mistaken for an animal by his frenzied wife and sisters-in-law, he was torn to pieces.

After this Ino disappeared for a while, leaving Athamas and her two small children by him, Learchus and Melicertes. After a certain lapse of time, he presumed her dead. He soon married Themisto, daughter of Hypseus, and she bore him twin sons, Orchomenus and Sphingius. It was not long, however, before Ino returned secretly. Still in love with her, Athamas disguised her as a servant and visited her when he could. Themisto learned Ino was still alive but did not know her whereabouts. She decided to have Ino's children killed and confided her plan to the new servant. The plan consisted of having the two pairs of sleeping children distinguished by black and white coverlets. The hired assassins were instructed to kill the ones covered in black, who were Ino's sons. Ino switched the coverlets, and Themisto's sons were thus murdered.

When Themisto learned what she had done, she hanged herself. Athamas went insane, and this condition was probably intensified by Hera, who still after many years deeply resented his role in bringing up Dionysus. Athamas killed Learchus and was about to kill Melicertes, but Ino fled with the boy across Megaris and jumped with him into the sea from the high cliffs.

The body of Ino washed onto the coast of Megara; it was found and buried by Tauropolis and Cleso, daughters of Cleson. Melicertes' body washed ashore at Corinth and was found and buried by Sisyphus, the boy's uncle. Both Ino and Melicertes, however, were transformed into marine divinities and named Leucothea and Palaemon.

As earlier stated, there were numerous variations on these interconnected stories. In one, Ino killed Melicertes in a fit of jealousy over a slave called Antiphera. Some said Athamas surrendered Ino and Melicertes to Phrixus to be killed but that Dionysus saved them. There was even a subsequent history of Athamas, in which Themisto played a part.

From the very beginning Ino was not painted as a particularly wholesome individual. One could make a case for her that she was only protecting herself and later her children, but her excesses were especially chilling. She appeared vindictive and ruthless. There seems to be no question that without Dionysus' affection for her she would not have become a goddess. [Apollodorus 1.9.5, 3.4.3; Hyginus, *Fables* 1–5; Ovid, *Metamorphoses* 4.520, 13.919; Apollonius Rhodius 1141; Pausanias 1.42.8, 2.44.11; Euripides, *Bacchanals* 99–102, *Medea* 1289; Plutarch, *Roman Questions* 13; Tzetzes on Lycophron 107.]

INTERCIDONA (*See* DEVERRA)

INTERDUCA was a surname of Juno, under which she was invoked by newly married people. [St. Augustine, *City of God* 7.3; Festus, "Interduca."]

INVIDIA was the personification of envy and described as a daughter of the giant Pallas. Pallas was one of the secondary Titans and married to Styx. Their other children were Zelus, Cratos, Bia, and Nice (Nike). Styx was the first of all the immortals who took her children to Zeus to assist him against the Titans. Zeus rewarded her by letting the children live on Olympus. [Hesiod, *Theogony* 376,383; Pausanias 7.26.5, 8.18.1; Apollodorus 1.2.2,4.]

IO and her wanderings constitute one of the great riddles of mythology. The basic story appears simple enough—another of Zeus' infidelities accompanied by Hera's retribution—but the long-drawn-out account took on geographical, religious, and quasi-historical aspects, each of which opened up realms of questioning and investigation.

Io was usually called a daughter of Inachus, the river-god who founded the worship of Hera at Argos. But she was also called the daughter of Iasus or Peiren. If she was a daughter of Iasus, that would have made Inachus her great-grandfather six times removed. In relation to her office as a priestess of Hera, it makes more sense that Inachus was her father. In that case, her mother was either a Melian nymph or Argeia, Inachus' own sister. Her brothers were Phoroneus, Aegialeus, Phegeus, and, according to some, Argus Panoptes.

The chronological tables of the priestesses of Hera at Argos placed Io at the head of the list of priestesses under the name of Callirrhoe or Callithyia. For some reason a nymph named Iynx cast a spell on Zeus and caused him to fall in love with Io. Zeus knew he was on dangerous ground tampering with a priestess of Hera, so he changed Io into a white cow and presumably mated with her either in manlike or bull-like form. Accustomed to these tactics, Hera set a guard over the white cow. This was Argus Panoptes, Io's brother, uncle, or grandfather, depending on the version of her genealogy. His hundred eyes had to be symbolic, since no face could accommodate so many. Io grazed mainly around Mycenae, but the watchful Argus followed her everywhere; even while he slept, some of his eyes kept guard.

Zeus was unhappy at what had befallen his lover. Maybe his unhappiness arose from deprivation. In any case, he commissioned Hermes to free Io. The ever-resourceful Hermes lulled Argus to sleep and then cut off his head. His eyes were transferred to the tail of the peacock, Hera's favorite bird. But Hera was not easily discouraged from her vindictiveness. She sent a gadfly to pursue the unfortunate cow, causing her to wander endlessly across mountains, streams, seas, and even whole countries.

Her route has been debated for centuries. It is perhaps simplest to say that it included Euboea, northern Greece, the Ionian Sea, Mount Haemus, the Danube delta, Scythia, the Caucasian Mountains, the Crimean and Thracian Bosphorus, Asia Minor, Media, Bactria, India, Arabia, Ethiopia, and finally Egypt. On her way she encountered the chained Prometheus, who told her the course she still had to take. She met the Amazons, the Graeae, and the Gorgons.

Itinerary aside, one of the puzzling things about Io was the fact that she continued to have children by Zeus during her gadfly-plagued wanderings. One of these was Ceroessa, who was born on the spot where Byzantium was afterward built. Again we have to wonder about the mechanics of birth. Did Io periodically reassume human shape, or was Ceroessa born from a cow's uterus? Was she born as a calf? Later she had a son, Byzas, by Poseidon, so we have to conjecture that she and her son had human forms. Io also bore a son called Iasus, but we know nothing of him. Some even mentioned Dionysus as her son by Zeus.

Epaphus was the son we know best. He was also a son of Zeus, and again we are not sure of when or how he was conceived. It seems Io bore him shortly after her arrival on the Nile River. It is most likely he was conceived during bovine coupling but delivered as a human after Io returned to her original state. Since neither Io nor Zeus were genuinely bovine, it was not the same situation as in the case of the Minotaur, in which one of the parents was a real bull.

Hera had not abandoned her vendetta, even though a great deal of time had elapsed from Zeus' first ecstasy with Io. Epaphus was stolen and concealed by the Curetes at Hera's direction, and poor Io had to undergo further wanderings before she at length found him in Syria. She finally found peace on the Nile and married Telegonus, a king of Egypt. Maybe she decided that the price for being Zeus' lover was much too high.

Io founded the worship of Isis. She was said to have invented the five vowels of the first alphabet (her name was already two of them). Her legends were ancient and mysterious. Her wanderings somehow suggested the phases of the moon, and indeed she was regarded by many as a lunar goddess.

Epaphus was the ancestor of Danaus, who went with his daughters from Egypt to Argos. Thus the circle was complete. Io had wandered by land all the way to Egypt; then her great-great-grandson returned and, in effect, reclaimed her father's kingdom. [Hyginus, *Fables* 145,149,275; Apollodorus 2.1.2–4,5.11; Stephanus Byzantium, "Byzas"; Diodorus Siculus 4.49; Antoninus Liberalis 3; Ovid, *Metamorphoses* 1.668,722; Aeschylus, *Prometheus* 548,703–705; Herodotus 1.1, 2.41; Suidas, "Io"; Euripides, *Iphigeneia in Taurica* 382; Eustathius on Dionysius Periegeta 92,143.]

IOCASTE (1) was, according to some, the mother of Agamedes by Zeus. Usually, though, Agamedes is recorded as the son of Erginus (no wife mentioned), king of Orchomenus, and brother of Trophonius.

IOCASTE (2), also called Epicaste, was a daughter of Menoeceus, and sister of Hipponome and Creon. She became a part of the ill-fated Theban dynasty when she married Laius, the son of Labdacus. This was for her a most advantageous marriage because it brought together two branches of the family of Cadmus and seemed to guarantee political strength. But disappointment came when she was not able to produce an heir. Laius went to Delphi and asked how the problem might be overcome. The oracle proclaimed that a child born to Iocaste would be his murderer, so he went home and moved into bachelor's quarters. To make matters worse,

Laius rejected all women and went off to Pisa and kidnapped Chrysippus, the son of Pelops. Not to be outdone, Iocaste contrived to get Laius drunk and sleep with him. She got pregnant, and Laius was both alarmed and angry. When a son was born, he snatched him up, pierced his feet, and exposed him. Of course, this caused Iocaste immeasurable distress. It is even doubtful Laius gave her a reason, and almost certainly he never slept with her again. The baby, of course, was Oedipus, who was rescued and reared in the house of Polybus of Corinth.

Years passed, and more trouble arrived. A terrible monster called the Sphinx arrived at Thebes and sat outside the gates of the city, forcing people to guess at a riddle she posed. Nobody could guess it, and she promptly killed those who tried or were caught passing beyond the city. Almost at the same time news reached the city that Laius had been killed by unknown assailants on the road between Delphi and Thebes. So the childless Iocaste also became a widow. Outside the gate the terror continued; Thebes was paralyzed, commerce was suffering, and the citizens were demanding that something be done.

Creon had become the regent upon Laius' death, and he decided to offer the kingdom and his sister, the queen, to anyone who could rid the city of the monster. Oedipus had been in the city a short time, and this offer stirred his ambition. He had left a legacy in Corinth because he too had received an oracle, even more horrifying than the one Laius had received. His said that he would murder his father and marry his mother. Believing the oracle referred to his foster parents (who had never told him the truth), he decided to seek his fortunes elsewhere. It is a mystery how he came up with the answer to the Sphinx's riddle, since there had been no survivors to pass the question along for private pondering. More than likely, the gods had revealed the answer to him in a dream. To the query "What creature walks on four legs, then two, then three and is strongest when it has fewest legs?" he answered "Man," and this being the correct answer, the Sphinx flew off in rage and was seen no more.

Oedipus was the hero of the city, and his coronation and marriage ceremonies were joyous occasions. It is hard to guess how the recently widowed Iocaste felt about this young stranger. It is doubtful Laius' demise caused her intense grief, since he had rejected her for many years. She probably felt that marriage to Oedipus was good for the civic morale. She was eager to have children, and this fearless young man probably looked as if he were able to give her several.

Iocaste was in her mid-thirties, and Oedipus was probably not much more than 18. It was probably whispered about the city more than once that she looked old enough to be his mother. Be that as it may, they had four children over the next few years—Antigone, Polyneices, Eteocles, and Ismene. Iocaste was truly happy during the period of their birth and growing up.

Then the unthinkable came to light. A plague came to Thebes; after much searching for causes and remedies, the blind seer Teiresias revealed the problem. Testimony was obtained here and there from those involved in Oedipus' supposed death and early upbringing. On learning the truth Oedipus seized ornamental pins from Iocaste's breast and stabbed out his eyes. Iocaste quietly withdrew and hanged herself.

Iocaste has always been pitied by countless generations of readers of tragedy. Actually her life could have been much worse. She had an indifferent first husband, who had reason to fear for his future, but many women had lived with unresponsive spouses and somehow managed. Laius probably would have looked the other way if she had chosen to take a lover. Life was not rosy when the city was besieged by the Sphinx. News of her husband's death, while unsettling, probably did not send her into an inconsolable state. Then there was the second plague and the unfolding of revelations that exposed the awful truth. And this last part has been the occasion for the pity for Iocaste. She was happiest during these years. She had a vigorous and devoted young husband, who gave her four handsome children. He was a good ruler, and the future looked extremely bright. Iocaste's despair at what she finally learned lasted all of a half-hour or so. Granted that she did not die on a happy note, it was over quickly. Pity was much more in order for Oedipus, who was obliged to live with the horrible knowledge for the rest of his life, and for the children, especially Antigone. Though a mere girl when the terrible events occurred, she felt obliged to care for her blind father the rest of his days. So her suffering was a matter of years, during which she was robbed of the joys of youth. The real villain was perhaps Laius, who should have told Iocaste of the oracle's dire prediction. Even in those days there were probably primitive means of birth control. [Apollodorus 2.4.5, 3.5.7; Homer, *Odyssey* 11.271; Herodotus 5.59; Pausanias 9.5.2.]

IODAMA was the daughter of Itonus, son of Amphictyon and the nymph Melanippe. Her brother was Boeotus and her sister, Chromia. Itonus was the founder of the cult of Athena Itonia at Coroneia, and Iodama was one of the priestesses at the temple. One night she entered the temple, and the goddess appeared. Iodama was turned into stone when she looked directly at the head of Medusa mounted on the shield of the goddess. Thereafter a flame was kindled on the altar of Iodama by a woman who intoned three times: "Iodama lives and demands fire." Before this event, Iodama had a daughter, Thebe, by Zeus. It is possible that this was the reason for her having been turned to stone by Athena. However, an obscure legend called Athena a daughter of Itonus and sister of Iodama, whom she accidentally killed. Thebe married Ogygus, after whom one of the gates of Thebes was named. [Pausanias 9.34.1; Tzetzes on Lycophron 355.]

IOLE was the daughter of Eurytus of Thessalian Oechalia and Antioche. Her brothers were Iphitus, Molion, Clytius, and Toxeus. Eurytus was a brilliant archer, as were his sons, and even instructed Heracles. Eurytus was so proud of his skill he decided to sponsor a contest open to everyone, with the hand of Iole as prize for the best archer, one who could outshoot him and his sons.

Heracles won the contest, but Eurytus and his sons refused to give him Iole because they knew his reputation for fits of madness. It was said that he had already killed one wife and some of his children. Iphitus was the only son who defended Heracles. Eurytus backed up his refusal with an army, so the angry Heracles went his way, vowing revenge. To add to the insult, Eurytus later accused Heracles of stealing cattle

from him. He might have had justification, for Heracles was a known cattle rustler, but it turned out the livestock were stolen by Autolycus. Iphitus again defended Heracles, whom he obviously fancied, and offered to help him clear his name by going with him to recover the animals. They came to Tiryns, and during a quarrel Heracles threw Iphitus from the high wall of the city. For this crime he was obliged to serve Omphale, queen of Lydia, for a certain period of time.

After this task ended, Heracles had other adventures. He had meanwhile married Deianeira of Calydon, and their home was Trachis. Eventually he returned to Trachis to raise an army to march on Oechalia to collect the long-overdue debt. He killed Eurytus and his remaining sons, collected Iole, and started home. News that he was bringing home a new bride caused Deianeira to resort to what she thought was a remedy of love but turned out to be a poisoned garment given to her by the dying Centaur Nessus. She sent the shirt to Heracles, who died miserably when he put it on for a sacrifice. As he died he commanded his son Hyllus to marry Iole as soon as he was old enough.

Iole was a beautiful woman who appeared to be something to be bartered with, passed around according to the wishes of the men in her life. She was not an individual but a property. One or two accounts said she resisted being taken by Heracles, even jumping from the wall of the city, but was saved from death by her billowing garments. There is no account of her history subsequent to her marriage to Hyllus. [Sophocles, *Trachiniae* 44–45; Antoninus Liberalis 32; Ovid, *Metamorphoses* 9.325; Apollodorus 2.6.1, 7.7; Pausanias 4.3.6, 27.4, 33.5.]

IONE was one of the NEREIDES. [Apollodorus 1.2.7.]

IONIDES was a name borne by four nymphs believed to possess healing powers. They had a temple on the Cytherus River in Elis and derived their name from a mythical Ion, a son of Gargettus, who was believed to have led a colony from Athens to those districts. The story undoubtedly arose from the existence of a mineral spring on the spot where their sanctuary stood. [Pausanias 6.22.4.]

IOPE (1) was a daughter of Aeolus and wife of Cepheus. The town of Joppa was said to have derived its name from her. In the legends of Perseus and Andromeda she was called CASSIEPEIA. [Stephanus Byzantium, "Iope."]

IOPE (2) was a daughter of Tirynthian Iphicles, twin brother of Heracles. She was one of the wives of Theseus, but nothing beyond that is known of her. [Plutarch, Theseus 29.]

IOPHOSSA was a daughter of Aeetes, commonly called CHALCIOPE. [Scholiast on Apollonius Rhodius 2.1115,1153; Hesychius, "Iophossa."]

IPHIANASSA (1) was one of the PROETIDES.

IPHIANASSA (2) was another name of IPHIGENEIA.

IPHIANASSA (3) was the mother of Aetolus by Endymion, according to some. The wife of Endymion was usually called NEIS. [Apollodorus 1.7.6.]

IPHIANASSA (4) was one of the NEREIDES. [Lucian, Dialogues of the Gods 14.]

IPHIANEIRA was a daughter of Megapenthes and married to Melampus, according to some, but usually his wife was called Iphianassa, one of the PROETIDES, or daughters of Proetus. [Diodorus Siculus 4.68l; Apollonius Rhodius 1.142.]

IPHIAS (1) was a patronymic for Euadne, daughter of Iphis and wife of Capaneus. [Ovid, Ex Ponto 3.1.111; Euripides, Suppliants 985.]

IPHIAS (2) was the name of a priestess mentioned in the story of the Argonauts. As Jason left the city of Iolcus to set sail, Iphias kissed his right hand in farewell. She was too ancient to utter any word. [Apollonius Rhodius 1.312.]

IPHIBOE was the mother of Augeas by Phorbas, according to some. Usually the mother of Augeas was called HYRMINE. [Tzetzes on Lycophron 41.]

IPHIGENEIA (1) is one of the most well known individuals in mythology. She has been the subject of plays, operas, orchestral works, paintings, and even modern cinema. Part of the reason for her artistic immortality was the dual character she portrayed, one having a pivotal role in the events of the Trojan War and the other involved in the story of Orestes 20 years later. There were two independent accounts of Iphigeneia, and they are so distinguished in artistic works—Iphigeneia at Aulis and Iphigeneia in Tauris. A third account, an extension of the second, could be called Iphigeneia at Brauron.

Iphigeneia was usually called one of the three daughters of Agamemnon and Clytemnestra, but one or two writers, as if trying to broaden her dramatic base and perhaps give credibility to her later worship in Attica, called her the daughter of Helen and Theseus. In this case, Clytemnestra and Agamemnon were considered foster parents, since they brought her up. This version, of course, lessens the poignancy of the sacrifice at Aulis.

While the Greek fleet lay at Aulis prior to sailing against Troy, Agamemnon killed a stag in the sacred grove of Artemis. The goddess caused a great calm to descend, and the fleet could not sail. Calchas the seer declared that the sacrifice of Iphigeneia was the only way of propitiating Artemis. This suggestion was totally abhorrent to Agamemnon. Once before he had refused to sacrifice Iphigeneia. The year she was born, for some reason he sought a favor from Artemis and vowed to sacrifice the most beautiful thing the year would produce. This, of course, turned out to be Iphigeneia, but he could not bring himself to carry out the promise. Now it was different; pressure came from all sides. In the harbor lay a thousand ships, most of them there because of his almost fanatical recruitment. Menelaus urged him to obey the oracle's command so that the campaign to recover Helen could proceed. At length he capitulated, and Odysseus and Diomedes were sent to Mycenae to bring Iphigeneia to Aulis under the pretext that she was to be married to Achilles.

It is interesting to think about what all this meant to Iphigeneia. She was probably about 16, the age at which romantic adventure was a constant daydream. Who had not heard of the startlingly handsome Achilles, whose participation in the war was necessary for its success? He had been hunted down by Odysseus and brought from Scyros, where he had been concealed by his immortal mother. He was already the father of a young son by the daughter of the king of Scyros. Iphigeneia must have jumped at the opportunity to become the wife of this glorious youth. Her mother Clytemnestra, a calculating woman, must have seen the political advantage of thus uniting the kingdoms of Mycenae and Phthia. So mother and daughter set off, probably congratulating themselves on their good fortune.

They were not long at Aulis before the terrible truth came out. One can only imagine Clytemnestra's hysteria and rage, her disbelief. Believing to the last that her magnificent young lover would emerge, Iphigeneia was led to the altar and hurriedly sacrificed.

This then was the awful story, which might have ended there. In fact, for some tragedians this heartless act was the basis on which Clytemnestra planned her revenge and carried it out on the return of Agamemnon from Troy. The story is complete in itself—blind ambition overcoming paternal and humanitarian considerations.

But the ancient writers, experts at cliffhanging literary devices, spared Iphigeneia from the knife and thus added a whole new series of events. At the last possible moment, a sacrificial victim appeared on the altar, and Iphigeneia was whisked away under a cloud cover to Tauris by Artemis. A spin-off of this miracle had Achilles, in collusion with Clytemnestra, spirit Iphigeneia to a remote place, where she became by the hero the mother of Neoptolemus.

The usual story is that Artemis made her a priestess at Tauris. Artemis, as the Taurian goddess, was dark and cruel. The miserably treated Iphigeneia was the perfect priestess for a misanthropic cult that sacrificed strangers who landed at Tauris. In this sinister place Iphigeneia held a deadly power for the next 20 years.

The war ended, Agamemnon returned home and was murdered by Clytemnestra and her lover, and Orestes emerged from hiding

and avenged his father. Iphigeneia was aware of none of this. Even the father who had allowed her supposed sacrifice must have been a dim memory. One curious story had her officiate at Tauris in the sacrifice of Helen and Menelaus, who happened to land there. In some respects this would have been a fitting retribution for the distress she had suffered because of them.

She did remember, however, that she had a young brother. This saved his life. An oracle instructed him to go with his friend Pylades to Tauris to bring back an image of Artemis to Attica. The two young men were snatched from their ship as soon as they landed. They were about to be killed on the altar of Artemis when Iphigeneia made a connection between the present and past, and realized Orestes was her brother. Risking her own safety, she stole the statue and fled from Tauris with her brother and their cousin.

They arrived in Attica and apparently needed some authentication of the statue, so they went to Delphi for advice from the oracle. Electra, the sister of Orestes and Iphigeneia, meanwhile had heard that Orestes and Pylades had been sacrificed at Tauris by a priestess of Artemis. She too journeyed to Delphi to get the truth of the report. While there, she had pointed out to her the very priestess who had allegedly given the order for her brother's death. She tried to put out Iphigeneia's eyes, but Orestes appeared in time to prevent her. The long-separated sisters were reunited, and everyone returned to Mycenae. Iphigeneia did not tarry but took the statue to Brauron in Attica.

She lived there many years as the priestess of Artemis Brauronia. Although her personal story ended rather happily, the worship she introduced at Brauron—and later Sparta—was involved with human sacrifice. It seems her years in Tauris had established a way of religious life that she was unable to relinquish. When worship of Artemis Orthia spread to Sparta, it at first embraced human sacrifice but was changed by Lycurgus into ritual scourging of youths. A feature of the Taurian worship was human blood on the altar, and in Sparta this was accomplished by the practice of the *diamastigosis*.

Iphigeneia died at Brauron. By that time the Atticans had recovered the old claim that she was the daughter of Theseus. After her death the costly garments of women who had died in childbed were offered to her. Some said her tomb was at Megara. Others said she did not die at all but was changed by Artemis into Hecate. Still others claimed the goddess made her immortal and that under the name of Oreilochia she became the wife of Achilles on the island of Leuce. This last would be a superb irony. It would also be somewhat awkward, since Achilles was also supposed to be the husband of Helen of Troy in the afterworld. [Hyginus, *Fables* 79,98,121; Tzetzes on Lycophron 133,183,1374; Euripides, *Iphigeneia in Taurica* 10–30,79,89–91,783,1446, *Electra* 14,542; *Iphigeneia at Aulis* 100,1540; Servius on Virgil's *Aeneid* 2.116; Diodorus Siculus 4.44; Pausanias 1.33.1, 2.22.7, 3.16.6; Apollodorus 3.10.6, *Epitome* 6.24,27; Dictys Cretensis 1.20; Homer, *Iliad* 9.145; Eustathius on Homer's *Iliad* 1187; Aeschylus, *Libation-Bearers* 232.]

IPHIGENEIA (2) was a surname of Artemis at Hermione, where she had a temple. It is likely that Iphigeneia at Tauris was considered a goddess in her own right but that when the Taurian goddess came to Attica, Argolis, and Sparta under the names of Brauronia and Orthia, the identities of the two goddesses became fused. [Pausanias 2.35.2,7.26; Herodotus 4.103.]

IPHIMEDEIA was a daughter of Triopas, son of Poseidon and Canace. Her father had a certain notoriety. He had a statue on horseback at Delphi, an offering from the Cnidians from the city he founded. Her brother was Erysichthon, who was afflicted with insatiable hunger because of violating a sacred grove of Demeter. He exhausted the resources of his kingdom to satisfy his hunger and eventually ate his own flesh.

Iphimedia was not altogether normal. She fell in love with Poseidon and walked longingly along the seashore, attempting to bring him to the surface. She must have been aware that he was her grandfather. She had to satisfy herself by dabbling seawater over her genitals, so that finally she became pregnant by the god, who might have been surprised at his *in absentia* paternity.

The offspring of this curious union were more curious still. They were the Aloeidae, so-called from Iphimedeia's husband Aloeus, who

was not aware of his wife's aquatic fixation. He, incidentally, was Iphimedeia's uncle. The Aloeidae, Otus and Ephialtes, were amazing twins. They caused no end of problems for the Olympians. Even before their beards grew they were gigantic in size. They attempted to scale Olympus and threatened the gods with war. They put Ares in chains and held him captive for 13 months; Hermes managed to free him.

Iphimedeia and Pancratis, the half-sister of the Aloeidae, were captured by pirates and carried to Strongyle (Naxos) but were rescued by the twins. Otus and Ephialtes later instituted the worship of the Muses on Mount Helicon. They then set out to sleep with Hera and Artemis, but Artemis, who had mastered the art of punishment, sent a stag between them so that they killed each other trying to spear the beast.

The tomb of Iphimedeia was shown at Anthedon along with that of her sons. She was worshipped as a heroine at Mylasia in Caria and immortalized by Polygnotus in the Lesche at Delphi. [Homer, *Iliad* 5.385, *Odyssey* 11.304; Apollodorus 1.7.4; Diodorus Siculus 5.50; Hyginus, *Fables* 28; Pausanias 9.22.2,5,29.1; Pindar, *Pythian Odes* 7.89; Stephanus Byzantium, "Aloium"; Parthenius, *Love Stories* 19.]

IPHIMEDUSA was one of the DANAIDES, daughter of Danaus by Atlantia or Phoebe. She married and murdered Euchenor. [Apollodorus 2.1.5.]

IPHINOE (1) was one of the PROETIDES.

IPHINOE (2) was the wife of Metion and mother of Daedalus, according to some. The mother of Daedalus is usually called ALCIPPE. [Scholiast on Sophocles' *Oedipus at Colonus* 468.]

IPHINOE (3) was a daughter of Nisus, son of Pandion. Her mother was Abrota, and her sister was Scylla. Aegeus had assigned the kingdom of Megara to Nisus, and Nisus had to defend this kingdom against Minos when the Cretan ruler attacked Attica in retribution for the death of his son Androgeus. Scylla fell in love with Minos and betrayed the kingdom, which thereafter along with Athens had to pay tribute to Crete.

Iphinoe married her uncle Megareus, brother to her mother. He succeeded his father-in-law (who was also his brother-in-law). Iphinoe's children by him were Euippus, Timalcus, Euaechme, and Hippomenes. Euippus was killed by the Cithaeronian lion, and Timalcus was killed, some said, by Theseus during the raid of the Dioscuri on Aphidna (not likely, since Theseus was in Hades at that time with Peirithous). Whatever the case, being without direct heirs, Megareus offered his kingdom and his daughter Euaechme to whoever should kill the Cithaeronian lion. Alcathous, son of Pelops, obliged and therefore became the next king of Megara.

Iphinoe had no particular distinction beyond being the necessary link in the royal line from Nisus to Ajax. She was called Merope by some writers. [Pausanias 1.19.3,39.5,41.1, 2.34.7; Apollodorus 3.15.8; Ovid, *Metamorphoses* 10.605; Hyginus, *Fables* 157.]

IPHINOE (4) was a daughter of Alcathous and Euaechme. Her father overcame the Cithaeronian lion and became king of Megara. He rebuilt the walls of the city. Iphinoe's brothers Echepolis and Callipolis died early. She herself was a virgin, so the royal line was carried forward by her sister Periboea. The Megarian women, previous to marriage, offered to her a funeral sacrifice of a lock of their hair. [Pausanias 1.42.1,7,43, 4.43.4; Apollodorus 2.4.1, 3.12.7.]

IPHINOE (5) was one of the women of Lemnos who received the Argonauts when they landed on the island. The women had killed their husbands some time before and were ready to entertain men once more. Iphinoe was the ambassador who invited the Argonauts ashore. [Apollonius Rhodius 1.702; Valerius Flaccus 2.162,327.]

IPHINOE (6), the daughter of Antaeus, was the mother of Palaemon by Heracles. Some called her AUTONOE. [Apollodorus 2.7.8; Tzetzes on Lycophron 662.]

IPHINOME was one of the AMAZONS. [Hyginus, *Fables* 163.]

IPHIS (1) was one of the THESPIADES. By Heracles she became the mother of Celeustanor. [Apollodorus 2.7.8.]

IPHIS (2) was the beloved of Patroclus, from the island of Scyros. Achilles gave Iphis to his friend when he took the city of Enyeus on the island. In the *Iliad* we see the two friends, after rejecting the offers from Agamemnon, bedding down in their tent on the same couch, Achilles with Diomede from Lesbos and Patroclus with Iphis. [Homer, *Iliad* 9.667; Philostratus, *Heroicus* 10.]

IPHIS (3) was a daughter of Ligdus and Telethusa of Phaestus in Crete. She was brought up as a boy because, previous to her birth, her father had ordered the child to be killed if it should be a girl. When Iphis grew up and became betrothed to Ianthe, the difficulty thus arising was removed by Isis, who had previously advised the mother to treat Iphis as a boy and now metamorphosed her into a youth. [Ovid, *Metamorphoses* 9.665.] (*See also* IANTHE.)

IPHITEA, the daughter of Prognaus, was the wife of Dion, a king in Laconia. Apollo, who had been kindly received by Iphitea, rewarded her by conferring the gift of prophecy upon her three daughters, Orphe, Lyco, and Carya. However, the conditions were that they should not betray the gods nor search after forbidden things. Afterward, Dionysus also came to the house of Dion; he was not only well received, like Apollo, but won the love of Carya, and therefore soon paid Dion a second visit under the pretext of consecrating a temple that the king had erected to him. However, Orphe and Lyco guarded their sister, and when in vain Dionysus reminded them of the command of Apollo, they were seized with raging madness. Having gone to the heights of Mount Taygetus, they were metamorphosed into rocks. Carya, the beloved of Dionysus, was changed into a nut tree, and the Lacedaemonians, on being informed of this by Artemis, dedicated a temple to Artemis Caryatis. [Servius on Virgil's *Eclogues* 8.30.]

IPHTHIME (1) was one of the NEREIDES and mother of the Satyrs. The Satyrs were a race of half-human, half-goat creatures. They were depicted as drunken, dancing followers of Dionysus, usually in pursuit of Maenads or nymphs. In earlier representations they were hairy and had long tails like that of a horse; their penises were usually erect and of enormous proportions. Curiously, Hermes, one of the handsomest of the gods, was called their father.

IPHTHIME (2) was a daughter of Icarius. He was one of the sons of Gorgophone, and brother to Aphareus, Leucippus, and Tyndareus. Driven from Sparta by his half-brother Hippocoon, Icarius went to Acarnania, where he married Asterodeia and became father of Alyzeus, Leucadius, Penelope, Iphthime, and others.

Iphthime married Eumelus, son of Admetus and Alcestis. He went to the Trojan War in 11 ships as commander of the men of Pherae, Boebe, Glaphyrae, and Iolcus. He was distinguished for his excellent horses. Apparently he returned safely from the war.

There is a hint that Iphthime stayed with her sister Penelope part of the time that the war was in progress. Athena assumed Iphthime's appearance once when she appeared to· Penelope; had her sister been remote, Penelope probably would have been less inclined to believe the message. [Homer, *Odyssey* 1.329, 4.791,797; Apollodorus 3.10.6.]

IPSIA was, according to some, the mother of Absyrtus by Aeetes. Most others called her ASTERODEIA.

IRIS can almost be regarded as the personification of personifications. The rainbow is the epitome of personifications, delicately beautiful, evanescent. As messenger of the gods, fleet-footed Iris, even exceeding Hermes, used her own symbol as a path of delivery. The rainbow, ever lying just beyond reach, even suggests the whole world of myth, hovering just beyond imagination, just beyond history.

Iris was the daughter of Thaumas, the Wonderful. Her mother was Electra, and her sisters were the fearful Harpies. Again, the incredible Greek sense of balance made her a messenger of light and her sisters messengers of darkness.

Iris cannot be visualized except by the ever-present rainbow. She was a function and not a personality. Only one reference gave her sexuality, and that was as the mother of Eros by Zephyrus. Otherwise she was at the will of the gods, setting in motion their wishes. Zeus sent by her a message to Demeter to be reconciled to the rape of Persephone. Hera sent her to Cheiron's cave to make Peleus ready for his marriage to Thetis. Hera also sent her to Menelaus in Crete with the news of Helen's elopement. Iris fetched a cup of water from the Styx River when the gods were taking oaths, part of which was pouring water from the cup.

She seemed to accomplish a few missions on her own. She roused Achilles from his lamentations and exhorted him to rescue the body of Patroclus. She carried the wounded Aphrodite from the Trojan War field of battle to Olympus. She assumed the appearance of Beroe, a Trojan captive, and persuaded the captured women to set fire to Aeneas' ships on the coast of Sicily. She commanded the Boreades to set free her sisters, the Harpies, if they promised to leave the seer Phineus in peace.

It is impossible to get a picture of this lightning-speed individual. She was surnamed Aellopus, or fleet-footed like the storm wind. Was she beautiful? Did she have feelings? She was frequently mentioned by the ancient playwrights but usually only in the context of messenger of the gods, particularly Hera. [Homer, *Iliad* 8.409, 18.166; Virgil, *Aeneid* 5.620; Diodorus Siculus 4.4; *Homeric Hymn to Demeter* 419; Hesiod, *Theogony* 266,775; Apollodorus 1.2.2,6; Pausanias 4.33.6; Ovid, *Metamorphoses* 4.479,845; Tzetzes, *Chiliades* 1.217.]

ISIS was not a Greek or Roman goddess, but she had altars and temples in Greek and Roman cities and a substantial cult following. She was the wife of the divine Osiris. When he was killed and his body scattered, Isis searched for him and thus became identified with the classical wanderers and searchers such as Io and Demeter. Inevitably she made her way into Greek myth, so that Artemis was considered by some to be her daughter by Dionysus. Io, originally an Argive, was said to have introduced the worship of Isis. The funereal emphasis of Egyptian mythology served to identify her with Persephone. Beyond these particular identities, Isis remained an

Egyptian divinity. [Herodotus 2.156; Plutarch, *Isis and Osiris*; Apuleius, *Golden Ass* 11.]

ISMENE (1) was a daughter of the Asopus River and Metope. According to some, she was married to Argus and was the mother of Iasus, who became the father of Io. The genealogy of Io is complicated; it is almost impossible to accept a single version and be consistent since father, brothers, and other relatives continue to turn up in unexpected relationships. Ismene, as a daughter of Asopus, could be expected to be in an ancestral role, since many of her sisters (e.g., Aegina) were kidnapped by gods and became mothers of dynasties. [Apollodorus 2.1.3.]

ISMENE (2) was one of the four children of Oedipus by his mother, Iocaste, and therefore was half-sister to her father. Her sister was Antigone, and her brothers were Polyneices and Eteocles. Ismene was still a little girl when her father/brother's unhappy story unfolded, and was probably only partially aware of the circumstances. She grew up amidst the contest of her two brothers for the throne of Thebes.

When the seven heroes marched on the city, Tydeus, the son of Oeneus and one of the principals, came to Thebes as ambassador in advance of the others and sought to reconcile the brothers. Eteocles would not listen to him. Tydeus then challenged the Thebans to a succession of single combats and managed to defeat one after another. He finally decided the Thebans were beyond convincing and departed. He was ambushed but killed all his assailants. This experience with the stubborn Thebans hardened his heart and made him doubly vindictive.

During the siege of the city, Athena advised him that Ismene was having an affair with a young Theban named Theoclymenus. He learned that the lovers were accustomed to meet in a secret place just outside the city (which seems a dangerous thing to do in a city under siege) and lay in wait. He surprised the couple in their lovemaking. Theoclymenus managed to escape (which does not say much for his integrity), but Ismene was taken prisoner. She begged for her life, but Tydeus was unrelenting and killed her.

This story is not generally known. It probably arose as an effort to include all the children of Oedipus in his doom-laden history. There appears to be no connection between her name and that of the Ismenus, one of the rivers of Thebes. Perhaps she was named for the river. Some accounts called Ismene and her brothers and sisters the children of Eurygeneia by Oedipus, which removed the incest focus of the story. [Apollodorus 3.5.8; Pausanias 9.5.5–10; Sophocles, *Antigone* 1, *Oedipus at Colonus* 321; Scholiast on Euripides' *Phoenician Maidens* 53,1760.]

ISSA was a daughter of Macareus in Lesbos, and the beloved of Apollo. He took the appearance of a shepherd and made love to her. She must have been exceedingly beautiful, since Hermes also slept with her. By him she became the mother of the seer Prylis. Perhaps the two gods collaborated in giving her name to the Lesbian town of Issa. In fact, the whole island of Lesbos was earlier called Issa. Macareus introduced written laws to the island even before the Trojan War. [Ovid, *Metamorphoses* 6.124; Tzetzes on Lycophron 220; Stephanus Byzantium, "Issa"; Strabo 1.3.19.]

ISSORIA was a surname of the Laconian Artemis. She was worshipped under this name on Mount Issorion in Sparta, where she had a sanctuary. [Pausanias 3.14.2,25.3.]

ITEA was one of the DANAIDES. She was married to Antiochus. [Hyginus, *Fables* 170.]

ITHOME was a nymph from whom the Messenian hill of Ithome derived its name. According to a Messenian tradition, Ithome and Neda, from whom a small river of the country derived its name, were said to have nursed Zeus and to have bathed the infant god in the spring of Clepsydra. [Pausanias 4.33.2.]

ITONE was the daughter of Lyctius. No one really knows anything about Lyctius and his daughter. Crete was populated before Zeus went there with Europa. Some of the population were probably families of those who had tended Zeus after his birth on Crete. Minos was one of the sons of Zeus by Europa and founder of the

Minoan dynasty. He married Itone, and she became by him the mother of Lycastus. Lycastus married Ida, the daughter of Corybas, and became by her the father of Minos II, the king under whose reign the famous labyrinth was built. [Diodorus Siculus 4.60; Stephanus Byzantium, "Itone."]

ITONIA, Itonias, or Itonis was a surname of Athena. This name came either from the town of Iton in the south of Phthiotis or from Itonus, who has been called her father. This Itonus was also father of Iodama, whom Athena was said to have killed accidentally. At Iton the goddess had a celebrated sanctuary and festival. From there her worship spread into Boeotia and especially the country around Lake Copais, where the Pamboeotia was celebrated. [Pausanias 1.13.2, 9.34.1; Plutarch, *Pyrrhus* 26; Polybius 4.25.]

IYNX (1) was a daughter of Pan and Echo or Peitho. For some reason she took it upon herself to make Zeus fall in love with Io. As a woodland nymph she shared with other nymphs a running battle with Hera. Nymphs were favorites of Zeus, and some of them often diverted Hera while Zeus romped with the others. Iynx's own mother, Echo, had been deprived of her ability to converse because she once detained Hera in idle chatter while Zeus dallied with another nymph. Perhaps Iynx caused Zeus to lust after Io in retaliation. But, as in the case of Echo, Hera caught up with her and changed her into a bird called the wryneck (*iynx torquilla*). [Scholiast on Theocritus 2,17, on Pindar's *Pythian Odes* 4.380, on Pindar's *Nemean Odes* 4.56; Tzetzes on Lycophron 310.]

IYNX (2) was one of the PIERIDES. Iynx was changed into a bird called the iynx, which became the symbol of passionate and restless love. Such a bird was given by Aphrodite to Jason, who used it to excite the love of Medea. [Pindar, *Pythian Odes* 4.380; Tzetzes on Lycophron 310; Antoninus Liberalis 9.]

JANA was an ancient Latin divinity who along with Janus was regarded as the highest of the gods. She was the moon and he was the sun. Jana was another form of Diana, but the ancients also connected the word with the word for door (*janua*). [Varro, *On Country Matters* 1.37.]

JUGA, or Jugalis, that is, the goddess of marriage, occurs as a surname of Juno in the same sense as the Greek Zygia. She had a temple under this name in the forum at Rome, and the street that started at the temple was called Vicus Jugarius. [St. Augustine, *City of God* 4.8,11, 6.9.]

JUNO was the female supreme being among the Romans. She was the wife of Jupiter and queen of the heavens. From an early time she was identified with the Greek Hera, but she had many attributes that were purely Roman. As queen of heaven she was surnamed Regina and had a temple by that name on the Aventine.

She protected everything connected with women, from birth to death. This matronage was reflected in such surnames as Virginalis, Opigena, Sospita, and Matrona. On their birthday women offered sacrifices to Juno Natalis. Of greatest concern to her was the ability of women to bear children. Consequently the whole realm of the menstrual cycle, courtship, and marriage were matters to which she devoted most of her attention. As goddess of marriage she had the surnames of Juga or Jugalis. Marrying couples invoked her under the names of Domiduca, Interduca, Pronuba, and Cinxia, all having to do with the ceremony itself. The names Prema and Pertunda referred to the sex act performed by newlyweds. Fluonia was a name by which young couples invoked Juno to cease the menstrual flow, thus signifying conception. The name Lucina or Luceria suggested that a fetus would soon perceive the light of life. The month of June was considered the most propitious time for marriage, and this notion survives even today. Juno Viriplaca restored peace among quarreling married couples. She even had a sanctuary on the Palatine for women who needed to address wrongs done to them by their husbands.

The sanctity of marriage was all-important to Juno. Fornication, adultery, and inordinate preoccupation with sexual pleasure were frowned on by the goddess. Under law a prostitute could not even touch an altar of Juno. Newborn children were under her protection, and in this capacity she was compared with

Artemis and Eileithyia. The whole process of the female's progression from puberty through motherhood was celebrated in a general festival called the Matronalia.

Juno also had public responsibilities. She was the guardian of finances, and under the name of Moneta she had a temple on the Capitoline Hill. The names Curiatia and Populonia also betokened her involvement in the affairs of state. She was especially worshipped at Talerii, Lanuvium, Aricia, Tibur, and Praeneste.

It is interesting that in the Roman Juno there appears to be little preoccupation with the clandestine affairs of Jupiter. Maybe the Greek stories were simply accepted as they were and superimposed by Roman mythographers. But the whole structure of Roman myth seems more sober, even austere. One feels that the Roman equivalent of Hera would be far less inclined to pettiness, and that the state itself and the Roman people were more important than a series of vindictive actions. This is not to say there was not an occasional display of such behavior. Juno cut out the tongue of Larunda, who told her Jupiter was having an affair with Juturna.

Juno had other functions, many of them reflected in identification with minor goddesses, whose worship was eventually absorbed by her. Some of these were Feronia, Empanda, Matuta, and Mephistis. [Livy 5.21.22, 22.1, 24.10, 27.37; Varro, *On the Latin Language* 5.67,159; Ovid, *Heroides* 6.43, *Fasti* 2.56, 6.33; Horace, *Odes* 3.4,59; Virgil, *Aeneid* 7.739, 8.84; St. Augustine, *City of God* 4.11, 6.7,11, 7.3; Arnobius, *Adversus Nationes* 3.7,25, 3.9,21.23, 6.7,25; Cicero, *On Divination* 1.2; Plutarch, *Roman Questions* 77; Propertius 4.1,95; Catullus 34.13; Dionysius of Halicarnassus, *Roman Antiquities* 1.21, 4.15; Valerius Maximus 2.1.6.]

JUTURNA was the nymph of a spring in Latium. This spring was famous for its healing qualities, and its water was used in nearly all sacrifices. Eventually a chapel was dedicated to Juturna in the Campus Martius, and sacrifices were offered to her on January 11 both by private individuals and by the state. She was said to have been a lover of Jupiter, who rewarded her with immortality and rule over waters. She was called the wife of Janus and the mother of Fontus.

Juturna was also called the daughter of Daunus and Venilia, and sister of Turnus and Canens. [Virgil, *Aeneid* 10.75; Servius on Virgil's *Aeneid* 12.139; Varro, *On the Latin Language* 5.71; Ovid, *Fasti* 1.463, 2.585,606, *Metamorphoses* 14.334.]

JUVENTAS was the personification of youth, corresponding to the Greek Hebe. At a very early time her chapel on the capital existed before the temple of Jupiter was built there. She had another temple in the Circus Maximus built as a result of the Roman defeat of Hasdrubal in 207 B.C. [Livy 5.54, 36.36; Dionysius of Halicarnassus, *Roman Antiquities* 4.23; St. Augustine, *City of God* 4.23.]

LACAENA was one of the female DOGS that killed Actaeon. [Hyginus, *Fables* 181.]

LACHESIS was one of the MOIRAE.

LACINIA was a surname of Juno, under which she was worshipped near Croton, where she had a famous sanctuary. The name was derived from Lacinius, a notorious robber who stole from Heracles some of Geryones' cattle. Heracles killed him and built a temple to Juno (Hera) Lacinia. Some claimed the temple was built by Lacinius, son of Cyrene and king among the Bruttians. [Servius on Virgil's *Aeneid* 3.552; Polybius 3.33; Livy 28.46; Diodorus Siculus 4.24.]

LAMACHE was the mother of Leucophanes by Euphemus. Her name is more often seen as MALACHE.

LAMIA (1) was a daughter of Poseidon who became by Zeus the mother of the Sibyl HEROPHILE. [Pausanias 10.12.1; Plutarch, *The Oracles at Delphi No Longer Given in Verse* 9.]

LAMIA (2) was a daughter of Belus and a queen in Libya. She was very beautiful and attracted the attention of the ever-watchful and far-seeing Zeus. He had children by her, but Hera discovered their involvement and kidnapped the children. Their ultimate fate is unknown. This loss drove Lamia insane; in revenge and despair she snatched up the children of others and murdered them. The cruelty, which became obsessive, caused her appearance to change, and she became ugly with distorted features. Perhaps in a well-intended gesture, Zeus inexplicably gave her the power to take out her eyes and then reinsert them.

She was used to frighten unruly children, and the vision of the eyeless bugaboo must have been quite effective. Some called Lamia the mother of Scylla. [Diodorus Siculus 22.41; Suidas, "Lamia"; Plutarch, *On Being a Busy-Body* 2; Scholiast on Aristophanes' *Peace* 757; Eustathius on Homer's *Odyssey* 1714.]

LAMIAE, obviously related to the persona of Lamia, the fearful child-snatcher, were handsome, ghostly women who by various sensuous means lured young men to their beds. There they enjoyed the fresh, youthful energy of their victims, then drank their blood and ate their flesh. They were in ancient times the equivalent of vampires in modern legends. [Philostratus, *Life of Apollonius of Tyana* 4.25; Horace, *Ars Poetica* 340; Apuleius, *Golden Ass* 1.57.]

LAMPADO was, according to some, one of the PLEIADES. [Scholiast on Theocritus 13.25.]

LAMPATHO was, according to some, one of the PLEIADES.

LAMPETIA was one of the daughters of Helios by the nymph Neaera. She was, therefore, halfsister to Phaethon and the Heliades. She and her sister, Phaethusa, were carried to Thrinacia, an island off Sicily, to watch over the valuable herds of their father. Before Odysseus came to Thrinacia with his very last ships, he had been warned by Circe to avoid at all costs any tampering with the cattle of the sun-god. Unfortunately, unknown to Odysseus, some of his men stole and ate some of the cattle. For this sacrilege they were pursued upon their departure by storms that wrecked the fleet and drowned everyone but Odysseus.

Lampetia married Asclepius, according to some, and bore several children by him. [Homer,

Odyssey 12.128,132,261; Propertius 3.12,29; Hyginus, *Fables* 154; Ovid, *Metamorphoses* 2.349; Apollonius Rhodius 4.965.]

LAMPETO was an Amazon queen who with Marpesia and Hippo seized a great part of Asia Minor and Syria, and helped found the cities of Ephesus, Smyrna, Cyrene, and Myrina. [Strabo 11.5.4; Justinus 2.4.]

LANASSA was the daughter of Cleodaeus, son of Hyllus and grandson of Heracles. She was carried off from the temple of the Dodonaean Zeus by Neoptolemus, son of Achilles. She became by him the mother of several children. The usual account is that Neoptolemus brought Andromache, Hector's widow, from Troy and had sons by her. He later left her and married Hermione, daughter of Helen and Menelaus. Shortly thereafter he was murdered at Delphi. It is unclear where Lanassa could fit into this chronology. One of her sons was Pyrrhus, which was Neoptolemus' original name, and he was the first in a long line of Molossian kings that reached all the way to Alexander the Great. So it appears that ancient biographers invented Lanassa to provide a link between the heroes Heracles and Achilles and the historical dynasty of Macedonia. [Justinus 17.3; Plutarch, *Pyrrhus* 1.]

LAOCOOSA was, according to some, the wife of Aphareus and mother of Idas and Lynceus. The wife of Aphareus is usually called ARENE. [Theocritus 22.206.]

LAODAMEIA (1) was the daughter of Bellerophon. She is usually called DEIDAMEIA.

LAODAMEIA (2) was a daughter of Acastus, son of Pelias. Her mother was probably Astydameia, although Acastus was recorded as having a second wife. He had participated both in the Argonaut and the Calydonian boar hunt, and after his father was killed by his sisters, he became king of Iolcus.

While Laodameia was still young, Peleus, later to become father of Achilles, went to Iolcus to be purified for a murder. Astydameia fell in love with him and, being rejected by him, accused him of attempted seduction. Acastus tried unsuccessfully to kill him; later Peleus returned to kill both of Laodameia's parents. She then married Protesilaus and moved to Phylace.

Not long after their marriage, Protesilaus went off to the Trojan War and was the first Greek killed at Troy. When his body was brought back, Laodameia begged the gods to allow her to converse with him for only a few hours. The request was granted, and Protesilaus lived a while longer. When it came time for him to die again, Laodameia threw herself on the funeral pyre and died with him. A later tradition says she made an image of her husband and worshipped it. Her father commanded her to burn the image. She did, but leapt into the fire and was herself consumed. The second version ignores the account of her father's death at the hands of Peleus.

The wife of Protesilaus was also called Polydora, daughter of Meleager by Cleopatra. Protesilaus had a magnificent temple at Eleusis and a sanctuary at Phylace, where funeral games were celebrated. It is not recorded that Laodameia shared any honors with him. [Ovid, *Heroides* 13, *Ex Ponto* 3.1,110; Catullus 64.74; Lucian, *Dialogues of the Dead* 23.1; Servius on Virgil's *Aeneid* 6.447; Hyginus, *Fables* 103,104; Eustathius on Homer's *Iliad* 325; Pausanias 3.4.5.]

LAODAMEIA (3) was a daughter of Amyclas and Diomede, and the mother of Triphylus by Arcas. Other writers called the wife of Arcas ERATO. [Pausanias 10.9.3.]

LAODAMEIA (4) was the nurse of Orestes. She was more often called ARSINOE. [Scholiast on Pindar's *Pythian Odes* 11.25.]

LAODAMEIA (5) was a daughter of Alcmaeon and wife of Peleus. More often the wife of Peleus was called ANTIGONE, daughter of Eurytion. [Scholiast on Homer's *Iliad* 2.684.]

LAODICE (1) was a Hyperborean maiden who, together with Hyperoche and five companions, was sent from the country of the Hyperboreans to carry sacrifices to the island of Delos. [Herodotus 4.33.] (*See also* HYPEROCHE.)

LAODICE (2) was a nymph, the second wife of Phoroneus. Some called her Europa. Phoroneus, son of the river-god Inachus, was the first ruler of Peloponnesus and the first to offer sacrifices to Hera at Argos. He also taught the use of fire and united the people. He first married Peitho, by whom he was the father of Car. Afterward he married Laodice and had Apis and Niobe. Both her children continued the Argive line, Apis giving his name to Apia, the earlier designation of Peloponnesus. [Apollodorus 2.1.1; Pausanias 2.22.6; Hyginus, *Fables* 143.]

LAODICE (3) was a daughter of Cinyras, the king of Cyprus. The accounts of Cinyras vary in regard to his offspring, and according to some of them Laodice would have been a sister of Adonis. She married Elatus, son of Arcas of Arcadia, and had by him four sons, Stymphalus, Aepytus, Cyllen, and Pereus. Elatus was also called father of Ischys and Dotis, but they could have been illegitimate children. Laodice at first resided on Mount Cyllen with her husband and children, but they later went to Phocis, where Elatus helped protect the Delphic oracle against the Phlegyans. He founded the town of Elateia in Phocis. He was honored by statues at Elateia and Tegea. Both Stymphalus and Aepytus died early, and Pereus continued the line. He was an ancestor of Telephus, who played an important role in the Trojan War. [Apollodorus 2.7.8, 3.9.1; Pausanias 8.4.3, 22.1,48.6, 10.34.3; Pindar, *Pythian Odes* 3.31; Stephanus Byzantium, "Dotion."]

LAODICE (4) was a daughter of Priam and Hecuba. According to Homer she was the wife of Helicaon, son of Antenor. Antenor had shown sympathy to the Greek cause, and it seems Helicaon was spared by Odysseus. Suspecting she might become one of the captive women, Laodice prayed to be swallowed up by the earth, and her prayer was answered on the night of the fall of Troy.

A better-known tradition had her becoming the lover of Acamas, the son of Theseus, when he accompanied Diomedes to Troy as one of the ambassadors seeking the return of Helen. She bore a son to Acamas, and the boy, Munitus, was reared by his great-grandmother Aethra, Theseus' mother and Helen's slave.

Pausanias saw a painting of Laodice in the Lesche at Delphi, but he felt she was represented not as a captive but as a free woman because of the debt the Greeks owed Antenor and his family. Hyginus called her the wife of Telephus, but he was confusing her with her aunt Astyoche, daughter of Laomedon. Munitus returned to Greece with his father and great-grandmother, but later died in Thessaly from a snakebite. Acamas succeeded to the throne of Athens. [Homer, *Iliad* 3.123; Pausanias 10.26.7; Tzetzes on Lycophron 513,547; Hyginus, *Fables* 101; Apollodorus, *Epitome* 5.23.]

LAODICE (5) was a name by which ELECTRA, daughter of Agamemnon, was often called.

LAODICE (6) was the daughter of Agapenor of Tegea. Agapenor was marginally involved in the story of the fatal necklace of Harmonia. When Phegeus' sons killed Alcmaeon, they gave their sister as a slave to Agapenor. It was at his house that the sons of Alcmaeon killed the sons of Phegeus. Agapenor received 60 ships from Agamemnon and led the Arcadians to Troy. He had been one of the suitors of Helen and was under oath to protect her. He survived Troy but on his way home was shipwrecked on the coast of Cyprus. He founded the town of Paphus and the famous temple of Aphrodite Paphia. Laodice, whom he fathered there, later sent a robe to Tegea as a gift for Athena Alea. Nothing at all is known of Laodice, but it is safe to suppose that she was a priestess of Aphrodite at the famous Paphian temple. [Pausanias 8.5.2,53.2; Homer, *Iliad* 2.609; Hyginus, *Fables* 81,97; Apollodorus 3.7.5,10.8.]

LAODICE (7) was the daughter of Iphis, son of Alector. She was the wife of Hipponous and mother of Capaneus. The mother of Capaneus was more often called ASTYNOME, daughter of Talaus. [Scholiast on Euripides' *Phoenician Maidens* 180.]

LAOGORE was a daughter of Cinyras in Cyprus, sister of Orsedice and BRAESIA, and, according to some, of Adonis.

LAOMACHE was one of the AMAZONS. [Hyginus, *Fables* 163.]

LAOMEDEIA was one of the NEREIDES. [Hesiod, *Theogony* 258.]

LAONOME (1) was the wife of Alcaeus and mother of Amphitryon, according to some. More often the mother of Amphitryon was called ASTYDAMEIA. [Pausanias 8.14.2.]

LAONOME (2) was a nymph who was married to Odoedocus. By him she was mother of Oileus and Calliarus. Oileus was an Argonaut but mainly famous for being the father of the Lesser Ajax. Calliarus was the founder of the Locrian town of Calliarus. [Apollodorus 5.10.8; Stephanus Byzantium, "Kalliaros."]

LAONOME (3) was a daughter of Amphitryon and Alcmena, and therefore half-sister of Heracles. Her relationship to her famous brother was never mentioned, but both her husbands were companions of Heracles. It would be interesting to know more about these associations and how both these men happened to marry Heracles' sister. Both, along with Heracles, were Argonauts. It is likely that Polyphemus, son of Elatus, was Laonome's first husband and that he and Heracles took the voyage as in-laws. When Hylas, Heracles' lover, got lost in Mysia, Polyphemus left the *Argo* with Heracles to help locate the boy. He founded Cius in Mysia and fell in a battle against the Chalybes, thereby leaving Laonome a widow. It was not common for widows to remarry (Gorgophone, daughter of Perseus, was supposed to have been the first to do so), but Laonome next married Euphemus, son of Poseidon and helmsman of the *Argo*. He was already father of a son by one of the Lemnian women with whom many of the Argonauts mated. Euphemus was quite unusual, having inherited from his father the ability to walk on water. By the Lemnian woman, not Laonome, he became the father of a line that eventually produced Battus, the founder of Cyrene. [Tzetzes on Lycophron 886; Apollonius Rhodius 1.182; Scholiast on Apollonius Rhodius 1.1241; Valerius Flaccus 1.457; Apollodorus 1.9.16; Scholiast on Pindar's *Pythian Odes* 4.76.]

LAOPHONTE, daughter of Pleuron, according to some was the wife of Thestius, and mother of Althaea and Leda. According to others Thestius' wife was EURYTHEMIS. [Apollodorus 1.7.7.; Scholiast on Apollonius Rhodius 1.146.]

LAOSOOS, Rouser of Nations, was one of the epithets of Athena, derived from her warlike character. The name was also applied to Eris, goddess of discord. [Homer, *Iliad* 13.128, 20.48.]

LAOTHOE (1) was a daughter of Altes, king of the Leleges. She was, according to some, the mother of two of Priam's illegitimate sons, Lycaon and Polydorus. There has always been a question about whether or not Hecuba was the mother of Polydorus and whether her final days had to do with getting revenge for his murder. But Priam had as many illegitimate sons and daughters as legitimate ones. The Homeric account called Polydorus the son of Laothoe. He challenged Achilles and was killed by him. At least one account had him stoned to death by the Greeks before the walls of Troy. As for Lycaon, he was also slain by Achilles. Thus Laothoe lost both her sons in the war. Polydorus, the younger, was still an adolescent. Laothoe was probably taken as a captive. [Homer, *Iliad* 3.333, 21.35,85, 22.46,406.]

LAOTHOE (2) was the mother of Echion by Hermes, according to some. Echion's mother was usually called ANTIANEIRA. [Orphica, *Argonautica* 134.]

LAOTHOE (3) was the wife of Idmon. He was a son of Apollo and one of the soothsayers who accompanied the Argonauts. Laothoe did not know when her husband left that she would never see him again, but he knew. His spirit of adventure overcame what he had divined as his certain fate. He indeed was killed by a boar in the country of the Mariandynians. Laothoe's son was Thestor. He became a priest in the service of his grandfather and was himself the father of the famous seer Calchas. [Homer, *Iliad* 1.69; Hyginus, *Fables* 128; Apollonius Rhodius 2.826.]

LAOTHOE (4) was one of the THESPIADES and by Heracles the mother of Antiphus. [Apollodorus 2.7.8.]

LAPHRIA was a surname of Artemis among the Calydonians, from whom the worship of the goddess was introduced at Naupactus and Patrae in Achaia. At Patrae it was not established until the time of Augustus, and its introduction was accompanied by a great festival. The name Laphria probably came from a hero named Laphrius, son of Castalius, who was said to have instituted the worship of Artemis at Calydon. Laphria was also a surname of Athena. Britomartis, who was closely identified with the worship of Artemis, went from Argos to Cephallenia, where she received divine honors under the name of Laphria. [Pausanias 4.31.6, 7.18.6; Scholiast on Euripides' *Orestes* 1087; Lycophron 356.]

LARISSA (1) was a daughter of Pelasgus from whom the citadel of Argos and two Thessalian towns, one on the Peneius River and one on the sea, were believed to have derived their name. [Pausanias 2.24.1.]

LARISSA (2) was a daughter of the Pelasgian ruler Piasus. He was a king at Phriconis (Cyme) on the Hermus River. He lusted after his daughter and overpowered her. In outrage she pushed him into a huge wine barrel, where he drowned. Larissa was said to have married Cyzicus, the king of the Doliones on the Propontis. His wife was usually called Cleite.

Larissa was also recorded as having two sons by Poseidon—Pelasgus, who founded Thessalian Argos, and Phthius. Phthia, in Thessaly, the home of Peleus and Achilles, derived its name from the second son. [Dionysius of Halicarnassus, *Roman Antiquities* 1.17; Eustathius on Homer's *Iliad* 321; Parthenius, *Love Stories* 28.]

LARISSAEA was a surname of Athena, who derived it from the Larissus River between Elis and Achaia, where the goddess had a sanctuary. [Pausanias 7.17.3.]

LARUNDA, daughter of Almon, was the nymph who gossiped to Juno that Jupiter was having an affair with Juturna. For this indiscretion Larunda was deprived of her tongue and condemned to the lower world as an infernal water nymph. Mercury, the messenger god and conductor of dead souls, fell in love with her on the way to Hades and impregnated her. From this union two Lares were born.

Larunda, being a nymph on reassignment, was not dead when these developments took place, although Mercury came close to an act of necrophilia. The birth of the twin Lares in the underworld was a unique occurrence. Larunda's name is close in meaning to the Latin words for talkative. She was identified with Muta and Tacita, but certainly not before her tongue was removed. [Ovid, *Fasti* 2.599; Lactantius 1.20.]

LARYMNA was a daughter of Cycnus, son of Opus. Her brother was Odoedocus, who became the father of Oileus. Cycnus in Locris derived its name from her father, while two Boeotian towns were named Larymna. [Pausanias 6.21.7, 9.23.4; Eustathius on Homer's *Iliad* 277.]

LATHRIA (*See* ANAXANDRA)

LATIVERNA (*See* LAVERNA)

LATONA (*See* LETO)

LAURENTIA (*See* ACCA LARENTIA)

LAURINA was the daughter of Latinus, the son of Faunus. When Locrus went to Italy from Scheria, island of the Phaeacians (modern Corfu), he was hospitably received by Latinus, who gave him Laurina in marriage. At a later time, Heracles went through Italy while driving the cattle of Geryones back to Greece, and Locrus warmly received him. Latinus, who was visiting his daughter, coveted the beautiful cattle and helped himself to some of them. Heracles killed him. Meanwhile, believing his father-in-law was going to get the better of Heracles, Locrus rushed to help his guest. Thinking Locrus was coming against him, Heracles slew him as well. When he realized the truth of the matter he mourned Locrus and performed sacrifices to his spirit. He was ordered by an oracle to found a

city on the spot where the tomb was and to call it after his unfortunate friend. Laurina thus lost her father and husband. There is no record of her subsequent fate. [Conon, *Narrations* 3.]

LAVERNA, or Lativerna, was the patron divinity of thieves. Her name probably was derived from *levare*, to steal. In Rome she had a sacred grove on the Via Salaria and an altar near Porta Lavernalis, the gate that derived its name from her. [Arnobius, *Adversus Nationes* 3.26; Varro, *On the Latin Language* 5.163; Festus, "Laverniones."]

LAVINIA was a daughter of Latinus, king of Latium, and Amata. She was named for her father's brother Lavinius, and it is interesting to see the complicated, repetitive system of Roman family names in evidence so early. Lavinia was betrothed to Turnus, king of the Rutuli, before the arrival of Aeneas. When Aeneas and his Trojans, including his son Ascanius, settled in Latium, a war seemed certain between them and the aborigines, but an alliance was concluded, and the allies conquered the Rutulians.

Aeneas sued for the hand of Lavinia. The marriage was opposed by Amata because she favored a political alliance with Turnus, to whom she had already promised Lavinia. When she saw her plans were not working out, she stirred up another war with Turnus. Aeneas meanwhile married Lavinia and named for her the town Lavinium, which he founded. The war continued until Turnus and Latinus both were killed. When Amata learned Turnus had fallen, she hanged herself. Aeneas became the sole ruler and united the two kingdoms into one.

We do not get a very clear picture of Lavinia. We do know she was possessive, perhaps a trait inherited from her mother. Once, Anna, the sister of Dido, went to Italy and was kindly received by her friend Aeneas, but Lavinia was jealous and planned to kill her. Anna was warned in a dream and escaped. One would have expected Lavinia to be jealous of her stepson Ascanius, particularly since she was slow in bearing Aeneas a son.

The Rutuli came back, this time supported by Etruscans, and Aeneas fell in battle against them. His body was not found. It was suspected that Aphrodite carried her son to heaven. A monument was erected to him, probably at the insistence of Lavinia.

Lavinia bore a posthumous son, Silvius, to Aeneas. When he grew up, Ascanius let him have Lavinium and went to found Alba. When he died, he also passed Alba to Silvius, although some accounts say he had been compelled to leave Lavinium because of the hostility of his stepmother. Through Silvius the Roman kings descended.

According to one account, Anius was called a son of Aeneas and Lavinia. In another, Lavinia was described as the daughter of the priest Anius in Delos. Anius was a soothsayer who followed Aeneas on his trip to the west and died in Lavinium. [Dionysius of Halicarnassus, *Roman Antiquities* 1.50,64,70; Livy 1.1,2; Virgil, *Aeneid* 7.47,52; Servius on Virgil's *Aeneid* 1.6, 3.80, 6.761; Plutarch, *Romulus* 3; Arnobius, *Adversus Nationes* 2.71.]

LEAENA was one of the DOGS of Actaeon. [Hyginus, *Fables* 181.]

LEAGORE was one of the NEREIDES. [Hesiod, *Theogony* 256.]

LEANEIRA was, according to some, the wife of Arcas. Usually his wife was called ERATO. [Apollodorus 3.9.1.]

LEDA is a name that immediately stirs the imagination, for who has not seen dozens of representations of this voluptuous woman being embraced by a gigantic swan? Who has not heard the irreverent schoolboy Tennysonian paraphrase: "After many a Leda dies the swan"? This famous coupling was not just a quick and soon-forgotten barnyard scuffle, for it produced the spark that ignited the most glorious war of all time.

Leda was a daughter of Thestius and Eurythemis, although there were a number of variations on her parentage. Among the names given to her mother were Laophonte, Deidameia, Leucippe, and Paneidyia. Her sisters were Althaea and Hypermnestra, and her brothers were Iphicles, Euippus, Plexippus, Eurypylus, and Prothous. Consequently, Leda was affected by the tragedy that overtook her brothers when her nephew Meleager, Althaea's son, killed them. However, she had probably left home long before that event occurred.

The Spartan prince Tyndareus had been driven into exile by his stepbrother and had been hospitably received by Thestius in Aetolia. He fell in love with the lovely Leda and carried her back to Sparta when Heracles restored him to the throne.

The beautiful Leda drew the attention of Zeus, who was expert at circumventing the interference of husbands. One night he assumed the appearance of a swan and ravished Leda as she walked in the palace garden. The scene, although depicted many times, defies the imagination. Swans and human beings are not genitally compatible, but the father of the gods was endlessly inventive, and at least one painting demonstrates a possibility. The story goes that she was impregnated by Tyndareus on the same night. That also arouses speculation. Tyndareus must have gone first, since being trodden by a huge swan must have been an experience so unnerving that nothing else would have been possible that same evening for Leda.

She not only became pregnant by both Zeus and Tyndareus but when her time came, she laid two eggs. It has always been a mystery why Tyndareus' comparatively prosaic performance should have produced an egg, but such is the story. The midwife must have gone into shock, since obviously the eggs had to be produced intact and then hatched. Over the years the contents of the eggs have been subject to endless dispute, but the combination that makes the best sense is the one in which Helen and Polydeuces hatched from one egg and Clytemnestra and Castor from the other. That would separate the mortals from the immortals. Some claimed there was only one egg. Others went even further and maintained that Helen, at least, came from an egg laid at Rhamnus by Nemesis after she was raped by Zeus in the disguise of a swan. Leda found the egg, hatched it, and claimed Helen as her own.

There are several questions to be asked about this most phenomenal of birthings. What was Tyndareus' reaction to this curious brood? It was reported that in the temple of the

Leucippidae at Sparta there were fragments of an enormous shell said to be part of the egg or eggs laid by Leda. Was Tyndareus ever made aware that he was not the father of all four of the quadruplets?

The childhood of these four must have been full of uncommon happenings. Their interrelationships could only have been provocative since two of them were immortal, thinking and reacting correspondingly. The Dioscuri, Castor and Polydeuces, were fiercely devoted, and there is no reason to believe Clytemnestra and Helen were any less so. There were three additional children born after the famous quartet—Philonoe (sometimes written Phylonoe), Timandra, and Phoebe—and their reactions to their unusual siblings can only be imagined.

Leda might have lived long enough to see Helen kidnapped by Theseus and her return by the Dioscuri, but it is likely she died before Helen's suitors swarmed into Sparta. She was not mentioned during either of these events nor after Helen's marriage to Menelaus. Odysseus saw her in the underworld, so certainly she was not alive when Helen returned from Troy and Clytemnestra was murdered. Some accounts say she was deified as Nemesis, but this is a curious claim in view of the prior existence of Nemesis, and particularly in relation to the story that makes Leda the surrogate mother of Nemesis' egg. [Apollodorus 1.7.7, 2.7.3, 3.10.5–7; Pausanias 1.33.7, 2.18.6, 3.13.8,16.1, 8.5.1; Homer, *Iliad* 3.426, *Odyssey* 11.293, 24.199; Hyginus, *Fables* 77,155; Ovid, *Heroides* 8.77, 17.55, *Fasti* 1.706; Horace, *Odes* 1.12,25, *Ars Poetica* 147; Lucian, *Dialogues of the Gods* 2.2, 24.2,26; Pindar, *Nemean Odes* 10.80; Euripides, *Helen* 254,1497,1680, *Iphigeneia at Aulis* 49,50; Tzetzes on Lycophron 511.]

LEDAEA was a name Virgil [*Aeneid* 3.328] called Hermione, the granddaughter of Leda.

LEIPEPHILENE was a daughter of Iolaus, son of Heracles. She was married to her cousin Phylas, son of Antiochus and grandson of Heracles. Leipephilene and Phylas were parents of Hippotes and Thero. Thero was mother of Chaeron by Apollo. Hippotes killed the seer Carnus at Naupactus when the Heracleidae

were on the point of invading Peloponnesus. This brought calamities on the army, and Hippotes was banished from its command. He was believed to be the founder of Cnidus in Caria. [Pausanias 9.40.6; Diodorus Siculus 4.54; Scholiast on Euripides' *Medea* 20.]

LEIRIOPE, Liriope, or Leirioessa was the mother of Narcissus by the river-god Cephissus. A seer told Leiriope, the first person ever to consult him, that Narcissus would live to a ripe old age as long as he never knew himself. We know Narcissus did not live to a ripe old age, but it is doubtful he could be said to have known himself. He was pursued by many lovers, male and female, but he rejected them all. One of the lovers killed himself and called upon the gods to avenge him. Narcissus fell in love with the beautiful youth he saw looking up at him from the depths of a pool. The fact that he pined away because this lover was unattainable suggests he had less than a strong grasp on reality. He was changed into the flower known as the narcissus. There is no record of Leiriope's reaction to her son's strange behavior and metamorphosis. She was probably a doting mother whose son could do no wrong. [Ovid, *Metamorphoses* 3.342; Conon, *Narrations* 24; Pausanias 9.31.6; Eustathius on Homer's *Iliad* 266.]

LEIS was a daughter of Orus, king of Troezen, and the mother by Poseidon of Althepus. A territory in Troezenia was called Althepia after him. In his reign Athena and Poseidon disputed the possession of Troezen with each other. [Pausanias 2.30.6.]

LENAE were one of the classes of women who accompanied Dionysus. As with the Maenades, they were represented as raging with madness or enthusiasm, with disheveled hair, and carrying thyrsus staffs entwined with ivy and headed with pine cones or other mystic paraphernalia. [Hesychius, "Lenai"; *Palatine Anthology* 9.248.]

LEONTIDES were the daughters of Leos. He was a son of Orpheus, and the phyle of Leontis derived its name from him. His daughters were Praxithea (or Phasithea), Theope, and Eubule. He also had a son, Clyanthus. Once, Athens was suffering from a famine, and the Delphic oracle stated that relief would come only with human sacrifice. It is not clear whether the oracle specifically named one of the daughters of Leos or whether the sacrifice of all three was required. In more than one account, the sisters chose to die together if one of them had to die. In any case, the three were sacrificed. They were afterward honored by the Athenians, who erected to them the Leocoreion in the Agora.

The sources indicate that Leos unhesitatingly obeyed the oracle. One wonders if perhaps he should not have offered himself instead. How did the sisters feel about this cruel fate, and did they beg for their lives or go willingly to the sacrificial altar? [Suidas, "Leos"; Pausanias 1.5.2, 10.10.1; Diodorus Siculus 15.7; Demosthenes, *Funeral Speech* 1398; Aelian, *Various Narratives* 12.28.]

LERNAEA was a surname of Demeter at Lerna. The mysteries of Lernaean Demeter were celebrated here, one of the places said to be the entrance to the underworld and the one taken by Hades when he abducted Persephone. [Pausanias 2.36.6–8, 37.1–3,5.]

LETHE, the personification of oblivion, was a daughter of Eris, the goddess of discord. Her name was given to the Lethe River in the underworld. The dead were required to drink from this river in order to forget everything about their earthly life. If for any reason one returned to the upper world, he or she had to drink from the Lethe to remove all memory of Hades. There was also a spring called Lethe at the oracle of Trophonius at Lebadeia.

In spite of her narcoleptic association (she was also sister of Thanatos and Hypnos, Death and Sleep), Lethe was visited by Zeus. Some claimed she was the mother by him of the Charites. Some said she was also the mother of Dionysus. [Plutarch, *Table-Talk* 7.5; Hesiod, *Theogony* 227; Scholiast on Pindar's *Olympic Odes* 3.177.]

LETO, next to Demeter, was the most celebrated mother in ancient myth. She was the mother of Apollo and Artemis, whose birth gave rise to a whole body of worship centered at Delos. Leto was the daughter of the Titans Coeus and Phoebe, and thus a cousin of Zeus. The cousins were lovers before Zeus married Hera, and Leto's tribulations were a result of this unfortunate timing. Apollo and Artemis might well have been the children of Asteria, Leto's sister, had she not outmaneuvered Zeus by being changed into a quail (*ortyx*) and then into the island named for the quail, Ortygia. Zeus, it seems, was not particular when it came to planting the divine seed. With Asteria out of the picture, he returned to Leto and made her pregnant. By that time Hera was on the scene, and she enlisted the help of two or three monsters to prevent Leto from finding a place to give birth. Chief among these was Python, the frightening denizen of Delphi, who pursued the hapless Leto from land to land and island to island. All the world was afraid to receive her on account of Hera, who could send plagues, famines, and other calamities on whole populations.

Finally Leto reached Ortygia. This island, the metamorphosed Asteria, floated just beneath the level of the sea, but it rose to receive Leto and became anchored on four pillars. Hera had also proclaimed that Leto would not be able to give birth in any place reached by sunlight. But Poseidon was able to cover the island with a film of water that screened out the rays of the sun. Thus Leto was finally able to give birth even though Eileithyia, the goddess of birth, had to be bribed to attend her. The labor lasted for nine days. The twins Apollo and Artemis were born while Leto clung to a palm tree by the shore of a small lake. Some claimed Artemis was born first and, anticipating her future role as patron goddess of midwifery, assisted Leto in delivering Apollo. The birth was attended by all the goddesses of Olympus except Hera.

By reason of the birth of Apollo, the name of the island was changed to Delos (the Brilliant). At once it became sacred, and from that time it was unlawful for any human to be born or die on the island. Pregnant women were conveyed to the neighboring island of Rheneia when time came for delivery.

Leto's troubles were by no means over. Delos had provided only temporary respite from Hera's persecution. She fled to Lycia, taking the children with her. This was after Apollo, at the age of a few days, slew Python and thus established Delphi as a second major center of his worship. In Lycia, Leto stopped at a spring to bathe the children, but local herdsmen tried to stop her. She turned them into frogs. Lycia, sometimes referred to as the country of wolves, gave Apollo an epithet as protector from wolves.

At a later time Leto was on her way to Delphi, presumably after Apollo was established there, and was pursued near Panopeus by the giant Tityus, who tried to rape her. Ironically, Tityus was another of Zeus' bastards, whose birth had taken place under the earth to escape Hera's wrath. But Hera used any means at her disposal to make life miserable for Leto. Tityus was immediately dispatched by Apollo.

Revenge for wrongs done to Leto became an early theme in the careers of Apollo and Artemis. They ruthlessly took vengeance even on innocent bystanders for real or imagined slights to their mother. The sons and daughters of Niobe were slaughtered when Niobe boasted of her superiority over Leto because of her own large number of children in contrast to Leto's two.

Leto was worshipped mostly in conjunction with her celebrated children. Attempts to extend her visibility made her also mother of Britomartis, Selene, and Hecate, but one can see immediately that these were among the identities of Artemis. As a rule, sacrifices to Artemis and Apollo were made to Leto as well. Achilles, for example, sacrificed to all three after killing Penthesileia. At least one case has been cited in which Leto alone was worshipped. At Phaestus, when she was approached to change a girl into a boy, she did so and consequently was offered sacrifices under the name of Leto Phytia, the Creator. Places other than Delos claimed the honor of the sacred birthplace, such as Ephesus in Asia Minor, Tegyra in Boeotia, and Zoster in Attica. [Hesiod, *Theogony* 406,921; Homer, *Iliad* 1.9, 5.447, 14.327, 20.40,72, 21.499, *Odyssey* 11.318,580; *Homeric Hymn to Apollo* 14,45,89; Apollodorus 1.2.2,4.1; Hyginus, *Fables* 63,93,140; Callimachus, *Hymn to Delos* 37,61, *Hymn to Artemis* 35,37,191; Servius on Virgil's *Aeneid* 3.72; Antoninus Liberalis 17,35; Pausanias 2.30.3; Orphica, *Argonautica* 975; Pindar, *Pythian Odes* 4.160; Ovid, *Metamorphoses* 6.155,370.]

LETOGENEIA was a matronymic of Artemis from her mother, Leto. [Aeschylus, *Seven against Thebes* 148.]

LEUCE was a nymph, a daughter of Oceanus, who was carried off by Hades. After her death she was changed into a white poplar in Elysium. The white poplar was sacred to Hades. When Heracles returned from the underworld, he was crowned with poplar leaves. [Servius on Virgil's *Eclogues* 7.61; Strabo 8.3.14.]

LEUCIPPE (1) was one of the nymphs with Persephone when she was abducted by Hades. [*Homeric Hymn to Demeter* 418; Pausanias 4.30.4.]

LEUCIPPE (2) was one of the MINYADES. When the sisters were driven mad by Dionysus, it was Leucippe who was chosen by lot to offer a sacrifice to Dionysus. She gave up her son Hippasus to be torn to pieces.

LEUCIPPE (3) was the wife of Ilus and mother of Laomedon. The wife of Ilus was usually called EURYDICE, daughter of Adrastus. [Hyginus, *Fables* 250.]

LEUCIPPE (4) was one of the daughters of Thestor and Laothoe. He was a son of the seer Idmon and, in addition to Leucippe, father of Theoclymenus, Theonoe, and Calchas, the famous seer of the Trojan War. As a young girl, Theonoe was kidnapped by pirates and sold to King Icarus in Caria, who made her a privileged concubine. Disconsolate at her disappearance, Thestor searched for her. His ship was wrecked in a storm off the coast of Caria, and he was taken prisoner and confined to the slave quarters of the king. It was then Leucippe's turn to search for her father and sister, but first she consulted the Delphic oracle, which directed her to conduct the search in the attire of a priest of Apollo. Leucippe cut her hair, posed as a man, and after much travel came to Caria. She was hospitably treated, and Theonoe fell in love with the beautiful stranger. She sent word to the young priest to join her in bed, but the offer was politely rejected. Theonoe went into a rage and ordered the priest to be locked up. She summoned a slave (who, of course, was none other than Thestor) to stab the uncooperative young man. Already reluctant to perform such a deed on a priest of Apollo (his own grandfather), Thestor lamented to the intended victim about his own sad state of affairs, then turned the sword on himself. Leucippe suddenly recognized her father, whom the years had changed, and seized the sword. Leucippe went looking for her would-be executioner. As Theonoe was about to be killed, she cried out her father's name, and he recognized her. So all three were united, and King Icarus sent them home with many presents.

This nice little story was most probably taken from a lost drama. It was hardly a tragedy, since everything turned out well. The tale would have been interesting mainly as a character study since Thestor and Leucippe certainly learned a lot about Theonoe, who was willing to use her power to kill an innocent young priest for refusing to go to bed with her. [Homer, *Iliad* 1.69; Hyginus, *Fables* 128,190.]

LEUCIPPE (5) was the wife of Thestius, according to some. His wife was usually called EURYTHEMIS. [Hyginus, *Fables* 14.]

LEUCIPPE (6) was the wife of Laomedon, according to some. She was more often called STRYMO. [Apollodorus 3.12.3.]

LEUCIPPE (7) was, according to some, a daughter of Pelops and wife of Sthenelus, son of Perseus. She was usually called NICIPPE. [Scholiast on Homer's *Iliad* 19.116.]

LEUCIPPE (8) was the mother of Teuthras. He was the rescuer of Auge and her son Telephus in Teuthrania. When Telephus was still a young man, he was hunting on Mount Teuthras and pursued a boar sacred to Artemis. In a human voice the boar begged to be spared, but Teuthras killed it anyway. Artemis inflicted a leprous condition on Teuthras that caused him great agony. Leucippe sought the help of the seer Polyidus, who helped appease Artemis with generous sacrifices. Teuthras was cured and built an altar to Orthosian Artemis. [Pseudo-Plutarch, *On Rivers* 21.]

LEUCIPPIDES were daughters of the Messenian king Leucippus and Philodice. He was the brother of Aphareus, Icarius, and Tyndareus. The Leucippides usually referred only to Hilaeira and Phoebe, but strictly speaking the designation would have to include Arsinoe, the other daughter of Leucippus.

Phoebe and Hilaeira were priestesses of Athena and Artemis and betrothed to their cousins Idas and Lynceus. But many will remember that Idas was the husband of Marpessa and father of Cleopatra. Consequently, it is necessary to set up a chronology that makes sense in the events that followed. The betrothal of the cousins was probably during their extreme youth. The Dioscuri, Castor and Polydeuces, cousins of Idas and Lynceus as well as of Hilaeira and Phoebe, were in love with their cousins; with youthful bravado (helped by Polydeuces being the son of Zeus) they simply carried them away and married them.

Many accounts related that the sons of Aphareus went after their intended brides, insults were exchanged, and a battle ensued that was fatal to Idas, Lynceus, and Castor. We find that the Dioscuri and Idas and Lynceus participated in both the Argonaut and the Calydonian boar hunt, and further that Idas was described in the latter adventure as the father-in-law of Meleager. So it makes more sense to believe that while the abduction of the Leucippides might have been the beginning of the rivalry between the cousins, it was by no means the occasion for a fatal battle. The more likely story of the conclusion of their hostilities was the one in which the four, still on friendly enough terms to steal cattle together, had a quarrel over a herd they had rustled and then killed each other (with the exception of the immortal Polydeuces).

Interestingly, the Leucippides appear mainly as a motive for the famous rivalry, and there are no separate stories about them. Some said the sons of Aphareus stole Helen in revenge for the abduction of their brides-to-be. Most accounts name Theseus as the abductor of Helen. In any case, the Dioscuri, at least, would have been too young at that time to have carried off the sisters, since Helen was only 12 when she was kidnapped, and they were of the same age.

By Castor, Hilaeira became the mother of Anogon. Phoebe was the mother by Polydeuces of Mnesileus. Nothing further is known of either of these sons. [Pausanias 1.18.1; Apollodorus 3.10.3,11.2,12.8; Hyginus, *Fables* 80; Lactantius 1.10; Ovid, *Heroides* 16.327, *Fasti* 5.709; Theocritus 22.137; Propertius 1.2.15; Pindar, *Nemean Odes* 10.60.]

LEUCONOE (1) was a daughter of Poseidon and Themisto. There is some confusion here. Themisto was the third wife of Athamas and bore him four sons, Leucon, Erythrius, Schoeneus, and Ptous. A daughter by Poseidon with a name almost identical to one of the sons raises the possibility that these two children were in fact only one. Hyginus, the incurable listmaker, even headed this particular list "Sons of Poseidon" but proceeded to use a feminine name form. Whatever the situation, neither Leuconoe nor Leucon achieved any important distinction, except that Agamemnon fell in love with Leucon's son Argennus and caused his death. [Hyginus, *Fables* 157; Apollodorus 1.9.2.]

LEUCONOE (2) was, according to some, one of the MINYADES, a daughter of Minyas, but she is elsewhere called Leucippe. [Ovid, *Metamorphoses* 4.168.]

LEUCONOE (3), daughter of Lucipher, was the mother of Philammon, according to some. His mother was usually called CHIONE. [Hyginus, *Fables* 161.]

LEUCOPHRYNE (1) was a surname of Artemis derived from Leucophrys, a town in Phrygia. She had a temple there, as well as one at Magnesia on the Maeander River. Because Themistocles had once ruled at Magnesia, his sons dedicated a statue to Artemis Leucophryne on the Acropolis. There was also a statue of her at Amyclae, carved by the famous Magnesian sculptor Bathycles, who was the artist for the celebrated throne of the Amyclaean Apollo. Hermogenes, the builder of her temple at Magnesia, wrote a work on the magnificent temple. [Xenophon, *Hellenica* 3.2.19; Tacitus, *Annals* 3.62; Athenaeus 15.683; Pausanias 1.26.4; Thucydides 1.138; Plutarch, *Themistocles* 29; Vitruvius 7.]

LEUCOPHRYNE (2) was a nymph or priestess of Artemis Leucophryne whose tomb was shown in the temple of the goddess at Magnesia. [Arnobius, *Adversus Nationes* 6.6.]

LEUCOSIA was, according to some, one of the SIRENS. An island in the Gulf of Paestum derived its name from her. [Aristotle, *On Marvelous Things Heard* 103; Strabo 6.1.1.]

LEUCOTHEA (1) was the name under which HALIA was worshipped after she became divine. [Diodorus Siculus 5.55.]

LEUCOTHEA (2) was the name of INO, wife of Athamas, after her transformation into a sea deity. Under this identity she was the goddess of the spray of the sea. She and her deified son Palaemon guided sailors in storms. In Rome she was identified with Mater Matuta, whose temple was situated not far from the port of Rome. [Pausanias 1.42.8; Plutarch, *Roman Questions* 13; Ovid, *Metamorphoses* 4.505,520; Tzetzes on Lycophron.]

LEUCOTHEA (3) was a sister of Cycnus. She was therefore the aunt of Tenes and Hemithea, who were cast adrift because of an accusation by Cycnus' second wife that Tenes had tried to seduce her. Leucothea was one of those mentioned-in-passing individuals who hint at the possibility of a more significant role in some lost version of the original story. [Scholiast on Homer's *Iliad* 1.33,38.]

LEUCOTHOE (1) was a daughter of the Babylonian king Orchamus and Eurynome, and was loved by Helios. Her secret meetings with the god were betrayed by the jealous Clytia to her father, who buried her alive, whereupon Helios metamorphosed her into an incense shrub. [Ovid, *Metamorphoses* 4.208.]

LEUCOTHOE (2) was one of the NEREIDES. [Hyginus, *Fables: Preface* 8.]

LEVANA was a Roman divinity. Her name came from the verb *levare,* to lift up. It was the custom for a Roman father to pick up a newborn child from the ground, thus symbolically declaring that his intention was to bring up the child instead of doing harm to it or having it destroyed. [St. Augustine, *City of God* 4.11.]

LIBENTINA, Lubentina, or Lubentia was a surname of Venus among the Romans, by which she was described as the goddess of sexual pleasure. [Varro, *On the Latin Language* 5.6; Cicero, *On the Nature of the Gods* 2.23; St. Augustine, *City of God* 4.8; Plautus, *Comedy of Asses* 2.2.2.]

LIBERA was an ancient Italian divinity worshipped in conjunction with her brother Liber. Their mother was Ceres, and they presided over the cultivation of the vine and fertility of the fields. Libera was identified with Core (Kore), daughter of Demeter. The festival of Liberalia was celebrated by the Romans every year on March 16 and was characterized by processions, feasting, and considerable licentiousness. [Cicero, *On the Nature of the Gods* 2.24; Ovid, *Fasti* 3.713; St. Augustine, *City of God* 7.21.]

LIBERTAS, a Roman divinity, was worshipped as the personification of liberty. Three temples were built to her at public expense at different times, and a statue was set up in the forum. The Atrium Libertatis, north of the forum, had a somewhat different function from the earlier temples. It was used as an office of the censors, criminal records were kept there, and hostages were retained in it. It was later used for public archives. It was rebuilt by Asinius Pollio and became the first public library in Rome.

Libertas was usually represented as a matron with a laurel wreath. Sometimes she wore or held a kind of skullcap, which seemed to be a symbol of liberty. [Dio Cassius 43.44; Livy 25.7, 43.16; Suetonius, *Deified Augustus* 29, *Nero* 57; Cicero, *Pro Milone* 22.]

LIBETHRIDES was a name of the Muses, that they derived from the spring Libethra in Thrace or from the Thracian mountain Libethrus, where they had a grotto sacred to them. Pausanias connected it with Mount Libethrias in Boeotia. [Pausanias 9.34.4; Virgil, *Eclogues* 7.21; Lycophron 275.]

LIBITINA was an Italian divinity presiding over the dead and their burial. Her temple at Rome was a warehouse for everything necessary for burials, and the bereaved might buy or rent those things there. Morticians were called *libitinarii*. The funeral utensils were called *libitina*. One king, in an effort to keep a running census of the dead, made it a law to have a piece of money deposited in the temple of Libitina. The Roman poets often used Libitina's name as a metaphor for death itself. Libitina was identified with Persephone because of her connection with the dead, but in a few cases with Aphrodite, because of a similarity with the word *libido*. [Plutarch, *Numa* 12, *Roman Questions* 23; Seneca, *De Beneficiis* 6.38; Pliny 37.3; Martial 10.97; Suetonius, *Nero* 39; Horace, *Odes* 3.30.6.]

LIBYA (1) was a daughter of Epaphus and Memphis. Epaphus was the son of Zeus and Io, and was born on the banks of the Nile River after the long wanderings of his mother. Memphis, from whom the city of Memphis derived its name, was the daughter of the Nile. Libya had a brother, Telegonus, according to some, but this same Telegonus was said to have married Io, which would make him her grandson. A sister, Lysianassa, was also mentioned.

Libya was loved by Poseidon and bore him three sons, Belus, Agenor, and Lelex, all progenitors of important dynasties in Thebes, Argos, and Megara. Thus Libya could be called the mother of the Argives, the Cadmeans, and the Leleges.

Like so many other eponymic beings, Libya is hard to imagine as an individual. Her name instantly becomes depersonalized, and one can only think of the vast indefinite area to which she gave her name. Even her offspring took on the character of geographical areas. She was sometimes called the wife of the sea-god Triton, but this association could have arisen from a lake by his name in Libya. [Apollodorus 2.1.3–5,11, 3.1.1; Pausanias 1.44.3,5; Hyginus, *Fables* 145,149; Herodotus 3.27,28; Scholiast on Euripides' *Orestes* 920.]

LIBYA (2) was the daughter of Palamedes. He was a son of Nauplius and a most creative inventor. He was enthusiastic in his efforts connected with the Trojan War and provided many benefits to the Greek soldiers during the conflict. He had incurred the wrath of Odysseus prior to the war and was unjustly charged with treason by him and stoned to death. Nothing is known of his daughter except that she became the mother of Libys by Hermes. Nor is anything known of Libys, not surprising since his name came from Hyginus, the list-maker. [Hyginus, *Fables* 160.]

LIBYA (3) was a daughter of Oceanus, a sister of Asia, and half-sister of Europa and Thrace. These names, of course, were personifications of vast land areas. This Libya went back in time to the formation of boundaries of the ancient world and the convention of assigning genealogical connections for everything, particularly topographical features. [Tzetzes on Lycophron 1277.]

LIGEIA (1), or Ligea, i.e., the Shrill-Sounding, occurs as the name of one of the SIRENS and of a nymph. [Eustathius on Homer's *Odyssey* 1709; Virgil, *Georgics* 4.336.]

LIGEIA (2) was one of the NEREIDES. [Hyginus, *Fables: Preface* 9.]

LILAEA was one of the NAIADES, a daughter of Cephissus, from whom the town of Lilaea in Phocis was believed to have derived its name. [Pausanias 10.33.4.]

LIMA, or Limentina, was a Roman divinity protecting the threshold (*limen*), the female counterpart of Limentinus, the god of thresholds. [Arnobius, *Adversus Nationes* 4.9.]

LIMENIA, Limenites, Limenitis, and Limenoscopus, i.e., Protector or Superintendent of the Harbor, occur as surnames of certain goddesses, such as Artemis and Aphrodite. [Callimachus, *Hymn to Artemis* 259; Pausanias 2.34.11; Servius on Virgil's *Aeneid* 1.724.]

LIMNADES were a species of nymphs associated with fresh bodies of water. [Theocritus 5.17.]

LIMNAEA, or Limnatis, i.e. Lake-Born or Lake-Dwelling, was a surname of Artemis, who had temples at Sicyon, near Epidaurus, on the frontiers between Laconia and Messenia, near Calamae, at Tegea, and at Patrae. [Pausanias 2.7.6, 3.2.6,7.4,23.10, 4.4.2,31.3, 7.20.7, 8.53.11.]

LIMNATIDES were a class of NAIADES who inhabited lakes. [Orphica, *Argonautica* 644.]

LIMNOREIA was one of the NEREIDES. [Apollodorus 1.2.7.]

LINDIA (1) was a surname of Athena derived from Lindus on the island of Rhodes, where she had a celebrated temple. On his flight from Egypt, Danaus first landed at Rhodes, where he set up an image of Athena Lindia. According to the story in Herodotus, a temple of Athena was built at Lindus by the daughters of Danaus, and according to Strabo, Tlepolemus built the towns of Lindus, Ialysus, and Cameirus, naming them after three of the Danaides. [Diodorus Siculus 5.58; Herodotus 2.182, Strabo 14.2.8.]

LINDIA (2) was a daughter of Danaus. Her name does not appear on the lists of DANAIDES by Apollodorus and Hyginus, but see the foregoing entry.

LINOS was a nymph, said by some to be the mother of Pelops by Atlas. Pelops is most often called the son of Tantalus by DIONE. [Lactantius, *Stories from Ovid's Metamorphoses* 6.6; Servius on Virgil's *Aeneid* 8.130.]

LIRIOPE (*See* LEIRIOPE)

LITAE were personifications of prayers offered in repentance. They were daughters of Zeus, and they endeavored to make amends for criminal actions and those intended to injure. However, if anyone refused to forgive a wrong, then he or she had to atone for the wrong as well. [Homer, *Iliad* 9.502; Eustathius on Homer's *Iliad* 768.]

LOCHEIA, Protectress of Women in Childbed, was a surname of Artemis. [Plutarch, *Table-Talk* 3.10; Orphica, *Hymns* 35.3.]

LONGATIS was a surname of Athena, which she derived from being worshipped in a Boeotian district called Longas, the location of which is still unknown. [Lycophron 520,1032; Tzetzes on Lycophron 520.]

LOTIS was a nymph who attracted the unwelcome attention of the god Priapus, the ugly offspring of Aphrodite and Dionysus. He was a fertility god, and with characteristic exaggeration the ancient Greeks described him as having a monstrous penis. He pursued Lotis, and she appealed for help from the gods. She was metamorphosed into a tree called after her *lotis*. [Ovid, *Metamorphoses* 9.347.]

LOXO was a daughter of Boreas, one of the Hyperborean maidens who brought the worship of Artemis to Delos, from which circumstance the name was also used as a surname of Artemis herself. [Callimachus, *Hymn to Delos* 292; Nonnos, *Dionysiaca* 5.168.]

LUA, also called Lua Mater, was an early Italian divinity about whom very little is known. We do know that the arms of defeated enemies were dedicated to her and burned as a sacrifice. Plagues were also called down in her name. [Livy 8.50, 45.33; Gellius 13.22; Varro, *On the Latin Language* 8.36.]

LUBENTIA (*See* LIBENTINA)

LUCANIA was the mother of Roma by Italus, a king of the Pelasgians, Siculians, or Oenotrians. Italy was said to have derived its name from him. According to some, he was the son of Telegonus, Circe's son, by Penelope. In one way or another Roma was involved with the founding of Rome. Accounts vary widely. [Dionysius Halicarnassus 1.72; Plutarch, *Romulus* 2; Servius on Virgil's *Aeneid* 1.6, 8.328; Aristotle, *Politics* 7.10.]

LUCERIA, or Lucetia, Giver of Light, was a surname of Juno (cf. Lucerius as a surname of Jupiter). It was used among the Oscans and most particularly might have had to do with Juno's role in childbirth. [Servius on Virgil's *Aeneid* 9.570; Macrobius, *Saturnalia* 1.15; Gellius 5.12.]

LUCINA, Light-Bringer, was a surname of Juno and Diana as goddesses who presided over the birth of children. Lucina was assisted in her functions by Nascio, the equivalent of the Greek Eileithyia. When women of rank gave birth to a son, a feast was prepared and an image of Juno Lucina was placed on a couch by a table in the atrium of the house. [Servius on Virgil's *Aeneid* 4.63; Cicero, *On the Nature of the Gods* 3.18.]

LUCRINA was a surname of Venus, who had a temple at Baiae near Lake Lucrine. [Statius, *Silvae* 3.1.150; Martial 11.81.]

LUNA was the Roman goddess of the moon. Her worship was introduced in the time of Romulus. As prevalent as was the worship of both the sun and moon among ancients of the known world, it is curious that at first the two divinities shared only a small chapel in the Via Sacra. Luna later had temples on the Aventine, Capitoline, and Palatine hills. Part of her greater popularity (than Sol) was the use of the moon by the Romans in their calculations. In her temple on the Palatine Hill she was called Noctiluca, and her temple was lighted each night. In Italy she was identified with Anna Perenna and Jana, and in Greece with Phoebe and Selene. [Varro, *On the Latin Language* 5.68,74; Dionysius Halicarnassus *Roman Antiquities* 2.50; Tacitus, *Annals* 15.41; Horace, *Odes* 4.6.38; Ovid, *Fasti* 3.657; Virgil, *Georgics* 1.431; Virgil, *Aeneid* 10.215.]

LUPERCA, or Lupa, an ancient Italian divinity, was the wife of Lupercus and, in the shape of a she-wolf, performed the office of nurse to Romulus and Remus. In some accounts she was identified with Acca Larentia, the wife of the shepherd Faustulus. The Luperci, a community of priests, celebrated an annual festival called the Lupercalia on February 15. On this occasion they paraded naked around the Palatine and struck young women with a scourge made from goat hair. This ritual was believed to make the women fertile. The festival was a distant antecedent of our present-day Mardi Gras. [Arnobius, *Adversus Nationes* 4.3; Livy 1.4; Dionysius of Halicarnassus, *Roman Antiquities* 1.22.4; Plutarch, *Romulus* 21; Suetonius, *Deified Augustus* 31.]

LUSIA was one of the HYACINTHIDES. [Stephanus Byzantium, "Lusia."]

LYCE was, according to some, the nymph who loved Daphnis. Most accounts call the nymph NOMIA.

LYCEIA, Wolfish, was a surname of Artemis, under which she had a temple at Troezen, built by Hippolytus. Its derivation is not known. Hippolytus might have destroyed wolves that ravaged Troezen, or Lyceia might have been a surname of Artemis among the Amazons, with whom Hippolytus was related through his mother. Most likely, as was so often the case with Artemis, it was the female equivalent of her brother's surname, Lyceius. [Pausanias 2.31.6.]

LYCIPPE was, according to some, the wife of Thestius. Usually her name was EURYTHEMIS. Lycippe was probably a misspelling of Leucippe, which was occasionally given as the name of the wife of Thestius.

LYCO was one of the daughters of Dion and Iphitea. (*See* CARYA.)

LYCOATIS was a surname of Artemis, who had a temple at Lycoa in Arcadia. [Pausanias 8.36.5.]

LYCORIAS was one of the NEREIDES. [Hyginus, *Fables: Preface* 8.]

LYGODESMA was a surname of Artemis at Sparta, whose statue had been found by the brothers Astrabacus and Alopecus under a bush of willows (*lygos*), by which it was surrounded so that it stood upright. The brothers, who were from the royal house, went insane at the sight of the statue. The surname Orthia was more commonly used. [Pausanias 3.16.7.]

LYNCESTE was one of the DOGS of Actaeon. [Hyginus, *Fables* 181.]

LYSE was one of the THESPIADES. She was mother of Eumedes by Heracles. [Apollodorus 2.7.8.]

LYSIANASSA (1), sometimes called Anippe, was a daughter of Epaphus and Memphis, a daughter of the Nile River; her sister was Libya. Epaphus was the son of Zeus and Io, and was born on the banks of the Nile after the long wanderings of his mother. Like her sister, Lysianassa was loved by Poseidon, and became by him the mother of Busiris. Busiris was king of Egypt, and was told by a seer that the only way a plague would end would be the sacrifice each year of a stranger. Heracles landed and was about to be sacrificed, but he broke his bonds and slew Busiris, his son, and all his attendants. He usually did not kill women, so Lysianassa was probably spared. [Apollodorus 2.1.3–5,11; Hyginus, *Fables* 145,149,275.]

LYSIANASSA (2), daughter of Polybus, was sometimes called the wife of Talaus and the mother of Adrastus. She was perhaps better known as LYSIMACHE. [Pausanias 2.6.3.]

LYSIANASSA (3) was one of the NEREIDES. [Apollodorus 1.2.7.]

LYSIDE was a daughter of Coronus. Coronus and his brother Leonteus were princes of the Lapithae. They were sons of Caeneus, who had been born a woman but was changed by Poseidon into a man. The Lapiths were at war with the Dorian king Aegimius, and unfortunately he was a friend of Heracles, who joined him as an ally. Heracles slew Coronus and many of his forces, and handed the whole country over to Aegimius without even asking recompense.

Lyside was called the wife of the Telamonian Ajax, and this was a good possibility. Much was written about Ajax but little about his love life, with the exception of his beloved Tecmessa after he reached Asia Minor. Glauce was also called his wife, but she was probably from Asia Minor as well. So Lyside was more than likely Ajax's wife or lover before he went to Troy. She bore him a son, Philaeus. The Attic deme of Philaidae received its name from this son. [Apollodorus 2.7.7; Stephanus Byzantium, "Philaidai"; Tzetzes on Lycophron 53.]

LYSIDICE (1) was a daughter of Pelops, the famous eponymic hero of Peloponnesus and founder of the Olympic games. Her mother, though not stated, was most certainly Hippodameia. Among her brothers were Atreus, Thyestes, and Pittheus. Her half-brother Chrysippus was kidnapped by Laius of Thebes, recovered by Pelops, and then killed by Atreus and Thyestes. This incident caused them to flee along with their mother, who instigated the murder. It is not hard to see that Lysidice had a most irregular upbringing.

Lysidice married Mestor, one of the sons of Perseus, and had a daughter, Hippothoe, by him. In a confusion of genealogical assignment, she was also called wife of Alcaeus and mother of Amphitryon, as well as wife of Electryon and mother of Alcmena. Alcaeus' wife was usually called Astydameia, and Electryon's wife was called Anaxo. Hippothoe was loved by Poseidon and became the mother of Taphius. The Taphians later waged war on Electryon in an effort to claim the kingdom that had belonged to Mestor. Lysidice was never mentioned again. [Apollodorus 2.4.5; Pausanias 8.14.2; Scholiast on Pindar's *Olympic Odes* 7.49; Plutarch, *Theseus* 7.]

LYSIDICE (2) was one of the THESPIADES. By Heracles she was the mother of Teles. [Apollodorus 2.7.8.]

LYSIMACHE (1) was a daughter of Abas, son of Melampus. Nothing is known of Abas, but he was almost certainly a seer and a medical practitioner, as his father and sons were. Lysimache's brothers were Coeranus, who became the father of the famous seer Polyidus, and Idmon, the soothsayer who accompanied the Argonauts. On this journey, one of Idmon's shipmates was his cousin Talaus, son of Bias and Pero. As in many other cases, this relationship perhaps introduced Talaus to his comrade's sister, although Idmon died on the voyage.

Lysimache married Talaus and bore him several children: Adrastus, Aristomachus, Parthenopaeus, Pronax, Mecisteus, and Eriphyle. After Adrastus was grown, a feud developed between his father and Amphiaraus, who jointly ruled in Argos. Amphiaraus killed Talaus, and Adrastus fled with his mother, sister, and brothers to Sicyon, where they lived for a long time under the protection of Polybus, the

king. Polybus was the father of Lysianassa, whom some called the wife of Talaus and mother of Adrastus. This would have put Adrastus in line for the throne as Polybus' grandson, but with Lysimache as his mother, Adrastus' succession to Polybus' throne must have been because of admiration or obligation.

The trouble between Adrastus and Amphiaraus became reconciled, and Adrastus and his family came back to Argos, where Adrastus gave his sister, Eriphyle, Lysimache's daughter, in marriage to Amphiaraus. Lysimache was not mentioned again, but by the time the war of the Seven against Thebes came about she would have been at least 60. It is doubtful she lived to see the devastation caused to her family by the war. Three sons, a grandson, and a son-in-law were in the campaign, and all were killed except Adrastus. Her daughter, Eriphyle, played a key role in the history of the fatal necklace of Harmonia, which was involved in the war of the Seven. After his death Adrastus was worshiped in several parts of Greece. Lysimache was occasionally called Lysianassa, as well as Eurynome. [Apollodorus 1.9.13, 3.6.3; Homer, *Odyssey* 11.326, *Iliad* 2.566; Pausanias 2.20.4, 9.18.4.]

LYSIMACHE (2) was a daughter of Priam. She and her sisters (or half-sisters), Medesicaste, Medusa, and Aristodeme, were illegitimate. There is no further reference to her. Unless she married and left home before the war, she became one of the captive women of Troy and ended up in Greece. There is always the possibility she died as a child or young woman. [Apollodorus 3.12.5.]

LYSIPPE (1) was one of the THESPIADES. By Heracles she became the mother of Erasippus. [Apollodorus 2.7.8.]

LYSIPPE (2) was one of the PROETIDES. [Apollodorus 2.2.2.]

LYSIPPE (3) was the mother of Ialysus, Lindus, and Cameirus by Cercaphus. She was also called CYDIPPE.

LYSIPPE (4) was one of the AMAZONS. She had a son, Tanais, who offended Aphrodite by his scorn of marriage and his devotion to war. In revenge Aphrodite caused him to fall in love with his mother. He was so shamed by this abnormal passion that he flung himself into the river called Amazon, whereupon its name was changed to the Tanais. Although she was probably unaware of his incestuous love for her, Lysippe feared the ghost of her son and led her daughters around the Euxine Sea to a plain near the Thermodon River. In that place they formed three tribes, each of which founded and settled a city. Lysippe built the city of Themiscyra and defeated every tribe as far as the Tanais River. From the spoils of her campaigns she was said to have raised temples to Ares and Artemis Tauropolos, whose worship she was believed to have established. [Pseudo-Plutarch, *On Rivers* 14.]

LYSIZONA, the Girdle-Loosener, was a surname of Artemis and Eileithyia, who were worshipped under this name at Athens. Loosening the girdle did not have the same meaning then as it does in modern times. It meant abandoning maidenly attire and preparing for marriage and motherhood. Both Artemis and Eileithyia were goddesses of childbirth. [Theocritus 17.60; Scholiast on Apollonius Rhodius 1.287.]

LYTAEA was one of the HYACINTHIDES. [Apollodorus 3.15.8.]

MA, meaning Mother, was a name the Lydians used in referring to Rhea. Bulls were sacrificed to her, and from this ritual the name of the town Mastaura was derived. The name also designated Gaea as the mother of all. According to some, Ma was a nymph in the service of Rhea to whom Zeus gave the infant Dionysus to be reared. [Aeschylus, *Suppliant Maidens* 890; Stephanus Byzantium, "Mastaura."]

MACARIA was the daughter of Heracles by Deianeira. After Heracles' immolation, she joined her brothers in Trachis, where they took refuge with King Ceyx. Eurystheus demanded that Ceyx expel them, which he did out of fear of the powerful Mycenaean king. They went to Athens, where Demophon, son of Theseus, received them, but Eurystheus immediately declared war on Athens. When fighting

commenced, an oracle declared that the Athenians would be victorious only if one of the children of Heracles voluntarily died. Macaria killed herself, some say at Marathon, although it is hard to explain how or why she happened to be there. A spring at Marathon on the road to Rhamnus was named for her. [Pausanias 1.32.6; Zenobius 2.61; Euripides, *Madness of Hercules* 406,488.]

MACETAE were among the beings who cared for the infant Dionysus and later joined his train. They were Macedonians, and equivalent to the Bacchantes and Mimallones. [Athenaeus 5.198; Eustathius on Homer's *Iliad* 989.]

MACHANITIS, the Deviser or Contriver, was a surname of Aphrodite at Megalopolis. It referred to the variety of items and forms of speech invented by man for the sake of love. Machanitis was also a surname of Athena at Megalopolis. In her case it had reference to her skill as an inventor of plans and devices of all kinds. [Pausanias 8.31.6,36.5.]

MACRIS was a daughter of Aristaeus of Euboea, the demigod who instructed men in agricultural pursuits. He was married to Autonoe, one of Cadmus' ill-fated daughters, and by her became father of Actaeon and Macris. Actaeon met a hideous death when his hunting hounds killed and ate him. Macris remained a virgin, and she and her father helped nurse Dionysus, much to the displeasure of Hera. Macris was finally obliged to flee from Euboea, taking Dionysus with her. She went to Scheria, the island of the Phaeacians, and lived in a grotto, where she gained a reputation for helping people. Heracles came to her to be purified after he had killed his wife and children. Macris probably left when Dionysus grew old enough to be passed to others to be educated. She probably took him to Ino and Athamas, her uncle and aunt.

Jason and Medea were married in the cave of Macris, which afterward was called by Medea's name. [Apollonius Rhodius 4.540,990,1131; Scholiast on Apollonius Rhodius 1131.]

MAENADES were female companions of Dionysus. The first Maenades were the nymphs who had nursed the infant god. When he grew to manhood, he inspired these women with a kind of divine madness, which they enhanced with drunkenness. They were naked or thinly clad and wore wreaths of ivy on their heads. They carried thyrsus staffs and played double flutes or struck tambourines. In their wanderings they were joined by local converts and caused great concern to the husbands of the countryside, since the worship included orgies with the male followers of the god. Pan, one of the train of Dionysus, boasted he had coupled with all the drunken Maenades. In their frenzied state the Maenades were quite dangerous. Orpheus had warned against the worship of Dionysus and had condemned the Maenades' promiscuity. The Maenades believed he was advocating homosexuality and luring their husbands from them, so some of them killed their husbands and tore Orpheus to pieces. Pentheus, the son of Agave, was similarly killed by his mother and her companions. They were synonymous with Bacchantes, or Bacchae, and Mimallones. [Euripides, *Bacchae*; Sophocles, *Antigone* 1150; Athenaeus 5.198; Diodorus Siculus 3.64,4.3; Hyginus, *Fables* 224, *Poetic Astronomy* 2.27; Ovid, *Metamorphoses* 3.356–401.]

MAEONIS was a name by which Omphale was called because she was a Lydian. Maeonia was an ancient name of the portion of Lydia in which Omphale lived. The same was true of Arachne, the maiden changed by Athena into a spider. [Ovid, *Metamorphoses* 6.103, *Fasti* 2.310.]

MAERA (1) was the dog of Icarius. Icarius was killed by his Attic countrymen for introducing them to wine, which they thought was poison when they became intoxicated. They buried him, and after a long search his daughter Erigone found his grave, to which she was led by Maera. She hanged herself on the tree under which he was buried. Zeus placed Erigone and Icarius among the stars, making Erigone the Virgin, Icarius Bootes, and Maera the dog star. [Hyginus, *Fables* 130, *Poetic Astronomy* 2.4.]

MAERA (2) was one of the NEREIDES. [Homer, *Iliad* 18.48.]

MAERA (3) was the daughter of Proetus and Anteia. Proetus had fled to Lycia from Argos because of a charge that he had molested his niece Danae. He ended up marrying the king's daughter, who bore him Maera. They returned to Greece, and Proetus ruled at Tiryns. Maera was probably old enough to have been aware of her mother's infatuation with the young hero Bellerophon, who had fled to Tiryns from Corinth to escape conviction for a murder.

These examples of moral decay caused Maera to become a companion of Artemis and shun the company of men. She would have died a virgin had not Zeus overpowered her. When she bore a son, Locrus, she was killed by Artemis. Maera was represented by Polygnotus in the Lesche at Delphi. She was never mentioned in connection with her sisters, the Proetides. Locrus helped Amphion and Zethus build the walls of Thebes. [Homer, *Odyssey* 11.325, *Iliad* 6.160; Eustathius on Homer's *Odyssey* 1688; Apollodorus 2.2.1; Pausanias 10.30.2.]

MAERA (4) was one of the four daughters of Erasinus of Argos. [Antoninus Liberalis 40.] (*See* ANCHIROE.)

MAERA (5) was a daughter of Atlas. She was married to Tegeates, son of Lycaon and founder of Tegea in Arcadia. Their sons were Leimon, Scephrus, Cydon, Archedius, and Gortys (but most accounts call Cydon the son of Apollo and Acacallis). Apollo and Artemis were taking vengeance on those who had mistreated their mother, Leto, and came to Tegea. When Apollo secretly questioned Scephrus, Leimon thought Scephrus was plotting against him and killed him. Artemis instantly chased and killed Leimon. Grieved and terrified, Maera and Tegeates immediately offered sacrifices, but the country was plunged into famine. The oracle of Delphi commanded that Scephrus be honored with funeral solemnities. From that time on, part of the festival of Apollo Agyieus at Tegea was dedicated to Scephrus. In a special ceremony, a priestess of Artemis pursued a man, just as Artemis had pursued Leimon. The meaning is not altogether clear but seems to be an attempt to explain the origin of an obscure ritual that continued into a late period.

Gortys, another of the sons, built the town of Gortyn in Crete, where he was regarded as the son of Rhadamanthys. The tombs of Maera and Tegeates were shown both at Tegea and Mantineia in Arcadia. It is generally agreed that it was this Maera seen by Odysseus in Hades. [Pausanias 8.12.4,48.4,53.1,2.]

MAERA (6) was the name of the bitch into which HECUBA was changed when she jumped overboard from the ship carrying her and other captive Trojan women. [Euripides, *Hecuba*; Ovid, *Metamorphoses* 13.536.]

MAEROPE (*See* MEROPE)

MAGARSIA was a surname of Athena, derived from Magarsos, a Cilician town near the mouth of the Pyramus River, where the goddess had a sanctuary. [Arrian, *Anabasis of Alexander* 2.5.]

MAIA was the eldest of the PLEIADES. As daughter of Atlas and Pleione, she was sometimes called either Atlantis or Pleias. One account called her a daughter of Atlas and Sterope, his own daughter. She was visited in a cave on Mount Cyllene in Arcadia by Zeus and became the mother of Hermes, one of the Olympian gods. He was surnamed Cyllenius from his birthplace. That is the extent of what we know of Maia. After Zeus had his affair with Callisto and she was changed into a bear, the baby, Arcas, was carried to Maia to be brought up. In a manner of speaking, he was her stepson, but so were scores of other sons of Zeus.

Maia is famous through her son, for her presence is felt in the nursery adventures of the god of thieves. Hermes escaped from his cradle and went to Pieria, carrying off some of Apollo's oxen, but was forgiven when he invented the lyre from a tortoise shell. He became the messenger of the other gods, and was notorious for his ingenuity and cunning. We lose sight of Maia after Hermes became adult. She was not even mentioned in the upbringing of Dionysus, in which Hermes took a part.

The Romans had a divinity called Maia, or Majesta, who was sometimes considered the wife of Vulcan, largely because a priest of Vulcan offered a sacrifice to her on May 1. Later, she became identified with the Greek Maia and was called the mother of Mercury. [*Homeric Hymn to Hermes* 3,17; Hesiod, *Theogony* 938; Apollodorus 3.10.2,8.2; Horace, *Odes* 1.10.1, 2.42; Macrobius, *Saturnalia* 1.12; Gellius 13.22; Servius on Virgil's *Aeneid* 8.130; Pausanias 8.17.1.]

MAJESTA (*See* MAIA)

MALACHE was one of the Lemnian women with whom some of the Argonauts mated in the early part of their journey. The Lemnian women had been afflicted by Aphrodite with an unpleasant body odor so that their husbands had turned away from them. The women slaughtered their mates, but by the time the Argonauts landed they were ready to entertain gentlemen callers. It is not clear whether their odor still lingered, but the Argonauts had been at sea long enough for it not to matter. Malache became by Euphemus the mother of Leucophanes. Euphemus was a son of Poseidon and among other talents, such as navigational ability, he could walk on water. He already had a wife, Heracles' sister Laonome, but like his father, he did not let this stand in his way. Leucophanes became the ancestor of Battus, the founder of Cyrene. Malache was also called Malicha or Lamache. [Pindar, *Pythian Odes* 4.1; Scholiast on Pindar's *Pythian Odes* 4.455; Tzetzes on Lycophron 886; Apollonius Rhodius 1.182.]

MALIADES, or Meliades, were nymphs who were worshipped as the protectors of flocks and fruit trees. They were also called Melides or Epimelides. The very same name was given to the nymphs of the district of Malis near Trachis on the Spercheius River. [Theocritus 1.22; Eustathius on Homer's *Odyssey* 1963; Sophocles, *Philoctetes* 715.]

MALICHA was, according to some, the mother of Leucophanes by Euphemus. Others called her MALACHE.

MALIS was one of Omphale's women. By her Heracles was father of Cleodaeus, or Cleolaus, and of Alcaeus. Malis is a good example of Heracles' insatiable sexual appetite. Deianeira was his wife, and he was being unfaithful by living with his mistress Omphale. While living with Omphale, he was sleeping with her domestics. Alcaeus was the founder of the Lydian dynasty, which Croesus deposed from the throne of Sardis. [Diodorus Siculus 4.31; Herodotus 1.7; Hellanicus 102; Eusebius, *Preparation for the Gospel* 2.35.]

MANA, or Mana Geneta, was an ancient Roman divinity concerned with generation and with beings who died at birth. The Romans sacrificed a female dog to her because of the ease with which a bitch gave birth. They prayed that none of those born in the house should become *good,* that is, that none should die. [Plutarch, *Roman Questions* 52.]

MANIA was an Italian divinity of the lower world. She was called the mother of the Manes, or souls of the dead. She was worshipped at the Compitalia, the festival of the spirits of the crossroads. A very ancient oracle had decreed that heads should be offered to her, and boys were sacrificed to her. Human sacrifice was later abolished, and garlic and poppy heads were substituted. Images of Mania were hung in doorways of houses to avert evil. In later times, the plural Maniae designated terrible, deformed specters with which parents and nurses threatened unruly children. [Varro, *On the Latin Language* 9.61; Arnobius, *Adversus Nationes* 3.41; Macrobius, *Saturnalia* 1.7.]

MANIAE were certain mysterious divinities who had a sanctuary in the neighborhood of Megalopolis in Arcadia, and whom Pausanias (8.34.1) considered to be the same as the EUMENIDES.

MANTO (1), also known as Daphne, was a daughter of Teiresias; her sister was Historis. Teiresias was the famous blind seer of Thebes who was able to unravel the terrible truth about Oedipus. In his younger years he had been changed to a woman for a period of seven years. Presumably Manto and Historis were born after this event.

Manto was a prophetess of the Ismenian Apollo at Thebes, where monuments of her were later shown. After the Epigoni conquered

Thebes, she was at first the concubine of Alcmaeon and bore him two children, Amphilochus and Tisiphone. They were almost necessarily twins, since very shortly after the fall of Thebes, Manto and other captives were dedicated to Apollo at Delphi, probably as temple servants. Her children were perhaps born at Delphi. Alcmaeon gave the children to Creon, king of Corinth, to educate.

Alcmaeon then murdered his mother, according to a deathbed promise he had made to his father, and had to flee the pursuit of the Erinyes. Along with the other captives, Manto was sent by Apollo to what later became Colophon in Asia Minor, where she founded the temple of the Clarian Apollo. She married Rhacius, a king of Caria, and bore him two sons, Mopsus and Melus. Mopsus founded Mallos in Cilicia, where his oracle existed for centuries. Melus founded the sanctuary of Apollo Malloeis in Lesbos.

The ultimate fate of Manto is not known. Her son Amphilochus was also a seer, and he founded Argos Amphilochium in Aetolia. He went to Troy and collaborated with Mopsus, his half-brother, in founding Mallos. The two seers later had a falling out and killed each other. Tisiphone incurred the jealousy of Creon's wife, who sold her as a slave. Alcmaeon bought her but found out she was his daughter before he had a chance to commit incest. [Apollodorus 3.7.4,7, quoting Euripides' *Alcmaeon;* Pausanias 7.3.1, 9.10.3,11.2,33.1; Strabo 14.5.16; Scholiast on Apollonius Rhodius 1.908; Diodorus Siculus 4.66; Tacitus, *Annals* 2.54; Virgil, *Aeneid* 3.360; Stephanus Byzantium, "Malloeis."]

MANTO (2) was a daughter of the soothsayer Polyidus and sister of ASTYCRATEIA. The tombs of these two sisters were shown at Megara near the entrance of the sanctuary of Dionysus. [Pausanias 1.43.5.]

MANTO (3), an Italian prophetess for whom the city of Mantua was named, was called by some the daughter of Heracles, although most writers consider that Heracles had only one daughter, Macaria. She was also woven by some into the story of Manto, the daughter of Teiresias, but inasmuch as that particular Manto was sent from Delphi to the area of Colophon in Mysia, she was not the same as the Italian Manto. Manto was a name usually associated with prophetesses, so it is understandable there was a certain amount of confusion among them. [Servius on Virgil's *Aeneid* 10.198.]

MANTO (4), a nymph, was a lover of the god of the Tiber River. By him she had two sons, Aulestes and Ocnus. Aulestes was a Tyrrhenian ally of Aeneas and slain by Messapus. Before that, he founded Perusia. Ocnus, also known as Bianor, built the town of Mantua, which he named for his mother. He later went to Gaul, where he founded Cesena. This Manto did not appear to have prophetic powers. [Virgil, *Aeneid* 10.207, 12.290; Servius on Virgil's *Aeneid* 10.198, on Virgil's *Eclogues* 9.60.]

MANTO (5), according to Diodorus Siculus (4.68), was a daughter of Melampus. Other writers assign Melampus a son, Mantius, so it appears that Manto was a mistake in transposition.

MARICA was a nymph who was worshipped at Minturnae in Italy in a sacred grove on the Liris River. She was a lover of Faunus, an early divinity and/or king of Latium, and became by him the mother of Latinus. Thus her grandson-in-law was Aeneas (husband of Lavinia). Some identified Marica with Aphrodite, but she was more often thought to be a deified Circe. [Virgil, *Aeneid* 7.47; Servius on Virgil's *Aeneid* 1.6; Arnobius, *Adversus Nationes* 2.71.]

MARPE was one of the AMAZONS. [Diodorus Siculus 4.16.]

MARPESIA was a queen of the AMAZONS. [Justinus 2.4; Orosius 1.15.]

MARPESSA was a daughter of Euenus and Alcippe. Euenus was said to be a son of Ares and Demonice. Alcippe was a daughter of Oenomaus and sister of Hippodameia. She was, of course, a witness to the contests waged by Oenomaus with the suitors of Hippodameia and as a young girl was often confronted with grisly reminders, such

as the heads of young men hanging at the entrance of the house. Undoubtedly she talked about the experience to Euenus, who thought it was not a bad idea. So when their daughter Marpessa grew up, Euenus decided to reenact his late father-in-law's idea.

There is no record of suitors who might have lost their heads to Euenus, but perhaps Apollo got there before anyone else. Marpessa was exceptionally beautiful, and the god was determined to have her as a wife, which was quite unusual for him. He accepted Euenus' challenge and was about to set off on a race with his prospective father-in-law when Idas, son of Aphareus, appeared on the scene. Idas was in love with Marpessa and had prayed to Poseidon for assistance in acquiring her. For reasons unknown Poseidon granted the plea and provided him with a winged chariot. It should be mentioned that, earlier, Idas and his brother Lynceus had been on the point of marrying their cousins Hilaeira and Phoebe but had them stolen away by Castor and Polydeuces, the Dioscuri.

So there were three Olympian gods involved in the suit for Marpessa—Ares, the father of Euenus, who provided his son's horses; Poseidon, who perhaps fancied Idas; and Apollo, a contender. Idas wasted no time and snatched up the lovely woman. Euenus pursued them but was unable to overtake the winged chariot. In despair he threw himself into the Lycormas River, which was thereafter called the Euenus.

Apollo was furious, and it took him only a short time to find the couple in Messene. He tried to take Marpessa, but Idas fought with him. Zeus intervened, probably more for the sake of Idas than for Apollo, since Apollo could not be killed and Idas could. Zeus left the decision up to Marpessa. Marpessa chose Idas because she feared Apollo would leave her when she grew old. This did not say a great deal for any love she might have had for Idas, but she was practical and did not believe in mincing words.

By Idas she became the mother of Alcyone (usually called Cleopatra), who became the wife of Meleager. Idas was identified as Meleager's father-in-law when the two went on the Argonaut. Later Idas and his son-in-law also participated in the Calydonian boar hunt. A short time after, Meleager was caused to die, and Cleopatra hanged herself. Idas and Lynceus had a quarrel with their old rivals, the Dioscuri, and were killed.

Marpessa's subsequent history is not known. She was left without a father, a husband, or children. The basis for her rejection of Apollo was fear of abandonment in old age, and it seems that was her fate regardless. On the chest of Cypselus, Idas was shown leading her from the temple of Apollo. [Homer, *Iliad* 9.557; Plutarch, *Greek and Roman Parallel Stories* 40; Apollodorus 1.7.8; Pausanias 4.2.5, 5.18.1; Hyginus, *Fables* 174.]

MARSE, one of the THESPIADES, was the mother of Bucolus by Heracles. [Apollodorus 2.7.8.]

MATER MATUTA (*See* MATUTA)

MATRONA was a surname of Juno. Juno was the protecting genius of the female sex in general, but accompanied every individual woman through life from the moment of her birth to the end of her life. [Horace, *Odes* 3.4.59; Silius Italicus 8.219.]

MATUTA, or Mater Matuta, was usually considered the goddess of the dawn of morning. Matuta was probably a surname of Juno. Her festival, the Matronalia, which took place on July 11, enjoined relatives to provide for the orphaned children of their deceased brothers and sisters as if the children were their own. Under no circumstances were they to be left at the mercy of slaves. No female slave was allowed to enter the temple of Matuta at her festival. Only a token slave was admitted, and she was boxed on the ears by the attendant matrons. There appeared to be a connection between this custom and the story of the Greek Ino who, according to some, went mad out of jealousy of a female slave, killed her own son, and was transformed into the marine divinity Leucothea, who similarly banned slaves from her temple. Consequently, some believed Matuta was a marine divinity. [Plutarch, *Roman Questions* 13,16,17, *Camillus* 5; Lucretius 5.655; St. Augustine, *City of God* 48; Ovid, *Fasti* 6.55; Cicero, *On the Nature of the Gods* 3.19; Livy 5.19,23, 25.7, 41.33.]

MECIONICE was, according to some, the mother of Euphemus by Poseidon. She is usually called EUROPA. [Tzetzes on Lycophron 886.]

MEDA (1), or Medeia, was the daughter of Phylas, the king of the Dryopes who succeeded Theiodamas. He led his people in an attack on the sanctuary of Delphi. Heracles made war on Phylas and killed him. He then expelled the Dryopes from their territory and gave it to the Malians, after which he appropriated Meda and made her pregnant. It is safe to assume he took her by force, since he had just killed her father and exiled her relatives and friends. She became the mother of Antiochus, who in turn became the ancestor of Hippotes and Aletes. Statues of Phylas as an eponymic hero of an Athenian tribe existed at Athens and Delphi. The one at Delphi was carved by Pheidias. The subsequent fate of Meda was never disclosed. [Philostratus, *Imagines* 2.24; Pausanias 1.5.2, 10.10.1.]

MEDA (2) was the wife of Idomeneus, the son of Deucalion, grandson of Minos, and king of Crete. Having been a suitor of Helen he was obliged to enter the Trojan War (but he was also a cousin of Menelaus). He took with him 80 ships and performed valiantly on the battlefield.

During his absence he left Leucas in charge of his kingdom. Leucas was the son of Talos, the infamous man of brass, and when he was abandoned at birth, Idomeneus brought him up. Meda did not have too much trouble seducing the ambitious young man. She was inspired to do this from stories brought to her by Nauplius, whose son Palamedes had been stoned to death by the Greeks for suspected treason. Nauplius told her that her handsome husband was being unfaithful to her and was planning to bring home a mistress at the conclusion of the war.

Little did she know that her lover had inherited his father's criminal disposition. One day he murdered her and Cleisithyra, her daughter by Idomeneus. He then proceeded to take over ten strategic cities of Crete and thereby control the island. Consequently, when Idomeneus returned, he was expelled from the island by Leucas and settled in Calabria in Italy.

There was another well-known story to explain his exile. On his way home from Troy he was in a violent storm and vowed to Poseidon that he would sacrifice to him the first thing he saw if he reached shore safely. The first thing he saw was his son, and true to his oath he sacrificed him. A plague broke out, and the consensus was that it was caused by the cruelty of Idomeneus. So he was forced to leave Crete. Meda was not mentioned in the variant story, and curiously no name was given to the sacrificed son (or daughter, in some accounts). [Apollodorus, *Epitome* 6.10; Tzetzes on Lycophron 384,1093,1218.]

MEDEA was one of the truly complex women in mythology. She was intelligent, passionate, cunning, and assertive. At the same time she was emotionally vulnerable. She was capable of unconditional love but just as capable of its opposite. Her heritage was distinguished but strange, starting with Helios, the sun, her grandfather. Her father was Aeetes, who was brother of Perses, Circe, and Pasiphae. So Medea came by her unusual powers quite naturally. Her mother was commonly called Idyia, daughter of Oceanus, but various writers suggested other possibilities, even Hecate, the divinity of witchcraft. Medea was sometimes called Aeaea from the country ruled by her father, and Aeetis from him. She had a sister, Chalciope, and a half-brother, Absyrtus. Chalciope was older and had become the wife of Phrixus, who flew to Colchis on a ram with golden fleece.

The Golden Fleece was the object of the Argonaut, the voyage ordered by King Pelias of Iolcus to eliminate Jason as a threat to his kingdom and, indeed, to his life. The quest was joined by the cream of the Greek heroes. After many adventures Jason and his companions arrived in Colchis, the seaport and capital of Aea.

They were hospitably received, although the Colchians had a reputation for sacrificing strangers. Medea and Aeetes had often disagreed on this practice, and for her opposition Medea was held in a kind of minimum security. Aeetes immediately learned from the Argonauts the nature of their visit, but his spies certainly must have preceded the landing of the Argonauts with the same information. Aeetes agreed to give them the Golden Fleece, but first Jason was expected to perform a series of seemingly impossible tasks. While Jason pondered a means of

tackling the problem he was approached by Medea, who wanted to strike a bargain with him. Because of irreconcilable differences with Aeetes, she wanted a means of leaving Colchis. She asked Jason to marry her and take her away, in return for which she would help him complete the formidable tasks assigned to him by her father. She did not tell him that the main reason for her offer was that she had fallen deeply in love with him.

Jason, on the other hand, was willing to make any deal that would get him through his ordeal. First he had to catch and yoke two enormous fire-breathing bulls with brazen hooves that had never before been yoked. With them he had to plow a field and sow the furrows with the teeth of the same dragon Cadmus had encountered at Thebes. Medea gave him a magical salve that would protect him from the ravages of the fiery brutes, and she also revealed that a crop of fully armed warriors would spring from the dragon's teeth. She told him to throw stones in their midst so they would turn on one another in anger.

All these things Jason successfully managed on the appointed day, after which he awaited the award of the Golden Fleece. He also told Aeetes that he was marrying Medea. Aeetes was no fool and saw immediately how Jason had escaped almost certain death in the arena. Of course, he had never had any intention of parting with the sacred fleece. He postponed his announcement while he summoned his troops, but Medea had anticipated his action. First entering the sacred grove and lulling the guardian dragon to sleep so the fleece could be taken, she hurried with Jason and his men to the *Argo,* which Aeetes was just about to burn. In the final moments of escape, Medea had also seized her young brother, Absyrtus, thinking perhaps she might use him for purposes of ransom.

The *Argo* was closely pursued by Aeetes and his forces, and it looked as if the Argonauts would be overtaken. Medea quickly slit her brother's throat, dismembered him, and dropped overboard a piece of him at a time, correctly guessing her father would stop to collect each part of the boy. We must assume the Argonaut was pursued by only one ship, since with more ships Aeetes could have managed his grisly harvest while sending other vessels to head off the fleeing *Argo*.

The return route of the *Argo* has been the subject of countless speculations and dissertations, but everyone seems to have agreed that eventually the travelers, by whatever route, came to Drepane (Corcyra), the island of the Phaeacians, where they were kindly received by King Alcinous and his wife, Arete. Aeetes had sent a number of Colchians in search of the Argonauts with the threat that they would be killed if they returned without Medea and the Golden Fleece. By chance the Colchians landed just after the Argonauts and demanded that Alcinous surrender Medea. Alcinous was in a dilemma, realizing it would be difficult to make a correct decision. On the one hand, he feared reprisals from Aeetes, but at the same time knew he would be signing Medea's death warrant if he surrendered her. Queen Arete, however, proposed to the Colchians that indeed Medea would be surrendered if she and Jason were not married.

This seemingly simple solution was far more complicated than it appeared. Some accounts made the condition one of intact virginity instead of marriage. Others tended to make the terms interchangeable. Medea swore she was still a virgin when she pleaded her case before Alcinous, but that would, in fact, have made her eligible for deportation. If she were not still a virgin but remained unmarried, she could only be viewed as a woman of loose morals deserving to be returned to her father. So marriage had to be the real issue, since it presupposed a sacred ritual. It becomes increasingly apparent that Jason did not love her and had only used her to gain possession of the Golden Fleece. At any time along the way, particularly after they had first eluded the Colchians, he could have kept his promise and married her, since among the sailors there were those who could officiate at a marriage ceremony.

Medea's claim about her virginity is highly suspect. It is hardly likely that her overpowering love for Jason did not result in sexual intercourse at the first opportunity. After all, Medea must have considered herself as good as married, since she had no reason to doubt Jason's solemn oath to her. She would have gained no particular

advantage in withholding sexual favors. For his part, Jason was a hot-blooded youth whose resistance must have diminished each day of the extended voyage, even though he was probably horrified at the ghastly slaughter of Absyrtus. Neither did he have anything to gain by postponing their coming together, even though conveniently he might have deferred a marriage ceremony because of the ever-present threat of the pursuing Colchians.

In fact, it is highly doubtful Jason ever intended to marry Medea. He might have decided to drop her off at Corinth, where Aeetes had first ruled, and consider that in part he had lived up to his obligation of getting her out of Colchis. But now he was more or less compelled to marry her to prevent an international incident. Consequently, he and Medea were secretly married that very night in the cave of Macris. In this cave, Macris, the daughter of the god Aristaeus, had nursed the infant Dionysus. The event of the marriage caused the name of the grotto to be changed to the Cave of Medea. The Colchians were obliged to accept the verdict. Since they could not return home under penalty of death, they settled in nearby islands. One major version of the story had Absyrtus leading the Colchians. He had not been abducted by Medea and, of course, he was not a child as in the more common versions.

The Argonauts left Drepane and continued their homeward voyage. They were blown off course rounding the straits of Malea and tried to land in Crete, but were prevented by Talos, the formidable man of brass who patrolled the coast. He cast boulders at the ship and nearly succeeded in sinking it. After praying to the gods, Medea managed to fix him with her gaze and hypnotize him, causing him to go mad, stumble, and tear open the single vein that supplied his life-giving fluid. It gushed forth and, thus depleted, he fell from a bluff into the sea.

After further wandering, the Argonauts got back to Iolcus and delivered the Golden Fleece to Pelias. He had meanwhile brought about the death of Jason's father, Aeson, his mother, and his brother. There were no witnesses, however, and Jason could only suffer in impotent rage and grief. Medea was not so easily put off. At once she set about befriending Pelias and his daughters. She seized on the universal desire for perpetual youth and gave a demonstration with an old ram, which, when cut up and thrown into a pot with magical herbs, sprang out of the seething mutton stew as a gamboling lamb. She convinced the Peliades, the daughters of Pelias, that the process was as simple as alpha-beta-gamma, and that Pelias could be made young again in the same fashion. The Peliades, with their father's consent, followed the same steps but succeeded only in parboiling their father's dismembered body.

Acastus, the son of Pelias, who had also been an Argonaut, expelled his sisters and Jason and Medea from Iolcus. Had he been aware of the goings-on, he would have prevented the slaughter, since he had seen what Medea could do to people who stood in her way. The couple fled to Corinth, where Medea reclaimed Aeetes' kingdom. Creon was on the throne, but apparently he and Jason entered into some form of bicameral government. This relationship has always posed an enigma (*see* GLAUCE). For all intents and purposes Medea still held the ultimate sovereignty in Corinth that dated back to Helios, her grandfather.

For ten years Jason and Medea lived happily, according to the usual account, and had several children. Some said they only had two, but the names and numbers of the children differed with different writers. The names on record are Alcimenes, Tisander, Mermerus (also called Mormorus or Macareus), Pheres, Thessalus, and Eriopis.

After ten years Creon proposed to Jason that he marry his daughter Glauce, probably for political reasons. Glauce had probably just come of age, and the king wanted to guarantee her future (and his own). There is a question whether Jason and Medea had lived as happily as some supposed. There is no record that Jason had been unfaithful up until then, but the casual way he walked out on Medea leads us to believe that he was awaiting an opportunity. According to some, Medea was banished, but that seems unlikely unless she had roused superstitious fear among the Corinthians because of her reputation for sorcery. She prepared to leave, but not before she completed two characteristically violent acts. First she sent a wedding gift to Glauce,

probably without Jason's knowledge. The gift was a robe and crown, ironically symbolizing Glauce's anticipated coronation. At once Glauce, probably a vain young woman, tried on the garment and the crown, and was immediately consumed in fire. Hurrying to her in response to her screams, her father was also consumed, as was the entire palace. Medea then bade her children farewell, killed them, and fled in a dragon-drawn chariot.

That was the most familiar account, but variations were inevitable. Some say she did not kill the children but left them in the temple of Hera, where they were stoned to death by the Corinthians. One account says Jason deserted her for trying to make the children immortal and went back to Iolcus. After that, Medea also quit Corinth and left the government in the hands of Sisyphus. Since descendants of Jason and Medea are mentioned, it would follow that if she did kill the children she killed only two of them. Pheres and Thessalus appear to have survived. Thessalus was said to have been the ancestor of the Thessalian race.

Medea first sought out Heracles, who had once promised to help her if ever Jason proved unfaithful. He was ill, however, of his recurrent madness and was not able to help her. She cured him of his malady and proceeded to Athens, where King Aegeus had also promised her sanctuary. It is not clear when exactly such a promise was made, but undoubtedly there were many occasions for diplomatic negotiations between Athens and Corinth. The promise had been made in exchange for another. Aegeus was almost certainly sterile, and Medea had told him that she could bear him a son. Now she was ready to prove her claim to Aegeus if he would marry her. He did so, and in due course a son, Medus, was born. Medea probably had in her pharmacopoeia a potion to overcome sterility, but her cunning did not rule out an extramarital affair if that became necessary. One or two accounts even make Medus a son of Medea by an Asian king after she fled Athens.

Everything seemed to be going well, but she had not planned on the sudden appearance of young Theseus from Troezen, who claimed to be the king's son and presented certain tokens in support. Nearly two decades earlier Aegeus had, in fact, slept with Aethra, daughter of King Pittheus, on a visit to Troezen, but Poseidon had slept with her on the same night. In view of Aegeus' inability to have children by a series of wives, it was generally conceded that the ever-fertile Poseidon was the father. Of course, this made no difference now, since Aegeus believed he was the father of Theseus and readily pronounced him his successor. At a feast shortly after the arrival of the young hero, Medea tried unsuccessfully to poison him. As a result, she had to flee once more.

She took Medus (sometimes called Polyxenus) and went to Asia, where, according to some, she married a king. Most accounts, though, had her returning to Colchis, where she contrived to overthrow her uncle Perses, who had usurped the kingdom of Aeetes. She restored Aeetes to the throne and reared her son, who after growing up gave his name to the Medes, the powerful Asian race. Some writers contended she went to Italy and taught the Marrubians the art of snake charming. She was deified by them as the somewhat obscure goddess ANGITIA. She was also identified with the Roman Bona Dea. Whatever the case, at length Medea became immortal and was honored with divine worship. She was said to have married Achilles in Elysium. If so, Achilles had a full plate, for he also was supposed to enjoy a postmortal marriage with both Iphigeneia and Helen.

As earlier stated, Medea was one of the most complex characters in ancient literature. Various renditions of her episodic career have added further complications. Some have tried to soften her image by making her innocent of the death of Absyrtus, her children, and even Glauce. Others presented her most heinous act, the murder of her children, with such pathos that blame for the deed appeared to rest on Jason. Modern translations and original works have presented new viewpoints. However, taking the main events of the basic story, we have to concede that Medea's destiny was directed by her obsessive love for Jason. The episode with Aegeus has all the appearance of afterthought and reluctance to end a completed story of love, rejection, and revenge. [Apollodorus 1.9.23–28; Hesiod, *Theogony* 961,1000; Diodorus Siculus 4.45,54, 55; Hyginus, *Fables* 23,25,239; Ovid, *Tristia*

3.9, *Metamorphoses* 7.9,296, *Heroides* 6.103; Apollonius Rhodius 3.1135, 4.338,1010–1169,1638–1688; Pausanias 2.3.6,7,11; Valerius Flaccus 8.233; Silius Italicus 8.498; Plutarch, *Theseus* 12; Euripides, *Medea*; Scholiast on Euripides' *Medea* 20; Cicero, *On the Duties of Office* 1.31; Ptolemaeus Hephaestion 2.]

MEDESICASTE (1) was a daughter of Laomedon. At the fall of Troy she was taken prisoner along with two of Priam's other sisters, AETHYLLA and Astyoche. [Apollodorus, *Epitome* 6.15.]

MEDESICASTE (2) was an illegitimate daughter of Priam, obviously named for his sister. Nothing is known of her except that she became the wife of Imbrius, son of Mentor, at Pedaeum. An interesting consideration about Priam's many illegitimate offspring is whether or not they were publicly acknowledged as his children. Medesicaste's marriage into an undistinguished family in a small town near Troy is an indication that she was no more than an ordinary citizen of Troy. Her husband was killed in the war. [Homer, *Iliad* 13.171; Pausanias 10.25.4.]

MEDITRINA was a Roman divinity of the art of healing in whose honor the festival of the Meditrinalia was celebrated in the month of October. Varro (*On the Latin Language* 6.21) connects the verb *mederi*, to heal, with the name, and this seems to accord well with the rites observed at the festival of the goddess.

MEDUSA (1), one of the GORGONS, was one of the major monsters of Greek mythology. Her career was almost exclusively tied to the story of Perseus, for we have no record of any trail of terror she blazed before encountering the hero. Almost all the damage she did to individuals took place after her head was severed and placed on Athena's shield. Vials of her blood were distributed for both beneficial and harmful purposes.

If we accept the story that she once had been a beautiful maiden who made the mistake of sleeping with Poseidon in one of Athena's temples and was thus transformed into the familiar monster with snaky locks, we must concede that she was a victim of circumstances. If Athena really wanted to blame someone, she should have taken out her spite on Poseidon, who should have respected his niece's temple just as he expected his own to be. This whole variation, though, was probably an addition by later writers to add credibility to the abundant assistance given by Athena to Perseus in his quest for the head of Medusa. [Hesiod, *Theogony* 287; Apollodorus 2.4.3; Ovid, *Metamorphoses* 4.792.]

MEDUSA (2) was one of the daughters of Sthenelus and Nicippe. Sthenelus was a son of Perseus, and Nicippe was a daughter of Pelops. The brother of Medusa was Eurystheus, who through Hera's intervention was born shortly before Heracles and thus gained sovereignty over him. Nothing is known of Medusa, but *see* ALCINOE and ADMETE, who were her sisters. [Pausanias 2.4.5.]

MEDUSA (3) was a daughter of Priam. Nothing further is known of her, except that she was depicted in the Lesche at Delphi. [Apollodorus 3.12.5; Pausanias 10.26.9.]

MEDUSA (4) was one of the PELIADES. [Hyginus, *Fables* 24.]

MEDUSA (5) was a daughter of Orsilochus, king of Pharae in Messenia. She was called by some the wife of Polybus, who brought up Oedipus. Polybus' wife was more often called PERIBOEA.

MEGAERA was one of the EUMENIDES.

MEGAMEDE, daughter of Arneus, was the mother of the THESPIADES, 50 daughters she was said to have borne to Thespius, son of Erechtheus and the eponymous hero of Thespiae in Boeotia. Even granted the tendency of ancient Greek storytellers to gross exaggeration, Megamede's fecundity is far beyond belief. Even if she began bearing children at the age of 12 and continued to bear one a year, she would have reached 62 before the last was born. That would make the oldest daughter 50—and about 63 when the youngest would have reached child-

bearing age. Since Heracles was said to have impregnated each of the daughters on 50 successive nights, his youngest bedmate would have been 13 and at least a dozen of the others would have been over 50. To make the story even more ludicrous, Heracles was said to have believed he was sleeping with the same woman each night. Of course, Megamede could have had a series of multiple births, but even so, the range in ages would still have been enormous. It is, of course, rather obvious that Thespius had a number of concubines, and Megamede simply claimed all the resultant bastards as her own. Fifty seemed to be a magic number among the hyperbolic Greeks. It probably meant "a great number," even though the Thespiades are named. Hecuba, wife of Priam, according to some had 50 children. Doris, the wife of Nereus, had 50 daughters, but she was a sea creature and more than likely spawned them. She was also immortal and not restricted to a biological clock. Megamede might have had as many as 15 daughters, thus confining them to a more realistic distance between youngest and oldest. [Apollodorus 2.4.10,7.8; Pausanias 9.27.5.]

MEGANEIRA (1) was a daughter of Crocon and Saesara, and the wife of Arcas, according to some. Others call Arcas' wife ERATO. [Apollodorus 3.9.1; Pausanias 1.38.2.]

MEGANEIRA (2) was, according to some, the wife of Celeus. His wife is usually called METANEIRA.

MEGARA was a daughter of Creon of Thebes, son of Menoeceus. Creon was one of the most elusive persons in Theban chronicles. He was involved with Heracles in a whole separate chronology separate from the events surrounding Oedipus and the Theban wars. It is almost as if there were two kings by his name. He has even been confused with Creon, son of Lycaethus, who was king of Corinth when Jason and Medea went there after their expulsion from Iolcus. It could be that he had two separate families, one during his youth and one later on. The first in this case would have been when he first became king and Heracles rid the city of the tribute imposed by Erginus of Orchomenus.

Creon was so grateful to Heracles for his great service that he gave him his daughter Megara in marriage. He also gave Iphicles, Heracles' brother, the hand of his youngest daughter. Heracles lived with Megara long enough to father three sons, although the number given was as high as seven. He then went off on the business of one of his labors. While he was gone, Lycus of Euboea, in an attempt to overthrow Creon, tried to kill Megara and her children, but Heracles returned in time to slay him. Hera, who favored Lycus and hated Heracles, caused Heracles to go mad and kill his wife and children. Some writers did not accept that Megara was killed but held instead that Heracles, after killing his children, knew the marriage was cursed and gave her to Iolaus, his nephew, even though Megara was at least double his age.

Various writers gave Megara's children different names and different numbers. A cumulative list of names included Therimachus, Deicoon, Ophites, Areas, Aristodemus, Deion, Democoon, Chersibius, Menebrontes, Mecistophanus, Patrocles, Toxocleitus, Oneites, Creontiades, Oxeus, Antimachus, Clymenus, Glenus, Polydorus, and Anicetus.

The best characterization of Megara is given by Euripides, who has her killed by Heracles. Thinking that she, her children, and Amphitryon, her father-in-law, are going to be killed by Lycus during Heracles' absence, she demonstrates admirable courage and urges Amphitryon to die with dignity, as she plans to do. Whichever version one follows, Megara emerges as a victim, even in the account that forces her into a marriage with her young in-law. [Homer, *Odyssey* 9.268, 11.269; Euripides, *Madness of Hercules*; Apollodorus 2.4.11,7.8; Pindar, *Isthmian Odes* 1.82; Hyginus, *Fables* 32; Pausanias 10.29.7; Tzetzes on Lycophron 38.]

MEGISTO was in some accounts another form of CALLISTO, mother of Arcas, who was also called Themisto. [Stephanus Byzantium, "Arkas"; Hyginus, *Poetic Astronomy* 2.1; Eustathius on Homer's *Iliad* 300.]

MEILINOE (*See* MELINOE)

MELAENA was a daughter of Cephissus and, according to some, the mother of Delphus by Apollo. More often the mother of Delphus was called CELAENO, daughter of Hyamus. [Pausanias 10.6.2,3.]

MELAENIS, the Dark, was a surname of Aphrodite under which she was worshipped at Corinth. This name was explained by the fact that men, unlike beasts that mated openly, usually had sexual intercourse under cover of night. [Pausanias 2.2.4, 8.6.5.]

MELANAEGIS, Black-Shielded, was a surname of the Erinyes. [Aeschylus, *Seven against Thebes* 700.]

MELANCHAETES was one of the DOGS of Actaeon. [Hyginus, *Fables* 181.]

MELANIPPE (1) was a daughter of Aeolus II, son of Hippotes and Melanippe. She was more often called ARNE. [Diodorus Siculus 4.67.]

MELANIPPE (2) was the daughter of Hippe, who was raped by Aeolus I. By Hippotes, the grandson of Aeolus I, Melanippe became the mother of Aeolus II, who in turn was the father of another Melanippe, better known as ARNE. Arne by Poseidon became the mother of twin sons Aeolus and Boeotus, eponymic heroes of the Aeolians and Boeotians. There are, of course, variations on this complicated genealogy. [Diodorus Siculus 4.67.]

MELANIPPE (3) was a nymph who by Itonus, son of Amphictyon, became the mother of Boeotus, Chromia, and Iodama. Itonus was said to have founded the cult of Athena Itonia. His daughter Iodama was a priestess of the goddess. Chromia, according to some, was the wife of Endymion. Boeotus gave his name to the region of Boeotia, according to some accounts. Though nowhere stated, it appears there were two people named Boeotus. It is significant that in this particular genealogy, Aeolus is not mentioned. Other accounts almost invariably call him a twin of Boeotus, in which case they are sons of Arne (confusingly called also Melanippe) by Poseidon. [Pausanias 5.1.2, 9.1.1,34.1.]

MELANIPPE (4) was a queen of the AMA-ZONS. She was a sister of Hippolyte, whose girdle Heracles had to acquire as one of his labors. She was captured by Heracles, but Hippolyte ransomed her by agreeing to Heracles' terms. In the fight that later took place, Melanippe was killed by Telamon, Heracles' companion. As usual with the Amazons, their history was full of variant accounts. On this same voyage Theseus was supposed to have received Antiope as his reward for participation in this embarrassing raid. [Diodorus Siculus 4.16; Scholiast on Pindar's *Nemean Odes* 3.64; Apollonius Rhodius 2.966.]

MELANIPPE (5) was the mother of Elephenor by Chalcodon. Elephenor's mother was more often called IMENARETE. [Tzetzes on Lycophron 1034.]

MELANIPPE (6) was one of the MELE-AGRIDES. [Antoninus Liberalis 2; Ovid, *Metamorphoses* 8.532.]

MELANTHEIA, daughter of the Alpheius River, was the mother of Eirene by Poseidon. The island of Calaureia (modern Paros) was in early times called Eirene. This Eirene is not to be confused with the goddess of the same name. [Plutarch, *Greek Questions* 19.]

MELANTHO (1) was a daughter of Dolius and sister of Melanthius. She was a slave in the house of Odysseus. Like her brother, or more likely coerced by him, she sided with the suitors who overran the house of Odysseus during his absence. She was among those hanged by Odysseus for collaboration with the enemies. [Homer, *Odyssey* 18.321; Pausanias 10.25.1.]

MELANTHO (2) was a daughter of Deucalion. She was the mother of Delphus by Poseidon, who took the form of a dolphin to seduce her. The question always needs to be asked whether the union took place between two different species or whether at the last moment Poseidon took his usual appearance. The city of Delphi took its name from Delphus. Another Delphus, for whom the same claim was made, was the son of Apollo by Celaeno. [Tzetzes on Lycophron 208.]

MELANTHO (3) was the wife of Criasus. He was one of the kings in the complicated Argolid line. Melantho bore to him Ereuthalion and Cleoboea. Ereuthalion was the founder of Ereuthalia, an untraceable place. Nothing is known of Cleoboea. It is not certain whether Melantho was the mother of Phorbas. He was the father of Arestor, who in turn became, according to some, the father of Argus Panoptes. [Scholiast on Euripides' *Phoenician Maidens* 1116, *Orestes* 920.]

MELEAGRIDES were daughters of Oeneus and Althaea and sisters of Meleager. The handsome and valiant Meleager, idol of his sisters, had been doomed from the day he was born. The Moirae (Fates) had appeared and warned his mother that a brand burning on the hearth controlled his life, which would end when the wood was consumed. Althaea hastily extinguished the flame and kept the splinter in a safe place. When in a fit of anger Meleager killed Althaea's brothers, she threw the wood into the fire and thus terminated her son's life.

His sisters—Eurymede, Melanippe, Phoebe, Eurydice, Menesto, Erato, Antiope, and Hippodameia—lamented his death unceasingly. Artemis took pity on them; turning them into guinea hens, she transported them to one of her temples on the small island of Leros in the Aegean Sea. Thereafter, guinea fowl were sacred birds in this precinct of Artemis. Deianeira and Gorge were also Meleager's sisters and mourned along with the others, but Dionysus prevented them from being transformed. Some said Deianeira was his daughter. [Antoninus Liberalis 2; Ovid, *Metamorphoses* 8.532; Hyginus, *Fables* 174; Suidas, "Meleagrides"; Athenaeus 14.655.]

MELETE was one of the MUSES. [Pausanias 9.29.2.]

MELIA (1) was one of the OCEANIDES. There were a great number of these marine nymphs (Hesiod listed 41), but very few of them had any special distinction. Melia, however, could be called the mother of the Argive nation. By her brother Inachus, god of the Inachus River, she became the mother of Phoroneus and Aegialeus. The part of Peloponnesus afterward called

Achaia derived its name, Aegialeia, from Aegialeus. Phoroneus, whose mother was sometimes called Archia, was the first to sacrifice to Hera at Argos. He also united the people from a nomadic existence into a social structure. Upon his death his sons distributed the kingdom of Argos among themselves.

Before this marriage with her brother, Melia had been carried off by Apollo. Abduction of nymphs was a common occurrence, and their fathers had to keep a watchful eye. In this case, Oceanus sent his son Caanthus to search for his sister. Caanthus soon found her at Thebes in the possession of Apollo, but he quickly learned that Apollo was not going to surrender her. Caanthus spitefully threw fire into the god's sacred grove called the Ismenion. Apollo shot Caanthus with an arrow, and the youth was buried near the Ismenus River. This river was named for Ismenus, son of Melia by Apollo. It had formerly been called the Ladon or Cadmus. Melia also became by the god the mother of Tenerus, who became a soothsayer and priest of Apollo Ptous.

Melia was worshipped at the Ismenion, probably in deference to her sons. After their birth she left Thebes. At some point she met Inachus (the waters of rivers continually blended with the waters of seas and oceans). The emergence of a whole nation from the watery element was somewhat uncommon. The progenitors were usually autochthonous, i.e., born directly from the earth, or they were the sons of gods. [Apollodorus 2.1.1; Pausanias 1.39.4, 2.5.5, 7.1.1, 9.10.5,26.1; Hesychius, "Ismenios"; Hyginus, *Fables* 143.]

MELIA (2), a Bithynian nymph, according to some was the mother of Amycus by Poseidon. Others called Amycus' mother BITHYNIS. [Apollonius Rhodius 2.4.]

MELIADES (*See* MALIADES)

MELIAE were the nymphs who sprang from the drops of blood from the severed genitals of Uranus, along with the Giants and the Erinyes. The nymphs who nursed Zeus were also called Meliae. [Callimachus, *Hymn to Zeus* 47; Eustathius on Homer's *Odyssey* 1963.]

MELIBOEA (1) was a daughter of Oceanus and, according to some, the mother of Lycaon by Pelasgus. Lycaon's mother is more often called CYLLENE. [Apollodorus 3.8.1.]

MELIBOEA (2) was the wife of Magnes. Magnes was one of the Aeolids, son of Aeolus and Enarete. Two sons by Meliboea were mentioned, Eioneus and Alector. Eioneus was one of the suitors of Hippodameia and therefore suffered an unpleasant death. Nothing further is known of this particular Alector. Magnes was also the father of Dictys and Polydectes, known chiefly for their part in the story of Perseus. They were sons by a Naiad. Another wife, Philodice, was mentioned, and it could be that she was a second wife. Magnes named the town of Meliboea in Magnesia after his wife and the region after himself. The town might have been named as a memorial to Meliboea. [Eustathius on Homer's *Iliad* 338.]

MELIBOEA (3) was a daughter of Amphion and Niobe. She was usually called CHLORIS because she turned white with fear when Artemis and Apollo killed her brothers and sisters. [Pausanias 2.21.10.]

MELIBOEA (4) was a young woman from Ephesus who was in love with a young man named Alexis. Unhappily her parents had someone else in mind for her, and no amount of pleading would deter them from committing her to their choice. Alexis decided to leave the scene and try to recover from his heartbreak, so he moved down the river to another town. On the day of the wedding, in despair Meliboea threw herself from the roof of her house but was not injured. A boat was near, and she decided to flee. The ropes came loose as she touched them, and she floated downstream to Alexis. The happy lovers dedicated a sanctuary to Aphrodite Automate. [Servius on Virgil's *Aeneid* 1.724.]

MELIBOEA (5) was said to be one of the wives of Theseus. She was also called the mother of Ajax, son of Telamon, but his mother was usually called PERIBOEA. There is no substantiation that Meliboea was a wife of Theseus, and Athenaeus probably confused Meliboea with

Periboea, who indeed was called a wife of Theseus. [Athenaeus 13.557.]

MELIBOEA (6) was a surname of Persephone, goddess of the underworld. Meaning Sweet-Voiced, this was one of the many euphemistic names of the goddess. [Lasus, quoted by Athenaeus 14.624.]

MELIDES (See MALIADES)

MELINAEA was a surname of Aphrodite, derived from the Argive town of Meline. [Stephanus Byzantium, "Melinaia"; Lycophron 403.]

MELINE was one of the THESPIADES. She became by Heracles the mother of Laomedon. [Apollodorus 2.7.8.]

MELINOE was an infernal divinity, sometimes called by the surname Chthonia. She was said to be the daughter of Zeus and Persephone. She was a frightening spectral being who left the underworld nightly to strike fear and confusion among people everywhere. [Orphica, Hymns 71.]

MELISSA (1) was one of the daughters of Melisseus, king of Crete, who nursed the infant Zeus. Her sister Amaltheia gave milk of a goat to the child, while Melissa fed him honey. Some said the bees themselves deposited honey in the baby's mouth. From Melissa the nymphs who nursed Zeus were called Melissae or Meliae. Melissa was probably the nymph who discovered and taught the use of honey and gave bees their name (melissae). [Scholiast on Pindar's Pythian Odes 4.104; Antoninus Liberalis 19; Callimachus, Hymn to Zeus 47; Apollodorus 1.1.3; Lactantius 1.22.]

MELISSA (2) was a surname of Artemis as the goddess of the moon, in which capacity she alleviated the suffering of women in childbed. [Porphyry, From the Cave of the Nymphs 261.]

MELISSA (3) was a daughter of Epidamnus. He founded Epidamnus, an Illyrian city on the Ionian Sea. Melissa was loved by Poseidon and bore a son to him called Dyrrhachius. He in turn named the city Dyrrhachium after himself. In

later times it was learned that actually there were two cities, Epidamnus and Dyrrhachium, quite close to each other. [Pausanias 6.10.8; Stephanus Byzantium, "Dyrrhachion."]

MELISSAE was a name originally given to nymphs, but later it was transferred to priestesses in general. According to some, priestesses received their name from the purity of the bee. The name especially applied to the priestesses of Demeter, Persephone, and the Delphian Apollo. The Pythia was even called the "Bee of Delphi." [Pindar, Pythian Odes 106; Scholiast on Pindar's Pythian Odes 4.104; Callimachus, Hymn to Apollo 110; Hesychius, "Melissai"; Scholiast on Theocritus 15.94.]

MELITE (1) was one of the NEREIDES. [Apollodorus 1.2.7; Hyginus, Fables: Preface 8.]

MELITE (2) was a Naiad, daughter of the river-god Aegaeus. The Aegaeus River was in the island of Drepane (or Scheria), land of the Phaeacians. After killing his children, Heracles went there to be purified by King Nausithous and Macris, the nurse of Dionysus. While there he took Melite by force, and she became the mother of Hyllus. This Hyllus is not to be confused with Hyllus the hero's son by Deianeira and leader of the Heraclids. This Hyllus eventually migrated across to the Illyrian peninsula on the Cronian Sea with a number of settlers and gave his name to the Hyllaeans. [Apollonius Rhodius 4.538.]

MELITE (3) was a daughter of Erasinus of Argos. She and her sisters, Byze, Moira, and ANCHIROE, were visited by Britomartis.

MELITE (4), daughter of Hoples, according to some was the first wife of Aegeus. She was more often called META.

MELITE (5) was the daughter of Myrmex, an obscure Attic hero. She was said to be the lover of Heracles. From her the Attic deme of Melite received its name. In this deme Heracles was initiated into the lesser Eleusinian mysteries, and he later had a temple there under the surname Alexicacus (Averter of Evil), since it was dedicated at the time of a plague. [Scholiast on Aristophanes' *Frogs* 501; Suidas, "Melite."]

MELITODES, Sweet as Honey, occurred as a euphemistic surname of Persephone, queen of the infernal regions. [Porphyry, *From the Cave of the Nymphs* 261; Theocritus 15.94.]

MELLONA, or Mellonis, was a Roman divinity who was believed to protect honey. She is otherwise unknown. [St. Augustine, *City of God* 4.34; Arnobius, *Adversus Nationes* 14.7,8,11.]

MELOBOSIS, or Melobote, was one of the OCEANIDES. [*Homeric Hymn to Demeter* 420; Hesiod, *Theogony* 354; Pausanias 4.30.3.]

MELPOMENE, the Singing, was one of the nine MUSES. In spite of her joyous-sounding name, she became the Muse of tragedy. She was said by some to be the mother of the SIRENS. [Apollodorus 1.3.4; Apollodorus, *Epitome* 7.18; Hesiod, *Theogony* 77.]

MEMNONIDES were phantom birds formed from the smoke of Memnon's funeral pyre. They rose from the fire and flew three times around the pile. The fourth time around they divided into two flocks, fought with beaks and talons, and fell back into the fire as a funeral sacrifice. Some said the Memnonides were Memnon's female companions, who wept so heavily after his death that they were changed into birds. They visited the grave beside the Hellespont annually, wet it with their water-dipped wings, and pecked at themselves until lacerations were produced.

Memnon was the son of Eos, goddess of the dawn, and Tithonus, brother of Priam of Troy. He reigned over the Ethiopians and was an ally to Priam during the Trojan War. He was slain by Achilles, whose destiny weighed more favorably on the scales of Zeus. Eos gained immortality for him, but even so, continued to cry daily for him, her tears becoming the familiar dew. [Ovid, *Metamorphoses* 13.578; Apollodorus 3.12.4; Servius on Virgil's *Aeneid* 1.493,755; Pausanias 10.31.2.]

MEMPHIS (1) was a daughter of the Nile River. She married Epaphus, the son of the long-suffering Io, who in the form of a cow had been pursued over the whole world by a gadfly sent by Hera as punishment for Io's affair with Zeus. Zeus and Io, not learning a lesson from the persecution, produced Epaphus after Io arrived in Egypt. He became king of Egypt, and Memphis bore him two daughters, Libya and Lysianassa. The city of Memphis was named for her. It is rather curious that in this obvious generation of eponyms Memphis should have become the mother of Libya, a vastly greater geographical entity. Some called Memphis a daughter of the river-god Uchoreus and made her mother of Aegyptus. [Diodorus Siculus 1.51; Apollodorus 2.1.3–5,11; Hyginus, *Fables* 145,149,275.]

MEMPHIS (2) was by Danaus the mother of three Danaides, who were paired with three sons of Aegyptus because of the similarity of their names. Cleite was married to Cleitus, Sthenele to Sthenelus, and Chrysippe to Chrysippus. [Apollodorus 2.1.5.]

MENDEIS was a nymph in Macedonia. She was loved by Sithon, a son of Poseidon and Ares. He was king of the Hadomantes in Macedonia. By him she became the mother of Pallene and Rhoeteia. Courted by two young men, Pallene loved one of them and managed to have his rival killed in a chariot race that would have decided the matter. She was about to be burned with her victim on his funeral pyre when Aphrodite sent rain to drench the flames. The peninsula of Pallene (Macedonia) and Rhoeteia (Thrace) were named for the sisters. [Conon, *Narrations* 10; Tzetzes on Lycophron 1356; Parthenius, *Love Stories* 5.]

MENE was a divinity presiding over the months. Nothing of significance is known of her. Mene was also a name given to Selene, goddess of the moon. The identities were probably interchangeable. [Apollonius Rhodius 3.533, 4.55; St. Augustine, *City of God* 7.2; *Homeric Hymn* 32.1.]

MENESTHO was one of the OCEANIDES. [Hesiod, *Theogony* 355.]

MENESTO was one of the MELEAGRIDES.

MENIPPE (1) was one of the CORONIDES. [Antoninus Liberalis 25.]

MENIPPE (2) was a daughter of the Peneius River. She was loved by Pelasgus and bore Phrastor to him. The descendants of Phrastor were driven out of Greece and settled in Italy in a country they called Tyrrhenia. In effect, Menippe was the mother of the Tyrrhenian race. [Dionysius of Halicarnassus, *Roman Antiquities* 1.28.]

MENIPPE (3) was a daughter of Thamyris and, according to some, the mother of Orpheus. His mother was more frequently called CALLIOPE. [Tzetzes, *Chiliades* 1.12.]

MENIPPE (4) was one of the NEREIDES. [Hesiod, *Theogony* 260.]

MENIPPIS was one of the THESPIADES. By Heracles she was the mother of Entelides. [Apollodorus 2.7.8.]

MENODICE, a daughter of Orion, was the wife of Theiodamas, king of the Dryopes. She suffered two great losses because of Heracles. Crossing the country of the Dryopes with his wife Deianeira and his son Hyllus, the hero once asked for food from Theiodamas, who refused. Heracles killed one of Theiodamas' oxen, roasted it, and gave it to his wife and son. Theiodamas went off and returned with a small army, and Heracles killed him in the resulting battle. Menodice and Theiodamas had a beautiful young son, and the bisexual Heracles did not fail to notice him. When Heracles decided to join the Argonauts, he also decided to take along a pretty bunkmate, so he returned to Dryopis and helped himself to Hylas. Hylas never returned home, so Menodice was twice bereaved. When the Argonauts landed on the coast of Mysia, Hylas went to fetch water for Heracles. His beauty excited the Naiads of the pool, and they pulled him into the water. He was never seen again. [Apollonius Rhodius 1.131,1213; Hyginus, *Fables* 14,271; Theocritus 13.72.]

MEPHITIS was a Roman divinity who had a grove-surrounded temple on the Esquiline Hill. It was considered fatal to enter the area. Mephitis was a very obscure deity. Her worship seemed to be connected with mephitic exhalations from the earth. She might have been one of the Italian SIBYLS. Some identified her with Juno, which is not unusual since most female Roman divinities eventually came to be associated in one way or another with her. [Pliny, *Natural History* 2.93; Varro, *On the Latin Language* 5.49; Servius on Virgil's *Aeneid* 7.84; Tacitus, *Annals* 3.33.]

MEROPE (1) was one of the OCEANIDES and by Clymenus the mother of Phaethon. Phaethon's mother was usually called CLYMENE and his father Helios. [Hyginus, *Fables* 154.]

MEROPE (2) was one of the HELIADES. [Ovid, *Metamorphoses* 2.340; Hyginus, *Fables* 154.]

MEROPE (3) was one of the PLEIADES. In the constellation of the Pleiades she is the seventh and least visible star because she was ashamed of having had intercourse with a mortal man. This mortal was Sisyphus, and Merope should have been ashamed not so much that he was mortal but because of the type of mortal he was.

He was the son of Aeolus and Enarete, and brother to Cretheus, Athamas, Salmoneus, Deion, Magnes, Perieres, and Macareus. He eventually reigned in Corinth, since Medea gave him the sovereignty when she left. He promoted commerce and helped make the city important. He was of bad character, however, as Merope was soon to discover. She bore him Glaucus, Ornytion, Thersander, and Halmus. Sisyphus meanwhile had twin sons by his niece Tyro, but she killed them at their birth. Of Merope's sons we know Glaucus best, not only as the father of Bellerophon but also as the breeder of flesh-eating mares.

When Sisyphus was on his deathbed, he begged Merope not to bury him. She complied, and when he got to the underworld he complained that he was neglected and needed to return to the upper world to punish his wife. Once there he refused to return, and Hermes, transporter of the dead, had to carry him back by force. [Apollodorus 1.9.3, 3.10.1; Ovid, *Fasti* 4.175; Homer, *Iliad* 6.153; Eustathius on Homer's *Iliad* 1155; Pausanias 2.4.3, 6.20.9, 9.34.5; Hyginus, *Fables* 60.]

MEROPE (4) was a daughter of Oenopion, son of Dionysus, and Helice in Chios. She was also called Haero, Aerope, Aero, and Maerope. The extraordinarily handsome giant Orion once came to Chios and was hospitably received by Oenopion. He fell instantly in love with Merope, and apparently she was not unpleased. Orion cleared the island of wild beasts and brought the spoils of the chase to his beloved. Oenopion was not as impressed with Orion as his daughter and kept putting off formal acknowledgment of the marriage proposal. His reluctance could have been a result of his own physical interest in his daughter.

One day Orion became drunk (not too difficult, since Oenopion was a son of Dionysus, and he and his own sons were wine makers) and raped Merope. Oenopion was afraid of Orion and implored Dionysus for assistance. The god threw Orion into a deep sleep, and Oenopion blinded him. In this pitiful state Orion left the island.

From such sparse detail it is hard to know how Merope reacted to this series of events. Certainly the rape was an outrage, but perhaps her love was strong enough to have forgiven him, considering he was in a state of diminished (mental) capacity when he committed the act. Did she have regrets at seeing Orion wander off remorseful and helpless? It is doubtful she ever saw him again, even though after he was cured he returned to Chios to seek vengeance on Oenopion. Oenopion hid and was thus saved. He probably hid his whole family as well, and Orion must have departed Chios for good. [Apollodorus 1.4.3; Hyginus, *Poetic Astronomy* 2.34.]

MEROPE (5) was, according to some, the wife of Megareus, by whom she became the mother of Hippomenes. The wife of Megareus is more often called IPHINOE. [Hyginus, *Fables* 185.]

MEROPE (6) was a daughter of Cypselus, son of Aepytus and king of Basilis on the Alpheius River in Arcadia. She married Cresphontes, son of Aristomachus and one of the Heraclid conquerors of Peloponnesus. Cresphontes obtained Messenia as his share of the invaded kingdom. During an insurrection by the Messenian nobles, he and two of his sons were killed. The youngest son, Aepytus, was away being educated at the house of his grandfather Cypselus and so escaped the danger.

Merope was not so lucky. The throne was immediately occupied by the Heraclid Polyphontes, who forced Merope to become his wife. Aepytus was able to communicate with his mother through messengers, and she begged him to punish the murderers of his father. When he was grown, he married a daughter of Holcas. With his father-in-law's help he managed to return to Messenia and kill Polyphontes and his fellow conspirators. Aepytus left a son, Glaucus, and through him gave his name (and that of his great-grandfather) to the Aepytids rather than the more general name of Heraclids. [Apollodorus 2.8.4,5; Pausanias 2.18.6, 4.3.3,31.9, 8.5.4,5; Hyginus, *Fables* 137,184.]

MEROPE (7) was, according to some, the wife of Polybus, king of Corinth, who reared Oedipus. She was more often called PERIBOEA. [Apollodorus 3.5.7.]

MEROPE (8) was a daughter of Pandareos. (*See* CAMEIRA.)

MEROPE (9) was a daughter of Erechtheus II and, according to some, mother of Daedalus. His mother is more often called ALCIPPE.

MESE was one of the MUSES worshipped at Delphi. [Plutarch, *Table-Talk* 9.14.]

MESSEMBRIA was one of the HORAE.

MESSENE was a daughter of Triopas, son of the Argive Phorbas, and her brothers were Iasus and Agenor. She married Polycaon, the youngest son of Lelex, king of Sparta. When Lelex passed the kingdom to his older son Myles, Messene urged Polycaon to set up a kingdom elsewhere. So with assistance from his Argive and Spartan relatives, Polycaon conquered a region he named Messenia for his wife. The capital of the area was Andania, and there Messene helped introduce the worship of Zeus and the Eleusinian mysteries. After her death she was honored with a temple and worshipped as a minor goddess. [Pausanias 2.16.1, 3.1.1, 4.1.2,3.6,27.4,31.9.]

MESSIA was a minor agricultural divinity among the Romans. Unfortunately no written accounts of her worship endure. [Tertullian, *On Spectacles* 8.]

MESTRA, or Hypermestra, was a daughter of Erysichthon. This man had incurred the wrath of Demeter for cutting down a grove sacred to her. The goddess condemned him to perpetual hunger. He eventually had to sell everything in his house to support his insatiable appetite. Mestra finally hit on the plan of selling herself as a slave to obtain food for her father. This worked quite well, for she had once been a lover of Poseidon, who gave her the power to change her shape at will. She could and did change herself into a man on several occasions in order to escape from her masters. Each time she would return home, only to start the whole process over again. In spite of her devoted efforts, Erysichthon finally went mad and consumed his own flesh. [Tzetzes on Lycophron 1393; Ovid, *Metamorphoses* 8.847; Antoninus Liberalis 17, who calls her Hypermestra.]

META, sometimes called Melite, was the daughter of Hoples, one of the sons of Ion, who gave his name to one of the major classes of individuals in Attica. She was the first wife of Aegeus, who became king of Athens. Aegeus desperately wanted an heir, but Meta did not become pregnant, so he divorced her and married Chalciope. She did not bear him any children either, so he consulted the Delphic oracle about the situation and received a cryptic reply. On his way home he slept with Aethra, daughter of King Pittheus at Troezen. From this union Theseus was thought to have been conceived, but Aethra also slept with Poseidon that same night. Twenty years afterward, Theseus went to Athens to claim his birthright, and Medea, who was being kept by Aegeus, tried to poison him. Medea had a son she claimed was fathered by Aegeus, and she wanted him on the throne. She was promptly exiled, of course.

It becomes rather apparent that Aegeus was sterile. If Meta and Chalciope could not give him a child, if (as most people believed) Theseus was Poseidon's son, and if 20 years passed without any woman becoming pregnant by him, then the problem lay with him. Medea was scheming and resourceful. Medus, Aegeus' alleged son, could easily have been the son of a palace guard. Meta needlessly suffered the disgrace of having a seemingly barren womb. She probably learned the truth soon enough if and when she married or took a lover, although it was not the custom for women to take a second husband. [Apollodorus 3.15.6; Scholiast on Euripides' *Medea* 668.]

METANEIRA, sometimes called Meganeira or another of several names, was the wife of Celeus, king of Eleusis. She was by him the mother of Demophon, Triptolemus, Demo, Callidice, and Callithoe. Some added Abas, who was changed into a lizard for making fun of Demeter, but this relationship would make no sense in terms of subsequent developments. Metaneira's daughters once encountered an aged woman at the public fountain; hearing her story about her misfortunes, they pitied her and invited her to their home. Metaneira hospitably received the woman, who was Demeter in disguise searching for the lost Persephone. Metaneira took a fancy to the sad-faced woman and decided to retain her to look after the infant Demophon. At the same time, everyone tried to cheer the melancholy visitor, particularly Iambe, one of Metaneira's slaves.

Demeter, still disguised, proved to be a very good nurse. She was profoundly grateful to Metaneira and her family and decided to repay their kindness. Over a period of several nights she held young Demophon in fire to make him immortal. The job was almost completed when Metaneira happened upon the scene one night and screamed in hysteria, causing Demeter to drop Demophon so that he was consumed by the fire. A great alarm went out, and Demeter had to reveal herself in her true form.

To make amends, Demeter gave the older son, Triptolemus, a chariot drawn by winged serpents and bade him travel over the world sowing grains of wheat. He introduced the festival of the Thesmophoria at Athens and was said by some to have become a judge of the dead in the underworld.

Celeus was the first priest of Demeter at Eleusis, and his and Metaneira's daughters were priestesses. [*Homeric Hymn to Demeter* 109, 161,202; Apollodorus 1.5.1; Antoninus Liberalis 23; Pausanias 1.38.3, 2.14.2; Ovid, *Fasti* 4.512; Hyginus, *Fables* 147.]

METER, meaning Mother, was a surname of Athena at Elis. After Heracles sacked Elis in revenge for his treatment by Augeas, the women of Elis saw that most of the young vigorous men had been killed, and they prayed to Athena that they might conceive the first time they had intercourse with their husbands. Athena answered their prayer, and they set up a sanctuary to Athena Meter. [Pausanias 5.3.1.]

METHARME was a daughter of King Pygmalion and Galateia, and wife of Cinyras, according to some. According to others, the wife of Cinyras was CENCHREIS. [Apollodorus 3.14.3.]

METHE was the personification of drunkenness. She was represented as a nymph in the train of Dionysus, accompanied by Seilenus and satyrs. Not much was written about her. In the city of Elis there was a temple of Seilenus, in which Methe was represented as offering him a cup of wine. In Epidaurus was a picture of her, the work of the artist Pausias, in which she herself drank from a cup. [Pausanias 2.27.3, 6.24.8.]

METHONE (1) was one of the ALCYONIDES. [Suidas, "Alkyonides."]

METHONE (2) was the mother of Peirene either by the Achelous or Asopus River. Nothing further is known of Methone, but Peirene was the nymph of the spring Peirene near Corinth. This spring was believed to have arisen from the tears Peirene shed when her son Cenchrias died. [Pausanias 2.2.3,3.5.]

METHONE (3) was the wife of Poeas and mother of Philoctetes. Philoctetes' mother was more often called DEMONASSA. [Eustathius on Homer's *Iliad* 323.]

METHYMNA was a daughter of Macar, son of Helios and king of Lesbos. After the Deucalionian flood, Macar went to Lesbos from Rhodes as leader of a group of Ionians and other settlers. The settlement was profitable and Macar became king. At nearly the same time, Lesbus, son of Lapithes, went to Lesbos in obedience to an oracle. He married Methymna. Thus the Thessalians who came with Lesbus and the Ionians who came with Macar inhabited the island jointly and intermarried. At that time the island was renamed Lesbos. The town of Methymna derived its name from Methymna. [Diodorus Siculus 5.81; Stephanus Byzantium, "Methymna."]

METIADUSA was a daughter of Eupalamus, one of the many sons of Erechtheus (II) and Praxithea. She married her uncle Cecrops (II) and became the mother of Pandion II. Pandion became king of Athens after the death of Cecrops but was expelled by the sons of Metion, his cousins. He went to Megara, and after marrying into the royal family obtained the government. He became the father of Aegeus, Pallas, Nisus, and Lycus. We never hear of Metiadusa again, but if she was alive at the time of the insurrection by the Metionidae, she probably fled to Megara with Pandion. [Apollodorus 3.15.1,5; Pausanias 1.5.2,3,29.5; Euripides, *Medea* 660.]

METIDICE (*See* MYTHIDICE)

METIOCHE was one of the CORONIDES.

METIS was one of the OCEANIDES, but she assumed a greater importance than her many sisters. She was the first love of Zeus, even though she tried not to be, changing herself into various shapes and sizes. After this failed, she succumbed, and she and Zeus lived together briefly. During this time Zeus was trying to recover his lost brothers and sisters swallowed by Cronus. Metis proposed, ironically as it turned out, that he give Cronus a vomitive. It is needless to dwell on the point that if Zeus was old enough to be chasing women, his siblings had been inside Cronus for many years.

Metis had tried to flee Zeus because she knew her own fate. Zeus learned that in the future Metis would give birth to a daughter. Then she would bear a son who would later dethrone him as he had dethroned Cronus. Following the lead of his father, Zeus swallowed Metis when she became pregnant. In due time, a female child grew inside Zeus' body and finally sprang, fully grown, from his head. This was Athena. A male did not follow as predicted, for when Metis was swallowed by Zeus all connubial relations had to end, of course.

It is not clear whether or not Metis ever emerged from the body of Zeus. She was said to have been the personification of prudence, but this would have been a short-lived office if it ended when she was ingested. She was also said to have had a son, Porus, the personification of expediency. For obvious reasons Zeus was not mentioned as his father. Metis must have had Porus before she became involved with Zeus, and he might have been born without a father, thus setting a precedent for Athena's parthenogenesis. [Apollodorus 1.2.1.,3.6; Hesiod, *Theogony* 471,886; Plato, *Symposium* 203.]

METOPE (1), also called Parnassa, was a daughter of the river-god Ladon and Stymphalis in Arcadia. She married the river-god Asopus in Phlius. Asopus fathered by her two sons, Pelasgus and Ismenus, and 12 daughters, Cercyra, Salamis, Aegina, Peirene, Cleone, Thebe, Tanagra, Thespeia, Asopis, Sinope, Ornia, and Chalcis. Ismenus went to Boeotia and settled near the river, which was called Ismenus after him. Sinope was carried off by Apollo to the place later called Sinope and became the mother of Syrus, who became king of the Syrians. Cercyra was carried off by Poseidon to the island he named for her, and her son Phaeax gave his name to the Phaeacians. Salamis was also seized by Poseidon and taken to the island later named for her. Aegina was abducted by Zeus and gave birth to Aeacus on the island later named for her. It is easy to see that most of the children of Metope had places named for them.

The carrying off of river nymphs was a convenient way to explain the origin of colonies of various tribes. In addition to the above named, other children of Metope and Asopus were Ismene, Pelagon, and seven unnamed daughters. [Apollodorus 2.1.8, 3.12.6; Pindar, *Olympian Odes* 6.144; Diodorus Siculus 4.72; Pausanias 2.5.2, 5.22.5, 9.1.2; Herodotus 11.51.]

METOPE (2) was a daughter of Asopus. Though not stated, her mother was Metope, the wife of Asopus. Metope was said to have borne 20 daughters to Asopus, and the second Metope was probably one of these. [Scholiast on Pindar's *Isthmian Odes* 8.37.]

METOPE (3) was the wife of the Sangarius River and named as one of the possible mothers of Hecuba. [Apollodorus 3.12.6.]

METOPE (4), also called Amphissa, was a daughter of Echetus, son of Euchenor and Phlogea and a king of Epeirus. She loved Aechmodicus and met him secretly. Echetus caught the lovers in naked embrace and castrated Aechmodicus, who probably died from the crude operation. Echetus blinded Metope and then gave her iron barleycorns, telling her that when she ground them to flour he would restore her vision. This tale was perhaps an example of stories told around the campfires for entertainment during the Trojan War. [Homer, *Odyssey* 18.83, 21.307; Apollonius Rhodius 4.1093.]

MIDEA was one of the DANAIDES. She was married to Antimachus. [Hyginus, *Fables* 170.]

MIDEATIS was a surname of Alcmena, derived from the town of Midea in Argolis, where her father Electryon ruled as king. [Pausanias 2.25.8; Theocritus 13.20, 24.1.]

MIDEIA (1), or Midea, was a Phrygian woman who was loved by Electryon, father of Alcmena. She bore a son to him after he had nine sons by his wife, Anaxo. This son, Licymnius, was the only one of Electryon's sons to survive the raid of the Taphians. He became a friend and companion of his half-sister Alcmena, accompanying her and Amphitryon to Thebes. He married

Perimede, the daughter of Amphitryon, and had several sons by her. He took part in the final battle with Eurystheus and later joined the first, but unsuccessful, expedition into Peloponnesus. He was killed accidentally by his grandnephew Tlepolemus. Though mother of the only direct heir of Electryon, Mideia was never heard of again. [Apollodorus 2.4.5; Pindar, *Olympian Odes* 7.29; Pausanias 2.22.8, 3.15.4.]

MIDEIA (2) was, according to some, a daughter of Phylas and by Heracles the mother of Antiochus. Antiochus' mother is more often called MEDA. [Pausanias 1.5.2, 10.10.1.]

MIDEIA (3) was a nymph loved by Poseidon, by whom she became the mother of Aspledon. An ancient Minyan town of Boeotia called Aspledon derived its name from him. Nothing further is known of Mideia and Aspledon. The city, whose site is uncertain, was mentioned by Homer. It was about 4 kilometers from Orchomenus and was abandoned in the time of Pausanias because the water supply was exhausted. [Pausanias 9.38.6; Homer, *Iliad* 2.510.]

MIEZA was a granddaughter of Macedon, a hero of uncertain ancestry, for whom Macedonia was said to be named. The city of Mieza (near modern Lefkadia) was named for Mieza. The city was made famous by establishment there of an Aristotelian school by Alexander the Great. [Stephanus Byzantium, "Mieza."]

MIGONITIS was a surname of Aphrodite, derived from Migonium, a place on the mainland near the island of Cranae in Laconia. Paris founded the sanctuary of Aphrodite Migonitis there when he eloped with Helen. [Pausanias 3.22.2.]

MILITARIS was a surname of Venus, probably equivalent to the Greek Aphrodite Areia. [Servius on Virgil's *Aeneid* 1.724; Macrobius, *Saturnalia* 3.8.]

MIMALLONES was the Macedonian name of the MAENADES. [Strabo 10.3.10.]

MINERVA was the Roman goddess identified with the Greek Athena. Since she was the daughter of the supreme god, a virgin goddess, and the patroness of domestic skills and arts useful and esthetic, the identification was an easy one, and the attributes of Athena were almost totally transferred to Minerva. She was the personification of thinking, calculating, and inventing. She was the third most important divinity at Rome, and joined Jupiter and Juno in a kind of trinity. They were sometimes united in a common temple.

Her festival, called Quinquatrus, was celebrated March 19–23. Among other things it featured rites of purification. Musical instruments, which played a prominent role in religious worship, were said to have been invented by Minerva. Instruments were purified annually. She also was said to have invented numbers. She was invoked by those who desired to enjoy prominence in sculpture, painting, poetry, pedagogy, medicine, or decorative arts. While she was particularly revered by women as patroness of domestic skills such as spinning and weaving, she was also worshipped by men who sought cunning, prudence, and courage in military affairs. For this reason she was often represented with a helmet, shield, and cuirass of mail. The number five was sacred to her, and her principal sacrificial victims were calves.

Even though an avowed virgin, she was at one time the object of the affection of Mars. With the help of a fellow divinity, Anna Perenna, she was able to make the god look foolish, and he abandoned his pursuit of her. One or two obscure accounts made her the mother of children—the Muses by Jupiter and Broteas by Vulcan. Being the mother of the Muses would make a certain amount of sense. Being mother of Broteas may recall the attempt of Hephaestus to penetrate Athena that ended with his dropping his sperm on the ground to produce Erichthonius. Broteas was extremely ugly, so much so that he burned himself to death.

Minerva's oldest temple was on the Capitoline Hill. She also had one on the Aventine Hill and a chapel on the Caelian Hill. Her surname in this chapel was Capta, a name of unknown origin. She also was surnamed Nautia. When Diomedes took the Palladium to

Italy from Troy, he was ordered by an oracle to restore it to the Trojans. He left it to be delivered by Nautes to Aeneas, but Nautes and his descendants kept the statue and by so doing were especially blessed by the goddess. This image was preserved at Rome in the temple of Vesta and was regarded as one of the safeguards of the state. [St. Augustine, *City of God* 4.10; Varro, *On the Latin Language* 6.14; Arnobius, *Adversus Nationes* 4.16, 7.22; Dionysius Halicarnassus, *Roman Antiquities* 1.69; Ovid, *Fasti* 3.809,849, 6.728; Livy 45.33; Virgil, *Aeneid* 2.615, 5.704; Servius on Virgil's *Aeneid* 2.166, 3.407, *Georgics* 1.277; Lucan 1.598; Valerius Maximus 2.1.2.]

MINTHA, or Mentha, was a nymph of the Cocytus River in the underworld. She was loved by Hades and might have been the only other woman besides Persephone in his life. He visited her secretly but was soon found out by Demeter. The goddess had been through too much during the loss and partial recovery of her daughter to tolerate any adulterous behavior. Either she or Persephone, after battering the rival, changed her into dust. From this pile of dust Hades caused the mint plant to grow. Some say Persephone changed her directly into a mint. Near Pylus in Triphylia there was a hill called Mintha. At its foot was a temple of Hades and a grove of Demeter. [Strabo 8.314; Ovid, *Metamorphoses* 10.729; Oppian 3.486.]

MINYADES were the daughters of Minyas, son of Chryses and king of the area around what later became Orchomenus in Boeotia. These daughters were Alcathoe, Leucippe, and Arsippe (or variations on these names). When the worship of Dionysus was introduced into Boeotia and other women flocked to Bacchic gatherings, the sisters remained at home and calmly went about their ordinary chores. Dionysus was outraged at having his sacred celebrations profaned. Visiting the women in the disguise of a young maiden, he urged them to take part in the mysteries. They not only refused but ridiculed the maiden. The god then changed himself successively into a bull, a lion, and a panther. The sisters went mad and expressed eagerness to honor the god. Leucippe was selected by lot to offer a sacrifice,

and she gave up her young son Hippasus to be torn to pieces. The sisters then roamed the hills in drunken frenzy, and Dionysus changed them into birds. A more familiar version says they were changed into bats and their weaving into vines. A festival, the Agrionia, was observed every year at Orchomenus to remind women of the consequences of neglecting Dionysiac worship. [Aelian, *Various Narratives* 3.42; Plutarch, *Roman Questions* 38; Ovid, *Metamorphoses* 4.1–40, 390–415.]

MISA was a mystic being in the Orphic mysteries, perhaps the same as Cybele or an attribute of her. [Orphica, *Hymns* 41; Hesychius, "Misatis."]

MISME was an Eleusinian woman who encountered Demeter when the goddess went to Eleusis on her search for Persephone. Misme felt sorry for the pathetic woman and gave her cold water mixed with grain and flavored with mint. Demeter was so thirsty she drained the vessel entirely. Ascalabus, the adolescent son who accompanied Misme, laughed at her and called for a whole barrel of water. Insulted by this insolence, Demeter sprinkled the remaining drops from the vessel on Ascalabus' head, and he was promptly changed into a lizard. One would think Demeter might have respected Misme's kindness enough to temper her rage and give Ascalabus only temporary punishment. [Antoninus Liberalis 24.]

MITHIDICE (*See* MYTHIDICE)

MITYLENE (*See* MYTILENE)

MIXOPARTHENOS, i.e., Half-Maiden, was a surname of the Erinyes, or Furies. [Lycophron 669; Herodotus 4.9.]

MNEIAE was a name by which the nine MUSES were known in some places. It meant Remembrances. [Plutarch, *Table-Talk* 9.14.]

MNEME, Memory, was one of three MUSES worshipped in early times at Ascra in Boeotia. [Pausanias 2.29.2.]

MNEMONIDES was a name given to the MUSES, suggesting to some that their mother was Mneme, who is otherwise known as one of the three Muses worshipped very early in Ascra. Mnemonides could be a variation on the designation for the daughters of Mnemosyne. [Ovid, *Metamorphoses* 5.268.]

MNEMOSYNE, Memory, was a daughter of Uranus and Gaea and therefore one of the Titanides. She was an aunt of Zeus, who fell in love with her. This probably happened quite early, before he married another aunt (Themis), a cousin (Metis), and finally his sister (Hera). By Mnemosyne he became the father of the nine MUSES, who were born at Pieria at the foot of Mount Olympus. Their conception occupied nine consecutive nights. The physiological ramifications of this phenomenon are endless.

Mnemosyne had a statue at Athens. She also had a sacred fountain and throne at Lebadeia near the oracle of Trophonius, and both played a part in the ceremonies that took place there. Mnemosyne was scarcely ever mentioned in mythological accounts. [Pausanias 9.39.4; Hesiod, *Theogony* 57,75,135,915; Homer, *Iliad* 2.491, *Odyssey* 1.10; Apollodorus 1.3.1.]

MNESIMACHE was, according to some, the daughter of Dexamenus. She is more often called DEIANEIRA. [Apollodorus 2.5.5.]

MNESTRA was one of the DANAIDES, daughter of Danaus and an Ethiopian woman. She was the wife and murderer of Aegius, son of Aegyptus. [Apollodorus 2.1.5.]

MOIRAE were the Fates, personification of the inescapable destiny of man. The Moirae assigned to every person his or her share in the scheme of things. Originally only one Moira was conceived, and not necessarily in a personified sense. Zeus, as father of gods and men, weighed out the "fate" of individuals, as he did in the case of Achilles and Memnon. Later there were two Fates, one at either pole of a person's life. Finally, the familiar trio of Fates came to be accepted, each with a specific function.

The three Moirae were Clotho, Atropos, and Lachesis. They were called variously daughters of Zeus, Nyx alone, Erebus and Nyx, Cronus and Nyx, Oceanus and Gaea, or Ananke (Necessity) alone. Depending on the identity of their parents, they were variously called sisters of the Horae, the Ceres, or Erinyes. They were described sometimes as aged and formidable women, often lame to indicate the slow march of fate. Clotho spun the thread at the beginning of one's life, Atropos wove the thread into the fabric of one's actions, and Lachesis snipped the thread at the conclusion of one's life. The process was absolutely unalterable, and gods as well as men and women had to submit to it.

As goddesses of fate the Moirae necessarily knew the future and therefore were regarded as prophetic deities. Thus their ministers were all the soothsayers and oracles. Then as now the concept of predestination presented the usual paradoxes, since if from one's birth he or she was destined to commit a crime, then punishment for the crime, itself preordained, placed good and evil beyond human control. Yet the Erinyes unfailingly fulfilled their function in a kind of obbligato to the inexorable hum of the spindle and thwack of the loom.

For all the claims made for the immutability of fate, there were a few questionable instances in which destinies appeared to be altered. Apollo induced the Moirae to grant Admetus delivery from death, if at the hour of his death his father, mother, or wife would die for him. Some said he made the Moirae drunk in order to accomplish this. The Moirae also joined Eileithyia in trying to delay the birth of Heracles.

They were identified with the somewhat obscure Heimarmene and Pepromene. Tyche, the goddess of luck, was by some considered one of the Moirae, as was Aphrodite Urania. They had sanctuaries in many parts of Greece, such as Corinth, Sparta, Olympia, and Thebes. [Homer, *Iliad* 5.613, 8.69, 20.5, 22.209, 24.29; Hesiod, *Theogony* 217,904; Pausanias 1.19.2, 2.4.7, 3.11.8, 9.25.4, 10.24.4; Cicero, *On the Nature of the Gods* 3.17; Lycophron 144; Tzetzes on Lycophron 406; Herodotus 1.9; Ovid, *Metamorphoses* 8.454, *Tristia* 5.3; Pindar, *Olympian Odes* 1.40; Plato, *Republic* 617.]

MOLAE were Roman divinities called the daughters of Mars. They could have been the same as the Camenae, but the name suggests they were connected with the pounding or grinding of grain. [Gellius 13.22.]

MOLIONE, or Moline, was a daughter of Molus, son of Ares. She had two sons, Cteatus and Eurytus, who she claimed were sons of Poseidon even though she was married to Actor, son of Phorbas and Hyrmine and brother of Augeas. The Greeks, in love with curiosities, later claimed the sons were born from an egg and joined in one body that had two heads, four arms, and four legs. While this freakish anatomy might be explained by what we call Siamese twins, the exploits later associated with these so-called Molionidae would not have been possible. Moreover, without the benefit of modern surgery, Molione could not have survived their delivery. So we are obliged to consider them as normal twins.

When yet boys the Molionidae took part in an expedition of the Epeians against Neleus and the Pylians. They also participated in the Calydonian boar hunt. When they were older they were commissioned by their uncle Augeas to take charge of the defense campaign against Heracles, who was demanding satisfaction for the refused payment for cleaning the Augean stables. Heracles became ill and concluded a separate peace with Augeas, but was attacked and beaten by the nephews. In vengeance he later killed them at Cleonae as they were on their way to sacrifice for the Eleians at the Isthmian games. The Eleians demanded that the Argives atone for the murder, but the Argives refused and continued to take part in the games.

Molione cursed any Eleian who should ever again participate in the games. Before they died, the Molionidae gave Molione grandchildren. Their tombs were shown at Cleonae near a temple of Heracles. [Homer, *Iliad* 11.709,750, 23.638; Eustathius on Homer's *Iliad* 882; Apollodorus 2.7.2; Pindar, *Olympian Odes* 11.33; Pausanias 2.15.1, 5.2.1,3.4, 8.14.6; Plutarch, *On Brotherly Love* 1; Athenaeus 2.58.]

MOLPADIA (1) was a daughter of Staphylus, the son of Dionysus and Ariadne, and Chrysothemis; her sisters were Rhoeo and Parthenos. Rhoeo was seduced by Apollo, became pregnant,

and was cast into the sea in a chest. The remaining two sisters never had a chance to learn that she landed safely on Delos and gave birth to Anius. But they learned from this incident not to go against their father's will. Unfortunately they did. They were put in charge of guarding their father's wine, but one day they fell asleep on the job. Their pigs overturned the vessels and ruined the vintage. The terrified sisters fled from the certain punishment and threw themselves over a cliff. Probably out of a kind of familial loyalty, Apollo saved them. He transported Molpadia to Castabus in the Thracian Chersonesus and changed her name to Hemithea. A temple was erected to her, and no one was allowed to enter who had so much as touched a pig. Libations of honey and water were poured to her. She was worshipped as a divinity affording comfort to women in labor. Some said she became by Lyrcus the mother of Basileus. Parthenos was similarly transferred to Bubastus in the Chersonesus. [Parthenius, *Love Stories* 1; Diodorus Siculus 5.52,63.]

MOLPADIA (2) was one of the AMAZONS. When these warrior women invaded Attica in an effort to recover Antiope from Theseus, they were too late to achieve that purpose. Antiope had already fallen in love with Theseus and borne him a son. When her sister Amazons besieged Athens, she fought at the side of her husband. Molpadia threw a javelin and killed Antiope, and was herself immediately run through by Theseus. Antiope's tomb was near the temple of Gaea. Molpadia's tomb was also shown at Athens; though never precisely located, it was probably near that of Antiope. [Plutarch, *Theseus* 27; Pausanias 1.2.1.]

MOLPE was one of the SIRENS. [Hyginus, *Fables: Preface* 30.]

MONETA, the Adviser, was a surname of Juno among the Romans. At the time of an earthquake, a voice came from Juno's temple commanding that a pregnant sow should be sacrificed to her. From that occasion the goddess was called the Adviser. There were various other explanations for the name as well, but they all had to do more or less with Juno's advisory function. One story was that during the war against Pyrrhus, the Romans were getting low on funds. They sought the advice of Juno Moneta, and she responded that they would always be solvent if their wars were carried out according to the principles of ethics. They won, and in gratitude decided that the minting of coins would be placed under the patronage of Juno Moneta. Subsequently she was characterized as the protectress of money. She had a temple on the Capitoline Hill that served as the mint. Her festival was celebrated on June 1. [Cicero, *On Divination* 1.45, 2.32; Ovid, *Fasti* 1.635, 6.183; Macrobius, *Saturnalia* 1.12.]

MONUSTE was one of the DANAIDES. She was married to Eurysthenes. [Hyginus, *Fables* 170.]

MORMO was a female specter that the Greeks used to frighten little children. She was one of the same class of frightful creatures as Empusa and Lamia. The Mormolyceia further were said to be able to assume the form of beautiful women for the purpose of luring young men to bed, where they then sucked their blood and consumed their flesh. [Philostratus, *Life of Apollonius of Tyana* 4.25; Aristophanes, *Acharnians* 582, *Peace* 474.]

MORPHO, or the Fair-Shaped, occurs as a surname of Aphrodite at Sparta. She was represented in a sitting position, with her head veiled and her feet chained. Tyndareus, king of Sparta, was said to have put the shackles on the feet of the statue either to symbolize the faithfulness of wives to husbands or to punish the goddess for her part in the shame of his daughters. [Pausanias 3.15.8; Lycophron 449.]

MOTHONE was a daughter of Oeneus by a concubine. Methone (called Mothone by Pausanias) in the extreme southwest of Messenia was said to have been named for her. The town was earlier called Pedasus. Pausanias believed the town was named for a rock called Mothon that formed the harbor. Mothone was born after Oeneus had taken refuge in Peloponnesus with his grandson Diomedes, so he was already of advanced age. [Pausanias 4.35.1.]

MUNYCHIA was a surname of Artemis derived from the Attic port town of Munychia, where she had a temple. She was the guardian deity of this citadel. The temple was famous as a place of asylum for state criminals. Her festival was celebrated at Athens in the month of Munychion (April). Artemis Munychia had a temple near Ephesus founded by Agamemnon, who was forced to remain for a time in the vicinity because his men were suffering from a disease of the buttocks. Munychia was also a surname of Athena and Hecate, but the reasons why are not clear. [Pausanias 1.1.4; Strabo 14.1.20, Eustathius on Homer's *Iliad* 331; Xenophon, *Hellenica* 4.11.]

MURCIA, Murtea, or Murtia was a surname of Venus at Rome, where she had a chapel in the Circus with a statue. The name probably was derived from a myrtle grove that stood in front of her sanctuary. [Varro, *On the Latin Language* 5.154; Livy 1.33; St. Augustine, *City of God* 4.16; Servius on Virgil's *Aeneid* 1.724; Plutarch, *Roman Questions* 20.]

MUSES were goddesses who presided over the arts and sciences and inspired those who excelled in these pursuits. The concept was so persuasive that even today an individual might refer in figurative language to a personal muse as a source of his or her inspiration.

There were not always nine Muses. Like so many ideas in Greek mythology, their number represented an evolution from earlier times. Originally three Muses were worshipped on Mount Helicon in Boeotia: Melete, Mneme, and Aoede, referring to their characterization of meditation, memory, and song. Their worship was said to have been established by Otus and Ephialtes, the so-called Aloeidae. Three Muses were worshipped also at Sicyon, but we have the name of only one of them, Polymatheia. Again, three were worshipped at Delphi; their names corresponded with the names of the three strings of the lyre—Nete, Mese, and Hypate. At Delphi they were alternately called Cephisso, Apollonis, and Borysthenis. Four Muses were at one time recognized—Thelxinoe, Aoede, Arche, and Melete—two of the names having been used before. One of the persons associated with the Muses was Pierus. By some he was called the father of a total of seven Muses, called Neilo, Tritone, Asopo, Heptapora, Achelois, Tipoplo, and Rhodia. At Athens, eight Muses were recognized before nine became the standard number.

Not only their number but their parentage varied among the most ancient writers. Most commonly they were called the daughters of Zeus and Mnemosyne, but other parents named were Uranus and Gaea, Pierus and Antiope, Apollo, Zeus and Plusia, Zeus and Moneta (probably a transposed reading of Mnemosyne), Zeus and Minerva, or Aether and Gaea. Their nurse was Eupheme, and she brought them up with her son, Crotus.

Their place of birth was generally acknowledged to be Pieria at the foot of Mount Olympus, from which location their worship was carried next to the vicinity of Mount Helicon and Mount Parnassus. Most say their worship was brought there by the above-mentioned Pierus, which somehow conflicts with the story that he had nine daughters whom he was presumptuous enough to name for the real Muses. The Muses changed them into birds after defeating them in a musical contest (*see* PIERIDES).

The nine Muses finally established in the worship and imagination of the Greeks were Clio, Euterpe, Thaleia, Melpomene, Erato, Polymnia, Calliope, Urania, and Terpsichore. They were sometimes referred to as the Mneiae, Remembrances. Once the full complement of Muses had settled in, the poets could not have enough of them. Sometimes they were on Olympus, singing songs at the table of the gods. Sometimes they were on Mount Helicon or its extension, Mount Libethrias. Other times they were on Mount Parnassus in the company of Apollo. Wherever they were they conferred the poetic gift, and invocations to them were deeply sincere. Later these invocations became conventions in opening sections of literary works. The Muses were given presence by inclusion in certain events such as the funeral of Patroclus, at which they sang lamentations. They performed at the weddings of Harmonia and Thetis. They were judges in the contest between Apollo and Marsyas. They helped teach Aristaeus the art of healing. They instructed Orpheus on the lyre,

and later they had him placed among the stars. Their companions were the Charites, the Horae, Eros, Dionysus, Apollo, Aphrodite, Harmonia, and other divinities.

The Muses were not all sweetness and light. In addition to punishing the Pierides, they deprived Thamyris of his sight and ability to sing when he claimed he could surpass them in song. Similarly they defeated the Sirens in a contest and took away their wings. One did not foolishly match artistic talents with those of the nine sisters.

The Muses were also considered to have prophetic power, partially as a result of their association with Apollo. Apollo was described as the leader of the choir of the Muses and consequently had the surname Musagetes. Among the surnames of the Muses themselves were Aganippides, from a spring sacred to them on Mount Helicon; Castalides, from a sacred spring on Mount Parnassus; Ilissides, from an altar at Athens on the Ilissus River; Libethrides, from Mount Libethrias, where they had a sacred grotto; Olympiades, as an expression of their heavenly (versus worldly) status; Pierides, from Pieria, where they were first worshipped; and Thespiades, from Thespiae, a town at the foot of Mount Helicon.

The role of the Muses as inspirers of poets and singers led to an even closer association with some of these creative individuals. Linus was called a son of Urania, Calliope, or Terpsichore. Clio was, according to some, the mother of Hyacinthus. Orpheus was also sometimes called her son, but more often Calliope was called his mother. Hymen was thought to be a son of Clio or Calliope. Curiously, Thamyris, who was blinded and muted by the Muses, was the son of Erato, according to some. Most people tended, though, to regard them as virgins, apparently equating their spiritual inspiration with sexual abstinence.

The worship of the Muses was centered in Boeotia, although it seems to have originated in the country around Mount Olympus. The Aloeidae offered the first sacrifices to them in the neighborhood of Mount Helicon. The Aloeidae were juvenile delinquents, and this juxtaposition affords yet another glimpse of the delightful Greek imagination. On Helicon were the sacred fountains Aganippe and Hippocrene. On neighboring Mount Libethrias was a sacred grotto. At the foot of Helicon was Thespiae, the place Pierus was supposed to have brought their worship from the north. There they had a temple and statues, and the Thespians celebrated a festival to them called Museia. Mount Parnassus was sacred to them, and they had a temple on the southern slope near the Castalian spring. At Athens they had a temple in the Academy. Interestingly, at Sparta, where bloody offerings were customary, sacrifices were made to them before soldiers entered battle. At Troezen, where Ardalus had introduced their worship, they shared sacrifices with Hypnos, the god of sleep. At Corinth, the spring Peirene was sacred to them. Here Pegasus was drinking when Bellerophon tamed him to the bridle. Pegasus, born from the blood of Medusa, was considered the Muses' horse. At Rome they shared an altar with Hercules, who was incongruously called Musagetes. Sacrifices to them consisted of libations of water, milk, or honey. [Hesiod, *Theogony* 52–54,77,915; Homer, *Iliad* 1.604, 2.491,484,594, *Odyssey* 1.10, 8.481, 24.60; Apollodorus 1.3.1–3; Pindar, *Nemean Odes* 3.1, *Pythian Odes* 6.49; Scholiast on Pindar's *Nemean Odes* 3.16; Pausanias 1.19.6,30.3, 2.31.3, 3.17.5,31.4, 9.29.2,30.1,33.3; Cicero, *On the Nature of the Gods* 3.21; Plutarch, *Table-Talk* 9.14, *Roman Questions* 59; Diodorus Siculus 1.18, 4.7; Arnobius, *Adversus Nationes* 3.37; Plato, *Republic* 116; Antoninus Liberalis 9; Ovid, *Metamorphoses* 5.300; Martial 7.11; Apollonius Rhodius 2.512.]

MUTA, a Roman divinity of silence, was identical to Tacita and LARUNDA. [Lactantius 1.20.]

MYCALESSIA was a surname of Demeter, derived from Mycalessus in Boeotia, where the goddess had a temple. It stood on the seacoast just south of the Euripus River and a little north of Aulis. [Pausanias 9.19.4.]

MYCALESSIDES were the mountain nymphs of Mycale, a promontory on the Ionian mainland directly opposite Samos. [Callimachus, *Hymn to Delos* 4.50; Pausanias 7.4.1.]

MYCENE was a daughter of Inachus and wife of Arestor. From her the town of Mycenae derived its name. Arestor was the son of Phorbas and, according to some, the father of Argus Panoptes. Inachus, the river-god, was thought by many to be the father of Io, and thus Mycene would be a sister to Io but not necessarily by the same mother. Melia was often called the mother of Io. [Homer, *Odyssey* 2.120; Pausanias 2.16.3.]

MYRINA (1) was a daughter of Cretheus and Demodice. Cretheus was one of the sons of Aeolus and founder of Iolcus. Myrina was married to Thoas, king of Lemnos. Not too long before the Argonauts arrived at Lemnos, the Lemnian women had killed all their husbands. Thoas escaped the slaughter with the help of his and Myrina's daughter Hypsipyle. Myrina was not mentioned in the account of the Argonauts, and it is most likely she had died by that time. The fact that the capital city was named for her could suggest that she was thus memorialized. Had she still been alive she would have been entertaining her nephew Jason. [Scholiast on Apollonius Rhodius 1.604; Hyginus, *Fables* 120; Homer, *Iliad* 14.230; Apollodorus 1.9.17.]

MYRINA (2) was one of the AMAZONS. Some claimed that the city of Myrina in Lemnos was named for her, but it is more likely that it was named for Myrina, wife of Thoas, king of Lemnos. [Strabo 12.8.6; Stephanus Byzantium, "Myrina."]

MYRINA (3) was a daughter of Teucer. According to some, she was the wife of Dardanus, but his wife was usually called BATEIA. [Homer, *Iliad* 2.814; Eustathius on Homer's *Iliad* 351.]

MYRMEX, or Myrmix, was an Attic maiden. By her industry and piety she came to the attention of Athena, who fell in love with her. Athena might have been hasty in her appraisal of the young woman. When the goddess invented the plow, Myrmex boasted that she had made the discovery herself. Pious and industrious as she might have been, she was not too bright in thinking this claim would go unchallenged or unpunished. Athena turned her into an ant, whose industry is proverbial. [Servius on Virgil's *Aeneid* 4.402.]

MYRMIDONE was one of the DANAIDES. She married and murdered Mineus. [Hyginus, *Fables* 170.]

MYRRHA, alternately known as Smyrna, was a daughter of Cinyras and Cenchreis, or of Theias and Oreithyia. This uncertainty comes from names given by different writers, but the circumstances are the same. Myrrha had been remiss in worshipping Aphrodite, and the goddess punished her by causing her to have lustful intentions toward her father. With the help of a servant she was able to carry out these intentions and soon was in her father's bed at every possible opportunity. All this time her father thought she was a woman of the town who was shy about revealing herself. One night his curiosity got the better of him, and he unexpectedly brought forth a light. The deception was bared, and Cinyras wanted to kill this unnatural daughter. But the gods made her invisible long enough to escape him. When she had reached the forest, they changed her into a myrrh tree. After nine months the tree burst and Adonis was born.

A variation on this story was that Aphrodite caused Myrrha to lust for her father because Cenchreis, her mother, had extolled the maiden's beauty above that of the goddess. When her father learned the location of the tree into which she had been changed, he split it with his sword, and Adonis came forth. Some even said a wild boar opened the tree with its tusks (which circumstance darkly predicted the future).

When the baby was born, the Naiades anointed him with the tears of his mother, which was the sap that oozed from the tree. Aphrodite was at once awed by the child's beauty. For some reason she gave the child to Persephone, the goddess of the underworld, to bring up. When the boy was in late adolescence, both goddesses were in love with him, and Persephone refused to return him. Finally Zeus or Calliope had to settle the argument, and Adonis lived alternately with the two goddesses. He excited the jealousy or wrath of Ares, Apollo, or Artemis (the reasons have never been clear) and was gored by a wild boar. A cult grew up around these tragic events,

and the worship of Adonis spread throughout the Mediterranean countries.

When the name Myrrha is used, we find that the myrrh tree was named for her. When Smyrna is used, we learn that the city of Smyrna was supposed to have derived its name from her. [Lucian, *Goddess of Surrye* 6; Hyginus, *Fables* 58,164,251,271; Ovid, *Metamorphoses* 10.300,435; Apollodorus 3.14.4; Antoninus Liberalis 34.]

MYRTEA (*See* MURCIA)

MYRTO (1) was a nymph of Euboea. According to some, the Myrtoan Sea off the coast of Euboea was named for her. Traditionally, Myrtilus, the charioteer of Oenomaus, was the one from whom it was called, but as one or two commentators point out, the events surrounding the murder of Myrtilus by Pelops took place all the way across Peloponnesus. [Pausanias 8.14.12; Apollonius Rhodius 1.752.]

MYRTO (2) was a daughter of Menoetius and therefore the sister of Patroclus. She was loved by Heracles and had a daughter, Eucleia, by him. Most accounts say he had only one daughter, Macaria, whose mother was Deianeira. Both daughters came to symbolize glory in one sense or another. Eucleia died quite young and was regarded as the personification of glory; she came to be worshipped as one of the attributes of Artemis. [Plutarch, *Aristides* 20.]

MYRTO (3) was an Amazon and called by some the mother of Myrtilus by Hermes. The mother of Myrtilus more often was called CLEOBULE. [Scholiast on Apollonius Rhodius 1.752.]

MYRTOESSA was the nymph of a spring of the same name in Arcadia. She was represented on a carved table at Megalopolis along with Anchiroe, Hagno, Anthracia, and Neda, all of whom had helped nurse the infant Zeus. Myrtoessa carried a watering pot with simulated water coming from it. [Pausanias 8.31.2.]

MYSIA (1) was a surname of Demeter, who had a temple called Mysaion between Argos and

Mycenae and at Pellene. The name was derived from an Argive, Mysius, who hospitably received her during her search for Persephone and built a sanctuary to her. [Pausanias 2.18.3,35.3, 7.27.4.]

MYSIA (2) was a surname of Artemis, under which she was worshipped in a sanctuary near Sparta. [Pausanias 3.20.9.]

MYSTIS was a Sidonian whom Cadmus had brought up from a girl to attend his daughter Ino. She was a nurse of Dionysus and also instructed him in mysteries. She was the mother of Corymbus, who was among the followers of Dionysus. [Nonnos, *Dionysiaca* 9.99–120, 12.292, 13.140.]

MYTHIDICE, Mithidice, or Metidice was a daughter of Talaus, sister of Adrastus, married to Nesimachus, and mother of Hippomedon. Usually Hippomedon was called the son of Aristomachus and therefore nephew to Mythidice. She was barely mentioned among the royal family at Argos. It is conceivable she had a son and died, and that the virtually unknown Nesimachus died or disappeared. Aristomachus might then have raised the boy as his own. This was not an infrequent happening in families of the day and often gave rise to confusion about one's parentage. [Hyginus, *Fables* 70.]

MYTILENE (1) was a daughter of Macareus, son of Helios and Rhodos, and sister to Methymna. Marcareus was a colonist from Rhodes to Lesbos, where eventually he became king. Each of the daughters gave her name to a town of Lesbos. Mytilene became by Poseidon the mother of Myton, about whom nothing further is known. Macareus is sometimes confused with Macareus, son of Aeolus, who had incestuous relations with his sister. [Stephanus Byzantium, "Mytilene."]

MYTILENE (2) was one of the AMAZONS, sister of Queen Myrina. Myrina subdued Lesbos and built the city, which she called Mytilene after her sister, who had shared in the campaign. [Diodorus Siculus 3.55.]

NAENIA was a personification of lamentation for the newly dead. At Rome she was worshipped as a goddess. Her chapel, like those of all other deities connected with death, was outside the walls of the city. Hers was near the Viminal Gate. [St. Augustine, *City of God* 6.9; Arnobius, *Adversus Nationes* 4.7, 7.32; Horace, *Odes* 3.28.16.]

NAIADES were nymphs of fresh water as distinguished from Nereides and Oceanides. Naiades were attached to rivers, lakes, brooks, or springs in much the same way Dryades were attached to trees. When a source of water dried up, the Naiad died. There were classes of Naiades, depending on the category of the body of fresh water they inhabited. For example, there were Crinaeae (of fountains), Pegaeae (of springs), Eleionomae (of marshes), Potameides (of rivers), and Limnades or Limnatides (of lakes). Even the rivers of the lower regions had Naiades, called Nymphae Infernae Paludis and, in Rome, Avernales.

Naiades had an inconsistent genealogy. Some writers took the easy way and called all nymphs daughters of Zeus. Others made them part of the vast family of Oceanus by calling them daughters of the river-gods of the rivers in which they lived or to which they were tributary. This second idea is the better one, since Zeus made regular sexual forays among the nymphs, and his being their father would make it appear that he had produced hundreds of daughters for this exclusive purpose.

Even as daughters of river-gods they were fair game for anyone who happened along and managed to catch one. They were particularly prey to the gods. The Asopus River, who had many daughters, lost several of them in this way. One may remember particularly the abduction of Aegina by Zeus.

Many Naiades presided over springs that were believed to inspire those who drank from them. Consequently they were considered to be endowed with prophetic powers and to inspire men with similar oracular gifts. Other Naiades were thought to have restorative powers and to be able to cure sick persons. The Anigrides in Elis, whose waters were sought for healing skin diseases, were among these. Because of their intimate association with water, the life-giving element, Naiades in general were worshipped along with divinities of fertility and growth. Some of their surnames in this connection were Carpotrophae, Aepolicae, Nomiae, Curotrophae, etc.

Some of the better-known Naiades are remembered from special stories. Aegle, a daughter of Zeus and Neaera, said to be the most beautiful of the Naiades, was called by some the mother of the Charites by Helios. Creusa, daughter of Oceanus and Gaea, was mother of Hypseus and Stilbe by the Peneius River. Nomia fell in love with the handsome shepherd Daphnis and blinded him when he became unfaithful to her. The Naiades of a spring in Bithynia fell in love with Hylas, the lover of Heracles, and pulled him down into their watery domain. The town of Lilaea in Phocis was named for Lilaea, daughter of the Cephissus River. Melite, a daughter of the Aegaeus River in Corcyra, became the mother of Hyllus by Heracles. Pandion was a son of Erichthonius by Praxithea. Lovers of Endymion, Magnes, Lelex, Oebalus, Icarius, Thyestes, and others were said to be Naiades, and most of them were therefore cofounders of important families. [Homer, *Odyssey* 17.240; Apollonius Rhodius 1.1225, 3.881,1219, 4.538,1218; Orphica, *Argonautica* 644; Ovid, *Metamorphoses* 5.540, *Fasti* 2.610; Pausanias 3.4.3, 4.27.2, 9.3.5; Plutarch, *Aristides* 11; Pindar, *Olympian Odes* 12.26, *Pythian Odes* 9.30; *Homeric Hymn to Aphrodite* 262; Horace, *Odes* 1.1.31, 2.19.3; Apollodorus 3.14.6,8.]

NANA was the mother of Atys. Zeus had a noctural seminal emission and spilled sperm on the earth (Gaea, his grandmother). From this accidental union grew a superhuman hermaphrodite called AGDISTIS. The gods feared it and severed its male genitals. From the severed penis grew an almond tree. Nana, the daughter of the river-god Sangarius, masturbated with some of the almonds, and she became impregnated by one of them. She gave birth to Atys, who was extraordinarily beautiful.

Atys became associated with the goddess Cybele, either as lover, priest, disciple, or all three. In all stories connecting him with her, he died; lamentations for and commemorations of him were prominent features in the worship of Cybele. [Pausanias 7.17.10; Arnobius, *Adversus Nationes* 5.5.12.]

NANAEA was another name for ANAITIS, the Asiatic divinity with whom Artemis was often identified. [Maccabees 2.1.13.]

NAPAEA were a class of forest nymphs who specialized in appearing suddenly to startle solitary travelers. [Apollonius Rhodius 1.1066,1227; Orphica, *Hymns* 50.7; Virgil, *Georgics* 4.535.]

NARCAEA was a surname of Athena at Olympia. The name was derived from Narcaeus, son of Dionysus by Physcoa. When Narcaeus grew up, he made war against the neighboring folk and rose to power. He set up a sanctuary of Athena, surnamed after his own name. Narcaeus and Physcoa were the first to pay tribute to Dionysus. [Pausanias 5.16.6,7.]

NASCIO was a Roman divinity who presided over the birth of children. She assisted Lucina in her functions and was analogous to the Greek Eileithyia. She had a sanctuary in the neighborhood of Ardea. [Cicero, *On the Nature of the Gods* 3.18.]

NATALIS was a surname of Juno at Rome. On their birthday women offered sacrifices to Juno Natalis. [Tibullus 3.12.1–20.]

NAUCRATE was the wife of Daedalus, a tremendously talented artisan who fled from Athens to Crete after murdering his nephew. He was employed by Minos to build a labyrinth to house the dreadful Minotaur, offspring of Minos' wife, Pasiphae, and a bull. Minos gave Daedalus Naucrate, one of the palace slaves, as a wife. Naucrate, then, was present during the construction of the labyrinth, and she certainly observed the succession of Athenian youths and maidens who periodically were fed to the monster. She bore a son, Icarus, to Daedalus, and the family lived secure and well regarded in Cnossus.

Theseus went to Crete as one of the would-be victims of the Minotaur, but Minos' daughter Ariadne fell in love with him. With the assistance of Daedalus she helped him overcome the monster and find his way out of the maze. After Theseus eloped with Ariadne, Minos discovered the part Daedalus had played and locked him and Icarus, who was probably 15 or so, in the labyrinth. Naucrate was either dead by that time or Minos reclaimed her as a slave. No further mention of her was ever made. Daedalus and Icarus escaped their prison by means of wings fashioned by Daedalus. But Icarus flew too near the sun, and the wax that held the wings together melted and he plunged into the sea. Daedalus managed to get all the way to Sicily, where later he helped kill Minos, who pursued him. [Apollodorus, *Epitome* 1.12; Tzetzes, *Chiliades* 1.498.]

NAUPIDAME, Naupiadame, or Nausidame was, according to some, the mother of Augeas. Some called her Iphiboe. Augeas was more often called a son of Phorbas and HYRMINE. [Tzetzes on Lycophron 41; Hyginus, *Fables* 14.]

NAUSICAA was the heroine of one of the best-known stories about Odysseus. It is interesting that this story is remembered by nearly everyone, but it can be told in very few sentences. Perhaps it is remembered because Nausicaa appeared in sweet contrast to the series of tribulations recently suffered by the hero. She and her companions were washing clothes on the beach in the kingdom of the Phaeacians, ruled by her father and mother, Alcinous and Arete. While the clothes were drying, the young ladies played ball, and their joyous screaming awakened the sleeping Odysseus, who, naked and bruised, had been cast ashore by a storm that destroyed his flimsy raft.

When Odysseus showed himself, the other maidens ran away in fright, but Nausicaa stayed to inquire if she might help him. She provided food and clothes, and arranged for him to come to the palace to be received by her parents, who were known for their generosity and hospitality.

Nausicaa was very much impressed with the stranger. She was by nature warm and tender-hearted, and these admirable attributes were heightened by her appreciation of the hero's bearing and good looks. It later turned out that she would willingly have become his wife and that Alcinous would gladly have given her. They learned about his love for his wife and son in Ithaca, and that was the end of any amorous intentions, even though in his recital of his adventures they certainly must have surmised what

had taken place between him and Circe. Assisted by the Phaeacians, he was able to get back to Ithaca with no further mishap.

Nausicaa's story was a simple one, and that is part of its charm even today. She displayed self-confidence and maturity in confronting the naked stranger. She showed compassion and was able to follow it up with action. Later writers were not able to let go of this admirable young woman, so they had Telemachus, the son of Odysseus, come to Scheria and marry her. A son, Ptoliporthus (or Perseptolis), was born to them. [Homer, *Odyssey* 6.12,16,62; Eustathius on Homer's *Odyssey* 1796; Dictys Cretensis 6.6.]

NAUSITHOE was one of the NEREIDES. [Apollodorus 1.2.7.]

NAUTIA was a surname of Minerva. It was believed to have originated from the following circumstance. Diomedes had carried the Palladium from Troy, but he found that it did nothing to prevent his series of misfortunes. An oracle commanded him to restore it to the Trojans, and he sought to do so when he wandered through Calabria. When he came to the Trojans, Aeneas was offering up a sacrifice, so the Palladium was left with Nautes, who kept it and passed it down to his descendants. Minerva thus bestowed many favors upon him, instructed him in many arts, and chose him for her servant. The family of Nautii afterward retained the exclusive knowledge of the manner in which Minerva Nautia was to be worshipped. [Virgil, *Aeneid* 5.704; Servius on Virgil's *Aeneid* 2.166, 3.407, 5.704; Dionysius of Halicarnassus, *Roman Antiquities* 6.69.]

NEAERA (1) was a nymph loved by Helios, god of the sun. She had two daughters, Lampetia and Phaetusa, by him. There is a suggestion that these daughters were twins, since the accounts said they were carried after their birth to the island of Thrinacia off the coast of Sicily to watch over their father's flocks. Neaera presumably did not accompany them. Helios' affair with her was of short duration. His daughters (and sons) called the Heliades were generally considered to be by Rhodos. His most famous son, Phaethon, was by Clymene. If, as some suggested, Lampetia became a wife of Asclepius, Neaera would then have been his mother-in-law. [Homer, *Odyssey* 12.133; Propertius 3.12,29; Hyginus, *Fables* 154; Ovid, *Metamorphoses* 3.49.]

NEAERA (2) was a daughter of Pereus, son of Elatus. She married Aleus, son of Apheidas and grandson of Arcas. He was king of Tegea, and founded the town of Alea and the first temple of Athena Alea at Tegea. Neaera became by him the mother of Auge, Cepheus, and Lycurgus. Cepheus' mother was occasionally called Cleobule.

The children of Neaera all became prominent. Cepheus was an Argonaut and returned home to father 20 sons and two daughters. Nearly all his sons perished in a raid on the Spartan usurper Hippocoon. The town of Caphyae derived its name from him. Auge, a priestess of Athena, was seduced by Heracles and became by him the mother of Telephus, a hero in the Trojan War. Lycurgus succeeded Aleus and was grandfather to Atalanta and her cousin Meilanion, whom she married. [Apollodorus 1.9.16, 2.7.3, 3.9.1; Apollonius Rhodius 1.161; Hyginus, *Fables* 14; Pausanias 2.3.3, 8.4.3,9,8.3,23.1.]

NEAERA (3), also called Ethodeia, was one of the daughters of NIOBE. [Apollodorus 3.5.6.]

NEAERA (4) was the wife of the Strymon River. River-gods often had two identities, and Strymon was also a king in Thrace. By Neaera he was father of Euadne. Euadne married Argus, the third king of Argos, and became the mother of several sons, including the eponymic founders of Epidaurus and Tiryns. Strymon apparently was quite handsome and was associated with the Muses. By either Euterpe or Calliope he fathered Rhesus. This event took place long after his marriage to Neaera, since Rhesus was a Trojan hero and Euadne's children had to do with the early history of Argolis. But river-gods were immortal and could father children in generations remote from one another. [Apollodorus 1.3.4, 2.1.2; Hesiod, *Theogony* 339; Conon, *Narrations* 4; Antoninus Liberalis 21.]

NEAERA (5) was a nymph who became by Zeus the mother of Aegle. Aegle was called the most beautiful of the Naiades. Some called her the mother by Helios of the Charites. [Virgil, *Eclogues* 6.20; Pausanias 9.35.1.]

NEAERA (6) was the wife of Aeetes, by whom she became the mother of Absyrtus, according to some. Absyrtus' mother was more often called ASTERODEIA. [Scholiast on Apollonius Rhodius 3.241.]

NEAERA (7) was, according to some, the wife of Autolycus, although most others called her AMPHITHEA. [Pausanias 8.4.3.]

NEDA was an Arcadian nymph who was among those who nursed the infant Zeus. Her companions were called Theisoa and Hagno. In a Messenian tradition she and Ithome nursed Zeus and bathed him in the fountain Clepsydra. A small river in Messenia derived its name from her. At Megalopolis in Arcadia she was represented on a carved table as carrying the infant Zeus. [Callimachus, *Hymn to Zeus* 38; Pausanias 4.33.2, 8.31.2,38.3,47.2.]

NEDUSIA was a surname of Athena under which she had a sanctuary on the Nedon River in Messenia and another at Poeeessa in Ceos. The latter was said to have been founded by Nestor on his return from Troy and to have derived its name from Nedon, a place in Messenia. [Strabo 8.4.4, 10.5.6; Stephanus Byzantium "Nedon."]

NEILO was one of seven MUSES. [Tzetzes on Hesiod's *Works and Days* 6; Arnobius, *Adversus Nationes* 3.37.]

NEIS (1) was a daughter of Amphion by NIOBE, from whom the Neitian gate at Thebes was believed to have derived its name. [Scholiast on Euripides' *Phoenician Maidens* 1104.]

NEIS (2) might have been a generic name, much in the sense of a Naiad, but some writers used it as the name of a specific individual. One such individual was Neis, the wife of Endymion. Endymion was the son of Aethlius and Calyce, and by Neis (or Asterodeia, Chromia, Iphianassa, or Hyperippe) the father of Aetolus, Epeius, Paeon, and Eurycyde. At the same time, we have to consider the highly romantic story in which, as a pretty youth, he was put into an eternal sleep by Selene, the goddess of the moon, by whom he became in this somnolent state the father of 50 daughters. Trying to bring these two quite separate accounts into conjunction makes no sense. If as a youth he was sent into perpetual slumber, then he could never have married and raised a family. If he married and had children who reached maturity, he could not have been a youth when Selene found him. Moreover, these separate existences occurred in places geographically remote from each other. A possible but really fanciful chronology might have been that as a young shepherd Endymion was seduced by Selene and taken to Mount Latmus in Caria, where the goddess suspended time and, while he slept, had her way with him, all the way to 50 daughters. After tiring of him and perpetual pregnancy, she deposited him back in Elis where she had found him, and set time in motion again. Still young and presumably unaware of his prodigious potency, he sought a wife and had a normal number of legitimate offspring. It is not inconceivable, too, that Endymion in later years invented the Selene story to enhance his own sexual appeal. The alternate names of wives give some indication that he was not exactly monogamous.

He also set about the business of being king by conquering and expelling Clymenus and introducing settlers from Thessaly into Elis. When finally he grew old, Endymion forced his sons to engage in a footrace at Olympia with the promise of the kingdom to the victor. Epeius won and succeeded Endymion. He in turn was succeeded by Aetolus, who was the eponymic hero of the Aetolians. Meanwhile, seeing no chance for the throne, Paeon migrated to the country he called Paeonia. The rule in Elis passed next to Eleius, son of Eurycyde, and finally to Augeas.

Neis was not mentioned again in any of these accounts, as was so often the case. But by looking at all the circumstances surrounding her marriage to one of the most recognized individuals in ancient legends, we can form some picture of her life and times. [Pausanias 5.1.3–5,8.1; Apollodorus 1.7.5–6.]

NELO was one of the DANAIDES, daughter of Danaus and an Ethiopian woman. She married and murdered Menemachus. [Apollodorus 2.1.5.]

NEMEA was a daughter of Zeus and Selene, the goddess of the moon. Her sisters were Pandeia and Ersa. Nothing is known of these three sisters except for their mention in a so-called Homeric hymn. [32.14.]

NEMERTES was one of the NEREIDES. [Homer, *Iliad* 18.46; Hesiod, *Theogony* 262.]

NEMESIS was the personification of divine vengeance. More properly, she directed human affairs in such a way as to maintain equilibrium. Happiness and unhappiness were measured out by her, care being taken that happiness was not too frequent or too excessive. If this happened, Nemesis could bring about losses and suffering. As one who checked extravagant favors by Tyche, or Fortune, Nemesis came to be regarded as an avenging or punishing divinity. This particularly applied to persons who rose above their condition, thus exposing themselves to reprisals from the gods, who were envious of excessive human happiness.

Nemesis was a daughter of Nyx (Night), Erebus (Darkness), or Oceanus. The first two assignments would make her part of the vast family of abstract beings who emerged from the chaotic beginning of things but also, unlike many of them, one who anticipated a role for individuals in a society. As a daughter of Oceanus she would have been, incongruously, a sister to the myriad Oceanides, rivers, and other watery beings.

She was usually represented as a virgin, but one must remember the curious story that Zeus pursued her and in the form of a swan coupled with the goose into which she had changed herself. She produced an egg, which Leda found and from which Helen and the Dioscuri emerged. This event took place at Rhamnus, which was the principal place of the worship of Nemesis. Rhamnus overlooks the strait between Euboea and Attica, and in the famous temple there Leda was depicted leading Helen to Nemesis.

Along with Dice and Themis, Nemesis was considered one of the assistants of Zeus, who was regarded as the founder of law and order. Her principal surnames were Rhamnusia and Adrasteia. Adrasteia probably referred to the founding near Thebes of a temple to her by Adrastus. [Hyginus, *Fables* 77, *Fables: Preface* 1; Tzetzes on Lycophron 88; Pausanias 1.33.2,7, 7.5.1; Hesiod, *Theogony* 211,223, *Works and Days* 183; Herodotus 1.34, 3.40; Pindar, *Pythian Odes* 10.67; Apollonius Rhodius 4.1043; Apollodorus 3.10.6; Callimachus, *Hymn to Zeus* 79, *Hymn to Artemis* 232; Sophocles, *Philoctetes* 518.]

NEOMERIS was one of the NEREIDES. [Apollodorus 1.2.7.]

NEPHELE (1) was one of the most curious beings in mythology. She was a personification of a cloud, yet human enough to have two children, Phrixus and Helle, by Athamas. It is not clear exactly where she came from. At Hera's insistence, it was said, she was given to Athamas as his first wife. It is difficult to imagine what she must have been like, but in view of later developments she was probably passive and ethereally aloof. Athamas was part of the large family of Aeolus and Enarete, and brother of Cretheus, Sisyphus, Salmoneus, and others. He fell in love with the more earthly Ino, daughter of Cadmus. Seeing that he had abandoned her, Nephele disappeared, probably assuming her original form.

Ino managed to discredit her stepson Phrixus to the extent that he was about to be sacrificed. Nephele, however, sent a magic ram with golden fleece, which rescued Phrixus and carried him and his sister, Helle, through the air on the way to Colchis. Why Colchis was chosen as a destination is not known. On the way, Helle fell into the body of water known later as the Hellespont. [Apollodorus 1.9.1; Aeschylus, *Persians* 70,875; Hyginus, *Poetic Astronomy* 2.20; Scholiast on Pindar's *Pythian Odes* 4.288.]

NEPHELE (2) was the phantom created by Zeus for Ixion, who lusted after Hera. Zeus had been the only god to take pity on Ixion when he murdered his father-in-law. Ixion repaid the kindness by trying to rape Hera. Zeus then shaped a cloud to resemble Hera, and Ixion lay with the phantom and became the father of Centaurus, who in turn produced the Centaurs. Others say Ixion fathered the Centaurs directly on the cloud, which was usually called Nephele.

Some say that this Nephele was the same as the first wife of Athamas, and that after playing the role of the false Hera, she remained an occupant of Olympus. Hera apparently felt a sense of indebtedness to her and demanded she be given as wife to Athamas. [Scholiast on Euripides' *Phoenician Maidens* 1185; Pindar, *Pythian Odes* 2.36,44; Diodorus Siculus 4.69.]

NEPTUNINE was a patronymic of Thetis from Neptune, her grandfather. [Catullus 64.28.]

NEREIDES were marine nymphs of the Mediterranean Sea, daughters of Nereus and Doris. Nereus was the son of Pontus and Gaea, and Doris was one of the Oceanides, daughter of Oceanus and Tethys. The Nereides were distinguished from the Oceanides by being confined to the seas around Greece. They were nymphs of the salty sea as opposed to Naiades, the myriad freshwater nymphs. Their number was said to be 50, but both their number and names varied from writer to writer. There were four principal lists of them, and it can be seen that some of the names remained the same in all the lists:

APOLLODORUS: Actaea, Agave, Amphitrite, Autonoe, Calypso, Ceto, Cranto, Cymo, Cymothoe, Dero, Dione, Doto, Dynamene, Eione, Erato, Euagore, Eucrante, Eudora, Eulimene, Eumolpe, Eunice, Galateia, Glauconome, Halia, Halimede, Hipponoe, Hippothoe, Ianeira, Ione, Limnoreia, Lysianassa, Melite, Nausithoe, Neomeris, Nesaea, Panope, Pherusa, Plexaure, Polynome, Pontomedusa, Proto, Psamathe, Sao, Speio, and Thetis. (45)

HOMER: Actaea, Agave, Amatheia, Amphinome, Amphithoe, Apseudes, Callianassa, Callianeira, Clymene, Cymodoce, Cymothoe, Dexamene, Doris, Doto, Dynamene, Galateia, Glauce, Halia, Iaera, Ianassa, Ianeira, Limnoreia, Maera, Melite, Nemertes,

Nesaea, Oreithyia, Panope, Pherusa, Proto, Speio, Thaleia, Thoe. (33)

HESIOD: Actaea, Agave, Alimede, Amphitrite, Autonoe, Cymatolege, Cymo, Cymodoce, Cymothoe, Doris, Doto, Dynamene, Eione, Erato, Euagore, Euarne, Eucrante, Eudora, Eulimene, Eunice, Eupompe, Galateia, Galene, Glauce, Glauconome, Halia, Hipponoe, Hippothoe, Laomedeia, Leagore, Lysianassa, Melite, Menippe, Nemertes, Neso, Nisaea, Panopea, Pasithea, Pherusa, Ploto, Polynoe, Pontoporeia, Pronoe, Proto, Protomedeia, Psamathe, Sao, Speio, Themisto, Thetis, Thoe. (51)

HYGINUS: Actaea, Agave, Amatheia, Amphinome, Amphithoe, Apseudes, Arethusa, Asia, Beroe, Callianassa, Clio, Clymene, Creneis, Cydippe, Cymodoce, Cymothoe, Deiopea, Dexamene, Doris, Doto, Drimo, Dynamene, Ephyra, Eurydice, Galateia, Glauce, Iaera, Ianassa, Ianeira, Leucothoe, Ligeia, Limnoreia, Lycorias, Maera, Melite, Nemertes, Nesaea, Opis, Oreithyia, Panope (Panopaea?), Pherusa, Phyllodoce, Proto, Speio, Thaleia, Thoe, Xantho. (47)

There were, in addition, a few Nereides mentioned by other writers, or so-named in inscriptions on vases, such as Cale, Choro, Eudeia, and Nao. These entire lists are presented here for purposes of comparison. Only two of them show Thetis, but this more or less identifies her as a Nereid and not an Oceanid as some have suggested (but it should be pointed out that neither Apollodorus nor Hesiod lists her among the Oceanides). These lists did not exactly conform in spelling, so very small alterations have been made to bring them into conformity. This is the only place in the English language that the lists are juxtaposed. A far more elaborate set of lists, complete with variant spellings, has been treated with Teutonic thoroughness by Roscher and Pauly-Wissowa.

The Nereides were described as beautiful, naked women dwelling at the bottom of the sea with Nereus. They were solicitous about the welfare of sailors, and they gave special assistance to the Argonauts, guiding them safely past Scylla and Charybdis and through the clashing rocks. They did not always stay submerged. Some of them surfaced to cohabit with mortals. The most famous of these, of course, was Thetis, who became the mother by Peleus of Achilles. It took considerable effort to mate with a Nereid, however, since like most marine beings they had the power to change to any form they chose. Their beauty and elusiveness gave rise to stories of mermaids told by men long at sea. The Nereides were worshipped in several parts of Greece, particularly in port cities like Cardamyle and those ports on the Corinthian isthmus. [Homer, *Iliad* 18.42–49; Hesiod, *Theogony* 240–262; Apollodorus 1.2.7; Hyginus, *Fables: Preface* 18; Pindar, *Pythian Odes* 6.8; Virgil, *Aeneid* 5.825; Apollonius Rhodius 4.859,930; Pausanias 2.1.7, 3.26.5.]

NEREIS, or Nerine, was a patronymic from Nereus as applied to individual NEREIDES.

NERIO was the wife of Mars. Little is known of her except that she was considered the personification of valor. The spoils of battle were dedicated to her and to Mars. The name was said to be of Sabine origin. [Gellius 3.22; Lydus, *On the Months* 4.42; Plautus, *Truculentus* 2.6.24.]

NESAEA was one of the NEREIDES. [Homer, *Iliad* 18.40; Hyginus, *Theogony* 249.]

NESO (1) was one of the NEREIDES. [Hesiod, *Theogony* 261.]

NESO (2) was the daughter of Teucer, the ancestor of the Trojan royal house, and by Dardanus the mother of Sibyl, the first of the famous SIBYLS. As daughter of Teucer, Neso's life was strongly involved with the art of prophecy. For one thing, her father founded the famous temple of Apollo Smintheus in the Troad, in which Neso was born. It was appropriate that she and Dardanus, who brought the Samothracian mysteries to Troy, should have produced the first Sibyl. [Lycophron 1465; Eustathius on Homer's *Iliad* 356.]

NESSA was one of the PIERIDES. [Antoninus Liberalis 9; Pausanias 9.29.2.]

NETE was one of the three MUSES worshipped at Delphi, whose names corresponded to the chords on the lyre. [Plutarch, *Table-Talk* 9.14.]

NICAEA was a daughter of the river-god Sangarius and Cybele. Her sister was Alce and her brother, Midas. She was loved by the shepherd Hymnus, but as a follower of Artemis she was distressed by his persistence and shot him through the heart. Eros, the god of love, was furious over this cruel display and swore vengeance. He therefore inspired his cousin/half-brother/stepfather, Dionysus, to fall in love with the defiant maiden. Dionysus pursued her unsuccessfully for a long time and grew almost mad with desire. She spurned him even more forcibly than she had Hymnus, and he vowed to have her. Even when she told him that if she wanted a man she would choose a virile one and not an effeminate one like him, he refused to desist. Finally he contrived to get her drunk, and had his way with her while she was in a stupor. From this union came Telete, after whose delivery Nicaea hanged herself in shame. Telete grew up to follow Dionysus in his orgiastic celebrations. Dionysus named the city of Nicaea in remembrance of his triumph of passion. [Nonnos, *Dionysiaca* 15.16.]

NICAGORA, according to Sicyonian tradition, brought the worship of Asclepius to Sicyon. She was the wife of Echetimus and the mother by him of Agasicles. She journeyed to Epidaurus in a cart drawn by mules and brought back an image of Asclepius that was in the form of a serpent. [Pausanias 2.10.3.]

NICE (1), commonly spelled Nike, was the goddess of victory. She was a daughter of Pallas and Styx, and sister of Zelus (Zeal), Cratus (Power), and Bia (Force). Pallas was a son of the Titan Crius, and Styx was a daughter of Oceanus. Nice and her brothers and sisters were allies of Zeus against the Titans, and in gratitude Zeus included them among the residents of Olympus. Victory was, of course, one of the primary forces in Greek society. It was part of religious obser-

vation, and statues of Aphrodite, Athena, and Zeus were carved holding an image of Nice. In particular the gigantic chryselephantine statue of Athena in the Parthenon held a human-sized image of Nice. She also had her own temple on the Acropolis, called the temple of Nice Apteros, the Wingless. Nice was usually represented with wings, as seen in the famous statue in the Louvre from Samothrace, and absence of them was intended to signify that she could never fly away. The temple stood at the exit from the Acropolis, and Nice's protection was sought by persons starting on hazardous missions. In appearance she resembled Athena. She was represented as carrying a palm or wreath, and sometimes she was shown guiding the horses of conquering heroes as well as raising a trophy or inscribing the victory of a conqueror on his shield. Euander was said to have introduced the worship of Nice into Italy. In Rome she was called Victoria. [Hesiod, *Theogony* 382; Apollodorus 1.2.2; Pausanias 1.22.4, 3.15.5, 5.10.2, 11.1,2, 6.18.1.]

NICE (2) was one of the THESPIADES and mother by Heracles of Nicodromus. [Apollodorus 2.7.8.]

NICE (3) was a surname of Athena. In the temple of Nice Apteros (Wingless) on the Acroplis at Athens, Athena was represented both in relief and by a statue. The relief showed a band of winged Victories attendant upon Athena and included the famous Victory adjusting her sandal. Thus Athena was strongly identified with Nice and came to be called Athena Nice. Under this name she had a sanctuary on the acropolis at Megara. [Pausanias 1.42.4; Euripides, *Ion* 1529.]

NICEPHORUS, Bringing Victory, occurred as a surname of several divinities, such as Aphrodite. [Pausanias 2.19.6.]

NICIPPE (1) is a name most people will not recognize, but she had a significant role in one of the great myths. She was the mother of Eurystheus, the king of Mycenae, who ordered all the labors of Heracles. She was a daughter of Pelops and Hippodameia, and sister of some of the most famous heroes in Greek legend. She was occasionally called Archippe, Antibia, Leucippe, or Astydameia. Her marriage to Sthenelus, son of Perseus, joined two of the great royal families of Peloponnesus. She was somewhat younger than her sister-in-law (and niece by marriage) Anaxo, for she and Alcmena, daughter of Anaxo and Electryon, became pregnant at the same time. It was this close timing that allowed Hera to win the promise from Zeus that the first son born to the race of Perseus after a certain time would have the sovereignty. Hera delayed the birth of Heracles and hastened the labor of Nicippe.

Nicippe had other children by Sthenelus. These were Medusa (Astymedusa?), Alcyone (Alcinoe?), and Iphis. She was only middle-aged when her son Eurystheus imposed the famous labors on her grandnephew-in-law. Her husband, Sthenelus, was slain by Hyllus, the son of Heracles, and it is likely she lived to witness her son's defeat and death by the Heracleidae. [Apollodorus 2.4.5; Hyginus, *Fables* 244; Scholiast on Euripides' *Orestes* 5.]

NICIPPE (2) was one of the THESPIADES and mother of Antimachus by Heracles. [Apollodorus 2.7.8.]

NICOSTRATE (1) was the original name of CARMENTA, one of the Camenae.

NICOSTRATE (2) was the wife of Oebalus and mother of Hippocoon. She was more often called BATEIA. [Scholiast on Euripides' *Orestes* 447.]

NICOTHOE was one of the HARPIES. [Apollodorus 1.9.21.]

NIOBE (1) was a daughter of Phoroneus, son of Inachus. Her mother was usually called Laodice. Her brother Apis became king of Argos and named the area later called Peloponnesus after himself Apia. Niobe was seduced by Zeus and became the mother of Argus and Pelasgus. Argus succeeded to the throne after Apis was killed by his son Thelxion and Telchis, another relative. He changed the name of the country from Apia to Argos, which included the region of Argolis as

well as the whole of Peloponnesus. Pelasgus gave his name to the earliest inhabitants of Greece, who were called Pelasgians. He established the worship of the Dodonaean Zeus, Hephaestus, and the Cabeiri. By the Naiad Cyllene he became the father of Lycaon, whose sons colonized many of the towns of Greece. Niobe was sometimes said to be the wife of Inachus and mother of Phoroneus. [Apollodorus 1.7.6, 2.1.1,21.1; Pausanias 2.22.6; Hyginus, *Fables* 143; Plato, *Timaeus* 22.]

NIOBE (2) is a name that almost everyone recognizes as virtually a symbol of despair. Niobe's story has stood for centuries as a warning of the penalty for excessive pride. She was a daughter of Tantalus by the Hyad Dione. This made her sister to Pelops, although one account called her his daughter. She was married to Amphion, king of Thebes. By him she became the mother of six sons and six daughters, and it can be expected that different writers gave them different names and numbered them as few as four to as many as 20. A collective list of names included sons Amphion, Amyclas, Archenor (Agenor?), Damasichthon, Eupinytus, Ismenus, Phaedimus, Sisyphus, and Tantalus; and daughters Astycrateis, Astynome, Astyoche, Cleodoxa, Ethodeia (or Neaera), Eudoxa, Homolois, Meliboea (later called Chloris), Ogygia, Pelopeia, and Phthia.

Niobe was inordinately proud of her children but made the most unfortunate mistake of boasting that she was superior to Leto in motherhood because Leto had only two children, Artemis and Apollo. The folly of this statement was not long in making itself felt. One day Apollo shot to death all the sons while they exercised or were hunting on Mount Cithaeron. At the same time Artemis emptied her quiver on the daughters while they went about their daily chores. Most accounts allowed for two survivors, thus evening the number of children of Leto and Niobe. Either Amyclas or Amphion was spared by praying to Apollo, and likewise Meliboea was spared by begging Artemis for her life. Meliboea turned completely ashen and remained so, and was thereafter called Chloris. Amphion, the father, either killed himself from grief or was killed by Apollo for assaulting the temple of the god.

Niobe, of course, went to the brink of insanity, having to blame herself for the slaughter. Most accounts said she went to Lydia to her father's house on Mount Sipylus. She wept unceasingly and begged Zeus to turn her into a stone. This he did, and a particular stone on the mountain was said to shed tears during the summer. For a long time people claimed they could see the petrified figure of Niobe. The tomb of her children was shown at Thebes. The most famous of artistic expressions of this tragic event was on the pediment of the temple of Apollo Sosianus at Rome.

Inevitably there were variations on the story. The most popular was one that made Niobe the daughter of Assaon and wife of an Assyrian called Philottus. She argued with Leto about the respective beauty of their children, and the goddess caused her husband to be torn to pieces during the chase. Afterward her father fell in love with her and tried to seduce her. When she rejected him in horror, he invited her 20 children to a feast and then set fire to the building in which they were gathered. All of them were destroyed. He killed himself in remorse, and Niobe threw herself from a cliff. [Homer, *Iliad* 24.605–617; Ovid, *Metamorphoses* 6.146–312; Hyginus, *Fables* 9.11; Pausanias 1.21.3; Parthenius, *Love Stories* 33.]

NIXI, or Nixi Dii, were Roman divinities who assisted women during the pain of childbearing. At Rome they were represented by three statues on the Capitoline Hill in front of the entrance to the temple of Minerva. [Ovid, *Metamorphoses* 294; Nonius 57.]

NOMIA (1), also referred to as Echenais, Xenia, or Lyce, was a shepherdess of Sicily who loved the extraordinarily handsome Daphnis, a shepherd son of Hermes. She was not alone, since Daphnis' looks attracted many persons and one or two gods. He reciprocated the love of Nomia, who made him vow fidelity to her at the risk of being blinded by her. This was a menacing threat and not the best note on which to begin a relationship. Daphnis tried to remain true, but one of his admirers was determined to have him. She was a princess, and Daphnis' fine looks must have been exceptional to cause her to go to

extremes for a lowly shepherd. She got the youth drunk and carried him to her bed. The story was not long in being told, and Nomia, true to her word, blinded the unfortunate young man. She also abandoned him and left him to wander about singing his sad songs, for he was said to have invented bucolic poetry. Eventually he threw himself from a cliff in despair, though some claimed he was changed into a rock or taken to heaven by his father. Hermes caused a fountain to gush forth at Syracuse in his memory, and annual sacrifices were offered to him. [Diodorus Siculus 4.84; Servius on Virgil's *Aeneid* 8.68, 10.26; Aelian, *Various Narratives* 10.18; Ovid, *Metamorphoses* 4.275.]

NOMIA (2) was an Arcadian nymph from whom Mount Nomia near Lycosura in Arcadia derived its name. She was included among those painted by Polygnotus in the Lesche at Delphi. [Pausianias 8.38.8, 10.31.10.]

NONACRIS was the wife of Lycaon, the infamous Arcadian king. Lycaon was the father of 50 sons, but Nonacris could not have been the mother of them all, even if she bore one every year. So she was stepmother to many of Lycaon's sons, who according to report were brutal and even engaged in cannibalism. The background of Nonacris is not known, consequently no idea of her can be formed. She could have been pious and refined, or she could have been a slattern content with her lot among her loutish stepsons. Her husband and his sons were turned into wolves for serving Zeus human flesh.

A less dramatic but more reasonable account said that Lycaon was a pious man like his father Pelasgus, and that his sons were the eponymous heroes of various towns in Peloponnesus. It is not known which of the sons belonged to Nonacris.

The Arcadian town of Nonacris was named for her. Above the site of the ancient town rises the Styx River (now the Mavroneria), which in falling over the rocks produces the highest waterfall in Greece. [Pausanias 8.17.5; Stephanus Byzantium, "Nonakris"; Ovid, *Fasti* 5.97.]

NORTIA was an Etruscan divinity worshipped mainly at Volsinii. Driving a nail into the wall was an annual ritual in this place and would appear to mark the passage of time. However, it more likely had to do with nailing down evil for the town for the foregoing year, suggesting the immutability of destiny. This last is more plausible, since Nortia was often identified with Fortuna. [Livy 7.3; Horace, *Odes* 1.35.17; Juvenal 10.74.]

NOX was the Latin counterpart of NYX, goddess of night.

NUMERIA was a Roman goddess to whom women in childbirth were accustomed to pray. [St. Augustine, *City of God* 6.11; Nonius 352.]

NYCTEIS was the daughter of Nycteus, son of Hyrieus or Chthonius. This made her a sister of Antiope, who from time to time was also confusingly called Nycteis as a patronymic. Nycteis became the wife of Polydorus, son of Cadmus, and mother of Labdacus. It is likely she had left home before Antiope's defection. Polydorus died when Labdacus was only a year old, and Nycteus became regent at Thebes. After his violent death, his brother Lycus became regent. The reign then passed finally to Labdacus, who was grandfather to Oedipus. It is doubtful that Nycteis had any role in the controversy over Antiope. She might have been on good terms with Dirce, since Lycus had served as regent for her son. [Apollodorus 3.5.5.]

NYCTIMENE was a daughter of Epopeus, king of Lesbos, or of Nycteus, a king of Ethiopia. Her outstanding beauty attracted her father, and he seduced her. Afterward she was miserably ashamed for having allowed this unspeakable act to occur, and she hid herself deep in the forest. Athena eventually took pity on her and changed her into an owl, a bird that hides by day and comes out only after dark. [Hyginus, *Fables* 204; Ovid, *Metamorphoses* 2.590; Servius on Virgil's *Georgics* 1.403.]

NYMPHES was one of the HORAE. [Hyginus, *Fables* 183.]

NYMPHS were a most perplexing class of minor divinities. Even ancient writers could not seem to agree on their nature, attributes, and genealogy. Nymphs seemed to constitute an almost infinite supply of lovely maidens, representing a kind of pantheistic expression of natural phenomena. They were everywhere—in trees, rivers, springs, seas, glades, mountains, caves, and even the underworld. They were also connected with certain races and localities. They represented powers and aspects of nature.

They were often called daughters of Zeus, but this collective disposition did not take into account whole groups designated as daughters of Nereus, Oceanus, Uranus, and the vast number of river-gods. We even find designated as nymphs a few young women with mortal fathers.

Nymphs were divided into classifications in accordance with the parts of nature they represented. The water nymphs fell into three large orders—OCEANIDES, NEREIDES, and NAIADES. Naiades, or nymphs of fresh water, were further divided into Potameides, Crinaeae, Pegaeae, Limnatides, etc., designating their habitats as rivers, springs, fountains, lakes, and so on. These were even further divided according to specific bodies of water—e.g., Acheloides, Anigrides, and inhabitants of other rivers, marshes, lakes, or streams. These were represented as daughters of the various gods of various rivers. It is not clear who were the fathers of nymphs of small bodies of water such as lakes or fountains. Perhaps these nymphs were thought to be associated with the nearest river. There were even nymphs of the lower world, and it seems evident their fathers were the infernal rivers. Water is a life-sustaining element, and thus nymphs of fresh water were worshipped with the major agricultural gods.

Nymphs of mountains and grottoes were called OREADES. We read little about them as a class, but we certainly find ample reference to them as inhabitants of certain mountains and caves, such as the Idaean, Cithaeronian, Corycian, etc.

Nymphs of trees were DRYADES and HAMADRYADES. They were subdivided according to the type of tree they lived in, but we seldom see references with this specificity. There was a suborder called Maliades, who were nymphs of fruit trees. It was commonly accepted that the life of a Dryad depended on the life of the tree she inhabited.

Nymphs were the earliest equivalent of sex symbols. They were usually depicted nude or attired in flimsy garments. As part of the pervasive fecundity of nature, they suggested sexual freedom unencumbered with institutionalized life. They had the reputation of promiscuity, mating freely with Seileni, Satyrs, and other beings who lived in the open. They were considered fair game for amorous males ranging from shepherds to kings. They were often the mates of eponymous heroes, and long family lines would be traced back to them. In many cases they produced children and then disappeared back into their native habitat, abdicating their domestic responsibility. Their reputation for unlicensed behavior has endured into modern times in the pejorative designation *nymphomania*. They were not always the quarry of lustful males, for they were sometimes the initiators of amatory pursuits, as in the case of the Bithynian nymphs who kidnapped Hylas or the Mariandynian nymphs who abducted Bormus.

They were involved with the gods, not only as sexual partners but also as ordinary companions. Apollo was accompanied by prophetic nymphs. Dionysus was followed by a train of bacchic nymphs, who lived up to their reputation as totally uninhibited. Artemis, on the other hand, had a large following of nymphs who were pledged to chastity and despised males. We find several stories in which persistent suitors of these Arcadian nymphs came to unhappy ends. Some nymphs performed services for the gods and their offspring. Aeneas was brought up by nymphs on Mount Ida. Dionysus was nursed and brought up by nymphs of Mount Nysa and elsewhere. Even Zeus himself was cared for as an infant by Cretan or Arcadian nymphs. Aetna, a Sicilian nymph, was arbiter between Hephaestus and Demeter in their contest over the possession of Sicily.

The worship of the nymphs was widespread, and usually their sanctuaries were near springs, groves, or grottoes. Some of their notable places of worship were Cyrtone, Athens, Olympia, Megara, and Sicyon. Amphissus, son of Apollo, founded a temple to them at Oeta. Sacrifices to them consisted of goats, lambs, milk, and oil, but never wine. [Homer, *Odyssey* 6.123, 12.318, 17.240, *Iliad* 20.8, 24.615;

Homeric Hymn to Aphrodite 259; Hesiod, *Theogony* 346, 364; Callimachus, *Hymn to Artemis* 13,15; Apollonius Rhodius 1.1066,1225, 3.1215, 4.1414; Virgil, *Aeneid* 1.168,500, 8.70, *Eclogues* 6.56; Pausanias 1.31.1, 2.11.3, 3.10.8, 5.5.6, 6.22.4, 9.3.5; Apollodorus 3.4.3; Antoninus Liberalis 31,32; Ovid, *Metamorphoses* 5.540, 6.16, *Fasti* 2.610, 3.769.]

NYSA was one of the NYSEIDES or HYADES. [Diodorus Siculus 3.69.]

NYSEIDES, or Nysiades, nymphs of Mount Nysa, reared the god Dionysus. Their names were Cisseis, Nysa, Erato, Eripha, Brome, and Polyhymno. They were identified with the HYADES. The location of Mount Nysa has never been determined with certainty. It was placed variously in Libya, Ethiopia, India, or Thrace. The Thracian location had a somewhat better claim, since the orgiastic worship of Dionysus was prominent among Thracian tribes. The relationship of these nymphs to one another is uncertain. Nysa, for example, was said to be a daughter of Aristaeus. [Hyginus, *Fables* 182, *Poetic Astronomy* 2.21; Apollodorus 3.4.3; Ovid, *Metamorphoses* 3.314, *Fasti* 3.769.]

NYX was night personified. She was among the very oldest of the gods, having been born fatherless from Chaos along with her brother Erebus. Some said she was the daughter of Eros, the cosmic unifying force of nature. She was regarded as the subduer of men and gods alike, and even Zeus stood in awe of her. She was conceived as winged and riding in a chariot. Her dress was dark, and stars blinked around her and perhaps through her. Her residence was the darkness of Hades.

With her brother she became the mother of Aether and Hemera, so from the dark womb of night came light of day. She was also the mother, without mating, of many dark and menacing individuals, such as the Ceres, Eris, the Eumenides, the Moirae (Fates), Nemesis, the Oneirata, Hypnos, Thanatos, and Oizys (Distress). Some cosmogonies assigned other parents to some of these, but it can be readily understood how these associations came to be made. She was somewhat inappropriately called the mother of the Hesperides and of Momus, the personification of mockery.

Nyx was not worshipped widely. A statue of her, carved by Rhoecus, was shown at Ephesus. She was represented on the chest of Cypselus as carrying in her arms Hypnos and Thanatos, who were depicted as young boys. [Homer, *Iliad* 14.259; Hesiod, *Theogony* 123, 211,748; Orphica, *Argonautica* 14; Cicero, *On the Nature of the Gods* 3.17; Euripides, *Ion* 1150; Virgil, *Aeneid* 5.721, 6.390; Pausanias 5.18.1, 10.38.7.]

OCALEIA was a daughter of Mantineus and, according to some, the wife of Abas and mother of Acrisius and Proetus. She was usually called AGLAIA. [Apollodorus 2.2.1.]

OCEANIDES were daughters of Oceanus and Tethys, and thus could be called nymphs of the ocean, except that unlike the Nereides they were not always exclusively confined to the watery element. Many have regarded them as part of the ocean beyond the Mediterranean, the preserve of the Nereides, but that would have put them at too remote a location to have been involved in many of the accounts that included them. A few seem to have been connected with bodies of fresh water.

Their names and number, as might be expected, varied from writer to writer. The number of listed Oceanides ranged from a mere seven (by Apollodorus) to 41 (by Hesiod), with other writers repeating or adding names. With typical extravagance some writers claimed there were as many as 3,000 of them. All the Oceanides on Apollodorus' list were famous—Asia, Styx, Electra, Doris, Eurynome, Amphitrite, and Metis. They all mated with gods or Titans and produced other divinities. Only two of them, Doris and Amphitrite, remained connected with the sea.

Hesiod's list included the following: Acaste, Admete, Amphirho, Asia, Callirrhoe, Calypso, Cerceis, Chryseis, Clymene, Clytia, Dione, Doris, Electra, Eudora, Europa, Eurynome, Galaxaure, Hippo, Ianeira, Ianthe, Idyia, Melobosis, Menestho, Metis, Ocyrrhoe, Pasithoe, Peitho, Perseis, Petraea, Plexaure,

Pluto, Polydora, Prymno, Rhodeia, Styx, Telesto, Thoe, Tyche, Urania, Xanthe, and Zeuxo. Other writers added Aethra, Argeia, Asterope, Beroe, Capheira, Dodone, Eidothea, Euagoreis, Iache, Leucippe, Melia, Meliboea, Melite, Menippe, Pasiphae, Phaeno, Pleione, Polyxo, Rhodope, Stilbo, and Theia. About a dozen of these names coincide with names of Nereides, which causes a certain amount of confusion. Several of the names reflected identification with the sea, but not necessarily with the great western ocean. Thus Xanthe referred to the turbidity of waters, Amphirho meant the surrounding flood, Ianthe was the delightful stream, and Ocyrrhoe was swift-flowing. Some Oceanides, such as Asia, Europa, Doris, and Ianeira (Lady of the Ionians) derived their names from the lands over which they presided.

Some of the Oceanides mated with mortals, as others had done with gods. Idyia was the mother of Medea by Aeetes. Pelasgus by Meliboea was father of Lycaon. Calypso had two sons by Odysseus. They were all supposed to be immortal except in the case of Metis, who was swallowed by Zeus to produce Athena, or in the story of Ocyrrhoe, who was killed by her son for adultery. They had no particular identity except for the few who were lovers of gods and men. The rest seemed to blend into the vast family of Oceanus and were accepted as part of the teeming world of sea deities. The Oceanides had no special worship and apparently no altars. Even the Nereides had more visibility. [Hesiod, *Theogony* 346–366; Callimachus, *Hymn to Artemis* 13; Apollonius Rhodius 4.1414; Apollodorus 1.2.2.]

OCHNE was the daughter of Colonus, a Tanagran hero. Her brothers were Echemus, Leon, and Bucolus. Ochne fell in love with Eunostus, son of Elinus, but he avoided her. As in many other instances of unreciprocated love, she accused Eunostus of trying to seduce her; her brothers, without looking into the truth of the matter, killed him. Later Ochne confessed she had lied about the young man, and then threw herself over a cliff. Eunostus had a sanctuary at Tanagra in a sacred grove that no woman was allowed to approach. [Plutarch, *Greek Questions* 40.]

OCYALE was one of the AMAZONS. [Hyginus, *Fables* 163.]

OCYDROME was one of the DOGS of Actaeon. [Hyginus, *Fables* 181.]

OCYPETE (1) was one of the DANAIDES, daughter of Danaus and Pieria. She married and murdered Lampus. [Apollodorus 2.1.5.]

OCYPETE (2) was one of the HARPIES.

OCYPETE (3) was one of the DOGS of Actaeon. [Hyginus, *Fables* 181.]

OCYPODE was an alternate name of Ocypete, one of the HARPIES. [Apollodorus 1.9.21.]

OCYRRHOE (1) was one of the OCEANIDES. By Helios, the sun-god, she was the mother of Phasis. Once after he was grown, Phasis surprised his mother with a lover and killed her. In despair he threw himself into the Arcturus River and drowned. Afterward the river was called the Phasis. [Pseudo-Plutarch, *On Rivers* 5.]

OCYRRHOE (2) was a daughter of Cheiron the Centaur and Chariclo. Her name was given to her because she was born by a swift-flowing stream. She grew up and inherited from her father the gift of prophecy. She was so skilled that she alienated the gods and was changed into a mare. In this form she was called Hippe or Hippo. [Ovid, *Metamorphoses* 2.635; Hyginus, *Poetic Astronomy* 2.18.]

OCYRRHOE (3) was the daughter of the river-god Imbrasus in Samos and of Chesias. She was raped by Apollo and when she tried to flee him by water, he changed the ship into a stone and the skipper Pompilus into a fish. [Apollonius Rhodius, quoted by Athenaeus 7.283.]

OCYRRHOE (4) was a nymph of Mysia, who became by Hermes the mother of Caicus. For some reason Caicus killed Timander and, fearing the vengeance of his victim's family and friends, threw himself into the Astraeus River, which was afterward called the Caicus. [Pseudo-Plutarch, *On Rivers* 21.]

OCYTHOE was another form of Ocypete, one of the HARPIES. [Apollodorus 1.9.21.]

OEAGRIDES were daughters of Oeagrus and sisters of Orpheus. Oeagrus was a king of Thrace and, according to some, father of Orpheus and Linus. [Apollodorus 1.3.2; Orphica, *Argonautica* 73; Ovid, *Ibis* 484; Moschus 3.37.]

OECHALIA was the wife of Melaneus, son of Apollo. Melaneus was a good archer and came to Perieres in Messenia. Perieres assigned him a dwelling in Carnasium, which later Melaneus named for his wife, Oechalia. Others, however, called Melaneus' wife STRATONICE, who bore to him the famous archer Eurytus. [Pausanias 4.2.3.]

OEME was one of the DANAIDES. Apollodorus called her a daughter of Danaus by Crino. She was married to Arbelus. Hyginus did not mention a mother and called her husband Polydectores. [Apollodorus 2.1.5; Hyginus, *Fables* 170.]

OENEIS was, according to some, the mother of Pan by Zeus or Aether. Pan's mother was more often called DRYOPE. [Aristippus, quoted by the scholiast on Theocritus 1.3.]

OENO was one of the OENOTROPAE.

OENOATIS was a surname of Artemis, who was worshipped at Oenoe in Argolis. [Euripides, *Madness of Hercules* 376.]

OENOE (1) was the name given by Antoninus Liberalis (16) to GERANA.

OENOE (2) was a sister of Epochus, from whom the Attic deme of Oenoe was believed to have derived its name. Nothing further is known of Oenoe or her brother, so it is curious they were represented on the pedestal of the statue of Nemesis at Rhamnus. [Pausanias 1.33.8.]

OENOE (3) was an Arcadian nymph said to have been one of those who brought up the infant Zeus. She was represented on the altar of Athena Alea at Tegea. [Pausanias 8.47.3.]

OENOE (4) was one of the followers of Dionysus. [Nonnos, *Dionysiaca* 29.253.]

OENOIE, a Naiad, was by Thoas the mother of Sicinus. Thoas was the father of Hypsipyle by Myrina. When the women of Lemnos killed their husbands, Thoas was spared by Hypsipyle. He fled from Lemnos and settled, according to some, in Tauris. He probably went first to the island of Oenoie, where the nymph by the same name bore Sicinus. When Sicinus grew up he changed the island's name to his own. [Apollonius Rhodius 1.626.]

OENONE was a daughter of the river-god Cebren, and sister of Asterope or Hesperia. She fell in love with a handsome shepherd on Mount Ida, and her love was reciprocated. Neither knew that he, Paris, was in reality the son of Priam and Hecuba, king and queen of Troy. Because of a direful prophecy that he would destroy Troy, he had been exposed as a newborn infant. He was rescued by one of the king's shepherds and grew up believing the man to be his father. Paris once took one of the royal bulls to a celebration in Troy. He could not know the celebration consisted entirely of funeral games of which he was the subject (his supposed death had been commemorated annually from the time of his exposure). He participated in the games and won the bull he had brought, which was his only reason for entering the contest. He was confronted by his bullying older brother, but was identified by his clairvoyant sister, Cassandra, before any harm came to him.

After that he was restored to a more than favored position in the court of Priam. Little by little he became spoiled by the attention lavished on him by his mother and father, and despite warnings from Cassandra and from Oenone, who also possessed prophetic powers, the old curse was ignored. Paris recalled the dreamlike visit to him of three Olympian goddesses, who compelled him to choose the fairest among them. One had promised him the most beautiful woman in the world, and he had awarded her the prize. Now the dream promised to be reality when affairs of state caused him to go to Sparta, where lived as queen the incredibly beautiful Helen.

Oenone could divine the outcome and begged Paris to remain in Troy (apparently she had joined him there after his restoration in the royal house). The brief stay among the princes and princesses of Troy must have been difficult for her since she, a simple and unassuming nymph, was out of place among her urban in-laws. But Paris left, for it was his destiny to do so. Oenone returned with their adolescent son, Corythus, to Mount Ida, promising Paris she would always be there for him and could be counted on to heal him if ever he should be wounded. She told him that was the most she could do for him.

It is doubtful if Oenone's in-laws took the trouble to let her know that Paris eloped with Helen and brought her to Troy, but word eventually reached her. She was abandoned and powerless to do anything but accept the unhappy reality that Helen had become the toast of Troy and that she herself was totally forgotten. When the Greeks started to arrive, she sent Corythus to guide them, vowing vengeance on the husband and the kingdom that had rejected her.

In her frustrated anger she even went so far as to have Corythus, in his capacity as the son of Paris, seek favor in the royal house and eventually, when Paris was totally preoccupied with the war, find his way into Helen's bed. Some said Paris found his son in bed with Helen and killed him. It is interesting he did not kill Helen as well, but apparently in adulterous relationships the aggressor was always the guilty party.

Shortly thereafter Paris was mortally wounded by Philoctetes with one of the poisoned arrows of Heracles. Paris remembered the promise Oenone had made to him and asked to be carried to Mount Ida. Oenone refused to heal him, and he was carried back to Troy. At the last moment Oenone relented and rushed to Troy with drugs that would have saved him, only to find he had died. She went into a frenzy of grief and hanged herself. Some said she leapt from the walls of the city or threw herself on her ex-husband's funeral pyre.

Oenone could quite easily be called the epitome of the abandoned wife, but one unwilling to accept her fate without resorting to a series of actions to recover her lost love. Her first attempt was reasoning, but that failed. Then she tried a thwarting tactic by providing her son as a weapon to end the war quickly. When that didn't work, she tried to discredit her rival. Finally, she allowed the death of her self-destructive ex-husband, but repented and in a final desperate action tried to save him. After that, there was nothing left but her own destruction. She loved as people should love, but her kind of love could not compete with the erotic fantasy the gods had decreed for her once-devoted husband. [Apollodorus 3.12.6;.Parthenius, *Love Stories* 4,34; Homer, *Iliad* 5.64; Lycophron 65; Tzetzes on Lycophron 57,61; Conon, *Narrations* 23; Ovid, *Metamorphoses* 11.769; Quintus Smyrnaeus 10.467; Dictys Cretensis 4.19.]

OENOPE was, according to some, the mother of Megareus by Poseidon or Hippomenes. He was brother of Abrota, wife of Nisus, and father of Euippus, Timalcus, Euaechme, and, some said, Hippomenes. According to Boeotian tradition, Megareus with his army went to the assistance of his brother-in-law Nisus, who was king of Megara, against Minos. He fell in battle and was buried at Megara, which was called after him, its early name having been Nisa. According to a Megarian tradition, Megareus was the husband of Iphinoe, daughter of Nisus, and succeeded his father-in-law/brother-in-law in the government of Megara, which he later left to Alcathous because his own sons had died before him. [Apollodorus 3.15.8; Pausanias 1.39.5,41.4; Plutarch, *Greek Questions* 16.]

OENOTROPAE, the Changers into Wine, was the name of the three daughters of Anius, king of Delos. Anius was a son of Apollo by Rhoeo. After Apollo made her pregnant, her father, Staphylus, son of Dionysus, put her in a chest and cast her adrift. By the time she landed on Delos she had given birth to Anius. He was immediately consecrated to the service of Apollo, who gave him prophetic power. Anius grew up on Delos and had sex with a convenient nymph called Dryope. She gave him three daughters, Oeno, Spermo, and Elais, whose names can be translated as wine, wheat, and olive oil. Dionysus decided to confer on his great-granddaughters special powers. They could at will convert water into wine, grass into wheat,

or berries into olives. They were a later version of the horn of plenty.

One can imagine the three women with their powerful gift. They sat on an island and could change anything to something else, but eventually they had to become bored with their special ability. The Trojan War came, and they were happy to stock the ships of the Greeks with provisions. Anius, who was prophetic, told the Greeks to weigh anchor and wait out the war, since nothing significant was going to happen for nine years. He probably had in mind to marry his daughters to deserving heroes, but the Greeks would not be persuaded. Agamemnon wanted to abduct the fruitful daughters, but they implored their great-grandfather to help them, and were metamorphosed into doves. Some said Odysseus kidnapped them but they escaped and were then changed into doves.

The Oenotropae were utterly sexless in spite of their luxuriant provision. They perhaps symbolized to the Greeks the last abundance they saw before being confronted with the barren landscapes of Asia Minor. However, the house of Anius was not devoid of nubile women. Aeneas was said to have landed on Delos and taken Lavinia, one of Anius' other daughters, to wed. She too had prophetic powers. She followed Aeneas to Lavinium, where she died. There was no indication she was able to supply the colonizing Trojans with an endless supply of food and wine. [Tzetzes on Lycophron 750; Ovid, *Metamorphoses* 13.643–674; Servius on Virgil's *Aeneid* 3.80; Diodorus Siculus 5.62; Conon, *Narrations* 41; Dionysius of Halicarnassus, *Roman Antiquities* 1.59.]

OEORPATA was the name given by the Scythians to the Amazonian women around the Black Sea. [Diodorus Siculus 2.451; Herodotus 4.110; Apollonius Rhodius 2.287–289.]

OGYGIA was a daughter of NIOBE and Amphion. [Apollodorus 3.5.6.]

OIZYS, daughter of Nyx, was the personification of woe. [Hesiod, *Theogony* 214.]

OLBIA was mother of Astacus by Poseidon. Astacus in Bithynia, afterward called

Nicomedeia, derived its name from him. [Stephanus Byzantium, "Astakos"; Pausanias 5.12.5.]

OLYMPIADES was a surname for the Muses as acknowledgment of their heavenly (versus earthly) state. [Homer, *Iliad* 2.491.]

OLYMPUSA was one of the THESPIADES. By Heracles she became the mother of Halocrates. [Apollodorus 2.7.8.]

OMA was one of the names by which BONA DEA was called.

OMPHALE, sometimes called Maeonides because she was a native of Maeonia, was daughter of the Lydian king Iardanus. Omphale was also called by the patronymic Iardanis. She was married to Tmolus, who already had a son, Tantalus, by the nymph Pluto. Tmolus died early. We are not sure that he was not the same Tmolus who was killed by Artemis for raping the nymph Arhippe in the temple of the goddess. In that case, Omphale might have been the mother of Theoclymenus, who buried his father and named for him the mountain Tmolus. In any case, she was a widow and ruled her late husband's kingdom. In this capacity she bought the services of Heracles, who was condemned to work for wages for a year or so for having killed Iphitus.

Omphale was a most unusual woman. It makes a certain amount of sense that her late husband had fancied nymphs. She bought Heracles as a sexual object, not as a servant. In a way she seemed to be evening the score with her husband by abasing Heracles, making him spin wool and dress in her clothes while she strode around in his lion's skin. These reversed sex roles apparently had the desired effect, although Heracles, the father of children by wives, lovers, and even the monster Echidna, did not need exotic stimulation. Maybe it was Omphale who needed to indulge herself in erotic games.

Heracles had a limited time in which he had to serve his penance, but he must have been in or out of service to Omphale for at least four years, since his children by her were Agelaus,

Lamius, Maleus, and Tyrrhenus. During one of her pregnancies, he even fathered Bargasus by Barge, a slave of Omphale. More than likely he occasionally indulged his fondness for boys. And to prove his masculinity after being forced to wear female attire, he cleaned up the kingdom of spiteful gnomes such as the Cercopes, serpents, and miscellaneous malefactors.

Then he left, and Omphale returned to ruling her kingdom. There is no record that she took a husband. Her son Agelaus started the line that produced Croesus, a historical king. Lamius gave his name to the Thessalian Lamia. Maleus invented the trumpet. Tyrrhenus led a Pelasgian colony from Lydia into Italy. [Apollodorus 1.9.19, 2.6.3,7,8; Sophocles, *Trachiniae* 253; Dionysius of Halicarnassus, *Roman Antiquities* 1.28; Lucian, *Dialogues of the Gods* 13.2; Antoninus Liberalis 2; Stephanus Byzantium, "Bargasa"; Ovid, *Fasti* 2.305,310, *Heroides* 9.53,103, *Metamorphoses* 11.157; Diodorus Siculus 4.31; Herodotus 1.7.]

ONCA was a surname of Athena, derived from Oncae in Boeotia, where she had a sanctuary. Actually, the name of the town was derived from Onga, a Phoenician goddess, whose worship resembled that of Athena. On his search for Europa, Cadmus was directed by an oracle to found a city at the spot on which a spotted cow should lie down. When this happened, he dedicated an altar to Athena under the name of Onga. The town of Onca stood just outside the gates of Thebes. [Aeschylus, *Seven against Thebes* 166,489; Pausanias 9.12.2; Scholiast on Euripides' *Phoenician Maidens* 1062.]

ONCAEA was a nymph on the island of Lesbos. She was loved by Poseidon, by whom she became the mother of Arion. Arion was the famous bard who was especially skilled on the cithara. Once, he was robbed on a sea voyage and was about to be thrown overboard. He begged to be allowed to play and sing one final time. Dolphins gathered around the ship and, when he was tossed into the sea, carried him to land. The musician then proceeded on land ahead of his assailants, and when they landed they were seized and crucified or impaled. Arion was called also the inventor of dithyrambic poetry. [Herodotus

1.23; Scholiast on Pindar's *Olympian Odes* 13.25.]

ONGA (*See* ONCA)

OPHTHALMITIS was a surname of Athena at Sparta, referring to her keen sight or to her role as patron goddess of eyesight. Lycurgus dedicated a temple to Athena when one of his eyes was struck out by Alcander, who believed Lycurgus' laws were unfavorable to him. The Lacedaemonians saved his other eye, and he rededicated the temple to Athena Ophthalmitis. [Pausanias 3.18.2; Plutarch, *Lycurgus* 11.]

OPIS (1) (*See* UPIS)

OPIS (2) was one of the NEREIDES. [Hyginus, *Fables: Preface* 8.]

OPS was the Roman goddess of plenty and fertility. She was the protectress of everything associated with agriculture. She was said to be the daughter of Peisenor, and she was the wife of Saturnus, regarded as the introducer of agriculture. She was thought to live in the earth, so people who invoked her or made vows to her were accustomed to touch the earth. She was worshipped as the nurturing goddess who gave shelter and food to individuals. Newborn children were commended to her care. In common with Saturnus she had temples and festivals, but she had one separate sanctuary on the Capitoline Hill. She also had an altar in common with Ceres in the Vicus Jugarius. Her festivals were called Opalia and Opiconsivia (from her surname Consivia, meaning "the Sower").

Despite her role in fertility, Ops herself had only two children, and curiously these children were not connected with a time beyond memory of men but with events as late as the Trojan War. Her son was Eurypylus, a suitor of Helen and consequently a participant in the war. He had a controversial genealogy, so Ops might not have been his mother at all. Interestingly, he was not represented as her son by Saturnus but by Euaemon. Her daughter was Eurycleia, the nurse of Odysseus, who recognized him when he returned home from his long years of wandering after the war. Saturnus was not identified as the father, but since no one else was mentioned, we can make the assumption that he was.

Because of her special function as goddess of the earth, plenty, and fertility, Ops was identified with a number of other divinities, such as Lua, Maia, Pomona, Rhea, and Tutelina. She was surnamed Patella as the stimulator of the wheat crop and Runcina as promoter of the harvest. [Macrobius, *Saturnalia* 1.10,12,16; St. Augustine, *City of God* 4.8,11,21; Livy 8.1, 39.22, 45.33; Hyginus, *Fables* 81; Gellius 13.22; Varro, *On the Latin Language* 5.74, 8.36; Arnobius, *Adversus Nationes* 4.1,7; Homer, *Odyssey* 2.38; Pliny, *Natural History* 18.2.]

OPTILETIS was a surname of Athena. (*See also* OPHTHALMITIS.]

ORBONA was a divinity at Rome. She had an altar in the Via Sacra near the temple of the Lares. Parents whose children had died came to her to pray for their other children. Those whose children had life-threatening diseases also appealed to her. [Cicero, *On the Nature of the Gods* 3.25; Pliny, *Natural History* 2.7; Arnobius, *Adversus Nationes* 4.7.]

OREADES were mountain NYMPHS, inhabiting grottoes on mountains as well. They were also called Orodemniades, but often they bore the names of mountains or caves they inhabited, such as Cithaeronides, Peliades, or Coryciae. Mountain nymphs were almost indistinguishable from tree nymphs or nymphs who frequented mountain streams. Seldom do we find any of them separately identified. Pan took part in the revels of the Oreades, and one of his famous loves was Echo, an Oread. [Theocritus 7.137; Virgil, *Aeneid* 1.168,500; Pausanias 5.5.6.]

OREASIDE was the mother of Xanthus by Triopas. Xanthus was at first king of the Pelasgians in Lycia but later settled on the island of Lesbos, which until then had been unpopulated. He divided the land among the settlers and called it Pelasgia. [Diodorus Siculus 5.81; Callimachus, *Hymn to Delos* 41.]

OREIA was one of the THESPIADES and by Heracles the mother of Laomenes. [Apollodorus 2.7.8.]

OREILOCHIA was the name of Iphigeneia on the island of Leuce. Some traditions said she did not die (at Brauron) but was changed by Artemis into Hecate, or was endowed with immortality and eternal youth under the name of Oreilochia and became the wife of Achilles on the island of Leuce. [Antoninus Liberalis 27.]

OREITHYIA (1) was one of the NEREIDES. [Homer, *Iliad* 18.48.]

OREITHYIA (2) was a daughter of Erechtheus and Praxithea and lived on the Acropolis with her dozen or so brothers and sisters. She was related in one way or another to just about everyone in the early history of Athens. She and her sisters, Protogeneia, Procris, Creusa, Otionia, Pandora, and Chthonia had formed an agreement to die together if any of them should die, but most of them were unable to fulfill this promise since their destiny lay in other directions. Oreithyia was a good case in point. Once, she frolicked with other maidens across the Ilissus River just outside the walls of the Acropolis. Boreas, the north wind, swept down and carried her away. He must have had his eye on her for some time and been waiting for an opportunity to catch her outside the palace.

Boreas was a son of Astraeus and Eos, and dwelled with his brother winds in a cave on Mount Haemus in Thrace. It was there that he carried Oreithyia. After her rich, royal life in Athens, this stark, drafty abode must have been a terrible ordeal. Her feelings about her savage abductor could scarcely have been anything but shrinking terror. He had ravaged her on a rock near the Erginus River on the way to Thrace. She became immediately pregnant and first bore the twins Zetes and Calais, and afterward Chione, Cleopatra, and Haemus. After this succession of children she probably became reconciled to her fate, even to Boreas' extramarital excesses. For example, he engaged in bestiality and impregnated 12 of the mares of the Trojan Erichthonius. He had a good side, however, offering assistance to the Greeks against the

Persians and to the Megalopolitans against the Spartans. For the latter service he was honored with annual festivals at Megalopolis. Oreithyia was dead by that time, since as a mortal her years were numbered.

Zetes and Calais were Argonauts and prominent in the story of Phineus, who had married their sister Cleopatra. They were later killed by Heracles. Haemus and his wife, Rhodope, were changed into mountains for impersonating Zeus and Hera. Chione became the mother of Eumolpus by Poseidon.

Oreithyia was shown on the chest of Cypselus as being carried off by Boreas, whose legs were depicted as tails of serpents. Boreas was honored with a temple by the grateful Athenians for assisting them against the Persians. Coincidentally, its site was close to the place from which he took Oreithyia. [Apollodorus 3.15.1,2; Apollonius Rhodius 211,215; Hesiod, *Theogony* 379; Callimachus, *Hymn to Delos* 63; Ovid, *Metamorphoses* 6.683; Pausanias 1.19.6,38.3; 5.19.1, 8.36.3; Servius on Virgil's *Aeneid* 1.321.]

OREITHYIA (3) was one of the AMAZONS. She swore vengeance on Theseus, and after concluding an alliance with the Scythians, she led a force of Amazons across the Cimmerian Bosphorus, crossed the Danube, and passed through Thrace, Thessaly, and Boeotia. At Athens she encamped on the Areiopagus. First she raided Laconia to discourage Pelops from reinforcing the Athenians. When the campaign proved unsuccessful, she escaped to Megara where, according to some, she died of grief. One writer said she was the queen after Antiope. There seems to be confusion between her and Hippolyte. [Justinus 2.4; Quintus Smyrnaeus 1.168; Hellanicus, quoted by Plutarch's *Theseus* 26,27; Apollodorus, *Epitome* 1.16; Diodorus Siculus 4.28.]

OREITHYIA (4) was the wife of Theias and mother of Smyrna. The mother of Smyrna (Myrrha) was more often called CENCHREIS. [Apollodorus 3.14.4; Ovid, *Metamorphoses* 10.435.]

OREITHYIA (5) was a daughter of Cecrops and wife of Macedon, a son of Zeus and Thyia. His sons by Oreithyia were all founders of places.

They were Pierus, Amathus, Beres, Atintan, Europus, and Oropus. [Stephanus Byzantium, "Beres," "Atintania," "Europos," "Oropos"; Scholiast on Homer's *Iliad* 14.226.]

ORESITROPHOS was one of the DOGS of Actaeon. [Hyginus, *Fables* 181.]

ORIAS was one of the DOGS of Actaeon. [Hyginus, *Fables* 181.]

ORIS was, according to some, the mother of Euphemus by Poseidon. She was a daughter of Orion. Usually the mother of Euphemus was called EUROPA. [Scholiast on Pindar's *Pythian Odes* 4.15; Tzetzes, *Chiliades* 2.43.]

ORMENIS was a patronymic of Astydameia, granddaughter of Ormenus. [Homer, *Iliad* 2.734, 9.448, *Odyssey* 15.413.]

ORNIS was the mother of the Stymphalides by Stymphalus. Stymphalus was a son of Elatus and the eponymic hero of the town of Stymphalus in northeastern Arcadia (now in Corinthia). Pelops was unable to overcome him in war and murdered him by a stratagem. The sons of Stymphalus were Agamedes and Gortys, and his daughter was Parthenope. They were nowhere referred to as the children of Ornis.

The Stymphalides were voracious birds with brazen claws, wings, and beaks. They used their feathers as arrows and ate human flesh. Their number was vast, and they killed men and beasts. The sixth labor of Heracles was ridding the vicinity of these dreadful creatures before they further multiplied.

Some more reasonably claimed that the Stymphalides were not birds but women, and were killed by Heracles for entertaining his enemies the Moliones but not welcoming him. In the temple of the Stymphalian Artemis, however, they were shown as birds. [Apollodorus 2.5.6; Hyginus, *Fables* 30; Pausanias 8.22.4,5.]

ORODEMNIADES (*See* OREADES)

ORPHE was one of the sisters of CARYA, who was a lover of Dionysus. [Servius on Virgil's *Aeneid* 8.30.]

ORPHNE was, according to some, the mother of Ascalaphus by Acheron. Ascalaphus was usually called the son of GORGYRA. [Ovid, *Metamorphoses* 5.540.]

ORSEDICE was a daughter of Cinyras and Metharme. (*See* BRAESIA.)

ORSEIS was a nymph who was loved by Hellen, son of Deucalion and Pyrrha. Hellen was among the first generation after the great flood and did his part in helping repopulate the earth. He was the mythical ancestor of the Hellenes, or Greeks, in distinction to the ancient Pelasgians, although presumably this distinction was unnecessary if the flood did indeed wipe out all mankind. No one has ever questioned the welfare of the lesser immortals, such as nymphs. Were they terminated, too, when the natural features to which their lives were attached disappeared in the deluge? Did their ranks see a repopulation after the flood?

Orseis became by Hellen the mother of Aeolus, Dorus, and Xuthus. Aeolus was the founder of the Aeolian branch of the Hellenes and began an important dynasty. Dorus was the ancestor of the Dorians and dwelled in the area of Parnassus. Xuthus was a king of Peloponnesus and started the races of the Achaians and Ionians. Hellen himself ruled at Phthia in Thessaly and left the kingdom to Aeolus. [Apollodorus 1.7.3,6; Diodorus Siculus 4.60; Herodotus 1.56; Homer, *Iliad* 2.684; Pausanias 3.20.6.]

ORSILOCHE was a name the Taurians used for IPHIGENEIA. [Euripides, *Iphigeneia in Taurica* 784,1045; Hesiod, *Catalogues of Women*, quoted by Pausanias 1.43.1.]

ORSINOME, sometimes called Hiscilla, was the daughter of Eurynomus, son of Magnes. She was married to Lapithes, son of Apollo and Stilbe, and became by him the mother of Phorbas, Triopas, Periphas, and Lesbus. Lapithes was regarded as the ancestor of the Lapithae in Thessaly. The sons of Orsinome achieved a certain amount of fame. Triopas was said to have founded the city of Cnidus. Phorbas was invited to Rhodes to rid the island of snakes, and was honored with heroic worship. He later had a share in the government of Elis for assisting Alector against Pelops. Periphas was the grandfather of Ixion, who became father of the Centaurs. Lesbus went to the island that later bore his name and became king. [Homer, *Iliad* 12.126; Diodorus Siculus 4.69, 5.58,61; Hyginus, *Poetic Astronomy* 2.14.]

ORSOBIA was the daughter of Hyrnetho, daughter of Temenus the Heraclid, by Deiphontes. Her brothers were Antimenes, Xanthippus, and Argeius. Hyrnetho and her husband, favorites of Temenus, were forced to abandon Argos when Hyrnetho's brothers killed Temenus and usurped the kingdom. They went to Epidaurus and ruled there, but even that rule was begrudged by Hyrnetho's brothers. Two of them kidnapped her, and she was killed in the struggle to recover her. In great sadness Deiphontes erected a sanctuary to her in Epidaurus.

Orsobia married Pamphylus, son of Aegimius, a former ally of Heracles and foster father of Hyllus after Heracles' death. The Dorian tribe of the Pamphylians was named for her husband. Pamphylus and his brother Dymas fought with the Heraclids against Tisamenus and both were killed. [Apollodorus 2.7.7,8.4; Pausanias 2.28.3.]

ORTHAEA was one of the HYACINTHIDES. [Apollodorus 3.15.8.]

ORTHIA was a surname of Artemis, who is also called Iphigeneia or Lygodesma. Her worship was said to have been brought to Sparta from Tauris by Iphigeneia and Orestes in the form of a statue. Two brothers, Astrabacus and Alopecus, sons of Irbus, found the statue in an upright position, thus gaining its name of Orthia, although some have maintained the name referred to an erect phallus. It was at the altar of Artemis Orthia that Spartan boys had to undergo ritual flogging. The goddess had temples at Brauron, in the Cerameicus at Athens, in Elis, and on the coast of Byzantium. [Scholiast on Pindar's *Olympian Odes* 3.54; Herodotus 4.87, 6.69; Pausanias 3.26.5.]

ORTHOSIA was one of ten HORAE mentioned by Hyginus (*Fables* 183).

ORTYGIA was a surname of Artemis, derived from the island of Ortygia, the ancient name for Delos. The goddess bore this name in various places, but the name always referred to the island on which she was born. [Ovid, *Metamorphoses* 1.694; Strabo 10.5.5.]

OSSA, the personification of rumor, was the Greek equivalent of Fama. She was called a messenger of Zeus, since all reports had to emanate from him. She was sometimes called a daughter of Elpis (Hope), and at Athens she had an altar. [Homer, *Odyssey* 1.282, 2.216, *Iliad* 2.93; Sophocles, *Oedipus the King* 158; Pausanias 1.17.1.]

OSSIPAGA, or Ossipanga, also written Ossilago and Ossipagina, was a Roman divinity who was invoked to harden and strengthen the bones of infants. [Arnobius, *Adversus Nationes* 3.30, 4.7.]

OTIONIA was the youngest daughter of Erechtheus. Her sisters were Protogeneia, Pandora, Procris, Creusa, Oreithyia, and Chthonia. Early in life the sisters took a kind of melodramatic oath that if any one of them should die by violence they all would destroy themselves. As time went on, enthusiasm for this noble declaration dwindled, and one by one the sisters drifted away to become married.

When it seemed they would no longer need to concern themselves with the oath, Eumolpus brought a large number of Thracians to assist Eleusis in its battle against Athens. The Athenians were greatly alarmed and bade the king to consult an oracle. The oracle said that Erechtheus must sacrifice one of his daughters if Athens hoped for victory. Otionia valiantly volunteered, and she was joined by the only sisters remaining at home, Protogeneia and Pandora. Patriotic suicide seemed to be fashionable at the time. They were probably imitating the daughters of Cecrops, who had died in a similar manner some years before. [Apollodorus 3.15.4; Hyginus, *Fables* 46; Suidas, "Parthenoi."]

OTRERA is one of the really mysterious women in mythology. She is generally accepted as the mother of the AMAZONS, but since they were a race of sufficient numbers to invade Attica, she must have been only the founding mother of these warrior women. She was said to be the mother of Hippolyte, Antiope, and Melanippe by Ares. This would make a certain amount of sense, since these three were considered queens of the Amazons, ruling either jointly or consecutively. She was again represented as a daughter of Ares, and this would not be surprising, since incest was common among the Olympians. It makes more sense when one realizes she had to be immortal to bear Ares children as far apart in time as Hippolyte and Penthesileia.

Hippolyte existed in the time of Heracles and Theseus, a whole generation before the Trojan War. Penthesileia was a young warrior in the war. Except as an immortal, Otrera's childbearing years could not have reached so far. Moreover, she was said to have built the temple of Artemis at Ephesus, and this edifice was already in place before the Amazons marched on Attica.

Like the other daughters of Ares, Otrera was born with a warlike spirit. Coupling with her father to produce the forebears of a warrior race seemed appropriate, since no mere mortal could have helped spawn this curious breed. It is not known who her mother was. Ares probably had to create his own family of killing, marauding warriors since his lover Aphrodite could only produce Harmonia, Deimos, and Phobus, the by-products of war. [Hyginus, *Fables* 112,225; Scholiast on Apollonius Rhodius 1.1033; Servius on Virgil's *Aeneid* 1.491; Dictys Cretensis 4.2.]

OXYDERCIS was an epithet of Athena because of her keenness of sight or the power of her intellect. (*See also* OPHTHALMITIS.)

OXYRHOE was one of the DOGS of Actaeon. [Hyginus, *Fables* 181.]

PAEONIA, the Healer, was a surname of Athena, under which she had a statue at Athens and an altar in the temple of Amphiaraus at Oropus. The serpent, symbol of perpetual renovation, was sacred to her. She shared the altar at Oropus with Panaceia, Hygieia, Iaso,

and Aphrodite. [Pausanias 1.2.4,23.5,31.3, 34.3; Aristophanes, *Plutus* 701.]

PAIS was a surname of Hera. (*See* CHERA.)

PALES was a Roman divinity of flocks and shepherds. Some described her as female, and others said male. Some even said he/she was a combination of both. While the religion of the Romans rejected a hermaphroditic god, the rites performed at the festival of Pales on April 21, the birthday of the city of Rome, suggested a female divinity. The god/goddess was connected with the Greek Pan. [Virgil, *Aeneid* 3.1,297, *Georgics* 3.1; Servius on Virgil's *Aeneid* 5.35; Ovid, *Fasti* 4.721,746,766; Dionysius of Halicarnassus, *Roman Antiquities* 1.88.]

PALLANTIA, according to some, was a daughter of Euander loved by Hercules. She died and was buried on the Palatine Hill in Rome, and this circumstance was supposed to have been the origin of the hill's name. Others said the name came from Pallas, the son of Hercules and Dyna, another daughter of Euander.. [Servius on Virgil's *Aeneid* 8.51; Dionysius of Halicarnassus, *Roman Antiquities* 1.32.]

PALLANTIAS was a patronymic by which Aurora, daughter of the giant Pallas, was sometimes designated. Pallantias also occurred as a variation for Athena. [Ovid, *Metamorphoses* 4.373, 6.567, 9.420; *Palatine Anthology* 6.247.]

PALLAS (1) was the most common surname of Athena. At first the name always appeared in double form, but later Pallas alone was used. There were different explanations for the name, ranging from etymological conjecture (e.g., *pallein,* to brandish, or *pallax,* a virgin) to events from Athena's early history. For one thing, she killed the giant Pallas and used his skin as her aegis. Then there was the story of her girlhood, when she accidentally killed her playmate Pallas and thereafter commemorated her friend by setting her name before her own. The celebrated Trojan Palladium was an image of Pallas Athena, but there were others revered as a pledge of safety to the places in which they existed. [Pindar,

Olympian Odes 5.21; Plato, *Cratylus* 406; Apollodorus 1.6.2; Tzetzes on Lycophron 355.]

PALLAS (2) was a daughter of the river-god Triton. This Triton was commonly thought to be in Libya, but many identified it with a small stream in Boeotia emptying into Lake Copais. Triton brought up Athena along with Pallas. The two girls were fascinated by war games and frequently had playful contests. One such grew into a quarrel, and Athena accidentally killed Pallas. Athena made a wooden image of her and left it in Zeus' keeping. This was the famous Palladium. Athena also honored her friend by joining her name with her own. [Apollodorus 3.12.3; Herodotus 4.180; Pausanias 9.33.7.]

PALLENE (1), or Pallenaea, was a daughter of Sithon, king of the Odomanti in Macedonia. Her sister was Rhoeteia. Pallene was remarkably beautiful and had a number of suitors. Her father, who was probably in love with her himself, invited the contenders for her hand to engage with him in single combat. He invariably overcame them, but finally realized this tactic was not going to produce any grandchildren for him, so he favored one Dryas over the surviving suitors. Pallene had fallen in love with Cleitus, so Sithon allowed the two young men to fight for her. She was not willing to let the contest be decided by a show of strength, since Cleitus might prove the weaker of the two. She prevailed on Persyntes, her teacher, to bribe the charioteer of Dryas to remove the pins from the wheels of his master's chariot. Consequently, Dryas' chariot broke down during the fight, and Cleitus was able to kill him.

Sithon soon learned of his daughter's perfidy and prepared to burn her on the same funeral pyre with the body of Dryas. Just after the torch was applied to the pyre on which Pallene lay bound and screaming, Aphrodite appeared, bringing with her a downpour of rain that extinguished the flames. Sithon thought it well to change his mind, so Pallene and Cleitus were united.

Lest it appear that Pallene did a cruel thing by guaranteeing Dryas' death, it should be pointed out she had little choice. Indications are that Aphrodite would have made Cleitus the victor, but Pallene did not know that. Unlike most Greek women in these circumstances, she took matters into her own hands. She knew it was useless to try to change her father's mind, and she seemed destined to spend her years with a man she did not love (and maybe even despised).

Both the town of Pallene and one of the three Macedonian peninsulas were named for her. [Stephanus Byzantium, "Pallene"; Tzetzes on Lycophron 583,1356; Conon, *Narrations* 10; Parthenius, *Love Stories* 5.]

PALLENE (2) was a daughter of the giant Alcyoneus and one of the so-called ALCYONIDES. [Eustathius on Homer's *Iliad* 776; Suidas, "Alkyonides."]

PALLENIS was a surname of Athena under which she had a temple between Athens and Marathon. Pallene, a celebrated deme of Attica, was involved in three important military operations in the mythological and early history of Athens. The site of the temple has so far not been discovered. [Herodotus 1.62.]

PANACEIA, the All-Healing, was a daughter of Asclepius and Epione. Like her sisters Hygieia, Aegle, and Iaso, she was almost purely personification, having no individual stories about her in mythology. On the other hand, two of her brothers, Machaon and Podaleirius, were involved in flesh-and-blood adventures and even managed to die in the Trojan War. Panaceia shared an altar with Iaso, Hygieia, Aphrodite, and Athena Paeonia in the temple of Amphiaraus at Oropus. [Pausanias 1.34.3.]

PANACHAEA, that is, the Goddess of all the Achaians, occurred as a surname of Demeter at Aegae and of Athena in the precinct of Laphria at Patrae. [Pausanias 7.20.2,24.2.]

PANCRATIS was the beautiful daughter of Iphimedeia and Aloeus in Phthiotian Achaia. Her mother had had an extramarital affair with the god Poseidon, and consequently Pancratis had two half-brothers, the infamous Otus and Ephialtes, the so-called Aloeidae. Aloeus probably never knew they were not his own.

Once, Iphimedeia and Pancratis were attending a celebration of Dionysus on Mount Drius, which probably meant they were drunk and riotous. About that time, a band of Thracian pirates happened upon them and probably concluded that these tipsy women would make excellent wives and lovers on the newly settled island of Strongyle (later Naxos). We will not debate how these men happened to be so far inland at the time. They carried the women, some of whom were probably quite willing, to Strongyle. Pancratis was the prize of the mass abduction, and two of the pirates, Sicelus and Hecetorus, had already killed each other over her possession. Agassamenus, the king of the island, made her his wife and gave Iphimedeia to one of his lieutenants.

Aloeus was not long in sending his stepsons to look for their mother and sister. The Aloeidae found them and made short work of the pirates. They were a little too late, since Pancratis died without ever seeing her homeland again. There is no record of how or why she died. Iphimedeia presumably was reunited with Aloeus. The twins occupied Strongyle and lived there until they were killed by Artemis.

Pancratis seemed to characterize women abducted for their beauty. There is no record that she did anything to change her unfortunate state. Even the intervention of her brothers did not save her from an almost predetermined state of submission. She was characterless but, as is always the case, we have only the barest of accounts. She might even have fallen in love with King Agassamenus. [Diodorus Siculus 5.50; Parthenius, *Love Stories* 19.]

PANDA (*See* EMPANDA)

PANDAEA became the mother of many sons and daughters by Heracles when he visited India. He thus was ancestor of the Indian kings. [Arrian, *Indica* 8,9; Diodorus Siculus 2.39, 17.85,96; Philostratus, *Life of Apollonius of Tyana* 3.46.]

PANDEIA was the daughter of Zeus and Selene, and her sisters were Ersa and Nemea. We know nothing of these three daughters. [*Homeric Hymn to Selene* 32.14; Plutarch, *Table-Talk* 3.]

PANDEMOS, Common to All the People, occurred as a surname of Aphrodite. The name might have described her as the goddess of low sensual pleasure, in contrast to Urania, or the heavenly Aphrodite. Another meaning might have suggested the power of Aphrodite in unifying all the inhabitants of a country into one social or political body. In this respect she was worshipped at Athens along with Peitho (Persuasion), and her worship was said to have been initiated by Theseus when he was trying to unite all the scattered demes into one body of citizens. Aphrodite Pandemos was also worshipped at Megalopolis and Thebes. A festival was held in her honor, and sacrifices to her consisted of white goats. [Plato, *Symposium* 180; Lucretius 4.1067; Pausanias 1.22.3, 6.25.2, 8.32.1, 9.16.2; Lucian, *Dialogues of the Courtesans* 7.]

PANDORA (1) over the centuries has become a kind of equivalent of Eve, the first created woman. Much blame was assigned to both because of a foolish mistake (provided we remove the element of destiny). Pandora, whose name literally meant All Gifts, came into being when Zeus had her created by the master artisan Hephaestus to punish Prometheus for stealing fire from heaven. Right there we have an anomaly, since the theft of fire presupposed an already existing population of the earth. But perhaps only males existed at that point, and Zeus had other ideas for propagation. It is interesting that he saw the creation of a woman as a punishment.

Whatever the reason, Pandora was created as the first woman, and all the gods came forward to endow her with gifts. Aphrodite gave her beauty, Hermes gave her cunning, and other gods and goddesses gave her various powers that Zeus had calculated to bring about the ruin of man. Finally he had Hermes deliver her to Epimetheus, the not-so-bright brother of Prometheus. Epimetheus was utterly charmed by this marvelous creation, although he had been warned by Prometheus never to accept a gift from Zeus. He forgot his promise to his brother to think before acting, because Aphrodite's gift had certainly included the ability of Pandora to give her husband ultimate sexual pleasure.

Life was happy for Pandora and especially so for Epimetheus. But already destiny was at work. In the house was a covered earthen vessel (or box or chest) that either had been placed in the safekeeping of Epimetheus or given to Pandora along with other gifts. In either case it was forbidden to open it. But its unknown contents plagued Pandora (she had been given curiosity along with everything else). One day while Epimetheus was away, she could stand the temptation no longer and peeked into the vessel. She found out soon enough why she should not have opened the pot, for out swarmed all the calamities of mankind—from tidal waves to premature balding. It was too late to stop them as they spread out through the window and across the world. Pandora dropped the lid back in time to prevent the escape of the final occupant of the vessel. This was Elpis, and no matter how bad things became for people then and in the future, there was always hope.

Pandora became the mother of Pyrrha by Epimetheus. Pyrrha married Deucalion, son of Prometheus, and these two people repopulated the earth when Zeus, finally disgusted with man, sent a flood to wipe out the human race. There is no record of Pandora's final history. It is not really certain whether or not she was considered immortal. In later writings she became associated with infernal divinities such as Hecate, Persephone, and the Erinyes.

In one or two versions of the allegory, Pandora brought the fatal vessel to Epimetheus and, using her newly fashioned wiles, prevailed upon him to open it. It is interesting to observe the parallel of this story to that of Eve in the garden of Eden urging Adam to taste the forbidden apple. Some said the vessel contained only benefits for mankind, but these were allowed to escape. In any case, the result was intended to be the same.

The birth of Pandora was represented on the pedestal of the statue of Athena in the Parthenon. [Hesiod, *Theogony* 571, *Works and Days* 30,50,96; Hyginus, *Fables* 142; Apollodorus 1.7.2; Ovid, *Metamorphoses* 1.350; Orphica, *Argonautica* 974.]

PANDORA (2) was a surname of Gaea, the earth, as the giver of all. [Scholiast on Aristophanes' *Birds* 970; Philostratus, *Life of Apollonius of Tyana* 6.39; Hesychius, "Pandora."]

PANDORA (3) was a daughter of Erechtheus and Praxithea. Her brothers were Cecrops, Orneus, Eupalamus, Alcon, Thespius, Metion, and Pandorus. Her sisters were Protogeneia, Procris, Creusa, Oreithyia, Chthonia, and Otionia. Otionia was sacrificed at the direction of an oracle when Eumolpus invaded Athens. Her sisters Protogeneia and Pandora also killed themselves, having once vowed that if one of them should die by violence they would die, too. It has never been clear whether or not Otionia was specifically designated by the oracle for this sacrifice, but when she volunteered, she sealed the fate of her sisters. Even if they had second thoughts, their vow was probably public knowledge and their defection would have brought disgrace on the family and the state. [Apollodorus 3.15.4; Hyginus, *Fables* 46; Suidas, "Parthenoi."]

PANDROSOS was one of the three daughters of Cecrops and Agraulos, and sister of Erysichthon, Herse, and AGRAULOS. According to some, she was the mother of Ceryx by Hermes. Hermes was also the father of Cephalus by Herse, so the two sisters had much in common. Following the part of the story of Cecrops' daughters that has them leaping from the Acropolis, Pandrosos was honored with special ceremonies as a heroine. Her worship was carried out in conjunction with that of Thallo, one of the Horae. Pandrosos was credited with the introduction of spinning. Her name, which for some unaccountable reason means All-Bedewing, is preserved in a street name of modern Athens. [Apollodorus 3.14.2; Pausanias 1.2.6,18.2; Ovid, *Metamorphoses* 2.558; Scholiast on Homer's *Iliad* 1.334; Pollux 8.103.]

PANOPE (1) was one of the NEREIDES. [Homer, *Iliad* 18.45; Hesiod, *Theogony* 250.]

PANOPE (2) was one of the THESPIADES. By Heracles she was the mother of Threpsippas. [Apollodorus 2.7.8.]

PAPHIA was a surname of Aphrodite, derived from the celebrated temple of the goddess at Paphos in Cyprus. [Strabo 14.6.3.]

PAPHOS, sometimes called Amathusa, was the mother of Cinyras by Apollo. That is all we know of her, except that Cinyras named for her the town of Paphos in Cyprus, where he ruled. He was also a priest of the Paphian Aphrodite, and after him the office became hereditary in the family known as the Cinyradae. He was said to have brought the worship of Aphrodite to Cyprus from Cilicia. He married Metharme, a daughter of Pygmalion, and had several children by her. He also committed incest with his daughter and became the father of Adonis. When he committed suicide, his daughters leapt into the sea and were changed to aquatic birds. [Pindar, *Pythian Odes* 2.26; Tacitus, *Histories* 2.3; Hyginus, *Fables* 58,242.]

PARCAE was the name the Romans gave to the MOIRAE, or Fates. [Gellius 3.16.10.]

PAREIA (1) was a surname of Athena, under which she had a statue in Laconia, perhaps so-called from its being made of Parian marble. [Pausanias 3.20.8.]

PAREIA (2) was a nymph on Crete who was loved by Minos. Minos was married to Pasiphae and had several children by her, including Ariadne and Phaedra. His affair with Pareia lasted over several years, and he produced four sons by her: Eurymedon, Nephalion, Chryses, and Philolaus. Unlike most nymphs, Pareia stayed in one place as the mistress of Minos and reared her children. There is no record that they ever appeared in the palace at Cnossus.

When the children were grown they migrated to the island of Paros, which they colonized. One of their cousins, Alcaeus, son of Rhadamanthys, already owned the island. When Heracles stopped at Paros on his way to fetch the girdle of Hippolyte, two members of his crew were killed by the sons of Minos. He immediately killed the brothers and laid siege to the capital city. He replaced the dead crew members with Alcaeus and Sthenelus, sons of Androgeus, who had also been part of the Cretan colony on Paros. No further mention was ever made of their mother. It is doubtful she accompanied her sons to Paros, since a nymph was almost always bound inextricably to her specialized environment. [Apollodorus 3.1.2, 2.5.9.]

PARNASSA was, according to some, the mother of Sinope by Asopus. Others called Sinope's mother METOPE. [Scholiast on Apollonius Rhodius 2.946.]

PARTHENIA (1) was a surname of Artemis, which designated her as a virgin. It was also a surname of Hera, but in her case it was probably derived from the Parthenius River in Samos, which, according to some, was her birthplace. [Callimachus, *Hymn to Artemis* 110; Scholiast on Apollonius Rhodius 1.187.]

PARTHENIA (2) was the wife of Samus, from whom the island of Samos was anciently called Parthenia. Samus, son of Ancaeus and Samia, was the eponymic founder of Samos. It is interesting to see that the island was called Parthenia before it was called Samos. Parthenia was almost certainly a nymph, which means she could have been on the island for decades before the arrival of Samus. There was also a Parthenius River near the temple of Hera. [Strabo 14.1.15.]

PARTHENIA (3) was one of the mares of Marmax, the first suitor of Hippodameia. She and her companion Eripha were butchered by Oenomaus and buried with their master. The Parthenias River in Elis was named for her. [Pausanias 6.21.7.]

PARTHENIA (4) was one of the PLEIADES. [Scholiast on Theocritus 13.25.]

PARTHENOPE (1) was the daughter of Stymphalus. He was one of the sons of Elatus and the eponymic hero of the town of Stymphalus in Peloponnesus. Parthenope's brothers were Agamedes, Gortys, and Agelaus. Stymphalus and his sons successfully defended Arcadia against Pelops, but Pelops pretended to observe a truce and treacherously murdered Stymphalus.

Stymphalus was also called the father of the Stymphalian birds, which from the original few had grown to vast numbers. Heracles was sent on one of his labors to exterminate these voracious birds. While he was in Stymphalus, he seduced

Parthenope. From this union came Eueres, about whom nothing further is known. [Apollodorus 2.7.8, 3.9.1; Pausanias 8.4.3,22.1.]

PARTHENOPE (2) was a daughter of Ancaeus and Samia. Ancaeus was a son of Poseidon and Astypalaea, and king of the Leleges on the island of Samos. Samia was a daughter of the Maeander River in the Troad. Parthenope was loved by Apollo, by whom she became the mother of Lycomedes. Unfortunately there are no further references either to mother or son. [Pausanias 7.4.2; Callimachus, *Hymn to Delos* 50.]

PARTHENOPE (3) was one of the SIRENS. At Naples her tomb was shown, and a torch race was held every year in her honor. [Tzetzes on Lycophron 732; Scholiast on Homer's *Odyssey* 12.39; Aristotle, *On Marvelous Things Heard* 103.]

PARTHENOPE (4) was loved by Oceanus, by whom she became the mother of Europa and Thrace. Her daughters were eponymous heroines of the vast contrasting areas of northern and southern Greece. [Tzetzes on Lycophron 894.]

PARTHENOS (1), the Virgin, was a surname of Athena at Athens, where the famous Parthenon was dedicated to her. [Pausanias 1.24.5,2, 8.41.5,10.34.]

PARTHENOS (2) was the daughter of Staphylus and Chrysothemis. Her sisters were Rhoeo and MOLPADIA.

PASIPHAE (1) provided the most bizarre story in Greek mythology. It was as though she was born to commit the most outrageous act we can think of; certainly her family history made her the perfect candidate. Her father was Helios, the sun, whose progeny were Aeetes, Perses, Circe, and Pasiphae, all in one way or another endowed with strange powers and dark passions. Even the children of these individuals, such as Medea and Phaedra, continued the gloomy heritage. It is ironic that the sun should produce such forbidding offspring.

Pasiphae married Minos, who by that time was king of Crete. Minos had claimed the throne when his father died; as confirmation of his right he prayed that a bull would appear from the sea, which he vowed to sacrifice. The beautiful white bull that appeared was so magnificent that Minos had an alternate sacrifice made and kept the marvelous animal. This angered Poseidon, who had sent the bull, and in time he exacted an awesome revenge.

Pasiphae bore several children to Minos—Androgeus, Catreus, Deucalion, Glaucus, Acacallis, Xenodice, Ariadne, and Phaedra. During this time she also bore another child, one who gave Crete an evil reputation and, in effect, brought about the ruin of the empire. Poseidon caused Pasiphae to fall in love with the beautiful bull he had obligingly sent from the sea as a token of Minos' sovereignty.

Pasiphae was struck by the obsessive notion that she wanted to be penetrated by the spectacular beast. She had at her disposal the gifted artisan Daedalus, who had fled from Athens because of his wanton murder of his nephew. Pasiphae knew she could trust this man, whose record was already tainted, since by a word she could have him deported or tortured and killed. So Daedalus had no choice. He was ordered to arrange the means by which Pasiphae could satisfy her lust with the gigantic animal. After much pondering he fashioned for her an artificial cow into which she could be concealed except for her exposed vagina.

Coupling with animals was no new thing. For years the gods had changed themselves into everything from ants to horses to achieve their amorous ends. Some had changed their women into various creatures and had sex with them in human form. Always, though, the pairing was with a woman and a smaller animal, or temporary metamorphosis took place to allow for biological compatibility. Pasiphae was ambitious. It was as though she sought to outstrip everyone who had explored the uncertain territory of human/animal relations.

The fateful night arrived. The artificial cow seemed to graze in a field. The great bull caught the scent of expectation on the wind and enthusiastically performed the destined activity. The building of the cow and the brutal coupling have been graphically described in the modern novel *The Maze Maker* by Michael Ayrton (New York: Holt, Rinehart and Winston, Inc., 1967).

From this unlikely union the famous Minotaur was born. This creature was half-bull and half-man, and from an early age showed a preference for human flesh. Minos was horrified by this grotesque being and probably would have destroyed it except for his fear of Poseidon, whose power he no longer doubted. He might also have destroyed Pasiphae, but he feared his father-in-law. The subsequent fate of Pasiphae is not known. It is likely that all the normal children of Pasiphae and Minos had already been born, since sexual relations with his wife must have been unthinkable after her supreme consummation.

Pasiphae did survive, we know. She put a curse on Minos, who had, after all, been the cause of her terrible lust. Whenever he had sexual relations he ejaculated serpents, scorpions, and poisonous insects, thus killing his partners. Even though Minos was aware of Daedalus' role in the scandalous affair, he had him build the celebrated labyrinth in which to house the monster, an endeavor that took several years. It was during this time that Minos declared war on Attica for the mysterious death of his and Pasiphae's son Androgeus. In time Attica had to pay a tribute, which consisted of sending periodically a certain number of youths and maidens to Crete to be locked into the labyrinth with the voracious Minotaur. Daedalus and his son Icarus were also locked in the labyrinth but apparently out of reach of the dreadful creature. Pasiphae felt responsible for Daedalus and tried to help him escape. Finally, on his own he constructed wings of feathers and wax for himself and his son, and they flew out of the labyrinth. Icarus flew too near the sun (Helios still had his revenge), his wings melted, and he fell into the sea. Daedalus escaped and flew to Sicily.

After that we hear of Pasiphae no more. Her children came mostly to unhappy ends. Minos himself, going in pursuit of Daedalus, was killed when he located him in Sicily. Pasiphae was immortal, to what degree we do not know. Some confused her with an oracular goddess at Thalamae. [Apollodorus 1.9.1, 3.1.2; Apollonius Rhodius 3.999; Ovid, *Metamor-*phoses 15.501; Cicero, *On the Nature of the Gods* 3.19; Pausanias 5.25.9.]

PASIPHAE (2) was an oracular goddess at Thalamae in Laconia. It is not at all clear who this goddess was. Her statue with that of Helios was in the sanctuary of Ino on the road between Oetylus and Thalamae. Some said she was one of the daughters of Atlas and that by Zeus she had a son called Ammon. Others said she was a deified Cassandra, daughter of Priam, who was said to have died at Thalamae. Still others said she was Daphne, daughter of Amyclas, who fled from Apollo and was turned into a laurel. Whichever one she was, her oracles were believed and followed, and were patronized by the kings of Sparta. People slept in her temple in order to receive revelations in dreams. [Plutarch, *Agis* 9; Cicero, *On Divination* 1.43.]

PASIPHAE (3) was one of the OCEANIDES. (Hyginus, *Fables: Preface* 6.]

PASITHEA (1) was one of the CHARITES. [Homer, *Iliad* 14.268,276; Pausanias 9.35.1.]

PASITHEA (2) was one of the NEREIDES. [Hesiod, *Theogony* 247.]

PASITHEA (3) was the wife of Erechtheus (II) and mother of Pandion. More often she was called PRAXITHEA. [Apollodorus 3.14.6.]

PASITHOE was one of the OCEANIDES. [Hesiod, *Theogony* 352.]

PATELLA, or Patellana, was a Roman divinity described as opening the stem on a stalk of wheat so that the ears might come forth and develop. It has been suggested that Patella might have been a surname of Ops. [St. Augustine, *City of God* 4.8; Arnobius, *Adversus Nationes* 4.1.]

PATRO was one of the THESPIADES and mother of Archemachus by Heracles. [Apollodorus 2.7.8.]

PAX was the personification of peace. She was worshipped at Rome, and a festival was celebrated annually in her honor. She shared this festival with Salus, the goddess of health and public welfare, and with Concordia and Janus. These observances took place on April 30. Pax had a magnificent temple built by Vespasian. Her Greek counterpart was Eirene. [Ovid, *Fasti* 1.711, 3.881; Juvenal 1.115; Pliny, *Natural History* 36.5; Gellius 16.8; Suetonius, *Vespasian* 9.]

PEDIAS was the daughter of Mynes (or of Menys) of Lacedaemon. She became the wife of Cranaus, who many claimed was an autochthon. He was a king in Athens, and Pedias bore to him three daughters: Cranae, Cranaechme, and Atthis. Atthis is commonly considered the origin of the name of Attica. Nothing further is known of Cranaechme. Cranae married Amphictyon, the son of Deucalion. The marriage was most likely for political reasons, because Amphictyon shortly usurped the kingdom of Cranaus. Since Pausanias saw the tomb of Cranaus at Lamptra, it seems rather evident that he and Pedias went there in exile. Pedias was not mentioned again, but there is no reason to doubt that she was also buried at Lamptra. [Apollodorus 3.14.5; Plutarch, *Themistocles* 14; Stephanus Byzantium, "Pedias."]

PEDILE was one of the HYADES. [Hyginus, *Poetic Astronomy* 2.21; Hesychius, "Pedile."]

PEGAEAE were nymphs of springs. [Orphica, *Hymns* 51.6.]

PEGASIDES was a name sometimes applied to the Muses. This association is clear enough. Pegasus, the famous winged horse, pawed the ground and produced the Hippocrene fountain, which was from that time sacred to the Muses. Nymphs of springs and brooks were also called Pegasides. [Moschus 3.78; Ovid, *Tristia* 3.7.15, *Heroides* 15.27; Propertius 3.1.19; Quintus Smyrnaeus 3.301.]

PEIRENE was a daughter of the river-god Achelous. She was loved by Poseidon, by whom she became the mother of Leches and Cenchrias, who were probably twins. Cenchrias was accidentally killed by Artemis, but we have no details of this event. The spring of Peirene at Corinth was said to have been formed by Peirene's tears

over his death. The two port cities of Corinth, Lechaeum and Cenchreae, were named for the sons of Peirene. Peirene was called by some the daughter of Oebalus of Sparta, but in view of her relationship with Poseidon, harbors, and springs, Achelous as her father was more appropriate. Others called her a daughter of the Asopus River and the nymph Metope, daughter of the Ladon River. [Pausanias 2.2.3,3.2,24.7, 3.1.3,15.7.]

PEISIDICE (1) was a daughter of Aeolus and Enarete, one of five daughters. She had eight brothers, who for the most part were founders of extensive families. Peisidice married Myrmidon. Her husband had a curious parentage. Zeus had disguised himself as an ant and crawled under the clothing of Eurymedusa, daughter of Cleitus. By some incredible feat of potency he impregnated her, and she bore Myrmidon, who was regarded as the ancestor of the Myrmidons in Thessaly.

Peisidice became by Myrmidon the mother of Antiphus and Actor. Nothing is known of Antiphus. Actor succeeded Myrmidon as king of Phthia, and was father of Eurytion and Philomela. It was the kingdom of Phthia into which Achilles was born. [Apollodorus 1.7.3; Apollonius Rhodius 1.56; Eustathius on Homer's *Iliad* 320; Clement of Alexandria, *Exhortation to the Greeks* 34.]

PEISIDICE (2) was one of the PELIADES. [Apollodorus 1.9.10.]

PEISIDICE (3) was a daughter of Nestor and Eurydice. Nestor was the famous hero of Pylus whose adventures spanned three generations. He led battles against the Epeians over several years. He killed the giant Eurythalion in Arcadia. He participated in the battle between the Lapiths and Centaurs, was a member of the crew of the Argonaut, and was a Calydonian hunter. He finally went to Troy with 60 ships, where he acted as mentor on several occasions. Peisidice had seven brothers, the most famous of whom was Antilochus, who was killed in the Trojan War. Her sister was Polycaste; she later produced a son by Odysseus' son Telemachus, who had come to Nestor's court in search of news about his father. Peisidice is a mystery. All we know is her name and, as usual, we can speculate that she died young. [Apollodorus 1.9.9; Homer, *Odyssey* 3.413,452,464, 11.285.]

PEISIDICE (4) was a daughter of the king of Methymna in Lesbos. When Achilles raided the islands off the coast of the mainland of Asia Minor during the Trojan War, the inhabitants of Methymna held out against him very well, and it looked as if he might have to leave them unconquered. Peisidice, however, had watched Achilles from the walls and fallen in love with him. She sent her nurse with a message that she would arrange for him to gain entrance to the city if he would marry her. Achilles was so surprised that he agreed to the terms. When Peisidice received the word, she managed to have the gates unbarred, so shortly the city was overrun with Greek soldiers. She was forced to see the result of her treasonable action. Men young and old were put to the sword, and the women enslaved. The bitter irony was that Achilles was contemptuous of anyone who could thus betray her country, and he signaled his men to stone her to death.

Peisidice was foolish in more ways than one. She was taking a chance on a man she knew only by sight. What she took to be love was infatuation and lust, and under the best circumstances she might have found Achilles impossible to live with. She knew what the fate of her family and friends would be when she made the fatal deal with the hero. As bad as she was, however, Achilles proved himself less than honorable for not keeping his part of the bargain, regardless of how appalled he was over her action. Peisidice worked on the principle that anything is fair in love, and Achilles on the one that anything is fair in war. [Parthenius, *Love Stories* 21.]

PEISINOE was one of the SIRENS. [Tzetzes on Lycophron 712.]

PEITHO (1) was the personification of persuasion. As with other abstract beings, her parentage was indefinite. Some claimed she was a daughter of Ate, or a sister of Tyche or Eunomia. She was one of the attendants of Aphrodite. At Athens, where Theseus had introduced her worship, the

statues of Peitho and Aphrodite Pandemos stood close together, and at Megara the statue of Peitho stood in the temple of Aphrodite. Peitho was also counted as one of the Gamelii, or divinities who protected marriage.

Pure personification that she was, she nevertheless was credited with two children, neither of them appropriate to her, however, and ascribed to others by most writers. Eros made love to her, and they became parents of Hygieia, who is almost invariably called the daughter of Asclepius. By Pan she was said to have given birth to Iynx. The mother of Iynx was nearly always called Echo. The Roman name for the goddess of persuasion was Suada, sometimes Suadela. [Herodotus 8.111; Pausanias 1.22.3,43.6, 2.7.7; Pindar, *Nemean Odes* 8.1; Horace, *Epistles* 1.6.38; Dionysius Chrysostomus, *Orations* 7.568.]

PEITHO (2) was one of the CHARITES. [Pausanias 9.35.1.]

PEITHO (3) was one of the OCEANIDES. [Hesiod, *Theogony* 349.]

PEITHO (4), also called Cerdo or Teledice, was the first wife of Phoroneus. He was a son of the Inachus River and the Oceanid Melia, and ruler of Peloponnesus. He was the first to offer sacrifices to Hera at Argos, and he united the people into a city. His tomb was shown at Argos. Peitho's son by him was Car, who became king of Megara. The citadel of Megara was called Caria after him, and his tomb was shown on the road from Megara to Corinth. One commentator, as if to complicate an already difficult genealogy, called Peitho the mother of Aegialeus and Apia, but it was commonly accepted that Aegialeus was the brother of Phoroneus. Apia obviously resulted from a confusion with Apis, the son of Phoroneus by Laodice, from whom Peloponnesus was originally called Apia. [Scholiast on Euripides' *Orestes* 920; Hyginus, *Fables* 143; Apollodorus 2.1.1; Pausanias 2.19.5.]

PEITHO (5) was the wife of Argus, son of Zeus and Niobe. Usually she was called EUADNE. [Apollodorus 2.1.1.]

PEITHO (6), Persuasion, was a surname of Aphrodite, whose worship was introduced at Athens by Theseus when he was in the process of unifying the various communities into towns. Peitho was also a surname of Artemis. At Argos was a sanctuary of Artemis Peitho, founded by Hypermnestra after she won the trial to which she was brought by her father for saving her husband's life during the mass murder committed by the Danaides. [Apollodorus 2.21.2; Pausanias 1.22.3.]

PELARGE was the daughter of Potnieus. Potnieus, one of Apollo's lovers, was the founder of Potniae in Boeotia. Pelarge married Isthmides, and the two established the Cabeirian mysteries at Cabeiraea near Thebes. At the time of the invasion of Thebes by the Epigoni, the mysteries at Cabeiraea had to be suspended, and Pelarge and her husband transferred them to a place called Alexiarus. This place was not considered sacred, however, and the worship moved back to the Theban site as soon as possible. For her services, the priests, in accordance with an oracle from Dodona, established various honors for her. [Pausanias 9.25.7,8.]

PELASGA, Pelasgis, or the Pelasgian (Woman or Goddess) was a surname of Hera at Iolcus in Thessaly. It was also a surname of Demeter, who had a temple under this name at Argos. The name was said to have come from Pelasgus, the son of Triopas, who founded the sanctuary. [Apollonius Rhodius 1.14, with the scholiast; Propertius 2.28.11; Pausanias 11.22.2.]

PELEIA was the wife of Melus, a Delian, who for one reason or another fled to Cinyras in Cyprus. Cinyras accepted him virtually as a son, giving him his own son Adonis as a companion. He also gave him Peleia, a relative, in marriage. The couple soon had a son, whom they called Melus after his father. When Adonis was killed, the older Melus hanged himself from grief over Adonis, and Peleia hanged herself from grief over both. Aphrodite changed Melus into an apple tree and Peleia into a dove. The younger Melus was commanded by the goddess to return with a colony to Delos, where he founded the town of Delos. [Servius on Virgil's Eclogues 8.37.]

PELIADES were the daughters of Pelias. Pelias and Neleus were the twin sons of Poseidon by Tyro, the wife of Cretheus. Their half-brothers were Pheres, Amythaon, and Aeson, the father of Jason. Pelias and Neleus fought for the rule of Thessaly, and Neleus was driven out. Pelias became king in Iolcus, and his half-brothers withdrew from any competition for power. Pelias married Anaxibia, daughter of Bias, and became by her the father of Acastus, Peisidice, Pelopeia, Hippothoe, Alcestis, Medusa, Amphinome, Euadne, Asteropeia, and Antinoe.

While Jason was in Colchis, where Pelias had sent him (believing thus to be rid of him for good), Pelias killed Aeson and later Promachus, Jason's young brother. Jason's mother hanged herself. When Jason returned and learned the terrible news, he knew he had to proceed with caution against the ruthless man, and pretended to believe his family had died by means other than murder by his uncle.

Medea, Jason's wife, took care of the program of revenge, contriving a magic trick to accomplish her purpose. She chatted with the daughters of Pelias and impressed them with tales of enchantment from Colchis. She said she had a rare old recipe for making older people young again and that she could even return their father to vigorous youth. When they expressed disbelief, she said she could easily demonstrate. She found an old ram, dismembered it, and threw its dissected body into a cauldron of boiling water. To this pot she added some strange-looking herbs, and before long out from the cauldron leapt a frisky lamb. The daughters were speechless at this awesome feat, and when they had recovered their voices they urged Medea to apply this process to Pelias.

Some said Pelias observed the miracle of the ram and lamb and consented to the transformation. Medea lulled him to sleep and then ordered the daughters to dismember their father. Alcestis refused to join in this gruesome enterprise, but the others proceeded. Medea threw the parts into the cauldron, but the only yield was a thin broth from Pelias' meaty joints. Medea made her escape before the awful truth struck the sisters.

Jason appeared then and explained to the populace the reason for the terrible vengeance. Technically he was now in charge of the kingdom, which had been usurped from his father and uncles, but he consigned the rule to Pelias' son Acastus, who had been one of his company on the Argonaut. Acastus said that his sisters were his responsibility. He gave Alcestis in marriage to Admetus, his cousin. He arranged for Amphinome to marry Andraemon, son of the Lapith Coronus, and for Euadne to marry Canes, son of Cephalus of Phocis. Pelopeia, it appears, had been visited by Ares and was mother of Cycnus. She might have been gone from Iolcus by the time of the foregoing events. The remaining daughters were exiled from Iolcus and ended their days in Mantineia in Arcadia, where their tombs were shown. [Euripides, *Medea* 9; Hyginus, *Fables* 24; Pausanias 8.11.2; Diodorus Siculus 4.52.]

PELLONIA was a Roman divinity who was believed to assist mortals in warding off their enemies. [St. Augustine, *City of God* 4.21; Arnobius, *Adversus Nationes* 4.4.]

PELOPEIA (1) was one of the PELIADES. She was perhaps the oldest of the sisters and was gone from Iolcus when Jason returned from the Argonaut. She was loved by Ares and became the mother of Cycnus. Cycnus figured in one of the stories about Heracles. When the hero came to Itonus in Phthiotis, he met Cycnus, the king, who offered a prize to anyone who would duel with him. He was in the habit of robbing wayfarers and offering sacrifices to Ares with the money thus acquired. Heracles, of course, made short work of him. Pelopeia most likely lived with her son and consequently might not have participated in the grisly mutilation of her father. [Apollodorus 2.7.7; Hesiod, *Shield of Heracles* 58,345.]

PELOPEIA (2) was a daughter of Amphion and NIOBE. [Apollodorus 3.5.6.]

PELOPEIA (3) played a most unhappy role in the tragic history of the house of Pelops, whose granddaughter she was. She was the daughter of Thyestes, who with his brother Atreus had fled to Mycenae after murdering their half-brother Chrysippus. There they raised families and vied for the throne vacated by their nephew Eurystheus. Thyestes seduced Aerope, the wife of Atreus, and almost succeeded in acquiring the throne with her assistance. Atreus acquired the sovereignty and punished Thyestes in the most hideously cruel way imaginable. He killed the sons of Thyestes, served their flesh to him, and then revealed what he had done. In grief and terror Thyestes fled to King Thesprotus in Epeirus, where Pelopeia lived and served as a priestess of Athena. She happened to be in Sicyon at the time, perhaps officiating at a special sacrifice to Athena. Thyestes learned from one of the Thesprotian oracles that the only way to avenge himself on his brother would be to have incest with his own daughter. He promptly left for Sicyon, found Pelopeia cleansing herself in a stream from the blood of a sacrifice, and in disguise raped her. Thyestes hastily departed, leaving his sword behind. Pelopeia carried this painful reminder with her when she returned to Thesprotia. Thyestes meanwhile departed to Lydia to escape any further harm from Atreus.

Atreus had been advised by an oracle to seek Thyestes in order to be absolved from the murder of the children. He went to Thesprotia on his search but found that Thyestes had left there. He fell in love with Pelopeia, whom he thought to be the daughter of the king. Thesprotus agreed to their marriage, afraid to reveal that she was the daughter of Thyestes or that Pelopeia was pregnant by a stranger from Sicyon. Atreus took her back to Mycenae. When a boy was born to Pelopeia, she exposed him, but he was found by shepherds and suckled by a goat. Atreus eventually learned about the child and adopted him. He named the boy Aegisthus from his having been suckled by a goat. It is not clear whether Atreus connected the child with Pelopeia's pregnancy. She more than likely managed to pass off the disappearance of her baby as a stillbirth. When Aegisthus was older, she gave him the sword she had taken from her rapist. It is not known how she explained she happened to have it.

Thyestes was found finally and taken back to Mycenae, where Atreus sought to put an end to him for once and all. He sent the very young Aegisthus to the cell in which Thyestes was imprisoned, with instructions to kill him. As the boy was about to plunge the sword into him, Thyestes recognized it as his own. He asked Aegisthus where he got the weapon, and the boy said his mother had given it to him. Thyestes asked to see Pelopeia; thinking she would finally learn something about the strange past occurrence, she came to the cell. When she heard the story of the sword and simultaneously recognized her father, she at once took the sword and plunged it into her bosom.

Aegisthus refused to kill his real father (and grandfather as well) and slew Atreus instead, having learned the horrible sequence of events in the accursed family. He and Thyestes jointly ruled Mycenae until Agamemnon overthrew them to become the most powerful king in Greece.

With a story as complex as that of Pelopeia, there were of course many variations and discrepancies. Her mother was never named. The murdered young sons of Thyestes were born from concubines, so a legitimate wife was implied. Atreus must have known of a daughter of his brother, since in their early career they were joint rulers at Midea. Nothing ever explained why Pelopeia went to the court of King Thesprotus. She must have been sent there as a tiny child, since otherwise she would have recognized Atreus as her uncle. It is almost as if she were an invention by later writers to intensify the horrible warfare between the brothers. The events surrounding the birth of Aegisthus are muddled. Did Pelopeia manage to conceal her pregnancy or pass off the unwanted child as a stillbirth? Unless she thoroughly despised this product of rape, she could have claimed premature delivery and passed the child off as the son of Atreus. How did she feel when Atreus rescued the exposed infant? Obviously she recognized it as her own, since she gave the boy the sword left by her attacker. She undoubtedly was unacquainted with the murder of her half-brothers. She was an adult and far away when this event occurred. Some said Thyestes did not realize Pelopeia was his daughter when he raped her. This would subtract dramatic impact. It would also mean the event would have taken place in the dark or that Thyestes was so disguised that nobody could recognize him. However, there is no certainty that he would have been recognized by Pelopeia

under any circumstances, since we have no way of knowing Thyestes ever saw her after she was sent while very young to Thesprotia. [Apollodorus 2.4.6, *Epitome* 2.10–15; Hyginus, *Fables* 88,253; Ovid, *Ibis* 359; Scholiast on Euripides' *Orestes* 14; Aelian, *Various Narratives* 12.42.]

PEMPHREDO, or Pephredo, was one of the GRAEAE. [Hesiod, *Theogony* 273; Apollodorus 2.4.2.]

PENELOPE would probably get the vote as the most admirable woman in mythology. Her sterling quality was evident long before the Trojan War—as soon as she met Odysseus, in fact. She was a daughter of Icarius and Polycaste, daughter of Lygaeus. Icarius and Tyndareus had fled to Acarnania when Hippocoon usurped the kingdom at Sparta. Heracles restored Tyndareus. Some said Icarius remained in Acarnania, where he married Polycaste and became father of Alyzeus, Leucadius, and Penelope. Others said he returned to Sparta, married Periboea, and became father of Thoas, Damasippus, Imeusimus, Aletes, Perileus, and Penelope. In the *Odyssey,* another daughter, Iphthime, was mentioned. In many ways it is easier to accept the second version, since later events made Sparta a more likely setting.

When Penelope grew up, Icarius promised his beautiful and sought-after daughter to anyone who could conquer him in a footrace. Odysseus won the race and thus won Penelope. A better story is that Tyndareus intervened with Icarius on Odysseus' account because Odysseus had been the author of the famous oath concerning the honor of Helen, the daughter of Tyndareus. Icarius might have deliberately lost the race to the young suitor. After the marriage, Icarius urged the couple to remain near him, probably offering whatever share in the kingdom he possessed. Odysseus said no, and with Penelope started to leave. Icarius followed and asked to hear how Penelope felt about the decision. She did not answer but merely dropped her veil over her face; this signified that she would follow her husband. Icarius built a statue of Modesty on the spot.

Penelope had only one child by Odysseus (although one writer added another son, Arcesilaus, or Acusilaus, about whom nothing else was mentioned, and others claimed that still another son, Poliporthes, was born after Odysseus returned to Ithaca following the war), and this was somewhat uncommon. Helen did not elope until about seven years after her marriage to Menelaus, so Odysseus was at home minding the affairs of Ithaca, and five or six children might have been possible. The son was named Telemachus. Actually, Telemachus was born after Odysseus and Penelope had been married for about seven years. In spite of his expansive gesture in behalf of Helen and the husband she selected, Odysseus was not ready to go to war for her. He was happily married, had finally managed to father a son, and was held in high esteem in Ithaca, where he ruled. But Palamedes, Menelaus, and Agamemnon came searching for him. He feigned madness by hitching an ass with an ox and plowing a field. Palamedes saw through his scheme and stopped the charade by placing the infant Telemachus in front of the plow. So Odysseus was forced to participate in the war, to which from that point he gave his full attention.

Penelope was left to deal with running the kingdom. Her father-in-law was too old, and those left in charge were not fully effective. Nevertheless, she managed, and during the war the problems of state and the rearing of Telemachus helped keep her busy enough to endure the absence of her beloved husband.

It was after the war ended and most of the surviving Greeks returned home that Penelope's troubles began. She was still exceedingly beautiful at the age of 35 or so. Her beauty was enhanced by the kingdom she held, and when word got around that Odysseus had left Troy and not been heard of since, over a hundred suitors started arriving from Dulichium, Same, Zacynthus, and Ithaca itself. This pursuit more than likely culminated in the two or three years before Odysseus' return. Homer gave the number of suitors as 108. Apollodorus said 136. At first these suitors kept a respectful distance, but eventually, as the prospects of the return of Odysseus grew slimmer and slimmer, they moved into the palace and wined and dined on

Penelope's dwindling resources. This wanton waste and flagrant violation of the laws of hospitality continued for years, and Penelope was faced with the almost insuperable task of putting off their importunity. There was no one of them she would have chosen under any circumstances, but she knew that, like other women in her position, she might have to make a choice. The choice would have to be among those from:

ITHACA: Amphialus, Amphimachus, Amphimedon, Antinous, Aristratus, Ctesippus, Dulicheus, Eurynomus, Helenus, Liodes, Promachus, Pronous

DULICHIUM: Acamas, Acarnan, Agenor, Agerochus, Agrius, Amphimachus, Amphinomus, Andraemon, Antigonus, Antimachus, Argius, Astylochus, Bias, Calydoneus, Ceraus, Clymenus, Clytius, Ctesius, Cycnus, Damastor, Demoptolemus, Diopithes, Echion, Euenorides, Euryalus, Eurypylus, Glaucus, Hagius, Hellanicus, Iphidamas, Lamas, Lestorides, Marpsius, Mecisteus, Medon, Megasthenes, Meneptolemus, Nicomachus, Ormenius, Paralus, Periphron, Philodemus, Polyidus, Polypoetes, Promus, Pseras, Ptolemaeus, Pylaemenes, Schedius, Telmius, Thersilochus, Thoas, Thrasymede

ZACYNTHUS: Agenor, Alcarops, Andromedes, Antenor, Archestratus, Barthas, Celtus, Clytius, Daemon, Daesenor, Euenorides, Euryalus, Eurylochus, Halius, Hippomachus, Indius, Indius, Laodicus, Laomedes, Laomedon, Leiocritus, Magnes, Minis, Molebus, Nisas, Nissaeus, Oloetrochus, Ormenus, Pellas, Periallus, Periclymenus, Periphas, Phrenius, Phrenius, Polybus, Polybus, Polydorus, Pronomus, Stratius, Thadytius, Theophron

SAME: Agelaus, Antisthenes, Archemolus, Cerberus, Clytius, Ctesippus, Cynnus, Elatus, Eteoneus, Eumelus, Eurystratus, Hippodochus, Hyperenor, Itanus, Ithacus, Lyammus, Lycaethus, Perimedes, Pheroetes, Pisander, Pisenor, Prothous, Thriasus

(The list has been reproduced here mainly because it has hardly ever been made available in an English-language reference work. The names are also interesting as examples of what Greek parents named their sons in those days. There are certain repetitions of names, even among the suitors from a single island, and this suggests there might have been faddish names even in ancient times. On the other hand, the repetition could be a result of the close kindredship of people on the islands, where the combination of a given name and a surname might make two men indistinguishable in address.)

Penelope hit on a plan to forestall the suitors. She could not plead with the least degree of certainty that Odysseus would return, so she had to use another tactic. She said she was weaving a shroud for her father-in-law, Laertes, and that when it was done she would make a choice from among the impatient suitors. So by day she wove, and at night she unraveled what she had done. This subterfuge, she was aware, could last only so long. There was also the frightening possibility that Laertes could ruin everything by suddenly dying.

The suitors, mostly young men, were gullible, fortunately, and they were having the time of their lives. Has anyone ever really looked at them closely? Were they really as bad as painted or merely an assortment of spoiled young men out for a free ride? They could not all have been wealthy, and during the time they importuned Penelope, some must have had obligations to keep their own property in order. So most likely the scene at Penelope's palace was a drop-in situation, with an especially large weekend crowd (since there must have been an equivalent of our day or so off each week for rest and relaxation). There was also the matter of peer pressure. It was perhaps considered almost socially negligent not to join one's fellows and swap stories about women and what they would do with Penelope if they were the lucky one. It did not matter that she was nearly old enough to be the mother of many of the men.

In fact, Telemachus, by now around 19, had been pushed around by some of these contemporaries, and began a series of trips to find out what he could about Odysseus. If anyone could tell him anything, especially if there was proof his father was dead, at least some kind of plans could be laid. The present situation was totally untenable.

Penelope showed herself periodically, mainly to keep the men under some kind of control. She must have envisioned their battering their way into her bedroom and gang-raping her. Some of them probably had been appointed to inspect the progress of her work on the shroud. So time went on. To bring her comfort, Athena once appeared to Penelope in a dream disguised as her sister Iphthime, but even then did not reveal the fate of Odysseus. There was also a curious story that Nauplius, in order to avenge the murder of his son Palamedes by Odysseus and others, had spread the rumor that Odysseus had been killed at Troy. Penelope was reported to have attempted suicide but was saved by ducks. Her name up until then, so some writers claimed, was Ameirace, but it was changed to reflect the nature of her rescuers.

The day finally came when there was a report of a stranger having arrived on Ithaca, but Odysseus did not yet reveal himself to Penelope. With the help of Telemachus, Athena, and servants who had remained loyal, he slaughtered the suitors one and all, along with the servants who had taken the part of the interlopers. Penelope's decision, proposed by Odysseus but announced by her, had come down to the choice of any person who could wield the bow of Odysseus that hung in the great hall. Afterward, he revealed himself, and the reunion was a blissful one.

This bliss could not last long. First, Odysseus had to deal with the irate relatives of the slain suitors. Athena, as usual, came to his rescue. From that time on, life settled down, and later adventures had to be invented by post-Homeric writers. It was time, of course, for the iconoclasts to come forward in attempts to discredit the long-suffering and thoroughly admirable Penelope. Some related that Penelope had sex with Hermes and produced Pan. Others, trying to excel in outrageous claims, said she was impregnated by all the suitors and thus produced Pan. For this reason Odysseus was said to have expelled her from Ithaca; from there she went to Sparta and then Mantineia, where her tomb was shown. One version even went so far as to say

Odysseus killed her for infidelity with one of the suitors.

Then there was the story of Odysseus' infidelity with Euippe, when he went to Epeirus to consult an oracle. From this union a son, Euryalus, was born, and when he was grown he was sent to Ithaca by his mother with tokens by which his father would recognize him. Knowing of the affair, Penelope received Euryalus while Odysseus was away. On his return, without identifying the youth, she persuaded him to kill the young man on the charge that he had come to rob them. Although she could be said to have been protecting the interests of her own son, her act was heartless and certainly uncharacteristic of a woman with the reputation of unsurpassed purity.

Odysseus was killed by another of his illegitimate sons, Telegonus, whom Circe had borne to him. For some reason Odysseus' body was carried by Telemachus, Telegonus, and Penelope to Aeaea, where they buried him. Telemachus married Cassiphone, the daughter of Circe, and Penelope married Telegonus, her stepson and killer of her beloved husband. This made her also the daughter-in-law of her husband's ex-lover. She bore to Telegonus a son, Italus, who later founded the towns of Tusculum and Praeneste. So it went with the soap-operalike additions, with Circe finally packing the unlikely couple off to dwell in immortal bliss in the Isles of the Blessed.

Over the years Penelope has come to symbolize the virtuous wife, prevailing over the wicked forces that would seek to corrupt loyalty to husband, home, and family. It was inevitable that inventive and possibly perverted writers would assail this image of perfection. [Homer, *Odyssey* 1.329, 2.121, 11.447, 17.103, 21.158, 23.205, 24.192; Apollodorus 3.10.6, *Epitome* 3.7, 7.26; Propertius 2.9.5, 3.12.23; Euripides, *Orestes* 588; Ovid, *Heroides* 1.83, *Tristia* 5.14; Lycophron 772; Tzetzes on Lycophron 805; Cicero, *On the Nature of the Gods* 3.22; Pausanias 3.1.4,12.1,20.10, 8.12.3,15; Hyginus, *Fables* 127; Plutarch, *Greek Questions* 48,302.]

PENETRALIS was an epithet given to the divinities at Rome who were worshipped in the *penetrale,* or central part of the house. Some of them were Jupiter, Vesta, and the Penates. [Seneca, *Oedipus* 265; Festus, "Herceus."]

PENIA was, according to some, the mother by Porus of Eros, begotten on Aphrodite's birthday. Porus was the personification of expediency, and Penia was the personification of poverty. It takes a certain amount of imagination to conceive of Love as a product of Poverty and Opportunism. Eros was usually called the son of APHRODITE. [Plato, *Symposium* 178; Sextus Empiricus, *Against the Professors* 1.540.]

PENTHESILEIA, as might be expected, offers several problems. Any story with which the Amazons were involved was bound to present discrepancies both in time and place. Penthesileia was said to be the daughter of Ares and Otrera, as were Hippolyte, Melanippe, Antiope, and others. This relationship would have made her more or less contemporary with Theseus, who was, according to some accounts, about 50 when he abducted Helen at the age of perhaps 13 from Sparta. This event preceded the Trojan War by a minimum of ten years, since Helen needed four years to reach 17, be courted by the suitors, and marry Menelaus. She needed six or seven additional years to have children, especially Hermione, who was about six when her mother eloped. Then the war took ten years. Penthesileia came to the assistance of Priam after Hector was killed, and this means the tenth year. Granted she could have been an infant when Theseus came to Themiscyra, she would still have to have been at least 40 when her encounter with Achilles took place. The story, however, does not suggest this but rather that she was full of youthful vibrancy and beauty.

Penthesileia was said to have inadvertently killed a relative, and gone to Priam for purification. It would be interesting to learn why she went to Priam, since he was a former enemy of the Amazons. Perhaps in payment for this service she became a Trojan ally. She and her forces entered the war just after Hector's death. She was a fierce warrior and slew many Greeks, including Podarces, brother of Protesilaus.

Her bravery on the battlefield attracted the notice of Achilles, who was occupied elsewhere, and he worked his way nearer to her. As he was about to close in, Chalcon of Cyparissus, having fallen in love with the beautiful woman, tried to intercept him. Achilles killed him, and later the Greeks nailed his body to a cross. Then Achilles fatally wounded Penthesileia, and when he saw how beautiful and valiant she was, lamented his act and fell in love with her. Some have hinted he engaged in necrophilia with her corpse, but that might have been difficult to manage in the middle of a battlefield. Thersites, the boorish and ugly troublemaker among the Greeks, jeered at him for his tenderness and flipped out the dead woman's eyes with the tip of his sword. Achilles killed him with a single blow. Diomedes, a relative of Thersites, instantly clamored for retribution, but not before dumping the body of Penthesileia into the Scamander River. One chronicler felt she had behaved in a foolhardy manner and had brought on herself this ignominious end for having transgressed the bounds of nature and her sex. Some said her body was later retrieved from the river and buried by Achilles or the Trojans. Some claimed she killed Achilles, who was later restored to life, and that she was killed by Neoptolemus, son of Achilles.

One commentator said she had a son, Caystrius, by Achilles, and it would be entertaining to know what his thinking could possibly have been. Achilles never laid eyes on Penthesileia until he killed her. Even night visits behind enemy lines and a resulting pregnancy would have meant nine months of gestation. Perhaps the writer (who did not elaborate) decided that Achilles raped what he thought was a corpse and that Penthesileia recovered and bore a child. Other writers made her the mother of Caystrius, but not by Achilles. Caystrius gave his name to the Caystrus River and became the father of Ephesus and also the legendary Semiramis.

The dying Penthesileia, supported by Achilles, was depicted on the throne of Zeus at Olympia. [Pausanias 5.11.2, 10.31.1; Hyginus, *Fables* 112; Servius on Virgil's *Aeneid* 1.491, 11.661; Justinus 2.4; Lycophron 997; Tzetzes on Lycophron 997–999; Dictys Cretensis 3.15, 4.2,3; Ovid, *Heroides* 21.118; Diodorus Siculus 2.46; Scholiast on Homer's *Iliad* 2.219; Eustathius on Homer's *Odyssey* 1696; Quintus Smyrnaeus 1.40; Apollodorus, *Epitome* 5.1,2.]

PEPHREDO (*See* PEMPHREDO)

PEPROMENE was the personification of the idea that every man and woman is bound to a destiny. As a proper name it had much the same meaning as Moira, or Fate. [Homer, *Iliad* 3.309.]

PERDIX was the sister of Daedalus, thereby becoming part of the same confusion that has always surrounded his parentage (*see* ALCIPPE). Perdix was the mother of Talos by an anonymous Athenian. She also was called Polycaste by one or two writers. Talos inherited his uncle's marvelous talent for invention and, among many other useful items, developed the saw, the potter's wheel, the chisel, and the compass. He was so skillful that he aroused fears in Daedalus that he would be overshadowed by him. Daedalus enjoyed considerable prestige in Athens, both because of his consummate craftsmanship and the privileges accorded him as a member of the royal family. He could not allow anyone to interfere with his enviable station, so one dark night he pushed Talos over the cliff of the Acropolis. Talos was saved by being metamorphosed into a partridge (*perdix*), which accounts for his being called Perdix by some writers. Daedalus was observed while disposing of the boy's mortal remains and had to flee Athens, ending up as Minos' architect at Cnossus in Crete. Perdix was overcome with grief and hanged herself. [Pausanias 1.21.6,26.5; Diodorus Siculus 4.76; Apollodorus 3.15.9; Ovid, *Metamorphoses* 8.241.]

PERENNA (*See* ANNA PERENNA)

PERIAPIS, daughter of Pheres, according to some was the wife of Menoetius and mother of Patroclus. Most writers, however, called STHENELE the mother of Patroclus. [Apollodorus 3.13.8.]

PERIBOEA (1) was, according to some, the wife of Icarius. Others called Icarius' wife POLYCASTE. [Apollodorus 3.10.6.]

PERIBOEA (2) was a daughter of Eurymedon, a king of giants who lived at the far end of the earth. He and his kingdom were destroyed because of his violent actions. His beautiful daughter, however, was loved by Poseidon, and she bore him a son, Nausithous, on the island of Hypereia in Thrinacia. Nausithous became the leader of the people on the island, and when they were threatened by the Cyclopes, he led them to Scheria in the Ionic Sea. They were the Phaeacians, and Nausithous became their king. His sons were Alcinous and Rhexenor. It is not known whether Periboea accompanied the Phaeacian colony. [Homer, *Odyssey* 6.7, 7.56, 8.564; Apollonius Rhodius 4.547.]

PERIBOEA (3) was a daughter of Acesamenus, the eponymic founder of Acesamenae in Macedonia. She was loved by the god of the Axius River and became by him the mother of Pelagon. Pelagon is unknown except for being the father of Asteropaeus, whose battle with Achilles is described in the *Iliad* (21.141,2).

PERIBOEA (4) was a daughter of Alcathous and Euaechme or Pyrgo. Alcathous, son of Pelops, was the famous slayer of the Cithaeronian lion and rebuilder of the walls of Megara after the city was sacked by the Minoans. He was married first to Pyrgo and later to Euaechme, daughter of King Megareus, and we have no record of which of his wives bore which children to him. His children were Echepolis, Callipolis, Iphinoe, Periboea, and Automedusa. Periboea lost one brother in the Calydonian boar hunt and the other when her father killed him in a fit of anger.

Periboea was listed among the wives of Theseus. She had been one of his companions on the voyage to Crete as part of the tribute due Minos for the mysterious death of his son Androgeus. The victims were intended to be fed to the half-human Minotaur in the famous Cretan labyrinth. When the ship reached Crete, Minos rode down to the harbor to survey the victims. Falling in love with Periboea (or Eriboea, as she was often called), he would have ravished her on the spot had Theseus not protested that it was his duty as Poseidon's son to defend victims against outrage by tyrants. Minos challenged him to prove this claim by tossing his ring into the sea and telling Theseus to recover it. With the help of Amphitrite, the hero was able to

oblige the request and deliver Periboea from Minos. There is virtually nothing beyond a brief statement that Theseus later married Periboea. If a marriage did take place, it was of short duration. Why Periboea happened to be selected as one of the sacrificial victims, and how she and Theseus happened to marry would make a great story. It is surprising no one ever wrote it.

Periboea married Telamon, son of Aeacus and Endeis and brother of Peleus. Telamon represented the heroic ideal. He had gone on the Argonaut and had participated in the Calydonian boar hunt. He had been married earlier to Glauce, daughter of Cychreus in Salamis, where he had fled from Aegina because of his murder of his half-brother. He inherited the kingdom from Cychreus. Glauce died shortly after that.

Telamon's adventures were not over. Even though married to Periboea, he set off on a quest with Heracles, his great friend and probably one-time lover. On this expedition he gained Hesione, Laomedon's daughter, as his booty and had by her a son, Teucer.

Periboea's son by Telamon was the famous Ajax. From the evidence available, she also reared Teucer, the son of Hesione, who disappeared soon after the child was born. Both of these sons of Telamon achieved great renown, especially Ajax. He was one of the most distinguished leaders in the Trojan War, but he incurred the wrath of the gods and finally even the Greeks. His life ended ignominiously when he went mad because he was not awarded the arms of Achilles. When Teucer tried to return to Salamis, he was forbidden by Telamon because he had not better protected Ajax nor avenged his death.

Periboea's life seemed to be lived around the comings and goings of men caught up in heroic endeavors. Her father, brother, husband, son, and stepson were involved in wars and the aftermaths of wars. Her reaction to Hesione and Teucer is not known. She probably incited her husband to ban Teucer from Salamis, or at least she must have strongly supported his decision, since most likely she had always resented her stepson. She was occasionally called Eriboea or Meliboea. [Apollodorus 2.4.11,6.4, 3.12.7; Pausanias 1.17.3, 42.2; Pindar, *Isthmian Odes* 6.65; Sophocles, *Ajax* 566; Plutarch, *Theseus* 29.]

PERIBOEA (5) was the daughter of Hipponous and the wife of Oeneus, by whom she became the mother of Tydeus. Tydeus was considered by many to be the son of Oeneus by his daughter GORGE. [Apollodorus 1.8.4.]

PERIBOEA (6) was the wife of Polybus of Corinth. Her parents are not known. She was sometimes called Medusa or Merope. When the oracle warned Laius of Thebes that he would die at the hands of any son he produced, he had his newborn son exposed. A shepherd of King Polybus found the child and brought him to the palace at Corinth. He was adopted by Polybus and his wife, Periboea, and brought up as their own son, which meant, of course, that he was heir to the throne. Some versions said Laius threw the baby into the sea in a chest that floated to Corinth and was found by the king. He took the baby to the palace and Perioboea pretended to give birth to it. Only Polybus knew the truth, since no midwives were present.

Oedipus grew up in Corinth, and was once taunted by a Corinthian for not being the king's son. Perhaps the old shepherd had revealed the truth to someone. So Oedipus proceeded to Delphi to learn what he could about this possibility. On the way he encountered Laius, fell into an argument with him, and killed him, thus fulfilling the first of the oracle's predictions. At Delphi he learned that he would kill his father and marry his mother. Fully believing Polybus and Periboea were his parents, he never went back to Corinth.

Periboea had, of course, loved him as a son, but she was morally obliged to state the truth when an inquiry reached her and Polybus from Thebes. [Apollodorus 3.5.7; Sophocles, *Oedipus the King* 770.]

PERIBOEA (7) was the mother of Aura by Lelantos. Nothing further is known of her or her husband, but Aura came to a terrible end. After having twins by Dionysus she went mad, tore one of the babies to pieces, ate it, and threw herself into the Sangarius River. [Nonnos, *Dionysiaca* 48,243–943.]

PERIBOEA (8) was the name by which the sea serpent CHARIBOEA was sometimes called.

PERICLYMENE, also called Clymene, was a daughter of Minyas and Clytodoro or Euryanassa. Her distinguished father was the ancestor of the Minyans, and his children were Orchomenus, Presbon, Athamas, Diochthondas, Eteoclymene, Periclymene, Leucippe, Arsinoe, and Alcithoe. He built the first treasury at Orchomenus, where his tomb was shown. Periclymene's sisters were changed into bats for not honoring the worship of Dionysus. It is not clear how she escaped the same fate. Perhaps she was older and had already left home.

She was married to Pheres, son of Cretheus, and had by him Admetus, Lycurgus, Eidomene, and Periapis. Pheres founded the city of Pherae, where he ruled. Her children were distinguished. Lycurgus became king of the country around Nemea and was the father of Opheltes, whose premature death was the occasion of the establishment of the Nemean games. Eidomene was the mother of Bias and Melampus, who became joint kings in Peloponnesus. Admetus was an Argonaut and a Calydonian hunter. He married Alcestis, one of the daughters of the tyrant Pelias, but had to rely on the help of his lover Apollo to achieve this advantageous match. Admetus failed to sacrifice to Artemis and was doomed to an early death unless a close relative agreed to die in his stead. Periclymene and Pheres loved their son and, being advanced in age, could have delivered him from death when his time came all too soon. But they loved life more than they loved their son and claimed to bow to the will of destiny. Alcestis volunteered but was later resurrected.

Periclymene was a loving parent, but when it came down to her life or the life of her son, she chose to live. She probably rationalized that the gods could not be so cruel and would deliver him in time. The gods did so, but Periclymene probably lived with guilt the rest of her life. [Apollodorus 1.8.2,9.14,16; Hyginus, *Fables* 14,173.]

PERIDIA was the wife of Lelex, according to some. Her children by him were Myles, Polycaon, Bomolchus, and Therapne. The wife of Lelex was usually called CLEOCHAREIA. [Apollodorus 3.10.3; Pausanias 3.1.1,12.4.]

PERIGUNE was the tall and beautiful daughter of Sinis, one of the brigands of the Corinthian isthmus. Her mother was Sylea. Sinis waylaid travelers, robbed them, and killed them by bending together two stout pines to which he tied them. When he let the trees spring upright again, the victim was torn in half. Thus Sinis was surnamed Pitycamptes, the Pine-Bender. When Theseus crossed the isthmus on his way from Troezen to Athens to claim his heritage, he encountered Sinis but quickly overpowered him and gave him the same cruel death Sinis had given to many others.

Perigune witnessed her father's death and fled into a marsh overgrown with rushes and wild asparagus, praying to the plants to conceal her, in return for which she would never trample or burn them. Theseus followed her and assured her he meant her no harm. He slept with her, and she became pregnant. She was his first lover, and he was probably no more than 18 at the time. It is doubtful he lingered until she bore their son, Melanippus. Conceivably, Theseus returned from Athens and, with her and their son's welfare in mind, gave her in marriage to Deioneus, son of Eurytus of Oechalia. Melanippus became the father of Ioxus, who helped colonize Caria. The descendants of Ioxus revered the rush and asparagus because of their ancestor's act of faith. [Plutarch, *Theseus* 8.]

PERIMEDE (1) was a daughter of Aeolus and Enarete. She shared in the good and bad fortune of her brothers and sisters, who included such controversial individuals as Salmoneus, Sisyphus, Athamas, Perieres, Canace, and Alcyone. Little is known of her except that she married the river-god Achelous and became the mother of Hippodamas and Orestes. Thus she was the great-grandmother of Oeneus of Calydon, in whose reign the Calydonian boar hunt took place. Both Oeneus and Orestes had some connection with early wine making. She was one of several wives of the immortal Achelous River, and it would be interesting to learn what might have been involved in being his wife or lover. [Apollodorus 1.7.3,10.]

PERIMEDE (2) was a daughter of Oeneus. This Oeneus cannot be the same as the father of Meleager and the Meleagrides, since Phoenix was the brother of Cadmus, whose daughter married Athamas, the brother of another Perimede who was the great-grandmother of Oeneus of Calydon. So four generations separated these two individuals. Perimede married Phoenix and had by him Astypalaea and, according to some, Europa. Europa is more commonly called Phoenix's sister, for whom he, along with Cadmus and Cilix, searched unsuccessfully when she was abducted by Zeus. Astypalaea became by Poseidon the mother of the Argonaut Ancaeus and of Eurypylus, king of Cos. The island of Astypalaea in the Cyclades was named for her. [Pausanias 7.4.2; Apollodorus 2.7.1, 3.1.1; Homer, *Iliad* 14.321.]

PERIMEDE (3) was a sister of Amphitryon, husband of Alcmena. This means she was the daughter of Alcaeus and Astydameia, unless she was illegitimate. Her sister was therefore Anaxo, mother of Alcmena, making her both Alcmena's aunt and sister-in-law. In fact, she was Alcmena's sister-in-law twice, since she married Licymnius, Alcmena's brother. When the sons of Taphius killed the sons of Electryon, Licymnius was the only survivor. He was a faithful ally of Amphitryon, his brother-in-law, and accompanied him and Alcmena to Thebes. Perimede went with him and bore three sons, Oeonus, Argeius, and Melas.

Perimede shared in the tragedy that seemed to follow in the wake of her celebrated nephew Heracles. Oeonus was killed by the sons of Hippocoon at Sparta, and his death was the reason for Heracles' expedition against Sparta. Argeius and Melas accompanied their cousin against Eurytus of Oechalia and were both killed. After Heracles' death, Licymnius—and presumably Perimede—took refuge in Trachis, where part of the battle against Eurystheus took place. Licymnius later joined Hyllus in the unsuccessful battle in Peloponnesus. The Argives invited him and Tlepolemus, one of Heracles' sons, to settle in Argos, and Perimede again accompanied him. Licymnius was killed by Tlepolemus either unintentionally or during a quarrel. The subsequent fate of Perimede is unknown. [Apollodorus 2.4.5,6,8.2; Pausanias 2.22.8, 3.15.4; Pindar, *Olympian Odes* 7.50.]

PERIMEDE (4) was, according to some, the mother of Jason by Aeson. Jason's mother was most often called POLYMEDE.

PERIMELE (1) was called a daughter of Hippodamas. The mother of Hippodamas was PERIMEDE, and his father was Achelous. According to Ovid (*Metamorphoses* 8.590–610), Perimele was deflowered by Achelous, and Hippodamas, enraged by this, threw her from a high cliff into the sea. Achelous prayed for Poseidon to let her become an island, which was granted. Perimele was supposedly one of the Echinades Islands in the delta of the Achelous River. It is not altogether beyond belief that Hippodamas might have reacted so violently because his daughter was seduced by his father. Usually, though, Perimele and Perimede are considered to be confused with each other.

PERIMELE (2) was a daughter of Admetus and Alcestis, and was therefore the sister of Eumelus and Hippasus. Her mother volunteered to die in place of her husband but was resurrected when Heracles brought her back from the underworld. It is not known whether Perimele and her brothers were old enough at the time to offer to die in place of their father.

Perimele married her cousin Argus, son of Phrixus. Argus was born in Colchis, where his father had been carried on the back of the flying ram whose fleece was the object of the voyage of the Argonauts. Perimele's son by Argus was Magnes, who settled in the part of Thessaly known as Magnesia. The original foundation of Magnesia was more properly attributed to Magnes, son of Aeolus and great-granduncle of Magnes, son of Perimele. [Antoninus Liberalis 23; Scholiast on Euripides' *Alcestis* 269; Tzetzes, *Chiliades* 2.787.]

PERIMELE (3) was a daughter of Amythaon, son of Cretheus, and Eidomene. Her brothers were Bias and Melampus, and she had a sister, Aeolia. Amythaon left Thessaly and journeyed with his wife and children to Messenia, where he settled at the court of Neleus, his half-brother. This meant he was also half-brother to Pelias, the twin of Neleus, who ruled in Iolcus and sent Jason on the perilous Argonaut. Amythaon went back to Iolcus to intercede for Jason. Perimele either stayed in Thessaly when her family moved to Messenia or returned with her father. In any case, she met Antion, the oldest son of Periphas and Astyageia, and slept with him. Their son was Ixion.

It was ironic that Perimele, accustomed to a benevolent father and two shrewd but compassionate brothers, should produce such a scoundrel as Ixion. He married Dia, daughter of Eioneus, but failed to keep his bargain regarding a dowry. When Eioneus tried to collect it, Ixion murdered him and was held in contempt by men and gods alike. Finally Zeus, who was having an affair with Dia, agreed to purify him from the murder, but Ixion repaid him by trying to seduce Hera. Zeus set a trap for him by creating a facsimile of Hera and then caught Ixion having sex with the phantom. Zeus chained him to a fiery wheel in the underworld. The phantom gave birth to the first of the Centaurs, and Dia gave birth to Peirithous. Thus Perimele was grandmother both of Peirithous and the Centaurs. [Diodorus Siculus 4.69; Scholiast on Pindar's *Pythian Odes* 2.39.]

PERINEICE was the daughter of Hippomachus. By Naubolus she was the mother of Iphitus, one of the Argonauts from Phocis. When Jason went to Phocis to consult the Delphic oracle about his impending voyage to Colchis, Iphitus received him hospitably. He also joined Jason on the voyage. He was the father of Schedius and Epistrophus, who led the Phocian army to the Trojan War. [Apollonius Rhodius 1.207–210; Homer, *Iliad* 2.517.]

PERIOPIS, a variation of Periapis, was said by some to be the mother of Patroclus, but his mother was more commonly called STHENELE, daughter of Acastus.

PERNIS was the wife of Lycus and, according to some, mother of Ialmenus. Usually his mother was called ASTYOCHE.

PERO (1) was the mother of the river-god Asopus by Poseidon. His parents were more often called Oceanus and TETHYS. [Apollodorus 3.12.6.]

PERO (2) was a daughter of Neleus and Chloris. The father of Chloris was Amphion, often confused with Amphion, husband of Niobe. Neleus was the brother of Pelias, the unscrupulous king of Iolcus. Exiled from Iolcus, Neleus took refuge in Messenia, where his cousin Aphareus gave him the rule of part of the kingdom, including Pylus. Neleus became one of the most powerful rulers of Greece.

Pero had 12 brothers, including Nestor. She was exceedingly beautiful and was sought by many love-stricken young men. In typical father fashion, Neleus wanted the best for his daughter, so he required the suitors, as a test of their virility and commitment, to bring her the cattle of Iphiclus from Phylace in Thessaly. This dowry discouraged the other suitors, but Melampus, brother of Bias and half-nephew of Neleus, persisted. Against overwhelming odds he brought back the cattle and bought Pero for his beloved brother. Neleus was unhappy because this meant losing his daughter and the lands of Melampus he had seized during his absence.

Thus Pero married Bias and had three sons by him, Talaus, Areius, and Laodocus. Talaus, by far the most prominent, was the father of Adrastus, Parthenopaeus, Pronax, Mecisteus, Aristomachus, and Eriphyle, all involved in the war of the Seven against Thebes. Areius, with his brothers, was an Argonaut. Laodocus took part in the battle of the Seven. He helped organize the funeral games of Opheltes (Archemorus), in which he excelled in spear thrusting.

Pero was abandoned by Bias, who married one of the daughters of Proetus, king of Argos. Melampus had cured the women of madness, for which service he asked in return two-thirds of the kingdom for himself and his brother. It is not known exactly when this happened, but it was probably at a late time in Bias' life, when a younger woman—and the daughter of a king, at that—could perhaps offer him royal heirs to the new kingdom he had inherited.

Pero's subsequent fate is not known. She was one of those women who was central to the heroic era that reached from the Argonaut to the first Theban war. It is doubtful she lived to see the expedition of the Epigoni, which involved her great-grandchildren. [Homer, *Odyssey* 11.281–286; Apollodorus 1.9.9, 3.6.5; Pausanias 10.31.2,36.4; Apollonius Rhodius 1.118.]

PERSE, Persea, or Perseis was one of the OCEANIDES. She was the wife of Helios, the sun, by whom she became the mother of Aeetes, Circe, Pasiphae, Perses, and Aloeus. Interestingly these offspring were designated as Perseides, the term Heliades seemingly reserved for the children of Helios by later wives. All the children of Perse were endowed with powers of enchantment, as were their own children. Aeetes was the father of Medea. Circe inhabited the island of Aeaea and turned those who landed there into swine. Pasiphae, Perses, and Aloeus had unusual careers in Crete, Asopia, and Tauris. Helios gave Corinth to Aeetes, Asopia to Aloeus, and Tauris to Perses. Aeetes later left Corinth to reign at Colchis. After that Perses usurped the kingdom of Colchis and held it until Medea restored it to her father. Nothing further is known of Perse or what caused her to produce for Helios, the source of light, such dark and mysterious children. [Homer, *Odyssey* 10.139; Hesiod, *Theogony* 354,956; Apollodorus 1.9.1, 3.1.2; Tzetzes on Lycophron 174; Apollonius Rhodius 4.591; Scholiast on Apollonius Rhodius 3.200; Valerius Flaccus 5.582.]

PERSEIS (1) was, according to some, the patronymic of Hecate from her father Perses. [Apollodorus 1.2.4; Apollonius Rhodius 3.478.]

PERSEIS (2) was one of the OCEANIDES. [Hesiod, *Theogony* 354.]

PERSEPHONE (1), though not one of the Olympian divinities, was a goddess of enormous importance. She was the goddess of death and the underworld.

> NATIVITY: Daughter of Zeus and Demeter. Daughter of Zeus and Styx.
>
> LOVERS: Zeus, Hades, Adonis.
>
> CHILDREN: Dionysus, Iacchus, Zagreus, Sabazius, Erinyes.
>
> PRINCIPAL SEATS OF WORSHIP: Eleusis, Thebes, Athens, Corinth, Megara, Ephyra (in Thesprotia), Sicily, Locri.

SACRED TO HER: Mint, pomegranate.

COMPANIONS: Cyane, Demeter, Ianthe, Leucippe, Pluto (Oceanid), Rhodeia, Rhodope, Tyche, Urania.

IDENTIFIED WITH: Artemis, Axieros, Bendis, Bona Dea, Daeira, Despoena, Gaea, Hecate, Hestia, Isis, Libera, Pandora, Proserpina, Rhea.

SURNAMES: Auxesia, Averna, Azesia, Brimo, Calligeneia, Carpophoros, Deione, Despoena, Eleusina, Epaine, Hermione, Meliboea, Melitodes, Soteira, Thesmia.

The story of the rape of Persephone by Hades and her eternally recurring return to the land of the living is a central theme in mythology. The worship that grew up around this story was the most important in ancient Greece. The Eleusinian mysteries were of very early origin and were observed until about A.D. 200. These rituals, probably fairly straightforward in the earliest times, became increasingly complex as time went on and the number of initiates grew. It should be pointed out, however, that the mysteries were not directed to Persephone as goddess of the lower regions but to Kore (Persephone) as daughter of Demeter.

Persephone was the daughter of Demeter by her brother Zeus. After Persephone became associated with the underworld, she was considered by some the daughter of Zeus by Styx, one of the daughters of Nyx (Night). Hades, the gloomy heir of the infernal kingdom, sought a companion to share his lonely empire but understandably did not have much success. He saw Persephone, his lovely niece, and was advised by Zeus to kidnap her, since her mother would never otherwise consent to her going to the melancholy subterranean world. So Hades in his dark chariot grabbed up the bright young girl while she gathered flowers one day with companions. Demeter was frantic with worry, and only after long, heartbreaking, and footsore wanderings did she learn of her daughter's whereabouts.

One can only guess at her rantings and railing at Zeus, the maiden's own father, for his part in the abduction. It was only after Demeter, as goddess of agriculture, began to carry out a threat of withholding nourishment to the plants of the earth that Zeus requested Hades to send Persephone back to the upper world. Hades complied, but one Ascalaphus, a hanger-on in the underworld, disclosed that Persephone had eaten part of a pomegranate. Therefore, she was doomed to spend part of every year in the lower regions. When this cycle of resurrection became fixed, she was represented as staying in Hades during the fall and winter, returning each spring to awaken the sleeping seeds. Therefore, the theme of death, resurrection, and fertility became interfused, and onto this corporate concept the multilevel symbolism of the Eleusinian mysteries was superimposed.

The scene of her abduction was claimed by many places—Athens, Boeotia, Lerna, Crete, and Sicily. The Eleusinians advanced a strong claim for Erineus near Eleusis, since the royal house of Eleusis had played a large role in Demeter's search. The Eleusinians capitalized on this association, and part of the elaborate secrecy of the rituals could have been due to jealousy over sharing the mysteries with any other place.

Persephone was worshipped in Arcadia under the name of Despoena. In this curious juxtaposition of divinities, Demeter in her wanderings came to Onceium and, pursued by Poseidon, changed herself into a mare to escape him. He changed himself into a stallion and engaged her in violent coupling. Despoena and the horse Areion were born from this union. Despoena was reared by the Titan Anytus. Really a separate goddess, she was later regarded as an extension of the Demeter/Kore myth and accepted as identical with Persephone.

The name Persephone was also seen as Persephoneia, Persephassa, Phersephassa, Persephatta, and other spellings. It probably had a meaning similar to "death-bringing." She did not have a great number of stories told about her after she became queen of the lower world. When Alcestis elected to die in place of her husband, Persephone was said to have been touched by this loving action and to have made it possible for her to return to the upper world. On the darker side, the Hyacinthides were sacrificed to her by the Athenians. The Coronides, who committed suicide for patriotic reasons, were metamorphosed into comets by

Persephone and Hades. Then there was the famous story of the descent of Theseus and Peirithous into Hades. Both had vowed to have a child by a daughter of Zeus. Theseus, according to some, accomplished his goal with Helen. Peirithous foolishly decided to aim for the impossible by trying to seduce Persephone. Why he chose the implacable and unrelenting queen of the dead was known only to the author of the idea. Persephone was not amused and had both men imprisoned in chairs from which they could not move and tortured by means readily available on all sides. Theseus was freed by Heracles, but Peirithous was doomed to remain forever in the grim kingdom of the dead. Plutarch contrived a rather silly account of this already ridiculous story in an attempt at a historical rationale.

Persephone was a mere girl when snatched up by Hades. Hades gratefully took her virginity but, lacking evidence to the contrary, was sterile and could produce no children. Again, only the Greek gift for contrasts could have juxtaposed the bringer of fertility with a sterile husband. Persephone was anything but promiscuous, but there was no way of avoiding the will of Zeus; even Hades had to give in to it. So Persephone became the mother of Dionysus/Sabazius/Zagreus. The explanation for this collective identity is tied up in the various mystical personae of Dionysus, who also underwent death and resurrection in the being of Zagreus. Zagreus was said to have been sired by Zeus in the form of a dragon even before Persephone went to Hades. Iacchus, another mystical being (i.e., one strongly associated with the celebration of the mysteries) was said to be her son also by Zeus. But some writers considered Iacchus her brother, a kind of male Persephone. Some called her also the mother of Melinoe, a nocturnal specter, by Zeus. Some writers appropriately thought of her as the mother of the Erinyes by Hades, but the Erinyes, divinities of infernal punishment, had been around long before Persephone was born.

The marriage between Hades and Persephone, apart from her command performances with Zeus, was tranquil enough. Probably needing a change from his dreary surroundings or during Persephone's summer residence, Hades once had a series of meetings with a subterranean nymph named Mintha. Assisted by Demeter, who was not fond of her son-in-law, Persephone made short work of the affair by changing Mintha into a mint plant. Persephone herself was not entirely without physical desires that extended beyond her husband/uncle and father/lover. Once Aphrodite brought to her the baby Adonis, who had been born from an incestuous relationship, inspired by Aphrodite, between mortals. She left the beautiful child with Persephone and apparently forgot about him until he grew into an extraordinarily handsome young man. At that point Persephone did not want to give him up, and Zeus was forced to intervene, so that Adonis spent a third of the year with Persephone, a third with Aphrodite, and a third for rest and relaxation. In effect, his story of seasonal appearances on earth ran a kind of parallel to Persephone's own early history. However, Adonis' days on earth were ended when he was killed by a boar. Some say a jealous Ares or Apollo engineered the fatal accident, but Persephone could well have become envious when Adonis started spending two-thirds of the year with Aphrodite. By having him killed, Persephone could have him for all time. [NATIVITY: Homer, *Iliad* 14.326, *Odyssey* 11.216; Hesiod, *Theogony* 912; Apollodorus 1.3.1,5.1; Pausanias 8.37.3,6.25.5—LOVERS: Hyginus, *Fables* 146, *Poetic Astronomy* 2.7; Ovid, *Metamorphoses* 10.300; Hesiod, *Theogony* 914—CHILDREN: Hesychius, "Zagreus"; Scholiast on Euripides' *Orestes* 952; Aristophanes, *Frogs* 326; Diodorus Siculus 4.4; Cicero, *On the Nature of the Gods* 3.23; Orphica, *Hymns* 29.6, 70.3—CHARACTERISTICS: Homer, *Odyssey* 10.494, 11.226,385,634, *Iliad* 9.457,569; Apollodorus 1.9.15; Scholiast on Theocritus 3.48; Cicero, *On the Nature of the Gods* 2.26; Lydus, *On the Months* 90,284; Orphica, *Hymns* 29.16; Tzetzes on Lycophron 708,1176—WORSHIP: Pausanias 1.31.1, 3.13.2, 9.25.5; Scholiast on Euripides' *Phoenician Maidens* 687; Pindar, *Nemean Odes* 1.17; Diodorus Siculus 5.2,4; Athenaeus 4.647; Livy 29.8,18.] (*See also* DEMETER.)

PERSEPHONE (2) was a daughter of Minyas. She was not mentioned in the usual accounts and was therefore probably illegitimate. She married Amphion, son of Iasus, and became the mother of Chloris. Chloris was the wife of Neleus, king of Pylus, and became by him the mother of many children, including Nestor and Pero. Nothing further is known of her or her husband. [Scholiast on Homer's *Odyssey* 11.281; Apollodorus 1.9.9.]

PERSO was called one of the GRAEAE. [Hyginus, *Fables: Preface* 9.]

PERTUNDA was a surname of Juno, under which she was invoked by newly married people in reference to piercing of the bride's maidenhead. [Tertullian 2.11; St. Augustine, *City of God* 6.9.]

PESSINUNTIA was a surname of Cybele, which she derived from the city of Pessinus in Galatia. [Livy 29.10; Herodian 1.11.]

PETRAEA was one of the OCEANIDES. It also occurred as a surname of Scylla, who dwelt in or on a rock. [Hesiod, *Theogony* 357; Homer, *Odyssey* 12.231.]

PHACE, also called CALLISTO, was a sister of Odysseus.

PHAEA was the name of the monstrous wild sow of Crommyon that terrorized the countryside. Crommyon (modern Agii Theodori) was a district between the isthmus of Corinth and Megara. The inhabitants were so terrified of the destructive beast that they no longer dared to till the fields. The creature, named for the crone who raised it, was thought to be one of the monsters produced by Typhon and Echidna. Theseus had to pass through Crommyon on his way from Troezen to Athens and was attacked by the sow but managed to kill her. Plutarch suggested a rationalistic approach by making Phaea a female robber, called a sow because of her slovenly habits. [Plutarch, *Theseus* 9; Hyginus, *Fables* 38; Apollodorus, *Epitome* 1.1.]

PHAEDRA was a daughter of Minos (II), and the younger sister of Ariadne. She was probably quite a few years younger than Ariadne, maybe even the last child born to Pasiphae before she produced the terrible Minotaur.

After Theseus killed the Minotaur, he left with Ariadne, who would never be seen again by her relatives. Crete, which then must have come under the sovereignty of Athens, was ruled by Catreus after the death of Minos. It is not certain whether Theseus occasionally journeyed there on diplomatic missions. If he did, he would have been acquainted with the king's sister Phaedra.

Theseus married Antiope after his journey to the country of the Amazons and became by her the father of Hippolytus. Antiope was killed when the Amazons marched on Athens, and Hippolytus was sent to Troezen to be reared by his grandmother Aethra and great-grandfather Pittheus. We do not know exactly when Theseus married Phaedra, but it was probably not too long after the death of Antiope. There was even a report that their marriage ceremony was interrupted by Antiope (!) and other Amazons, all of whom were killed by Theseus. (This would presuppose that he had abducted and married Hippolyte, the sister of Antiope, as some have contended.) In any case, he was still relatively young and dashing, and probably quite appealing to Phaedra when he came to Crete to fetch her.

Back in Athens, Phaedra gave birth to two sons, Acamas and Demophon. She was otherwise busy with affairs of court. She also had a temple built to Aphrodite Zerynthia in Thrace. It is quite possible that she never beheld young Hippolytus or, if so, it had been while he was a mere boy. He was meanwhile growing up in Troezen and, unlike his father, showed no interest in women. Like his Amazonian mother, he embraced the worship of Artemis and while still in early manhood built a temple to Artemis Lyceia in Troezen. None of this pleased Aphrodite, and her eventual reprisal for Hippolytus' virtuous conduct took an indirect route. Hippolytus once was present in Eleusis during the celebration of the mysteries. Phaedra beheld him dressed in white and participating in an athletic event. Aphrodite caused her to fall desperately in love with him.

Phaedra contained herself fairly well at first. However, when Theseus killed the sons of Pallas and went to Troezen for purification, she jumped at the opportunity to accompany him. She spent several days of frustration, since the window of her quarters overlooked the stadium in which Hippolytus daily exercised stark naked. The Troezenians later pointed out a myrtle with pierced leaves. They said it did not grow that way but that Phaedra, while watching her stepson, out of frustration had punched holes in the leaves with her hairpin. On this spot later was found the temple of Artemis Catascopia (Spying).

Phaedra finally wrote Hippolytus a letter in which she declared her love, making references to the unhappy treatment the women in her family had received from men, not forgetting to mention her own sister Ariadne and her abandonment by Theseus. She begged him to come to her and not worry about the appearance of incest. Hippolytus was appalled, and raged at her for her scandalous behavior. It is not clear what happened then. Some said Phaedra screamed that she was being raped and then hanged herself. Others said that after Hippolytus reproached her and left, she hanged herself and left in plain sight the letter she had sent him and which he had brought back to her quarters. Still others said she killed herself after Hippolytus died.

Theseus appeared and cursed Hippolytus, who fled the scene in his chariot along the treacherous cliffs above the coast of Troezen. A bull appeared from the sea and frightened the horses so that they overturned the chariot and dragged the innocent youth to his death.

It is not certain Theseus ever learned the real story. Some said Artemis revealed the truth to him and made it possible for him to be reconciled with the dying Hippolytus. Hippolytus' tomb was shown at Troezen, ironically near the tomb of Phaedra.

Phaedra's son Acamas was one of the ambassadors to Troy who tried to recover Helen. He fell in love with one of Priam's daughters and had a son by her. He was later killed in Cyprus, and had a promontory and town named for him. Demophon assisted Heracles against Aegisthus before the Trojan War and gained the Palladium after the war when Diomedes landed by chance on the shores of Attica.

Phaedra is considered by many as a lustful and wholly unscrupulous woman. This seems hardly fair. Up until her obsession with Hip-

polytus she had been a good wife, mother, and citizen. She had shown devotion to the gods. Even in the matter of her lust for her stepson she was a victim of a goddess's jealousy and received a punishment not really designed specifically for her. Hippolytus was the object of Aphrodite's wrath, and Phaedra, unhappily, was the agent for his destruction. [Apollodorus 3.1.2, *Epitome* 1.18,19; Homer, *Odyssey* 11.325; Euripides, *Hippolytus*; Pausanias 1.22.1–3, 2.27,4, 31.4,32.1–4; Cicero, *On the Nature of the Gods* 3.31; Tzetzes on Lycophron 449,958; Hyginus, *Fables* 47; Seneca, *Phaedra*.]

PHAENNA was one of the CHARITES. [Pausanias 3.18.4, 9.35.1.]

PHAENO was one of the OCEANIDES. [*Homeric Hymn to Demeter* 416.]

PHAEO was one of the HYADES. [Scholiast on Aratus' *Phenomena* 254.]

PHAESYLE was one of the HYADES. [Hyginus, *Fables* 192.]

PHAETHONTIADES, Phaethontides, or Phaethonides were the daughters of Helios and sisters of the unfortunate Phaethon. They were also called HELIADAE. [Virgil, *Eclogues* 6.62; *Palatine Anthology* 9.782.]

PHAETHUSA (1) was a daughter of Helios, half-sister of the Heliadae, and sister to LAMPETIA. [Homer, *Odyssey* 12.132; Apollonius Rhodius 4.971.]

PHAETHUSA (2) was, according to some, the mother of Myrtilus by Hermes. Myrtilus' mother was more often called CLEOBULE. [Scholiast on Apollonius Rhodius 1.752.]

PHANOSYRA was, according to some, the wife of Minyas. More often his wife was known as EURYANASSA. [Pausanias 9.36.4.]

PHANOTHEA, or Phemonoe, was the wife of the Athenian Icarius and mother of Erigone. Her husband was hospitable to Dionysus, who gave him skins of wine in gratitude, but was murdered by his neighbors with whom he shared the wine because when they became intoxicated they thought he had poisoned them. Erigone, the daughter, went in search of her father and hanged herself to the tree under which she found him buried. Thus in a short time Phanothea lost both husband and daughter, who were changed into constellations. Apparently she turned for solace to the arts. She became a priestess of Apollo and was said to have invented the hexameter. [Clement of Alexandria, *Miscellanies* 1.366; Stobaeus, *Anthology* 21.26.]

PHARMACEIA was the nymph of a spring with poisonous powers near the Ilissus River in Athens. It was near this spring that Oreithyia, daughter of Erechtheus, was abducted by Boreas. Pharmaceia was one of Oreithyia's playmates. [Plato, *Phaedrus* 229.]

PHARMACIDES was the name of the witches who assisted Hera and Eileithyia in delaying the birth of Heracles. These witches, probably local Theban sorceresses, appeared to have been summoned on occasions when their knowledge of drugs was required. It is not really clear why their presence was needed in the case of Alcmena. Perhaps Hera called in all the forces she could muster. These witches were sometimes called divinities, but that seems unlikely unless they were of a very low order. In any case, they were never mentioned in any other connection. [Pausanias 9.11.2.]

PHARNACE was a daughter of Megassares, a king of Syria. She married Sandacus, son of Astynous and grandson of Phaethon. Sandacus migrated from Syria to Cilicia and founded the town of Celenderis. Their son was Cinyras, who founded Paphos in Cyprus and was the father of Adonis by his own daughter Myrrha. This sketchy genealogy has been the subject of a great deal of speculation, and more than anything shows how the Adonis legend had its origin in Semitic tradition and was carried eventually to Cyprus. [Apollodorus 3.14.3.]

PHARTIS was one of the DANAIDES, a daughter of Danaus and an Ethiopian woman.

She married and murdered Eurydamas. [Apollodorus 2.1.5.]

PHARYGAEA was a surname of Hera, derived from the town of Pharygae in Locris, where she had a temple. [Stephanus Byzantium, "Pharygai"; Strabo 9.4.6.]

PHASITHEA, more often seen as Praxithea, was one of the LEONTIDES. [Pausanias 1.5.2.]

PHEMONOE was a daughter of Apollo and his first priestess at Delphi. She was a poetess and invented hexameter verse. She was also called PHANOTHEA, who was not, however, identified as a daughter of Apollo. [Pausanias 5.5.7,6.7; Clement of Alexandria, *Miscellanies* 1.323,334.]

PHENO was a daughter of Clytius of Athens. She was the wife of Lamedon, son of Coronus. Lamedon became king of Aegialeia after Epopeus was killed and surrendered Antiope to her uncle Lycus. By Lamedon, Pheno became the mother of Zeuxippe. War arose with the sons of Achaeus, and Lamedon brought in Sicyon from Attica as an ally. He gave Zeuxippe to Sicyon in marriage, and thus Sicyon became king of Aegialeia, the name of which he changed to Sicyon. [Pausanias 2.6.5.]

PHERAEA (1) was a surname of Artemis at Pherae in Thessaly, Argos, Athens, and Sicyon, as well as in Dalmatia, where she had temples. Pheraea was also a surname of Hecate because she was said by some to be a daughter of Zeus and Pheraea (others said Zeus and Asteria), because she had been brought up by the shepherds of Pheres, or because she was worshipped at Pherae. [Callimachus, *Hymn to Artemis* 259; Pausanias 2.10.6,23.5; Tzetzes on Lycophron 1180.]

PHERAEA (2) was a daughter of Aeolus and, according to some, the mother of Hecate by Zeus. Hecate's mother was usually called ASTERIA. Pheraea as a daughter of Aeolus is otherwise unknown. [Tzetzes on Lycophron 1180; Scholiast on Theocritus 2.36.]

PHEREBOEA was included as a wife of Theseus. She was almost certainly the same as PERIBOEA, although Plutarch included both names. [Plutarch, *Theseus* 29.]

PHERUSA (1) was one of the NEREIDES. [Homer, *Iliad* 18.43; Hesiod, *Theogony* 248.]

PHERUSA (2) was one of the HORAE. [Hyginus, *Fables* 183.]

PHIALO was the daughter of Alcimedon, an Arcadian who lived in a cave on Mount Ostracina above a plain called Alcimedon between Mantineia and Methydrium. Heracles went that way once and seduced Phialo. She concealed her pregnancy from her father, but he found out when the baby was born and exposed both mother and baby on the mountain. He tied Phialo so she could not go for help. The baby cried for its mother and was overheard by a jay, which imitated the child's wailing. By some miracle Heracles happened to be passing along the road and heard the jay. He followed it and came to where Phialo was bound. He set her free and saved the baby. The nearby spring was called Cissa (Jay) after the bird. The boy was called Aechmagoras. In spite of this pretty story and his being the son of the great Heracles, Aechmagoras was never heard from again. [Pausanias 8.12.2–4.]

PHIGALIA was a Dryad from whom the town of Phigalia in Arcadia was believed to have derived its name. [Pausanias 8.39.2.]

PHILA was one of the DANAIDES and married to Philinus. [Hyginus, *Fables* 170.]

PHILIA (1) was a personification of friendship. She had an altar in Athens. Nothing is known of her except that she was in one way or another associated with Peitho, the personification of persuasion. [*Palatine Anthology* 12.163.]

PHILIA (2) was a nymph of Naxos who cared for Dionysus in his infancy. [Diodorus Siculus 5.52.]

PHILIA (3) was a surname of Aphrodite. [Tzetzes, *Chiliades* 70,72.]

PHILIPPIS was one of the AMAZONS. [Diodorus Siculus 4.16.]

PHILLO (*See* PHIALO)

PHILLYRA was, according to some, the mother of Hypseus. Usually her name was given as CREUSA. [Scholiast on Pindar's *Pythian Odes* 9.26.]

PHILOBIA was the wife of Perseus, a governor of Dardanus in the neighborhood of Troy. When Acamas went to Troy with Diomedes and Menelaus to ask for the restoration of Helen, Laodice, a daughter of Priam, was smitten with his youth and good looks and wanted to go to bed with him. She was shy, and he was standoffish, so Laodice appealed to Philobia to help her. Philobia appealed to Perseus, who invited Acamas to a feast; separately he also invited Laodice and other Trojan women. He put Laodice in Acamas' bed, telling the grateful young man she was a royal concubine. Munitus was born from the union. [Parthenius, *Love Stories* 16.]

PHILODAMEIA was one of the daughters of Danaus. He is usually thought of only as the father of the so-called Danaides, but this name was applied solely to the 50 daughters who murdered their husbands at Argos on the night of their mass marriage. In spite of having fathered 50 daughters by various wives, Danaus was still reasonably young, willing, and able to father additional ones. Philodameia was born after Danaus arrived in Argos. She was loved by Hermes, and they had a son, Pharis, who was the reputed founder of the town of Pharae in Messenia. The line thus begun by Philodameia reached all the way to the Trojan War. [Pausanias 4.30.2, 7.22.3.]

PHILODICE (1) was a daughter of the Inachus River. She became the wife of Leucippus, son of Perieres and Gorgophone and king of Messenia. The Inachus River did not flow into Sparta or Messenia, so it would be interesting to learn how Leucippus happened to find Philodice. By him she was the mother of Hilaeira, Phoebe, and Arsinoe. Arsinoe's lover was none less than

Apollo, and by him she had a daughter, Eriopis. The Messenians also claimed that she was by the god the mother of Asclepius, but most other people regarded Coronis as his mother. In any case, Arsinoe had a sanctuary at Sparta and was worshipped as a heroine.

Hilaeira and Phoebe became priestesses of Athena and Artemis. They were betrothed to their cousins Idas and Lynceus, sons of Aphareus, but were stolen away by the Dioscuri, Castor and Polydeuces, who were also their cousins. As a result of this, the sons of Aphareus and the sons of Tyndareus became enemies and eventually killed one another (with the exception of the immortal Polydeuces). It would be interesting to learn how Philodice felt about the abduction and with whom she sided. It was not every day that one's son-in-law was a son of Zeus. [Apollodorus 3.10.3; Pausanias 2.26.6, 3.12.7.]

PHILODICE (2) was the wife of Magnes, and mother of Eurynomus and Eioneus. The wife of Magnes was more often seen as MELIBOEA. [Scholiast on Euripides' *Phoenician Maidens* 1760.]

PHILOMACHE (*See* PHYLOMACHE)

PHILOMEDUSA (*See* PHYLOMEDUSA)

PHILOMELA (1) was a daughter of Pandion in Attica. Her story is one of the most familiar in mythology, and her name was frequently used as a metaphor by the English Romantic poets. Pandion succeeded Erechtheus (I), his father, as king of Athens and was married to Zeuxippe, by whom he had twin sons, Erechtheus (II) and Butes, and two daughters, Philomela and Procne. Pandion needed help against Labdacus of Thebes in a boundary dispute. He appealed for assistance, and the call was answered by Tereus. This Tereus was a son of Ares and from all appearances a kind of mercenary. It appears he was king of a colony of Thracians who had settled in Phocis. Thanks to him, Pandion won the war and gratefully gave his daughter Procne to him in marriage. Tereus took her to Daulis, which lay in the high pass between Delphi and Chaeroneia, where she soon became the mother of Itys.

Tereus grew restless after Itys was born. He remembered the lovely sister back in Athens and found a reason to visit Pandion. According to some, he told Pandion that Procne had died and that he wanted to marry her sister. Others said he brought the news that Procne wanted to see her sister and had sent him to bring her back with him. She came willingly in either case. On the way back to Daulis, he raped her and then cut out her tongue so she could not tell anyone what had happened. Back in Daulis he kept her imprisoned so he could enjoy her whenever he felt like it. Philomela was miserable in her confinement and powerlessness, but she finally hit on a plan to warn her sister. She wove the story of her abduction and mutilation into a garment she sent to Procne. How she managed to convey all this by a piece of clothing is a puzzle. Maybe she merely wove her name and whereabouts, trusting the messenger to do the rest. Thus Procne found her and learned the terrible truth about her husband. The sisters contrived to get revenge by killing Itys and cooking his flesh for Tereus' dinner.

After he had eaten, Philomela appeared, and Procne told him the nature of his meal. He was horrified, and seizing an ax pursued the sisters. The gods were also appalled with what had taken place and changed Tereus to a hoopoe (some said a hawk), Procne to a nightingale, and Philomela to a swallow.

The Megarians claimed Tereus was a native of nearby Pagae. They also stated that when he could not overtake the sisters he killed himself. They further claimed that Procne and Philomela went back to Attica and wept themselves to death. For some reason, the Megarians also sacrificed to Tereus and showed his tomb.

The late Latin poets reversed the birds into which Procne and Philomela were changed, perhaps because the irony of having a tongueless woman transformed into a sweet singer was too much to resist. Actually the name Philomela meant nightingale in ancient Greek. [Apollodorus 3.14.8; Zenobius 3.14; Conon, *Narrations* 31; Pausanias 1.5.4,41.8; Hyginus, *Fables* 45; Ovid, *Metamorphoses* 5.426–674.]

PHILOMELA (2) was, according to some, the mother of Patroclus. She was usually called

STHENELE. [Scholiast on Homer's *Odyssey* 4.343, 17.134.]

PHILOMELA (3) was a daughter of Actor, son of Myrmidon, and according to some the wife of Peleus, by whom she was the mother of Achilles. It was rumored that Cheiron the Centaur wanted to make Peleus more celebrated and spread the report that he was married to THE-TIS. [Scholiast on Apollonius Rhodius 1.558, 4.816.]

PHILOMELA (4) was mentioned as one of the daughters of Priam, but nothing further is known of her. [Hyginus, *Fables* 90.]

PHILOMELA (5) was one of the DANAIDES and married to Panthius. [Hyginus, *Fables* 170.]

PHILONIS (1), daughter of Daedalion, according to some, was the mother of Autolycus by Hermes and of Philammon by Apollo, both conceived on the same night. Their mother was more often called CHIONE. [Hyginus, *Fables* 200.]

PHILONIS (2) was the mother of Ceyx by Eosphorus. Ceyx was married to Alcyone, daughter of the Thessalian Aeolus. The couple was so happy that they compared themselves to Zeus and Hera and were changed into sea birds. Philonis, who was a nymph, has been confused with Philonis, daughter of Daedalion and, according to some, the mother of Autolycus and Philammon. [Hyginus, *Fables* 65; Ovid, *Metamorphoses* 11.271.]

PHILONOE (1), or Phylonoe, was a daughter of Tyndareus by Leda, and sister of Timandra, Clytemnestra, and Castor, as well as half-sister to Helen and Polydeuces. Philonoe was the only daughter of Leda who did not commit adultery. In fact, she was never given a chance, since Artemis for some unknown reason rendered her immortal, which probably means she died as a child. Artemis, never particularly fond of Aphrodite, probably made sure that at least one of Tyndareus' daughters would not be subject to the curse of adultery placed on them by Aphrodite. [Apollodorus 3.10.6.]

PHILONOE (2) was a daughter of Iobates and wife of Bellerophon. She was usually called ANTICLEIA. [Apollodorus 2.3.2.]

PHILONOME (1), sometimes called Polyboea, was a daughter of Tragasus of the Troad. She was the second wife of Cycnus, son of Poseidon and Calyce. Cycnus was first married to Procleia, daughter of Laomedon, by whom he had Hemithea and Tenes. Philonome fell in love with her handsome stepson and tried to seduce him. He rejected her advances, but she accused him of trying to seduce her. She even produced a witness, Eumolpus (or Molpus), a flute player. Cycnus was enraged; putting his son and daughter (who probably defended her brother) into a chest, he cast them into the sea. Long after they were gone, Cycnus learned the truth and, after stoning the flute player to death, buried Philonome alive. Philonome was one of a long list of women who falsely accused stepsons or guests when their own seduction failed. Many times this accusation came from wounded pride, but more often probably from fear that the object of their desires would reveal them to their husbands. Particularly this must have been true where stepsons were concerned, although it is hardly likely the young men would have been believed. [Apollodorus, *Epitome* 3.25.]

PHILONOME (2), daughter of Nyctimus, was usually seen as PHYLONOME.

PHILOZOE was the wife of Tlepolemus, son of Heracles. Her name was more often seen as POLYXO.

PHILYRA (1) was a daughter of Oceanus. She was not mentioned in the usual lists of Oceanides, so Tethys was probably not her mother. Philyra attracted the attention of her uncle Cronus. He was afraid of being discovered by his wife, Rhea, so he changed himself into a horse and had sex with Philyra. In this particular version of the story she willingly complied. Another version says she resisted by changing herself into a mare, but Cronus changed himself into a stallion and raped her. This mixture of species during the mating process accounted for the strange appearance of the child that was born. He was

Cheiron, who had the upper torso of a human and the body and four legs of a horse. Some said Philyra hated the child and prayed to Zeus for a solution. She was changed into a linden tree on the island of Philyra in Thrace. But this version was not accepted by most writers.

Somehow Philyra ended up in Thessaly, where she brought up Cheiron. Meanwhile she had another son, Dolops, by Cronus; this one seemed to be human in form, so the parents must have made love in the conventional way. Nothing further is known of Dolops. Philyra lived with Cheiron in a cave on Mount Pelion, where he had been expelled by the Lapiths.

A curiosity exists in regard to Cheiron's relationship to other Centaurs. He was not remotely related to them, yet he was always grouped with them because of his appearance. He even shared their history and their disenfranchisement from the Lapiths. Cheiron was immortal, a further difference between him and the other Centaurs. Philyra helped Cheiron bring up and educate the young sons of kings and heroes who were entrusted to his care. They were on particularly friendly terms with Peleus and Achilles.

There is no record of what happened to Philyra when Cheiron gave away his immortality and died. She might have rejoined her father, but we are not sure that she was a nymph of the watery element. [Pindar, *Nemean Odes* 3.43,47; Apollonius Rhodius 2.1231,1241; Scholiast on Apollonius Rhodius 2.392; Hyginus, *Fables: Preface* 14.]

PHILYRA (2) was the wife of Nauplius, according to some, but usually his wife was called CLYMENE. [Apollodorus 2.1.4.]

PHINEIS was betrothed to Enalus. She was thrown into the sea to appease Amphitrite, who had somehow been offended by the colonists who were following the sons of Penthilus to Lesbos. Enalus dived overboard to join Phineis and was rescued by a dolphin. The dolphin's mate rescued Phineis. [Plutarch, *Dinner of the Seven Wise Men* 20; Pausanias 10.13.5.]

PHLOGEA was the mother of Echetus by Euchenor. Echetus was a cruel king of Epeirus. His daughter Metope had a secret affair with Aechmodicus. Echetus found them out and had Aechmodicus castrated. He then blinded Metope and gave her iron barleycorns to grind, saying he would restore her sight if she ground them into flour. [Homer, *Odyssey* 18.83, 21.307; Apollonius Rhodius 4.1093.]

PHOEBE (1) was a daughter of Uranus and Gaea, and was one of the Titanides. By her brother Coeus she became the mother of Asteria and Leto, and thus was the grandmother of Apollo and Artemis. Asteria was the wife of Perses, cousin of the sun, and, according to some, the mother of Hecate. Later she was pursued by Zeus but eluded him by changing into a quail and then into the island Asteria, later called Delos. This was where Leto came to give birth to Apollo and Artemis. So Phoebe was fundamental in the story of the oracular Apollo. In fact, she was said to be in possession of the Delphic oracle before Apollo, to whom she bequeathed it. Apollo's surname Phoebus probably came from her. [Hesiod, *Theogony* 136,404; Apollodorus 1.1.3,2.2; Aeschylus, *Eumenides* 6.]

PHOEBE (2) was said to be a daughter of Tyndareus and Leda. She was mentioned only by Euripides and Ovid, and only then in passing. She could have died very young and thus missed being included in the curse that overhung her sisters Clytemnestra, Helen, and Timandra. Another sister was Philonoe, who was made immortal by Artemis, which probably means she also died young. [Euripides, *Iphigeneia at Aulis* 50; Ovid, *Heroides* 8.77.]

PHOEBE (3) was a Hamadryad nymph by whom Danaus had several daughters. Her sister nymph was Atlantia, who also had daughters by Danaus, so it is not certain which daughters were by which nymph. The daughters were Hippodameia, Rhodia, Cleopatra, Asteria, Hippodameia, Glauce, Hippomedusa, Gorge, Iphimedusa, and Rhode. It is certain that Phoebe had a daughter named Hippodameia. [Apollodorus 2.1.5.]

PHOEBE (4) was one of the LEUCIPPIDES. [Apollodorus 3.10.3.]

PHOEBE (5) was one of the AMAZONS slain by Heracles. [Diodorus Siculus 4.16.]

PHOEBE (6) was a surname of Artemis in her capacity as the goddess of the moon, the moon being regarded as the female Phoebus, or sun. [Virgil, *Georgics* 1.431, *Aeneid* 10.215; Ovid, *Heroides* 20.229.]

PHOENICE was by Poseidon the mother of Torone. Nothing is known of Phoenice except that she might have been a daughter of Phoenix by Telephe, thereby being part of the family of Agenor that went searching for Europa. Torone became the wife of Proteus, and mother of Tmolus and Telegonus. [Scholiast on Euripides' *Phoenician Maidens* 5; Stephanus Byzantium "Torone."]

PHORCIDES, Phorcydes, or Phorcynides were daughters of Phorcys and Ceto. They were the GORGONS and the GRAEAE. [Aeschylus, *Prometheus* 794; Hyginus, *Fables: Preface* 9.]

PHORONIS was a surname of Io, being a descendant of Phoroneus, according to some, or his sister, according to others. [Ovid, *Metamorphoses* 1.668; Hyginus, *Fables* 145.]

PHOSPHOROS, Bringing Light, was a surname of Artemis, probably relating to her role as goddess of birth. It was also a surname of Eos, relating to her function as bringer of dawn. It was also a name of Hecate, who was frequently depicted bearing a torch. [Pausanias 4.31.8; Euripides, *Ion* 1157, *Helen* 569.]

PHRASIMEDE was, according to some, the mother of Daedalus. Usually his mother was called ALCIPPE. [Scholiast on Plato's *Republic* 7.529.]

PHRONTIS was the wife of Panthous. Panthous was a son of Othrys and a priest of Apollo. Priam, king of Troy, had raised him to this rank, probably because he had originally come from Delphi. He had been taken to Troy as a youth by Antenor because of his remarkable beauty, which suggests he was Antenor's lover until he reached manhood. He and Phrontis were secure as citizens of Troy, and Panthous was one of the elders. Their sons were Euphorbus, Polydamas, and Hyperenor. Polydamas was a close friend of Hector. Hyperenor was killed in the Trojan War by Menelaus. Euphorbus, the best known, was also killed by Menelaus, who took his shield to the temple of Hera at Argos. It was through recognition of this shield that the philosopher Pythagoras claimed to have been Euphorbus in a previous life. [Homer, *Iliad* 11.57, 16.808, 17.1,40; Virgil, *Aeneid* 2.319; Pausanias 2.17.3; Diogenes Laertius, *Lives of Eminent Philosophers* 8.1.4.]

PHRYGIA was a name used for Cybele as the goddess who was worshipped above all others in Phrygia, and as a surname of Athena because of the Palladium, which was brought from Phrygia. [Pliny, *Natural History* 5.32; Virgil, *Aeneid* 7.139; Ovid, *Metamorphoses* 13.337.]

PHTHIA (1) was a daughter of Amphion and NIOBE. [Apollodorus 3.5.6.]

PHTHIA (2) was thought to be a daughter of Phoroneus. Zeus desired her and changed himself into a dove to achieve his purpose. Presumably he changed back in time to consummate the affair, since we have no record of egg-laying by Phthia. The son born from this union was Achaeus, who founded Phthiotian Achaea. The parents of Achaeus are most often called Xuthus and Creusa. [Servius on Virgil's *Aeneid* 1.242.]

PHTHIA (3) was the beloved of Apollo in the country of the Curetes. She bore him three sons, Dorus, Laodocus, and Polypoetes. They were leaders there until Aetolus, son of Endymion, arrived and killed them. Dorus was one of those said to have given his name to the Dorian race. If he was killed by Aetolus, he must have had sons who escaped and survived to carry on the race. The ancestor of the Dorian race was usually called the son of Hellen and brother of Aeolus. [Apollodorus 1.7.6; Pausanias 5.1.6.]

PHTHIA (4) was the mistress of Amyntor. Most writers called her CLYTIA. [Apollodorus 3.13.8.]

PHTHONIA was one of the ALCYONIDES.

PHYLACEIS was the patronymic of AL-CIMEDE as daughter of Phylacus. [Apollonius Rhodius 1.47.]

PHYLEIS was one of the THESPIADES and mother by Heracles of Tigasis. [Apollodorus 2.7.8.]

PHYLLIS was the daughter of a Thracian king, possibly Phyleus (though other names have been suggested). On his way back from Troy, Theseus' son Demophon was detained on the coast near the town of Ennea Hodoi (Nine Roads), and was kindly received by the king and his daughter. Phyllis fell in love with Demophon, and the king gave him part of the kingdom when the young man married her. It was not long until he grew homesick and begged to visit Athens, with promises to return shortly. Phyllis reluctantly consented, and they agreed on a certain day, after which if he did not return it would be assumed that some misfortune had befallen him.

He was delayed, however, and on the appointed day Phyllis went nine times to the landing place. This was said to have accounted for the name of the city Ennea Hodoi (modern Amfipoli), though its position at the confluence of nine roads was a more likely explanation. When Demophon failed to show up, Phyllis hanged herself and was metamorphosed into a leafless almond tree. Demophon arrived shortly afterward and embraced the tree in a spasm of grief and sexual deprivation. The tree then burst into full leaf and bloomed with flowers. From the name Phyllis came the Greek name for leaves, *phylla*. Some said the tree had leaves to begin with, but when Demophon embraced it they fell to the ground in sympathy.

Another version of the story, which confuses Demophon with his brother Acamas, says that on their farewell Phyllis gave her lover a cask that he should open at an appointed time if he realized he would not return. He did not return, and did as she instructed. When he saw the contents of the cask (which were never revealed but probably had to do with some kind of curse), he galloped away on his horse and was thrown headlong onto the point of his sword, which had wedged between rocks as he fell. [Lucian, *On the Dance* 40; Apollodorus, *Epitome* 5.16; Hyginus, *Fables* 59; Tzetzes on Lycophron 495; Servius on Virgil's *Eclogues* 5.10; Ovid, *Heroides* 2, *Art of Love* 3.38.]

PHYLLODOCE was one of the NEREIDES. [Hyginus, *Fables: Preface* 8.]

PHYLO was a companion of Helen after she returned to Sparta from Troy. When Telemachus went there in search of news of his father, Helen joined him and Menelaus with her three maidservants. Phylo brought a silver basket filled with yarn that she placed beside Helen. This was a very minor incident, but was significant because during this audience Helen admitted her shamelessness and irresponsibility in the Trojan conflict. [Homer, *Odyssey* 4.124.]

PHYLOMACHE was a daughter of Amphion and, according to some, the wife of Pelias and mother of Acastus. Usually she was called ANAXIBIA.

PHYLOMEDUSA was the wife of Areithous, king of Arne in Boeotia. He was called Corynetes because he fought with no weapon but a club. He fell by the hand of the Arcadian Lycurgus, who drove him into a narrow defile where he could not swing his club. These events took place some time before the Trojan War. The tomb of Areithous was shown in Arcadia. Erythalion, friend of Lycurgus, wore the armor of Areithous in the war. The son of Phylomedusa and Areithous was Menesthius, one of the Greeks at Troy. It is curious he was allied with his father's killer, one who openly wore his father's armor. Menesthius was killed by Paris. [Homer, *Iliad* 7.9,136.]

PHYLONOE was a variant spelling of PHILO-NOE, daughter of Tyndareus and Leda.

PHYLONOME, or Philonome, was a daughter of Nyctimus and Arcadia. Nyctimus was the only son of Lycaon who survived Zeus' wrath. Lycaon and his other sons were changed into wolves when they placed human flesh before Zeus. Nyctimus was reigning when the Deucalionian flood took place. Phylonome was a companion of Artemis, but was seduced by Ares in the guise of a shepherd and became pregnant by him. She concealed her condition from Nyctimus, and when twin sons were born, she set them adrift in the Erymanthus River. They were carried by the river-god into the hollow of a tree, where they were found by a she-wolf. The wolf put her own cubs into the stream and suckled the twins until they were found by a shepherd, Gyliphus, who named them Lycastus and Parrhasius. Later, Parrhasius and Lycastus succeeded to the throne of Arcadia. [Plutarch, *Greek and Roman Parallel Stories* 36.]

PHYSADEIA was a daughter of Danaus from whom the spring of Physadeia near Argos was believed to have derived its name. Along with several other daughters, Physadeia was born after Danaus went to Argos. She and these sisters were not part of the mass murder committed by the so-called Danaides. In fact, she might not even have been born at the time, or was a very young child. [Callimachus, *Bath of Pallas* 47.]

PHYSCOA was a woman from Orthia in Elis who mated with Dionysus and bore him a son, Narcaeus. When he grew to manhood, he waged successful wars against hostile neighbors and became quite powerful. He founded a sanctuary of Athena Narcaea at the city of Olympia. He and his mother were also the first to pay worship to Dionysus, both with very good reason. Physcoa received various honors. There was a choral dance named for her by the Sixteen Women, a group that managed the quadrennial Heraean games at Olympia. [Pausanias 5.16.6,7.]

PHYTIA, Creator, was a surname of Leto at Phaestus in Crete. She earned this epithet by changing a maiden into a male to protect her from her father, who had ordered that any female child born to his wife should be killed. The Phaestians celebrated a festival to Leto Phytia called Ecdysia to commemorate the maiden having taken off her female attire. [Antoninus Liberalis 17.]

PHYTO (1) was one of the HYADES. [Hyginus, *Poetic Astronomy* 2.21.]

PHYTO (2) was one of the SIBYLS. [Eratosthenes, quoted by Lydus, *On the Months* 4.47.]

PIERIA (1), probably a nymph, was the wife of Oxylus, son of Haemon. Oxylus was descended from a family of Elis but lived at first in Aetolia. When the Dorians invaded Peloponnesus, they were instructed to choose him as one of their leaders. After he conquered Elis, he became king. He married Pieria and had by her two sons, Aetolus and Laias. Aetolus died at a very early age, and an oracle told his parents to bury him neither in nor out of the city of Elis. There was nothing left to do but bury him under the gate. The managers of the Olympic games from Elis offered an annual sacrifice on his tomb at the gate, from which ran the road to Olympia. [Pausanias 5.4.1; Aristotle, *Politics* 6.2.]

PIERIA (2) was the mother by Danaus of the Danaides Actaea, Podarce, Dioxippe, Adite, Ocypete, and Pylarge. [Apollodorus 2.1.5.]

PIERIA (3) was a daughter of Pythes and Iapyia, prominent citizens of Myus in Caria. Myus had been settled by Ionians who revolted from the rule of the Neleids in Miletus. The Milesians continued to persecute them for their defection, but a kind of truce seemed to be in effect on days of religious festivals. Pythes allowed Pieria and Iapyia to attend a festival at Miletus in honor of Artemis. There Pieria was observed by Phrygius, son of Neleus, who promptly fell in love with her. In subsequent communications with her, he wanted to know what he could do to please her most. She answered that she would like to be able to come to Miletus often and bring others with her. Phrygius understood she was asking for peace, and he promptly stopped hostilities. Pieria was honored in both cities. Women of Miletus prayed that their husbands would love them as much as Phrygius loved Pieria. [Plutarch, *Bravery of Women* 16.]

PIERIDES were the nine daughters of Pierus, an autochthonous king of Emathia (Macedonia), and Euippe or Antiope. Pierus named them after the nine Muses, and we are not sure whether he did this presumptuously, or out of reverence and admiration. The daughters, probably without prompting, entered a contest with the Muses and were defeated. The Muses metamorphosed them into birds called Colymbas, Iynx, Cenchris, Cissa, Chloris, Acalanthis, Nessa, Pipo, and Dracontis. These names were taken from actual names of birds including the wryneck, hawk, jay, duck, goldfinch, and four with no recognizable modern equivalents.

Pierides was also a surname of the MUSES, which they derived from Pieria near Mount Olympus, where they were worshipped. Pierus migrated from Emathia into Boeotia and established the worship of the Muses at Thespiae. [Pausanias 9.29.2; Hesiod, *Theogony* 53; Antoninus Liberalis 9; Ovid, *Metamorphoses* 5.295; Cicero, *On the Nature of the Gods* 3.21.]

PIERIS, or Tereis, an Aetolian, was one of Menelaus' slaves. She shared her bed with him, either from lack of choice or because she sought to improve her unenviable lot. Pieris became the mother of Megapenthes. Some said she was also the mother of Nicostratus by Menelaus, but many others called him the son of Helen.

It is not clear whether this affair went on prior to Helen's leave-taking, but it would not be too surprising if that were the case. While attending his grandfather's funeral in Crete, Menelaus got the nymph Cnossia pregnant, and for all intents and purposes he was still happily married (although Helen was at that very time in the process of eloping).

Megapenthes was born after Helen left. Because of the curious circumstances, he most probably had a favored upbringing, even though Menelaus shortly went off to prepare for war and then to the war itself. Megapenthes did not see his father for many years and was nearly an adult when he returned from Troy (considerably adult if the stories of the difficult and delayed return can be accepted).

Menelaus set about finding a suitable marriage for his son. He helped arrange a liaison between Megapenthes and one of the daughters of Alector, son of Argeius. It would be extremely interesting to know what prompted this choice. Alector was probably a Spartan nobleman. When Menelaus died, the Spartans were unwilling to have an illegitimate king, so the rule went

to Orestes, the husband of Hermione, Menelaus' daughter.

Some said that Orestes could not succeed to the throne at first, since he was still suffering from madness caused by his matricide. So Megapenthes ruled as regent for a while. During this time he and his half-brother Nicostratus drove Helen into exile. No one has ever explained why Nicostratus did not inherit the throne. Perhaps there was some truth to the story that he was not Helen's son.

Pieris was not heard from again. It is conceivable she continued as Menelaus' mistress. On the other hand, she might have died before Menelaus and Helen returned to Sparta. [Homer, *Odyssey* 3.188, 4.11, 15.100; Apollodorus 3.11.1; Pausanias 3.18.7, 19.2.]

PIETAS was the personification of duty toward one's family, the state, and the gods. At Rome she at first had a small sanctuary but later a larger one, built in 191 B.C. at the foot of the Capitoline Hill. She was often depicted on coins, usually as a matron. She was also represented offering her breast to an aged parent. The stork was sacred to her, and children were considered to be under her protection. [Pliny, *Natural History* 7.36; Cicero, *On Laws* 2.28; Livy 40.34.]

PIMPLEIDES was a surname of the Muses derived from Pimpleia (modern Litohoro) in Pieria, which was sacred to them. [Horace, *Odes* 1.26.9.]

PIPLEIA, or Pimpleia, was a nymph loved by Daphnis. The nymph was more often called NOMIA. [Servius on Virgil's *Eclogues* 8.68.]

PIPO was one of the PIERIDES.

PIRENE was one of the DANAIDES, daughter of Danaus and an Ethiopian woman. She married Agaptolemus. According to Hyginus, she married Dolichus. [Apollodorus 2.1.5; Hyginus, *Fables* 170.]

PISIDICE (*See* PEISIDICE)

PISINOE (*See* PEISINOE)

PITANATIS was a surname of Artemis, derived from the little town of Pitane in Laconia, where she had a temple. [Callimachus, *Hymn to Artemis* 172; Pausanias 3.16.9.]

PITANE was a daughter of the Eurotas River in Laconia. She became by Poseidon the mother of Euadne. As soon as Euadne was born, Pitane sent her to the Arcadian king Aepytus to be reared. Euadne was the mother of Iamus by Apollo. The town of Pitane, a hamlet of Sparta and a fashionable place of residence, was named for Pitane. There was never an explanation of why Pitane sent her daughter to Arcadia. [Pindar, *Olympian Odes* 6.28,30,46; Hyginus, *Fables* 175.]

PITYS was a nymph loved by Pan. One day when she fled from his embraces she was changed into a pine tree. Thereafter the pine was sacred to Pan, and he used sprays of pine needles as chaplets. Some said both Pan and Boreas, the north wind, loved Pitys, and that she chose Pan. In a jealous rage Boreas blew her over a cliff. Gaea took pity and changed her into a pine, which still weeps when the north wind blows through its branches. [Lucian, *Dialogues of the Gods* 2; Propertius 1.18.20; Nonnos, *Dionysiaca* 2.108.]

PLACIA was, according to some, the wife of Laomedon. Her name was usually given as STRYMO. [Apollodorus 3.12.3.]

PLATAEA was a daughter of the Asopus River. She had a sanctuary at Plataea, which derived its name from her. She had an indirect role in a famous confrontation between Zeus and Hera. Hera once retreated to Euboea in a fit of jealousy, and Zeus asked his friend King Cithaeron of Plataea to help him get her back. Cithaeron was a very clever man; he told Zeus to dress a wooden statue in wedding attire and pretend he was marrying Plataea, the daughter of Asopus. Zeus did this, and Hera appeared and tore off the dress. When she saw the situation, she was both pleased and ashamed. A festival called Daedala grew from this incident. [Pausanias 9.1.2,3.1.]

PLAUCIA was, according to some, one of the PLEIADES. [Scholiast on Theocritus 13.25.]

PLEIADES were the daughters of Atlas by Pleione, although the usual meddlers in ancient cosmogony suggested the Oceanid Aethra or the queen of the Amazons as their mother. They were the sisters of the Hyades. Their names were Electra, Maia, Taygete, Alcyone, Celaeno, Sterope, and Merope. Again, one writer saw fit to depart from tradition and called them Coccymo, Plaucia, Protis, Parthenia, Maia, Stonychia, and Lampatho (or Lampado). Additionally we find Asteria, Calypso, and Dione occasionally listed as Pleiades. Sterope sometimes appeared as Asterope.

For the most part the Pleiades mated with gods. Taygete, Maia, and Electra were lovers of Zeus, and Alcyone and Celaeno were lovers of Poseidon. The two who did not have gods for lovers managed to pick two of the worst scoundrels of ancient story. Sterope married Oenomaus, who killed 20 of his daughter's suitors because he wanted Hippodameia for himself. Merope married Sisyphus, who had to suffer special torture in Hades for his many sins.

The Pleiades were transformed into a constellation, and the story goes that they and their mother Pleione were pursued by the giant Orion for a very long time until the gods intervened and placed them in the sky. Another story says they mourned so deeply when Atlas was punished by having to bear the heavens on his shoulders that they were transformed into doves and then into stars. Merope was said to be the least visible of these stars, since she hid her face in shame for having married a mortal. This did not take Sterope into account, but many claimed she was the mother (by Ares) of Oenomaus, not the wife. [Apollodorus 1.9.3, 3.10.1; Diodorus Siculus 4.27; Servius on Virgil's *Aeneid* 8.130; Ovid, *Fasti* 4.175.]

PLEIONE was one of the OCEANIDES and mother of the PLEIADES by Atlas. Atlas was the son of Iapetus and Clymene, and leader of the Titans in the war against Zeus and the Olympians. He was condemned to bear the heavens on his head and shoulders. Pleione had to share him with Aethra, who, according to some, became the mother of the Hyades and Hesperides by him. He had children by other women as well. The Pleiades mated with gods for the most part, but interestingly only one of Pleione's grand-children—Hermes—was one of the immortal Olympian gods. An interesting question might be why he was different, since Zeus, his father, had sons by two of the other Pleiades. [Apollodorus 3.10.1; Diodorus Siculus 4.27; Scholiast on Homer's *Iliad* 18.486, *Odyssey* 5.272; Hyginus, *Fables* 192,248.]

PLEXAURE (1) was one of the OCEANIDES. [Hesiod, *Theogony* 353.]

PLEXAURE (2) was one of the NEREIDES. [Apollodorus 1.2.7.]

PLOTO was one of the NEREIDES. [Hesiod, *Theogony* 242.]

PLUTO (1) was one of the OCEANIDES and one of the playmates of Persephone. [Hesiod, *Theogony* 355; *Homeric Hymn to Demeter* 422.]

PLUTO (2) was a daughter of Cronus or Himantes (also called Mimas but thought to be a surname of Atlas). She slept with Zeus and became the mother of Tantalus. Some said his father was Tmolus, a Lydian king. If so, this could not be the same Tmolus who was married to Omphale, since his grandson Pelops would need to be contemporary with Perseus, instead of five generations later as in the latter case.

Tantalus was one of the miscreants of mythology, practicing theft, deception, and even sacrilege. He started out as a favorite of the gods, often joining them at their banquets, but after revealing their secrets, sharing their nectar and ambrosia with his mortal friends, and even serving his son to them for dinner, he was imprisoned under Mount Sipylus in Lydia. Later he was condemned to torture in the underworld by being placed in view of bountiful food and drink that withdrew when he reached for them. [Pausanias 2.22.4; Scholiast on Euripides' *Orestes* 5; Scholiast on Pindar's *Olympian Odes* 3.41; Hyginus, *Fables* 155.]

PODARCE was one of the DANAIDES, daughter of Danaus and Pieria. She married and murdered Oeneus. [Apollodorus 2.1.5.]

PODARGE was one of the HARPIES. By Zephyrus, the west wind, she was mother of Xanthus and Balius, the horses of Achilles. [Homer, *Iliad* 16.150; Quintus Smyrnaeus 3.750.]

POENE was the personification of retaliation. The name sometimes appeared in the plural, which suggested punishing beings similar in function to the Eumenides, but their sphere of influence appeared to be narrower. They were part of the train of Dice (Justice).

As an individual divinity, Poene was once sent in the form of a monster by Apollo to punish the inhabitants of Argos because of the murder of Psamathe by her father when she bore Linus to the god. Young Coroebus slew the monster, but another scourge was sent. Coroebus had to make further amends for his people and in the process founded Megara.

Obviously Poene as an abstract notion was not destroyed. She apparently had no altars or temples, but she did appear on vases and in inscriptions. [Aeschylus, *Libation-Bearers* 936, 947; Pausanias 1.43.7, 2.19.7.]

POLEMUSA was one of the AMAZONS. [Quintus Smyrnaeus 1.42.]

POLIAS, Guardian of the City, was a surname of Athena at Athens. The name distinguished Athena in her oldest temple on the Acropolis. In times of war, towns, fortresses, and harbors were under her care. Among many other things, the temple boasted a rare folding seat made by the artist Daedalus. Though the name Polias was mainly associated with Athens, Athena had the same name in other cities. [Apollodorus 2.14.2; Pausanias 1.2.5,27.1,3.]

POLIUCHOS, Protecting the City, was a surname of Athena Chalcioecos at Sparta. [Pausanias 3.17.2.]

POLYBE was one of the DANAIDES. She was married to Iltonomus. [Hyginus, *Fables* 170.]

POLYBOEA (1) was the daughter of Amyclas and Diomede. Her brother was the beautiful boy Hyacinthus, who was condemned to an early death as the object of rivalry between two gods. Nothing is known of Polyboea except that she died a virgin and was depicted along with her brother on the famous throne of the Amyclaean Apollo. [Pausanias 3.19.4.]

POLYBOEA (2) was the first wife of Actor, son of Myrmidon. Actor was king of Phthia and, according to some, welcomed Peleus to his kingdom when the young man came to be purified of the murder of his brother. Some said he died childless and left the rule to Peleus, but others said that by Polyboea or a second wife he had Eurytion, who befriended Peleus. The friends were fellow Argonauts and Calydonian hunters. Peleus married Eurytion's daughter and succeeded to the kingdom of Phthia when he accidentally killed his father-in-law during the Calydonian hunt. [Eustathius on Homer's *Iliad* 321; Apollodorus 1.7.3,8.2.]

POLYBOEA (3) was, according to some, the second wife of Cycnus and the stepmother of Hemithea and Tenes. Cycnus' second wife was usually called PHILONOME. [Scholiast on Homer's *Iliad* 1.38.]

POLYBOEA (4) was a daughter of Oicles and Hypermnestra and sister of Iphianeira and Amphiaraus. While a great deal is known about Amphiaraus, one of the great seers of his day and a principal in the war of the Seven against Thebes, we know nothing of his sisters. Again, the very fact they were mentioned at all suggests there was more to know about them, and perhaps there were written accounts that were lost. [Diodorus Siculus 4.69.]

POLYBOULOS, Exceedingly Wise, was a surname of Athena. [Homer, *Iliad* 5.260.]

POLYBULE was, according to some, the wife of Alector and mother of Leitus. More often she was called CLEOBULE. [Homer, *Iliad* 17.602; Hyginus, *Fables* 97.]

POLYCASTE (1) was one of the two daughters of Nestor and Eurydice. She had seven brothers, one of whom, Antilochus, was killed in the Trojan War. Nestor had returned home safely from

the war and, apparently favored by the gods, was living in full enjoyment of old age after an adventurous and fulfilling life. He had two lovely daughters and six intelligent and brave sons. Telemachus, son of Odysseus, went to Pylus in search of news of his father, and Nestor received him hospitably. Telemachus stayed a very short time, since he learned nothing of sufficient importance, but before supper he was given a bath and an oil rubdown by Polycaste, which somehow made the trip worthwhile. The next day he left for Sparta, but he did not forget Polycaste. He later married her and had a son, Persep(t)olis. Nothing is known of this son, and we never hear of Polycaste again. We know Telemachus later had a child by Nausicaa and then married the daughter of Circe. Polycaste could have died in childbirth, and the child Persep(t)olis might have died as well. [Homer, *Odyssey* 3.464; Scholiast on Homer's *Odyssey* 16.118.]

POLYCASTE (2) was the daughter of Lygaeus, about whom nothing is known. Polycaste married Icarius, son of Perieres and Gorgophone. He had fled to Acarnania with his half-brother Tyndareus when their stepbrother Hippocoon usurped the kingdom of Sparta. The brothers remained in Acarnania for many years. Tyndareus married Leda, daughter of Thestius, and Icarius married Polycaste. By her he had three children, Leucadius, Alyzeus, and Penelope. Heracles overthrew Hippocoon and restored Tyndareus to the throne of Sparta. Icarius also returned to Sparta, taking with him Polycaste and Penelope. The two sons were old enough to make their own way in the world. They remained in Acarnania, where Leucadius gave his name to the island of Leucas, and Alyzeus his name to the city of Alyzeus.

Penelope was very lovely and sought by many suitors. Finally, Icarius reluctantly gave her to Odysseus. It is not known how Polycaste felt about the match. Mothers worried about the character of their prospective sons-in-law, and Odysseus was, after all, the grandson of the notorious thief Autolycus. Moreover, Odysseus had spent much of his boyhood in the company of his grandfather.

Both Icarius and Polycaste had disappeared by the time the culminating events in the *Odyssey* occurred, but one scandalous post-Homeric account said Penelope was seduced by the leader of the suitors and that Odysseus sent her back to her father.

It is necessary to point out that Periboea, a Naiad, was also called the wife of Icarius and the mother of Thoas, Damasippus, Imeusimus, Aletes, and Perilaus. It is not inconceivable that Periboea could have been a second wife. Both Polycaste and Periboea were called the mother of Penelope. Periboea's sons had no particular distinction. Perilaus was mentioned as wanting to exact revenge on Orestes for the murder of Clytemnestra, Perilaus' cousin. The wife of Icarius was also called Dorodoche or Asterodeia. [Homer, *Odyssey* 2.132,133; Apollodorus 3.10.4–6,9, *Epitome* 7.38; Pausanias 8.34.4.]

POLYCASTE (3) was a sister of Daedalus and mother of Talos. Most called her PERDIX.

POLYDAMNA was the wife of King Thon in Egypt. When Helen and Menelaus were forced to spend time in Egypt, Polydamna gave Helen a remedy by which she could soothe any grief or anger. Helen mixed this drug with wine when Telemachus visited Sparta. The communal way in which the drug was used suggests recreational drugs were not uncommon in the ancient world. Helen reported to the others that Egypt rendered the greatest store of drugs and that there every person was a physician. [Homer, *Odyssey* 4.228.]

POLYDORA (1) was one of the OCEANIDES. [Hesiod, *Theogony* 354.]

POLYDORA (2) was called by some the mother of Idas and Lynceus. Their mother was more often known as ARENE. [Scholiast on Apollonius Rhodius 1.151.]

POLYDORA (3) was a daughter of Danaus after he arrived in Argos. He had several daughters— never a son—after fathering the famous Danaides, who accompanied him from Egypt. Polydora was loved by the river-god Spercheius and had a son, Dryops. He became king of the Dryopes, who occupied the country from the valley of the Spercheius and Thermopylae all the way to Mount Parnassus. Polydora was consequently the mother of the Dryopian race. The Dryopes were driven out by the Dorians and settled in various places, notably the Argolid peninsula, where Dryops himself led some of them to Asine. [Antoninus Liberalis 32; Scholiast on Apollonius Rhodius 1.1212; Tzetzes on Lycophron 480.]

POLYDORA (4), according to some, was the daughter of Meleager and Cleopatra, who married Protesilaus. More often she was called LAODAMEIA. [Pausanias 4.2.5.]

POLYDORA (5) was the daughter of Peleus and Antigone, and half-sister to Achilles. Her mother committed suicide when she received a spiteful message from Astydameia, wife of Acastus, that Peleus was about to marry the daughter of Acastus. (Astydameia had tried to seduce Peleus but failed.) After that, Polydora was motherless for awhile. Peleus then pursued Thetis, the Nereid, until he was able to convince her to become his wife. The wedding was a grand affair, attended by both gods and mortals. Achilles was born, and Thetis came and went. Polydora was probably intimidated by her regal stepmother.

Polydora was loved by the river-god Spercheius and by Borus, son of Perieres. By one or the other she had Menesthius. It is likely she married the mortal Borus, but the son was probably by the river-god.

Menesthius was one of Achilles' commanders in the Trojan War. He was probably about the same age as his uncle. [Homer, *Iliad* 2.3.142, 16.173–177; Apollodorus 3.13.1–4; Pausanias 1.37.2.]

POLYDORA (6) was one of the AMAZONS. [Hyginus, *Fables* 163.]

POLYHYMNIA (*See* POLYMNIA)

POLYHYMNO was one of the NYSEIDES.

POLYMATHEIA was one of three MUSES in Sicyon. [Plutarch, *Table-Talk* 9.14.]

POLYMEDE was a daughter of Autolycus, the famous thief and son of Hermes, and Neaera. She and her sister Anticleia spent a lonely youth growing up on Mount Parnassus in the carefully chosen hideouts their father was forced to use to elude pursuers. Polymede was considerably older than Anticleia and married as soon as she was able in order to escape the isolation imposed by her father's occupation.

She married Aeson, son of Cretheus and Tyro, and they lived in Iolcus. It was not long before Aeson was excluded by his half-brother Pelias from his rightful share in the kingdom. After that, Pelias grew more and more tyrannical. When a son was born to Aeson and Polymede, they had reason to believe Pelias would destroy the baby, so Polymede called on trusted friends to weep over him as though he were stillborn. Then the parents of the child they called Diomedes sent him in secret to Mount Pelion, where he was reared by Cheiron the Centaur.

So Polymede became acquainted early with sadness. She longed for the child she had to surrender, and would not see him for nearly two decades. When he did reappear he had a different name, Jason. He had lost a sandal in a river on his way, and Pelias knew immediately that he had much to fear from this youth from the mountains, for an oracle had warned him to beware of a man with a single shoe. He was even more alarmed when he learned Jason was his nephew. He soon devised a plan to be rid of this threatening young man by trapping him into a commitment to fetch for him the fabled Golden Fleece from the kingdom of Colchis, a quest that was certain to be fatal.

He might have been disquieted, though, when the idea caught on and heroes from all over Greece came forth to join in this most glorious of adventures. He was particularly distressed when his own son Acastus decided to join the expedition. Polymede saw Jason constantly during the building of the *Argo* and his preparations, but her heart was heavy. She joined Pelias in believing that the voyage would be perilous and maybe final. She must have tried to dissuade him, but the decision was made. Incidentally, she must have been doubly miserable in her belief that the voyage would be unsuccessful since her own father, Autolycus, was among the crew.

Finally, the Argonauts, as they were called, set off, and Polymede could not know that in-deed she would never see her son again. Occasional rumors came back to Iolcus, finally one that the quest had ended in disaster. In spite of his own imagined loss in the person of Acastus and perhaps even more intensely maddened by it, Pelias had awaited this opportunity to destroy the whole house of Aeson, thus removing any contenders for the throne. He first killed Aeson, though some said Aeson begged to be allowed to end his own life, which he did by drinking bull's blood(!). Then Pelias sent men to murder Polymede and Promachus, a son born to the couple several years after Jason's first departure. They murdered Promachus first in plain view of Polymede. When they turned to her, she slipped past and ran to the hearth of Pelias. To his face she cursed him to suffer the same fate he had so relentlessly brought on her and her family. She then plunged a dagger in her heart and died with the curse on her lips.

Polymede received more than her due share of unhappiness in life. First of all, she grew up in isolation and perhaps some embarrassment because of her father's outlaw ways. She married early to escape this solitary life but was immediately plunged into the intrigue of big-city politics. Her husband was unfortunately unassertive and did not even have the initiative to move beyond the reach of his ruthless half-brother. He had connections in the powerful but sometimes dissolute Aeolid line from which he descended. Indeed his brother Amythaon had even come from Messenia to attempt to intercede for Jason when Pelias announced he was sending him on the suicidal voyage. When the voyage became a fact and Jason left, Polymede had only seen him for a few months. She never saw him again, and during his absence she must have imagined for him a thousand horrible deaths. She was told, incorrectly as it turned out, that he was not coming back, and added to her grief was terror at the certain fate for herself and her family. She then learned Aeson was dead, and after that she saw Promachus killed before her eyes. Her own death was if anything an anticlimax. Her only two triumphs were hiding Jason when he was born and pronouncing the powerful curse on the superstitious Pelias. It is unfortunate she could not have seen the grisly manner in which the curse had its effect.

The mother of Jason was also variously called Alcimede, Amphinome, Perimede, Polypheme, Scarphe, Arne, Periclymene, Polymela, and Rhoeo. [Apollodorus 1.9.16,27; Ovid, *Heroides* 4.105; Hyginus, *Fables* 13,14; Diodorus Siculus 4.50; Valerius Flaccus 1.777.]

POLYMELA (1) was, according to some, the daughter of Peleus and wife of Menoetius, by whom she became the mother of Patroclus. The mother of Patroclus was more often called STHENELE. [Apollodorus 3.13.8.]

POLYMELA (2) was a daughter of Phylas. She was a joyous maiden given to dancing and singing, and she tended to lean toward service to Artemis. But Hermes observed her among all her companions and decided to change her mind about chastity. Endowed with great sex appeal, the god did not have much difficulty in getting into bed with Polymela. The result of this union was Eudorus. Eudorus was adopted by Echecles, son of Actor, who had long been in love with Polymela. Polymela decided it was time to settle down, and accepted him. Her father took charge of rearing the boy. It is easy to see that Polymela was blessed with a tolerant father and husband.

When Eudorus grew up, he was especially fleet-footed and showed talent in military affairs. When the Trojan War came along, he made a perfect captain for Achilles, and was one of the five leaders of the Myrmidons. Achilles sent him out to prevent Patroclus from venturing too far behind Trojan lines, but Eudorus was slain by Pyraechmes. [Homer, *Iliad* 16.179–193; Eustathius on Homer's *Odyssey* 1697.]

POLYMELA (3) was one of the six daughters of Aeolus, son of Hippotes and king of the winds. It was Aeolus' custom to marry his sons to their sisters, but somehow Polymela had not married when Odysseus arrived on their island. Aeolus meanwhile extended every courtesy to the hero, whom he very much admired. Odysseus repaid this kindness by secretly meeting Polymela for sexual intercourse. When Aeolus finally sent the voyagers on their way, with winds shut up in a bag for future emergencies, Polymela was heartbroken. Aeolus found her fondling objects left behind by Odysseus. Not only was he furious

with Odysseus, but he planned to punish Polymela. Her brother Diores, who had been waiting for the right moment, begged him not to harm her and to let him marry her at once. Seeing the extent of her father's wrath, Polymela agreed that she would remain with family tradition, and married Diores. [Parthenius, *Love Stories* 2.]

POLYMELA (4) was the daughter of Actor and, according to some, married to Peleus. His wife was usually called ANTIGONE.

POLYMELA (5) was, according to some, the mother of Jason. His mother was more often called POLYMEDE.

POLYMNIA was one of the nine MUSES. She presided over lyric poetry and was believed to have invented the lyre. She was called by some the mother of Orpheus by Oeagrus and of Triptolemus by Celeus or Cheimarrhous, son of Ares. She was even called sometimes the mother of Eros. [Hesiod, *Theogony* 78; Scholiast on Apollonius Rhodius 1.23, 3.1; Scholiast on Homer's *Iliad* 10.425; Plato, *Symposium* 187.]

POLYNOE was one of the NEREIDES. [Hesiod, *Theogony* 258.]

POLYNOME was one of the NEREIDES. [Apollodorus 1.2.7.]

POLYPHEME was, according to some, the mother of Jason. His mother was usually called POLYMEDE.

POLYXENA (1) has always presented problems for scholars, mainly because of post-Homeric writers telling not one but several stories about the relationship between her and Achilles. This was the result of there being no Homeric story on which to comment and offer variations. The principal versions might fall into two parts, one in which Polyxena did not love Achilles and the other in which she did.

Polyxena was one of the daughters, probably the youngest, of Priam and Hecuba. She had virtually grown up with the Trojan War, having been born only a few years before its commencement. She saw her brothers go into battle, and she saw funeral ceremonies performed for most of them. It is likely that she defended Helen, as did her father and mother, in spite of the great havoc her presence had caused.

Once, Polyxena was at a fountain where her brother Troilus was watering his horse. Achilles suddenly appeared and killed him, but Polyxena fled before he could seize her. He could not forget her, however, and when next he saw her realized he was in love with her. This was, according to some, the occasion of her visit with Priam to ransom the corpse of Hector. Achilles stubbornly refused the entreaties of Priam but yielded when Polyxena offered to be his slave in return for the body. Some said she did not come with Priam but threw down her gold bracelets from the walls when the ransom, set at Hector's weight in gold, fell short. Achilles then asked Priam what he could do to win Polyxena, and this certainly must have meant Priam's blessing, not Polyxena's love. He had killed her younger brother in a surprise attack and, though he had killed her older brother honorably, he had refused to surrender the corpse. He told Priam he would swap Hector's body for Polyxena and would undertake to bring about peace between the Greeks and Trojans, the only condition being that Helen would have to be returned. Priam, who had vowed never to surrender Helen, said he would gladly give him Polyxena if Achilles would persuade the Greeks to leave without Helen. It is not difficult to see Priam's priorities, offering a virgin daughter in lieu of an adulteress who had brought down a whole nation.

So far Polyxena had not shown the least flicker of love or admiration for Achilles. If anything, her hostility toward him increased. But as negotiations for a marriage were entered into, she pretended love for him and managed to learn of his vulnerable heel. Finally she sent for him to meet her and her brother Deiophobus in the temple of the Thymbraean Apollo to finalize the marital arrangement. He came barefoot and unarmed as was the custom in this neutral zone. As he approached Polyxena, he was shot in his heel by Paris, who was hiding behind a post. About that time, Odysseus, Ajax, and Diomedes rushed in. They had followed Achilles, suspecting him of treasonable motives. As he died in their arms,

he implored them to sacrifice Polyxena on his tomb as soon as Troy should fall.

The principal version that contended Polyxena loved Achilles said the two fell in love when Hector's body was delivered up to Priam. There was no mention of the murder of Troilus. This love, though of brief duration, was intense. When Achilles was eventually killed by Paris, Polyxena fled to the Greeks and killed herself with a sword on the tomb of her beloved.

The common story was that she was sacrificed by the Greeks on Achilles' tomb unwillingly. As already stated, Achilles had begged that Polyxena be sacrificed, and one could suppose his motive was revenge, since certainly he knew she had betrayed him. However, the prevalent notion among the Greeks was that Achilles wanted to be united with Polyxena after her death. He had appeared in dreams, particularly those of his son Neoptolemus, renewing his request that she be sacrificed. Without this, the dreamers were warned, there would be no favorable winds, and there were many among them who remembered an almost identical situation at Aulis ten years earlier. Agamemnon was opposed to killing Polyxena, but he was, after all, sleeping with Polyxena's sister Cassandra and certain to be prejudiced, everyone agreed. Polyxena was fetched by Odysseus and then stabbed on Achilles' grave by Neoptolemus in view of the whole army. Immediately, favorable winds sprang up. Another version said the Greeks sailed with Polyxena but that the ghost of Achilles appeared as they reached Thrace and threatened them with a calm. They drew ashore and killed her then and there.

These somewhat confusing stories collectively tell us more than perhaps was intended. Except for a single story, Polyxena did not love Achilles. She had every reason. Often when a man "fell in love" with a beautiful woman it meant he wanted to go to bed with her. Achilles might have admired Polyxena's valor and love for her brother Hector, but he scarcely had an opportunity to really fall in love with her. He was young and what we call romantic. He had had tender feelings for Iphigeneia. He withdrew from the war because his beloved Briseis was taken from him. He fell in love with Helen when he beheld her on the walls of Troy. He fell in love with Penthesileia. In addition, he had a steady boyfriend, Patroclus. His request to have Polyxena sacrificed on his tomb could have been partly from this romantic idealism, partly from revenge, and partly for self-aggrandizement.

It is a miracle that some of these post-Homeric writers did not come up with a child for Achilles and Polyxena. They missed a golden opportunity. Under much more difficult circumstances, Achilles was even reported by one writer to have fathered a child by Penthesileia.

Polyxena's sacrifice was represented in the Pinakotheke on the Acropolis. If indeed she joined Achilles after death, she had to share him with Helen, Iphigeneia, and Medea, all of whom were reported to be married to him in the afterlife. [Apollodorus 3.12.5; Euripides, *Hecuba* 40; Ovid, *Metamorphoses* 13.448; Tzetzes on Lycophron 307,323; Hyginus, *Fables* 110; Philostratus, *Heroicus* 19.11; Pausanias 1.22.6; Dares of Phrygia 34; Quintus Smyrnaeus 3.50.]

POLYXENA (2) was one of the DANAIDES and married to Aegyptus, son of Aegyptus. [Hyginus, *Fables* 170.]

POLYXO (1) was one of the lovers of Danaus. By him she had Autonoe, Theano, Electra, Cleopatra, Eurydice, Glaucippe, Anthelia, Cleodora, Euippe, Erato, Stygne, and Bryce. This was by far the greatest number of daughters borne to him by one individual. This means she was either the most desirable of his concubines or the most fertile. Polyxo was a Naiad, and it was uncommon for a Naiad to carry on a sustained relationship. Polyxo could almost be considered the wife of Danaus instead of a concubine. [Apollodorus 2.1.5.]

POLYXO (2) was the wife of Nycteus, son of Hyrieus and Clonia. Her own background is unknown, but she was likely the daughter of the Asopus River in Boeotia. She had two daughters by Nycteus called Antiope and Nycteis. Antiope, the younger one, was quite beautiful and was loved by Zeus. From fear of her doting father she fled when she discovered she was pregnant. She took refuge with King Epopeus of Sicyon, who refused to surrender her on Nycteus' command. Nycteus declared war, and both he and Epopeus

died in the ensuing battle. Antiope was taken prisoner by her uncle Lycus, who swore to his dying brother that he would deal with her. She gave birth to Amphion and Zethus on the way back to Thebes. The twins grew up to avenge their mother for all the wrongs she suffered from Lycus and his cruel wife, Dirce. Polyxo was heard from no more. If she remained in Thebes, she probably was mistreated by Dirce because she was Antiope's mother and therefore expected to be protective of her daughter. Antiope later married Phocus, grandson of Sisyphus. It is possible that Polyxo joined them in Phocis if she was still alive. [Pausanias 3.10.1, 9.17.4.]

POLYXO (3) was one of the HYADES. [Hyginus, *Fables* 182.]

POLYXO (4) was the nurse of Hypsipyle. She convinced the Lemnian women, who had murdered their husbands, that their race would become extinct without men. She urged them to offer themselves to the well-born Argonauts, who had recently landed on the island and were being repelled by the inhabitants. Polyxo insisted they welcome them and breed new stock for the island. [Apollonius Rhodius 1.668; Hyginus, *Fables* 15.]

POLYXO (5) was an Argive woman married to Tlepolemus. She has also been called Philozoe. Tlepolemus was a son of Heracles by Astyoche, daughter of Phylas, king of Ephyra in Thesprotia. Tlepolemus and his granduncle Licymnius settled in Argos after Heracles' death, but Tlepolemus killed Licymnius either accidentally or during the heat of a quarrel. Consequently, he was forced to leave Argos, and with Polyxo he settled in Rhodes, became king, and founded the cities of Lindus, Ialysus, and Cameirus.

When the Greeks sailed against Troy, Tlepolemus had to join them, for as a former suitor of Helen he was bound to the oath taken in common with the other suitors. He commanded nine ships. He left Polyxo as regent in Rhodes, and she continued in this capacity after the war, since Tlepolemus was killed. She was to hold this office, apparently, until one of her sons became old enough to succeed to the throne.

Polyxo instituted funeral games in commemoration of the death of Tlepolemus. Victors received chaplets of white poplar.

When Menelaus died in Sparta, Helen was driven into exile by her stepson Megapenthes. She fled to Rhodes to the court of Polyxo, as the two had been friends during the years before the war. Helen naively assumed they could resume their friendship, and although she was hospitably received, she could not know just how much Polyxo hated her. First of all, Tlepolemus had been one of Helen's suitors, so Polyxo was not his first choice of wives. Second, Helen had been the cause of the Trojan War, in which Polyxo lost her husband.

Polyxo feigned friendship but secretly planned Helen's destruction. Once while Helen was bathing, Polyxo sent servants disguised as Erinyes, the goddesses of retribution. They took Helen and hanged her on a tree until she was dead. Strictly speaking, this should not have been possible since as a daughter of Zeus Helen was supposed to be immortal, but ancient writers seemed obliged to dispose of her, even in this sordid anticlimactic way. There is no record that Polyxo suffered any punishment for this act, but apparently the Rhodians were nervous about being a party to the murder of the celebrated beauty and built a sanctuary to Helen Dendritis, Helen of the Tree. [Pausanias 3.19.10; Apollodorus 2.8.2; Homer, *Iliad* 2.653; Tzetzes on Lycophron 911.]

POLYXO (6) was one of the OCEANIDES. [Hyginus, *Fables: Preface* 6.]

POMONA was the Roman divinity of fruit trees. She was loved by several rustic divinities. Silvanus, god of fields and forests, sought her favors, although he was usually represented as advanced in years. Picus, a prophetic divinity, loved her but in the process rejected Circe, who loved him. Circe, whose affections were not to be spurned, used her powers of transformation and turned him into a woodpecker. That left Vertumnus, the god of seasons and the growth of plants. He could change into various shapes, which he did in trying to woo Pomona. Finally, after everything else failed, he changed into a blooming youth, and that seemed to be the answer. Vertumnus and Pomona became lovers, and their union seemed to be an ideal one, since it embodied the cycle of seasons and the fruition of trees and crops.

Pomona's worship was of considerable importance, and there was a special priest appointed to her service. She had a sacred grove called the Pomonal, which was situated on the road from Rome to Ostia. It is quite appropriate that she was often identified with Ops, the goddess of plenty. [Ovid, *Metamorphoses* 14.623; Propertius 4.2.21; Servius on Virgil's *Aeneid* 7.190; Horace, *Odes* 3.8, *Epodes* 2.21.]

PONTOMEDUSA was one of the NEREIDES. [Apollodorus 1.2.7.]

PONTOPOREIA was one of the NEREIDES. [Hesiod, *Theogony* 257.]

PORRIMA was one of the CAMENAE.

POSTVERTA, Postvorta, or Prorsa was one of the CAMENAE.

POTAMEIDES were the whole class of river nymphs, who were further classified by specific rivers. [Apollonius Rhodius 3.1219.]

POTINA was a Roman divinity who blessed the drink of children. Her companions, Edulica and Cuba, blessed their food and sleep. [St. Augustine, *City of God* 4.11.]

PRAENESTINA was a surname of the Roman Fortuna, who had a temple and oracle at Praeneste. [Ovid, *Fasti* 6.62; Suetonius, *Domitian* 15.]

PRAXIDICAE were demigoddesses who saw to it that justice was carried out, particularly when oaths were given. Oaths were not to be taken rashly or thoughtlessly, but once sworn had to be followed. Frequently a single goddess, Praxidice, was mentioned, as in the case of Menelaus when he returned with Helen. As a token of just requital of the old wrong done to him, he set up a statue of Praxidice near Gythium, the port of Sparta, not far from the place where Paris had founded a sanctuary of Aphrodite Migonitis in gratitude for her assistance in his elopement with Helen.

The Praxidicae were particularly worshipped near Haliartus in Boeotia. There they were considered the daughters of Ogygus. We are not certain who Ogygus was, but some have given him descent from the Titans. He was a king in Boeotia, some said, ruling over the earliest inhabitants of the world. During his reign was a flood earlier than the one in the time of Deucalion. He had three daughters, Alcomenia, Thelxinoea, and Aulis. They had a temple at the foot of Mount Tilphossium near Haliartus. Statues of these divinities were bodiless, having only heads. Sacrifices to them were restricted to heads of animals. The singular, Praxidice, might have been a surname of Persephone. [Pausanias 9.33.2,4; Suidas, "Praxidike"; Orphica, *Argonautica* 31.]

PRAXITHEA (1), or Pasithea, was a water nymph, probably daughter of the Cephissus River in Attica. She was loved by Erichthonius (Erechtheus I). According to Attican genealogy, Erichthonius was the half-serpent, half-human being produced when Hephaestus, in attempting to rape Athena, spilled his sperm onto the earth and fertilized his great-grandmother Gaea. Athena took the monstrous child to the daughters of Cecrops to be guarded. When against orders they looked into the chest or basket that held the snaky baby, they went mad and flung themselves over the cliff of the Acropolis. Athena brought up Erichthonius in her temple on the Acropolis. He inherited the throne of Cecrops. His serpentine features did not inhibit him from acquiring a wife. Perhaps only a water nymph was able to deal with the extraordinary physical properties possessed by this curious hybrid. They had a son called Pandion, and from all appearances he seemed human enough.

Pandion became king after Erichthonius died. He was the father of Procne, Philomela, Butes, and Erechtheus II. During his reign Athens warred with Thebes and was assisted by Tereus, who became Pandion's son-in-law. There is no record of what happened to Praxithea. She probably returned to her native element even before the death of Erichthonius,

maybe even after the birth of Pandion. [Apollodorus 3.14.6.]

PRAXITHEA (2) was a daughter of Phrasimus and Diogeneia. Phrasimus was probably a provincial king of Attica, and Diogeneia was a daughter of the Cephissus River in Attica. Praxithea married Erechtheus, son of Pandion. By him she had 15 or more children: Cecrops (II), Orneus, Thespius, Eupalamus, Alcon, Pandorus, Metion, Protogeneia, Pandora, Procris, Creusa, Chthonia, Oreithyia, Otionia, and Merope. We know quite a bit about some of these offspring but very little about Praxithea. We can only surmise that her life was probably a gratifying one during the years her children were being born and growing up. She was busy with them and the court life at Athens. As queen she must have entertained important visitors and been influential in the state-sponsored religious observances. Erechtheus was credited with the introduction of the celebration of the Panathenaea, the principal sacred festival.

It was when the children reached adulthood that Praxithea's troubles began. Oreithyia was kidnapped by Boreas, the god of the north wind. Procris was killed accidentally by her husband, Cephalus. Three of Praxithea's daughters committed joint suicide when an oracle declared that sacrifice of one of them was necessary for Athens to win its war with Eleusis. Her grandsons the Metionidae were troublesome and lay in wait for Erechtheus to abandon the throne. Another grandson, according to some, was Daedalus, who killed his nephew and was exiled from Athens. Finally, Erechtheus was killed in the war with Eleusis, and Pandion occupied the throne. Immediately the succession was contested and another war commenced. Praxithea, whose life was not a happy one, probably survived Erechtheus only a short time. [Apollodorus 3.14.6,15.1; Pausanias 1.5.3.]

PRAXITHEA (3) was one of the THESPIADES. By Heracles she was mother of Nephus. [Apollodorus 2.7.8.]

PRAXITHEA (4) was one of the LEONTIDES. [Aelian, *Various Narratives* 12.28.]

PREMA was a surname of Juno, referring to her invocation by newly married people to assist in an easy labor at the birth of a child. [Tertullian, *On Being Born* 2.11; St. Augustine, *City of God* 6.9.]

PRIMA was the daughter of Romulus and Hersilia. Hersilia was the wife of Romulus and mother of Aollius, or Avillius, and Prima. Hersilia was the only married woman carried off by the Romans in the rape of the Sabine maidens. [Plutarch, *Romulus* 14.18.]

PROCLEIA was the daughter of Clytius, son of Laomedon of Troy and one of the Trojan elders. Her brother was Caletor. She married Cycnus, son of Poseidon and Calyce, who was king of Colonae in the Troad. Her children by him were Tenes and Hemithea. She died when they were adolescents, so she could not have known of the unhappy lot that befell her children when Cycnus remarried. (*See* HEMITHEA or PHILONOME.)

PROCNE was a daughter of Pandion, king of Athens, and the wife of Tereus. She killed her small son Itys and served him to her husband for dinner when she learned he had raped her sister PHILOMELA. [Apollodorus 3.14.8.]

PROCRIS (1) was one of the daughters of Erechtheus (II) and Praxithea. Having married and left home, she was not held to the suicide pact that took the lives of three of her sisters, although she indeed at one time might have agreed to die with them if any one of them should have to die. But she was courted by Cephalus, the son of Deion, and had moved to Phocis. They were very much in love and swore eternal fidelity to each other. It is doubtful Procris had any notion of her husband's earlier reputation as the father of Iphiclus by his sister-in-law Clymene. According to some, Procris and Cephalus had a son, Arceisius, the father of Laertes, but Arceisius was more often called the son of Zeus and Euryodia (although some even claimed Cephalus fathered him by a bear after the death of Procris).

The exceedingly handsome Cephalus was once out hunting and was approached by Eos, the goddess of the dawn. She tried to seduce him, but he rejected her advances. Eos had had an affair with another Cephalus, son of Herse and Hermes, but in that case she had simply snatched him from Mount Hymettus and lived with him in Asia. That Cephalus was about the same age as Procris' great-grandfather Erichthonius, since Herse was one of Cecrops' daughters in whose charge Erichthonius had been left.

Never ceasing in her search for beautiful young men, Eos was practiced in matters of the heart. She told Cephalus no one was immune from infidelity and challenged him to test Procris. He was so certain of her love for him that he agreed. Eos metamorphosed him into a handsome stranger and gave him rich presents to tempt Procris. The glamorous young man with his persuasive gifts finally caused Procris to go to bed with him. Cephalus was transformed back into his customary appearance, and Procris was in despair over what she had done and fled to Crete, where she attached herself to the train of Artemis. She remained there for some time but longed for her husband and the happy life she had led. One strange story said that while in Crete she cured Minos of a loathsome curse placed on him by Pasiphae. He could not have sexual relations without killing his partner since, instead of semen, he ejaculated deadly scorpions and insects.

Finally Artemis sent her back to Phocis with a wonderful dog that always tracked down its quarry and a magical spear that never missed its mark. Procris disguised herself as a youth and soon enough fell into company with Cephalus, who loved the chase. It is not clear whether Eos had taken advantage of the absence of Procris and seduced Cephalus but, judging from his passionate nature, she probably had no trouble in doing so. Cephalus was entranced with the young man's spear and dog and tried to buy them, but the youth said Cephalus would have to make love to him first. Cephalus was not given to this form of lovemaking but agreed to go along if there was no other way. As he readied himself to perform the act, Procris revealed herself, and they both had to admit the score was even.

The husband and wife were reconciled, but Procris was never at ease again. She had seen how both of them had been lured by material things to the extent that they proved unfaithful, and she knew it could happen again. Cephalus undoubtedly told her the part Eos had played, and she was particularly afraid that Eos would return with other, more attractive offers. So she started to spy on Cephalus during the hunt. Once, he spotted her in a thicket. He threw the never-erring spear at what he thought was an animal, and Procris was pierced through the heart.

Cephalus was exiled for this accidental death. He joined Amphitryon against the Taphians and was given the island of Cephallenia as his reward. He remarried and had several sons. Some said he never recovered from his despair over Procris and, after having built as atonement a temple of Apollo on the steep cliff of Cape Leucas, he leapt from there into the sea to his death. [Apollodorus 1.9.4, 3.15.2; Eustathius on Homer's *Odyssey* 1961; Hyginus, *Fables* 48,125,189; Ovid, *Metamorphoses* 7.394; Antoninus Liberalis 41; Pausanias 1.37.4.]

PROCRIS (2) was one of the THESPIADES. She became by Heracles the mother of twins, Antileon and Hippeus. [Apollodorus 2.7.8.]

PRODROMIA, Advance-Guard, was a surname of Hera. Phalces, son of Temenus and father of Rhegnidas, was one of the Heracleidae. He took possession of the government of Sicyon and there founded the temple of Hera Prodromia. He was said to have killed his father and his sister Hyrnetho. [Strabo 8.8.5; Pausanias 2.6.4,11.2,13.1,29.3.]

PROETIDES were the daughters of Proetus by Anteia. They were usually called Lysippe, Iphinoe, and Iphianassa or Iphianeira (though one writer called the last two Hipponoe and Cyrianassa, and another writer mentioned only two daughters, Elege and Celaeno). These daughters were probably born in Lycia, where their father fled when he was expelled from Argos by his twin brother, Acrisius, the father of Danae, who claimed Proetus had molested her. Proetus married Anteia, the daughter of the Lycian king Iobates. By armed force his father-in-law helped him regain his share of the kingdom in Argolis, so Proetus thus acquired Tiryns, the Heraion (temple of Hera), Midea, and the coast of Argolis. The famous walls of Tiryns were built by the Cyclopes, who followed Proetus to Peloponnesus.

The sisters offended Dionysus, according to some, by rejecting his worship. Others said they set their beauty above Hera's or stole gold from her statue. The last is more likely the case, since the famous Heraion was in their father's territory. Whatever the reason, they were stricken with madness and, in spite of their father's efforts to deal with the problem, left home and wandered through Peloponnesus.

Melampus, the famous seer, offered his services, but his price was high—one-third of the kingdom. Proetus refused to talk to him. But his daughters' madness increased, and reports came back that the disease was spreading to other Argive women, who ran about in frenzy and even murdered their children. Finally, Proetus agreed to listen to Melampus, but the price for his services had gone up. Now he asked for another third of the kingdom for his brother Bias. Proetus had little choice but to agree. His own safety was being threatened by the Argives, who regarded the king as absolute in matters of public welfare.

Melampus chose the strongest among the young men of Tiryns and pursued the women. They caught up with them in the territory of Sicyonia. During the pursuit Iphinoe died, but Melampus managed to catch Lysippe and Iphianassa. He purified them at one of the sacred springs of Arcadia and returned them to their father. Proetus wisely founded a sanctuary of Hera between Sicyon and Titane and, to be on the safe side, one of Apollo at Sicyon. Melampus married Iphianassa, and Bias married Lysippe. [Apollodorus 2.2.2; Diodorus 4.68; Servius on Virgil's *Eclogues* 6.48; Aelian, *Various Narratives* 3.42; Herodotus 9.3; Pausanias 2.7.7,12.1; Ovid, *Metamorphoses* 3.25; Scholiast on Pindar's *Nemean Odes* 9.30.]

PROMACHORMA, Protectress of the Bay, was a surname of Athena under which she had a sanctuary on Mount Buporthmus near Hermione. [Pausanias 2.34.9.]

PROMNE was the wife of Buphagus at Pheneus in Arcadia. Buphagus was a son of Iapetus and

Thornax, and an Arcadian hero. He and Promne received the wounded Iphicles, the brother of Heracles, into their house and took care of him until he died. Iphicles had been wounded in the battle with the Molionides at Cleonae. The Buphagus River on the boundary between Megalopolis and Heraea was named for him. He was afterward killed by Artemis for trying to rape her. This incidental information was the sort often thrown out by ancient writers with no further explanation. Perhaps Promne was an invalid or died. [Pausanias 8.14.9,27.17.]

PRONAEA, Fore-Temple, was a surname of Athena, under which she had a temple at Delphi in front of the temple of Apollo. The surname is often found as Pronoea, Forethought, but the reference is the same. This temple played a part in two major accounts. Menelaus consulted the Delphic oracle about his expedition against Troy and then dedicated Helen's necklace to Athena Pronaea. The sons of Alcmaon, Amphoterus and Acarnan, similarly dedicated the necklace of Harmonia there. [Herodotus 1.92; Aeschylus, *Eumenides* 21; Pausanias 9.10.2.]

PRONOE (1) was one of the NEREIDES. [Hesiod, *Theogony* 261.]

PRONOE (2) was the daughter of Phorbus. Nothing is known of Phorbus (which is not a misreading of Phorbas), but it is reasonable to assume he was an Aetolian, perhaps one of the Curetes. Pronoe married Aetolus, son of Endymion, when he was exiled from Elis for an inadvertent murder. Her sons by him were Pleuron and Calydon, each of whom founded the city named for him. Pronoe can be called the mother of the Aetolian royal line, which included Oeneus, Meleager, Hypermnestra, Leda, and others. [Apollodorus 1.7.7; Pausanias 3.13.5.]

PRONOE (3) was a Naiad in Lycia. When Caunus, son of Miletus, wandered to Lycia to escape the incestuous passion he felt for his sister Byblis, he was followed by his sister, who shared the illicit love. She could not cope with her feelings and hanged herself, and from her dying tears a fountain gushed forth. Pronoe, who knew the story from other Naiades, came forth from her watery world and told Caunus what had happened to Byblis. She persuaded him to live with her, telling him that he not only would obtain her love but also the kingdom to which she was heiress. He married her and became by her the father of Aegialus. Aegialus became king after the death of Caunus, united the far-flung population, and founded on the river shore a large and prosperous city, which he called Caunus. Pronoe remained nearby, since Naiades were immortal, to give assistance to her son and his descendants. [Conon, *Narrations* 2.]

PRONOE (4) was a daughter of Melampus and Iphianassa. Her brothers were Abas, Mantius, and Antiphates. Melampus was one of the great seers of his time. He predicted events, even those that adversely involved him. He effected cures and thus was regarded as one skilled in the medical art. His greatest medical feat was curing the daughters of Proetus of insanity. His charge for this service, two-thirds of Proetus' kingdom, undoubtedly set a precedent for exorbitant medical fees for all time to come. He married Proetus' daughter Iphianassa, one of his patients. Melampus was not a seer for nothing. He knew that this way he would get the remaining third of the kingdom when Proetus died, and that is what happened.

Pronoe and her brothers were barely mentioned in ancient writings, but it is reasonable to guess that some or all of them inherited the prophetic (and healing) gift. This ability usually ran in families and was passed on to successive generations. [Diodorus Siculus 4.68; Apollodorus 1.9.13.]

PRONOEA (*See* PRONAEA)

PRONUBA was a surname of Juno among the Romans, describing her as the divinity presiding over marriage. [Virgil, *Aeneid* 4.166, 7.319; Ovid, *Heroides* 6.43.]

PRORSA was one of the CAMENAE. [Tertullian, *On Being Born* 2.11.]

PROSERPINA was the Roman PERSEPHONE. Before her worship was combined with that of the Greek goddess of the underworld, she had been a rustic goddess presiding over the germination of seeds. [St. Augustine, *City of God* 4.8.]

PROSPICIENS, Gazing, was a surname of Venus. Anaxarete was a maiden of the island of Cyprus, a descendant of Teucer. She remained unmoved by professions of love by Iphis, who finally hanged himself at her door. Venus punished her by changing her into a stone statue, preserved at Salamis in Cyprus in the temple of Venus Prospiciens. [Ovid, *Metamorphoses* 14.698.]

PROSYMNA (1) was one of the daughters of the river-god Asterion near Mycenae. She and her sisters, Acraea and Euboea, acted as nurses to Hera. Her name was given to the town Prosymna, called "lofty," near the Heraion, the temple of Hera. [Pausanias 2.17.1.]

PROSYMNA (2) was a surname of Demeter in Lerna, where she had a statue in a grove on the Amymone River. [Pausanias 2.37.1.]

PROTE, a daughter of Neleus, was the mother of Phaethon by Helios, according to some. Phaethon's mother was usually called CLYMENE. [Tzetzes, *Chiliades* 4.363.]

PROTHOE was one of the AMAZONS. [Diodorus Siculus 4.16.]

PROTIS, according to some, was one of the PLEIADES. [Scholiast on Theocritus 13.25.]

PROTO was one of the NEREIDES. [Apollodorus 1.2.7.]

PROTOGENEIA (1) was the daughter of Deucalion and Pyrrha. She was married to Locrus but had no children. Zeus, however, abducted her and took her to Mount Maenalus in Arcadia, where she became the mother of Opus. Opus became king of the Epeians. Apparently Zeus found Protogeneia worthy of visiting again, since she bore him a second son, Aethlius, who in turn became the father of Endymion, the father of the Aetolian race. [Apollodorus 1.7.2,5; Scholiast on Pindar's *Olympian Odes* 9.85;

Scholiast on Apollonius Rhodius 4.1780; Hyginus, *Fables* 155.]

PROTOGENEIA (2) was a daughter of Calydon and Aeolia. Calydon was a son of Aetolus, and Aeolia was a daughter of Amythaon. Aetolus and his sons, Calydon and Pleuron, started the Aetolian dynasty. Protogeneia's sister was Epicaste, who married her cousin Agenor, son of Pleuron. Protogeneia was loved by Ares, who frequented the area because of the constant strife of the Aetolians with the Curetes, and her son by him was Oxylus. It would be interesting to know how she felt when her lover began an extended affair with her niece Demonice, daughter of Epicaste and Agenor. By her Ares had four sons, which made them stepsons and grandnephews of Protogeneia. One of them, Thestius, was the father of Leda. Oxylus, her own son by Ares, was undistinguished. [Apollodorus 1.7.7; Stephanus Byzantium, "Kalydon."]

PROTOGENEIA (3) was the eldest daughter of Erechtheus and Praxithea. Most of her brothers and sisters were distinguished in Athenian mythological history. She herself was pathetically but nobly immortalized by her patriotic suicide with her sisters Pandora and OTIONIA, when an oracle said that one of them must die to save the state. [Apollodorus 3.15.4.]

PROTOMEDEIA was one of the NEREIDES. [Hesiod, *Theogony* 249.]

PROVERSA was one of the CAMENAE.

PRYMNO was one of the OCEANIDES. [Hesiod, *Theogony* 349.]

PSAMATHE (1) was one of the NEREIDES. She was pursued by Aeacus on the island of Aegina and, being capable of transforming herself, changed into a seal. Aeacus persisted and waited for her to change back to her usual appearance, then made love to her. She bore a son, Phocus, to him and afterward, although remaining in the vicinity, she left Aeacus. He married Endeis, who bore him Telamon and Peleus, but Phocus remained his favorite. When the sons grew up, Phocus was aware of the hostility of his stepmother and half-brothers. He was already married to Asterodeia, by whom he had two sons, Panopeus and Crisus. He decided to relocate his family in Phocis, where he remained for some time, enjoying a friendship with Iaseus so intimate that it was later captured in a painting in the Lesche at Delphi. Ultimately Phocus returned to Aegina, where he again received preferred treatment by Aeacus. He was exceedingly skilled in athletics and war exercises, and Endeis persuaded her sons to engage him in a contest and then cause him to have a fatal accident. Accordingly, Peleus deliberately threw a discus that bashed in his skull. The brothers were obliged to flee. Peleus went to Thessaly and, after losing his first wife by suicide, married Thetis, the sister of Psamathe.

Psamathe knew what had taken place and sought to punish Peleus by sending a wolf among his flocks. She was persuaded by her sister to desist and, after changing the wolf to stone, she disappeared back into the sea.

Her grandsons Panopeus and Crisus returned to Phocis, where they founded cities that they named for themselves. [Diodorus Siculus 4.72; Pausanias 2.29.7, 10.30.2; Apollodorus 3.12.6; Tzetzes on Lycophron 901; Antoninus Liberalis 38.]

PSAMATHE (2) was the daughter of Crotopus, son of King Agenor of Argos. She was loved by Apollo and became by him the mother of Linus. Terrified of her father, she exposed the child at birth. The boy was rescued by shepherds but was later killed and eaten by dogs. Psamathe was so devastated when she learned the fate of her child that she collapsed in grief before her father and told him everything. He refused to believe that Apollo was the father and had her put to death. Apollo was furious that his lover and his son had been killed, and sent a famine to Argos and the surrounding area. When the Argives consulted an oracle, they learned that in order to have the famine lifted they would have to expel Crotopus and propitiate Psamathe and Linus. Crotopus went to the region of Megaris. The Argives instituted periodic sacrifices and ceremonies that featured the singing of dirges (*linae*).

Another version says Apollo sent the monster Poene to terrorize the population and that a certain Coroebus slew her. For this service, Coroebus had to flee for fear of Apollo. He was said to have founded Megara, and sometimes he was confused with Crotopus.

Linus was sometimes called the son of Calliope, Chalciope, or Urania. Some said Apollo killed him because, son or not, he challenged his father to a musical contest and threatened to outplay him. As might be expected, several cities claimed to possess his tomb, such as Thebes, Argos, and Chalcis in Euboea. Psamathe's tomb was probably in Argos. [Pausanias 1.43.7, 2.19.8, 9.29.3; Servius on Virgil's *Eclogues* 4.56; Conon, *Narrations* 19; Ovid, *Ibis* 573.]

PSAMATHE (3) was, according to some, the wife of Proteus, son of Poseidon. Proteus' wife was more often called TORONE. [Apollodorus 2.5.9.]

PSOPHIS (1) was the daughter of Xanthus, son of Erymanthus. Nothing is known of her except that the city of Psophis in Arcadia was said by some to have been named for her. [Pausanias 8.24.1.]

PSOPHIS (2) was the daughter of Eryx, the despot of Sicania. Eryx was the son of Aphrodite and Butes. He is chiefly remembered for having founded the temple of Aphrodite Erycina in Sicily. When Heracles was driving the cattle he had stolen from Geryones, Eryx challenged him to a fight, hoping to get the valuable animals. Heracles killed him, of course, but turned the kingdom over to the inhabitants, saying that in time one of his descendants would arrive to take possession. Before going on, though, he had intercourse with Psophis, which as usual with the ever-potent Heracles resulted in pregnancy. When twin sons were born, Heracles refused to take them to his home (since his wife would certainly cause a problem) but left them in the care of his friend Lycortas, who lived in Phegia in Arcadia. The sons, Echephron and Promachus, changed the name of Phegia to Psophis in honor of their mother. They both later had shrines there. [Pausanias 8.24.1; Stephanus Byzantium, "Psophis."]

PSYCHE was a personification of the soul, but she did not start out as such. She was the youngest of three daughters of an unidentified king of Miletus and exceedingly beautiful. Her beauty was such that she incurred the jealousy of Venus when men neglected the worship of the goddess just to catch sight of Psyche. Psyche's beauty became a burden to her when would-be suitors turned to maidens they considered more available. Venus finally enlisted her son Cupid to cause Psyche to fall in love with some contemptible man, but Cupid himself was stricken by her loveliness and fell immediately in love with her. Up to that time he had never been in love, even though by then he was about 17. Cupid, the Greek Eros, was a puzzling divinity with at least a half-dozen possible genealogies. Some Roman writers finally decided to call him the son of Jupiter by his own daughter Venus. Descriptions of him ranged from a mischievous child to an extremely handsome young man. Like his mother he inflicted wounds in the hearts of men with his erotic arrows.

Through an oracle Cupid commanded the king to set his daughter atop a lonely mountain, where she would be wed to an evil spirit. The frightened girl was led away and abandoned by her sorrowing father and friends. But no monster came to claim her. Instead, she was transported to a magic, wood-surrounded castle. When she entered, she was awed by the opulence of her surroundings and the provision of food and comforts by invisible hands. She was guided to a bedroom when darkness came, and she lay down fearfully to await what she was sure was an unhappy end to her wonder-filled day. She felt someone beside her and began to panic. A man's voice soothed her, and his hands caressed her. Before long she not only was ready to surrender her virginity, but eager. She fell then into a dreamless and untroubled slumber. When she awoke, her wonderful lover was gone.

He was back the next night and the next. He told her that the greatest of loves could be theirs and that a beautiful child would be born to them but at the price of her never learning his identity. She could only marvel at this strange request. She could not know that he had asked this because he was concealing their affair from his mother, who, if she knew, would bring the whole thing to an end.

As time went on she began to miss her family and requested her lover's permission to visit them. He reluctantly agreed but begged her not to be induced to try to seek his identity. If she did, he said, she would lose him forever. She made promises and left.

Her father was astonished and overjoyed to see her. The joy of her sisters, on the other hand, soon gave way to envy. They began to suspect something most unusual when Psyche was unable to describe her lover. Although Cupid continued to visit her nightly and to renew his admonition, she eventually admitted to her sisters that she indeed had no idea what her lover looked like, only what he felt like. The sisters told her not to be a fool, that this passionate lover was hiding some awful truth. He could even be a monster in disguise who would devour her and her unborn child. Psyche was sufficiently alarmed by this possibility to hide by her bed a knife and a shrouded lamp.

When Cupid came to her that same night, he made love as usual, and the lovemaking was better than ever. Psyche was almost discouraged from her intention, but then remembered that the sleeping man could even at that moment be changing into a serpent or worse. She leaned over him with the lamp and found herself looking at a youth of astonishing beauty. She had never even imagined a man could look that way. She started to withdraw, but a drop of hot oil fell on the youth's bare shoulder, and he awoke. He gave her a mournful and accusing look, and instantly was gone.

Psyche was inconsolable. She knew now that her ecstasy had been provided by none other than the god of love. His wings identified him (although it is strange that if during their lovemaking her hands had explored his body, she would not have found out in more ways than one that she was in bed with someone heavenly). She wandered about seeking to right the wrong she had done. She prayed at the temples of Juno and other goddesses, all except Venus. Help was not forthcoming, since the other goddesses did not care to offend the one goddess who was capable of wounding immortals as well as mortals. Venus was livid that her son had failed to carry out her orders, and then got the silly girl pregnant. She pursued Psyche and enslaved her, imposing seemingly impossible tasks on her that somehow Psyche was able to complete. Psyche, though unaware of it, had Cupid to thank for the successful fulfillment of these chores, since he lent invisible assistance. A final chore sent her to the underworld to procure some of Proserpina's beauty balm. This was a terrifying journey, but Psyche managed to deliver the ointment to the upper world. Unfortunately she felt an urge to sample the preparation, perhaps with the hope of making herself irresistible to her lost lover. She instantly fell into a coma when a stupefying vapor came from the box Proserpina had given her.

Cupid came to her rescue and put the vapor back into the box. He then begged Jupiter to let him marry Psyche. Jupiter, wise in affairs of the heart, readily agreed and made Psyche immortal in the bargain. Venus grudgingly became reconciled to her daughter-in-law. Not long after, a beautiful daughter, Volupta (Pleasure), was born to the happy couple.

This tale, to which fairy tales ever since have owed a debt, tells us something of ancient attitudes about the nature of woman. Some of these views, both complimentary and unflattering, persist today. For example, among a woman's negative characteristics were shown insatiable curiosity, willingness to gossip and believe the worst, and stubborn insistence on spoiling an enviable situation. On the positive side, she was seen as one willing to admit a mistake and undergo the most humiliating tasks of atonement. It showed her as determined to suffer a descent to hell to keep the affection of the man she loved.

On a deeper allegorical level, Psyche was the embodiment of the triumphant emergence of the soul after its journey through the dark trials of the world. She was represented, after her apotheosis, as winged. Her symbol was a butterfly, itself an example of a glorious metamorphosis. It is curious that in all classical literature this story is the only reference to the butterfly, which is prominent everywhere in the Mediterranean. [Apuleius, *Golden Ass* 4.28–6.26.]

PSYLLA, Springer, was one of the mares given to Oenomaus by his father, Ares. The mares were offspring of Boreas, the north wind. Oenomaus used them in racing with the suitors of his daughter Hippodameia. He decapitated the inevitable losers. [Hyginus, *Fables* 84; Scholiast on Apollonius Rhodius 1.752.]

PUDICITIA was the personification of modesty. She was worshipped both in Greece and at Rome. She had an altar at Athens and two sanctuaries at Rome, one called Pudicitia Patricia and the other Pudicitia Plebeia. The second one was founded by a patrician woman who had married a plebeian and was driven out of the first. No woman who had married twice was allowed to touch a statue of Pudicitia. She was often considered identical with Fortuna Muliebris. In Greece she was called Aedos. [Pausanias 1.17.1; Livy 10.23.]

PYLAITIS, Gate-Keeper, was a surname of Athena, referring to her role as protectress of towns. [Lycophron 356.]

PYLARGE was one of the DANAIDES, daughter of Danaus and Pieria, and wife of Idmon. [Apollodorus 2.1.5.]

PYLIA was the daughter of Pylas, son of Cteson and king of Megara. She married Pandion of Athens, who had been expelled from his kingdom by his cousins, the Metionidae. When Pylas had to flee Megara in consequence of murdering his uncle, he consigned the kingdom to Pandion. Pylia's children by Pandion were Aegeus, Pallas, Nisus, and Lycus. Pandion also had a bastard son, Oeneus, and a daughter, who married Sciron.

After Pandion's death, his sons invaded Athens and regained their father's legacy. Aegeus was the eldest and received the largest share of the kingdom. Nisus kept Megara, Lycus got the east coast of Attica, and Pallas was given the south coast. Pylia most likely remained in Megara, having already assisted two kings in its governance. Pandion's tomb was shown in the territory of Megaris near the rock of Athena Aethyia on the coast. He had a hero shrine at Megara, and he had a statue in Athens as an eponymic hero. [Apollodorus 3.15.1–5; Pausanias 1.5.2,29.5,41.6.]

PYRANTE was one of the DANAIDES and the wife of Athamantes. [Hyginus, *Fables* 170.]

PYRANTIS was one of the DANAIDES and married to Plexippus. [Hyginus, *Fables* 170.]

PYRENE (1) was the mother of Cycnus by Ares. Cycnus was a king in Macedonia. When Heracles was on his way to the garden of the Hesperides, he crossed the Echedorus River, which probably meant he invaded the territory of Cycnus. He was challenged to a duel by Cycnus. Ares, who happened to be present, championed the cause of Cycnus and even entered the combat. Not willing to allow his sons to bloody each other, Zeus intervened by hurling a thunderbolt between them. He was also certainly aware that a battle to the death would mean Heracles' only, since Ares was immortal. The battle was thus a draw, and Pyrene did not lose her son. Ares later changed Cycnus into a swan when it came time for him to die. Some writers confused this Cycnus with another of Ares' sons, also called Cycnus, who was in fact killed by Heracles. [Apollodorus 2.5.11; Scholiast on Pindar's *Olympian Odes* 11.19; Eustathius on Homer's *Iliad* 254.]

PYRENE (2) was the daughter of Bebryx, king of a Gaulish people. Heracles crossed their country on his way to bring back the cattle of Geryones. At the court of Bebryx he overindulged in wine and raped Pyrene. He continued his expedition, and Pyrene became pregnant. When her time came, she gave birth to a serpent, which so terrified her that she ran into the mountains where she was torn to pieces by wild animals. When Heracles returned through the country, he found what was left of her body and buried it with funeral solemnities. In her memory he called the overhanging mountain range the Pyrenees. [Silius Italicus 3.420.]

PYRGO was the first wife of Alcathous, a son of Pelops and Hippodameia. He lived probably in the vicinity of Pisa and Olympia, where Pelops reigned. He was most courageous and responded promptly to the call for help that came from King Megareus of Megara, who wanted someone to kill the fierce Cithaeronian lion that had terrorized the area and even killed his son. Megareus also promised the hand of his daughter to the one who should kill the lion.

Pyrgo was doubly unhappy to see Alcathous leave. On the one hand, she wanted him to succeed because she wanted him alive. On the other hand, she risked losing him to Euaechme, the king's daughter. Even so, she had confidence in her husband, especially since they had children.

Her worst fears were realized when the ambitious Alcathous was successful in killing the lion and acquiring the king's daughter and the throne of Megara. He unceremoniously abandoned Pyrgo and probably took the children. We know the names of his children—Echepolis, Callipolis, Iphinoe, Periboea, and Automedusa—but we do not know which of them belonged to Pyrgo and which to Euaechme. It is entirely possible Alcathous compensated Pyrgo with some kind of settlement. Perhaps he had no choice but to marry Euaechme if he wanted the kingdom of Megara. In any case, Pyrgo must have gone to Megara, since her tomb was shown there alongside that of Alcathous and a daughter, Iphinoe. [Pausanias 1.43.4.]

PYRIPPE was one of the THESPIADES and mother by Heracles of Patroclus. [Apollodorus 2.7.8.]

PYRRHA (1) was a daughter of Creon, and sister of Haemon and HENIOCHE.

PYRRHA (2) was the daughter of Epimetheus and Pandora. She married Deucalion, son of Prometheus and Clymene and king in Phthia. About this time, after the barbaric treatment he received from Lycaon and his sons, Zeus angrily resolved to destroy the human race. Prometheus learned of this intention and hastily advised Deucalion to build a ship and stock it with provisions. When Zeus sent a flood over all the world, Deucalion and Pyrrha managed to float to safety on Mount Parnassus.

When the waters subsided, Deucalion and Pyrrha offered sacrifices to Zeus Phyxius, and Zeus, perhaps regretting his precipitous action, sent Hermes to Deucalion, offering to grant him any wish he might have. Deucalion prayed that Zeus might restore mankind. He and Pyrrha reiterated the request in the temple of Themis on Parnassus. The goddess, acting in conjunction with Zeus, told them to cover their heads and throw the bones of their mother behind them when walking away from the temple.

It took them a little while to figure out that Themis referred to the stones of the earth (Gaea) as the bones of their mother. They did as told, and from the stones men and women sprang up. Since the voyage to Parnassus took only nine days, the world was without population for less than two weeks.

Deucalion and Pyrrha descended from Parnassus and built a home at Opus. They had several children, including Hellen, Amphictyon, and Protogeneia. Zeus was probably reminded that by depleting the world of humans he would have cut off his supply of mortal women, and he gratefully abducted Protogeneia, by whom he became the father of Opus. Hellen became by Orseis the father of Aeolus, Xuthus, and Dorus, and was subsequently called the father of the Hellenes. Amphictyon usurped the kingdom from the autochthonous Cranaus and ruled Attica for 12 years until expelled by Erechtheus. He introduced the worship of Dionysus Orthus and the nymphs. He founded the amphictyony of Thermopylae.

Pyrrha was to Greek mythology what Noah's wife was to biblical legend. Her tomb was shown at Cynus (near Opus) in later times. [Scholiast on Pindar's *Olympian Odes* 9.64; Servius on Virgil's *Eclogues* 6.41; Hyginus, *Fables* 153; Strabo 9.4.2; Conon, *Narrations* 27; Apollodorus 1.7.2; Ovid, *Metamorphoses* 1.260.]

PYTHIA was the title of Apollo's prophetess in his temple at Delphi. In the temple the Pythia sat on a tripod and gave her prophecies. She was an old woman except in the earliest times. Her prophecies were given under a trancelike spell, during which she was believed to be possessed by the god. The trance might have been induced by mephitic vapors rising from deep inside the earth through a cleft in the rock or from the chewing of laurel leaves, though both conjectures have been largely disproven by modern geological and medical analysis. The prophecies, probably disjointed babblings, were recorded by attendant priests and rendered into verse. They were cleverly ambiguous and, like biblical scriptures,

open to endless interpretations. [Pausanias 10.24.7; Plutarch, *The Obsolescence of Oracles* 50, *The Oracles at Delphi No Longer Given in Verse* 17; Diodorus Siculus 16.26.]

QUERQUETULANAE VIRAE were nymphs presiding over green oak forests near the Porta Querquetulana in Rome. They were thought to possess prophetic powers. [Pliny, *Natural History* 16.10,15.]

QUIES was the personification of tranquillity. She was worshipped as a divinity by the Romans. A chapel dedicated to her was located on the Via Lavicana, and travelers probably used it as a rest stop. Quies had another sanctuary outside the Porta Collina. [Livy 4.41; St. Augustine, *City of God* 4.16,21.]

RAIDNE was one of the SIRENS. [Hyginus, *Fables: Preface* 30.]

RHAMNUSIA was a surname of Nemesis, who had a celebrated temple at Rhamnus in Attica. According to some, Zeus begot by Nemesis at Rhamnus an egg that Leda found and from which Helen and the Dioscuri were hatched. Thus Helen herself was called Rhamnusia. On the pedestal of the Rhamnusian Nemesis, Leda was represented as leading Helen to Nemesis. [Pausanias 1.33.2,7, 7.5.3; Strabo 9.1.17; Stephanus Byzantium, "Rhamnusia"; Callimachus, *Hymn to Artemis* 232.]

RHARIAS was a surname of Demeter, which she derived from the Rharian Plain in the vicinity of Eleusis, the principal seat of her worship. [Pausanias 1.38.6; Stephanus Byzantium, "Rharias."]

RHEA (1), the so-called mother of the gods, has always posed many problems for mythographers, mainly because her worship underwent a number of evolutions whereby she was strongly identified with Thracian and Asiatic goddesses. The most basic account, as outlined in the *Theogony* of Hesiod, was that she was a daughter of Uranus and Gaea, with Oceanus, Coeus, Hyperion, Crius, Iapetus, and Cronus as brothers and Theia, Themis, Mnemosyne, Phoebe, and

Tethys as sisters. She married Cronus and became by him the mother of Hestia, Demeter, Hera, Hades, Poseidon, and Zeus. Cronus learned from an oracle that he would be overthrown by one of his children. Accordingly, he swallowed each child as soon as it was born. He thus made his way through five of them. When Zeus was about to be born, on the advice of her parents Rhea went to Crete, some say accompanied by the giant Hopladamus. She bore Zeus in a cave on Mount Ida or Mount Dicte and left him in the care of the Curetes, Dactyls, and certain nymphs. She went back to the mainland, where she gave Cronus a stone wrapped as an infant. He swallowed it as he had done with the children.

When Zeus grew up, he gave his father an emetic that caused him to vomit up the children he had devoured, along with the stone he had believed to be Zeus. The stone was later shown and worshipped at Delphi. Presumably the brothers and sisters had continued to grow and mature in the body of Cronus, since as soon as they were disgorged they joined Zeus in declaring war on their father. Cronus was supported by his brothers, and this war with the Titans lasted ten years. The Titans were finally overcome, and Cronus and the other Titans were confined in Tartarus.

Crete is usually considered the original seat of the worship of Rhea. She had an ancient temple at Cnossus. This claim was disputed, however, by various other localities. Some said Rhea gave birth to Zeus at Thebes, at Chaeroneia, at Plataea, or in Arcadia. The Athenians claimed to be the first among the Greeks to have adopted her worship, and they pointed out her temple called the Metroon.

After Cronus was gone, Rhea, who had taken no part in the war between her children and her husband and brothers, came to be considered an earth goddess in much the same way as Gaea, her mother, and Demeter, her daughter. Her worship moved beyond Crete to Thrace, where she became a divinity of greater importance than she had been on the island. She was incorporated into the earlier worship of Bendis or Cotys (Hecate). The mysteries in the neighboring islands of Lemnos and Samothrace borrowed the concept of Rhea-Hecate. In Phrygia,

where her worship was next carried by Thracian colonists, Rhea was identified with Cybele, at the same time incorporating the worship of Dionysus along with its orgies. Following down the coast, we find an important center of her worship at Pessinus in Galatia, where her sacred image was thought to have fallen from heaven. Her name at Pessinus was AGDISTIS. From Pessinus her image was carried to Rome, but Pessinus remained her religious center, and from there her worship extended as far as Bactriana. At Rome she had a temple on the Palatine Hill, and Roman matrons celebrated her festival called Megalesia. A significant feature of her worship was castration of all her priests.

Rhea's sex life might have ended when Cronus was imprisoned, but as Rhea-Cybele she blossomed anew and became the mother of Sabazius, whose father was unknown. By Olympus, god of the Phrygian mountain by that name, she became the mother of Alce and Midas, the famous wealthy king.

There were not many accounts about Rhea beyond the birth of Zeus. She took Hera to her sister Tethys to be educated, and she entrusted Poseidon to the Telchines to be brought up. She restored Pelops when he was dismembered, boiled, and served to the gods. She changed Sangas, who had offended her, into the Sangarius River. By this same Sangarius she became the mother of Nicaea. As her worship fused with that of Cybele she became involved in the death and regeneration accounts of the Phrygian religions.

The Corybantes, who danced in full armor, were her priests, and their celebrations were accompanied by drums, cymbals, and horns. The lion was sacred to her, as was the oak, both symbols of strength. Rhea was generally represented as sitting, usually with lions on either side, or riding in a chariot drawn by lions. [Hesiod, *Theogony* 133,446; Apollodorus 1.1.3,5, 3.5.1; Diodorus Siculus 3.57, 5.66,70; Orphica, *Hymns* 13,25,26; Pausanias 1.18.7, 8.32.4,36.2,41.2, 9.2.5,25.3,41.3, 10.24.5; Tzetzes on Lycophron 1194; Scholiast on Apollonius Rhodius 1.1124; Herodian 1.35; Julian, *Orations* 5; Strabo 10.3.14, 12.5.3.]

RHEA (2) was a priestess and mother of Aventinus by Hercules. Aventinus was a king of the Aborigines; he was killed and buried on the hill afterward called the Aventine. [Virgil, *Aeneid* 7.656.]

RHEA SILVIA, sometimes called Ilia, was a Vestal virgin. One day she went into the sacred grove to draw water for the service of the goddess and encountered a wolf. She fled into a cave for safety. There she was raped by Mars, but he assured her that she would be the mother of heroic children. When she delivered twins, her father Amulius doomed her and her babies to be drowned in the river. The god of the Anio River caused her to become a goddess. He then guided the cradle of the newborn infants into the Tiber, and it was stranded finally at the foot of the Palatine Hill. A wolf nursed them until they were found by Faustulus and reared by him and his wife, Acca Larentia. They were called Romulus and Remus. [Servius on Virgil's *Aeneid* 1.274; Dionysius of Halicarnassus, *Roman Antiquities* 2.56; Plutarch, *Romulus* 27.]

RHENE was a nymph and, according to some, the mother of Ajax by Oileus. More often she was called ERIOPIS. Rhene was, however, the mother of Medon by Oileus. He commanded the Pythians in the Trojan War and later the Methonians when Philoctetes was wounded. He was slain by Aeneas. His mother was occasionally called Alcimache. [Homer, *Iliad* 2.727; Hyginus, *Fables* 97.]

RHODE (1) was a daughter of Poseidon by Amphitrite, and the sister of Triton and Benthesicyme. She was also called sometimes a daughter of the Asopus River. She was said to be married to Helios, but this was probably the result of confusion with RHODOS, another daughter of Poseidon, by Halia, who was the mother of the Heliades. Rhode was also called by some the mother of Phaethon by Helios, but Phaethon's mother was more often called CLYMENE. [Diodorus Siculus 5.55; Apollodorus 1.4.4.]

RHODE (2) was one of the DANAIDES, daughter of Danaus and Atlantia or Phoebe. She married and murdered Hippolytus. [Apollodorus 2.1.5.]

RHODEIA was one of the OCEANIDES and a playmate of Persephone. [Hesiod, *Theogony* 351; Homer, *Hymn to Demeter* 451.]

RHODIA (1) was one of the MUSES. [Tzetzes on Hesiod's *Works and Days* 1.]

RHODIA (2) was one of the DANAIDES, daughter of Danaus and Atlantia or Phoebe, and married to Chalcodon. [Apollodorus 2.1.5.]

RHODOPE (1) was the daughter of the Strymon River and was one of the playmates of Persephone. After Persephone was abducted, Rhodope had a quick physical encounter with Apollo, which resulted in the birth of Cicon, the ancestor of the Cicones in Thrace who gave assistance to Priam during the Trojan War. Then Rhodope married Haemus, son of Boreas and Oreithyia, and they had a son, Hebrus. Rhodope and Haemus initiated a cult in Thrace and called themselves Zeus and Hera. As punishment they were metamorphosed into mountains that were thereafter called by their names. Their son Hebrus (Ebro) gave his name to the river that today is one of the boundaries of Greece. [*Homeric Hymn to Demeter* 423; Lucian, *Dance* 51; Scholiast on Virgil's *Aeneid* 1.321; Ovid, *Metamorphoses* 6.87.]

RHODOPE (2) was, according to some, the wife of Amythaon, and mother of Melampus and Bias. Their mother was usually called EIDOMENE. [Scholiast on Theocritus 3.43.]

RHODOPE (3) was one of the OCEANIDES. [Hyginus, *Fables: Preface* 6.]

RHODOPIS was a beautiful maiden from Ephesus who swore eternal chastity and was thus a favorite of Artemis, who made her a close companion. Aphrodite despised chastity and decided to change this situation. She found a shy but exceedingly handsome young Ephesian named Euthynicus, who had also vowed chastity. Aphrodite then arranged to have the two meet in the woods during the hunt, which they both dearly loved. As they beheld each other, Eros, at his mother's command, sent arrows into both of them. The initial flicker of interest when first they encountered each other grew into a warm glow and then into violent passion. They threw down their bows and arrows, entered a cave, and engaged in extended lovemaking. Rhodopis had to pay. Artemis turned her into a spring on the very spot where she had lost her virginity. It is a miracle that something horrible did not happen to Euthynicus.

Thereafter this spring became a test for young girls whose chastity was in doubt by their parents. A tablet on which the girl had written that she was a virgin was hung on a chain around her neck. She stood in knee-deep water, and if the vow was false the water rose as high as her chin, thus covering the tablet. [Achilles Tatius 8.12.]

RHODOS was a daughter of Poseidon and Halia, though some called her mother Amphitrite, Aphrodite, or a wife of Oceanus. Rhodos was said to have given her name to the island of Rhodes. When the gods distributed the various countries, the island was still under water. Halia's brothers, the Telchines, had fled when they knew the island would be inundated. Helios was absent, and no one drew a lot for him, so he was about to miss out on the distribution of lands. However, the island of Rhodes suddenly rose from the sea, and Zeus gave Helios permission to possess it. Rhodos, the nymph of the island, became his wife and bore him seven sons and a daughter—Cercaphus, Actis, Macareus, Tenages, Triopas, Candalus, Ochimus, and Electryone. These individuals were called HELIADAE, and confusingly the same name was given to the children of Helios by Clymene.

Ochimus later became king of Rhodes. According to some, Triopas founded the city of Cnidus. Macareus helped kill his brother Tenages and fled from Rhodes to Lesbos, where he became king. Cercaphus married the daughter of his brother Ochimus and followed him on the throne. Actis was the founder of the city of Heliopolis. Candalus became king of Cos. Electryone died as a maiden and was honored as a heroine. [Diodorus Siculus 5.55–57; Pindar, *Olympian Odes* 7.24,100; Tzetzes on Lycophron 923; Ovid, *Metamorphoses* 4.204; Apollodorus 1.7.4.]

RHOEO (1) was a daughter of Staphylus and Chrysothemis. Staphylus was a son of Dionysus and Ariadne, and was one of the Argonauts. We know nothing further of Chrysothemis. The couple had three daughters, Molpadia, Rhoeo, and Parthenos. Rhoeo was loved by Apollo and became pregnant by him. When she was found out, her father demanded to know who the father was. When Rhoeo told him, he was certain she was lying to protect one of the local youths, and he put her in a chest and cast it into the sea. Rhoeo floated to Delos and there gave birth to Anius. She placed him on the altar of Apollo, and Apollo concealed him and taught him the art of prophecy.

Anius by Dryope became the father of the three Oenotropae, who could convert things into wine, oil, or wheat. He was said also to have had another daughter, Lavinia, whom Aeneas married.

Rhoeo went on to marry Zarex, son of Carystus and grandson of Cheiron. She had other sons by him. There was even one story that Rhoeo became by Aeson the mother of Jason, but there were at least ten other women for whom this claim was made.

A different story had Rhoeo and her sister Hemithea (an alternate name of Molpadia) quarreling over who would sleep with Lyrcus, a friend and guest of their father. In this instance, Staphylus was eager to have male heirs. Hemithea ended up in bed with Lyrcus. Rhoeo, not to be outdone, attracted the attention of Zeus and became pregnant by him. This time Staphylus became an outraged father, and the story developed as in the first version. [Diodorus Siculus 5.62; Tzetzes, *Chiliades* 6.979, on Lycophron 570,580; Apollodorus 1.9.16; Dionysius of Halicarnassus, *Roman Antiquities* 1.59.]

RHOEO (2) was a daughter of the Scamander River. According to some she became the mother of Tithonus by Laomedon. Tithonus' mother was usually called STRYMO. [Tzetzes on Lycophron 18.]

RHOETEIA was a daughter of the Thracian king Sithon and a nymph, Mendeis. Her sister was Pallene, who led a far more exciting life than she did, so nothing is known of her except that the Trojan promontory of Rhoeteium was said to have derived its name from her. [Tzetzes on Lycophron 583,1161; Stephanus Byzantium "Rhoiteia."]

RHYTIA was the mother of nine Corybantes by Apollo. They lived in Samothrace. Sacrifices were offered to the Corybantes along with the Cabeiri of Lemnos and Imbros. Rhytia was perhaps a daughter of Proteus and has been identified with Rhoeteia, also in this connection called a daughter of Proteus, though usually called a daughter of Sithon. [Pherecydes, quoted by Strabo 10.3.19.]

ROMA (1) was the personification of the city of Rome, in which identity she was called Dea Roma. She had temples not only in Rome but in other cities of the empire as far away as Smyrna. These temples appeared only during and after the time of Augustus. Her statues depicted her as tall and stately, reminiscent of Athena. She wore a long robe and a helmet. [Tacitus, *Annals* 4.37,56; Livy 43.5.]

ROMA (2) was a Trojan captive of noble birth and rank. When the Greek ships reached the banks of the Tiber, where they were driven by a storm, Roma persuaded her fellow captives to set fire to them, which put an end to the trip. The voyagers settled on the Palatine Hill, and the settlement proved so prosperous that they honored it with the name of the heroine. [Plutarch, *Romulus* 1; Tzetzes on Lycophron 921.]

ROMA (3) was a daughter of Italus and Lucania, or of Telephus, son of Heracles. Italus was an ancient king of one or another of the ancient Italian tribes, and it was from him that Italy received its name. Some called him the son of Telegonus by Penelope. Some called Roma the wife of Aeneas, but others said she was the daughter of Ascanius, son of Aeneas. She was one of those said to have given her name to the city of Rome. [Plutarch, *Romulus* 2; Servius on Virgil's *Aeneid* 1.6, 8.328; Aristotle, *Politics* 7.10.]

ROMA (4) was a daughter of Euander and sister of Pallas and Dyna. Euander was an Arcadian

who migrated to Italy. He settled on the Palatine Hill and was a benevolent ruler who helped civilize the rough inhabitants. He taught them the arts of writing and music and many other skills. He was responsible for introducing certain of the Greek gods and goddesses to Italy. When Aeneas arrived in the country, he was warmly received by Euander, who assisted him against the Rutulians. At his death an altar was dedicated to him at the foot of the Aventine. His mother was worshipped under the name of Carmenta. Roma was one of those from whom Rome was said to have received its name. [Virgil, *Aeneid* 8.574; Servius on Virgil's *Aeneid* 1.277; Dionysius of Halicarnassus, *Roman Antiquities* 1.32.]

ROMA (5) was a daughter of Telemachus, son of Odysseus. She was said to have married Aeneas. Obviously she was confused with Roma, the daughter of Italus, who was the granddaughter, according to some, of Telegonus, the other son of Odysseus. [Servius on Virgil's *Aeneid* 1.273.]

RUMINA was one of three Roman divinities worshipped as protectors of infants sleeping in their cradles. Libations of milk were offered to her. Her sisters were Cuba and Cunina. The names of her sisters referred to beds or cradles, and her name meant a mother's breast. [St. Augustine, *City of God* 4.10; Lactantius 1.20,36.]

RUNCINA was a divinity to whom the people of Italy prayed to help prevent weeds from overtaking their crops and to promote the harvest. Runcina was probably a surname of Ops. [St. Augustine, *City of God* 4.8; Arnobius, *Adversus Nationes* 4.7.]

SABBE, a daughter of Berosus and Erymanthe, was mentioned among the SIBYLS. [Pausanias 10.12.8; Aelian, *Various Narratives* 12.35.]

SAESARA was a daughter of Celeus, king of Eleusis, and Metaneira. During the reign of Celeus, Demeter went to Eleusis in search of Persephone. Saesara and her sisters invited the goddess to their home, not knowing she was divine. Demeter tried to express her appreciation by making immortal the prince Demophon, their brother, but was interrupted at a crucial point and inadvertently caused him to die. She compensated by giving Saesara's other brother, Triptolemus, a flying chariot and a commission to sow grain throughout the world. The whole family of Celeus then became connected with the priesthood of Demeter. Saesara married her nephew Crocon, son of Triptolemus and a king in the territory of Eleusis. As Triptolemus' son he was, of course, part of the cult of Demeter, which grew ultimately into the famous Eleusinian mysteries.

Meganeira was the daughter of Saesara and Crocon. Some have confused her name with that of her grandmother Metaneira. According to some she was the wife of Arcas and mother of Elatus and Apheidas, but Arcas' wife was more often called Erato. [Apollodorus 3.9.1; Pausanias 1.38.2.]

SAGARITIS was a Hamadryad and a secret lover of Attis. Attis, however, was loved by the goddess Cybele. There were many variations to his melancholy history. In one of them, Cybele swore the beautiful youth to celibacy, and he was managing quite well until Sagaritis enticed him to have sex with her. They were found out, and Cybele caused Sagaritis to die by cutting down the tree on which her life depended. Cybele made Attis go mad, and in this state he castrated himself. It was never wise to go against the will of the powerful mother goddesses. [Ovid, *Fasti* 4.229.]

SAGNOS was one of the DOGS of Actaeon. [Hyginus, *Fables* 181.]

SAITIS was a surname of Athena, under which she had a sanctuary on Mount Potinus near Lerna in Argolis. The name was traced to Egypt, where Athena was called Sais. [Pausanias 2.36.8; Tzetzes on Lycophron 111.]

SALACIA was a female divinity of the sea among the Romans. She was the wife of Neptune and probably the equivalent of the Greek Amphitrite. She was akin to Venilia, the goddess of coastal waters, but distinguished from her as the goddess of the deeper saline seas. Some said Salacia might be used for Venus as well, not for the resemblance of the word to *salacious* but because Venus was born from the foam of the sea. [St. Augustine, *City of God* 7.22; Varro, *On the Latin Language* 1.720; Gellius 13.22.]

SALAMIS was one of the daughters of the Asopus River. Like several of her sisters she was pursued by a god. This was the salacious Poseidon. He took her to the island that he later allowed to be called Salamis in her honor. On the island she bore a son, Cychreus, who became king. He renamed the island Cychreia after he had rendered the inhabitants the great service of delivering them from a dragon. For this public benefit he also received heroic worship. He himself gained the epithet of Dragon because of his savage nature, and this undesirable quality caused him to be expelled from Salamis-Cychreia by one Eurylochus, who then became king. He went to Eleusis, where Demeter appointed him as a priest. His granddaughter Endeis was the mother of Telamon, who later was king of Salamis. Nothing further was heard of the nymph Salamis. After giving birth to Cychreus, she might have left him with the islanders and returned to her river home. [Pausanias 1.35.2; Apollodorus 3.12.7; Diodorus Siculus 4.72.]

SALMACIS was a nymph who at her request became united with the youth HERMAPHRODITUS in a single body.

SALPINX, Trumpet, was a surname of Athena at Argos. She was said by some to have herself invented the trumpet, but the claim was also made by Tyrsenus, the son of Heracles. Hegeleos, son of Tyrsenus, taught the Dorians with Temenus how to play the instrument. He founded the sanctuary of Athena Salpinx in gratitude for her inspiration. [Pausanias 2.21.3.]

SAMIA (1) was a daughter of the Maeander River. She became the wife of Ancaeus, son of Poseidon and Astypalaea and king of the Leleges on the island later called Samos. Ancaeus was famous for the proverb that originated at the time of his death. He had a large vineyard of which he was quite proud. A seer told him he would not live to taste the wine of his vineyard, and when Ancaeus later was about to drink a cup of his wine, he derided the seer. The seer answered: "There is many a slip between the cup and the lip." At that moment a disturbance arose outside, and Ancaeus was told that a wild boar was rooting up his vines. He put down his cup, went out to dispatch the animal, and was impaled on its tusks.

Samia's children by Ancaeus were Perilaus, Enodus, Samus, Alitherses, and Parthenope. The island was named either for her or for her son. [Pausanias 7.4.2; Callimachus, *Hymn to Delos* 50.]

SAMIA (2) was a surname of Hera, derived from her temple and worship on the island of Samos. There was a tradition that she was born on Samos or at least brought up there. [Herodotus 3.60; Pausanias 7.4.4; Scholiast on Apollonius Rhodius 1.187.]

SAO was one of the NEREIDES. [Apollodorus 1.2.7.]

SARDO (1) was a daughter of Sthenelus and sister of Cycnus, the lover of Phaethon. The scene of Phaethon's fall from heaven was placed along the Pactolus River, and that is where the grieving Cycnus was changed into a swan. Of Sardo nothing is known beyond her giving her name to the Lydian city of Sardis, which was located on the Pactolus River. Ovid tranferred the scene of Phaethon's crash to Italy. [Hyginus, *Fables* 275; Ovid, *Metamorphoses* 2.368.]

SARDO (2) was the wife of Tyrrhenus, son of Agron, with whom she migrated from Asia Minor to Italy. The island of Sardinia was said to have been named for her. Before she left Asia, she gave her name, according to some, to the city of Sardis. [Scholiast on Plato's *Timaeus* 25.]

SARONIA, or Saronis, was a surname of Artemis at Troezen. Saron was a mythical king of Troezen who built a sanctuary of Artemis Saronia on the seacoast. While chasing a stag into the sea he drowned, and his body, which was washed on shore in the grove of Artemis, was buried there. From this circumstance the gulf between Attica and Argolis was called the Saronic Gulf. Every year in honor of Artemis the Troezenians held a festival called Saronia. [Pausanias 2.32.10.]

SARPEDONIA was a surname of Artemis taken from Cape Sarpedon in Cilicia, where she had a temple with an oracle. [Strabo 14.5.19.]

SATURNIA was a patronymic given to Juno and Vesta as daughters of Saturnus. [Virgil, *Aeneid* 1.23; Ovid, *Fasti* 1.265.]

SCAEA was one of the DANAIDES, a daughter of Danaus and Europa. She married and murdered Daiphron. She was later married to Archander, son of Achaeus, who with his brother Architeles went from Phthiotis in Thessaly to Argos. After the Danaides killed their husbands, Danaus had understandable difficulty in marrying them off. Scaea and her sister Automate, who married Architeles, were just about the only two whom we discover to have remarried. Perhaps the others had to settle for more lowly mates not considered worth mentioning. The sons of Achaeus, on the other hand, were of noble stock. Scaea's son by Archander was Metanastes. [Pausanias 7.1.3; Apollodorus 2.1.5.]

SCAMANDRODICE was, according to some, the mother by Poseidon of Cycnus. His mother was usually called CALYCE. [Scholiast on Pindar's *Olympian Odes* 2.147.]

SCARPHE was the mother of Jason by Aeson, according to some accounts. Jason's mother was most frequently called POLYMEDE. [Scholiast on Homer's *Iliad* 2.532.]

SCIRAS was a surname of Athena, under which she had a temple in the port of Phaleron in Attica and on the island of Salamis. In the month of Scirophorion (June), a festival called Sciraphoria was celebrated at Athens in her honor. This temple was said to have been founded by a soothsayer, Scirus from Dodona, during the time of the war between Erechtheus and the Eleusinians. [Pausanias 1.36.3; Stephanus Byzantium, "Skiros"; Strabo 9.1.9.]

SCYLLA (1) was perhaps the most loathsome monster in mythology. The Lamiae and

Mormolyceia, even though they cannibalized their young male victims after seducing them, were beautiful to look at and gave their victims some final ecstatic moments. Medusa, in spite of her snaky locks and stony stare, was remotely located and harmful only if one met her gaze. Even Echidna, though half-serpent, was not so repulsive that Heracles could not find something about her to arouse him long enough to father triplets by her. But Scylla was another story. She had 12 feet, six long necks, mouths with rows of sharp teeth, and she barked like a dog. Some said her six heads were from different animals.

This horrible creature was said by some to be the daughter of Crateis by Phorcys or Triton. Others said her mother was Hecate, and still others called her parents Typhon and Echidna, who specialized in producing monsters. As in the case of Medusa, it was told that Scylla had originally been a beautiful maiden who frolicked with the sea nymphs. The marine god Glaucus fell in love with her and asked the enchantress Circe how to make Scylla return his love, not realizing that Circe entertained warm thoughts about him. She threw magic herbs into a pool where Scylla bathed and thus caused her to turn into the frightful creature with whom we are familiar. A similar story said Poseidon was the lover and that Amphitrite in jealousy transformed the maiden.

Whatever the case, Scylla took up residence on one of the rocks overlooking the strait between Italy and Sicily. Across from her was a fellow monster, the voracious whirlpool called Charybdis. Ships going from Greece to the west coast of Italy had to pass between these unpleasant women, steering just right to avoid being sucked into the maelstrom or else providing Scylla with six succulent sailors for supper. Scylla tended to profit from her placement near Charybdis, since skippers were more likely to sacrifice a half-dozen men than a whole ship. Odysseus said that watching her devour his men before his eyes was perhaps the most horrible thing that happened to him up until then. Sometimes other marine beings helped ships steer a safe course between the monsters, as in the case of the Argonauts. The phrase "between Scylla and Charybdis," though seldom heard now, continued into modern times as descriptive of a choice between two equally hazardous alternatives.

Heracles was reported to have killed Scylla because she stole some of the oxen of Geryones, but Phorcys was said to have restored her to life. [Homer, Odyssey 12.78,235; Eustathius on Homer's Odyssey 1714; Apollonius Rhodius 4.828; Tzetzes on Lycophron 45,650; Ovid, Metamorphoses 13.732,905, 14.40; Servius on Virgil's Aeneid 3.420.]

SCYLLA (2) was a daughter of Nisus, king of Megara, and Abrota. Nisus, the brother of Aegeus, had to suffer a siege by the Minoans, along with the rest of Attica, because of the mysterious death of Androgeus, son of Minos, while he was attending the Panathenian festival. When Minos was storming Megara, Scylla fell in love with him. She needed to demonstrate this love but could think of no good way. Then she remembered the family secret that Nisus was invulnerable as long as a certain gold (some say purple) lock of hair grew on his head. Scylla reached Minos to tell him that she would cut the lock if he would marry her. Minos decided she was imagining things but told her to go right ahead. She slipped into her father's bedroom and cut the magic lock, as a result of which he died. Immediately Minos' forces began to win the victory. After Megara fell and Minos learned how heartless the daughter had been, he tied her by the feet to the stern of his ship and when out to sea cut her loose so that she drowned. Her body washed ashore at a promontory later called Scyllaeum, the most easterly point of Peloponnesus. Some said Minos simply left in disgust but that she swam after the ship. At his death Nisus had been changed into a hawk, and he swooped down on her just as she herself was being changed into an aquatic bird. [Apollodorus 3.15.8; Ovid, Metamorphoses 8.6; Pausanias 1.19.4; Hyginus, Fables 198.]

SCYLLA (3) was one of the DANAIDES and married to Proteus. [Hyginus, Fables 170.]

SECIA (See TUTILINA)

SEGESTA (See EGESTA)

SEGETIA (*See* TUTILINA)

SEIRENES (*See* SIRENS)

SEJA (*See* TUTILINA)

SELENE, also called Mene, was the goddess of the moon. She was a daughter of Hyperion and Theia, and the sister of Eos (dawn) and Helios (sun). As usual, other parents were mentioned, such as Hyperion and Euryphaessa, Pallas, Zeus and Leto, or Helios. She was sometimes called Phoebe, as sister of Phoebus, when in late times Phoebus Apollo was called the sun-god. This caused her also to be identified with Artemis. But neither Artemis nor Apollo was, properly speaking, a deity of either of these heavenly bodies.

Selene was mainly known for her extended love affair with the beautiful youth Endymion, the son of Aethlius. Like her sister Eos she was fond of young men, but unlike Eos, who abducted them because of their adolescent vigor, she put Endymion into a somnolent state and visited him nightly. Being immortal she had no biological clock to worry about and thus took her time in producing by him 50 daughters and, according to some, a son, Naxus. Endymion's narcoleptic state apparently did not affect his potency. Since he had another separate history that could not allow for perpetual slumber, a far-fetched speculation about the phenomenon of this relationship is discussed under NEIS.

Endymion was not the only man in Selene's life. By Zeus she became the mother of Pandeia, Ersa, and Nemea. Pan changed himself into a white ram and had his way with her.

In keeping with her heavenly role, Selene was described as very beautiful. She was often shown with wings, and on her head was a diadem, sometimes featuring horns as in a crescent moon. Like Helios she rode across the heavens in a chariot, and her steeds were snow-white. In Rome she was called Luna. [Hesiod, *Theogony* 371; Apollodorus 1.2.2,7.5; *Homeric Hymn* 31.5, 32.14, *Homeric Hymn to Hermes* 99; Scholiast on Euripides' *Phoenician Maidens* 175; Hyginus, *Poetic Astronomy* 10; Cicero, *Tusculan Disputations* 1.38; Pausanias 5.1.2; Plutarch, *Table-Talk* 3; Virgil, *Georgics* 3.391; Ovid, *Fasti* 4.374; Callimachus, *Hymn to Artemis* 114,141.]

SEMELE was the first in line for the series of tragedies that beset the house of Cadmus. She was the daughter of Cadmus and Harmonia, and sister of Ino, Agave, Autonoe, and Polydorus. It was not long before Zeus noticed her and started to visit her in secret. Semele was flattered by the attention of the god, who, if she stopped to reckon, was her great-grandfather. But Semele did not stop to think very often. She boasted to her sisters, who believed her only to the extent that they were envious of her for having so attentive a lover that she dared compare him with Zeus. Hera, who knew about the affair, appeared in the disguise of Semele's old nurse, Beroe, and easily talked the gullible young woman into a foolish scheme. She said that Semele was not experiencing the full benefit of having a divine lover, since Zeus visited her in the guise of an ordinary man. On the other hand, said Beroe, there was Hera, to whom he appeared, on the nights he was not with Semele, in his full glory and majesty. Why should not Semele be granted the same respect, especially since the god had found her body so satisfying that he had quite early promised to grant any wish she might make known? Semele thought about it and decided Beroe was right, so she made her desire known to Zeus on his next visit. He would have refused except for the strength of his promise. So the next time he came to call he changed before her eyes into the great thunderer, the great wielder of lightning. Semele, who was pregnant with Dionysus, became wrapped in flames from the sheet of lightning that shimmered around her, and fell into a burning heap. Zeus barely had time to rescue the fetus, which he carried in his thigh until the baby came to full term.

All this happened without the knowledge of her family, until they found her smoldering corpse. Successive calamities began when the three sisters circulated the rumor that Semele had had an affair with a mortal and tried to cover her misconduct by claiming to have had intercourse with the father of the gods. Semele deserved to be punished, they said, for this sacrilege.

The sisters were under a curse from then on. According to one story, trouble had developed even earlier when Actaeon, Autonoe's son, supposedly fell in love with Semele. He was pledged to the service of Artemis, who caused his 50 dogs to go mad and tear him to pieces. Usually, though, this calamity was brought about by Actaeon's accidental (but probably deliberate) spying on Artemis while she was bathing in the nude. (The misfortunes of the sisters can be followed under entries for their names.)

One variation on Semele's demise had Cadmus going into a rage when she gave birth to a baby. He put her and Dionysus into a chest and cast them into the sea. Semele died and was buried by the inhabitants when the chest drifted to Brasiae in Laconia. Dionysus survived and was brought up at Brasiae.

It is not altogether clear, in the usual story, whether or not Ino was fully aware that she was bringing up her nephew, since none of Semele's family was present when she was incinerated or when Zeus sewed Dionysus into his thigh. Zeus put the baby into Hermes' hands, and Hermes later brought him to Ino and Athamas to rear. Hermes could have deliberately concealed the fact that he and his half-brother were sons of Zeus. So it is not certain that Ino knew who Dionysus was. She certainly was not aware of his divine nature, since Dionysus had to travel over the world to prove his divinity. Interestingly, through Dionysus, Semele reached beyond the grave to avenge the wrong done to her by her sisters. Dionysus was the cause of terrible disasters for Agave and Ino.

After his full recognition by the other gods, Dionysus directed his energies to retrieving Semele from the underworld. He descended by way of the Alcyonian lake of Lerna, the quickest route to the nether regions, and with a certain amount of difficulty he recovered Semele from the infernal divinities. They climbed back to the upper world, where Semele was apotheosized into the goddess Thyone.

A statue of Semele was shown at Thebes. At Rome she was sometimes identified with Bona Dea. She was also called Stimula there, probably a mispronunciation of her Greek name. Dionysus' descent to and return from Hades was celebrated every year at Lerna in nocturnal rites. One part of the ritual was most peculiar. In order to find the entrance to the lower world, Dionysus had to ask directions from a man

named Prosymnus, who would only tell him if he allowed him to sodomize him. Dionysus told him that if his trip was successful, he would oblige him on the way back. While Dionysus was in the underworld, Prosymnus died, but back at Lerna, Dionysus performed a ritual that, if she observed it, must have astonished Semele/Thyone. He shaped a smooth piece of wood to resemble a phallus, thrust the sharpened end in the man's grave, and sat down on the protruding rounded end. Thus he fulfilled his promise. [Homer, *Iliad* 14.323; *Homeric Hymn to Dionysus* 6.57; Apollodorus 3.4.3,5.3; Ovid, *Metamorphoses* 3.260, *Fasti* 503; Hyginus, *Fables* 179; Pausanias 2.31.2,37.5, 9.2.3, 11.12.3,16.4; Pindar, *Olympian Odes* 2.44, *Pythian Odes* 11.1; Cicero, *On the Nature of the Gods* 3.23; Livy 39.12; St. Augustine, *City of God* 14.11,16.]

SEMONIA (*See* TUTILINA)

SETIA (*See* TUTILINA)

SIBYLLA was the name of the first of the SIBYLS.

SIBYLS were certain women of ancient times who prophesied under the influence of a deity. The deity was most often Apollo, and in many respects Sibylline predictions resembled the utterances of the Pythia at Delphi. Their origin and number varied from writer to writer, but ten came to be a generally accepted number. They were the Babylonian Sibyl, the Libyan, the Cimmerian, the Delphian, the Erythraean, the Samian, the Cumaean, the Hellespontian, the Phrygian, and the Tiburtine. The most famous was the Cumaean, who was consulted by Aeneas before he went to the underworld.

We know the names of many of the Sibyls, since both mythological stories and historical accounts referred to them. The first Sibyl was named Sibylla, and it was she who established the designation for those who followed her, regardless of their given names. She was said to be a daughter of Dardanus and Neso in the Troad. This parentage makes sense, because it was Dardanus who brought the Samothracian mysteries to the Troad, and Neso, daughter of Teucer, was involved with the art of prophecy from an early age. Some claimed that Sibylla was born in Libya and was the daughter of Zeus and Lamia.

The second Sibyl was Herophile, also born in the Troad, a daughter of a nymph and a mortal. She predicted the fall of Troy. Some said she interpreted Hecuba's famous dream about producing from her womb a firebrand that would destroy the city. She was based in Troy but visited various centers of Apollonian worship, such as Clarus. She gave her prophecies in verse, which she delivered standing on a stone she always carried with her. In later times this stone was pointed out to pilgrims who visited Delphi. Other Sibyls of note were Phyto, the Samian Sibyl, and Sabbe, the Hebrew Sibyl. Mephitis, a Roman divinity, was considered by some to be one of the Sibyls.

The most famous Greek Sibyl was from Erythrae in Lydia, daughter of Theodorus and a nymph. She was variously called Demo, Phemone, Deiphobe, Demophile, and Amaltheia. She prophesied in verse almost as soon as she was born. While very young she was dedicated to Apollo. She was said to have lived for about a thousand years. She was the same as the Cumaean Sibyl, according to some accounts. She migrated to Cumae in Campania, where she remained, since longevity had been accorded her on the condition that she never return to Erythrae. She would also have been granted youth for the duration of her long life, but she refused to pay the price, which was sleeping with Apollo. She died when she received a letter sealed with clay from the earth of Erythrae, the soil of which she was forbidden to touch.

During the long career of the Sibyls, a body of prophetic literature was accumulated. This corpus constituted the so-called Sibylline books. It was related that the Cumaean Sibyl came to Rome during the reign of Tarquinius with an offer to sell him nine of the books. It is not clear why she was willing to part with them; perhaps she had retained copies. Her price was very high, and Tarquinius refused their purchase. She promptly burned three of them and offered him the remaining six at the same price. He still refused, and she burned three more. He then decided to take the remaining three. He deposited them in the temple of Jupiter on the Capitoline Hill. These books, which were written in hexameter Greek verse, had a strong influence on Roman religion well into the reign of the Caesars. They were consulted on occasions when something unusual occurred or when advice was needed on unforeseen events. Special curators were appointed as custodians and interpreters. As time went on, they were influential in synthesizing the Greek and Roman deities, and paved the way for the introduction of foreign divinities and rites that eventually characterized Rome's array of officially recognized gods. The books disappeared in A.D. 83, when the temple burned. [Clement of Alexandria, *Miscellanies* 1.108; Lactantius 1.6; Pausanias 10.12.1; Aristotle, *On Marvelous Things Heard* 95; Virgil, *Aeneid* 6.10; Servius on Virgil's *Aeneid* 3.441, 6.3.21; Petronius 48; Dionysius of Halicarnassus, *Roman Antiquities* 4.62; Ovid, *Metamorphoses* 14.130; Aelian, *Various Narratives* 12.35; Gellius 1.19; Strabo 14.1.34.]

SIDE (1) was the wife of Orion, the handsome young Boeotian giant, son of Hyrieus. Orion is usually called a giant, but perhaps this should not be taken literally. He was probably tall, well-muscled, and prodigiously strong, instead of having an abnormal pituitary gland. He was married to Side, who, perhaps trying to compete with her husband, whose beauty was celebrated, became quite vain. She made the mistake of comparing her beauty with that of Hera, a serious error, as others had found. Hera unceremoniously consigned her to Hades. This event more than likely signaled the downfall of Orion, who left shortly afterward on a series of amorous encounters, one of which resulted in his death. [Apollodorus 1.4.3.]

SIDE (2) was a daughter of Danaus from whom the town Side in Laconia was believed to have received its name. [Pausanias 3.22.11.]

SIDE (3) was, according to some, the wife of Belus and mother of Aegyptus and Danaus. She was said to have given her name to the city of Sidon. The mother of Danaus and Aegyptus more often was called ACHIROE. [John of Antioch, *Fragments* 6.15.]

SIDE (4) was a young maiden who killed herself on her mother's grave rather than submit to incestuous relations with her father. A pomegranate tree grew from the blood she shed on the grave. Her father was changed into a kite, and it was widely held that this bird would not settle on the branches of a pomegranate. [Dionysius, *On Birds* 1.7, paraphrase of Oppian.]

SIDE (5) was the daughter of Taurus, a king in Pamphylia, whose name was given to a mountain range. Side married Cimolus, after whom one of the Cyclades was named. She gave her name to the city of Side in Pamphylia. [Stephanus Byzantium, "Side."]

SIDERO was another example of an evil stepmother who was ultimately made to pay for her cruelty. Her background is not known, but she was conceivably a nymph of the region. She married Salmoneus, son of Aeolus and brother to Cretheus, Athamas, Sisyphus, Deion, Perieres, Magnes, and Macareus. Salmoneus migrated from Thessaly to Peloponnesus, where he married Alcidice of Tegea. They settled in Elis, where Salmoneus founded the city of Salmone near the source of the Enipeus River. They had a daughter, Tyro. Alcidice died while Tyro was still quite small, and Salmoneus married Sidero.

Sidero was extremely hostile to her stepdaughter and forced her to perform all manner of demeaning chores. Tyro became very withdrawn and in her adolescent daydreaming decided she was in love with the Enipeus River. Taking the appearance of the river-god, Poseidon ravished her, and she became pregnant. She managed to conceal her condition but exposed her twin sons from fear of Sidero, who continued to torture her.

Salmoneus meanwhile had grown strange. Perhaps it had to do with the shock he received when his unbalanced brother Sisyphus got Tyro pregnant with twins whom she immediately killed when they were born. Sisyphus took their dead bodies to the marketplace and accused Salmoneus of incest and murder. Salmoneus became arrogant and tyrannical. He declared himself equal to Zeus, dragging empty kettles behind his chariot to simulate thunder and throwing torches aloft to give the appearance of lightning.

Zeus did not tolerate this for very long and shortly destroyed both Salmoneus and the town. Salmoneus' brother Cretheus married Tyro. It is not clear what happened during this interval to Sidero.

Several years passed and Tyro bore three sons to Cretheus. The twins, Neleus and Pelias, who had been found and reared by a shepherd, grew up and learned the identity of their real mother. They were reunited with her and adopted by Cretheus, who was the king of Iolcus. The twins learned of the cruel treatment their mother had received from Sidero, and they hunted her down. She fled to a temple of Hera, but Pelias followed her inside and killed her on the altar. It is unfortunate we do not know which temple of Hera this was, since its location would reveal Sidero's whereabouts during the years after the death of Salmoneus. [Apollodorus 1.7.3,9.8; Lucian, *Timon or Misanthrope* 2; Virgil, *Aeneid* 6.585; Hyginus, *Fables* 60,61,250; Diodorus Siculus 4.68.]

SILVIA (*See* RHEA SILVIA)

SINOE, an Arcadian nymph, helped bring up the god Pan, who derived from her the surname Sinoeis. [Pausanias 8.30.2.]

SINOPE was a daughter of Asopus by Metope, or of Ares by Aegina or Parnassa. Apollo kidnapped her from Boeotia and carried her to Paphlagonia on the Black Sea, where she gave birth to Syrus and where the town of Sinope was named for her. Another story said that Zeus fell in love with her and promised her any gift she might choose. To his surprise she chose virginity. This, of course, is at odds with her being the mother of Syrus. [Diodorus Siculus 4.72; Scholiast on Apollonius Rhodius 2.946.]

SIRENS, or Seirenes, are among the most familiar beings of mythology. They have appeared, singly or in numbers, in later folklore and even today provide a word defined as a temptingly beautiful woman or one who sings seductively.

They were said to have been daughters of Achelous by Sterope, Gaea, or one of the Muses. From Achelous they were often called Acheloides. Because they fell into the class of beings dangerous to men, they were said to be part of the family of monsters sired by Phorcys. Not surprisingly their number and names were inconsistent. Some said there were only two, Aglaopheme and Thelxiepeia. Others said three: Peisinoe, Aglaope, and Thelxiepeia, or Parthenope, Ligeia, and Leucosia. Variations on these names were given, such as Aglaophonos, Thelxiope, Thelxione, and Molpe. And there were two, Teles and Raidne, not in the usual lists.

Their description was somewhat vague. They were reported to have the body of a woman to the waist and of a bird below, sometimes with wings and sometimes without. Their possession of wings has always been a point of argument. Originally, it was said, they were companions of Persephone. When she was abducted, some claimed that they asked to be provided with wings so they could help search. Others claimed they already had wings and were deprived of them for failing to help in the search. Still others said they had wings but were stripped of them when they lost a singing contest with the Muses, whom they had challenged. They were skilled musicians both vocally and instrumentally. According to the writers who described three of them, one sang, one played the lyre, and one played the flute. They lived on a rocky island generally considered to be near the southwestern coast of Italy between the island of Aeaea and the rock of Scylla.

On this lonely, rocky island they awaited passing ships. When one came into view they played so exquisitely that the sailors lay on their oars or failed to mind their sails, and their crafts would crack up on the rocks. Some even leapt overboard, only to be mangled on the rocks. It is not clear what the Sirens' motive was, but it has been suggested that the shipwrecked sailors were devoured by them.

The Argonauts got safely by them because Orpheus, their own musician, outperformed the Sirens. Even so, one of the men, Eryx, jumped overboard and swam toward the temptresses; he was saved by Aphrodite. Warned by Circe, Odysseus put wax in his men's ears and had himself lashed to the mast of his ship. He tried to break free when he heard the wonderful music, but fortunately could not. The Sirens were so frustrated at their failure that they hurled

themselves into the sea and drowned, as so many of their victims had.

The idea of Sirens, heavenly voiced seductresses, has been almost as alluring as the birdmaidens themselves. It is easy to believe that on long voyages lonely sailors could be brought to imagine alluring females, even though part bird or part fish, and burn to embrace them even if the consequence might be death. There was a temple of the Sirens near Surrentum (Sorrento), and the tomb of Parthenope was believed to be near Neapolis (Naples). [Homer, *Odyssey* 12.39,166; Eustathius on Homer's *Odyssey* 1709; Tzetzes on Lycophron 712; Servius on Virgil's *Eclogues* 4.562, *Aeneid* 5.364; Plutarch, *Table-Talk* 9.14; Orphica, *Argonautica* 1284; Apollodorus 1.3.4,7.10,9.25; Ovid, *Metamorphoses* 5.552; Apollonius Rhodius 4.893–896; Hyginus, *Fables* 141.]

SITO was a surname of Demeter, describing her as the giver of food or grain. [Athenaeus 3.109, 10.416; Aelian, *Various Narratives* 1.27.]

SMILAX was the beloved of Crocus, but she did not love him in return. He was changed by the gods into a saffron plant (crocus), and she was changed into the plant bearing her name. [Ovid, *Metamorphoses* 4.283.]

SMYRNA (1) was a daughter of Theias and Oreithyia, or of Cinyras and Cenchreis. She was also called MYRRHA and was said to have given her name to the city of Smyrna. [Apollodorus 3.14.4; Antoninus Liberalis 34.]

SMYRNA (2) was one of the AMAZONS. [Strabo 14.1.4.]

SORORIA was a surname of Juno under which an altar was erected to her in common with Janus Curiatis. When Horatius fought with and killed the Curiatii for the supremacy of Rome over Alba, he returned home in triumph and was met at the Capene Gate by his sister, who recognized on his shoulders the mantle of her betrothed lover, one of the Curiatii. Her hysterical grief caused Horatius to stab her, exclaiming that thus every woman should die who lamented for a foe.

He was acquitted, but an altar was raised to Juno Sororia, and the Horatian family had to make special sacrifices for years to come. [Livy 1.26.]

SOSIS, or Sois, was the mother of the twins Iasus and Pelasgus by Triopas. Later she bore Agenor and Xanthus. Pelasgus was said to have founded Argos and to have taught people agriculture. The brothers shared the Peloponnesian territory; Iasus held the west, which included Elis, and Pelasgus had the east. Agenor inherited his father's cavalry and overthrew both brothers. Pelasgus then migrated to the north and founded Larissa. [Pausanias 1.14.2, 2.22.2; Scholiast on Euripides' Orestes 920.]

SOSPITA, Saving Goddess, was a surname of Juno at Lanuvium and at Rome, and she had temples in both these places. [Cicero, On the Nature of the Gods 1.29, On Divination 1.2.]

SOTEIRA, Saving Goddess, occurred as a surname of several divinities in Greece, such as Artemis at Pegae in Megaris, at Troezen, at Boeae in Laconia, and at Pellene; Persephone in Laconia and in Arcadia; Athena; and Eunomia. [Pausanias 1.40, 2.31.1,44.7, 3.13.2,22.9, 7.27.1, 8.31.1; Aristotle, Rhetoric 3.18; Pindar, Olympian Odes 9.25.]

SOTERIA was the personification of safety or recovery (Latin, salus) and was worshipped as a divinity in Greece. She had a temple and statue at Patrae. Eurypylus dedicated a sanctuary to her at Patrae after he was cured of madness incurred when he beheld an ancient image of Dionysus that fell to him as part of the booty at the sack of Troy. [Pausanias 7.21.2,24.2.]

SPARTA was a daughter of Eurotas by Cleta. Eurotas, son of Myles, had a channel dug that carried the waters of the Laconian plain to the sea. Afterward, this waterway was called the Eurotas River. Cleta was probably a Laconian nymph, though it should not be overlooked that Cleta was also the name of one of the Spartan Charites.

Sparta married Lacedaemon, son of Zeus and Taygete, one of the Pleiades. The country was called Lacedaemon after him, and its capital was called Sparta. Lacedaemon built the sanctuary of the Charites between Sparta and Amyclae. He later had a hero shrine at Therapne, a suburb of Sparta. The children of Sparta and Lacedaemon were Amyclas, Eurydice, and Asine. Amyclas became king of Laconia after Lacedaemon and was regarded as the founder of the town of Amyclae, where the famous throne of the Amyclaean Apollo was located. He was the father of the renowned Hyacinthus. Eurydice married Acrisius of Argos and was thus grandmother of the hero Perseus of Gorgon-killing fame.

Sparta as an individual had virtually no importance, but as the name of a city she ranked with the goddess Athena as one of the two most important namesakes of Greece. [Apollodorus 3.10.3; Pausanias 3.1.3,18.4,5,20.3; Stephanus Byzantium, "Asine."]

SPEIO was one of the NEREIDES. [Homer, Iliad 18.40; Hesiod, Theogony 245.]

SPERMO was one of the OENOTROPAE.

SPES was the personification of hope and was worshipped at Rome, where she had several temples. The most ancient of these was built in 354 B.C. by the consul Atilius Calatinus near the Porta Carmentalis. The Greeks also worshipped the personification of hope, Elpis. [Livy 2.51, 21.62, 24.47, 25.7; Tacitus, Annals 2.49.]

SPHINX was another monster who, as an enigmatic being, made her way into modern languages. We know the Sphinx best as the monster who terrorized Thebes and, in effect, was responsible for the incestuous marriage of Oedipus and his mother.

The Sphinx, older than the pyramids of Egypt, was said to have been a daughter of Orthrus and Chimaera, or of Typhon and Echidna, or of Typhon and Chimaera. Any one of these combinations would have made her extraordinarily deadly. In spite of her ability to wreak havoc, she was not known before her Theban episode except as one of a number of replicated guardians of approaches to Egyptian tombs or temples. She had the winged body of a lion and the breast and upper part of a woman. She also had the tail of a serpent and the wings of an eagle.

Only such a beast could punish Thebes. The reasons are not clear. According to some, Ares still harbored a grudge against the ancient wrong done to his dragon by Cadmus. Others claimed Hera sent the Sphinx because King Laius had kidnapped and molested young Chrysippus from Pisa. Or Dionysus sent her. Or Hades did. It could have been that the Sphinx was sent by the gods in general to fulfill the destiny of Oedipus.

Whatever the case, she appeared one day without warning and started to harass the Thebans. She perched outside one of the gates of the city and proceeded to stop passersby. She posed impossible riddles, then killed and devoured people when they were unable to provide the correct answers. Needless to say, all traffic to and from the area halted, and Thebes was like a city under siege.

Finally, a brash young newcomer to the city decided it was time to put a stop to this terrorism. He was inspired to do this by the reward, offered by the regent, of control of the kingdom and the hand of the recently widowed queen. Oedipus was, unknown to himself, the murderer of the king and the son of the widowed queen.

He met the Sphinx and heard the famous riddle that now any schoolboy can answer: What walks on four legs in the morning, two at noon, and three in the evening, and the fewer legs it has the stronger it is? Oedipus answered that it was a human being, and the Sphinx, cheated out of supper, had to agree this was the correct reply. In frustration she dive-bombed into a cliff and was silenced forever.

She could not be aware that she had really accomplished more evil than she intended. Oedipus became king, married his mother, and had four children by her. Whatever god sought vengeance through the Sphinx certainly achieved it. One rather inane story said she was actually a daughter of Laius who used the riddle to advance her claim to the throne, disposing of her brothers when they could not answer it. [Hesiod, *Theogony* 306; Apollodorus 3.5.8; Scholiast on Euripides' *Phoenician Maidens* 46,810,1760; Pausanias 9.26.2; Hyginus, *Fables* 67; Tzetzes on Lycophron 7; Sophocles, *Oedipus the King* 391; Diodorus Siculus 4.63.]

SPHRAGITIDES was the name of a class of prophetic nymphs on Mount Cithaeron in Boeotia, where they had a grotto. [Plutarch, *Aristides* 9; Pausanias 9.3.9.]

SPONDE was one of the HORAE. [Hyginus, *Fables* 183.]

STATA MATER was a Roman divinity whose statue at one time stood in the forum, where fires were kept burning every night. When the forum was paved, the fires were kindled in other parts of the city in order not to spoil the stones. Inscriptions called this goddess Stata Mater, but this was most probably another name for Vesta. [Festus 317.]

STEROPE (1) was one of the PLEIADES, daughter of Atlas and Pleione. Like her sister Merope she married a mortal. He was Oenomaus, son of Ares and Harpinna, and king of Pisa in Elis. Sterope's children by Oenomaus were Leucippus, Hippodameia, and Alcippe. One writer also listed Dysponteus, who founded the city of Dyspontium.

Sterope suffered the loss of Leucippus. He fell in love with a nymph who followed Artemis. He could find no other way to be near her, so he dressed as a maiden and became close friends with her. He was found out, however, and killed by her companions. Alcippe married Euenus, who unhappily imitated his father-in-law and forced contenders for the hand of their daughter Marpessa to compete with him in a chariot race.

When Hippodameia grew up, reports of her beauty attracted many suitors. Oenomaus took a dim view of them, since he was in love with his daughter. We do not know whether or not Sterope was aware of this development. Oenomaus agreed to give Hippodameia to anyone who could beat him in a chariot race, but the price of losing was death to the contender. In spite of the grim probability of death, about 20 young men came forward and failed. Sterope and her daughters must have been horrified by the severed heads of recent losers strung over the doorway.

Finally Pelops defeated Oenomaus, who died in the contest. He married Hippodameia and assumed Oenomaus' kingdom. That meant that Sterope had a choice of remaining with them or going elsewhere. It is difficult to consider Sterope's story as Oenomaus' wife together with the story of the collective Pleiades, who were said by some to have been changed into doves when pursued by Orion or into stars as a result of grief for their father's punishment by Zeus. Several other Pleiades had independent lives as well, so their metamorphosis must be considered as having come about after their separate careers had ended.

Sterope was called by some the mother of Oenomaus by Ares, which would have concurred with the statement that only one of the Pleiades married a mortal. To support this contention, the wife of Oenomaus was by some called Euarete or Eurythoe. [Apollodorus 3.10.1; Pausanias 5.10.5,22.5, 6.21.6.]

STEROPE (2) was a daughter of Pleuron and Xanthippe. Pleuron was a son of Aetolus, who migrated to central Greece from Peloponnesus, and brother of Calydon. He founded the town of Pleuron in Aetolia. Sterope's brother was Agenor, and her sisters were Stratonice and Laophonte. Nothing further is known of her or Stratonice, but Laophonte married Thestius and became mother of Leda and Althaea. [Apollodorus 1.7.7.]

STEROPE (3) was a daughter of Acastus and Astydameia. Acastus, son of Pelias, was an Argonaut and a Calydonian hunter, and after his father's death reigned in Iolcus. He had been a special friend of Peleus on the Argonaut and readily agreed to purify him when Peleus accidentally killed his father-in-law and came to the court of Acastus. Sterope's mother fell in love with Peleus, but could not get him to respond to her various seductions. She became quite angry with him and secretly sent a message to Antigone, the wife of Peleus, telling her that Peleus was on the point of marrying Sterope. In despair Antigone killed herself, but Peleus did not know this before he returned home. Astydameia meanwhile accused him before her husband, who could not violate laws governing hospitality and the purification rite by killing him outright, so he took his guest on a hunt on Mount Pelion and made off with his weapons during the night,

leaving him defenseless. Peleus was almost killed by Centaurs but managed to escape. He returned and killed both Acastus and Astydameia. Sterope had no part in any of this, even though reference to her had prompted Antigone's suicide. There is no record of what happened to her after she was orphaned. [Apollodorus 3.13.3.]

STEROPE (4) was a daughter of Cepheus of Tegea. He was a son of Aleus and took part in the Argonaut. Like so many other Laconians he was sorely opposed to Hippocoon, illegitimate son of Oebalus, who had usurped the throne from his half-brother Tyndareus. When Heracles asked for his alliance, he was ready to agree, except he was certain that once he left with his 20 sons, the town would be invaded by other enemies. Heracles said not to worry and produced an urn that held a lock of Medusa's hair. He instructed Sterope that if the occasion arose she should hold the lock aloft on the walls of the city, since the mere sight of it would put an enemy to flight.

Sterope was the sister of Auge, who was the mother of Telephus by Heracles. Nothing further is known of her. [Pausanias 8.47.4; Apollodorus 2.7.3.]

STEROPE (5) was a daughter of Porthaon and Euryte. Porthaon, son of Agenor and Epicaste, was king of Pleuron and Calydon in Aetolia. Sterope's brothers were Oeneus, Agrius, Laocoon, Alcathous, Melas, and Leucopeus. She grew up amidst hostility between two of her brothers. Oeneus succeeded to the kingdom but was deprived of it by Agrius and his sons. By the time that event had occurred, however, Sterope had become the lover of the Acheron River and produced, according to some, the Sirens. These strange creatures were subject to many variations in number and names and, for that matter, parentage. They had once been companions of Persephone but were given wings to help locate her when she was lost. Eventually they were consigned to a rocky island off the coast of Italy, where their ethereal singing and playing enticed sailors to their death on the jagged rocks. Sterope was never heard from again, so we do not know how she was affected by the murderous conduct of her daughters. Her own nephew Meleager was an Argonaut and risked death by his cousins, the Sirens, when the *Argo* passed near their island. [Apollodorus 1.7.10,8.5; Homer, *Iliad* 14.115; Pausanias 4.35.1, 6.20.8,21.7; Hyginus, *Fables* 175.]

STEROPE (6) was called the mother of Aspledon by Presbon, but Aspledon's mother was more often called MIDEIA. [Scholiast on Homer's *Iliad* 2.511.]

STEROPE (7) was a daughter of Helios, the god of the sun. Consequently, she was sister or half-sister to Circe and Pasiphae. She married Eurypylus, the son of Poseidon and Celaeno, who ruled over Cyrene in Libya. Eurypylus gave Euphemus a clod of earth when the Argonauts passed through Lake Tritonis. This clod gave claim by his descendants to sovereignty in Cyrene, which had been so named when Apollo brought the nymph Cyrene there. By Eurypylus, Sterope had two sons, Lycaon and Leucippus, but there is no record of anything they did. [Scholiast on Pindar's *Pythian Odes* 4.57; Tzetzes on Lycophron 886.]

STHEINO was one of the GORGONS. [Apollodorus 2.4.2.]

STHENEBOEA was a daughter of Iobates or Amphianax or Apheidas and, according to some, the wife of Proetus. For love of Bellerophon she killed herself. She is usually called ANTEIA. [Apollodorus 2.2.1, 3.9.1.]

STHENELE (1) was one of the DANAIDES, daughter of Danaus and Memphis. She married and murdered Sthenelus. [Apollodorus 2.1.5.]

STHENELE (2) was a daughter of Acastus and Astydameia. Her sister was Sterope. At about the age of 16 Sthenele married Menoetius, son of Actor, who was some 20 years older. He was the half-brother of Aeacus, both having the same mother, Aegina. Shortly after they married, Peleus, son of Aeacus, came to the court of Acastus at Iolcus to be purified of the accidental murder of his father-in-law. He, Acastus, and Menoetius had been fellow sailors on the famous *Argo*. Astydameia, Acastus' wife, became infatu-

ated with Peleus and tried to seduce him. When he refused her, not only did she send a letter to Antigone, Peleus' wife, telling her that Peleus was going to marry her daughter Sterope, but she also accused Peleus of making improper advances. As a result of all this, Peleus nearly lost his life when Acastus left him without weapons on Mount Pelion during a hunt, and Antigone hanged herself. Peleus avenged the wrong done to him by killing Acastus and strewing Astydameia's dismembered body about the city.

Sthenele's marriage was definitely not off to a good start. Not long after his wife's death, Peleus courted and married the Nereid Thetis. Rather close together were born Patroclus, Sthenele's son, and Achilles, Thetis' son. Menoetius and Sthenele lived at Opus, and Menoetius was the first to worship Heracles as a god. Part of the reason might have been that Heracles had provided Menoetius and Sthenele with a granddaughter by their daughter Myrto. This granddaughter, Eucleia, was later afforded divine honors and associated with the worship of Artemis.

While still a boy Patroclus quarreled with Clitonymus, son of Amphidamas, over a game of dice and killed him. Whatever rancor Sthenele might have harbored in regard to Peleus, she readily agreed to send Patroclus to his older cousin at Phthia to be brought up. She perhaps saw Patroclus intermittently during his developing years, but he did not return to Opus. He and Achilles grew up together as cousins, friends, and almost certainly lovers. Patroclus was a suitor of Helen but went to the Trojan War more out of love of Achilles than loyalty to Helen and the Greek cause. In the war, both greatly distinguished themselves, both died, and both were buried in a common grave with their ashes mingled.

The mother of Patroclus was also called Periapis (or Periopis), Polymela, and Philomela. [Apollodorus 3.2.8,13.8; Homer, *Iliad* 11, 608,770, 16.14, 23.87; Ovid, *Heroides* 1.17; Diodorus Siculus 4.39.]

STILBE (1) was a daughter of the Peneius River and Creusa, daughter of Oceanus and Gaea and sister of Hypseus and Daphne. The valley of the Peneius was a favorite haunt of Apollo, who soon discovered there the beautiful Stilbe. She bore him three sons, Centaurus, Lapithes, and Aeneus. During this rather extended affair with her, Apollo noticed that the young sister, Daphne, was developing most interestingly. He pursued her in an attempt to rape her but was thwarted when she was changed into a laurel tree. It is not known how Stilbe reacted to this turn of events.

Nothing can be learned of Centaurus, although his name anticipated the race of Centaurs created a few generations later. Lapithes was regarded as the ancestor of the Lapithae. He lived near the Peneius River and ruled over the region. Aeneus became father of Cyzicus, who ruled on the coast of the Propontis until unintentionally killed by the Argonauts. The city of Cyzicus was named for him. [Diodorus Siculus 1.69, 4.69; Apollonius Rhodius 1.9.18; Scholiast on Apollonius Rhodius 1.40; Ovid, *Amores* 3.6.31; Hyginus, *Fables* 203; Conon, *Narrations* 41.]

STILBE (2) was a daughter of Eosphorus and by some called the mother of Autolycus by Hermes. The mother of Autolycus was usually given as CHIONE. It is not certain whether or not this same Stilbe was called the mother of Callisto by Ceteus. [Scholiast on Homer's *Iliad* 10.267; Scholiast on Euripides' *Orestes* 1642.]

STILBO was one of the OCEANIDES. [Hyginus, *Fables: Preface* 6.]

STIMULA was the name of SEMELE, according to the pronunciation of the Romans. [Livy 39.12; St. Augustine, *City of God* 4.11.16; Ovid, *Fasti* 6.503.]

STONYCHIA was one of the PLEIADES. [Scholiast on Theocritus 13.25.]

STRATONICE (1) was one of the THESPIADES and mother of Atromus by Heracles. [Apollodorus 2.7.3.]

STRATONICE (2) was a daughter of Pleuron and Xanthippe in the city of Pleuron. Her brother was Agenor, and her sisters were Sterope and Laophonte. Laophonte married Thestius and became the mother of Leda and Althaea. Stratonice and Sterope are otherwise unknown. [Apollodorus 1.7.7.]

STRATONICE (3) was called the wife of Melaneus, although his wife was also called Oechalia. The confusion arose apparently from traditions in two separate places in Greece. Melaneus was a son of Apollo and a skilled archer. According to Messenian tradition, he came to Perieres in Messenia and was assigned a dwelling in Carnasium, which later Melaneus named Oechalia for his wife. Others claimed Melaneus dwelled in Thessaly, where he married Stratonice, by whom he became the father of Eurytus, the celebrated archer.

Eurytus succeeded his father as king of Oechalia, and by Antioche became the father of Iole and several sons. He was said to have instructed Heracles in the use of the bow, but this sharing of expertise resulted in the murder of Eurytus and his sons by Heracles, who fought for possession of Iole. [Hesiod, *Fragments* 48; Pausanias 4.3.6,27.4,33.5; Theocritus 24.105; Apollodorus 2.4.9.]

STRATONICE (4) was the wife of Chaeresilaus, son of Iasius and grandson of Eleuther. Their son was Poemander, who founded a city that he first called Poemander and later changed to the name of his wife, Tanagra, daughter of Aeolus or Asopus. The inhabitants refused to have any part in the Trojan War, and Achilles attacked them for this (in spite of his own draft-dodging history). He carried off Stratonice and killed her grandson. Poemander escaped and hastily began fortifying the city. At one point he grew angry with the builder and threw a large stone at him. It killed Leucippus, his own son, instead. Poemander had to leave Boeotia, and the besieging army under Achilles allowed him to pass through their lines in safety. Achilles even sent him to Elephenor at Chalcis for purification. Poemander gratefully built a shrine to Achilles outside Chalcis. Presumably Achilles also restored Stratonice to her son, but the record does not say. [Pausanias 9.20.2; Plutarch, *Greek Questions* 37,299; Lycophron 326.]

STRYMO was a daughter of the Scamander River and wife of Laomedon. Some called his wife Rhoeo, Placia, Thoosa, Zeuxippe, or Leucippe. Several of the early kings of Troy married daughters of river-gods. Laomedon followed his father Ilus as king of Troy and had several children by Strymo. The sons were Priam, Tithonus, Lampus, Clytius, Hicetaon, and Bucolion. The daughters were Hesione, Cilla, Astyoche, Aethylla, Medesicaste, and Procleia. During his reign he built the massive walls of the city, and he was fortunate to have the assistance of Poseidon and Apollo, who, having revolted from Zeus, had to work for Laomedon for wages. He was unfortunate in thinking he could get out of paying their wages. In punishment for this rash oversight, Poseidon sent a marine monster to terrorize the coast. The only way to appease it, an oracle declared, was to sacrifice a maiden. Laomedon tried to dodge his responsibility, but the citizens finally agreed that his own daughter, Hesione, should be the victim. Strymo must have hated her husband for causing this horrible thing to happen to her beloved daughter. There seemed no way out, though, until Heracles happened to land just as the monster was about to satisfy its appetite for virgins. He killed the beast and brought the terrified girl back to Laomedon. For this service Heracles asked for the horses Zeus had given to Tros, Laomedon's grandfather, in compensation for stealing Ganymede. Laomedon again refused to pay and backed up his refusal with an army. Once more Strymo had a chance to see what a chiseler her husband was, and she was probably not too unhappy when Heracles took Hesione with him when he left. He gave her to Telamon, his companion. After a certain time, Heracles returned with his own army and killed Laomedon and all his sons except Priam, whom Hesione ransomed. So Strymo saw her husband buried near the Scaean gate, which itself had been built on his false promises.

Priam then became king of Troy and developed the mighty fortress of Troy that later resisted ten years of siege by the Greeks who came to recover Helen of Sparta. Strymo lived perhaps long enough to see these calamitous events set in motion. Most of the Trojan heroes were her grandsons, who died one at a time because of her son's steadfast refusal to surrender Helen. In her son she saw a reflection of the disastrous stubbornness of her late husband. [Homer, *Iliad* 5.265,640, 6.23, 7.452, 20.236, 21.446, 23.348; Scholiast on Homer's *Iliad* 20.145, 21.442; Apollodorus 2.5.9,6.4, 3.12.3; Tzetzes on Lycophron 232,467; Diodorus Siculús 4.32,49; Hyginus, *Fables* 89.]

STYGNE was one of the DANAIDES, daughter of Danaus and Polyxo. She married and murdered Polyctor. [Apollodorus 2.1.5.]

STYMPHALIA was a surname of Artemis at Stymphalus in Arcadia, where she had a temple. [Stephanus Byzantium, "Stymphalos"; Eustathius on Homer's *Iliad* 302.]

STYMPHALIDES were rapacious birds that infested Lake Stymphalus in northeastern Arcadia. They were said to be the daughters of King Stymphalus and Ornis, but this was probably local propaganda that expressed the neighboring community's displeasure with a terrible nuisance. The birds had overrun the area, dropping feathers and guano over fields and meadows. The rumor spread that they ate human flesh. Eurystheus imposed their eradication as one of the labors of Heracles. This was one of his easier labors. Athena provided him with a bronze rattle with which he startled the birds and killed them as they tried to fly away. Some of them, it was told, escaped to the island of Aretias in the Euxine Sea, where they were encountered by the Argonauts.

Some said they were not birds but women, daughters of Stymphalus and Ornis. They were killed by Heracles because they did not receive him hospitably, as they had done in the case of Heracles' enemies, the Molionidae. In the temple of Artemis at Stymphalia they were represented as birds. Behind the temple were white marble statues of maidens with the feet of birds. This representation must have given rise to the whole legend of the Stymphalides. [Pausanias 8.22.5; Scholiast on Apollonius Rhodius 1054.]

STYX was another ancient being whose name has become a part of modern vocabulary. She was a nymph of the underworld, one of the daughters of Oceanus and Tethys, who became associated, not with a free-flowing upper world river, but a sluggish infernal river. She was a stream into which the Cocytus flowed. She dwelled at the entrance of Hades, and her grotto was supported by silver beams. She probably earned this geographical advantage by having given assistance to Zeus during his battle with the Titans. She was married to Pallas, son of Crius and Eurybia, and therefore a second-generation Titan like herself. When Zeus battled the Titans, she brought him her children—Zelus (Zeal), Nice (Victory), Bia (Force), and Cratus (Power)—and offered their assistance against the enemy. Zeus was extremely grateful and gave them a home on Olympus. Styx, who retired to her customary home, became the divinity in whose name the most solemn oaths were sworn. Even a god who took an oath by Styx was subjected to a fixed ritual. Iris, the early messenger of the gods, fetched a cup of water from the Styx River and, while the oath was taken, slowly poured out the water.

For all her somber surroundings Styx was not unattractive to Zeus, whose appetite embraced women, boys, and beasts alike. There were those who could not resist the notion that Persephone was the daughter of Styx by Zeus, but it was rather well established that Persephone was the daughter of Zeus by his sister Demeter. Styx was also said to be the mother of Echidna by Peiras, but as an underworld being she could be expected to be called a mother of monsters. Echidna was usually called the daughter of Phorcys and Ceto. Her daughters by Pallas probably represented the extent of her maternity, although the Romans added Invidia, the personification of envy, to her brood. [Hesiod, *Theogony* 361,383,778; Apollodorus 1.2.2, 5,3.1; Homer, *Odyssey* 5.185, 15.37; Apollonius Rhodius 2.191; Virgil, *Aeneid* 6.324, 12.816; Ovid, *Metamorphoses* 2.760, 3.290; Pausanias 7.26.5, 8.18.1.]

SUADA was the Roman personification of persuasion. She was sometimes called by the diminutive Suadela. Her Greek counterpart was Peitho. [Horace, *Epistles* 1.6.38; Cicero, *Brutus* 15.]

SYLEA, daughter of Corinthus, was the mother of Sinis by Polypemon or Poseidon. One is never sure of the father's identity when a choice of husbands was given, since it was convenient for a young woman to claim that a god had slept with her, when in reality she had had intercourse with a local. If a son turned out bad, a god could be claimed, instead of a mortal, to account for abberant behavior. Sinis was such a one. He dwelled on the isthmus of Corinth and preyed on travelers. He disabled them, then bent two pines down and tied the legs of a victim to each pine. When he let the trees spring apart, they tore the victim in half. Theseus met and conquered this villain but had to be purified, since Sinis was one of his relatives. Theseus instituted the Isthmian games in his honor. One can never be sure to what extent one of these criminals' mothers was involved in their dark deeds. Sylea might have been unaware of her son's grisly career, or she might have assisted him. Her daughter Perigune was the first female sexual partner of Theseus, and she bore him a son. Sylea was not mentioned by most chroniclers of this deadly encounter between Theseus and Sinis. [Apollodorus 3.16.2; Plutarch, *Theseus* 8; Pausanias 1.37.3, 2.1.3.]

SYLLIS was a nymph and wife or lover of Zeuxippus, son of Apollo and king of Sicyon. At the time of Zeuxippus the throne of Sicyon was not acquired by normal royal succession. Zeuxippus probably came to the throne by show of strength or by popular demand, or he could have been a duly appointed regent. Before him was Phaestus, a son of Heracles, and after him Hippolytus, son of Rhopalus and grandson of Phaestus. Nothing further is known of him or Syllis. [Pausanias 2.6.7.]

SYMAETHIS was the mother of Acis by Faunus, protector of flocks and shepherds. Acis was loved by the nymph Galateia; jealous of him, Polyphemus the Cyclops crushed him under a rock. His blood was changed by the nymph into a spring that became the Acis River at the foot of Mount Aetna. [Ovid, *Metamorphoses* 13.750.]

SYME was a daughter of Ialysus and Dotis. Ialysus was the eponymous hero of the city of

Ialysus on Rhodes. He was descended from the sun. Syme was carried off by the marine divinity Glaucus to an island near the coast of Caria. The island received its name from her. [Athenaeus 7.296; Stephanus Byzantium, "Syme."]

SYRIA DEA, the Syrian Goddess, was a name by which the Syrian Astarte was often designated. Astarte resembled the Greek Aphrodite, and her epithet followed her absorption into the Greek pantheon. The route by which Astarte entered Greece was from Asia to Cyprus (an especially important site of Aphrodite's worship) to mainland Greece. [Lucian, *Goddess of Surrye;* Pausanias 1.14.6; Aeschylus, *Suppliant Maidens* 562.]

SYRINX was an Arcadian nymph. Unlike most of her sisters, she was not impressed by the attention she attracted from Pan, the son of Hermes and god of fields and flocks. His inherited cunning from his father, his determined courtship, and his enormous phallus did nothing to change her mind; when pursued by him she ran away. Once when he nearly caught her, she fled into the Ladon River, the god of which was probably her father, and prayed to be rid of the importunate god. She was metamorphosed into a clump of reeds, which Pan impotently embraced. He fashioned them into a musical instrument, known to this day as Pan's pipes. [Ovid, *Metamorphoses* 1.690.]

TACITA, the Silent, was one of the CAMENAE. Her worship was introduced by Numa, who considered her the most important of the Camenae. She was sometimes identified with Muta and Larunda. [Plutarch, *Numa* 8.]

TANAGRA was a daughter of Aeolus or Asopus and wife of Poemander, son of Chaeresilaus and STRATONICE. Her husband named the town of Tanagra after her. [Plutarch, *Greek Questions* 70.]

TANAIS was a variant form of the name of the divinity ANAITIS. [Clement of Alexandria, *Exhortations to the Greeks* 43.]

TANAQUIL was a woman of the highest nobility in Tarquinii in Etruria. She married Lucumo, a son of Demaratus, a Corinthian of the noble family of Bacchiadae. He had inherited the great wealth of his father but found that he and his wife were excluded from any promise of power or influence because of the alien status of his father. Tanaquil influenced him to move to Rome, where he might have a better chance of distinction, and they set out with a large retinue. When they came within sight of Rome, an eagle seized Lucumo's cap, carried it very high in the heavens, then returned and placed it once again on his head. Tanaquil, skilled in augury, predicted the highest honor for her husband from this omen. True enough, Lucumo was accorded a high-ranking position by the Romans and eventually succeeded to the throne under the name of Tarquinius Priscus, the fifth king of Rome. Tanaquil bore him two sons and two daughters, all of whom married into noble families. One son, Tarquinius Superbus, succeeded his father. Tanaquil, more formally known as Caecilia, was later connected with the worship centered around the hearth and domestic life. [Livy 1.34–41; Dionysius of Halicarnassus, *Roman Antiquities* 3.46–73, 4.1; Plutarch, *Roman Questions* 271.]

TARPEIA was the daughter of Tarpeius, the governor of the Roman citadel on the Capitoline Hill. When the Sabines made war on Rome as a result of the abduction of their women, Tarpeia observed the Sabine king Tatius encamped with soldiers at the foot of the Capitoline. She fell in love with him and managed to get word to him that she would open the gates to him if he would marry her. Tatius agreed, but when Tarpeia opened the gates, on Tatius' orders the soldiers crushed her beneath their shields. Another version said she bargained for what the soldiers wore on their left arms, meaning their gold jewelry. Tatius pretended she meant their shields and had his men pile them on top of her. In the opinion of many, the Sabines killed her rather than bargain with her because they did not want anyone to believe their success was due to treason.

She was buried on the hill, and her memory was preserved by the name of the Tarpeian Rock, from which criminals were thrown. Tarpeia was called by some a Vestal virgin. [Livy 1.11; Plutarch, *Numa* 10; Varro, *On the Latin Language* 5.41.]

TAUROPOLIS (1), Tauro, Taurione, or Tauropos was the name given to the Taurian goddess (Taurica Dea), who presided over the bloody and savage worship at Tauris on the Black Sea. She was identified with Artemis, and the name was explained by some as referring to the bull as the symbol of the Taurian worship. Iphigeneia, daughter of Agamemnon, was conveyed to Tauris by Artemis just when the Greeks were about to sacrifice her at Aulis. Iphigeneia became the high priestess of the Taurian worship and very nearly sacrificed her brother Orestes and his friend Pylades when they came to fetch the image of Artemis in response to an oracle given by Apollo. They were spared, and with Iphigeneia brought the statue to Brauron in Attica, where it introduced the worship of Artemis Brauronia. The worship spread later to Sparta, where Artemis Orthia was characterized as demanding bloody sacrifices, which were accommodated by the ritual flogging of Spartan youths. The worship was carried to Aricia in Italy, according to some, by the resurrected Hippolytus, son of Theseus. Whichever name was later adopted, the dark worship could be traced back to that of the Taurian goddess. Appropriately enough, she and Ares were the principal gods worshipped by the Amazons. Thoantea was a surname of the Taurian Artemis, derived from Thoas, who had escaped the mass murder of Lemnian males to become king of Tauris. [Hesychius, "Tauropolai"; Scholiast on Sophocles' *Ajax* 172; Euripides, *Iphigeneia in Taurica* 1457; Valerius Flaccus 8.208; Pausanias 3.16.6; Herodotus 4.103; Ovid, *Ibis* 386.]

TAUROPOLIS (2) was a daughter of the Megarian Cleson, son of Lelex, and sister of Cleso. The sisters found the body of Ino washed up on the coast of Megara and buried it. Either fleeing from her husband (who had been driven mad by Hera) or in a state of insanity herself, Ino leapt into the sea with her son Melicertes. Both were converted into sea deities, but their mortal remains were still in evidence until found and disposed of. The Megarians first recognized Leucothea, the apotheosized Ino, by annual sacrifices. [Pausanias 1.42.7.]

TAYGETE, from whom Mount Taygetus in Laconia derived its name, was one of the PLEIADES. By Zeus she became the mother of Lacedaemon, even though she fled from the god's embraces. Artemis tried to help by changing her into a cow, but Zeus found no problem with cows, bears, geese, swans, or other animals, and the question would really be one of whether he was willing to wait for Taygete to resume her original form or go right ahead with what was at hand. Whichever he chose, Lacedaemon was conceived. Still, Taygete felt obliged to Artemis and presented her with the famous Ceryneian hind with golden antlers that Heracles later captured as one of his labors.

Lacedaemon became king of the region of his same name. He founded the sanctuary of the Charites between Sparta and Amyclae. Taygete was also called by some the mother of Eurotas by Myles. His mother was more often called Cleochareia. [Apollodorus 3.10.1,3; Pausanias 3.1.2,18.7,20.2; Stephanus Byzantium, "Taygeton"; Scholiast on Pindar's *Olympian Odes* 3.53; Hyginus, *Fables* 9,82; Ovid, *Metamorphoses* 6.174.]

TECMESSA (1) was the daughter of Teuthras, or Teleutas, a king of Phrygia. During the Trojan War the Telamonian Ajax, like Achilles, made excursions into neighboring countries. Once, he went into Phrygia, where he slew King Teuthras in single combat. He carried away rich spoils, not the least of which was Tecmessa, the king's daughter, who became his mistress.

It would be interesting to know whether she was his mistress unwillingly or by choice. It is hard to believe that a captive woman whose father he killed and whose house he looted could entertain too much affection for her captor. Ajax was strong, large, and very handsome, and he was characterized as calm, self-controlled, benevolent, and god-fearing. Nevertheless, he was still a man of war and rough-edged. His remarkable shield was made of seven layers of oxhides and a final layer of bronze. Perhaps Tecmessa came to accept her lot as part of the fortunes of war and looked at the positive attributes of Ajax, whose beauty and bravery put him in a class with the great Achilles. She bore him a son, Eurysaces. Their mating almost certainly took place in the Greek camp, where privacy was at a premium. Eurysaces was named after his father's broad shield.

Ajax was among the greatest of the Greeks at Troy, but there was a strain of insanity that had lain submerged until triggered by an unexpected turn of events. When Achilles was killed, his armor was supposed to go to the one who was considered by the rest of the men as inspiring the greatest fear among the Trojans. The men, many of whom were jealous of Ajax, agreed on Odysseus as the recipient. This drove Ajax mad, and that night he slaughtered the herds of sheep that provided food for the soldiers, thinking the animals were the enemy. The next morning he realized the extent of his madness and plunged the sword into himself.

Ajax was buried by Teucer, his half-brother. Teucer then attempted to return to Salamis, but Telamon, his and Ajax's father, refused to receive him because he had not avenged Ajax and had not brought his remains home. He had also left Tecmessa and her son in Troy. Teucer was not given a chance to answer to these charges and, forced into exile, settled in Cyprus.

Tecmessa apparently came later with Eurysaces to Salamis. Or she might have died before they left Troy. If she came with him to Salamis, she would have found that Ajax already had a wife and a son, Philaeus, there. How the matter of succession or inheritance was handled is only partially known. For some reason Eurysaces and Philaeus gave up to the Athenians the property rights to Salamis, which they had inherited from their grandfather. They received property in Attica in return. One settled in Brauron and the other at Melite. The Attic deme of Philaidae was named for Philaeus, and Eurysaces was honored at Athens with an altar. [Plutarch, *Solon* 10; Pausanias 1.35.2; Dictys Cretensis 2.18; Sophocles, *Ajax* 210,480; Quintus Smyrnaeus 500; Philostratus, *Heroicus* 11.3; Herodotus 6.35.]

TECMESSA (2) was one of the AMAZONS. [Diodorus Siculus 4.16.]

TELAUGE was, according to some, the mother of Autolycus by Hermes or Daedalion. The mother of Autolycus was usually called CHIONE. [Apollodorus 1.9.16; Hyginus, *Fables* 201.]

TELCHINIA was a surname of Athena at Teumessus in Boeotia and at Cameirus on Rhodes, where she had temples. The name indicates that the worship of the goddess in these places was joined in some way with that of the mysterious Telchines, who were regarded as cultivators of the soil and ministers of the gods. Telchinia was also a surname of Hera on Rhodes at Ialysus. [Pausanias 9.19.1.]

TELECLEIA, daughter of Ilus and wife of Cisseus, was by many called the mother of Hecuba and Theano. [Scholiast on Euripides' *Hecuba* 3; Eustathius on Homer's *Iliad* 1083.]

TELEDICE was a nymph who by Phoroneus was, according to some, the mother of Apis and Niobe. Their mother was more often known as LAODICE. [Apollodorus 2.1.1.]

TELEGONE was the daughter of Pharis, son of Hermes and Philodameia. Pharis was the founder of Pharae (modern Kalamata) in Messenia. By the river-god Alpheius, Telegone became mother of Orsilochus. Since Pharae was founded by Pharis and Orsilochus' son Diocles later ruled there, it is rather curious that Telegone journeyed all the way to Arcadia to mate with Alpheius (Alpheius could not very well travel to Pharae for the purpose). Diocles' descendants included Machaon, Nichomachus, and Gorgasus, members of the medical profession. [Homer, *Iliad* 5.545, *Odyssey* 3.489, 15.187, 21.15; Pausanias 4.30.2, 7.22.3.]

TELEIA was a surname of Hera. (*See* CHERA.)

TELEPHASSA was the wife of Agenor, son of Poseidon and Libya. His twin brother was Belus. He was considered the ancestor of the Phoenicians, including those who migrated to Carthage, such as Dido. By Agenor, Telephassa had Europa, Cadmus, Phoenix, Cilix, Thasus, and Phineus.

When Europa was barely pubescent she was abducted from the coast of Phoenicia. According to eyewitnesses, her kidnapper was a great white bull that swam out to sea with her on its back. Agenor sent his sons in search of the girl and told them not to return without her. None returned home, because nobody found her. Her abductor was Zeus, and he carried her to Crete, where she became the mother of the Minoan race. It is curious that the searchers went in just about every direction but Crete, the direction in which the bull swam.

Telephassa joined Cadmus in the search. They stopped at Rhodes and Thera, and then arrived in Thrace, where, having been hospitably received by the Edones, they decided to remain. It is interesting to speculate on why Telephassa did not choose to return to her husband. Surely he did not expect her to search for their missing daughter, and certainly the consequences of returning from a search empty-handed did not apply to her.

Telephassa died in Thrace, and after Cadmus buried her he went to Delphi to consult the oracle. The rest of his story was the saga of the Theban dynasty. Phoenix settled in Phoenicia on the site of the future city of Sidon and gave his name to the Phoenicians. Cilix settled in the country named Cilicia for him. Thasus settled in the island he called Thasos. Phineus settled in Salmydessus in Thrace. [Apollodorus 3.1.1; Hyginus, *Fables* 178; Scholiast on Euripides' *Phoenician Maidens* 5; Pausanias 5.25.7; Scholiast on Apollonius Rhodius 2.178, 3.1185; Virgil, *Aeneid* 1.338; Diodorus Siculus 5.49.]

TELEPHE presents something of a problem. In one place she was called the daughter of Epimedusa, wife of Phoenix, and mother of Peirus, Astypalaea, and Europa. Phoenix was usually called the brother of Europa, joining Cadmus and Cilix in search of her when she was abducted by Zeus. This Europa could have been, of course, a namesake of the other Europa. Other accounts said Telephe was the wife of Thasus and mother of Galepsus. Thasus founded the island in the north Aegean that he named for himself. A city of the island was named for Galepsus. Thasus is often included with the sons of Agenor and Telephassa. It is quite likely that the names

of Telephe and Telephassa became confused over the years and referred to the same person, even though resultant family relationships consequently became blurred. [Scholiast on Euripides' *Phoenician Maidens* 5.]

TELES was one of the SIRENS. [Hyginus, *Fables: Preface* 30.]

TELESTO was one of the OCEANIDES. [Hesiod, *Theogony* 356.]

TELETE (1) was one of the HORAE. [Hyginus, *Fables* 183.]

TELETE (2) was the daughter of Nicaea by Dionysus. Nicaea was a daughter of the river-god Sangarius and Cybele. She was loved by a shepherd, Hymnus, and killed him, but Eros took vengeance on her. Dionysus, who first intoxicated her, made her the mother of Telete, whereupon Nicaea hanged herself. Dionysus called the town of Nicaea after her. Telete became the personification of consecration, and there was a statue of her on Mount Helicon. [Pausanias 9.30.3.]

TELETHUSA was the mother of Iphis by Ligdus of Phaestus in Crete. Iphis was brought up as a boy because, previous to her birth, her father had ordered the child to be killed if it should be a girl. When Iphis had grown up and was betrothed to Ianthe, the difficulty arising was removed by Isis, who had before advised the mother to treat Iphis as a boy and now metamorphosed her into a youth. [Ovid, *Metamorphoses* 9.665.] (*See also* IANTHE.)

TELLUS, sometimes called Terra Mater, was the personification of the earth among the Romans, corresponding with the Greek Gaea. She was, however, somewhat more associated with the nether world than her Greek counterpart. When oaths were sworn by her, people stretched their hands downward in contrast to turning them upward in swearing by Jupiter. Sacrifices were offered to her at the time of sowing and the harvest, especially when a member of the family had died without due honors having been paid to him or her. It was Tellus who received the departed into her bosom. A public festival called the Fordicidia or Hordicalia was celebrated in her honor on April 15. At this festival priests also prayed to a male divinity of the earth called Telumno. Tellus had a temple at Rome in the street leading to the Carinae. Tellus, in the persona of Terra, was called by some the mother of the Harpies. By Aether she had a son, Luctus, personification of grieving or mourning. This being, who wasted the energies of man, was placed by the poets at the entrance of the lower world. [Varro, *On Country Matters* 1.1,15; Macrobius, *Saturnalia* 3.9; Livy 2.41, 8.9, 10.29; Dionysius of Halicarnassus, *Roman Antiquities* 8.79; Ovid, *Fasti* 4.629,633; Arnobius, *Adversus Nationes* 7.22; Virgil, *Aeneid* 6.274; Silius Italicus 13.581.]

TELPHUSA (1) was a nymph of the fountain of the same name at the foot of Mount Tilphossium. The fountain, located between Haliartus and Alalcomenae in Boeotia, was sacred to Apollo. The seer Teiresias was said to have died here after fleeing from Thebes when the Epigoni took the city. [Apollodorus 3.7.3; Pausanias 9.33.1.]

TELPHUSA (2) was a daughter of the Ladon River from whom the city of Telphusa (Thelpusa) in Arcadia was named. [Stephanus Byzantium, "Telphousa."]

TELPHUSIA was one of the Erinyes, by whom Ares became the father of the dragon that was slain by Cadmus. He sowed the dragon's teeth, from which sprang armed men who fought among one another until only five were left. With these five Cadmus founded and populated the city of Thebes. [Scholiast on Sophocles' *Antigone* 126.]

TEREIS by some was called the mother of Megapenthes by Menelaus. His mother was more often called PIERIS. [Acusilaus, quoted by Apollodorus 3.11.1.]

TERPSICHORE was one of the MUSES. She presided over choral song and dancing. Some said she was the mother of the Sirens, of Linus by Amphimarus, of Rhesus by the Strymon River, and of Hymen by Apollo. [Hesiod, *Theogony* 78; Pindar, *Isthmian Odes* 2.7; Apollonius Rhodius 4.893; Alciphron, *Letters* 1.13; Scholiast on Euripides' *Rhesus* 346; Suidas, "Rhesos."]

TERPSICRATE was one of the THESPIADES and by Heracles was the mother of Euryopes. [Apollodorus 2.7.8.]

TERRA (*See* TELLUS)

TETHYS was one of the Titanides, daughter of Uranus and Gaea. Her brothers, the Titans, were Cronus, Oceanus, Coeus, Crius, Hyperion, and Iapetus. Her sisters were Rhea, Themis, Phoebe, Mnemosyne, and Theia. With her brother/husband Oceanus she was given dominion over the seas by Cronus when the Titans overthrew Uranus. Possession of the seas was wrested, it appears, from the earlier generation of the Uranids, when they were the domain of Pontus and Thalassa. Tethys became by Oceanus the mother of the river-gods, said to be about 3,000 in number, and she was also the mother of the Oceanides, also numbering in the thousands, according to some. Conception and birth of these beings would necessarily resemble the spawning process carried out by marine animals such as fish, even though Titans were immortal and could breed as leisurely as they chose. But the forming of the world's rivers could scarely wait for conventional birthing.

When Cronus was overthrown by Zeus, he and his brother Titans were imprisoned in Tartarus, but Oceanus apparently was the exception. He assisted Zeus, as did the firstborn of the Oceanides, Styx. Consequently, Oceanus did not lose his sovereignty over the seas even though Poseidon, in the next generation of godheads, acquired the sea as his domain. Poseidon's territory was probably confined to the Aegean. There was also Nereus, who with his daughters the Nereides held the Mediterranean. It would seem that the overall dominion was accorded Oceanus, and indeed the great western ocean to which the Mediterranean and ultimately the Aegean were subsidiary was called his habitat.

This dominion was held jointly with Tethys. None of the Titanides were involved in the war between the Olympians and the Titans, so they continued to interact with the later gods and goddesses. Hera, for example, was brought up by Tethys until the time came for her to marry Zeus. This was about the only time in ancient accounts that Tethys was given consideration as an individual instead of a personification. Her corresponding divinity in Rome was called Salacia. [Hesiod, *Theogony* 136,337; Apollodorus 1.1.3; Plato, *Timaeus* 40; Ovid, *Fasti* 5.81; Virgil, *Georgics* 1.31.]

THALASSA was a personification of the Mediterranean, according to some. She was described as a daughter of Aether and Hemera, which made her emerge as one of the two earliest beings identified with the physical mass of the sea. Aether was the upper sky, and Hemera was the day. The other being was Pontus, son of Aether and Gaea, which suggested that the sea was the offspring of the earth instead of the usual reverse. Pontus' principal mate was Gaea rather than Thalassa, although she did have by him the fish of the sea. From her the mysterious Telchines were also said to have descended.

In contrast to Tethys, Doris, and Amphitrite, Thalassa appears to have been the vast and lonely primitive sea, heaving her bosom against unpopulated shores. She had no role in the descent of the gods, and references to her seemed to be in a metaphorical sense rather than in the sense of an actual being. [Hyginus, *Fables: Preface* 2,5; Lucian, *Dialogues of Sailors* 11; Diodorus Siculus 5.55.]

THALEIA (1), or Thalia, was one of the nine MUSES. She was regarded as the Muse of comedy. She became the mother of the Corybantes by Apollo, according to some. [Hesiod, *Theogony* 77; Apollodorus 1.3.4; Plutarch, *Table-Talk* 9.14.]

THALEIA (2) was one of the NEREIDES. [Homer, *Iliad* 18.39; Hesiod, *Theogony* 248.]

THALEIA (3) was a daughter of Hephaestus. No mother was mentioned, which is unusual since Hephaestus had very few physical contacts, and a daughter by anyone would seem to have been a special event. Thaleia became pregnant by Zeus, but was terrified of Hera and prayed to be swallowed by the earth. Zeus granted her request, and in due time twin sons, the Palici, emerged from the earth. These divinities were considered as protectors of solemn oaths, and they were worshipped in the vicinity of Mount Aetna near Palice. It was said that in earliest times they were offered human sacrifices. Later their sanctuary was an asylum for runaway slaves. Nearby were two springs called the Deilloi. Sacred oaths were sworn here, written on tablets. If the tablet floated, the oath was accepted as sincere; if it sank, the oath was false, and the one who swore it was punished by blindness or death by the Palici. [Stephanus Byzantium, "Paliki"; Aristotle, *On Marvelous Things Heard* 58; Cicero, *On the Nature of the Gods* 3.22; Virgil, *Aeneid* 9.585.]

THALEIA (4) was one of the CHARITES. [Hesiod, *Theogony* 909; Apollodorus 1.1.3.]

THALESTRIS was one of the AMAZONS. [Diodorus Siculus 17.17.]

THALLO was one of the Attic HORAE. She was believed to grant vitality to the young shoots of plants. She was also invoked by Athenian youths on being admitted among the ephebi. They took a political oath in the temple of Agraulos and called on Thallo along with other gods. [Pausanias 9.35.1; Pollux 8.106.]

THEANO (1) was one of the DANAIDES, daughter of Danaus and Polyxo, and wife and killer of Phantes. [Apollodorus 2.1.5.]

THEANO (2) was a daughter of Cisseus and Telecleia, which made her, according to some, the sister of Hecuba. She was a priestess of Athena at Troy. Being a priestess of Athena did not include a vow of chastity. Theano was married to Antenor, son of Aesytes and Cleomestra. He was the wisest of the Trojan elders and received Menelaus and Odysseus as ambassadors when they came to seek the return of Helen to Menelaus. Antenor advised the Trojans to restore Helen to her husband. He had a strong sense of justice and felt friendly to the Greeks, although this sense of fraternity might have been overplayed by later writers. Before the Trojan

War he had been sent by the Trojans to Greece to claim Hesione, but even then he felt that the Greeks had a rightful claim since Laomedon had defected on his promise to compensate Heracles for delivering Hesione from a sea monster. His friendship for the Greeks might also have been inspired by his love for Panthous, a youth whom he took with him back to Troy. In any case, Menelaus and Odysseus might have been killed except for the intervention of Antenor.

Theano had a large number of sons by Antenor, all of them loyal Trojans. Most writers included Iphidamas, Archelochus, Acamas, Glaucus, Eurymachus, Helicaon, and Polydamas. Others added Coon, Medon, Thersilochus, Antheus, Agenor, Polybus, Demoleon, Erymanthus, Laodocus, Hippolochus, and a daughter, Crino. Like all good Trojan mothers, Theano lost most of her sons in the war.

However, the liberal Antenor was maligned by his fellow citizens, and after one too many insults he did indeed betray Troy. He was said to have devised a plan for the taking of the city and delivery of the protecting Palladium to the Greeks. As a result, when Troy fell, the house of Antenor had a skin of a panther hung above its door, a sign for the Greeks not to commit any outrage on it. So any surviving sons were protected by the signal.

Some say Antenor founded a new Troy on the remnants of the old. Others said he embarked with Menelaus and Helen, and remained at Cyrene when they touched there. Still others had him go first to Thrace, then to the west coast of the Adriatic, where he founded several towns.

Some say Theano collaborated in the theft of the Palladium. It is rather certain that she and her surviving sons were allowed to go free. She was painted with two of them, Glaucus and Eurymachus, with the hanging panther skin, in the Lesche at Delphi. The daughter, Crino, was shown standing next to her father and carrying a baby. [Homer, *Iliad* 3.146,203, 5.70, 6.298, 7.348, 11.224; Dictys Cretensis 1.11, 5.8; Pausanias 10.27.3; Virgil, *Aeneid* 7.720; Servius on Virgil's *Aeneid* 1.246,651, 2.15; Euripides, *Hecuba* 3; Tzetzes on Lycophron 339; Suidas, "Palladion"; Hyginus, *Fables* 91; Pindar, *Pythian Odes* 5.110.]

THEANO (3) was, according to some, the stepmother of Boeotus and Aeolus. Usually their stepmother was called AUTOLYTE. [Hyginus, *Fables* 186.]

THEANO (4) was the mother of Mimas by Amycus. He was born the same night as Paris, which suggests he was potentially subject to eradication by Priam, since he and Hecuba looked for a suitable substitute to satisfy the prediction that any son born that night would cause the downfall of Troy. There is, however, no suggestion that this was the case. He was a companion of Aeneas and slain by Mezentius, a king of the Tyrrhenians in Italy. [Virgil, *Aeneid* 10.702.]

THEBE (1) was a daughter of Prometheus, from whom the Boeotian Thebes was believed to have derived its name. [Stephanus Byzantium, "Thebe."]

THEBE (2) was a daughter of Asopus and Metope, who by Zeus became the mother of Zethus and Amphion. Usually, though, she was called ANTIOPE. [Apollodorus 3.5.6.]

THEBE (3) was the daughter of Cilix, brother of Cadmus and Europa, who during his search for his abducted sister founded Cilicia. Thebe married Corybas, who along with Dardanus and Cybele had carried the sacred rites of the mother of the gods to Phrygia. Thebe had no particular distinction. It is not even clear whether or not she was the mother of the Corybantes, whom Corybas was supposed by some to have fathered. The Corybantes were male attendants of Cybele who danced in full armor and clashed their shields together. [Diodorus Siculus 5.49; Herodotus 7.9.]

THEIA (1) was one of the Titanides, daughter of Uranus and Gaea. She was wife to her brother Hyperion and became by him the mother of Helios (sun), Eos (dawn), and Selene (moon). There is a faint quality of anachronism about this splendid family, since the basic functions of sun, moon, and dawn might more appropriately have been established by the antecedent Uranids. Be that as it may, Theia was considered as the goddess from whom light emanated. She and her husband can be considered as especially beautiful. Her daughters had a reputation for being abductors of young men. Her resplendent son Helios owned magnificent herds of white cattle on the island of Thrinacia, and these were tended by some of his daughters, who were called Heliades. [Hesiod, *Theogony* 135,371; Pindar, *Isthmian Odes* 5.1; Apollodorus 1.1.3,2.2; Catullus 66.44.]

THEIA (2) was one of the OCEANIDES and mother of the Cercopes. These creatures were thievish gnomes who robbed and killed passersby. Although warned by their mother against a hero called Melampygus (Black-Bottom), they once tried to rob Heracles while he slept near Thermopylae. Apparently they failed to notice his excessively suntanned behind. Heracles was amused by them, so he either gave them to Omphale or set them free. They did not learn their lesson, so Zeus finally changed them into monkeys and confined them on the island of Pithecusa (Ischia) in the bay of Neapolis. [Eustathius on Homer's *Odyssey* 1864; Tzetzes on Lycophron 91; Ovid, *Metamorphoses* 14.90; Pomponius Mela 2.7.]

THEISOA was one of the nymphs who brought up the infant Zeus. She was worshipped at Theisoa in Arcadia. [Pausanias 8.38.3,7.47.2.]

THELPUSA was a daughter of the Ladon River from whom the town of Thelpusa in Arcadia derived its name. Thelpusa was near the site of the rape of Demeter by Poseidon, when she changed herself into a mare and he turned himself into a stallion. Demeter had a temple and a sanctuary at this location. [Stephanus Byzantium, "Telphusa."]

THELXIEPEIA, Thelxiope, or Thelxepeia was one of the SIRENS.

THELXINOE was called one of the earliest MUSES. [Pausanias 9.29.2.]

THELXINOEA was one of the PRAXIDICAE.

THEMIS (1) was one of the Titanides, daughter of Uranus and Gaea. She was the personification of the order of things established by law, custom, and ethics. By the command of Zeus she convened the assembly of the gods, and she was invoked when mortals assembled. She was also described as an ancient prophetic divinity and was said to have possessed the Delphic oracle after Gaea and prior to Phoebe, who bequeathed it to Apollo.

According to some writers, she was mother of the Horae, Eunomia, Dice, Eirene, Astraea, the Moirae, the Hesperides, and even Prometheus. Most of these beings were called her children by Zeus, who was represented as her husband after his marriage to Metis and before his marriage to Hera. Several of these children had to do with the order of events and the regulation of society.

Themis was said to dwell on Olympus, and her presence commanded respect. She was reported to be on good terms even with Hera. It was Themis who bade Deucalion and Pyrrha to repopulate the earth after the flood by throwing the bones of their mother (stones of the earth) behind them as they walked away from her temple at Delphi. It was she who told Thetis that her son would be more powerful than his father, thus causing Zeus to desist in his pursuit of her. She gave Apollo nectar and ambrosia when Leto was unable to nurse him.

Her worship was established at Thebes, Olympia, Athens, Tanagra, and Troezen. At Thebes she had a sanctuary in common with the Moirae and Zeus Agoraeus. The surname Ichnaea, the Tracing Goddess, was derived from the town of Ichnae in Phthiotis, where she was worshipped. In her representation on coins she resembled Athena. Symbols accompanying her were often a cornucopia or scales. In Rome she was often identified with Anna Perenna. [Hesiod, *Theogony* 135, 901; Apollodorus 1.3.1,4.1; Homer, *Odyssey* 2.68, *Iliad* 15.87, 20.4; Pausanias 1.22.1, 5.14.8, 9.22.1,25.4, 10.5.3; Diodorus Siculus 5.67; Ovid, *Metamorphoses* 1.321, 4.642; Apollonius Rhodius 4.800; Servius on Virgil's *Aeneid* 4.246; Gellius 14.4.]

THEMIS (2), an Arcadian nymph, daughter of the Ladon River, was sometimes called the mother of Euander by Hermes. Euander's mother was more often known as CARMENTA.

THEMISTAGORA was one of the DANAIDES and married to Podasimus. [Hyginus, *Fables* 170.]

THEMISTE was a daughter of Ilus and Eurydice, and sister of Laomedon. She married her cousin Capys, son of Assaracus, and became by him the mother of Anchises. This son grew up to be stunningly beautiful, so much so that there were those who said Zeus was his father. It is a miracle that Zeus did not abduct Anchises as he had done in the case of Ganymede, Anchises' granduncle. But this beauty, said to be equal to that of the immortal gods, did not go unnoticed. Aphrodite herself became his lover, and things were going well for the young man. Aphrodite made him promise to keep their affair private, but Anchises could not manage this and consequently was lamed by the goddess, who then abandoned him. She did leave him a son, the famous Aeneas.

Themiste had another son by Capys, Ilus, but there was nothing exceptional about him. Anchises survived the Trojan War and escaped with Aeneas as far as Arcadia, where he died at the age of 80. [Apollodorus 3.12.2; *Homeric Hymn to Aphrodite;* Homer, *Iliad* 22.239; Hyginus, *Fables* 270; Virgil, *Aeneid* 1.617, 2.687.]

THEMISTO (1) was one of the NEREIDES. [Hesiod, *Theogony* 261.]

THEMISTO (2) was a daughter of the Lapith king Hypseus and Chlidanope. Her sisters were Cyrene, Alcaea, and Astyageia. According to most writers, Themisto was the third wife of Athamas, son of Aeolus, but the chronology became quite confused with the disappearance and reappearance of his second wife, Ino. In effect, there were two versions of Themisto's story.

In the first one, Athamas married Themisto when he was convinced that Ino would not return. In due time Themisto bore him twin sons, Sphingius and Orchomenus, and things seemed to be going well. Then Athamas heard that Ino was still living as a Bacchant in the valleys of Mount Parnassus. He was still in love with her and sent for her. She dwelled with him in the guise of a servant, but Themisto soon found out and resolved to kill the two young sons Ino had left behind when she first disappeared. She placed black coverlets over Ino's sons and white ones over her own, then ordered her servants to kill the children under the black covers. Ino anticipated this action and switched the coverlets. Thus Themisto's children were killed; when she discovered the mistake, she hanged herself.

The other version said that after Ino's death and the death of his sons by her, one of whom he murdered, Athamas fled to Boeotia. An oracle told him to settle where he was treated hospitably by wild beasts. He happened upon wolves devouring sheep, and they ran away, leaving their feast for Athamas. He settled on the spot. Afterward he married Themisto and had several sons by her.

These sons were Leucon, Schoeneus, Ptous, and Erythrius. A daughter, Eurycleia, was also mentioned. Leucon gave his name to Leuconis, the old name of Lake Copais. Schoeneus gave his name to the Boeotian town of Schoeneus. Mount Ptoum and the sanctuary of Apollo Ptous got their names from Ptous. Erythrius' name was perpetuated in the town of Erythrae. Eurycleia married her nephew Melas, son of Phrixus, and became mother of Hyperes.

It can be seen that the two versions are incompatible. Themisto could have lived with Athamas long enough to have six sons and a daughter before Ino's return, but the subsequent events after Ino's return—that is, the insanity of Athamas, his murder of Learchus, and the death and apotheosis of Ino and Melicertes—would have closed out any subsequent attention to Themisto. The murder of her own children was an artificial circumstance created, it seems, to heap horror upon horror in the story of the accursed Athamas. One can even believe that in order to make the coverlet story acceptable, we would have to insert a mistress who happened to be named Themisto. It probably would have been better if the unfortunate woman had remained nameless, serving only to satisfy Athamas' needs until he could be finished entirely with the dreadful events prior to his settling in Athamania. [Apollodorus 1.9.1, 3.9.2;

Athenaeus 13.560; Pindar, *Pythian Odes* 9.13; Scholiast on Pindar's *Pythian Odes* 4.221; Diodorus Siculus 4.69; Hyginus, *Fables* 1–5,157; Pausanias 2.23.3, 6.21.7, 8.35.8, 9.34.5.]

THEMISTO (3) was the mother of Arcas, according to some. More often she was called CALLISTO. [Apollodorus 1.9.2; Athenaeus 13.560.]

THEOBULE (1) was the mother of Arcesilaus and Prothoenor by Archilycus, son of Itonus. Both sons were leaders of the Boeotians in the Trojan War and both were slain. The remains of Arcesilaus were brought back to Boeotia, where a monument was erected to his memory in the neighborhood of Lebadeia. [Homer, *Iliad* 2.495, 15.329; Hyginus, *Fables* 97; Pausanias 9.39.2.]

THEOBULE (2) was, according to some, the mother of Myrtilus by Hermes. More often Myrtilus' mother was called CLEOBULE. [Hyginus, *Fables* 224.]

THEOGONE was the mother of Tmolus by Ares. Tmolus was a Lydian king and perhaps the Tmolus who was married to Omphale. If so, he was unfaithful and had a fondness for nymphs that proved his undoing. He pursued Arhippe and had sex with her on the altar of Artemis, who had him gored by an enraged bull. [Pseudo-Plutarch, *On Rivers* 7.]

THEONOE (1) was a daughter of Proteus and Psamathe or Torone. Proteus was a son of Poseidon and king of Egypt. He kindly received Dionysus during his wanderings, and he also was rumored to have kept the real Helen after her abduction, giving Paris only a phantom to carry with him to Troy. He was said to have restored the true Helen to Menelaus after his return from Troy. Theonoe fell in love with Canobus, the helmsman of Menelaus, but Canobus was bitten by a snake and died. Theonoe was also called Eido or Eidothea. [Euripides, *Helen* 11; Aristophanes, *Thesmophoriazusae* 897; Plato, *Cratylus* 407; Homer, *Odyssey* 4.363.]

THEONOE (2) was a daughter of Thestor and sister of LEUCIPPE, with whom she fell in love, believing her sister to be a handsome young priest.

THEOPE was one of the LEONTIDES.

THEOPHANE was a daughter of Bisaltes. She was exceedingly beautiful and attracted many suitors. Poseidon, however, seized the first opportunity and carried her off to the island of Crumissa. The frustrated lovers found the location of the place and followed her there. Poseidon changed her into a ewe and himself into a ram, a ploy he knew well. He also changed the inhabitants into other kinds of animals. The suitors began slaughtering the animals for food while they searched for Theophane, so Poseidon changed the suitors into wolves. In due time Theophane gave birth to the ram with the golden fleece that carried Phrixus to Colchis. There is no record that Poseidon restored Theophane to her original form. [Hyginus, *Fables* 188; Ovid, *Metamorphoses* 177.]

THERAPHONE, daughter of Dexamenus, was the mother of Thalpius by Eurytus, one of the Molionidae. The Molionidae, Eurytus and Cteatus, were sons of Actor by Molione. While yet boys they went with the Epeians against Neleus and the Pylians. When Heracles marched against Augeas to punish him for refusing to pay the wages he had promised, Augeas entrusted the conduct of the war to the Molionidae. In the series of skirmishes that followed, the Molionidae were killed by Heracles. Their tomb was shown at Cleonae.

The Greeks delighted in monstrosities. Cteatus and Eurytus were described by some as what today we might call Siamese twins. If that were the case, sexual relations between them and their wives, Theraphone and her sister Theronice, would have proven to be quite awkward. It is more likely that the brothers were just ordinary twins; otherwise, not only would sexual relations have been difficult but their participation in battles would have been next to impossible. [Apollodorus 2.7.2, Athenaeus 2.58; Eustathius on Homer's *Iliad* 882.]

THERAPNE was a daughter of Lelex and the Naiad Cleochareia. Lelex, one of the original inhabitants of Laconia, called it Lelegia. Therapne's brothers were Myles, Polycaon, Eurotas, and Bomolchus, though some called Eurotas her nephew, son of Myles. Therapne had no story, except that the town of Therapne was named for her. The town of Therapne was immediately across the Eurotas River east of Sparta. [Pausanias 3.19.9; Scholiast on Euripides' *Orestes* 615.]

THERIDAMAS was one of the DOGS of Actaeon. [Hyginus, *Fables* 181.]

THERIOPE was one of the DOGS of Actaeon. [Hyginus, *Fables* 181.]

THERIPHONE was one of the DOGS of Actaeon. [Hyginus, *Fables* 181.]

THERMODOSA was one of the AMAZONS. [Quintus Smyrnaeus 1.46.]

THERO (1) was the nurse of Ares from whom he was believed to have received the surname of Thereitas. A sanctuary of Ares Thereitas stood on the road from Sparta to Therapne with a statue that the Dioscuri were said to have brought from Colchis when they returned from the Argonaut. [Pausanias 3.19.8.]

THERO (2) was the daughter of Phylas and Leipephilene, daughter of Iolaus, and her brother was Hippotes. The beauty of Thero was compared with moonbeams, and she was embraced by Apollo. She bore to him Chaeron, from whom the town of Chaeroneia in Boeotia was named. [Pausanias 9.40.5; Stephanus Byzantium, "Chaironeia."]

THERONICE was the mother of Amphimachus by Cteatus. Amphimachus was among the suitors of Helen and one of four chiefs who led the Epeians against Troy. He was slain by Hector. Theronice was the sister of THERAPHONE, mother of Thalpius by Eurytus, the twin brother of Cteatus. [Apollodorus 3.10.8; Pausanias 5.3.4; Homer, *Iliad* 2.620, 13.185.]

THESEIS was one of the AMAZONS. [Hyginus, *Fables* 163.]

THESMIA, or Thesmophoros, the Law-Giver, was a surname of Demeter and Persephone, in honor of whom the Thesmophoria was celebrated at Athens in the month of Pyanepsion (October). Sanctuaries were erected to them at Megara, Troezen, Pheneus, and other places. It was related that the Danaides had brought the mysteries of Demeter Thesmophoros from Egypt to Peloponnesus, and from them the Pelasgian women learned the mysteries. [Pausanias 1.42.7, 2.32.7, 8.15.1, 9.16.3.]

THESPEIA was a daughter of the Asopus River from whom the town of Thespiae in Boeotia was said to have received its name. [Pausanias 9.26.4.]

THESPIADES (1) were the 50 daughters of Thespius, son or descendant of Erechtheus, and MEGAMEDE, daughter of Arneus. Their story is one of the most titillating in mythology, since it established Heracles' reputation as the all-time champion in sexual indefatigability. The herds of his stepfather, Amphitryon, and those of Thespius, king of Thespiae, were being harassed by the notorious Cithaeronian lion, a sly and seemingly unconquerable beast. Heracles, only 18 at the time, volunteered to hunt down the brute, which had moved its hunting territory close to Thespiae. Thespius entertained him for 50 days, which period happened to coincide not only with the number of days it took to get rid of the lion but also with the number of Thespius' daughters.

Thespius liked Heracles' looks and wanted grandchildren by him. Each night after the exhausting hunt, Thespius planted one after another of his daughters in Heracles' bed. Heracles thought he was sleeping always with the same one, and a combination of fatigue and youthful ardor must have been responsible for his not recognizing anatomical and tactile variations. Eventually he worked his way through all 50 (although some claim that one refused to bed with him).

Even though these daughters had to be the offspring of a number of different women in addition to Megamede, they must have represented a wide range of ages. Selection of a nightly bed partner had to take into account the monthly estrous cycle of each of them. In spite of Heracles' incredible fertility, the risk was run that one or two of them might have been barren. The most baffling consideration is that none of these daughters already had a husband. Early marriages for women was a way of life in Greek society, especially in rural areas such as Thespiae. What was the problem with the daughters of Thespius? Surely he was not so obsessed with having grandchildren by Heracles that he sneaked them away from their husbands to have them impregnated. Certainly in so large a group of young married women some of them would already be pregnant.

Whatever the case, the result was 49 pregnant women. The ensuing scene of mass morning sickness, cravings, swollen uteruses, differing times and durations of labor, and lying-in of 49 women must have been something to behold. Heracles was long gone, but he left 50 sons. Although one of the daughters (Anthea?) would not sleep with him, another one, Procris, who happened to be the eldest, made up for her by bearing twins.

The mothers and their sons were:

Aeschreis	Leucones
Aglaia	Antiades
Anthea	—
Anthippe	Hippodromus
Antiope	Alopius
Argele	Cleolaus
Asopis	Mentor
Calametis	Astybies
Certhe	Iobes
Chryseis	Onesippus
Clytippe	Eurycapys
Elachia	Buleus
Eone	Amestrius
Epilais	Astyanax
Erato	Dynastes
Euboea	Olympus
Eubote	Eurypylus
Eurybia	Polylaus
Eury(ce)?	Teleutagoras
Eurypyle	Archedicus
Eurytele	Leucippus
Exole	Erythras
Heliconis	Phalias
Hesychia	Oestrobles
Hippo	Capylus
Hippocrate	Hippozygus
Iphis	Celeustanor
Laothoe	Antiphus
Lyse	Eumedes
Lysidice	Teles
Lysippe	Erasippus
Marse	Bucolus
Meline	Laomedon
Menippis	Entelides
Nice	Nicedromus
Nicippe	Antimachus
Olympusa	Halocrates
Oreia	Laomenes
Panope	Threpsippas
Patro	Archemachus
Phyleis	Tigasus
Praxithea	Nephus
Procris	Antileon and Hippeus
Pyrippe	Patroclus
Stratonice	Atromus
Terpsicrate	Euryopes
Tiphyse	Lyncaeus
Toxicrate	Lycurgus
Xanthis	Homolippus
?	Creon

Some said Heracles slept with all the daughters in seven nights or even in a single night, but even the mighty Heracles might have been unequal to this challenge. Even at the rate of one per night, the performance has appropriately been called his thirteenth labor.

Most of the boys were, on Heracles' instructions, taken by Iolaus to Sardinia, where they colonized the island. Two came back to Thebes, and seven never left Thespiae. The subsequent fate of the daughters of Thespius is unknown. [Apollodorus 2.4.9,7.6; Pausanias 1.29.5, 7.2.2, 9.23.1,27.6, 10.17.5,6; Diodorus Siculus 1.29.]

THESPIADES (2) was a surname of the Muses, derived from Thespiae, where they were especially honored. [Pausanias 9.29.3; Varro, *On the Latin Language* 7.70.]

THESTIAS was a patronymic of Leda as the daughter of Thestius. [Euripides, *Iphigeneia at Aulis* 49; Aeschylus, *Libation-Bearers* 606.]

THETIS was the most famous of the NEREI-DES. Only one commentator suggested that instead of being a Nereid she was a daughter of Cheiron the Centaur. Her identity with the sea, though, was established with the Latin poets. She was called Neptunine by one of them. She was brought up by Hera until she reached maturity, then like her sisters lived in the depth of the sea with her parents, Nereus and Doris. She was in intermittent contact with other divinities. She received Dionysus when he fled from Lycurgus, and she was hospitable to Hephaestus when he was thrown from heaven. In both instances she risked censure from the Olympian gods. Poseidon and Zeus both tried to seduce her, but when the prophetic Themis declared that a son of Thetis would be more illustrious than his father, they withdrew. Some said Thetis rejected the advances of Zeus because she had been brought up by Hera. Zeus was not happy with the situation, so he condemned Thetis to marry a mortal.

The mortal was Peleus, son of Aeacus, who had a somewhat checkered career. Peleus had been married to Antigone but when Astydameia, the wife of his friend Acastus, fell in love with him and tried unsuccessfully to seduce him, Antigone killed herself when false reports by Astydameia reached Phthia, the city in which Peleus ruled. After that, Peleus' friend and teacher Cheiron spread the report that Peleus was married to Thetis. He was not, but Cheiron thought it would make the young man more celebrated. At some point Peleus decided to give validity to Cheiron's reports and set about possessing the lovely Nereid. Cheiron gave Peleus advice on how to manage this, since like most marine divinities Thetis could transform herself into any shape she chose. Peleus then lay in wait and seized her. In spite of all the forms she changed to, some of them frightening, he held on, and eventually she returned to her usual appearance.

An alternate version held that Thetis sought Peleus, but he accidentally observed her playing with dolphins and knew her to be immortal. When he avoided her presence, she came looking for him and reminded him of other marriages between mortals and immortals, such as Aphrodite and Anchises, Eos and Tithonus, and Selene and Endymion.

The wedding was one of the most celebrated events in mythology. It was attended by mortals and divinities alike but, unknown to anyone at the time, provided the occasion that set in motion the Trojan War. The ensuing home life of Thetis and Peleus is difficult to imagine. Phthia was a considerable distance from the sea, and Thetis undoubtedly missed her native element, her sisters, and the sea creatures with which she usually frolicked. It was not long before she was pregnant, though, and her time was occupied in preparing for the son whose fame, she knew, would follow him down the ages. She knew also that he would die at a young age. Even so, she attempted to alter destiny by her efforts to make him immortal. Soon after his birth she put Achilles in fire to destroy the mortal parts he inherited from Peleus and followed the procedure with anointment in ambrosia. Some said she dipped him in the Styx River or in boiling water to achieve this purpose but failed to remember the heel she held him by, which consequently remained vulnerable. Peleus caught her in this strange ritual and cried out, so the process was not completed. One commentator said she had experienced accidents with six earlier children by Peleus, so that they perished. It is easier to believe Achilles was an only child and that the marriage broke up as a result of Peleus' outrage at what Thetis appeared to be doing with his son. Thetis went back to the sea, so the widely celebrated marriage lasted for only about a year.

Achilles was sent to Cheiron to be reared and educated. Cheiron was in the business of serving as foster father and pedagogue to budding heroes. While still a boy, Patroclus, a cousin of Achilles, had killed a friend and was exiled. He joined the family of Peleus, and he and Achilles went through adolescence together. Patroclus was a suitor of the exquisite Helen, but Thetis, knowing how events would develop, again attempted to change destiny by hiding her son among the daughters of King Lycomedes on the island of Scyros. She also acquired a grandson, Neoptolemus, when Achilles, long blonde hair and female attire notwithstanding, impregnated Diomedeia, the king's daughter.

Achilles was found out and forced to come out of hiding to join the Greeks against Troy.

From that time on, Thetis was somehow always in the background of events involving Achilles. When Agamemnon took away Briseis from Achilles, Thetis prevailed on Zeus to side with the Trojans until Agamemnon redressed the wrong to her son. She gave Achilles advice on how to conduct himself in the war, and her overprotectiveness was certainly her way of denying to herself the inevitable outcome. When Achilles battled with Memnon, son of Eos, the two immortal mothers hastened to Zeus, who weighed the destinies of the two heroes on a divine scale and found that Memnon's weighed more. Thus Achilles was spared a while longer. It was claimed by some that the Amazon Penthesileia killed the hero, who was recalled to life by Zeus at Thetis' tearful request.

Ultimately, of course, Achilles had to meet his preordained doom, which came from an arrow that struck his vulnerable heel. Thetis had no choice but to accept the sad evidence of her son's human mortality. Even then she did not disappear back into the sea. She offered his armor to the most courageous Greek left alive at Troy. She left the decision to the Greeks, and ironically the armor went to Odysseus, who had been among those who found Achilles in disguise among the daughters of Lycomedes and by a ruse forced him to reveal himself.

Apart from Achilles and the Trojan War, we do not read a great deal about Thetis, although she is usually mentioned among the Nereides. She pitied Aesacus, son of Priam, when he lost his beloved Asterope and leapt into the sea. She changed him into an aquatic bird. With other Nereides she guided the Argonauts safely by Scylla and Charybdis. When Zeus was threatened by the other gods, she induced the giant Briareus or Aegaeon to come to his assistance. When Psamathe, to avenge the murder of Phocus by Peleus, sent a wolf to destroy Peleus' flocks, Thetis turned it to stone.

There was enough mention of Thetis to form a picture of her. She was beautiful, cool, compassionate, and serene. Her garments were reminiscent of seaweed or sea fern. She moved gracefully on land and in the sea alike. She had a temple, the Thetideion, near Pharsalus (modern Farsala) in Thessaly. She was likewise worshipped in Sparta and Messenia. [Statius, *Achilleid* 1.269; Homer, *Iliad* 1.359,500, 18.395,434, 24.60,535, *Odyssey* 11.495; Apollodorus 1.2.2, 3.13.5; Apollonius Rhodius 4.793–816; Scholiast on Apollonius Rhodius 4.816; Catullus 64.28; Lycophron 178; Ptolemaeus Hephaestion 6; Pindar, *Isthmian Odes* 8.58, *Nemean Odes* 3.60; Hyginus, *Fables* 54; Servius on Virgil's *Eclogues* 6.42; Pausanias 3.14.4,22.2, 8.18.1; Philostratus, *Heroicus* 19.1; Ovid, *Metamorphoses* 11.225,350, 15.856.]

THISADIE was the sister of Peirithous and therefore daughter of Ixion and Dia. Very little is known of her. Her glorious brother was a close friend of Theseus. Peirithous' wedding to Hippodameia was one of the great events of the day, since it touched off the battle between the Lapithae and the Centaurs. Certainly Thisadie was in attendance at this memorable affair. We hear of her first as a companion of Helen at Aphidna, where Theseus and Peirithous brought their captive. Both heroes had vowed to go to bed with a daughter of Zeus before they died, and Helen was the choice of Theseus. It was then his turn to accompany Peirithous in the attempted kidnapping of Persephone. Theseus left his mother, Aethra, in charge of Helen at Aphidna, and apparently Peirithous volunteered Thisadie to keep her company. When Helen's brothers, the Dioscuri, freed Helen, they took Aethra and Thisadie with them to Sparta. When Helen eloped with Paris, she took both Aethra and Thisadie with her to Troy. We know of Aethra's subsequent fate, but we never hear of Thisadie again. We do know she never saw her brother again, since he was permanently imprisoned in Hades. [Hyginus, *Fables* 92.]

THISBE (1) was a beautiful Babylonian maiden loved by Pyramus. The lovers had to communicate secretly since their parents were very much opposed to any thought of marriage. They accomplished this by speaking to each other through an opening in the wall that separated their houses. This frustrating situation could continue just so long, and the lovers burned to embrace each other. They daringly made plans to meet one night at the tomb of Ninus. Thisbe arrived first and while waiting for Pyramus saw a lioness eating an ox she had just killed. Thisbe ran from the scene, dropping her shawl, and the lioness nuzzled the garment with her bloody nose. Pyramus arrived, found the garment covered with blood, thought Thisbe had been murdered, and in despair stabbed himself. Thisbe then cautiously emerged; finding her dead lover, she in turn stabbed herself. Their blood stained forever after the fruit of the mulberry tree under which these tragic events occurred. The story was famous in antiquity and provided inspiration for similar stories in much later times. Shakespeare liked the theme well enough to use it twice. [Ovid, *Metamorphoses* 4.55–165.]

THISBE (2) was a Boeotian nymph from whom the town of Thisbe on the south of Mount Helicon derived its name. [Pausanias 9.32.2.]

THOANTEA was a surname of the Taurian Artemis, derived from Thoas, king of Tauris, who was said to have reigned there after fleeing from Lemnos when all the Lemnian men were murdered by their wives. [Virgil, *Fasti* 8.208; Ovid, *Ibis* 386.]

THOE (1) was one of the NEREIDES. [Hyginus, *Fables: Preface* 8; Homer, *Iliad* 18.40.]

THOE (2) was one of the OCEANIDES. [Hesiod, *Theogony* 353.]

THOOSA (1) was called by some the wife of Laomedon. His wife was more usually called STRYMO.

THOOSA (2) was a daughter of Phorcys, which classed her along with other monstrous offspring called the Phorcides, such as the Gorgons and the Graeae. She was a kind of personification of the stormy waves of the sea. Perhaps she was less terrifying in appearance than her sisters since Poseidon mated with her to produce Polyphemus, the celebrated Cyclops, who tried to eat Odysseus and his men. The wily Odysseus managed to blind the one-eyed monster and escape with his men from the island cave in which they were imprisoned. Because of this act of self-defense Odysseus experienced the wrath of Poseidon and was prevented from returning home for many years. [Homer, *Odyssey* 1.71,

5.286,366,423, 11.101, 13.96,345; Ovid, *Tristia* 1.2,9; Nonnos, *Dionysiaca* 39.293.]

THOOSA (3) was the personification of velocity or swiftness. [Empedocles, *Fragments* 122.]

THORNAX was the mother of Buphagus by Iapetus. Buphagus was an Arcadian hero and husband of Promne. He received the wounded Iphicles, the brother of Heracles, into his house and took care of him until he died. Buphagus was afterward killed by Artemis for having pursued her. [Pausanias 8.14.6,27.11.]

THRACE was the daughter of Parthenope by Oceanus, and her sister was Europa. Thrace was the eponymous heroine of the vast and barbarous area called Thrace. Her sister Europa was probably intended to symbolize the more civilized region to the south. Thrace was also said to be the mother of Doloncus and Bithynia by Cronus and Zeus, respectively. Another son, Trierus, was fathered by Obriareus. Like many other Thracian women, human and divine, Thrace had a reputation for sorcery. [Stephanus Byzantium, "Thrake," "Bithynia," "Dolonkoi"; Arrian, quoted by Stephanus Byzantium, "Trieres."]

THRIAE were three prophetic nymphs on Mount Parnassus by whom Apollo was reared. They were believed to have invented the art of prophecy by means of little stones that were thrown into an urn. They were said also to have taught Hermes the same art, from which he got the idea for the game of knucklebones. [*Homeric Hymn to Hermes* 552; Scholiast on Callimachus' *Hymn to Apollo* 45.]

THYADES (*See* THYIA)

THYENE was one of the HYADES.

THYIA (1) was a daughter of the Cephissus River or of Castalius, one of the original inhabitants of Delphi. She was said to have been the first to have sacrificed to Dionysus and to have celebrated orgies in his honor. Therefore the Attic women, who every other year went to Mount Parnassus to celebrate the Dionysiac orgies with the Delphian Thyiades, themselves received the name of Thyiades. It was the custom for these Thyiades to hold dances on the road between Athens and Delphi at places such as Panopeus. Thyia was by some called the mother of Delphus by Apollo, but Delphus' mother was usually known as Celaeno. [Pausanias 10.4.3,6.2,22.5.]

THYIA (2) was a daughter of Deucalion (and presumably Pyrrha). By Zeus she was the mother of Macedon and Magnes. Macedon gave his name to Macedonia and in turn produced several sons whose names also were given to geographical areas. Magnes, who founded Magnesia, was usually called a son of Aeolus. It seems apparent that in the first generation following the flood, it was necessary to assign as many names as possible. It is interesting that Zeus, who had been eager to destroy mankind, was quite willing to help repopulate the earth. [Stephanus Byzantium, "Makedonia," "Magnes."]

THYIADES (See THYIA 1)

THYMBRIS was one of the nymphs designated as mother of Pan by Hermes. Pan's mother was more often called DRYOPE. [Apollodorus 1.4.1; Scholiast on Theocritus 1.3.]

THYONE was the name given to SEMELE when she was fetched from Hades by her son Dionysus and made immortal. Thyoneus was a surname given to Dionysus.

THYRIA was the mother of Cycnus by Apollo. His mother was more often called HYRIA. [Antoninus Liberalis 12.]

TIBURTIS, daughter of the Ladon River, was called in Roman tradition the mother of Euander. She was more often known as CARMENTA. [Plutarch, Roman Questions 53; Dionysius of Halicarnassus, Roman Antiquities 1.31.]

TILPHUSA (See TELPHUSA)

TILPHUSIA (See TELPHUSIA)

TIMANDRA (1), like her sisters Helen and Clytemnestra, was included in the curse laid on the daughters of Tyndareus. He had neglected a sacrifice to Aphrodite, and the goddess resolved to make his daughters notorious for their adulteries. We know in detail about the infidelity of Helen and to a somewhat lesser degree about that of Clytemnestra, but we know very little about Timandra's life and times. We do not know, for example, whether she was older or younger than her famous sisters. It is likely that she was older, the first child of Tyndareus and Leda. Philonoe and Phoebe, the other sisters, probably died very young and were thus delivered from the curse.

Timandra married Echemus, son of Aeropus and grandson of Cepheus of Tegea. Echemus succeeded Lycurgus on the throne of Tegea, so that is where Timandra resided. Echemus was said by some to have accompanied the Dioscuri on their expedition to Aphidna to bring back Helen, who had been abducted by Theseus. This makes sense, and it also suggests he was already married to Timandra, thus causing the rescue to be something of a family affair.

After the Trojan War, Echemus became a principal in the so-called Dorian invasion of Peloponnesus. In single combat he slew Hyllus, the son of Heracles. After the fall of Hyllus, the Heracleidae were obliged not to repeat their attempts on Peloponnesus for at least 50 years. The Tegeatans were honored with the privilege of overseeing all expeditions against foreign enemies, and for the duration of his reign Echemus was in charge of seeing that the contract was carried out.

Some said a son, Euander, was born to him and Timandra. Euander's genealogy was controversial. Most claimed he was the son of Hermes and a nymph, and that he migrated to Italy, where his mother was deified as Carmenta. Timandra had no connection with the god Hermes, and certainly there was no suggestion she was ever worshipped in Italy.

She was said to have left her husband for Phyleus, son of Augeas. Phyleus championed Heracles against his father, when Augeas refused to pay Heracles for cleansing his stables. Phyleus married Ctimene, according to most records, and had by her Meges, who was killed in the

Trojan War. Again, Timandra seems to have been an afterthought.

Meges could not have been her son, as some claimed. He was said to have been one of Helen's suitors. Of course, this would have been a little odd, considering that Helen would have been his aunt, and by even the most generous reckoning he would have been 15 or more years younger.

It really appears that Timandra was a victim of the reputation gained by her sisters. If Aphrodite's curse included her, it was only by association. It is conceivable she was a lover of Phyleus, but even that is unlikely, since Phyleus would have been in the Echinades Islands, a place remote from Tegea. There was also a lack of any evidence to support a love affair between them, although they could have been about the same age. It is more likely Timandra remained a faithful wife to Echemus, even though she might not have given him heirs. [Apollodorus 2.5.5, 3.10.6; Pausanias 8.4.7,5.1,45.2,53.5; Servius on Virgil's *Aeneid* 8.130; Scholiast on Pindar's *Olympian Odes* 10.79; Herodotus 9.26; Diodorus Siculus 4.58; Plutarch, *Theseus* 32; Homer, *Iliad* 12.625.]

TIMANDRA (2) was the mother of Neophron. He discovered she was having a love affair with his friend Aegypius, son of Antheus. Aegypius was his same age, and Neophron was distressed at this liaison and thought of a way to end it. He made overtures to Boulis, Aegypius' mother, who though married to Antheus consented to be his lover. Having spied on his mother and his friend, Neophron knew the exact time of their frequent meetings and contrived to place Boulis in bed in the dark chamber. He told her he would be with her shortly, then detained his own mother on some kind of pretext. Soon Aegypius joined his mother in bed and coupled with her, suspecting nothing at all. They fell asleep, but Boulis awakened to find her son beside her. She took a dagger and dug out his eyes, then plunged it into her bosom. Apollo restored Aegypius' vision long enough for him to realize what had happened. All four were thereupon changed into birds. The young men became vultures, Timandra a tit, and Boulis a long-beaked bird that pecks out the eyes of fish. [Antoninus Liberalis 5.]

TIPHYSE was one of the THESPIADES and mother by Heracles of Lynceus. [Apollodorus 2.7.8.]

TIPOPLO was, according to some, one of the MUSES.

TIRYNS was a daughter of Alcaeus and sister of Amphitryon. The city of Tiryns was named for her. This is all we know about her, but she was the sister-in-law of Alcmena, the aunt of Heracles, and granddaughter of Perseus. It is questionable that Tiryns was named for her; more likely it was the opposite. Tiryns had long been in existence and, presumably, long called by the name we know. Her nephew Heracles eventually took over the kingdom from the Argolids, who already had named the place for one of their own line. [Stephanus Byzantium, "Tiryns."]

TISIPHONE (1) was one of the EUMENIDES.

TISIPHONE (2) was the daughter of Alcmaeon and Manto, daughter of Teiresias. Alcmaeon, the son of Amphiaraus and Eriphyle, became famous for having murdered his mother. Before this happened, he was triumphant at Thebes in the battle of the Epigoni. He acquired Manto as part of his spoils and became by her the father of Tisiphone. Manto was sent to Colophon in Asia Minor as a priestess of Apollo, but Tisiphone was left with her father.

Alcmaeon took her to Creon in Corinth to be brought up. Creon's wife tolerated her well enough until she matured into an extraordinarily beautiful young woman. At that point Creon's wife had Tisiphone sold into slavery.

As it turned out, Alcmaeon himself, compelled by the beauty of the exquisite Tisiphone, bought her at auction. He was on the point of committing incest with her but found out just in time that she was his daughter who had mysteriously disappeared from the house of Creon. [Apollodorus 3.7.7; Diodorus Siculus 4.66; Pausanias 7.3.1, 9.33.1.]

TITANIDES were the daughters of Uranus and Gaea. They were Theia, Rhea, Themis, Mnemosyne, Phoebe, and Tethys. All but

Mnemosyne and Themis mated with their brothers, the Titans, and their offspring constituted another generation of divinities. After Cronus castrated Uranus, the Titans seized power and attempted to hold it with Cronus as their leader. Cronus had been warned that he would be overthrown by one of his children and swallowed them as soon as they were born, but Rhea managed to deceive him into believing that the swaddled stone he swallowed was his youngest son, Zeus. Zeus grew up to liberate his brothers and sisters from Cronus and, with their help, overthrew him. Oceanus helped Zeus dethrone Cronus, and none of the Titanides took part in the battle between the Olympians and the Titans.

The Titanides were probably given residence on Olympus. Mnemosyne and Themis were lovers of Zeus and had offspring by him. We see one or another of the Titanides mentioned from time to time. Tethys, for example, brought up Hera. Phoebe willed the oracle at Delphi to Apollo. Rhea, the most important, became interfused with Thracian and Phrygian goddesses and took on a different identity.

Sometimes the name Titanides was broadened to include certain children of the Titans, such as Selene, Dione, Eos, etc. [Hesiod, *Theogony* 132,531; Apollodorus 1.1.2; Hyginus, *Fables: Preface* 3; Homer, *Iliad* 15.224.]

TITANIS was one of the HORAE. [Hyginus, *Fables* 183.]

TITHOREA was a nymph of Mount Parnassus from whom the town of Tithorea, previously called Neon, was believed to have derived its name. This town was the burial place of Antiope and her husband, Phocus, from whom the territory of Phocis derived its name. [Pausanias 10.32.9.]

TORONE, sometimes called Chrysonoe, was the daughter of Cleitus, king of the Sithones in Thrace, and Pallene, daughter of Sithon. Cleitus gave her to Proteus, who had come to Thrace from Egypt. Proteus was a son of Poseidon and had quit Egypt from fear of his brother Busiris. He assisted Cleitus against his enemies and, as a reward, came to have his own kingdom. His sons

by Torone were Telegonus and Polygonus, brutal louts who challenged passing strangers to combat and always killed them. They met their match when Heracles passed by after one of his labors and killed them. Proteus had been so ashamed of his sons' behavior that he even offered to purify Heracles of the murders.

Eventually Proteus prayed to Poseidon to take him back to Egypt. Poseidon accordingly opened a chasm in Pallene that created an undersea passage, and Proteus was able to walk back to Egypt. Torone must have remained in Thrace, and just as well, since according to some, Proteus already had a wife, Psamathe, in Egypt. [Conon, *Narrations* 32; Apollodorus 2.5.9; Tzetzes on Lycophron 115,124.]

TOXICRATE was one of the THESPIADES. By Heracles she was the mother of Lycurgus. [Apollodorus 2.7.8.]

TRAGASIA was the daughter of Celaeneus in Caria. Miletus, son of Apollo and Areia, fled from Crete with his lover Sarpedon to escape persecution from Minos, who also loved him. Either he or Sarpedon founded Miletus, and later he married Tragasia, by whom he became the father of Caunus and Byblis. Byblis fell in love with Caunus (some say the reverse was true or that the love was mutual), and Caunus fled to Lycia. According to some, Byblis followed him and died either by her own hand or from total exhaustion. In either case, she was said to have been changed into a fountain. Caunus was said to have settled in Lycia, where he married Pronoe and fathered a son called Aegialus. Nothing further was written about Tragasia, who was also called Eidothea, Areia, or Cyane. The subsequent history of Miletus is not known. [Parthenius, *Love Stories* 11; Conon, *Narrations* 2; Antoninus Liberalis 30.]

TRICLARIA was a surname of Artemis in Achaia. Melanippus, a youth of Patrae, was in love with Comaetho, a priestess of Artemis Triclaria. They were forbidden to marry by their parents, so they began to have sex in the temple. The goddess punished the offenders with instant death, and brought a plague and famine to the country. An oracle said that in order to avert these calamities the handsomest youth and love-liest maiden must be sacrificed each year. The oracle also said that the population would be released from this obligation if a foreign divinity should be brought to them by a stranger. Eu-rypylus, son of Euaemon, had received a myste-rious chest among his share of spoils from Troy. When he opened it and beheld the statue within, he was stricken with fits of madness. An oracle told him he would be cured when he came to a place on his way home where an unusual sacrifice was taking place. He stopped at Patrae as the citizens were carrying out their annual sacrifice, and produced the chest with its statue of Dionysus Aesymnetes. Thus the people of Patrae were able to end the practice of the cruel sacrifice to Artemis Triclaria. [Pausanias 7.19.2–9.]

TRIGONEIA, or Tritogeneia, was a daughter of Aeolus and, according to some, the wife of Minyas, although his wife was more commonly called EURYANASSA, daughter of Hyperphas. [Tzetzes on Lycophron 874.]

TRITE was one of the DANAIDES and married to Enceladus. [Hyginus, *Fables* 170.]

TRITEIA was a daughter of Triton and priestess of Athena. By Ares she bore a son, Melanippus. When he grew up, Melanippus founded a city in Achaia and named it for his mother. Sacrifices were offered at Triteia (modern Kato Vlassia) to Ares and Triteia alike. [Pausanias 7.22.8.]

TRITO, Tritonis, or Tritogeneia was a surname of Athena. Some said the name came from Lake Tritonis in Libya, near which she was said to have been born. Others said she received the surname from a stream called Triton near Alalcomenae in Boeotia, where she was worshipped and might have been born. Still others said the name might have come from an Aeolian word for head, so that Tritogeneia would mean "head-born," refer-ring, of course, to her being born from the head of Zeus. [Homer, *Iliad* 4.515, *Odyssey* 3.378; Hesiod, *Theogony* 924; Apollodorus 1.3.6; Eu-ripides, *Ion* 872.]

TRITONE was mentioned among the early MUSES. [Epicharmus, *Fragments* 41.]

TRIVIA was the Latin equivalent of the Taurian Artemis (cf. TAUROPOLIS, DICTYNNA, OR-THIA, THOANTEA, and BRAURONIA).

TUCCIA was a Vestal virgin who, when accused of incest, appealed to the goddess to prove her innocence. Vesta gave her the power to carry a sieve of water from the Tiber to the temple without spilling a drop. [St. Augustine, *City of God* 10.16.]

TUTILINA was an agricultural divinity among the Romans or, perhaps, rather an attribute of Ops. She was described as the goddess protecting the fruits brought in from the fields at harvest time. Tutilina, Secia, and Messia had three pillars with altars in the Circus. Tutilina seemed to incorporate the worship of several minor agricul-tural divinities, such as Segetia, Seja, and the ones mentioned. [St. Augustine, *City of God* 4.8; Macrobius, *Saturnalia* 1.16; Varro, *On the Latin Language* 5.74.]

TYCHE (1) was the personification of luck or chance. The Romans called her Fortuna. She was said to be the daughter of Zeus Eleuthereus. She was variously represented, since the concept of fortune had many aspects. Sometimes she was seen with a rudder, and this indicated that she guided the affairs of the world. With a ball, Tyche was seen perhaps as unsteady and capable of rolling in any direction. She was often repre-sented with Plutus, the god of plenty, or the horn of Amaltheia, since fortune was viewed optimis-tically. She was surnamed Automatia, a name that characterized her as managing things ac-cording to her own will without regard to man's merit. She also was surnamed Meilichios, the Gentle or Soothing, perhaps as a placatory invocation or a name to offset the somewhat negative effect of Automatia. Nemesis was cau-tiously regarded as the downside of Tyche, one who provided a check on extravagant favors conferred by Tyche.

Tyche was worshipped widely—at Pharae in Messenia, Smyrna in Asia Minor, Sicyon and Aegeira in Achaia, Elis, Thebes, Lebadeia, Olym-pia, and Athens. It was said that when Palamedes invented dice he dedicated the first set in the temple of Tyche at Argos. [Pindar, *Olympian*

Odes 12, *Fragments* 75; Artemidorus 2.37; Pausanias 2.7.5, 4.30.2,4, 5.15.4, 6.25.4, 7.26.3, 9.16.1,39.4; Aelian, *Various Narratives* 9.39; Orphica, *Hymns* 71.2.]

TYCHE (2) was a nymph, one of the playmates of Persephone. [*Homeric Hymn to Demeter* 421.]

TYCHE (3) was one of the OCEANIDES. [Hesiod, *Theogony* 358.]

TYRIA was the mother by Aegyptus of Cleitus, Sthenelus, and Chrysippus, who were married to and murdered by three of the DANAIDES. [Apollodorus 2.1.5.]

TYRO was the daughter of Salmoneus and Alcidice. Her mother died not long after she was born, and her father married Sidero. This woman hated Tyro and used her as a kind of slave. Tyro drew closely within herself and experienced curious fantasies. In one of these she was the lover of the god of the Enipeus River, along whose banks she walked whenever she could escape Sidero's clutches. The ever-watchful, ever-lustful, ever-optimistic Poseidon observed this obsessive behavior and decided to fulfill the girl's wish. He took the appearance of Enipeus and had no trouble thoroughly satisfying his (and her) appetite. Tyro became pregnant immediately but somehow managed to conceal her condition. When her time came, she exposed the twins who were born because she knew they would have to suffer their whole lives from the same kind of indignities she did.

Meanwhile Sisyphus, who hated his brother Salmoneus, consulted an oracle as to how to be rid of him. The oracle told him that if he fathered sons by Tyro, his niece, they would avenge him. It is difficult to imagine that Apollo would give any encouragement to someone as unscrupulous as Sisyphus, but perhaps the god saw things that mortals could not. Sisyphus proceeded to corrupt Tyro, who perhaps listened to and obeyed her uncle as someone sympathetic to her wretched state. She bore him twins, but found out they were products of a scheme and not of love. She did not even bother to expose them but killed them outright. Sisyphus seized the opportunity to put his brother over the edge

of an already serious mental condition by declaring that the twins were products of incest between father and daughter, and he displayed their bodies in the marketplace of Salmone.

Indeed this did serve to finish Salmoneus. He had already shown symptoms of insanity, but now he became unmanageable. He declared himself equal to Zeus, and rode about the city dragging empty kettles behind his chariot to simulate thunder. He hurled torches in the air for make-believe lightning. Zeus, although recognizing a pathological personality, had to intervene. He destroyed Salmoneus and the city of Salmone with a single thunderbolt.

Tyro was taken in by Deion, another uncle. Meanwhile Cretheus, still another uncle, had discovered that his wife, Demodice, had tried to seduce Phrixus, Tyro's cousin, and failing, had tried to have him killed. Cretheus dispatched Demodice and married the still quite young Tyro, already mother of two sets of twins.

Tyro very shortly became pregnant by him, and in rapid succession had Aeson, Pheres, Amythaon, and Hippolyte. Life became quite different for her after her years of oppression. Everything seemed to be going well, and she had settled into the role of motherhood. About that time, her long-lost sons Pelias and Neleus appeared. They had been found, as was so often the case, by shepherds and reared without knowledge of their beginnings. In time, though, they learned they had a mother and made a determined effort to seek her out. It appears that even then throwaway children sought out their biological mothers, even though these mothers had abandoned them and for all intents and purposes consigned them to death. They finally located Tyro and soon learned what she had suffered at the hands of Sidero. They could even blame their own abandonment on their cruel stepgrandmother, and they swore vengeance. They hunted her down and found her at an altar of Hera, where she had fled in terror. Not one to worry about sacrilege, Pelias unceremoniously killed her.

Cretheus had already willed his throne to his oldest son, Aeson, but it was not long before Pelias began a methodical takeover of the government of Iolcus and its surrounding territory. When Neleus tried to interfere, Pelias drove him out of the kingdom. Neleus went to Messenia with his half-brother Amythaon. Aeson's claim was totally overturned, and Pelias became king as soon as Cretheus died. Pheres, who became king in nearby Pherae, was probably subject to Pelias. Aeson continued to live apart. He realized his half-brother was unscrupulous and dangerous, so when a son, Jason, was born to him and Polymede, they told everyone he was stillborn, held a wake, and spirited him to Mount Pelion to be reared by Cheiron the Centaur.

After Jason grew up and revealed himself, Pelias realized that Jason and his whole family posed a threat to him, and sent him off on the perilous Argonaut. Pelias was certain the expedition would prove fatal to all of them, including his own son. As soon as the adventurers left, he started to kill Aeson but spared him when Tyro pleaded with him. Aeson was imprisoned instead.

Tyro might not have lived to see the Argonauts return. In that case she would not have known of the assassination of Jason's entire family. The murders might well have come about as a result of Tyro's death, since she could no longer intervene with her son. Had she lived, she might have taken a certain satisfaction in the ghastly death of Pelias. Her other children produced notable offspring, including Admetus, Bias, and Melampus. [Homer, *Odyssey* 2.120, 11.235; Apollodorus 1.9.7; Diodorus Siculus 4.68; Lucian, *Timon or Misanthrope* 2; Virgil, *Aeneid* 6.585; Hyginus, *Fables* 60,239,254; Strabo 8.3.32; Propertius 1.13.21.]

UOLATOS was one of the DOGS of Actaeon. [Hyginus, *Fables* 181.]

UPIS was a name closely associated with Artemis in a variety of connections. It was one of her surnames at Ephesus. Her statue was set up by the Amazons, and Ephesus was a rallying place for the belligerent women warriors. They established a walled shrine, the original temple of Artemis, and fiercely defended it against enemies.

Upis was also said to be a being who reared Artemis, and some considered her one of the nymphs in Artemis' train. A male Upis was mentioned as her father(!).

Upis (Opis) was also a Hyperborean maiden, who together with Arge or Hecaerge carried to Eileithyia at Delos an offering that had been vowed for the birth of Apollo and Artemis. This offering was later incorporated into the cult worship of the twins, particularly Apollo. Delian brides dedicated their hair to Upis or Hecaerge. [Pausanias 1.4.4,43.4, 5.7.8; Cicero, *On the Nature of the Gods* 3.23; Callimachus, *Hymn to Artemis* 240; Herodotus 4.35.]

URANIA (1) was one of the nine MUSES and called the Muse of astronomy. She was represented with a celestial globe to which she pointed with a staff. She was said to have been the mother by Apollo of Hymen, and by Apollo or Amphimarus of Linus. The mothers of Hymen and Linus were usually considered to be one or another of the Muses, but opinions varied widely as to which. [Catullus 61.2; Hyginus, *Fables* 161; Pausanias 2.29.3.]

URANIA (2) was one of the OCEANIDES. She was in the train of Persephone. [Hesiod, *Theogony* 350; *Homeric Hymn to Demeter* 424.]

URANIA (3) was a surname of Aphrodite. This name described her as the Heavenly to distinguish her from the earthy Aphrodite PANDEMOS. She was represented as a daughter of Uranus, begotten without a mother. Wine was not used in libations poured to her. [Plato, *Symposium* 180; Xenophon, *Symposium* 8.9; Herodotus 1.105; Suidas, "Nephalia."]

URANIA (4) was one of the DOGS of Actaeon. [Hyginus, *Fables* 181.]

VACUNA was a Sabine divinity, probably identical with Victoria. She had an ancient sanctuary on the Tiber River near the villa of Horace and a second one at Rome. According to some, her name had to do with the word *vacuus,* meaning to be at leisure or free from duties. Apparently country people offered sacrifices to her when the labor of the fields was over. She was identified with Diana, Ceres, Venus, or Minerva. As was so often the case, the most ancient divinities of Rome underwent an evolution in identities and had a primitive worship contemporary with an urbanized one. [Ovid, *Fasti* 6.307; Pliny, *Natural History* 3.17; Scholiast on Horace's *Epistles* 1.10.49.]

VALERIA (1) was a virgin from the city of Falerii. Because of a plague that continued to ravage the city, an oracle decreed that a virgin should sacrifice herself every year to Juno. This practice continued until Valeria was about to kill herself. An eagle flew to the altar and carried away the sword she was about to use. It flew over a neighboring field and let the sword fall on a heifer. Valeria understood the meaning and sacrificed the heifer. She took the ritual hammer that also lay on the altar and touched those afflicted with the pestilence. They were immediately cured. [Plutarch, *Greek and Roman Parallel Stories* 35.]

VALERIA (2) was the daughter of Valerius of Tusculum. She fell in love with her father, and with the help of her nurse slept with him. He thought she was a woman of the town. Valeria became pregnant and retreated into the woods. When her time neared she tried to abort the baby by jumping over a cliff, but both she and the fetus survived. She then returned home; Valerius learned the truth and killed himself. The child was born and called Aegipan, whom the Romans identified with Silvanus, god of fields and forests. [Plutarch, *Greek and Roman Parallel Stories* 22.]

VENILIA was a Roman divinity connected with the winds (Venti) and the sea. She was called a sister of Amata, the wife of Latinus and subsequently mother-in-law to Aeneas.

Venilia married Daunus, a son of Pilumnus and Danae, and king of Daunia. She bore to him Juturna and Turnus. Turnus became king of the Rutulii about the time of the arrival of Aeneas in Italy. He fought Aeneas because Latinus had given the Trojan hero his daughter Lavinia, who had previously been promised to Turnus. He finally was killed by Aeneas. Juturna was the nymph of a spring in Latium, the water from which was used in nearly all sacrifices. She was said to have been a lover of Jupiter even though she was the wife of Janus and mother of Fontus, divinity of fountains. One account called Venilia the mother of the nymph Canens by Janus.

[Varro, *On the Latin Language* 5.72; Virgil, *Aeneid* 7.408, 9.4, 10.75; 12.138; Servius on Virgil's *Aeneid* 9.148; Ovid, *Metamorphoses* 14.334.]

VENUS was the goddess of love among the Romans, especially of sensual love. Before her identification with the Greek Aphrodite, she had been quite unimportant and identified mainly with vegetation and gardens, thus ranking with several other minor fertility divinities. She had no festival. The Vinalia, celebrated in April and August by courtesans, seems to have been mistakenly consigned to her.

Things changed rapidly when the worship of Aphrodite came in by way of Sicily. Part of the worship stemmed from patriotism, since Venus/Aphrodite through Aeneas was considered the mother of the Roman people. Once the worship took root, sanctuaries were established widely. There was a sanctuary at Lavinium and a stone chapel at Rome in the Circus. This chapel had a statue of Venus Murtea, which in some way connected her with myrtle. A statue of Venus Cloacina was set up in a temple near the forum. A legend persisted that the statue had been found in the *cloaca* (sewer system of Rome), but the word was better explained in characterizing Venus as the goddess presiding over and purifying sexual intercourse in marriage.

Venus had two temples in the area of the Capitoline Hill under the surname of Calva. There have been various speculations about the origin of this name, but most likely it had to do with the dedication to Venus of a lock of hair by women on their wedding day. Surnames proliferated as the worship of Venus was extended. Some of these were Verticordia, Acidalia, Obsequens, Salacia, Erycina, Libentina, Postvorta, Genetrix, Militaris, Barbata, and Equestris. Sanctuaries of Venus Rhamnusia, Placida, and Alma were built at a very late date.

Festivals honoring Venus were held in April as a rule, in the belief that the beginning of spring was particularly sacred to the goddess of love. She was sometimes identified with Vacuna, a divinity associated both with victory and with leisure at the end of harvest.

The very well known story of Cupid and PSYCHE is about the only one that deals with

Venus in narrative instead of symbolic terms. [Macrobius, *Saturnalia* 1.12, 3.8; Ovid, *Fasti* 4.135,160,865, *Remedies of Love* 549; Plutarch, *Numa* 19, *Roman Questions* 20; Lydus, *On the Months* 4.45; Apuleius, *Golden Ass;* Tertullian, *On Spectacles* 8; Varro, *On the Latin Language* 5.154, *On Country Matters* 1.1; St. Augustine, *City of God* 4.16; Livy 1.33; Servius on Virgil's *Aeneid* 1.724; Pliny, *Natural History* 15.29, 19.4; Persius, *Saturae* 2.70; Valerius Maximus 8.15.12.]

VESTA was one of the 12 great Roman divinities. She was almost identical with the Greek Hestia in concept, but her worship naturally reflected Roman history and various embellishments such as the Penates and the institution of Vestal virgins. Like Hestia she was goddess of the hearth, but her worship included due reverence to the household gods called Penates, images of which were believed to have been brought from Troy along with the eternal Vestal fire. In houses of ancient Romans, the hearth was the central part, and the residents met daily at mealtimes to sacrifice to Vesta and the Penates, thereby strengthening their own familial bonds. This caused every dwelling to be in effect a temple of the goddess. A public sanctuary, which stood in the forum, served to unite all individual citizens of the state into one large family. Under the dome-shaped roof an eternal fire burned on the hearth.

The temple of Vesta was attended by the Vestals, her virgin priestesses. Every year on March 1, her sacred fire and the laurel tree that shaded her hearth were renewed. On June 9, the Vestalia was celebrated; on that day only women could come into the temple, and then only if they were barefoot. On June 15, her temple was cleaned and purified.

Vesta had several obvious surnames, such as Aeterna, Felix, Ignea, Mater, Sacra, and Tutela. She was occasionally identified with Stata Mater. [Virgil, *Aeneid* 2.296, 5.744, 10.259; Servius on Virgil's *Aeneid* 1.734; Macrobius, *Saturnalia* 1.12, 3.4; Ovid, *Fasti* 3.143, 6.269,282,305; St. Augustine, *City of God* 4.11; Dionysius of Halicarnassus, *Roman Antiquities* 2.65; Plutarch, *Numa* 11.]

VICTORIA was the personification of victory among the Romans, as was Nice among the Greeks. The first temple of Victoria was dedicated by Euander on the Palatine Hill. At length there were four sanctuaries to her at Rome. She was almost identical with the Sabine divinity Vacuna. [Livy 10.33, 29.14, 35.9.]

VICTRIX, the Victorious, was a surname of Venus, and her worship was founded by Julius Caesar. [Servius on Virgil's *Aeneid* 1.724.]

VIRILIS was a surname of Fortuna, under which she was worshipped by women who prayed to her that she might conceal their blemishes and cause them to remain exciting to their husbands. [Ovid, *Fasti* 4.145.]

VIRIPLACA, Placater, was a surname of Juno, describing her as the restorer of peace between married people. She had a sanctuary on the Palatine Hill into which women went when they thought themselves wronged by their husbands. They frankly told the goddess their grievances, and the priestesses gave them advice on how to become reconciled. [Valerius Maximus 2.1.6; Festus, "Conciliatrix."]

VIRTUS was the Roman personification of manly valor. She was represented with a short tunic, her right breast uncovered, a helmet on her head, a spear in her left hand, a sword in the right, and standing with her right foot on a helmet. There was a golden statue of her at Rome, which Alaric, king of the Goths, melted down. [Livy 27.25, 29.11; Valerius Maximus 1.1.8; Cicero, *On the Nature of the Gods* 2.23.]

VOLUPIA was the personification of sensual pleasure among the Romans. She was honored with a temple near the Porta Romanula. She was also called Voluptas. Interestingly, a statue of Angerona, the goddess of anguish, stood in the temple of Volupia. [Varro, *On the Latin Language* 5.164; Cicero, *On the Nature of the Gods* 2.23.]

XANTHE (1) was one of the OCEANIDES. [Hesiod, *Theogony* 355.]

XANTHE (2) was one of the AMAZONS. [Hyginus, *Fables* 163.]

XANTHIPPE was the daughter of Dorus. Dorus, Laodocus, and Polypoetes were sons of Phthia and Apollo and lords of the country of the Curetes. A report said that Aetolus came there after exile from Elis and killed his "hosts." This suggests he was received kindly at first, later turning against those who offered him hospitality (since the Greek translation does not imply hostility). It is unfortunate no more is known about this incident, since the subsequent history of the city of Pleuron concerned war with the Curetes. In the usual fashion Aetolus named the area Aetolia. His sons were Pleuron and Calydon, and the two Aetolian cities they founded were named for them. Xanthippe married Pleuron, the son of her father's murderer. This liaison might have signaled the end to trouble between the cities of Pleuron and Calydon and the Curetes, but it did not. Pleuron was probably an Aetolian stronghold built on the site of the older Curetean town. Xanthippe's children by Pleuron were Agenor, Sterope, Stratonice, and Laophonte. Agenor married Epicaste, the daughter of Calydon. Laophonte married Thestius and became the mother of Althaea and Leda, but the other two daughters were not notable. Nothing further is known of Xanthippe. Pleuron had a hero shrine at Sparta erected by his great-granddaughter Leda. [Apollodorus 1.7.7; Pausanias 3.13.5.]

XANTHIS was one of the THESPIADES. She became by Heracles the mother of Homolippus. [Apollodorus 2.7.8.]

XANTHO was one of the NEREIDES. [Hyginus, *Fables: Preface* 8.]

XENIA (1) was a nymph in love with the shepherd Daphnis. His lover was most often called NOMIA.

XENIA (2) was a surname of Athena, describing her as presiding over the laws of hospitality and protecting strangers. [Pausanias 3.11.11; Homer, *Odyssey* 14.389.]

XENODICE (1) was a daughter of Minos and Pasiphae. It seems rather certain that she died young. The family of Minos was a gold mine of stories, but the only record of Xenodice was as above. It is surprising that one of the imaginative commentators did not invent a life for her. [Apollodorus 3.1.2.]

XENODICE (2) was a captive Trojan woman depicted in the Lesche at Delphi. Pausanias knew of no writer who had identified her. It would be gratifying to tie her to the equally mysterious daughter of Minos, but the time period is not compatible. [Pausanias 10.26.1.]

XENODOCE was a daughter of Syleus of Aulis. Syleus and his brother Dicaeus, sons of Poseidon, were very different. Dicaeus was honest and just, while Syleus was arrogant and cruel. He would waylay passersby and force them to work in his vineyard before killing them. Heracles was thus stopped and, after seeing what Syleus planned to do, killed him with a hoe.

Instead of being angry with the hero, Dicaeus thanked him and entertained him. During this time, Heracles saw Xenodoce, who had been brought up by her uncle, and fell in love with her. As usual, Heracles had to leave not long after consummating the affair. Xenodoce pined during his absence to the extent that she became ill and died. When Heracles returned, he was so disconsolate he wanted to throw himself on the funeral pyre, but was restrained. The inhabitants afterward built a temple of Heracles over the tomb of Xenodoce. [Apollodorus 2.6.3; Conon, *Narrations* 17.]

ZEPHYRITIS was a surname of Aphrodite, derived from the promontory of Zephyrium in Egypt. [Athenaeus 7.318; Stephanus Byzantium "Zephyritis."]

ZERYNTHIA was a surname of Aphrodite from the town of Zerynthus in Thrace, where she had a sanctuary said to have been built by Phaedra. [Tzetzes on Lycophron 449,958; Stephanus Byzantium, "Zerynthia."]

ZEUXIPPE (1) was the sister of the Naiad Praxithea, mother of Pandion, whom she married. Her nephew/husband succeeded his father Erechtheus on the throne of Athens. Zeuxippe bore him two sons, Erechtheus (II) and Butes, and two daughters, Procne and Philomela. The two daughters were ill-fated. Pandion needed assistance in a war and called on Tereus, who helped win the victory. Pandion gave him Procne in marriage. Tereus gave her a son, Itys, but raped Philomela and cut out her tongue so she could not tell. The daughters managed to communicate, served Tereus his son Itys for dinner, and fled, pursued by Tereus. All were changed into birds.

Both Zeuxippe's sons turned out very well. On the death of Pandion, his estate was divided between the brothers. Erechtheus received the succession, and Butes the priesthood of Athena and Poseidon, an office that carried many rewards and privileges.

Zeuxippe's life was a mixture of happiness and extreme unhappiness. Her daughters came to a grievous end, but her sons rose to positions of great influence. From Zeuxippe the royal line of Athens could be traced well beyond the Trojan War. [Apollodorus 3.14.8.]

ZEUXIPPE (2) was a daughter of Lamedon, son of Coronus and king of the territory later called Sicyon(ia). Lamedon married Pheno, daughter of Clytius, and their daughter was Zeuxippe. During Lamedon's reign, war arose between him and the sons of Achaeus, and as an ally he brought in a hero named Sicyon from Attica. The identity of the father of Sicyon was uncertain; Marathon, Metion, Erechtheus, and Pelops have all been named. It is reasonable to suppose Marathon was the father, since there was an already established connection between the two families. Lamedon gave Zeuxippe to Sicyon in marriage, and Sicyon became king. He called the region Sicyonia and its capital Sicyon.

Chthonophyle was the only child from this union. She had Hermes as a lover and became the mother of Polybus, who succeeded Sicyon.

Polybus was said to have found the infant Oedipus, who had been exposed, and to have reared him as his own son. [Pausanias 2.1.1,6.2, 6.2.3.]

ZEUXIPPE (3) was the daughter of the god of the Eridanus River. He was called the king of rivers, and on the banks of the Eridanus amber was found. No one is certain of the location of the river. Zeuxippe married Teleon, a son of Ion, and their son was Butes. This Butes is occasionally confused with Butes, son of Pandion, but the second Butes was a great-grandnephew of the first.

This Butes was an Argonaut, the only one to succumb to the enchanting music of the Sirens. Before his companions could prevent him, he jumped overboard and swam toward certain death. But Butes was extremely good-looking, and the goddess Aphrodite decided to save him. She transported him to Sicily, where she became by him the mother of Eryx, who, according to some, was responsible for introducing the worship of Aphrodite into Italy. [Hesiod, *Theogony* 338; Hyginus, *Fables* 14,260; Apollodorus 2.5.10; Virgil, *Georgics* 1.482; Ovid, *Metamorphoses* 2.324; Apollonius Rhodius 4.910.]

ZEUXIPPE (4) was called by some the wife of Laomedon. Usually his wife was known as STRYMO. [Scholiast on Homer's *Iliad* 3.250.]

ZEUXO was one of the OCEANIDES. [Hesiod, *Theogony* 351.]

ZOSTERIA, Girded (for Battle), was a surname of Athena among the Epicnemidian Locrians. On his return from his battle with the Minyans, Heracles dedicated two stone images to Athena Zoster. [Pausanias 9.17.3; Stephanus Byzantium, "Zoster."]

ZYGIA, Joiner or Yoker, was a surname of Hera, describing her as presiding over marriage. [Hesychius, "Zygia."]

The Men in Their Lives

ABAS (s. Celeus?): Metaneira

ABAS (s. Lynceus): Abantias, Aglaia (4), Eidomene, Hypermnestra (2), Idomene, Ocaleia

ABAS (s. Melampus): Lysimache (1)

ABAS (s. Poseidon): Arethusa (4), Arethusa (5)

ABSYRTUS: Asterodeia (3), Eurylyte, Hecate, Ipsia, Medea, Neaera (6)

ACAMAS (s. Antenor): Theano (2)

ACAMAS (s. Theseus): Aethra (1), Clymene (3), Laodice (4), Phaedra, Philobia, Phyllis

ACAMAS (of Dulichium): Penelope

ACARNAN: Callirrhoe (2), Pronaea

ACASTUS: Anaxibia (1), Astydameia (1), Hippolyte (2), Laodameia (2), Peliades, Phylomache, Sterope (3), Sthenele (2)

ACERBAS: Dido

ACESAMENUS:. Periboea (3)

ACESTES (*See* EGESTUS)

ACHAEUS: Automate (2), Creusa (2), Phthia (2)

ACHELOUS: Acheloides, Amaltheia (1), Callirrhoe (2), Castalia, Deianeira (1), Methone (2), Peirene, Perimede (1), Perimele (1), Sirens

ACHERON: Gaea, Gorgyra, Orphne, Sterope (5)

ACHILLES: Arce, Artemis, Astynome (1), Calliope, Deidameia (2), Diomede (1), Helen (1), Helen (6), Hemithea (1), Hippodameia (3), Iphigeneia (1), Medea, Oreilochia, Peisidice (4), Penthesileia,

Philomela (3), Polyxena (1), Stratonice (4), Thetis

ACIS: Galateia (1), Symaethis

ACONTIUS: Cydippe (1)

ACRAGAS: Asterope (1)

ACRIAS: Hippodameia (1)

ACRISIUS: Acrisioneis, Aganippe (2), Aglaia (4), Danae, Euarete, Eurydice (4), Ocaleia

ACTAEON: Alce, Arcena, Arethusa (3), Argo, Artemis, Aura (2), Autonoe (1), Chediaetros, Cyllo, Dioxippe (4), Gorgo (4), Harpyia, Lacaena, Leaena, Lynceste, Melanchaetes, Ocydrome, Ocypete (3), Oresitrophos, Orias, Oxyrhoe, Sagnos, Semele, Theridamas, Theriope, Theriphone, Uolatos, Urania (4)

ACTIS: Rhodos

ACTOR (s. Azeus): Astyoche (1)

ACTOR (s. Deion?): Aegina, Diomede (2), Eurydice (10)

ACTOR (s. Myrmidon): Peisidice (1), Philomela (3), Polyboea (2), Polymela (4)

ACTOR (s. Phorbas): Hyrmine, Molione

ACTOR (s. Poseidon): Agamede (1)

ACUSILAUS (*See* ARCESILAUS, s. Odysseus)

ADANUS: Gaea

ADMETUS: Alcestis, Artemis, Clymene (6), Moirae, Periclymene, Perimele (2)

ADONIS: Alphesiboea (1), Aphrodite, Beroe (3), Calliope, Cenchreis, Myrrha, Persephone (1)

ADRASTUS: Adrastine, Aegiale (1), Amphithea (1), Argeia (4) Deipyle, Demonassa (2), Demonassa (3), Eriphyle, Eurydice (3), Eurynome (2), Lysianassa (2), Lysimache (1), Nemesis

AEACUS: Aegina, Endeis, Psamathe (1)

AECHMAGORAS: Phialo

AECHMODICUS: Metope (4)

AEETES: Aeaea (1), Aeaea (2), Aeetias, Antiope (6), Asterodeia (3), Chalciope (3), Euryale (3), Eurylyte, Hecate, Idyia, Iophossa, Ipsia, Medea, Neaera (6), Perse

AEGAEON: Gaea, Thetis

AEGAEUS: Melite (2)

AEGESTUS (See Egestus)

AEGEUS: Aethra (1), Aphrodite, Apteros, Autochthe, Chalciope (1), Medea, Melite (4), Meta, Pylia

AEGIALEUS (s. Adrastus): Amphithea (1), Archia, Demonassa (3), Melia (1)

AEGIALEUS (s. Phoroneus): Peitho (4)

AEGIALUS: Pronoe (3)

AEGICORES: Helice (2)

AEGIPAN: Aega, Valeria (2)

AEGISTHUS: Cassandra (1), Clytemnestra, Electra (4), Erigone (2), Helen (3), Pelopeia (3)

AEGIUS: Mnestra

AEGYPIUS: Timandra (2)

AEGYPTUS (s. Aegyptus): Dioxippe (1), Gorgo (3), Polyxena (1)

AEGYPTUS (s. Belus): Achiroe, Argyphia, Atlantia, Caliadne, Danaides, Gorgo (3), Hephaestine, Memphis (1), Side (3), Tyria

AELIUS: Hippodameia (1)

AENEAS: Alecto, Andromache, Anna Perenna, Aphrodite, Artemis, Caieta, Charybdis, Creusa (2), Deiopea (1), Deiphobe, Dido, Erycina, Eurydice (8), Lavinia, Roma (3), Roma (5), Sibyls

AENETUS: Diomede (2)

AENEUS: Aenete, Stilbe (1)

AEOLIUS: Hippodameia (1)

AEOLUS (s. Hellen): Aegiale (2), Aeolis, Alcyone (2), Antiope (4), Calyce (1), Canace, Cleobule (4), Enarete, Hippe (4), Iope (1), Melanippe (2), Orseis, Peisidice (1), Perimede (1), Pheraea (2), Tanagra, Trigoneia

AEOLUS (s. Hippotes): Arne (1), Cyane (2), Deiopea (1), Melanippe (1), Melanippe (2), Polymela (3)

AEOLUS (s. Poseidon): Antiope (4), Arne (1), Autolyte, Theano (3)

AEPYTUS (s. Cresphontes): Merope (6)

AEPYTUS (s. Elatus): Euadne (1), Laodice (3)

AESACUS: Alexirrhoe, Arisbe (1), Asterope (2), Hecuba, Hesperia, Thetis

AESEPUS: Abarbarea

AESON: Alcimede, Amphinome (1), Arne (3), Perimede (4), Polymede, Rhoeo (1), Scarphe, Tyro

AESYETES: Cleomestra

AESYMNETES: Artemis

AETHALIDES: Eupolemeia

AETHER: Caligo, Dione (1), Gaea, Hemera (1), Muses, Nyx, Oeneis, Tellus, Thalassa

AETHIOLAS: Helen (1)

AETHLIUS: Calyce (1), Protogeneia (1)

AETOLUS (s. Endymion): Asterodeia (1), Chromia, Cleobule (4), Hyperippe (1), Iphianassa (3), Neis (2), Pronoe (2)

AETOLUS (s. Oxylus): Pieria (1)

AGAMEDES: Epicaste (5), Iocaste (1)

AGAMEMNON: Aerope (1), Artemis, Astynome (1), Cassandra (1), Chrysothemis (1), Cleola, Clytemnestra, Electra (4), Helen (1), Hippodameia (3), Iphigeneia (1), Laodice (5), Munychia, Oenotropae

AGANUS: Helen (1)

AGAPENOR: Arsinoe (1), Helen (1), Laodice (6)

AGAPTOLEMUS: Pirene

AGASICLES: Nicagora

AGASSAMENUS: Pancratis

AGATHYRSUS: Echidna

AGDISTIS: Gaea, Nana

AGELAUS (s. Heracles): Omphale

AGELAUS (s. Oeneus): Althaea

AGELAUS (of Same): Penelope

AGELAUS (slave of Priam): Hecuba

AGENOR (s. Aegyptus): Cleopatra (2), Euippe (1)

AGENOR (s. Antenor): Theano (2)

AGENOR (s. Pleuron): Demonice, Epicaste (2), Xanthippe

AGENOR (s. Poseidon): Agriope (1), Antiope (7), Europa (4), Libya (1), Telephassa

AGENOR (s. Triopas): Sosis
AGENOR (of Dulichium): Penelope
AGENOR (of Zacynthus): Penelope
AGEROCHUS: Penelope
AGRIUS (s. Odysseus): Circe
AGRIUS (s. Porthaon): Dia (6), Euryte (1)
AGRIUS (of Deulichium): Penelope
AJAX (s. Oileus): Athena, Cassandra (1),
    Eriboea (2), Eriopis (1), Helen (1),
    Rhene
AJAX (s. Telamon): Eriboea (3), Glauce (7),
    Helen (1), Lyside, Meliboea (3), Periboea
    (4), Tecmessa (1)
ALABANDUS: Callirrhoe (5)
ALALCOMENES: Alalcomeneis, Athena,
    Athenais
ALASTOR: Chloris (2), Harpalyce (3)
ALCAEUS (s. Heracles): Malis
ALCAEUS (s. Perseus): Anaxo (1),
    Andromeda, Astydameia (3),
    Hipponome, Laonome (1), Lysidice (1),
    Perimede (3), Tiryns
ALCAROPS: Penelope
ALCATHOUS (s. Aesyetes): Hippodameia (2)
ALCATHOUS (s. Pelops): Agrotera,
    Automedusa, Euaechme (1),
    Hippodameia (1), Iphinoe (4), Periboea
    (4), Pyrgo
ALCATHOUS (s. Porthaon): Euryte (1),
    Hippodameia (1)
ALCES: Glauce (2)
ALCIMEDON: Phialo
ALCIMENES: Medea
ALCINOUS: Arete, Medea, Nausicaa
ALCMAEON: Alphesiboea (2), Arsinoe (1),
    Callirrhoe (2), Eriphyle, Eumenides,
    Laodameia (5), Manto (1), Tisiphone (2)
ALCMENOR: Hippomedusa
ALCON (s. Erechtheus II): Praxithea (2)
ALCON (s. Hephaestus): Cabeiro
ALCYONEUS: Alcyonides, Pallene (2)
ALECTOR: Cleobule (3), Meliboea (2),
    Polybule
ALETES: Electra (4)
ALEUS: Alcidice, Alea, Auge (1), Cleobule
    (2), Neaera (2)
ALEXANOR (s. Asclepius): Epione
ALEXANOR (s. Machaon): Anticleia (4)
ALEXIARES: Hebe
ALEXIDAMUS: Alceis

ALEXIS: Aphrodite, Meliboea (4)
ALITHERSES: Samia (1)
ALMON: Larunda
ALMOPS: Helle (1)
ALOEIDAE: Elate, Eriboea (1), Iphimedeia,
    Muses, Pancratis
ALOEUS: Antiope (6), Canace, Elate, Eriboea
    (1), Iphimedeia, Pancratis, Perse
ALOPECUS: Lygodesma, Orthia
ALOPIUS: Antiope (5)
ALPHEIUS: Alphaea, Alpheias, Arethusa (1),
    Artemis, Eumenides, Melantheia,
    Telegone
ALTES: Laothoe (1)
ALTHAEMENES: Apemosyne
ALTHEPUS: Leis
ALYZEUS: Polycaste (2)
AMALEUS: Aedon (1)
AMARYNCEUS: Diogeneia (2)
AMARYNTHUS: Artemis
AMATHUS: Oreithyia (5)
AMESTRIUS: Eone
AMISODARUS: Chimaera (1)
AMMON: Acacallis, Amalthei; (3),
    Pasiphae (2)
AMPHIALUS (s. Neoptolemus): Andromache
AMPHIALUS (of Ithaca): Penelope
AMPHIANAX (See IOBATES)
AMPHIARAUS: Alexida, Demonassa (2),
    Eriphyle, Eurydice (11), Hypermnestra
    (1), Hypsipyle
AMPHICTYON: Chthonopatra, Cranae,
    Gaea, Pyrrha (2)
AMPHIDAMAS: Antibia, Antimache,
    Antinoe (1), Cleophile, Eurynome (3)
AMPHILOCHUS: Eriphyle, Helen (1),
    Manto (1)
AMPHIMACHUS (s. Cteatus): Helen (1),
    Theronice
AMPHIMACHUS (s. Electryon): Anaxo (1)
AMPHIMACHUS (of Dulichium): Penelope
AMPHIMACHUS (of Ithaca): Penelope
AMPHIMARUS: Terpsichore, Urania (1)
AMPHIMEDON: Penelope
AMPHINOMUS (s. Nisus): Penelope
AMPHINOMUS (?): Hyria
AMPHION (s. Amphion): Niobe (2)
AMPHION (s. Hyperasius): Hypso
AMPHION (s. Iasus): Chloris (2),
    Persephone (2)

AMPHION (s. Zeus): Antiope (1), Astycrateia, Astynome (2), Astyoche (5), Chloris (1), Cleodoxa, Dirce (1), Ethodaia, Homolois (1), Meliboea (3), Neaera (3), Neis (1), Niobe (2), Ogygia, Pelopeia (2), Phthia (1), Phylomache, Thebe (2)

AMPHISSUS: Dryope (1)

AMPHITHEMIS: Acacallis

AMPHITRYON: Alcmena, Anaxo (1), Astydameia (3), Comaetho (1), Hipponome, Laonome (1), Laonome (3), Megara

AMPHOTERUS: Callirrhoe (2), Pronaea

AMPYCUS: Aregonis, Chloris (4)

AMULIUS: Rhea Silvia

AMYCLAS (s. Amphion): Niobe (2)

AMYCLAS (s. Lacedaemon): Daphne (4), Diomede (3), Laodameia (3), Polyboea (1), Sparta

AMYCUS: Bithynis, Melia (2), Theano (4)

AMYNTOR (s. Aegyptus): Damone

AMYNTOR (s. Ormenus): Astydameia (2), Cleobule (1), Clytia (4), Hippodameia (5), Phthia (4)

AMYTHAON: Aeolia, Aglaia (3), Eidomene, Idomene, Perimele (3), Rhodope (2), Tyro

ANACTOR: Anaxo (1)

ANAX: Gaea

ANCAEUS: Alta, Antinoe (1), Astypalaea, Cleophile, Eurynome (3), Parthenope (2), Samia (1)

ANCHEMOLUS: Casperia

ANCHISES: Aphrodite, Egesta, Eriopis (4), Hippodameia (2), Themiste

ANCUS: Acca Larentia

ANDES: Gaea

ANDRAEMON (of Aetolia): Dryope (1), Gorge (1)

ANDRAEMON (of Dulichium): Penelope

ANDREUS: Euippe (5)

ANDRODAMAS: Chthonophyle

ANDROGEUS: Crete (1), Pasiphae (1)

ANDROMACHUS: Hero (1)

ANDROMEDES (of Crete): Britomartis

ANDROMEDES (of Zacynthus): Penelope

ANDRON: Dorippe (2)

ANDROPOMPUS: Anchiroe (2), Henioche (5)

ANICETUS I (s. Heracles): Megara

ANICETUS II (s. Heracles): Hebe

ANIO: Rhea Silvia

ANIUS (s. Aeneas): Lavinia

ANIUS (s. Apollo): Creusa (3), Dorippe (2), Lavinia, Oenotropae, Rhoeo (1)

ANOGON: Leucippides

ANTAEUS: Alceis, Barce (2), Gaea, Iphinoe (6)

ANTANDRUS: Alexirrhoe

ANTEIAS: Circe

ANTENOR (s. Aesyetes): Cleomestra, Theano (2)

ANTENOR (of Zacynthus): Penelope

ANTEROS: Aphrodite

ANTHAS: Alcyone (1)

ANTHEUS: Theano (2)

ANTHUS: Hippodameia (6)

ANTIADES: Aglaia (5)

ANTIGONUS: Penelope

ANTILEON: Procris (2)

ANTILOCHUS: Anaxibia (2), Helen (1)

ANTIMACHUS (s. Aegyptus): Midea

ANTIMACHUS I (s. Heracles): Megara

ANTIMACHUS II (s. Heracles): Nicippe (2)

ANTIMACHUS (of Dulichium): Penelope

ANTIMENES: Hyrnetho

ANTINOUS: Penelope

ANTIOCHUS (s. Aegyptus): Itea

ANTIOCHUS (s. Heracles): Meda, Mideia (2)

ANTION: Astyageia, Perimele (3)

ANTIPAPHUS: Critomedeia

ANTIPHAS: Chariboea

ANTIPHUS (s. Heracles): Laothoe (4)

ANTIPHUS (s. Myrmidon): Peisidice (1)

ANTIPHUS (s. Priam): Hecuba

ANTIPHUS (s. Thessalus): Chalciope (5)

ANTIPOENUS: Alcis (2), Androcleia

ANTISTHENES: Penelope

ANXURUS: Feronia

ANYTUS: Demeter, Despoena, Gaea

AOLLIUS: Hersilia

AORIS: Araethyrea

APHAREUS: Arene, Arne (4), Gorgophone (1), Laocoosa

APHEIDAS: Chrysopeleia, Erato (1), Stheneboea

APIS: Apia, Laodice, Teledice

APOLLO: Acacallis, Aethusa, Antianeira (1), Apanchomene, Aphrodite, Areia (3),

Arge (2), Arsinoe (3), Artemis, Asteria
(6), Astynome (1), Athena, Borysthenis,
Calliope, Carya, Cassandra (1), Castalia,
Celaeno (4), Cephisso, Chariboea,
Chariclo (1), Charites, Chione (2),
Chrysorthe, Coronis (1), Corycia, Creusa
(2), Creusa (3), Cyrene, Daphnaea,
Daphne (2), Daphne (3), Delia,
Delphinia, Delphyne, Dia (3), Dryope
(1), Eileithyia, Epicaste (5), Eriopis (2),
Euadne (1), Euanthe, Eumenides, Gryne,
Hestia (1), Hyria, Issa, Leto, Maera (5),
Marpessa, Melaena, Melia (1), Melissae,
Moirae, Molpadia (1), Muses, Niobe (2),
Nymphs, Ocyrrhoe (3), Paphos,
Parthenope (2), Phanothea, Phemonoe,
Philonis (1), Phoebe (1), Phthia (3),
Poene, Psamathe, Pythia, Rhodope (1),
Rhoeo (1), Rhytia, Sibyls, Sinope, Stilbe
(1), Telphusa (1), Terpsichore, Thaleia
(1), Themis, Thero (2), Thriae, Thyria,
Urania (1)
APOLLO AMAZONIUS: Amazons (1)
APOLLO CLARIUS: Manto (1)
APOLLO MUSAGETES: Muses
APOLLO SMINTHEUS: Herophile
ARABUS: Cassiepeia
ARAS: Araethyrea
ARATUS: Aristodeme (1), Epione
ARBELUS: Oeme
ARCAS: Callisto (1), Chrysopeleia,
    Diomeneia, Erato (1), Helice (1),
    Laodameia (3), Leaneira, Maia,
    Meganeira (1), Megisto, Themisto (3)
ARCEISIUS: Chalcomedusa, Euryodia
ARCEOPHON: Arsinoe (5)
ARCESILAUS (s. Archilycus): Theobule (1)
ARCESILAUS (s. Odysseus): Penelope
ARCHANDER: Automate (2), Scaea
ARCHEDICUS: Eurypyle
ARCHEDIUS: Maera (5)
ARCHELAUS (s. Aegyptus): Anaxibia (4)
ARCHELAUS (s. Electryon): Anaxo (1)
ARCHELOCHUS: Theano (2)
ARCHEMACHUS: Patro
ARCHEMOLUS: Penelope
ARCHEMORUS (*See* OPHELTES)
ARCHENOR: Niobe (2)
ARCHESTRATUS: Penelope
ARCHILYCUS: Theobule (1)

ARCHITELES: Automate (1), Automate (2)
ARDALUS: Ardalides, Muses
ARDEAS: Circe
AREAS: Megara
AREION: Demeter, Despoena, Gaea, Harpies
AREITHOUS: Phylomedusa
AREIUS: Pero (2)
ARES: Achiroe, Aegina, Aerope (2), Agraulos
    (2), Alcippe (1), Althaea (1), Amazons
    (1), Androdice, Antiope (2), Aphrodite,
    Astyoche (1), Chryse (2), Demonice,
    Dotis, Enyo (1), Eos, Eris, Harmonia (1),
    Harmonia (2), Harpinna (1), Hera,
    Lysippe (4), Otrera, Pelopeia (1),
    Penthesileia, Phylonome, Protogeneia (2),
    Sinope, Sterope (1), Telphusia,
    Theogone, Thero (2), Triteia
ARESTOR: Mycene
ARETUS: Anaxibia (2)
ARGADES: Helice (2)
ARGAEUS: Aspalis
ARGALUS: Diomede (3)
ARGEIUS (s. Deiphontes): Hyrnetho
ARGEIUS (s. Licymnius): Perimede (3)
ARGEIUS (s. Pelops): Hippodameia (1)
ARGENNUS: Argennis
ARGES: Gaea
ARGIUS (s. Aegyptus): Euippe (1)
ARGIUS (of Dulichium): Penelope
ARGONAUTS: Arete, Athena, Circe, Cleite
    (1), Dindymene, Dryope (4), Hera,
    Hypsipyle, Iasonia, Idaea (3), Iphinoe
    (5), Medea, Nereides, Polyxo (4), Sirens,
    Thetis
ARGUS (s. Phrixus): Argeia (3), Chalciope
    (3), Perimele (2)
ARGUS (s. Zeus): Euadne (3), Ismene (1),
    Niobe (1), Peitho (5)
ARGUS PANOPTES: Echidna, Gaea, Hera,
    Io, Mycene
ARION (s. Poseidon): Oncaea
ARION (king of Miletus): Hesione (1)
ARISTAEUS: Autonoe (1), Cyrene, Dryades,
    Eurydice (1), Gaea, Macris
ARISTODEMUS (s. Aristomachus): Argeia (5)
ARISTODEMUS (s. Heracles): Megara
ARISTOMACHUS (s. Talaus): Lysimache (1)
ARISTOMACHUS (?): Hippodameia (1)
ARISTONOUS: Celaeno (5)
ARISTRATUS: Penelope

ARMENIUS: Henioche (5)
ARNEUS: Megamede
ARRHON: Budeia (2)
ARSINOUS: Hecamede
ARUNS: Camilla
ASCALABUS: Demeter, Misme
ASCALAPHUS (s. Acheron): Demeter, Gorgyra, Orphne, Persephone (1)
ASCALAPHUS (s. Ares): Astyoche (1), Helen (1)
ASCANIUS: Caieta, Creusa (3), Roma (3)
ASCLEPIUS: Aegle (5), Arsinoe (3), Aristodeme (1), Coronis (1), Epione, Hygieia (1), Iaso, Lampetia, Nicagora, Panaceia
ASIUS: Arisbe (1)
ASOPUS (River of Boeotia): Antiope (1), Euboea (1), Pero (1), Plataea, Polyxo (2)
ASOPUS (River of Peloponnesus): Aegina, Asopis (2), Cegluse, Cercyra, Chalcis, Cleone, Euanthe, Harpinna (1), Ismene (1), Methone (2), Metope (1), Metope (2), Parnassa, Peirene, Pero (1), Rhode (1), Salamis, Sinope, Tanagra, Thebe (2), Thespeia
ASPLEDON: Mideia (3), Sterope (6)
ASPONDUS: Cleopatra (6)
ASSAON: Niobe (2)
ASSARACUS: Callirrhoe (3), Hieromneme
ASTACUS: Olbia
ASTERIDES: Chrysothemis (2)
ASTERION (s. Oceanus): Acraea (1), Euboea (2), Prosymna (1)
ASTERION (s. Pyremus): Antigone (4)
ASTERIUS (s. Aegyptus): Cleo
ASTERIUS (s. Minos): Androgeneia
ASTERIUS (s. Neleus): Chloris (2)
ASTERIUS (s. Teutamas): Crete (1), Europa (4)
ASTRABACUS: Lygodesma, Orthia
ASTRAEUS (s. Crius): Astraea, Eos, Eurybia (1)
ASTRAEUS (Macedonian youth): Alcippe (2)
ASTYANAX (s. Hector): Andromache
ASTYANAX (s. Heracles): Epilais
ASTYBIES: Calametis
ASTYGETES: Aspalis
ASTYLOCHUS: Penelope
ATHAMANTES: Pyrante
ATHAMAS (s. Aeolus): Alos, Antiphera,

Enarete, Eurycleia (1), Helle (1), Hera, Ino, Leucothea (2), Nephele (1), Themisto (2)
ATHAMAS (s. Oenopion): Helice (5)
ATHLETES: Europome
ATINTAN: Oreithyia (5)
ATLAS: Aethra (2), Asia (2), Asteria (4), Asterope (3), Atlantides, Atlantis, Calypso, Clymene (1), Dione (3), Electra (2), Gaea, Hesperides, Hesperis, Hyades, Maera (5), Maia, Pasiphae (2), Pleiades, Pleione, Sterope (1)
ATRAX: Caenis, Hippodameia (4)
ATREUS: Aerope (1), Anaxibia (3), Artemis, Cleola, Hippodameia (1), Pelopeia (3)
ATROMUS: Stratonice (1)
ATTIS: Agdistis, Sagaritis
ATYS: Callithea, Cybele, Nana
AUGEAS: Agamede (1), Ambracia (3), Epicaste (3), Hyrmine, Iphiboe, Naupidame
AULESTES: Manto (4)
AUSON: Calypso, Circe
AUTESION: Argeia (5)
AUTOLYCUS (s. Hermes): Amphithea (2), Anticleia (1), Chione (2), Neaera (7), Philonis (1), Polymede, Stilbe (2), Telauge
AUTOLYCUS (s. Phrixus): Chalciope (3)
AUTONOUS: Hippodameia (6)
AVENTINUS: Rhea (2)
AXIUS: Periboea (3)
AZAN: Chrysopeleia, Deianeira (2), Erato (1)
AZEUS: Budeia (2)
BALIUS: Podarge
BARGASUS: Barge
BARTHAS: Penelope
BASILEUS: Molpadia (1)
BEBRYX: Pyrene (2)
BELLEROPHON: Aethra (1), Amazons (1), Anteia, Anticleia (3), Asteria (5), Athena, Chalinitis, Chimaera (1), Deidameia (1), Eurymede (1), Eurynome (8), Hellotia (2), Hippia, Laodameia (1), Philonoe (2), Stheneboea
BELUS: Achiroe, Agamede (1), Anna Perenna, Antiope (7), Lamia (2), Libya (1), Side (3)
BERECYNTHUS: Berecynthia
BERES: Oreithyia (5)
BEROSUS: Erymanthe, Sabbe
BIAS (s. Amythaon): Aglaia (3), Alphesiboea

(3), Anaxibia (1), Eidomene, Idomene, Pero (2), Proetides, Rhodope (2)

BIAS (of Dulichium): Penelope

BISALTES: Theophane

BITIAS: Iaera (2)

BITON: Cydippe (2), Hera

BOEOTUS (s. Itonus): Melanippe (3)

BOEOTUS (s. Poseidon): Antiope (4), Arne (1), Autolyte, Hermippe, Theano (3)

BOMOLOCHUS: Peridia

BOREAS: Chione (1), Cleopatra (6), Eos, Hecaerge (1), Loxo, Oreithyia (2), Pitys

BORUS (s. Penthilus): Anchiroe (2)

BORUS (s. Perieres): Polydora (5)

BRANCHUS: Argiope (3)

BRIAREUS: Aetna, Gaea, Thetis

BRISEUS: Briseis (1), Hippodameia (3)

BROMIUS: Caliadne, Erato (6)

BRONTES: Gaea

BROTEAS (s. Tantalus): Artemis, Dione (3), Eurythemistra

BROTEAS (s. Vulcan): Minerva

BUCOLION: Abarbarea, Calybe (1), Strymo

BUCOLUS: Marse

BULEUS: Elachia

BUNOMUS: Helen (1)

BUNUS: Alcidameia, Bunaea

BUPHAGUS: Artemis, Promne, Thornax

BUSIRIS (s. Aegyptus): Automate (1)

BUSIRIS (s. Poseidon): Anippe, Lysianassa (1)

BUTES (s. Boreas): Coronis (4)

BUTES (s. Pandion): Athena, Chthonia (4), Zeuxippe (1)

BUTES (s. Teleon): Aphrodite, Zeuxippe (3)

BYZAS: Ceroessa

CABARNUS: Demeter

CABEIRI: Anchinoe, Cabeiria, Cabeiriae, Demeter, Electra (2), Hecate

CACUS: Caca

CADMILUS: Axieros, Axiocersa, Cabeiriae, Cabeiro, Hyades

CADMUS: Agave (1), Antiope (7), Athena, Autonoe (1), Electra (3), Europa (4), Harmonia (1), Ino, Mystis, Onca, Semele, Telephassa, Telphusia

CAENEUS: Hippe (5)

CAICUS: Ocyrrhoe (4)

CALAICARPUS: Autonoe (1)

CALAIS: Cleopatra (6), Harpies, Oreithyia (2)

CALCHAS: Briseis (2), Iphigeneia (1)

CALLIARUS: Laonome (2)

CALLIPOLIS: Euaechme (1)

CALYDON: Aeolia, Epicaste (2), Pronoe (2), Protogeneia (2)

CALYDONEUS: Penelope

CAMEIRUS: Cydippe (3), Lysippe (3)

CANDALUS: Rhodos

CANES: Euadne (4)

CANETHUS: Henioche (4)

CANOBUS: Theonoe (1)

CANTHUS: Eurydice (2)

CAPANEUS: Astynome (3), Euadne (2), Laodice (7)

CAPETUS: Hippodameia (1)

CAPYLUS: Hippo (1)

CAPYS: Egesta, Hieromneme, Themiste

CAR: Callirrhoe (5), Peitho (1)

CARCAPHUS: Cydippe (3)

CARMANOR: Alexirrhoe

CARNEIUS: Europa (4)

CARPUS: Chloris (3)

CARUTIUS: Acca Larentia

CARYSTUS: Chariclo (1)

CASIPHONES: Circe

CASSANDRUS: Creusa (5)

CASSUS: Helicta

CASTALIUS: Thyia (1)

CASTOR: Electra (4), Leda, Leucippides

CATREUS: Aerope (1), Apemosyne, Clymene (4), Crete (1), Europa (6), Pasiphae (1)

CAUCON: Astydameia (5)

CAUNUS: Byblis, Cyane (3), Eidothea (2), Pronoe (3), Tragasia

CAYSTRIUS: Penthesileia

CEBREN: Asterope (2), Oenone

CECROPS (son of Erechtheus II): Metiadusa, Oreithyia (5), Praxithea (2)

CECROPS (autochthon): Agraulos (1), Agraulos (2), Athena, Herse (2), Pandrosos

CEISUS: Araethyrea

CELAENEUS (s. Electryon): Anaxo (1)

CELAENEUS (of Caria): Tragasia

CELEUS: Demeter, Demo (3), Diogeneia (3), Meganeira (2), Metaneira, Polymnia, Saesara

CELEUSTANOR: Iphis (1)

CELEUTOR: Dia (6)

CELTUS: Penelope

CENCHRIAS: Peirene

CENTAURS: Dia (1)
CENTAURUS: Stilbe (1)
CEPHALUS (s. Deion): Eos, Procris
CEPHALUS (s. Hermes): Artemis,
    Chalcomedusa, Clymene (2), Creusa (2),
    Diomede (2), Eos, Hemera (1), Herse (2)
CEPHEUS (s. Aleus): Antinoe (1), Cleobule
    (2), Neaera (2), Sterope (4)
CEPHEUS (s. Belus): Achiroe, Aerope (2),
    Andromeda, Cassiepeia, Iope (1)
CEPHISSUS (River of Attica): Diogeneia (1),
    Praxithea (1)
CEPHISSUS (River of Boeotia): Euippe (5),
    Lilaea, Melaena, Thyia (1)
CERAUS: Penelope
CERBERUS (s. Typhon): Echidna
CERBERUS (of Same): Penelope
CERCAPHUS: Rhodos
CERCETES: Dorium
CERCOPES: Theia (2)
CERCYON (s. Agamedes): Epicaste (5)
CERCYON (s. Branchus): Alope, Argiope (3)
CERYNES: Hyrnetho
CERYX: Agraulos (2), Pandrosos
CESTRINUS: Andromache
CETEUS: Callisto (1), Stilbe (2)
CEYX: Alcyone (2), Philonis (2)
CHAERESILAUS: Stratonice (4)
CHAERON: Thero (2)
CHAETUS: Asteria (3)
CHALCODON (s. Abas): Imenarete,
    Melanippe (5)
CHALCODON (s. Aegyptus): Rhodia (2)
CHALCODON (?): Hippodameia (1)
CHALCON: Penthesileia
CHAMYNUS: Chamyne
CHAOS: Caligo
CHARMUS: Autonoe (1)
CHAROPUS: Aglaia (2)
CHEIMARRHOUS: Polymnia
CHEIRON: Chariclo (1), Euippe (4), Hippe
    (4), Ocyrrhoe (2), Philyra (1), Thetis
CHERSIBIUS: Megara
CHIMAEREUS: Celaeno (1)
CHIRIMACHUS: Anaxo (1)
CHORAEUS: Callithea
CHREMETES: Anchiroe (3)
CHROMIS: Dryope (3)
CHRYSAOR: Callirrhoe (1), Echidna
CHRYSES (s. Agamemnon): Astynome (1)

CHRYSES (s. Minos): Pareia (2)
CHRYSES (priest of Apollo): Astynome (1)
CHRYSIPPUS (s. Aegyptus): Chrysippe (1),
    Demoditas, Tyria
CHRYSIPPUS (s. Pelops): Astyoche (7),
    Axioche, Danaia, Hippodameia (1)
CHTHONIUS: Bryce, Caliadne
CICON: Rhodope (1)
CILIX: Europa (4), Telephassa, Thebe (3)
CINYRAS: Amathusa, Braesia, Cenchreis,
    Laodice (3), Laogore, Metharme, Myrrha,
    Orsedice, Paphos, Pharnace, Smyrna
CISSEUS (s. Aegyptus): Anthelia, Caliadne
CISSEUS (river-god): Hecuba, Telecleia,
    Theano (2)
CLARUS: Deidameia (1)
CLEINIS: Artemicha, Harpe
CLEITOR: Eurymedusa
CLEITUS (s. Aegyptus): Cleite (2), Tyria
CLEITUS (king of Sithonia): Chrysonoe,
    Pallene (1), Torone
CLEOBIS: Cydippe (2), Hera
CLEOCHUS: Areia (3)
CLEODAEUS (s. Heracles): Malis
CLEODAEUS (s. Hyllus): Lanassa
CLEOLAUS: Argele
CLEON: Hippodameia (1)
CLEOPOMPUS: Cleodora (2)
CLESON: Cleso, Tauropolis (2)
CLYMENUS (s. Helios): Merope (1)
CLYMENUS (s. Heracles): Megara
CLYMENUS (s. Oeneus): Althaea (1)
CLYMENUS (s. Orchomenus): Eurydice (5)
CLYMENUS (s. Phoroneus): Chthonia (2)
CLYMENUS (s. Schoeneus): Harpalyce (3)
CLYMENUS (s. Teleus): Epicaste (4)
CLYMENUS (king of Orchomenus):
    Budeia (2)
CLYMENUS (of Dulichium): Penelope
CLYTIUS (s. Alcmaeon): Arsinoe (1)
CLYTIUS (s. Eurytus): Antioche (1),
    Antiope (3)
CLYTIUS (s. Laomedon): Procleia, Strymo
CLYTIUS (of Athens): Pheno
CLYTIUS (of Dulichium): Penelope
CLYTIUS (of Same): Penelope
CLYTIUS (of Zacynthus): Penelope
CLYTIUS (a giant): Hecate
CLYTONEUS: Arete
CLYTUS (s. Aegyptus): Autodice

CLYTUS (s. Mantius): Eos
CODRUS: Anchiroe (2), Henioche (5)
COEUS: Asteria (1), Gaea, Leto, Phoebe (1)
COLAENUS: Colaenis
COLONTAS: Chthonia (3)
COLONUS: Ochne
COMETES (s. Sthenelus): Aegiale (1)
COMETES (a Thessalian): Antigone (4)
COON: Theano (2)
CORAX: Arethusa (6)
CORESUS: Callirrhoe (4)
CORINTHUS: Hippodameia (1), Sylea
COROEBUS (s. Mydon): Cassandra (1)
COROEBUS (of Argos): Poene, Psamathe (2)
CORONEUS: Coronis (2)
CORONUS (s. Apollo): Anaxiroe, Asteria (6),
    Chrysorthe
CORONUS (s. Caeneus): Lyside
CORYBANTES: Calliope, Chalcis, Rhea (1),
    Rhytia, Thaleia (1), Thebe (3)
CORYBAS: Ida (1), Thebe (4)
CORYMBUS: Mystis
CORYTHUS (s. Paris): Helen (1), Oenone
CORYTHUS (king of Tuscia): Electra (2)
COTTUS: Gaea
CRAMBIS: Cleopatra (6)
CRANAUS: Atthis, Cranae, Cranaechme,
    Gaea, Pedias
CRANTOR: Cleobule (1)
CRATAIGONUS: Anchiroe (3)
CRATIEUS: Anaxibia (2)
CRATUS: Gaea, Styx
CREON (s. Lycaethus): Creusa (4), Glauce
    (5), Medea, Tisiphone (2)
CREON (s. Menoeceus): Antigone (1),
    Eurydice (7), Henioche (1), Henioche
    (3), Iocaste (2), Megara, Pyrrha (1)
CREONTIADES: Megara
CRESPHONTES: Abia, Merope (6)
CRETHEUS: Biadice, Cretheis, Demodice,
    Enarete, Myrina (1), Tyro
CRIASUS: Cleoboea (1), Euadne (3),
    Melantho (3)
CRIMISUS: Egesta
CRISUS: Antiphateia, Asteria (9),
    Asterodeia (5)
CRIUS: Eurybia (1), Gaea
CROCON: Meganeira (1), Saesara
CROCUS: Smilax
CRONIUS (s. Zeus): Himalia

CRONIUS (?): Hippodameia (1)
CRONUS: Aphrodite, Crete (3), Demeter,
    Dione (1), Eumenides, Euonyme, Gaea,
    Hera, Hestia (1), Moirae, Philyra (1),
    Pluto (2), Rhea (1), Thrace
CROTALUS: Hippodameia (1)
CROTOPUS: Psamathe (2)
CROTUS: Eupheme (1), Muses
CTEATUS: Molione, Theraphone, Theronice
CTESIPPUS I (s. Heracles): Astydameia (2)
CTESIPPUS II (s. Heracles): Deianeira (1)
CTESIPPUS (of Ithaca): Penelope
CTESIPPUS (of Same): Penelope
CTESIUS: Penelope
CUPID: Psyche, Venus
CURETES (of Aetolia): Althaea (1)
CURETES (of Crete): Adrasteia (1), Rhea (1)
CYCHREUS: Chariclo (2), Demeter, Glauce
    (6), Salamis
CYCLOPES: Gaea
CYCNUS (s. Apollo): Hyria, Thyria
CYCNUS (s. Ares): Pelopeia (1), Pyrene (1)
CYCNUS (s. Opus): Larymna
CYCNUS (s. Poseidon): Calyce (2), Glauce
    (7), Harpale, Hemithea (1), Philonome
    (1), Polyboea (3), Procleia, Scamandrodice
CYCNUS (of Dulichium): Penelope
CYDNUS: Anchiale (1)
CYDON: Acacallis, Maera (5)
CYLLARUS: Hylonome
CYLLEN: Laodice (3)
CYNNUS: Penelope
CYNORTAS: Diomede (3)
CYNOSURUS: Hippodameia (1)
CYPARISSUS: Euryanassa (2)
CYPRUS: Eune
CYPSELUS: Merope (6)
CYTISSORUS: Chalciope (3)
CYTUS: Himalia
CYZICUS: Aenete, Cleite (1), Larissa (2)
DACTYLS: Anchiale (2), Ida (3), Rhea (1)
DAEDALION: Chione (2), Phrasimede
DAEDALUS: Alcippe (1), Aphrodite,
    Ariadne, Artemis, Athena, Iphinoe (2),
    Merope (9), Naucrate, Pasiphae (1),
    Polycaste (3)
DAEMON: Penelope
DAESENOR: Penelope
DAIPHRON: Adiante, Scaea
DAMASICHTHON: Niobe (2)

DAMASICLUS: Erimede
DAMASTOR: Penelope
DANAUS: Achiroe, Atlantia, Crino,
    Danaides, Elephantis, Europa (7),
    Eurythoe, Herse (1), Hesione (2), Hippe
    (3), Hypermnestra (2), Lindia (1), Lindia
    (2), Memphis (2), Philodameia, Phoebe
    (3), Physadeia, Pieria (2), Polydora (3),
    Polyxo (1), Side (2), Side (3)
DAPHNIS: Chimaera (2), Echenais, Lyce,
    Nomia (1), Pipleia, Xenia (1)
DARDANUS: Arisbe (2), Bateia (1), Chryse
    (1), Electra (2), Idaea (3), Myrina (3),
    Neso (2), Sibyls
DAUNUS: Danae, Euippe (3), Juturna, Venilia
DEICOON: Megara
DEILEON: Chalciope (3)
DEIMACHUS (s. Cleon): Glaucia
DEIMACHUS (s. Neleus): Chloris (2)
DEIMAS: Chryse (1)
DEIMOS: Aphrodite
DEION (s. Aeolus): Asterodeia (4), Diomede
    (2), Enarete, Tyro
DEION (s. Heracles): Megara
DEIONEUS (s. Eurytus): Perigune
DEIONEUS (?): Dia (1)
DEIPHOBUS: Athena, Hecuba, Helen (1)
DEIPHONTES: Hyrnetho, Orsobia
DEIPYLUS: Iliona
DELPHINEUS: Amphitrite
DELPHUS (s. Apollo): Celaeno (4), Melaena
DELPHUS (s. Poseidon): Melantho (2)
DEMARCHUS: Eubule (2)
DEMOCOON: Megara
DEMOLEON (s. Antenor): Theano (2)
DEMOLEON (s. Phrixus): Chalciope (3)
DEMOPHON (s. Celeus): Demeter,
    Metaneira
DEMOPHON (s. Theseus): Alcmena,
    Phaedra, Phyllis
DEMOPTOLEMUS: Penelope
DEUCALION (s. Hyperasius): Hypso
DEUCALION (s. Minos): Crete (2),
    Pasiphae (1)
DEUCALION (s. Prometheus): Asia (3),
    Axiothea, Hesione (5), Melantho (2),
    Protogeneia (1), Pyrrha (2), Themis,
    Thyia (2)
DEXAMENUS: Ambracia (1), Deianeira (2),
    Hippolyte (3), Mnesimache, Theraphone

DIAS: Cleola, Hippodameia (1)
DICAEUS: Xenodoce
DICTYS (s. Magnes): Danae
DICTYS (s. Poseidon): Agamede (1)
DIOCLES: Anticleia (4)
DIOCORYSTES: Hippodameia (7)
DIOMEDES (s. Ares): Cyrene,
    Hippodameia (11)
DIOMEDES (s. Atlas): Asteria (4)
DIOMEDES (s. Diomedes): Euippe (3)
DIOMEDES (s. Tydeus): Aegiale (1),
    Anemotis, Aphrodite, Athena, Briseis (2),
    Callirrhoe (6), Deipyle, Euippe (3),
    Helen (1)
DION: Iphitea, Lyco
DIONYSUS: Agave (1), Alexirrhoe,
    Alphesiboea (4), Althaea (1), Amaltheia
    (3), Amazons (2), Antheia, Aphrodite,
    Araethyrea, Arge (1), Ariadne, Artemis,
    Aura (1), Bassarae, Beroe (1), Brisa,
    Brome, Callirrhoe (4), Carya, Charites,
    Clodones, Coronis (4), Coronis (5),
    Cotys, Cybele, Deianeira (1), Demeter,
    Dione (1), Eripha (2), Hera, Hippe (1),
    Hyades, Ino, Io, Iphitea, Lenae, Lethe,
    Leucippe (2), Macetae, Macris,
    Maenades, Minyades, Muses, Mystis,
    Nicaea, Nymphs, Nyseides, Oenoe (4),
    Persephone (1), Philia (2), Physcoa,
    Proetides, Rhea (1), Semele, Telete (2),
    Thyia (1), Thyone
DIOPITHES: Penelope
DIORES: Polymela (3)
DIOSCURI: Asia (1), Clytemnestra,
    Helen (1), Leda, Leucippides, Nemesis,
    Thisadie
DODON: Europa (4)
DOLICHUS: Pirene
DOLIUS: Melantho (1)
DOLONCUS: Thrace
DOLOPS: Philyra (1)
DORUS (s. Apollo): Phthia (3), Xanthippe
DORUS (s. Hellen): Orseis
DORUS (s. Xuthus): Creusa (2)
DRYANTIS: Hecabe (1)
DRYAS (s. Aegyptus): Caliadne, Eurydice (2)
DRYAS (a Macedonian): Pallene (1)
DRYOPS: Dia (3), Dryope (1), Dryope (3),
    Polydora (3)
DULICHEUS: Penelope

DYMAS: Euagore, Eunoe, Hecuba

DYNASTES: Erato (5)

DYRRHACHIUS: Melissa (3)

DYSPONTEUS: Euarete, Sterope (1)

ECBASUS: Euadne (3)

ECHECLES: Polymela (2)

ECHEMUS: Timandra (1)

ECHEPHRON (s. Heracles): Psophis (2)

ECHEPHRON (s. Nestor): Anaxibia (2)

ECHEPOLIS: Euaechme (1)

ECHETIMUS: Nicagora

ECHETUS: Metope (4), Phlogea

ECHION (s. Hermes): Antianeira (2),
    Laothoe (2)

ECHION (of Dulichium): Penelope

ECHION (one of the Sparti): Agave (1),
    Cybele

ECNOMINUS: Achamantis

ECPHAS: Eurycleia (3)

EETION: Andromache

EGESTUS: Egesta, Entella

EIONEUS: Hippodameia (1), Meliboea (2),
    Philodice (2)

ELATUS (s. Arcas): Amphictyone,
    Chrysopeleia, Dotis, Erato (1), Erimede,
    Hippe (5), Laodice (3)

ELATUS (of Same): Penelope

ELECTRYON: Alcmena, Anaxo (1),
    Andromeda, Electryone (2), Eurydice (9),
    Lysidice (1), Mideia (1)

ELEIUS: Eurycyde

ELEPHENOR: Helen (1), Imenarete,
    Melanippe (5)

ELEUSIS: Cothonea, Cyntinea, Daeira, Hyona

ELEUTHER: Aethusa

EMATHION: Eos

ENALUS (an Ethiopian): Benthesicyme

ENALUS (a Lesbian): Amphitrite, Phineis

ENCELADUS (s. Aegyptus): Amymone, Trite

ENCELADUS (giant): Gaea

ENDYMION: Asterodeia (1), Calyce (1),
    Chromia, Eurycyde, Hera, Hyperippe
    (1), Iphianassa (3), Neis (2), Selene

ENIPEUS: Tyro

ENODUS: Samia (1)

ENORCHES: Daeto

ENTELIDES: Menippis

ENYALIUS: Enyo (1)

EOSPHORUS: Eos, Hesperides, Hesperis,
    Philonis (2), Stilbe (2)

EPAPHUS: Io, Libya (1), Lysianassa (1),
    Memphis (1)

EPEIUS (s. Endymion): Anaxiroe, Asterodeia
    (1), Hyrmine, Neis (2)

EPEIUS (s. Panopeus): Aphrodite, Athena

EPHIALTES (s. Aegyptus): Arsalte

EPHIALTES (s. Poseidon) (See ALOEIDAE)

EPIDAMNIUS: Helen (4)

EPIDAMNUS: Melissa (3)

EPIDAURUS: Euadne (3), Hippodameia (1)

EPILAUS: Chloris (2)

EPIMETHEUS: Asia (2), Clymene (1),
    Ephyra (1), Pandora (1), Pyrrha (2)

EPISTROPHUS: Helen (1), Hippolyte (4)

EPOCHUS: Antinoe (1), Cleophile,
    Eurynome (3)

EPOPEUS (s. Aloeus): Antiope (1), Athena,
    Canace

EPOPEUS (king of Lesbos): Nyctimene

ERASINUS: Anchiroe (1), Maera (4), Melite (3)

ERASIPPUS: Lysippe (1)

EREBUS: Caligo, Chaos, Hemera (1), Moirae,
    Nemesis, Nyx

ERECHTHEUS I: Agraulos (2), Athena,
    Atthis, Gaea, Herse (2), Hyades (?),
    Praxithea (1)

ERECHTHEUS II: Chthonia (4), Creusa (2),
    Hyacinthides, Merope (9), Oreithyia (2),
    Otionia, Pandora (3), Praxithea (2),
    Procris (1), Protogeneia (3), Zeuxippe (1)

EREUTHALION: Melantho (3)

ERGINUS (s. Clymenus): Budeia (2)

ERGINUS (s. Poseidon): Celaeno (3)

ERICHTHONIUS (s. Dardanus): Astyoche
    (4), Bateia (1)

ERICHTHONIUS (s. Poseidon) (See
    ERECHTHEUS I)

ERIDANUS: Zeuxippe (3)

EROS: Aphrodite, Artemis, Chaos, Charites,
    Eileithyia, Hygieia, Iris, Muses, Nicaea,
    Peitho (1), Penia, Polymnia

ERYMANTHUS (s. Antenor): Theano (2)

ERYMANTHUS (s. Apollo): Aphrodite

ERYSICHTHON (s. Cecrops): Agraulos (1),
    Eileithyia

ERYSICHTHON (s. Triopas): Demeter,
    Hypermestra, Mestra

ERYTHRAS (s. Heracles): Exole

ERYTHRAS (s. Leucon): Hippodameia (1)

ERYTHRIUS: Themisto (2)

ERYX: Aphrodite, Erycina, Psophis (2), Sirens

ETEOCLES (s. Cephissus): Charites, Euippe (5), Hesione (2)

ETEOCLES (s. Oedipus): Antigone (1), Astymedusa, Euryganeia, Iocaste (2)

ETEONEUS: Penelope

EUAEMON (s. Amyntor): Cleobule (1), Ops

EUAGORAS: Chloris (2)

EUANDER (s. Hermes): Carmenta, Demeter, Dyna, Nice (1), Pallantia, Roma (4), Themis (2), Tiburtis, Timandra (1), Victoria

EUANDER (s. Sarpedon): Deidameia (1)

EUANTHES (s. Dionysus): Ariadne

EUANTHES (s. Oenopion): Helice (5)

EUBULUS: Carme

EUCHENOR (s. Aegyptus): Iphimedusa

EUCHENOR (of Epeirus): Phlogea

EUDAEMONES: Erato (6)

EUDORUS: Polymela (2)

EUENORIDES (of Dulichium): Penelope

EUENORIDES (of Zacynthus): Penelope

EUENUS: Alcippe (4), Demonice, Marpessa

EUERES (s. Heracles): Parthenope (1)

EUERES (descendant of Udaeus): Chariclo (3)

EUIDEAS: Helice (3)

EUIPPUS (s. Megareus): Iphinoe (3), Oenope

EUIPPUS (s. Thestius): Eurythemis

EUMAEUS: Anticleia (1)

EUMEDES: Lyse

EUMELUS (s. Admetus): Alcestis, Ethemea, Helen (1), Iphthime (2)

EUMELUS (of Same): Penelope

EUMOLPUS (s. Poseidon): Benthesicyme, Chione (1), Deiope, Demeter

EUMOLPUS (a flute player): Philonome (1)

EUNEUS: Hypsipyle

EUNOSTUS: Eunoste, Ochne

EUPALAMUS: Alcippe (1), Metiadusa, Praxithea (2)

EUPHEMUS: Celaeno (3), Europa (3), Lamache, Laonome (3), Malache, Malicha, Mecionice, Oris

EUPHORBUS: Phrontis

EUPINYTUS: Niobe (2)

EUROPUS: Oreithyia (5)

EUROTAS: Cleochareia, Cleta (2), Pitane, Sparta, Taygete

EURYALUS (s. Odysseus): Euippe (6), Penelope

EURYALUS (of Dulichium): Penelope

EURYALUS (of Zacynthus): Penelope

EURYALUS (?): Hippodameia (1)

EURYBIUS: Chloris (2)

EURYCAPYS: Clytippe

EURYDAMAS (s. Actor): Demonassa (1)

EURYDAMAS (s. Aegyptus): Phartis

EURYLOCHUS (s. Aegyptus): Autonoe (4), Caliadne

EURYLOCHUS (of Zacynthus): Penelope

EURYMACHUS (s. Antenor): Theano (2)

EURYMACHUS (?): Hippodameia (1)

EURYMEDON (s. Hephaestus): Cabeiro

EURYMEDON (s. Minos): Pareia (2)

EURYMEDON (king of giants): Periboea (2)

EURYMENES: Chloris (2)

EURYNOMUS (s. Magnes): Orsinome, Philodice (2)

EURYNOMUS (of Ithaca): Penelope

EURYOPES: Terpsicrate

EURYPYLUS (s. Dexamenus): Soteria

EURYPYLUS (s. Euaemon): Helen (1), Ops, Triclaria

EURYPYLUS (s. Poseidon): Astypalaea, Celaeno (1), Chalciope (2), Sterope (7)

EURYPYLUS (s. Telephus): Argiope (4), Astyoche (3), Cassandra (1)

EURYPYLUS (s. Thestius): Eurythemis

EURYPYLUS (of Dulichium): Penelope

EURYSACES: Tecmessa (1)

EURYSTHENES (s. Aegyptus): Monuste

EURYSTHENES (s. Aristodemus): Argeia (5)

EURYSTHEUS: Admete (1), Admete (2), Alcmena, Antibia, Antimache, Arcippe, Nicippe (1)

EURYSTRATUS: Penelope

EURYTION (s. Actor): Antigone (2), Polyboea (2)

EURYTION (s. Irus): Demonassa (1)

EURYTION (Centaur of Achaia): Deianeira (2)

EURYTION (Centaur of Thessaly): Hippodameia (4)

EURYTIUS: Galateia (2)

EURYTUS (s. Actor): Theraphone, Theronice

EURYTUS (s. Hermes): Antianeira (2)

EURYTUS (s. Melaneus): Antioche (1), Antiope (3), Dryope (1), Iole, Oechalia, Stratonice (3)

EURYTUS (s. Poseidon): Molione

EUSEIRUS: Eidothea (4)

EUSORUS: Aenete

EUTHYNICUS: Rhodopis

EUXANTHIUS: Dexithea

FAUNUS: Bona Dea, Diana, Dryope (2),
Faula, Marica, Symaethis

FAUSTULUS: Acca Larentia, Helen (5),
Luperca

FAUSTUS: Entoria

FELIX: Entoria

FONTUS: Venilia

GALEPSUS: Telephe

GANYMEDE: Callirrhoe (3), Eos, Hebe

GARAMAS: Acacallis

GELEON: Helice (2)

GELONUS: Echidna

GENII: Aphrodite

GERYMBAS: Cleopatra (6)

GERYONES: Callirrhoe (1), Erytheia (2)

GIANTS: Apaturia (2), Gaea

GLAUCOPUS: Athenais

GLAUCUS (s. Antenor): Theano (2)

GLAUCUS (s. Anthedon): Circe, Deiphobe,
Deliades, Euboea (3), Scylla (1)

GLAUCUS (s. Hippolochus): Demonassa (5)

GLAUCUS (s. Sisyphus): Aphrodite,
Eurymede (1), Merope (3)

GLAUCUS (of Dulichium): Penelope

GLENUS: Deianeira (1), Megara

GOLGOS: Aphrodite

GORGASUS: Anticleia (4)

GORGOPHONUS: Anaxo (1)

GORTYS: Maera (5)

GRANICUS: Alexirrhoe

GYGES: Gaea

HADES: Demeter, Eumenides, Leuce,
Mintha, Persephone (1), Rhea (1)

HAEMON: Antigone (1), Eurydice (7)

HAEMONIUS: Amaltheia (3)

HAEMUS: Oreithyia (2), Rhodope (1)

HAGIUS: Penelope

HALESUS: Hera

HALIOS: Arete

HALIRRHOTHIUS: Alcippe (1), Euryte (2)

HALIUS: Penelope

HALMUS: Chryse (2), Chrysogeneia,
Merope (3)

HALOCRATES: Olympusa

HARCUS: Eris

HARPALYCUS: Harpalyce (1)

HARPASUS: Harpe

HEBRUS: Rhodope (1)

HECATON: Calyce (2)

HECETORUS: Pancratis

HECTOR: Andromache, Aphrodite, Hecuba,
Polyxena (1)

HEGELEOS: Salpinx

HELEIUS: Andromeda

HELENUS (s. Priam): Andromache, Arisbe
(3), Cassandra (1), Deidameia (2),
Hecuba, Helen (1)

HELENUS (of Ithaca): Penelope

HELICAON: Laodice (4), Theano (2)

HELIOS: Aega, Aegle (1), Antiope (6),
Calypso, Circe, Clymene (1), Clytia (5),
Crete (1), Demeter, Dirce (1), Electryone
(1), Euryphaessa, Gaea, Heliadae,
Lampetia, Leucothoe (1), Neaera (1),
Neaera (5), Ocyrrhoe (1), Pasiphae (1),
Perse, Phaethontiades, Phaethusa (1),
Rhode (1), Rhodos, Selene, Sterope (7),
Theia (1)

HELLANICUS: Penelope

HELLEN (s. Deucalion): Orseis, Pyrrha (2)

HELLEN (s. Phthios): Chrysippe (2)

HELLEN (s. Poseidon): Antiope (4)

HEPHAESTUS: Aetna, Aglaia (1), Anticleia
(2), Aphrodite, Athena, Atthis, Cabeiro,
Celedones, Charis, Demeter, Eurynome
(1), Gaea, Hera, Pandora (1), Thaleia (3)

HERACLES: Abia, Admete (2), Aegophagus,
Aella, Alcestis, Alcippe (5), Alcmena,
Alcyone (4), Amaltheia (1), Amazons (1),
Amazons (2), Antioche, Antiope (2),
Apaturia (2), Artemis, Asteria (8),
Astydameia (2), Astydameia (5), Astyoche
(2), Athena, Auge (1), Autonoe (2),
Axiopoenos, Barge, Bolbe, Celaeno (6),
Chalciope (2), Charybdis, Deianeira (1),
Deianeira (2), Deianeira (4), Dyna,
Echidna, Eileithyia, Eleusina, Epicaste
(3), Epione, Eriboea (2), Eucleia (1),
Eurybia (3), Galinthias, Glaucia,
Gorgons, Hebe, Hera, Hesione (1),
Hesperides, Hippolyte (1), Iole, Iphinoe
(6), Lacinia, Macaria, Malis, Manto (3),
Meda (1), Medea, Megamede, Megara,
Melanippe (4), Melite (2), Melite (5),
Menodice, Mideia (2), Moirae, Myrto (2),

HERACLES *(continued)*
  Omphale, Pandaea, Pharmacides, Phialo, Phoebe (5), Psophis (2), Pyrene (1), Pyrene (2), Scylla (1), Sterope (4); Stilbe (2), Stymphalides, Thespiades, Xenodoce, Zosteria
HERCULES: Acca Larentia, Caca, Cyane (1), Faula, Pallantia
HERCULES MUSAGETES: Muses
HERILEUS: Arethusa (4)
HERMAPHRODITUS: Aphrodite, Salmacis
HERMES: Acacallis, Agraulos (2), Alcidameia, Amaltheia (1), Antianeira (2), Apemosyne, Aphrodite, Artemis, Carmenta, Charites, Chelone, Chione (2), Chthonophyle, Cleobule (4), Creusa (2), Daeira, Dryope (5), Erytheia (2), Eupolemeia, Hermaphroditus, Herse (2), Iphthime (1), Issa, Laothoe (2), Libya (2), Maia, Myrto (3), Ocyrrhoe (4), Pandora (1), Pandrosos, Penelope, Phaethusa (2), Philodameia, Philonis (1), Polymela (2), Telauge, Themis (2), Theobule (2), Thriae, Thymbris
HERMOCHARES: Ctesylla
HERMUS: Caliadne, Cleopatra (3)
HEROPHILUS: Aphrodite
HESPERUS *(See* EOSPHORUS)
HIARBAS: Dido
HICETAON: Strymo
HIMANTES: Pluto (2)
HIMERUS (s. Lacedaemon): Aphrodite, Cleodice
HIMERUS (companion of Eros): Aphrodite
HIPPALCIMUS: Asterope (4)
HIPPALMUS: Hippodameia (1)
HIPPASUS (s. Pelops): Hippodameia (1)
HIPPASUS (?): Leucippe (2)
HIPPEUS: Procris (2)
HIPPOCOON: Bateia (2), Nicostrate (2)
HIPPOCORYSTES: Hyperippe (2)
HIPPODAMAS: Euryte (1), Perimede (1), Perimele (1)
HIPPODAMUS: Euarete
HIPPODOCHUS: Penelope
HIPPODROMUS: Anthippe
HIPPOLOCHUS (s. Antenor): Theano (2)
HIPPOLOCHUS (s. Bellerophon): Anticleia (3), Deidameia (1), Demonassa (5)

HIPPOLYTUS (s. Aegyptus): Rhode (2)
HIPPOLYTUS (s. Theseus): Aegeria, Aethra (1), Antiope (2), Aphrodite, Aricina, Artemis, Diana, Hippolyte (1), Lyceia, Phaedra, Tauropolis (1)
HIPPOMACHUS (of Zacynthus): Penelope
HIPPOMACHUS (?): Perineice
HIPPOMEDON: Mythidice
HIPPOMENES (s. Megareus): Atalanta, Iphinoe (3), Merope (5), Oenope
HIPPOMENES (s. Poseidon): Oenope
HIPPONOUS (s. Oicles?): Astynome (3), Laodice (7)
HIPPONOUS (s. Priam): Hecuba
HIPPONOUS (king of Olenus): Periboea (5)
HIPPOTES: Leipephilene, Melanippe (2)
HIPPOTHOON: Alope
HIPPOTHOUS: Gorge (2)
HIPPOZYGUS: Hippocrate
HODITES: Deianeira (1)
HOMADUS: Alcyone (4)
HOMOLIPPUS: Xanthis
HOPLES: Helice (2), Melite (4), Meta
HORATIUS: Sororia
HOSTILIUS: Hersilia
HOSTUS: Hersilia
HYACINTHUS: Clio, Diomede (3), Hyacinthides
HYAMUS: Celaeno (4)
HYAS: Boeotia, Hyades
HYDIS: Asteria (5)
HYDISSUS: Asteria (5)
HYDRA: Echidna
HYLAS: Menodice
HYLLUS I (s. Heracles): Abia, Alcmena, Deianeira (1), Euaechme (2), Iole
HYLLUS II (s. Heracles): Melite (2)
HYLLUS (s. Thersander): Arethusa (7)
HYLLUS (river-god): Gaea
HYMEN: Aphrodite, Calliope, Clio, Terpsichore, Urania (1)
HYMNUS (s. Saturn): Entoria
HYMNUS (shepherd): Nicaea, Telete (2)
HYPERANTUS: Electra (6)
HYPERASIUS: Hypso
HYPERBIUS: Celaeno (5), Eupheme (2)
HYPERENOR (s. Panthous): Phrontis
HYPERENOR (s. Poseidon): Alcyone (1)
HYPERENOR (of Same): Penelope
HYPERES (s. Melas): Eurycleia (1)

HYPERES (s. Poseidon): Alcyone (1)

HYPERION: Aerope (4), Eos, Euryphaessa, Gaea, Selene, Theia (1)

HYPERPHAS: Euryanassa (2), Euryganeia

HYPNOS: Muses, Nyx

HYPSEUS: Alcaea, Astyageia, Chlidanope, Creusa (1), Cyrene, Phillyra, Themisto (2)

HYRIEUS: Alcyone (1), Clonia (1), Euryale (1), Histiaea

HYRTACUS (a Trojan): Arisbe (1)

HYRTACUS (relative of above): Ida (4)

IACCHUS: Baubo, Demeter, Persephone (1)

IALEMUS: Calliope, Clio

IALMENUS: Astyoche (1), Helen (1), Pernis

IALYSUS: Cydippe (3), Dotis, Lysippe (3), Syme

IAMUS: Euadne (1)

IANISCUS: Epione

IAPETUS: Anchiale (1), Asia (2), Clymene (1), Gaea, Thornax

IARDANUS: Iardanis, Omphale

IASION: Demeter, Electra (2), Hemera (2)

IASO: Epione

IASON (See JASON)

IASUS (s. Argus): Ismene (1)

IASUS (s. Lycurgus): Antinoe (1), Atalanta, Cleophile, Clymene (2), Eurynomé (3)

IASUS (s. Triopas): Callithyia, Io, Sosia

IASUS (s. Zeus): Io

ICARIUS (s. Perieres): Aedos, Aletis, Asterodeia (2), Dorodoche, Gorgophone (1), Iphthime (2), Penelope, Periboea (1), Polycaste (2)

ICARIUS (of Athens): Erigone (1), Maera (1), Phanothea

ICARUS: Leucippe (4), Naucrate

IDAEUS (s. Dardanus): Chryse (1), Cybele

IDAEUS (s. Paris): Helen (1)

IDAS (s. Aegyptus): Hippodice

IDAS (s. Aphareus): Arene, Arne (4), Cleopatra (1), Helen (1), Laocoosa, Leucippides, Marpessa, Polydora (2)

IDAS (s. Clymenus): Epicaste (4)

IDMON (s. Aegyptus): Gorgo (3), Pylarge

IDMON (s. Apollo): Antianeira (1), Asteria (6), Cyrene, Laothoe (3)

IDMON (a Lydian): Arachne

IDOMENEUS: Athena, Cleisithyra, Helen (1), Meda (2)

IDRIEUS: Callirrhoe (5)

ILLYRIUS: Harmonia (1)

ILTONOMUS: Polybe

ILUS (s. Capys): Themiste

ILUS (s. Dardanus): Bateia (1)

ILUS (s. Tros): Callirrhoe (3), Eurydice (3), Leucippe (3), Telecleia, Themiste

IMBRASUS: Ocyrrhoe (3)

IMBRIUS: Medesicaste (2)

IMBRUS: Caliadne, Euippe (2)

INACHUS: Archia, Argeia (2), Callithyia, Inachia, Io, Melia (1), Mycene, Niobe (1), Philodice (1)

INDIUS I (of Zacynthus): Penelope

INDIUS II (of Zacynthus): Penelope

IOBATES: Anteia, Anticleia (3), Cassandra (2), Philonoe (2), Stheneboea

IOLAUS: Alcmena, Automedusa, Leipephilene

ION (s. Apollo): Bura, Creusa (2), Helice (2),

ION (s. Gargettus): Ionides

IPHICLES (s. Amphitryon): Alcmena, Iope (2), Promne, Thornax

IPHICLES (s. Thestius): Eurythemis

IPHICLUS: Astyoche (6), Clymene (2), Diomedeia, Harpalyce (2)

IPHIDAMAS (s. Antenor): Theano (2)

IPHIDAMAS (of Dulichium): Penelope

IPHIS (s. Alector): Euadne (2), Ianeira, Iphias (1), Laodice (7)

IPHIS (s. Ligdus): Ianthe (2), Telethusa

IPHIS (s. Sthenelus): Nicippe (1)

IPHIS (a Cypriot): Anaxarete

IPHITUS (s. Eurytus): Antioche (1), Antiope (3)

IPHITUS (s. Naubolus): Eurynome (4), Hippolyte (4), Perineice

IRUS: Chrysippe (2), Demonassa (1)

ISANDER: Anticleia (3), Deidameia (1)

ISCHEPOLIS (See ECHEPOLIS)

ISCHYS: Artemis, Coronis (1)

ISMENUS (s. Amphion): Niobe (2)

ISMENUS (s. Apollo): Melia (1)

ISMENUS (s. Asopus): Metope (1)

ISTHMIDES: Pelarge

ISTRUS: Hippodameia (7)

ITALUS: Lucania, Roma (3)

ITANUS: Penelope

ITHACUS: Penelope

ITONUS: Athena, Iodama, Itonia, Melanippe (3)

ITYLUS: Aedon (1)

ITYS (s. Polytechnus): Aedon (2)
ITYS (s. Tereus): Philomela (1), Procne
IULUS (*See* ASCANIUS)
IXION: Dia (1), Hera, Nephele (2),
    Perimele (3)
JANUS: Cardea, Entoria, Jana, Juturna, Venilia
JASON: Alcimede, Amphinome (1), Arete,
    Arne (3), Charybdis, Creusa (4), Eriopis
    (3), Glauce (5), Hera, Hypsipyle, Iphias
    (2), Iynx (2), Medea, Peliades, Perimede
    (4), Polymede, Polymela (5), Polypheme,
    Rhoeo (1), Scarphe, Tyro
JUPITER: Baucis, Cura, Domiduca, Juno,
    Juturna, Minerva
LABDACUS: Nycteis
LACEDAEMON: Asine, Cleodice, Eurydice
    (4), Sparta, Taygete
LACINIUS: Lacinia
LADON (s. Phorcys): Ceto (1), Gaea,
    Hesperides
LADON (River): Daphne (3), Metope (1),
    Syrinx, Telphusa (2), Thelpusa, Themis
    (2), Tiburtis
LAERTES: Anticleia (1), Chalcomedusa,
    Ctimene, Penelope
LAIAS: Pieria (1)
LAIUS: Eurycleia (3), Iocaste (2)
LAMAS: Penelope
LAMEDON: Pheno, Zeuxippe (2)
LAMIUS: Omphale
LAMPRUS: Galatea (2)
LAMPUS (s. Aegyptus): Gorge (3), Ocypete (1)
LAMPUS (s. Laomedon): Strymo
LAMPUS (horse): Eos
LAOCOON: Antiope (9), Athena, Cassandra
    (1), Chariboea, Curissia
LAODAMAS (s. Alcinous): Arete
LAODAMAS (s. Hector): Andromache
LAODICUS: Penelope
LAODOCUS (s. Antenor): Theano (2)
LAODOCUS (s. Apollo): Phthia (3)
LAODOCUS (s. Bias): Pero (2)
LAOMEDES: Penelope
LAOMEDON (s. Heracles): Meline
LAOMEDON (s. Ilus): Aethylla, Antigone
    (3), Astyoche (3), Calybe (1), Cilla,
    Hesione (1), Leucippe (3), Medesicaste
    (1), Placia, Rhoeo (2), Strymo, Thoosa
    (1), Zeuxippe (4)
LAOMEDON (of Zacynthus): Penelope

LAOMENES: Oreia
LAPHRIUS: Laphria
LAPITHES (s. Apollo): Orsinome, Stilbe (1)
LAPITHES (of Sparta): Diomede (3)
LARES: Acca Larentia, Larunda
LASIUS: Hippodameia (1)
LATINUS: Amata, Circe, Faula, Laurina,
    Lavinia
LATRAMYS: Ariadne
LAVINIUS: Lavinia
LEANDER: Hero (3)
LEARCHUS: Ino
LECHES: Periene
LEIMON: Artemis, Maera (5)
LEIOCRITUS: Penelope
LEITUS: Cleobule (3), Helen (1), Polybule
LELANTOS: Aura (1), Periboea (7)
LELEX: Cleochareia, Libya (1), Peridia,
    Therapne
LEONTEUS: Helen (1)
LEOS: Eubule, Leontides
LEPREUS: Astydameia (5)
LESBUS: Orsinome
LESTORIDES: Penelope
LEUCADIUS: Polycaste (2)
LEUCAS: Cleisithyra, Meda (2)
LEUCIPPUS (s. Eurypylus): Sterope (7)
LEUCIPPUS (s. Heracles): Eurytele
LEUCIPPUS (s. Lamprus): Galatea (2)
LEUCIPPUS (s. Oenomaus): Daphne (3),
    Euarete, Sterope (1)
LEUCIPPUS (s. Perieres): Arsinoe (3),
    Gorgophone (1), Leucippides,
    Philodice (1)
LEUCIPPUS (s. Thurimachus): Calchinia
LEUCON: Euippe (5), Themisto (2)
LEUCONES: Aeschreis
LEUCOPEUS: Euryte (1)
LEUCOPHANES: Lamache, Malache,
    Malicha
LIBER: Ceres, Libera
LIBYS: Libya (2)
LICHAS: Deianeira (1)
LICYMNIUS: Alcmena, Mideia (1),
    Perimede (3)
LIGDUS: Iphis (3), Telethusa
LIMUS: Eris
LINDUS: Cydippe (3), Lysippe (3)
LINUS: Aethusa, Calliope, Clio, Psamathe
    (2), Terpsichore

LIODES: Penelope
LIPARUS: Cyane (2)
LIXUS: Caliadne, Cleodora (3)
LOCRUS (s. Locrus): Cabya, Cambyse
LOCRUS (s. Physicus): Cabya, Cambyse
LOCRUS (s. Zeus): Maera (3), Protogeneia (1)
LOCRUS (?): Laurina
LUCOMO: Tanaquil
LUCTUS: Tellus
LUPERCUS: Acca Larentia, Luperca
LYAMMUS: Penelope
LYCAETHUS: Penelope
LYCAON (s. Azeus): Deianeira (3)
LYCAON (s. Eurypylus): Sterope (7)
LYCAON (s. Pelasgus): Callisto (1), Cyllene
    (1), Deianeira (3), Dia (3), Helice (1),
    Meliboea (1), Nonacris
LYCAON (s. Priam): Laothoe (1)
LYCASTUS (s. Ares): Phylonome
LYCASTUS (s. Minos I): Ida (1), Itone
LYCHNUS: Athena
LYCIUS: Harpe
LYCOMEDES (s. Apollo): Parthenope (2)
LYCOMEDES (king of Scyros): Deidameia (2)
LYCOPEUS: Dia (6)
LYCORUS: Corycia
LYCOTHERSES: Agave (1)
LYCTIUS: Itone
LYCURGUS (s. Aleus): Antinoe (1),
    Cleophile, Eurynome (3), Neaera (2)
LYCURGUS (s. Heracles): Toxicrate
LYCURGUS (s. Pheres): Amphithea (3),
    Eurydice (6), Hypsipyle, Periclymene
LYCURGUS (?): Hippodameia (1)
LYCUS (s. Aegyptus): Agave (3)
LYCUS (s. Hyrieus): Antiope (1), Clonia (1),
    Dirce (1)
LYCUS (s. Pandion): Arene, Demeter, Pylia
LYCUS (s. Poseidon): Celaeno (1), Celaeno (3)
LYCUS (of Euboea): Dirce (2), Megara
LYCUS (king of Libya): Callirrhoe (6)
LYCUS (?): Pernis
LYDUS: Callithea
LYGAEUS: Polycaste (2)
LYNCAEUS: Tiphyse
LYNCEUS (s. Aegyptus): Argyphia, Danaides,
    Hypermnestra (2)
LYNCEUS (s. Aphareus): Arene, Arne (4),
    Helen (1), Laocoosa, Leucippides,
    Polydora (2)

LYNCUS: Demeter
LYRCUS: Molpadia (1), Rhoeo (1)
LYRNUS (See LYRUS)
LYRUS: Aphrodite
LYSINOMUS: Anaxo (1)
MACAR: Methymna
MACAREUS (s. Aeolus): Amphissa (1),
    Canace, Enarete
MACAREUS (s. Helios): Mytilene (1), Rhodos
MACAREUS (priest of Dionysus): Arisbe (3),
    Issa
MACEDON (s. Zeus): Oreithyia (5), Thyia (2)
MACEDON (?): Mieza
MACHAON: Anticleia (4), Arsinoe (6),
    Coronis (1), Epione, Helen (1)
MAEANDER: Callirrhoe (5), Cyane (3),
    Samia (1)
MAEON: Cybele, Dindyme
MAGNES (s. Aeolus): Clio, Enarete,
    Meliboea (2), Philodice (2)
MAGNES (s. Argus): Perimele (2)
MAGNES (s. Zeus): Thyia (2)
MAGNES (of Zacynthus): Penelope
MALEUS: Omphale
MALUS: Cleophema, Erato (2)
MANES: Callirrhoe (1)
MANTINEUS: Aglaia (4), Ocaleia
MARAPHIUS: Helen (1)
MARIANDYNUS: Eidothea (3), Eurytia,
    Idaea (3)
MARMAX: Eripha (1), Hippodameia (1),
    Parthenia (3)
MARPSIUS: Penelope
MARS: Anna Perenna, Bellona, Discordia,
    Minerva, Molae, Nerio, Rhea Silvia
MARSYAS: Muses
MECISTEUS (s. Talaus): Lysimache (1)
MECISTEUS (of Dulichium): Penelope
MECISTOPHANUS: Megara
MECON: Demeter
MEDON (s. Antenor): Theano (2)
MEDON (s. Oileus): Rhene
MEDON (s. Pylades): Electra (4)
MEDON (of Dulichium): Penelope
MEDUS (s. Aegeus): Medea
MEDUS (s. Dionysus): Alphesiboea (4)
MEGAPENTHES: Anteia, Iphianeira, Pieris,
    Tereis
MEGAREUS: Euaechme (1), Ipinoe (3),
    Merope (5), Oenope

MEGASSARES: Pharnace
MEGASTHENES: Penelope
MEGES: Ctimene, Helen (1), Timandra (1)
MEILANION: Aphrodite, Atalanta
MELAMPUS: Aglaia (3), Cyrianassa, Dorippe
(1), Eidomene, Idomene, Iphianeira,
Manto (5), Pero (2), Proetides, Pronoe
(4), Rhodope (2)
MELANEUS: Ambracia (2), Oechalia,
Stratonice (3)
MELANIPPUS (s. Agrius): Dia (6)
MELANIPPUS (s. Ares): Triteia
MELANIPPUS (s. Theseus): Perigune
MELANIPPUS (of Patrae): Comaetho (2),
Triclaria
MELANTHUS: Henioche (5)
MELAS (s. Licymnius): Perimede (3)
MELAS (s. Oenopion): Helice (5)
MELAS (s. Phrixus): Chalciope (3),
Eurycleia (1)
MELAS (s. Porthaon): Euryte (1)
MELEAGER: Alcyone (3), Althaea (1),
Artemis, Atalanta, Cleopatra (1),
Eumenides, Meleagrides, Polydora (4)
MELICERTES: Ino
MELISSEUS: Adrasteia (1), Aega, Amaltheia
(2), Hyades, Ida (2), Melissa
MELUS (s. Melus): Aphrodite, Peleia
MELUS (s. Rhacius): Manto (1)
MELUS (of Delos): Aphrodite, Peleia
MEMNON: Cissia, Eos, Hemera (1),
Memnonides
MENACLES: Adite, Gorgo (3)
MENEBRONTES: Megara
MENELAUS: Aerope (1), Cleola, Cnossia,
Eidothea (1), Helen (1), Hermione (1),
Pieris, Praxidicae, Pronaea, Tereis
MENEMACHUS: Nemea (2)
MENEPHRON: Blias, Cyllene (2)
MENEPTOLEMUS: Penelope
MENES: Creusa (5)
MENESTHEUS: Helen (1)
MENESTHIUS (s. Areithous): Phylomedusa
MENESTHIUS (s. Spercheius): Polydora (5)
MENETUS: Antianeira (2)
MENOECEUS: Hipponome, Iocaste (2)
MENOETIUS: Aegina, Asia (2), Clymene (1),
Damocrateia, Myrto (2), Periapis,
Polymede (1), Sthenele (2)
MENTES: Athena

MENTOR (s. Alcimus): Athena
MENTOR (s. Heracles): Asopis (1)
MERCURY: Baucis, Larunda, Maia
MERMERUS: Medea
MEROPS (f. Epione): Epione
MEROPS (king of Cos): Cos, Ethemea
MEROPS (king of Ethiopia): Clymene (1)
MEROPS (king of Rhindacus): Arisbe (1),
Cleite (1)
MESOLAS: Ambracia (1)
MESTOR: Andromeda, Hippothoe (5),
Lysidice (1)
METABUS: Camilla
METALCES: Cleopatra (4)
METANASTES: Scaea
METION: Alcippe (1), Iphinoe (2),
Praxithea (2)
MIDAMUS: Amymone
MIDAS: Rhea (1)
MILETUS (Carian, s. Apollo): Areia (3),
Deione (2)
MILETUS (Cretan, s. Apollo): Areia (4),
Byblis, Tragasia
MIMAS: Theano (4)
MINEUS: Myrmidone
MINIS: Penelope
MINOS (s. Lycastus): Acacallis, Androgeneia,
Ariadne, Arne (2), Crete (1), Dexithea,
Eriboea (3), Ida (1), Itone, Naucrate,
Pareia (2), Pasiphae (1), Periboea (4),
Phaedra, Procris (1), Scylla (2),
Xenodice (1)
MINOS (s. Zeus): Britomartis, Crete (1),
Europa (4), Itone
MINOTAUR: Ariadne, Pasiphae (1)
MINYAS: Callirhoe (1), Clymene (2),
Clytodora, Elara, Eteoclymene,
Euryanassa (2), Leuconoe (2),
Minyades, Periclymene,
Persephone (2), Phanosyra,
Trigoneia
MNESILEUS: Leucippides
MOLEBUS: Penelope
MOLION: Antioche
MOLIONIDAE: Stymphalides
MOLOSSUS: Andromache
MOLUS: Demonice, Molione
MOMUS: Nyx
MOPSUS (s. Ampycus): Aregonis, Chloris (4),
Himantis

MOPSUS (s. Nicodamas): Gerana

MOPSUS (s. Rhacius): Manto (1)

MULIUS: Agamede (1)

MUNIPPUS: Cilla, Hecuba

MUNITUS: Aethra (1), Laodice (4)

MUSAEUS: Astyanassa

MUTTO: Dido

MYGDON: Alexirrhoe, Amazons (1)

MYLES: Cleochareia, Peridia

MYNES (s. Euenus): Hippodameia (3)

MYNES (of Lacedaemon): Pedias

MYRMEX (?): Ephyra (1)

MYRMEX (an Athenian): Melite (5)

MYRMIDON: Eupolemeia, Eurymedusa,
    Peisidice (1)

MYRTILUS: Cleobule (4), Clytia (1),
    Hippodameia (1), Myrto (3), Phaethusa
    (2), Theobule (2)

MYSIUS: Demeter, Mysia (1)

MYTON: Mytilene (1)

NARCAEUS: Narcaea, Physcoa

NARCISSUS: Echo, Leiriope

NAUBOLUS: Perineice

NAUPLIUS (s. Clytoneus): Ameirace, Auge
    (1), Clymene (4), Hesione (3), Penelope,
    Philyra (2)

NAUPLIUS (s. Poseidon): Amymone

NAUSIMEDON: Clymene (4), Hesione (3)

NAUSINOUS: Calypso

NAUSITHOUS: Calypso, Periboea (2)

NAUTES: Minerva, Nautia

NEBROPHONUS: Hypsipyle

NELEUS: Arene, Chloris (2), Pero (2), Prote,
    Sidero, Tyro

NEOPHRON: Timandra (2)

NEOPTOLEMUS: Andromache, Deidameia
    (2), Hermione (1), Lanassa, Penthesileia,
    Polyxena (1)

NEPHALION: Pareia (2)

NEPHUS: Praxithea (3)

NEPTUNE: Neptunine, Salacia

NEREUS: Doris, Gaea, Nereides, Nereis

NESIMACHUS: Mythidice

NESSUS: Deianeira (1)

NESTOR: Anaxibia (2), Chloris (2), Eurydice
    (5), Hecamede, Nedusia, Peisidice (3),
    Polycaste (1)

NESTUS: Callirrhoe (9)

NIAUIUS: Glaucippe (2)

NICODAMAS: Gerana

NICODROMUS: Nice (2)

NICOMACHUS (s. Machaon): Anticleia (4)

NICOMACHUS (of Dulichium): Penelope

NICOSTRATUS: Helen (1), Pieris

NILUS: Achiroe, Anippe, Argiope (2), Chione
    (3), Euanthe, Memphis (1)

NIREUS: Aglaia (2)

NISAS: Penelope

NISUS: (s. Hyrtacus): Ida (4)

NISUS (s. Pandion): Abrota, Iphinoe (3),
    Pylia, Scylla (2)

NISSAEUS: Penelope

NORAX: Erytheia (2)

NOTUS: Eos

NUMA: Aegeria

NYCTEUS (s. Hyrieus): Antiope (1), Clonia
    (1), Nycteis, Polyxo (2)

NYCTEUS (s. Poseidon): Celaeno (3)

NYCTEUS (an Arcadian): Callisto (1)

NYCTEUS (king of Ethiopia): Nyctimene

NYCTIMUS: Arcadia (1), Philonome (2),
    Phylonome

NYSUS: Eurynome (8)

OARTHUS (See ORYITHUS)

OAXUS: Acacallis, Anchiale (2)

OBRIAREUS: Thrace

OBRIMUS: Hippothoe (2)

OCEANUS: Aetna, Creusa (1), Daeira, Dione
    (1), Ephyra (1), Gaea, Europa (2), Leuce,
    Libya (3), Meliboea (1), Moirae, Naiades,
    Nemesis, Oceanides, Parthenope (4),
    Philyra (1), Styx, Tethys, Thrace

OCHIMUS: Cydippe (3), Hegetoria, Rhodos

OCNUS: Manto (4)

ODOEDOCUS: Laonome (2)

ODYSSEUS: Anticleia (1), Arete, Athena,
    Callidice (1), Calypso, Cassiphone,
    Charybdis, Circe, Euiippe (6), Eurycleia
    (2), Hecuba, Helen (1), Heurippe,
    Melantho (1), Nausicaa, Oenotropae,
    Penelope, Polymela (3), Scylla (1), Sirens,
    Sphinx

OEAGRUS: Calliope, Polymnia

OEAX: Clymene (4), Hesione (3)

OEBALUS: Arene, Bateia (2), Gorgophone
    (1), Nicostrate (2), Peirene

OEDIPUS: Antigone (1), Astymedusa,
    Eumenides, Eurycleia (3), Euryganeia,
    Iocaste (2), Ismene (2), Merope (7),
    Periboea (6)

OENEUS (s. Aegyptus): Gorgo (3), Podarce

OENEUS (s. Porthaon): Althaea (1), Artemis, Deianeira (1), Euryte (1), Gorge (1), Meleagrides, Mothone, Periboea (5)

OENEUS (?) Perimede (2)

OENOMAUS: Alcippe (4), Euarete, Eurythoe, Harpinna (1), Harpinna (2), Hippodameia (1), Parthenia (3), Psylla, Sterope (1)

OENOPION: Ariadne, Helice (5), Merope (4)

OEOCLUS: Ascra

OEONUS: Perimede (3)

OESTROBLES: Hesychia

OGYGUS: Daeira, Praxidicae

OICLES: Hypermnestra (1), Polyboea (4)

OILEUS: Eriopis (1), Laonome (2), Rhene

OLENUS: Aega, Anaxithea, Helice (4)

OLOETROCHUS: Penelope

OLYMBRUS: Gaea

OLYMPUS: Alce (1), Rhea (1)

OLYNTHUS: Bolbe

ONCHESTUS: Abrota, Dia (6)

ONCUS: Demeter

ONEIRATA: Gaea, Nyx

ONEIRUS: Deidameia (2)

ONEITES: Megara

ONESIPPUS: Chryseis (2)

OPHELTES: Amphithea (3), Eurydice (6), Hypsipyle

OPHION: Eurynome (1)

OPHITES: Megara

OPUS: Cabya, Protogeneia (1)

ORCHAMUS: Eurynome (5), Leucothoe (1)

ORCHOMENUS (s. Athamas): Ino, Themisto (2)

ORCHOMENUS (s. Eteocles?): Elara, Hermippe, Hesione (2)

ORCHOMENUS (s. Minyas): Euryanassa (2)

ORESTES (s. Achelous): Perimede (1)

ORESTES (s. Agamemnon): Anaxibia (3), Areia (2), Arsinoe (2), Artemis, Athena, Boulaia, Clytemnestra, Diana, Electra (4), Erigone (2), Eumenides, Geilissa, Helen (1), Helen (3), Hermione (1), Iphigeneia (1), Laodameia (4), Tauropolis (1)

ORION: Artemis, Clonia, Coronides, Eos, Euryale (1), Menodice, Merope (4), Oris, Pleiades, Side (1)

ORMENIUS: Penelope

ORMENUS (s. Cercaphus?): Ormenis

ORMENUS (of Zacynthus): Penelope

ORNEUS: Praxithea (2)

ORNYTION: Merope (3)

OROPUS: Oreithyia (5)

ORPHEUS: Agriope (2), Aphrodite, Calliope, Eurydice (1), Maenades, Menippe (3), Muses, Oeagrides, Polymnia, Sirens

ORSILOCHUS: Dorodoche, Medusa (5), Telegone

ORTHOPOLIS: Chrysorthe, Demeter

ORTHRUS: Chimaera (1), Echidna, Sphinx

ORTYGIUS: Harpe

ORUS: Leis

ORYITHUS: Cleopatra (6)

OSIRIS: Isis

OSTASUS: Gaea

OTHRYONEUS: Cassandra (1)

OTREUS: Amazons (1)

OTUS: Artemis

OXEUS: Megara

OXYLUS (s. Ares): Protogeneia (2)

OXYLUS (s. Haemon): Hamadryades, Hamadryas, Pieria (1)

PAEON (s. Endymion): Asterodeia (1), Neis (2)

PAEON (s. Poseidon): Helle (1)

PALAEMON (s. Heracles): Autonoe (2), Iphinoe (6)

PALAEMON (sea deity): Leucothea (2)

PALAMEDES: Clymene (4), Epipole (1), Hesione (3), Libya (2), Tyche (1)

PALICI: Aetna, Thaleia (3)

PALLAS (s. Crius): Bia, Eos, Eurybia, Invidia, Nice (1), Selene, Styx

PALLAS (s. Heracles): Dyna

PALLAS (s. Lycaon): Chryse (1)

PALLAS (s. Pandion): Pylia

PALLAS (Giant): Athena, Pallantias, Pallas (1)

PAMMON: Hecuba

PAMPHILUS: Demophile (1), Orsobia

PAN: Aega, Amaltheia (1), Callisto (1), Dryope (5), Echo, Erato (1), Gaea, Hybris, Iambe, Iynx (1), Maenades, Oeneis, Oreades, Pales, Peitho (1), Penelope, Pitys, Selene, Sinoe, Syrinx, Thymbris

PANDAREOS: Aedon (1), Cameira (2), Cleodora (1), Cleothera, Demeter, Eumenides, Harmothoe, Merope (8)

PANDARUS: Iaera (2)
PANDION (s. Aegyptus): Callidice (2),
    Hephaestine
PANDION (s. Cecrops): Metiadusa
PANDION (s. Erechtheus I): Philomela (1),
    Praxithea (1), Procne, Zeuxippe
PANDION (s. Erechtheus II): Pylia
PANDION (s. Phineus): Cleopatra (6),
    Idaea (3)
PANDORUS: Praxithea (2)
PANOPEUS: Aegle (4), Asteria (9),
    Asterodeia (5), Athena
PANTHIUS: Philomela (5)
PANTHOUS: Phrontis
PAPHUS (s. Belus): Galateia (3)
PAPHUS (s. Cephalus): Aphrodite
PARALUS: Penelope
PARIS: Aphrodite, Arisbe (3), Athena,
    Cassandra (1), Hecuba, Helen (1),
    Helen (2), Hera, Herophile, Migonitis,
    Oenone
PARIUS: Demeter
PARNASSUS: Cleodora (2)
PARRHASIUS: Phylonome
PARTHENIUS (s. Cydnus): Anchiale (1)
PARTHENIUS (s. Phineus): Cleopatra (6)
PARTHENOPAEUS: Atalanta, Clymene (5),
    Lysimache (1)
PATROCLES: Megara
PATROCLUS (s. Heracles): Pyrippe
PATROCLUS (s. Menoetius): Helen (1), Iphis
    (2), Muses, Periapis, Periopis, Philomela
    (2), Polymela (1), Sthenele (2)
PEDASUS: Abarbarea
PEGASUS: Chalinitis, Chimaera (1), Eos,
    Gorgons, Muses, Pegasides
PEIRANTHUS: Callirrhoe (8), Euadne
PEIRAS: Echidna, Styx
PEIREN: Callithyia, Io
PEIREUS: Autonoe (2)
PEIRITHOUS: Deidameia (3), Dia (1),
    Eumenides, Hippodameia (4),
    Persephone (1), Thisadie
PEIRUS: Telephe
PEISENOR: Ops
PEISISTRATUS: Anaxibia (2)
PELAGON (s. Axius): Periboea (3)
PELAGON (?): Hippodameia (1)
PELASGUS (s. Apollo): Larissa (1)
PELASGUS (s. Asopus): Metope (1)

PELASGUS (s. Poseidon): Larissa (2)
PELASGUS (s. Triopas): Pelasga, Sosis
PELASGUS (s. Zeus): Meliboea (1), Niobe (1)
PELASGUS (autochthon): Cyllene (1), Gaea
PELASGUS (?): Menippe (2)
PELEUS: Antigone (2), Astydameia (1),
    Demonassa (1), Endeis, Laodameia (5),
    Philomela (3), Polydora (5), Polymela
    (1), Polymela (4), Psamathe (1), Sterope
    (3), Sthenele (2), Thetis
PELIAS: Alcestis, Alphesiboea (3), Anaxibia
    (1), Asteropeia, Medea, Peliades, Pelopeia
    (1), Phylomache, Polymede, Sidero, Tyro
PELLAS: Penelope
PELOPS (s. Agamemnon): Cassandra (1)
PELOPS (s. Tantalus): Arcippe, Astydameia
    (3), Astyoche (7), Axioche, Clotho,
    Clytia (3), Danais, Demeter, Dia (5),
    Dione (3), Euryanassa (1), Eurydice (9),
    Eurythemista, Hippodameia (1),
    Leucippe (7), Linos, Lysidice (1), Nicippe
    (1), Niobe (2), Rhea (1)
PELOPS (of Opus): Hippodameia (1)
PENATES: Vesta
PENEIUS: Chlidanope, Creusa (1), Daphne
    (2), Menippe (2), Stilbe (1)
PENELEUS: Asterope (4), Helen (1)
PENTHEUS: Agave (1), Autonoe (1), Ino,
    Maenades
PENTHILUS (s. Orestes): Erigone (2)
PENTHILUS (s. Periclymenus): Anchiroe (2)
PEPARETHUS: Ariadne
PERATUS: Calchinia
PEREUS: Laodice (3), Neaera (2)
PERGAMUS: Andromache
PERIALLUS: Penelope
PERICLYMENUS (s. Neleus): Chloris (2)
PERICLYMENUS (s. Poseidon): Chloris (5)
PERICLYMENUS (of Zacynthus): Penelope
PERIERES: Enarete, Gorgophone (1)
PERILAUS (s. Ancaeus): Samia (1)
PERIMEDES (s. Eurystheus): Antimache
PERIMEDES (of Same): Penelope
PERIPHAS (s. Aegyptus): Actaea (2),
    Gorgo (3)
PERIPHAS (s. Lapithes): Astyageia, Orsinome
PERIPHAS (s. Oeneus): Althaea
PERIPHAS (of Zacynthus): Penelope
PERIPHETES: Anticleia (2)
PERIPHRON: Penelope

PERISTHENES: Caliadne, Electra (6)
PERMESSUS: Aganippe (1)
PERSEPTOLIS: Polycaste (1)
PERSES (s. Crius): Asteria (1),
    Eurybia (1), Hecate, Perseis (1)
PERSES (s. Helios): Medea, Perse
PERSES (s. Perseus): Andromeda
PERSEUS (s. Nestor): Anaxibia (2)
PERSEUS (s. Zeus): Andromeda, Athena,
    Autochthe, Cassiepeia, Clymene (7),
    Danae, Gorgons, Gorgophone (1),
    Graeae, Medusa (1)
PHAEAX: Cercyra
PHAEDIMUS: Niobe (2)
PHAETHON (s. Cephalus): Aphrodite,
    Hemera (1)
PHAETHON (s. Helios): Clymene (1), Eos,
    Heliadae, Merope (1), Phaethontiades,
    Prote, Rhode (1)
PHALAECUS: Agrotera, Artemis
PHALAIS: Helioconis
PHALCES: Hyrnetho, Prodromia
PHALERUS: Chalciope (4)
PHANTES (s. Aegyptus): Caliadne
PHANTES (s. Antenor): Theano (1)
PHAON: Aphrodite
PHARIS: Philodameia, Telegone
PHASIS (s. Helios): Ocyrrhoe (1)
PHASIS (river-god): Aea
PHEGEUS: Alphesiboea (2), Arsinoe (1)
PHEIDIPPUS: Chalciope (5)
PHERES (s. Cretheus): Antianeira (1),
    Antigone (4), Clymene (6), Eidomene,
    Eriopis (1), Periapis, Periclymene, Tyro
PHERES (s. Jason): Medea
PHEROETES: Penelope
PHILAEUS: Lyside
PHILAMMON: Argiope (1), Artemis,
    Chione (2), Philonis (1)
PHILEMON: Baucis
PHILINUS: Phila
PHILOCTETES: Chryse (3), Chryse (4),
    Demonassa (4), Helen (1), Methone (3)
PHILODEMUS: Penelope
PHILOLAUS: Pareia (2)
PHILOMELUS: Demeter
PHILOTTUS: Niobe (2)
PHINEUS (s. Agenor): Cleopatra (6), Dia (4),
    Eidothea (3), Eurytia, Harpies, Idaea (3),
    Telephassa

PHINEUS (s. Belus): Achiroe, Andromeda,
    Cassiepeia
PHLEGYAS: Chryse (2), Cleophema, Coronis
    (1), Dotis, Gyrtone
PHLIAS: Araethyrea, Ariadne, Chthonophyle
PHLOGIUS: Chalciope (3)
PHOBOS: Aphrodite
PHOCUS (s. Aeacus): Asteria (9),
    Psamathe (1)
PHOCUS (s. Ornytion): Antiope (1)
PHOCUS (of Glisas): Callirrhoe (10)
PHOENIX (s. Agenor): Agriope (1),
    Alphesiboea (1), Astypalaea, Europa (4),
    Perimede (2), Telephassa, Telephe
PHOENIX (s. Amyntor): Cleobule (1),
    Hippodameia (5)
PHOENODAMAS: Egesta
PHORBAS (s. Argus): Euboea (5)
PHORBAS (s. Criasus): Melantho (3)
PHORBAS (s. Helios): Ambracia (1),
    Astydameia (5)
PHORBAS (s. Lapithes): Chariclo (3),
    Diogeneia (2), Hermione (3), Hyrmine,
    Iphiboe, Orsinome
PHORBAS: (s. Triopas): Hiscilla
PHORBAS (of Lesbos): Diomede (1)
PHORBUS: Pronoe (2)
PHORCYS: Ceto (1), Crateis, Gaea, Gorgons,
    Graeae, Hecate, Hesperides, Phorcides,
    Scylla (1), Sirens, Thoosa (2)
PHORONEUS: Apia, Archia, Cerdo,
    Chthonia (2), Europa (5), Hera, Laodice
    (2), Melia (1), Niobe (1), Peitho (4),
    Phoronis, Phthia (2), Teledice
PHRASIMUS: Diogeneia (1), Praxithea (2)
PHRASIUS: Chloris (2)
PHRASTOR: Menippe (2)
PHRENIUS I (of Zacynthus): Penelope
PHRENIUS II (of Zacynthus): Penelope
PHRIXUS: Biadice, Chalciope (3), Demodice,
    Helle (1), Ino, Nephele (1)
PHRONIUS: Chalciope (3)
PHRONTIS: Chalciope (3)
PHRYGIUS: Pieria (3)
PHTHIUS: Chrysippe (2), Larissa (2)
PHYLACUS: Alcimede, Clymene (2),
    Diomede (2), Phylaceis
PHYLAS (s. Antiochus): Leipephilene, Thero (2)
PHYLAS (king of Dryopes): Meda (1),
    Mideia (2)

PHYLAS (king of Ephyra): Astyoche (2)
PHYLAS (of Thessaly): Polymela (2)
PHYLEUS (s. Augeas): Ctimene, Eustyoche, Timandra (1)
PHYLEUS (of Thrace): Phyllis
PHYLONOMUS: Anaxo (1)
PHYSCUS: Chthonopatra
PHYTALUS: Demeter
PIASUS: Larissa (2)
PICUS: Canens, Circe, Pomona
PIELUS: Andromache
PIERUS (s. Macedon): Oreithyia (5)
PIERUS (king of Emathia): Antiope (8), Clio, Euippe (7), Muses, Pierides
PILUMNUS: Danae, Deverra
PISANDER: Penelope
PISENOR: Penelope
PITTHEUS: Aethra (1), Dia (5), Henioche (4), Hippodameia (1)
PLEISTHENES (s. Atreus): Aerope (1), Anaxibia (3), Cleola, Cydragora
PLEISTHENES (s. Menelaus): Helen (1)
PLEISTUS: Coryciae
PLEURON: Laophonte, Pronoe (2), Sterope (2), Stratonice (2), Xanthippe
PLEXIPPUS (s. Aegyptus): Amphicomone, Pyrantis
PLEXIPPUS (s. Phineus): Cleopatra (6), Idaea (3)
PLEXIPPUS (s. Thestius): Eurythemis
PLUTO: Averna
PLUTUS: Amaltheia (1), Demeter, Eirene (1), Ergane
PODALEIRUS: Arsinoe (6), Epione, Helen (1)
PODARCES: Astyoche (6), Helen (1)
PODASIMUS: Themis (2)
POEAS: Demonassa (4), Methone (3)
POEMANDER: Stratonice (4), Tanagra
POLEMOCRATES: Anticleia (4)
POLIPORTHES: Penelope
POLITES: Hecuba
POLYBUS (s. Antenor): Theano (2)
POLYBUS (s. Dryas): Alcinoe (2)
POLYBUS (s. Hermes): Chthonophyle, Lysianassa (2)
POLYBUS (s. Larymnus?): Argeia (3)
POLYBUS (king of Corinth): Medusa (5), Merope (7), Periboea (6)
POLYBUS (king of Thebes in Egypt): Alcandra
POLYBUS I (of Zacynthus): Penelope
POLYBUS II (of Zacynthus): Penelope

POLYCAON: Cleochareia, Euaechme (2), Messene, Peridia
POLYCTOR: Caliadne, Stygne
POLYDAMAS (s. Antenor): Theano (2)
POLYDAMAS (s. Panthous): Phrontis
POLYDAMAS (s. Priam): Hecuba
POLYDECTES: Danae
POLYDECTORES: Oeme
POLYDECTUS: Cleopatra (6)
POLYDEUCES: Leda, Leucippides
POLYDORUS (s. Cadmus): Harmonia (1), Nycteis
POLYDORUS (s. Heracles): Megara
POLYDORUS (s. Phineus): Cleopatra (6)
POLYDORUS (s. Priam): Hecuba, Helen (1), Iliona, Laothoe (1)
POLYDORUS (of Zacynthus): Penelope
POLYGONUS: Torone
POLYIDUS (s. Coeranus): Astycrateia (1), Manto (2)
POLYIDUS (of Dulichium): Penelope
POLYLAUS: Eurybia (2)
POLYMESTOR: Electra (4), Hecuba, Iliona
POLYNEICES: Antigone (1), Argeia (4), Astymedusa, Eriphyle, Euryganeia, Iocaste (2)
POLYPEMON: Sylea
POLYPHEMUS (s. Elatus): Hippe (5), Laonome (3)
POLYPHEMUS (s. Poseidon): Thoosa (2)
POLYPHONTES: Merope (6)
POLYPOETES (s. Apollo): Phthia (3)
POLYPOETES (s. Odysseus): Callidice (1)
POLYPOETES (s. Peirithous): Helen (1), Hippodameia (4)
POLYPOETES (of Dulichium): Penelope
POLYTECHNUS: Aedon (2)
POLYXENUS: Helen (1)
PONTUS: Ceto (1), Eurybia (1), Gaea, Harpies
PONUS: Eris
PORPHYRION: Aphrodite, Gaea
PORTHAON: Epicaste (2), Euryte (1), Sterope (5)
PORUS: Metis, Penia
POSEIDON: Aethra (1), Aethusa, Agamede (1), Alcyone (1), Alope, Alta, Amphitrite, Amymone, Anippe, Anticleia, Antiope (4), Apaturia (1), Aphrodite, Arethusa (4), Arne (1), Arne (5), Ascra, Asia (2),

POSEIDON *(continued)*

Asia (3), Assa, Athena, Benthesicyme, Bithynis, Caenis, Calchinia, Callirrhoe (1), Calyce (2), Canace, Capheira, Cegluse, Celaeno (1), Cercyra, Ceroessa, Charybdis, Chione (1), Chrysogeneia, Coronis (2), Crateis, Demeter, Eirene (2), Erinys, Euadne (1), Euagore, Euboea (1), Europa (3), Euryale (1), Eurycyde, Eurynome (8), Euryte (2), Gaea, Halia (2), Harpale, Harpies, Helle (1), Hera, Hesione (1), Hestia (1), Hippothoe (5), Iphimedeia, Lamia (1), Leis, Leuconoe (1), Libya (1), Lysianassa (1), Mecionice, Medusa (1), Melantheia, Melantho (2), Melia (2), Mideia (3), Mytilene (1), Oenope, Olbia, Oncaea, Oris, Pasiphae (1), Peirene, Periboea (2), Pero (1), Phoenice, Pitane, Rhea (1), Rhode (1), Rhodos, Scamandrodice, Sylea, Theophane, Thetis, Thoosa (2), Tyro

POSEIDON HIPPIUS: Demeter, Despoena

POSENA: Cloelia

POTAMON: Caliadne, Glaucippe (2)

POTHOS: Aphrodite

POTNIEUS: Pelarge

PRESBON: Sterope (6)

PRIAM: Alexandra, Alexirrhoe, Amazons (1), Arisbe (1), Aristodeme (2), Cassandra (1), Cilla, Creusa (3), Hecuba, Helen (1), Henicea, Hero (2), Iliona, Laodice (4), Lysimache (2), Medesicaste (2), Medusa (3), Penthesileia, Philomela (4), Polyxena (1), Strymo

PRIAPUS: Aphrodite, Chione (4), Hestia (1), Lotis

PRIAS: Hippodameia (1)

PROCAS: Cardea

PROCLES: Anaxandra, Argeia (5)

PROETUS: Aglaia (4), Anchinoe, Anteia, Danae, Elege, Maera (3), Ocaleia, Proetides, Stheneboea

PROGNAUS: Iphitea

PROMACHUS (s. Aeson): Polymede

PROMACHUS (s. Heracles): Psophis (2)

PROMACHUS (of Ithaca): Penelope

PROMETHEUS: Axiothea, Bia, Clymene (1), Hesione (4), Thebe (1), Themis (1)

PROMUS: Penelope

PRONAX: Amphithea (1), Lysimache (1)

PRONOMUS: Penelope

PRONOUS: Penelope

PROTESILAUS: Aethylla, Astyoche (6), Helen (1), Laodameia (2), Polydora (4)

PROTEUS (s. Aegyptus): Argyphia, Gorgophone (2)

PROTEUS (s. Poseidon?): Cabeiro, Chrysonoe, Eido, Eidothea (1), Eurynome (6), Helen (1), Psamathe (3), Rhytia, Theonoe (1), Torone

PROTEUS (a Theban): Galinthias

PROTEUS (king of Egypt): Helen (1)

PROTHEON: Hipparete

PROTHOENOR: Theobule (1)

PROTHOUS (s. Agrius): Dia (6)

PROTHOUS (of Same): Penelope

PRYLIS: Issa

PSERAS: Penelope

PSYLLUS: Anchiroe (3)

PTERELAUS: Comaetho (1)

PTOLEMAEUS: Penelope

PTOLIPORTHUS: Nausicaa

PTOUS: Themisto (2)

PYGMALION (s. Mutto): Dido

PYGMALION (a Cypriot): Aphrodite, Galateia (3), Metharme

PYGNONES: Daplice

PYLADES: Anaxibia (3), Astyoche (8), Electra (4), Helen (1), Iphigeneia (1), Tauropolis (1)

PYLAEMENES: Penelope

PYLAON: Chloris (2)

PYLAS: Pylia

PYLEUS: Budeia (2)

PYLON: Antioche (1), Antiope (3)

PYLUS: Demonice

PYRAMUS: Thisbe (1)

PYREMUS: Antigone (4)

PYRRHUS (s. Achilles) (*See* NEOPTOLEMUS)

PYRRHUS (s. Neoptolemus): Lanassa

PYTHES: Pieria (3)

PYTHON: Artemis, Delphinia, Delphyne, Gaea, Leto

REMUS: Acca Larentia, Ilia, Luperca, Rhea Silvia

RHACIUS: Manto (1)

RHADAMANTHYS: Alcmena, Europa (4)

RHESUS: Arganthone, Calliope, Euterpe, Terpsichore

RHEXANOR: Arete
RHEXENOR: Chalciope (1)
RHOETUS: Casperia
ROMULUS: Acca Larentia, Hersilia, Ilia,
    Luperca, Prima, Rhea Silvia
ROMUS: Circe
SABAZIUS: Cybele, Persephone (1), Rhea (1)
SAGARIS: Alexirrhoe
SALAGUS: Helice (5)
SALMONEUS: Alcidice, Enarete, Sidero, Tyro
SAMUS: Parthenia (2), Samia (1)
SANDACUS: Pharnace
SANGARIUS: Hecuba, Metope (3), Nana,
    Nicaea, Rhea (1), Telete (2)
SANGAS: Rhea (1)
SARON: Saronia
SAROS: Gaea
SARPEDON (s. Euander): Deidameia (1)
SARPEDON (s. Zeus): Europa (4)
SATURNUS: Demeter, Entoria, Ops,
    Saturnia
SATYRS: Iphthime (1)
SCAMANDER (s. Deimachus): Acidusa,
    Glaucia
SCAMANDER (s. Oceanus): Glaucia,
    Callirrhoe (3), Idaea (1), Rhoeo (2),
    Strymo
SCAMANDRIUS (See ASTYANAX)
SCEPHRUS: Maera (5)
SCHEDIUS (s. Iphitus): Helen (1),
    Hippolyte (4)
SCHEDIUS (of Dulichium): Penelope
SCHOENEUS: Atalanta, Themisto (2)
SCIRON (s. Canethus): Henioche (4)
SCIRON (s. Pelops?): Hippodameia (1)
SCIRON (s. Pylas): Chariclo (2), Endeis
SCOTUS: Eumenides, Euonyme
SEILENUS: Methe
SELEMNUS: Argyra
SELINUS: Helice (2)
SICELUS: Pancratis
SICINUS: Oenoie
SICYON: Chthonophyle
SILVANUS: Deverra, Pomona, Valeria (2)
SILVIUS: Lavinia
SIMOIS: Astyoche (4), Hieromneme
SINIS: Perigune, Sylea
SISYPHUS (s. Aeolus): Anticleia (1), Enarete,
    Merope (3), Tyro
SISYPHUS (s. Amphion): Niobe (2)

SITHON: Achiroe, Assa, Mendeis, Pallene
    (1), Rhoeteia
SORANUS: Feronia
SOSIPOLIS: Amaltheia (1), Eileithyia
SPARTAEUS: Himalia
SPERCHEIUS: Polydora (3), Polydora (5)
SPHINGIUS: Ino, Themisto (2)
SPHYRUS: Anticleia (4)
STAPHYLUS: Ariadne, Chrysothemis (3),
    Molpadia (1), Parthenos (2), Rhoeo (1)
STEROPES: Gaea
STHENELUS (s. Aegyptus): Sthenele (1),
    Tyria
STHENELUS (s. Capaneus): Euadne (2),
    Helen (1)
STHENELUS (s. Perseus): Alcinoe (1),
    Alcyone (4), Andromeda, Arcippe,
    Astymedusa, Hippodameia (1), Leucippe
    (7), Medusa (2), Nicippe (1)
STHENELUS (king of Lydia): Sardo (1)
STRATICHUS: Anaxibia (2)
STRATIUS (s. Clymenus): Budeia (2)
STRATIUS (of Zacynthus): Penelope
STRATOBATES: Anaxo (1)
STROPHIUS (s. Crisus): Anaxibia (3),
    Antiphateia, Astydameia (4)
STROPHIUS (s. Pylades): Electra (4)
STRYMON: Calliope, Euadne (3), Neaera
    (4), Rhodope (1), Terpsichore
STYMPHALIDES: Stymphalus
STYMPHALUS: Laodice (3), Ornis,
    Parthenope (1)
SYCHAEUS: Barce (1)
SYLEUS: Xenodoce
SYRUS: Sinope
SYTHES: Echidna
TAENARUS: Erimede
TALAUS: Astynome (3), Eriphyle, Eurynome
    (2), Lysianassa (2), Lysimache (1),
    Mythidice, Pero (2)
TALOS (nephew of Daedalus): Perdix,
    Polycaste (3)
TALOS (of Crete): Medea
TANAIS: Lysippe (4)
TANTALUS (s. Amphion): Niobe (2)
TANTALUS (s. Thyestes): Clytemnestra
TANTALUS (s. Zeus): Dione (3), Eupryto,
    Euryanassa (1), Eurythemistra, Niobe (2),
    Pluto (2)
TAPHIUS: Hippothoe (5)

TARPEIUS: Tarpeia

TARQUINIUS: Amaltheia (4), Caecilia, Sibyls, Tanaquil

TARQUITUS: Dryope (2)

TARTAROS: Aspalis

TARTARUS: Echidna, Gaea, Hecate

TATIUS: Tarpeia

TAURUS (s. Neleus): Chloris (2)

TAURUS (king of Pamphylia): Side (5)

TAUS: Herse (3)

TEGEATES: Acacallis, Maera (5)

TEIRESIAS: Alcmena, Athena, Cale (1), Chariclo (3), Chloris (5), Daphne (1), Hera, Historis, Iocaste (2), Manto (1), Telphusa (1)

TELAMON: Endeis, Eriboea (3), Glauce (6), Hesione (1), Melanippe (4), Meliboea (5), Periboea (4)

TELCHINES: Artemis, Rhea (1), Telchinia

TELEDAMUS: Cassandra (1)

TELEGONUS (s. Odysseus): Calypso, Cassiphone, Circe, Penelope

TELEGONUS (s. Proteus): Torone

TELEGONUS (king of Egypt): Io

TELEMACHUS: Athena, Cassiphone, Circe, Nausicaa, Penelope, Polycaste (1), Roma (5)

TELEON: Zeuxippe (3)

TELEPHUS: Argiope (4), Astyoche (3), Auge (1), Hiera, Roma (3)

TELES: Lysidice (2)

TELESTES: Ianthe (2)

TELEUTAGORAS: Eury(ce)?

TELEUTAS: Tecmessa (1)

TELMIUS: Penelope

TELUMNO: Tellus

TEMENUS: Chera, Hera, Hyrnetho

TENAGES: Rhodos

TENERUS: Melia (1)

TENES: Hemithea (1), Philonome (1), Polyboea (3), Procleia

TERAMBUS: Eidothea (4)

TEREUS: Philomela (1), Procne

TEUCER (s. Scamander): Arisbe (2), Asteria (7), Bateia (1), Idaea (1), Myrina (3), Neso

TEUCER (s. Telamon): Eune, Helen (1), Hesione (1), Periboea (4)

TEUTHRAS: Argiope (4), Artemis, Auge (1), Leucippe (8), Tecmessa (1)

THADYTIUS: Penelope

THALPIUS: Helen (1), Theraphone

THALUS: Helice (5)

THAMYRIS: Argiope (1), Menippe (3), Muses

THANATOS: Nyx

THASUS: Europa (4), Telephassa, Telephe

THAUMAS: Arce, Electra (1), Gaea, Harpies, Iris

THEIAS: Myrrha, Oreithyia (4), Smyrna

THEIODAMAS: Menodice

THEMON: Deidameia (1)

THEOCLYMENUS (s. Tmolus): Omphale

THEOCLYMENUS (Theban youth): Ismene (2)

THEODORUS: Sibyls

THEOPHRON: Penelope

THERAGER: Epicaste (4)

THERIMACHUS: Megara

THERSANDER (s. Agamididas): Anaxandra, Argeia (4)

THERSANDER (s. Polyneices): Demonassa (2), Eriphyle

THERSANDER (s. Sisyphus): Merope (3)

THERSANDER (a Cretan): Arethusa (7)

THERSILOCHUS (s. Antenor): Theano (2)

THERSILOCHUS (of Dulichium): Penelope

THERSITES: Dia (6), Penthesileia

THESEUS: Aegle (4), Aethra (1), Amazons (1), Amphitrite, Anaxo (2), Antiope (2), Aphrodite, Ariadne, Artemis, Athena, Epitragia, Eriboea (3), Eumenides, Hecale, Helen (1), Hippe (2), Hippodameia (10), Hippolyte (1), Iope (2), Iphigeneia (1), Medea, Meliboea (5), Molpadia (2), Pandemos, Peitho (6), Periboea (4), Perigune, Phaea, Phaedra, Phereboea

THESPIEUS: Hyle

THESPIUS: Megamede, Praxithea (2), Thespiades

THESPROTUS: Pelopeia (3)

THESSALUS (s. Heracles): Chalciope (2), Chalciope (5)

THESSALUS (s. Jason): Medea

THESTALUS: Epicaste (3)

THESTIUS: Althaea (1), Androdice, Deidameia (4), Demonice, Epicaste (2), Eurythemis, Hypermnestra (1), Laophonte, Leda, Leucippe (5), Lycippe, Thestias

THESTOR: Leucippe (4), Theonoe (2)
THOAS (s. Andraemon): Gorge (1)
THOAS (s. Dionysus): Ariadne, Hypsipyle, Myrina (1), Oenoie, Tauropolis (1), Thoantea
THOAS (of Dulichium): Penelope
THON: Polydamna
THRASYMEDES (s. Nestor): Anaxibia (2)
THRASYMEDES (of Dulichium): Penelope
THREPSIPPAS: Panope (2)
THRIASUS: Penelope
THYESTES: Aerope (1), Artemis, Daeto, Hippodameia (1), Pelopeia (3)
THYMBRAEUS: Chariboea
THYMOETES: Cilla
THYNUS: Eidothea (3), Eurytia, Idaea (3)
THYREUS: Althaea (1)
TIBER: Manto (4)
TIGASIS: Phyleis
TIMALCUS: Iphinoe (3), Oenope
TIMANDER: Eurytione, Hellotia (1)
TIPHYS: Hyrmine
TIRYNS: Euadne (3)
TISAMENUS: Demonassa (2), Hermione (1)
TISANDER: Medea
TITANS: Aega
TITHONUS: Eos, Rhoeo (2), Strymo
TITYRUS: Helen (6)
TITYUS: Artemis, Elara, Europa (3), Gaea, Leto
TLEPOLEMUS: Astydameia (2), Astyoche (2), Perimede (3), Philozoe, Polyxo (5)
TMOLUS: Arrhippe, Artemis, Omphale, Pluto (2), Theogone
TOXEUS (s. Eurytus): Antioche (1)
TOXEUS (s. Oeneus): Althaea (1)
TOXOCLEITUS: Megara
TRACHION: Epipole (1)
TRAGASUS: Philonome (1)
TRAMBELUS: Hesione (1)
TRICOLONUS: Hippodameia (1)
TRIERUS: Thrace
TRIOPAS (s. Helios): Rhodos
TRIOPAS (s. Lapithes): Orsinome
TRIOPAS (s. Poseidon): Canace, Iphimedeia, Messene, Oreaside, Sosis
TRIPHYLUS: Laodameia (3)
TRIPTOLEMUS: Cothonea, Cyntinea, Deiope, Demeter, Gaea, Hyona, Metaneira, Polymnia

TRITON (river-god): Athena, Pallas (2)
TRITON (sea-god): Amphitrite, Celaeno (1), Scylla (1), Triteia
TROEZEN: Hippodameia (1)
TROILUS: Briseis (2), Hecuba, Polyxena (1)
TROPHONIUS: Epicaste (5), Europa (1), Hercyna (1)
TROS: Astyoche (4), Callirrhoe (3), Cleopatra (5)
TURNUS: Alecto, Calybe (2), Lavinia, Venilia
TYCHIUS: Euboea (1)
TYCHON: Aphrodite
TYDEUS: Athena, Deipyle, Gorge (1), Ismene (2)
TYNDAREUS: Aphrodite, Arene, Chalcioecos, Clytemnestra, Gorgophone (1), Helen (1), Leda, Morpho, Philonoe (1), Phoebe (2), Timandra (1)
TYPHON: Chimaera (1), Delphyne, Echidna, Gaea, Gorgons, Harpies, Phaea, Scylla (1), Sphinx
TYRIMMAS: Euippe (6)
TYRRHENUS (s. Agron): Sardo (2)
TYRRHENUS (s. Atys): Callithea
TYRRHENUS (s. Heracles): Omphale
TYRSENUS: Salpinx
UCHOREUS: Memphis (1)
UPIS: Artemis, Glauce (4), Upis
URANUS: Aetna, Aphrodite, Dione (1), Eumenides, Gaea, Meliae, Muses, Phoebe (1), Rhea (1), Tethys, Theia (1), Themis (1), Titanides
VALERIUS: Valeria (2)
VENTI: Venilia
VERTUMNUS: Pomona
VIRBIUS: Aegeria, Artemis, Diana
VULCAN: Caca, Maia, Minerva
XANTHIPPUS: Hyrnetho
XANTHUS (s. Aegyptus): Arcadia (2)
XANTHUS (s. Erymanthus): Psophis (1)
XANTHUS (s. Oceanus): Eurythemistra, Glaucippe (1)
XANTHUS (s. Triopas): Oreaside
XANTHUS (a Samian): Alcinoe (2)
XANTHUS (horse of Achilles): Podarge
XENODAMUS: Cnossia
XUTHUS: Creusa (2), Diomede (2), Helle (2), Orseis
ZAGREUS: Persephone (1)
ZAREX: Rhoeo (1)

ZELUS: Styx
ZEPHYRUS: Chloris (3), Eos, Iris, Podarge
ZETES: Cleopatra (6), Harpies, Oreithyia (2)
ZETHUS: Aedon (1), Antiope (1), Dirce (1),
    Thebe (2)
ZEUS: Acacallis, Adamanteia, Adrasteia (1),
    Aega, Aegina, Agdistis, Alcinoe (3),
    Alcmena, Amaltheia (1), Amaltheia (2),
    Amaltheia (4), Anaxithea, Antiope (1),
    Aphrodite, Arce, Arche, Arge (1),
    Artemis, Asteria (1), Asterope (1),
    Astraea, Ate, Athena, Bia, Britomartis,
    Calliope, Callisto (1), Campe, Carme,
    Ceroessa, Charites, Cynosura, Danae,
    Deidameia (1), Delphyne, Demeter, Dia
    (1), Dice, Dindymene, Dione (1),
    Dodonides, Eidothea (5), Eileithyia,
    Elara, Electra (2), Enyo (1), Eos, Eris,
    Ersa, Europa (4), Eurydomene,
    Eurynome (1), Euryodia, Gaea, Glauce
    (3), Hagno, Harmonia (1), Hebe,
    Hecate, Helen (1), Helice (1), Helice (4),
    Hemera (2), Hera, Herse (3), Hesione
    (2), Hesperides, Hestia (1), Horae,
    Hyades, Hybris, Ida (2), Ida (3), Io,
    Iocaste (1), Ithome, Iynx (1), Lamia (1),
    Lamia (2), Leda, Lethe, Leto, Litae,
    Maera (3), Maia, Meliae, Melinoe,
    Melissa (1), Melissa (3), Metis,
    Mnemosyne, Moirae, Muses, Myrtoessa,
    Naiades, Neaera (5), Neda, Nemea,
    Nemesis, Nephele (2), Nice (1), Niobe
    (1), Nymphs, Oeneis, Oenoe (3),
    Pandeia, Pandora (1), Pasiphae (2),
    Persephone (1), Pheraea (2), Phthia (2),
    Plataea, Pluto (2), Protogeneia (1),
    Rhamnusia, Rhea (1), Rhoeo (1), Selene,
    Semele, Sibyls, Sinope, Styx, Taygete,
    Thaleia (3), Thebe (2), Theisoa, Themis
    (1), Thetis, Thrace, Thyia (2), Trito
ZEUS ELEUTHEREUS: Tyche (1)
ZEUS HOMOLOIUS: Homolois
ZEUXIPPUS: Syllis

REFERENCE